REF.
E
840.6
.P64
V. 5

Political profiles

DATE DUE			
		REF.	
	REF.		
		REF.	
	ı		
			REF.
REF.			

POLITICAL
PROFILES

☆ ☆ ☆

The
Nixon/Ford
Years

CONTRIBUTING EDITORS

EDITORIAL ADVISORY BOARD

POLITICAL
PROFILES

The
Nixon/Ford
Years

EDITOR:

Eleanora W. Schoenebaum, Ph.D., Columbia University

Facts On File, Inc.
119 West 57th Street, New York, N.Y 10019

POLITICAL PROFILES
The Nixon/Ford Years

Library of Congress Catalog Card No. 76-20897
ISBN 0-87196-454-6
9 8 7 6 5 4 3 2 1

Contents

POLITICAL PROFILES
The Nixon/Ford Years

Preface

The Nixon/Ford Years is the fifth volume in the *Political Profiles* series. It contains biographies of the varied men and women who played a significant role in U.S. politics during the 1970s. When completed *Political Profiles* will consist of six volumes which include detailed biographies of those individuals prominent in American politics since the end of World War II. This volume, unlike its predecessors, spans two presidencies. The Administrations were combined because the two were so intertwined.

As in the case of the profiles in the earlier volumes, each entry is a detailed account of the individual's career during a particular presidential administration. It also includes his social and political background, his early career and major accomplishments as well as an assessment of his impact on the social, political or cultural life of the nation. Individuals with long careers, such as Hubert Humphrey and George Meany, appear in several volumes of the series. In these cases each volume's entry briefly summarizes the subject's entire career but concentrates on his activities during the Administration under consideration. For example, Sen. William Fulbright's profile in *The Nixon/Ford Years* focuses on the role he played in reorienting U.S. policy toward the Soviet Union. Fulbright's profile in *The Eisenhower Years* traces his opposition to Sen. Joseph McCarthy. This unique organizational structure enables us to update the series by tracing an individual's career through *The Truman Years* to *The Carter Years* if necessary. It provides a richness of detail and historical perspective unavailable in other biographical reference works.

Each entry begins with a headnote giving the individual's name, date and place of birth and death, and major offices held during the period covered in the volume. In the case of men and women in political office, the years— and if important the months—in office are given. We have chosen to list the date of Senate confirmation as the beginning of service to maintain consistency. Thus George Bush is listed in this volume as "Ambassador to the U.N. February 1971–December 1972." Jane Fonda, however, is recorded simply as "Actress, political activist."

The body of the entry then follows, its size commensurate with the individual's importance or the significance of the issue he or she was involved in. If the individual is profiled in another volume, this is indicated in a bracketed notation in the text. The notation [*q.v.*] (i.e., quod vide) follows the names of other men and women who have entries in the same volume. (The notation does not follow the names of Presidents.) Each profile concludes with the initials of the author and, in many instances, brief suggestions for further reading.

One of the most difficult tasks in compiling a new biographical reference work is choosing the individuals to be covered. A large portion of the entries are self-evident: the President and Vice President, members of the Supreme Court and cabinet, and chairmen of important congressional committees. Beyond these individuals we have been guided by two questions: Did the man or woman have a lasting impact on politics broadly defined? Or did the individual capture the political attention of the nation? We have, therefore, included not only political officeholders but also influential business and labor leaders, journalists and intellectuals as well as civil rights activists.

i

Because of the importance of the executive branch during the postwar period, we have included important figures in the executive departments, particularly Defense and State, as well as the President's aides and advisers. We have been selective in choosing members of Congress. Only those associated with a major issue or interest have been included. Specific governors have been chosen to focus on the main problems facing states during the period.

Choosing among the numerous journalists and intellectuals of the period has been one of the most difficult tasks. We have included a number of those, such as John Kenneth Galbraith and William F. Buckley, who had an influence on the general body politic. Left out are those academics who, while important in their fields, are little known to the general public. Finally, we have profiled a number of figures who achieved brief fame or notariety. These include Rabbi Baruch Korff, who defended Nixon during Watergate; Lt. William Calley, who was involved in the My Lai massacre; and William Shockley, whose racial theories generated controversy.

Because *Political Profiles* deals with those individuals who dominated the visible surface of public affairs during the postwar period, we have not attempted to provide a political or ethnic balance. The selection of individuals included reflects the nature of national politics under each President. Our series does not purport to be a reference work on the American political and economic elite. There has been little attempt to profile members of the so-called American establishment who may have had profound influence on policy but who chose to work behind the scenes. Similarly, while we have profiled business leaders, such as Stuart Saunders and C. Arnholt Smith, who played a role in politics during the period, *The Nixon/Ford Years* contains no representatives of the Mellon or DuPont dynasties.

Almost all of the entries in this volume were researched and written by trained historians, either graduate students or Ph.Ds. A distinguished editorial board helped us select those profiled. Edward W. Knappman, executive editor of Facts on File, conceived the series and reviewed most profiles included in the volume. Martha Sobel undertook the arduous task of assemblying the appendix.

The Nixon/Ford Years contains several useful references found in the appendix. It has a complete chronology of the period, the membership list of the 91st–94th Congresses, a list of Supreme Court members, the membership of the most important regulatory agencies and a list of state governors. The volume also contains an extensive bibliography covering the Nixon/Ford era. We thought it useful to include a career index within the appendix for the convenience of those seeking information on individuals in similar fields. The volume also contains an extensive subject and name index.

The Nixon/Ford Years: An Introduction

Public discontent with the Democratic Administration of congressional wheeler-dealer Lyndon Johnson helped bring another Washington "old hand" into office—Republican Richard Nixon. From Lyndon Johnson through Richard Nixon to Gerald Ford, the public looked to experienced national politicians for leadership. Yet by the end of the Nixon-Ford years, the nation's bicentennial, the country was disillusioned and disappointed in the record of the recent presidency (regardless of party) and in a mood to experiment with men untainted by big government service. Richard Nixon came to office faced with problems of the war in Vietnam, inflation and a crisis in public confidence, which was generally referred to as the "credibility gap." When the Republicans left office in 1976, only the Vietnam war was no longer an issue. Inflation and flagging public confidence not only remained, but had become even more acute.

Narrowly elected to office and representing the minority Party of the nation, President Nixon soon embarked on a course to broaden his support base with "Middle America" (later christened the "Silent Majority") and to revitalize the Republican Party that had been badly fragmented since the presidential candidacy of Barry Goldwater in 1964.

To help unify the Party, the President named Rep. Rogers C.B. Morton of Maryland as Republican National Committee chairman. Morton gave up a chance to be nominated as a senatorial candidate in 1970 to continue his work for the Party. By the end of that year, Morton had put the Republicans in good financial shape, led them through the midterm elections with a creditable showing and begun extensive preparations for the 1972 presidential campaign. The President not only praised Morton for uniting "the Party as no chairman in my memory has been able to do . . . in recent years," but also rewarded his faithful and effective service by appointing him Secretary of Interior in January 1971.

In putting together his "official family," President Nixon chose a group of men much like himself—the sons of small-town America, self-made men and political middle-of-the-roaders. All the cabinet secretaries were white, male, middle-aged, business-minded Republicans. There were no token representatives of the Democratic Party or of either the Goldwater or the Rockefeller wings of the Republican Party. The composition of the cabinet raised considerable interest because of Nixon's announced intention of abandoning the JFK-LBJ operating style of powerful White House staffs and of returning to the Eisenhower style of "running the government through a strong cabinet."

The cabinet that President Nixon presented to a television audience of millions in mid-December 1968 was comprised of a few close friends, a couple of academics and a number of practical politicians. He put friends in command of the strategic Departments of State (William P. Rogers), Justice (John Mitchell), and Health, Education and Welfare (HEW) (Robert Finch). In addition to Rogers, he brought in another veteran of the Eisenhower Administration—Maurice Stans—as Commerce Secretary. Both George Shultz as Labor Secretary and Clifford Hardin as Agriculture Secretary were academics with practical administrative experience. Most of the other cabinet members were elective officials. Politically astute Congressman Melvin Laird (R, Wis.) was named Defense Secretary and three Republican governors joined the Administration: George Romney of Michigan as Secretary of Housing and Urban Development (HUD), John Volpe of Massachusetts as Secretary of Transportation and Walter Hickel of Alaska as Secretary of Interior. The President repaid a campaign debt by naming David Kennedy as Treasury Secretary in reward for his fund-raising assistance. Finally, the appointment of conservative Alabama Republican Winton Blount as Postmaster General appeared to be one of the Administration's first moves in its Southern Strategy. At 43 Finch was the youngest cabinet member; most of the others were in their 50s or 60s. There were at least seven millionaires—Blount, Hickel, Kennedy, Rogers, Romney, Stans and Volpe—but all had worked their way up from middle-class backgrounds.

Despite the fact that they seemed to fit the Nixon mold, few fared well in the Administration. Postmaster General Blount presided over the transformation of the Post Office from a cabinet department to a government corporation and then left the Administration in 1971. Interior Secretary Hickel was fired in the autumn of 1970 after publicly complaining that he could not penetrate the "Berlin Wall," the layer of insulation that White House assistants John D. Ehrlichman and H.R. Haldeman had thrown up around the President. Midway through the term, Finch, Kennedy and Hardin were eased out as their policy preferences and the President's began to diverge. Labor Secretary Shultz also left the cabinet in midterm to assume the directorship of the newly reorganized Office of Management and Budget (OMB). As part of this first major personnel shuffle of the Administration, Undersecretary of State Elliot Richardson replaced Finch at HEW; Undersecretary of Labor James D. Hodgson was promoted to fill George Shultz's cabinet spot; Rogers C.B. Morton replaced Hickel at Interior; and former Texas Gov. and Democrat John Connally replaced David Kennedy at the Treasury Department.

Secretaries Romney, Volpe and Laird lasted through the first term, but did not continue into the second. The President's oldest friend in the cabinet—William Rogers—held onto the title of Secretary of State until the summer of 1973, even though National Security Affairs Assistant Henry Kissinger had long since become the chief foreign policy adviser and negotiator. Finally, Maurice Stans and John Mitchell resigned from the cabinet to become respectively campaign fundraiser and manager for the reelection effort.

Despite Nixon's avowed intention of relying on a strong cabinet, it soon became evident that power and influence were gravitating toward the White House staff. The "Teutonic Trio" of Kissinger, H.R. Haldeman and John D. Ehrlichman were soon envied for their access to and influence with the President. Also prominent among the staff were congressional strategist Bryce Harlow and domestic policy advisers like the liberal Daniel Patrick Moynihan and the conservative Arthur Burns.

As the staff grew in prominence, it also grew in numbers. Clearly Nixon had learned during his years as Eisenhower's vice president that reliance on an extensive staff system helped conserve the President's time and energy. The buffering function of the staff was particularly important to Nixon because he had a low threshold for fatigue and was uneasy with most people. As a result of these factors, the President quickly acquired the largest staff in history—over 150 members, not counting secretaries and stenographers.

As a means of gaining support for the Administration and enlarging the Republican Party's base, the White House evolved its Southern Strategy. The results of the 1968 election seemed to indicate that the Democratic hold on the "Solid South" was weakening and that the region held great potential for Republican gains. Therefore the Administration undertook several actions designed to attract Southern support. In 1969, in one of the first moves, Attorney General John Mitchell presented and won congressional support for a voting rights proposal that extended the provisions of the 1965 Voting Rights Act to the entire nation, rather than just targeting those states (primarily Southern) that had a history of de jure discrimination against blacks.

Another major element of the Southern Strategy was the development of a more restrained policy regarding school desegregation enforcement, particularly through the use of busing. Beginning in the late summer of 1969, the Administration, through HEW and the Justice Department, began to delay implementation of various desegregation orders. During 1970 the President made it clear that in his opinion, "education not integration" was the primary concern of the schools and that it was impossible to achieve "instant integration." He went on to state that his policy would be one of "cooperation, rather than coercion." In October 1970 the Solicitor General, in oral argument before the Supreme Court, pointed out that white students in the South might abandon public education if desegregation efforts were pressed too strongly, thus reinforcing Nixon's stated position opposing busing and favoring the "neighborhood school" concept.

While these moves won the applause of the Southern conservatives, blacks and other minority groups and civil rights activists strongly disapproved. Indeed the U.S. Commission on Civil Rights reported a "major breakdown" in federal efforts to fight discrimination and a number of HEW officials and attorneys with the Civil Rights Division of the Justice Department resigned in protest of the Administration's policies. Overall the White House position on civil rights issues from school desegregation and voting rights to housing and employment seemed to fit a policy proposed by one of the President's major domestic affairs advisers, Daniel Patrick Moynihan, which he described as one of "benign neglect."

Another tactic in the Southern Strategy was the use of the President's appointment power. As Nixon staffed his new Administration, the *Baltimore Sun* estimated that a "higher number of Southerners had received patronage appointments . . . than ever before." However Nixon's first two attempts to name Southerners to the Supreme Court met bitter congressional opposition and eventual disapproval.

To replace Justice Abe Fortas, the President initially nominated South Carolina federal Circuit Court Judge Clement F. Haynsworth. Criticized as a "racist" and a "laundered segregationist" and as "antilabor," Haynsworth faced questions at his Senate confirmation hearings about possible conflict-of-interest improprieties. On Nov. 21, 1969, his nomination was rejected by the Senate. Two months later Judge G. Harrold Carswell of the Fifth Circuit Court of Appeals in Florida was nominated and he also encountered intense opposition. Like Haynsworth, Carswell was accused of being a racist and a segregationist, but to these criticisms were added objections that he was a mediocre jurist and thus not of the caliber befitting a member of the Supreme Court. When Carswell's nomination was also rejected, the President lashed out at the Senate, saying that "it [was] not possible to get confirmation for a judge on the Supreme Court of any man who believes in the strict construction of the Constitution . . . if he happens to come from the South . . . ." The President finally succeeded in filling the vacancy on the Court with the nomination of Circuit Court Judge Harry A. Blackmun of Minnesota, who was unanimously confirmed in May 1970.

Far less controversial, but perhaps more important, was the nomination and confirmation of a new Chief Justice—Judge Warren E. Burger of the U.S. Circuit Court of Appeals for Washington, D.C. In contrast to the controversy surrounding the associate justice nominations, Burger easily won Senate confirmation to replace the retiring Earl Warren in 1969. By the end of his first term in office, the President had had the opportunity to appoint four men to the Court who he hoped would direct its constitutional philosophy toward a more conservative stance than that of the preceding Warren Court.

In 1971 President Nixon succeeded in naming a Southerner, former American Bar Association President Lewis F. Powell, Jr., to the Supreme Court. The same year he placed Assistant Attorney General William H. Rehnquist on the Court. Observers of the judicial process soon began to perceive a trend towards less "lenient" decisions in criminal matters, which was more in keeping with the Nixon Administration's "law and order" campaign.

Along these lines the Administration had submitted various crime control proposals to Congress in 1969, and in 1970 Nixon declared a "war on crime" and won legislative approval for four major crime bills—the Comprehensive Drug Abuse Prevention and Control Act, the Omnibus Crime Control Act, the Organized Crime Control Act and the District of Columbia Court Reorganization and Criminal Procedure Act (designed as a "model anti-crime package" to redress Washington's reputation as the nation's "crime capital").

The war in Southeast Asia was a prominent issue throughout Nixon's first term of office. Committed to ending the conflict he had inherited from the Johnson Administration, President Nixon initially encountered a lull on this front. During 1969 peace negotiations in Paris were stalemated. At home congressional criticism was restrained during the Administration's "honeymoon period" and anti-war activity had decreased. But in the fall of 1969, issues of war and defense reemerged and were attended by heated debate, both congressional and public. Controversy over the funding and deployment of a Safeguard anti-ballistic missile (ABM) system culminated in a dramatic 50-50 Senate vote with a tie-breaking ballot cast by Vice President Spiro Agnew that allowed development of the ABM to continue. As the conflict in Vietnam dragged on, Senate criticism of the Administration's war policies became more pronounced.

With students returning to school for the fall semester, campus protest increased. On Oct. 15, 1969, the Vietnam Moratorium staged protests around the country and, a month later, brought 250,000 people to Washington for the largest demonstration in the capital's history. In an effort to extricate American forces from Vietnam and thereby quiet domestic dissent, President Nixon proposed a policy of "Vietnamization" of the war that involved a gradual shifting of military responsibility from U.S. combat troops to the South Vietnamese. The new policy, announced on Nov. 3, 1969, marked the beginning of U.S. troop withdrawals from Vietnam. Vietnamization was an elaboration of an earlier foreign policy statement by Nixon. In his "Asian Doctrine" of July the President had called for the maintenance of American commitments to Asian allies, but with a greater stress on self-help and economic development in the region and the avoidance of U.S. participation in future wars on the Asian mainland.

The President further developed this policy direction with the promulgation of the "Nixon Doctrine." Embodied in a 40,000-word "State of the World" message to Congress in February 1970, the Nixon Doctrine called for a change in U.S. relations with its allies, from one of American "predominance" to one of "partnership." Under this policy the U.S. would "participate in the defense and development of allies and friends but . . . cannot—and will not—conceive all the plans, design all the programs, execute all the decisions and undertake all the defense of the free nations of the world."

Despite the apparent intent to limit American military commitments around the world and withdraw from Vietnam, the President acted to broaden U.S. military involvement in Southeast Asia in 1970 by sending U.S. forces into Laos and Cambodia. Initially the Administration had cloaked its Laotian activities in a secrecy designed to help maintain that country's official neutrality. However hearings by a Senate Foreign Relations subcommittee under Stuart Symington (D, Mo.) elicited an explanatory statement from the President in March 1970.

The revelation about the Laotian involvement generated apprehensions that the U.S. was still bogged down in the Southeast Asian war with no end in sight and thus set the stage for quick, strong reaction against the President's decision to send American troops into Cambodia to clean out Communist sanctuaries along the Vietnamese border. Nixon's action revived congressional concern about the extent of presidential war-making and foreign policy powers and set off an outburst of public anti-war sentiment. As a result the Senate engaged in a two-month debate over the Cooper-Church Amendment, which sought to restrain presidential authority to launch, expand or sustain military activity in Cambodia without the concurrence of Congress. While the Senate on June 20 approved (58-37) the attachment of the Cooper-Church Amendment to a foreign military sales bill, opposition from conferees resulted in a six-month delay and finally the amendment was dropped.

The Cooper-Church Amendment controversy was, however, only one example of renewed congressional concern about executive war powers. Sens. George McGovern (D, S.D.), Mark Hatfield (R, Ore.), Alan Crantson (D,

Calif.), Harold Hughes (D, Iowa) and Charles Goodell (R, N.Y.) proposed an end-the-war amendment that would have cut off funds for use in Vietnam after Dec. 31, 1970 except for troop withdrawal purposes. In July the Senate passed a concurrent resolution repealing the 1964 Gulf of Tonkin Resolution, which many war critics considered a presidential carte blanche to wage the war in Vietnam. (The House failed to pass a similar resolution.) The White House did not oppose the repeal of the Gulf of Tonkin Resolution, maintaining that the President had sufficient constitutional authority to continue the war. In effect the Senate resolution was merely a symbolic act, expressive of congressional dissatisfaction with a continuing, and apparently expanding, war.

The invasion of Cambodia also rekindled anti-war activity. Immediately following President Nixon's announcement of an American troop offensive into Cambodia, the Vietnam Moratorium Committee issued a call for a nationwide student strike. A strike at Kent State University in Ohio ended in the killing of four students by National Guardsmen. This tragedy galvanized the anti-war forces and helped produce a turnout of between 60,000 and 100,000 demonstrators in Washington on May 9. Althought the President had labeled anti-war protesters "bums," he did greet the Washington group with a conciliatory predawn appearance at the Lincoln Memorial. However the effort proved fruitless. As public dissent tapered off, the scene of protest shifted again to Congress.

Despite public and congressional pressure for a quick end to U.S. involvement, the Administraion continued its policy of gradually removing American troops from Southeast Asia. Through 1971 the Paris peace talks remained stalled. Meanwhile both Houses of Congress finally approved a weakened version of the Mansfield Amendment, another measure calling for the withdrawal of U.S. troops from Indochina.

In keeping with the developing sentiment for a retrenchment of U.S. commitments around the world, and in response to the dissatisfaction over the course of the Vietnam war, the President moved toward fulfilling his campaign promise to replace the military draft with an all-volunteer force. Although the President's Commission on an All-Volunteer Army reported that the draft could be abolished by mid-1971, Nixon set June 30, 1973, as the target date for the change. In the meanwhile draft quotas were reduced and for a time the draft was suspended.

In its battle against anti-war dissent at home, the Administraion lost a 1971 Supreme Court decision to prevent *The New York Times* and other newspapers from publishing the *Pentagon Papers*, a Defense Department study of U.S. involvement and decisionmaking in Southeast Asia, particularly in Vietnam. Although the information revealed in the *Papers* focused on policies followed under previous Administrations, the Court's ruling rankled the President.

The Administration's principal diplomatic concern at this time was the reopening of diplomatic contact with the People's Republic of China. In a sudden shift of foreign policy, the U.S. made a diplomatic approach to the Chinese, abandoning more than two decades of hostility between the two nations. During the summer of 1972 Nixon announced three major steps that radically altered America's position on China and shocked U.S. allies and adversaries. In June the U.S. ended its 21-year trade embargo of mainland China; a month later it was announced that Nixon would pay a state visit to Peking in February 1972; and in August the State Department reported that it would back the admission of the People's Republic into the U.N. These moves won the President accolades as a statesman working for world peace and boosted his popularity at home, but aroused uneasiness among America's allies, particularly Japan and the Nationalist Chinese government on Taiwan. The fears of the Nationalist Chinese and their conservative supporters in the U.S. were partially realized in October 1971. That month, while national security adviser Kissinger was in China preparing the agenda for Nixon's forthcoming trip, the U.N. voted to admit Communist China and to expel Taiwan, refusing to adopt the "two Chinas" policy proposed by the United States to retain Nationalist China while admitting the People's Republic.

The U.N. decision was greeted by angry suggestions that the United States retaliate by reducing its financial support of the organization to a more reasonable and appropriate sum. Such threats, however, were soon drowned out by the chorus of praise that accompanied the first visit of an American President to China, which was the highlight of the Nixon presidency. The Peking trip ended with the issuance of the Shanghai Communique, which committed both the U.S. and China to "a peaceful settlement of the Taiwan question" and to a provision that neither nation "should seek hegemony in the Asia Pacific region and each is opposed to efforts by any other country or group of countries to establish such hegemony." Eventually diplomatic contact was reestablished between the U.S. and China. Opening the lines of communication marked American recognition of China's emergence as a central figure in world power politics.

A significant problem that confronted Nixon during his first term in office was the troubled state of the U.S. economy. In its initial efforts to curb inflationary growth without triggering recession, the Administration followed a policy of "gradualism" that included the trimming of governmental expenditures, but determinedly eschewed wage and price controls. After more than a year of cautious restraint, anti-inflation strategy shifted in late 1970 towards efforts to spur economic recovery. By this time the President's handling of the economy was criticized not only by congressional Democrats and many private economists, but also by the public. Speculation arose that if Nixon did not take strong measures to improve the economic situation he might lose the presidential election of 1972.

In a major economic speech delivered on Dec. 4, 1970, President Nixon announced changes in federal spending, monetary and tax policies. Abandoning hopes of achieving a balanced budget, he announced the adoption of deficit spending to stimulate growth. He stressed that he had secured the agreement of Federal Reserve Board (FRB) Chairman Arthur Burns, to "provide fully for the increasing monetary needs of the economy," thus easing the "tight money" situation created by previous FRB policies. He also tentatively entered the area of wage and price controls, warning that the government would take measures to offset oil price increases and would intervene in construction industry wage negotiations if salary demands and rising costs were not restrained.

Finally after two and a half years of tenuous attempts to curb inflation and unemployment, the President took bold action in 1971, not only to improve the economic condition of the nation, but also to improve his standing with the public and therefore guarantee his prospects for reelection in 1972. On Aug. 15, 1971, President Nixon froze wages and prices for 90 days; called for a variety of tax revisions to stimulate growth and investment; imposed a 10% surcharge on imports; cut the dollar loose from the traditional $35-an-ounce fixed price for gold and established a Cost of Living Council to administer these policies.

Phase Two of the stabilization program, announced on Oct. 7, terminated the wage-price freeze and replaced it with a Pay Board and a Price Commission to regulate wage and price increases under specific guidelines. The President also asked for and received congressional approval of a tax cut proposal and a year's extension of his economic stabilization authority. The final step in this initiative was the devaluation of the dollar (Dec. 18, 1971) as part of a general realignment of currency values among the major industrial nations. This move was designed to improve America's international trading position by eliminating the disadvantage created by an overvalued dollar against the undervalued currencies of other nations.

The initial overall effect of these efforts was generally favorable: the gross national product (GNP) increased and wages rose faster than prices. But unemployment continued to be a problem, remaining well above the Administration's goal of 4%. In September 1972 the unemployment rate stood at 5.5%, representing 4.8 million Americans out of work, or 2 million more than when President Nixon had assumed office. In addition to its economic implications the unemployment situation was a troublesome political problem since the jobless might easily turn into a dissatisfied voting bloc in 1972.

The Nixon Administration sought to address the unemployment problem within the context of its overall domestic policy orientation by trimming back "Great Society" programs started by the Johnson Administraion and by instituting a "New Federalism" approach. The major thrust of the New Federalism was to shift some power and program responsibility from the federal government to state and local governments. One of the first proposals in this strategy was a broad reform of the welfare system that would set minimum annual payments for welfare recipients (the Family Assistance Plan) and would link welfare to job-training programs administered by the states. Funding for these programs would come from a projected revenue-sharing system under which a portion of federal tax revenues would be returned to the state and local governments.

However, the Administration's reform efforts, as well as other domestic initiatives in education, health and labor, encountered substantial opposition in Congress. Although the House and Senate approved a 15% increase in basic Social Security payments in 1969, none of the Administration's proposed reforms of the system were adopted. The Family Assistance Plan died in Congress during 1970. The two branches of government battled over health and education programs and revenue-sharing schemes, with the President vetoing various educational funding bills three years in a row and Congress voting to override his vetoes. Although the Administration's manpower revenue-sharing program of 1971 was rejected, the seriousness of the unemployment situation elicited cooperation between the two branches on the passage of a $2.25 billion Democratic-sponsored program to create public service jobs at the state and local levels.

In his 1971 State-of-the-Union message, President Nixon proposed "six great goals" to restructure government and to turn power "back to the people." These six goals were revenue sharing; executive department reorganization; initiatives to reduce pollution and preserve the environment; prosperity through a federal budget based on full-employment spending to stimulate the economy and efforts by labor and management to control wages and prices; major reform of the welfare system; and improvement of America's health care system.

The President's environmental proposals received favorable acceptance, because they coincided with a growing public concern about the environment, symbolized by the celebration of Earth Day in April 1970. During 1970 Congress approved Administration bills to curb air and water pollution, as well as to establish the National Oceanic and Atmospheric Administration within the Commerce Department and an independent Environmental Protection Agency. Another presidential success was the establishment of a five-year revenue-sharing program, approved in 1972, to return $30 billion in federal revenues to state and local governments for spending as they saw fit.

One of the most politically controversial goals was reorganization of the executive departments, reducing them from 12 to 8, with most of the changes occurring in the domestic, constituency-oriented departments. State, Treasury, Defense and Justice were to remain untouched, and Congress had already approved the conversion of the Post Office from a cabinet department into a quasi-public corporation in 1970. President Nixon proposed that the remaining seven departments be consolidated into four: Natural Resources (primarily Interior, with parts of Commerce and Agriculture); Human Resources (based on HEW, with parts of Agriculture and Labor); Economic Development (primarily Transportation, with parts of Labor, Commerce and Agriculture); and Community Development (based on HUD, with parts of Agriculture). Congressional reaction to governmental reorganization of such scope was guarded and beyond hearings in both houses, no action was taken.

Midway through the first term, Nixon and his advisers began to plan for the next presidential election. Dan Rather in *The Palace Guard* contended that immediately after the 1970 midterm elections Nixon became concerned about political threats from both the right and the left. On the left President Nixon feared Sen. Edward Kennedy (D, Mass.) might rise above the potentially damaging Chappaquiddick incident to become a presidential contender. In addition Sen. Edmund Muskie (D, Me.) was becoming a potentially formidable contender and a spokesman for the Democrats. On the right George Wallace loomed as a potential third-party candidate who could seriously damage the Republicans' Southern Strategy and who might cut into the President's support from conservatives who favored lax desegregation efforts and strong law and order measures.

In the domestic area the Nixon Administration had relatively little to show in the way of tangible accomplishments. Although the Administration could point to "the most advanced environmental program in American history" and to a new revenue-sharing plan, inflation and unemployment remained serious problems. Relations with the Democratic controlled Congress were strained and often antagonistic. During his first term Nixon vetoed 30 pieces of major authorizing or appropriating legislation and saw his veto challenged 11 times and overridden 14 times. In addition many of his legislative proposals were significantly modified and his spending proposals were generally increased by Congress. On occasion, such as with Haynsworth and Carswell, the Senate had been not only unreceptive but hostile to the President's nominee. Clearly he had little hope of building himself a "monument" in domestic affairs, where the collaboration of Congress was so necessary. Thus his best opportunities for securing reelection, and a place in history, rested in the arena of foreign affairs, where the President had the ability to act without legislative approval and where he was confident of his abilities and those of his aides.

Early Administration ventures in the field of foreign affairs met with limited success. A serious policy blunder occurred during the December 1971 Indo-Pakistani war when the U.S. decided to back Pakistan against India, which joined with East Pakistan in its struggle to gain independence. India beat Pakistan and East Pakistan became the independent nation of Bangladesh. The Soviet Union, which had supported India in the conflict, claimed a victory over the U.S. But the Administration's failure soon faded in the shadow of the China rapprochement. The President's visit to Peking in early 1972 was not only a diplomatic plum but also a most effective political maneuver. Major events of the trip were scheduled to coincide with prime time television in the U.S. and to provide a statesmanlike contrast to the Democratic Party primary squabbles. The China trip constituted the launching of Nixon's reelection bid.

Soon after returning from China, Nixon flew to Moscow for a summit in May, becoming the first American President to set foot on Soviet soil since Franklin Roosevelt visited Yalta in 1945. During the Moscow Summit Nixon and Soviet Party Secretary Leonid Brezhnev signed two agreements—one limiting each country to construction of two ABM missile sites and another freezing the deployment of new offensive strategic missiles on both sides. The ABM treaty was submitted to the Senate for ratification and was approved by an 88-to-2 vote in August. The executive agreement on offensive arms, while not requiring congressional action, was submitted to both Houses. After weeks of debate and the adoption of several modifying amendments, the Senate and the House granted approval in September.

Yet the foundation for a strong record in foreign affairs had to encompass significant progress in ending the Vietnam war. Nixon had been elected in 1968 because of voter disenchantment with the Democratic Administration's handling of the war and its failure to end U.S. participation in it. He had promised to bring the war to a close with an honorable peace, and after four years in office he would have to show major achievements towards that goal.

The Administration's Vietnamization policy was a step in that direction, as was the scheduled abolishment of the draft. But given the intensity of anti-war sentiment in the country, more substantial accomplishments were needed.

The Democratic presidential candidate, Sen. George McGovern, made the war his major campaign issue. McGovern maintained that the Nixon Administration had not gone far enough or fast enough in resolving the war. The attendant issue of the release of American prisoners-of-war (POWs) became a volatile and emotional topic in the campaign. Nixon considered his opponent the "most extreme of the anti-war candidates"—one who saw the war not as an issue but as a cause.

After three years of stalled peace talks, prospects of capitalizing on the Vietnam issue appeared dim until shortly after the President's return from his trip to Moscow. Following some hopeful signs in the summer of 1972, a breakthrough in the peace talks seemed possible, perhaps because of Nixon's meetings with the leaders of both Communist China and the Soviet Union, or because of his decision to bomb prime military targets in the Hanoi area and to mine Haiphong harbor. In mid-October, Kissinger reported that major progress had been made in the Paris peace talks. By the end of the month, the North Vietnamese broadcast the general provisions of a tentative agreement over Radio Hanoi, and Kissinger announced that "peace [was] at hand" and that "an agreement [was] within sight . . . ." McGovern called the announcement a "cynical effort" to win the election.

Although subsequent events showed that peace was not quite "at hand," it was within reach and evidence of the diplomatic breakthrough was enough to give President Nixon another major foreign policy achievement on the eve of the election. It also seriously undercut the single-issue campaign of his opponent. McGovern had run as the peace candidate and yet mere days before the election, Nixon seemed to be delivering a peace agreement. Not only was the Administration apparently delivering on the Vietnam peace promise, but it had recognized and played to the Silent Majority that was developing to the right of the Democratic Party. Author Theodore White maintained that starting in 1952 "the more liberal the Democratic candidate, the better Nixon did against him," until in 1972 his margin swelled to a landslide. The June break-in at the Democratic National Committee's headquarters in the Watergate office complex in Washington and the subsequent indictments of White House employees Howard Hunt and Gordon Liddy did not develop into a significant campaign issue, despite Democratic efforts to make it one.

Nixon waged a restrained campaign in which he minimized his own participation and left much of the public appearances to his family, Vice President Agnew, and select political supporters like John Connally, who organized "Democrats for Nixon." The election results provided Richard Nixon with his first overwhelming victory in the national political arena. In a landslide victory of near record proportion, Nixon carried 49 states for a total of 521 Electoral College votes—the third largest vote in the nation's history. His 60.7% of the popular vote tally had been surpassed only twice before—by Franklin Roosevelt in 1936 and Lyndon Johnson in 1964. It also marked the defection of the Solid South from the Democratic Party—all the states of the Old Confederacy plus all the border states had swung into the Republican column for the first time since the Reconstruction era. The Republican presidential mandate did not extend through the congressional or gubernatorial ranks of the party, however. While the GOP gained 12 seats in the House, it lost two seats in the Senate as well as one statehouse.

President Nixon began his second term of office riding a wave of popularity that was unprecedented in his political career. The economy seemed to prosper and shortly before his second inauguration, the President announced Phase Three of his economic plan, which relaxed wage and price controls except in the food, health and construction industries. Three days after his inauguration, the President announced a Vietnam peace agreement that included plans for the return of American POWs.

Following the election a major Administration shake-up took place. Since Congress had displayed little interest in cooperating with his first-term proposals for governmental reorganization, the President now embarked on revamping the Administration by executive fiat. According to his *Memoirs*, Nixon approached his second term with three major goals in mind—"to reform the budget and terminate wasteful and ineffective programs"; to initiate "a massive reorganization and reduction of the federal bureaucracy and White House staff" and "to revitalize the Republican Party along New Majority lines."

Even before his second inauguration, Nixon began to construct the "administrative presidency" as a means of gathering in the reins of bureaucratic control. To avoid the typical "downhill" nature of second-term presidencies, Nixon felt he had "to change not only some of the players but also some of the plays . . . ." The keystone of his reorganization plan was the construction of a supercabinet of seven functional area coordinators. Presidential assistants Henry Kissinger and John D. Ehrlichman would preside over foreign affairs and U.S. intergovernmental affairs respectively. In addition Roy Ash, former head of the President's Advisory Council on Executive Organization, was appointed director of OMB and presidential assistant for executive management.

Meanwhile Treasury Secretary Shultz was accorded concurrent status as assistant to the President for economic affairs and Agriculture Secretary Earl Butz was given a similar White House title and responsibility for natural resources. In other cabinet changes George Romney was replaced at HUD by James Lynn, who was also named presidential assistant for community development. Elliot Richardson was moved from HEW to the Defense Department and replaced at HEW by former OMB Director, Caspar Weinberger, who was given overall responsibility for human resources. These attempts to centralize bureaucratic control also included the appointment of new Secretaries of Labor (Peter J. Brennan) and of Transportation (Claude S. Brinegar). In all, the changes seemed to highlight men of known managerial ability and low public profiles. How successful the "administrative presidency" might have been as a tool of executive control became a moot point since such efforts were soon sidetracked and overwhelmed by the emerging Watergate scandal.

Events during 1973 seesawed between diplomatic drama and the tragic revelations of White House political abuses that eventually brought down the Nixon Administration. Announcement of the Vietnam "peace with honor" agreement was soon followed by the creation of a Senate select committee to investigate Watergate. Confirmation hearings for a new FBI director, L. Patrick Gray III, revealed presidential counsel John Dean's involvement in the Bureau's investigation of Watergate and led the trail of suspicion closer to the White House. In the midst of the hearings, the Administration announced the opening of liaison offices between the United States and China to handle cultural and trade exchanges.

The Nixon Administration received a staggering blow in April when two of the President's closest White House aides, H.R. Haldeman and John D. Ehrlichman, were forced to resign because of their apparent implication in the widening Watergate scandal. The following month two former members of the Nixon cabinet—John N. Mitchell and Maurice Stans—were indicted for illegal campaign finance activities during the 1972 elections. The President was also forced to agree to the appointment of an independent special prosecutor to handle the Watergate investigation in order to obtain confirmation of a new Attorney General, Elliot Richardson, after Richard Kleindienst had resigned the post following controversy over the settlement of a Justice Department anti-trust suit against International Telephone and Telegraph.

In June the White House scored another foreign policy success with the week-long visit of Soviet Communist Party leader Leonid I. Brezhnev to the United States. The meeting was hailed as symbolic of the new spirit of detente between the two nations and several agreements were concluded. Although most of these agreements were rather minor in nature (regarding oceanographic, commercial and cultural exchange matters), declarations of principles designed to accelerate the Strategic Arms Limitation Talks (SALT) and to avoid nuclear war were noteworthy.

However, on the domestic scene, both political and economic affairs continued to deteriorate. Inflation continued to soar and the dollar weakened further on the international money market despite Phase Three of the President's economic efforts, which had included the imposition of a price ceiling on certain meats in response to a spring shoppers' boycott against record high prices. Acknowledging that neither voluntary wage and price guidelines nor the limited price control on meats had been effective, President Nixon, on June 13, reimposed a price freeze for 60 days. Meanwhile Congress, criticized for both inflation and the continuing war in Cambodia, took advantage of the President's preoccupation with Watergate to reassert itself and challenge the executive's war-making powers. On June 29 it passed the War Powers Act, which imposed an Aug. 15 deadline for ending combat activities in Indochina and sought to impose limitations on the ability of Presidents to exercise their war-making powers unilaterally and without consultation and consent of Congress. Although the President vetoed the bill, Congress succeeded in overriding his veto.

For the rest of the summer of 1973, Watergate dominated the news. The surprise revelation of a White House taping system by a former White House assistant, Alexander P. Butterfield, to the Senate Watergate Committee touched off a nine-month political and legal battle for the release of these tapes. Throughout the summer the televised Watergate hearings brought the testimony of numerous former Administration officials, such as Haldeman, Ehrlichman, Richard Helms and L. Patrick Gray, III, into the homes of millions of Americans.

There was also controversy over the nomination of national security adviser Henry Kissinger to succeed William Rogers as Secretary of State. The nomination should have been welcomed by the Senate as an indication of better access to foreign policy-making information with Kissinger in a position of formal responsibility and of greater accountability to the Congress. Beclouding the confirmation hearings, however, was concern over Kissinger's role in authorizing the wiretapping of 17 government officials and newsmen from May 1969 to February 1971, in a search for the source of national security leaks. Despite this controversy Kissinger was confirmed and assumed the position of Secretary of State late in September 1973.

Although untouched by the Watergate scandal, Vice President Spiro Agnew added another dimension to corruption within the Administration. Under investigation for alleged conspiracy, extortion and bribery, the Vice President resigned on Oct. 10 as part of a plea bargain that involved his pleading nolo contendere to a charge of income tax evasion. After accepting his sentence of three years unsupervised probation and a $10,000 fine, Agnew made a farewell television address professing his innocence, denouncing witnesses as "self-confessed bribe brokers, extortionists and conspirators" and attacking government prosecutors for "improperly and unconscionably" leaking grand jury proceedings to a press that published "scurrilous and inaccurate reports." He maintained that he had resigned because "the American people deserve to have a vice president who commands their unimpaired confidence and trust" and because he did not want to "subject the country to a further agonizing period of months without an unclouded successor for the presidency."

Two days later in a television ceremony, President Nixon announced his selection of a replacement for Agnew. Invoking for the first time the procedure in the 25th Amendment for filling a vacancy in the vice presidency, Nixon announced his nomination of House Minority Leader Gerald R. Ford (R, Mich.). Ford's confirmation hearings moved quickly in both Houses. Although he repeatedly stated that he did not seek "personal political aggrandizement" and did not intend to seek the presidency in 1976, his confirmation created considerable interest because of speculation that he would become President as a result of either the resignation or impeachment of President Nixon.

The drama surrounding the vice presidency was, however, only the beginning of Administrative problems. On the same day that Gerald Ford's nomination as vice president was announced, the U.S. Circuit Court of Appeals for the District of Columbia upheld an earlier ruling by Judge John Sirica directing President Nixon to surrender Watergate-related tapes. The President, hoping to effect a compromise, offered to supply transcripts of the tapes verified by Sen. John C. Stennis (D, Miss.) if Special Watergate Prosecutor Archibald Cox agreed not to subpoena additional tapes or documents.

Cox refused Nixon's compromise of tape transcripts, saying it would "defeat the fair administration of criminal justice." The President felt that Cox had "deliberately exceeded his authority" and that such a challenge to presidential authority would reflect badly on his prestige at a time of an imminent diplomatic showdown with the Soviets. Hence Nixon decided to fire the special prosecutor and directed Cox's immediate superior, Attorney General Richardson, to carry out his order. Richardson, feeling he had pledged himself to guarantee the independence of the special prosecutor, refused and tendered his resignation. Deputy Attorney General, William Ruckelshaus also resigned rather than carry out the order. Finally the third ranking official at the Justice Department, Solicitor General Robert H. Bork, now acting Attorney General, fired Cox.

Public reaction to what became known as the "Saturday night massacre" was swift and intensely adverse. Characterized by White House Chief of Staff Alexander M. Haig as a "firestorm" of protest, the move precipitated the initiation of impeachment hearings and marked the beginning of the end of the Nixon presidency. Within two days of the firings, House Democratic leaders had tentatively agreed to have the House Judiciary Committee begin an inquiry into the grounds for impeaching the President. Realizing how badly he had underestimated public reaction to the dismissal of the special prosecutor, the President agreed to release the nine subpoenaed tapes and to allow the continuation of the special prosecutor's office under Texas trial lawyer Leon Jaworski, Cox's successor.

In the midst of the Administration's domestic troubles, war had erupted in the Middle East between Egypt and Israel. In response to a U.S. announcement that it would supply Israel with military equipment, the Arab oil-producing nations imposed a ban on oil exports to the U.S. On Oct. 25 American military forces were put on a worldwide nuclear alert in reaction to the possibility of Soviet troop movement into the area. Within hours the situation was eased through Soviet agreement to a proposal for an international peace-keeping force without big power participation. Response to the alert varied widely. Sen. Henry Jackson (D, Wash.) thought the incident had brought the world "right at the brink again." On the other hand there was considerable public skepticism that the crisis was real and it was suggested that the alert was merely an Administration tactic to divert attention from the Watergate scandals. Secretary of State Kissinger denied such speculation, calling it symptomatic of the "crisis of authority" the country was undergoing, and Nixon called it "the most difficult crisis we've had since the Cuban confrontation in 1962."

In the aftermath of the October 1973 Middle East war, Kissinger embarked on a round of "shuttle diplomacy" that brought the Egyptians and the Israelis to their first face-to-face diplomatic encounter in over two decades. The meeting led to an agreement for the exchange of prisoners of war and eventually to an Arab-Israeli peace conference in Geneva in late December 1973.

Dominating the first half of 1974 was the possibility that because of the Watergate scandal Nixon would become the first American President removed from office through impeachment. Probes into the affair had re-

vealed additional campaign illegalities in which the Administration was allegedly involved. In February the House Judiciary Committee began hearings into possible impeachment charges against the President. In March sev-
en former Nixon aides, including Mitchell, Haldeman and Ehrlichman, were
indicted for conspiracy to cover up the Watergate burglary. In April the
Internal Revenue Service (IRS) reported that Nixon owed over $450,000 in
back taxes and interest for the period from 1969 through 1972.

Also during this month the House Judiciary Committee and the special
prosecutor subpoenaed tapes and documents relating to more than 60 presidential conversations. Nixon responded by releasing a 1308-page edited transcript of these materials, but he declined to release the actual tapes and
other documents claiming these were protected by executive privilege. In
the face of mounting congressional, legal and public sentiment against him,
the President continued to deny both knowledge of the Watergate burglary
and participation in the subsequent cover-up.

On July 24 the Supreme Court, in response to a motion by the special
prosecutor, handed down an 8-0 decision against the President's claim that
executive privilege justified his withholding of the subpoenaed tapes. Nixon
then announced, through his attorney James St. Clair, that he would turn
over the tapes. Within a week the House Judiciary Committee approved
three articles of impeachment charging Nixon with obstructing justice in the
Watergate cover-up, misuse of presidential powers, and contempt of Congress for refusing to comply with congressional subpoenas. Bipartisan support within the Committee for the articles strongly indicated that the House
was likely to adopt at least one article of impeachment and thus send the
President to trial in the Senate.

A week after the adoption of the articles of impeachment, Nixon provided
the "smoking gun" in surrendering tapes of conversations on June 23, 1972,
that clearly showed he had participated in the cover-up. With this evidence
remaining congressional support for the President collapsed. On Aug. 8 in a
televised speech, Richard M. Nixon tendered his resignation as President of
the United States, effective at noon of the following day. He thus became
the first President in American history to resign from office.

At 12:03 Vice President Gerald Ford was sworn in as the 38th President
of the United States. He declared that the "long national nightmare" was
now over, and the nation rallied behind him with a strong showing of popular and congressional support. Since he had been a generally well-liked Congressman, it was hoped that under Ford interbranch relations would improve. The new President, in addressing à joint session of Congress, called
for an "era of good feelings" between the executive and the legislature and
expressed confidence that the Congress would be both his "working partner"
and a "most constructive critic."

One of President Ford's earliest actions was to provide for the line of
succession by nominating Nelson A. Rockefeller as vice president. Earlier in
his career Rockefeller had twice turned down the job of vice president,
calling it "standby equipment." Three times before, in 1960, 1964 and 1968,
Rockefeller had made a run for the White House and various political observers believed that he was going to make a fourth attempt in 1976. When

the fall of Richard Nixon brought Gerald Ford to the White House and made him the de facto Republican front-runner for 1976, the former New York governor finally put aside his presidential ambitions and accepted the nomination as vice president.

The choice of this moderate veteran politician who had experience in both state and federal administrations won widespread praise both from Republicans and Democrats as being complimentary to the conservative, congressionally experienced President Ford. Despite this initially favorable reaction to the nomination, the topic of Rockefeller's wealth generated considerable controversy during his confirmation hearings. During four months of grueling hearings, Congress questioned Rockefeller's habit of making loans and gifts to former members of his New York state administrations as well as the wisdom of placing the power of such wealth "only a heartbeat away" from the power of the presidency. Confirmation was finally secured, however, and Nelson Rockefeller was sworn in as vice president on Dec. 19, 1974. Thus, for the first time in its history, the United States had both a President and a vice president selected under the provisions of the 25th Amendment rather than by national election.

Less than three weeks after nominating his new vice president, Ford made a much more controversial decision. He granted former President Nixon a "full, free and absolute pardon . . . for all offenses against the United States which he . . . has committed or may have committed" during his years as President. Seeking to put an end to the "bitter" and "divisive national debate" that had raged for over 18 months and to show the measure of mercy that his conscience dictated was "the right thing to do," Ford exercised his constitutional pardoning power and, in the process, ended his "honeymoon" period with the nation and the Congress. Ford was strongly criticized for circumventing the judicial process and his credibility and popularity suffered. The House Judiciary Committee's Subcommittee on Criminal Justice convened hearings to investigate the reasons for the pardon, and in October Ford became the first sitting President to formally testify before a congressional committee. During that testimony Ford vigorously denied that he had made any secret arrangement with Nixon to grant a pardon in return for the former President's resignation.

The pardon had the effect of tainting Ford with the Watergate scandal. He was further criticized during 1974 for not moving quickly or decisively to replace the Nixon staff with choices of his own. Initial changes were slow and focused on the core members of the White House. Under a new chief of staff, Donald Rumsfeld, the mood in the White House began to relax from the tension and suspense that had permeated the Nixon Administration. Cabinet changes trickled through Ford's first year in office as Attorney General William Saxbe was replaced by Edward H. Levi; Transportation Secretary Claude Brinegar by William Coleman; Commerce Secretary Frederick Dent by Rogers C.B. Morton, who was moved from Interior and replaced there by Stanley Hathaway; and HEW Secretary Caspar Weinberger by F. David Mathews. Since these changes were spread out over a year's time, their impact was fragmented. Thus although President Ford made significant changes in the Administration he had inherited, the public found it difficult to appreciate the extent of the turnover because of its piecemeal character.

Ford also inherited severe economic problems, which had been exacerbated by the sense of drift and the internal battling over economic policy that had occurred as President Nixon became more preoccupied with the Watergate affair. In October 1975 Ford unveiled his WIN ("Whip Inflation Now") program, which consisted of a 5% tax surcharge, voluntary efforts to hold down energy consumption and a tight money policy accompanied by reduced federal spending. The WIN program was severely criticized in Congress as "misdirected and insufficient" and the program soon faded as the Administration shifted attention, early in 1975, from inflation to unemployment, which hovered above 7%.

Criticized for inadequacy in dealing with administrative and domestic problems, Ford found his public popularity declining steadily and his relations with Congress just as troubled (though less acerbic) as those of President Nixon. In reaction to the Watergate scandals, the public had sent a record number of Democrats to Congress in the 1974 midterm elections. The resultant number of liberal and reform-minded Democratic congressmen were dissatisfied and often at odds with the President. With inadequate congressional support, Ford's legislative strategy turned negative as he resorted to the frequent use of the veto and the veto threat. Although Congress frustrated many of the Administration's economic, energy and even foreign policy proposals, it was, however, unable to forge its own policy alternatives.

In contrast with its economic and political problems at home, the Administration found the area of foreign affairs more rewarding. During the autumn of 1974 Ford traveled to Vladivostok to sign an arms limitation agreement with the Soviet Union. The following year he went to Europe three times and ended 1975 with a seven-day visit to China, Indonesia and the Philippines. The European trips dealt with North Atlantic Treaty Organization (NATO) affairs, the formalization of territorial boundaries and the Declaration of Rambouillet, which pledged Western nations and Japan to mutual economic cooperation.

The Ford Administration presided over the final chapter of U.S. involvement in Southeast Asia. A series of military victories by the Communists in March and April brought down the South Vietnamese and Cambodian governments. With the final evacuation of Americans from the area in late April, Ford declared the war "finished as far as America is concerned." There was, however, another episode in the long American saga in Indochina. In response to the May seizure of an American merchant ship, the *Mayaguez*, by Cambodian Communists in the Gulf of Siam, the President ordered U.S. troops to recapture and free the ship and its crew. Despite questions as to whether Ford had fully complied with the congressional consultation provisions of the War Powers Act in sending in American troops, the *Mayaguez* incident prompted an overwhelming rally of congressional and public support for the President.

More troublesome issues emerged in the Middle East and Turkey. During Secretary of State Kissinger's efforts at shuttle diplomacy in the Middle East in the spring and summer of 1975, the Administration announced a "total reassessment" of U.S. policy in the area. The announcement was viewed as an unsubtle form of pressure on Israel to agree to negotiating concessions that would facilitate the search for peace. The Administration further fueled Israeli and Jewish-American opposition by trying to establish better relations with moderate Arab nations such as Jordan and Egypt. Despite these problems Kissinger finally succeeded in working out an agreement between Israel and Egypt that called for Israeli withdrawal from the Sinai mountain passes and oil fields in return for political concessions from Egypt.

Another major problem was the dispute between Turkey and Greece over Cyprus. Following Turkey's July 1974 invasion of Cyprus, congressional sentiment turned against Turkey and, as a result, Congress sought to cut off U.S. military aid to that nation. Although Ford twice vetoed such efforts, Congress imposed an embargo on arms shipments to Turkey, which went into effect on Feb. 5, 1975. The action did nothing to encourage a settlement of the Cyprus issue and worsened U.S.-Turkish relations. Turkey retaliated by taking over U.S. and NATO bases considered essential for Western intelligence gathering. Convinced that its hard-line policy was proving ineffective, Congress eased the embargo in October.

As 1975 ended, Ford reshuffled his national security team, appointed a new member of the Supreme Court, and began to assess his chances for nomination and reelection in 1976. As part of a sweeping personnel change in November, both Defense Secretary James R. Schlesinger and Central Intelligence Agency (CIA) Director William E. Colby were dismissed and replaced by Donald Rumsfeld and George Bush respectively. Although the dismissal of Schlesinger was called a "Kissinger coup," Kissinger did not emerge from the shuffle unaffected. He lost his position as national security assistant, which was assumed by his assistant, Brent Scowcroft. Ford insisted that the changes were prompted by his desire to put together his "own team," but he also admitted that he had not been comfortable with Schlesinger.

Other personnel developments included the retirement of Supreme Court Justice William O. Douglas and the nomination of U.S. Circuit Court Judge John Paul Stevens as his replacement. Vice President Rockefeller withdrew from a potential Republican ticket headed by Ford in 1976. Rockefeller's withdrawal was interpreted as an effort by the President to strengthen his position with the conservatives of the Party, who were opposed to Rockefeller and who were mounting a serious campaign for the nomination of their candidate, former California Gov. Ronald Reagan.

Ford's final year in office was preoccupied by the presidential nomination and election contests. Challenged on the right by Reagan's candidacy and pressured from the left by congressional Democrats, Ford found he had few of the usual advantages of an incumbent seeking reelection. The state of the economy, again a major issue of the campaign, was unstable and far from prosperous. Although the economic system seemed to be slowly recovering from the worst recession since the 1930s, the growth rate of the gross national product was low and the unemployment rate remained above 7%.

In the aftermath of Watergate, the question of ethics and honesty in government became another major issue. Ford's strategy was to cultivate the idea that his Administration had done much to heal the divisive wounds caused by White House scandals and a loss of the public's confidence in government. Yet the taint of Watergate came back to haunt him because of his pardon of former President Nixon.

In the post-Watergate era, the American public wanted not only honest government but also strong leadership, after years of drift and disillusionment. President Ford's record of conflict with Congress, as well as his evident vulnerability within his own Party, cast serious doubts about his ability to lead. Realizing that he was not an incumbent in the traditional sense and that he had never won a national elective constituency, Ford began campaigning in the fall of 1975 and made a good showing in the early primaries of 1976. His campaign organization, however, was weak and disrupted in late March by the resignation of his campaign manager, Howard H. (Bo) Callaway, who was accused of influence peddling.

Because of these problems and a highly effective television campaign by Reagan, the tide began to turn against Ford with Reagan's success in the March North Carolina primary. Throughout the remaining primaries, Reagan and Ford ran neck and neck, with Ford emerging in June with only a slight delegate lead. As the Republican Convention convened in Kansas City in mid-August, the Party was more evenly divided than it had been in over two decades. Ford threw all the status of the presidency into a last-minute push for the nomination, while Reagan overplayed his hand in an attempt to win wider appeal. Trying to woo liberal and middle-of-the-road Republicans to his banner (and to corner a large state delegation vote), Reagan announced his choice of a running mate just before the Convention met. His selection of liberal Pennsylvania Sen. Richard Schweiker, however, backfired, alienating some of his conservative supporters and repelling, rather than attracting, some uncommitted delegates.

When the Convention voted, Ford won on the first ballot with a thin margin of 1187 to Reagan's 1070. As a running mate Ford chose Kansas Sen. Robert Dole, an outspoken, aggressive political fighter. Furthermore, selection of the conservative Dole was designed to appeal to Reagan and his backers and thus promote Party unity.

Meanwhile the Democratic side produced a multitude of candidates ranging from Alabama's Gov. George Wallace to Arizona Rep. Morris Udall. Yet out of a field that included many well-known national and Party figures, a dark-horse candidate, former Georgia Gov. Jimmy Carter, emerged as the front-runner. Carter's campaign did not so much emphasize issues as personal qualities like honesty, competence and trustworthiness. Throughout the primaries Carter engineered and benefited from a process of elimination of the other contenders. Finally, as the indisputable leader in June, Carter won the Democratic nomination on the first ballot, amidst the rallying of the various Party segments behind him. After a long deliberative process, Carter selected Minnesota Sen. Walter Mondale, a protege of Hubert Humphrey and the preference of labor and liberals, as his running mate.

The election campaign of 1976 presented an acutely undecided electorate with the prospect of a return to normalcy after the traumas of Vietnam and

Watergate. While the issue of trust in government dominated the campaign, neither candidate seemed particularly able to generate or hold the public's confidence. Gerald Ford, the unelected incumbent, had been bloodied in the primaries and still carried the stigma of the Nixon pardon. Jimmy Carter, the "outsider," promised never to lie to the public and campaigned against the Washington establishment, yet he still appeared an unknown and untested leader. In such a climate of public uncertainty, both candidates needed to sharpen and improve their images. Hence both Ford and Carter saw advantages to engaging in the first televised debates between presidential candidates since those of Kennedy and Nixon in 1960.

After an initial lead in the popularity polls, Carter's rating dropped precipitously in late September. Contributing to this decline were an interview with Carter published in *Playboy* magazine and his poor showing in the first TV debate. The *Playboy* interview was Carter's most serious blunder and his statements there came back to haunt him repeatedly during the campaign. He eventually apologized to Lady Bird Johnson for having said that Lyndon Johnson had lied, cheated and distorted the truth. He never did quite live down the notoriety of his admission in *Playboy* to having "looked on a lot of women with lust" and to having "committed adultery in my heart many times." Carter, however, staged a comeback in the second and third debates. Particularly damaging to Ford was his assertion during the Oct. 6 debate that "there is no Soviet domination of Eastern Europe," a statement he later recanted.

As the American voter went to the polls on Nov. 2, 1976, the election contest was considered too close to call. When the votes were counted, Carter beat Ford narrowly by less than two million popular votes and by an Electoral College vote of 297 to 240.

The nation's bicentennial election contest produced a rural, Southern Baptist ex-governor as the 39th President of the United States. For some Carter's election became a symbol for a South risen again and finally reintegrated into the Union. Carter began the country's third century with a call for "a new beginning, a new dedication . . . and a new spirit among us all" linked to the pursuit of "an old dream," that of "faith in our country—and in one another."

Carter's inauguration marked the end of the Nixon/Ford years. Those years had seen war, peace and extensive diplomatic activity; nagging domestic problems, particularly those related to the economy; and scandal that had produced high political drama and tragedy. The eight Republican years, starting with Richard Nixon's election as President in 1968, had confronted the issues of peace, prosperity and public confidence in government. When the Republican Administration left office in 1976, the Vietnam war was ended, detente with the Soviet Union had been nurtured and relations with Communist China had been reopened. Its record on the other two issues was, however, less commendable.

The economic situation was certainly no better, and probably worse, than eight years earlier. Inflation and unemployment seemed intractable problems, and over the years the American public had become less optimistic about the state of the economy and the prospects that better days were just around the corner. Public confidence had declined even further in the wake of the Watergate scandals and the resignation of both a President and a vice president disgraced in office. Thus after eight years only the issue of war had changed; the search for prosperity and for confidence in government and its officials continued.

ABEL, I(ORWITH) W(ILBUR)
b. Aug. 11, 1908; Magnolia, Ohio.
President, United Steelworkers of
America, 1965-77.

The son of a small town blacksmith, Abel attended Canton Ohio Actual Business College before working in a local steel-rolling mill in 1925. In 1936, while a foundryman for the Timken Roller Bearing Co., Abel joined the Congress of Industrial Organizations (CIO). That same year he helped establish the Timken plant's first local of the Steel Workers Organizing Committee, the predecessor of the United Steelworkers of America (USW).

He played an active role in union affairs, and in 1937 he was appointed staff representative by the president of the Steel Workers Organizing Committee, Phillip Murray. In 1952 when David J. MacDonald became president of the United Steelworkers, Abel assumed the post of secretary-treasurer.

In 1965 he became president after defeating MacDonald in one of the most bitter campaigns in the union's history. He strengthened ties with other unions in the AFL-CIO and sided with its conservative president, George Meany [q.v.], during Meany's dispute over foreign policy matters with United Automobile Workers President Walter Reuther [q.v.]. When Reuther quit the labor federation, Abel was given Reuther's position as head of the AFL-CIO Industrial Union Department.

In 1969 Abel was reelected by a surpris-

ingly thin margin considering his national reputation and the relative obscurity of his opponent, union lawyer Emil E. Narick. Major steel-making districts such as Pittsburgh and Chicago were particularly anti-Abel, reflecting discontent with the 1968 contract, which had not included a cost-of-living clause or stronger guarantees of job security. Many local union officials felt that Abel's promises of greater consultation with the rank and file were largely unfulfilled.

In July 1970 President Nixon named Abel and five other national labor leaders to the National Commission on Productivity. The purpose of the Commission was to "seek a balance between costs and productivity which would stabilize prices."

In September, Abel opened the union's national convention with a fiery condemnation of the "Republican inflation program" and of the corporate "greed for profits." He accused the Nixon Administration of expecting the workers to bear the burden of the anti-inflation campaign through pay cuts and increased unemployment. Union delegates to the convention pressed Abel to make major demands at the 1971 contract talks with the steel industry. Abel announced that the USW would seek a "very, very substantial wage increase," and a new cost-of-living clause.

In April of 1971, following a warning to the steel industry from the President's Council of Economic Advisers against "excessive wage increases," Abel responded that the steelworker was the victim, not the cause, of inflation and characterized the economic policies of the Nixon Administration as "disastrous."

In the summer of 1971 Abel negotiated a new contract with the steel industry. The agreement included a wage increase and a cost-of-living provision. Abel called the agreement the "best ever," while chief steel industry negotiator R. Heath Larry said that the agreement was inflationary but necessary to avert a strike. The contract also included a clause linking future wages and benefits to increased productivity, which was to become a point of controversy within the union.

On Aug. 15 President Nixon, in a complete reversal of previous policies, imposed a 90-day wage-price freeze, dubbed "Phase One" of an overall economic program. In October, Abel was one of five union leaders named to a federal Pay Board that consisted of representatives from labor, industry and the general public. The Board was designed to regulate wage increases, limiting them to 5.5%. But differences with the Administration grew and in March 1972 Abel joined George Meany, Floyd Smith of the International Association of Machinists and Leonard Woodcock [q.v.] of the United Automobile Workers in quitting the Board. In a joint statement Abel, Meany and Smith declared that the Board offered labor "no hope for fairness, equity or justice." Nixon condemned the walkout as "selfish and irresponsible" and hastily restructured the Board.

Abel supported the candidacy of Sen. Henry M. Jackson (D, Wash) [q.v.] for the Democratic presidential nomination in 1972. At the Miami convention in July, he delivered Jackson's seconding speech. When the nomination went to Sen. George McGovern [q.v.], Abel joined George Meany in withholding his support for the campaign.

In March 1973 Abel signed the Experimental Negotiating Agreement (ENA) with the steel industry, an accord that granted various wage and cost-of-living guarantees to steelworkers in return for a no-strike clause in which unresolved issues would be submitted to binding arbitration. The agreement was to apply to all contract talks until 1980. Despite some opposition to the ENA, Abel was elected to a third term on June 1.

In January 1974 dissident members of Abel's union filed a class action to void the ENA on the grounds that the agreement had been reached without its submission to the general membership for approval. But the suit was rejected on March 26 by a federal district court in Pittsburgh, which stated that inasmuch as the union was a "representative democracy" and not "a pure democracy," the agreement was "legally irreproachable."

A new three-year steel contract was reached in April following negotiations conducted under the ENA for the first time. The new pact included wage increases and left no unresolved issues.

Abel was barred by the union constitution from running for a fourth term, and he ignored the suggestions of his followers that he seek to amend the constitution at the August 1976 union convention. However he remained active in union politics and helped his supporter Lloyd McBride win the presidency in 1977.

[MDQ]

ABERNATHY, RALPH D(AVID)
b. March 11, 1926; Linden, Ala.
President, Southern Christian
Leadership Conference, 1968-77.

The grandson of a slave, Ralph Abernathy was raised on his parents' 500-acre farm in Alabama. He was ordained a Baptist minister in 1948, and received his B.S. from Alabama College in 1950 and an M.A. in sociology from Atlanta University the following year. In 1951 Abernathy was appointed pastor of the First Baptist Church in Montgomery and became close friends with the Rev. Martin Luther King, Jr., whom he accompanied in the early civil rights demonstrations. He and King, with several other black ministers, established the Southern Christian Leadership Conference (SCLC) in 1957 to end segregation and win full civil rights for Southern blacks through nonviolent protest. [See EISENHOWER Volume]

During the 1960s Abernathy was King's closest friend and adviser. Their protest campaign in Selma, Ala., attracted national attention and helped win enactment of the Voting Rights Act of 1965. During the late 1960s the SCLC leadership became interested in other economic and social issues affecting the poor, both black and white. After King was assassinated in Memphis on April 4, 1968, Abernathy, who was with him at the time, became president of SCLC and led the Poor People's Campaign in Washington. For several weeks in May and June, thousands of poor people camped out in "Resurrection City" in Potomac Park, attended sessions of Congress to present their demands and demonstrated outside government buildings. [See KENNEDY, JOHNSON Volumes]

Under Abernathy's leadership, the SCLC concentrated on broad social and economic issues other than civil rights. Still firmly committed to nonviolence, Abernathy was especially concerned with forging a coalition of all the disaffected groups rising to speak out. He regularly appeared at anti-war rallies, endorsed the grape pickers boycott sponsored by Cesar Chavez [q.v.] and the United Farm Workers (UFW) and participated in a week-long UFW march through California in May 1969. The defense efforts of anti-war activists in the Chicago and Harrisburg conspiracy trials also received his support.

Targeting unemployment and poverty as the major civil rights issues, Abernathy took a leading role in the 1969 strike of hospital workers in Charleston, S.C. The strike began on March 20 after 12 union organizers were fired from their jobs. After a court injunction was issued against picketing, Abernathy led daily marches through the city, resulting in several hundred arrests. The strikers' demands for union recognition and a living wage were endorsed by major civil rights spokesmen, liberal senators and representatives, and union leaders. The demonstrations continued into June, when Abernathy was indicted on charges of inciting to riot

after some protesters had damaged property. The strike was settled, however, on June 27 when the hospitals agreed to rehire all of the workers dismissed earlier and to recognize the union.

Abernathy, meanwhile, was organizing a second Poor People's Campaign, which began on May 12. Throughout the spring and summer, delegations of poor people from all races met with congressional officials, held small demonstrations in Washington and lobbied intensively for social and economic welfare legislation. Their demands included jobs for all, a guaranteed annual income, a comprehensive health care program, quality education for all children and a shift from defense expenditures to government spending on basic human needs.

In 1969 SCLC sponsored an intensive voter registration drive in Greene County, Ala., that resulted in the election of six blacks to local office and a black majority on the school board. It initiated demonstrations in Chicago during the summer of 1969 to protest the discriminatory hiring policies of the city's construction unions. In May 1970, after police in Augusta, Ga., killed five young blacks during a protest march, Abernathy led 10,000 people on a 100-mile march to protest police violence against blacks. He supported the efforts of welfare recipients in Nevada to have arbitrary welfare cuts rescinded, and in April 1971 he was arrested in New York City during a demonstration against A & P hiring practices.

Abernathy found himself increasingly at odds with the Nixon Administration. In January 1969 he and several other black leaders met with the President, who promised to do "more for the underprivileged and more for the Negro" than any other President. Four months later Abernathy met with Nixon again and later told the press that it was "the most disappointing and most fruitless of all the meetings we have had up to this time." He opposed the Administration's proposed relaxation of school desegregation guidelines, the nominations of Clement Haynsworth [q.v.] and G. Harrold Carswell [q.v.] to the Supreme Court and the White House attempt to weaken the 1965 Voting Rights Act. By the summer of 1970 Abernathy was so disillusioned with Nixon's policies that he termed the Administration "a repressive, anti-black, anti-poor, anti-youth national government" under "fascist domination."

With other militant civil rights leaders and anti-war activists, Abernathy helped form the People's Coalition for Peace and Justice. In April and May 1971, the Coalition sponsored a series of daily demonstrations against the war, poverty, and government repression. On April 29 Abernathy conducted a "teach-in" at HEW and led a mule train from the Department's offices to the White House. The following day he read a "poor people's bill of particulars" against the Justice Department. The police began making mass arrests a few days later and held over 7,000 demonstrators in make-shift jails. The arrests and convictions were later overturned because of widespread violations of constitutional rights.

Despite Abernathy's energetic leadership, the SCLC was plagued by internal difficulties during the 1970s. In December 1971, its board of directors suspended the Rev. Jesse Jackson [q.v.], head of SCLC's Operation "Breadbasket," in a dispute over the use of funds. Jackson responded by resigning, announced the formation of his own organization, Operation PUSH (People United to Save Humanity), and took most of SCLC's Chicago chapter with him. The following year SCLC fired 21 workers at its national headquarters in Atlanta due to budget difficulties. Although in the late 1960s the SCLC had easily raised over $2 million a year, by 1973 income had fallen to half a million dollars. On July 9, 1973 Abernathy announced his resignation as the organization's president. He blamed SCLC's problems on middle-class blacks who "feel they have 'arrived' simply because they now occupy high positions, but will not support SCLC financially." When the board of directors rejected his resignation Abernathy agreed to stay on. By the mid 1970s, however, SCLC was only a shadow of its former self and had ceased to play a leading role in the struggle for racial justice.

In 1977 Abernathy ran unsuccessfully to fill the Georgia congressional seat vacated when President Carter appointed Representative Andrew Young [q.v.] as U.S. ambassador to the United Nations. He continued to serve as SCLC president.

[JD]

ABPLANALP, ROBERT H.
b. 1923, New York, N. Y.
Businessman.

The son of Swiss immigrants, Abplanalp attended Villanova College for a short time before dropping out during World War II to open a machine shop in Yonkers, N.Y. There he perfected the aerosol valve and began manufacturing his invention at the Precision Valve Co. in 1949. The invention made Abplanalp a millionaire. By 1971 the company was grossing $50 million a year and Abplanalp's personal fortune was estimated at $100 million.

Abplanalp contributed to Richard Nixon's 1960 presidential contest and was introduced to Nixon in 1963. Soon thereafter Nixon's New York law firm began representing Precision Valve Co. overseas. In 1966 Abplanalp bought the island of Grand Cay in the Bahamas and built a luxury compound. Nixon, by now a fast friend, paid frequent visits to the island, visits that became more frequent after Nixon became President.

The island was a refuge for the troubled President during the Watergate period. Often, Nixon and Abplanalp were in one another's company as Nixon prepared a new defense or recovered from new charges. In the worst days of Watergate, when impeachment loomed and Nixon withheld information even from his lawyers, a source close to Nixon said "the only people he will talk to candidly about Watergate are Bebe Rebozo [q.v.] and Bob Abplanalp." Rebozo was another millionaire who often joined Grand Cay fishing trips.

Abplanalp was also involved in Nixon's personal financing. Nixon's home in San Clemente, Calif., was purchased with the help of a $625,000 loan from Abplanalp, a financial arrangement that was revealed after a California newspaper charged that Nixon financed San Clemente with $1 million in unreported 1968 campaign funds.

In 1973 the General Services Administration reported that $10 million in new security arrangements ordered by Nixon and paid for by the government were detailed for Nixon's own homes in San Clemente and Key Biscayne, Fla., and at the Abplanalp complex at Grand Cay. The figures showed that $160,000 in communications equipment had been installed at Grand Cay and a $16,000 bunk house for secret service agents was built for use during Nixon's visits.

Abplanalp was investigated by special Watergate prosecutor Archibald Cox [q.v.] after a 1971 Justice Department decision to drop anti-trust charges against Precision Valve Co. was revealed. Presidential critics said the charges were dropped because of Nixon's friendship with Abplanalp, but Cox found no evidence of price violations or presidential influence.

Abplanalp and Nixon remained friends following the President's resignation.

[BO]

ABRAMS, CREIGHTON W(ILLIAM), (JR)

b. Sept. 15, 1914; Springfield, Mass.
d. Sept. 4, 1974; Washington, D.C.
Commander, U.S. Military Assistance Command, Vietnam, June 1968-June 1972; Army Chief of Staff, June 1972-September 1974.

Creighton Abrams graduated from West Point in 1936 and during World War II distinguished himself as the commander of the 37th Tank Battalion. He served as chief of staff of several Army corps in Korea in 1953 and 1954. While assigned to the Pentagon in the early 1960s, he was in charge of the federal troops that were placed on alert in the deep South to prevent racial violence during desegregation. A general since 1956 Abrams was elevated to the rank of four star general in 1964. He was deputy commander of the U.S. Military Assistance Command in South Vietnam in 1967 and 1968.

In June 1968 Abrams succeeded Gen. William Westmoreland [q.v.] as commander of the half-million American troops stationed in South Vietnam. Abrams' handling of the war was dictated in large measure by Johnson's decision in March 1968 to place a limit on U.S. military involvement in South Vietnam at its present level, to deescalate the fighting and to renew efforts for a negotiated end to the conflict.

In May preliminary peace talks between the U.S. and North Vietnam began in Paris. The negotiations took a more substantive form in January of the following year when, at Abrams' urging, the South Vietnamese entered the talks. He arranged for weapons aid and helped to overcome the Saigon government's reluctance to join negotiations that included the National Liberation Front. [See JOHNSON Volume]

Abrams continued as the U.S. commander in Vietnam under President Nixon. With the new Administration came a change in war policy. No longer did the initiative for running the war come from the U.S. command in Saigon; it now came from the White House and Henry Kissinger [q.v.]. The Nixon Administration had decided to "wind down" the war. While strengthening South Vietnamese forces in the difficult task of Vietnamization, a term to describe the goal of making South Vietnam capable of defending itself, Abrams was also charged with breaking contact with a still-able enemy and withdrawing U.S. forces. Troop withdrawals began in August 1969.

To carry out his new mission, Abrams modified Westmoreland's tactics. He deemphasized Westmoreland's search-and-destroy missions, designed to engage the enemy's large units in a war with no fronts. Abrams replaced ground forces with planes as troop reductions proceeded. He relied upon large deployments of artillery and precision B-52 strikes to defeat the enemy in medium- and large-scale engagements. Abrams gave subordinate commanders unusually wide latitude and increased night patrols and ambushes, favoring "spoiler" patrols of four or five men sent out to disrupt the enemy.

Abrams and other top military leaders resisted but went along with the Nixon Administration's "orderly scheduled timetable" for the disengagement of U.S. forces from South Vietnam. The exact timetable was based on the pace of Vietnamization, progress at the Paris peace talks and the extent of the Communist military threat.

In May 1970 President Nixon, in a move proposed since 1965 by a series of defense and foreign affairs advisers and strongly advocated by Abrams, ordered U.S. combat forces to attack North Vietnamese sanctuaries in Cambodia along the South Vietnamese border. The goal, which was accomplished, was to buy one year of grace from an enemy attack against South Vietnam to allow Vietnamization needed time. Domestic political reaction against the incursion prompted the Administration to limit it to eight weeks. In pursuit of the same military results, the U.S. command furnished much of the logistical, air and artillery support for the movement of South Vietnamese troops into Laos in February 1971.

Abrams was named Army chief of staff in June 1972. His confirmation was delayed as the Senate Armed Services Committee looked into allegations by Lt. Gen. John D. Lavelle [q.v.] that Abrams shared responsibility with him for unauthorized air strikes against North Vietnam in late 1971 and early 1972. Abrams denied the allegations before the Committee. He said he did not know that Lavelle's raids were unauthorized, nor that false postaction reports had covered up the nature of the missions. The Committee's investigation

supported Abrams' claims and his nomination was approved in October. Abrams appeared before the Committee again in 1973 to answer charges that he had taken part in the cover-up of secret Cambodian bombing operations in 1969 and 1970. While acknowledging that he was fully informed of the secret B-52 raids, he denied responsibility for the falsification of reports, saying that special reporting procedures, authorized by the Joint Chiefs of Staff, had been used in the operation.

Abrams returned from Vietnam convinced that the Army needed to reduce its "support tail." He abolished seven Army headquarters around the world, reduced desk jobs in favor of more fighting strength and worked to update the training of the reserve forces. As peace talks in Paris entered a new serious phase in October 1972, Abrams was ordered to South Vietnam to discover what additional arms would be needed by Saigon to make a cease-fire acceptable. Before the end of the month a massive airlift of planes, tanks and ammunition began, based in part on Abrams' recommendations. After the Paris peace accords of 1973, Abrams, in his role as Army chief, sought to stimulate subordinates to make the new volunteer Army work.

Abrams supported the Nixon Administration's pursuit of a policy of detente. However the Strategic Arms Limitation Talks (SALT) I agreement between the U.S. and the Soviet Union, signed by Nixon in Moscow in 1972, caused some dissent among the Joint Chiefs. There were fears that the Administration had given too much away. Abrams broke the silence of the military about detente in October 1973, during the Yom Kippur war in the Mideast, declaring, "the word 'detente' for some people evidently colors everything rose and turns their perceptions away from even obvious threats." He cautioned that it was necessary to keep the military's strength up to par. Abrams died in September 1974 of complications following lung cancer surgery.

[SF]

ABZUG, BELLA (STAVISKY)
b. July 24, 1920; New York, N.Y.
Democratic Representative, N.Y.,
1971-77.

Bella Stavisky, the daughter of a butcher, graduated from Hunter College in 1942. She then worked in a shipbuilding factory to help in the war effort. She met Maurice Abzug and married him in June 1944. After the war she returned to Columbia Law School and graduated in 1947. While at Columbia she was editor of the *Columbia Law Review.*

Abzug worked as a labor lawyer during the 1950s, representing fur workers, restaurant workers, auto workers, longshoremen and civil rights workers. She was active in opposing Sen. Joseph McCarthy's anti-Communism and defended people accused of subversive activities, including several groups of New York school teachers.

Abzug won a reputation as a leader of liberal and radical causes during the 1960s. In 1961 after the failure of the nuclear test ban treaty, she and several other women founded the Women's Strike for Peace, which urged worldwide disarmament and an end to nuclear testing. In 1967 and 1968 she was active in the Democratic Party's "dump Johnson" politics, and in 1968 she was one of the founders of both the "Coalition for a Democratic Alternative," which supported the candidacy of Sen. Eugene McCarthy [q.v.] and the Coalition for an Open Convention. After Richard M. Nixon was elected President in 1968, she joined with other Democrats to found the New Democratic Coalition.

In 1970 Bella Abzug won a House seat from New York City's 19th ward, a polyglot district including the Lower East Side, Chinatown, Little Italy, Greenwich Village and the Upper West Side. From her first moment in Washington, her unrestrained enthusiasm and flamboyance won her many enemies who felt that new representatives, and especially women, should be seen and not heard. In her first

confrontation with her Democratic colleagues, she tried to have herself assigned to the House Armed Services Committee. Rep. F. Edward Hebert (D, La) [q.v.], the chairman of that Committee, refused the request, and she was assigned to the Public Works Committee and the Government Operations Committee. On her first day in office after being sworn in, she introduced a bill calling for the withdrawal of troops from Vietnam by July 4, 1971. It was tabled within a week by the deft political maneuvering of conservative House members who were offended by her "brashness."

After the 1970 census returns verified that New York City had lost population and would therefore lose one of its four Representatives, a struggle arose among New York politicians over which district would be gerrymandered. The state legislature led by a Republican majority decided that Abzug's district would be carved up. That left her with the option of challenging John Murray, a conservative from Staten Island; senior House member Edward Koch [q.v.] from the upper East Side; William Ryan [q.v.] an outstanding liberal candidate whose 20th district included 30% of Abzug's old district; or Charles Rangel, one of the few blacks in the House. She decided to challenge the ailing Ryan.

Abzug's decision split the district's liberal Democratic vote. Since both she and Ryan agreed on the issues and both had comparable liberal records, the contest came down to their personalities. In June Ryan won the primary. When Ryan died eight weeks before the November election, his supporters refused to concede to Abzug and ran Ryan's wife, Patricia, instead. In the general election Abzug won handily.

Bella Abzug made her impact felt on the House as an impassioned anti-war critic and as a feminist. She supported and spoke at many of the anti-war rallies both in Washington, D.C. and New York City. She and four other Representatives were castigated by their more conservative House colleagues for "inciting to riot" a number of anti-war protesters whom they had invited to speak on the House steps during the May Day demonstrations of 1971. In April 1971 after the My Lai massacre had been exposed, she planned to head a war atrocities probe. Again in January 1972 after the bombings of Hanoi and the mining of Haiphong harbor, she introduced a motion to censure President Nixon. On May 10 she offered an impeachment resolution based on Nixon's conduct of the war.

As a feminist Abzug supported the Equal Rights Amendment and spoke at and helped form the National Women's Political Caucus in July 1971. A month later she encouraged one of her staff members, Cynthia Edgar, to bring suit against the FBI, Attorney General John Mitchell [q.v.] and FBI Director J. Edgar Hoover [q.v.] for sex discrimination. An FBI agent had told Edgar that women need not apply to the FBI for employment because they "do not command enough respect" and because they "could not handle combat situations."

During that same year she sponsored a $5 billion child care bill, eventually vetoed by President Nixon. In 1973 and 1974 she continued to champion such feminist causes as a women's credit rights bill, abortion rights, a national women's convention, equalization of pay between men and women and welfare reform. Although her politics won her a 100% rating for both 1973 and 1974 from the liberal Americans for Democratic Action, they also earned her a place on President Nixon's "enemies list."

Close to the end of her term, Abzug decided, with four other Democrats, to seek the nomination for U.S. senator from New York. She lost the Democratic nomination to Patrick Moynihan [q.v.] by less than 1% of the vote in a hard fought and often rancorous battle. In 1977 she lost the Democratic primary for mayor of New York City to Edward Koch.

[SJT]

ACKLEY, (HUGH) GARDNER
b. June 30, 1915; Indianapolis, Ind.
Economist.

Gardner Ackley earned his doctorate in economics from the University of Michigan in 1940. A supporter of the New Deal, he worked for the Office of Price Administration during World War II and served for a year with the Office of Strategic Services. After the war he taught economics at the University of Michigan.

Ackley became a member of the President's Council of Economic Advisers (CEA) in 1962 and chairman of the CEA in 1964. Ackley was an enthusiastic proponent of the Keynesian "new economics," which held that the federal government could promote economic growth and maintain price stability through an activist fiscal policy. During the late 1960s, a period of economic boom and large budget deficits incurred to finance the Vietnam war, Ackley fought the inflation accompanying the war by pressuring business and labor to remain within the Administration's wage-price guidelines. He also urged a 10% tax surcharge, finally passed in 1968. That year President Johnson appointed Ackley ambassador to Italy. He remained there until August 1969 when he returned to the University of Michigan as a professor of economics. [See JOHNSON Volume]

In January 1970 Ackley was named chairman of the Democratic Policy Council's Committee on Economic Affairs, a post he held until 1972. At that post Ackley emerged as a major critic of the Nixon Administration's economic policies. He criticized Nixon's goal of balancing the federal budget as a means of reducing the nation's unemployment rate. He deplored, for example, the President's veto of a Health, Education and Welfare appropriations bill in 1970 as "a gross oversimplification for political purposes." Ackley asserted that White House policies had allowed productivity to stagnate while inflation continued. He called for wage-price guidelines to control inflation and said that the nation could tolerate a budget deficit of up to $10 billion to check a long period of "chronic and creeping paralysis."

In 1971 he denounced the Administration's liberalization of business depreciation allowances as part of a "lamentable set of priorities" and reemphasized the need for a more expansionary fiscal policy. Ackley, however, praised the President's wage-price freeze, the opening of a three-phase program introduced in 1971 as a "vital first step." He urged that the freeze be followed by a "social compact" among business, labor and other groups limiting further price increases and spreading out cost-of-living wage hikes over time. He also said that a proposed excess profits tax would further dampen productivity since profits were already at a low level.

In 1973 Ackley reacted favorably to the lifting of mandatory wage-price controls except in the food, health and construction fields, but warned that the voluntary controls of phase three required the vigorous use of "standby" government authority when necessary to control inflation. But Ackley asserted that President Ford's proposed budget cuts in 1974 would only further weaken an already shaky economy. The federal budget, he argued, was not the main source of inflation and federal, state and local budgets must be viewed together.

As a columnist Ackley continued to criticize the nation's economic policies.

[FLM]

ADDONIZIO, HUGH J(OSEPH)
b. Jan. 31, 1914; Newark, N.J.
Mayor, Newark, N.J., 1962-70.

After graduating from Fordham University in 1939, Addonizio returned to Newark to work for his father's clothing business. The son of Italian immigrants, Addonizio was elected to the U.S. House in 1948 and repeatedly reelected thereafter with the strong support of black and Italian voters. In 1962 Addonizio resigned from the House to run for mayor of Newark and defeated the incumbent Leo P. Carlin.

Newark experienced racial violence twice while Addonizio was mayor: first in the summer of 1967 and again in the spring of 1969. Sparked by the fatal shooting of a black youth by a black policeman on May 19, 1969, ensuing riots forced the mayor to impose a curfew on the city and close all bars and liquor stores. Order was restored two days later after Addonizio met with black and white community leaders. [See JOHNSON Volume]

On Dec. 18, 1969, Addonizio and nine present or former municipal administrators were indicted by a federal grand jury on charges of payoff extortion, conspiracy and tax evasion. The defendants allegedly extorted nearly $253,000 in kickbacks from an engineering firm, Constrad Inc., under contract to Newark's Municipal Utilities Authority. Addonizio pleaded not guilty to the charges and declared that he had no intention of resigning his office despite demands for his immediate removal by the Newark *Star-Ledger* and the Greater Newark Chamber of Commerce.

In the 1970 mayoral race, Addonizio campaigned as a moderate, calling himself the logical choice while characterizing his strongest opponent, Kenneth Gibson [q.v.], as a representative of the radical elements in Newark. On May 12, 1970, Addonizio received only half as many votes as Gibson, coming in a distant second in the seven-candidate race. While Addonizio campaigned for a June 16 runoff election, his trial opened in federal district court in Trenton. Gibson defeated Addonizio in the runoff, becoming Newark's first black mayor.

After deliberating for nearly six hours on July 22, 1970, the jury returned guilty verdicts against Addonizio and four other defendants on 64 counts of conspiracy to extort over $250,000 in kickbacks. Key testimony came from Paul Rigo, head of Constrad Inc., who said that he made specific payments to each of the defendants, fearing that if he did not cooperate with them, his life as well as his contract with the city would be in jeopardy. Addonizio was released on his own recognizance until sentencing.

On Sept. 22, 1970, Addonizio was sentenced to 10 years in prison and fined $25,000. He remained free pending appeal, but the court later refused to hear his appeal on Feb. 22, 1972. Addonizio began serving his sentence in Lewisburg, Pa., in March. He was refused parole by the U.S. Parole Board in July 1975. His second appeal for release was also rejected by the U.S. Parole Board in February 1976.

[AFB]

AGEE, PHILIP
b. July 19, 1935; Tacoma Park, Fla.
Central Intelligence Agency critic.

The Florida-born son of a businessman, Philip Agee attended a Jesuit high school before graduating from Notre Dame University in June of 1956. Recruited into the Central Intelligence Agency (CIA) in 1957, Agee swore to "be a warrior against Communist subversive erosion of freedom and personal liberties around the world—a patriot dedicated to the preservation of my country and our way of life." Following three years of military training taken under CIA auspices, Agee was assigned to the Western Hemisphere Division, serving in Ecuador, Uruguay and Mexico from 1960 to 1968. That year he resigned as the result of his growing disillusionment over U.S. Latin American policies. He later defined the CIA as "nothing more than the secret police of American capitalism, plugging up leaks in the political dam . . . so that shareholders of U.S. companies operating in poor countries can continue enjoying their rip-off." Writing retrospectively, Agee explained that "Once out of the CIA . . . I began to feel I could make a contribution to the campaign against the Vietnam war by showing how Vietnams germinate wherever the CIA is at work."

In early 1970 Agee began work on his best-seller, *Inside the Company: CIA Diary.* An expose of the Agency's day-to-day South American operations, the book covered a period of 18 years. It listed nearly 250 persons, referred to as officers, local agents, informers or collaborators of the CIA, whose main objective was defined as the counteraction of Cuban influence in the Western Hemisphere. It also offered a description of CIA infiltration of local political parties, cooperation with local police forces to eliminate leftist subversives, tampering with local mail services and the wiretapping of embassies of Communist countries.

Agee was first published in London by Penguin Books in early 1975 due to fear of censorship in the United States. He maintained that he had experienced various forms of CIA harassment during the research and writing of the book. Although the CIA refused comment on the book's veracity, Miles Copeland, a former CIA official of high rank, reported that as an "account of how an ordinary American or British case officer operates . . . all of it . . . is presented with deadly accuracy."

To further inform the public of CIA operations, Agee wrote articles and gave speeches and lectures. His testimony before the second Bertrand Russell Tribunal—reconvened in Brussels, Belgium, from Jan. 11 to Jan. 18, 1975—was in part responsible for the court's verdict "morally condemning" President Gerald Ford and former President Richard Nixon for "encouraging and favoring" foreign economic domination of Latin America and for causing the military coup against the late Chilean President Salvador Allende. Agee maintained that the CIA had kept personal name checks of Venezuelan employees of the Creole Petroleum Corp., a subsidiary of the U.S. Exxon Corp., and that the CIA performed this service customarily for subsidiaries of large U.S. corporations.

In November 1976 Agee, who had been living in England since 1972, was ordered expelled as a security risk, allegedly because he had been meeting regularly with foreign agents, primarily Cubans. Agee became a cause celebre among journalists, civil libertarians and members of Parliament who hinted that CIA pressure was responsible for the move. Agee left Great Britain in June 1977, and after being expelled from France as "undesirable," he went to Belgium. He then moved to the Netherlands, where he was asked to leave at the end of 1977.

During the 1970s Agee edited the magazine *Counterspy*. In 1975, when CIA station chief Richard Welch was assassinated in Athens, the Agency blamed Agee because he had identified Welch as a CIA official in the magazine. Three years later Agee published *Dirty Work*, which reprinted a number of anti-CIA articles published elsewhere. The most distinctive feature of the book was a 415-page appendix, a dossier of over 700 CIA operatives.

[SBB]

AGNEW, SPIRO T(HEODORE)
b. Nov. 9, 1918; Baltimore, Md.
Vice President of the United States, January 1969-October 1973.

Agnew, whose father was a Greek immigrant, attended Johns Hopkins University and the Baltimore Law School before serving in the Army during World War II. He received his law degree in 1947. Agnew became active in Maryland politics during the 1950s. He was appointed to the Baltimore County Zoning Board of Appeals in 1957 and was elected county executive in 1962, the first Republican to hold that post since 1895.

In 1966 Agnew ran for governor of Maryland. The strong segregationist views of his opponent, George Mahoney, led many normally-Democratic blacks and liberals to cast their ballots for Agnew, who won the election handily. In his first year in office, Agnew secured passage of several liberal measures, including an open-housing law, a graduated income tax and an expanded state-financed anti-poverty program. However, he shifted direction abruptly in 1968 when he took a tough line against demonstrators, slashed state welfare spending and won new police powers as head of the state militia. [See JOHNSON Volume]

Agnew was an early supporter of the undeclared candidacy of New York Gov. Nelson Rockefeller [q.v.] for the 1968 Republican presidential nomination. When Rockefeller firmly announced that he would not run, Agnew became a favorite-son candidate and eventually backed Richard Nixon, whose name he placed in nomination at the Republican National Convention. Nixon announced that Agnew was his choice for a running mate and the Convention accepted Nixon's wishes.

During the campaign, while Nixon sounded the statesmanlike themes of peace, prosperity and a healing of the nation's wounds, Agnew spoke bluntly as a champion of "law and order." He attacked what he called "stylish forms of discontent," lashed into the "pie-in-the-sky" wastefulness of the Johnson Administration's War on Poverty and labeled Democratic candidate Hubert Humphrey, [q.v.] "squishy soft on Communism." In the November balloting he and Nixon won a narrow plurality of the total vote.

Once in office Agnew toned down his rhetoric and for a few months of the Nixon Administration spoke in a conciliatory manner. At the National Governors Conference in February 1969, he successfully urged the rejection of a resolution sponsored by California Gov. Ronald Reagan [q.v.] to have the Justice Department thoroughly investigate the sources of campus unrest. In April he voiced acceptance of nonviolent dissent as within "the limits of permissibility." Agnew told businessmen to increase their commitment to minority employment and business opportunities, and promised the U.S. Conference of Mayors that Nixon's revenue-sharing plan would provide big cities with an "equitable and fair share" of federal funds. A strong supporter of the anti-ballistic missile (ABM), Agnew nonetheless cautioned the Republican Governors Conference against endorsing the ABM, saying that it should not become a divisive partisan issue.

Nevertheless Agnew's comments were soon at odds with the policy statements of liberal administration officials. Shortly after the Apollo moon landing in July 1969, for example, Health, Education and Welfare (HEW) Secretary Robert Finch [q.v.] and Housing and Urban Development (HUD) Secretary George Romney [q.v.] both urged a shift in spending from the space program to domestic needs. Agnew responded by declaring "we do not need a transfer of dollars from the space program to other programs. We need a transfer of its spirit—an infusion of American dedication to purpose and hard work." In September Agnew told the Southern Governors Conference that the Nixon Administration opposed the use of busing to achieve school integration. Finch, a few days later, announced that HEW would use busing to bring school districts in compliance with desegregation guidelines.

By the autumn of 1969 Agnew's public comments had become outspokenly strident in their attacks on anti-war protestors, student radicals and any group or individual who dissented vocally from the Administration's policies. Over the next few years Agnew became a symbol of the tough law-and-order position of the Nixon presidency. He appealed to the millions of Americans who felt threatened by the social turbulence of the 1960s, playing upon their fears and confusion. With the repeated backing of the President, Agnew injected a level of vitriolic rhetoric seldom seen in American politics.

Administration concern over the impact of the anti-war demonstrations planned for the fall by the Vietnam Moratorium Committee provided the setting for Agnew's renewed attacks on dissenters. At a Republican fundraiser in New Orleans shortly after the Oct. 15 nationwide anti-war rallies, Agnew described the protestors as an "effete corps of impudent snobs who characterize themselves as intellectuals." Despite the overwhelmingly peaceful nature of these demonstrations, Agnew predicted that the November protests would be "wilder, more violent." Speaking against the dissenters at another fundraiser on Oct. 30, Agnew declared: "America cannot afford to divide over their demagoguery or to be deceived by their duplicity or let their license destroy liberty. We can, however, afford to sepa-rate them from our society—with not more regret than we should feel over discarding rotten apples from a barrel."

The following month, Agnew extended his attacks to the national television networks, accusing them of "a form of censorship" in their coverage of the Administration's Vietnam policy, and attacking the networks' executives as "a small and unelected elite." The response to Agnew's comments was immediate. FCC member Nicholas Johnson feared that "serious and permanent harm to independent journalism and free speech" might result, and the ACLU called Agnew's speech a "clear and chilling threat" of censorship. A few days later Agnew extended his criticism to the press, saying it had "grown fat and irresponsible" and singling out *The Washington Post* and *The New York Times* for their anti-Administration stands. The Vice President received considerable praise from President Nixon who told the press on Dec. 8 that Agnew had "rendered a public service" by his comments on the media.

Agnew's tough rhetoric stimulated an on-going reaction. At the February 1970 hearings of the Senate Foreign Relations Committee on Nixon's Vietnamization policy, Sen. Harold Hughes, (D, Iowa) deplored the inhibiting effect that Agnew's comments were having on public debate. "First you pistol-whip the mass media," he said, "and then you commandeer it for political purposes." A report on student unrest issued by the American Council on Education in April 1970 concluded that "repressive and provocative pronouncements" by Administration officials had an "inflammatory effect" on the campuses and warned against the "political exploitation of campus problems by some public figures." The United Automobile Workers and the Amalgamated Clothing Workers of America, at their spring 1970 conventions, attacked Agnew by name.

The Vice President nonetheless persisted in his attacks on dissenters and his defense of Administration policies in Vietnam. He defended the May 1970 invasion of Cambodia as "the finest hour in the

Nixon presidency." After four students at Kent State University in Ohio were killed by the National Guard during a demonstration against the invasion, Agnew called the tragedy "predictable and avoidable" and blamed it on "the new politics of violence and confrontation." Agnew's remarks provoked a reaction even within the Administration. Interior Secretary Walter Hickel, [q.v.] wrote to the President asking him to bring an end to Agnew's attacks on the nation's youth; Robert Finch declared that the Vice President's rhetoric "contributed to heating up the climate in which the Kent State students were killed."

No restraints, however, were placed on Agnew who soon extended his barbs to Senate opponents of the war. He described as "reprehensible" the Cooper-Church Amendment to cut off funds for operations in Cambodia and accused Sens. Fulbright (D, Ark.), Kennedy (D, Mass.) and McGovern (D, S.D.) of having a "psychological addiction to an American defeat." Agnew called the McGovern-Hatfield Amendment "a blueprint for the first defeat in the history of the United States."

When the President's Commission on Campus Unrest issued a report that condemned "divisive and insulting rhetoric," Agnew turned his fire on Nixon's personal appointees and labeled the conclusions "more pablum for the permissivists." Meanwhile, he defended the assault on anti-war demonstrators by construction workers in New York City as "a wave in defense of the country."

Agnew became the chief Administration spokesman in the 1970 congressional elections. In his first campaign speech in San Diego on Sept. 11, he said that the "great question" in the upcoming elections was "Will America be led by a president elected by a majority of the American people or will we be intimidated and blackmailed into following the path dictated by a disruptive radical and militant minority—the pampered prodigies of the radical liberals in the United States Senate?" The attack on "radical liberals" remained Agnew's central theme, and he

campaigned heavily against liberal Democrats up for reelection.

He reserved special fire, however, for New York's Republican Sen. Charles Goodell who was an outspoken opponent of the war in Vietnam. Agnew's attack on a fellow Republican provoked a heated response in Party circles. Nelson Rockefeller, [q.v.] himself running for reelection, wrote to Nixon and asked him to "please let us handle our own political problems" in New York. "Outside intervention," he said, would be "prejudicial" to the state Republican ticket. Repudiating Agnew's position 18 Republican senators, including Minority Leader Hugh Scott [q.v.] and Minority Whip Robert Griffin, [q.v.] signed a public letter of endorsement for Goodell.

Agnew's attacks on Democratic candidates were so vitriolic that prominent Democrats purchased prime television time on the eve of the election to respond to his charges. Speaking for his Party, Maine Sen. Edmund Muskie [q.v.] asked voters to repudiate the "politics of fear." Pointing to the generally conservative legislative proposals of the Administration, he told the working people of America that Nixon and Agnew "really believe that if they can make you afraid enough or angry enough . . . you can be tricked into voting against yourself."

For whatever reason the election returns demonstrated that Agnew's rhetoric was not as effective as the Administration had hoped. Although Goodell and Democratic Sen. Albert Gore [q.v.] of Tennessee, another Agnew target, were defeated, and the Republicans gained two Senate seats, the Democrats increased their margin in the House and won an additional 11 governorships. Perhaps in reaction there was a notable lack of inflammatory rhetoric on the Vice President's part during the following year. In April 1971 Agnew actually praised the organizers of a massive anti-war demonstration in Washington, D.C., for "a very well-controlled rally."

Agnew served as an emissary of the Nixon Administration to foreign governments during 1971. In June and July he made a month-long 10-nation tour of Asia, Africa and Europe in which he reassured America's allies that the United States would not drift into isolationism. In October Agnew took another extended trip abroad.

In 1972, Nixon again chose Agnew as his running mate. While the President did little campaigning, Agnew became by far the most visible spokesman for the Administration. Trying to cultivate a new image, he told the National Newspaper Association that "we all, whether government official or editor, might do well to forego harangue and cliche in favor of discussion based on reason." Agnew refrained from attacking most Democratic candidates and instead reserved his sharpest criticism for presidential aspirant Sen. George McGovern [q.v.], whom he called "one of the greatest frauds ever to be considered as a presidential candidate by a major American Party." When the ballots were counted in November, Nixon and Agnew had won an unprecedented landslide victory.

Nixon's second term had scarcely begun when it was overtaken by the deepening Watergate scandal. During the spring of 1973, as the Senate Watergate Committee conducted its nationally televised hearings on the affair, Agnew defended the President and attacked the investigation. In April he declared his "full confidence in the integrity of President Nixon." He called the press treatment of Watergate "a very short jump from McCarthyism," and said of the Senate hearing that they "can hardly hope to find the truth and can hardly fail to muddy the waters of justice beyond repair."

Agnew, however, was soon preoccupied with serious troubles of his own. On August 7 the *Wall Street Journal* reported that Agnew was the target of an investigation by U.S. Attorney George Beall [q.v.] in Maryland concerning allegations of kickbacks by contractors, architects and engineers to officials of Baltimore County. The alleged violations of conspiracy, extortion and bribery, and tax statutes were supposed to have extended from the time Agnew was Baltimore County executive through his years in the vice presidency. In a news conference on Aug. 8, Agnew vehemently denied the charges, labeling them "false, scurrilous and malicious" and saying that he had "no expectation of being indicted." On Aug. 21, in a nationally televised statement, Agnew denounced "leaks" to the press. "Some Justice Department officials have decided to indict me in the press whether or not the evidence supports their position," he said. Attorney General Elliot Richardson [q.v.], who was watching the investigation closely, hurriedly denied Agnew's charges, but promised to investigate the source of the leaks.

News reports subsided early in September as the grand jury recessed, but on Sept. 25 it was scheduled to begin hearing evidence against Agnew. The Vice President, in an attempt to squelch rumors of his impending resignation and to block the investigation, contended that he could not be indicted while in office and asked the House of Representatives to begin its own inquiry under the impeachment provisions of the Constitution. When House Speaker Carl Albert [q.v.] rejected the request the next day, the grand jury began hearing evidence. Agnew's lawyers filed suit in federal district court on Sept. 28 to stop the proceedings, but Judge Walter E. Hoffman allowed the grand jury to continue its hearings pending a decision. On Oct. 3, in an unusual action, he authorized Agnew's attorneys to investigate the alleged news leaks with full subpoena power.

With the investigation continuing in the courts, Agnew renewed his appeals to the public. In a speech delivered in Los Angeles on Sept. 29, he repeated the charges of deliberate news leaks designed to indict him in the press and promised that he would not resign even if indicted. Agnew's options, however, were rapidly dwindling as he became increasingly isolated. Meetings with the President on Sept. 20 and 25 failed to get a strong, unequivocal statement of support and rumors circulated that Nixon, buffeted by the Watergate revelations, asked Agnew to resign. On Oct. 1, the White House confirmed that presidential counsel J. Fred Buzhardt, Jr. [*q.v.*] was involved in plea-bargaining negotiations between Agnew's lawyers and the Justice Department.

On Oct. 10, 1973, Agnew announced his resignation from office. Under the agreement reached with the Justice Department, Agnew was to resign office and plead nolo contendere (no contest) to a single charge of federal income tax evasion. In return the Justice Department would not proceed with indictments against Agnew on multiple charges of conspiracy, extortion and bribery, although government lawyers did present the court with a 40-page document outlining alleged misconduct by Agnew. When Agnew appeared in court on Oct. 10, Judge Hoffman informed him that the no contest plea was the "full equivalent of a plea of guilty." Hoffman fined Agnew $10,000 and sentenced him to three years unsupervised probation.

Agnew delivered a farewell address to the nation on Oct. 15 in which he continued to protest his innocence and blame news leaks for his predicament. His decision to plead no contest, however, rather than simply resign and have his innocence judged in court, cast serious doubt on his claims. Coming in the midst of the Watergate revelations, moreover, Agnew's resignation deepened the shadow around the Nixon Administration. By the time he left office, Agnew had lost virtually all credibility except among some die-hard supporters.

In January 1974 a special three-judge panel in Maryland unanimously recommended Agnew's disbarment on the grounds that he was "unfit to continue as a member of the bar." In May the Maryland Court of Appeals carried out the recommendation, saying that "it is difficult to feel compassion for an attorney who is so morally obtuse that he consciously cheats for his own pecuniary gain that government he has sworn to serve."

After leaving public office Agnew became a lobbyist for Mideastern oil interests.

[JD]

For more information:
Richard M. Cohen and Jules Witcover, *A Heart-Beat Away: The Investigation and Resignation of Vice President Spiro T. Agnew* (New York, 1974).
Jules Witcover, *White Knight, The Rise of Spiro Agnew* (New York, 1972).

AIKEN, GEORGE D(AVID)
b. Aug. 30, 1892; Dummerston, Vt.
Republican Senator, Vt., 1941-74.

Raised on a farm near Brattleboro, Vt., George Aiken opened a nursery business after graduating from high school. He was elected to the Vermont House of Representatives in 1930, became its speaker in 1933 and won the election for lieutenant governor two years later. Aiken was elected governor of Vermont in 1937 and was a successful candidate for the U.S. Senate in 1940. Because of his popularity with the state's voters, he had little difficulty winning reelection in the succeeding decades.

Throughout his Senate career Aiken was generally associated with the moderate wing of the Republican Party, though his voting record proved difficult to categorize, and he remained an unpredictable figure. Aiken voted for the Civil Rights Act of 1964 and the Voting Rights Act of 1965, but opposed the use of federal funds to aid school desegregation. In 1962 he voted against medical care for the aged, but reversed himself three years later. As a member of the Agriculture and Forestry Committee since he entered the Senate in 1941, Aiken supported legislation to increase the prosperity of rural Americans.

During the Nixon years, Aiken's voting record continued to be unpredictable. He sometimes supported the Administration on key issues, and at other times broke ranks with the Party. He voted to confirm conservatives Clement Haynsworth [*q.v.*] and G. Harrold Carswell [*q.v.*] to the Supreme Court, and in favor of extending the President's authority to control wages and prices in 1971, but opposed continued funding of the controversial SST and voted against a federally guaranteed loan for the Lockheed Corporation in 1971.

Aiken, the ranking Republican on the Senate Foreign Relations Committee, was critical of U.S. involvement in Vietnam. As early as 1965 he spoke out against U.S. bombing of North Vietnam, and in 1966 won national recognition when he said that the United States should declare that it had won the war and begin a pullout of troops. Aiken spoke out strongly in favor of troop withdrawal and the cessation of hostilities throughout Nixon's Administration. He denounced the invasion of Cambodia in 1970 and was a cosponsor of the Cooper-Church amendment to cut off funds for combat operations in Cambodia. Later that year Aiken deplored the President's decision to intensify the bombing of North Vietnam and criticized Nixon for not consulting with Congress on foreign policy. In February 1971 he proposed an all-Asian conference of belligerents to make peace among themselves. In May 1972 when Nixon announced the mining of North Vietnam's harbors, Aiken called the decision an example of "brinkmanship."

Despite his criticism of the war, Aiken generally opposed congressional efforts to cut off funds for troops in Vietnam, arguing that it would leave U.S. soldiers vulnerable to attack. Thus he voted against the McGovern-Hatfield end-the-war amendment in 1970 and was the sole opponent of a similar effort by the Senate Foreign Relations Committee in 1972. Instead Aiken urged that the President set a firm date for the final withdrawal of all U.S. troops and then keep to the timetable.

Aiken generally favored an easing of cold war tensions and a lowering of the U.S. profile in world affairs. In 1969 he introduced, with Senator Alan Cranston (D, Calif.), a resolution stating that diplomatic recognition of a foreign government by the U.S. "does not imply that the United States approves of the form, ideology, or policy" of that government. The resolution, which was approved in September 1969, was designed to hasten recognition of Communist China. In 1971 Aiken supported a proposal by Senate Majority Leader Mike Mansfield to cut the number of U.S. troops stationed in Europe.

Despite his increasing attention to foreign affairs, Aiken's concern for rural America continued. He supported extensions of the food stamp program as a way both to aid low-income families and to increase farm income, and in 1972 won a one-year extension of the rural environmental assistance program. That year he also cosponsored a bill to preserve wilderness areas in the East from real estate developers and land speculators.

Aiken retired from the Senate in 1974 at the age of 82.

[JD]

ALBERT, CARL (BERT)
b. May 1 , 1908; McAlester, Okla.
Democratic Representative, Okla., 1947–77; Majority Leader, 1962–71; Speaker of the House, 1971–77.

The son of a miner, Albert graduated from the University of Oklahoma in 1931. A Rhodes scholar, he received two law degrees from Oxford University. Albert practiced law from 1934 to 1941 and served in the Army during World War II. In 1946 he was elected to the U.S. House from Oklahoma's third congressional district, where he established a record as a liberal on social welfare legislation and a hawk on defense policy. Working under the tutelage of Speaker Sam Rayburn, he was elected Democratic whip in 1955 and rose to majority leader in 1962. [See EISENHOWER, KENNEDY, JOHNSON Volumes]

During the early Nixon years Albert maintained his moderate record, supporting the 18-year-old vote, the Equal Rights Amendment, the Philadelphia Plan, family assistance, tax reform and consumer legislation. He supported strong controversial "no-knock" entry legislation. Despite ties to the petroleum industry, important in his district, he voted for a decrease in the oil depletion allowance from 27% to 20%, although he opposed efforts to reduce it further. In most other cases he backed the oil industry. Until 1973 Albert supported the Administration's Vietnam war policy. That year, however, he backed a cutoff of funds for the bombing of Cambodia.

Albert succeeded John McCormack (D, Mass.) [q.v.] as Speaker in 1971. The selection was automatic and unchallenged, a reflection of the continuation of the tradition that the majority leader rose to Speaker upon the retirement of his predecessor. Albert's rise took place despite dissatisfaction with his leadership. Albert was generally viewed as a weak Speaker, unable to direct his Party in opposition to the Administration. The Speaker was a frequent critic of the Nixon Administration, but he failed to develop Democratic alternatives to the President's programs.

Albert had risen through the House during a period when the Democratic Party was deeply divided between Northern liberals and Southern conservatives. His reputation as a conciliator and his penchant for compromise had been important in keeping the Party together during the 1950s and 1960s. However during the early 1970s when Albert was Speaker, the Democrats were overwhelmingly dominated by liberals. Rather than leading the Party, marshaling its power in Congress and galvanizing it into an effective legislative force, Albert preferred to work quietly behind the scenes, letting others take the headlines and guide the Party. His natural reticence and desire for compromise was combined with an inability to use his staff or the media effectively. His power, therefore, was limited.

Nevertheless he did occasionally wield power effectively. In 1973 Albert insisted that the members of the powerful Rules Committee be loyal to him. By appointing a few friendly members to the panel, he became the first Speaker in nearly four decades to have control over the House's legislative agenda. Albert also cooperated with the reformers in the House to shift the power base in the chamber away from the committees and to the majority party caucus and its steering and policy committee. This action resulted in the removal of three chairmen by the Democratic Caucus.

On two occasions Albert was second in line to become President because of vacancies in the vice presidency—once when Spiro Agnew [q.v.] resigned and again when Gerald Ford succeeded to the presidency. It was said of Albert that he was "running from the presidency" because he made every effort to avoid becoming President.

Albert encountered some personal criticism. At times he fell asleep while presiding over the House. It eventually became public that he had a drinking problem. In 1972 a car he was driving hit two cars, and some witnesses reported he had been drinking. However, no charges were brought against him.

At the time of his election as Speaker, Albert announced that he would retire at age 70 in 1978. (That was also the year in which he was eligible for maximum pension benefits.) However because of growing opposition to his leadership, he decided not to seek reelection in 1976.

[HML]

ALIOTO, JOSEPH L(AWRENCE)
b. Feb. 12, 1916; San Francisco, Calif.
Mayor, San Francisco, 1968-76.

Joseph Alioto was born and raised in an Italian section of San Francisco. His father, a Sicilian immigrant, was the founder of the prosperous International Fish Co., where Alioto worked while still a boy. He received his B.A. in 1937 from St. Mary's College in Moraga, Calif., and his law degree in 1940 from Catholic University in Washington, D.C. After working for the Department of Justice and the Board of Economic Warfare during World War II, he returned to San Francisco and opened his own law practice. Alioto became one of the most successful anti-trust lawyers in the country. He was also a successful businessman, served as president of the San Francisco Board of

Education in 1953 and 1954 and later became chairman of the San Francisco Development Agency.

In September 1967 State Sen. Eugene McAteer, the favored candidate in the upcoming mayoral election, died unexpectedly. Alioto entered the race and put together a coalition that included support from business interests, organized labor and the city's racial minorities. Campaigning as a moderate Democrat who supported both social justice and law and order, he won a landslide victory in November. During his first year in office, he confronted a number of crises, including a newspaper strike already in progress before his inauguration and the shutdown of San Francisco State College by militant black students. Alioto appointed a mediator to negotiate a settlement in the newspaper strike and the walkout ended on Feb. 25, 1968. In the student strike, which began in November 1968, Alioto supported the efforts of acting president S.I. Hayakawa to keep order on campus.

During his first term Alioto won recognition as a strong advocate for the needs of the nation's troubled cities. San Francisco was one of the few major cities to escape serious urban riots, and Alioto received credit for this. Like New York Mayor John Lindsay [q.v.], he frequently toured the city's ghettos and slum areas and met with community leaders. He substantially increased the proportion of minority workers in city jobs, and his high standing with the city's labor leaders helped increase minority representation in local unions. A proponent of urban redevelopment, Alioto succeeded in obtaining large federal and state grants that vastly increased jobs in the construction industry. [See JOHNSON Volume]

Alioto's success in avoiding major urban disorders raised speculation that he would seek higher office. He was widely mentioned as a possible gubernatorial candidate against Ronald Reagan [q.v.], or as a future vice-presidential nominee. His political future received a serious blow, however, when Look magazine published an article in September 1969 alleging that Alioto was "enmeshed in a web of alliances with at least six leaders of La Cosa Nostra." Alioto immediately denied the accusation, charged that it was politically motivated and initiated a libel suit against the publisher. Although the courts eventually ruled in his favor in 1977, Alioto announced in January 1970 that he would not run for governor.

Alioto sought reelection for a second term as mayor in 1971. He retained the support of organized labor and business leaders, but other sectors of the population had grown disenchanted with him. Some middle-class voters objected to his encouragement of new commercial and residential construction, charging that skyscrapers and high-rise apartments were destroying the traditional charm of San Francisco. Some minority leaders objected to the destruction of low-income neighborhoods in the name of urban renewal, while the city's increasingly militant homosexual population accused Alioto of condoning police harassment.

In March 1971, moreover, Alioto was indicted by a Seattle grand jury on charges of conspiracy to bribe public officials in an anti-trust case (Alioto was later acquitted of the charge.) A 12-candidate race, however, made it difficult for any one opponent to rally the opposition, and Alioto won a plurality of the votes in the November election.

During his second term Alioto became more outspoken in his advocacy of federal aid to the nation's cities. In 1971, with Mayor John Lindsay of New York, he led a fact-finding tour of major urban areas for the U.S. Conference of Mayors. He attacked Nixon's 1972 budget as a "severe setback" for the cities and charged that the President's revenue sharing proposals would hurt urban areas. In 1972 he helped launch and then headed "Mayors for McGovern." Elected president of the U.S. Conference of Mayors in 1974, Alioto lobbied hard for federal funds for mass transit, a proposal finally enacted by Congress in November 1974. The following year he spoke strongly in favor of federally guaranteed loans to help New York City avert bankruptcy.

Alioto's last years in office were

plagued by labor disputes. In March 1974 city hospital, sewage and transit workers struck for higher wages, and were followed shortly thereafter by San Francisco's teachers. The following year police and fire fighters also went on strike, and Alioto had to invoke emergency powers under the city charter to impose a settlement. Alioto came under heavy criticism in 1974 for his handling of the "Zebra" killings, a series of random murders of whites. His order to the police to stop, search, and question all young black men matching the killer's description was termed "a racist outrage and a massive violation of constitutional rights" by the American Civil Liberties Union, and the courts issued an injunction against carrying out the order.

In 1974 Alioto ran for the Democratic gubernatorial nomination but was defeated by Edmund Brown, Jr. Prevented by city law from serving more than two terms as mayor, he returned to the private practice of law in 1976.

[JD]

ALLEN, JAMES B(ROWNING)
b. Dec. 28, 1912; Gadsden, Ala.
d. June 1, 1978; Foley, Ala.
Democratic Senator, Ala., 1969-78.

Following graduation from the University of Alabama and its Law School, Allen began to practice law in Gadsden, Ala., in 1935. He was elected to the Alabama House of Representatives in 1938 but resigned in 1942 to enter the Navy. In 1946 he was elected to the Alabama State Senate, serving until 1950. He was Alabama's lieutenant governor from 1951 to 1955 and again from 1963 to 1967. In his 1968 race for the U.S. Senate, Allen based much of his campaign on his ties with George Wallace [q.v.], and he charged his opponent in the Democratic primary, Armistead I. Selden, Jr., with being part of "the Washington crowd." Allen went on to win the seat with 70% of the vote.

In the Senate, Allen established an image of an "old-fashioned Southern Sena-

tor", a "champion of the filibuster" and "master parliamentarian," according to *The New York Times*. A hard-line conservative in both domestic and foreign affairs, Allen, in 1971, voted with the Senate's conservative coalition 93% of the time. The following year he earned an 86 rating from the conservative Americans for Constitutional Action. He supported legislation to restrain federal involvement in busing and school integration and supported curbs on pornography. He fought the creation of a federal consumer protection agency; public financing of political campaigns and legislation that would have permitted voter registration by postcard; reform of the Senate's filibuster rule; and federal funding of the SST. Allen was a strong supporter of the Vietnam war and vigorous opponent of detente with the Soviet Union. He opposed foreign aid in general and resisted granting financial assistance to countries opposed to the white minority regime in Rhodesia.

Allen voted for the Supreme Court nominations of Clement Haynsworth [q.v.] and G. Harrold Carswell [q.v.], which were rejected by the Senate, and the nomination of William Rehnquist approved in 1971. Following the disclosure of possible improprieties involving financial payments to Supreme Court Justice Abe Fortas [q.v.] in 1969, Allen became the second Democratic senator to urge Fortas to resign. At the same time he called for the resignation of the Court's leading liberal, William O. Douglas [q.v.]. In both 1971 and again in 1975, Allen used his knowledge of parliamentary rules, particularly the filibuster, to block action on proposals to reform the cloture rule. He was successful in 1971 but not in 1975, when the Senate changed its rules reducing from two-thirds to three-fifths the number of senators required to invoke cloture or cut off debate.

Allen was a vigorous opponent of busing. He criticized the Supreme Court and other federal courts for what he saw as their use of discretionary powers over public school systems to force the achievement of racial balance. In a March 1969 effort to stop the federal government's usurpation of power over public school systems, Allen proposed a constitutional amendment returning control of public education to local and state governments. In 1972 Allen was a supporter of legislation designed to bar courts from ordering long-distance busing to desegregate public schools. In further criticism of the courts, he often contended that the judiciary was assuming the powers of the legislative branch. In February 1971 he introduced a Senate resolution that proposed a constitutional amendment limiting the terms of appointment and method of selection of federal judges. He called for court judges to be subject to reappointment and reconfirmation.

In his work as a member of the Agricultural and Forestry Committee, Allen was a supporter of legislation assisting rural community development and providing federal cost-sharing for small watershed protection and resource conservation projects.

During the Carter Administration Allen was the Senate's most adamant opponent of the Panama Canal treaties. He died of an apparent heart attack on June 1, 1978, while attending a reception in Alabama.

[GMS]

ALLOTT, GORDON (LLEWELLYN)
b. Jan. 2, 1907; Pueblo, Colo.
Republican Senator, Colo., 1955-73.

Son of a federal meat inspector, Gordon Allott received his law degree from the University of Colorado in 1929 and five years later entered politics as chairman of the Colorado State Young Republican League. During World War II Allott saw action with the Army Air Force in the South Pacific. He was elected lieutenant governor of Colorado in 1950 and upset a popular Democrat for the U.S. Senate four years later. Allott compiled a conservative record in the Senate, voting against most of the Kennedy and Johnson Administration domestic programs except civil rights legislation.

On the Vietnam war Allott allied staunchly with the "hawks," arguing for a vigorous military effort to avoid another "Korean stalemate." In 1968 Allott helped lead the eventually successful Senate opposition to the nomination of Associate Justice Abe Fortas [q.v.] for Chief Justice of the Supreme Court. [See EISENHOWER, KENNEDY, JOHNSON Volumes]

In January 1969 Allott won the chairmanship of the Senate Republican Conference (Policy) Committee, making him the third ranking member of the Party's Senate power structure. During President Nixon's first term of office, Allott remained a firm supporter of the war in Vietnam and helped rebuff anti-war legislation. In June 1970 Allott engineered the defeat of the McGovern-Hatfield Amendment to cut off war funds after the end of 1971 by introducing the bill to the Senate floor before its sponsors had had sufficient time to muster public and Senate support. That same month he voted against the Cooper-Church anti-war Amendment. Allott originally supported an amendment introduced by Sen. Mike Mansfield (D, Mont.) [q.v.] in 1971, requiring all U.S. troops to be out of South Vietnam within nine months if Hanoi first released its American POWs. However after the Administration promised to back a military pay proposal that he was sponsoring, Allott withdrew his endorsement, and support for the measure collapsed.

In 1972 Allott supported Nixon's decision to resume the bombing of North Vietnam, which, during the Senate debate on the issue in April, he called a necessary warning to "the reckless rulers in the Kremlin for fueling Hanoi's war machine." Allott voted for the War Powers Act of 1972 in which Congress for the first time further defined the constitutional war powers of the President, but he resisted attempts to apply its restrictions to the conflict in Indo-China.

On other issues of foreign policy Allott voted with fellow conservatives. In 1971 he opposed a Mansfield amendment to reduce NATO troop levels in Europe, and that same year cosponsored with Sen. Frank Church (D, Ida.) [q.v.] a successful bill passed to reduce the monies available to the Development Loan Fund. He opposed the repeal that year of the 1955 Formosa Resolution which granted the President authority to use U.S. troops to defend Taiwan.

In domestic matters Allott generally supported the President. However, he voted with the majority to override the President's veto of an aid to education bill in 1970. On transportation issues he favored development of the supersonic transport plane. He opposed an $800 million mass transit bill introduced by Sen. Jacob Javits (R, N.Y.) [q.v.], arguing that it would encourage "the worst systems to continue their bad practices."

Although his seat was considered a "safe" one for the Republicans, Allott was upset in his bid for reelection in 1972 by Floyd Haskell, a former Republican turned Democrat, who campaigned against the Vietnam war. Contributing to his defeat was the issue of the 1976 Winter Olympics scheduled to be held in Denver. Allott had strongly backed Denver as a site and had sponsored a bill authorizing $15 million in federal funds to be spent on sports facilities. But Colorado voters, in an unprecedented move, struck down a bond issue for the games and forced them to move elsewhere.

In 1973 Allott worked as a general council for the Interstate Commerce Commission and in 1976 was defeated as a delegate for President Ford to the Republican National Convention.

[FLM]

ANDERSON, JACK (NORTHMAN)
b. Oct. 19, 1922; Long Beach, Calif.
Newspaper columnist.

The son of "straight-laced, honest, salt-of-the-earth Mormons," Anderson was brought up in Salt Lake City. While still a teenager, Anderson began his journalism career as a reporter for the *Deseret News*. By 1939 he was a staff reporter for the *Salt Lake Tribune*. He studied for a short time at the University of Utah and then served two years during the early 1940s as a Mormon missionary. At his request, Anderson began work as a war correspondent for the *Deseret News* in 1945. Two years later he moved to Washington, D.C., to begin work for Drew Pearson, who wrote the widely syndicated muckraking column "The Washington Merry-Go-Round." With Pearson he uncovered such important influence-peddling scandals as the "Five Percenters" in the 1940s, the Sherman Adams-Bernard Goldfine case in the 1950s and the Thomas Dodd incident in the 1960s. In 1965 Anderson was finally granted an equal by-line with Pearson. [See JOHNSON Volume]

Anderson inherited the column after Pearson's death in 1969. His approach to the news was very different from that of Pearson. While the older man frequently reported personal gossip about public figures, Anderson attempted to uncover important problems in government.

During the Nixon Administration, Anderson made headlines with several scoops revealing duplicity or wrong doing in the White House. In 1972 the columnist published secret government documents revealing that despite the Administration's public policy of neutrality, Nixon wanted to "tilt" U.S. support toward Pakistan in the war between that nation and India over Bangladesh. Although several critics opposed Anderson's publication of secret documents, his action was praised and he received the Pulitzer Prize that year.

In February 1972 Anderson, using a memo reportedly written by International Telephone & Telegraph (ITT) lobbyist Dita Beard [q.v.], revealed that the Justice Department had settled a pending antitrust suit against ITT at a time when the giant conglomerate had pledged $400,000 to the 1972 Republican National Convention. He later revealed ITT attempts to stop the election of Marxist Salvador Allende in Chile.

During the Nixon Administration, Anderson also uncovered evidence that the FBI had kept dossiers on persons opposed to Administration policies and that the Central Intelligence Agency (CIA) had made attempts to assassinate foreign leaders, including Fidel Castro. In April 1973 Anderson began a series of columns that included a verbatim account of Watergate grand jury transcripts he had obtained during the jury's probe of the break-in. It was later revealed through White House sources that his access to these minutes was a factor in the President's decision to allow an open investigation of the case.

Other Anderson columns raised doubts about Sen. Edward M. Kennedy's (D, Mass.) [q.v.] account of events surrounding the accident at Chappaquiddick in which an aide drowned, revealed that Attorney General Robert F. Kennedy had known about FBI wiretapping of Martin Luther King, Jr., and made public the CIA's large-scale spending in an unsuccessful attempt to raise a sunken Soviet submarine. Anderson was often criticized during this period for his methods, particularly his use of secret documents and his failure to check his sources adequately. In 1972 he publicly apologized to Sen. Thomas Eagleton (D, Mo.) [q.v.], then the Democratic vice-presidential candidate, for reporting false charges that the Senator had been arrested for drunken driving.

[SBB]

ANDERSON, JOHN B.
b. Feb. 15, 1922; Rockford, Ill.
Republican Representative, Ill.,1961–.

Anderson, the son of Swedish-American parents who operated a small grocery store in Rockford, graduated from the University of Illinois in 1942. After serving in the Army during World War II, he received his law degree from the university in 1946. From 1952 to 1955 he served as an adviser to the U.S. High Commissioner for Germany while a member of the Foreign Service. Returning to Rockford he was elected State's Attorney for Winnebago County in 1956. He held the post until 1960, when he was elected to the House of Representatives from a predominantly agricultural and solidly Re-

publican district in northwestern Illinois.

Anderson began his House career as a conservative Republican. He opposed funding what he called "warmed-over New Deal panaceas" like the anti-poverty and Model Cities programs of the 1960s. Instead he favored greater involvement by the private sector in meeting social goals. He regularly opposed efforts to cut defense expenditures.

During the Nixon and Ford terms, Anderson generally supported the Administration's legislative positions and regularly voted to sustain Nixon-Ford vetoes of spending legislation. At the same time, however, he began to shift away from his earlier conservatism on some issues. In 1971, for example, he supported the creation of an independent legal services corporation to aid the poor, a move the Administration opposed. In 1973 he supported the successful effort to override Nixon's veto of the War Powers Resolution, which limited the President's authority to commit U.S. troops abroad. And even though he had been elected Republican Conference chairman in 1969, the third highest Republican leadership post in the House, Anderson opposed his fellow Republicans almost as often as he supported them on party line votes, which pit a majority of Republicans against a majority of Democrats. Anderson's changing viewpoints angered many conservative Republicans in the House. In contrast to his 1969 victory of the Conference chairmanship by a 122–65 vote, he was elected chairman in 1971 by only eight votes, when he faced conservative Rep. Samuel L. Devine (R, Ohio), who charged that Anderson's voting record was too liberal on domestic issues.

Anderson strongly supported "good government" reform efforts. In 1971 he and Rep. Morris K. Udall (D, Ariz.) [q.v.] headed the bipartisan campaign reform movement in the House. They cosponsored a four-part election reform package that called for tax credits on media expenditures by candidates and an agency to enforce campaign spending limits. The Federal Election Campaign Act of 1971, the first major federal election reform in

47 years, included many of the Anderson-Udall proposals.

Anderson and Udall advocated public financing for House and Senate races, as well as for presidential contests, when Congress was revising the 1971 law after the spending abuses of the 1972 campaigns had pointed out its many loopholes. Anderson and Udall favored public financing of elections as a way of limiting the increasing political influence of campaign contributions. Nixon and many in Congress opposed the concept, however, claiming that government financing undermined the democratic electoral process. The House refused to enact the Anderson-Udall proposal for public financing of House and Senate races, but it passed the Election Campaign Act Amendments of 1974, which provided for public financing of presidential primary and general election campaigns.

Anderson angered many Republicans when he called for a complete explanation of the unfolding Watergate scandal even before many Democrats had reacted. He quickly objected to the broad claims of executive privilege advanced by Administration officials to restrict congressional inquiries into the Watergate affair. In May 1973 he cosponsored a resolution calling for the appointment of a special Watergate prosecutor as the only effective way to ensure an impartial and complete investigation of the scandal.

When the House Judiciary Committee formally opened its impeachment probe in early 1974, Anderson at first opposed the suggestion that Nixon resign so that impeachment could be avoided. He stated that the impeachment process was the only way to clear or convict the President and told Republicans that impeachment was "a Republican problem and we can't turn away from it." But he changed his position after reading the edited transcripts of taped White House conversations that were released to the Judiciary Committee in April 1974. Although Nixon always claimed he had not been aware of the cover-up until March 21, 1974, Anderson pointed out that the "transcripts make it quite clear he [Nixon] was

deeply involved in Watergate on the 13th of March 1973." He then predicted the President would be impeached if he did not resign and called for Nixon's resignation so the nation could avoid the agony of impeachment.

Anderson's candor about Watergate did not damage him politically. He retained his Conference chairmanship by a solid 85-52 margin after the 1974 elections swept many conservatives out of office. During the 1976 presidential primary campaign, he strongly supported Ford's candidacy over the more conservative Ronald Reagan [q.v.]. During the Carter presidency, Anderson continued to advocate "good government" reforms, like reducing government regulation of business and televising House debates.

[AE]

ANGLETON, JAMES J(ESUS)
b. 1917; Boise, Ida.
Chief of Counterintelligence, Central Intelligence Agency, 1954-73.

Angleton attended Yale and in 1943 joined the Office of Strategic Services, the nation's wartime intelligence agency. He remained in intelligence work following World War II, eventually becoming a member of the Central Intelligence Agency (CIA) after it was formed in 1947. Angleton was involved in clandestine activities in Italy during the late 1940s and set up the Agency's counterintelligence staff in 1954. By the late 1950s he had put together a large counter-intelligence section, divided into security, operations, research and analysis, liaison and such special sections as a Communist Party unit. The counterintelligence staff became part of the Directorate for Plans (later the Directorate for Operations), the Agency's clandestine operations branch. Counterintelligence, however, was highly segregated from the rest of the CIA. During the 1950s the staff concentrated on the Soviet Union and its intelligence bureau, the KGB. In 1956 Angleton was responsible for obtaining a copy of Nikita Khrushchev's secret speech denouncing Stalin before the Soviet Communist Party congress. It was reported that Angleton was responsible for the transfer of secret nuclear technology to Israel in the late 1950s.

In 1967 Angleton was put in charge of Operation Chaos, a program established by Lyndon Johnson to discover whether there was any foreign financing or manipulation behind the anti-war movement or any of the radical groups associated with it. Radical groups were infiltrated, computer files on subjects and individuals were established and extensive liaison with a similar office in the FBI was set up. The operation continued until 1974, although the CIA reported to Presidents Johnson and Nixon that it could find no direct foreign involvement in the anti-war movement. The Rockefeller Commission investigation in 1975 determined that Angleton had been responsible for the operation, but that he had had little contact with its actual functioning. The Commission documented several instances where the momentum of the operation had carried it beyond Director Richard Helms's [q.v.] instruction to limit the investigation to foreign aspects of the anti-war movement.

In the early 1970s the CIA's executive director-comptroller, William E. Colby [q.v.], became concerned over Angleton's handling of counterintelligence. He began to question whether Angleton's ultracareful approach, with its concern about KGB penetration in the U.S., allowed for a sufficient recruitment of agents from Communist countries. When James R. Schlesinger [q.v.] became the CIA's Director in February 1973, Colby became head of the Directorate for Operations. During Schlesinger's extensive reorganization of the Agency, Colby recommended Angleton's removal, reiterating his belief that the super-secretive style of operation used by Angleton was no longer effective. Angleton was retained, but Colby removed from counterintelligence such functions as the CIA's liaison with the FBI and thereby reduced its large staff.

In 1952 in New York the CIA had started a program of examining mail between the U.S. and the Soviet Union and opening select letters. Eventually the program grew into a major operation involving also the FBI. Thousands of letters were scrutinized and a computerized record system was kept. Angleton and the counterintelligence staff considered the operation crucial to their work. Colby recommended to Schlesinger that the program be terminated. He noted that opening first-class mail was a direct violation of a criminal statute and he claimed that he could get nothing more than "vague generalities" from the counterintelligence staff when he asked about the operation's accomplishments. Angleton countered with a strong appeal to Schlesinger that the program be continued. Schlesinger reviewed the project and had it "suspended," deciding that the intelligence derived was not worth the risk of CIA involvement.

Colby's selection as CIA director led to Angleton's resignation and retirement in December 1974. That same month Seymour Hersh in *The New York Times* charged the CIA with conducting "a massive, illegal domestic intelligence operation during the Nixon Administration against the anti-war movement and other dissident groups." Angleton was identified in the story, but he denied the allegations. He later testified before the Rockefeller Commission and other congressional panels.

[SF]

ARENDS, LESLIE C(ORNELIUS)
b. Sept. 27, 1895; Melvin, Ill.
Republican Representative, Ill., 1935-74.

Arends left Oberlin College during World War I to enlist in the Army. After the war he became a leading farmer and banker in his home town just outside of Chicago. In 1934 he was elected to the

U.S. House of Representatives from the largely agricultural district that became a Chicago suburb. Arends emerged to be one of the House's leading conservative critics of the New Deal. In 1943 he became Republican minority whip and served in this position until 1974 except when his Party controlled the House (1947-49, 1953-55) when he moved up to become majority leader.

Arends enthusiastically favored the defense and foreign policies of both the Democrat and Republican Administrations in the postwar period. A fiscal conservative who deplored excessive spending, Arends opposed most liberal domestic legislation of the Democratic Presidents. However he backed the civil rights measures of the Johnson presidency. During the late 1960s Arends also supported President Johnson on the Vietnam War. [See EISENHOWER, KENNEDY, JOHNSON Volumes]

During the Nixon presidency Arends, in his position of whip, served as Minority Leader Gerald Ford's (R, Mich.) [q.v.] chief legislative assistant. His most important function was to see that all House Republicans voted the Party line on key legislation. Although Arends maintained a low profile as a leader, he made his presence felt through his knowledge of the Party's House members and of House procedure. He kept tabs on the locations of all Republicans absent from the floor. Arends had legislative profiles of all his colleagues in the House to help determine how they would vote. Frequently Arends took informal polls of his peers before a key vote took place.

Aside from his position as minority whip, Arends was the ranking Republican on the Armed Services Committee. He worked with Committee Chairman F. Edward Hebert (D, La.) [q.v.] to line up votes for the funds requested by the Pentagon. Throughout the Nixon presidency in response to those who called for defense cuts, Arends raised the theme that the Russians should not be permitted to "bury us." Arends frequently expressed outrage at those in Washington who advocated the reallocation of defense money to social programs. He considered this a serious betrayal of the national defense.

In 1971 Arends voted against efforts to reduce the defense budget. Two years later he voted against an amendment introduced by Rep. Les Aspin (D, Wisc.) [q.v.] to establish a defense ceiling of $20.5 billion. Arends avidly backed the Pentagon's desire to continue spending for new weapons systems. In 1971 he voted for the B-1 Bomber, the F-14 fighter and the anti-ballistic missile program.

Although a member of the congressional leadership, Arends was one of the leading defenders of the executive's right to conduct a foreign policy free from congressional interference. He voted to uphold Nixon's veto of the war powers bill designed to limit the President's authority to commit troops abroad. Arends opposed all attempts to end U.S. intervention in the Vietnam war by witholding funds from the executive. A member of the top secret committee overseeing the operations of the Central Intelligence Agency (CIA), Arends never questioned any CIA operation or the allocation of funds to the agency.

In domestic legislation Arends consistently voted conservative. He fought efforts to expand the federal contribution for increased local health services. During the 1973-74 recession Arends opposed measures to allocate funds for public works employment and to increase and expand unemployment insurance benefits in areas where the unemployed rate exceeded 6.5%. An opponent of proconsumer legislation, Arends resisted efforts to strengthen the powers of the Consumer Protection Agency.

With his seniority in Congress and his position in the House leadership, Arends kept up a close relationship with his constituency. Through his connections with the Pentagon, he obtained key defense contracts and an air force base for his district. In 1972 Arends faced a Republican challenger in the primary who campaigned on the issue of Arends's age. Arends easily defeated him but decided to retire in 1974.

[JB]

ARMSTRONG, ANNE (LEGENDRE)
b. Dec. 27, 1927; New Orleans, La.
Counselor to the President 1972–74;
Ambassador to Great Britain 1976–77.

The daughter of a well-to-do New Orleans coffee importer, Anne Legendre received her B.A. from Vassar College in 1949. The following year she married Tobin Armstrong, a wealthy Texas ranch owner. During the 1950s and 1960s she became active in Republican politics. From 1968 to 1973 Armstrong served as Republican national committeewoman from Texas. Acting on Richard Nixon's suggestion, the Republican National Committee made Armstrong its first female cochairman in January 1971. She was put in charge of special programs. Armstrong worked to promote the Party's "Open Door" policy, to make the GOP and its leaders more accessible and prominent to the public. Working to recruit feminists into the Party, she joined other Republican women in a successful effort to win a pledge from the GOP for an attempt to increase the number of women participating in the next Party convention and to expand the anti-discrimination clause in the Party's rules to include a prohibition on sexual bias. During the 1972 Republican Convention, Armstrong became the first woman to deliver a keynote speech for either Party.

President Nixon named Armstrong counselor to the President on Dec. 18, 1972. She was the first woman to assume the post. The appointment, coming at a time of growing bitterness toward the Administration for its failure to assign women to positions of high authority, was labeled tokenism by many women's groups. As counselor, Armstrong was liaison between the White House and the GOP National Committee. In 1973 she described her function: "I have a rather generalist role, with diffuse responsibilities. That has advantage in that I don't have a special interest, or special department to take care of, as do other Cabinet officers, and I can advise the President in a broader way." At the White House she served as chairman of the Property Review Board, was a member of the Domestic Council and became liaison with the cabinet committee on the Spanish-speaking, youth groups and the Bicentennial Commission.

Armstrong supported the Equal Rights Amendment (ERA) and urged the use of more women in high-level positions. But she defended the Administration's refusal to push the ERA in the states on the grounds that the federal government had no right to interfere in states' affairs. She was pleased that under Nixon there was a three-fold increase over past administrations in the number of women placed in top-level jobs.

Armstrong was a staunch supporter of Nixon during the White House Watergate controversy. She reported in May 1974: "I don't see an impeachment offense. . . . I think he has the guts to see it through in the proper way." But during the final days of the Administration, she joined Sen. Barry Goldwater (R, Ariz.) [q.v.] in urging the President to resign.

Armstrong remained at the White House during the early months of the Ford Administration. She resigned in November 1974 "because of unforeseen and pressing family responsibilities."

On Jan. 28, 1976, the Senate announced its unanimous approval of Armstrong to fill the post of ambassador to Great Britain. In February she was sworn in as envoy to the Court of St. James, becoming the 14th woman since World War II to hold an ambassadorship. Possessing the required wealth and sense of social graces necessary to maintain the position, Armstrong was welcomed in Great Britain. Before she resigned in March 1977, she was credited by the *London Times* "an assiduous ambassador . . . responding with womanly warmth to both our established habits and our changing ways."

[SB]

ARMSTRONG, NEIL (ALDEN)
b. Aug. 5, 1930; Wapakoneta, Ohio
Astronaut.

Armstrong, a naval pilot during the Korean war, received a B.S. degree in aeronautical engineering from Purdue University in 1955 and a M.S. degree from the University of Southern California in 1970. In 1955 Armstrong became a civilian research pilot for the National Advisory Committee for Aeronautics, the predecessor of the National Aeronautics and Space Administration (NASA). Armstrong was selected in the second group of NASA astronauts in September 1962. In March 1966 Armstrong, as command pilot of the Gemini 8 space mission with Air Force Major David R. Scott, performed the first manual space-docking in history.

In July 1969 Armstrong commanded the moon flight with Col. Edwin E. Aldrin, Jr., and Lt. Col. Michael Collins. While Collins maintained the command ship in lunar orbit, Armstrong and Aldrin descended to the moon's surface in the landing module on July 19, 1969. Before a worldwide television audience estimated at more than 500 million people, Armstrong stepped on the moon's surface and said, "That's one small step for man, one giant leap for mankind." Armstrong, joined by Aldrin, placed an American flag on the moon, collected soil and rock samples, performed several scientific tests and received the first earth to moon "phone call" from President Nixon. He left a plaque signed by the astronauts and President Nixon with the message: "Here men from the planet earth first set foot on the moon. July, 1969 A.D. We came in peace for all mankind."

Armstrong and the other two astronauts returned to worldwide acclaim. They received the Galabert International Astronautics Prize for 1969 before they had even splashed down on earth. Parades in major cities welcomed them as national heroes, and they received Medals of Freedom from President Nixon. They addressed a joint session of Congress and were received at the United Nations. Armstrong, Aldrin and Collins went on a 38-day, 44,650-mile trip, which President Nixon called the most successful goodwill tour in history. The three were received by 20 heads of state and were decorated nine times.

The Apollo 11 mission to the moon added fuel to the controversy over the reordering of U.S. priorities. Numerous critics of the Johnson and Nixon Administrations claimed that too much of the nation's money was being wasted on space and the military, particularly the war in Vietnam and reaching the moon. By comparison too little money was being spent to combat poverty, hunger, discrimination, disease and other problems on earth. There was also hostility over the relationship of the space program to the military industrial complex, because the aerospace industry, which had produced most of the Apollo equipment also produced military hardware. Critics speculated that Apollo was really a quasi-military venture. Many scientists said that the space program received the largest share of the declining federal budget for non-defense research at the expense of other vital research.

The threat of Soviet competition in space, which had helped gain support for the U.S. space program in the beginning, faded as the moon landing was achieved. At the time of Armstrong's mission to the moon, the space program was being subjected to financial cuts and relegated to the status of a lesser national priority. The goal set by President Kennedy to land a man on the moon before the end of the decade had been attained and national attention turned elsewhere. The space program, however, continued, although with a reduced budget.

In 1970 Armstrong retired as an astronaut and became NASA deputy associate director, coordinating research and technology between government and private industry. The following year he resigned from NASA to become the first university professor of engineering at the University of Cincinnati. Yet Armstrong continued to serve NASA as a consultant.

[CLC]

ASH, ROY L(AWRENCE)
b. Oct. 20, 1918; Los Angeles, Calif.
Chairman, President's Advisory
Council on Executive Organization,
1969-71; Director, Office of
Management and Budget, 1973-75.

Ash began his career at the Bank of America, where he worked from 1936 to 1942, and again from 1947 to 1949, attaining the rank of chief financial officer. Although he never attended college, he earned an MBA at Harvard in 1947. Ash worked at Hughes Aircraft from 1949 to 1953, when he left to participate in the founding of Litton Industries, Inc. Ash served as director and later as president of Litton from 1953 until 1972, and during his tenure the firm grew from a small defense contractor to a controversial holding company listed among the 50 largest corporations in the United States.

In April 1969 Ash became chairman of the President's Advisory Council on Executive Organization, known as the "Ash Commission."

The first recommendations of the Ash Commission were sent to Congress in March 1970. The plans involved a reorganization of the White House, including the creation of a new Domestic Council and the supercession of the Bureau of the Budget by an Office of Management and Budget (OMB). The reforms, suggested in the Commission's final report submitted in November 1970, were addressed to growing domestic discontent with government bureaucracy. In the government's view the reforms gave regional civil servants more power in funding and decision making and rendered the federal apparatus more responsive to local pressure groups. Ash's Commission further recommended the elimination of the Office of Economic Opportunity (OEO) and the distribution of its functions among four new agencies. Ash proposed, among other things, to transfer the OEO's legal services to a congressionally-chartered, non-profit organization. This move would, in his view, insulate the services

from politics and avoid the confusion engendered by OEO lawsuits against other government agencies.

Ash also proposed to transform the Departments of Labor, Agriculture, Commerce, Transportation, Housing and Urban Development, and Health, Education and Welfare into four "super agencies," the Departments of Human Resources, Economic Affairs, Community Development and Natural Resources.

In November 1972, shortly after his re-election, Nixon appointed Ash to head the Office of Management and Budget, which had replaced the Bureau of the Budget on Ash's recommendation. Shortly thereafter Ash was also appointed to a newly created Council on Economic Policy headed by Secretary of the Treasury George Shultz [*q.v.*].

Ash's appointment, however, became the center of a confrontation between Congress and the White House. In early January 1973 *The Washington Post* alleged that Ash, while working for Hughes Aircraft, had falsified affidavits resulting in a $43 million overpayment on a defense contract. Admiral Hyman G. Rickover charged that Litton had "grossly exaggerated" the costs on a nuclear submarine. Two days after the *Post*'s charges, Nixon announced that he was moving ahead with all aspects of Ash's reorganization plan not requiring formal congressional approval, with the reduction of the White House staff from 4,000 to 2,000 a top priority.

In late January the conflict escalated when the Senate demanded formal review of appointees to the OMB directorship. Rep. Les Aspin (D, Wisc.) called for an investigation of Ash's sale of 85,000 shares of Litton stock in 1970 to determine if Ash had acted on "inside information." On Feb. 5 Ash informed Congress that the Nixon Administration was impounding $8.7 billion in federal appropriations from past legislation, citing the President's obligation to observe the legal limit on the national debt. Sen. Edmund Muskie (D, Me.) charged Ash with "a determined effort to butt back Congress's constitutional authority." On the same day the Senate legislated itself the right to review appointment to the OMB directorship, although Ash had been sworn in three days before. Nixon vetoed the measure, which the House overrode in May 1973. Nixon waited until March 1974 to sign the bill, which exempted the incumbent Ash.

In April 1974, as the Nixon Administration was being paralyzed by the Watergate scandal, Ash had one of his last confrontations with Congress during his appearance there to promote alternative legislation to a pending bill establishing a Consumer Protection Agency (CPA). In the view of most supporters of the bill, the Nixon-backed alternative stripped the CPA of almost all effective power. On the day before Ash's testimony, consumer advocate Ralph Nader [q.v.] released a White House memo telling Ash to "signal hard veto from here on" unless the bill was "cleaned up," a move that gave more credence to congressional charges that the Administration was "knuckling under to business lobbyists."

Despite his close association with the Nixon "inner circle," Ash survived Nixon's departure in August 1974. He helped to prepare Gerald Ford's September 1974 economic summit, and was named to the Council on Wages and Prices, established to fight inflation. At the Sept. 27-28 summit meetings, Ash was appointed to the Economic Policy Board.

After helping to ease the transition to a new Administration, Ash announced his resignation in December 1974. He had participated in the Ford Administration's policy turnabout from deflation to stimulation in November and December 1974, when the rapid collapse of U.S. production forced such a shift. Ash remarked that "the conditions of the economy are changing faster than we can change the budget." He left the OMB in February 1975 and returned to Litton Industries.

[LG]

ASHBROOK, JOHN M(ILAN)
b. Sept. 21, 1928; Johnstown, Ohio.
Republican Representative, Ohio, 1961-.

John Ashbrook was the son of a newspaper publisher and conservative, anti-New Deal Democratic Representative. After graduating from high school in 1946, he enlisted in the Navy for a two-year tour of duty and then entered Harvard in 1948. Receiving a B.S. degree four years later, Ashbrook entered law school at Ohio State University. While in law school he took over the publishing of the family's weekly newspaper. Admitted to the bar in 1955, Ashbrook was elected as a Republican to the state legislature in 1956 and again in 1958. He was active in Republican Party organizations, becoming chairman of the Ohio League of Young Republicans in 1955 and chairman of the Young Republican National Federation in 1957. In 1960, in his first bid for national office, Ashbrook was elected to the House of Representatives.

A staunch conservative, Ashbrook quickly became a spokesman for the right-wing traditionalists of the Republican Party. Throughout the 1960s he consistently opposed the social welfare measures of the Kennedy and Johnson Administrations, voting against federal aid to education, "war-on-poverty" funds and other domestic spending programs. Although he opposed deficit spending and big government at home, Ashbrook nonetheless was a strong advocate of huge defense budgets.

One of the earliest supporters of Barry Goldwater's [q.v.] presidential bid, he was a founder in 1963 of the Draft Goldwater organization. After Goldwater's defeat, Ashbrook helped found the American Conservative Union and served as its chairman from 1966 to 1971. In 1968 he surprised some right-wing Republicans when he came out in support of Richard Nixon's campaign for the Republican presidential nomination. [See JOHNSON Volume]

During the Nixon years, Ashbrook

maintained his conservative voting record. He opposed giving enforcement powers to the Equal Employment Opportunity Commission and voted against extension of the Office of Economic Opportunity and against the federal minimum wage. Ashbrook was also one of the most outspoken foes of busing to achieve racial balance in schools and supported every anti-busing measure in Congress. In 1974 he proposed an amendment to the Health, Education and Welfare appropriations bill to prohibit the use of any federal funds for busing, even if ordered by the courts. Although it was accepted in the House, the Senate-House conference adopted a much weaker provision that allowed the funding of court-ordered busing.

Initially a supporter of President Nixon, Ashbrook became increasingly disenchanted with the Administration's policies. A Congressional Quarterly study found that in 1972 Ashbrook voted against the President more than half the time. In December 1971 he accused Nixon of breaking 1968 campaign pledges and announced his candidacy for the Republican presidential nomination. Angered over continued deficit spending, the imposition of wage and price controls and the Administration's diplomatic initiatives toward Communist China, Ashbrook said that he intended his candidacy to halt the dangerous "leftward drift" of the Nixon Administration. With the support of conservative writer William F. Buckley, Jr., [q.v.] he entered the New Hampshire primary, but received only 11% of the vote. Ashbrook fared badly in every primary he entered, never winning more than 10% of the vote. His effort had little impact upon the President who easily won renomination at the Republican National Convention in August.

Ashbrook was critical of Nixon's handling of the Watergate affair. At a conference held by the American Conservative Union in January 1974, he cautioned against supporting the President out of personal or Party loyalty. After reading the partial transcripts of the White House tapes released by the President in April 1974, Ashbrook announced that he no longer believed Nixon's version of his involvement. On July 30 he called for the President's impeachment.

Ashbrook opposed President Ford's selection of Nelson Rockefeller [q.v.] as vice president, arguing that Rockefeller had "continually been rejected nationwide by the majority of the Republican Party." In 1975 he served on a committee sponsored by the American Conservative Union and Young Americans for Freedom to explore the possibility of a third party for the 1976 presidential elections. Abandoning that option Ashbrook joined with other conservative Republicans in Congress in issuing a statement in June 1975 that called for an "open" convention in 1976. After Ronald Reagan's [q.v.] entry into the Republican race, Ashbrook announced his support of Reagan, only to be disappointed by Reagan's choice of liberal Sen. Richard S. Schweiker (R, Pa.) [q.v.] as his running mate. Ashbrook called the decision "the dumbest thing" he had ever heard and said that he had become a "former" Reagan supporter. Remaining aloof from the presidential campaign, Ashbrook was elected in 1976 to his ninth term in Congress.

[JD]

ASHLEY, THOMAS L(UDLOW)
b. Jan. 11, 1923; Toledo, Ohio
Democratic Representative, Ohio, 1955–.

Born into a rich, old Republican family, Ashley earned his B.A. at Yale in 1948 and his LL.B. at Ohio State in 1951. After working briefly for Radio Free Europe, Ashley ran for the U.S. House as a Democrat in 1954. He won by a narrow margin in Ohio's ninth district, a heavily industrial and ethnic area that includes most of Toledo. Reelected without difficulty through the 1960s, Ashley served on the Banking and Currency Committee and became a specialist in housing legislation. He promoted a national urban growth policy and was able to secure funds for the re-building of downtown Toledo.

During the Johnson years Ashley voted for all major Great Society legislation and maintained a solid liberal record. He did not, however, criticize Johnson's Vietnam policies. As a member of the Banking and Currency panel, Ashley helped to write the 1966 amendments to the Bank Merger Act of 1960 and win congressional approval of U.S. Export-Import Bank financing of a Fiat automobile plant in the Soviet Union. [See JOHNSON Volume]

Ashley maintained a solidly liberal record during the Nixon Administration, winning a 100% rating on selected issues from the Americans for Democratic Action in both 1968 and 1970. A member of the Banking Committee's Housing Subcommittee, he helped draft the Housing and Urban Development Act of 1970. He worked for passage of an amendment to fund urban renewal and aid new communities, spoke in favor of a national urban growth policy and advocated the establishment of a three-member urban growth council in the executive branch. President Nixon opposed the council as an encroachment on executive prerogative. The provision was deleted from the final bill, but the act as passed did include a federal crime insurance program and an extensive Model Cities and metropolitan development program. Ashley's work on the bill was rewarded by the government's decision to build a new Model Cities town near Toledo.

During the early 1970s Ashley often teamed with Banking Committee Republican Garry Brown of Michigan to develop housing legislation acceptable to the Administration. Ashley voted for the Housing Act of 1974, although he opposed the bill's special housing subsidy provisions for the elderly. The Act, the first major piece of housing legislation since 1968, revised the nation's housing and urban aid programs. It provided block grants for development and established new programs of rental assistance for low- and middle-income families. The measure permitted communities to spend grants as they chose with only a few fed-

eral requirements for community development.

During 1975 and 1976 Ashley advocated new construction as the best way to stimulate the sagging housing industry and fought for the allocation of funds for new construction and public housing, a position opposed by the Ford Administration. Ashley joined Republicans, however, in opposing a low-interest mortgage loan program for middle-income home buyers and was instrumental in developing the compromise emergency housing bill signed by President Ford in July 1975.

Ashley continued to win reelection through the 1970s, though his margin of victory dropped from 69% in 1972 to 53% in 1974, following his arrest for drunk driving in Toledo in 1973.

[DAE]

ASPINALL, WAYNE N(ORVIEL)
b. April 3, 1896; Middleburg, Ohio.
Democratic Representative, Colo., 1949–73; Chairman, Interior and Insular Affairs Committee, 1959–73.

The son of a fruit grower, Aspinall grew up in the small town of Palisade, Colo. He studied law at the University of Denver, receiving an LL.B. in 1925. Aspinall worked as a fruit grower, a school teacher and administrator, and as legal representative for local farmers and marketing associations before entering Colorado politics in 1930. He served in both houses of the state legislature until 1948.

Elected to the U.S. House of Representatives from a small rural district in 1948, Aspinall was immediately appointed to the Public Lands Committee, later called the House Interior and Insular Affairs Committee. He ruled the Committee with an autocratic hand, appointing staff members and setting the agenda of every meeting of every subcommittee. He soon became a powerful figure in natural resources policies, advocating land reclamation projects and a "multiple-use" approach to resources development. Many of the measures he advocated, including major water reclamation projects, directly benefitted Aspinall's district. During his 24 years in the House, he sent over $1 billion in projects to his home district. A strong opponent of what he called "conservation extremists," he helped delay and then weaken a wilderness preservation bill during the early 1960s. One environmentalist maintained that Aspinall "did more damage to the American earth than any other human being in this century." [See KENNEDY, JOHNSON Volumes]

In 1963 Aspinall created the Public Land Law Review Commission (PLLRC), an executive-legislative commission authorized to decide how the country's public lands should be used. The panel's report issued in June 1970 reflected Aspinall's views. It recommended the maximum possible development of public land by mining and logging interests, while limiting the Secretary of the Interior's power to withdraw public lands from multiple-use development. Aspinall spent his last years in Congress trying unsuccessfully to enact the panel's recommendations into law, despite strenuous opposition by environmentalists and the Nixon Administration.

Aspinall's powers in his Committee were curbed by the Reorganization Act of 1970. As a result of the measure, the Democratic Caucus was empowered to veto the selection of subcommittee chairman, and subcommittees gained authority to set agendas. In an attempt to maintain his control, Aspinall created a Subcommittee on the Environment with jurisdiction to consider any bill referred to the Committee. Aspinall still had power because he could withold legislation from his subcommittee if he so chose, but because of continued opposition from within the Committee and pressure from the "Young Turks" in the 92nd Congress, his power began to erode.

Aspinall's influence in Colorado also declined as a result of redistricting that increased the urban, liberal and pro-conservation elements in his constituency. He lost further popularity at home in 1970 because of the way he handled the problem of radioactive uranium tailings used in housing foundations in his district. Aspinall delayed reporting the health hazard to the Atomic Energy Commission (AEC) and defended the AEC's failure to enlist federal aid in cleaning up the tailings. He was defeated in the 1972 Democratic primary by Alan Merson, a University of Denver law professor strongly supported by environmental and anti-war groups.

[DAE]

BAKER, HOWARD H(ENRY), Jr.
b. Nov. 15, 1925; Huntsville, Tenn.
Republican Senator, Tenn., 1967-.

Howard Baker comes from a political family. His grandfather was a judge, and his father was a representative from the second Tennessee district from 1951 to 1964. He married the daughter of Sen. Everett Dirksen (R, Ill.) [q.v.]. Baker received his law degree from the University of Tennessee in 1949. He engaged in private law practice, banking and business activities before running for the Senate in 1964 on what was essentially a conservative platform. He lost to a moderate Democrat. Adopting a more moderate political stance, he ran again in 1966 and defeated Democratic Gov. Frank G. Clement to become the first popularly elected Republican Senator in the state's history.

In the Senate Baker compiled a relatively conservative record, voting to give state governors the power to veto federal grants in aid and supporting increased military spending. However he backed major civil rights initiatives. [See JOHNSON Volume]

Baker remained a conservative on matters pertaining to the courts and justice during the Nixon years. He voted for the nomination of conservatives Clement F. Haynsworth [q.v.] and G. Harrold Carswell [q.v.] to the Supreme Court. He also voted for the District of Columbia crime bill's "no-knock" and preventive detention clauses.

The Senator continued supporting civil rights legislation. He backed extension of the Voting Rights Act in 1970 and 1972 and endorsed the nomination of Judge Ben Hooks to be the first black member of the Federal Communications Commission. He was, however, a strong opponent of forced busing to promote racial integration in the schools. He backed amendments to the Education Act of 1972 that limited the use of federal funds for busing.

He supported several environmental protection laws. He played an important role in the Senate Public Works Committee in the development of the clean air and water bills of 1970 and 1972 and the highway bill that permitted the trust fund to be used for mass-transit projects. But, he voted in favor of the supersonic transport program and the construction of the Alaska pipeline. Baker was sponsor of every major revenue sharing measure to come before the Senate from 1967 until the successful enactment of the Revenue Sharing Act of 1972 in which the federal government distributed part of its revenues to state and local governments with few strings attached.

In foreign and national security policy, Baker generally sided with the Nixon and Ford Administrations. He supported United States policy in Indochina until 1973, when he voted to force the United States to stop the bombing of Cambodia and Laos. He was a partisan of the president's prerogatives in foreign affairs and voted against the Cooper-Church amendment of 1970, the McGovern-Hatfield amendments of 1970 and 1971, and the Mansfield and Brooke amendments of 1971 and 1972 to withdraw American troops from Indochina. He joined with most of his colleagues in 1973, however, in voting to override Nixon's veto of the war powers bill. He supported high military expenditures and voted in favor of the anti-ballistic missile system and the Trident submarines.

Baker rose to national prominence during the Watergate affair. He served as co-chairman of the Senate Select Committee on Presidential Campaign Activities. More than any other committee member, Baker probed the motives of those in-

volved in Watergate. Nixon had earlier been a supporter of Baker and had campaigned for him in 1966. Nixon staffers had expected Baker to be their friend on the committee. Baker, however, won praises from Democrats and Republicans for his impartiality and critical questions to Watergate witnesses. Baker served as a member of the Senate select committee investigating the Central Intelligence Agency. His attacks on a Republican President and the CIA drew criticism from some conservative Republicans.

Baker's name was mentioned as a possible vice president from the time that it seemed that Spiro Agnew [q.v.] would step down. He supported Gerald Ford in 1976 and served as Ford's campaign manager in Tennessee. Baker was keynote speaker at the Republican national convention in 1976.

Baker sought to become the Senate Minority Leader—a post once held by his father-in-law, Everett Dirksen. He lost in two attempts for the post in 1969 and 1971. Seeking a new image and a more forceful opposition voice, his party elected him to the post in January 1977. [See CARTER Volume]

[HML]

BALL, GEORGE W(ILDMAN)
b. Dec. 21, 1909; Des Moines, Iowa
Foreign policy critic.

Following graduation from Northwestern University Law School in 1933, George Ball moved to Washington to accept a position with the Farm Credit Administration and the Treasury Department. Two years later he returned to Chicago to join Adlai Stevenson's law firm. During World War II, Ball was an administrator in the Office of Lend-Lease administration and then director of the U.S. Strategic Bombing Survey. A specialist in international economic policy, Ball advised France in its recovery efforts after the war. He also participated in the steps taken that led to the creation of the

European Coal and Steel Community and the European Common Market. During the 1950s Ball was one of Stevenson's closest advisers. He served as undersecretary of state from 1961 to 1966. He then returned to private law practice and investment banking in New York. [See TRUMAN, KENNEDY, JOHNSON Volumes]

Ball was one of the leading Democratic critics of the Nixon Administration's Vietnam policy. In a 1969 *Foreign Affairs* article he wrote that the lesson of the Vietnam War was that "there are regions in the world where modern arms cannot be effectively used and thus should never have been committed." "We must never again be beguiled by the false assumption," Ball continued, "that whenever the Western presence is withdrawn . . . a power vacuum is created." Ball recommended in the *New York Times Magazine* that the U.S. "de-escalate the importance of Vietnam." Nixon's Vietnamization policy disturbed Ball. He suggested that the phased withdrawal of American troops would be responsible for the U.S. losing its bargaining strength in possible negotiations and would be interpreted by Hanoi as a signal that Washington could not win the war. Nevertheless, Ball believed that the withdrawal could be a positive step if Washington made it clear that it was now Saigon's responsibility to win the war. If the South Vietnamese failed, the U.S. would thus be absolved from complicity in its defeat.

Ball was equally critical of Nixon's China policy. He supported the Administration overture to Communist China but questioned the need for Nixon's trip in 1972. Arguing that summit conferences tended to accomplish very little, Ball suggested that it would have been better if Secretary of State Henry Kissinger [*q.v.*] negotiated the normalization of relations with China. He was also angered by the Administration's failure to consult Japan. By refusing to involve Tokyo, Ball warned, the U.S. had insulted the proud, fiercely nationalistic Japanese. This blunder could encourage Japan to embark on its own China policy which could be detrimental to American interests.

In his book, *In Diplomacy For A Crowded World* (1976), Ball expressed displeasure with Kissinger for his personal style of diplomacy. He accused the Secretary of State of reducing the importance of the State Department, Congress, and, most important, the European alliance. Ball also criticized detente. He feared that the overselling of detente would lull the West into minimizing the Soviet threat. This would substantially weaken the North Atlantic Treaty Organization. Nevertheless, Ball did endorse the efforts to reach a strategic arms limitation agreement.

In the 1976 presidential campaign, Ball advised a number of presidential aspirants including Jimmy Carter.

[JB]

BARKER, BERNARD L.
b. March 17, 1917; Havana, Cuba.
Convicted Watergate conspirator.

Cuban-American Bernard Barker worked for Central Intelligence Agency (CIA) contact E. Howard Hunt [*q.v.*] during the CIA's early campaigns against Fidel Castro. Prior to the 1972 Presidential election, Hunt and G. Gordon Liddy [*q.v.*] put together a program of electronic surveillance, covert entry and other dirty tricks for the Committee to Re-Elect the President (CREEP). Hunt sought Barker for various covert entry projects in connection with the program. In September 1971 Barker and two cohorts broke into the office of Dr. Louis Fielding, Daniel Ellsberg's [*q.v.*] psychiatrist, in an effort to find information damaging to the antiwar activist. Ellsberg had been indicted on federal charges in connection with his release of the *Pentagon Papers,* a secret study compiled by the Rand Corp. documenting the history of United States involvement in Southeast Asia. They found no evidence, however.

In May 1972 Barker was one of several individuals who broke into the Democratic National Committee's (DNC) headquarters in the Watergate office building in Washington, D.C., to "plant" electronic "bugs" and photograph files. Because of an error in the placement of a phone tap, the team had to redo the job on June 17. During this second break-in, Barker and the other members of the entry team were discovered by a guard and arrested. Barker was carrying incriminating documents that led police investigators immediately to Hunt.

On Sept. 15, 1972, Liddy, Hunt, Barker and the other members of the entry team were indicted on charges in connection with the Watergate break-in. Barker pleaded not guilty and was released on bond.

The trial of the Watergate burglars started on Jan. 10, 1973, with Judge John Sirica [q.v.] presiding. The following day Hunt pleaded guilty to all charges and a week later Barker and the others followed suit. On March 23, Judge Sirica sentenced Barker and the other entry team members to a provisional maximum term of 40 years. He said he would not promise leniency but urged full cooperation with the federal grand jury and the Senate Select Committee investigating Watergate. During his testimony before the Senate Select Committee, Barker claimed that his motivation for committing the break-ins flowed from his belief that he was helping the anti-Castro movement. On Nov. 9, 1973, Barker was sentenced to 18½ months to six years in prison. In July 1974, Judge Sirica reduced the sentence to time already served.

Barker and five other persons involved in the Fielding break-in were indicted for conspiring to deprive Dr. Fielding of his civil rights in March 1974. He and the others pleaded not guilty. In July Barker was convicted and given a maximum sentence of 10 years and a $10,000 fine. However on July 22, the sentence was reduced to probation. On May 17, 1976, the court of appeals in the District of Columbia reversed Barker's conviction for his role in this incident. The court cited the failure of the trial judge to instruct the jury that Barker believed the break-in was legal because it had White House approval.

[RLN]

BAYH, BIRCH E(VANS), JR.
b. Jan. 22, 1928; Terre Haute, Ind.
Democratic Senator, Ind., 1963–.

Following graduation from Purdue University, Birch Bayh settled on a 340-acre farm outside Terre Haute in 1951. He entered politics in 1954 when he successfully ran as a Democrat for a seat in Indiana's House of Representatives. While serving in the legislature, he studied law at night at Indiana University, which awarded him a degree in 1960. In 1962 Bayh won a seat in the U.S. Senate. As chairman of the Judiciary Committee's Subcommittee on Constitutional Amendments, Bayh gained national prominence when, in January 1965, he sponsored the 25th Amendment outlining the steps to be taken in case of a presidential disability and rearranging the order of succession in the event of the death of a President. [See KENNEDY, JOHNSON Volumes]

During the Nixon and Ford Administrations, Bayh, as chairman of the Constitutional Amendments Subcommittee, dealt with many of the major issues of the period. In 1970 Bayh's subcommittee held hearings and approved the Equal Rights Amendment and the 26th Amendment giving 18-year-olds the vote. Following the Supreme Court's 1973 decision striking down restrictive state abortion laws, Bayh's subcommittee received testimony on a constitutional amendment that would have permitted the states to ban abortions. With the vote deadlocked at 4 to 4, Bayh cast the deciding vote in 1975 that prevented the reporting of the amendment to the full committee and the Senate floor for consideration. Bayh introduced an "alternatives to abortion" package of legislation that would have provided a variety of social and medical services for young mothers and prohibited discrimination against unmarried mothers seeking health insurance benefits. Although Bayh personally opposed abortions, he pushed through the Senate a procedural vote that again barred a vote on the abortion amendment in 1976.

Bayh compiled a solid liberal record on

domestic legislation. He was especially concerned with the passage of laws expanding day care centers and programs to help juvenile offenders. He backed legislation to control hand guns. Bayh joined other liberals in the Senate to prevent the passage of legislation severely restricting the use of busing to facilitate integration. In 1969 and 1970 Bayh led the fight in the Senate that denied President Nixon's Supreme Court nominees, Clement Haynsworth [q.v.] and G. Harrold Carswell [q.v.], appointment to the high bench. It was Bayh and a number of staff members who publicized the conflict of interest charge that doomed the Haynsworth nomination. Bayh argued that Haynsworth's opposition to civil rights and the fact that so many of his decisions were overruled by an appeals court revealed he was not competent to sit on the nation's highest court. In foreign affairs Bayh supported the cutback of American troops in Europe and a reduction in defense spending for such projects as the Safeguard anti-ballistic missile system, the B-1 bomber and the Trident submarine.

In 1971 Bayh tested the waters for the Democratic Party's presidential nomination. He toured the nation, concentrating on the states with future primaries, to raise money and make political contacts. He was usually well received because his staff did excellent advance work, and Bayh, who had always been a favorite of the AFL-CIO, received strong labor encouragement. Bayh ran on an anti-Nixon platform stressing his opposition to the Vietnam war and his support for domestic liberal legislation. The fight against the Carswell-Haynsworth nominations also became a central issue in the campaign. Bayh unexpectedly withdrew from the race in October 1971 because his wife had undergone "critical" surgery for breast cancer and he wanted to be at her side to help her recover.

In 1974 Bayh won a third term with a narrow victory over Mayor Richard Lugar [q.v.] of Indianapolis. The economy was the dominant issue in the contest. Lugar accused Bayh of contributing to inflation by supporting excessive federal spending and refusing to go along with President Ford's budget cuts. Bayh's victory resulted primarily from an effective get-out-the-vote campaign by the state's unions.

In late October 1976 Birch Bayh became the ninth Democrat to declare his candidacy for the presidency. Running as a liberal, Bayh announced plans to be the front-runner of the left-of-center by the time of the April New York primary. He began his campaign with $150,000 supplemented by matching federal funds, but by the time of the New Hampshire primary, Bayh had run out of money. He and his staff had miscalculated the amount of donations they would receive. Bayh had planned large campaigns in Massachusetts and New York, where he had strong local support, but he did not have enough money. Following poor showings in New Hampshire and Massachusetts, Bayh withdrew from the race. [See CARTER Volume]

[JB]

BEAM, JACOB D(YNELEY)
b. March 24, 1908; Princeton, N.J.
Ambassador to the Soviet Union, March 1969-January 1973.

Jacob Beam, a university professor's son, received a bachelor's degree from Princeton University in 1929. After a year of study at Cambridge University in England, he entered the Foreign Service, and served mostly in Europe. His first ambassadorial position was in Poland from 1957 to 1961, a period in which he negotiated with representatives of Communist China. At the time Richard Nixon assumed the presidency, Beam had already been serving as U.S. ambassador to Czechoslovakia for nearly three years. [See EISENHOWER Volume]

Appointed to the post of ambassador to the Soviet Union in March 1969 Beam, who had considerable experience in both arms-control matters and Eastern European affairs, was expected to play an important role in U.S. foreign policy formulation and negotiations with the Soviet leadership. The Moscow post had previously been held by people vigorously involved in policy: W. Averell Harriman, Llewellyn E. Thompson, George F. Kennan and Foy D. Kohler.

Beam played a minor role in policymaking and negotiating, however. In an Administration in which foreign policy formulation was dominated by Henry Kissinger [q.v.], Beam's influence was peripheral. Kissinger, as national security adviser to the President and as Secretary of State, preferred to deal directly with Anatoly F. Dobrynin, the Soviet ambassador to the United States, rather than work through formal United States diplomatic channels. In practice, Kissinger was the U.S. ambassador to the Soviet Union.

So minimal was Beam's role that he did not take part in a sit-down meeting with Soviet leader Leonid Brezhnev until three years after he began his Moscow tour. Kissinger once quietly visited Moscow for talks with Soviet officials. Beam did not learn of the visit until Kissinger was preparing to depart. On another occasion Kissinger arrived in Moscow with his own aides, leaving all embassy officials—including Beam—uninvited to private meetings with the Soviet's.

Beam resigned his post in January 1973 and retired from the Foreign Service after a career that lasted more than 40 years. In November 1974 he became chairman of Radio Free Europe, succeeding Lucius D. Clay.

[HML]

BEAME, ABRAHAM D(AVID)
b. March 19, 1906; London, England.
Mayor, New York, N.Y., 1974-77.

The son of Polish-Jewish immigrants who had fled their native land to escape political persecution, Abraham Beame was born in London. His parents migrated to the United States while Beame was still an infant, and he grew up on Manhattan's Lower East Side. Attending New York public schools and City College, he received an accounting degree in 1928

and founded a small accounting firm with a close friend. Beame moved to the middle-class Crown Heights section of Brooklyn in 1928 and became active in local Democratic Party politics. He attracted the attention of Party leaders for his diligent work as an election-district captain. In 1946 he was appointed assistant director of New York City's budget bureau, and in 1952 he became budget director, a position he held until 1961.

In 1961 Beame won election as city comptroller on an "anti-machine" ticket headed by Mayor Robert F. Wagner. Encouraged by the respect he had won for his conservative approach to monetary matters, Beame unsuccessfully sought election as mayor in 1965. After his re-election to the post of comptroller in 1969, Beame became the focus for the "regular" Democrats opposed to Mayor John Lindsay [q.v.]. He entered the mayoral primary in 1973 and, after winning a plurality of the votes, defeated Herman Badillo (D, N.Y.) in the runoff. Presenting himself as an experienced administrator and budget expert, Beame won a landslide victory in November.

Beame took office at a time when cities across the nation were experiencing serious fiscal woes. The country's deepest recession in the postwar era had raised unemployment to near-depression levels and increased the demand for social services at a time when local revenues were in decline. Double-digit inflation, particularly the high cost of energy caused in part by the quadrupling of oil prices in 1973, placed a further drain on municipal budgets.

In May 1974 Beame presented an $11.1 billion "austerity" budget that eliminated low-priority programs and raised taxes. He opposed the Ford Administration's effort to curb inflation by reducing federal expenditures, arguing that it would only worsen the plight of the nation's cities. He also lobbied hard for congressional approval of federal aid for mass transit.

Beame soon found himself in the midst of a fiscal crisis far worse than what other cities faced. By April 1975 New York City's publicly-held debt totaled a staggering $14 billion. On April 2, the Standard and Poor's Corp. suspended its "A" rating for New York City bonds. The city's cash-flow problems were so bad that state officials loaned the city $400 million. Beame promised a new austerity budget that included plans to fire 4,000 workers and to slash many city services. But he warned that even with these cuts the city still faced a $641 million deficit.

The crisis deepened in May when New York commercial banks refused to buy $280 million in city notes. Citing an immediate need for $1.5 billion by June 30 to meet the city's short-term debt obligations, Beame sought financial assistance from federal and state officials. He was rebuffed in Washington by President Ford, who instead urged the adoption of "sound budget policies" and the curtailing of "less-essential services and subsidies." Ford's response was echoed by Treasury Secretary William E. Simon [q.v.] and Federal Reserve Board Chairman Arthur Burns [q.v.].

Although Republican leaders in the State Senate initially rejected Beame's request, the threat of default was too serious to ignore. With the strong support of Gov. Hugh Carey [q.v.], Beame won approval of a rescue plan. On June 10 the legislature created a new state agency, the Municipal Assistance Corp. (MAC), designed to alleviate the immediate cash-flow crisis and to supervise the city's long-range borrowing plans. "Big Mac," as it became known, was authorized to refinance New York's short-term debt of $3 billion, which was due for repayment in September, by floating long-term bonds guaranteed by the state. In return, MAC could limit the city's borrowing power and impose new, stringent budgetary procedures on the city. Although Beame was reluctant to relinquish control over the budget, New York's desperate financial situation left him with no alternative.

The state's rescue plan, however, was only the first in a long series of last minute rescue operations designed to stave off bankruptcy. For months Beame presided over a city government periodically on the brink of insolvency and forced to make drastic cuts in essential services in order to survive. On June 30, 1975, Beame announced that 40,000 city workers, including firefighters, police and sanitation workers, would be laid off. Sanitation workers struck, laid-off police conducted demonstrations and firefighters called in "sick." The conflict eased on July 3 when Beame won agreement from state officials for a plan to increase the city's taxing authority in order to rehire some of the workers.

Meanwhile MAC officials declared that Beame's austerity measures were insufficient. Accusing the agency of trying to "humiliate" him by becoming a "shadow government," he was nonetheless forced to comply with its demands. On July 31 Beame announced a wage freeze for all city workers, increases in mass transit and commuter rail fares and a $375 million reduction in the city's capital budget. Despite these measures MAC failed to find buyers for its August bond issue, and the state again had to rescue the city. In a special session the state legislature passed a $2.3 billion aid bill, which also set stringent financial curbs on the city and gave control of city revenues to a newly created Emergency Financial Control Board. Beame angrily broke with Gov. Carey over the measure, charging that it destroyed the city's independence as a self-governing municipality. Another crisis was narrowly averted in October when the municipal teachers' union agreed to purchase $250 million in MAC bonds with pension fund money.

The inability of state and local efforts to permanently avert a financial collapse led to a concerted attempt aimed at securing federal assistance. In October the Congressional Budget Office released a study concluding that default by the city was a near certainty unless new aid was obtained. On Oct. 12, Vice President Nelson Rockefeller [q.v.] broke ranks with the Administration and urged aid for New York City. Arthur Burns warned that if New York's "financial crisis is not resolved, it could injure the recovery process underway in our national economy." On Oct. 29, however, President Ford delivered a strong speech in which he vowed to veto any bill providing federal loans for New York. Blaming the crisis on "fiscal mismanagement," he said that federally guaranteed loans would allow New York City officials to "escape responsibility for their past follies" and warned that only additional austerity measures would lead him to reconsider his stand.

Ford's tough position forced state and city officials to take further actions. Beame announced more cutbacks in municipal employment and services, and in late November the state approved a new tax package to raise city revenues. Pressure began to mount for congressional action. The U.S. Conference of Mayors supported federal aid for New York, and the Bank of America warned that if New York defaulted, "the entire nation would suffer." The House and Senate Banking Committees both initiated hearings on loan legislation.

On Nov. 26, the day after New York state approved its latest rescue operation, Ford ended his opposition to federal aid and asked Congress to approve legislation making up to $2.3 billion a year in direct federal loans available to New York City. Congress quickly complied and on Dec. 9 Ford signed the three-year loan package.

Although federal legislation virtually eliminated the danger of default or bankruptcy, the crisis had a continuing impact on New York City. The price of federal and state aid was the imposition of austerity budgets for the remainder of Beame's administration. The Mayor was forced to curtail city services drastically, reducing police and fire protection to dangerously low levels. He also had to order the closing of schools, hospitals, libraries, and day-care centers; cutback funds for the city's parks; and end free tuition at the City University. The quality of life in the nation's largest city deteriorated badly.

Beame sought reelection in 1977. He was opposed by several candidates, including liberal Democratic Reps. Bella Abzug [q.v.], Herman Badillo and Edward Koch [q.v.], and New York Secretary of State Mario Cuomo. Beame was the target of all the candidates and in the Sep-

tember primary, in which no one received the required 40% of the vote, he failed to make the runoff. He was succeeded as mayor by Rep. Edward Koch.

[JD]

BEARD, DITA D(AVIS)
b. November 1918; Fort Riley, Kan.
Lobbyist.

Dita Beard's father was an Army colonel. Beard held various odd jobs following high school. With the onset of World War II, she went to work for the Board of Economic Warfare before joining the Red Cross. During the late 1940s and early 1950s, she was married and divorced twice.

After her second divorce Beard went to Washington, D.C. with her five children. With no child support payments from either of her former husbands, she was forced to find work as a secretary for the National Association of Broadcasters. She was actively involved in Richard Nixon's 1960 campaign for the presidency.

The following year, she began working for the International Telephone and Telegraph's (ITT) new Washington, D.C. office, initially as a secretary. But because of her extensive experience with D.C.'s social and political life, ITT president Harold Geneen [q.v.] promoted her to lobbyist and general troubleshooter. Beard's professional relationship with Geneen remained close. Indeed she occasionally aroused the ire of her superiors by going over their heads and reporting directly to the president. In 1966 *Fortune* magazine identified her as one of Washington's major lobbyists, noting her penchant for blunt language and actions and her keen knowledge of "what makes congressmen tick." She was particularly adept at establishing contacts with politicians by making various ITT services available to them free of charge.

During the Nixon administration her influence increased even further—as a lifelong Republican, she was on friendly terms with a number of the new faces at the White House, such as Defense Secretary Melvin Laird [q.v.].

In the first half of 1971, the Republican Party was searching for a city to host its 1972 National Convention. President Nixon strongly favored San Diego because of its proximity to his home in San Clemente. Local leaders, however, were far from convinced that the business the Convention would bring to the city was worth the great expense required. But the Republican Party continued to show an interest—White House staffers visited in June, long after the deadline for convention bids had passed without any action on San Diego's part.

ITT, whose subsidiary, Sheraton Hotels, had recently opened a new hotel in San Diego, was also interested in having the Republican Convention there. In May ITT's annual general meeting was held in San Diego. Dita Beard, who had been in San Diego for the past few months, gave a dinner party in which White House aides, local politicians and ITT officials discussed the Convention question. Out of this informal gathering came a quiet ITT pledge of considerable support, in money and services, to defray the cost of the Convention. In July the Republican National Committee, meeting in Denver, chose San Diego as the Convention site.

Later that same month a government anti-trust suit against ITT was settled out of court. The settlement, which permitted a merger between ITT and the Hartford Insurance Group, was largely along the lines ITT had desired. As word of ITT's support for the San Diego Convention site circulated, suspicions of a "deal" between ITT and the Republican Party emerged in Washington. In December Democratic Party Chairman Lawrence O'Brien [q.v.] wrote to Richard Kleindienst [q.v.] of the Justice Department, questioning the implications of the settlement. Rumors of a deal were emphatically denied.

But in February of 1972 Washington columnist Jack Anderson [q.v.] obtained an ITT memorandum written by Dita Beard to William Merriam, head of ITT's Washington office, during the height of the San Diego Convention negotiations in June of 1971. Beard stated in the memo that ITT's promise of financial support for the Convention had "gone a long way toward our negotiations on the mergers eventually coming out as Hal (Harold Geneen) wants them." The memo not only confirmed a connection between ITT's proposed contribution to the San Diego Convention and the ITT Hartford Insurance merger, but indicated that President Nixon and Attorney General John Mitchell [q.v.] were aware of the arrangement.

Anderson passed the document to his associate, Brit Hume, who contacted Dita Beard and arranged two meetings during which she reportedly confirmed the authenticity of the memorandum. Hume told Anderson that Beard took the credit for finalizing the ITT committment with John Mitchell in May 1971 at a Kentucky Derby social gathering held by Republican Gov. Louis Nunn. Both Nunn and Mitchell denied the allegations when Hume confronted them with Beard's statements.

Nonetheless the substance of Brit Hume's investigations appeared in the Feb. 29 edition of Anderson's column. Two days later another column implicated Richard Kleindienst in the ITT settlement, directly contradicting Kleindienst's December 1971 assurances to Lawrence O'Brien. The Senate was then considering the confirmation of Kleindienst to replace Attorney General Mitchell, who had stepped down to run President Nixon's re-election campaign. Kleindienst immediately requested a chance to appear before the Senate Judiciary Committee to refute the claims of Anderson and Hume.

When the hearings began on March 2, Dita Beard figured prominently in the testimony of such witnesses as Mitchell and Gov. Nunn. Nunn portrayed Beard as unreliable, stating that she had been intoxicated at the Kentucky Derby social. Harold Geneen testified that his connection with Dita Beard was a distant one, and denied any knowledge of the events described in the memo.

Meanwhile Dita Beard had vanished

from Washington, D. C. at about the time the hearings began. The FBI eventually located her in the coronary ward of a Denver hospital, where she had apparently gone after being taken out of Washington by G. Gordon Liddy [q.v.], who would play a key role in the Watergate scandal later that year. Her personal physician, Dr. Victor Liska, told the FBI that she was too ill to give evidence to the Committee. Dr. Liska testified at the hearing that Beard had been suffering from a heart ailment for sometime—implying that her physical and mental condition affected her competency at the time she wrote the memo. Liska's own credibility, however, was damaged when it was learned that the Justice Department was investigating him and his wife on charges of medicare fraud.

It was not until March 17 that Beard made her first public response to the proceedings in Washington. In a sudden reversal she released a statement through her lawyer that referred to the memo as "a forgery, a fraud and a hoax." Several members of the Judiciary Committee then flew to Denver to take testimony from Beard in her hospital room. Although she conceded that some of the less controversial passages did sound familiar, intensive questioning was prevented when Beard's attending physicians cleared the room, claiming she was showing symptoms of a relapse. In April two independent physicians associated with the hospital stated there was no evidence, except her own complaints of chest pains, that Beard suffered from any heart ailments. In any event there was no further testimony from Beard.

The balance of the hearings involved more conflicting testimony, various experts with differing opinions on the memo's authenticity, the introduction of yet another memo, which ITT claimed was the "real" Dita Beard memorandum—in short, a bewildering array of evidence that made a clear determination of the facts increasingly difficult. Ultimately the Committee and the full Senate confirmed the nomination of Kleindienst as Attorney General.

Dita Beard never returned to her old post in Washington. She was transferred by ITT to Denver and retired in June of 1975 to a farm near Shepardstown, W. Va.

[MDQ]

BEIRNE, JOSEPH A(NTHONY)
b. Feb. 16, 1911; Jersey City, N.J.
d. Sept. 2, 1974; Washington, D.C.
President, Communications Workers of America, 1947-74.

Beirne, the son of Irish immigrants, was raised in a tenement district of Jersey City. He began working for the Western Electric Co. in 1928 and soon became active as a union organizer. He was elected president of the National Federation of Telephone Workers in 1943. Three years later he negotiated the first national contract with the American Telephone and Telegraph Co. (AT&T). After a nationwide strike in 1947 that severely disrupted telephone service, Beirne became president of the reorganized Communications Workers of America (CWA), which affiliated with the Congress of Industrial Organizations (CIO) in 1949. Beirne became a CIO vice president that same year, and after the AFL-CIO merger in 1955, a vice president and member of the Executive Council of that organization, positions he held until his death. [See TRUMAN Volume]

Beirne helped expel the International Brotherhood of Teamsters from the AFL-CIO in 1957. A staunch supporter of Presidents Kennedy and Johnson, he served on several presidential commissions. Beirne was a strong advocate of U.S.-sponsored training programs for Latin American trade unionists as a means of resisting communist influence in the labor movement there. In April 1968 he gave in to rank-and-file pressure and called the first nationwide telephone strike in 21 years. The following month the Bell System agreed to a three-year contract with a 19% wage increase. [See KENNEDY, JOHNSON Volumes]

On July 14, 1971, Beirne led his

400,000 member union in another telephone strike. Inflation had eaten into the living standards of telephone workers, and the union membership was determined to win protection against further inflationary pressures. Although telephone service was hardly impaired due to widespread automation in the industry, the Bell System management did not want a long strike. On July 20 Beirne announced that a settlement had been reached with AT&T. The contract provided for an immediate 12.8% wage hike, increases of 29.5% over the life of the three-year contract and cost-of-living raises pegged to the Consumer Price Index. It also stipulated that wage differentials between male and female employes be reduced, and guaranteed a modified agency shop (a provision requiring employes either to join the union or pay union dues after 30 days on the job).

While most CWA members voted to approve the pact and return to work, more militant locals in New York rejected the contract in defiance of the national leadership. Although Beirne declared their continued strike unwise, the national union provided over $11 million in strike benefits to its New York members. A contract was finally reached with New York Telephone in February 1972 after seven months.

In 1972 Beirne broke with AFL-CIO President George Meany [q.v.] over the presidential elections. On July 19 the Executive Council of the labor federation voted to remain neutral in the campaign, refusing to support George McGovern [q.v.]. It was the first time in 17 years that the AFL-CIO failed to endorse the Democratic candidate. The following month 25 leaders of individual unions within the Federation announced the formation of the National Labor Committee for the Election of McGovern-Shriver. Beirne, who served as secretary-treasurer, explained that McGovern had "a 12-year record in the Senate that is 93% right" according to the ratings of the AFL-CIO's Committee on Political Education. Nixon, he said, had a "zero-minus record." Beirne announced that the organization's

goal was to inform trade unionists of McGovern's record and "hope they listen and accept it and support it." The CWA contributed substantially to the McGovern campaign.

Beirne and the CWA came under criticism in 1973 for opposition to a job discrimination settlement with AT&T. On Jan. 18, 1973, AT&T reached an agreement with the Labor Department and the Equal Employment Opportunities Commission under which the company agreed to pay $15 million in back pay to women and minority males in compensation for past discrimination and $23 million a year in raises to compensate for discrimination in promotions. The settlement was the largest to date in a job bias case. In February the CWA petitioned in U.S. district court against the settlement and requested that it be admitted as a party in the dispute. The CWA charged that its collective bargaining rights had been ignored and that the agreement entailed "preferential treatment constituting discrimination against certain of its members." On Oct. 14 a federal judge dismissed the union's petition, saying the union's failure to participate in the settlement was "willful and by choice," and charging the CWA with consistently failing to challenge discriminatory practices by the telephone company.

Beirne retired from the presidency of the CWA in June 1974 for reasons of poor health. He died of cancer on Sept. 2, 1974 in Washington, D.C.

[JD]

BENNETT, WALLACE F(OSTER)
b. Nov. 13, 1898; Salt Lake City, Utah.
Republican Senator, Utah, 1951-75.

A graduate of the University of Utah in 1919, Bennett began an apprenticeship in his father's paint-manufacturing and glass-distributing firm the following year. Under his father's tutelage he rose from office clerk to company president by 1938. In 1939 he founded the Bennett Motor Company, a Ford dealership. In addition during these years he was active civically and served on the board of a number of Western banks. Bennett's business acumen and leadership ability became widely recognized, and in 1950 he was urged to run for the Senate. After an energetic campaign he defeated the Democratic incumbent, Elbert D. Thomas, who had been a key figure in the New Deal. Bennett was subsequently reelected in 1956, 1962 and again in 1968. [See TRUMAN, EISENHOWER, KENNEDY, JOHNSON Volumes]

A steadfast fiscal conservative and ardent supporter of the free enterprise system, Bennett gained prominence as a leading monetary expert. The ranking Republican on the Senate Finance Committee, he stressed the necessity of building a more flexible international monetary system that would determine the value of the dollar based on supply and demand in world markets. Bennett regarded the U.S. gold reserve for domestic currency as an anachronism, since the gold standard had been abandoned in 1934. Based on Finance Committee recommendations, Nixon suspended convertibility between gold and the dollar in 1971 and instead permitted the international market to decide dollar value.

As a member of the Senate Banking, Housing and Urban Affairs Committee, Bennett opposed the increasing number of bank acquisitions by industrial conglomerates and in 1969 introduced the Bank Holding Company Act. The bill broadened the existing definition of bank holding companies, thus reducing loopholes that enabled multibillion dollar corporations or banks to acquire large and diverse financial and nonfinancial businesses. The bill was enacted into law in a modified form in 1970. Bennett played a key role in the shaping of revenue-sharing legislation which provided local and state governments with federal funds based on population, local tax revenues and per capita income. Thus funds to impoverished areas would exceed funds to wealthy suburban comunities. The State and Local Fiscal Assistance Act passed in 1972.

An opponent of anti-poverty programs during the Johnson Administration, Bennett advocated responsible legislation structured to effectively meet the needs of the poor and avoid excessive drain of revenue at the taxpayer's expense. In 1972 he introduced the Allied Service Act, which was designed to coordinate federally financed social service programs on a state and local level. The bill was rejected by Congress, however. He also cosponsored a bill that provided funds for bilingual job-training programs and the Minority Business Equity Investment Act, which established investment opportunities in minority businesses.

Bennett staunchly supported the anti-busing legislation passed by the House in 1972 because it provided federal aid to disadvantaged students, retained the neighborhood school concept and offered remedies to help achieve equal educational opportunities.

A vociferous foe of organized labor, Bennett supported a 1973 Senate resolution giving union employes the right to end a strike by secret ballot vote. He also backed legislation that increased presidential power to end strikes. In 1972 he opposed a bill to increase the minimum wage because he considered it inflationary in its recommendation for an immediate wage increase.

Throughout his final senatorial term Bennett provided unwavering support of Nixon Administration policies. "Nixon," he stated, "has raised the level of our leadership to new and greater heights and made America the symbol of hope for peace among all nations in all the world."

Bennett decided against a fifth term in office and retired from the political arena at the age of 77.

[DGE]

BENTSEN, LLOYD(MILLARD),(JR.)
b. Feb. 11, 1921; Mission, Tex.
Democratic Senator, Tex., 1971-.

Lloyd Bentsen grew up in the citrus country of the Rio Grande Valley, in southern Texas, where his father and uncle had a real estate business. Bentsen took his LL.B. degree at the University of Texas in Austin in 1942. He served in the U.S. Army Air Corps during World War II.

After discharge from the Army in July 1945, Bentsen returned to McAllen, Tex., and entered private law practice. He was elected judge of Hidalgo County in 1946. In December 1948, the last day of the 80th Congress, he was sworn in as the youngest member of the U.S. House of Representatives, after winning a special election. During his years in the House Bentsen generally supported the interests of Texas farmers and fruit growers. He was a militant anti-Communist, favoring U.S. involvement in Indochina and opposing alleged Communist domination of U.S. labor unions.

Bentsen decided not to run for reelection in 1954. Instead he returned to Texas to become a businessman. With his father's multimillion dollar financial help, he founded Lincoln Consolidated, a holding company that owned Lincoln Liberty Life Insurance Co. and controlled stocks worth hundreds of millions of dollars.

Bentsen challenged liberal Sen. Ralph Yarborough (D, Tex.) in the May 1970 Democratic senatorial primary. With the support of former Gov. John B. Connally [q.v.] and others of the conservative Democratic establishment in Texas, Bentsen waged a heavily funded, highly organized campaign. Associating Yarborough with the domestic disorders of the late 1960s, he managed to defeat the incumbent, who had the backing of a coalition of liberals, blue-collar workers, blacks and Mexican Americans.

Bentsen and George Bush [q.v.], the Republican candidate for the Senate in 1970, differed little in their general positions. Both supported Nixon's Vietnam policies and measures to aid the oil industry while opposing social welfare programs. Bentsen was helped by a large voter turnout. Two proposed amendments to the state constitution allowing saloons throughout the state and giving tax breaks to undeveloped land turned out the conservative Democratic vote enabling Bent-

sen to win with 53% of the ballots. Bentsen classified himself as part of the loyal opposition to the President. He criticized the Nixon Administration for its neglect of education, health and the environment and for economic policies that resulted in inflation and high unemployment. Bentsen declared support for a limited form of national health insurance and supported allocation of federal funds to promote medical education, scientific research, rural area development and improved daycare programs.

The federal budget deficit was an issue of utmost importance to the Senator. He demanded cuts in government spending and tax reform as an alternative to increased taxes. In keeping with his conservative fiscal stand, Bentsen voted against the Revenue Sharing Act of 1972. His reason was that he knew of no revenue to share, only federal deficits, and he believed that in the long run revenue sharing would not improve local government. Bentsen also supported welfare reform, although he opposed the guaranteed income plan proposed by the Nixon Administration because he believed it lacked sufficient work incentives. In another effort to stop needless federal spending Bentsen proposed an unsuccessful amendment to cut increased expenditures on the Trident nuclear submarine.

Bentsen was concerned about the erosion of power from the Congress to the executive branch of the federal government. He objected to the tendency of U.S. Presidents to enter into executive agreements rather than to make treaties, which must be ratified by a two-thirds vote of the Senate. In 1972 Bentsen cosponsored a Senate resolution asking the executive branch to comply with the Constitution and submit such agreements to the Senate as treaties. When the Administration did not comply, the Senate voted to deny the money needed to implement such agreements unless they were resubmitted as treaties. He also supported the War Powers Act of 1973, which limited the President's power to commit U.S. forces to combat without consent of Congress.

Bentsen supported measures that

would allow Congress to make its own evaluation of social programs and budgets. He advocated one measure, a national goals and priorities bill, which would have created a three-man President's council of social advisers that would submit an annual report to the Congress evaluating social programs. The measure would have also created an office of national goals and priorities to advise Congress on social programs. Bentsen also worked for the adoption of the Congressional Budget and Impoundment Act of 1974. The Act provided for the staff and information needed by Congress to make independent decisions on budget policies.

Bentsen continued his early career interest in the American farmer. The Senator disapproved of the handling of the 1972 United States-Soviet Union grain trade. He stated that a few giant trading companies made immense profits while many farmers in early harvest areas actually lost money. He introduced legislation that would have authorized the Secretary of Agriculture to make special deficiency payments to wheat farmers. The measure was defeated.

In February 1975 Bentsen announced his candidacy for President in the 1976 election. He stated that the paramount issue of the election was economic recovery. He pledged to "restore the meaning of America's two great promises: opportunity at home and moral leadership." Bentsen's campaign raised a lot of money but little popular support. He was reelected to the Senate in 1976.

[CLC]

BEN-VENISTE, RICHARD
b. 1943, New York, N.Y.
Watergate Assistant Special
Prosecutor, 1973-75.

Upon completion of Columbia Law School, Ben-Veniste joined the Special Prosecutions Section of the U.S. Attorney's Office in New York City. After a year he was promoted to chief of the Official Corruption Section, and was

credited with the successful prosecution of a number of organized crime figures for income tax fraud and collusion with union officials in kick-back schemes. In 1973 Archibald Cox [q.v.] special Watergate prosecutor recruited Ben-Veniste for his staff. Assigned to the Watergate Task Force in mid-July, his responsibilities included investigating allegations of hush money, destruction of documents and illegal wiretapping as well as charges that Nixon had advance knowledge of Watergate activities.

Ben-Veniste was the attorney who subpoenaed the White House tapes during July. When Nixon refused to supply the tapes on the grounds of national security and executive privilege, Ben-Veniste helped prepare the prosecution's case, which was argued before Judge John Sirica [q.v.]. Sirica ruled in the prosecution's favor.

Ben-Veniste was involved in further legal battles for additional tapes and was one of the attorneys responsible for analyzing them once turned over to the Watergate prosecutor. His analysis helped develop the case for Nixon's complicity in the Watergate cover-up. Ben-Veniste later presented evidence of complicity by high Administration officials to various grand juries investigating the affair, evidence which led to the indictment of several former members of the Nixon Administration. He continued to probe the case until the special prosecutor's office was officially disbanded in the latter part of 1975, soon after Nixon's resignation.

[DJE]

For further information:
Richard Ben-Veniste and George T. Frampton, *Stonewall* (New York, 1977).

BERGSTEN, C. FRED
b. April 23, 1941; New York, N.Y.
Economist.

Bergsten obtained his B.A. in 1961 from Central Methodist College in Fayette, Mo., and between 1961 and 1969 received his M.A. and Ph.D. from the

Fletcher School of Law and Diplomacy. Bergsten began his career in government while still a graduate student, working as an economic adviser for the State Department from 1963 to 1967. In 1967-68, he was a visiting fellow with the Council on Foreign Relations (CFR). When Richard Nixon assumed the presidency in 1969, Bergsten became assistant for international economic affairs to Henry Kissinger [*q.v.*], who was then head of the National Security Council (NSC).

During Bergsten's tenure with the NSC, international economic questions were largely subordinated to the Vietnam war. As a consequence Bergsten emerged as a public spokesman only after leaving the NSC in May 1971 to become part of Washington's "think tank" world of advisers as a senior fellow at the Brookings Institute. In June 1971 Bergsten stated that, in spite of the "hot money" movements of the previous month, which had forced the countries of Western Europe into a joint float against the dollar, the world monetary system was not in fact in disequilibrium. At that time Bergsten proposed a plan to alter and diminish the reserve currency role of the dollar.

Like many other economists, Bergsten was concerned that the currency turmoil of 1971 would accelerate a global drift into protectionism. Immediately after the December 1971 signing of the Smithsonian Agreements, which set new fixed exchange rates following the collapse of the old Bretton Woods system in August 1971, Bergsten, with 11 other prominent international economists, signed a statement calling for the elimination of all remaining tariffs on industrial goods over a 10-year period. In the immediate wake of President Nixon's Aug. 15, 1971, speech on the economy, Bergsten told a House subcommittee that Nixon's 10% surcharge on foreign imports could have "disastrous" effects on overall U.S. foreign policy and challenged the need for the $13 billion turnaround in the U.S. trade deficit being promised by the Administration as unrealizable and unnecessary.

In September 1972 Bergsten drafted a plan on behalf of the CFR for the reform of the international monetary system. Bergsten argued that the issue confronting the world's major financial powers was whether "the reform will be negotiated and rational," or result solely from the interplay of market forces and uncoordinated exercise of national economic and political power. Bergsten's plan emphasized the wider use of special drawing rights (SDRs), international reserve instruments issued by the International Monetary Fund (IMF), and the use of wider "bands" in which currencies would be allowed to float. In the discussion prompted by Bergsten's plan, he called on the Nixon Administration to take the initiative in negotiations for a reform of the international monetary system, and in late December 1972, he again warned that the U.S. might adopt tougher trade policies if reforms were not achieved.

During the crisis of February-March 1973, which ended the fixed-rate system established by the Smithsonian Agreements, Bergsten strongly supported Federal Reserve Board Chairman Arthur Burn's [*q.v.*] call for international monetary reform. In August 1973 he published an article in *The New York Times* summarizing his analysis of the ongoing monetary crisis. In Bergsten's view, worldwide confidence in the ability of the U.S. and Europe to readjust the monetary system was virtually gone, and both sides were to blame for the impasse. Bergsten argued that a replacement for U.S. "stewardship" of the system had to be found, given changed world conditions and the apparent lack of U.S. interest in reform.

At the heart of the problem, Bergsten felt, was the $100 billion "overhang," or U.S. dollars held abroad, which was a constant source of monetary instability as it moved in and out of different national currencies. Bergsten suggested that Japan and Europe, which held most of the overhang, should agree to cancel this U.S. indebtedness in a "Marshall Plan in reverse" to rectify the world economic situation. The IMF, in Bergsten's view, should issue new SDRs in exchange for the excess dollars, thereby converting the U.S. overseas debt into international reserves. He cited the Hoover Moratorium and the Marshall Plan as precedents for such international financial cooperation.

With the 1973-74 oil crisis and the subsequent problems raised by "petrodollar recycling," the question of the dollar overhang was posed with renewed urgency. Bergsten criticized the many "Cassandras" then predicting the imminent collapse of the international monetary system, and continued to propose a funding of U.S. overseas indebtedness. In 1975 Secretary of the Treasury William Simon [q.v.] attacked Bergsten's SDR conversion plan, stating that the deeper issue was the need to improve U.S. economic performance and eliminate the nation's chronic deficits.

In June 1975 Bergsten published an article in the influential quarterly *Foreign Policy* analyzing the 1974-75 slide of the dollar as the result of the transfer of massive amounts of petrodollars from friendly Western nations to potentially hostile OPEC countries. In response to this article Simon again attacked Bergsten's overhang thesis. In June 1976 Bergsten went before a subcommittee of the House Banking Committee to urge that the U.S. adopt effective methods of surveillance of foreign exchange fluctuations to protect itself from actions by other nations.

In December 1976 president-elect Jimmy Carter appointed Bergsten assistant secretary of the Treasury for international affairs.

[LG]

BERNSTEIN, CARL
b. Feb. 14, 1978; Washington, D.C.
Journalist, Author

The son of labor and political activists, Carl Bernstein grew up in Silver Springs, Md., and attended the local public schools. At age 16, Bernstein worked as a copy boy for the *Washington Star*, and at 19 was named to the *Star*'s reporting staff as a summer replacement. His by-lined, human interest stories dominated the front page of the *Star*'s local news section. In 1965 Bernstein dropped out of the University of Maryland to work at the Elizabeth (N.J.) *Daily Journal*, where he covered the November 1965 New York City blackout and won several prizes in local press association competitions.

Landing a job on the metropolitan staff of *The Washington Post* in 1966, Bernstein covered the police department, City Hall and the Virginia state legislature. On his own initiative, Bernstein wrote discursive articles on Washington's ethnic neighborhoods, investigative pieces on slum landlords and rock music reviews.

Although not initially assigned to cover the Watergate break-in, Bernstein produced a sidelight story on the five apprehended suspects, and later "polished" Bob Woodward's [q.v.] piece identifying James W. McCord, Jr. [q.v.], as a salaried security adviser for the Committee to Re-Elect the President (CREEP). In July 1972 the *Post*'s editors named Bernstein to the Watergate team, where he combined his efforts with Woodward.

Woodward and Bernstein ("Woodstein") relied on two principal investigative techniques to solve the Watergate riddle. They attempted to trace the "money chain" all the way from the apprehended burglars to higher officials in CREEP, and they located employees in the White House and CREEP who might be persuaded to provide them with small pieces of the puzzle. "The thing is to work from the bottom up," Bernstein told journalist Leonard Downie.

In pursuit of his story, Bernstein on several occasions employed methods that he questioned in others, such as using clandestine sources to get telephone and credit card records of major figures in the case. Woodward and Bernstein were also criticized for their surreptitious attempt to contact members of the special Watergate grand jury hearing evidence in U.S. district court in Washington. But through persistent and imaginative questioning of disgruntled CREEP employees, arduous checking of records and tiring legwork, Woodward and Bernstein followed the "money chain" of secret funds all the way up to former Attorney General John N. Mitchell [q.v.], the director of CREEP at the time of the break-in.

Woodward and Bernstein provoked angry denunciations from White House spokesmen for their Oct. 10, 1972, scoop tying campaign "dirty tricks" and financial irregularities to the President's reelection team. The *Post* was accused of printing stories based on "third-hand information" and the "shabbiest journalistic techniques." The attacks intensified after Woodward and Bernstein incorrectly reported on Oct. 25, 1972, that CREEP Treasurer Hugh W. Sloan, Jr. [q.v.] had named H.R. Haldeman [q.v.] in grand jury testimony as the head of a secret slush fund that financed the Watergate break-in and other illegal operations. To prevent further blunders, the *Post*'s editors tightened their control over the reporting team. In addition to requiring two cross-checks for every fact, the editors subjected the team to intensive cross-examinations.

For the first nine months, the *Post* had pursued the Watergate case virtually alone. Following McCord's letter to Judge John J. Sirica [q.v.] in March 1973, however, other news media joined the hunt. Sharpened by the competition, Woodward and Bernstein compiled an impressive record of scoops, including E. Howard Hunt's clandestine visit to International Telephone and Telegraph (ITT) lobbyist Dita Beard and CREEP's manipulation of TV public opinion polls after the mining of Haiphong harbor. From April 1973 until Nixon's resignation, the team concentrated on uncovering the President's involvement in Watergate.

Woodward and Bernstein's "story within the story" was told in *All the President's Men*. Written in the third person, the book traced the two reporters' steps from the break-in to the Senate Ervin Committee hearings in May 1973. Published in late spring 1974, *All the President's Men* was an immediate best-seller.

Urged to continue the story begun in *All the President's Men*, Woodward and Bernstein next focused on Nixon's last 15 months in office, paying particular attention to the final two weeks. The result was *The Final Days*, published simultaneously with the release of the film version of *All the President's Men* in April 1976. Gossipy, titillating selections in *Newsweek* excerpts of the book provoked strong criticism from former Nixon associates, particularly from Henry Kissinger [q.v.], who was outraged by their version of a drunken, tearful Nixon. The book shot to the top of *The New York Times* best-seller list within days of its publication, hovering around the top for more than six months.

Bernstein returned to his desk at the *Post* in June 1976 after an extended leave of absence, during which he wrote a long article on McCarthy-era Washington for the *New Yorker*. In December 1976 Bernstein resigned from the *Post* to pursue full-time free-lance investigative journalism.

[JAN]

For further information:
Carl Bernstein and Bob Woodward, *All the President's Men (New York, 1974)*.
—, *The Final Days* (New York, 1976).
Leonard Downie, Jr., *The New Muckrakers* (Washington, D.C., 1976).

BERRIGAN, DANIEL
b. May 9, 1921; Virginia, Minn.
Anti-war activist.

Berrigan's father was a socialist and union organizer. Berrigan entered a Jesuit seminary near Poughkeepsie, N.Y., in 1939 and was ordained a Roman Catholic priest in 1952. He was attracted to social activism, being influenced by French worker-priests. He became a staunch critic of the Catholic Church's views on social consciousness and of American political and social institutions. He taught and lectured on college campuses and served as an editor of *Jesuit Missions*, a liberal publication. He was active in the civil rights movement and participated in civil rights teach-ins and sit-ins. In 1965 Berrigan founded the Clergy Concerned About

Vietnam (later Clergy and Laymen Concerned About Vietnam). He went to Hanoi in 1968 to help gain the release of three American prisoners of war. An ardent anti-war activist, he and his brother Philip (also a Catholic priest) became leading critics of the war and were once described as "the shock troops of the peace movement." In May 1968 the two brothers and seven others raided the Selective Service office in Catonsville, Md.–outside of Baltimore–and destroyed the draft board's files. [See JOHNSON Volume]

In October 1968 Daniel Berrigan was tried and sentenced to three years in prison for the Catonsville raid. He immediately went into hiding. Berrigan was captured in Rhode Island in August 1970 and served 18 months in a federal prison in Danbury, Conn. As a poet and writer, he dramatized the anti-war activities of himself and his associates in his play, *The Trial of the Catonsville Nine*. He described his attempt to avoid imprisonment in his book *No Bars to Manhood*.

Berrigan was named by a federal grand jury in 1972 as an unindicted coconspirator in a case in which his brother Philip was charged with conspiracy to kidnap Henry Kissinger [q.v.] and to blow up the heating systems of federal buildings in Washington. The conspiracy charges against Philip and six other defendants in the case were eventually dropped by the government.

Berrigan continued his anti-war protests. He became the center of a storm of protest when in late 1973 he addressed a meeting of the Arab University Graduates Association in Washington, D.C. In that talk he blasted Israel as a "nightmare military-industrial complex . . . the creation of millionaires, generals and entrepreneurs." He was sharply criticized for his anti-Israel views. Accusations were made that he was anti-Semitic, a charge he ardently denied. Some leading anti-war activists, such as Donald Harrington, Nat Hentoff and Arthur Hertzberg, condemned Berrigan for his anti-Israel position.

With the ending of the war in Vietnam,

Berrigan dropped out of the national spotlight. Only his Middle East views catapulted him to prominence again. He continued to teach, write and lecture. He was arrested several times for protest activities after 1973. Berrigan turned his attention to the nuclear arms race and was arrested at a Pentagon protest in 1976.

[HML]

BIBLE, ALAN D.
b. Nov. 20, 1909; Lovelock, Nev.
Democratic Senator, Nev., 1954-75.

Bible received his B.A. degree from the University of Nevada in Reno in 1930 and his law degree from Georgetown University in Washington in 1934. He practiced law and served in various state posts until elected to the Senate in 1954. Throughout the Eisenhower, Kennedy and Johnson Administrations, Bible voted as a moderate Democrat and established himself as a very effective but "low-profile" senator. Bible had a broad range of committee assignments, in which he quietly worked for Nevada's interests. He backed civil rights legislation, although he voted against imposing cloture during Southern Democratic attempts to filibuster the major bills. Bible also took an active interest in policy on land management and parks and recreation. Bible had a mixed record of support for the liberal measures of the Johnson era. [See EISENHOWER, KENNEDY, JOHNSON Volumes]

Although Bible was not a particularly outspoken opponent of the Vietnam war, he did support much of the anti-war legislation that came out of the Senate. In 1970 he voted for the Cooper-Church Amendment to curtail American military activity in Cambodia. In September 1970 he was one of 14 senators, including both hawks and doves, to sign a letter urging President Nixon to negotiate a cease-fire in Vietnam. In 1971 Bible voted for the Mansfield Amendment calling for the withdrawal of all U.S. forces from Indochina within nine months of the bill's enactment provided that the Communists had released U.S. prisoners of war. However in a May 1972 Democratic Caucus debate over a resolution criticizing President Nixon's escalation of the war, Bible joined conservative Southern and Border state senators in arguing that Nixon should be given more time to "luck out" in Indochina, as Sen. Gale McGee (D, Wyo.) put it.

In domestic affairs Bible was more conservative. He voted for the Supreme Court nominations of both G. Harrold Carswell [q.v.] and Clement Haynsworth [q.v.]. Bible registered his opposition to busing, establishment of a consumer protection agency, the volunteer army and modification of penalties for the use of marijuana. He supported federal funding of the controversial SST.

Bible continued his interest in land management, recreation and parks into the Nixon Administration and took issue with the Administration's funding proposals for forest, mine and conservation programs in September 1973, criticizing them as insufficient. As a member of the Public Land Law Review Commission, in 1970 he opposed the Commission's recommendation that no further land grants be made by the federal government to the states.

Bible was a supporter of the direct election of Presidents. In 1969, speaking in support of a constitutional amendment abolishing the Electoral College, he said that "nothing less than a direct popular presidential contest in which the ballot of every citizen carries equal weight can satisfy the demands of a truly participatory democracy."

As chairman of the Select Committee on Small Business, Bible continued his efforts to aid that segment of the economy. In 1970 he moved unsuccessfully to have his Committee's powers extended from advisory status to enable it to hear and report on legislation affecting small business. No action was taken on the proposal. The following year he backed an unsuccessful amendment to the fiscal 1972 supplemental bill providing $100 million for the Small Business Administration's loan and investment fund.

In 1970 press reports revealed that Bible was one of 14 senators or former senators whose offices were used for possible abuse of private immigration bills. Although no senators were implicated, it was suggested that Senate employees demanded bribes in return for submission of the bills. Choosing not to seek reelection in 1974, Bible retired at the end of his term.

[GMS]

BIEMILLER, ANDREW J(OHN)
b. July 23, 1906; Sandusky, Ohio.
Director, Department of Legislation, AFL-CIO, 1956-.

A Cornell graduate, Andrew Biemiller taught history before becoming a labor relations counselor and organizer for the Wisconsin State Federation of Labor. He served six years in the Wisconsin legislature and in 1942 went to work for the War Production Board. During the 1940s he served two terms in Congress as Democratic Representative from Wisconsin's fifth district.

Biemiller joined the American Federation of Labor (AFL) in 1953 as a legislative lobbyist and helped AFL President George Meany [q.v.] negotiate the merger with the Congress of Industrial Organizations that led to the AFL-CIO in 1955. The following year Biemiller became director of the organization's legislative department.

As AFL-CIO legislative director, Biemiller headed a staff of professional lobbyists and representatives from major labor unions. While he often opposed the Eisenhower Administration, Biemiller maintained close contact with both the Kennedy and Johnson White Houses, whose policies coincided more closely with the AFL-CIO's political goals. [See EISENHOWER, KENNEDY, JOHNSON Volumes]

In 1968 Biemiller worked actively in Vice President Hubert H. Humphrey's [q.v.] campaign for the presidency. After the election of President Richard M. Nixon, Biemiller lobbied for anti-poverty programs, the Utility Consumers Counsel Act and controls on foreign investment of U.S. money. He presented to Congress a statement by AFL-CIO President Meany that outlined measures to increase government revenues through taxation of unearned income, while reducing the tax burden on low- and-middle-income taxpayers. Several of Meany's suggestions were included in the 1969 tax bill, the most comprehensive tax reform bill ever passed by Congress.

During the Nixon Administration Biemiller worked largely behind the scenes, lending labor's support to the unsuccessful welfare reform bill of 1970 and helping to pass a federal grant program to aid urban mass transit while instituting environmental controls. He was perhaps most successful in efforts to block the appointments of conservative Southern Judges Clement R. Haynsworth and G. Harrold Carswell [q.v.] to the Supreme Court.

In August 1969 President Nixon nominated Haynsworth, chief judge of the U.S. Circuit Court of Appeals in Greenville, S.C., to the Supreme Court to "restore proper balance" in the Court. Liberal critics attacked Haynsworth for his consistent opposition to labor and civil rights causes while on the bench. Biemiller and Thomas E. Harris, general counsel to the AFL-CIO, compiled a dossier against Haynsworth that exposed his anti-labor bias and his conflict of interest in several judicial decisions involving businesses in which he owned stock. The defeat of Haynsworth's nomination in November 1969 by a vote of 55-45 marked the first time since 1930 that the Senate had failed to approve a Supreme Court candidate. Early in 1970 Nixon nominated G. Harrold Carswell to the vacant Supreme Court seat. Again Biemiller led labor's attack on Carswell, whose alleged racism and reputation as a mediocre jurist led the Senate to defeat his appointment by a vote of 51-45.

In November 1971 Biemiller tried unsuccessfully to block the appointment of Assistant Attorney General William H. Rehnquist [q.v.] to the Supreme Court.

Spokesmen for the NAACP and Americans for Democratic Action (ADA) charged Rehnquist with racism and obstructing blacks from voting in his home city of Phoenix. Testifying before the Senate Judiciary Committee, Biemiller termed Rehnquist a "right-wing zealot" who would try to write archconservative political views into the Constitution. Rehnquist denied all charges of racism and insisted that he would totally disregard his personal beliefs in interpreting the Constitution. On December 11, 1971, the Senate approved Rehnquist's appointment 68 to 26.

In a pamphlet entitled "Labor Looks at Congress 1971," Biemiller accused Nixon of trying, with some success, to pass legislation favoring the "narrow conservative concerns of big business," rather than social legislation beneficial to most Americans. Biemiller remained legislative director for the AFL-CIO through the Ford and into the Carter Administration. [See CARTER Volume]

[DE]

BLACK, HUGO L(A FAYETTE)
b. Feb. 27, 1886; Harlan, Ala.
d. Sept. 25, 1971; Bethesda, Md.
Associate Justice, U.S. Supreme Court, 1937-71.

Black grew up in rural Clay Co., Ala., and received his law degree in 1906 from the University of Alabama Law School. He practiced in Birmingham and held several local offices there before his election to the U.S. Senate in 1926. Reelected in 1932, Black proved to be an ardent New Dealer. He became Franklin Roosevelt's first Supreme Court appointee in August 1937. On the bench Black supported federal and state economic and social welfare legislation and favored strong enforcement of national labor and antitrust laws.

More important, Justice Black developed a judicial philosophy that was to have a significant impact on American law. As he explained in a June 1947 dissent, Black believed that the 14th Amendment had "incorporated," or made applicable to the states, all the guarantees of the first eight amendments to the Constitution. The Justice also argued that the provisions in the Bill of Rights should be interpreted literally. As a result of that approach, he viewed the scope of most criminal rights very broadly. Black considered the First Amendment "the heart of our government" and was especially ardent in its defense. He believed its guarantees of free thought and expression were fundamental to all other liberties, and he insisted that the Amendment prohibited all goverment interference with freedom of speech and of the press. [See TRUMAN, EISENHOWER Volumes]

Until the 1960s Black frequently voiced these positions in dissents in criminal rights, loyalty-security and other First Amendment cases. When a liberal majority emerged on the Warren Court, however, many of Black's views finally prevailed. Few justices adopted his absolutist position on the First Amendment, but the Warren Court gave significantly greater protection to its guarantees in areas such as free press, libel, obscenity and loyalty-security. Similarly, though a majority never accepted Black's "total incorporation" doctrine, the Court applied most of the Bill of Rights to the states on a case-by-case basis. The Court also took an expansive view of the criminal safeguards in those amendments and broadened the rights afforded defendants in federal and state courts. During the 1960s a majority also adopted Black's long-held views on legislative reapportionment and ordered congressional and state redistricting according to a one-man, one-vote standard.

Just when Black seemed vindicated and at the height of his influence, he began taking "conservative" positions that surprised many observers. He dissented, for example, when the majority invalidated a Connecticut anti-contraceptive law in June 1965. The Justice also voted in a series of cases beginning in 1964 to uphold the convictions of civil rights demonstrators. [See KENNEDY, JOHNSON Volumes]

During his last years on the bench,

Black continued in this vein. He dissented in February 1969 when the Court held that public school students had a right to nondisruptive political expression. He also objected to a June 1971 ruling in which the majority overturned the conviction of a demonstrator who had entered a courthouse wearing a jacket inscribed with a vulgarism condemning the draft.

Black protested when the Court in June 1969 limited the area that police could search without a warrant incident to a suspect's arrest. In March 1970 his opinion for the Court held that a disruptive defendant could be expelled from the courtroom and could even be bound and gagged, if necessary, to maintain order during a trial.

Justice Black also resisted efforts to expand the rights of debtors and of illegitimate children through the courts. He considered welfare a "gratuity," not an entitlement, and dissented from rulings in April 1969 and March 1970 that broadened the rights of welfare recipients. Black cast the deciding vote in a set of December 1970 cases in which the Court held that Congress could lower the voting age to 18 for federal elections but not for state and local elections. For a five man majority in June 1971, the Justice ruled that Jackson, Miss., officials had not violated the Constitution when they closed all public swimming pools rather than desegregate them.

Based on such decisions, some observers charged that Black was backsliding and "going conservative" in his old age. Others, including Black himself, said the Justice had not changed and that his views were consistent with those expressed years before. Black had always maintained, for example, that government could regulate the time and place of speech, though never its content. Thus he believed it could forbid political expression and demonstrations in schools or on other public or private property. In contrast to his broad approach to most criminal rights guarantees, the Justice had repeatedly taken a narrow view of the Fourth Amendment's prohibition on unreasonable searches and seizures and had frequently voted against expanding the scope of this provision. Similarly Black had long inveighed against policymaking by judges. He had objected when the court's conservative majority in the 1930s read its own economic notions into the Constitution, and he protested late in his life when he thought liberal justices, using the due process and equal protection clauses, were attempting to graft their personal social and political ideas onto the Constitution. Black's literalism, as some commentators pointed out, limited him to the express provisions of the Constitution and kept him from recognizing any new constitutional rights such as a right to privacy. Other analysts remarked that Black's conservatism demonstrated simply that the judicial revolution he had started had passed him by. Many of Black's goals had essentially been achieved. When a younger generation sought to move beyond them, Black tried to confine constitutional change within the bounds he had originally set.

For all the talk of Black's alleged conservatism, the Justice remained in the forefront in his defense of certain rights, even in his final years on the bench. In a March 1969 majority opinion, Black held that the *Miranda* ruling applied once a suspect was taken into custody, not just before questioning at a police station. He dissented in February 1971 when a new majority authorized the use of incriminating statements obtained in violation of *Miranda* at trial to impeach a defendant's credibility on the witness stand. Black voted in June 1969 to make the provision against double jeopardy applicable to the states and in June 1970 to extend the right to counsel to preliminary hearings. He objected in June 1971 when the majority ruled that juveniles had no right to trial by jury.

In February 1970 Justice Black's majority opinion extended the one-man, one-vote rule to state and local elections for specialized bodies such as school boards. In June 1969 he upheld a federal district court order requiring the Montgomery, Ala, school board to desegregate faculty and staff according to a specific numerical ratio. In a majority opinion in a January 1970 case, the Justice held that the Selective Service System lacked authority to reclassify a youth with a valid student deferment as punishment for turning in his draft card to protest the Vietnam War. Five months later Black's opinion of the Court ruled that a person was entitled to conscientious objector status when he possessed deeply held moral or ethical beliefs against war, even if his beliefs were not religiously based.

Black adhered to his absolutist views on freedom of speech and of the press. In a May 1970 majority opinion, he overturned, as a violation of the First Amendment, a federal law making it a crime for an actor to wear a U.S. military uniform in a production critical of the armed forces. In three February 1971 suits he voted to invalidate state requirements that applicants for admission to the bar take a loyalty oath or disclose membership in subversive organizations. On June 30, 1971, Black joined the majority to deny the government's request for an injunction prohibiting newspaper publication of a classified study of U.S. involvement in Vietnam known as the *Pentagon Papers.* In a separate opinion the Justice insisted that freedom of the press, like other First Amendment rights, was unassailable and that no judicial restraint on the press was permissible.

The opinion was Justice Black's last. On Aug. 28, 1971, he entered the hospital, and on Sept. 17, after 34 years on the Court, Black resigned because of ill health. Two days later he suffered a stroke. Within a week he was dead at the age of 85.

Throughout his life Black had been a man of enormous energy and drive. Extremely hard working on the bench, he had largely educated himself through a program of extensive reading begun during his Senate years. He was an aggressive man with a zest for confrontation and argument that was generally devoid of any personal animosity or hostility towards his opponent. "The paradox of Hugo Black," John P. Frank once remarked, was "steel and softness, the sharp cutting edge balanced with kindliness."

At his death all commentators agreed that Black had been the most influential justice of his day and one of the most significant in the history of the Supreme Court. He lived to see his dissents become established law in fields as varied as free expression, criminal procedure and reapportionment. Although he did not get the Court to accept all the tenets of his constitutional philosophy, he helped it reach the goals he had set forth regarding nationalization of the Bill of Rights and individual liberties. Black, wrote constitutional scholar Paul Freund, "exhibited to a singular degree an intense moral commitment, concentrated through the focus of an unwavering vision, and brought to bear with immense prowess. One thinks of Justice Brandeis's confident formula for achievement: brains, rectitude, singleness of purpose, and time."

[CAB]

For further information:
"Mr. Justice Black: Thirty Years in Retrospect," *UCLA Law Review*, 14 (1967). pp. 397-552.
Gerald T. Dunne, *Hugo Black and the Judicial Revolution* (New York, 1977).
John P. Frank, "Hugo Black," in Leon Friedman and Fred L. Israel, eds., *The Justices of the United States Supreme Court, 1789-1969* (New York, 1969), Vol. 3.
Stephen P. Strickland, ed., *Hugo Black and the Supreme Court* (New York, 1967).

BLACKMUN, HARRY A(NDREW)
b. Nov. 12, 1908; Nashville, Ill.
Judge, U.S. Eighth Circuit Court of Appeals, 1959-70; Associate Justice, U.S. Supreme Court, 1970-.

Blackmun grew up in St. Paul, Minn., and graduated from Harvard College, Phi Beta Kappa, in 1929. He received a degree from Harvard Law School in 1932 and then clerked for a year for a judge on the U.S. Eighth Circuit Court of Appeals. From 1934 to 1950 Blackmun practiced with a large Minneapolis law firm, where

he specialized in taxation and estate planning and became a general partner in 1943. He also taught part-time at several area law schools. In 1950 he began serving as resident counsel at the Mayo Clinic in Rochester, Minn.

A Republican, Blackmun was named a judge on the Eighth Circuit Court in 1959 by President Dwight D. Eisenhower. On the circuit bench he developed a reputation as a cautious and basically conservative judge who respected precedent and favored a policy of judicial restraint. An expert on taxation, Blackmun was a moderate on civil rights and civil liberties issues and a conservative on criminal rights. He was well-regarded within his circuit and was considered a fair and scholarly jurist of complete integrity who wrote thorough and careful opinions.

On April 14, 1970 President Richard Nixon appointed Blackmun to the Supreme Court seat vacated by Abe Fortas [q.v.] in May 1969. The Senate had rejected Nixon's two previous nominees for the post, Clement Haynsworth [q.v.] and G. Harrold Carswell [q.v.]. However Blackmun's record withstood close scrutiny, and his nomination was well-received. He was confirmed by the Senate, 94-0, on May 12, 1970. Blackmun was sworn in on June 9 by Chief Justice Warren Burger [q.v.], with whom he had been friends since childhood.

As most observers had expected, Justice Blackmun was generally conservative in his interpretation of the Constitution and restrained in the use of judicial power, especially in criminal cases. He voted in favor of the prosecution in almost all Fourth Amendment cases. He also took a very narrow view of the Fifth Amendment's privilege against self-incrimination. In an opinion for the Court in June 1971, Blackmun ruled that juvenile defendants were not guaranteed the right to trial by jury. Two years later the Justice held that a defendant's counsel did not have to be present during a pretrial display of photographs to witnesses for the purpose of identifying the accused. Although personally opposed to capital punishment, Blackmun voted in June

1972 and July 1976 to sustain state death penalty laws against the charge that they violated the constitutional ban on cruel and unusual punishment.

On racial issues Blackmun followed a moderate course. He spoke for the Court in February 1973 when it upset a suburban swim club's policy of excluding all blacks from membership, and he participated in decisions interpreting provisions of the 1964 Civil Rights Act favorably to blacks. However, the Justice also joined in several rulings that limited the scope of remedies for school segregation and in a June 1971 decision allowing a city to close its public swimming pools rather than desegregate them.

Blackmun voted to overturn most laws discriminating against women and illegitimate children and to hold most forms of state aid to parochial schools unconstitutional. In other areas, however, he was wary of invalidating federal or state statutes. For a five man majority in April 1971, he upheld a federal law revoking the citizenship of individuals born abroad of one American parent who failed to meet a U.S. residency requirement. Although he joined in a March 1972 decision upsetting a one year state residency requirement for voting, Blackmun supported a 50 day state registration requirement in March 1973 and several laws establishing lengthy registration requirements for voting in party primaries. He backed most state welfare regulations and voted to sustain laws authorizing the seizure of goods or wages from an allegedly delinquent debtor without notice or hearing. In his first few years on the Court, Blackmun almost always voted in favor of the government in First Amendment cases. He dissented in June 1971 when the Court refused to grant an injunction against newspaper publication of the *Pentagon Papers,* and he joined in several June 1973 decisions giving the states greater leeway to suppress allegedly obscene materials.

In January 1973 Blackmun made a notable departure from his policy of judicial restraint and, for a seven-man majority, held laws prohibiting abortions during the first six months of pregnancy an unconstitutional violation of women's right to privacy. During the 1974 and 1975 Court terms, commentators detected in Blackmun signs of greater self-confidence and independence. In March 1975, for example, he spoke for the majority to hold that officials in Chattanooga, Tenn., had violated the First Amendment by denying the use of a municipal theater for a production of the controversial rock musical *Hair.* In June 1975 and May 1976, the Justice overturned on First Amendment grounds Virginia laws prohibiting advertisements for abortion services and of drug prices. As the justice overseeing the Eighth Circuit, Blackmun acted independently in November 1975 to invalidate parts of a Nebraska judge's "gag" order restricting media coverage of a mass murder case. In June 1976 he joined with the rest of the Court to overturn the remaining portions of the order. Blackmun once again spoke for the majority in July 1976 to upset state laws requiring women to get the consent of a spouse or parent before having an abortion. He protested a June 1977 ruling holding that states and municipalities were not constitutionally required to fund elective abortions for indigent women.

Despite such rulings, Blackmun remained, overall, a largely conservative jurist who was closely aligned in his votes with the other Nixon appointees on the Court. Personally quiet and reserved, Blackmun was not an outstanding justice or a leader on the Court. His opinions offered detailed, scholarly considerations of all aspects of a case, and he was considered a diligent, conscientious and fair-minded jurist.

[CAB]

BLAKE, EUGENE, C(ARSON)
b. Nov. 7, 1906; St. Louis, Mo.
Secretary General, World Council of Churches, 1966-72.

Educated in private schools in the East and reared in biblical instruction from an early age, Blake graduated from Princeton in 1928 with a degree in philosophy. After a year teaching at Forman Christian College in Pakistan, he attended the theological college of the Church of Scotland until 1930. In 1932 he received a Th.B. from Princeton Theological Seminary. From 1932 to 1935 he served an assistantship at St. Nicholas Collegiate Church in New York City. He then became pastor of the First Presbyterian Church in Albany for a period of five years. From 1938 to 1940 he taught theology at Williams College. Blake relocated in 1940 to Pasadena, where he remained at the Pasadena Presbyterian Church for 10 years. The church thrived under his ministry and was soon regarded as one of the strongest and largest of its denomination in the country. Blake regularly broadcast from the church-owned radio station.

When the U.S. Conference to the World Council of Churches (WCC) was formed in 1948 Blake became one of the organization's first delegates. He was also elected clerk of the Presbyterian Church's General Assembly in 1951 and retained this post until 1966, when he was elected General Secretary to the WCC.

Having spearheaded the church's participation in civil rights struggles during his parish ministry, Blake sought to expand the WCC constituency to include a greater representation of underdeveloped nations. Under his administration the organization placed emphasis on Third World concerns and racial justice in particular. The extent of the WCC commitment was evident after the Program to Combat Racism was created to fund political liberation movements in Africa. In response to widespread criticism of the program by a variety of church organizations, Blake merely stated that the program was grounded in the gospel.

Through the WCC he attempted to further his proposal that a "truly catholic, truly evangelical and truly reformed" church be established to unify Presbyterians, Methodists, Episcopalians and the United Church of Christ. He also worked toward a closer relationship with the Roman Catholic Church. [See EISENHOWER, KENNEDY, JOHNSON Volumes]

An active opponent of the Vietnam War, Blake publicly endorsed liberal attempts to focus on wartime ravages and the destruction caused by U.S. intervention. In 1972 when U.S. planes bombed dikes in North Vietnam, Blake appealed to Nixon to "use your authority as commander in chief of the military forces of the U.S.A. immediately to cease this bombing." He also urged Nixon "to stop the bombing in the region of the dikes in order that the people of North Vietnam can make the urgent necessary repairs to avoid catastrophe of unthinkable proportions." Since the White House refused direct comment on Blake's remarks, he then became embroiled in a heated exchange with White House religious adviser Father John McLaughlin over the issue. Blake retired from the WCC in 1972.

In 1974 he was appointed president of the Board for Bread for the World, a Christian citizen movement established to combat world hunger through grass roots lobbying efforts and the encouragement of agricultural production in developing nations. He remained at the post until 1977.

[DGE]

BLATNIK, JOHN A(NTON)
b. Aug. 17, 1911; Chisholm, Minn.
Democratic Representative, Minn., 1947-75.

A former high school chemistry teacher and Minnesota state senator from 1940 to 1946, John Blatnik was elected to the U.S. House in 1947 on the Democratic-Farmer-Labor ticket. His heavily industrial ore-mining district in northeastern Minnesota bordered on Lake Superior and included Duluth and the iron-rich Mesabi Range. Beginning with his vote against the Taft-Hartley Bill in 1947, Blatnik compiled a strongly pro-labor, liberal record during the Truman and Eisenhower Administrations. He voted for all of the civil rights legislation of the late 1950s and advocated a foreign policy based on economic aid and cultural exchange rather than on armament.

During the 1950s Blatnik became known as a conservationist and a crusader for clean water legislation. As chairman of the Public Works Committee's Rivers and Harbors Subcommittee, he sponsored the Federal Water Pollution Control Act of 1956, steering it through the pro-industry committee and a hostile Congress.

Blatnik maintained his liberal record on most issues during the 1960s. But he ceased to be a vigorous proponent of pollution control legislation. In 1968, when Interior Secretary Stewart Udall ordered an investigation of pollution in Lake Superior, a task force of five Interior agencies found the beginning of widespread pollution by mining wastes being dumped into the lake by the Reserve Mining Co. The task force recommended that Reserve Mining's permit to dump be revoked within three years. Blatnik, on close terms with officials of the company which provided more than 3,000 jobs in his district, spoke out publicly against the report, saying that it had "no official status" and later denouncing it as "completely false." In 1968 Blatnik tried unsuccessfully to block a plank in the Minnesota Democratic-Farmer-Labor party's platform declaring Lake Superior off-limits as a dumping ground for mining and industrial wastes. [See EISENHOWER, JOHNSON Volumes]

At a water pollution enforcement conference in 1969 in Duluth, government scientists were unable to develop an indisputable case of interstate pollution against Reserve Mining. Findings as early as 1967 by the Duluth National Water Quality Laboratory, opened through Blatnik's efforts, had shown the ill effects of Reserve Mining's dumping, but the results of studies were suppressed by Washington headquarters and a Blatnik supporter, known to be sympathetic to the interests of Reserve Mining, appointed assistant director of the laboratory. By 1971 every Lake Superior polluter had been given a clean-up deadline except for Reserve Mining.

In 1971 Blatnik acceded to the chairmanship of the powerful Public Works Committee. While his leadership on pollution control matters within the strongly pro-industry committee continued to be weak, he still retained something of his old reputation as an environmentalist. His committee helped write a new Water Pollution Control Act, which was passed in 1972 over President Richard Nixon's veto. When the President announced his plan to cut by more than half the congressional allocations for state waste treatment plants, Blatnik joined Sen. Edmund S. Muskie (D, Me.) [q.v.] in denouncing the President's move as indicative of his "halfhearted commitment to the cause of clean water."

Blatnik announced his retirement from Congress in February, 1974.

[DAE]

For further information:
David Zwick, *Water Wasteland* (New York, 1971).

BLOUNT, WINTON M(ALCOLM)
b. Feb. 1, 1921; Union Springs, Ala.
U.S. Postmaster General, January 1969-December 1971; Chairman, Postal Board of Governors, July 1971-December 1971.

Blount left the University of Alabama in his sophomore year to manage his father's asphalt plant. After serving in the Army Air Force during World War II, he took over his father's failing sand and gravel business. With his brother's help Blount invested in war surplus equipment and built the Blount Brothers Corp. of Montgomery into one of the nation's largest general contractors, moving into the field of nuclear energy, missile bases, and space development projects. He served as director of the Central Georgia Railway Company and of the First National Bank of Montgomery and had numerous other business affiliations.

Blount was elected 41st president of the U.S. Chamber of Commerce in April 1968 after serving for several years as director and chairman of the manpower training panel. Responsible for studying and defining national economic problems, he warned against inflation, which he blamed in part on excessive wage increases, and declared that the most effective way to end urban rioting was to crack down on the "lawless hoodlums" who threatened the rights of businessmen and ghetto residents.

Originally a Democrat, Blount supported the presidential candidacy of Dwight D. Eisenhower and helped lead the Southern campaign of Richard M. Nixon in his 1960 bid for the presidency. He joined the Republican Party in the early 1960s and by 1968 termed himself "conservative." Blount's position as president of the Chamber of Commerce prevented him from taking part in Nixon's successful 1968 campaign.

When President-elect Nixon designated him Postmaster General in December 1968, Blount announced that he would sever all business connections in accepting the position. Acting upon the 1968 recommendations of the President's Commission on Postal Organization, Blount put forward a plan in early 1969 for converting the Post Office Department into a nonprofit, nonpolitical government-owned corporation. He also planned to end post office patronage by filling vacancies on a strict merit system.

In March 1970 an eight-day postal workers' strike for higher wages, the first in the history of the federal postal system, stopped mail in New York and other cities across the country. President Nixon declared a national emergency and ordered in federal reserve troops to help move the mail, while Blount ordered a mail stoppage to New York and obtained a federal court injunction to bar the illegal strike of federal workers. AFL-CIO President George Meany [q.v.] condemned the use of troops but urged the strikers to return to work. The Administration promised to enter negotiations with the postal unions once the strike ended. After meeting with the heads of seven postal unions, Blount pledged that President Nixon was committed to obtaining congressional approval of any agreement reached in negotiations. Within a few weeks Congress passed a 6% pay raise for all postal and civil service employees and military personnel.

In July 1970 Congress approved the plan to make the U.S. postal system a semi-autonomous federal agency. The new system was to be financed by its own revenues and congressional appropriations, and governed by a board of nine presidential appointees, who in turn would appoint the Postmaster and deputy postmaster general. A special five-member Postal Rate Commission would make recommendations on rates, classifications of mail and services. Blount presided over the transition and agreed to stay on as chairman of the postal service governing board after the change occurred in July 1971. At a press conference in January 1971, Blount cited as his accomplishments the abolition of the patronage system for appointing the Postmaster, the passage of anti-obscenity laws to help curb the distribution of pornographic mail and the recruitment of businessmen to improve postal services. Repeated postal rate increases and continued poor service, however, provoked much criticism of the system. Democratic Party National Chairman Lawrence F. O'Brien charged that the post office was "bogged down in partisan politics, service cutbacks and financial ineptitude," while Sen. Jennings Randolph (D, W.Va.) accused officials of bypassing the commission authorized by Congress to establish postal rates.

In a move he had apparently been planning for six months, Blount resigned as chairman of the postal service board in October 1971 to run against incumbent Democratic Sen. John J. Sparkman of Alabama. Political observers considered this a test of Nixon's "Southern strategy" to gain congressional seats for the Republican Party by wooing the traditionally Democratic deep South with conservative stances. Blount's campaign was managed by Allison, Treleaven and Rietz, a Washington firm who had worked for Nixon in 1968, and the former postmaster received strong Administration support. During the campaign, Blount emphasized his ties with the Nixon Administration and focused his criticism on the Democratic presidential ticket headed by liber· al Sen. George McGovern of South Dakota [*q.v.*]. Sparkman, who wielded great power as chairman of the Senate Banking and Currency Committee, was as critical of Sen. McGovern as his Republican opponent. With the support of banking interests and an endorsement by former Alabama Gov. George Wallace [*q.v.*], the 72-year-old Sparkman swept to an easy victory over Blount, providing a major setback for the Republican effort to win Southern congressional seats.

After the election Blount returned to private business.

[DAE]

BOGGS, (THOMAS) HALE
b. Feb. 15, 1914; Long Beach, Miss.
d. Oct. 16, 1972; Alaska.
Democratic Representative, La., 1941-43, 1947-72; Majority Whip, 1962-71; Majority Leader, 1971-72.

Boggs studied journalism and law at Tulane University, from which he graduated in 1937. In 1941 he won a seat in the U.S. House. After being defeated in 1943, he joined the Navy. He returned to the House in 1947, where he was a protege of Speaker Sam Rayburn. In 1962 he became majority whip under John McCormack (D, Mass.) [*q.v.*], Rayburn's successor. Boggs was also a ranking Democrat on the Ways and Means Committee. The Louisiana Representative compiled a moderate record, liberal by Southern standards. Although he voted against early civil rights measures, he supported the voting rights and open housing legislation of the late 1960s and helped direct Great Society legislation through the House in the Johnson years. [See EISENHOWER, KENNEDY, JOHNSON Volumes]

Boggs maintained his moderate stand during the Nixon years. He voted for the amendment lowering the voting age to 18,

tax reform and family assistance programs as well as the Philadelphia Plan, revenue sharing and the "no-knock" entry legislation. He opposed busing, environmental legislation and, although backed by labor, efforts to aid migrant workers. Many of Boggs's votes were based on the specific needs of his district. As a representative of a large urban area, he introduced bills designed to provide tax incentives to builders for slum clearance and rehabilitation. Because New Orleans had several important defense and space industries, he backed large-scale spending by the Defense Department and the National Aeronautics and Space Administration. Although he voted against the Cooper-Church Amendment of 1970, Boggs eventually became a critic of the war.

Boggs played a major role in the passage of the measure extending the income surtax in 1969. Because of the illness of Chairman Wilbur Mills (D, Ark.) [*q.v.*], Boggs pushed the bill through the Ways and Means Committee and the House. He met heavy opposition from liberals who attempted to prevent passage of the surtax unless the House took up general tax reform. Boggs, the floor leader for the measure, urged bipartisan support for the bill, which he argued was needed to limit inflation. He also promised that the House would consider tax reform. The surtax passed by five votes.

In 1971 Boggs waged a difficult campaign to win the post of majority leader. He was opposed by liberals Morris Udall (D, Ariz.) [*q.v.*] and James O'Hara (D, Mich.), both of whom had the backing of labor, and by moderate B.F. Sisk (D, Calif.), who had the support of the California delegation as well as much of the South. His critics termed Boggs haughty and aloof, called his personal behavior erratic and described his performance as whip as minimal. However as a House leader and member of the Ways and Means Committee, Boggs used his ability to deliver choice committee assignments to parlay votes, and he won the post in January.

In 1971 Boggs became embroiled in the growing controversy over the conduct of J. Edgar Hoover [*q.v.*] and the FBI. He delivered a speech on the House floor accusing the FBI of tapping telephones of members of Congress and calling for Hoover's resignation. His allegations were later proven correct following Administration and congressional probes of the Agency. Boggs himself came under criticism because he had permitted a wealthy builder to perform $40,000 worth of improvements on his Bethesda home at a fraction of the cost.

In 1972 Boggs was killed in a plane crash in Alaska.

[HML]

BOLLING, RICHARD W(ALKER)
b. May 17, 1916; New York, N.Y.
Democratic Representative, Mo., 1949- .

Bolling graduated from the University of the South in 1939. After service in the Army during World War II, Bolling became active in liberal politics. In 1948 he was elected to represent Missouri's fifth (Kansas City) district in the House of Representatives. Although a liberal, he became a protege of Speaker of the House Sam Rayburn (D, Tex.) [q.v.] during the latter years of the Eisenhower Administration. In January 1961 he led Democratic insurgents in their successful effort to reform the Rules Committee through expanding that panel from 12 to 15 members. Bolling supported the anti-poverty and civil rights legislation of the Johnson Administration. In contrast to many liberals who grew disenchanted with the Vietnam War, Bolling remained one of Johnson's most enthusiastic supporters. [See KENNEDY, JOHNSON Volumes].

Throughout his legislative career Bolling championed reform of the procedures of the House to make it more democratic and reduce the influence of special interests on the members. He wrote two critical studies of that body, *House Out of Order* (1964) and *Power in the House* (1968). In both works he recommended full financial disclosure of members' holdings, limitations on conflict of interests

and a weakening of the seniority system. On Jan. 31, 1973 the House of Representatives asked Bolling to chair a bipartisan special subcommittee charged with reforming the House rules. The following December his panel made tentative proposals to strip the House Ways and Means Committee of non-tax related authority, delegate to committees specific jurisdiction, reduce the power of the Rules Committee to initiate floor action on legislation and permit members to serve on one major committee.

Republicans and Democrats with low seniority welcomed Bolling's recommendations while those Democrats with long periods of House service opposed them. In addition interest groups that had established relationships with existing committee members and chairpersons objected to the plan because of a possible reduction in their influence. On May 9 the Democratic Caucus voted 111 to 95 to sidetrack the Bolling proposal and instructed Rep. Julia Butler Hansen (D, Wash.) [q.v.] to head a committee to prepare an alternative. The Hansen Plan, presented to the full House in September, was less ambitious than Bolling's. It recommended the committee system remain intact but suggested the Ways and Means Committee establish four subcommittees to handle specific matters and proposed a reduction of the power of the Rules Committee. On Oct. 8, by a vote of 203 to 165, the House rejected the Bolling proposal. It adopted the Hansen Plan by a vote of 359 to 7.

In both foreign policy and defense spending, Bolling supported the Administration. Although he voted to limit the Safeguard anti-ballistic missile system to two sites and opposed the appropriations of funds for the B-1 bomber, Bolling resisted attempts to cut defense spending. He backed the Administration's Vietnam war policy and in 1972 successfully thwarted an attempt by the anti-war coalition in the House to cut off funds for the war.

In domestic legislation Bolling compiled a liberal record. He cosponsored bills to establish national health insurance, public works programs, legal aid to the poor and tax reform. In December 1976 Bolling unsuccessfully sought the position of House majority leader. With nearly 30 years of seniority, he continued during the early Carter years to press for rules reform and liberal legislation. A minor heart attack in the summer of 1977 curtailed his activities.

[JB]

BOMMARITO, PETER
b. May 17, 1915; Detroit, Mich.
Vice President, AFL-CIO, 1969-;
President, United Rubber Workers, 1966-.

Bommarito began his career in the rubber industry before World War II, working in the plants of the U.S. Rubber Co. In 1940 he took his first union post as shift committeeman for United Rubber Workers (URW) Local 101, and held that position until 1942. In 1948 he became the local's treasurer and an executive board member, moving up in 1955 to the position of vice president, and finally to the local presidency from 1957 to 1960. In that year he became an international vice president of the URW, and in 1966, the union's president.

Bommarito's role as URW president differed to some extent from that of other leaders of major national unions because the URW was relatively decentralized and adapted to local and regional conditions, with significant local control over collective bargaining and different settlements in different parts of the U.S. Partly for this reason the URW under Bommarito was involved in 12 major rubber strikes in the years between 1966 and 1976. The ability of regions and localities to break ranks and negotiate separately often made centralized conduct of strikes quite difficult. Consequently the 1967, 1970 and 1973 contract negotiations involved a strike against one or more of the "Big Four"

rubber companies–Goodyear, Firestone, B.F. Goodrich and Uniroyal.

Troubles for the URW began in earnest in 1973 when Bommarito and his negotiating team had to deal with the Nixon Administration's Wage and Price Commission, which had powers to enforce guidelines on labor settlements. In keeping with the Commission's desire to limit wage increases to "noninflationary" levels, the URW leadership under Bommarito accepted a contract that provided for a mere 6% wage increase in the first year of the contract and, more importantly, contained no cost-of-living allowance, which would adjust wages to inflation. The difficulties of the situation were underlined when the traditional URW strategy of striking one Big Four company and then making the same settlement with the other three broke down. The employees of B.F. Goodrich rejected the URW national settlement and struck on their own to obtain a better deal.

The double-digit inflation of 1974 drove home to the URW rank and file their vulnerability in the absence of a cost-of-living allowance. Around the country URW officials attempted to persuade rubber companies to reopen the 1973 contracts, but the companies declined. As a result, when the URW negotiations for the 1976 contracts opened, it was estimated that a $1.65-per-hour increase in the basic wage rate would be necessary to "catch-up" on the purchasing power lost from 1973 to 1976 due to inflation. This catch-up demand, presented by Bommarito in the opening round of negotiations, clashed directly with the Ford Administration's "moral suasion" attempts to control inflation. Because no less than 15 URW local presidents had been deposed after the 1973 settlement, the Bommarito leadership was under great pressure to deliver.

The significance of the 1973 settlement, which would influence the United Auto Workers' negotiations scheduled for the fall of 1976, was highlighted by the Ford Administration's concerted attempt, in 1975, to oversee a merger of the URW with the Oil, Chemical and Atomic Workers (OCAW). In collaboration with Secretary of Labor John T. Dunlop [q.v.] and Federal Mediation and Conciliation Director W.J. Usery, Jr., the two unions held extended merger talks aimed at consolidating the memberships of both organizations under Bommarito. The government's hope was that consolidation would eliminate the local and regional autonomy that had disrupted the bargaining process in previous contracts, and thereby avert a long strike. The negotiations failed, and in April 1976 Bommarito and the URW leadership called a nationwide rubber strike, the first since 1967.

The structural changes in the U.S. rubber industry that necessitated the regional bargaining arrangements threatened to render impossible a coherent national strike strategy. The rubber companies showed every sign of wanting to move the bulk of production from Akron, Ohio, to Southern states with lower labor costs. There was little solidarity between Northern and Southern URW members against such an eventuality. The bargaining broke down several times, with Bommarito characterizing the Big Four's offer as "substandard" and the Ford Administration considering invocation of a Taft-Hartley injunction to force the strikers back to work. After more than four months Bommarito and the URW leadership obtained a 36% wage increase over the three years of the contract, a cost-of-living allowance, and additional pension and benefit increases. The Ford Administration took pains to point out the "special" quality of the URW settlement, emphasizing the poor 1973 contract, and urged other industries not to view the 36% wage increase as any precedent. Due to the length of the strike and the intransigence of both sides, Ford Administration officials pointed to the possibility of a "real donnybrook" over the 1979 contract.

Bommarito remained president of the URW and a vice president of the AFL-CIO into the late 1970's.

[LG]

BORK, ROBERT H(ERON)
b. March 1, 1927; Pittsburgh, Pa.
Solicitor General, October
1973-March 1977.

Robert Bork attended the University of Chicago Law School, where he graduated as managing editor of the law review in 1953. From 1955 to 1962 he practiced law with a Chicago firm. During the 1960s he taught at Yale Law School, where he was a leading expert in the field of antitrust law and the most conservative member of the law faculty. A believer in free market economics, Bork favored an aggressive antitrust policy on the part of the government. He served the Johnson Administration as a member of the presidential task force on antitrust in 1968.

Bork was a critic of the Warren Court, which he believed "represented a sharp challenge to the traditional relationship of the judiciary to the process of democratic government." He was a strong supporter of the presidential candidacy of Richard Nixon in 1968 and 1972 and considered Nixon an "intellectual politician." Bork assisted in drafting the Nixon Administration's proposal for a moratorium on busing to achieve racial balance in public schools and defended the constitutionality of the proposals in testimony before Congress. He disagreed with the Administration's antitrust policy, however, on the grounds that it was insufficiently activist in promoting competition.

In June 1973 Nixon appointed Bork Solicitor General of the United States. As head of the small but prestigious Solicitor General's office in the Justice Department, Bork controlled the flow of cases through the appellate system, deciding which cases the government would appeal and what line of argument its appeals would follow. Bork himself often argued the important cases before the U.S. Supreme Court. Bork's first major public act was the filing of a brief in Baltimore federal court on Oct. 5 arguing that a sitting vice-president could be indicted and tried on criminal charges. Vice President Spiro T. Agnew [q.v.], under investigation for taking bribes, had tried to block a grand jury investigation with the argument that criminal proceedings could not be commenced against a sitting vice president until he had been impeached. Agnew resigned on Oct. 10 and pleaded nolo contendere to income tax evasion.

Bork's most dramatic and controversial official act occurred a few weeks later as part of the so-called "Saturday Night Massacre" of Oct. 20. On that night President Nixon attempted to fire Watergate Special Prosecutor Archibald Cox [q.v.], who had refused to obey Nixon's command to drop his legal effort to secure certain White House tapes for the Watergate grand jury's investigation. After Attorney General Elliot Richardson [q.v.] resigned rather than carry out Nixon's order to fire Cox, and Deputy Attorney General William Ruckelshaus [q.v.] was fired for his refusal to discharge Cox, Bork, third in command in the Justice Department, became acting Attorney General and dismissed Cox. "I believe a President has the right to discharge any member of the Executive branch," Bork said in defense of his act.

Two days later Bork placed Henry Petersen [q.v.], assistant attorney general in charge of the criminal division, in direct charge of the Watergate case. In response to an avalanche of public criticism over his removal of Cox, however, Nixon on Oct. 26 announced that Bork would appoint a new special prosecutor. On Nov. 1 Bork announced the appointment of Houston lawyer Leon Jaworski [q.v.] to the post. Bork said Jaworski would have the same charter as Cox, the "full cooperation" of the Executive Branch, and no restrictions placed on his freedom of action if he sought additional presidential documents. Nixon also appointed Sen. William Saxbe (R, Ohio) [q.v.] as attorney general; with Saxbe's confirmation, Bork returned to his position as solicitor general. He remained the government's chief advocate until early 1977, when he returned to Yale as Chancellor Kent Professor of Law.

[TO]

BORMAN, FRANK
b. March 14, 1928; Gary, Ind.
Astronaut; Chairman, Eastern Air Lines, 1975-.

Frank Borman grew up in Tucson, Ariz. where he began taking flying lessons at the age of 15. Upon graduation from West Point in 1950, he joined the Air Force. After serving in a fighter bomber squadron in the Philippines, Borman earned an M.A. degree in aeronautical engineering at the California Institute of Technology in 1957 and returned to teach at West Point.

In September 1962 Borman was chosen to become an astronaut and three years later was promoted to the rank of colonel. In December 1965 he and James Lovell orbited the earth for 14 days in a Gemini 7 spacecraft, setting a record for the duration of a manned flight into space. After the completion of its Gemini projects, the National Aeronautics and Space Administration (NASA) inaugurated the $23 billion Apollo program, aimed at putting a man on the moon. In 1967, when three astronauts were killed in a fire aboard an Apollo 204 test spacecraft at Cape Kennedy, Borman served on the review board that investigated the accident. The board's suggestions for extensive redesign of the translunar vehicle were incorporated in the Apollo 8, which Borman, Lovell and William A. Anders were assigned to pilot to the moon and back.

The Apollo 8 was sent into orbit on Dec. 21, 1968, with Borman in command of the three-man crew. In a special Christmas Eve telecast from the lunar craft, the crew sent to earth live pictures of the moon's landscape and, at Borman's suggestion, read from the story of creation in Genesis. The craft splashed into the Pacific six days later, after having orbited the moon 10 times. Following their debriefing the astronauts received heroes' welcomes in Washington, D.C. and New York City.

Although assured of participation in future space flights, Borman chose a desk job as deputy director of flight crew operations for NASA. In addition he traveled the world as a goodwill ambassador and briefly considered entering politics. In 1970 Borman joined Eastern Air Lines as a vice president and soon showed his ability as a tough, able executive. He was promoted to executive vice president in charge of operations in 1974, to president and finally to chairman in 1975, and played a major role in solving the airline's financial problems. Although Eastern had been one of the most profitable airlines during the 1950s and early 1960s, managerial mistakes combined with an inefficient route structure and inflated costs had brought the carrier close to bankruptcy by 1975. Borman reversed this trend, cutting 3,000 employees from the payroll and enlisting the aid of the airline's unions in getting the remaining employees to accept a wage freeze for 1976. He was also able to persuade the 70 lending institutions carrying Eastern's long-term debts to defer $75 million in repayments due in 1976.

Borman, who was on close terms with the Ford Administration, proved an ideal advocate for the new profitable air routes assigned by the Civil Aeronautics Board (CAB). In testimony during March 1976 before two House subcommittees concerned with aviation, he described the airlines as swamped by rising fuel and service costs, unable to attract investment capital and therefore deprived of new cost-saving technology. Calling the airlines a "quasi utility," Borman made a strong case for continued regulation of the industry by the CAB.

Borman's tactics succeeded in bringing Eastern back into the black. While the airline lost $50 million in 1975, under Borman's leadership the company's profits hit a record $46.2 million in 1976. Eastern employees were given a delayed wage hike of 8% in 1977, as well as the chance to join a profit-sharing plan. Concerned that U.S. airlines would not be able to afford replacements for their existing fleets, Borman sought in the late 1970s to secure the cooperation of other airlines

and the federal government in developing a more economical jet aircraft for the 1980s.

[DAE]

BOYLE, WILLIAM A(NTHONY)
b. Dec. 1, 1904; Bald Butte, Mont.
Labor leader.

The son of a coal miner, "Tony" Boyle attended public schools in Montana and Idaho before he began working as a miner. In 1922 he joined the United Mine Workers of America (UMW) and soon became active in union issues involving improved working conditions and upgraded health and pension benefits. His unflinching commitment to the goals of the UMW brought him widespread recognition throughout the rank and file, and he was eventually elected president of District 27 in Montana. His local presidential tenure extended until 1948. During this period Boyle also represented four Western states as regional director for the Congress of Industrial Organizations (CIO) and was a member of several wartime government and industry committees.

From 1948 to 1960 Boyle served as an assistant to UMW President John L. Lewis. He then held the post of international vice president from 1960 to 1963 with a year as acting president. As assistant and protege to the mighty Lewis, Boyle's ascendancy in the bureaucratic UMW hierarchy was assured. At the age of 80, Lewis was reluctantly beginning to loosen the grip on his 40-year presidential rule. In 1960 he passed on his legacy to Thomas Kennedy, his immediate successor. When Kennedy died in 1963, Boyle was handed the union reins and the following year he was elected to his first five-year term.

Unlike the flamboyant and impetuous Lewis, Boyle, a soft-spoken and cautious man, maintained a low profile during his first term in office. His public statements were invariably supported by affidavits he held within reaching distance. But it soon became apparent that he had every intention of fashioning his administration after that of his predecessors. Although his style and demeanor were a significant departure from the union's former president, Boyle shared Lewis's dictatorial bent.

In the late 1960s, despite earlier predictions that the coal industry would face an irreversible decline, the demand for coal dramatically increased due in part to an emerging export market. The ranks of the UMW swelled as production expanded, and union assets doubled. In order to retain tight control on the union's membership, Boyle began to consolidate his power over both working miners and pensioners. He kept district offices in trusteeships, which prevented the rank and file from voting for their district officers. He appointed district heads who carried out policies enacted by the international executive board, which Boyle oversaw. Over the years, the rank and file had grown increasingly disgruntled with what they regarded as complacency on the part of the UMW leadership. Charges of nepotism, acquiescence to management and manipulation of pension funds had been frequently lodged against Lewis and his executive board, and as Boyle's first term came to a close, the same allegations were made.

As the union's presidential election of 1969 approached, Boyle structured his platform to secure reelection. Since all of the 80,000 retired members were eligible to vote, Boyle vowed to increase pension benefits to coincide with inflation trends, thereby assuring himself of the support of almost half the UMW voters. Joseph "Jock" Yablonski [q.v.], a veteran miner who rose to become president of District Five in Pittsburgh, was Boyle's only opposition. Critical of Boyle's autocratic rule and refusal to account for union holdings and assets, Yablonski was convinced he could beat Boyle in a fair election. With his supporters he set forward an 11-point program that included a pledge to improve safety standards, provide acceptance for district office elections and establish an "open administration" with no relatives on the payroll. He also vowed to "keep the coal companies at arm's length."

Boyle, who did not anticipate any stiff opposition, was surprised by Yablonski's declared candidacy, but he viewed it publicly as merely token opposition that posed no real threat to his reelection. Yablonski, despite numerous threats and hostile confrontations with Boyle supporters, was determined to campaign across the country. During the height of the campaign in June 1969, John L. Lewis died. Boyle immediately took measures to have himself appointed to Lewis's seat on the Welfare and Pension Fund board. He then hastily voted a $35-a-month pension increase, thereby ensuring his support from the retirees.

Yablonski, meanwhile, secured the necessary 50 nominations to guarantee him a place on the ballot. Boyle, forced to recognize Yablonski's increasing popularity, hired a public relations staff and, admitting that he had "tremendous catching up to do," began promising a fight for better wages and open district elections. Yablonski retaliated by informing the rank and file that "it is indicative of Mr. Boyle's imagination that it took three months and the counsel of a high-priced political adviser before he realized I had a good idea."

Two weeks before the December election, the Labor Department made public its investigation into the UMW's financial affairs. The report stated that Boyle and two other top union officials maintained a $400,000 yearly budget for the salaries of relatives. All three union officers had established a fund that guaranteed them full salary at retirement. The fund had never been fully accounted for in financial reports to the government, and as a result the UMW executive board was faced with "possible criminal prosecution." Yablonski viewed the report as a substantiation for his continual charges of nepotism and cronyism, but added that the Labor Department had barely uncovered the tip of the iceberg.

On the day of the election, Yablonski supporters were positioned at the polls and subsequently sighted numerous violations that rendered the election results questionable. Boyle, not surprisingly, received over 65% of the vote. Yablonski re-fused to concede the election and stated publicly that the polls had been rigged. He brought his charges to the Department of Labor, which began an investigation. Within three weeks of his vow to continue the fight against Boyle, Yablonski and his wife and daughter were shot to death.

Boyle, who deplored the killings and denied any connection between Yablonski's murder and the union, announced the establishment of a fact-finding commission to investigate the deaths. The commission, regarded by Yablonski's sons as "Tony Boyle's show trial," lasted two days and failed to produce any significant testimony.

Miners for Democracy, a rank-and-file group that had consolidated its support and backed Yablonski, continued to demand that the Department of Labor intervene and declare the 1969 election void. In early 1970, UMW records were subpoenaed to determine if allegations of fraud could be documented. In addition the FBI began an intensive investigation into the Yablonski murders. Within 10 days of the labor leader's death, three suspects were apprehended. Although no immediate link between the union and the suspects was established, after careful scrutiny of over 1,000 pieces of UMW accounting sheets, a special prosecutor was able to determine that funds had, in fact, been set aside for Yablonski's murder.

In 1971 all three suspects in the case were convicted, although the evidence needed to point an accusing finger at Boyle required further substantiation. After exhaustive research and the collaborative testimony of several retired miners who had received checks from the UMW fund only to secretly return the money, the case against Boyle became conclusive.

In 1972 the Department of Labor through a court order invalidated the results of the 1969 election. The Boyle administration, which had all but lost any semblance of credibility, suffered a decisive setback as a result of the election invalidation. Boyle had barely regained his composure when in 1973 he was charged and convicted of the illegal use of UMW funds for political contributions. Boyle received a three-year sentence, which he began serving in December 1973. That same month he was indicted for conspiring to murder Yablonski. After a lengthy trial and conviction in September 1975, Boyle was sentenced to three life terms for his role in the Yablonski murders.

[DGE]

For further information:
Stuart Brown, *A Man Named Tony* (New York, 1976).

BRADEMAS, JOHN
b. March 2, 1927; Mishawaka, Ind.
Democratic Representative, Ind., 1959-.

Born near South Bend, Ind., Brademas attended local public schools and, after service in the Navy, graduated from Harvard University magna cum laude in 1949. As a Rhodes Scholar, he earned a doctoral degree in social studies from Oxford University in 1954. Brademas gained political experience through two unsuccessful campaigns for the U.S. House in 1954 and 1956 and by working as an assistant to Democratic presidential candidate Adlai Stevenson in the 1956 primary campaign. He was elected to the House in 1958. From that time Brademas, a liberal, was the unusually popular choice to represent the blue-collar third congressional district in Indiana, which included the cities of South Bend and Elkart.

During the Kennedy and Johnson Administrations, Brademas sat on the House Education and Labor Committee. He co-sponsored the Elementary and Secondary Education Act of 1965, which nearly doubled the amount of federal outlays for education. He also led the floor fight for the Headstart program and vigorously supported the other Great Society programs of the Johnson Administration. [See JOHNSON Volume]

During the Nixon-Ford years, Brademas fought to preserve and extend federal aid to education. He sponsored the Environmental Education Act of 1970 and the

Drug Abuse Education Act of 1970, providing federal support for such instruction particularly at the secondary level. He was the chief sponsor of the National Commission on Libraries and Information Science of 1970 and the principal architect of the National Institute for Education in 1972. Among his other accomplishments were the Omnibus Education Act of 1972, the Elementary and Secondary Education Amendments of 1974 and the Higher Education Amendments of 1976. A 1975 *Change* magazine poll of 4,000 college and university presidents, foundation executives, journalists and government officials named Brademas one of the four most influential leaders of higher education in the United States.

Brademas worked to extend federal aid to children, the elderly and the handicapped. In 1969 and 1975 he sponsored amendments to the Older Americans Act that expanded programs for the elderly. He pressed for extension and expansion of the Rehabilitation Education Act in 1973 and sponsored the Child Abuse Prevention Act of 1974 and the Education for All Handicapped Children Act of 1974.

With Sen. Claiborne Pell (D, R.I.) [*q.v.*], Brademas mobilized congressional support for the arts during the Nixon-Ford years. He was the chief House backer of bills to extend the National Foundation for the Arts and Humanities in 1970, 1973 and 1976. These extensions included the formation of an advisory National Council for the Arts and the Museum Services Act of 1975, through which the King Tutankhamen exhibit later came to the United States. In December 1976 *The New York Times* called Brademas "Congress's most articulate and effective spokesman for aid to culture."

Brademas increasingly opposed the Nixon Administration and, after publicly attacking the Nixon record, was added to the President's "enemies list" in January 1973. In the aftermath of Watergate, Brademas wrote major sections of the Federal Election Campaign Amendments of 1974 and 1976. In 1976 Common Cause gave him "special thanks" for his role in saving the Federal Election Commission from being dismantled by congressional opponents of election reform.

Brademas took an increasingly anti-war position on the Vietnam war after 1970, but he demanded the return of U.S. prisoners of war as the condition for American withdrawal. He voted against the Safeguard anti-ballistic missile system and the supersonic transport. A Greek-American, Brademas led the congressional drive to suspend U.S. arms aid to Turkey following the Turkish invasion of Cyprus in 1974. In 1976 Brademas criticized the signing of long-term military aid accords with both Greece and Turkey as a possible surrender of the right of Congress to review all such agreements annually.

The only controversy of Brademas's career arose over his acceptance of $5,000 in campaign contributions from Park Tong Sun, a South Korean businessman under federal investigation for alleged influence peddling in Congress. Brademas in October 1976 admitted having received the contributions and noted that they had been properly reported according to the new federal campaign contribution laws. He also pointed out his long record of opposition to the repressive policies of the South Korean government. In January 1977 Brademas became majority whip of the House of Representatives. [See CARTER Volume]

[AB]

BRADLEE, BENJAMIN C.
b. Aug. 26, 1921; Boston, Mass.
Journalist, author.

Bradlee developed an early interest in politics and news reporting through his family, staunch Massachusetts Republicans, and at his prep school, St. Mark's in Southborough, Mass., where Bradlee landed his first newspaper job, copyboy on the Beverly (Mass.) *Evening Times.* He entered Harvard College in 1939 and wrote for the *Harvard Crimson*. After graduation and a stint in the U. S. Navy, he helped launch the *New Hampshire*

Sunday News in Manchester, N. H. He sold his interest in the paper in 1948 and became a police reporter for *The Washington Post*. In 1951 he left the *Post* to become a press aide at the U. S. embassy in Paris, but returned to journalism in 1953 when he was hired by *Newsweek* as chief European correspondent.

In 1957 Bradlee was transferred to Washington, D. C., where he became a lasting friend of then-Sen. John F. Kennedy. The relationship boosted Bradlee's career and *Newsweek's* circulation. The *Post*, in the midst of reorganization under publisher Katherine Graham [*q.v.*], persuaded Bradlee to return as deputy managing editor.

He soon became the paper's managing editor and hired such political reporters as David Harwood and former *New York Times* newsman David Broder to enliven the sometimes colorless product. On Sept. 30, 1968, Bradlee was named vice president and executive editor.

His plan to enhance the *Post's* image and make it the nation's most-respected paper suffered a sharp blow in 1971 when the *Times* became the first paper to publish the *Pentagon Papers*, a secret study of the Vietnam war. The *Post* obtained a copy of the classified Defense Department documents three days after the *Times*.

The paper's image improved after a police report about a break-in at the Democratic National Committee's Watergate headquarters set in motion a story that would topple the Nixon Administration and bring a Pulitzer Prize to the *Post*. Bradlee pushed his senior editors to get complete details on the break-in from the beginning, despite the Administration's characterization that the incident was just a "third-rate burglary." The *Post* ran 80 column inches about the burglary on June 18, 1972, the day after the break-in.

Bradlee was not dismayed when others, both on the *Post* and outside it, disagreed with his emphasis on the story. "Editors throughout the country really downplayed the story," Bradlee said, "as a vagary of the *Post*." He allowed two young reporters, Bob Woodward [*q.v.*] and Carl

Bernstein [*q.v.*], to work full time on the story and defended them inside the hierarchy of the paper as the complex details of their story linked the break-in to the President. In May 1973 the *Post* broke the details of the cover-up that followed the break-in and of White House involvement in several other scandals. The *Post* named top Administration officials in connection with the illegal acts.

The White House retaliated by limiting *Post* contacts and denouncing both the paper and Bradlee. Sen. Robert Dole (R, Kan.) [*q.v.*], head of the Republican National Committee, called Bradlee a "Kennedy coat-holder" and White House Press Secretary Ron Zeigler [*q.v.*] said the *Post* practiced "shabby journalism" based on "hearsay and innuendo." As the Administration sank, however, *Post* stories held up, and the paper received the Pulitzer Prize for public service in 1973.

Bradlee continued to support controversial stories in the years following Watergate. He was the author of two books: *That Special Grace* (1964), a eulogy of President Kennedy; and *Conversations with Kennedy* (1975), an informal record of encounters with the former President from 1959 to 1963.

[BO]

BRENNAN, PETER J(OSEPH)
b. May 24, 1918, New York, N.Y.
Secretary of Labor, January
1973–February 1975.

Brennan was born in a New York City tenement. Following his graduation from high school, he became a painter and jointed the Painters, Decorators, and Paperhangers of America. During this period he began attending the City College of New York on a part-time basis, receiving a degree in business administration in the early 1950s. Brennan saw action in the Navy during World War II and then resumed his career in the painting trade. He rose gradually in the union movement, eventually becoming head of the Building and Construction Trades Council of Greater New York by the late 1950s.

Brennan came to national prominence as a result of a series of violent confrontations between student demonstrators and New York "hard hats" in May 1970. Following the Cambodian invasion, a series of anti-war demonstrations occurred protesting the fatal shootings at Kent State and Jackson State colleges. At a rally in Wall Street on May 8, 200 well-organized construction workers violently broke up the student protest, leaving 70 bloody victims, including three policemen; six workers were arrested. Brennan was credited with organizing the attack and a series of confrontations that occurred over the next five days. His efforts culminated on March 20 when approximately 100,000 construction, longshore, and office workers rallied at City Hall in support of President Richard Nixon's war policies. The demonstration was officially sponsored by Brennan's Building and Construction Trades Council. Brennan supported Nixon in the 1972 presidential election and rallied traditional Democratic Labor support behind the Republican incumbent.

Three weeks after his overwhelming victory, on Nov. 29, 1972, Nixon nominated Brennan to be Secretary of Labor to succeed J. D. Hodgson [q.v.]. Not since Martin P. Durkin, former president of the plumbers' union, held the position under Eisenhower, had a trade unionist been Secretary. The nomination received only lukewarm approval by George Meany [q.v.], president of the AFL-CIO. It was strongly criticized by civil rights leaders who felt that Brennan had obstructed integration of the building trades in New York. Nevertheless, Brennan was overwhelmingly confirmed by the Senate on Jan. 31, 1973.

During the two years Brennan held his post, he became fully embroiled in the major issues affecting the Nixon Administration. His stand on wage-price control policies and support of Nixon during the Watergate crisis alienated him from many leaders of organized labor.

Despite his initial opposition to the plan, Brennan supported the President's program to raise the minimum wage but set a lower rate for youth during 1973. He alienated labor further by recommending that the public employment program established by the Emergency Employment Act of 1971 be phased out as unemployment dropped. Yet in 1974 he introduced Administration plans to find summer jobs for youths and presented a minimum wage bill that contained a compromise on the issue of substandard wages for youth.

On April 31, 1974 federal wage-price controls, which had been in effect since August 1971, were suspended, precipitating the greatest strike wave since World War II. Brennan urged workers not to strike and accept voluntary wage restraint in the face of mounting inflation.

Brennan favored collective bargaining and voluntary arbitration as a major tool in cutting down strike activity. He did, however, strongly oppose compulsory arbitration. While he supported workers' right to strike, he also endorsed the management-labor collaboration efforts of the President's Commission for Industrial Peace.

The Watergate crisis put Brennan in a difficult position. The AFL-CIO called repeatedly for Nixon's impeachment because he had created a "special and personal secret police" and in Meany's words, used "tools of repression" to violate individual rights. Brennan sought to neutralize this criticism by insisting that "labor should not lead these attacks" against the President. He implored organized labor to stand by Nixon, insisting that the President "could make mistakes like anyone else" and that until Nixon was proven guilty "we have to work within the Administration."

During the early months of the Ford presidency, Brennan helped formulate the Administration's plans to create jobs as unemployment rose. He served on the newly-created Council of Wage and Price Stability, formed to help consolidate Administration anti-inflation policy. In September 1974 Brennan outlined Administration plans to launch public service jobs if unemployment topped 5.5%. He announced that the government would double existing outlays of $500 million to create 100,000 jobs and increase the funding for job creation as unemployment rose. If unemployment rose to 7% a $4 billion program would be launched. He also urged workers to accept voluntary wage guidelines as their contribution to fighting inflation. Organized labor opposed these proposals as insufficient to deal with unemployment. They also insisted that they could not comply with the guidelines and keep pace with inflation. As a result of this pressure, Brennan began speeding up dispersal of funds to finance 85,000 public sector jobs and dispatch monies to communities hardest hit by unemployment.

Out of a September economic summit to deal with "stagflation," Ford announced the creation of two special commissions with Brennan actively connected to both. The top-level Economic Policy Board was established to coordinate federal economic affairs. The second commission, the White House Labor-Management Committee, was a bipartisan group of 16 labor-management representatives which sought to "help assure effective collective bargaining and promote sound wage and price policies."

Brennan resigned as Secretary of Labor in February 1975 and reassumed his position as President of the Building and Construction Trades Council.

[DR]

BRENNAN, WILLIAM J(OSEPH) JR.
b. April 25, 1906; Newark, N.J.
Associate Justice, U.S. Supreme Court, 1956-.

Brennan graduated from the Wharton School of Finance in 1928 and from Harvard Law School in 1931. A labor law specialist who practiced in Newark, N.J., he served as a state court judge from 1949 until September 1956, when he was named to the U.S. Supreme Court.

From the start Justice Brennan voted with the Court's liberals. Although not an absolutist or literalist in his approach to the Constitution, Brennan was deeply committed to procedural fairness by the government, and he believed the protection of individual rights from government intrusion to be a primary function of the Court. He took an expansive view of most of the criminal safeguards in the Bill of Rights and favored extending those guarantees to the states. The Court's main spokesman in obscenity cases, Brennan wrote opinions which liberalized this area of the law. He also broadened freedom of the press in a series of rulings which put limits on libel judgments against the media. Justice Brennan was a key member of the Warren Court's activist and liberal majority and the author of some of its most significant opinions. [See EISENHOWER, KENNEDY, JOHNSON Volumes]

On the Burger Court, Brennan's role changed significantly. He became a frequent and vocal dissenter from the decisions of a new, more conservative Court majority. In most of the Court's terms after 1970, Brennan ranked second only to Justice William O. Douglas [q.v.] in the number of dissents he entered, and he was identified with Douglas and Thurgood Marshall [q.v.] as part of a liberal trio that protested majority rulings on criminal rights, reapportionment, racial discrimination and free expression. Because of the anti-libertarian trend he perceived on the Supreme Court, Brennan urged litigants to turn to the state courts and state constitutional provisions to secure greater expansion and protection of individual rights.

In criminal cases Brennan opposed Court decisions sanctioning warrantless searches and arrests. He spoke out strongly against limitations on the exclusionary rule, which barred the use of illegally obtained evidence in court. He dissented from February 1971 and December 1975 decisions cutting back on the 1966 *Miranda* ruling. Brennan also protested a May 1972 judgment permitting non-unanimous jury verdicts in state courts, but he did join in June 1970 and June 1973 decisions authorizing juries of less than 12 members. In June 1970 Brennan's opinion for the Court extended the right to counsel to preliminary hearings, and he dissented from a June 1972 ruling limiting the right to counsel at police lineups to those conducted after a defendant's indictment or arraignment. A strong proponent of equal justice for rich and poor, Brennan's majority opinion in a March 1971 case overturned a Texas law limiting punishment for traffic violations to fines for those able to pay but allowing imprisonment of those who could not pay. In June 1972 and July 1976 cases, Brennan argued that the death penalty violated the Eighth Amendment's ban on cruel and unusual punishment because, under current moral standards, it did not comport with human dignity.

Justice Brennan took a broad view of the equal protection clause and voted to overturn laws discriminating against the poor and illegitimate children. In an April 1969 majority opinion, he overturned state residency requirements for welfare as a denial of equal protection and an unconstitutional restriction on the right to travel. Brennan urged a strict standard of review in cases alleging sex discrimination. He wrote the opinion of the Court in several cases in the 1970s invalidating distinctions between men and women in military dependency benefits, in social security law and in state laws governing the sale of liquor. In racial discrimination cases, Brennan maintained an activist position. His opinion in a March 1976 case held that under the 1964 Civil Rights Act, an individual denied employment by a company because of race and then later hired by the company may be awarded seniority retroactive to the date of his initial job application.

Brennan insisted that the government use fair procedures in taking away from an individual any benefit or entitlement. In a March 1970 majority opinion, he ruled that welfare recipients were entitled to a hearing before their benefits could be cut off. He also voted to grant hearings to debtors before their wages or property was seized by creditors, to drivers before revocation of their licenses for involvement in an accident, to federal civil service and municipal employes before dis-

missal and to public school students before a disciplinary suspension.

The Justice supported the one-man, one-vote standard for legislative apportionment and, in an April 1969 majority opinion, ruled that no deviation from that standard, no matter how small, was acceptable in congressional districting without strong justification. He objected to February and June 1973 decisions that held that state legislative apportionment did not have to meet the same exacting degree of compliance.

In First Amendment cases Brennan continued to vote in favor of individual rights. In a plurality opinion in a June 1976 suit, he held patronage firings of public employes a violation of their rights of freedom of belief and association. The Justice further expanded the protection of the press from libel judgments in a June 1971 ruling and objected in June 1974 and March 1976 when the majority narrowed this protection in cases involving private citizens rather than public figures or officials. Brennan also dissented from several June 1973 decisions in which the Court gave the states greater leeway to regulate allegedly obscene material. In a significant departure from his earlier position in such cases, Brennan said that the Court's attempts to establish a clear, workable definition of obscenity had failed. Rejecting his own past opinions, he urged the Court to abandon the effort and to overturn all obscenity laws for willing adult audiences. The only Roman Catholic on the bench, Brennan advocated strict separation of church and state and repeatedly voted against state aid to parochial schools.

After the Abe Fortas [q.v.] affair in 1969, Brennan gave up virtually all off-the-bench activities. He became the senior Justice on the Court following William O. Douglas's retirement in 1975. As a Justice, he had a reputation for being an extremely hardworking and painstaking legal technician. He wrote intricate and scholarly opinions that explored all aspects of an issue in detail and was considered much better at explaining and rationalizing his decisions than other liberal members of the Court. During his more than 20 years on the bench, Brennan made a significant contribution by writing key opinions in the fields of reapportionment, First Amendment law and criminal and civil rights. Highly regarded by legal scholars, the Justice was widely recognized as a defender of individual freedoms and, in the words of Paul Freund, as "a redoubtable champion of a free, open and just society."

[CAB]

For further information:
"Mr. Justice Brennan." *Rutgers-Camden Law Journal*, 4 (Fall, 1972), pp. 1-102.

BRIDGES, HARRY (ALFRED) (RENTON)
b. July 28, 1901; Melbourne, Australia
President, International
Longshoremen's and
Warehousemen's Union, 1937-77.

Harry Bridges was the son of a prosperous Melbourne realtor. After spending five years as a seaman, he began working on the San Francisco docks in 1922. Close to the Communists in the early 1930s, he emerged in 1934 at the head of the San Francisco Longshoremen's strike and the citywide general strike which it triggered off. By 1937 Bridges had brought a group of Pacific Coast locals out of the American Federation of Labor's International Association of Longshoremen (ILA) and organized them into the International Longshoremen's and Warehousemen's Union (ILWU), which affiliated with the Congress of Industrial Organizations (CIO). While never a member of the Communist Party himself, Bridges made the ILWU an important base of Communist strength in the CIO during the 1930s and 1940s. As a result, the federal government waged an unsuccessful 16-year-long campaign to have Bridges deported, and in 1949 the ILWU was expelled from the CIO. [See TRUMAN Volume]

The ILWU's isolation in the 1950s induced Bridges to adopt a friendlier attitude toward the employers. In 1960 he signed a collective bargaining agreement with the Pacific Maritime Association (PMA) that brought far-reaching changes to the nature of longshore work and to the future of the ILWU itself. Known as the Mechanization and Modernization Agreement (M&M), the new contract traded long-standing ILWU work rules and production standards for a $29 million pension fund. Bridges himself sought respectability by becoming a registered Republican and establishing close ties with conservative business and political figures in the San Francisco Bay Area. [See EISENHOWER, KENNEDY, JOHNSON Volumes]

The effects of the M & M Agreement produced growing discontent among the ILWU rank and file. Thousands of jobs were lost as a result of the displacement of traditional cargo work by containers— huge metal boxes that could be loaded at a factory or warehouse and shipped to any destination without their contents ever being reloaded. In addition, the union allowed the employers to hire operators for the new mechanized equipment on a full-time, or "steady" basis. This represented a major departure from the use of the equal-rotation hiring hall, which the ILWU had established in 1934 as a means of equalizing work and earnings among longshoremen. The new "steady men" were able to work long hours at high earnings, while most union members who were dispatched through the hiring hall worked only a few days a week.

Despite Bridges' behind-the-scenes opposition, the ILWU struck all 24 West Coast ports on July 1, 1971. To the amazement of observers, it was revealed that the union had no strike fund; instead, longshoremen divided up military cargo work, which was exempted from the strike, to support themselves. In addition, Canadian ILWU members in British Columbia, who did not strike, handled a large amount of U.S.-bound cargo, which was then funneled across the border by land. Bridges' reluctance to lead a more aggressive strike was apparently linked to his expectations of support from the ILA on the East Coast, and possibly even merger between the two unions. At the beginning of October ILA men walked off their jobs in the Atlantic, Gulf, and Great Lakes ports, creating the first nationwide dock strike in U.S. history.

On Oct. 6 President Nixon forced the ILWU back to work with an 80-day Taft-Hartley injunction. Voting in government-supervised elections in December, union members overwhelmingly rejected the PMA's final offer. However, although the injunction expired on Christmas, Bridges postponed resumption of the strike until mid-January while he tried to get ILA agreement to a second nationwide shutdown. By the time the membership was called out there were very few ships vulnerable to strike action on the West Coast. Hopes of support from the ILA collapsed on Feb. 1, when it announced a 30-day contract extension following the expiration of its own federal injunction.

On Feb. 9 Congress passed special legislation ordering the ILWU back to work, and thus the strike ended after 134 days. The contract signed with the PMA called for increases in pay and fringe benefits totalling 21.5%, more than three times the 5.5% ceiling set by the Administration's Pay Board. In asking for the Board's approval, Bridges stressed his record of cooperation with the employers in mechanizing port operations and increasing labor productivity. Nonetheless, on March 17 the panel cut the settlement by about one third. The Pay Board's action prompted four of its five labor members to resign in protest. But although he had threatened a third strike if even a penny were cut off the increase, Bridges did not order his longshoremen out again.

Growing criticism of Bridges' leadership, both from rank and file longshoremen and from other ILWU officers, marked the last years of his presidency. He retired on April 23, 1977.

[TLH]

For further information:
Charles P. Larrowe, *Harry Bridges: The Rise and Fall of Radical Labor in the U.S.* (New York, 1972).

BRINEGAR, CLAUDE S(TOUT)
b. Dec. 16, 1926; Rockport, Calif.
Secretary of Transportation, January 1973-February 1975.

Claude Brinegar was born in California and joined the Air Force in 1945 for a two-year tour. He graduated from Stanford in 1950 and received his Ph.D. there four years later. Brinegar was an economic consultant before joining the Union Oil Company of California in 1953. He worked at Union Oil for 20 years, rising to president of the gasoline division and member of the company's board of directors.

At the start of his second term in 1972, President Nixon nominated Brinegar to be the nation's third Secretary of Transportation, succeeding John Volpe [q.v.]. Brinegar was considered an unknown political quantity, but observers, citing his association with Union Oil, saw him as a conservative addition to the cabinet. The Highway Action Coalition, an anti-highway lobby, said it was "outraged" at the nomination because of Union Oil's involvement in the oil spill off Santa Barbara in 1966. The lobby also pointed out that the oil company had contributed $30,000 in the early 1970s towards the defeat of propositions in California that would have allowed the state's gasoline taxes to be used for mass transit. At his confirmation hearings, however, Brinegar pleaded unfamiliarity with the issues and declined to say whether federal highway funds should be used for mass transit or to comment on oil pollution. The Senate confirmed his nomination in January 1973.

During his tenure, Brinegar was deeply involved in the question of mass transit subsidies. In 1973 both Houses of Congress passed different versions of a bill authorizing $800 million of the Highway Trust Fund to provide operating subsidies for deficit-ridden urban mass transit systems. Brinegar testified that he supported the use of Highway Trust Fund monies for capital expenditures, but he reiterated the Administration's opposition to the federal underwriting of operating expenses, saying this would be the "easy way out" and merely encourage inefficiency and an "accelerating subsidy program." The House-Senate conference, fearing a presidential veto, postponed further action until the following year.

Congress began consideration of the same measure in 1974. Brinegar, though he now agreed to the principle of subsidized operating expenses, unexpectedly denounced the bill as "heavily weighted to a handful of big cities with large and expensive rail transit systems" and said he had urged the President to veto the measure. After a series of complex legislative maneuvers, the House Public Works Committee returned a bill that apportioned more funds to smaller cities wishing to expand their transit facilities, while sharply cutting funds to the larger cities, especially New York. The bill broadened the scope of the earlier proposal, extending it from two to six years as the Administration had urged, but it authorized $20.4 billion, which Brinegar said was excessive. In the first major success of President Ford's policy of fighting inflation by curbing federal spending, Congress reduced the appropriation to $11.3 billion, and Ford signed the bill in November.

Faced in 1973 with the near bankruptcy of several railroads, including the Penn Central, serving the populous Northeast, Brinegar proposed a reorganization plan that depended on private financing. Declaring that the problem must "be solved within the broad framework of the private sector," Brinegar advocated a pruning of unprofitable lines and the establishment of a board, whose members would be named by the President, that would select the carriers to serve the remaining "essential" routes. Later in the year he modified his plan to include more public funding and participation in the new system. In the meantime the Federal Railroad Administration announced a $17 million loan to the Penn Central.

In December Congress passed a version of the Administration bill, reorganizing the Penn Central and six other bankrupt railroads in the Northeast into one profitable system. A Federal National Railway Association would plan and finance the network and have the authority to raise $1 billion in federally backed bonds. Brinegar first opposed some provisions as too expensive, but faced with deteriorating trackage and a larger role projected for railroads because of the energy crisis, he reversed himself and endorsed the measure. Labor organizations objected to the proposed abandonment of more than 15,000 miles of track, and industry spokesmen said that the plan was a step towards nationalization. Brinegar replied that the remaining trackage could handle 96% of the traffic currently carried and that although the government might eventually have to take over the railroads, they should not "be permitted to slide into the morass of nationalization."

In other financially troubled areas of public transportation, Brinegar tried to follow a policy of government support short of direct subsidies or takeover. In September 1974 he announced the government's refusal to pay a monthly subsidy of $10.2 million to Pan American Airways, which had lost $174 million since 1968. Instead he outlined a strategy of belt tightening, international fare hikes and consolidation of competitive routes with other airlines. Later in 1974 Brinegar met with auto industry officials to work out a long-range program for increasing fuel efficiency. Although the plan was a voluntary one, Brinegar said it was no "sweetheart deal." Gasoline usage in 1974, he said, was five million barrels per day, a per auto average of 14 miles per gallon (mpg). The Administration's goal was 19.6 mpg for 1980 model cars, which he said could be accomplished by smaller automobiles and engines and simple design changes.

In December, as part of a gradual transition from a Nixon to a Ford cabinet, Brinegar resigned effective February 1975 and returned to Union Oil. He was replaced by William T. Coleman [q.v.], a Philadelphia transportation lawyer.

[FLM]

BROOKE, EDWARD W(ILLIAM)
b. Oct. 26, 1919; Washington, D.C.
Republican Senator, Mass., 1967 -.

Brooke was the son of a prosperous Veterans Administration lawyer. He received a bachelor of science degree from Howard University in 1941, served in the Army during World War II, and graduated from Boston University's Law School with LL.B. and LL.M. degrees in 1948 and 1949 respectively. During the 1950s Brooke practiced law and made several unsuccessful attempts for state office.

Brooke was elected attorney general of Massachusetts in 1962 and reelected two years later with a plurality of almost 800,000 votes, the largest margin of victory of any Republican in the country that year. He was a speaker at the 1964 Republican National Convention in San Francisco, but declined to endorse presidential candidate Barry Goldwater [q.v.].

In 1966 Brooke became the first black in history to be elected to the U.S. Senate by popular vote. His success in defeating liberal Endicott Peabody by more than 4,000 votes was widely attributed to a singular ability to defuse the issue of his race. As a senator, Brooke was mildly critical of the Johnson Administration's Vietnam policies. In January 1967, in a move that puzzled his critics and admirers alike, he stated after a visit to Indochina that suspension of the U.S. bombing in North Vietnam would not produce fruitful negotiations. It was widely thought at the time that Brooke had succumbed to the famous Johnson "treatment" of persuasion and pressure. [See JOHNSON Volume]

Although Brooke had campaigned vigorously for the Nixon-Agnew ticket in 1968, he soon found himself clashing with the Administration on substantive issues. In 1969 he opposed the Supreme Court nomination of Clement W. Haynsworth [q.v.] and was considered a significant force in Haynsworth's ultimate rejection by the Senate in November of that year. He also opposed the nomination of G. Harrold Carswell [q.v.] to the high

court in 1970. Carswell's "self-proclaimed conservatism," Brooke said, "cannot excuse the behavior and decisions which tend more to confirm than to contradict the thrust of his initial views on racial supremacy." Using a similar argument, Brooke unsuccessfully challenged William H. Rehnquist's [q.v.] appointment to the Court in 1971.

In January 1970 Brooke strongly criticized the Nixon Administration's civil rights record. He stated that the Administration had not acted vigorously enough on desegregation of public schools. He charged that the decision not to seek an extension of the 1965 Voting Rights Act represented a step backwards for the cause of civil rights.

In March of the same year, Brooke declared that the White House had made a "cold, calculated political decision" to shun the needs of blacks in the U.S. in favor of pursuing a "Southern strategy" of wooing Southern whites to ensure reelection in 1972. Brooke further stated that he and other Republicans who had worked for Nixon's election in 1968 because of his promise to "bring us together" were now "deeply concerned about the Administration's lack of commitment to equal opportunities."

It was Brooke's belief that his clashes with the Administration over its civil rights record and Supreme Court nominations had greatly damaged his effectiveness as a senator, and resulted in cutbacks and impoundments of his housing legislation.

Throughout his career Brooke was particularly interested in housing legislation, which became the cornerstone of his work in the Senate. Brooke's most important achievements in housing were the proposals he offered to a 1969 housing bill. As passed in the 1970 Housing and Urban Development Act, the Brooke Amendment provided that tenants in federally assisted public housing would have to pay to no more than 25% of their income for rent. The Act also required the federal government to pay the difference between the 25% ceiling and the housing authorities' operating expenses and provided $75 million for the management of housing facilities to improve maintenance and services. Under an amendment introduced by Brooke to the 1972 Housing Act, low-income tenants of government-subsidized housing in Massachusetts received extended allowances to assist them in buying standard housing.

As a legislator, Brooke also showed a special interest in reforming the nation's system of justice. In 1971 alone, he sponsored eight bills that included provisions for establishing training centers for prison officials, for accelerating court trials, for orienting prisons toward manpower and community correctional programs and for rehabilitating juvenile delinquents.

In foreign policy matters Brooke voted a generally liberal line. He supported every anti-war amendment from 1970 until the end of the Vietnam war. In 1972 Brooke introduced an amendment calling for the withdrawal of U.S. troops from Indochina within four month's of the bill's passage pending release of U.S. prisoners of war. The Senate adopted the measure in August.

On April 22, 1973, Brooke spoke out for the first time on the Nixon Administration's deepening Watergate crisis. He stated that Nixon could not escape the responsibility for Watergate "under any circumstances." On Nov. 4 Brooke became the first Republican senator to publicly call for Nixon's resignation. "There is no question that President Nixon has lost his effectiveness as the leader of this country, primarily because he has lost the confidence of the people of the country, and I think . . . that he should step down, should tender his resignation." Brooke added that he did not know of anything that the President could do to reverse the situation.

On May 22, 1974, Brooke publicly questioned the wisdom of Nixon's planned summit meeting with Soviet leader Leonid Brezhnev in June when "the question of impeachment could be coming to a head in the House of Representatives." Four months later, on Aug. 8,

Brooke and Republican Rep. John H. Buchanan, Jr., of Alabama introduced companion resolutions expressing "a sense of Congress" that Nixon should not be prosecuted after he left office but that the measure would not be binding on the prosecution or the courts. Brooke explained the next day, however, that he would not press for passage of the resolution because of the lack of contrition and confession in Nixon's televised resignation announcement.

Brooke maintained cordial relations with President Ford, and was viewed as a possible running mate in 1976 until he removed his name from consideration. Brooke seconded Ford's nomination for President at the Republican National Convention in Kansas City on Aug. 19, 1976. Brooke lost his reelection bid in 1978, in part as a result of his controversial divorce which revealed possible perjury in statements over loan dispositions during the proceedings. The Senate Ethics Committee discussed the possibility of hearings into Brooke's financial affairs. But with this defeat the Committee announced it would not institute a probe because the panel had lost its jurisdiction over Brooke.

[FHM]

BROWER, DAVID (ROSS)
b. July 1, 1912; Berkeley, Calif.
President, Friends of the Earth, 1969-.

Brower's lifelong love of nature stemmed from hikes in the hills around his Berkeley home and family camping trips in the Sierra Nevadas. After dropping out of the University of California, he worked at Yosemite National Park. From 1941 to 1952 Brower was an editor at the University of California Press. In 1952 he was named executive director of the Sierra Club, the conservation organization, which he had joined in 1933.

Under Brower's leadership the Club greatly increased its membership and assumed a more active political role in preserving wilderness areas. Among the areas saved from development partly by the Sierra Club's efforts were the Grand Canyon and what is now Redwoods National Park. Brower personally supervised the publication of a series of Sierra Club books that helped awaken the public to the splendor of American wilderness and the need to preserve it. [See KENNEDY, JOHNSON Volumes]

By 1969, however, Brower was at odds with the board of directors, who claimed he was dictatorial and financially irresponsible. Brower maintained his measures were necessary to enable the club to become involved in the entire global environmental scene. In May 1969 he was forced to resign.

By September Brower announced the formation of two new organizations to fight what he called "cirrhosis of the environment." Friends of the Earth (FOE) was established as a nonprofit membership organization lobbying for legislative and political action in the environmental arena. The John Muir Institute for Environmental Studies was founded to concentrate on research and education. Brower became president of FOE and director of the John Muir Institute.

FOE lobbied aggressively against the proposed Alaskan oil pipeline, one of the major environmental issues of the early 1970s. The pipeline would cut through what Brower identified as "America's last great wilderness." In newspaper articles, lectures and testimony before Congress, Brower criticized the Administration's support of the pipeline. He said the Interior Department had not seriously considered alternative means of transporting the oil or adequately judged the need for developing the Alaskan oil fields based on projected energy use and the availability of other sources.

The Alaska pipeline was eventually approved by Congress and built, but the oil companies later admitted that the questions raised by FOE and other environmental groups had resulted in a safer, better pipeline. However in a second major fight, the testimony of Brower and others convinced Congress to reject the proposed building of the SST.

FOE also took a strong stand against nuclear proliferation. Brower was worried by President Nixon's energy address in 1971 because of its emphasis on fusion power and fast breeder reactors. In 1973 he charged that the Atomic Energy Commission (AEC) was operating more as a nuclear reactor salesman than as a regulatory agency protecting the public. The AEC continued to give provisional operating licenses to new nuclear power plants despite the increasing volume of anti-nuclear testimony and the insufficient testing of backup cooling systems. Later in the year, FOE joined with Ralph Nader [q.v.] in a suit to close 20 nuclear power plants across the nation because their safety systems were "crude and untested."

Over the years Brower aided new conservation organizations, and expanded Friends of the Earth to include FOE International and FOE Foundation. He also supervised FOE's publishing program.

During the mid 1970s David Brower continued the work—lecturing, lobbying, writing—that has led to his description as the "single most effective conservationist in the world today." Under his direction, FOE stepped up its campaign against nuclear power, and mounted a major effort in 1978 on behalf of a bill before Congress to set aside 120 million acres of Alaskan land as parks and wilderness, free from commercial exploitation or private development.

[TD]

BROWN, EDMUND G(ERALD), JR.
b. April 7, 1938; San Francisco, Calif.
Governor, Calif., 1975-.

Edmund Jr., the only son of California Gov. "Pat" Brown, attended parochial schools and spent four years at a Jesuit seminary in California. He obtained his B.A. degree from Berkeley in 1961 and his law degree from Yale in 1964. After spending a year as a law clerk for the California Supreme Court, Brown took an extensive trip through Central and South America. Upon his return in 1966 he joined the Los Angeles law firm of Tuttle and Taylor.

During the late 1960s Brown became active in efforts to organize migrant workers and anti-war groups. In 1970 he won the election for secretary of state in California and was the only Democrat to survive a Republican sweep of state offices that year.

Over the years the position of secretary of state had become unimportant, but Brown used his powers in a series of bold, highly publicized reform campaigns that soon made his nickname, "Jerry," as well known among voters as his father's had been. He filed suit against three major oil companies—Standard Oil, Gulf and Mobil—charging that they had made illegal contributions of up to $95,000 to politicians who opposed diverting gasoline tax revenues into rapid transit development funds. He issued new, stricter regulations on the reporting of campaign funds by candidates for office in California. Angry legislators responded by cutting Brown's budget, but this only made him more popular with the voters.

In March 1972, Brown initiated a court action against the International Telephone and Telegraph Corp. ITT had become involved in a major scandal following reports by columnist Jack Anderson [q.v.] that the corporation had offered to contribute to the upcoming Republican Convention in San Diego in return for a favorable settlement of an anti-trust suit. Brown's suit sought to prohibit ITT from sponsoring the Convention and to return the funds already committed. Eventually the Republicans decided to hold their convention in Miami instead of San Diego.

In January 1974 Brown's office charged that a deed for President Richard M. Nixon's gift of his vice-presidential papers to the National Archives had been falsely predated to avoid a federal law prohibiting tax deductions for such gifts. It was not the first confrontation between Brown and the President. He had already become one of the first politicians demanding the impeachment of Richard Nixon on the grounds that the President had lied to Congress about the conduct of the war in Southeast Asia.

In January 1974 Brown announced his candidacy for California's Democratic gubernatorial nomination. His platform called for restrictions on campaign spending and lobbying activities. Brown won the primary against such prominent opponents as San Francisco Mayor Joseph Alioto [q.v.] and California State Assembly Speaker Robert Moretti. In the general election campaign against Republican State Controller Houston Flournoy, Brown pledged to bring a "new spirit" to state government.

Brown's positions were a curious amalgam of liberal and conservative themes. He supported abortion rights for women and aid to California's farm workers and poor. But Brown also expressed doubts about increased government spending to solve social ills. He adopted a strict law-and-order stand, stating at one point that prisons were for punishment not rehabilitation. In November Brown was elected by a narrow margin.

Brown swiftly set a new, austere image in his administration. He dispensed with elaborate inauguration ceremonies, turned down the customary chauffeured limousine and refused to occupy the new governor's mansion. He canceled a raise for himself and cut the salary of his staff. Brown selected his staff not from the established Party functionaries, but from generally young, well-educated poverty lawyers and consumer advocates.

Brown established a liberal reputation as governor. In the spring of 1975 he personally oversaw the passage of a major bill of his administration, the farm labor relations measure. It set up the machinery for secret ballot elections of worker representatives who were to monitor the labor practices of growers. The bill also sanctioned consumer boycotts, one of the key strategies of the United Farm Workers. Later Brown signed a bill reducing to a misdemeanor the possession of an ounce or less of marijuana. In 1976 Brown signed into law a right-to-die bill permitting adult patients suffering from terminal illness or injury to make a "living will" that would authorize doctors to turn off life-sustaining equipment if it was evident that death was inevitable. In 1977 Brown vetoed a death penalty bill, but the veto was successfully overridden by the legislature.

Brown's theme of limited governmental powers and his image of thrift and austerity struck a responsive chord with voters. In December 1975 they gave him an approval rating of 84%. Critics, however, including some former members of his staff, claimed that behind his media image Brown was an indecisive leader who avoided grappling with the state's more complex problems. Yet as the 1976 presidential election year began, Brown was one of the most popular politicians in the country.

That year Brown entered several presidential primaries. In Maryland he called for "a new generation of leadership" and a foreign policy with a "moral base." He characterized the campaign of former Georgia Gov. Jimmy Carter [q.v.] as "all just smiles." Carter accused Brown of "not really running for President," but merely acting as part of a "stop Carter" movement organized by the Democratic Party establishment. In May Brown defeated Carter in Maryland by a substantial margin. Later that month in Nevada he defeated the state's former governor, and placed a strong third in Oregon, considered a good showing since Brown had conducted only a write-in campaign in that state. After Brown visited New Jersey, pledging a presidency that "would restore honesty to the White House and put a paycheck in every pocket," the state's uncommitted delegates threw their support to him and Hubert Humphrey [q.v.].

Victories in California and New Jersey in early June brought Brown's total delegate count to 225, after a campaign that cost $1 million. Carter had done poorly in the final series of primaries, but his early lead was so strong that his opponents withdrew one by one and announced their support for Carter's candidacy.

Brown was one of the few holdouts. In a paid national TV address in June, Brown repeated his familiar themes but added that he would "enthusiastically support" Carter should the governor win the nomination. In July Brown finished third at the Democratic Convention. During the fall he campaigned across California with Carter, referring to the former governor as a "fine, dedicated human individual" and predicting Carter would be "a great President." Although Carter was victorious in the November election, California gave its electoral votes to his opponent, Gerald Ford.

In 1978 Brown ran for governor and was reelected. [See CARTER Volume]

[MDQ]

BROWN, GEORGE S(CRATCHLEY)
b. Aug. 17, 1918; Montclair, N. J.
Air Force Chief of Staff, July 1973-July 1974; Chairman, Joint Chiefs of Staff, July 1974-June 1978.

George Brown graduated from West Point in 1941 and was commissioned a second lieutenant in the Army Air Force. In World War II he rose to the rank of colonel as a bomber pilot with the Eighth Air Force in Europe. During the conflict in Korea he directed the operations of the Fifth Air Force. After graduate study at the National War College in the late 1950s, Brown served as assistant to the Secretary of Defense from 1956 to 1963 and to the chairman of the Joint Chiefs of Staff, Gen. Earle Wheeler [q.v.], from 1966 to 1968. In that year he was promoted to general and placed in command of the Seventh Air Force, with jurisdiction over all Air Force operations in Southeast Asia. He returned to the U.S. in September 1970 to take charge of the Air Force Systems Command, the service's research and development program.

In July 1973 President Nixon named Brown Air Force chief of staff. Senate hearings on Brown's appointment raised the issue of his role in the secret bombing of Cambodia in 1969 and 1970, when Brown was in command of air operations in Indochina. In his Senate testimony Brown acknowledged that reports from his office had concealed the bombing missions. He explained that this had been done on instructions from higher authority as a "special security precaution."

As Air Force chief of staff, Brown orchestrated the extensive U.S. airlift of military supplies to Israel during the October 1973 Yom Kippur war. The following spring, in response to concern over the buildup of a new line of Soviet missiles armed with multiple warheads, he expressed confidence that the Soviet Union could not destroy his service's deterrent force of land-based Minuteman missiles. At the same time Brown warned about the much greater expenditures and more forceful momentum of Soviet military research and development, which, he asserted, was the crucial groundwork for future military strength. On the recommendation of Secretary of Defense James Schlesinger [q.v.], Nixon in May 1974 nominated Brown to replace the retiring Adm. Thomas H. Moorer [q.v.] as chairman of the Joint Chiefs of Staff.

Shortly after taking charge, Brown addressed a forum of law students at Duke University. In answering questions from the audience, he said that in the face of another oil embargo, Americans might "get tough-minded enough to set down the Jewish influence in this country and break that lobby." Citing the influence Israel had in Congress, the General continued: "This is somebody from another country, but they can do it. They own, you know, the banks in this country, the newspapers. Just look at where the Jewish money is." Brown's remarks were disclosed by *The Washington Post* on Nov. 13. Public reaction was instantaneous, with several Jewish organizations and members of Congress demanding his dismissal. President Ford personally reprimanded Brown, and Brown made a public apology for his remarks. Ford later declared at a news conference that he had no intention of asking Brown to resign.

Brown took an active part in the Ford Administration's final attempts to save South Vietnam in March 1975. The Administration advocated sending military aid to that country in response to the North Vietnamese offensive, but found itself constrained by recent congressional legislation limiting the President's authority to act abroad. In a speech at the end of March, Brown linked the collapse of Saigon's forces before the North Vietnamese offensive to congressional cutbacks in military aid. He stressed that aircraft, tanks and armored personnel carriers lost in battle had not been replaced by the U.S. and claimed that for lack of spare parts and proper maintenance, Saigon had been unable to keep large numbers of aircraft and helicopters in the air.

In October 1976 Brown was again criticized for remarks quoted in an interview with the Israeli journalist Ranan R. Lurie. Asked by Lurie whether Israel was more of a military blessing or burden to the U.S., Brown had replied, "I think it's just got to be considered a burden." He went on to deprecate Great Britain's military strength and questioned the Shah of Iran's motives in enlarging his country's armed forces. Both Ford and Secretary of Defense Donald Rumsfeld [q.v.] rebuked Brown for his remarks, but they defended him as a good officer. Ford noted that he had recently recommended Brown for another two-year tour of duty as chairman of the Joint Chiefs and that the Senate had confirmed the appointment. Brown held a news conference at which he regretted making the remarks. Ford and Democratic presidential candidate Jimmy Carter [q.v.] later argued in their third televised debate about the propriety of Brown's remarks and their subsequent censure by Ford.

Brown strongly supported the Carter Administration's successful drive for Senate ratification of the Panama Canal treaties. He was an advocate of both the B-1 bomber and the cruise missile. In 1977 President Carter canceled production of the B-1 and chose the cruise missile as its strategic alternative. Brown served as chairman of the Joint Chiefs until May 1978, when he was replaced by Gen. David C. Jones, Air Force chief of staff. Jones had been serving as acting chairman since earlier in the year when Brown was discovered to have cancer.

[SF]

BROWN, SAM(UEL) (WINFRED).
b. July 27, 1943; Council Bluffs, Iowa.
Political activist, public official.

Sam Brown was raised in Council Bluffs, Iowa, where his family owned a retail shoe outlet. He received a B.A. in 1965 from the University of Redlands, and an M.A. in government in 1966 from Rutgers University. He entered Harvard Theological Seminary in the autumn of 1966, and became increasingly active in the growing student movement against the war in Vietnam. He narrowly lost the election for president of the National Student Association at its August 1967 annual convention, but out of that meeting came a decision by Brown and other student leaders to try to organize a "Dump Johnson" movement in 1968.

When anti-war Sen. Eugene McCarthy [q.v.] announced his intention to challenge President Lyndon B. Johnson in the Democratic primaries, Brown joined the campaign as coordinator of student volunteers. For the New Hampshire primary, Brown brought in hundreds of college students who rang doorbells and canvassed voters throughout the state. Dubbed the "children's crusade" by the media, the student volunteer effort received a large amount of the credit for McCarthy's impressive showing in the primary. Brown repeated the tactic in subsequent primaries.

Brown continued his anti-war activities after McCarthy failed to win the Democratic presidential nomination. In 1969 he helped found and became coordinator of the Vietnam Moratorium Committee, (VMC), an umbrella organization of anti-war activists. Endorsed by almost 500 college student body presidents and editors of campus newspapers, the Committee took out a full-page ad in *The New York Times* of Sept. 21 to announce a nationwide "moratorium" against the war to

be held on Oct. 15. Stressing local educational activities against the war, the VMC won the support of politicians, civic, religious and labor leaders and many community organizations. Protests took place across the country on a large scale and revealed that opposition to the war extended far beyond the ranks of college students.

Immediately afterward, Brown announced a two-day moratorium for Nov. 13 and 14, and endorsed the anti-war rally planned for Nov. 15 in Washington, D.C., by the New Mobilization Committee to End the War in Vietnam, a more radical anti-war group. Brown pledged that the demonstrations would be "legal and nonviolent." Together the November actions were the largest demonstrations against the war up to that time.

The Vietnam Moratorium Committee disbanded in April 1970 with Brown citing financial pressures and the end of "the need for which we came together." Settling in Colorado he devoted his time to writing. In 1970 he edited, with Len Ackland, *Why Are We Still in Vietnam,* a collection of articles against the war. In 1972 he published *Storefront Organizing,* a how-to-do-it manual, based on his experience, for community organizers. Brown also became active in the growing environmental movement and helped organize the successful campaign to defeat plans to bring the 1976 Winter Olympics to Colorado.

In 1974 Brown won election as a Democrat to the position of Colorado state treasurer. Campaigning on a populist platform, he used the normally routine post to push for social and economic reforms. Vowing to get the profits "away from the banks and into the community," he placed state deposits in banks with a record of improving lending and employment opportunities for minorities, women and rural dwellers. In 1976 he served on the Democratic Party's National Platform Committee, where he won acceptance for a plank endorsing a pardon for those in "legal or financial jeopardy" because of their opposition to the Vietnam war. As worded, the plank opened the possibility of pardons for armed forces' deserters as well as for draft resisters.

In February 1977, President Carter named Brown director of ACTION, the federal agency in charge of all volunteer programs, including Vista and the Peace Corps.

[JD]

BRUCE, DAVID K(IRKPATRICK) E(STE)

b. Feb. 12, 1898; Baltimore, Md.
d. Dec. 5, 1977; Washington D.C.
Chief Negotiator, Paris Peace Talks, July 1970 - July 1971; Chief Liaison Officer to the People's Republic of China, March 1973 - September 1974; Ambassador to the North Atlantic Treaty Organization November 1974 - January 1976.

Born into one of Maryland's most prominent families, David K. E. Bruce enjoyed a comfortable childhood. He left Princeton University in 1917 during his sophomore year to enlist in the Army. After completing his law studies at the University of Maryland, Bruce was admitted to that state's bar in 1921, and elected to the Maryland state legislature in 1924. During the 1930s Bruce became a "gentleman farmer" in Virginia and was elected to Virginia's House of Delegates in 1939. Bruce helped in the formation of the Office of Strategic Services (OSS) during World War II and commanded the OSS in Europe from 1943 to 1945. Following the war Bruce became an important diplomat in Europe and was the only ambassador to hold three major posts: France from 1949 to 1952; West Germany 1957 to 1959; and Great Britain from 1961 to 1969. [See TRUMAN, EISENHOWER, KENNEDY, JOHNSON Volumes]

In July 1970 President Nixon called Bruce out of retirement to replace Henry Cabot Lodge, Jr. [q.v.] as chief negotiator at the Paris peace talks. At his first session with the Communists on Aug. 6, Bruce expressed confidence that an agreement could be reached provided that both sides negotiated with sincerity and quiet re-

solve. On Sept. 17 the chief delegate of the National Liberation Front, Mme. Nguyen Thi Binh, made the first Communist initiative in 16 months. Although pressing for a reunified Vietnam, the Communists suggested a June 1971 deadline for American troop withdrawal, rather than their oft-repeated demand for an immediate pullout. Once the United States accepted this deadline, Binh would agree to discuss the prisoner-of-war issue. The Communists also expressed a willingness to negotiate the fate of Saigon's government, provided Nguyen Van Thieu, Nguyen Cao Ky and Premier Tran Thien Khiem were excluded. Bruce interpreted these proposals as "old wine in new bottles."

On Oct. 8 Bruce submitted President Nixon's five-point peace plan to the Communist delegation in Paris. Describing the plan as an effort to deceive world opinion, the Communists rejected the proposals which called for a cease-fire in place, expansion of the peace conference to include Laos and Cambodia, negotiation of a timetable for U.S. troop withdrawal, a political settlement to meet the needs of all South Vietnamese, and an immediate release of all prisoners of war. Bruce continued as chief negotiator until July 31, 1971, when he resigned for health reasons. Throughout his stay in Paris, Bruce continually blamed the Communists for not negotiating in good faith and attacked their treatment of war prisoners. Bruce was replaced by William J. Porter.

During his historic 1972 visit to mainland China, Nixon found the Communist Red Chinese reluctant to establish liaison offices because of the Vietnam war. In February 1973, three weeks after a cease-fire was declared in Vietnam, Secretary of State Henry Kissinger [q.v.] was again in Peking. Many observers found it no coincidence that Chou En-lai issued a communique stating that the time was now "ripe for accelerating normalization of relations."

On March 15, 1973, Nixon summoned Bruce to head the United States liaison office in Peking. Bruce's staff of 20 included two notable China hands: Kissinger's adviser John Holdridge and the State Department's Director of Asian Communist Affairs, Alfred Jenkins. Bruce remained in Peking from May 1973 to September 1974 when President Gerald R. Ford replaced him with Republican Party National Chairman George Bush [q.v.]. While in China, Bruce dealt mainly with cultural exchanges and trade matters. A major unresolved issue during this period was the recovery of $78 million in Chinese assets that were frozen in the United States and approximately $195 million in U.S. claims for private property confiscated by the Communists in 1949.

With a sense of duty that made virtually any call to public service obligatory, Bruce accepted President Ford's request in November 1974 to serve as ambassador to the North Atlantic Treaty Organization at its Brussels headquarters, where he remained until his retirement from the Foreign Service in January 1976. On Feb. 10, 1976, President Ford presented Bruce with the nation's highest civilian honor, the Medal of Freedom, for his 50 years of distinguished diplomatic service. Bruce died of a heart attack on Dec. 5, 1977, at the age of 79.

[TML]

BUCHANAN, PATRICK J(OSEPH), (JR.)
b. Nov. 2, 1938; Washington, D.C.
Special Assistant to the President, 1969–73; Consultant to the President, 1973–74.

Patrick Buchanan was born in Washington, D.C. He graduated with a B.A. in English from Georgetown University in 1961 and received his M.S. in journalism from Columbia the following year. He then became an editorial writer with the St. Louis *Globe Democrat*. He was named the paper's assistant editorial editor in 1964. In 1966 Buchanan became an assistant to Richard M. Nixon in New York. At the time the former Vice President, who was a partner in a Wall Street law firm, was campaigning for Republican victories in congressional and state elections in

anticipation of a run for the presidency in 1968. In 1967 Buchanan accompanied the future candidate on a trip to Africa and the Middle East, one of four such foreign study tours Nixon made to prepare for the 1968 election. During the campaign Buchanan worked as a speechwriter.

Buchanan came to the White House with the new Administration as a senior writer on the research and writing staff headed by James Keogh [q.v.]. Nixon would turn to Buchanan for his generally conservative analysis and hard-hitting style. He prepared the President's tough speech defending the military service from "unprecedented attack," which was delivered at the Air Force Academy in June 1969. In April 1970 he drafted Nixon's address explaining the U.S. military incursion into Cambodia.

A strong critic of the press, Buchanan wrote Vice President Spiro Agnew's [q.v.] blistering Nov. 13, 1969, attack on the three major TV networks' news coverage in which he protested the kind of "instant analysis and querulous criticism" that had followed the President's speech to the nation on Vietnam 10 days earlier. Agnew questioned the validity of a "small band of network commentators and self-appointed analysts" inheriting an audience of 70 million Americans gathered to hear the President's address. Again during the 1970 campaign Buchanan was enlisted to assist the Vice President in his carefully articulated criticism of press coverage of the Administration.

Buchanan played an important conceptual role in the off-year elections. He helped to design a Republican campaign strategy aimed principally at disaffected Democrats including blue-collar workers and working-class white ethnics. In 1971 Buchanan drew up a provocative memorandum warning that on such traditional Republican issues as balancing the budget and reducing the federal bureaucracy, President Nixon was not doing enough and risked being labeled a liberal. He urged the Administration to concentrate on constructing "the new majority," which, in his 1973 book of the same name, he identified as an alliance of disparate political groups moving away from New Deal-type coalitions and toward the decentralization of power from the federal to the local level.

In 1973 Buchanan was named a consultant to the President. His time became increasingly devoted to Watergate. In April of that year he stated in a memorandum to Nixon that aides H.R. Haldeman [q.v.] and John D. Ehrlichman [q.v.] should voluntarily leave if they could no longer maintain their effectiveness. He later pushed for their resignation. Buchanan was the first witness when the Senate Watergate Committee opened the second phase of its probe, in September 1973, focusing on alleged political sabotage during the 1972 presidential campaign. The Committee majority set out to show that the policy groundwork for alleged campaign sabotage in 1972 had been firmly laid in early political strategy memorandums. The Committee produced memos revealing Buchanan's urgings to Nixon supporters to knock out one Democratic contender—Sen. Edmund Muskie (D, Me.) [q.v.]—and to elevate another—Sen. George McGovern (S.D.) [q.v.], considered a weaker challenge to the President.

Buchanan denied any illegal or unethical tactics. He told the Committee that he had been willing to use "anything that was not immoral, unethical, illegal or unprecedented in previous Democratic campaigns." He asserted that he had neither suggested nor participated in anything beyond acceptable political operations. He declared that Nixon had won his record landslide reelection not because of Watergate and dirty tricks but in spite of them.

The Supreme Court on July 24, 1974, ordered President Nixon to surrender the tapes of 64 conversations subpoenaed by the special prosecutor. A review of the tapes by White House lawyer J. Fred Buzhardt, Jr. [q.v.], led several aides to believe that the transcripts of discussions between Nixon and Haldeman on June 23, 1972, were sufficiently damaging to cause the President to resign. Buchanan was among the aides who successfully argued that it would be better to release the transcripts first and then evaluate the

reaction. He reasoned in that way there would be no doubt about whether the resignation was necessary.

After Nixon's resignation, Buchanan stayed on briefly in the Ford White House as an adviser. He left in November and became a nationally syndicated columnist.

[SF]

BUCHEN, PHILIP W(ILLIAM)
b. Feb. 27, 1916; Sheboygan, Wis.
Council to the President, August 1974-January 1977.

Philip Buchen received his A.B. from the University of Wisconsin in 1939 and remained at that university to earn his J.D. two years later. He was admitted to the Michigan bar soon after graduation. In November 1941 he opened a law office with fraternity brother Gerald R. Ford. As novices, their clients were primarily indigents whose cases had been referred by local courts. The partnership was short-lived, however; when Ford joined the Navy in April 1942, Buchen joined one of Grand Rapid's leading law firms, Butterfield, Keeney and Amberg. (Buchen had been crippled by polio as a child and was unable to serve in the armed forces during World War II.) He remained in private practice in Grand Rapids through 1974, entering political affairs only as part of the original "Ford for Congress" group in 1948. Buchen also assisted Ford politically in preparing for the proposed-vice president's confirmation hearings in 1973.

In March 1974 Buchen came to Washington, D.C., as counsel for the Domestic Council's Committee on the Right of Privacy, a group chaired by Vice President Ford. Two months later Buchen began working with the head of the Office of Telecommunications, Clay Whitehead, for what Ford's old friend saw as the eventual move of the Vice President to the presidency. Whitehead and Buchen initially worked without Ford's knowledge. But as the Watergate crisis deepened, they were forced to involve the Vice President.

On July 24 the Supreme Court ruled

that President Nixon must give potentially damaging tape recordings pertaining to the Watergate burglary to the special prosecutor. Following the release of tape transcripts detailing Nixon's intricate knowledge of and participation in the subversion of efforts to investigate the burglary, Buchen worked closely with Ford on the likely transition. It was Buchen who helped assemble Ford's White House staff and prepare his initial speech on the assumption of office.

Buchen was appointed presidential counsel shortly after Ford became President in August 1974. Immediately after assuming his new position, Buchen became immersed in legal proceedings involving the Watergate burglary investigation and upcoming trial. He and Ford ordered the retention of Nixon's tapes and documents pending the resolution of legal issues raised by the special prosecutor. Buchen at first denied the defendants access to their files; he later permitted them to see the documents, but would not allow notes or copies to be made.

Buchen also helped work out an agreement with Nixon's attorney giving the former President ownership and control of material still stored in the White House. The pact was soon challenged by the Reporters' Committee for Freedom of the Press and the American Political Science Association, which sought to keep the papers available for public use. The suit argued that the material was "prepared on government time by government employees in the discharge of their public duties." The material was ultimately put in the permanent custody of the General Services Administration.

On Sept. 8, 1974, Ford granted "a full, free and absolute pardon" to ex-President Nixon. Buchen acted as a liaison between the White House and the various other parties involved; he queried Special Prosecutor Leon Jaworski [q.v.] on the possible timing of a Nixon trial and asked a friend of Ford's to go to San Clemente and meet with Nixon's counsel. Buchen told the press that no demands had been made upon Nixon as a condition for the pardon, which he described as an "act of mercy." Although an admission of guilt was not requested of Nixon, Buchen said that the granting of a pardon "can imply guilt–there is no other reason for granting a pardon."

Buchen served as the President's counsel until Ford left office.

[RB]

BUCHER, LLOYD M(ARK)
b. Sept. 1, 1927; Pocatello, Ida.
Naval officer.

Lloyd Bucher spent much of his early childhood in a Mormon orphanage in Boise, Ida. and a Catholic mission and orphanage in the northern part of the state. After graduating from high school he enlisted in the Navy. He rose through the ranks and by December 1966 was named commanding officer of the USS *Pueblo*, a surface ship in the light-freighter class. Shortly thereafter the ship was refitted and recommissioned as an intelligence ship designed to take part in Operation "Clickbeetle." This was the code name for a secret program of electronic and radio surveillance by small, unarmed navy vessels operating independently in areas close to potential enemies. In January 1968 the *Pueblo* received orders to conduct electronic surveillance in international waters outside the 12-mile territorial limit along the eastern coast of North Korea.

On Jan. 23, two days after a North Korean infiltration attack on Seoul, the *Pueblo* was fired on, boarded and seized by four North Korean torpedo boats and two subchasers. The nearest possible U.S. military assistance was hundreds of miles and hours away. The ship was taken to the North Korean port of Wonson. The U.S. immediately demanded both the release of the crew and ship and an apology, insisting that the *Pueblo* had been in international waters. North Korea maintained that the ship had been spying within its waters. Public reaction in the U.S. ranged from calls for caution to demands for action. During the 1968 presidential campaign, Republican nominee Richard M. Nixon made frequent reference to the *Pueblo*'s capture, questioning how it happened and attacking the fact that North Korea had been able to seize a U.S. vessel on the high seas.

The crew was held hostage in North Korea for 11 months. During this period U.S. representatives met 27 times with the North Koreans at Panmunjom to negotiate for the crew's release. This was eventually accomplished on Dec. 22 when the U.S., acceding to North Korean demands, admitted in a signed statement that the *Pueblo* had intruded into North Korean waters and apologized for the intrusion. Gen. Gilbert H. Woodward, chief U. S. negotiator at the Panmunjom talks, read into the record, before signing the agreement, a statement disavowing the admission.

At a news conference in Seoul on Dec. 23, Bucher said that he and other crew members had been tortured and forced to sign confessions written by the North Koreans. After his release Bucher steadfastly claimed that he had no choice but to surrender when faced with the North Korean seizure, because the ship had only light weapons and the Navy had ignored his requests for a mechanism to scuttle the *Pueblo* in case of such a circumstance. While Bucher stated that he was "totally accountable" for the loss of classified documents and electronic equipment to North Korea, he noted that he had not been provided with the necessary means for their destruction.

In March 1969 a Navy court of inquiry recommended general courts-martial for Bucher and the ship's intelligence officer and letters of reprimand for several other members of the crew. It recommended court-martialing Bucher because he had not taken immediate and aggressive action when the ship was attacked and because he had "negligently" failed to complete the destruction of secret material.

Because in his opinion the crew had "suffered enough," Secretary of the Navy John H. Chafee [*q.v.*] announced on May 6 that "no disciplinary action" would be taken against any crew members of the *Pueblo.* He also rejected the recommendation for letters of reprimand, asserting that the responsibility for the conse-

quences of "the *Pueblo*'s lonely confrontation by unanticipatedly bold and hostile forces" must by borne by all involved in the chain of command.

Bucher resigned from the Navy in 1973.

[SF]

For further information:
Lloyd M. Bucher, *Bucher: My Story* (New York, 1970).

BUCKLEY, JAMES L(ANE)
b. March 9, 1923; New York, N. Y.
Conservative Senator, N.Y., 1971-77.

James Buckley attended Yale College and graduated in 1943. After serving in the Navy during World War II, he studied at Yale Law School and completed his degree in 1949. He practiced law in New Haven, Conn.

Buckley entered political life by managing the unsuccessful campaign of his brother, William F. Buckley, Jr. [*q.v.*], when the latter sought the post of mayor of New York City in 1965.

In 1968 James Buckley ran unsuccessfully as a Conservative Party candidate for the United States Senate. He ran again in 1970 and succeeded in defeating Charles Goodell, the Republican incumbent, and the Democratic candidate Richard Ottinger. Buckley only received 38.7% of the vote — but that was enough to gain him the victory. He was aided in his campaign by Richard Nixon whose support in the election had probably been decisive.

Buckley immediately became a leading conservative figure in the Senate. Both in domestic and foreign policy, he spoke for and voted for conservative programs. He was opposed in principle to government programs designed to strengthen the welfare state and to intervene in the management of a free-enterprise economy. He voted against government guarantees to the Lockheed Corp. He fought against federally financed and controlled day-care centers. Buckley voted against a federal bail-out of New York City and suggested that New York City would be better off if it went into bankruptcy. He cast his ballot against the minimum wage bill of 1974, and opposed increased social security benefits and vocational rehabilitation for the handicapped.

Buckley backed strong anti-crime measures and drug abuse laws. He opposed the Equal Rights Amendment in 1972 and introduced a constitutional amendment to outlaw abortions except when the mother's life is in danger.

Buckley supported the Nixon and Ford Administrations in their Indochina policy. He opposed the McGovern-Hatfield amendment calling for the withdrawal of United States troops from Vietnam by the end of 1971. He was also an advocate of high defense spending. A staunch critic of communism, he advocated a hard-line American foreign policy to deal with the Soviet Union and her allies. He endorsed the preservation of the President's foreign policy prerogatives and voted against the war powers bill and other measures which would weaken the president in the conduct of foreign policy.

On a number of issues, Buckley gathered the support of some liberals. He joined with former Sen. Eugene J. McCarthy to file a federal court lawsuit challenging the Federal Election Campaign Act Amendments of 1974. In that suit, they contended that the federal financing provisions of the act violate constitutional restrictions on federal taxing and spending power, prevent taxpayers from supporting candidates or parties, and discriminate against minor parties and independent candidates.

Buckley supported legislation, moreover, to protect student rights. The "Buckley Amendment" of 1976 gave parents and adult students the right to inspect school records and restricted the rights of institutions to pass on the content of students' files to outsiders.

Buckley became the first conservative to call for Nixon's resignation. He suggested that Nixon resign as "an extraordinary act of statesmanship and courage" because of the Watergate scandals. This statement undermined Nixon-supporters who argued that the liberals wanted Nixon to resign.

In 1976 Buckley lost his reelection bid to Daniel Patrick Moynihan.

[HML]

BUCKLEY, WILLIAM F(RANK), JR.
b. Nov. 24, 1925; New York, N.Y.
Editor-in-Chief, *National Review*, 1955-.

The son of wealthy Roman Catholic parents, Buckley attended private schools in Great Britain, France and the United States. After a year at the University of Mexico, Buckley served two years in the U.S. Army and was discharged in 1946 with the rank of second lieutenant. He entered Yale University, became chairman of the *Yale Daily News*, and graduated with honors in 1950.

Buckley's literary career began in 1951 with the publication of *God and Man at Yale*, a critically acclaimed attack on the political and religious liberalism of his former university. In 1954 Buckley co-authored *McCarthy and His Enemies*, which defended the anti-Communist activity of Sen. Joseph R. McCarthy (R, Wis.). *Up from Liberalism*, a critical survey of liberal reform, followed in 1959.

Buckley emerged in the 1960s as the intellectual leader of white-collar conservatives who combined resistance to Communism abroad with opposition to liberalism at home. To promote the conservative point of view, Buckley launched the biweekly *National Review* in 1955, which soon attracted more subscribers than both of its counterparts on the left, *The New Republic* and *The Nation*. In 1962 Buckley began writing a nationally syndicated newspaper column, "On the Right." Beginning in 1966 a syndicated television interview program, "Firing Line," exposed public figures to Buckley's sarcastic questioning. "Firing Line" received an Emmy Award for Outstanding Program Achievement in 1969.

Buckley supported the 1964 presidential candidacy of Sen. Barry M. Goldwater (R, Ariz.) [q.v.], but he denounced the influence of the extreme right-wing John Birch Society. Although he lost a conservative third party campaign for mayor of New York in 1965, Buckley supported the nomination and election of Republican Richard Nixon in 1968. He also managed the unsuccessful 1968 Senate campaign of his brother James L. Buckley [q.v.] on the New York Conservative Party ticket.

From 1969-72 William F. Buckley served on the five-member Advisory Committee of the U.S. Information Agency, a largely honorary presidential appointment. However in protest of the Administration's policies of detente with the Soviet Union and deficit spending at home, Buckley announced a "suspension of support" for President Nixon in 1972. The indictment and subsequent resignation of Vice President Spiro Agnew [q.v.] in 1973 surprised Buckley and his followers, who had supported Agnew's criticism of the American press and his calls for law and order. In April 1974 Buckley endorsed Sen. James L. Buckley's call for the resignation of President Nixon.

William F. Buckley's youthful opposition to social welfare programs, federally enforced school desegregation and U.S. membership in the United Nations mellowed during the Nixon-Ford years. In *Four Reforms* (1973), Buckley called for federal welfare assistance but only to those states with an income per capita below the national average. Buckley also advocated simplified federal taxation to exemptions, "noncoercive" education to permit state aid to private schools as well as nondiscriminatory admission to all public schools, and revision of the Fifth Amendment to ensure swift justice and eliminate plea bargaining.

Buckley served as a member of the delegation to the United Nations in 1973. In his book *United Nations Journal* (1974), Buckley defended U.S. membership in the world organization but attacked the General Assembly for its anti-American sentiment and for its condemnation of right-wing but not left-wing oppression.

Buckley's lifelong opposition to Communism did not diminish in the Nixon-Ford era. He welcomed the arrival in the U.S. of the recently exiled Soviet dissident Alexander Solzhenitsyn in the summer of 1975. He condemned President Ford's refusal to receive Solzhenitsyn in Washington that fall.

Buckley supported the presidential candidacy of former Gov. Ronald Reagan [q.v.] in 1976 but endorsed Ford in the election.

In 1968 Buckley published a selection of his articles entitled *The Jeweler's Eye.* Books entitled *The Governor Listeth* (1970), *Cruising Speed* (1971), *Inveighing We Will Go* (1972), and *Execution Eve* (1975) followed. In a sentimental book, *Airborne* (1976), Buckley recounted his crossing of the Atlantic Ocean in a sailboat the previous summer with his wife and son. Buckley's first novel, *Saving the Queen,* also appeared in 1976 and became a best-seller, as did its sequel, *Stained Glass,* in 1978.

[MDB]

BUNDY, McGEORGE
b. March 30, 1919; Boston, Mass.
President, Ford Foundation, 1966–79.

Bundy graduated first in his class from Yale in 1940. Following service in World War II, he worked briefly in the Truman Administration in 1948 for the agency responsible for implementing the Marshall Plan. In 1949, after having worked for Thomas Dewey's presidential campaign, Bundy went to Harvard as a lecturer in government. A brilliant teacher, Bundy attained full professorship by the age of 34, when he was appointed dean of arts and sciences.

Although a nominal Republican, Bundy had campaigned for John F. Kennedy in 1960 and served in the Kennedy Administration as a close adviser to the President on foreign policy issues. After the Kennedy assassination Bundy remained in Washington as an adviser to Lyndon B. Johnson. He became a leading spokesman for the Administration's policy in Vietnam and was an important force in policy formation. In December 1965, unable to accommodate himself to Johnson's style of dealing with advisers, Bundy resigned. [See KENNEDY, JOHNSON Volumes]

Following his resignation from the White House staff, Bundy became president of the Ford Foundation. He brought changes in the policies of the Foundation, which until that time had employed relatively conservative funding practices. Foremost among these was making the fight against racism a top-priority concern. In June 1966 the board of trustees formally agreed that the issue of equal opportunity should be the first domestic concern of the Foundation. The Foundation became involved in higher education for blacks and other minorities. One of its major efforts, started in 1972, was a $100 million, five-year program to strengthen those black institutions with the highest chance of survival. Through the Michele Clark program and a community news service—"Race Relations Reporter"—the Foundation made an effort toward getting more minorities into the media, especially broadcasting. Foundation money also provided "core" and "experimental" support for community development corporations.

In 1974 Bundy announced a 50% cutback in the Foundation's program budget, reducing it from $200 million to $100 million, because of an inability to sustain the high rate of grantmaking that had been set for the 1960s and early 1970s. The Foundation sharply reduced work in the arts and broadcasting while maintaining support of education and environmental programs.

In March 1973 Bundy was a prominent witness for the defense in the case of Daniel Ellsberg [q.v.], accused of espionage in leaking the *Pentagon Papers.* Considered to have been a chief architect of American policy in Vietnam, the former special assistant for national security to Presidents Kennedy and Johnson testified that several documents revealed had not damaged the U.S. nor aided Hanoi and that many had lost their importance with the change in Administration.

Bundy remained with the Foundation until June 1979.

[MLB]

BUNKER, ELLSWORTH
b. May 11, 1894; Yonkers, N.Y.
Ambassador to South Vietnam, April 1967-March 1973.

Ellsworth Bunker was the son of a wealthy sugar manufacturer. After graduating from Yale in 1916, Bunker worked for his father's firm, the National Sugar Refining Company until 1948. Three years later he left business to accept an appointment as ambassador to Argentina.

Through the 1950s and into the 1960s, Bunker handled his diplomatic duties skillfully and gained a reputation as a formidable mediator. He served as ambassador to Italy and to India under President Eisenhower and undertook two special assignments for President Kennedy, mediating armed confrontations in Indonesia and Yemen. Kennedy designated Bunker U.S. representative to the Organization of American States (OAS), and President Johnson approved the appointment, which became official in 1964. [See TRUMAN, EISENHOWER, KENNEDY Volumes]

Bunker approved of OAS programs "designed to enhance the internal security capabilities of the military and police forces of Latin America," and supported U.S. intervention in situations involving threats to the security of the hemisphere. After armed U.S. intervention in the civil war-torn Dominican Republic in 1965, Bunker undertook a year-long assignment as head of a three-man OAS peace mission.

In 1967, President Johnson named Bunker to succeed Henry Cabot Lodge as ambassador to South Vietnam. The appointment was applauded by both "hawks" and "doves." Bunker became one of the strongest supporters of the war in the Johnson Administration, severely damaging his reputation as a disinterested mediator. As the number one American in Vietnam, he gave final approval to all important military and political decisions and, according to *The New Republic*, was in large part responsible for the continued U.S. presence in Indochina during the Nixon era. Bunker took an optimistic view of U.S. involvement in the war, asserting that progress was being made even after the disastrous Tet offensive of January 1968. He favored border incursions into Laos and Cambodia and was a strong supporter of the repressive regime of South Vietnamese President Nguyen Van Thieu, whom he regarded as "an extremely reasonable, open-minded man." [See JOHNSON Volume]

In January 1969 Bunker agreed to stay in his Saigon post at the request of President-elect Richard M. Nixon. He continued to favor U.S. participation in the war and spoke publicly of the progress of the South Vietnamese against the Communists. Bunker supported the 1970 invasion of Cambodia by South Vietnamese and U.S. troops as part of the Administration's policy of Vietnamization of the war. The destruction of North Vietnamese bases in that country, he stated, would give "more time to develop the South Vietnamese forces." Fearing political repercussions at home and in Vietnam if the government of Nguyen Van Thieu failed to win a democratic mandate from the Vietnamese people, Bunker worked to give the October 1971 presidential elections in South Vietnam the appearance of a free contest. He urged South Vietnamese Vice President Nguyen Cao Ky and General Duong Van Minh to run against Thieu, and reportedly offered to finance Minh's campaign. Both men withdrew from the elections, charging U.S. interference and a conspiracy by President Thieu to rig the elections. Thieu ran unopposed and was reelected.

Bunker resigned his Saigon post in March 1973, returning to Washington as ambassador-at-large. He worked closely with Secretary of State Henry Kissinger [q.v.], accompanying Kissinger to Saudi Arabia in a futile effort to seek lower oil prices. In November 1973 Bunker took charge of the deadlocked Panama Canal treaty negotiations. He left in December to head the U.S. delegation to the Geneva Mideast Peace Conference.

Bunker continued his Panama negotiations through the Ford Administration, maintaining steady progress at the bargaining table. By the time Sol Linowitz joined Bunker in Panama at the beginning of the Carter Administration, most of the work had been done. Bunker won Pentagon support for the treaty by separating the issues of canal operations and canal defense. On August 10, 1977, the negotiators announced that they had reached an "agreement in principle," and Bunker devoted himself to achieving Senate ratification of the pact. After accompanying President Carter to Panama in June 1978 for ceremonies accompanying the signing of the treaty, the 84-year-old diplomat announced his retirement to his Vermont farm. [See CARTER Volume]

[DAE]

BURCH, DEAN
b. Dec. 20, 1927; Enid, Okla.
Chairman, Federal Communications Commission, October 1969-February 1974; Special Counselor to the President, February 1974-August 1975.

The son of a federal prison guard, Dean Burch worked his way through the University of Arizona law school, graduating in 1953. From 1955 to 1959 he was administrative assistant to conservative Sen. Barry M. Goldwater (R, Ariz.) [q.v.] and then entered private law practice. In 1963 Burch left his practice to serve on Goldwater's presidential campaign staff. Following Goldwater's nomination for President at the 1964 Republican National Convention, the Senator named Burch chairman of the Republican National Committee (RNC). Burch, who never served in a national campaign, knew little about the Committee's operations, but Goldwater felt that his position as chairman would help keep the GOP national organization in conservative hands even if Goldwater lost the election.

As RNC chairman Burch was responsible for running Goldwater's campaign and made most of the major strategy decisions. Unprepared for his leadership role, however, he proved a poor campaign director and failed to efficiently organize the RNC. He antagonized liberal-moderate Republicans by packing the RNC executive committee with conservative loyalists, and brought in his own aides to run the national organization, shattering morale among permanent RNC employees. In the 1964 elections the Republican Party suffered its worst defeat since 1936. Under pressure from Richard M. Nixon and other influential moderate Republicans, Goldwater agreed to Burch's replacement by the nonideological Ray C. Bliss of Ohio. Burch returned to his Phoenix law practice and in 1968 directed Goldwater's successful campaign for reelection to the U.S. Senate. [See JOHNSON Volume]

In September 1969 President Nixon appointed Burch chairman of the Federal Communications Commission (FCC). Before announcing Burch's appointment, the President had cleared it with broadcasting executives, who expected the new chairman, with his conservative ties, to uphold their interests. At first Burch supported the large broadcast companies, who were being threatened for the first time in 42 years by private groups seeking to wrest their licenses. However, Burch soon challenged the power of broadcast industry chiefs in the area of television news commentary. Instead of waiting the customary 30 days, he requested immediate transcripts of network commentaries on President Nixon's Nov. 3 speech on Vietnam. Broadcast executives saw this move as a subtle threat of federal censorship of TV news presentations. On November 14, 1969 Burch again surprised industry chiefs when he endorsed Vice President Spiro T. Agnew's [q.v.] attack on the biases of TV news coverage. Democratic congressional leaders protested that Burch was trying to suppress criticism of the Nixon Administration and to stifle open news coverage and analysis. Burch denied the charges of federal censorship, stating that he hoped news coverage would change as a result of public pressure and decisions within the industry. Burch's position was supported by liberal Democrats on the FCC, who feared the potential influence of network power and corporate control in biasing news reportage.

In October 1971 Burch and Nicholas Johnson, a liberal FCC member who often opposed Burch's views, appeared together before the Senate Subcommittee on Constitutional Rights to defend the FCC against broadcasters' charges that the commission had interfered with news programming. When Dr. Frank Stanton, president of the Columbia Broadcasting System (CBS), stated that there was "ample evidence" of attempts by government officials to intimidate the press, Burch cited cases in which the FCC had purposely avoided judging controversial news journalism, including the coverage of the 1968 Democratic National Convention and two CBS documentaries, "Hunger in America" and "The Selling of the Pentagon." Burch and Johnson saw the real threat of news censorship as coming from the networks and their attempts to maximize profits. Burch's criticism of the major networks was welcomed by opponents of the Pastore bill, legislation that would have made it even more difficult for small private groups to apply for broadcast licenses.

Burch left the FCC in the winter of 1974 to become presidential counselor for domestic affairs. Political observers saw the move as an attempt by the President, whose involvement in the Watergate scandal had deepened, to shore up his defenses against impeachment. Through the spring of 1974, while Nixon refused to turn over subpoenaed tapes and documents dealing with Watergate to Special Prosecutor Leon Jaworski [q.v.], Burch urged Republicans to remain loyal to the President and to link their political futures to his. In April 1974 Burch assured the RNC that Nixon would soon turn over to the House Judiciary Committee a "massive body of evidence" which would establish the truth of the Watergate affair.

When, in May, the White House finally released edited transcripts of the Watergate tapes, Burch defended their tone and content to a public appalled by the revelation of the inner workings of the White House. In a letter to the *Chicago Tribune* Burch argued that the transcripts showed "life as it is" in "government, politics, industry and business." He continued to denounce the deliberations of the House Judiciary Committee as a "black spot on jurisprudence," even as it became clear that both Democrats and Republicans believed Nixon guilty of impeachable offenses.

After Nixon's resignation in August 1974, Burch remained on the White House staff as President Gerald R. Ford's campaign coordinator for the 1974 elections. Although Burch left the President's staff in 1975, he filed the organizing papers for the President Ford Committee with the Federal Elections Commission in June 1976. His major role during the 1976 Ford presidential campaign consisted of his efforts to dissuade his former boss, Sen. Goldwater, from supporting California Gov. Ronald Reagan [*q.v.*] for the Republican presidential nomination. From 1975 Burch worked for the Washington law firm of Pierson, Ball and Dowd, which specialized in communications.

[DAE]

BURGER, WARREN E(ARL)
b. Sept. 17, 1907; St. Paul, Minn.
Judge, U.S. Court of Appeals for the District of Columbia, 1956-69; Chief Justice of the United States, 1969-.

Warren Burger worked his way through the St. Paul College of Law, graduating third in his class in 1931. A partner in a St. Paul law firm from 1935 to 1953, he maintained a varied general practice while teaching part-time at his alma mater. Burger, a Republican, worked to elect Harold Stassen governor of Minnesota in 1938. He was floor manager for Stassen's unsuccessful presidential bids at the 1948 and 1952 Republican National conventions and shifted his support to Dwight D. Eisenhower at an important moment during the 1952 gathering. Burger was named assistant attorney general in charge of the Civil Division of the Justice Department in 1953. In June 1955 Eisenhower nominated him to a judgeship on the U.S. Court of Appeals for the District of Columbia. Burger was sworn into office in April 1956.

In his 13 years as a circuit judge, Burger developed a reputation as a conservative, particularly in criminal cases. In often articulate, quotable opinions, he opposed the reversal of convictions for what he considered legal technicalities and was a critic of the *Durham* rule which broadened the definition of criminal insanity. Off the bench Burger challenged various aspects of the American criminal justice system, criticized the Warren Court's approach in criminal rights cases and urged reform of the penal system. Active in the American Bar Association (ABA), he was a leader in efforts to improve the management and efficiency of the courts.

On May 21, 1969 President Richard Nixon nominated Burger as Chief Justice to replace the retiring Earl Warren. Nixon had made the Warren Court's criminal rights rulings a target during his 1968 campaign and had promised to appoint "strict constructionists" to the bench. He selected Burger for the Court largely because the Judge's record demonstrated a philosophy of judicial conservatism, especially on criminal issues. Burger's appointment was confirmed by the Senate on June 9 by a 74-3 vote. He was sworn in on June 23, 1969, at the end of the Court term.

In criminal cases Chief Justice Burger usually took a conservative stance. He voted to uphold searches and arrests made without a warrant and vigorously attacked the exclusionary rule that prohibited the use of illegally seized evidence at trial. He took a narrow view of the Fifth Amendment's privilege against self-incrimination and joined in several decisions limiting the scope of the 1966 *Miranda* ruling. Although he voted to guarantee indigent defendants free counsel in certain misdemeanor cases, Burger opposed extending the right to counsel to preliminary hearings, pre-indictment lineups and displays of photographs of a suspect to witnesses. He supported the use of six-member juries and non-unanimous jury verdicts and voted repeatedly to uphold the death penalty against constitutional challenge. In December 1971, however, Burger ruled that prosecutors must adhere to their part of plea bargaining agreements. He joined in several decisions banning the imposition of jail terms on convicts solely because they could not pay fines.

In July 1974 Burger spoke for the Court in the celebrated case of *U.S. v. Nixon*. He ordered the President to surrender the tapes and documents subpoenaed by special prosecutor Leon Jaworski [*q.v.*] for the pending Watergate cover-up trial of six former presidential aides. Nixon's claim of executive privilege, Burger ruled, had to yield in this case to the demonstrated need for evidence in a pending criminal trial. Conversations recorded on several of the tapes that Nixon surrendered in response to the Court's order led directly to his resignation from office on Aug. 9, 1974.

In free speech cases the Chief Justice generally sustained government action against individual rights claims. For a five man majority in June 1973, he reversed a 16-year Court trend lowering restrictions on pornography and set new guidelines for obscenity laws that gave the states greater leeway to regulate pornographic materials. He dissented in June 1971 when the Court denied the government's request for an injuction to halt newspaper publication of the *Pentagon Papers*. Burger joined the majority a year later in holding that journalists had no First Amendment right to refuse to testify before grand juries about information obtained from confidential sources. However, he spoke for the Court in June 1974, to invalidate as an infringement on free-

dom of the press, a Florida law requiring newspapers to print replies from political candidates whom they criticized. He also overturned a judicial "gag" order restricting pretrial news coverage of a Nebraska mass murder case in June 1976 as an unjustified prior restraint on the press.

Burger wrote several significant opinions on government and religion. In May 1972 he ruled that the application of a state law for compulsory secondary education to the Amish denied the sect their right to free exercise of religion. His May 1970 majority opinion held that tax exemptions for church property used solely for religious purposes did not violate the First Amendment's ban on government establishment of religion. However, Burger overturned several programs for direct state aid to parochial schools in June 1971, because they would result in excessive government entanglement with religion. In later cases he voted to sustain state aid programs in which the benefits went to the individual parents or children rather than directly to the religious schools.

In a widely publicized April 1971 case, Burger spoke for a unanimous Court to uphold court-ordered busing as one means of eliminating state-imposed school segregation. In July 1974, however, he overturned a plan to remedy segregation in Detroit's school system by merging it with suburban districts. For a five man majority, Burger held such an interdistrict plan inappropriate when segregation had been established only in one district and there was no evidence showing that school district lines had been drawn in a discriminatory way. In other racial discrimination cases, Burger followed a moderately conservative course.

The Chief Justice applied the constitutional guarantee of equal protection of the laws to women for the first time in November 1971, when he invalidated an Idaho law favoring men over women in the administration of estates. In later sex discrimination suits and other equal protection cases, however, Burger again took moderate to conservative positions. He concurred in January 1973 when the Court upset state laws prohibiting abortions within the first six months of pregnancy as a denial of due process. However, he was otherwise wary of invalidating government action on due process grounds. Burger usually upheld the states' power to establish voting requirements. Nevertheless for a unanimous Court in March 1974, he ruled that states requiring political candidates to pay a filing fee had to provide some alternative means of access to the ballot for individuals too poor to pay the charge. The Chief Justice joined in numerous rulings limiting the Court's jurisdiction to hear cases. He voted, for example, to set restrictive requirements for bringing federal class action suits, to tighten standing requirements and to limit state prisoners' right of appeal in federal courts in certain instances.

As Chief Justice, Burger took a leading role in promoting administrative efficiency and reform in the courts. He publicized the problems of the courts through annual State of the Judiciary addresses given before the ABA, press interviews and public speeches. He suggested a variety of administrative improvements and successfully urged establishment of state-federal judicial councils, a national center for state courts and an institute to train court managers. Burger devoted special attention to what he considered an excessive workload in all of the federal courts. To remedy it, he urged Congress to remove certain cases from federal jurisdiction and to consider the impact of all new legislation on the courts before passage. He also favored studying the possibility of limiting the right of appeal and of having certain types of cases, such as family law problems or prisoner complaints, settled in some other forum than the courts. Burger appointed a seven man committee in the fall of 1971 to study the Supreme Court's caseload. In a controversial December 1972 report, the committee recommended establishment of a new national appeals court to screen all the petitions for review of cases currently filed in the Supreme Court. Burger also promoted

penal reform and proposed special training and certification for trial attorneys.

Assessments of Burger varied, depending in part on commentators' agreement with his judicial views. It was generally accepted, however, that the Chief Justice did not dominate his colleagues on the bench but was an articulate, sometimes pungent, advocate of restraint by the Court. He maintained a high level of agreement with Nixon's other Court appointees and argued that judicial decisions should not play a major role in promoting reform. A hardworking man with a pragmatic mind, Burger may make a more lasting impact, according to some observers, as a judicial administrator rather than as a jurist.

[CAB]

For further information:
John P. MacKenzie, "Warren E. Burger," in Leon Friedman and Fred L. Israel, eds., *The Justices of the U.S. Supreme Court, 1789-1968* (New York, 1969), Vol 4.

BURNS, ARTHUR F(RANK)
b. April 27, 1904; Stanislau, Austria.
Counselor to the President, January 1969-January 1970; Chairman, Board of Governors, Federal Reserve System, January 1970–January 1978.

Arthur Burns was born in Austria and immigrated to the United States with his parents prior to World War I. After growing up in Bayonne, N.J., he attended Columbia University, where he took his B.A., his M.A. and finally, in 1934, his Ph.D. in economics. While still a graduate student, Burns began teaching at Rutgers University, and in 1930 he was hired as a research associate at the National Bureau of Economic Research (NBER), a private institute established for the study of business cycles. In 1941 Burns returned to Columbia as a visiting professor, becoming a full professor in 1944. The following year he was appointed director of research at the NBER, and became NBER president in 1957.

Burns's early career was not limited to teaching and research. Through his association with the NBER, he had served as a consultant to various government agencies and departments. In 1953 President Eisenhower appointed Burns chairman of the Council of Economic Advisers (CEA). Burns, in his three-year tenure as chairman, was widely credited with bringing the Council to the center of U.S. economic policymaking. [See EISENHOWER Volume]

Because of his early critique of Keynesian economics and other writings, Burns was generally viewed as a conservative, but repeatedly proved to be, above all, a pragmatist who could shift policies as the situation demanded. Thus to combat the recessions of the 1950s, he on occasion pressed for more extensive credit policies against the tight money bias of the Eisenhower Administration. In the early 1970s, reversing a position he had taken in an influential 1965 article, Burns emerged as a leading spokesman for wage and price controls.

Burns's career first became interwoven with that of Richard Nixon when he correctly informed the Vice President in 1960 that without adequate economic stimulus the Republicans would lose the upcoming presidential elections. After Nixon's defeat Burns served on the Advisory Committee on Labor-Management Policy under Kennedy and Johnson. When Nixon was elected to the White House in 1968, Burns became counselor to the President, with cabinet status. In January 1970 he succeeded William McChesney Martin [q.v.] as chairman of the Federal Reserve Board.

Burns took over the Fed at an auspicious moment. The Nixon Administration had come into office amid promises to combat inflation and to balance the federal budget, and under Martin, the Federal Reserve had pursued what some observers felt was a draconian credit policy. Just before Burns took office, the nation's money supply had been held to an unprecedented five months of zero growth, prompting Nixon, at Burns's inauguration, to end his introductory remarks with the plea: "Dr. Burns, please give us more money!"

Burns was in fact preparing to ease monetary conditions. In his Senate confirmation hearings in December 1969, he had stated that he was in favor of a relaxation of current tight money "under normal conditions," although he had gone on to say that conditions at the time were by no means "normal."

Burns was under pressure from many quarters, including the White House. In appointing Burns, Nixon had acclaimed the chairman's "independence" but added his hope that "independently he [Burns] will conclude that my views are the ones that should be followed." Burns admitted at a May 1970 convention of the American Bankers' Association (ABA) that the Administration's exclusive reliance on monetary and fiscal policy to combat inflation could cause "a very serious business recession." In the same speech he voiced support for a "modest" incomes policy, though not for full-fledged wage and price controls. Two weeks later, at a White House dinner for top U.S. businessmen, Burns alluded to the widespread concern about U.S. corporate liquidity, and promised action by the Fed to avert any liquidity crisis.

Events quickly put Burns to the test. In June 1970 congressional opposition to government-guaranteed loans for the Penn Central Railroad forced the company into bankruptcy, despite initial support by Burns and the Administration for such loans. Over the weekend prior to the Penn Central's public declaration of bankruptcy, Burns mobilized the Federal Reserve System for the largest rescue operation in its history.

Burns correctly feared that the Penn Central's default on $80 million in commercial paper might produce a general panic in the financial markets, forcing numerous other corporations into default and bankruptcy. The Federal Reserve Bank notified all member banks that it was prepared to issue standby credits through its discount window to enable capital markets to function smoothly, and a panic was thereby averted. In July 1970, testifying before the Joint Economic Committee (JEC) of Congress, Burns proposed the creation of a new federal lending corporation to guarantee loans to creditworthy corporations cut off from normal borrowing channels.

In December 1970, with the U.S. economy in serious recession and inflation still at high levels, Burns proposed an 11-point anti-inflation plan. Among his proposals were more vigorous use of antitrust regulations, expanded federal training programs to produce more skilled workers in high-wage sectors of the economy, a liberalized depreciation allowance for corporations, a suspension of the Davis-Bacon Act requiring union wages to be paid on federal construction projects and compulsory arbitration of public interest labor disputes. Burns also voiced his support for a wage-price review board, intensifying his campaign for controls that were still officially anathema to the Nixon Administration.

Burns's relations with the Administration entered a crisis in July 1971. In testimony before the JEC, Burns had stated that there had been "very little progress" in the fight against inflation. Widespread rumors began to circulate that Nixon was furious at Burns's remarks and exasperated by his repeated calls for wage-price controls. Other rumors, which were somewhat coolly denied by White House Press Secretary Ronald Ziegler [q.v.], implied that Nixon was considering steps to double the size of the Federal Reserve Board with his own appointees. Two days after Ziegler's remarks, Treasury Secretary John Connally [q.v.], countering Burns, stated that "very substantial" progress had been made against inflation. Finally rumors appeared in the press asserting that Burns was hypocritically seeking a $20,000-per-year increase in his own salary.

These rumors were later traced to White House aide and future Watergate figure Charles Colson [q.v.]. The *Wall Street Journal* editorialized that the White House wanted to embarrass Burns "either to diminish his impact on public opinion or to force him to resign and make room for a more docile central bank head." In early August Nixon himself was compelled to "set the record straight" about the rift, calling Burns "the most responsi-

ble and statesmanlike" Fed chairman in memory.

Behind this atmosphere of rumor and denial, however, a policy struggle of the gravest consequences was at stake. The U.S. economy remained stagnant, and the international crisis of the dollar had forced America's Common Market trading partners into a joint currency float in May 1971. According to Charles Coombs, who managed the foreign exchange desk for the Federal Reserve Bank of New York and was thus in charge of defending dollar parity, communication had virtually ceased between the Administration and Connally's Treasury Department on one side and the Federal Reserve on the other.

In Coomb's view, Burns "alone of Washington officialdom . . . had recognized the danger inherent in the Treasury policy stance." On the weekend of Aug. 14-15, 1971, Burns participated with Connally, Office of Management and Budget Director George Shultz [q.v.], Nixon and other leading Administration figures in the "Camp David II" talks, where Burns's long-advocated domestic wage-price controls were adopted in the drafting of Nixon's "New Economic Policy (NEP)" announced on national television on the evening of Aug. 15. Although victorious on wage-price controls, Burns fought and lost to Connally on the plan to end legal gold backing of the dollar in international settlements. Burns was aware that such a unilateral action by the U.S. would only fuel the criticisms that the Nixon Administration, with Connally, was practicing a "malign neglect" policy in international monetary matters. Nevertheless, Connally carried the day.

With the end of Phase One and the 90-day wage-price freeze, more permanent control mechanisms were established for Phase Two. President Nixon appointed Burns to head a newly created Government Committee on Interest and Dividends, whose purpose was to keep bank and other interest rates and stock dividend increases at appropriate levels. His appointment drew fire from critics who either feared Burns's increased power to influence capital markets, or who saw a possible conflict of interest between

Burns's functions on the committee and his role as Fed Chairman.

Nixon's NEP launched the U.S. economy on a two-year boom that was later criticized as hyperinflationary and politically motivated by the President's desire to be reelected in 1972. This criticism necessarily rebounded to Burns, who permitted the domestic money supply to expand through 1972 at unprecedented rates. Burns later admitted that the 1972 monetary expansion had been too rapid.

Burns also played a key role in the international arrangements related to the NEP. In the intense international negotiations in the fall of 1971 over the establishment of new fixed parities for the world's currencies, Burns represented the U.S. at the International Monetary Fund (IMF) Group of 10 meeting in London in September. With Connally and Paul Volcker, undersecretary of the Treasury for Monetary Affairs, Burns negotiated the final articles of the Smithsonian Agreements, signed in Washington in December 1971 most important monetary agreement in the history of the world."

Sixteen months later, the Smithsonian Agreements collapsed. Burns, more than most U.S. officials, had understood the fragility of the new accords, and was more adamant than most that the United States should take some of the responsibility for maintaining the stability of the dollar, which in the 1971 crisis had devolved largely onto foreign central banks who sought to save their own currencies from unnecessary appreciation.

In May 1972, at an American Bankers' Association convention in Montreal, Burns elaborated a 10-point program for monetary stability that appeared to many to contain gestures of conciliation towards U.S. trading partners, particularly in its acceptance of a continued role for gold and its emphasis on a "symmetrical" division of responsibilities. Immediately after Burns's speech, Undersecretary Volcker took the floor and emphatically reminded the convention that Burns "was not speaking for the U.S. government." Thus the Fed-Treasury rift on international questions continued into the second dollar crisis of 1973. In the interim,

with Burns's support, the Federal Reserve Bank of New York continued to make limited interventions to bolster the dollar in foreign exchange markets.

The end of Phase Two controls in January 1973 initiated a new period of intense international pressure on the dollar from foreigners, who correctly anticipated a new wave of U.S. inflation. In early February Burns told the Senate Banking Committee that enforcement of Phase Three guidelines would be "very tough indeed" and called for presidential standby authority to reimpose wage-price controls. Nevertheless, intense selling of the dollar on foreign exchanges forced a new dollar devaluation by mid-March. In early March Burns attended a crisis session with President Nixon on the matter and several days later told the House Banking Committee that he wanted a prompt international solution to the crisis. Burns then flew to Paris for the international meetings that ended the Smithsonian Agreements, realigned currencies and established a floating-rate system of international exchange.

The takeoff of inflation in early 1973 brought the Government Committee on Interest and Dividends into a showdown with the banking system. In February 1973 Burns had forced the major commercial banks to roll back an increase in the prime lending rate. In March, with increased pressure from inflation, Burns and the banks negotiated a "split" rate system of one rate for nationally known borrowers and another for small businesses dependent on local capital markets. In April Burns, acting in his capacity as Fed chairman, sent a letter to all Federal Reserve member banks urging them to "avoid a credit crunch" and to be cautious in their lending. A week later, however, he was forced to concede that his "jawboning" efforts had resulted in artificially low rates, and by the end of 1973, the prime commercial rate had risen from approximately 6.5% to 10%.

The problem of accelerating domestic inflation, compounded by the quadrupling of oil prices in the fall of 1973, confronted the Federal Reserve with the possibility of a new U.S. recession, of which many observers considered Burns to be a major architect. In April 1974 congressional testimony, Burns defended the Fed's application of the monetary brakes, which had begun to deeply depress the housing and mortgage markets. "To shape monetary policy with an eye to the fortunes of home building and to neglect the grave and very dangerous problem of inflation would be extremely unwise," said Burns. "We're having a veritable explosion of business loans." In July 1974 Burns told the House Banking Committee that inflation was the result of "loose fiscal policies," and defended the slowing of monetary growth by the Fed. In August he urged the JEC to channel $4 billion into the creation of 800,000 public service jobs if unemployment passed the 6% mark.

By the fall of 1974 U.S. industrial production entered the worst downturn since the Depression years of 1929-33, and Burns increasingly devoted his public statements to detailed analyses of its causes. In October he told the JEC that the U.S. was in "a most unusual recession" with "no precedent in history." Burns pointed to the potential illiquidity of the international banking system brought about by "petrodollar recycling," saying that such recycling was "piling debt upon debt, and more realistically, bad debt on top of good debt." Attempting to quiet fears in the wake of the bankruptcy of the Franklin National Bank, Burns revealed that the Fed had made some temporary loans to "a few other institutions" in order to allow financial markets to "function in an orderly manner."

Burns recognized that long-term trends were at work in the recession. He addressed an ABA convention in late October 1974, pointing to the long-term deterioration of U.S. bank liquidity and indicating that "the capital cushion which plays such a large role in maintaining confidence in banks has become thinner, particularly in some of our largest banking organizations." He went on to say that the federal regulatory system had "failed to keep pace" with these changes and called for a sweeping overhaul of the

Federal Reserve, the Federal Deposit Insurance Corporation (FDIC) and the Comptroller of the Currency, whose overlap was "indeed a jurisdictional tangle that boggles the mind."

When economic recovery began in mid-1975, Burns attempted to keep the U.S. money supply expanding at a 5%-7% rate, adequate to fuel a "modest" increase of production. Rep. Henry Reuss (D, Wis.) had used the collapse as an opportunity to introduce legislation forcing the Fed to expand the money supply at a 6% annual rate, a measure that Burns vehemently opposed as tying the hands of the central bank to a mechanical target. Reuss's measure was eventually turned into a sense of Congress resolution, but under congressional pressure, Burns made the unprecedented concession of revealing Federal Reserve Board monetary targets a year in advance on a quarterly basis.

In a September 1975 speech, Burns proposed a series of sweeping "structural reforms" to eradicate the inflationary bias of the U.S. economy. He called on the U.S. government to act as the "employer of last resort" with public works programs, at the same time calling for a reduction of unemployment insurance payment periods from 65 to 13 weeks and a modest set of voluntary wage and price controls. He also urged policymakers to stretch out environmental and job safety goals because of their "dampening" effect on business.

Burns repeatedly had to weather criticism of the Federal Reserve, particularly from labor leaders and liberal congressional opponents of his monetary policies. In 1971, in opposition to Burns's advocacy of wage-price controls, AFL-CIO President George Meany [q.v.] charged that "Chairman Burns . . . [and others] . . . have been engaged in the shocking and blatant use of a double standard while providing subsidies and aid for the banks and big business." As the U.S. entered the 1974-75 recession, Meany called for the ouster of Burns and other Nixon appointees.

Similarly, congressional advocates of

tighter governmental control of the Fed and the banking system, such as Rep. Wright Patman (D, Tex) [q.v.] and Rep. Henry Reuss, repeatedly attempted to push through legislation making the Fed more accountable to Congress. In 1971 when Congress was considering two bills that authorized the government to regulate interest rates, credit flows, and wages and prices and to permit the Fed to channel credit into desired sectors of the economy with variable reserve requirements, Burns opposed this increase of the Fed's powers, arguing that such legislation would put the central bank "in the political arena in a big way."

In May 1976, Burns vehemently opposed a watered down Reuss bill that made a Fed chairman's term roughly concurrent with a presidential term and introduced other measures to effectively "politicize" Fed policy. Burns also opposed attempts by Reuss and Patman to use the January 1976 leak of the Comptroller of the Currency's "problem list" of commercial banks to force greater disclosure practices

Burns played an important role in the 1975 New York City fiscal crisis. With Secretary of the Treasury William Simon [q.v.] and CEA Chairman Alan Greenspan [q.v.], Burns emerged as an opponent of federally guaranteed loans to the city in the summer and fall of 1975. In May, like many critics, he stated that the city had lost its credibility and that default was inevitable. However, by November 1975 national and international opinion had begun to sense that a New York City default might do serious damage to U.S. capital markets and hence to the shaky world economic recovery. Thus, while telling the Senate Banking Committee in early November that a default would not set off a chain reaction, he began to express growing concern over its effects. On Nov. 12, Felix Rohatyn [q.v.] of the Municipal Assistance Corp., established to oversee the city's finances, announced that Burns had given "an A-minus" to New York state Gov. Hugh Carey's [q.v.] rescue plan for the city. At the same time top U.S. officials, including Simon and Greenspan, were also beginning to favor some form of aid. Neverthe-

less, in a December 1975 meeting with Carey over the imminent bankruptcy of the state's Housing Finance Association, Burns denied Federal Reserve aid to the agency.

After the election of Jimmy Carter to the White House, Burns stayed on as Federal Reserve chairman. He clashed openly with Carter on several occasions over monetary policy, and when his term expired in January 1978, he was replaced by William Miller.

[LG]

BURNS, JOHN A(NTHONY)
b. March 30, 1909; Fort Assineboine, Mont.
d. April 5, 1975; Kaiwi, Oahu, Hawaii.
Democratic Governor, Hawaii, 1963–75.

During World War II Burns, who spent part of his youth in Hawaii, was a member of the Honolulu police department working to restore the morale of Japanese Americans who, under martial law, had been placed in detention camps. Following the war he began to reorganize Hawaii's Democratic Party. Burns was elected territorial delegate to Congress in November 1956, and became recognized as the architect of Hawaiian statehood. He lost the July 1959 gubernatorial election to the incumbent territorial governor, Republican William F. Quinn, but in a November 1962 rematch, Burns easily defeated the governor.

As governor, Burns followed a middle-of-the-road policy encouraging tourism and rapid economic growth. A practitioner of the "consensus" politics of his mentor Lyndon B. Johnson, Burns maintained close ties with business, labor and Hawaii's ethnic minorities and helped to reduce the state's Republican Party to one of the weakest in the nation. However because of the increased taxes and government expenditures accompanying Hawaii's economic boom, his 1966 reelection victory was a difficult one. [See EISENHOWER, KENNEDY, JOHNSON Volumes]

During Burns's second term, divisions arose within the Democratic ranks. His critics, led by Lt. Gov. Thomas P. Gill, argued that Burns encouraged the islands' economic expansion at the expense of environmental concerns and the needs of Hawaiians. Among the problems cited by Gill were industrial smog, unchecked land speculation, a critical housing shortage, the rise of organized crime and the highest cost of living in the U.S. He charged Burns with failing to utilize housing development laws and called for a tax on tourists.

Although Gill mounted a serious challenge in the 1970 primary, Burns won the race and easily beat his Republican opponent in the general election. Stung by criticism, however, he established an environmental quality control center during the campaign and assumed a tougher stand on land speculation. In 1972 he authorized the establishment of a commission that would make annual recommendations to the legislature on the maximum number of automobiles to be permitted on each island. Although a devout Catholic, in 1970 Burns favored and allowed a liberal abortion measure to pass without his signature.

After learning that he had cancer, Burns decided not to run in 1974, but his chosen successor was elected. Burns died on April 5, 1975.

[FLM]

For further information:
Tom Coffman, *Catch A Wave: A Case Study of Hawaii's New Politics* (Honolulu, 1973).

BURTON, PHILLIP
b. June 1, 1926; Cincinnati, Ohio.
Democratic Representative, Calif., 1964-.

Following military service during World War II, Burton received his B.A. from the University of Southern California in 1947 and his LL.B. from the Golden Gate Law School in 1952. He began practicing law in San Francisco, and emerged as one of the city's leading Dem-

ocratic liberals. In 1956 Phillip Burton won a seat in the California Assembly, where he served until 1964. While in the Assembly he labored for the enactment of progressive legislation. His most notable accomplishment was a reapportionment plan that increased the power of California's cities. Burton won a special election in 1964 to the House of Representatives from a liberal district that comprised part of San Francisco and its suburbs.

One of the most ambitious and hardworking members in the House, Burton quickly assumed a leadership role in Congress. In 1971 he won the chairmanship of the Democratic Study Group (DSG) and three years later was elected chairman of the House Democratic Caucus, the body responsible for planning upcoming legislation. In both positions Burton pressed for reform of House rules to reduce the power of the committee chairmen, replace the seniority system of appointing committee chairmen and members with a more flexible method and make it easier for legislation to reach the floor of the House.

Burton worked vigorously for the passage of bills to improve the working conditions of Americans. He cosponsored the Federal Coal Mine Health and Safety Act of 1969, which improved procedures for monitoring the working conditions and health of the nation's coal miners. Burton was responsible for inserting in the bill a section that granted federal money for the treatment of miners with black lung disease and provided for aid to their widows. The following year he actively backed the Occupational Safety and Health Act, which established comprehensive job safety programs for over 55 million Americans.

To aid the poor and the unemployed, Burton supported public works programs and the extension of unemployment insurance benefits in states where the jobless rate exceeded 6.5%. Responding to the needs of the rural poor in his state, Burton inserted in the 1973 minimum wage bill an amendment that would increase the minimum wage for farm workers from $1.30 an hour to $2.20 by 1976. But President Nixon vetoed the bill.

Phillip Burton was one of the leading House opponents of the Vietnam war. He wrote the minority plank of the 1968 Democratic Party platform opposing the war, voted consistently against funds for the war and supported Sen. George McGovern's [q.v.] quest for the Democratic presidential nomination in 1972. Burton led the anti-war forces in the House which rejected a bill that would have allowed the use of troops to aid the final evacuation of Saigon in the spring of 1975. He pointed out that President Johnson, whom he called an "honorable man," had in 1964 asked for and received authority to use troops in Vietnam. To now permit President Ford to make the same mistake would be "a mindless act."

Burton was also one of the foremost advocates of defense cuts. He voted against the Safeguard anti-ballistic missile, the B-1 bomber and the Navy F-14 fighter. He also opposed the SST. But when asked to aid the foundering California-based Lockheed aircraft company with a $250 million government loan, Burton voted for the loan in response to both union and corporate pressure from his home state.

In December 1976 Phillip Burton unsuccessfully sought the position of House majority leader. He remained chairman of the Democratic Caucus during the early Carter Administration.

[JB]

BUSH, GEORGE H(ERBERT) W(ALKER)
b. June 12, 1924; Milton, Mass.
Ambassador to the United Nations, February 1971-December 1972; Chief, Liaison Office, People's Republic of China, September 1974-December 1975; Director, Central Intelligence Agency, January 1976-January 1977.

The son of Sen. Prescott Bush (R, Conn.), George Bush attended the Phillips Academy and joined the U.S. Naval Reserve upon his graduation in 1941. After the war, Bush majored in economics at Yale University, graduating in 1948. Bush declined a position with his father's banking firm in New York, and instead, he became an oilfield supply salesman in Texas. In 1954 he founded the Zapata Off-Shore Co., a contract oil-drilling firm. This enterprise expanded rapidly and made Bush a millionaire in his own right.

Bush entered politics in 1964 with an unsuccessful run for a U.S. Senate seat. He won election in 1966 to the U.S. House from Houston's wealthy seventh congressional district. In his two terms in the House, Bush served on the Ways and Means Committee and earned a 77% rating from the conservative Americans for Constitutional Action. Although Bush favored state "right-to-work" laws and "freedom of choice" alternatives to school desegregation, he supported the Johnson Administration's open-housing legislation in 1968 over intense opposition among his constituents. Bush also supported the 1969 voting rights amendment and the Nixon Administration's 1970 Family Assistance Plan. Although Bush defended the interests of the oil companies, he favored stringent environmental legislation.

Bush was considered for the 1968 Republican vice presidential nomination on the strength of his Southern constituency and reputation as a Nixon backer, but Nixon chose Spiro Agnew [q.v.]. Bush launched a second unsuccessful campaign for the Senate in 1970.

President Nixon appointed Bush as U.S. ambassador to the United Nations in December 1970. Although initially regarded with skepticism as a politician, Bush earned the admiration of the other delegates in 1971 with his informal style and access to the White House. Bush advocated the Middle East peace proposals of Secretary of State William Rogers [q.v.] and called for stronger world action to control the illegal narcotics trade. In October 1971, he guided the Nixon Administration's attempt to admit Communist China to the U.N. under a "two Chinas" proposal that would have continued Nationalist Chinese membership in the General Assembly. The U.N. rejected the

American proposal, however, and expelled Taiwan. Bush defended the Administration's "tilt" toward Pakistan in the Indo-Pakistani war of December 1971, but pledged U.S. relief aid to Bangladesh in May 1972. He also defended the Administration's decision to blockade North Vietnam in May 1972.

Following the 1972 elections, Nixon appointed Bush chairman of the Republican National Committee. Bush sought to translate the Republican "new majority" of 1972 into greater Republican congressional power by broadening the party base to include workers and ethnic groups. The unfolding Watergate scandal soon absorbed most of Bush's attention, however, throwing the Republican Party on the defensive. Although maintaining that Nixon would survive the scandal, Bush resisted Administration pressure to involve the Republican Party in the President's defense. The crisis nevertheless slashed financial contributions to the Party by one-third and produced a series of bi-election losses to the Democrats, who won a landslide victory in the congressional elections of 1974.

In September 1974 President Ford appointed Bush to head the U.S. Liaison Office in Peking. Bush impressed the Chinese with his friendly informality by touring Peking on a bicycle and by holding hamburger and hot-dog parties in the American compound. He helped to host President Ford's state visit to China in December 1975.

In November 1975 Ford appointed Bush to replace William Colby [q.v.] as Director of the Central Intelligence Agency (CIA). Although at first suspected as a "political" director, Bush stayed out of the 1976 campaign. He helped the Agency to improve its professionalism by making structural reforms and by promoting younger personnel. In response to previous disclosures of CIA misconduct, Bush carried out President Ford's executive order of February 1976 to reform the intelligence community. The order prohibited abuses, upgraded the interagency committee on covert operations to cabinet-level, tightened measures to prevent unau-

thorized disclosures, and enlarged the responsibilities of the CIA director for overall management of the intelligence community.

George Bush was again considered for the Republican vice presidential nomination in 1976 but President Ford chose Sen. Robert Dole (R, Kan.) [q.v.] instead. After leaving office in 1977, Bush served as chairman of the First National Bank of Houston. He announced his candidacy for the Republican presidential nomination in the spring of 1979. [See CARTER Volume]

[GB]

BUTZ, EARL L(AUER)
b. July 3, 1909; Albion, Ind.
Secretary of Agriculture,
November 1971-October 1976.

Butz grew up on his family's 160-acre farm. He attended Purdue University and received a doctorate in agricultural economics in 1937. Nine years later he became a full professor at Purdue. From 1954-57 Butz served as assistant secretary of agriculture in the Eisenhower Administration. He was dean of Purdue's school of agriculture during the late 1950s and early 1960s and a director of the Ralston Purina company and several other agribusiness corporations.

In response to declining agricultural income and rising discontent among farmers, President Nixon, in November 1971, announced the resignation of Secretary of Agriculture Clifford Hardin [q.v.] and the appointment of Butz to replace him. The nomination aroused strong opposition because of Butz's association with the conservative policies of the Eisenhower Administration. For the first time the National Farmers Union opposed a presidential nominee for Agriculture Secretary. The Senate Agriculture Committee narrowly voted in favor of confirmation, 8-6, with two Republican farm-state Senators voting against Butz. On December 2 the Senate approved Butz's nomination 51-44.

Although he favored a return to free

market forces and a minimum of federal support for agriculture, Butz released agricultural appropriations impounded by the Nixon Administration. In December he announced the purchase of large amounts of corn and other grains on the open market to bolster farm prices. He also increased the subsidies paid to farmers to retire land from production and raised environmental conservation payments. In a gesture to congressional liberals he announced in January 1972 a reversal of planned cutbacks of $200 million in the food stamp program.

Butz advocated improved income levels for the nation's farmers. In a February 1972 speaking tour of farm states, he opposed controls on farm prices and blamed middlemen for rising food costs. His statements, however, were at odds with the Administration's wage and price controls and quickly provoked dissenting reactions. C. Jackson Grayson [q.v.], head of the federal Price Commission, deplored Butz's comments, saying that if other federal officials thought only of their own constituents, "the efforts to achieve price stability would be wrecked."

Butz looked to foreign sales of U.S. grain and other agricultural products as a way of bolstering farm income. At the urging of the White House, which was concerned about the persistent balance of payments deficit, Butz visited the Soviet Union in April 1972. In July he announced a three-year agreement with the Russians for the purchase of a "minimum" $750 million of U.S. wheat, corn and other grains on the open market. The Soviet Union would be eligible for long-term credits from the Department of Agriculture's Commodity Credit Corporation, and the domestic sellers would be eligible for government subsidies to bring the market price of the grain up to parity.

The Soviet grain deal, which was timed to coincide with the 1972 presidential campaign, quickly embroiled Butz in a storm of controversy that lasted two years. The sale also played a major part in wrecking the Administration's efforts to achieve price stability.

On August 30 the Consumers Union asked the Justice Department to investigate possible conflict of interest by two Agriculture Department officials who were involved in the negotiations and then left the department to take jobs with major grain-exporting firms. A Senate Agriculture Committee staff memo reported evidence of a "coziness between the Department of Agriculture and private grain exporters" that led to windfall profits for the corporations. On September 8 Democratic presidential candidate Sen. George McGovern attacked the deal as "another example of the big business favoritism" of the Nixon Administration, and charged the big grain companies with acquiring huge stocks of grain, based on inside information, early in July when prices were low. A few days later Butz called McGovern's charges "a bald-faced lie."

Despite Butz's denial the public outcry was so great that the Justice Department and the General Accounting Office began formal investigations. In July 1973 the GAO reported that the Department of Agriculture's mismanagement of the sale had resulted in $300 million in unnecessary subsidies paid to grain exporters and the escalation of food prices. That same month the Justice Department concluded no evidence of criminal fraud or conflict of interest existed. Nevertheless the final report of an inquiry by the permanent investigations subcommittee of the Government Operations Committee in the summer of 1974 severely criticized Butz for a "$300 million error in judgment." "At virtually every step," the report declared, "from the initial planning of the sales to the subsidy that helped support them, the grain sales were ineptly managed."

Although the grain sale eventually led to higher prices paid to farmers, it had a disastrous impact on domestic inflation, driving up the cost of feed grains for cattle producers and the retail price of food. The skyrocketing price of beef led consumer groups to declare in March 1973 a national meat boycott, but prices remained firm. Butz placed temporary export curbs on 41 commodities in July to prevent domestic shortages and ended all production controls to increase supplies. In June the Administration, over Butz's opposition, froze food prices for a month and beef prices for three months. In response cattle producers refused to bring steers to market, leading to widespread meat shortages in many parts of the country. Consumer food prices rose 22% in 1973 and another 14% in 1974. In September 1974 Butz warned consumers that prices would rise another 8-10% before leveling off.

Butz announced in January 1973 that the Administration would impound $1.2 billion in funds appropriated for agriculture, including monies for disaster loans and food stamps. In March, however, a federal district court in Minneapolis ordered the restoration of disaster aid, and the following year issued a similar ruling on $278 million in food stamp funds.

Despite the furor surrounding the 1972 Soviet grain sale, Butz, in October 1974, reported a $500 million sale to the Russians, but President Gerald Ford canceled the purchase because of its inflationary impact. A smaller export agreement was announced later.

In December 1974 cattle producers from South Dakota organized a "cross-country beef-in" to protest Butz's policies. Widespread evidence of corruption and bribe-taking among grain inspectors licensed by the Department of Agriculture was uncovered by the Department of Justice in May 1975. Grand juries in Houston and New Orleans handed down over 50 indictments. In August 1975 the General Accounting Office charged that faulty crop forecasting by the Department had resulted in policy decisions that led to $1.67 billion in unnecessary federal expenditures.

Butz's tenure as Agriculture Secretary ended abruptly during the 1976 presidential campaign when former White House counsel John Dean related in a magazine article a slur against blacks made by an unidentified Administration official. "I'll tell you why [The Republicans] can't attract coloreds. Because coloreds only

want three things. You know what they want? . . . first, a tight pussy; second, loose shoes; and third, a warm place to shit. That's all." A few days later another magazine revealed Butz as the source of the comment.

Reaction to Butz's remark was swift and furious. On October 1 President Ford gave Butz a "severe reprimand" for making a "highly offensive remark." Ford was forced to accept Butz's resignation when no one came to his defense and the public outcry continued to mount. On October 4 Butz resigned, admitting merely to a "gross indiscretion" and "unfortunate choice of language." He later resumed his professorship at Purdue University.

[JD]

BUZHARDT, J. FRED, JR.
b. Feb. 21, 1924; McCormick, S. C.
d. Dec. 16, 1978; Hilton Head Island, S. C.
Counsel to the President, May 1973-August 1974.

Raised in South Carolina, Buzhardt graduated from the U. S. Military Academy in 1946. He served in the Air Force until 1950 and received his law degree from the University of South Carolina in 1952. He practiced law until 1958 when he became administrative assistant to Sen. Strom Thurmond (R, S.C.) [q.v.]. He became chief aide to Secretary of Defense Melvin Laird [q.v.] following the 1968 election.

In 1970 Buzhardt was appointed general counsel to the Defense Department. From 1971 to 1973 he represented the Department of the Army in the prosecution of two Rand Corp. consultants accused of leaking the classified Pentagon Papers, which detailed the U. S. entry into the Vietnam war. The consultants, Daniel J. Ellsberg [q.v.] and Anthony J. Russo, were charged with conspiracy to obtain classified government documents, theft, espionage and receiving unauthorized government property. On May 11, 1973, after 89 days of trial, charges were dropped.

Following the *Pentagon Papers* trial Buzhardt became counsel to the President and was put in charge of the Watergate defense. For the next 16 months Buzhardt tried to coordinate the myriad of presidential legal battles, spending most of his time protecting presidential documents. He invoked "executive privilege" in numerous court appearances. His argument was based on a July 7, 1973, letter in which Nixon informed the Senate Watergate Committee that he would cooperate fully with its investigation "except in those instances where I determine that meeting the Committee's demands would violate my constitutional responsibility to defend the office against encroachment by other branches."

Buzhardt first used the argument shortly after existence of the White House tapes was discovered and special prosecutor Archibald Cox [*q.v.*] subpoenaed them. He lost in the court of appeals on Oct. 12. The court ruled that criminal prosecution took precedence over executive privilege. Later that year Buzhardt informed the court that two of the subpoenaed tapes were missing and that there was an 18 minute gap in another.

In October 1973 Buzhardt played the role of go-between in the resignation of Vice-President Spiro Agnew [*q.v.*]. Buzhardt, representing the Administration, met with Agnew's lawyers on Oct. 5. Agnew, it was agreed, would be free to deny criminal charges submitted by the Justice Department and would be able to review the government's evidence against him. Following the review, Agnew entered a plea of no contest to one count of tax evasion and resigned Oct. 10.

On Jan. 4, 1974, Buzhardt was removed as chief Watergate counsel but remained Nixon's chief legal adviser. When Nixon agreed to provide the House Judiciary Committee with edited transcripts of subpoenaed tapes, Buzhardt was put in charge of the project. He turned over 1,254 pages of text on April 30. In June Buzhardt was assigned to protect presidential papers against former aide John D. Ehrlichman's [*q.v.*] attempt to use them in his own defense. Buzhardt suf-

fered a heart attack June 13, but continued to advise the President. Following the July 24 Supreme Court decision ordering that all the subpoenaed tapes be turned over to the special prosecutor, Buzhardt urged the President to resign.

Buzhardt resigned as presidential counsel Aug. 15, 1974, a week after Nixon's departure. He returned to South Carolina and private legal practice. He died of a heart attack on Dec. 16, 1978.

[BO]

BYRD, HARRY F(LOOD), JR.
b. Dec. 20, 1914; Winchester, Va.
Democratic Senator, Va., 1966–.

Byrd was the son of Sen. Harry. F. Byrd (D, Va.), whose organization dominated Virginia politics from the late 1920s to the mid-1960s. Upon the elder Byrd's retirement in 1965, his son, known as "Little Harry," assumed the vacant seat and was elected to the Senate one year later. One of the staunchest conservatives in the upper house, Byrd opposed civil rights measures and large government expenditures, especially for social welfare programs. [See JOHNSON Volume]

During the Nixon Administration, Byrd maintained his conservative record, voting against establishment of a consumer protection agency, government aid for abortions and busing and for farm subsidy legislation and Nixon's conservative nominations to the Supreme Court. In foreign and defense affairs, he voted against foreign aid and attempts to limit troop commitments abroad. In 1974 he received a 100 rating from the conservative Americans for Constitutional Action. Byrd remained a staunch supporter of American policy in Vietnam. In 1972 he sponsored an amendment to prohibit U.S. assistance to North Vietnam without prior congressional consent. The amendment banned expenditures of any funds from the Defense Department or other federal budgets for any kind of assistance, direct or indirect, to North Vietnam.

In the belief that he would have difficulty winning the 1970 Democratic primary in Virginia because of opposition to the Byrd machine, Byrd ran and was re-elected as an Independent. Nixon strategists hoped that if the Republicans gained control of the Senate, Byrd would be free to switch Parties and lead an exodus of Southern conservatives to the GOP. When the Democrats won, Byrd was able to maintain his seniority on the powerful Armed Services and Finance Committees by voting with the Party when it organized the Senate.

In September 1971 Byrd spoke out in opposition to the U.N. embargo of the white supremacist government of Rhodesia, a measure that prohibited the importing of chrome needed by American defense industries. He presented an amendment to a defense procurement bill providing that the President could not regulate the amount of goods imported from any non-Communist country as long as the U.S. was importing the same material from a Communist country. Since approximately 60% of America's chromium ore came from the Soviet Union, the measure required the U.S. to end the embargo. Byrd stated that the purpose of his proposal was "simply to end the dependence of the United States upon the Soviet Union for chrome ore." The measure passed and was implemented in January 1972. However in December 1973, the Senate passed a bill that brought the U.S. back into compliance with U.N. sanctions.

In the 1976 general election, Byrd, running as an Independent, defeated the Democratic candidate, retired Adm. E.R. Zumwalt [q.v.], by over 200,000 votes.

[FHM]

BYRD, ROBERT C(ARLYLE)
b. Nov. 20, 1917; North Wilkesboro, N.C.
Democratic Senator, W. Va., 1959 – .

The son of an itinerant West Virginia coal miner, Robert Byrd drifted with his family from one mining town to another. Raised in poverty, he worked his way through high school but could not afford to go to college; instead he became a butcher in his home town. He eventually received a law degree from American University in 1963. In the early 1940s Byrd moved to Baltimore to be a welder in a shipyard. He then returned to West Virginia after the war to open a grocery store and teach a bible class. A born-again Baptist with an intense evangelical fervor, Byrd became so popular that he was invited to broadcast his sermons. In 1946 he won a seat in the state legislature and six years later won a seat in the U.S. House. In 1959 Byrd moved over to the Senate, where he established a conservative record. During the Kennedy and Johnson years, Byrd opposed efforts to end the Cold War with the Soviet Union. He also voted against civil rights and welfare legislation but supported regional redevelopment, labor and education measures. [See EISENHOWER, KENNEDY, JOHNSON Volumes]

In 1967 Byrd's colleagues elected him secretary of the Democratic Conference, a minor post with a great deal of potential. Byrd was responsible for the scheduling of debates, informing senators about votes on the Hill, polling his peers, pairing votes when necessary, stalling a roll call to accommodate a delayed senator, and keeping tabs for the majority leader of senators' birthdays and other celebrations. Because Sens. Russell Long (D, La.) [q.v.] and Edward Kennedy (D, Mass.) [q.v.], the two whips Byrd served until 1971, focused most of their attention on legislative issues, Byrd inherited their routine responsibilities as the majority leader's deputy. He was, in essence, Mike Mansfield's (D, Mont.) [q.v.] de facto whip. Holding such power, Byrd ingratiated himself with most of his colleagues. Many owed him favors; others were simply impressed with him for mastering the intricasies of running the day-to-day operations of the Senate. Thus, in January 1971, Byrd challenged Edward Kennedy for the position of whip. Support for Byrd crossed ideological lines and he defeated the Massachusetts Senator.

During the early years of the Nixon Administration, Byrd generally supported the President on most issues. He backed defense spending including funding for the Safeguard anti-ballistic system and development of the supersonic transport. Byrd supported the war in Vietnam and opposed many of the end-the-war amendments during the period. On domestic issues he voted for the confirmation of conservative nominees Clement Haynsworth [*q.v.*] and G. Harrold Carswell [*q.v.*] to the Supreme Court. Nixon even considered appointing Byrd to the high court, but the American Bar Association suggested that the West Virginian was not qualified. Byrd was a staunch law-and-order advocate and favored anti-riot, preventive detention and "no-knock" entry legislation. Nevertheless he voted with the liberals to preserve the major social service programs, such as Social Security, unemployment, housing and education. In 1972 he supported the Equal Rights Amendment.

After becoming the whip, Byrd became more moderate and started to break frequently with the Administration. As a member of the Judiciary Committee, Byrd expressed doubts in the spring of 1972 about appointing Richard Kleindienst [*q.v.*] Attorney General. His staff joined with Sen. Kennedy's in investigating the Kleindienst link to the ITT scandal. Byrd was one of 19 Democratic senators who voted against confirmation. He also led the opposition to the appointment of L. Patrick Gray [*q.v.*] as FBI director. He obtained secret material questioning Gray's controversial handling of an air hijacking attempt in which Gray had ordered agents to fire on the plane's tires.

Byrd also moderated his strident anti-Communist posture. He called for a review of American relations with Cuba as a step towards possible normalization of relations. Byrd proposed that the U.S. withdraw from the Southeast Asia Treaty Organization, and after visiting China in the fall of 1975, he recommended that the U.S. normalize relations with the Peking regime.

Byrd remained a conservative on civil rights, however. He vigorously opposed busing and in 1971 supported a constitutional amendment to permit the desegregation of schools based on a freedom-of-choice principle. Byrd also supported the Gurney Amendment aimed at restricting the courts' right to desegregate schools. In 1975 he secured passage of an amendment that would partially repeal the 1964 Civil Rights Act's prohibition of racial discrimination in federally funded projects.

In January 1977 Byrd succeeded Mansfield as majority leader. His only serious contender, Hubert Humphrey (D, Minn.) [*q.v.*], who was seriously ill, withdrew when it became apparent that he could not win. During the early Carter presidency, Byrd supported the Administration on most issues. He helped steer the Panama Canal treaties through the Senate. On a number of occasions, however, Byrd criticized the President for his failure to develop a coherent anti-inflation and energy policy. [See CARTER Volume]

[JB]

BYRNE, BRENDAN T(HOMAS).
b. April 1, 1924; West Orange, N.J.
Governor, N.J., 1974-.

After serving in the Air Force during World War II, Byrne graduated from Princeton University and obtained his law degree from Harvard in 1951. He served as assistant counsel to New Jersey Gov. Robert Meyner from 1955 to 1959, Essex County prosecutor for nine years and president of the New Jersey Public Utilities Commission for two years. Republican Gov. William Cahill [*q.v.*] appointed Byrne to the New Jersey Superior Court in 1970. He handed down the decision in 1971 that declared the state's 78-year-old law on capital punishment unconstitutional on the grounds that it violated the Fifth and Sixth Amendments.

In 1973, when the Watergate scandal was erupting in Washington and several members of Gov. Cahill's administration were being indicted, New Jersey Democratic Party leaders sought a gubernatorial candidate of unquestioned integrity. Byrne was picked because he had prosecuted underworld figure Anthony Boiardo and had been described by racketeers as a "man who couldn't be bought." He won the three-way Democratic primary for governor and easily beat conservative Republican Charles Sandman [q.v.] in the November election.

Despite campaign remarks that he saw no immediate need for a state income tax, Byrne proposed such a measure within a few months after assuming office. He said it was the only feasible answer to the New Jersey Supreme Court's decision mandating an end to reliance on local property taxes for funding municipal school systems. The issue dominated state politics and was rejected repeatedly by a number of Democrats as well as Republicans in the state Senate. Byrne's lack of rapport with legislators was considered instrumental in prolonging the tax fight until 1976. Even after the income tax bill finally passed the Senate in July of that year and was signed into law, it played a part in President's Ford's New Jersey victory over Jimmy Carter in the November 1976 presidential election. The issue finally began to subside following Byrne's reelection in 1977.

Fulfilling an inaugural promise, Byrne successfuly promoted passage of a strict "sunshine" law requiring that 250 top state officials disclose their personal finances. In addition New Jersey became the first state to provide for public financing of gubernatorial campaigns. The Governor also signed legislation in 1974 establishing the nation's first Department of the Public Advocate, designed to serve as ombudsman for citizen complaints of action or inaction by the state and provide legal representation for citizens in a wide range of public interests.

Byrne's record also reflected a restrained commitment to the environment, mass transit, and urban aid. He opposed offshore oil leasing in early 1975 and helped to defeat the controversial Tocks Island dam project. In June 1977 Byrne signed a law making New Jersey the only state in the nation other than Nevada with legalized casino gambling.

In 1977 Byrne, despite public resentment over the income tax law, won reelection by 300,000 votes.

[GWB]

CAHILL, WILLIAM T(HOMAS)
b. June 25, 1912; Philadelphia, Pa.
Governor, N.J. 1970-74.

The son of Irish immigrants, William Cahill received his law degree from Rutgers University in 1937. After one year as a special agent with the FBI he went into private law practice. For several years he was a prosecutor for Camden and Camden County, N.J., and served one term in the New Jersey Assembly beginning in 1951. Seven years later he won the first of six elections to the House of Representatives. His voting record was sympathetic to many of President Johnson's programs, including the "war on poverty."

With strong state Party support, notably from the New Jersey Republican Chairman Nelson Gross [q.v.], Cahill ran for the Republican gubernatorial nomination in 1969 and easily beat his opponent Rep. Charles Sandman [q.v.]. In November he faced former Gov. Robert Meyner. The powerful Hudson County Democratic organization actually backed Cahill, and President Nixon made a campaign appearance on the candidate's behalf contributing to the nearly unanimous county sweep and 61% vote total compiled by Cahill.

Gov. Cahill proposed and signed many reforms into law during his tenure including a migrant labor bill in 1971 that provided minimum wage requirements, money for interpreters and sanitary working condition requirements for the thousands of mostly Puerto Rican workers attracted to the seasonal work on New Jersey farms. In 1972, the Governor approved a consumer protection bill, a no-fault insurance bill and the first noise control bill in the country. He had successfully sponsored legislation reducing the sentence for possession of small amounts of marijuana in 1970. His religious convictions, however, precluded his support for abortion reform. Cahill created the state's first Department of Environmental Protection in 1970 and in 1973 fought the proposed deepwater oil port off the New Jersey coast.

One of Cahill's difficult problems was finding an alternative method to the local property tax for financing education in the state. In a momentous decision (Robinson v. Cahill 1973) the New Jersey Supreme Court had voided the reliance on local property taxes for providing funds for education. Cahill attempted to pass a state income tax bill but was forced to settle for raising the sales tax to 5% due to widespread opposition to the tax by labor unions and members of both political parties.

Although he was never personally implicated in scandal, Cahill's reelection drive in 1973 was doomed by the indictment and subsequent conviction on extortion and bribery charges of his close friend and political associate, Secretary of State Paul Sherwin. In the same year the Watergate scandal was surfacing, Cahill lost the primary to conservative Rep. Charles Sandman [q.v.]. Cahill retired to practice law at the end of his term.

[GWB]

CALLAWAY, HOWARD (BO)
b. April 2, 1927; La Grange, Ga.
Secretary of the Army, May 1973-July 1975.

Born into a prominent Georgia textile family, "Bo" Callaway received a B.S. degree from West Point in 1949. He was commissioned and served as a platoon leader in Korea for a year. As a civilian Callaway was active in various business, educational and civic affairs before turning to politics in the early 1960s.

Abandoning the party of his family, Callaway became a registered Republican and a delegate and fund raiser for Sen. Barry Goldwater [q.v.] in 1964. That same year he was elected to represent Georgia's third congressional district, thus becoming the state's first Republican Congressman since Reconstruction. Callaway spent his one term in Congress compiling a near-perfect conservative voting record; he staunchly opposed most Great Society programs, particularly bills pertaining to civil rights.

In 1966 Callaway ran for governor of Georgia. Although he won a narrow plurality of the popular vote in a three-way contest, he lost the governorship when the Democratic legislature decided the election in favor of Lester Maddox. During 1968 he was Nixon's chief preconvention scout in the South and then his Southern campaign director. His comment during the campaign in Mississippi that "perhaps we can get Gov. George C. Wallace [q.v.] on our side, that's where he belongs," reportedly angered Nixon who refused Callaway any significant appointment during his first Administration. Callaway was relegated to a three-man Advisory Commission on Inter-governmental Relations to "foster better federal-state-local relations."

In mid-1973 Callaway was nominated secretary of the Army. The major objection at his Senate confirmation hearing concerned his racial views. At a time when the Army was experiencing racial tensions, it was suggested that Callaway would "lack credibility . . . in dealing with the service's race relations." Such objections, however, were offset by support for his nomination from Georgia Rep. and civil rights activist Andrew Young [q.v.].

During his two-year tenure as secretary of the Army, Callaway's major accomplishment was to "sell" the concept of an all-volunteer Army and then preside over its implementation. He resigned from this post in June of 1975 to become President Ford's campaign manager. Reportedly Callaway was chosen because Ford needed an "enthusiastic advocate" with strong conservative credentials capable of countering "the Reagan threat from the right" and with "only limited ties to the 1972 Republican campaign."

Almost immediately Callaway became a controversial figure. His repeated public insistence that Vice President Nelson Rockefeller [q.v.] was the President's biggest problem enraged Republican liberals and moderates. Callaway, however, was encouraged to voice such sentiments by Ford's chief of staff, Donald Rumsfeld [q.v.] who had his own eye on the vice presidential nomination.

Although he bore the title of campaign manager, much of the actual strategy was decided at the White House first by Rumsfeld and his deputy, Richard Cheney, and later by Cheney and Jerry Jones, who headed a "scheduling committee." In addition to alienating the Vice President, Callaway also encountered problems with the White House press staff over "communications lapses" and "resistance in the government to his repeated efforts to establish a program that would coordinate public appearances by 'appropriate' cabinet and Administration officials to help sell Mr. Ford's candidacy to the voters."

Within the Party organization Callaway was criticized for courting conservatives "instead of managing the overall campaign," lacking "experience in presidential politics," and having "no organizing ability." Republican director of organization Lee Nunn resigned in October of 1975 accusing Callaway of outright incompetence, while finance chairman David Packard [q.v.] implied that fundraising was lagging because of Callaway's interference.

Despite such complaints President Ford retained Callaway and tried to "paper over his deficiencies" with the appointments of former Reagan political technician Stuart Spencer as Callaway's deputy and Rogers C.B. Morton [q.v.] as White House counselor and campaign advisor. The President finally became convinced that Calloway was a political liability after the disclosure that as secretary of the Army he had furthered his family's interests in a Colorado ski resort by "persuading" the U.S. Forest Service to drop environmental objections to the resort's expansion plans.

Callaway announced in March 1976 that he would "step aside until the air cleared." In January 1977 a Senate investigation subcommittee found Callaway guilty only of "poor judgment," while a Justice Department investigation cleared him of any conflict-of-interest charges.

[MJW]

CALLEY, WILLIAM L(AWS), JR.
b. June 8, 1943; Miami, Fla.
Army officer.

Calley worked as a bellhop, dishwasher and railroad switchman until 1966, when he enlisted in the Army. He graduated from Officers Candidate School and was then ordered to Hawaii to join Company C, First Battalion, 20th Infantry, under the command of Capt. Ernest L. Medina. Calley was given charge of the rifle company's first platoon.

Company C arrived in Vietnam in December 1967 and was assigned to the American Division in the northern I Corps zone as part of the new 11th Infantry Brigade. On March 16 it was part of a task force that swept through the South Vietnamese village district of Son My in an effort to destroy a suspected Vietcong stronghold in the hamlet of My Lai.

No Vietcong were encountered in either engagement. However helicopter pilots who circled the area during the action reported massive civilian casualties. Both Col. Oran K. Henderson, the new commander of the 11th Brigade, and Maj. Gen. Samuel W. Foster, commanding officer of the American Division, looked into the reports and decided nothing unusual had occured at Son My.

In April 1969 a Vietnam veteran, Ronald L. Ridenhour, reported alleged war crimes by U.S. soldiers at Son My in the operation a year before. In November the Army appointed Lt. Gen. William R. Peers to head a board of inquiry into the events of March 16 and to determine whether there had been a deliberate cover-up by the Americal Division command.

That same month Calley was charged with the premeditated murder of 102 civilians at My Lai. His court-martial, postponed several times, began a year later. In his defense Calley argued that he had been ordered by Medina at a briefing the day before the attack to destroy My Lai and kill every living being in the hamlet because "they were all enemy." Medina rebutted Calley's testimony.

On March 29 an Army court-martial jury found Calley guilty of the premeditated murder of at least 22 South Vietnamese civilians. He was sentenced to life imprisonment at hard labor, dismissal from the Army and forfeiture of his pay and allowances, pending the outcome of an automatic review of the case by another command.

Eventually Calley believed that he was made a scapegoat for the Army, taking the blame while his superiors escaped responsibility. Chief of Staff Gen. William C. Westmoreland [q.v.] later stated the Army's position: "Judging from the events at My Lai, being an officer in the U.S. Army exceeded Lt. Calley's abilities. Had it not been for educational draft deferments, which prevented the Army from drawing upon the intellectual segment of society for its junior officers, Calley probably never would have been an officer. Denied that usual reservoir of talent, the Army had to lower its standards."

Calley's conviction provoked an immediate and sharply divided outcry. Jimmy Carter [q.v.] and George Wallace [q.v.] were among the governors and other public officials who expressed indignation at the verdict. On April 1 President Nixon ordered Adm. Thomas H. Moorer [q.v.], chairman of the Joint Chiefs of Staff, to release Calley from the stockade and return him to his apartment on the base while his conviction was under review. Two days later Nixon announced that he would personally review Calley's case.

In August of the same year, Calley's sentence was reduced to 20 years. In 1973 both the Army Court of Review and the Court of Military Appeals upheld his con-

viction. Calley was released on bail in March 1974. In April Secretary of the Army Howard H. Callaway [q.v.] reduced his sentence to 10 years. The following month the Pentagon announced that Nixon had reviewed the case and decided that no further action was "necessary or appropriate." Calley's conviction was overturned on technical grounds by a U.S. district court in September but was reinstated a year later by a circuit court of appeals. He was released on parole in November and given a dishonorable discharge. The Supreme Court refused to hear Calley's appeal in 1976.

The Peers Report, released in 1972, was critical of the entire command structure of the Americal Division. Calley was not the only individual charged in the incident. Several other officers and enlisted men were investigated and tried. However Calley was the only one found guilty.

[SF]

For further information:
Richard Hammer, *One Morning in the War* (New York, 1970).
Seymour M. Hersh, *My Lai 4* (New York, 1970).
John Sack, *Lieutenant Calley His Own Story* (New York, 1971).

CANNON, HOWARD W(ALTER)
b. Jan. 26, 1912; St. George, Utah
Democratic Senator, Nev., 1968-.

Cannon worked on his father's ranch as a cowboy before entering Arizona State Teacher's College. He earned his B.E. in 1933 and an LL.B. in 1937 from the University of Arizona. Prior to entering military service in March 1941, Cannon worked as an attorney in Utah. He served with distinction as an Air Force pilot during World War II. After the war Cannon became a partner in a Las Vegas, Nev. law firm until his election to the Senate in 1959. Supporting most of President Kennedy's programs in the early 1960s, Cannon became identified as a moderately liberal Democrat. After winning reelection in 1964 by 48 votes, Cannon's support of liberal programs dropped. [See KENNEDY, JOHNSON Volumes]

In the late 1960s and early 1970s Cannon supported legislation to preserve natural resources. A representative from a silver-producing state, he urged Congress to take steps to conserve the diminishing U.S. silver supply and provide for future needs through industry incentives and other inducements to encourage producers. In April 1969 he spoke out on behalf of the lead-zinc quota which he hoped to be the beginning of a natural minerals policy. According to Cannon the major issue of the 1970s was man's ability to reverse the environment's deterioration. He cosponsored the Water Quality Improvement Act of 1970 and introduced a bill to establish a world environment institute. In 1971 Cannon cosponsored the Federal Water Pollution Control Act Amendment which established the federal government's commitment to clean up all navigable rivers by 1985. He also supported the 1971 Wild Mustang Protection Act empowering the federal government to protect, manage and control an estimated 17,000 remaining mustangs. On the international scene, Cannon supported the President's "Vietnamization" policy. He voted for the Cooper-Church amendment of 1970 to limit U.S. military involvement in Cambodia. In June 1971 he supported the Mansfield end-the-war amendment calling for withdrawal of all U.S. forces from Indochina within nine months in return for the phased release of American war prisoners. He also backed the Senate's refusal to authorize continued foreign aid programs in October 1971. Cannon believed it was time to reassess foreign aid in light of the world's changing political, economic and social conditions.

Cannon was chairman of the Senate Rules and Administration Committee in October 1973 when President Nixon nominated Rep. Gerald R. Ford (R, Mich.) to succeed Spiro T. Agnew [q.v.]. Although Cannon criticized the Justice Department's restrictions on the Committee's access to FBI files, he gained access to a wide range of documents. In this manner Cannon's committee was credited with rebuilding public confidence in government. The panel approved Ford's nomination in November. When President Nixon's Watergate induced resignation made Ford President in August 1974, Cannon's committee conducted an inquiry into Ford's vice-presidential nominee Nelson A. Rockefeller [q.v.]. Cannon expressed concern over Rockefeller's gifts to associates over the years but in the end supported his confirmation.

Because of Watergate, Cannon maintained that campaign spending reform was still unexplored territory despite the 1971 Federal Elections Campaign Act which he cosponsored. Subsequently, Cannon's Rules and Administration Committee hammered out a revised campaign spending bill, known as the 1974 Federal Election Campaign Act Amendments. The act imposed overall limitations on campaign expenditures and contributions, procedures for filing campaign expense reports and for public financing of presidential nominating conventions and presidential primary elections.

Throughout the remainder of Ford's Administration, Cannon received attention for his inquiries into the airline industry. In 1974, he charged that the Civil Aeronautics Board (CAB) had the power to deal with the problem of unfair foreign competition with American international air carriers, particularly over the North Atlantic. He criticized foreign governments for violating bilateral capacity agreements and the World Bank for subsidizing foreign owned air carriers. In October 1976 he proposed that the CAB approve air carriers to service routes on which present carriers charge too much or offer poor service. This was designed to help Pan-American Airways compete in the domestic market for routes finding their way into overseas lines.

Cannon continued to be an influential member of Congress in the Carter Administration.

[TML]

CAREY, HUGH L(EO)
b. April 11, 1919; New York, N.Y.
Democratic Representative, N.Y.,
1961–74; Governor, N.Y., 1975–.

Born and raised in New York City, Hugh Carey earned a Bronze Star during World War II. Following his graduation from St. John's University Law School in 1951, he worked for his family's oil company. A political unknown in New York's 12th congressional district, Carey challenged Rep. Francis E. Dorn in 1960. Carey, running on a liberal platform, narrowly defeated the incumbent in the Kennedy landslide of that year. During the Kennedy-Johnson years Carey emerged as a leading urban liberal in the House of Representatives. As a member of the Education and Labor Committee, he was a principal architect of bills providing federal aid to education and to the handicapped. [See JOHNSON Volume]

In 1969 Carey ran unsuccessfully for the Democratic nomination for New York City Council president. During the 1970s he continued his focus on social welfare legislation and aid to cities. He recommended that Congress shift more funds from Nixon's revenue-sharing program to urban areas, and in 1971 suggested that Congress double the revenue-sharing grants to the cities. In addition he lobbied for national health insurance and for the removal of the Social Security tax burden from the middle and working class. However, few of Carey's proposals became law.

Initially a supporter of U.S. involvement in Vietnam, by the 1970s Carey was an opponent of the war in Indochina. In 1971 he voted for the Fraser Amendment barring the assignment of draftees to Vietnam; the Mansfield Amendment calling for a pullout from Vietnam within nine months subject to a prisoner-of-war release; and the Boland Amendment cutting off funds for the war after June 1. Carey also supported attempts to cut defense spending and to limit the deployment of anti-ballistic missiles. Despite his liberal stance, Carey worked well with the established leaders in the House and opposed efforts to modify the seniority or committee systems.

In 1974 Carey campaigned for New York's Democratic gubernatorial nomination. Relatively unknown in upstate New York, he challenged the popular Howard Samuels, who had the support of Party bosses and many liberals. Carey ran as a reformer against a coalition of liberals and the Democratic machine. In November he won a surprise victory. His success was due to determination; generous campaign donations, including a substantial contribution by his brother Edward, the sole owner of an oil company; and excellent media work by Dave Garth. In the November election Carey crushed the lackluster incumbent, Malcolm Wilson. Carey's victory margin exceeded that of Al Smith and Franklin D. Roosevelt, the two most popular Democratic governors of the state.

During his first two years in office, Carey was primarily concerned with the impending bankruptcy of New York City. In May 1975 New York City officials announced an immediate need for $1.5 billion by June 1975 to meet the city's short-term debt obligation. Carey, Mayor Abraham Beame [q.v.] and other city officials sought assistance on many fronts but met rejections from President Ford, the New York state legislature and the city's leading commercial banks. After meeting with the President on May 14, Carey announced that Ford's response showed a "level of arrogance and disregard for New York that rivals the worst days of Richard Nixon and his gang of cutthroats." However he finally convinced the legislature to approve on June 10, one day before the bankruptcy date, a bill to create the Municipal Assistance Corp. (Big Mac). Its first task was to gradually refinance the city's current short-term indebtedness and then work with city hall to supervise budget cuts to bring spending in line over a three-year period.

During the summer Carey worked to prevent a possible default in October by persuading large municipal unions to invest in Municipal Assistance Corp. bonds and by lobbying for government loans. The city escaped default at the last hour when the New York City teachers' union agreed with the other municipal unions to invest its pension funds. Carey's pleas for federal aid met with little success. Ford continued to insist that federal aid would create a dangerous precedent. Only after Carey persuaded the legislature to pass a tax increase, for which he assumed full personal responsibility, did Ford relent. On Nov. 26, he asked Congress to approve the legislation making up to $2.3 billion in direct federal loans available annually.

Carey's skill as a negotiator with the bankers, unions, upstate Republicans and the Administration, as well as his forceful presentation of the city's case through the media, earned him national praise for salvaging what appeared to be a hopeless situation. That same year Carey helped organize aid for the Urban Development Corp., the nation's largest builder of public housing.

Carey inherited a state that was also in financial trouble. During the Rockefeller and Wilson administrations, state spending had increased by $1 billion a year and the area was losing its tax base. Carey therefore increased taxes and put curbs on spending increases. During the recession of 1975–76, he was forced to hold down spending on social services. He successfully reduced the number of state workers by 7%. Although he had championed free tuition in the City University system, Carey was forced to impose tuition on that institution, a step that angered city residents.

Conditions in the state improved in 1976, and the unemployment rate declined. Still Carey kept a lid on spending and instituted a tax cut to stimulate business. Because he was occupied with the state's financial problems, Carey was unable to institute the sweeping program he wanted in criminal justice, corrections and mental health. He was also unable to give guidance to his own administrators. Although he remained popular, his aloof, arrogant style and his distaste for state legislators alienated politicians in the state.

He was unable to project a clear image to the public. Conservatives were outraged with him for opposing the restoration of the death penalty, although he did sponsor legislation instituting mandatory sentencing and punishments for juvenile offenders.

In the summer of 1978 Carey faced challengers in his own Party for reelection. He won the primary by a narrow margin, and waged an uphill fight against his Republican opponent, Perry Duryea, in the general election campaign. Helped by an effective media blitz that focused on his accomplishments, Carey defeated his rival with 53% of the vote. [See CARTER Volume]

[JB]

CARSWELL, G(EORGE) HARROLD
b. Dec. 12, 1919; Irwinton, Ga.
Judge, Court of Appeals, 5th Circuit, 1969-70.

Harrold Carswell graduated from Duke University in 1941, and served in the Navy during World War II. Following his graduation from Mercer University Law School in 1948, Carswell, raised in a family active in Georgia Democratic politics, ran unsuccessfully for the state legislature. He then moved to Florida and opened his own law practice. In 1969, after serving appointments as U.S. District Attorney and District Judge for Northern Florida, Carswell was named Judge of the U.S. Court of Appeals for the 5th Circuit (Georgia, Florida, Alabama, Mississippi, Texas, Louisiana).

In keeping with his stated objective to nominate a conservative Southern jurist to fill the Supreme Court seat vacated by Abe Fortas [q.v.] Richard Nixon, on January 19, 1970, sent Harrold Carswell's name to the Senate for confirmation. Because the Senate had just emerged from a bitter fight resulting in the defeat of Clement Haynsworth [q.v.] to fill the Fortas seat, the appointment was expected to be approved with minimal opposition. But controversy developed immediately when the press publicized a Carswell statement made in 1948 supporting white supremacy and later attempts to circumvent integration of public facilities. These accusations and testimony of witnesses reviewing Carswell's hostile behavior towards civil rights lawyers and questionable rulings in voting rights and desegregation cases monopolized the hearings of the Senate Judiciary Committee which finally voted their approval in February.

Confirmation still seemed assured despite the growing opposition of the legal community which was reacting to the results of research on Carswell's judicial record: 60% of Carswell's published opinions had been reversed by higher courts; his decisions in all areas of law were characterized as mediocre, confused, and ignorant of precedent.

But after William Saxbe (R, Ohio) [q.v.] released a letter from Richard Nixon which in effect claimed that the Senate was usurping the power of the President to appoint justices, and evidence was produced to show that Carswell had lied during his confirmation hearings about his role in attempts to forestall desegregation at private facilities, the appointment was threatened. A number of senators became convinced that Carswell's nomination was an act of vengeance by Nixon for not confirming Haynsworth. Carswell was defeated on April 8th by a vote of 51-45. Nixon blamed the defeat on anti-Southern prejudice.

Carswell did not return to the bench; he ran for and lost the Florida Republican Senatorial primary in September 1970, returned to private law practice, and served as a bankruptcy referee to become eligible for a federal pension. In 1976 Carswell, semi-retired, was hospitalized with a nervous condition after having been arrested on vice charges.

[JMP]

For further information:
Richard Harris, *Decision* (New York, 1971).

CARTER, JIMMY
b. Oct. 1, 1924; Plains, Ga.
Governor, Ga., 1971-75.

Jimmy Carter's father, James Earl Carter, was the most prominent citizen of Plains, Ga., a small junction farm town. The elder Carter owned a farm supply store, was a peanut trader, and, after the birth of his son acquired large tracts of farmland. Carter studied for a year at Georgia Southwest College and Georgia Institute of Technology before being admitted to the United States Naval Academy at Annapolis in 1943. Three years later he graduated 10th in his class. Following the death of his father in 1953, Carter left the Navy to run his father's numerous business enterprises. In 1962 Carter won a seat in the state Senate. He ran unsuccessfully for governor in 1966 but won four years later.

As governor, Carter took a strong stand on civil rights. He opened up more state political positions to blacks than any governor before him. A number of Carter's programs, especially in education, health and prison reform, greatly helped the blacks of his state. For such endeavors Carter was applauded as the representative of the "New South," the new brand of Southern politician who sought to unify the races rather than divide them.

Carter's administrative reforms impressed the nation. He reduced the number of state agencies from 65 to 22, increasing efficiency and saved the taxpayer money. However, a number of Carter's critics claimed these reforms were more cosmetic than real. But they did concede that he improved the quality of service by Georgia's civil servants. Carter also introduced a "sunshine law" that opened most government deliberations to the people. His "zero based budgeting" program made all departments accountable for money spent. Carter expanded state programs to help the mentally ill. His prison reform activities received national praise. Conservationists were impressed with his interest in protecting Georgia's environment, especially the state's threatened swamps.

The publicity Carter enjoyed as governor catapulted him into national prominence as a Southern alternative to conservatives George Wallace [*q.v.*] and Lester Maddox [*q.v.*]. Efforts were made to win him the vice presidential nomination in 1972. In 1974 Carter served as the Democratic Party's national campaign committee chairman. He traveled throughout the nation speaking on behalf of many candidates and making himself valuable contacts. Carter served on the Trilateral Commission, an international think tank of leaders from the United States, Western Europe and Japan who engaged in economic forecasting and planning. On Dec. 12, 1974 Carter announced his candidacy for the Democratic nomination for the presidency. He proclaimed himself the Southern liberal alternative to George Wallace who would restore honesty and integrity to government.

Throughout the spring of 1976 Carter ran on a platform promising to end inflation and high unemployment, expand aid to the cities and the poor, and implement a national health insurance program. Even with these programs Carter promised to attain a balanced budget. Calling the American tax program a national disgrace, he promised to plug the loopholes. He pledged to maintain a rigid control of the FBI and the Central Intelligence Agency. In foreign policy Carter endorsed the substance of the Nixon-Kissinger diplomacy but objected to the style as secretive, manipulative, and unilateral. The obscure, one term, Southern governor astounded the nation by proceeding to defeat his rivals in most of the primaries. In July the Democratic convention gave him the nomination on the first ballot.

In the fall the Carter lead in the polls began to evaporate. In comparison to the exciting primary campaigns, Carter made a number of strategic errors, and his style appeared lackluster. He barely won the election with 51% of the vote. During his Administration, Carter concentrated on energy and economic problems in the domestic sphere. In foreign affairs he helped negotiate treaties with Panama and peace agreements between Israel and Egypt. [See CARTER Volume]

[JB]

CARTER, RUBIN "HURRICANE"
b. May 15, 1937; Clifton, N.J.
Prize fighter.

Rubin Carter was born in 1937 in Clifton, N.J., the third youngest of seven children. At the age of 10 he was sent to a reformatory for stabbing a man, who, he said, had attacked him sexually. Carter escaped when he was 15 and lied about his age and name to join the Army. While stationed in West Germany he developed into a skillful boxer. When Carter returned to the U.S. in 1956, his identity was discovered, and despite his excellent military record, he was sent back to prison.

In 1961 Carter became a professional boxer, and his aggressive, fast-punching style earned him the nickname "Hurricane." By 1966 he was considered one of the top contenders for the middleweight crown and signed a contract in August to fight the reigning champion, Dick Tiger. The bout never happened, however, because on Oct. 14, 1966, Rubin Carter and a friend, John Artis, were arrested for the murder of three men in a white working-class bar in Paterson, N.J.

The prosecution's case was based on the testimony of two convicted burglars who said that while they were robbing the factory across the street, they saw Carter and Artis leave the scene of the bar shootings. Despite some contradictory evidence the all-white jury found Carter and Artis guilty after a six-week trial, which was widely publicized. Both men were sentenced to three terms of life imprisonment.

New York Times reporter Selwyn Raab spent a year investigating the case and in 1975 reported that both key prosecution witnesses had recanted. After extensive publicity and a fund-raising campaign, Carter and Artis were granted on Dec. 21,

1976, a second trial by the New Jersey Supreme Court. But during the trial one of the witnesses accused Raab of having offered him a bribe to recant and again pointed to Carter and Artis as the men he had seen leaving the bar. They were found guilty a second time and returned to prison.

Both men still claim innocence and plan to appeal their case.

[DGE]

CASE, CLIFFORD P(HELPS)
b. April 6, 1904; Franklin Park, N.J.
Republican Senator, N.J., 1955-79.

Case was born the son of a Dutch Reformed Minister and the nephew of a future New Jersey Supreme Court Chief Justice, Clarence Case. He graduated from Rutgers and Columbia University Law School, joined a Wall Street law firm in 1928 and soon began winning local political office as a Republican. He served in the U.S. House of Representatives from 1945 to 1953, and after a brief stint as President of the Fund for the Republic, retained a seat in the Senate for 24 years.

Case was long viewed as one of the most liberal Republicans in the Senate. The senator's voting record on domestic issues reflected the interests of the most urbanized state in the union, where a heavy concentration of labor union members existed, along with teeming ghettos and a chaotic transportation system. Case consistently earned ratings of between 80% and 100% from the liberal Americans for Democratic Action and ratings of from 0% to 18% approval from the conservative Americans for Constitutional Action. He also won the support of labor unions. He was not considered personally magnetic or particularly activist in introducing legislation. Unusual to the Senate, he had no press secretary, although he retained a loyal and competent staff. He was often thought to be reclusive. His liberalism put him firmly in the political camp of Govs. Nelson Rockefeller [q.v.] and William Scranton [q.v.] in the 1964 Republi-

can presidential contest. He eventually withheld his endorsement of the convention designated candidate, Barry Goldwater [q.v.]. Four years later Case allowed his own pro-Rockefeller, favorite-son candidacy to continue long after the likelihood of Richard Nixon's nomination became evident. [See EISENHOWER, KENNEDY, JOHNSON Volumes]

The Senator voted against three of President Nixon's choices for the Supreme Court—Clement Haynsworth [q.v.], G. Harrold Carswell [q.v.], and William Rehnquist [q.v.]. He voted against the federal funding of the SST in 1971 and for various attempts to extend minimum wage provisions to include domestic household employees. In 1972 the New Jersey lawmaker voted for the mass transit bill that allocated $11.8 billion over six years and provided for federal funds to be available as operating subsidies for mass transit. During the Ford Administration Case voted for the Consumer Protection Agency, and against a prohibition on the use of food stamps for the families of those on strike in November 1974.

Perhaps the heart of Case's political philosophy and legislative interests can be appreciated by his belief that an educated public requires the maximum feasible public disclosure of the financial and political affairs of those involved in political decision making. Towards that end he introduced full disclosure bills in every session of the Senate since 1957. The legislation would have revealed the sources of income of public officials as well as their official written communications with other governmental functionaries. He proposed amendments to open up the appropriations of Radio Free Europe and Radio Liberty to public scrutiny rather than retaining them under needlessly secretive CIA auspices. In 1974 he also voted for 17 amendments to the Freedom of Information Act that made government held information more accessible to the public. The President vetoed the measure but the Senate overrode him.

The New Jersey legislator was appointed to the Foreign Relations Committee in

1965 and was the ranking Republican member in his last years in the Senate. His influence became important in the reassertion of congressional power during the two Republican administrations. In 1969 he voted against the anti-ballistic missile, then the following year voted for a narrowly defeated appropriations reduction for Pentagon public relations and for a $5.2 billion cut in a Defense Department appropriations bill. In February 1971 Case sponsored a bill, which eventually became law in 1972, requiring that the text of all international agreements accepted by the President be presented to both houses of Congress within 60 days for their approval.

Although becoming critical of the levels of American involvement in Vietnam during the Johnson Administration, Case, along with many other members of Congress, held off on his criticism of the Nixon Administration's policies for a number of months. His dissatisfaction mounted so that by June of 1970 he voted for the Cooper-Church Amendment that limited Presidential.authority to conduct ground operations in Cambodia. In January 1973, after the renewal of bombing of Hanoi and Haiphong, Case presented an amendment with Sen. Frank Church (D, Idaho) [q.v.] that mandated a deadline to cut off all funds for U.S. military involvement in Indochina. It passed the Senate but was defeated in the House.

The war was still an important issue in 1975 when the Ford Administration attempted to procure new aid for the American evacuation of Vietnam. Case rejected such aid saying "there was an inevitability about what happened that no change in our policy or amount of money could have affected significantly." Case ran for reelection in 1978 at the age of 74 but was defeated in the primary by a narrow margin. The Senator had relied on his standing in public opinion polls and with Republican county chairmen to win and had not campaigned extensively until the last two weeks before the election. The Republican nominee, Jeffrey Bell, was a national organizer for conservative Republicans who ran an effective, well financed campaign that concentrated on taxpayers' frustrations and Case's vote in support of the Panama Canal Treaty. The Senator's brand of liberalism seemed to be increasingly less welcome within the Republican Party.

[GB]

CELLER, EMANUEL
b. May 6, 1888; Brooklyn, N.Y.
Democratic Representative, N.Y., 1923-1973; Chairman, Judiciary Committee, 1949-53, 1955-73.

Emanuel Celler received his B.A. in 1910 and LL.B. in 1912 from Columbia University and then practiced law in New York. In 1922 he was elected for the first of 25 consecutive terms to represent Brooklyn's 10th district, a largely Jewish area of Flatbush. In the House, Celler compiled a liberal record. He was a lifetime advocate of liberalized immigration and naturalization laws and voted consistently for the social welfare legislation of Democratic Administrations. During his quarter of a century tenure as chairman of the Judiciary Committee, Celler became an authority on anti-trust, civil rights and civil liberties legislation.

During the 1950s Celler amassed a prodigious legislative record in the field of anti-trust. He coauthored the 1950 Celler-Kefauver Anti-Merger Act and his Anti-trust Subcommittee conducted extensive investigations into the monopolistic practices of American industry. Celler also opposed the creation and extension of the House Un-American Activities Committee and fought to temper the political hysteria of the McCarthy period. [See TRUMAN, EISENHOWER Volumes]

Celler's most notable legislative efforts in the 1960s were in the field of civil rights. He sponsored or managed the passage of all the major Civil Rights Acts, guided the 24th Amendment (abolishing the poll tax) through the House and managed the 1965 Voting Rights Act. In the area of civil liberties, Celler warned against and opposed the inclusion of court-supervised wiretapping and anti-riot provisions in the legislation of the late 1960s. [See KENNEDY, JOHNSON Volumes]

Celler's last years in Congress were marked by repeated conflict with an Administration attempting to win the loyalty of the South. In June 1969 he fought Administration attempts to weaken enforcement provisions of the 1965 Voting Rights Act extension by applying its sanctions to the North as well as the South. Celler held hearings in an attempt to undermine the momentum behind the support of the proposed changes but was unsuccessful at that time. However, he managed the extension of the original bill the following year, after the Senate had succeeded in striking out the Administration's proposed change.

In April 1970, Rep. Gerald Ford reflected the Administration's bitterness over the defeat of their nominee to the Supreme Court, conservative Southerner G. Harrold Carswell [q.v.], by calling for an impeachment investigation of Justice William O. Douglas [q.v.], whom Ford termed a "hippie-yippie type" revolutionary with ties to the "underworld." Celler fought the resolution, and after it passed, he defeated impeachment by appointing himself to head the five-man investigating panel and dragging out the process until December when he released a report that cleared Douglas of all charges.

In February and March of 1972, Southern Democrats introduced a constitutional amendment to prohibit the busing of school children to achieve racial integration. In an attempt to appease the Southerners but head off a protracted emotional battle across the country, the Nixon Administration proposed a busing moratorium and introduced statutory anti-busing provisions. Celler, clearly opposed to this whole movement, successfully killed approval of the proposed constitutional amendment by conducting hearings, but was less successful in defeating the Administration's proposals, which he termed "an unconstitutional interference with the judicial power" in view of the 1971 Supreme Court decision which ruled that busing was a legal means to achieve racial integration.

Celler also found himself in conflict with some of the favorite issues of the left in the 1970s. He refused to consider abortion reform legislation and proposals of amnesty for Vietnam war resisters. Charging that the Equal Rights Amendment would invalidate laws which protected women and that "there is more difference between a male and female than between a horse chestnut and a chestnut horse," Celler held up the ERA for 20 years until a discharge petition forced its release in 1970.

Criticism was also leveled at the way Celler ran his Committee, particularly his propensity to delay or refuse to hold hearings on proposals that he did not like. And although Celler's staff issued a report in 1971 that called for more effective anti-trust laws and he conducted hearings on six major conglomerates, Celler was accused of neglecting anti-trust issues. Intimations were also made that Celler was protecting corporate interests who were also clients of his New York law firm.

In 1972 Celler was up for reelection at the age of 84. When Elizabeth Holtzman [q.v.], a young New York lawyer, announced her candidacy for Celler's seat, Celler remarked, "She doesn't exist, as far as I'm concerned." Celler did not campaign, did not have an office in his district, and chose to remain in Washington and rely on his past record and the Democratic machine for reelection.

In a campaign largely ignored by the press, Holtzman covered the district on foot, with leaflets and through a small army of volunteers. She attacked Celler's record in opposition to the ERA and his reluctant support for the 25th Amendment, which gave 18 year olds the right to vote, and charged Celler with accepting legal fees from defense contractors. But most importantly, she argued that Celler had neglected his constituency and taken it for granted. Celler received no help from the Brooklyn Democratic machine, which was preoccupied with the reelection of Rep. John Rooney (D, N.Y.) [q.v.], and lost the primary by 609 votes.

Although Celler remained the Liberal Party candidate, he conceded the November election to Holtzman after conducting an unsuccessful court suit to declare the primary void on grounds of fraud and voting irregularities.

On his 90th birthday in 1978, Celler was still practicing law in New York. The bulk of his practice consisted of lobbying in Washington for his clients.

[JMP]

CHAFEE, JOHN H(UBBARD)
b. Oct. 22, 1922; Providence, R.I.
Secretary of the Navy, January 1969-May 1972.

Chafee was born into a family long active in Rhode Island politics. He graduated from Yale in 1947 after service with the Marines during World War II. Three years later Chafee earned a law degree from Harvard. After another tour with the Marines in Korea, he began a law practice in Providence in 1953.

A liberal Republican, Chafee won election to the Rhode Island House of Representatives in 1956. He was reelected in 1958 and 1960 and House minority leader from 1958-62. Chafee served as governor of Rhode Island from 1963-68. He worked closely with a Democratic legislature to pass liberal legislation, including a state medicare program, which earned recognition as "a state version of the Great Society." Chafee was defeated for reelection in 1968 largely due to advocacy of a state income tax. He supported George Romney for the 1968 Republican Presidential nomination and backed Nelson Rockefeller after Romney's withdrawal. Following the nomination of Richard Nixon, Chafee sought unsuccessfully to block the vice presidential nomination of Spiro Agnew in the hope of gaining the nomination for himself.

In January 1969 President Nixon appointed Chafee secretary of the Navy. The appointment was intended as a gesture of reconciliation toward the more liberal Republicans of the Northeast.

Chafee's duties included carrying out Nixon's Vietnamization program and modernizing the U.S. fleet. He provoked a controversy in May 1969 by overruling a naval court of inquiry that had recommended courts-martial for officers of the *U.S.S. Pueblo*, an electronic intelligence-gathering ship captured by North Korean gunboats in January 1968. He also supported the service reforms of Chief of Naval Operations Elmo Zumwalt.

Chafee resigned in May 1972 to challenge incumbent Sen. Claiborne Pell (D,R.I.). He won the Republican nomination but lost the election in November. In 1976, however, he won the U.S. Senate seat vacated by retiring Democrat John Pastore.

[DB]

CHAPIN, DWIGHT
b. Dec. 2, 1940; Wichita, Kan.
Watergate figure.

In 1959 Dwight Chapin enrolled as a freshman at the University of Southern California (USC) in Los Angeles. He was active in student politics and belonged to a student group, the Trojans for Representative Government. The Trojans distributed false campaign literature, stuffed ballot boxes and planted spies in the opposition camp. In 1962, a year before their graduation, Chapin and his friend Gordon Strachan [q.v.] were asked by a former Trojan and USC graduate, Ronald Ziegler [q.v.], to join him and H. R. Haldeman [q.v.] in Richard Nixon's 1962 campaign for governor of California. Although Nixon lost Haldeman was impressed with Chapin's style and initiative and offered him a job at J. Walter Thompson advertising agency after graduation in June 1963.

When Richard Nixon decided to run for the Presidency in 1965, he asked Haldeman to be his chief of staff. Haldeman's proteges Ziegler and Chapin became respectively Nixon's press secretary and his personal aide. After the election Ziegler stayed on as Nixon's press secretary, and

Chapin was named the President's appointments secretary. However since all of Nixon's appointments were cleared through Haldeman, Chapin was as much Haldeman's aide as Nixon's.

Chapin, like the rest of the people Haldeman gathered about him, was an ambitious corporate functionary with little political experience. As a Haldeman aide his official duties included preparing the itinerary and seeing to the details of the President's domestic and foreign trips. As was the case with most of the White House staff, however, he had political duties too. At the beginning of 1971 when Haldeman was forming the strategy for the reelection campaign, Chapin and Gordan Strachan were tapped to organize a "dirty tricks" unit to harrass the Democrats in the 1972 primaries.

In the spring of 1971 Chapin and Strachan contacted Donald Segretti [q.v.], another USC classmate, to have him organize a "non-Charles Colson" [q.v.] dirty tricks operation in the field. In June 1971 they flew Segretti to Washington and formally offered him a job as a political prankster working for Richard M. Nixon's reelection. In August Segretti met with Herbert Kalmbach [q.v.], President Nixon's personal lawyer, and was offered a salary of $16,000 a year plus expenses.

Segretti assembled an "intelligence unit" of 28 people in 17 states who devoted themselves to wreaking chaos in the Democratic candidates' primary campaigns. Chapin told Segretti to concentrate on Sen. Edmund Muskie's [q.v.] campaign since he was considered the President's most formidable rival. The dirty tricks campaign involved forging letters and distributing them under the candidates' letterheads, making dossiers on the candidates' personal lives and seizing confidential campaign files. The tricksters leaked false statements, manufactured items for the press and threw the candidates' campaign schedules into disarray by phoning ahead to cancel appearances and/or schedule appearances that the candidates could never make.

In October 1972 *Time* magazine and *Washington Post* reporters began to make the connections between the Watergate burglary, the Committee to Re-Elect the President (CREEP) and the Segretti operation. After Haldeman, John Ehrlichman [q.v.] and John Dean [q.v.] agreed that the cover-up had to be maintained to protect the President and "the presidency," they decided that Chapin would have to leave his White House job. In January 1973 Chapin resigned from the White House staff and accepted an executive position with United Airlines.

When called before the Watergate grand jury in April 1973, Chapin denied specifically encouraging Segretti to concentrate his activities on Sen. Edmund Muskie. In March 1974 Chapin with other former Nixon aides was indicted on four counts of perjury stemming from his April 1973 testimony. On April 5, 1974, Dwight Chapin was convicted of two counts of perjury, and on May 15 he received a jail sentence from 10 to 30 months. In December 1975, after his appeals had been exhausted, his sentence was reduced to from six to 30 months at the federal prison in Lampoc, Calif.

[SJT]

CHARREN, PEGGY
b. March 9, 1928; New York, N.Y.
Founder, Action for Children's Television.

The daughter of a New York furrier, Peggy Walzer graduated from Connecticut College in 1949. She worked in film syndication at WPIX television in New York before moving to Newton, Mass. Married to an engineer, Stanley Charren, in 1951, she was once described as a "casually chic, upper middle-class Boston matron."

Appalled by the violence and commercialism of many of the television shows available to children, Charren formed Action for Children's Television (ACT) in 1968 to push broadcasters for change. ACT demanded that networks end violence in the media or at least confine it to late-night hours and provide a minimum of 14 hours per week of children's programming. Charren was particularly disturbed by commercials that tried to convince young children, unable to understand and evaluate advertising, to buy unnecessary products or food products harmful to their health. During ACT's early years the organization concentrated on convincing networks to schedule better programs, but after 1970 Charren redirected its efforts to commercials, reasoning that "the fewer the commercials the less reason to put on rotten programs." Because the networks failed to change their programming voluntarily, Charren also worked to impose government regulations on them.

In 1971 the Federal Communications Commission (FCC) ruled that it would accept ACT's guidelines as the basis of a future ruling on children's television. These guidelines included the group's demand for a ban on all commercials and a minimum of 14 hours a week of children's programming. However no ruling was made. Three years later the National Association of Broadcasters (NAB), bowing to ACT's pressure, agreed to reduce advertising by 40% during weekend children's TV shows.

In 1972 ACT filed petitions with the Federal Trade Commission (FTC) to end the advertising of children's vitamins as candy and to ban the advertising of highly sugared snack foods, candy and soft drinks during children's TV programs. The FTC held hearings in June 1972 but failed to decide the issue. However the offending pharmaceutical companies voluntarily withdrew all their vitamin advertising from children's programs. During this period Charren also lobbied with both the FTC and the FCC to stop the practice of using cartoon characters in TV commercials. The NAB agreed in 1973 to drop this method of advertising, although neither the FTC nor the FCC ruled on the issue.

Charren was not content merely to petition the agencies and took ACT's message to Congress. In March 1972 before the Senate Commerce Committee's Communications Subcommittee, Charren denounced violence on children's shows and maintained that it was put there simply "because it sells." Three years later she chastized the FCC and the FTC for being "detached observers of the scene they have been empowered to govern."

In 1978 the FCC issued a report recommending a ban on all television advertising aimed at children under the age of eight and limiting the ads for sugared products likely to cause tooth decay.

[DBH]

CHAVEZ, CESAR E(STRADA)
b. March 31, 1927; Yuma, Ariz.
President, United Farm Workers
Organizing Committee, 1966–.

When Chavez was 10 years old, the foreclosure of his family's farm forced them to move on, to travel among labor camps in search of work. Although officially schooled through the seventh grade, he finally taught himself to read and write in his 20s and 30s. He served in the U.S. Navy in 1944–45.

In 1952 Chavez was recruited into Saul Alinsky's Community Service Organization (CSO), a Mexican-American self-help group. Chavez became general director of the CSO in 1958; he resigned four years later after the board of directors voted down his plan to organize farm workers. He then founded the National Farm Workers Association (NFWA) and over the next few years attempted to organize the migrant workers of southern and central California. In 1966 the NFWA merged with the Agricultural Workers Organizing Committee (AWOC), an AFL-CIO affiliate, to form the United Farm Workers Organizing Committee (UFWOC). The union's name was later shortened to the United Farm Workers of America (UFA). [See JOHNSON Volume]

From 1965 to 1970 Chavez and the union conducted a strike against the California grape growers. The long and bitter strike had elements of both a labor dispute and a crusade for migrant workers. Chavez led his workers in long marches similar to those used by black civil rights groups. In 1966 he called for a national boycott of table grapes that lasted into the late 1970s. These tactics and Chavez's personality brought together a coalition of liberal supporters including Robert F. Kennedy and Walter Reuther [q.v.]. The strike ended in 1970 when growers signed a three-year contract.

Jurisdictional disputes between the UFWOC and the International Brotherhood of Teamsters (IBT) often stymied Chavez's attempts to negotiate. The first pact marking the unions' territories was signed in July 1967; the Teamsters would represent workers in the commercial sheds, while the UFWOC would handle the field workers' affairs. Three years later, however, the IBT announced they had signed contracts for field workers with Salinas, Calif., fruit and vegetable growers. Another agreement was worked out between the unions in August 1970 that essentially followed the tenets of the earlier pacts. This "peace pact" lasted only two and a half years; late in 1972 the director of the Western Conference of Teamsters (WCT) announced his union's renegotiation of contracts with lettuce growers. As UFW contracts expired the following year, the WCT reported signed contracts or in-progress negotiations.

Chavez denounced the WCT agreements as "sweetheart contracts," favoring the growers rather than the workers, and pressed for secret ballot elections to allow the workers to choose their representation. Secret ballot elections did begin in September 1975, but only following passage of the California Agricultural Labor Relations Act (CALRA) earlier in the year. So many elections were contested that the newly formed state Agricultural Labor Relations Board (ALRB) ran out of funds in February 1976. Pressure from a grower-supported coalition of Republicans and rural Democrats in the state legislature stalled the governor's recommended supplemental appropriation for the Board. The ALRB received its annual budget in July 1976 and reopened the following November. A five-year territorial pact was signed between the WCT and

the UFW in March 1977; under the agreement the Teamsters represented all workers covered under the National Labor Relations Act (which specifically excluded farm workers) and the UFW received jurisdiction over laborers covered under the CALRA.

Use of pesticides became a major bargaining point for Chavez in 1969. Early that year, in a letter to the growers' organization, he emphasized the discussion of "economic poisons . . . even if other labor relations problems have to wait." The UFWOC filed suit in Delano demanding access to public records on pesticide use kept by the Kern County Agricultural Commission (KCAC). A Kern County Superior Court judge, while noting that "many commonly used pesticides . . . are highly toxic and can constitute a hazard to human health and welfare," refused the union permission to see the KCAC files. He claimed the union's primary purpose was "to keep alive controversy with the growers . . . and to force unionization." The union appealed the decision and filed several suits to end the use of DDT in California. This pressure, plus national publicity on the pesticide's harmful effects, resulted in a statewide ban of DDT effective Jan. 1, 1970.

Chavez served as president of the 30,000-member UFW through the 1970s.

[RB]

CHISHOLM, SHIRLEY (ANITA) (ST. HILL)
b. Nov. 30, 1924, New York, N.Y.
Democratic Representative, N.Y. 1968–.

Shirley Anita St. Hill, the daughter of an unskilled laborer, emigrated from the West Indies to Brooklyn when she was 11. She graduated cum laude from Brooklyn College in 1946. While she was in college, she became active in the Urban League and the NAACP. In 1952 she received her master's degree from Columbia in childhood education. In October 1948 she married Conrad Q. Chisholm.

From 1953 to 1959 Chisholm worked as

the director of the Hamilton-Madison Child Care Center in New York, and from 1959 to 1964 she served as an educational consultant in New York City's Bureau of Child Welfare. She was also active in the Brooklyn branch of the NAACP, the Democratic Women's Workshop, the League of Women Voters and the Bedford-Stuyvesant Political League. Chisholm served in the New York State Assembly from 1964 to 1968, where she was recognized as a feminist and a black leader.

In 1968 Chisholm ran against James Farmer [q.v.], the founder of the Congress of Racial Equality, for a seat in the U.S. House. Since they both agreed on basic issues, Farmer unwisely chose to base his campaign on male chauvinism. He charged that the black community needed "a strong male image" and "a man's voice in Washington" to counteract sociologists' claims that blacks suffered from "matriarchal dominance." That November Chisholm defeated Farmer by a margin of two to one.

As the first black woman ever elected U.S. Representative, Chisholm quickly found herself at odds not only with the Nixon Administration, but with her fellow Democrats and black male colleagues as well. Her initial encounter with the Democratic leadership came during her first month in the House when she refused to sit on the Agriculture Committee after having requested the Education and Labor, the Post Office and Civil Service, or the Foreign Affairs Committees. In a perhaps unprecedented reversal Rep. Wilbur Mills (D, Ark.) [q.v.], chairman of the Ways and Means Committee, placed her on the Veterans Affairs Committee.

Chisholm's voting record from 1969 to 1973 established her as a liberal, anti-war feminist. In her first year in the House, she voted against such Nixon proposals as the anti-ballistic missile system and the SST, the "no-knock" provision of the anti-crime bill and jet fighter planes for Taiwan. She also opposed Nixon's nominations of Clement F. Haynsworth [q.v.] and G. Harrold Carswell [q.v.] to the Supreme Court.

The same year Chisholm supported a full employment bill, appointment of a national commission on Afro-American history and culture, enlargement of the powers of the Department of Housing and Urban Development, establishment of a cabinet-level department of consumer affairs and federal reimbursement (up to 90%) of state welfare programs. She cosponsored with her colleague and friend Bella Abzug (D, N.Y.) [q.v.] a comprehensive bill to establish day care facilities in most major cities at a cost of $5 billion. President Nixon, however, vetoed the day care bill. In 1970 she opposed Nixon's welfare bill, charging that it was totally inadequate and demeaning to the poverty-stricken applicant.

As an anti-war activist, Shirley Chisholm backed and spoke at several of the marches on Washington in the late 1960s and early 1970s. She voted for the Cooper-Church Amendment following the Cambodian invasion of 1970 and supported legislation for an all-volunteer Army. A dedicated feminist, she spoke in favor of the Equal Rights Amendment, the right of all women to abortion, day care centers and the equalization of pay between men and women. In July 1971 she joined with other national women political leaders to form the National Women's Political Caucus. On other social issues she consistently voted for equitable health, education and welfare benefits for the poor, worked to establish a national SEEK program (a remedial education project for minority students) and continued to press for passage of full employment legislation. In 1971 Chisholm and Ronald Dellums (D, Calif.) held a series of hearings to investigate racism in the Army.

In December 1971 Chisholm announced that she would seek the Democratic nomination for president in 1972. She entered almost all of the primaries and went to the National Convention in Miami Beach with 152 delegates. However, during the convention she withdrew and threw her support behind George McGovern [q.v.].

In 1973 Chisholm launched a legisla-

Church—125

tive effort that for the first time united blacks, women and labor behind an amendment to include domestics in the minimum wage bill. Congress passed the bill in June 1973, and overrode Nixon's veto in March 1974.

In the mid-1970s Chisholm continued to oppose large defense budgets, to actively support federally funded abortions for welfare recipients and to lobby for a department of consumer affairs. Amidst criticism that she was not responding to the needs of her disadvantaged constituency, Chisholm won a difficult election in 1976.

[SJT, JMP]

CHOMSKY, NOAM A(VRAM)
b. Dec. 7, 1928; Philadelphia, Pa.
Professor of Linguistics, Massachusetts Institute of Technology, 1955–.

Noam Chomsky received his bachelor's degree from the University of Pennsylvania in 1949. He received his M.A. in linguistics from Penn in 1951 and took a Ph.D. there in 1955. He immediately joined the faculty of linguistics at the Massachusetts Institute of Technology, and first presented his linguistic theories for public scrutiny with the 1957 appearance of *Syntactic Structures.*

In the late 1950s and through the 1960s, Chomsky became the leading theoretician in linguistics. During that period he taught at Columbia, UCLA and the University of California at Berkeley, in addition to giving lecture appearances at universities in England and France. He became a fellow of both Princeton's Institute for Advanced Studies and Harvard's Center for Cognitive Studies.

By the late 1960s Chomsky had become a controversial political figure. As early as 1965 he emerged as one of the most articulate university critics of the Vietnam war, and his 1967 essay "The Responsibility of Intellectuals" made him an international figure. [See JOHNSON Volume] In his 1969 book *American Power and the*

New Mandarins, Chomsky indicted intellectuals who served as ideologues for the ends of government and big business, calling them the "new mandarins." In the same year Chomsky was one of 24 professors who publicly announced their support for the Oct. 15 nationwide moratorium against the war in Vietnam. In 1971 he participated in the formation of an anti-war Labor-University Alliance with students, professors and such trade union leaders as United Auto Mobile Workers President Leonard Woodcock [q.v.] and International Brotherhood of Teamsters Vice President Harold Gibbons. The Alliance condemned the "widening of the war into Laos" and accused the Nixon Administration of obfuscating its real purpose—the military conquest of Vietnam. In the same year Chomsky, with David Dellinger of the "Chicago Seven" and Daniel Ellsberg [q.v.], issued a statement calling for the release of the anti-war activist Berrigan brothers and all other political prisoners. These activities won Chomsky a place on President Nixon's enemies list.

In 1973 he signed a statement, addressed to the Soviet government, denouncing "a campaign to silence not only . . . intellectuals, but any Soviet citizen who seeks to express their rights." During the 1978–79 mass demonstrations in Iran, Chomsky became deeply involved in the agitation against the Shah conducted in the U.S. He continued to teach linguistics at MIT.

[LG]

CHURCH, FRANK (FORRESTER)
b. July 25, 1924; Boise, Ida.
Democratic Senator, Ida., 1957–.

After a bout with cancer, in which doctors only gave him six months to live, Frank Church earned his law degree from Stanford University in 1950. Running as a Democrat in a traditionally Republican state, Church lost a number of elections for local offices. In 1956 he upset archconservative Sen. Herman Welker (R,

Ida.) in a bitterly contested election. Church championed public ownership and development of power facilities and conservation against his rival who was supported by the private utilities and lumber and mining interests. Throughout the Kennedy-Johnson years Church compiled one of the most liberal records in the Senate, voting for civil rights acts, War on Poverty programs, Medicare, and conservation legislation. [See EISENHOWER, KENNEDY, JOHNSON Volumes]

It was in foreign policy that Church broke with the Johnson Administration. A member of the Foreign Relations Committee, Church became one of the Senate's most vocal critics of the Vietnam War. In 1965 Church called for direct negotiations with the Communists, free elections in South Vietnam, and American disengagement from the conflict. Yet Church continued to vote for appropriations bills for the war.

During the Nixon Administration, Church, fearing an expansion of the war, began to campaign to get Congress to use its funding power to force the President to seek peace in Asia. In the spring of 1970, Church and Sen. John Sherman Cooper (R, Ky.) [q.v.] introduced an amendment to a foreign military sales bill barring funds for future military operations in Cambodia. Capitalizing on the outrage many in the nation expressed toward the escalation of the war into Cambodia, Church and his supporters got the amendment passed by the Foreign Relations Committee. After a seven week filibuster, the Senate passed it in late June by the vote of 58 to 37. The House, however, rejected the measure. A watered down version was passed in December as part of a defense appropriation bill. The rider prevented the introduction of ground troops into Laos or Thailand. The adoption of the Cooper-Church amendment represented the first limitation ever voted on the President's power as commander-in-chief during a war situation.

In April 1972 Church, this time joined by Sen. Clifford Case (R. N.J.) [q.v.] introduced an amendment to a State Department appropriations bill authorizing a cutoff of funds for all U.S. combat operations in Indochina after Dec. 31 subject to an agreement for the release of American prisoners of war. The Foreign Relations Committee and the Democratic Party Caucus approved the Church-Case Amendment, but the Senate reduced its effectiveness by attaching a rider which made it effective only if an internationally supervised ceasefire was negotiated.

Church also questioned other Administration defense and foreign policies. He called for a reduction of American troops in Western Europe. Church voted against the deployment of the anti-ballistic missile system, backed ending the construction of the C5A plane, and opposed arms aid to repressive regimes.

In January 1975 the Senate created a bipartisan, select committee to investigate alleged abuses by the Central Intelligence Agency, the Federal Bureau of Investigation and other government intelligence and law enforcement agencies. Church was selected chairman. Over the next year and a half the Church committee heard testimony from cabinet heads, top military officials, the leadership of the CIA and the FBI, retired intelligence operatives and those Americans who felt victimized by the unconstitutional activities of both organizations. Among other things, the probe revealed CIA involvement in plots to assassinate world leaders and in the coup against Chile's Marxist president Salvador Allende. It also uncovered a series of covert operations by the FBI against organizations J. Edgar Hoover had considered radical.

In a November 1975 letter to Church, President Ford requested that the panel not make its assassination report public because it would "do grievous damage to our country," and be "exploited by foreign nations and groups hostile to the United States." Church responded that the Committee's intention to make the report public had "long been clear." Moreover, he felt the national interest would be "better served by letting the American people know the true and complete story" behind the death plots. The committee's report charged the U.S. government had ordered the assassination of two foreign leaders—Fidel Castro and Patrice Lumumba—and had been involved in assassination plots against three other foreign officials—Raphaelo Trujillo, Ngo Dinh Diem and Rene Schneider. Although four of the five leaders were assassinated, none of them died as the direct results of the plans initiated by U.S. officials.

In its April 26 report on the CIA, the Church Committee described the U.S. intelligence community as routinely engaged in covert operations that were often without merit and frequently initiated without adequate authorization. Two days later the Committee charged the FBI had conducted investigations, often employing illegal or improper methods, not only against individuals and political groups on the right and left but also against religious groups, prominent politicians, advocates of nonviolence and racial harmony and supporters of women's rights. The report astonished the American people by listing such FBI targets as Dr. Martin Luther King, Jr., Adlai Stevenson, and Justice William O. Douglas [q.v.]. In its final recommendation, the Church Committee advocated greater oversight of the agencies by Congress and the White House to prevent future excesses.

Frank Church decided to enter the 1976 Democratic primaries using his investigation as his major issue against the Ford Administration. Declaring his candidacy in March 1976, he hoped to rally liberals who had been disappointed with Morris Udall (D, Ariz.) [q.v.] and fearful of Jimmy Carter [q.v.] and Sen. Henry Jackson (D, Wash.) [q.v.]. For two months Church actively campaigned, running on his solid liberal record during the Nixon-Ford presidencies. Church supported conservation, opposed placing limits on busing, and voted to override the vetoes of Nixon and Ford of appropriations to cities and poverty programs. Although Church won the Nebraska, Idaho and Oregon primaries, it appeared certain to him by June that Carter would obtain the nomination. Church, therefore, endorsed the former Georgia governor.

During the early Carter presidency, Frank Church became one of the President's closest foreign policy advisers. He worked with Carter for the ratification of the Panama Canal treaties. A staunch pro-Zionist, Church broke with the Administration on its desire to sell arms to Israel's enemies to secure a military balance of power in the Middle East. [See CARTER Volume]

[JB]

CLARK, (WILLIAM) RAMSEY
b. Dec. 18, 1927; Dallas, Tex.
Lawyer.

Ramsey Clark was the son of Attorney General and Supreme Court Justice Tom Clark. Following service in the Marines during World War II, he entered an accelerated program that gave him a bachelors degree from the University of Texas in 1949 and a masters in history and a law degree from the University of Chicago in 1950. After practicing law in Dallas from 1951 to 1960, Clark joined the Justice Department as an assistant attorney general. He became deputy attorney general in 1965 and Attorney General in 1967. While at the Justice Department Clark implemented school desegregation orders, helped draft civil rights legislation, coordinated the White House response to the urban riots and reorganized the Department's efforts against organized crime. [See JOHNSON Volume]

Following Richard Nixon's election Clark joined the prestigious N.Y. law firm of Paul, Weiss, Rifkind, and Garrison. He also began to lecture throughout the country on crime. In 1970 Clark published *Crime in America,* an appeal to Americans to understand that poverty produced most crime. The former Attorney General called for prison reform and accused the judicial system of practicing a double standard by severely punishing the poor while being lenient on white-collar crime. Clark defended the Supreme Court decisions that expanded the rights of the accused against criticism by the law enforcement establishment, who thought the rulings responsible for permitting more criminals to go free. Liberal legal thinkers praised Clark for a book conservatives treated as a sentimental tract that tried to rationalize crime.

Clark grew increasingly involved in the anti-war movement. At both the 1969 and 1970 mass demonstrations in Washington, Clark served on a lawyers committee to insure that the civil liberties of the participants would be protected. He frequently addressed anti-war rallies and campaigned for anti-war candidates. In the summer of 1972 Ramsey Clark visited North Vietnam. He told the press that he decided to accept the invitation to assess the damage of U.S. bombing and said "if I could save one Vietnamese child on either side of the DMZ or help one prisoner of war get home, or explain to the people here what is being done in their name, I had to go." For two weeks Clark toured North Vietnam examining the effect of the bombing and speaking to prisoners of war. He found himself in a number of embarrasing situations when "off the cuff" comments he made criticizing U.S. war policy were picked up for broadcast by Radio Hanoi.

Upon his arrival home Clark accused the United States of bombing dikes and civilian areas. In response the Nixon Administration began a campaign to discredit Clark for, in the words of Attorney General John Mitchell [q.v.], being "naive" and a "dupe" of Hanoi. Administration spokesmen specifically cited his reputed broadcasts on Radio Hanoi as evidence that Clark was an alleged traitor. Clark defended himself by reiterating that he had obtained objective evidence of the bombing of the north and repeatedly warned that the escalation of the war would stiffen the will of the North Vietnamese to persist.

Clark became active in a number of controversial legal cases during the period. In 1972 he was part of the legal team that defended the Rev. Philip Berrigan and five other Catholic anti-war activists against charges that they conspired to kidnap Henry Kissinger [q.v.] and plotted to blow up the heating system of federal buildings in Washington, D. C. Clark also represented a number of inmates in cases stemming from the riots in New York's Attica prison.

In May 1974 Ramsey Clark announced his candidacy for the Democratic senatorial nomination in New York. Clark announced he would not accept donations over $100. By September he was able to raise over $100,000 more than his rival Lee Alexander, mayor of Syracuse, who had the Party's organizational support. Alexander lost to Clark in a lackluster campaign.

Clark ran an aggressive liberal campaign against the Republican incumbent Jacob Javits [q.v.]. He called for a cut in defense spending of over $25 billion, advocated the implementation of wage and price controls, and announced his support for proconsumer legislation, such as no-fault insurance, the creation of a federal Consumer Protection Agency and the easing of restrictions against class-action suits. He also raised the issue of Javits's "failure of moral leadership" by accepting large campaign donations from special interests.

Although most professionals felt Clark had no chance of winning, he made an unexpectedly strong showing in the early public polls. After Clark's aggressive campaign narrowed the gap originally held by the incumbent in early September, Javits went on the attack. He denounced Clark's stand on Israel because the Democrat endorsed the possibility of creating a Palestinian state in the future. Javits also charged that Clark's trip to Hanoi hurt the morale of the U.S. prisoners of war. Always friendly with the unions Javits obtained the endorsements of the state's AFL-CIO and the powerful teacher's union, which both looked upon Clark as a radical. Javits's popularity with the Jewish voters and his strength in upstate New York enabled him to defeat Clark by 130,000 votes in an election that was expected to be even more of a landslide.

Following the election Clark resumed his law practice and remained active in liberal causes.

[JB]

CLAUSEN, ALDEN W(INSHIP)
b. Feb. 17, 1923; Hamilton, Ill.
President, Bank of America, 1969-.

After serving three years in the Army Air Corps during World War II, Clausen obtained an LL.B. from the University of Minnesota in 1949. He began work for the Bank of America in the same year, and quickly ascended the executive hierarchy. As president of the world's largest commercial bank, Clausen emerged, like Chase Manhattan's David Rockefeller [q.v.] and Citibank's Walter Wriston [q.v.], as a major spokesman for the private business sector.

In the spring of 1970, amidst the 1969–70 credit crunch resulting from the Nixon's Administration's initial tight money, anti-inflationary policies, Clausen stated that a drop in interest rates would be "in the public interest." In April 1970 just before the near-panic of the May-June period, Clausen warned the New York City Economic Club that a liquidity shortage might become chronic in the U.S. economy and outlined a seven-point program to deal with it. In July 1970, after the Penn Central bankruptcy and its aftermath had forced a government policy reversal, Clausen told the congressional Joint Economic Committee that the short-term crisis was over, but that the U.S. economy faced a long-term capital shortage.

Clausen's public visibility involved him in various controversies. In March 1970 students of the University of California at Santa Barbara burned the Bank of America's Isla Vista branch to the ground, citing the bank as a major beneficiary of the U.S. war effort in Vietnam. Clausen issued a public statement denying that the bank was a "capitalist" organ involved in war profiteering. He again had to deal with the war issue when the bank's 1971 stockholders' meeting was disrupted by a guerrilla theater intervention and by stockholders criticizing the bank's role in Vietnam. Clausen denied that the bank had contributed to lengthening the war by financing government military expenditures.

Clausen continued to offer policy advice when he testified in May 1970 against the pending One-Bank Holding Company Act. Earlier he had urged the formalization of the "Quadriad" of economic policymakers (Secretary of the Treasury, Federal Reserve Board chairman, Council of Economic Advisers chairman, and director of the Bureau of the Budget) into a body capable of coordinated policy and action.

As monetary conditions eased late in 1971, Clausen's public policy statements emphasized the new dangers that an expanded budget deficit posed to control of the money supply. In October he anticipated the development of the 1974–75 hyperinflation when he urged a floating prime rate for commercial banks. With the onset of recession in 1974, Clausen stated that no government would be willing to take the draconian monetary and fiscal measures necessary to eradicate inflation, and in October 1974 he ordered Bank of America loan officers to stop seeking new loan customers and took steps to slow down the bank's growth.

Clausen also became involved in various aspects of foreign economic policy. In late May 1973 it was announced that he would head an international trade delegation to the Soviet Union for negotiations on East-West trade. In early August Clausen was appointed, with other leading bank presidents and former Treasury Department officials, to the President's advisory commission on international monetary reform issues. In September 1973 he attended the annual meeting of the International Monetary Fund (IMF) in Nairobi, Kenya. At the meeting Clausen created a stir when he endorsed the demands of various developing countries that the IMF's creation of special drawing rights be linked to aid for the Third World. Secretary of the Treasury George Shultz [q.v.] exploded at Clausen's remarks, charging that he had undermined the entire U.S. position at the conference.

Clausen took the lead in U.S. business support for detente and East-West trade after approval of the Jackson Amendment tying trade to Jewish emigration prompted the Soviet government to repudiate its 1972 trade agreement with the U.S. Clausen announced in a March 1975 speech to the U.S.-USSR Trade and Economic Council that the Bank of America would form a $500 million syndicate to finance U.S. exports to the Soviet Union.

Clausen also became involved in the 1975 New York City fiscal crisis. In October of that year, he appeared, with David Rockefeller and Walter Wriston, before the Senate Finance Committee to urge federal aid for New York. In his remarks Clausen urged the formation of a federal agency to serve as a "lender of last resort" to financially troubled cities and warned of "grave and enduring" damage to the U.S. economy if New York City defaulted.

Clausen returned to the public spotlight in January 1976 when the Comptroller of the Currency's "problem list" of banks was leaked to the press. Clausen called for increased disclosure by banks to ensure continued public confidence.

After Jimmy Carter's [q.v.] election in November 1976, Clausen was widely rumored to be Carter's choice for Secretary of the Treasury. However the post went to W. Michael Blumenthal.

[LG]

CLEAVER, (LEROY) ELDRIDGE
b. 1935; Wabbaseka, Ark.
Black Panther Party leader, 1967–71.

Cleaver grew up in the Watts section of Los Angeles, where his mother was a school janitor. He became involved in a series of legal offenses, including rape, that landed him in reformatories and jails for various periods of time until his self-imposed exile from the United States in 1968. While in prison he became attracted to the discipline and self-pride of the Black Muslims and became one of its ministers. He also began writing on radical subjects. Many of his magazine articles were included in his book *Soul on*

Ice, published in 1968, which became one of the best-selling radical works in the United States in the late 1960s and early 1970s. In 1966 Cleaver was released from prison. He joined the Black Panther Party the following year and was the Party's presidential candidate in 1968. In April 1968 Cleaver was involved in a gun battle with police. His parole was immediately revoked and he was returned to jail. He was later released by a superior court judge, but the state appealed the ruling and in November 1968 higher courts ordered Cleaver back to jail. He refused to comply, went underground and finally fled the country. He lived in Cuba until July 1969, when he moved to Algeria. He was in exile for six years during which time he visited North Korea and several other countries. [See JOHNSON Volume]

Cleaver attempted to keep his identification with the revolutionary struggle within the United States during his exile. He wrote an article for the Black Panther Party newspaper in 1969 in which he asserted: "in order to transform the American social order, we have to destroy the present structure of power in the United States. . . . The only means possible is the violent overthrow of the machinery of the oppressive ruling class." That same year he also wrote, "I love the angels of destruction and disorder as opposed to the devils of conservation and law and order." In October 1970 he made a broadcast through Radio Hanoi to the U.S. forces in Vietnam in which he called on black soldiers to dissent from the policies of the armed forces.

In 1971 Cleaver was expelled from the Black Panther Party as a result of conflicts within the Party's leadership over ideology and personality clashes with Party Chairman Huey P. Newton. The official reason given for the expulsion was that Cleaver still championed a violent position for the Party which was shifting toward a nonviolent approach to change. Cleaver's expulsion symbolized the decline in the fortunes of the Party, which henceforth contained its activities to electoral contests and the social needs of the few communities in which it operated.

Relations grew uncomfortable between Cleaver and the Algerian government after hijackers associated with the Panthers arrived in the country in August 1972. Cleaver therefore moved to Paris. In the early 1970s he began to tire of exile. He wanted his children to know the United States. He also thought that after Nixon's resignation from the presidency in 1974, the political climate in the United States would be less repressive. Cleaver had, in his own words, undergone a religious conversion while he was in France and became a "born-again Christian."

On November 18, 1975, Cleaver ended his self-imposed exile by surrendering to the FBI at Kennedy Airport in New York. He spent the first nine months in the United States in prison before being released on $100,000 bail. Upon his return Cleaver altered his ideology almost completely. He expressed faith in "the limitless possibilities of the American dream." He asserted that "I'm having a love affair with the U.S. military" and apparently meant it. Cleaver praised Henry Kissinger's [q.v.] policy on South Africa, eschewed even the NAACP and found Secretary of Agriculture Earl Butz's [q.v.] controversial remarks on blacks "sort of funny, nothing much to get excited about."

Cleaver published *Soul on Fire* in 1978, describing much of his more recent thoughts. The book was widely thought to be inferior to his earlier *Soul on Ice*. Aside from writing and lecturing, Cleaver began to travel on the evangelical circuit with the Rev. Billy Graham [q.v.].

[GWB]

COHEN, WILLIAM S.
b. Aug. 24, 1940; Bangor, Me.
Republican Representative, Me., 1973-.

William Cohen, the son of a baker, graduated in 1962 from Bowdoin College. He earned his law degree from Boston University Law School in 1965 and be-

came a partner in a Bangor law firm. He was active in the Maine Trial Bar Association and served as assistant editor-in-chief of the *Journal of the American Trial Bar Association* from 1965 to 1966. He was an instructor at Husson College in 1968 and at the University of Maine from 1968 to 1972. He was mayor of Bangor in 1971–72. In 1972 he ran for the U.S. House, conducting a 600-mile walking campaign through his congressional district. He won the seat that had been vacated when Democratic Rep. William D. Hathaway successfully challenged long-time Maine Sen. Margaret Chase Smith (R, Me.) [q.v.] in the 1972 election. Cohen's victory was considered an upset.

In the House Cohen compiled a moderate record. He supported the Nixon and Ford Administrations' only slightly more than 50% of the time. He usually voted to override Nixon-Ford vetoes of spending and social welfare measures. Cohen frequently backed consumer and labor legislation. His support of Administration defense policy was mixed. He opposed Nixon's program to develop the B-1 bomber and voted against increasing military assistance for South Vietnam and the continued funding of the Safeguard antiballistic missile system. He backed the Administration's demands to maintain defense appropriations budget spending levels and opposed cutting military aid for South Korea.

Cohen gained national attention when he became one of the most outspoken Republicans favoring impeachment during the House Judiciary Committee's impeachment proceedings in 1974. Shortly before the panel held public hearings, Cohen said, "If we are to have confidence in the concept of even-handed treatment under the laws, then we simply cannot condone" the kind of conduct the Committee had discovered during its investigation. Five other Republicans were also thought to be leaning toward impeachment, while 10 Republicans were firmly opposed. It was not easy for a freshman Republican to support impeachment. At the time the strategy of the Republican

House leadership was to brand impeachment as a purely partisan affair, supported mostly by the President's liberal political enemies. The Party position was that Nixon, a Republican President, deserved the support of Republicans in Congress.

Cohen took a leading role in the impeachment debate during the Committee's public hearings. He challenged Nixon's chief Committee defender, Rep. Charles E. Wiggins (R, Calif.) [q.v.], by pointing out how Wiggins had quoted selectively from the tape transcripts when he was making out the case for the President. Cohen helped revise the proposed impeachment articles so they more closely reflected Republican views on impeachable conduct and on the evidence.

Cohen was one of six Republicans who joined all 21 Democrats to vote for the first two articles of impeachment adopted by the Committee. The first article accused President Nixon of obstructing justice and the second accused him of misusing federal agencies to violate the rights of citizens. The Committee adopted a third article that Cohen opposed. The article accused Nixon of failing to comply with the Committee's subpoenas. Cohen also opposed the two articles the Committee rejected. The articles accused Nixon of waging an illegal war in Cambodia and of income tax evasion. Cohen never had to defend the difficult political choice he had made. After the White House was forced to release the contents of tapes which showed that Nixon had discussed using the CIA to halt the FBI's Watergate probe, almost everyone in the House supported impeachment.

Cohen's leading role in the impeachment hearings established him as a strong statewide candidate in Maine. He briefly considered challenging Sen. Edmund Muskie (D, Me.) [q.v.] in 1976 but decided against it. Two years later Cohen won a Senate seat from incumbent Sen. William D. Hathaway (D, Me.), the man Cohen replaced as the second district's representative.

[AE]

COLBY, WILLIAM E(GAN)
b. Jan. 4, 1920; St. Paul, Minn.
Director of Central Intelligence,
August 1973-January 1976.

Colby, the son of a career Army officer, graduated from Princeton in 1940. He served as a member of the Office of Strategic Services during World War II and received his law degree from Columbia in 1947. He then practiced law in New York City. Colby joined the Central Intelligence Agency (CIA) in 1950. Under cover of diplomatic title he served the Agency in Sweden and Italy during the 1950s. Colby played a major role in CIA attempts to block the expansion of the Italian Communist Party.

Colby became CIA station chief and first secretary of the American embassy in South Vietnam in 1959. Three years later he was appointed head of the Far East division of the clandestine services, where he presided over the CIA's expanding programs throughout Southeast Asia. He played an important role in social development programs designed to win the allegiance of the South Vietnamese people as well as in Operation Phoenix, an effort to coordinate American and Vietnamese attacks on the Communist infrastructure. [See JOHNSON Volume]

The latter program proved extremely controversial. Critics charged that American officials condoned and participated in the torture of political prisoners and that during its first two and a half years over 20,000 suspected Communists had been killed. In 1970 and 1971 Colby was called before congressional committees to explain and justify the program. He pointed out that many of the dead had been killed in battle, but when asked to state categorically that there had been no assassinations under the program, he refused. His testimony failed to quiet criticism of the program, which was generally accounted a failure.

In June 1971 Colby resigned his post and returned to Washington because of the serious illness of his eldest daughter. He became executive director-comptroller of the CIA, its third ranking position, in 1972. He had no direct influence on policy, but because he had control of the budget, Colby could influence the development of various programs. He refined the Agency's budgeting procedures to permit financing of unanticipated projects and presented budget requests to Congress.

Colby was aware of various high level CIA programs including "Track I," the Agency's efforts to prevent the election of marxist Salvador Allende in Chile in 1970. He was also aware of Track II, the top level program authorized by Nixon and revealed to no one outside the CIA, designed to prevent Allende from assuming office. The program failed. He also knew of the existence of Operation Chaos, an effort to investigate possible foreign links with domestic anti-war groups. In 1972, as a result of prompting by Colby, the focus of the operation was turned from the anti-war movement to anti-terrorist activities. However no effort was made to destroy the illegal information gathered.

Colby was deeply involved in the Agency's reaction to Watergate, following identification of the burglars as former CIA agents. Director of Central Intelligence Richard Helms [q.v.] spelled out the Agency's fundamental strategy: distance the CIA from the event to every extent possible. He also asked Colby to coordinate the Agency's efforts in the case. The CIA provided responses to what it considered legitimate demands from law enforcement agencies but would not volunteer information.

Shortly after James Schlesinger [q.v.] was named Director of Central Intelligence in January 1973, Colby became deputy director for plans. (He later changed the title to deputy director of operations to clarify to the public what his functions were.) At this post he reformed the clandestine services, paring down its staff and reducing its influence. Colby also reorganized the division to limit the power of James Angleton [q.v.], a cold warrior who opposed detente and had been active in supervising some of the illegal domestic operations. (After Colby

became DCI in 1974, he succeeded in forcing Angleton's retirement.) Colby reoriented the service, moving it from traditional clandestine operations to the use of sophisticated technology to collect intelligence. He also placed greater stress on the area of economic intelligence.

Under Schlesinger's direction, Colby compiled a list of what were termed the Agency's "family jewels," questionable or illegal operations. In addition to CIA actions in Chile and operations against the anti-war movement, they included the opening of domestic mail, attempts to assassinate or have assassinated such foreign leaders as Patrice Lumumba and Fidel Castro, experimentation with mind-control drugs on unknowing subjects and exchanges with domestic agencies of information on possible subversives. The list was compiled in an effort to identify potentially dangerous issues and reform internal procedures.

President Nixon named Colby DCI in May 1973. He was confirmed in August. Colby attempted to continue the reforms he had initiated as deputy director of operations. In an effort to establish better communications and interchange between policymakers and analysts, he abolished the Office of National Estimates and replaced it with a group of 11 specialists in functional and geographical areas known as National Intelligence Officers. These individuals were responsible for intelligence collection and production in their designated fields and reported directly to Colby.

Soon after Colby's appointment, the Agency became the focus of public and congressional attention as its illegal activities became public. Therefore, most of Colby's time was absorbed in responding to these developments. During 1974 and 1975 the Agency was investigated by a presidential commission led by Vice President Nelson Rockefeller [q.v.], a Senate committee under the direction of Sen. Frank Church (D, Ida.) [q.v.] and a House panel headed by Rep. Otis Pike (D, N.Y.) [q.v.]. It also became the target of a number of investigative reporters. Against the advice of such individuals as

Henry Kissinger [*q.v.*], Colby chose to cooperate with these panels, revealing information that he thought would not damage national security or endanger CIA agents. He did, however, unsuccessfully attempt to prevent an investigation of assassination plots on the grounds that the Agency had assassinated no one and that the probe would only damage the reputation of the U.S. He also failed to prevent revelation of the CIA's efforts to use the *Glomar Explorer,* a technically advanced ship built by Howard Hughes's [*q.v.*] interests, to salvage a Soviet submarine.

During September 1975 Colby was threatened with contempt of Congress for refusal to give the Pike Committee classified documents unless permitted to delete passages he felt jeopardized national security. A settlement was reached under which disputes between the Committee and Colby over deleted passages would be mediated by the President.

In testimony before the various committees, Colby reiterated his contention that the CIA's domestic misdeeds were few and that they had been stopped in 1973. He also repeated his statements that the CIA had assassinated no one and argued that certain aspects of the probes could damage national security. In September he revealed that the Agency possessed a poison cache in direct opposition to a presidential order given by Richard Nixon to destroy it. This last revelation proved the catalyst for President Ford to demand Colby's resignation. The White House had been disturbed by the continuing probes and revelations, Colby's handling of the situation and the impression given that the CIA was an unsavory world of cloak and dagger spies.

Colby announced his resignation in November. His departure was delayed until January 1976 to give his replacement, George Bush [*q.v.*], time to return from his diplomatic assignment in Peking. After he left government service, Colby set up law practice in Washington, D.C.

[ES]

For further information:
William Colby, *Honorable Men: My Life in the CIA* (New York, 1978).

COLEMAN, JAMES S(AMUEL)
b. May 12, 1926; Bedford, Ind.
Sociologist.

Coleman attended Emory and Henry College and received a bachelor of science degree from Purdue University in 1949. He worked as a chemical engineer, but an interest in sociology brought him to Columbia University, where he received his doctorate in sociology in 1955. He was the author of numerous books dealing with adolescence, mathematical sociology, social change, education and other subjects. He taught sociology at the University of Chicago from 1956 to 1959 and at Johns Hopkins University from 1959 to 1963.

Coleman rose to public attention as a result of his work as the principal author of *Equality of Educational Opportunity,* which came to be known as the Coleman Report. Research for that study was carried out under the Civil Rights Act of 1964 and was completed in 1966. The report involved tests and surveys of about 600,000 students and 60,000 teachers in 4,000 schools around the country. It showed that lower-class black children enrolled in schools with a majority of middle-class white students scored higher on standardized tests than did similar children enrolled in all-black schools. The report also indicated that there was little decrease in the achievement of whites in these integrated schools. Coleman concluded from the study that integration would bring about achievement benefits.

The Coleman Report became the basis for school integration efforts in many cities and was influential in President Nixon's educational programs. In his special message on educational reform on March 3, 1970, Nixon emphasized a finding of the Report that the economic and social background of a child had a direct bearing on his or her educational performance. Coleman himself helped to compose Nixon's message of March 24, 1970, in which the President called for the allocation of money to school districts to deal with the effects of racial segregation.

Coleman continued to advise the Nixon Administration on educational policy.

In 1975 Coleman changed his mind about some aspects of the Report. He concluded that based on a large number of analyses of the effects of desegregation on student achievement, there were no overall gains from integration of schools.

Although Coleman remained an ardent supporter of integration, he became a vocal critic of the means used to promote it. He concluded on the basis of his new statistical studies that "programs of desegregation have acted to further separate blacks and whites rather than bring them together." He particularly criticized massive forced busing of students in the big cities. He argued that white middle-class families chose to move to the suburbs or enroll their children in private schools when confronted with forced busing.

Coleman's new research was sponsored by the Urban Institute, a Washington, D. C., research organization, and was based upon an analysis of racial data and trends in United States schools from 1968 to 1973. According to Coleman, busing worked reasonably well when it involved small numbers of students, but massive busing in the big cities was counterproductive to integration.

Coleman was criticized for his new report. Some civil rights advocates argued that he was being used to sway blacks away from seeking court help as an instrument of promoting integration. Coleman was also challenged by some social scientists who contended that his criticism of busing went beyond the scope of his research findings. These critics argued that white flight preceded desegregation.

Coleman advocated alternatives to court-ordered massive busing. He urged consideration of interdistrict voluntary transfers (in which children would be permitted to transfer not merely to a school in another district but to a school anywhere in the metropolitan area that had space); vouchers for education (whereby students could decide which accredited school, public or private, to attend); and a system of incentives combined with choice (in which postsecondary tuition for attendance in an integrated school would be offered).

In addition to his other work, Coleman sat on the top advisory bodies of both the National Institute of Education and the National Institute of Mental Health. In 1973 he returned to the University of Chicago as professor of sociology.

[HML]

COLEMAN, WILLIAM T(HADDEUS), JR.,
b. July 7, 1920; Germantown, Pa.
Secretary of Transportation, March 1975-January 1977.

Born into a middle-class family with connections to many of America's most distinguished black leaders, William T. Coleman was educated in the public schools of Philadelphia and at the University of Pennsylvania. Following service in the Army Air Corps during World War II, Coleman received degrees from Harvard Law School, where he edited the *Law Review* and graduated first in his class. Admitted to the Pennsylvania bar in 1947, Coleman became a law clerk in 1948 for Supreme Court Justice Felix Frankfurter. He was the first black ever to hold such a post. In 1952 Coleman joined the Philadelphia law firm of Dilworth, Paxson, Kalin, & Levy, becoming a senior partner in 1956.

Although specializing in corporate and anti-trust litigation, Coleman acquired a reputation as an expert in transportation law. He represented Philadelphia, Cincinnati and other cities in mass transit and labor matters, in time becoming special counsel and negotiator for both the Philadelphia Transportation Authority and the Southeast Pennsylvania Transportation Authority. Coleman's corporate directorships included, among others, Pan Am World Airlines and the Penn Mutual Life Insurance Corporation, as well as membership on the board of governors of the American Stock Exchange.

Deeply involved in civil rights law, Coleman coauthored the brief presented to the Supreme Court in the *Brown* v *Board of Education* case, which led to the 1954 decision banning school segregation. In 1971 he was elected President of the NAACP's Legal Defense and Education Fund, of which he had been a member for years.

A long-standing member of the Republican Party, Coleman entered government during the Eisenhower Administration, serving from 1959 to 1961 on the President's Commission on Employment Policy. In the 1960s and 1970s Coleman was a consultant to the U.S. Arms Control and Disarmament Agency, an assistant counsel to the Warren Commission, and a member of the U.S. delegation to the United Nations General Assembly. On Jan. 14, 1975, Coleman accepted President Ford's offer to become Secretary of Transportation. Sworn into office March 7, 1975, Coleman succeeded Claude S. Brinegar [*q.v.*] as head of the fourth largest federal agency.

Coleman's priorities upon taking office were to settle transportation problems during a period of retrenchment in government spending. Several months of study produced *A Statement of National Transportation Policy,* which Coleman sent to Congress in September 1975. The 53-page document set forth measures that Coleman believed would lead to "a more safe, efficient, diverse, and competitive transportation system." In general Coleman recommended less governmental interference in the operation of railroads and airlines, an extensive reformation of federal regulations pertaining to rate structures and a more equitable distribution of federal funds among the various branches of transportation policy. Although it contained few new ideas, the *Statement* marked the first serious effort by the federal government to formulate a comprehensive national transportation policy.

An architect of the Ford Administration's efforts to change regulations in the transportation industry, Coleman recommended that financial aid be provided to airlines to help defray the cost of modifying old planes to meet new FAA noise standards. Under the Coleman proposal such aid would have been funded by diverting 2% of the 8% airlines-ticket tax. However Coleman took a tough stance against certain other transportation subsidies, such as free use of waterways by barge operators. Similarly Coleman approved a new $378 million federal budget allocation for Amtrak in 1976, higher than the $350 million of the previous year but considerably less than what Amtrak had requested.

Coleman's most controversial decision as Secretary of Transportation was his ruling on Feb. 4, 1976, to allow limited service by the British-French supersonic transport Concorde to New York and Washington on a 16-month basis. Although the decision stirred environmental opposition, President Ford announced that he would "stand by" Coleman's ruling. Excluding noise Coleman said that he did not consider the environmental consequences of the decision "to be substantial." The Concorde decision was found to be legal and reasonable on May 19, 1976, by a three-judge panel of the U.S. Court of Appeals for the District of Columbia.

Despite demands for increased safety controls on automobiles, Coleman ruled on Dec. 6, 1976, against requiring auto manufacturers to equip all new cars with air bags as a protective device against accidents. Instead of mandatory air bags, Coleman proposed a demonstration project, declaring his concern over the public's rejection of "unfamiliar and controversial technology." Coleman returned to private life at the end of the Ford Administration.

[JAN]

COLMER, WILLIAM M(EYERS)
b. Feb. 11 1890; Moss Point, Miss.
Democratic Representative, Miss., 1933–73; Chairman, Rules Committee, 1967–73.

William Colmer was elected to the U.S. House in the Democratic landslide of 1932. He supported Franklin D. Roosevelt's New Deal program but subsequently became an opponent of social welfare and civil rights measures. In the 1960s Colmer generally voted with the Southern Democratic-Republican conservative coalition against the Democratic Administration's domestic programs but supported the Vietnam war. In January 1967 he rose to chairman of the powerful House Rules Committee through which most bills had to pass before reaching the House floor. [See KENNEDY, JOHNSON Volumes]

With a nine-to-six liberal majority on the Rules Committee, Colmer was less successful than his predecessor in blocking liberal legislation, but as chairman, he nonetheless continued to wield considerable influence throughout President Nixon's first term. In 1970 he refused to schedule hearings on a bill that would have increased the power of the Equal Employment Opportunity Commission to combat racial discrimination in industry and craft unions, effectively killing it for that year. The same year he blocked in committee the creation of an independent consumer protection agency. John Gardner [q.v.], head of Common Cause, testifying on hearings on the seniority system in Congress in 1971, gave high priority to Colmer's ouster because the chairman had used his power "to kill important consumer protection and equal employment legislation." In 1972 Colmer managed to delay for several months a measure to raise the minimum wage from $1.60 to $2.00 an hour. However Congress eventually passed the legislation.

Although Colmer generally backed the President, especially in foreign affairs, he was unable to support some of Nixon's more liberal domestic proposals. He opposed the President's plan for revenue sharing in 1972 and voted against the Family Assistance Plan in 1971. About the latter, which provided for increases in Social Security and medicare-medicaid as well as other programs for the poor and disabled, Colmer asserted, "I would rather have that [the chaos of the present welfare system] than have what we are asked to take in this bill."

In March 1972 Colmer, at the age of 82, announced his retirement from political life at the end of his current term. His administrative assistant, Trent Lott [q.v.], 31, ran as a Republican for Colmer's seat and won with the Representative's backing.

[FLM]

COLSON, CHARLES (WENDELL)
b. Oct. 16, 1931; Boston, Mass.
Special assistant to the President 1970-71.

Charles Colson was born and raised in a comfortable home in Boston, where his father worked for the Securities and Exchange Commission. When he was 18, he turned down a full scholarship to Harvard because he thought the school was too radical and because a shocked admissions officer told him that no one had ever done that before. Colson went to Brown University and graduated in 1953. He served in the Marines from 1953 to 1956. After his discharge he went to Georgetown Law School and graduated in 1959. The following year he became Sen. Leverett Saltonstall's (R, Mass.) campaign manager and then served as his administrative assistant on Capitol Hill. From 1961 to 1969 he enjoyed a prominent law practice in Washington and continued to be active in Republican politics, working for Sen. Barry Goldwater [q.v.] in 1964 and Richard Nixon in 1968.

In 1968 Colson joined the Republican presidential campaign as an "issues man," helping Nixon think through his position on various issues. In 1969 he was brought to the White House to work as a political strategist under H. R. Haldeman [q.v.], the President's chief of staff. Colson worked out the Nixon strategy to court the potentially conservative, ethnic labor vote away from the Democrats on the issues of Vietnam, public school integration and birth control. Colson's influence was seen in Nixon's pardon of Teamster President James Hoffa [q.v.] and in his appointment of Peter J. Brennan [q.v.] of the New York Building Trades as Secretary of Labor.

Colson liked to describe himself as a "flag-waving, kick-em-in-the-nuts, anti-press, anti-liberal Nixon fanatic." He was known at the White House for his insensitivity and ruthlessness and had once exclaimed to astonished reporters, "I would walk over my grandmother if necessary" to ensure Richard Nixon's reelection.

The year 1970 proved to be a turning point for both the Nixon White House and for Charles Colson. In May 1970 after the Cambodian invasion and the resulting student strikes culminating in the public outcry over the shooting of college students at Ohio's Kent State and Mississippi's Jackson State Colleges, the Nixon Administration found itself increasingly on the defensive. Its response, carried out by the White House staff under H. R. Haldeman, John Ehrlichman [q.v.], John Dean [q.v.] and Colson, was a series of deceptive letter-writing campaigns designed to convince the public and government officials that the American people supported Nixon's policies.

Colson and Jeb Stuart Magruder [q.v.] set up a White House letter-writing campaign to influence citizens and politicians about the correctness of the President's foreign policy. Colson's office used Republican National Committee lists of editors, governors, congressmen, and media representatives and sent them letters and telegrams that expressed concern about their positions on Nixon policies. The letters and telegrams appeared to come from private citizens, but in fact came from the White House. Colson specialized in the establishment of dummy "citizens committees" organized to give the impression to both people in influential positions and to voters that Nixon policies had a broad base of support. He also supported the so-called Huston Plan to create a domestic security group to spy on "disruptive elements" within the society. Nixon approved the project, but J. Edgar Hoover [q.v.] vetoed it.

After the 1970 elections Colson moved to a key position with Haldeman and Ehrlichman as a special assistant to the President. For the next two years Colson was in daily contact with the President, speaking with him often as many as five or six times a day, and had a key role in creating the "Plumbers" unit, drawing up the "political enemies list" and establishing the security operation of the Committee to Re-Elect the President (CREEP).

The White House special investigations unit, or the Plumbers (as it was known in the White House), was established in June 1971 at Richard Nixon's directive that the White House "plug the leaks." The directive arose from the publication of the secret *Pentagon Papers*. John Ehrlichman and Colson served as supervisors of the unit, which was to identify people suspected of leaking information and harass, intimidate and embarrass them publicly.

In 1971, in response to Nixon's growing fear and hostility to criticism from Democrats and liberals, Charles Colson had his staff draw up elaborate lists in categories like "political enemies" and "media enemies," with suggestions about which government agencies might appropriately deal with them.

In addition to the enemies project, Colson was involved in a myriad of other clandestine and illegal activities. These included having E. Howard Hunt [q.v.] forge a cable implicating the Kennedy Administration in the 1964 assassination of President Diem of South Vietnam, which Colson then leaked to *Life* magazine. In the spring of 1972 during the International Telephone and Telegraph (ITT) scandal that erupted during the Richard Kleindienst [q.v.] confirmation hearings, Colson dispatched Hunt to discuss the case with Dita Beard [q.v.], who had written a memo suggesting that a "deal" had been worked out between the Nixon Administration and ITT to end an anti-trust suit against the company in return for funding the Republican National Convention planned for San Diego, near President Nixon's San Clemente, Calif., home. After Hunt had met with her, Dita Beard issued a statement claiming her memo was a fraud. Then in the summer of 1971, Colson suggested to John Caulfield, a member of John Dean's staff, that he arrange for the firebombing of the liberal

Washington-based Brookings Institute.

By winter 1972 when the Nixon Administration started gearing up for the 1972 reelection effort, a pattern of widespread illegalities under the direction of H. R. Haldeman, John Ehrlichman and Charles Colson had been well established. The Committee to Re-Elect the President, established as a Haldeman operation to circumvent the influence of John Mitchell [q.v.], was staffed by the young men from the White House who had been involved in these questionable activities for two years or more.

Although Colson was not involved in the formation of G. Gordon Liddy's [q.v.] "Gemstone" plan for electronic surveillance of Lawrence O'Brien [q.v.], chairman of the Democratic National Committee, he provided encouragement and support for the project. After the burglars were caught in June 1972, Colson supervised the destruction of the contents of E. Howard Hunt's White House safe, which included a psychological study of Daniel Ellsberg [q.v.], and the forged Diem cable. Colson promised Hunt clemency for his continued silence and urged that the White House continue its financial support of the defendants.

After Nixon's reelection in the fall of 1972, when people in the media and in Congress began to make connections between the Watergate burglary, the CREEP staff and the White House staff, Colson announced that he was submitting his resignation. In early 1973 he left the White House and returned to his lucrative law practice, bringing to the firm a $100,000-a-year retainer from the Teamsters Union.

In spring 1973 James McCord [q.v.], one of the Watergate burglars, broke his silence and wrote a letter to Judge John Sirica [q.v.], who had tried the Watergate case, charging that the defendants had been paid for their silence and that the deeds of wrongdoing extended far beyond those committed by the burglars or those traceable to CREEP.

In spite of his eleventh hour announcement that he had been "converted to Christ" and would dedicate himself to "working for the Lord," Colson was among seven top Nixon officials—including John N. Mitchell, H. R. Haldeman and John Ehrlichman—indicted by the Watergate grand jury in March 1974 for conspiracy to "commit offenses against the United States," for obstruction of justice, for their political activities from 1969 to 1972 and for lying to investigative officials and agencies about those activities.

In lieu of facing a possible 15 years in prison and citing his recent Christian conversion, Colson promised to plead guilty and to be a cooperative witness in the other investigations and lawsuits provided the most serious charges against him were dropped. On June 3, 1974, he pled guilty to a charge of obstructing justice and was sentenced to one to three years in a minimum security prison. In February 1975, after serving seven months of his sentence, Colson was released from jail and returned to private life in Washington.

[SJT]

CONNALLY, JOHN B(OWDEN), JR.
b. Feb. 27, 1917; Floresville, Tex.
Secretary of the Treasury, February 1971–May 1972.

The son of a tenant farmer, Connally attended the University of Texas at Austin, where he earned his law degree in 1941. His introduction to state and national politics, however, took place in 1938 when Lyndon B. Johnson, a freshman Democrat in Congress, invited him to Washington to serve as Johnson's aide. Connally joined the U.S. Naval Reserve in 1941 and worked in the office of the chief of naval operations and on the planning staff of Gen. Dwight D. Eisenhower. Later as a fighter plane director aboard the aircraft carrier USS *Essex* in the Pacific, he was awarded the Bronze Star. Connally returned to civilian life in 1946 and two years later managed Johnson's successful bid for the U.S. Senate. Connally worked as Johnson's administrative assistant in

1949. Thereafter he remained active in Texas Democratic Party politics and helped Johnson take over the Party machine in 1956. In 1960 Connally managed Johnson's unsuccessful campaign for the Democratic Party's presidential nomination. Connally also worked as an attorney representing the oil interests of his state.

In early 1961 President John F. Kennedy appointed Connally secretary of the Navy on the recommendation of Johnson and Secretary of Defense Robert S. McNamara [q.v.]. Connally resigned his post in December 1961 to enter the Texas gubernatorial race, in which he defeated his Republican opponent the following year.

On Nov. 22, 1963, Connally was riding in the presidential limousine in Dallas at the time of the assassination of John F. Kennedy and was himself seriously wounded. Connally's near-martyrdom made him a nationally known political figure and facilitated his re-election as governor of Texas in 1964 and 1966. Connally was generally a conservative, probusiness governor, stressing the need for economic growth and promoting expansion of the Texas educational system.

In 1968 Connally headed the Texas delegation to the Democratic Party Convention in Chicago, where Hubert Humphrey [q.v.] was nominated for President. Although his own hopes for a place on the ticket were dashed, Connally played a key role in mobilizing the Party apparatus behind Humphrey and pushing through a prowar plank in the face of liberal challenges inside the Convention and massive rioting in the streets outside. Connally gave Humphrey only modest support in the subsequent election and, in 1969, returned to his private legal practice in Texas. [See KENNEDY, JOHNSON Volumes]

In December 1970 President Nixon appointed Connally to succeed David Kennedy [q.v.] as Secretary of the Treasury. Connally's appointment was seen on all sides as a shrewd political move by Nixon. The incipient economic recession and Democratic gains in the off-year elections of November 1970 prompted Nixon to shake up his Administration. Connally had attracted Nixon's attention while serving on the President's Advisory Commission on Executive Organization, headed by Roy Ash [q.v.], which had been set up to streamline the executive branch. At a March 1970 cabinet meeting in which Ash had made a rather listless and unconvincing presentation of the Commission's recommendations, Connally had come to Ash's rescue with an impromptu summary of the advantages of the reorganization and had put at ease cabinet officials who feared their own jobs were being downgraded. On Dec. 1, 1970, Nixon appointed Connally to the prestigious Foreign Intelligence Advisory Board, and days later, when David Kennedy offered to step down to facilitate a revamping of the Administration, Nixon offered the Treasury post to Connally.

The reaction to the appointment of a Democrat to Nixon's cabinet was swift. Connally had not even consulted former President Lyndon B. Johnson, with whom he had discussed every previous move of his political career. Johnson was shocked at Connally's decision. One Washington commentator stated, "To my dirty mind, this appointment means only one thing: the start of 'Democrats for Nixon in 1972.'" Speculation that Nixon would replace Spiro Agnew [q.v.] with Connally as his running mate in 1972 began to circulate. A newspaper story concerning $225,000 in executor's fees that Connally had allegedly received from the estate of a former employer, Sid Richardson, while serving as governor of Texas created some friction at his Senate confirmation hearings, but Connally nonetheless assumed office in early February 1971.

Connally took over the Treasury while the U.S. was mired in recession. His appointment had been greeted with some skepticism by observers who questioned his ability to handle a post usually given to a banker. "I can add," Connally told a reporter who had asked him about his qualifications in economic matters. Connally imposed a grinding schedule on himself, reading widely to deepen his grasp of day-to-day Treasury operations and economics in general. In one of his first public actions, he attacked the Chase Manhattan Bank for boosting the prime interest rate at a time when credit for industry was already tight.

Connally's style was widely seen as a refreshing contrast to the rest of the Nixon Administration. In September 1971 *New York Times* columnist James Reston described Connally as "the spunkiest character in Washington these days. . . . He is tossing away computerized Treasury speeches, and telling American business and American labor off the cuff to get off their duffs if they want more jobs, more profits and a larger share of the increasingly competitive world market."

Connally quickly emerged as the main spokesman in Congress for the Administration's economic program. One of his first assignments was the promotion of the $250-300 million White House bailout plan for Lockheed Aircraft before a skeptical Congress. The issue had extensive international ramifications. The bankruptcy of Rolls Royce, the British-owned maker of jet engines, was threatening to bankrupt Lockheed, which had spent millions designing its new L-1011 jet with Rolls Royce engines. Connally's credibility in these matters was already strained by his statement that development of the supersonic transport (SST) by the U.S. would provide "$22 billion in the nation's foreign trade account over the next 20 years," a figure that caused even Council of Economic Advisers (CEA) Chairman Paul McCracken [q.v.], to criticize Connally for "numerical science fiction."

Sen. Joseph Montoya (D, N.M.) [q.v.] argued that Connally, in advocating a loan for Lockheed, was effectively asking the Congress to bail out a British firm. Connally replied that it would cost Lockheed $50 million to redesign the L-1011 to use different engines and emphasized how many jobs would be created by the firm's rescue. "The impact on the economy by the bankruptcy of Lockheed would be enormous, in my judgement," Connally told the Senate Finance Committee. Connally's personal sponsorship of the Lockheed loan drew the fire of economist John Kenneth Galbraith [q.v.], who used the incident to assert that "the military-industrial complex is alive in Washington and doing well." Galbraith saw Connally as "a new boy in town and a Democrat in a Republican Administration . . . needing to prove himself with the President." In contrast to Connally, Federal Reserve Chairman Arthur Burns [q.v.] and Deputy Secretary of Defense David Packard [q.v.] were cool to the Lockheed bailout.

In addition to numerous appearances before congressional committees to promote the Administration's domestic economic policies, Connally played a key role in U.S. foreign economic policy in 1971-72, a time of the worst monetary crisis since World War II.

In May 1971 Connally entered the arena that was to occupy his attention for the rest of his tenure at the Treasury. President Nixon sent him as the ranking representative to the International Banking Conference of the American Bankers Association in Munich, where Connally spoke on the international monetary crisis that had just forced the European countries into a joint currency float earlier that month. In his speech Connally articulated the archnationalist tone that characterized his stance with Europe and Japan over the following year. Connally attributed the exchange crisis to a shift of economic power from the U.S. to Europe and Japan. He complained about restrictions on U.S. industrial and agricultural exports to foreign nations and underlined the failure of other countries to share the defense burdens of the West. The "unalterable position" of the U.S. concerning the dollar, as expounded by Connally, was: "We are not going to devalue. We are not going to change the price of gold."

The position of the U.S. dollar and the U.S. economy continued to deteriorate throughout the summer of 1971, however, and by early August, it was obvious that drastic action was necessary. On August 13-15, Connally, Nixon, Office of Management and Budget Director George Shultz [q.v.], Federal Reserve Board Chairman Arthur Burns [q.v.], Council of

Economic Advisers Chairman Paul McCracken [q.v.] and New York Federal Reserve Bank President Paul Volcker [q.v.] conferred on the situation at Camp David, Md. Connally throughout the conference was an advocate of aggressive action, including the "closing of the gold window," or an end to the U.S. legal obligation to exchange its gold reserves for dollars held by foreign central banks.

When Arthur Burns, Connally's major opponent on the gold question, argued that such a move would severely tax the good will of the major U.S. trading partners, Connally replied, "We'll go broke getting their good will." Connally's views prevailed, and on the night of Aug. 15, in a nationwide television broadcast, Nixon announced his "New Economic Policy" (NEP), which included a closing of the gold window, a 10% surcharge on foreign imports and an 8% devaluation of the dollar.

Throughout the fall and winter of 1971, Connally was chief U.S. representative in all economic negotiations over the realignment of exchange rates. His first foreign appearance after his May 1971 speech in Munich was at the Group of Ten meeting of Sept. 15-16 in London, which Connally chaired. He reiterated the Administration's general policy, announcing the U.S. intention to promote a $13 billion swing in its balance-of-payments deficit over the next year, a figure whose dimension frightened the European representatives because they saw a shift for the worse in their own trade positions as a result. Connally also repeated his demands that U.S. trading partners reduce their tariff barriers to U.S. goods and share defense expenses more equally.

On Sept. 26, at a second Group of Ten meeting, Connally said that appropriate currency revaluations by foreign countries would make it easier for the U.S. to drop the 10% import surcharge. At the annual meeting of the International Monetary Fund in Washington on Sept. 27-30, Connally again defended the U.S. position and, in a closed session, attacked Latin American countries who encouraged U.S. investment and then expropriated

U.S. companies. In October, Connally said that the surcharge "is going to stay on for awhile because it is frankly to our advantage to keep it on for awhile." Shortly thereafter he went to Japan for top-level talks about a revaluation of the yen. He was widely referred to as "Typhoon Connally" in the Japanese press because of the hard bargaining position he took.

Connally's actions in the international economic sphere created serious tension in the high echelons of the Nixon Administration. Both Arthur Burns and Henry Kissinger [q.v.], National Security Council adviser, were appalled by Connally's apparent lack of concern for the sensibilities of America's allies. Rep. Henry Reuss (D, Wis.) [q.v.] had publicly called on Nixon to replace Connally with Arthur Burns as the top U.S. negotiator abroad. Kissinger, who had only a limited interest in economic matters, was equally worried about Connally's impact on U.S. foreign relations in general, a concern complicated by a certain rivalry growing out of Connally's intrusion into what Kissinger considered his domain.

Burns and Kissinger allied to convince Nixon of the dangers posed by Connally's behavior, and Burns urged Nixon to allow Dr. J. Zijlstra, president of the Bank of International Settlements, to draw up a currency realignment plan without Connally and to present the plan to the November 1971 meeting of the Group of Ten in Rome. Connally became incensed at Burns's intrusion into his activities and refused to have anything to do with Zijlstra's plan. At the time of his departure for Rome, Connally also refused to include any State Department officials in his delegation, a direct slap at Secretary of State William Rogers [q.v.], who was a passive ally of Burns and Kissinger in the struggle for Nixon's allegiance. Finally, on Nov. 24, Burns and Connally met with Nixon to discuss the situation, and at that meeting, in one observer's comment, Connally "got the message."

At the December 1971 Smithsonian monetary meeting Connally, confronted by a uniformly hostile group of foreign finance ministers alienated by six months of his unilateral actions and pressure tactics, pulled perhaps the most dramatic coup of his period in office. Tensions were mounting in the negotiations after long hours during which Connally had coaxed the European and Japanese representatives for greater revaluations of their own currencies against the dollar, without the slightest hint that the U.S. would reverse its refusal to readjust the dollar against the price of gold. After a French negotiator had snapped at Connally, "If that is your position, we can all go home," French Finance Minister Giscard d'Estaing asked the Secretary what the U.S. contribution to realignment would be. Connally answered laconically: "Well, we leave that up to you. What change in the gold price do you want, eight, nine, ten percent?"

After the stunned Europeans and Japanese had digested this first hint that the U.S. would raise the gold price, a British representative remarked that Connally's negotiating tactics were "not economics, but jujitsu." After the conclusion of the Smithsonian conference, at which the U.S. obtained much greater revaluations, particularly from Japan, than anyone thought possible, British Chancellor of the Exchequer Anthony Barber remarked that "a lesser man, a man less tough than Connally, could not have done it."

Connally's relations with Congress showed more mixed results in the period of the New Economic Policy (NEP). In late November the Emergency Loan Guarantee Board (ELGB), established by Congress to oversee loans to Lockheed, approved further credits to the ailing corporation, a victory for Connally. Connally was briefly embarrassed by the discovery that he owned a large amount of stock in an insurance company destined to benefit significantly from tax legislation pending before Congress. Connally denied any personal knowledge of the bill, however, and the incident had no further consequences.

In spring 1972 the Lockheed affair again complicated Connally's relations with Congress. General Accounting Office (GAO) Controller General Elmer B. Staats told a Senate subcommittee that Connally was obstructing the GAO's authority by refusing to provide documents and records of the aircraft company, making review of the loans impossible. Connally replied that "it was not the intent of Congress that the decisions of the ELGB be reviewed by the GAO," prompting Sen. William Proxmire (D, Wis.) [q.v.] to accuse Connally of defying the authority of Congress.

Connally's relations with labor suffered during his last months at the Treasury. He carried on a verbal battle with George Meany [q.v.] over the need to limit wage demands, in reference to which Meany stated that Connally knew nothing about the problems of labor.

Even Connally's relations with U.S. business deteriorated. In January 1972 he addressed the U.S. Chamber of Commerce, defending the Nixon Administration's new shift to anti-recessionary deficit spending and predicting a $35-40 billion deficit for the current fiscal year after almost balanced budgets in the previous two years. He went on to chide U.S. businessmen for not taking advantage of the investment tax credit included in Nixon's NEP package: "You asked for it. You got it. What have you done with it? Nothing." A week later Connally went before a hostile House Ways and Means Committee to ask for a $50 billion increase in the federal debt ceiling.

During the months before he left the Treasury, Connally began to move toward open identification with the Republican Party, feeding new rumors that he would be Nixon's choice for vice president in the November 1972 elections, in preparation for a Connally run at the presidency in 1976. On April 30 Connally received Nixon at his Texas ranch where he introduced the President to 200 members of the state's political and business elite in a show of his own regional power base. He also moved closer to the inner circle of Nixon's advisers, supporting Nixon in the decision to mine Haiphong harbor on May 10. The announcement of Connally's resignation on May 16 took most observers by surprise, particularly in view of an imminent meeting of the Organization of Economic Cooperation and Development (OECD), where critical negotiations on international monetary questions were to take place. Indirectly acknowledging recognition of his problematic role during the previous year, Connally said, "Charging up that hill to do battle hasn't been as exciting the last nine months as it was during the first six." Nixon said that Connally had initially agreed to serve at the Treasury for only a year, but had stayed on "because of the very, very sensitive monetary negotiations that were taking place."

Connally began campaigning for Nixon in the early summer of 1972 and, on Aug. 9, announced the founding of "Democrats for Nixon" in response to the Democratic Party's nomination of Sen. George McGovern [q.v.]. "[McGovern] . . . is so far out of the mainstream of American politics," said Connally, "he has no business being President of the United States." In September, Nixon kicked off his campaign with a dinner on Connally's ranch, and the McGovern forces seized the occasion to announce that "John Connally and his oil billionaire friends" were lining up behind the President and his "special interest Administration." In October, Connally made a 30-minute television plug for Nixon that, in the view of many observers, came close to red-baiting the Democratic candidate.

Immediately after the Nixon landslide, Connally met with the President at Camp David but denied he was seeking a cabinet post, amidst rumors he would be Secretary of State. In his 1977 television interviews with David Frost, Nixon admitted that he had almost given that post to Connally, but, fully aware of National Security Council adviser Henry Kissinger's intense rivalry with Connally and weary of the feud between Kissinger and outgoing Secretary of State Rogers, Nixon gave the portfolio to Kissinger.

On May 1, 1973, Connally announced that he was switching to the Republican Party, and on May 10 the White House announced that Connally would serve as a special adviser to the President on domestic and foreign affairs. By early June, however, Connally was already thinking about resigning, and on June 20 he held a press conference at which he announced his departure: "Obviously, I'm not being fully utilized in an advisory capacity. I have no operational responsibilities. . . ."

By this point, however, Connally was already becoming associated with the political scandals of the Nixon Administration, which ultimately destroyed his chances to run for President in 1976. As early as Nov. 10, 1972, the Watergate special prosecutor had focused on Connally's alleged role in facilitating higher federal price supports for the dairy industry in exchange for contributions to Nixon's 1972 presidential campaign. In March 1973 a House subcommittee charged that Connally had been a key Administration figure in delaying a Securities and Exchange Commission (SEC) probe of the International Telephone and Telegraph Corp. (ITT) and had interfered in government appeals of three anti-trust cases against the corporation. In June 1973 former White House Counsel John Dean [q.v.] testified that Connally had participated in top-level discussions on how to "turn off" the Watergate probes, suggesting ways to pressure Wright Patman (D, Tex.) [q.v.] into canceling the hearings. In August the Senate Watergate Committee made public a memo by White House staff member Charles Colson [q.v.], dated March 30, 1972, warning that the confirmation hearings for Attorney General-designate Richard G. Kleindienst [q.v.], then in progress, might link Nixon and many top Administration officials, including Connally, with the controversial out-of-court settlement of an anti-trust suit against ITT. A week later *Business Week* alleged that Connally had personally halted U.S. aid to Ecuador pending settlement of that country's expropriation of an ITT subsidiary.

The controversy over milk price supports refused to die. On Nov. 15 Connally testified before the Senate Watergate Committee that he had always favored higher price supports for the dairy industry, but he refused to discuss the question of campaign contributions by the dairy lobby. On Dec. 27 the Justice Department filed a civil anti-trust suit against the Mid-American Dairymen, Inc., for political contributions made in exchange for a relaxation of government price controls on milk. In Nov. 7 testimony that led to the suit, a dairy spokesman admitted he had personally discussed the issue with Connally in 1972 and that Connally had assured him "he would do all he could."

In January 1974 the White House was obliged to issue a 17-page paper explaining its 1971 increase in price supports for milk. The report indicated that Connally had called the Administration's attention to the power of the milk lobby in March 1971 and had urged action to appease the dairymen. On May 31, 1974, the Senate Watergate Committee issued its report on the dairy lobby question, concluding that there had indeed been a link between the government's decision on price supports and the millions of dollars in dairy association contributions to Nixon's 1972 presidential campaign. The Committee's report also alleged that Connally had received a $10,000 bribe from the Associated Milk Producers, Inc. (AMPI).

On July 19 the House Judiciary Committee released a report on the March 1971 increase in milk price supports. Included in the report was a transcript of a White House meeting of Nixon, his aides and Connally at which Connally had argued that there were excellent political reasons for the increase. At that meeting Connally urged swift action on price supports.

On July 28, 1974, the Watergate grand jury indicted Connally on five counts of accepting a bribe, conspiring to obstruct justice and committing perjury in connection with his acceptance of $10,000 in two cash payments from dairy lobbyists in 1971. In the following week two former AMPI officials pleaded guilty to charges of bribing Connally, but on Aug. 9 Connally entered a not-guilty plea at his own trial. In April 1975 Connally was acquit-

ted on the charge of accepting a bribe after his defense attorney had successfully convinced the court that the guilty pleas of the AMPI officials were made solely for plea-bargaining purposes.

Within weeks of his acquittal, Connally plunged back into Republican Party politics. President Gerald Ford had deemed it acceptable to pay a private visit to Connally even before his acquittal. Yet in his May 1975 appearance on the TV program "Meet the Press," Connally mildly criticized Ford while denying that he planned to run for any elective office in 1976. In April 1976 Ford in turn denied that Connally would be his new Secretary of State if he were reelected. At election time Connally merely endorsed Ford's candidacy.

Connally resumed his legal practice and business activities and remained active in Republican Party politics throughout the late 1970s.

[LRG]

For further information:
Charles Ashman, *Connally: The Adventures of Big Bad John* (New York, 1974).
A. F. Crawford and J. Keever, *John B. Connally: Portrait in Power* (Austin, 1973).

CONTE, SILVIO O(CTTAVIO)
b. Nov. 9, 1921; Pittsfield, Mass.
Republican Representative, Mass., 1959-.

Conte graduated from Pittsfield Vocational High School and apprenticed as a machinist for General Electric before enlisting in the Navy. He served in the South Pacific during World War II and with his G.I. benefits earned a law degree from Boston College in 1949. From 1950 to 1958 Conte held a seat in the Massachusetts state Senate in addition to practicing law in his own firm in Pittsfield, Mass.

Conte gave up his law practice in 1958 when he was elected to the U.S. House from his state's first congressional district. During his House career Conte gained a reputation for bucking Republican leadership to advocate his liberal views. [See JOHNSON Volume]

In the Nixon Administration Conte battled the President and the Republican leadership on ceilings for federal farm subsidies and oil-import quotas. He contended that farm subsidies fattened the incomes of the huge agricultural combines while discriminating against the small independent farmers. In both 1968 and 1969 he supported a $20,000 per crop limitation on individual farm subsidy payments, opposing the House Appropriations Committee's Agriculture Subcommittee leadership and Minority Leader Gerald Ford (R, Mich.) [q.v.], in addition to President Nixon and Secretary of Agriculture Clifford Hardin [q.v.]. In both years the House approved the ceiling only to have it defeated in the Senate or deleted during joint conference.

In 1970 Conte fought passage of the Administration's three-year omnibus farm bill, which included a sliding ceiling for payments up to $330,000 per farm. In a surprise reversal the Senate approved Conte's $20,000 limitation on a rider to the Administration appropriations bill. However the ceiling was dropped in a joint committee conference. Conte again tried unsuccessfully in 1971 and 1972 to win approval of subsidy limitations, citing figures that 63% of the total federal payments aimed at persuading farmers to practice voluntary crop control went to the wealthiest 7% of the nation's farm owners, while the poorer farmers received only 9.1% of the federal benefits. Finally in June 1973 both the House and Senate overruled the Appropriations Committee's agricultural budget and passed a rigid $20,000 per farmer ceiling on federal payments to wheat, feed grains and cotton growers.

Conte battled Nixon Administration policies on oil-import quotas, working to lift the quotas and to eliminate market manipulations by oil producers that artificially raised oil prices. He testified in both Senate and House hearings against anti-competitive practices in the oil industry. However in response to the start of the Arab oil embargo in the fall of 1973, Conte supported President Nixon's mandatory fuel-allocation program, stating that the legislation was needed to avert imminent fuel shortages in the event of an Israeli-Arab War. The bill authorizing the President to regulate the allocation of crude oil and oil products was passed on Nov. 14.

Other issues on which Conte fought President Nixon's position included the 1970 incursion into Cambodia and the continuation of the Vietnam war, which he denounced as "senseless." He voted against the anti-ballistic missile system and was a principal opponent of funding for the supersonic transport. He supported the unsuccessful 1973 House attempt to override President Nixon's veto of a minimum wage increase. He also voted to use federal funds for integration and backed busing to achieve racial balance in the schools.

In 1976 Conte served on the platform committee at the Republican National Convention. During preconvention meetings supporters of California Gov. Ronald Reagan [q.v.] ousted Conte as chairman of the human rights subcommittee. Conte won reelection that year and in 1978. Because of his liberalism he held little sway over Party policy.

[DAE]

CONYERS, JOHN, JR.
b. May 16, 1929; Detroit, Mich.
Democratic Representative, Mich., 1965-.

The son of an official of the United Automobile Workers in Detroit, Conyers served in the Army in Korea. After the war he enrolled in Wayne State University and received his B.A. in 1957 and a law degree in 1958. Admitted to the Michigan bar the following year, Conyers served as general counsel for the Trade Union Leadership Council, an organization of black trade unionists.

Conyers won election to the House of Representatives in 1964. One of only six blacks in the House in 1965, Conyers compiled a consistently liberal voting record. He was especially active in civil rights and was an early opponent of the Vietnam war. [See JOHNSON Volume]

During the Nixon-Ford years, Conyers played an active part in efforts to resist attempts to weaken civil rights legislation and dismantle the social welfare programs of the Johnson Administration. He also worked to preserve an activist, pro-civil rights Supreme Court.

His first major clash with the Nixon Administration came in 1969 over the question of extending the 1965 Voting Rights Act. In June Attorney General John Mitchell [q.v.] presented the House Judiciary Committee with a substitute proposal in place of a simple extension of the Act, which was due to expire in 1970. Mitchell urged the Committee to drop the requirement that states file election-law changes with the Justice Department for approval and to shift jurisdiction over voting rights cases from District of Columbia federal courts to federal courts in the affected states. He also proposed that the Act be extended to cover all states and not merely those in the Deep South.

Conyers, a member of the Judiciary Committee, as well as other Northern liberals, opposed these changes, arguing that they would dilute the effectiveness of a law that was already being enforced only minimally. Conyers proposed instead that loopholes in the law be closed, that criminal penalties be instituted for intimidation of campaign workers and that Congress appropriate money for nonpartisan voter registration drives in the South. Although his proposals were not adopted, the Judiciary Committee rejected the Administration's amendments. The full House, however, followed the recommendations of the Attorney General, and it was only through the efforts of Senate liberals that a simple five-year extension of the Act was finally passed in 1970.

Conyers was also at odds with Nixon's welfare reform proposals. After a presidential task force recommended a complete overhaul of the welfare system, Nixon in August 1969 announced a major welfare reform package called the Family Assistance Plan. It would have guaran-

teed federal payments of $1,600 a year for a family of four as well as requiring employable family members to seek work. At a National Welfare Rights Organization convention that same month, Conyers criticized the plan as a "step backward." He urged a $3,200 minimum income and the elimination of any mandatory work requirements. In the House, Conyers attacked the legislation for being based on the "ridiculous" assumption that "welfare recipients would deny themselves better lives rather than work." Although Nixon had made welfare reform a major priority, it faced widespread opposition in Congress and by 1971 was a dead issue.

Conyers and other black members of Congress were also aroused by Nixon's Supreme Court nominations. He signed a statement criticizing Clement Haynsworth's [q.v.] views as revealing "too much discord" with the civil rights record of the Warren Court. Conyers also opposed Nixon's nomination of G. Harrold Carswell [q.v.] and urged the Senate Judiciary Committee "to establish the basic principle that any person of a racist or segregationist perspective is per se unqualified to serve on the Supreme Court."

Distressed by the failure of the Nixon Administration to adequately enforce and extend civil rights legislation, Conyers and other black representatives announced on Oct. 14, 1970 the formation of a "shadow cabinet" to oversee federal enforcement of civil rights laws. The following January they reorganized themselves into the Congressional Black Caucus.

Conyers remained outspoken in his criticism of the Vietnam war. After the conviction in March 1971 of Lt. William Calley, Jr., on charges of murder stemming from the My Lai massacre, Conyers urged the House Armed Services Committee to investigate alleged U.S. war crimes in Vietnam. When the Committee refused, Conyers, with Reps. Bella Abzug (D, N.Y.) [q.v.], Ronald Dellums (D, Calif.), and Parren Mitchell (D, Md.) conducted their own ad hoc public hearings.

In May 1972 he introduced a resolution to impeach Nixon for conducting an illegal war. Conyers was one of a small number of anti-war members of Congress who voted against the 1973 War Powers Act, urging that it actually expanded the war-making powers of the President.

As a member of the House Judiciary Committee that conducted impeachment hearings against Nixon in 1974, Conyers pushed to have Nixon held in contempt of Congress for his refusal to hand over the White House tapes. Conyers voted in favor of all five of the impeachment articles offered in the Committee (only three articles were approved) and personally introduced an article, rejected by the Committee, to impeach the President for the secret bombing of Cambodia. After President Ford pardoned Nixon, Conyers urged an investigation of the action. He also voted against confirmation of Nelson Rockefeller [q.v.] as Vice President.

Conyers was active in the areas of crime and the judicial system. In 1974 he introduced legislation which Congress enacted to ensure a speedy trial for persons charged with federal crimes. In 1975 and 1976 he sponsored gun-control legislation, though heavy lobbying by the National Rifle Association defeated his efforts. In 1976 he won a liberalization of federal guidelines to allow community organizations to apply for federal anti-crime funds from the Law Enforcement Assistance Administration.

In 1977, with other members of the Black Caucus, Conyers criticized President Carter for not living up to his campaign promises to blacks.

[JD]

COOK, G(EORGE) BRADFORD
b. May 10, 1937; Lincoln, Neb.
Chairman, Securities and Exchange Commission, February-May 1973.

Cook, a member of a prominent Nebraska family, graduated from Stanford University in 1959, and then obtained his law degree from the University of Nebraska in 1962. He joined the prestigious Chicago law firm of Winston and Strawn, which specialized in corporate and securities law, and later became a partner in the firm, handling mergers, contracts and securities issued by corporations. Cook had long been active in Republican politics. He was a member of the Young Republicans while attending law school. He actively supported Nixon's 1960 presidential campaign and again worked for Nixon during the 1968 election.

Cook left his Chicago law firm in 1971 to become general counsel for the Securities and Exchange Commission (SEC). He took the job after the SEC's chairman convinced him it was a stepping stone to the chairmanship, the post Cook wanted. Later he headed the newly formed Division of Market Regulation, which was primarily responsible for regulating stock exchanges. In February 1973 Cook realized his ambition when he was appointed chairman of the five-member Commission, the youngest man ever to head the SEC.

Cook was chairman of the Commission for only 74 days, however. He resigned on May 16, 1973, after it was alleged that he had deleted references in an SEC suit to a secret $200,000 contribution from financier Robert Vesco [q.v.] to the 1972 Nixon presidential campaign. After the wording had been changed, the SEC filed a civil suit against Vesco on Nov. 27, 1972, charging him with defrauding four mutual funds of $224 million.

Cook's role in the Vesco case became public on May 10, 1973, when a federal grand jury indicted John Mitchell [q.v.] and Maurice Stans [q.v.] on charges of perjury and conspiracy to obstruct justice in connection with the Vesco suit. The indictment charged that Cook and former SEC Commission Chairman William Casey [q.v.] had met with Vesco associates on April 10, 1972, to discuss the case the Commission was developing against Vesco; that the meeting occurred only a few hours after Vesco associates had delivered a $200,000 contribution in $100 bills to Stans's office at the Nixon reelection headquarters; and that Cook had deleted from the SEC suit all specific references to that contribution. Cook defended himself, claiming that the references to the contribution in the suit were "unprofessional sensationalism," but he admitted in his letter of resignation that "the web of circumstances that I find myself confronted with has made me feel that the effectiveness of the agency might be impaired" if he remained chairman.

Cook was one of the three major government witnesses during the 1974 Mitchell-Stans trial. He testified that he had first discussed the Vesco case with Stans during a Nov. 11–13 goose hunting trip in Texas, which Cook's father, a Nixon fund-raiser, had arranged to promote his son's ambitions of becoming SEC chairman. Cook admitted he had told Stans of his ambitions while they were discussing Vesco's unreported cash gift. He claimed that Stans had asked him on four occasions to limit the SEC's investigation of Vesco's contribution and to conceal the circumstances surrounding the cash gift. Cook also admitted lying to the grand jury that investigated the matter and to two congressional committees.

Stans, however, denied Cook's charges, claiming that Cook had offered to delete the references without any urging. The trial jury acquitted Mitchell and Stans. One of the jurors said of Cook's testimony: "How could we believe him when he lied so many times before? And he admitted his perjury on the stand."

On July 24, 1974, the Nebraska Supreme Court suspended Cook from the practice of law for three years. The special Watergate prosecutor, however, declined to press charges against Cook for lying to the congressional committees, citing insufficient evidence to warrant prosecution.

[AE]

COOPER, JOHN S(HERMAN)
b. Aug. 23, 1901; Somerset, Ky.
Republican Senator, Ky., 1946–49, 1952–55, 1956–73.

Following graduation from Yale University and Harvard Law School, Cooper won election to the state legislature. He became a local judge in 1928 and a district judge in the 1930s. He held these positions in intervals throughout the 1940s and 1950s. Cooper also served as a consultant to Secretary of State Dean Acheson and sat on the American delegation to the United Nations during that period. He was ambassador to India and Nepal in the Eisenhower Administration. Cooper won special elections to the U.S. Senate in 1946, 1952 and 1956, although he lost two regular elections during the period. He won his first full term in 1960.

During the Truman, Eisenhower and Kennedy Administrations, Cooper established himself as a liberal Republican with an interest in foreign affairs. In domestic concerns he was a defender of small business and agriculture. Cooper was a moderate on civil rights. [See EISENHOWER, KENNEDY, JOHNSON Volumes]

Cooper was one of the Senate's earliest critics of the Vietnam war. Starting in January 1966 he began to criticize the bombing of North Vietnam, and at the time of the Tet offensive in February 1968, he warned against an escalation of the conflict. In 1969 he introduced an amendment to a procurement bill barring the President from using funds for U.S. combat support in Laos and Thailand. The bill passed the Senate 86-0 in September. Cooper teamed with Sen. Frank Church (D, Ida) [q.v.] to introduce in May 1970 another amendment to an appropriations bill barring the President from spending any funds without congressional approval after July 1 for American troops fighting in Cambodia, for support of advisers or troops from other countries aiding Cambodia or for air combat operations. The measure barred the introduction of U.S. ground troops into Thailand and Laos and forbade the spending of funds for "free-world forces" used to provide military support for the Laotian or Cambodian governments. The stipulation did not restrict the use of funds for action to safeguard the withdrawal of U.S. troops. The Senate passed the measure but the House deleted the Cooper-Church Amendment from its bill. A modified version of the Amendment restricting the powers of the President in the Vietnam war passed both houses of Congress in December. In 1971 Cooper charged that the Administration violated this Amendment by ferrying South Vietnamese troops into battle in Cambodia and providing air cover for them.

Cooper abstained in 1972 in the vote on the Church-Case Amendment that provided for a cutoff of funds for all U.S. combat operations in Indochina subject to an agreement for the release of American prisoners of war. Instead he supported the Nixon-sponsored bill that tied this proposal to an internationally supervised cease-fire. The Senator explained his opposition to the original Amendment was based on fear that it would undercut Nixon's bargaining position in the upcoming peace talks.

Cooper, a long-time opponent of the Cold War, opposed the Administration-sponsored Safeguard anti-ballistic missile (ABM) system. In 1969 he charged that this system would provoke an arms race. Cooper supported Sen. Mike Mansfield's (D, Mont) [q.v.] call for a moratorium on both sides in weapons development projects. In seeking a compromise on this issue, Cooper and Sen. Philip Hart (D, Mich.) [q.v.] introduced an amendment to the ABM bill that would have provided funds for research but not the deployment of the system. The Senate defeated this measure by a vote of 51 to 49. In 1971 he backed an ABM system deployed at a low level just to give the U.S. bargaining strength at the SALT negotiations.

Cooper also voted against the Administration on a number of domestic issues. In 1969 he opposed the nomination of conservative Judge Clement Haynsworth [q.v.] to the Supreme Court, but the following year he backed the nomination of G. Harrold Carswell [q.v.] to the high bench. Rather than support the Administration's voluntary health plan program, Cooper joined the bipartisan Senate group that introduced a federally financed national health insurance plan in September 1970.

Cooper retired from the Senate at the end of his term in 1973. From 1974 to 1976 he served as ambassador to East Germany during the period that witnessed the opening of the Communist state to Western trade. He retired at the end of the Ford Administration.

[JB]

CORNFELD, BERNARD
b. Aug. 17, 1927; Istanbul, Turkey.
Chairman, Investors Overseas
Services, 1958–71.

Cornfeld came to the U.S. with his immigrant parents at the age of five and grew up in New York City. During World War II, he served in the U.S. Merchant Marine. Following his graduation from Brooklyn College in 1951, Cornfeld went to Paris, where he created the embryo of his later mutual fund empire, Investors Overseas Services (IOS), Ltd. IOS started by selling shares in its fund to Americans living abroad. The fund in turn invested the money in a growing portfolio of stocks, banks, insurance companies and real estate.

Cornfeld's real innovation was a "fund of funds"—a mutual fund that invested in other mutual funds—and by the mid-1960s IOS controlled $420 million in assets. Under Cornfeld's leadership, IOS had become by the late 1960s a bonanza in the complex world of "offshore" (unregulated) money that resulted from a massive flow of U.S. dollars overseas. Although IOS and Cornfeld were viewed with considerable suspicion by the Securities and Exchange Commission (SEC), which investigated IOS thoroughly in the 1966–68 period, no major legal trouble developed. The long SEC investigations of IOS did, however, compel Cornfeld to reorganize IOS as a Canadian offshore operation in 1969.

Like many other businessmen, such as Jimmy Ling [q.v.], Roy Ash [q.v.] and C. Arnholt Smith [q.v.], who benefited from the boom atmosphere of the late 1960s to build up vast financial holdings, Cornfeld was a major victim of the 1969–70 credit crunch that resulted from the Nixon Administration's tight money policies, aimed at halting inflation. In December 1968, the last month of an eight-year bull market on Wall Street, Cornfeld and his advisers planned a major issue of IOS stock, an issue that was caught in the 18-month bear market which took the Dow Jones Industrial average from over 1,000 in January 1969 to a 631 low in June 1970.

The poor performance of the IOS stock issue led Cornfeld and his staff to seek a new strategy of securing cash for IOS operations. In December 1969, IOS announced, with much publicity, the "sale" of 10% of its rights in Canadian Arctic gas and oil exploration. However the sale was exposed as little more than a series of paper transfers among companies associated with IOS, and investors interpreted the maneuver as a sign that IOS, like many other corporations in early 1970, was facing a shortage of cash.

By March 1970 thousands of IOS mutual fund shareholders were redeeming their shares for cash, plunging the company into a liquidity crisis. In April 1970 an IOS attorney in Washington, D.C., informed Cornfeld that "President Nixon himself" had called the SEC to discuss the implications of an IOS failure in a very jittery stock market. Some observers saw in the IOS crisis a potential bust of 1929 proportions.

At the May 1970 meeting of the IOS board of directors, Cornfeld was forced to step down as chairman as a precondition for an outside rescue of IOS. At that time Robert Vesco [q.v.], who had carefully followed the IOS crisis from afar, implemented a shrewd strategy, built on a masterful combination of financial maneuvers, whereby he seized control of IOS and over the next year looted the company's assets. In January 1971 he succeeded in buying Cornfeld's 6 million IOS shares at 92 cents per share, down from $13 per share in the fall of 1969. Later in 1971 Cornfeld was named in a multimillion dollar gold-trading suit by the U.S. government, which charged that IOS had violated laws prohibiting U.S. citizens from owning gold during the 1968 dollar crisis.

Cornfeld and IOS were later cleared of this charge.

In 1973 the Swiss government arrested Cornfeld and charged him with criminal fraud and incitement to speculation. A year later he was released on $1.5 million bail, the highest bail in Swiss history. Five years later the legal threads surrounding IOS were still being unraveled.

[LG]

For further information:
Bert Cantor, *The Bernie Comfeld Story* (New York, 1970).
Robert A. Hutchinson, *Vesco* (New York, 1974).

COX, ARCHIBALD
b. May 17, 1912; Plainfield, N.J.
Watergate Special Prosecutor, May 1973-October 1973.

Archibald Cox attended St. Paul's, Harvard College, and Harvard Law School. After a year's service as clerk to Judge Learned Hand, he practiced law with the Boston firm of Ropes, Gray, Best, Coolidge & Rugg. During World War II he worked in Washington, D.C., first for the National Defense Mediation Board, then in the office of the Solicitor General of the Department of Justice, and from 1943 to 1945 in the Department of Labor as associate solicitor. After the war Cox returned to Harvard Law School, becoming in 1946 a full professor, one of the youngest men in the school's history to attain that rank.

An expert in labor law, Cox was frequently called away from the university to arbitrate labor disputes or accept temporary government positions. During the Korean War he served as co-chairman of the Construction Industry Stabilization Commission and as head of the Wage Stabilization Board. In the late 1950s Cox served as an adviser on labor legislation to Sen. John F. Kennedy (D, Mass.). During the 1960 presidential campaign he was a member of Kennedy's brain trust, directing an academic team that researched and drafted speeches on major issues for the candidate. After his election Kennedy appointed Cox Solicitor General, the third highest official in the Justice Department and the government's chief advocate before the Supreme Court. [See KENNEDY Volume]

Cox served as Solicitor General until 1965, when he returned to teaching at Harvard. He returned to the Supreme Court on occasion to argue cases as a private attorney, as in 1966 when he urged the Court to uphold the constitutionality of the 1965 Voting Rights Act. He also served as a special mediator in the 1967 New York City school strike and as chairman of a five-man commission investigating the violent disturbances at Columbia University in the spring of 1968. In 1969 Cox represented three welfare clients before the Supreme Court challenging the constitutionality of the one-year residency requirement for welfare benefits in Connecticut, Pennsylvania and the District of Columbia. The Supreme Court declared the residency requirement unconstitutional in a landmark decision on April 21.

In May 1973, under public and congressional pressure to appoint an independent special prosecutor to take command of the Watergate investigation, Attorney General-designate Elliot Richardson [q.v.], a former student of Cox, chose the Harvard professor for the post. Cox was given jurisdiction over the investigation of the Watergate burglary and coverup, as well as "all allegations involving the President, members of the White House staff or presidential appointees," and endowed with the full range of prosecutorial powers, including the power to contest in court any refusal by the White House to produce subpoenaed evidence. On May 21 Richardson assured the Senate Judiciary Committee that Cox would have full independence and support and would be fired only for "extraordinary improprieties." *Newsweek* characterized the appointment of Cox as a "master stroke," which brought "an infusion of unshakable integrity to the Administration's sometimes suspect handling of Watergate and related scandals."

Before long Cox chose a staff of about 30 lawyers, averaging about 30 years in age, mostly graduates of Ivy League law schools. He divided the Special Prosecutor's office into a series of task forces, each covering a major area of suspected criminality: the Watergate break-in and coverup, the main case, the activities of the White House "Plumbers" unit, the "dirty tricks" of White House functionaries during the 1972 elections, the alleged special treatment of an anti-trust suit against the International Telephone & Telegraph Co. (ITT) in return for campaign contributions, and assorted violations of campaign finance laws. Throughout the summer of 1973 the Special Prosecutor's office quietly went about its task of amassing evidence for presentation to the grand jury.

The startling revelation on July 16, 1973 that President Nixon had been tape-recording his White House conversations since 1971 set in motion the dramatic chain of events that led to Cox's firing three months later. On July 18 Cox wrote to the White House requesting eight tapes of conversations important to the Watergate probe. On July 26 Nixon announced that he would not surrender any tapes to the grand jury or the Senate Watergate Committee. Cox then requested that U.S. District Judge John Sirica [q.v.] issue a subpoena compelling production of the requested tapes.

White House lawyer Charles Wright [q.v.] attempted to quash the subpoena by arguing that the President was not subject to the ordinary processes of law and that the doctrine of executive privilege was a barrier to the demand for any evidence from the conversations of the President. During his oral argument before Judge Sirica on Aug. 22, Wright added the claim that some tapes contained sensitive "national security" information, the disclosure of which would harm the national interest. Cox contended that the President was subject to legal processes and that executive privilege did not cover possible evidence of criminal conduct. His brief stressed that the tapes were necessary for the grand jury to determine the criminal culpability of the President's aides, not the President himself. One week later Judge Sirica ordered Nixon to turn over the eight tapes to him for the judge's determination of whether or not they were covered by executive privilege.

On Oct. 12 the U.S. Court of Appeals affirmed Sirica's decision that Nixon must turn over the tapes. Rather than seek Supreme Court review, Nixon offered Cox a "compromise" plan, whereby Nixon would provide the special prosecutor with "summaries" of the taped conversations rather than the tapes themselves. Nixon selected Sen. John Stennis (D, Miss.) [q.v.] to listen to the tapes in question and verify the accuracy of the summaries. A final part of the compromise was that Cox would agree to make no further attempt to subpoena any more tapes or presidential papers.

On Oct. 19 Cox rejected the Nixon proposal. The proposed summaries would violate the court order and destroy the evidentiary value of the tapes, for summaries of the tapes would be inadmissible as evidence at trial. The President's order to forego any further attempts to obtain presidential tapes and other papers violated the pledge of independence given to Cox by the attorney general at his confirmation, Cox said. Acceptance of the President's directive, he said, would "defeat the fair administration of criminal justice. It would deprive prosecutors of admissible evidence in prosecuting wrongdoers who abuse high government office. . . . I cannot be party to such an arrangement."

On Oct. 20 Nixon ordered the Attorney General to discharge Cox. Richardson resigned rather than carry out the order, and Deputy Attorney General William Ruckelshaus [q.v.] was fired for his refusal to do so. Solicitor General Robert Bork [q.v.], then appointed acting Attorney General, finally discharged Cox. Nixon announced that he had abolished the special prosecutor's office and transferred the investigation back to the Justice Department. Cox issued a one-sentence statement: "Whether ours shall continue to be a government of laws and not of men is now for Congress and ultimately for the American people [to decide]."

The public response to what was dubbed the "Saturday Night Massacre" was a deluge of criticism of the President's act. Western Union in Washington was inundated with a record 220,000 telegrams of protest by Oct. 24, while public figures called for Nixon's resignation or impeachment. Nixon soon reversed his position on the tapes and on Oct. 23 announced he would obey the subpoena to turn them over to Judge Sirica. On Oct. 26 he announced that Bork would appoint a new special prosecutor. A week later Bork announced the appointment of Texas lawyer Leon Jaworski [q.v.] to fill the position.

Almost unnoticed amid the furor over the tapes and the dismissal of Cox was Cox's first major accomplishment as special prosecutor: the plea of guilty on Oct. 19 by former counsel to the President, John Dean [q.v.]. As part of a bargain negotiated with Cox, Dean pleaded guilty to a single count of conspiring to cover up the truth about the Watergate break-in and agreed to be a prosecution witness in return for Cox's promise not to bring other charges, with the exception of perjury, against him. Two of Cox's assistant prosecutors wrote that Dean's guilty plea was a result of Cox's "personal determination that Dean be prosecuted no matter what. Dean became an *idee fixe* for Cox."

Cox's firing gave him heroic stature in the eyes of the many, who saw him as the embodiment of integrity and dedication to constitutional principles, in addition to being a distinguished legal scholar. Returning to Harvard after his dismissal, he continued to play an occasionally prominent role in public affairs. In July 1976 Cox gave the nominating speech for Rep. Morris Udall (D, Ariz.) [q.v.] at the Democratic National Convention.

In October 1978 Cox appeared before the Supreme Court to defend the University of California's affirmative action program in the important Bakke case.

[TO]

For further information:
Richard Ben-Veniste and George Frampton, Jr., *Stonewall: The Legal Case Against the Watergate Conspirators* (New York, 1977).

CRAMER, WILLIAM C(ATO)
b. Aug. 4, 1922; Denver, Colo.
Republican Representative, Fla.,
1955-1971.

Cramer served in the Navy during World War II and graduated Phi Beta Kappa from the University of North Carolina in 1946. He earned his law degree in two years at Harvard and returned to St. Petersburg to lead the successful revitalization of the long-dormant Pinellas County Republican Party. In 1950 he won election to the state House of Representatives and served as minority leader. Four years later the 32-year-old Cramer became the first Republican Representative elected from Florida since 1875. He easily won reelection through the 1960s. His early success and statewide partisan labors made him, as journalist Neal Peirce observed, "virtually the founding father of the present-day Republican Party in Florida."

In the House Cramer almost always voted with the conservatives. He opposed President Johnson's Great Society programs and voted against civil rights legislation with the singular exception of the 1965 Voting Rights Act. After three consecutive summers of racial rioting, Cramer introduced in 1966 an amendment to the Civil Rights Act on open housing aimed at "those professional agitators" who travel interstate to incite riots. Cramer, who had not originally intended to support the open-housing law, voted for the final version passed in 1968 because it contained his anti-riot provision. [See JOHNSON Volume]

Cramer continued his opposition to civil rights during the Nixon Administration. He had been outraged at the presence of Resurrection City, a civil rights protest set up near the Washington Monument during May and June of 1968. The next year to forstall any similar incident that he said would be "potentially explosive and potentially disruptive" to the government, Cramer sponsored a bill banning any future encampment or overnight sit-in on federal property or in public parks and requiring protest leaders to post bond if officials considered it appropriate. The bill passed overwhelmingly in the House but died in the Senate.

Cramer clashed with environmentalists in the debate over the Water Quality Improvement Act of 1970. The issue was the extent of an oil company's responsibility in the event of an oil spill at sea. The Senate passed a version of "absolute liability," i.e., exempting the company from paying cleanup costs only if the spill were the result of an act of God, war or governmental negligence. The looser House version, strongly backed by Cramer, held the companies liable only in the event of willful negligence. Cramer held fast, and it seemed that in the House-Senate conference his version would prevail until a series of oil spills in California and the Gulf states swung the House over to the tougher doctrine of "absolute liability."

In 1969 Cramer joined the House Republican leadership when he was elected unopposed as Conference vice chairman. At that time he all but dominated the Party in his home state. A year later, at President Nixon's "personal" urging, Cramer entered the race for the U.S. Senate. In April of that year, less than two weeks after the Senate had refused to appoint him to the Supreme Court, Judge G. Harrold Carswell [q.v.] resigned from the U.S. Court of Appeals for the 5th Circuit to run for the same seat. Although Carswell was backed by the state's top Republicans, Gov. Claude R. Kirk, Jr. [q.v.], and Sen. Edward Gurney [q.v.], Cramer soundly defeated him in a primary that severely split the state's GOP.

In the general election Cramer ran a "law and order" campaign, inviting voters "to join the fight to stop cop killers, bombers, burners and racial revolutionaries who would destroy America." Although Nixon visited Florida twice on his behalf, Cramer lost in November to Lawton Chiles, who ran a low-key campaign stressing the economy and large cutbacks at Cape Kennedy. Cramer then retired to private life.

[FLM]

CRONKITE, WALTER (LELAND), JR.
b. Nov. 4, 1916; St. Joseph, Mo.
CBS News correspondent.

Cronkite grew up in Kansas City, Mo., and Houston, Tex. He attended the University of Texas at Austin for two years (1935–36) and during that period worked as state capitol reporter for the Scripps-Howard newspapers. During World War II Cronkite worked for United Press International and was one of the first newsmen on the scene after the Normandy invasion.

Cronkite began his broadcasting career in Washington, D.C., after the war and joined the Columbia Broadcasting System (now CBS Inc.) in July 1950 as a member of the network's Washington bureau. He rose quickly and was the network's anchorman for the 1952 political conventions. Cronkite subsequently became anchorman and then managing editor of the prestigious "CBS Evening News" broadcast, the most watched television news program (1973 estimated audience of 26 million). He received an Emmy Award in 1970 from the Academy of Television Arts and Sciences. [See KENNEDY, JOHNSON Volumes]

President Nixon was sensitive to the effects of television on public opinion. In Nixon's first 18 months in office, he used as much television time as had Eisenhower, Kennedy and Johnson combined. Nixon, however, did not like the "instant analysis" by network commentators just after the completion of his speeches. He also objected to newscasts considered critical of the President. Charles Colson [q.v.], when talking to CBS Vice Chairman Frank Stanton before the 1972 election, accused CBS of broadcasting three times as much pro-McGovern as pro-Nixon material.

Cronkite and the CBS News staff came into direct conflict with the Nixon Administration over coverage of Watergate. According to Daniel Schorr [q.v.], former CBS correspondent, "Only CBS News among the networks had taken it upon itself to raise Watergate from a newspaper story to a television story—and therefore a national story." Despite attempts by the Nixon Administration to avoid news stories about Watergate before the November 1972 elections, Cronkite in October 1972 aired a two-part feature about Watergate on the "CBS Evening News." The newscast resulted in a protest from the White House and continued efforts to suppress negative reporting about Nixon by the networks. According to Schorr, a conspiracy against the news media and CBS in particular became an extension of the Watergate cover-up and included such tactics as threats to institute antitrust suits and to withhold the licenses of network affiliates. Nevertheless Cronkite and his CBS colleagues, as well as reporters from the other networks, continued to cover the unfolding Watergate scandal. As much as 14 minutes of Cronkite's half-hour evening news show were at times devoted to the Watergate story. But Cronkite and his staff maintained there was no need to slant or alter the news to make the White House look bad because Nixon and his Administration members did that all by themselves.

Throughout and after the Watergate scandal, Cronkite reigned as America's preeminent newscaster. A poll in 1973 by the Oliver Quayle organization showed that 73% of those surveyed trusted Cronkite, an unusually high percentage for a public figure. Cronkite was described as a "father figure" to millions of Americans who preferred to learn both good and bad news from his broadcasts, delivered in a relaxed and lucid style. By 1973 Cronkite's program was carried by over 200 affiliated CBS stations and seen by an estimated audience of 26 million people. In a business constantly rocked by meteoric rises and equally sudden declines, Cronkite's longevity and his continued and substantial influence remained unequaled.

[PC]

CURRAN, JOSEPH E(DWIN)
b. March 1, 1906; New York, N.Y.
President, National Maritime Union,
1937-73.

Curran, whose father was a cook, went to sea at the age of 16. In 1935 he led a wildcat strike of the crew onboard the SS *California.* The action, although defeated, eventually led to the formation of the National Maritime Union (NMU). Curran was elected its first president in 1937, a position he held for 36 years. After World War II Curran initiated a successful purge of Communists from NMU leadership posts, thereby solidifying his control of the union. In 1960 the Labor Department brought suit under the 1959 Landrum-Griffin Act to challenge Curran's 1960 reelection on the basis of irregularities, but the suit was later dropped. [See TRUMAN, EISENHOWER Volumes]

During the 1950s and 1960s Curran was concerned about the deterioration of the passenger and merchant fleet, a decline that limited the employment opportunities of NMU members. In 1964 President Johnson appointed Curran to the Maritime Advisory Committee, a group charged with formulating proposals to regenerate the nation's merchant marine. Curran dissented sharply from the Committee's conclusions, however. During the Johnson Administration Congress failed to take action to strengthen the shipping industry. [See KENNEDY, JOHNSON Volumes]

By the end of the 1960s, Curran faced a serious challenge to his leadership. His 1968 reelection to the NMU presidency was set aside by the Labor Department because of serious irregularities, and a new election was ordered for January 1969. The dissidents, led by union members James M. Morrissey and Richard J. Haake, accused Curran and other union officials of receiving inordinately high salaries and of misusing the union's pension funds. Morrissey also charged the union leadership with obstructing distribution of the dissidents' campaign literature. When the votes were counted, Curran easily won reelection. Morrissey

appealed the results in federal court, but in April 1969 a district court judge upheld the outcome.

Curran supported the Nixon Administration's legislative proposals to strengthen the nation's merchant marine. In a basic revision of recent federal maritime policy, Nixon proposed in October 1969 a 10-year, $3.8 billion program of subsidies to rebuild the U.S. merchant fleet. The amount requested represented a threefold increase in operating subsidies for the shipping industry. Curran lavishly praised the initiative and in March 1970 testified in support of the legislation at Senate hearings. However, despite heavy lobbying by shippers, the NMU and other maritime unions, the legislation approved by Congress in September and signed by President Nixon was significantly weaker than the original proposal. Only one billion dollars was appropriated for a 10-year period, and the law stipulated that government subsidies be gradually reduced.

Still faced with a weak bargaining position and declining job opportunities for its membership, a situation exacerbated by the phasing out of America's involvement in Vietnam, the NMU and five other maritime unions announced in February 1972 an agreement to work toward labor stability in the shipping industry as a way of stemming the flow of jobs to foreign ships. The agreement, which in effect constituted a no-strike pledge, followed the settlement of a West Coast longshoremen's strike, the longest maritime strike in history.

In March Curran announced that the NMU had reached agreement on a new labor contract well in advance of the June 15 expiration date. The contract provided able seamen with a base pay of $529 a month (leaving them the lowest paid maritime workers) and a $300 a month pension for seamen who retired after the age of 55 with 20 years of service. Dissidents in the union attacked the provisions as a sellout of the union's membership.

Early in 1973 Curran announced that he would not seek another term as president. When it was revealed that he would receive about $1 million in severance pay and lump-sum pension benefits, his opponents in the union seized upon this as evidence of the leadership's corruption. Morrissey, again running for office, accused Curran and other union officials of "raiding" the union treasury. Forced to back down Curran eventually retired with $419,000 in benefits.

The campaign to choose Curran's successor was a heated one, however. One candidate, Andy Dinko, was shot and seriously injured on May 1. Dinko later revealed that he had received an anonymous threat and demand that he abandon his campaign. When the ballots were counted in June 1973, Curran's handpicked choice, Shannon J. Wall, was declared the winner.

[JD]

CURTIS, CARL T(HOMAS)
b. March 15, 1905; Minden, Neb.
Republican Senator, Neb., 1955-79

After attending the University of Nebraska and teaching school for a short time, Curtis studied law and was admitted to the bar in 1930. He was elected to the House of Representatives in 1938, where he served for 16 years before moving to the Senate in 1955. During his career, Curtis was widely viewed as one of the Senate's most conservative members on social, economic and foreign policy issues. Coming from a state considered the most Republican in the Union, he frequently joined Southern Democrats in thwarting spending programs for the disadvantaged. He was a strong supporter of President Johnson's Vietnam policies. [See EISENHOWER, KENNEDY, JOHNSON, Volumes]

Curtis favored Richard Nixon in 1968 for the Republican presidential nomination and backed the new President's handling of the Vietnam war as well as his defense policy. He voted for most major military spending programs including the Safeguard anti-ballistic missile system. Curtis sought to avoid tying the hands of the President in the execution of foreign policy, opposing a 1973 appropriations bill that prohibited the use of funds for bombing Cambodia, as well as the Cooper-Church Amendment in 1970 restricting presidential authority to conduct military operations in Cambodia.

Curtis held no such reservations when it came to funding for domestic programs. He was one of the most powerful members of the Finance Committee because of his attendance record. (Many liberal Dememocrats on the Committee were frequently absent). He opposed deficit spending and supported legislation to put the federal government on a pay-as-you-go basis in the absence of war or a grave national emergency. Curtis voted against the 20% increase in Social Security payments proposed in 1972, despite the fact that Nebraska had a high proportion of elderly people. He went on record against Nixon's 1973 budget proposal because of its $25.5 billion deficit.

Curtis resigned his post on the Government Operations Committee in 1969 to accept a position on the Agriculture and Forestry Committee. In that capacity he favored the generous spending of federal funds aimed at raising farm income, although he objected to such programs as food stamps. He sought a limitation on meat imports as well as legislation to create a rural affairs council. He helped write the Rural Development Act of 1972 to assist rural communities in their search for new industries.

Curtis voted for the nominations of William Rehnquist [q.v.], Clement Haynsworth [q.v.] and G. Harrold Carswell [q.v.] to the Supreme Court, cosponsored anti-abortion legislation in 1973 and voted against extension of the Office of Economic Opportunity. Generally considered anti-labor, Curtis sought to exempt businesses having 25 or fewer employees from provisions of the Occupational Safety and Health Act, which was designed to protect workers against hazardous job conditions.

During the Watergate controversy Curtis was a firm supporter of Nixon and in July 1973 he led a delegation of 10 Republican senators who met with Nixon in a show of their support. After Nixon resigned, Curtis approved of his pardon by President Ford. He also endorsed the elevation of Nixon's rival, Nelson Rockefeller [q.v.], to the vice presidency.

Curtis voted for the resumption of aid to Turkey in 1975. The same year he opposed legislation allowing striking workers eligibility for food stamps and establishing a federal consumer protection agency. He lauded President Ford's decision to attack Cambodia to facilitate the release of the merchant ship *Mayaguez*. Curtis beat Senator Jacob Javits [q.v.] by a vote of 23 to 14 for the chairmanship of the Senate Republican Conference, a party policy-making body. At the Republican Convention in 1976, Curtis was a major proponent of the platform plank calling for morality in foreign policy— seen as a not-so-subtle jab at the leadership of Henry Kissinger [q.v.].

Curtis chose not to run for reelection in 1978 and retired at the end of his term.

[GWB]

CUSHMAN, ROBERT E(VERTON), JR.

b. Dec. 15, 1914; St. Paul, Minn.
Deputy Director, Central Intelligence Agency, April 1969-December 1971; Commandant, U.S. Marine Corps, December 1971-May 1975.

Robert Cushman graduated from Annapolis in 1935 and was commissioned a second lieutenant in the Marines. He saw action in World War II as a battalion commander. After the war Cushman spent 12 years in a succession of school, staff and training positions. From 1949 to 1951 he was assigned to the Central Intelligence Agency (CIA). Cushman began a four-year association with Richard M. Nixon in February 1957, when he became Vice President Nixon's assistant for national security affairs. During those years Cushman, then a brigadier general, worked closely with the CIA in addition to advising Nixon on security matters.

Cushman went to Vietnam in April 1967 to succeed Lewis W. Walt as commanding general of the Third Marine Amphibious Force. For the next two years he commanded 163,000 Army and Marine troops in the I Corps Area located in the northernmost provinces of South Vietnam. This was the largest battle command ever given to a Marine officer. During his tour of duty Cushman strongly advocated tactical mobility instead of static seige warfare. He and the Marine command believed that the major goal in Vietnam was the achievement of the pacification program and the primary task of the military was the protection of pacification areas.

In April 1969 President Nixon named Cushman deputy director of the CIA. The Agency's director was Richard M. Helms [q.v.], a civilian and career CIA officer. The law provided that a civilian must hold the position of either director or deputy director, and the traditional practice was to divide the two posts between the civilian and the military. Cushman's major responsibility was to represent the CIA on the United States Intelligence Board, the National Security Council's central coordinating committee for the intelligence community. In 1971 following the reform of the CIA, Helms turned over many of the operating responsibilities to Cushman.

In December 1971 Nixon chose Cushman to replace the retiring Gen. Leonard F. Chapman, Jr., as commandant of the Marine Corps. When he took command, the armed services had suffered a decline in morale because of the Vietnam war, and defense spending cutbacks had made decisions about priorities all the more difficult. At the time the nation was heading toward volunteer military service, forcing each branch to do more to attract recruits. Cushman joined many Marine leaders in advocating a return to the traditionally smaller, more elite Corps. He identified one of his most serious tasks as that of assuring fair treatment for blacks. Recent years had witnessed persistent racial problems between black and white military personnel. In July 1972 Cushman issued a sweeping order that banned segregation practices in the Corps, even where segregation was voluntary.

In early May 1973 E. Howard Hunt, Jr. [q.v.] testified before a Washington grand jury investigating the Watergate break-in that the CIA had given him and G. Gordon Liddy [q.v.] assistance in preparing for the September 1971 burglary of the office of Daniel Ellsberg's [q.v.] former psychiatrist, Lewis J. Fielding, in Los Angeles. *The New York Times* reported May 7 that Cushman, as deputy director of the CIA, provided Hunt and Liddy with false identification papers, disguises, a tape recorder and a miniature camera. This aid, *The Times* said, came at the request of the President's domestic adviser John D. Ehrlichman [q.v.], who had been ordered by Nixon in 1971 to investigate a series of national security leaks.

On May 9 CIA Director James Schlesinger [q.v.] told a Senate subcommittee the Agency had been unaware that Hunt and Liddy were preparing to break into Fielding's office. He noted that aid to Hunt and Liddy had been discontinued one week before the break-in occurred because Cushman was becoming "increasingly concerned" over Hunt's repeated requests for assistance. Two days later Cushman confirmed before a series of House and Senate panels that he had provided aid in July 1971 to Hunt at the request of Ehrlichman.

Later in the month Ehrlichman denied before a Senate subcommittee having called Cushman about Hunt. In response to the Ehrlichman denial, Cushman told a news conference that a search of records had turned up minutes of a daily CIA staff meeting for July 8, 1971. Cushman said he had mentioned at the meeting a conversation with Ehrlichman the day before about giving aid to Hunt. In August, Cushman produced for the Senate Watergate Committee the transcript of a conversation he had had with Hunt in his CIA office on July 22. The conversation indicated that Ehrlichman had made the call to Cushman. In his testimony Cushman insisted that he did not know that Hunt intended to use the equipment to break into Fielding's office. He contended

that he did not learn of the break-in until it was made public on April 27, 1973, during Ellsberg's trial for releasing the *Pentagon Papers* to the press.

Cushman retired in May 1975.

[SF]

DALEY, RICHARD J(OSEPH)
b. May 15, 1902; Chicago, Ill.
d. Dec. 20, 1976; Chicago, Ill.
Mayor, Chicago, Ill. 1955–76.

Born in a blue-collar district of Chicago, Daley worked his way up the city's Democratic political machine. At the age of 21, he was a precinct captain for Chicago's Democrats. He rose to head the Cook County Democrat organization, the machine that dominated Chicago politics. In 1955 he was elected mayor of Chicago, a post which he successfully won in six consecutive elections. He held jointly the positions of mayor of Chicago and head of the Cook County Democratic organization. He was responsible for encouraging a revitalization of downtown Chicago. Funds from local, state and national government agencies and private sources poured into Chicago's development projects. At the time that other cities were experiencing immense decay, Chicago was undergoing a rebirth.

By 1968 Daley's power had begun to ebb; he was frequently labeled "the last of the bosses" by the media. In that year he reacted strongly to the riots that took place in Chicago in the aftermath of the assassination of Dr. Martin Luther King [q.v.] and gave his famous "shoot to kill" order to police in dealing with arsonists. Daley's role at the Democratic Party Convention in Chicago gave him further national attention. He was blamed by critics for creating the conditions that led to fighting between police and anti-war activists outside the convention hall. It was the television coverage given to this conflict that contributed to the defeat of Hubert Humphrey [q.v.], the Party's presidential standard-bearer. [See JOHNSON Volume]

Although he had exercised an important role in national politics, the 1968 Democratic National Convention was the high mark of his national influence. In part because of the reaction against the manipulations of Daley during the 1968 Convention, reforms were instituted in the Democratic Party nominating procedures requiring representation of minorities in state delegations. Daley refused to comply with the new rules for selecting delegates to the 1972 Democratic Convention. As a result his delegation was not seated. Instead a group led by William Singer, an independent Democrat, and Rev. Jesse Jackson [q.v.], the black leader of Operation PUSH, unseated the Daley-dominated delegation. Daley could not get along with the Democratic presidential nominee George McGovern [q.v.], and his liberal supporters, and the antagonism was mutual. Daley, however, supported McGovern in the election.

After the disastrous McGovern defeat of 1972, Daley was welcomed back into national Democratic Party influence. He played a major role at the Democratic miniconvention in Kansas City in 1974. At the meeting the Party adopted a charter that proscribed mandatory quotas for delegations to the 1980 National Convention and limited the ability of groups to challenge delegations on the basis of delegation composition or primary results. In 1976 his support of Jimmy Carter [q.v.] for the presidential nomination was slow in coming, although he actively endorsed him in the election. However, Gerald Ford carried Illinois in the contest against Carter.

From the time he rose to power as Cook County chairman in 1953, Daley always exercised an important role in state and local matters. His power even in these areas showed signs of deteriorating after 1968. In the Democratic primary of 1972, Dan Walker defeated the mayor's choice for gubernatorial candidate and went on to win the election. In that same year, moreover, Daley's choice for state's attorney also lost.

When the Nixon Administration assumed power, it appointed James Thompson as U.S. Attorney for the Chicago dis-

trict. Many of Daley's closest lieutenants were indicted and convicted on federal and county charges of conspiracy and bribery. The news that Daley's youngest son may have been involved in receiving local government insurance contracts for his firm further weakened the reputation of the mayor. In 1976 Thompson defeated the Daley-backed gubernatorial candidate.

In 1974 Daley suffered a stroke and was out of any active involvement in politics for four months. It was believed that he would not run for reelection. He did, in fact, run again and despite the opposition of Chicago newspapers, was reelected handily. He died of a heart attack in December 1976 after serving 22 years as mayor of Chicago.

In the Nixon years, Daley was a controversial figure. His activities in the 1968 Chicago riots and at the Democratic Convention identified him in the public mind as a "law and order" man. Those who admired Daley argued that because of him "Chicago works." Streets would be cleaned, potholes filled and vast new construction projects undertaken. His opponents, however, blamed him for presiding over a corrupt city government, weakening civil liberties, neglecting the needs of Chicago's black population and making Chicago the most segregated big city in America.

[HML]

DASH, SAMUEL
b. Camden, N.J.
Chief Counsel, Senate Watergate Committee, 1973–74.

The son of immigrant Russian Jews, Dash graduated from Temple University in 1947 and Harvard Law School in 1950. Following a year as a teaching associate at Northwestern University, he served as a trial lawyer for the Justice Department. Dash was appointed district attorney of Philadelphia in 1955. The next year he went into private practice. In 1959 he published *The Eavesdroppers,* a study of electronic surveillance. In 1965 Dash joined the faculty of the Georgetown University Law Center.

In February 1973 Dash was chosen by Sen. Sam Ervin (D, N.C.) [q.v.] to serve as chief counsel of the Senate Select Committee established to investigate the Watergate incident. Dash was given considerable independence to select his own staff, eventually numbering over 40, and investigate the facts wherever they led. Dash, for the first time in a congressional investigation, used a computer to keep track of the massive amounts of information generated by the Watergate inquiry.

The first break in the investigation came at the end of March when Judge John Sirica [q.v.] disclosed the contents of a letter from James McCord [q.v.], one of the Watergate burglars. Dash met secretly with McCord who informed him that Jeb Magruder [q.v.], second in command of the President's reelection campaign, had perjured himself when testifying that he knew nothing about Watergate. In an effort to get other participants to come forward with information, Dash informed the press that McCord had identified more persons involved in the scandal.

In May, Dash began meeting secretly with John Dean [q.v.], former counsel to President Nixon, to determine if the Committee should offer him immunity in return for testifying. In an unorthodox procedure Dash promised Dean he would tell no one, except Ervin, what was said in the interviews. This meant that the Committee would have to follow Dash's recommendation concerning immunity without any other information. Dash recommended immunity. The Committee approved it over the opposition of Sens. Howard Baker (R, Tenn.) [q.v.] and Edward Gurney (R, Fla.) [q.v.]. Baker and Gurney subsequently changed their votes in order to present a unified image to the public.

Working closely with Ervin, Dash began planning for public hearings to begin in May 1973. They hoped to educate as many people as possible on the threat that Watergate posed to the democratic proc-

ess. Dash wanted television coverage. He proposed they start with little-known witnesses who could gradually provide the necessary background for the public to understand the testimony of the major witnesses.

The nationally televised hearings opened on May 17. Dash helped Ervin prepare his opening statement, which warned of the threat to democracy posed by the affair and stressed that the purpose of the hearings was broadly educational, not prosecutorial. Throughout the hearings Dash was well prepared on the complex facts of the case and usually began cross-examination of witnesses. He also supplied senators on the Committee with questions ahead of time.

In the first week of June, Archibald Cox [q.v.], special Watergate prosecutor, requested a suspension of the Watergate Committee's hearings, arguing that they jeopardized the pending criminal proceedings. Dash strongly opposed this move, asserting that the Committee had a much broader responsibility than the courts, namely, to publicly expose all the facts and recommend remedial legislation. The Committee voted to refuse Cox's request. A few days later Dash argued before Judge Sirica against a motion by Cox to limit the hearings. Dash won. Sirica denied Cox's motion and granted Dean and Magruder immunity before the Committee.

At the end of June, Dean began his testimony by reading a 245-page statement that Dash had helped him prepare. This statement linked President Nixon directly to a cover-up of Watergate. At the beginning of Dash's cross-examination, he forced Dean to admit that he had personally participated in the cover-up. (Later Dash wrote a letter to Judge Sirica recommending a lenient sentence for Dean because of his cooperation with the Committee.)

In the first week of July, Dash secretly agreed to share the mountain of information collected by his staff with the House Judiciary Committee, which was considering an impeachment inquiry.

In the middle of July, Dash's staff uncovered the existence of a taping system at the White House, a fact subsequently revealed in the public hearings. After Nixon rejected a request for certain tapes, the Committee issued a subpoena. When Nixon refused to comply, the Committee filed suit in federal district court to force the President to relinquish the tapes. In October, Judge Sirica ruled against the suit on the grounds that the Committee had failed to prove the amount in controversy exceeded $10,000, a requirement for a civil suit to be tried in federal court. Dash appealed the decision but lost. Even though the Committee subpoenaed many more conversations, they never succeeded in obtaining a single presidential tape. (Eventually the special prosecutor, Cox, and the House Judiciary Committee did succeed.)

The first phase of the hearings ended on Aug. 7, 1973, after 33 witnesses had been heard and 7,537 pages of testimony had been compiled. At the end of September the Committee reopened hearings covering questionable campaign contributions and "dirty tricks" during the 1972 elections. Since Dash's staff was still in the midst of these investigations, the evidence was fragmentary, and the procedures never captured the public's attention like the summer hearings. The second phase of hearings adjourned in late November. In February 1974 the Committee voted to end public hearings on Watergate, yielding to the courts and the House impeachment inquiry.

Dash played an important role in writing the final report of the Committee, which was made public in July 1974. The report summarized the factual evidence of wrongdoing and made over 40 recommendations for legal and institutional reform. Among the Committee's major proposals were: an independent and permanent office of "public attorney" with powers similar to those of the Watergate special prosecutor; a federal elections commission with supervisory and enforcement powers; limits on cash campaign contributions by individuals, reforms in reporting procedures and restrictions on solicitation of campaign funds by presidential staff; and tightening of laws involving use of federal agencies to aid the election of candidates. A year later Dash testified before the Senate Government Operations Committee recommending Watergate reform legislation. In a book on Watergate published in 1976 Dash expressed strong disappointment that more had not been done to prevent future Watergates.

After his service on the Committee, Dash went back to his position as professor of law and director of the Institute of Criminal Law and Procedure at the Georgetown University Law Center.

[TFS]

For further information:
Samuel Dash, *Chief Counsel: Inside the Ervin Committee - The Untold Story of Watergate* (New York 1976).

DAVIS, ANGELA Y(VONNE)
b. Jan. 26, 1944; Birmingham, Ala.
Political activist.

The daughter of schoolteachers, Angela Davis grew up in a segregated neighborhood in Birmingham, Ala. With her mother she took part in civil rights demonstrations during the mid-1950s. In 1959 she moved to New York City to attend a private high school on an American Friends Service Committee scholarship. Davis recieved her B.A. from Brandeis University in 1965. After two years of graduate study in West Germany she enrolled in 1967 in the philosophy department of the University of California at San Diego to study under the Marxist philosopher Herbert Marcuse. Within two years Davis, whose gifted intellect was widely acknowledged by her professors, had completed all of the requirements for a doctorate except her dissertation.

Throughout these years of study Davis was steadily becoming more radical politically. While in Paris, she was friendly with Algerian revolutionaries. Strongly influenced by Marcuse's criticism of industrial capitalist society, Davis became increasingly active in the militant black power movement in California. In June 1968 she joined the Communist Party.

Immediately after Davis was hired by the philosophy department of the University of California at Los Angeles in 1969, she became the focus of controversy. When a Los Angeles newspaper revealed that she was a member of the Communist Party, the California Board of Regents refused to approve her appointment despite the favorable recommendation of the faculty and the university chancellor. In October 1969 she was reinstated by court order, but the Regents would not renew her contract at the end of the year, and this time the courts upheld their decision.

Davis, meanwhile, had thrown herself into the work of the Soledad Brothers Defense Committee. The "Soledad brothers" were three black convicts, including prison activist George Jackson, who was accused of murdering a white prison guard. After receiving numerous threats to her life, Davis legally bought several guns. On Aug. 7, 1970, Jackson's younger brother Jonathan entered the Marin County courthouse in San Rafael, Calif. where a black convict was on trial. With the guns purchased by Davis, he freed the defendant and seized five hostages including the judge and district attorney. A shootout followed and Jackson, the judge and two inmates were killed.

Because the guns were owned by her, Davis was indicted on charges of murder, kidnapping and conspiracy (under California law, an accessory to a capital crime is considered as equally guilty as the perpetrator). After going into hiding, she was placed on the FBI's 10-most-wanted list and became the object of a nation-wide search. Arrested in a New York City motel on Oct. 13, 1970, she was extradited to California.

Davis's trail quickly became an international cause celebre, with demonstrations in her support occurring around the world. After several procedural delays the trial finally began in March 1972. The prosecutor charged that Davis's motive in supplying the fatal weapons was "a passion for George Jackson" that "knew no bounds," but Davis dismissed the argu-

ment as evidence of "male chauvinism." On June 4, 1972, the jury acquitted her on all counts.

Davis continued to be a controversial figure. Elected to the Central Committee of the Communist Party (the Party's governing body) in 1972, she undertook a worldwide speaking tour during which she denounced the U.S. criminal justice system and called for socialism in the United States. In 1975 she taught at Claremont College in California, and in 1976 at Stanford. In both cases angry alumni threatened to withdraw their financial support.

Davis was actively involved in support of Joanne Little, a North Carolina black woman accused of murdering a white prison guard, and of the "Wilmington 10," civil rights activists appealing their 1972 convictions on charges of arson and conspiracy. In 1974 she published *Angela Davis: An Autobiography*.

[JD]

For further information:
Bettina Aptheker, *Morning Breaks: The Trial of Angela Davis* (New York, 1975).

DEAN, JOHN (WESLEY) III
b. Oct. 14, 1938; Akron, Ohio.
Counsel to the President, July
1970-April 1973.

John Dean lived with his family in Akron and in Evanston, Ill., before they settled down in Greenville, Pa., where his father was president of the Jamestown Manufacturing and Machine Co. Dean attended Staunton Military Academy in Virginia, Colgate University and Wooster College in Ohio, graduating from Wooster in 1961. He enrolled in American University's Graduate School in government and married the daughter of Sen. Thomas Hennings (D, Mo.) before he entered Georgetown Law School in 1962. After receiving his law degree in 1965, Dean became an associate with Welch and Morgan, a Washington law firm specializing in communications law. After six months Dean was fired for an outside business involvement that his employer considered a conflict of interest.

Following this mishap, Dean acquired a succession of political jobs and became known as a capable staff man who, according to Patrick Anderson in *The New York Times*, "always, always pleased the boss" and "never, never exceeded his authority." His first position was chief counsel to the Republican minority on the House Judiciary Committee. In mid-1967, under the sponsorship of Rep. Richard Poff (R, Va.), Dean became associate director of the National Commission on the Reform of Federal Criminal Law. In the 1968 presidential campaign Dean helped write position papers on crime for candidate Richard Nixon's "law and order" campaign. Brought into the Justice Department by Deputy Attorney General Richard Kleindienst [q.v.] after Nixon's election, Dean worked closely with Attorney General John Mitchell [q.v.] in the Administration's drug-control and crime bills.

In July 1970 Dean moved to the White House with the title of Counsel to the President, the post formerly held by John Ehrlichman [q.v.]. Dean did not inherit Ehrlichman's power and prominence, however. He had little authority, rarely saw the President, and was originally confined to dealing with relatively trivial matters. Dean sought to expand his little "law firm," he recounted in his book, *Blind Ambition*, by making his office's advice available to White House staff members on any subject they requested, from the technicalities of divorce and immigration laws, and possible conflicts of interest on the part of White House staffers to the propriety of suing or otherwise harassing certain magazines critical of the Nixon Administration.

The counsel's office built up a reputation for intelligence investigations as well. "I became the White House collecting point for anti-war intelligence reports, and I funneled information directly to the President during emergencies," particularly during the May 1971 "Mayday" demonstrations when thousands of anti-war protestors descended on Washington and disrupted government functions. By 1972 Dean had won the confidence of Nixon assistants Ehrlichman and H. R. Haldeman [q.v.] and was regularly chosen to handle important and sensitive assignments, such as interviewing potential nominees to the Supreme Court. Dean also sought to discover evidence that a memo written by Dita Beard [q.v.], an International Telephone and Telegraph Co. lobbyist, was a forgery. The memo stated that ITT had contributed $400,000 to the Republican Party in return for a favorable antitrust settlement. However the FBI confirmed the authenticity of the document.

Soon after the break-in on June 17, 1972 by agents of the Committee to Reelect the President (CREEP) at the Watergate offices of the Democratic National Committee, Dean became engaged in the strenuous effort by the White House to conceal the responsibility of high CREEP officials for the planning of the crime. The White House strategy was to contain the criminal investigation at a low level—the high-level CREEP officials denied any involvement while the seven men caught and ultimately convicted for the break-in did not reveal the source of their orders in the CREEP hierarchy.

Under the general direction of Haldeman and Ehrlichman, Dean orchestrated the day-to-day cover-up of responsibility for the Watergate break-in. As the White House liaison with the Justice Department investigators, he passed along information to CREEP officials and coordinated their denials and cover stories. He also supervised payments of "hush money" to the arrested burglars. "The cover-up blistered on," he wrote, "with me throwing water on it. Each day brought threats, dramas and more legal strategies. Clandestine conversations with [Herbert] Kalmbach [q.v.] and [Fred] LaRue [q.v.] about hush money . . . Constant messages between [John] Mitchell and the White House. Crisis calls from [Charles] Colson [q.v.] and [Robert] Mardian [q.v.]. Coaching sessions for the witnesses being interviewed by FBI agents or paraded before the grand jury." Dean wrote: "I was not the source of authority for the cover-up, yet I became the linchpin." In October Dean worked vigorously to block an investigation of the break-in by Rep. Wright Patman's (D, Tex.) [q.v.] Banking and Currency Committee. The effort succeeded, ending any chance of a congressional inquiry before the elections. By the time of Nixon's reelection in November Dean had managed to keep a lid on the Watergate investigation.

Dean was first propelled into the public spotlight in February 1973 during Senate confirmation hearings on the nomination of Acting FBI Director L. Patrick Gray [q.v.]. Gray revealed to the Judiciary Committee that he had passed FBI investigative reports to Dean and that Dean had sat in on FBI interviews with White House personnel. The Committee asked Dean to appear and testify before it, but Nixon refused to allow his aide to appear in person, citing the doctrine of executive privilege on which Dean had been his chief adviser. The jockeying between the Committee and the President over Dean's appearance ended with Gray's withdrawal of his name from nomination on April 5.

In February and March Dean, for the only time in his career as Counsel, met frequently with Nixon. The two discussed, among other things, the cover-up and the criminal liabilities of White House and CREEP officials. Facing the probability of eventual prosecution for his own heavy involvement in the cover-up, Dean began meeting secretly with prosecutors in April, relating his knowledge of cover-up to them, except for Nixon's involvement. During this period Dean in effect broke from his White House superiors. On April 19 the *Washington Post* published a letter from Dean in which he declared he would not become a "scapegoat" in the Watergate case. On April 30 Nixon announced that he had accepted the resignations of Haldeman, Ehrlichman, Dean, and Kleindienst. In contrast to his praise of Haldeman and Ehrlichman as "two of the finest public servants it has been my privilege to know," Nixon merely said of Dean that he

had "requested and accepted" the resignation of his counsel.

On June 12 Judge John Sirica [q.v.] granted Dean "testimonial" immunity for his upcoming testimony before the Senate Watergate Committee, meaning that no evidence derived from Dean's testimony could be used in prosecuting him. The prosecutors consistently rebuffed Dean's attempts to gain complete immunity from prosecution, however. At a subsequent appearance before the grand jury, Dean repeatedly invoked the Fifth Amendment to protect himself from self-incrimination.

Dean was the star witness of the Watergate Committee, the first to accuse Nixon of involvement in the cover-up. From June 25-29 he testified before the Committee and a national television audience in a dry monotone that belied the startling nature of his testimony. Dean commenced his testimony by reading a 245-page account detailing his own involvement in the cover-up conspiracy, the involvement of his colleagues, and his discussions with Nixon. He testified that on Sept. 15, 1972, Nixon had congratulated him for containing the investigation of the break-in. In February and March, Dean related, he had discussed with Nixon the possibility of executive clemency for some of the conspirators and "hush money" payments to maintain the cover-up. Nixon told him the money was "no problem" on March 13. On March 21, Dean said, he told Nixon there was a "cancer growing on the Presidency" and that he doubted whether continued perjury and payments could maintain the cover-up, but Nixon did not appear concerned.

Dean calmly refuted attacks on his credibility by the White House and hostile Committee members. The White House charged Dean with being the "mastermind" of the cover-up, but Dean insisted that his main role was as a conduit between Haldeman and Ehrlichman and CREEP. Under questioning by Sen. Edward Gurney (R, Fla.) [q.v.], Dean admitted that he had used, and replaced, Republican funds from his safe to finance his honeymoon. Gurney's hostile questioning, however, was unable to shake Dean's account of Nixon's knowledge of the cover-up. Gurney called Dean a "shoddy turncoat," but Sen. Joseph Montoya (D, N.M.) [q.v.] voiced the majority opinion that Dean was "a very credible witness."

Along with his testimony Dean submitted 47 documents to the Committee. One, the Nixon "enemies list," created a minor sensation in the press. The enemies list contained names of individuals, largely liberal Democrats, deemed "enemies" of the Nixon Administration for their political postures and activities. In an August 1971 memo Dean had suggested to his superiors ways in which "we can use the available federal machinery to screw our political enemies." Techniques included denial of federal grants and contracts, litigation, prosecution, and harassment by the Internal Revenue Service, among others.

Through the rest of the summer former Nixon Administration officials appeared before the · Committee and disputed Dean's version of events. On July 16 it was first revealed that Nixon had been taping his White House conversations. The tapes, played subsequently during the trial of the Watergate conspirators and the House impeachment hearings, ultimately confirmed Dean's account down to the smallest details.

On Oct. 19, Dean pleaded guilty to a single count of conspiring to obstruct justice. The plea was part of a bargain with Special Prosecutor Archibald Cox [q.v.] whereby Dean agreed to be a prosecution witness in return for Cox's promise not to bring further charges against him, except in the case of perjury. On Aug. 2, 1974 Judge Sirica sentenced Dean to one to four years in prison. He began serving his sentence on Sept. 3. On Oct. 2 Dean was barred from practicing law by the District of Columbia Court of Appeals.

Most of Dean's prison sentence was spent either in preparing to testify at the Watergate conspirators' trial, testifying, or waiting to be called to the stand. Two of the prosecutors wrote that he was "the most conscientious witness anyone connected with Watergate had ever seen" and marvelled at his retentive memory. In October 1974 Dean, the key witness, testified for eight days at the cover-up trial of Ehrlichman, Haldeman, John Mitchell, Robert Mardian, and Kenneth Parkinson [q.v.]. He told the same basic story he had related before the Watergate committee. The jury convicted all the defendants except Parkinson on Jan. 1, 1975.

On Jan. 8 Judge Sirica ordered Dean and two other Watergate figures, Herbert Kalmbach and Jeb Stuart Magruder [q.v.] freed from prison, having reduced their sentences to time already served. No longer able to practice law, Dean embarked upon a career as a writer. In October 1976 he published *Blind Ambition*, a regretful account of his White House years that presented an unflattering picture of Dean and his associates and quickly became a best-seller. In the same month Dean once again shook up a Republican Administration with a scandalous revelation. Covering the Republican National Convention for *Rolling Stone* magazine, Dean reported a conversation with a Cabinet officer, soon revealed to be Secretary of Agriculture Earl Butz [q.v.], in which Butz made jocular racial slurs against blacks. The story generated a storm of criticism against Butz, who resigned a few days later.

[TO]

For further information:
Richard Ben-Veniste and George Frampton, Jr., *Stonewall: The Legal Case Against the Watergate Conspirators* (New York, 1977).
John Dean, *Blind Ambition: The White House Years* (New York, 1976).

DENT, FREDERICK B(AILY)
b. Aug. 17, 1922; Cape May, N.J.
Secretary of Commerce, January 1973–March 1975.

Dent took his B.A. at Yale in 1943 and served the following three years in the Navy. After completing his military service he took a job with a family firm, the

Joshua A. Baily Co. of New York, and in 1947 went to work for Mayfair Mills, a textile company in South Carolina.

As the U.S. textile industry began to feel the increasing pressure of foreign imports, Dent became an industry spokesman and a critic of prevailing laissez-faire attitudes. In 1970, while serving as chairman of the Committee on International Trade of the American Textile Manufacturers' Institute, Dent attacked trade negotiations then underway between the U.S., Japan and other textile-producing nations, calling for an immediate termination of the talks and for legislation establishing an "effective, comprehensive, qualitative limitation on imports of all textile articles." A year later, when Japan agreed to voluntarily curtail textile exports to the U.S., the textile trade association called the move "worse than no agreement at all," and Dent called on President Nixon and Congress "to disavow and disregard the proposal and continue working for a real solution."

Dent's appointment to the post of Secretary of Commerce, in late 1972, represented a concession to domestic producers eager for tariff protection against foreign competition. After assuming office in January 1973, however, Dent was plunged immediately into the growing raw material and agricultural shortages that surfaced in the hyperinflationary boom conditions of that year. In June 1973, with Secretary of Agriculture Earl Butz [q.v.], Dent placed export controls on soybeans and cottonseed to prevent a domestic livestock feed shortage. In July Dent extended the controls to 41 other farm commodities. Several weeks later he was one of two cabinet-level officials to attend the annual conference of the Joint Japan-United States Committee on Foreign Affairs, at which the Japanese delegation attempted to assure Japan of a "stable supply" of key commodities.

Dent was also involved in the wider aspects of the Administration's economic policy. In August 1973 President Nixon instituted the Phase 4 plan which ended the price freeze then in effect and instituted a system of mandatory compliance with a regimen of price controls. Shortly afterward Dent told a conference of U.S. businessmen that Phase 4 would be a "phase out" of controls and announced an imminent return to a free market economy. He accompanied Secretary of Treasury George Shultz [q.v.] to Belgrade for trade talks in October 1973 and held further talks in Moscow and Sofia as part of the Administration's overall detente effort. In March 1974 Dent became briefly embroiled in a legal battle with the General Accounting Office (GAO) when it questioned the legality of certain Export-Import Bank loans to Eastern European countries, leading to a suspension of the loans on March 11. Dent stated that the GAO's action was endangering jobs in the U.S., and on March 22 the loans were declared legal. As the U.S. economy slid into recession in the fall of 1974, President Ford appointed Dent to the Council on Wage and Price Stability and later to the Economic Policy Board.

In February 1975 Dent was named a U.S. trade negotiator and one month later stepped down as Secretary of Commerce. Once again he became immersed in the protectionist issue. In March 1976 President Ford threatened to impose three-year quotas on U.S. imports of specialty steels unless an "orderly market agreement" could be negotiated with the nation's trading partners. In announcing the move Dent, who had also been appointed a U.S. representative to the General Agreement on Trade and Tariffs in Geneva, expressed the hope that Ford's decision would not "kick off a trade war." A month later Dent announced the President's decision not to implement a similar restriction on nonrubber shoe imports. When in June 1976 Ford did approve import quotas on specialty steel imports, Dent was sent to negotiate an "orderly market agreement" with Japan, after failing to win voluntary export restraint from Sweden and the European Economic Community (EEC) in the same areas.

In 1976 Dent also served on a cabinet-level task force to review U.S. corporate payoffs in overseas operations.

When President Ford left office, Dent stepped down as U.S. trade negotiator and returned to private business.

[LG]

DIGGS, CHARLES C(OLE), JR.
b. Dec. 2, 1922; Detroit, Mich.
Democratic Representative, Mich., 1955-.

Diggs, the first black congressman from Michigan, was the son of a wealthy Detroit undertaker who also served for many years in the Michigan state Senate. His father's popularity in the community boosted Diggs's own political career.

Diggs attended the University of Michigan and Fiske University before entering the Army Air Force in World War II. After the war Diggs entered the family business, one of the state's largest black funeral establishments. He also worked as a disc jockey and news commentator on the family's weekly radio show. In 1950 Diggs won a seat in the state Senate, and four years later he was elected to the U.S. House.

During the 1960s Diggs's success in winning reelection in the poor, black downtown Detroit district he represented depended less on his voting record, which reflected a high rate of absenteeism, than on services he offered his constituents. His office expedited the delivery of Social Security checks, speeded the processing of Small Business Administration loans and performed numerous minor legal services for voters. [See JOHNSON Volume]

During the Nixon/Ford Administrations, Diggs maintained that he was particularly concerned with legislation designed to protect and extend the rights of minorities. Yet his continued absenteeism limited his effectiveness. He became chairman of the Senate Foreign Relations Committee's African Subcommittee in 1969. As chairman he was an outspoken critic of U.S. policy towards southern Africa, which he felt supported the status quo of white racism and Portugese colo-

nialism. By 1971 Diggs began to push openly for changes in U.S. policy. After being denied a visa to visit Rhodesia, he denounced that government as the "new world's light-heavyweight champion of racism." He warned the Democratic Platform Committee in 1971 that "Southern Africa holds the frightening, but real, potential for another Vietnam." He said that the U.S. must act to avoid a racial holocaust and that U.S. business involvement formed a "bulwark for the status quo for apartheid."

As part of his U.S.-African relations activities, Diggs was involved in a congressional effort to repeal the 1971 "Byrd Amendment," which allowed the U.S. to import chrome from Rhodesia despite United Nations mandatory sanctions for which the U.S. had voted.

In 1971 Diggs's subcommittee made an extensive inquiry into the conduct and nature of American business in South Africa. As a result of the probe, it proposed a resolution to "protect United States domestic and foreign policy interests by making fair employment practices in the South African enterprises of U.S. firms a criteria for eligibility for government contracts." This proposal was reintroduced in the 93rd and 94th Congresses, but was never passed. In 1973, 1974 and 1975 Diggs introduced bills in Congress to prevent U.S. companies in South Africa from practicing racial discrimination with respect to wages, fringe benefits, hiring, and training and advancement opportunities.

As subcommittee chairman, Diggs liberally used his prerogatives to travel, making several trips to Africa and to Europe. After a trip to South Africa and the Portugese colonies of Guinea-Bissau and Cape Verde in 1972, Diggs issued an "Action Manifesto," which he sent to Secretary of State Kissinger [q.v.], urging the U.S. to condemn the use of violence by Portugal and the South African government to remain in power. Among its 55 specific proposals the Manifesto suggested ending Export-Import Bank loan guarantees to South Africa, terminating a U.S. sugar quota for South Africa and a justifying agreement with Portugal over the leasing of a military base in the Azores.

In October 1974, at Diggs's insistence, the House International Relations Committee agreed to hold closed hearings on CIA activities in southern Africa and to include in the hearings investigation of U.S. policy towards the Portugese colonies since the Portugese military coup in the spring of 1974.

In a 1976 interview with *Africa* magazine Diggs commented that "the record of the Ford Administration and its predecessor, the Nixon Administration, in the field of African affairs has left much to be desired, to put it in a kindly context."

In October 1978 Diggs was convicted of mail fraud and falsification of congressional payroll data. He was sentenced the following month to a maximum of three years in prison. Nevertheless in the November 1978 elections, he was returned to the House for a 12th term. [See CARTER Volume]

[MLB]

DIRKSEN, EVERETT McKINLEY
b. Jan. 4, 1896; Pekin, Ill.
d. Sept. 7, 1969; Washington, D.C.
Republican Senator, Ill., 1951–69;
Senate Minority Leader, 1959–69.

A son of German immigrants, Dirksen grew up in the farming town of Pekin, Ill. He entered the University of Minnesota in 1914, but left in 1917 to serve in the Army. He was general manager of the Cook Dredging Co. from 1922 to 1925, when he joined his brothers in a bakery business.

Dirksen was Pekin commissioner of finance from 1927 to 1931. He was elected to the U.S. House in 1932 and served there until 1948. Although opposed to many New Deal domestic measures, Dirksen favored Social Security and minimum wage laws. He was an isolationist in the years prior to American entry into World War II but supported the Marshall Plan during the Truman Administration. Dirksen supported the presidential candidacy of Sen. Robert A. Taft and was a bitter-end supporter of Wisconsin Sen. Joseph McCarthy, opposing that Senator's censure in 1954. Elected to the U.S. Senate from Illinois in 1950, Dirksen rose to become minority whip in 1957 and minority leader in 1959. [See TRUMAN, EISENHOWER Volumes]

The leading conservative in Congress after Sen. Taft's death in 1953, Dirksen insisted upon government economy and devoted his energies to reducing President Eisenhower's budgets. During Eisenhower's second term, he became more cooperative with the moderates in the Republican Party. Known as the "Wizard of Ooze" for his grandiose oratory, Dirksen gained new respectability as Republican leader and "political soothsayer" during the Democratic Administrations of Kennedy and Johnson. In 1963 his support carried the nuclear test-ban treaty through the Senate, and in 1964 he pushed through the epoch-making Civil Rights Act, reversing his previous opposition. He backed the Voting Rights Act of 1965 and the Housing Act of 1968. Despite his opposition to much Democratic social legislation, Dirksen remained a strong supporter of the Presidents' foreign policies, including the Vietnam war. [See KENNEDY, JOHNSON Volumes]

Dirksen was seldom consulted by the President during Nixon's first months in office, and his influence declined during his last months in the Senate. Manifesting an increasingly rigid attitude, he was confronted by "Young Turk" liberal Republicans who sought to displace him from leadership of the Party. He was unanimously reelected minority leader in 1969 but suffered a personal defeat when his candidate for minority whip, conservative Roman L. Hruska [q.v.], was defeated by liberal Hugh Scott [q.v.].

Dirksen generally proved a devoted advocate of the President's domestic and foreign policies. As a member of the Senate Finance Committee, he supported Nixon's efforts to extend the income tax surcharge and, after initial opposition, backed his expensive Safeguard anti-ballistic missile project. He joined the Nixon

Administration's clandestine campaign to force the resignation of Supreme Court Justice Abe Fortas [q.v.] after *Life* magazine disclosed Fortas had accepted a $20,000 fee from the Wolfson Foundation. Dirksen suggest that the Senate Judiciary Committee, to which he belonged, inquire into the matter.

A steadfast supporter of Nixon's Vietnam policy, Dirksen favored a gradual de-escalation of the war and praised the President's announcement in June 1969 that 25,000 U.S. troops would be withdrawn from Vietnam as "the first tangible, specific, immediate step to de-Americanize" the war. He opposed Senate passage of the Fulbright Resolution of June 25, 1969, which prohibited the President from sending troops or money to foreign countries without congressional approval. Serving as a Nixon spokesman, Dirksen announced the President's opposition to any resolution limiting the executive's war powers, but indicated that Nixon preferred the Republican-sponsored Mundt Resolution, which gave the president independent authority in cases of "a direct and immediate threat to the national security." Following Nixon's trip to Rumania and the Far East in August 1969, Dirksen, after meeting with the President, expressed confidence that American involvement in the Vietnam war was drawing to a close. Although he said the President had informed him that further U.S. troop withdrawals were imminent, White House Press Secretary Ronald Ziegler [q.v.] commented that this decision had not yet been made.

Dirksen was less accommodating to Nixon's civil rights policies, regarding them as too liberal. He attacked the Labor Department's decision that a federal program to guarantee jobs for blacks in the construction trades (the "Philadelphia Plan") was legal. On July 8, 1969, he told Nixon that the program violated the Civil Rights Act of 1964 by imposing employment quotas and urged him to postpone its implementation.

Entering Washington's Walter Reed Hospital on Aug. 31 for treatment of a malignant lung tumor, Dirksen died of cardiac arrest on Sept. 7, 1969. The Senate passed a resolution that his body lie in state in the Capitol Rotunda, an honor which until then had been bestowed on only one other senator, Robert A. Taft, in the 20th century. Nixon delivered a 12-minute eulogy there on Sept. 9.

[AES]

For further information:
Neil MacNeil, *Dirksen: Portrait of a Public Man* (New York, 1970).
Charles Roberts, "The Other Ev Dirksen," *Newsweek* (June 16, 1969), pp. 26–28.

DOAR, JOHN M(ICHAEL)
b. Dec. 3, 1921; Minneapolis, Minn.
Special counsel, House Judiciary Committee, 1973-74.

John Doar grew up in New Richmond, Wisconsin, where his father had a successful law practice. He served in the Air Force and attended Princeton University and the University of California at Berkeley's law school. From 1950 to 1960 Doar worked in the family firm. He then joined the Justice Department's Civil Rights Division. Four years later he became assistant attorney general and chief of the division. Doar played a major role in the civil rights movement. [See KENNEDY, JOHNSON Volumes]

In 1968 Doar left government and made his home in New York City. He was elected president of the New York Board of Education that October. A proponent of decentralization, Doar, a Republican, opposed the United Federation of Teachers' (UFT) demands for the same job security standards in the demonstration district as applied in the rest of the city. The episode somewhat tarnished Doar's reputation, since, as some city officials complained, he dragged out the resulting teachers' strike through his intransigence and rigid belief in the morality of his own position. Doar's term as board president ended in 1969. In December 1973, Rep. Peter Rodino (D, N.J.) [q.v.] asked him to join the House Judiciary Committee as special majority counsel.

The Judiciary Committee and Chairman Rodino were about to consider the evidence for the impeachment of President Nixon on Watergate and other matters. It was Doar's responsibility to compile the evidence, working with his own staff and the special counsel to the committee's Republican minority, Albert Jenner. Seeking to avoid publicity and any show of partisanship, Doar carefully put together his case. He preferred to use documents and existing records rather than witnesses. Doar was almost universally considered fair, although some Democrats found him too cautious.

By February 1974 the Committee's work was in full operation with broad subpoena powers from Congress. The two counsels told the committee that violation of criminal law need not be the basis for impeachment. Since the Constitution set no standards, they adopted a general standard from English history, which could include "constitutional wrongs that subvert the structure of government, or undermine the integrity of office and even the Constitution itself." The President's "entire course of conduct in office" as well as individual acts were to be considered. Although some Republicans on the committee believed that only criminality should constitute the basis for impeachment, Doar argued that to confine the case to criminal offenses "may well be to set a standard so restrictive as not to reach conduct that might adversely affect the system of government." For that reason Doar's staff examined not only the Watergate burglary and cover-up—which Nixon always insisted was the only issue at stake—but also the President's taxes and personal finances, "dirty tricks," domestic surveillance activities, the use of federal agencies for political purposes, the secret bombing of Cambodia and the impounding of Congressionally mandated funds.

Doar skillfully directed preparations for the committee's investigation. He successfully opposed a delay in the probe and got the Watergate grand jury's secret report despite the objections of the indict-ed men's lawyers. He would not allow the President's counsel, James D. St. Clair [q.v.], to sit in on pre-hearing staff proceedings. Nonetheless, Doar restrained some committee Democrats who wanted to pressure the White House by an immediate subpoena of White House tapes. He preferred to patiently seek Nixon's compliance and use subpoenas only as a last resort. And in April Doar's firm stance softened enough to allow St. Clair to state his client's case at panel meetings, although cross-examination, which Doar deemed inappropriate to the panel's function (he compared it to that of a grand jury's), was forbidden.

On May 9 Doar began to present the Committee with the evidence for impeachment, deliberately speaking in a boring monotone in order to underscore his nonpartisanship and emphasize the sheer weight of the facts. His performance lasted six weeks, covered 7200 pages of eivdence and listed 650 findings of fact. In early July the first witnesses were heard. By mid-July the committee members were visibly bored and exhausted by the whole process. The presentation of evidence had apparently not been so overwhelming as to move the majority of committee Republicans to favor impeachment. Therefore, although all the evidence had still not been presented, Rodino pressured Doar to present his 306-page summary of evidence with analysis, forcefulness and even some passion.

On July 19 Doar, seconded by Jenner (who would be replaced as minority counsel two days later by a lawyer friendlier to the President's cause), urged a Senate trial of the President on one or more of five impeachment charges: obstruction of justice in the Watergate cover-up; abuse of presidential powers through the invasion of the privacy and civil rights of citizens and the manipulation of government agencies; contempt of Congress and the courts through his defiance of subpoenas for Watergate tapes; denigration of the office of the Presidency through income tax evasion and the use of federal money for personal purposes; and the usurpation of Congress's power (as in the bombing of Cambodia). Doar admitted that, based on the available evidence, it could not be precisely ascertained at what point the President knew about Watergate, but the "enormous crime" at issue was Nixon's "conduct of his office." The counsel asserted that he had "not the slightest bias against President Nixon . . . I would not do him the smallest, slightest injury. But I am not indifferent . . . to this matter of Presidential abuse of power by whatever President." The evidence showed such a systematic "subversion of constitutional government," that "reasonable men acting reasonably would find the President guilty." Doar's speech was uncharacteristically passionate. Many Republicans criticized Doar, but when the committee voted at the end of July, a number of the GOP members joined the Democratic majority to approve three impeachment articles (on the obstruction of justice, the abuse of powers and subpoena defiance). The House impeachment debate was then scheduled for Aug. 18, but on the 9th Nixon resigned.

In 1975 Doar became a partner of the New York law firm of Donovan, Leisure, Newton and Irvine.

[JCH]

For further information:
Elizabeth Drew, *Washington Journal: The Events of 1973-1974* (New York, 1974).
Theodore H. White, *Breach of Faith: The Fall of Richard Nixon* (New York, 1975).

DODD, THOMAS J(OSEPH)
b. May 15, 1907; Norwich, Conn.
d. May 24, 1971; Old Lyme, Conn.
Democratic Senator, Conn., 1959-71.

Thomas Dodd graduated from Providence College in 1930 and Yale Law School three years later. He worked for two years as an FBI agent and then served in the Justice Department as a special assistant to the Attorney General, helping to establish the Department's first Civil Rights Division. After World War II he was named executive trial counsel at the Nuremberg war crimes tribunal.

Twice Dodd unsuccessfully sought the Connecticut gubernatorial nomination in the late 1940s. He was elected to the U.S. House of Representatives in 1952, but lost a U.S. Senate election to incumbent Sen. Prescott Bush (R, Conn.) in 1956. Two years later he won a Senate seat, running on a strong anti-Communist platform and was reelected in 1964. Named to the Judiciary and Foreign Relations Committees, Dodd supported Kennedy Administration legislation on over 60% of all major issues. [See KENNEDY Volume]

Dodd was among the first to call for an expansion of the Vietnam war against the North, and he denounced the war's "fainthearted" critics. In domestic politics Dodd was a liberal, voting for medicare and civil rights legislation and favoring limited control on the sale of firearms. In 1966 the Senate opened hearings on charges of official misconduct by Dodd that had first been alleged in the newspaper columns of Drew Pearson [q.v.] and Jack Anderson [q.v.]. The investigating committee found him guilty of accepting and performing favors, double-billing the Senate for travel expenses and converting over $100,000 in tax-free contributions to his private use. In June 1967 the Senate, in only the seventh such action in its history, voted 92-5 to censure Dodd. However, he retained his seniority and chairmanship of the Juvenile Delinquency Subcommittee and vice chairmanship of the Internal Security Subcommittee. [See JOHNSON Volume]

During the Nixon Administration Dodd maintained his staunch anti-Communist stance and firm support for the war in Vietnam. Considering Greece crucial to the NATO defense network, Dodd successfully opposed in 1969 efforts to cut off military aid to that country's right-wing government. He also opposed moves toward the warming of relations with Peking. In 1970 he voted against both the McGovern-Hatfield and Cooper-Church anti-war Amendments, saying of the former, "This is the same kind of fateful illusion that led Neville Chamberlain and other well-intentioned appeasers of the pre World War II period to believe that they could save human lives by avoiding war in 1938."

Although Dodd's voting record generally supported the Administration's policies, he voted against Nixon's nominees to the Supreme Court, Clement Haynsworth [q.v.] in 1969 and G. Harrold Carswell [q.v.] in 1970. In 1970 he cosponsored with Hugh Scott (R, Pa.) [q.v.] an amendment to the 1965 Voting Rights Act that suspended literacy tests until 1975 and set uniform state residence requirements for voting in presidential elections.

In his position as chairman of the Juvenile Delinquincy Subcommittee, Dodd investigated drug abuse in the military and drug addiction among veterans returning to civilian life. In 1970 he sponsored an omnibus drug-control bill, which was passed by the Senate, designed to reduce the penalities for minor violations while increasing federal powers against illicit narcotics trafficers. The measure contained the controversial "no-knock" provision that allowed agents to enter without warning or identification if they feared evidence would otherwise be destroyed.

In December 1969 the Justice Department had announced that no criminal prosecution was warranted against Dodd on the allegations that resulted in his censure by the Senate. Claiming the decision cleared him of any wrongdoing Dodd decided to run for reelection in 1970. After state Party leaders openly opposed his nomination, Dodd withdrew as a Democratic candidate but ran as an independent. With the liberal Rev. Joseph D. Duffey running on the Democratic ticket, the three-way election was won by Rep. Lowell P. Weicker [q.v.], a moderate Republican. Dodd died in May 1971 at age 64.

[FLM]

DOLE, ROBERT J(OSEPH)
b. July 22, 1923; Russell, Kan.
Republican Senator, Kan., 1969-;
Republican vice-presidential
candidate, 1976.

The son of a grain elevator manager, Dole attended the University of Kansas for two years before enlisting in the Army during World War II. He rose in rank to captain, and was seriously wounded while leading a combat platoon in Italy. Doctors thought that he would never walk again. Despite this prognosis, a combination of will power and physical therapy enabled Dole to walk out of a Veterans Administration hospital, but his right arm remained immobile. Dole received his B.A. from the University of Kansas in 1949 and earned his law degree from the same university in 1952. While in law school, he won a seat as a Republican in the Kansas State House of Representatives. Nine years later he was elected to the U.S. House. He focused his attention on the problems of his farm district, fought to preserve rural domination of the legislature and supported legislation to aid the handicapped. A conservative on most issues, he backed civil rights measures and tax incentives for business to help rebuild cities. In 1968 Dole moved up to the Senate after carrying his state with 60.5% of the vote.

Robert Dole emerged in the early years of the Nixon presidency as the Administration's leading defender. Often known to be arrogant, abrasive and brash, he frequently launched sarcastic attacks on liberals. He once termed Ramsey Clark [q.v.] a left-leaning marshmallow. His biting sarcasm and insulting humor won him few friends on the opposite side of the aisle but did earn him the praise of his conservative colleagues and the White House. Dole took it upon himself to be the most persistent Republican defender of the Vietnam war, the anti-ballistic missile and Nixon's conservative nominations to the Supreme Court. In gratitude for such loyalty, the President appointed Dole chairman of the Republican National Committee in 1971. The selection angered a number of Senate moderates. Republican Sen. William Saxbe [q.v.] of Ohio called Dole "a hatchet man" who was so arrogant he "couldn't sell beer on a troop ship." Throughout 1971 Dole toured the nation speaking for the Party, defending the President's war policies and collecting funds for the upcoming election campaign. He soon found to his dismay that the White House had shut him out of any decision-making role in the 1972 presidential campaign. Thus Dole was able to prove ignorance when responding to any charge that he knew of the Watergate break-in. Following the President's reelection, Dole's relationship with the White House staff was so strained that he resigned in January 1973. During the Watergate controversy Dole warned Nixon against hiding from the people but attacked the press for hounding the President.

In 1974 Dole ran for reelection in a race that emphasized the abortion issue. Dole opposed abortions and favored a constitutional amendment giving the states the right to restrict them. His opponent, Dr. William R. Roy, a Catholic physician who had performed abortions, supported abortions. Right to Life forces descended on Kansas to aid Dole in this test case. Leaflets such as one showing dead fetuses were widely circulated. Dole disclaimed any knowledge of this part of his supporters' campaign, but he refused to disassociate himself from the anti-abortion forces. He carried the state in a close election by 13,000 votes.

Robert Dole had always been on good terms with Gerald Ford, although he had broken with the President over the Nixon pardon in 1974 and Ford's veto of a consumer protection agency bill. At the 1976 Republican Convention, Ford chose Dole to be his vice-presidential running mate. Behind in the polls, the President hoped Dole's abrasive debating style would add color to the campaign. In addition Dole was close to the conservative forces, and Ford hoped his choice would reunite the Party. In the fall campaign Dole, more than Ford, went on the offensive in at-

tacking Jimmy Carter's [q.v.] and Walter Mondale's [q.v.] liberalism.

At Dole's historic Houston debate with his Democratic counterpart, the candidates exchanged verbal jabs on domestic issues. Dole accused the Democratic Party of bankrupting the nation, while Mondale tried to portray his adversary as a heartless conservative who showed no compassion for the poor, the unemployed or the elderly. It is generally believed that Mondale won the debate. Following the defeat of the Republican ticket in November, Dole returned to the Senate. During the first years of the Carter Administration, he led the opposition to the Panama Canal Treaties. [See CARTER Volume]

[JB]

DOUGLAS, WILLIAM O(RVILLE)
b. Oct. 16, 1898; Maine, Minn.
Associate Justice, U.S. Supreme Court, 1939-75.

After an impoverished childhood in Yakima, Wash., Douglas worked his way through Columbia Law School, graduating second in his class in 1925. He became a leading corporate and financial law expert while teaching at Columbia and Yale law schools. As chairman of the Securities and Exchange Commission from 1937 to 1939, Douglas effected a reorganization and reform of the stock exchange. Named to the Supreme Court in March 1939, Douglas used his financial law background over the years to write significant court opinions in the fields of bankruptcy, antitrust and patent law.

Justice Douglas became best known, however, as one of the foremost defenders of individual liberties in the Court's history. He gave a preferred position to the First Amendment and insisted that its guarantees of freedom of belief and expression could not be breached by government. He favored extension of the criminal safeguards in the Bill of Rights to the states and interpreted those rights, such as the right to counsel or the privilege against self-incrimination, very broadly. The Justice also took an expansive view of the guarantee of equal protection. Underlying many of his views was a strong concern for protecting the individual from the power and intrusiveness of big government, especially if the individual was socially or economically disadvantaged and powerless. Any changes in Douglas's position while on the Court were all in the direction of giving greater scope to constitutional liberties. [See TRUMAN, EISENHOWER, KENNEDY, JOHNSON Volumes]

Douglas shared many of his views with Justice Hugo Black [q.v.], and during the 1960s, the two men saw the Court adopt positions they had earlier espoused in dissent. In the late 1960s, however, Douglas surpassed even Black in his protection of individual freedoms, voting, for example, to protect the rights of anti-war and civil rights protesters, of debtors, of welfare recipients and illegitimate children, and of criminal defendants. Outspoken and personally nonconformist, Douglas became a symbol of the liberal judicial activism that characterized the Warren Court. Partly because of that position, he was the target of an impeachment attempt in 1970. On April 15, after the Senate had rejected two of President Richard Nixon's nominees for the Court, House Minority Leader Gerald R. Ford (R, Mich.) launched a move to impeach Douglas for alleged improprieties in his professional conduct. Ford challenged the Justice's association with the Albert Parvin Foundation prior to 1969 and with the Center for the Study of Democratic Institutions. He criticized the views Douglas expressed in his book, *Points of Rebellion*, the publication of excerpts from the book in an allegedly pornographic magazine, and Douglas's participation in several cases in which Ford detected a conflict of interest. A special House Judiciary subcommittee began investigating the charges on April 21. In a report released Dec. 15, the subcommittee cleared Douglas of all the allegations and declared there were no grounds for impeachment.

On the Burger Court Douglas resumed the role he had played earlier in his judicial career of dissenter from the rulings of a more conservative majority. From the 1969 Court term on, he entered far more dissents than any other justice, and he staked out a position as the most liberal member of the high bench. Especially notable were Douglas's numerous dissents from Court decisions refusing to hear cases such as those challenging the legality of the Vietnam war. Douglas favored making the Court an accessible forum where the aggrieved could obtain a remedy for deprivations of their civil and constitutional rights. He urged the Court to take more cases, and he opposed rulings that limited the Court's jurisdiction to decide lawsuits.

Douglas also dissented from many Burger Court criminal decisions. He objected to all rulings that in any way limited the scope of the 1966 *Miranda* decision and to judgments sanctioning warrantless searches and electronic surveillance. In May 1971 and May 1972 dissents, he maintained his position that the Fifth Amendment's privilege against self-incrimination barred the government from compelling anyone to confess to a crime, even with an immunity guarantee. Douglas did join the majority in June 1970 to validate six member juries in state courts, but he opposed a May 1972 decision allowing nonunanimous jury verdicts. He urged the Court to extend the right to a jury to all trials and to juvenile court proceedings. In a June 1972 opinion for the Court, Douglas held that an indigent defendant could not be jailed, even for a misdemeanor, unless given free counsel.

Justice Douglas continued to express his concern for those who were disadvantaged and different from the rest of society. A longtime critic of vagrancy laws, he wrote the majority opinion in a February 1972 case overturning a municipal vagrancy ordinance because it was vague and subject to arbitrary enforcement. The Justice voted to overturn the death penalty in June 1972, largely because under existing laws, judges and juries could discriminate against the poor and minorities in imposing the death sentence. Douglas retained a predominantly activist stance in racial discrimination cases and opposed all forms of discrimination against illegitimate children, the poor and women. In a June 1969 opinion he overturned state laws permitting garnishment of a debtor's wages prior to any hearing. In subsequent cases Douglas voted to guarantee hearings to welfare recipients before termination of their benefits, to parolees before revocation of their parole, and to public employees prior to dismissal. He also favored removing restrictions on the right to vote based on age, residency or status.

In First Amendment cases Douglas adhered to his absolutist position. He opposed all loyalty oaths and obscenity laws in these years and favored giving constitutional protection to a wide variety of symbolic forms of expression such as wearing a black armband or putting a peace symbol on the flag to protest the Vietnam war. He believed freedom of the press was unassailable and voted against the government's request for an injunction to halt newspaper publication of the *Pentagon Papers* in June 1971. Douglas also opposed all state aid to parochial education as a violation of the First Amendment. He was the lone dissenter in May 1970 when the Court upheld tax exemptions for church property used solely for religious purposes.

A dedicated conservationist and naturalist, Douglas wrote several important environmental law opinions. In an April 1973 case he ruled that the states could establish stiffer penalties for maritime oil spills than the federal government. A year later Douglas sustained a municipal zoning ordinance which barred communal living groups. He believed the ordinance a legitimate land use law aimed at preserving a quiet, uncongested residential area. When the majority ruled in April 1972 that the Sierra Club did not have the necessary legal interest to challenge the building of a ski resort in Sequoia National Forest, Douglas entered a widely discussed dissent which argued that inanimate objects such as trees and rivers should be accorded legal standing and be allowed to sue in their own name for their preservation.

Douglas was known to the public not only for his constitutional views but for his many off-the-bench activities. A colorful and controversial figure, he disputed the notion that the Court was overworked and used his free time to travel, to hike and mountain climb and to write and lecture. A vigorous, energetic man when well into his seventies, Douglas suffered a stroke on Dec. 31, 1974. He retired from the Court on Nov. 12, 1975 when he found that the aftereffects of the stroke kept him from performing his share of the Court's work.

By the time of his retirement, Douglas had served more than 36 years on the bench, longer than any other Justice in the Court's history, and had written over 1,200 opinions. His critics attacked many of them, especially in his later years, as brief, often idiosyncratic essays that were devoid of legal analysis and exposition. Douglas himself was charged with being too subjective and doctrinaire and too result-oriented in his approach to cases. The Justice's defenders, however, maintained that he had brought a sense of realism to the Court's work and had tried to keep it from losing sight of important problems in the midst of legal formalities. His opinions, they said, made clear what was at stake in a case and what the Court was doing about it. Whether critical or admiring of Douglas's work, all commentators recognized that he had grown tremendously while on the bench and had a significant impact on the law in fields as varied as citizenship and criminal rights, equality and privacy. A man of powerful intellect, he helped bring the Court to a broader view of First Amendment rights and worked to make the law responsive to the needs of a changing society. Douglas's role "in shaping the Constitution into a more effective shield for the rights of individuals," law professor William Beaney wrote, "and in stressing the Bill of Rights as essential to the maintenance of a free society, will give him a strong claim to a place in the gallery of outstanding American jurists."

[CAB]

For further information:
Vern Countryman, ed., *The Douglas Opinions* (New York, 1977).
Vern Countryman, *The Judicial Record of Justice William O. Douglas* (Cambridge, Mass., 1974).
"Mr. Justice Douglas," *Columbia Law Review*, 74 (April 1974), pp. 341-411.

DUNLOP, JOHN T(HOMAS)
b. July 5, 1914; Placerville, Calif.
Director, Cost of Living Council (CLC), January 1973-April 1974; Chairman, CLC, April 1974-March 1975; Secretary of Labor, March 1975-January 1976.

John Dunlop received his A.B. and Ph.D. from the University of California at Berkeley. He joined the Harvard faculty in 1938 and served at one time as dean of the Harvard Faculty of Arts and Sciences. During the postwar period, he participated in numerous boards and committees in and out of government as a mediator, arbitrator, and advisor—mostly in the construction industry.

In 1971 Dunlop was named chairman of the Nixon Administration's Construction Industry Stabilization Committee (CISC). As chairman of that panel, Dunlop fought many open and bitter battles with Nixon's Pay Board formed to monitor wages. The Board had insisted that Dunlop adhere to its guidelines in judging construction industry contracts. Dunlop, however, demanded to have autonomy for his committee and, in fact, retained the authority he sought. It was generally believed that he brought some order to the collective bargaining process in the construction industry. He was acclaimed for deflating wage pressures in that industry.

Dunlop became head of the Cost of Living Council (COLC) in January 1973 and was, consequently, responsible for directing Nixon's price and wage controls. He encouraged the federal government to use its power as a major buyer and seller to help keep market prices down. He played a role in convincing Nixon to speed up the sale of government-owned metals and rubber. When the price of steel scrap surged upward, he encouraged the Maritime Administration to double its sales of scrap from obsolete ships. Dunlop presided over the easing, and then ending, of price and wage controls in Phases 3 and 4 of Nixon's economic policy. His role was limited, however, because he ruled over a dying program.

In March 1975, President Ford appointed Dunlop to be his Secretary of Labor. Dunlop came to his post with strong support from organized labor. He took the job with the assurance by Ford that he would be given a role in the formulation of economic policy. Although he only served for nine months in this cabinet post, he was a strong Secretary. He staged a major shake-up in the Labor Department's Occupational Safety and Health Administration. He set up the Department's first office for enforcing the new federal pension law. He began an investigation of the Teamsters Union Central States Pension Fund. He helped to steer legislation through Congress which would increase permanently the number of workers eligible for unemployment insurance. He successfully mediated the dispute between the AFL-CIO and the White House that eventually allowed a long-term Soviet-American grain agreement. He played a role in formulating Ford's tax cut in 1975.

Dunlop put much of his energy into bringing peace to the construction industry. His solution for an industry plagued by unemployment and high wages was composed of two elements which he hoped would be enacted into law. First, a Construction Industry Collective Bargaining Committee composed of employer and employee representatives would get involved in local disputes to try to solve them without inflationary pressures emerging from local unions. Second, to get union support for the first part of his program, Dunlop included provisions which would have permitted a union to picket an entire construction site even if the union was only having a conflict with one of several contractors working at the site. President Ford had promised to sign the bill which contained this package. When Ford vetoed it, Dunlop felt that his usefulness as Labor Secretary had come to an end. He believed he would no longer have the confidence of organized labor. He resigned in January 1976.

After Jimmy Carter was elected president, Dunlop's name emerged as a possible Labor Secretary in the new Administration. Civil rights and women's groups objected. They were critical of the orders he had given as Labor Secretary under Ford for the new enforcement regulations governing the contract compliance program in which federal money could not be spent in those enterprises where workers face discrimination on the job. Dunlop had objected to employment goals and timetables. Although the AFL-CIO had favored Dunlop for the post, he was not named by Carter.

[HML]

EAGLETON, THOMAS (FRANCIS)
b. Sept. 4, 1929, St. Louis, Mo.
Democratic Senator, Mo, 1969-.

The son of a local St. Louis politician and prominent lawyer, Eagleton earned his B.A. from Amherst University in 1950. In 1953 he received his LL.B. from Harvard, graduating cum laude and editor of the *Law Review*. Eagleton then returned to St. Louis to join his father's law firm and pursue a career in politics. In 1956, running as a Democrat, he became the youngest circuit court attorney in St. Louis history. In 1960 he was elected state attorney general. Besides introducing administrative reforms that facilitated the processing of cases, Eagleton earned a liberal reputation by opposing the death penalty, championing consumer protection, and endorsing Supreme Court decisions protecting the rights of the accused.

In 1968 Eagleton entered the Democratic primary for a U.S. Senate seat. He defeated the incumbent, Edward V. Long (D, Mo.) and then narrowly won the election running on an anti-war, liberal platform in a conservative state.

Eagleton emerged as one of the leading liberal freshman in the Senate. He opposed the Vietnam war, voting for both the Cooper-Church and McGovern-Hatfield end-the-war Amendments, and questioned excessive defense spending. He successfully led the fight to ban funds for the development of the MBT-70 tank, a weapon he deemed obsolete. In domestic legislation he lobbied for programs to assist the elderly, protect the consumer, encourage clean air and water, improve the nutrition of Americans and plug up tax loopholes. He also opposed the development of the SST.

At the 1972 Democratic National Convention, presidential nominee George McGovern [q.v.], impressed with Eagleton's record, offered him the vice-presidential nomination. He did so after only a cursory check of the Senator's background which revealed that he had been hospitalized for "fatigue and exhaustion." McGovern and his staff thought that Eagleton, an urban Catholic, would strengthen the ticket in the ethnic neighborhoods suspicious of the anti-war movement. Eagleton gladly accepted the offer and delivered to the Convention an impassioned acceptance speech calling for an end to the war and a renewal of liberalism.

Rumors immediately began to spread suggesting that Eagleton had been hospitalized for a nervous breakdown. McGovern was aware of this, and when discussing the issue with Eagleton, both had agreed it would not hurt the ticket. Perhaps, they thought, the matter might even help them because of Eagleton's underdog status. However shortly after the Convention, two reporters for the Knight newspaper chain learned that Eagleton had been institutionalized on a number of occasions. Before they released the story to the press, they reported it to McGovern's campaign manager Frank Mankiewicz [q.v.]. In order to blunt the impact of this revelation, McGovern and Eagleton held a joint press conference at Sylvan Lodge, S.D. Eagleton announced that he had voluntarily checked himself into a hospital three times in the 1960s for nervous exhaustion. He admitted that he had undergone shock therapy and drug treatments and conceded that the breakdowns occurred after undertaking three grueling campaigns. McGovern announced that he was 1000% behind Eagleton and was satisfied with the Senator's explanation.

Soon after this press conference, Jack Anderson [q.v.] stated that Eagleton had been apprehended for drunken and reckless driving. Eagleton angrily denounced Anderson's charges. The columnist then retracted the story as completely false because his informant had proven to be unreliable. Nevertheless Eagleton's credibility was severely challenged. The leading newspapers of the nation, including *The New York Times* and *The Washington Post*, called for him to step down or be ousted from the ticket. They questioned his ability to assume the vigorous duties of the presidency if necessary and criticized his dissembling to McGovern. Leading Democratic officials also began to pressure McGovern to remove Eagleton. They feared that by having him on the ticket, the Party, already in trouble, would do even worse in the polls. Contributors to the Party treasury declined. Yet McGovern persisted in publicly claiming that he would keep Eagleton on the ticket, and Eagleton continued to campaign, trying to exploit his underdog image.

After several days of uncertainty, however, McGovern leaked reports that he was going to drop Eagleton to the press. Eagleton picked up these signals and announced on July 31 that he would leave the ticket. He reiterated that he considered himself mentally fit and explained that he made this decision because he feared questions concerning his health would divert discussion from the issues in the campaign.

In analyzing the Eagleton affair, critics accused McGovern of showing little cour-

age when he leaked those reports rather than confronting Eagleton and personally requesting his resignation. McGovern and his staff were also charged with failing to do a proper background check. Eagleton recalled McGovern asking him only, "Do you have any old skeletons rattling around your closet." Eagleton said no; he believed that what McGovern was asking referred to something sordid. However his critics wrote that Eagleton should have been honest with McGovern.

Eagleton returned to the Senate and remained one of the leading critics of the Administration's Southeast Asia and defense policies. In 1973 Eagleton introduced an amendment to an appropriations bill barring funds for military operations in Cambodia and Laos. He further lobbied for a cutoff of military aid to Turkey after that nation's invasion of Cyprus. In 1973 the liberal Americans for Democratic Action gave Eagleton a 90% rating. As one of the Senate's most important liberals, Eagleton supported appropriating more funds for urban mass transit and nutritional programs. In February of 1973, he was floor manager of the Older American Act, a bill designed to assist the elderly. Eagleton advocated tighter regulation by the federal government of the cosmetic industry, especially to protect the consumer from hazardous products. Only in the area of busing did Eagleton break from his liberal colleagues. He supported an effort in 1974 to restrict busing.

During the Carter presidency, Eagleton continued to be one of the leading liberals in Congress. He supported the President on the Panama Canal treaties and the SALT initiative. Eagleton continued to press for legislation to help the elderly.

[JB]

EASTLAND, JAMES O(LIVER)
b. Nov. 28, 1904; Doddsville, Miss.
Democratic Senator, Miss., 1943-79.

A Mississippi native, Eastland practiced law, managed the family's 5,400-acre cotton farm and served briefly in the state's House of Representatives until

1941 when he was appointed temporarily to the U.S. Senate. Two years later Eastland was elected to the Senate. During his tenure he compiled one of the most conservative records in the Senate, opposing federal social welfare and civil rights legislation. In the early 1970s the conservative Americans for Constitutional Action gave him a cummulative rating of 73. Eastland strongly supported agricultural programs, particularly cotton interests important to his state. In 1956 he became chairman of the Judiciary Committee. He also served on the Agriculture and Forestry Committee, chairing the Immigration and Naturalization Subcommittee. In July 1972 Eastland was elected President Pro Tempore of the Senate. [See EISENHOWER, KENNEDY, JOHNSON Volumes]

Although Eastland shunned publicity and was little known outside of Congress, he was one of the most powerful men on Capitol Hill. Because of his seniority and committee positions, he was able to block the flow of much liberal legislation. As chairman of the Judiciary panel, Eastland had control over all civil rights, crime and gun-control legislation, as well as judicial appointments. Eastland waged a continuing fight against all civil rights legislation and saw to it that no civil rights bill or resolutions received a favorable report from the Judiciary Committee. A staunch anti-Communist, he contended that Communists had infiltrated civil rights organizations and were seeking to destroy communication and cooperation between persons of good faith of all races. As chairman of the Immigration and Naturalization Subcommittee, he attempted to check many State Department policies regarding foreign travel, passports and admission of undesirable aliens. During his career Eastland introduced more than 30 bills aimed at increasing internal security, including one to control travel by "subversives" from the United States to other countries such as North Vietnam.

During the Nixon Administration, Eastland voted against the majority of Democrats in the Senate more often than he voted with them. He backed the President's position 3 out of 4 times in 1970 and supported the conservative coalition 99% of the time. Eastland defended the civil rights record of President Nixon's controversial Supreme Court nominees: Clement F. Haynsworth, Jr. [q.v.], G. Harrold Carswell [q.v.] and William H. Rehnquist [q.v.]. He opposed federal aid to primary and secondary schools. The Senator maintained that such aid was unconstitutional and that control of education belonged to state and local authorities. He warned that continued federal interference with education would result in "one conglomerate mass of people." In 1969 and 1970 Eastland spoke against busing plans to achieve racial balance in schools. He asserted that the plans were particularly aimed at the South and ignored racial discrimination in the North.

Despite the poverty of his home state, where the median income was the lowest in the nation, Eastland opposed federal programs for the poor. He voted against increasing appropriations for food stamps in 1970 and authorization of funds for anti-poverty programs in 1971. The Mississippi lawmaker believed that persons trafficking in narcotics should be severely punished. He supported proposed legislation mandating life imprisonment without parole for sellers of hard drugs. In February 1973 Eastland introduced a bill calling for a reduction of sentences for those dealers who revealed to law enforcement officials their source of narcotics.

By virtue of his seniority on the Agriculture and Forestry Committee, he was appointed adviser to the Senate Appropriations Committee. He proved effective in restoring funds for research, Extension Service and school lunch and milk programs. His record was unsurpassed in the protection of minimum cotton allotments for small farmers. In 1970 the Senator, who owned a large plantation, opposed a measure limiting farm subsidies to a maximum of $55,000.

As Chairman of the Senate Forestry and Soil Conservation Subcommittee, Eastland played a significant role in drafting legislation to salvage areas laid waste by silt, flood or mismanagement. In 1975

Eastland offered a Senate resolution to provide all government aid possible for the protection of the U.S. coastal fishing industry against excessive foreign encroachment.

On the international scene, Eastland maintained that, as a free nation, the entire U.S. population was responsible for foreign policy. As an ardent anti-Communist, Eastland believed that every weapon needed for victory should be made available to U.S. troops in Vietnam and thus "rattle the teeth of the Reds" in Moscow and Peking. On June 30, 1970, Eastland voted against the Cooper-Church Amendment to halt American military action in Cambodia. He also opposed the Administration's economic sanctions against Rhodesia and described Nixon's 1970 decision to close the U.S. consulate in Salisbury, Rhodesia as a "colossal folly." He charged that Americans ignored international law and followed the emotional dictates of African politics.

In 1971 Eastland endorsed congressional action permitting the importation of Rhodesian chrome ore into the U.S., a break in the U.N. mandated economic sanctions against the country. He observed that Communist China's admission to the U.N. demonstrated the futility of using foreign aid to buy votes. When he voted against the continuance of all foreign aid in October 1971, Eastland charged that such assistance had degenerated into a wasteful and inefficient program. He remained a staunch advocate of military aid to assist free nations vigorously resisting the spread of communism. Eastland opposed attempts to limit defense appropriations and supported construction of the Safeguard anti-ballistic missile system and the C-5A aircraft. He voted against the Nuclear Nonproliferation Treaty of 1969, the volunteer army in 1971 and the reduction of U.S. troop levels in Europe in 1971.

In May 1978 Eastland announced he would not seek reelection, thus ending a 35-year congressional career.

[TML]

EDWARDS, DON
b. Jan. 6, 1915; San Jose, Calif.
Democratic Representative, Calif.
1963-.

Don Edwards received his B.A. from Stanford University in 1936 and spent two years at Stanford's law school. Although he never received a law degree, Edwards passed the California bar. In 1940-41 he served as an FBI special agent and after World War II founded the Valley Title Company, eventually becoming a millionaire. In 1962 Edwards won a seat in the U.S. House from a predominantly blue-collar district.

During the 1960s Edwards compiled one of the most liberal voting records in Congress. In 1965 and 1966 he served as national chairman of Americans for Democratic Action (ADA). A consistent supporter of President Lyndon B. Johnson's Great Society programs and civil rights measures, Edwards opposed the Administration's escalation of U.S. military involvement in Southeast Asia. [See JOHNSON Volume]

During the Nixon Administration Edwards continued to oppose U.S. involvement in Vietnam, voting to restrict funds to withdrawal and aid efforts after 1971 and to cut off all funds in June 1972, pending release of American prisoners of war. Both proposals were defeated.

A member of the House Judiciary Committee, Edwards was appointed chairman of Sub-committee Number Four in 1971. Under Edwards the panel became known as the Civil Rights Oversight Committee, responsible for checking the enforcement of civil and constitutional rights legislation.

During the early 1970s Edwards' subcommittee held hearings on the enforcement of the Voting Rights Act of 1965, on federal employment of Spanish-speaking people and on the civil rights responsibilities of the Federal Power Commission. He led the effort to prohibit the FBI's dissemination of arrest information to employers. In 1971 Edwards opposed funding for the House Internal Security Committee, stating that the Committee violated the civil rights of those under investigation.

In 1971 Edwards pressed for passage of the constitutional amendment guaranteeing equal rights to women, the Equal Rights Amendment. He guided the bill through committee hearings and managed it on the House floor, where he fought the Wiggins amendment, which called for maintenance of laws exempting women from the draft and laws relating to health and welfare. Stating that the Wiggins amendment "would effectively kill the bill," Edwards helped defeat it by a House vote of 87 to 265. The ERA resolution passed 354 to 23.

Edwards won a 100% rating from the ADA for 1972, 1973 and 1974. A longtime advocate of conservation Edwards proposed in 1968 and again in 1971 the creation of a 21,000-acre South San Francisco Bay National Wildlife Refuge. The bill became law in 1972. During the 1974 House Judiciary impeachment hearings, Edwards was one of the senior Committee members to vote against President Nixon on all five articles of impeachment. After President Gerald R. Ford's pardon of Nixon, Edwards urged continuation of the impeachment proceedings. On Nov. 22, 1974, the House Judiciary Committee voted 6-3 against further inquiry into the Ford pardon, with Edwards one of the dissenting minority.

Edwards served briefly in 1975 on a special House Select Committee on Intelligence, formed to investigate illegal intelligence activities by government agencies. He easily won reelection in 1976 and 1978.

[DAE]

EHRLICHMAN, JOHN D.
b. March 20, 1925; Tacoma, Wash.
Counsel to the President, January 1969–November 1969; Assistant to the President for Domestic Affairs, November 1969–April 1973.

John D. Ehrlichman's family originally emigrated from Austria to Seattle in the late 19th century and soon thereafter abandoned their Orthodox Jewish faith to become Christian Scientists. His father was a land developer. Ehrlichman grew up in Santa Monica, Calif., and attended the University of California at Los Angeles (UCLA). In 1943 after his freshman year at UCLA, he enlisted in the Army Air Corps and flew 26 missions over Europe as a B-24 navigator.

After World War II he returned to UCLA on the GI Bill. Ehrlichman attended Stanford Law School, from which he received a law degree in 1951. Thereafter he joined a Los Angeles law firm for a short time before setting up his own law firm in Seattle. He built on his family's substantial connections in the real estate business community and established a prosperous specialization in zoning and land use law.

As a legal expert in land use, Ehrlichman had frequent dealings with state and local officials of both Parties, and it thus behooved him to sustain a low level of partisan involvement. Even during his years on President Nixon's White House staff, Ehrlichman was virtually unknown to many of his state's leading Republicans. This was largely because Ehrlichman never had a strong ideological/partisan commitment; instead his political commitment was to a single man—Richard M. Nixon.

Ehrlichman was drafted into Nixon's political career by his old college friend H.R. Haldeman [q.v.], who had been a fervid Nixonite since the late 1940s. In 1959 when Haldeman became chief advance man for the 1960 Nixon presidential campaign, he called on his friend to help out. During the course of that campaign, Ehrlichman was captivated by the excitement and scale of national politics and also became a committed Nixonite. He returned after the 1960 defeat to help in Nixon's unsuccessful 1962 race for the California governorship. Convinced that his candidate's career was finished, Ehrlichman returned to Seattle and his law practice.

Republican intraparty strife during the mid-1960s revived Nixon's political fortunes. In an effort to win the presidential nomination, Nixon and his forces actively campaigned for Republican candidates across the country and in the process tested the political waters for a possible comeback. As part of this 1966 campaign effort, Ehrlichman assisted in training some advance men. Thereafter he (and Haldeman) helped direct some of Nixon's early comeback and primary campaign efforts, although he maintained an attitude of reserve and incomplete commitment until he was convinced that Nixon was on a winning course.

After signing on full time, Ehrlichman set up Nixon's headquarters for the 1968 Miami Beach Republican Convention and played a role in carrying out Convention strategy. After Nixon secured the presidential nomination, he was appointed tour director and put in charge of the logistics of the campaign.

After his November victory the grateful Nixon offered Ehrlichman the position of Counsel to the President. The President recognized in him qualities that he valued: "diligence, caution, an open mind, an absence of distracting personal flair, and above all, orderliness and efficiency." Ehrlichman accepted, feeling that this was exactly the kind of unpretentious and uncontroversial job he could handle and yet not get shunted off into the executive branch's bureaucratic maze.

His first two projects as counsel were the composition of a conflict-of-interest code for the new Nixon appointees and the management of the President's personal finances, which included the purchase of the Nixon homes at San Clemente and Key Biscayne. Gradually he emerged as something of the "White House fireman," dampening political fires and anticipating bureaucratic blazes. As presidential counsel, he assumed a prominent role in reconciling interagency disputes and in turning legislative ideas into specific proposals. Without firm policy opinions or an inclusive ideological frame of reference, Ehrlichman was well suited to the role of idea broker. Furthermore as an unpresupposing character, he could interface with the President's more flamboyant domestic advisers, the liberal Daniel Moynihan [q.v.] and the conservative Arthur Burns [q.v.]. Indeed the President experimented with Ehrlichman as a domestic policy referee in mid-1969 when he returned from his European tour. Ehrlichman remembered that at that time the White House was "long on advocates and short on honest brokers" and that "the President himself was often left as the only honest broker . . . [which] was inefficient and wasteful of his time."

Clearly the President had neither the time, the personal disposition or the political interest to referee most domestic policy quarrels. But in order to delegate that task, he needed to find someone he knew and trusted and who was likeminded. On both counts Ehrlichman fitted the bill. He was regarded as a cautious, nonideological pragmatist who had the leanings of an "instinctive conservative." Furthermore, as one White House colleague observed, "He is a guy the President knows, trusts and likes to work with," which was particularly important to a President like Nixon who did not "like to work closely with too many people."

In November 1969 the President institutionalized Ehrlichman's role as domestic policy coordinator by naming him assistant to the President for domestic affairs. The change in Ehrlichman's title (although not his duties) came as part of a series of staff changes designed to streamline the President's domestic policymaking machinery and strengthen his grip on the executive branch. The moves were touched off by the impending departure of one of the President's chief domestic policy advisers, Arthur Burns, to assume the chairmanship of the Federal Reserve Board. As part of the change, both presidential assistants Daniel Patrick Moynihan and Bryce N. Harlow [q.v.] were accorded cabinet rank and named counselors to the President. The post of assistant for domestic affairs was also created and bestowed on Ehrlichman.

Ehrlichman viewed his new assignment as "essentially operational"—"to serve as a strainer" or as an "honest broker between warring points of view" on domestic policy issues. He was expected to coordinate the development of policy alternatives and specific programs. The White House announcement of his appointment stated that "advice and policy guidance will be channeled to the domestic affairs staff from the Urban Affairs Council, the Cabinet Committee on Economic Policy, the Environment Quality Council and the counselors to the President, as well as the departments and agencies." Thus all of the President's messages to Congress, his speeches, administrative policy statements and specific legislative proposals on domestic affairs had to be cleared through Ehrlichman's office.

Comparison was immediately made to the advisory/administrative setup under Henry Kissinger [q.v.] for foreign affairs. If the comparison was valid, then Ehrlichman was much more than a mere technician with minimal policy influence. And in fact, a *Newsweek* story on the staff changes called Ehrlichman a "domestic czar" with powers roughly equivalent to those of Joseph Califano in the Johnson presidency.

Certainly the President hoped that from this new position Ehrlichman could bring an order and neatness to domestic policy formulation and execution that would be comparable to Kissinger's system for foreign affairs. Yet despite the apparent similarities between Ehrlichman in domestic affairs and Kissinger in foreign affairs, there were two important differences.

Foremost, Kissinger was a theoretician, an idea generator in his area, whereas Ehrlichman laid "no great claim to creativity in policymaking" for domestic affairs. Instead Ehrlichman had to work with two other White House assistants of equal, if not superior, status who were to act as the substantive policy advisers in the domestic arena. It was Moynihan and Harlow who were given the responsibility to "anticipate events, think through the consequences of current trends, question conventional wisdom, address fundamentals and stimulate long-range innovation." From this perspective Ehrlichman's task was "essentially manageri-

al and judicial." He acted "like an editor, trimming, revising, expanding or compelling a complete overhaul of the literary products" of the idea men. Thus the combination of influential staff competition and a projected administrative function seemed to indicate that the new assistant for domestic affairs would be destined for a less significant role than the assistant for foreign affairs.

A second important difference between these two presidential assistants and their bailiwicks concerned presidential attitudes and interests. Foreign affairs were the focal point of the President's personal and political interests, and they were the topic of the creatively innovative policy impulses of his presidency. In contrast domestic affairs were generally less interesting to President Nixon and more often the target of negative policy impulses to cut back, consolidate or retrench. Thus, since Kissinger acted as major domo and confidential adviser in the area of major presidential concern, his influence with the President and over policy formulation was quite evident. On the other hand, since Ehrlichman acted in less of a substantive capacity over an area of less intense presidential interest, the President may have been more inclined to delegate affairs to him. It is therefore difficult to pinpoint the character and extent of Ehrlichman's influence over domestic policy. Although comparable in a formal sense, Kissinger's influence was more in the character of a pilot, while Ehrlichman's was that of a steward.

To achieve his coordinating task, Ehrlichman established a pyramidal organizational structure to channel ideas. First he assembled six aides to perform two essential roles: to determine how well government bureaus were executing the President's instructions and to supervise interagency "project teams" that would conduct research, develop legislative programs and "present policy options to the President." At a secondary level he collected a "pool of technicians organized into groups to solve specific problems and run specific programs." Through this system Ehrlichman became a "traffic manager," directing ideas up to the President and passing down policy choices made by the President for implementation.

Criticism of Ehrlichman in this position generally followed two themes. On the one hand comment focused on his inexperience. One White House aide said that Ehrlichman's relentlessly linear mind could not comprehend the untidiness of getting things accomplished in Washington. "He has not been around here long enough to understand that when Congress seems to make little sense to an orderly mind, that is frequently when Congress makes the most sense."

While admitting that he was not an expert, Ehrlichman saw certain advantages to his inexperience. He remarked: "My knowledge of the kind of things we're dealing in here is very limited and I'm the first to realize that. . . . Sometimes it helps to be uneducated, so you can ask stupid questions that need to be asked and get some hard answers—questions like, 'Do we have to do this at all?' and 'Why can't the states do this?'" This process may have been considered particularly useful to an Administration convinced that many federal programs which were a legacy of the New Deal and Great Society eras needed pruning, weeding and consolidating.

The other critical theme contended that instead of being a traffic manager, Ehrlichman (as well as other members of the White House staff) was acting more like a roadblock, cutting off direct access to the President and isolating him from political realities. As the character of the Nixon White House began to evolve, the Teutonic trio of Haldeman, Ehrlichman and Kissinger were accused of building a "Berlin Wall" around the President. Ehrlichman, in particular, incurred the enmity of domestic cabinet officers since, in operational details, he had broad authority to place the key domestic departments directly under his control.

With few exceptions, domestic cabinet secretaries were forced to adjust to the idea that they had to deal with Ehrlichman before they could reach the President and, frequently, instead of the President. One cabinet member who felt particularly estranged was Interior Secretary Walter Hickel [q.v.], whose frustration finally erupted into the public domain when his letter to the President protesting the handling of the Kent State demonstration strongly implied that the President was being isolated both from the public and from his Administration. Hickel suggested in the letter that Nixon "consider meeting on an individual and conversational basis with members of . . . [the] cabinet."

Despite the complaints of an occasional Hickel or the grumblings about "Von" Ehrlichman's "Berlin Wall," Ehrlichman's importance was implicit and played down during President Nixon's first term, when he was portrayed as merely a middleman—a conduit between the President and his domestic administrators. Within weeks of Nixon's reelection in 1972, however, the extent of Ehrlichman's influence in domestic affairs became more evident.

In mid-December of 1972 Ehrlichman was relieved of his responsibilities for supervising the day-to-day activities of the Domestic Council. These operational duties were assumed by his former deputy, Kenneth B. Cole, Jr., in order to free Ehrlichman "for additional responsibilities beyond being the President's chief domestic adviser." Given the President's desire to avoid most domestic affairs, he was glad to merely indicate what he wanted in broad, vague terms and leave Ehrlichman to handle the specifics. This virtually made Ehrlichman a surrogate President for domestic affairs, and as his power grew and became more evident, he outgrew the rather unpretentious and unassuming style he had brought to Washington. Instead he became arrogant in his power, regarding the cabinet and agency heads as irrelevant nuisances who wasted his and the President's time.

Once the Administration had been reelected, Ehrlichman helped develop a bureaucratic reorganization plan that displayed his disdain for the cabinet, his suspicions of the permanent bureaucracy and his new-found enjoyment and thirst for power. In all these things he was empathetic with the President's preferred style of dealing with a minimum of people and his view that something had to be done to bring a generally recalcitrant bureaucracy under presidential control.

Ehrlichman furthered the Administration's earlier reorganizational study, the Ash Commission Report, by coordinating a task force effort with the Justice Department and the Office of Management and Budget to develop the "administrative presidency." His approach was to find effective ways of gathering the reins of bureaucratic control into the President's hands without having to go to the Democratically-controlled and often uncooperative Congress to ask for new laws. An important part of his scheme was for the President to elevate four cabinet members to concurrent status as assistants to the President. This quartet was to be given coordinating responsibilities for the areas of economic affairs, human resources, natural resources and community development. In addition Ehrlichman was to assume direction of the Office of Intergovernmental Relations, thereby dealing with the mayors and governors of the nation. Meanwhile Henry Kissinger would continue to preside over the foreign affairs sphere.

These six individuals would constitute a supercabinet and the core of the projected "administrative presidency." A second step in the process of gaining control of the bureaucratic behemoth was the installation of loyal, White House-experienced personnel in each agency and bureau to establish an informal network of "old boys" who could help the President and his supercabinet.

Yet in attempting to grasp control of the bureaucratic machinery for domestic affairs, Ehrlichman projected the President's negative disposition towards this policy area. As Dan Rather in *The Palace Guard* observed, Ehrlichman and Haldeman "had a clear understanding of what the Nixon White House was *against* [but] they were never quite certain what it should be for. As a result, domestic policy under Ehrlichman's reign was essentially negative, both in tone and substance."

Another problem with Ehrlichman's supervision of domestic policy was his style of dealing with Congress. Not only was he inexperienced in the ways of Capitol Hill but he also chose to cloak his deficiencies with an arrogance of power—both his own and the President's. He used to like to say that "the President is the government." He dealt with Congress as if it were the enemy, and his favorite tactic was the veto. His approach finally resulted in a series of stalemates and setbacks that caused the defeat of the President's policies for welfare reform, national health insurance and the SST. Indeed the Administration's second term record on domestic issues was conspicuously lackluster and in contrast to the modest achievements of the preceding term (such as revenue sharing and environmental legislation). It seemed that as his self-assurance and influence with the President grew, his concern to get along with others, i.e., Administration members and Congressmen, lessened.

Ultimately the most damaging exhibition of Ehrlichman's arrogance in power, his inexperience in public affairs and his loyalty to the President was his involvement in establishing the White House "Plumbers" unit. The unit was initially created to deal with the *Pentagon Papers* leaks and eventually perpetrated the break-in at Democratic National headquarters in the Watergate office building and the burglary of Dr. Daniel Ellsberg's [q.v.] former psychiatrist's office. Although Ehrlichman claimed that he did not order the Watergate break-in, he admitted learning of it soon after the fact, at which time his response was to instruct the "Plumbers," like Egil Krogh [q.v.], E. Howard Hunt [q.v.] and Gordon Liddy [q.v.] that he "did not agree with this method of investigation" and that they should not repeat such tactics.

Thereafter, as subsequent investigations revealed the scandal, Ehrlichman's prominent role in the cover-up effort was exposed, and he came under considerable public criticism. Within four months of

Nixon's second inauguration, Ehrlichman and other major Administration figures were seriously implicated in a number of possibly illegal and unethical political activities ranging from the actual Watergate break-in through secret "hush money" payments and the Ellsberg burglary to obstruction of justice. Two days after the Hunt and Liddy connection to the Ellsberg break-in had been uncovered, it became clear that the scandalous trail led straight into the White House and directly to John Ehrlichman. Thus the President regretfully announced the acceptance of the resignations of Ehrlichman and Haldeman, as well as that of Attorney General Richard Kleindienst [q.v.].

In his letter of resignation, Ehrlichman wrote: "For the past two weeks it has become increasingly evident that, regardless of the actual facts, I have been a target of public attack. The nature of my position . . . has always demanded that my conduct be both apparently and actually beyond reproach. I have always felt that the appearance of honesty and integrity is every bit as important to such a position as the fact of one's honesty and integrity." He went on to complain that given his circumstances he was forced "to conclude that [his] present usefulness . . . and ability to discharge [his] duties [had] been impaired by these attacks, perhaps beyond repair."

From one perspective Ehrlichman's resignation appeared as the ultimate proof of his loyalty. To deflect some of the controversy directed at the White House and to help keep the Nixon presidency afloat, Ehrlichman and Haldeman had resigned. From the President's perspective it was a bitter loss of "two of [his] closest friends and most trusted assistants" and "two of the finest public servants it [had] been [his] privilege to know."

In a deposition made public on June 7, Ehrlichman placed much of the blame for Watergate on John Dean [q.v.], former counsel to the President, and on Jeb Stuart Magruder [q.v.], former deputy director of the Committee to Re-Elect the President. He also implicated former Attorney General John Mitchell [q.v.], in

contradiction to H.R. Haldeman's statement issued the same day.

Six weeks later, in late July 1973, Ehrlichman testified before the Senate Watergate Committee. Unlike most other witnesses, Ehrlichman, according to *The New York Times,* came across as "a tough, unapologetic Nixon stalwart who obviously felt that a good offense was the best defense." He vigorously denied John Dean's contention that a Watergate cover-up had preoccupied the White House between June 17 and Sept. 15, 1972. He stated that during the latter part of 1972, the President had been busy with domestic policy issues and that only "about one-half of 1% [of his time] was spent on politics and campaigning." He also disputed Dean's testimony concerning the possibility of executive clemency for the Watergate defendants.

In further testimony Ehrlichman defended the Ellsberg break-in as a valid exercise of the President's constitutional powers to protect the welfare of the nation by preventing the betrayal of national security secrets. This line of constitutional interpretation brought Ehrlichman into heated argument with the Senate Committee chairman, Sen. Sam Ervin (D, N.C.) [q.v.], who insisted that the break-in violated the Fourth Amendment. Later Ehrlichman also clashed with the majority counsel, Samuel Dash [q.v.], "over definitional matters," such as whether he had administered the Plumbers in a "literal sense" or an "actual sense." Ehrlichman's exchanges with Dash elicited the most obvious public display of partisan differences on the Committee when Sen. Howard Baker (R, Tenn.) [q.v.] and the minority counsel accused Dash of improper questioning and of interpreting the witness's answers.

The resignations of Ehrlichman and Haldeman from the White House staff late in April 1973 indicated that the Administration's efforts to ride out the Watergate storm by "stonewalling" it were not proving very successful. Shortly thereafter the revelation of a White House taping system and the halting release of taped conversations between the President and various aides increased public indignation and helped propel the impeachment inquiry.

The depth and seriousness of the Watergate scandal was further highlighted by the March 1974 indictment of Ehrlichman, Haldeman and John Mitchell [q.v.] for conspiracy and obstruction of justice with regard to the Watergate break-in and cover-up. In addition Ehrlichman was charged with lying to both the grand jury and the FBI. He was also indicted in the Plumbers case for conspiracy and perjury to both a grand jury and the FBI.

The Plumbers trial opened in Washington on June 28 with the prosecution contending that the burglary of Dr. Lewis Fielding's office was "a willful, arrogant act of men who took the law into their own hands and felt above the law." While Ehrlichman maintained that he had agreed to a "covert operation, not a break-in or illegal operation," the prosecution argued that he was clearly "implicated in knowledge of and approval of the break-in."

Considering the importance of the defendants and the political ramifications of the hearing, the trial was speedily concluded. On July 12 the jury found Ehrlichman guilty of three counts of perjury and one of conspiracy. In sentencing him to serve at least 20 months in prison, Judge Gerhard Gesell [q.v.] told Ehrlichman that he must bear "major responsibility for this shameful episode in the history of our country." The conviction of the Plumbers, in combination with the progress of the House impeachment hearings and the Supreme Court's ruling against the President on the tapes, demonstrated both the precarious and culpable position of the President and his men. Ten days later President Nixon resigned and, on Sept. 8, 1974, was pardoned by President Ford for all federal crimes that he "committed or may have committed or taken part in" during his time in office. Thus by the time Ehrlichman and other former Administration officials came to trial in October for the Watergate cover-up, the President was free and clear of any legal sanctions.

At the trial, which opened on Oct. 14, 1974, the defendants pursued a go-it-alone strategy, and Ehrlichman openly broke with his former colleagues and with the President. Ehrlichman's counsel contended that "Richard Nixon deceived, misled, lied to and used John Ehrlichman to cover up his own knowledge and his own activities. . . . In simple terms John Ehrlichman has been had by his boss, who was the President of the United States."

The climax of the trial occurred on Dec. 10, Ehrlichman's second day on the witness stand. According to his version of the Watergate affair, he had been deceived by the President and unaware of the extent of the cover-up until late March 1973. In recounting the circumstances of his resignation as the President's chief domestic adviser, the composure of the usually assured Ehrlichman cracked and he momentarily broke into tears.

On New Year's Day 1975, the jury turned in a verdict of guilty against the three former top political aides of President Nixon. Ehrlichman was convicted of conspiracy, of obstruction of justice and of making false declarations to a grand jury. In addition to these convictions, he was subsequently disbarred.

Of the nearly 30 former Nixon aides who pleaded guilty to or were convicted of Watergate-related crimes, Ehrlichman was one of the most visibly changed by the experience. He left his wife, moved from Seattle to Santa Fe, and abandoned his cleancut image for a bearded and more relaxed demeanor. In addition to his novel based on his White House years, *The Company,* Ehrlichman undertook some low-profile activities in civic projects in Santa Fe, where he felt "his knowledge of government" would be helpful.

[MW]

EISENHOWER, JULIE NIXON
b. July 5, 1948; Washington D.C.

Julie Nixon was the youngest daughter of Richard Nixon. She graduated from Smith College in 1970 and received a masters degree from Catholic University in 1971. In 1968 she married Dwight David Eisenhower, II, the grandson of President Dwight D. Eisenhower.

Mrs. Eisenhower campaigned for Nixon in his presidential election efforts of 1968 and 1972. She was his most ardent supporter and continued to speak on behalf of her father's Administration in over 40 states after his 1972 reelection. She supported her father's decision to bomb Cambodia, despite the psychological effect on the nation's campuses, believing, as the President did, that it would bring the war to a more rapid conclusion. Eisenhower respected conscientious objectors who chose to go to jail rather than fight in Vietnam, but she opposed any kind of amnesty for those who had left the country to avoid the draft. She agreed with the feminist movement that women should be able to choose their own role in society but considered the movement "too strident" and oppressive. She argued that the most important role in life was to be a successful parent. Eisenhower thought the pressure to conform was a real threat to the individual and criticized those who took drugs as "tuning out" on life. She believed her generation had an active role to play in the American political system and argued for the 18-year-old vote.

Eisenhower was a strong defender of her father during the Watergate crisis. Watergate, she told reporters, was a tragedy and a mistake made by seven men, and her father was innocent of any wrongdoing. Her sincerity and willingness to talk with reporters and to the public earned her the distinction of being "the only credible Nixon" according to the White House press corps; while the Administration's press office likened her speeches to sending in the Marines. She was the first member of the Nixon family to acknowledge that Nixon had considered resigning in May 1973. Eisenhower argued against resignation. Later Nixon said that she was the "one who never conceded."

[DBH]

ELLENDER, ALLEN J(OSEPH)
b. Sept. 24, 1890; Montegut, La.
d. July 27, 1972; Bethesda, Md.
Democratic Senator, La., 1953–72.

After serving as district attorney of Terrebonne Parish, Ellender was elected to Louisiana's House of Representatives in 1924. He soon allied himself with the political machine of Huey Long. Shortly after Long's assassination in 1953, Ellender won his seat in the U.S. Senate, and was reelected five times with almost no serious opposition. A prosperous potato farmer while still in his twenties, he soon dissociated himself from Long's populism to become a champion of the state's wealthy sugar, rice and cotton growers. Ellender was a leader of the filibuster campaigns aimed at defeating civil rights legislation proposed by the Kennedy and Johnson Administrations. On most issues he voted with the conservative Southern Democrats, but on occasion turned maverick. Throughout his Senate career Ellender traveled the globe at government expense, and his remarks about some of the nations he visited caused the State Department embarrassment. [See TRUMAN, EISENHOWER, KENNEDY, JOHNSON Volumes]

Ellender supported President Nixon on the Vietnam war and other military matters. In 1970 he voted against the Cooper-Church and Hatfield-McGovern Amendments designed to end the war, opposed attempts to cut U.S. troop levels abroad, and backed a 1971 bill extending the draft for two years. Ellender also sided with the President on key defense appropriations bills, although he opposed deployment of the Safeguard anti-ballistic missile in March 1969. None of Nixon's annual foreign aid proposals received Ellender's support.

The Louisiana Senator backed the Administration's "no-knock" entry legislation and opposed the reduction of penalties for certain marijuana offenses. In other domestic areas, Ellender was usually sympathetic toward big business. Always protective of his state's economy, he offered an unsuccessful amendment in

December 1969 to restore the oil depletion allowance to its original 27.5% level after Senate liberals had succeeded in lowering it to 23%. In 1971 he supported the financial rescue of the Lockheed Aircraft Corp. and initially favored continued development of the SST but changed his position because of mounting cost projections.

During Nixon's first term, Ellender stood fast in his resistance to integration. He endorsed the President's Supreme Court nominations of conservatives Clement Haynsworth [q.v.] and G. Harrold Carswell [q.v.] but refused to back the Administration's Philadelphia Plan requiring the hiring of minorities on federally financed construction projects. He was also an opponent of forced busing. Despite his pronounced conservatism on most social issues, Ellender was a proponent of the food stamp program dating back to the Johnson years. In 1969, as chairman of the Agriculture and Forestry Committee, he advocated increasing the Administration's $610 million request for the program to $700 million or possibly $800 million. In June of the following year, he pushed through an amendment providing $300 million to keep the program operating until enactment of the 1971 agricultural appropriations bill. Yet he opposed free food stamps, saying, "People should have to pay something, if only a very little bit, for the stamps."

During his 20-year reign over the Agriculture Committee, Ellender consistently sought to advance Louisiana's farm interests. In 1970 he attempted to block the Administration's program establishing three-year price supports for wool, wheat, cotton and feed grains. The legislation also limited subsidy payments to $55,000 per producer per crop for 1971–73 wheat, feed grain and cotton crops. In addition to opposing the subsidy ceiling, Ellender particularly objected to the bill's provision leaving cotton acreage allotments to the discretion of the Secretary of Agriculture. This discretionary power, he contended, could eventually lead to reductions in acreage and price supports, with disastrous repercussions

for the South. On Oct. 9 he refused to sign a House-Senate conference report on the bill and managed to stall its consideration by the full Senate until after mid-November. Despite his efforts Congress passed the bill Nov. 19 and President Nixon signed the Agricultural Act of 1970 on Nov. 30.

Ellender succeeded Richard Russell (D, Ga.) [q.v.] as chairman of the Appropriations Committee and as President Pro Tempore of the Senate following Russell's death on Jan. 21, 1971. Shortly thereafter he and three other Southern Democrats led off the successful six-week opposition to another of the myriad proposals aimed at relaxing the rule for cutting off filibusters. In the end reformers were thwarted by the target of their efforts—the filibuster—when the fourth attempt to choke off debate of the issue failed on March 9.

As chairman of the Appropriations Committee, Ellender attacked the unified budget concept employed by President Nixon to calculate the federal deficit projected in his fiscal 1973 budget proposal to Congress on Jan. 24, 1972. Under this concept surpluses from trust funds, those collected for specific purposes such as Social Security, were used to balance anticipated shortfalls in federal funds, those available for all government spending. Ellender said the device was an attempt to deceive the American public about the true cost of government and claimed that the actual 1973 deficit would be $11 billion more than the $25.2 billion estimated in Nixon's budget message.

At age 81 Ellender died of a heart attack in July 1972 following a day of campaigning for his seventh successive term.

[JR]

ELLSBERG, DANIEL
b. April 7, 1931; Chicago, Ill.
Economist, political scientist.

Daniel Ellsberg grew up in Chicago and Detroit, where he attended an exclusive prep school on a scholarship. He received a B.A. in economics from Harvard in 1952, and studied in England for a year. In 1954 he enlisted in the Marines. Returning to Harvard after two years in the service, he wrote as his dissertation an analysis of strategic military planning. In 1959 Ellsberg joined the Rand Corp. the West Coast "think tank," where he researched game theory and the risks involved in nuclear warfare. He was a consultant to governmental officials during the early 1960s and joined the staff of John T. McNaughton, an assistant secretary of defense, in 1964. Touring Vietnam in 1965 Ellsberg was decidedly "hawkish" on the war and lobbied on behalf of the Johnson administration's policy of escalation.

After returning to the Rand Corp., Ellsberg participated in the research for a massive history of United States involvement in Southeast Asia commissioned by Secretary of Defense Robert S. McNamara [q.v.] in 1967. Ellsberg's work convinced him that the war was unjust, the result of several Presidents' unwillingness to bear responsibility for the loss of South Vietnam to the Communists. After reading the entire study, he decided that from the start, it had been an "American war" in which the U.S. was guilty of "foreign aggression." Believing that he could be most useful by "working within the system," Ellsberg sent numerous memos and position papers to government officials in which he urged immediate withdrawal from Vietnam, wrote magazine articles urging an end to the war, and spoke at anti-war rallies.

By the autumn of 1969 Ellsberg was prepared to take drastic action to stop the war. Using his top secret clearance to obtain a copy of the Pentagon study, he rented a copying machine and reproduced the study with the aid of a Rand colleague, Anthony J. Russo, Jr. He sent a copy to Sen. J. William Fulbright (D, Ark.) [q.v.], who declined to use it, and approached other prominent opponents of the war, who likewise were unwilling to take action. Finally Ellsberg approached Neil Sheehan, a *New York Times* reporter, who, in March 1971, accepted the docu-

ments on behalf of the *Times*. On June 13 the *Times* began publishing excerpts of the study. When the government obtained an injunction against the paper, *The Washington Post,* the *Boston Globe,* and other newspapers continued to print excerpts. On June 30 the Supreme Court ruled in favor of the *Times's* right to publish the documents.

Ellsberg, meanwhile, had gone into hiding. Indicted by a Los Angeles grand jury on charges of theft of government property and violation of the Espionage Act, he surrendered to federal marshals in Boston on June 28. Ellsberg readily admitted that he was the source of the *Pentagon Papers,* as they were called, but denied he had broken any laws. In December 1971 twelve additional charges of theft, violation of the Espionage Act and conspiracy were lodged against Ellsberg. Anthony Russo was also named in the indictment.

After several unexpected procedural delays, Judge Matthew Byrne, Jr., declared a mistrial on Dec. 8, 1972. A new jury was selected, and the trial began on Jan. 18, 1973. The defense based its case on the argument that no laws had been broken, claiming that Ellsberg's clearance allowed him access to the study and that nothing in the documents endangered national security. The defense called as witnesses several prominent former government officials, including McGeorge Bundy [q.v.], Arthur M. Schlesinger, Jr. [q.v.], and John Kenneth Galbraith [q.v.], who testified that the top secret classification assigned to the Pentagon study was routinely used and indiscriminately applied to documents regardless of their contents.

In late April and early May, before the case went to the jury, Judge Byrne made a series of shocking revelations. On April 27 he released a Justice Department memo that G. Gordon Liddy [q.v.] and E. Howard Hunt [q.v.], convicted Watergate conspirators, had burglarized the office of Ellsberg's former psychiatrist, Lewis J.

Fielding, in September 1971, to find evidence that would embarrass and discredit Ellsberg. A few days later it was revealed that John Ehrlichman [q.v.], Nixon's domestic affairs adviser, had ordered the investigation of Ellsberg that led to the break-in. Byrne also announced that Ehrlichman had recently offered him the post of FBI director. Finally on May 9 came the disclosure that the FBI had wiretapped the home of Morton Halperin, head of the *Pentagon Papers* study and a close friend of Ellsberg, and had made tapes of Halperin's conversations with Ellsberg. When Byrne ordered the prosecution to turn over transcripts of the conversations, the government announced that it had lost all the relevant records.

Incensed at the government's action, Byrne declared a mistrial on May 11, 1973, and dismissed all the charges against Ellsberg and Russo. He accused the government of "gross misconduct" that disgraced the judicial system. In September 1973 indictments were handed down against Ehrlichman, Liddy and several others for the burglary of Fielding's office, and in July 1974 all were found guilty.

Ellsberg remained active in the antiwar movement, writing extensively and speaking at rallies and on college campuses across the country. After the Communist victory in South Vietnam in 1975, he turned his attention to other causes, becoming especially active in the growing movement against nuclear weapons and in favor of disarmament. In October 1976 Ellsberg was arrested with 40 others at a demonstration in front of the Pentagon. In March 1978 he organized and led a protest march on the nuclear weapons plant at Rocky Flats, Nevada.

[JD]

For further information:
Daniel Ellsberg, *Papers on the War* (New York, 1972).
Peter Schrag, *Test of Loyalty: Daniel Ellsberg and the Rituals of Secret Government* (New York, 1974).

ERVIN, SAM(UEL) J(AMES), JR.
b. Sept. 27, 1896; Morganton, N.C.
Democratic Senator, N.C.,
1954–1975; Chairman, Government Operations Committee, 1972–75; Chairman, Senate Select Committee on Presidential Campaign Activities, 1973–74.

Sam Ervin, a descendant of Scotch-Irish Calvinists, was born one of 10 children of parents living in Morganton, N.C., a community in the foothills of the Blue Ridge Mountains. He received his B.A. from the University of North Carolina in 1917 and his LL.B. from Harvard University Law School in 1922. Ervin then returned to Morganton to practice law intermittently for the next three decades. He served three terms in the State Assembly in the 1920s and 1930s. From 1935 to 1937 he was a judge in the Burke County Criminal Court and later served in the North Carolina Supreme Court from 1948 to 1954. When in the early summer of 1954 U.S. Sen. Clyde Hoey died, Gov. William B. Umstead named Ervin to fill his seat. He won election in November 1954 and was handily reelected to three full terms. Although he had no formal power base in the state, his folksy political style and dramatic use of the Bible and the works of Shakespeare appealed to his constituents.

During the 1950s and 1960s Ervin's strict constructionist view of the Constitution was the basis for his opposition to many important Administration policies. He opposed numerous civil rights bills that he found to be invasions of states rights. He opposed aid to education bills and voted against such programs as medicare, Model Cities, aid to mass transit, child care and Project Headstart. He did, however, build a record supporting environmental legislation and attempted on numerous occasions to strengthen the civil liberties of various types of citizens, such as Indians, mental patients and federal employees. [See EISENHOWER, KENNEDY, JOHNSON Volumes]

During the Nixon Administration, Ervin continued his policy of fully supporting the President and the military in the prosecution of the Vietnam war, and he voted against legislation such as the Cooper-Church Amendment to limit presidential authority to conduct military operations in Cambodia. Ervin attempted to keep the levels of military spending at what he considered to be adequate levels. But in August 1969 he voted for the amendment to the defense appropriations bill to delete funds for research and development of the Safeguard anti-ballistic missile system.

On domestic issues Ervin continued his conservative voting pattern except on matters of personal liberty that he saw to be transgressed by the power of government. His father, the Senator once said, had instilled in him the idea that "the greatest threat to our liberties comes from government, not from others." Government, Ervin believed, has "an insatiable thirst for power and is never satisfied." He opposed the Equal Rights Amendment when it came to a vote in March 1972, and in proposing nine changes to the Amendment aimed at narrowing the impact of its coverage, he warned that adoption of the measure unchanged would destroy the social fabric of America. Women would be crucified "upon the cross of dubious equality and specious uniformity." All of his amendments were rejected by substantial margins.

Reflecting both his political constituency and his constitutional beliefs, Ervin voted against the use of federal funds for the busing of school children to achieve racial balance. Never a strong labor advocate, he opposed the Nixon Administration's Philadelphia Plan giving the federal government power to force the hiring of minority workers on federally financed construction projects. He supported the nomination of fellow-Southerner G. Harrold Carswell [q.v.] to the Supreme Court in April 1970. The nomination was a controversial one because of allegations that Carswell was a racist and had a poor record as a lower court judge. A firm believer in free enterprise, Ervin voted against legislation appropriating an additional $289

million for the development of the SST. However he opposed any limitation on the amount of farm subsidies paid out by the government.

Aside from serving on the Armed Services Committee, Ervin spent his last three years in Congress presiding over the Government Operations Committee and was chairman of three subcommittees of the Judiciary Committee. These positions gave him considerable power that he used with great effectiveness. In 1971 he effectively challenged Nixon's impoundment of funds allocated by Congress for federal programs. In hearings called to investigate the right of the President to spend money only where he desired, the Senator said that "what concerns me is the use of impounding practice to void or nullify congressional intent." Ervin surprised many observers by obtaining a list of the impounded funds from the Office of Management and Budget and then publishing it in the Congressional Record to give a clearer and broader appreciation of the differing priorities of the President and Congress.

Ervin fervently opposed the concept of preventive detention under which certain types of individuals charged with "violent" or "dangerous" crimes or with threatening a witness or juror could be held for 60 days without being brought to trial. The Senator admonished that "such flagrant violation of due process smacks of a police state." In 1970 he said of the model District of Columbia Court Reform and Criminal Procedure Act (the D.C. Crime Bill) sponsored by the Nixon Administration that "this . . . is as full of unconstitutional, unjust and unwise provisions as a mangy hound dog is full of fleas . . . a garbage pail of some of the most repressive, nearsighted, intolerant, unfair and vindictive legislation that the Senate has ever been presented . . . an affront to constitutional principles and to the intelligence of the American people. . . ."

Alarmed at the increase in surveillance of civilians by government and private industry, the Senator held hearings in 1969 addressing the problems of government coercion of citizens into supplying personal information for statistical data banks. Two years later he presided over hearings that addressed an allegation by CBS newsman Daniel Schorr [q.v.] that an investigation into his activities by the FBI was an attempt to quiet his criticism of Nixon Administration policies. The Administration denied the charges by responding that Schorr was actually being considered for a position in the government and the FBI was merely engaged in a background clearance check. The issue died down but suspicions of improper intimidation remained.

In 1970 Ervin's Constitutional Rights Subcommittee looked into revelations first published in *Washington Monthly Magazine* that the Army had conducted "surveillance" on 800 Illinois citizens including many considered to be liberal politicians. The public cleansing that followed was supposed to limit collection practices, but it possessed, Ervin said, "qualifications, exceptions, and ambiguities which permit surveillance even within the confines of an otherwise restrictive policy."

Ervin was catapulted into national prominence early in 1973 after he had been chosen to head the seven-member committee to investigate the Watergate affair. The panel was formally labeled the Senate Select Committee on Presidential Campaign Activities. The main reason that he was chosen to lead the investigation was the fact that his advanced age precluded any potential charges of his grandstanding because of presidential ambitions. But Ervin's reputation for honesty and his skill as an interpreter of the Constitution were also in his favor. The probe by the Watergate Committee was soon to parallel the investigation of the special prosecutor, Archibald Cox [q.v.], but the panel had the unofficial, broader mission of educating the public about the nature of the crimes committed. After choosing Samuel Dash [q.v.], professor of law at Georgetown University Law Center, as chief counsel, the members settled on a strategy of calling witnesses before televised hearings on an ascending scale of political importance. The Committee sought to create a detailed basis of understanding before the major witnesses close to the President were called to testify.

Some of the earlier testimony involved numerous revelations of illegal espionage directed from the White House. Jeb Stuart Magruder [q.v.], the first major witness and former deputy director of the Nixon reelection campaign, not only admitted his own role in various illegal actions but implicated nearly every important person around the President. He was soon followed by former White House Counsel John Dean [q.v.] who not only corroborated much of Magruder's testimony but also said that Nixon himself had known of the cover-up activities as early as Sept. 27, 1972. Ervin was probably best remembered for his questioning of Maurice Stans [q.v.], the former Secretary of Commerce and finance director of the Nixon campaign committee. After Ervin berated Stans for not following ethical guidelines on campaign contributions, which Ervin implied should have been superior to the minimum requirements of the criminal law, the single Nixon loyalist on the Committee, Sen. Edward Gurney (R, Fla.) [q.v.], objected to the North Carolinian's harassing manner. In reply Ervin, ever the actor with a mask of innocence and a skilled sense of rhetoric, responded: "I am an old country lawyer and I don't know the finer ways to examine the witness. I just have to do it my way."

One minor witness, White House aide Alexander Butterfield, testified in July that a secret taping system had recorded most presidential conversations in the White House. Ervin and the Committee soon agreed to subpoena five tapes of conversations between the President and Dean. Ervin then told television viewers that the country was more interested in finding out the facts about Watergate than in "abstruse arguments about the separation of powers or executive privilege." And he concluded: "I think that Watergate is the greatest tragedy this country has ever suffered. I used to think the Civil War was the greatest tragedy, but I do remember some redeeming features in the Civil War in that there was some spirit of sacrifice and heroism displayed on both sides. I see no redeeming features in Watergate." In the fall of 1973 controversy over the tapes continued. Ervin at one time agreed to a compromise whereby Mississippi Sen. John Stennis [q.v.] would authenticate White House summaries of the tapes, but Special Watergate Prosecutor Cox refused, thereby causing his own dismissal in what became known as the "Saturday night massacre" in which Attorney General Elliot Richardson [q.v.] and Deputy Attorney General William Ruckleshaus [q.v.] were forced to resign rather than fire Cox.

Although the Committee unearthed widespread abuses of campaign activities, it faded from existence in early 1974 as the main attention shifted to the newly appointed special prosecutor, Leon Jaworski [q.v.], and the House Judiciary Committee, where formal impeachment hearings were to begin. Ervin and his colleagues demonstrated, in the words of historian Alonzo Hamby, "that Nixon had surrounded himself with operators who were ruthless, unprincipled, and authoritarian in their attitude toward opposition, possessed by a paranoia which made them distrustful even of one another, and convinced that they were exempt from the rule of law. . . ."

In the final Committee report submitted in July 1974, the question was raised whether there had been a genuinely fair election in 1972. Ervin, in a separate section setting forth his own views, wrote that the first objective of the "various illegal and unethical activities" studied by the Committee was to "destroy insofar as the presidential election of 1972 was concerned the integrity of the process by which the President of the United States is nominated and elected." Among the proposals of the Ervin Committee was the establishment of a public attorney to be appointed by the judiciary and confirmed by the Senate. Further curbs on intelligence-gathering activities in the White House and a ban on the examination of tax returns by anyone in the executive office were among the many other recommendations submitted.

Ervin declined to run for reelection in 1974 and retired to his home in Morganton.

[GWB]

For further information:
Samuel Dash, *Chief Counsel: Inside the Ervin Committee—The Untold Story of Watergate* (New York, 1976).

EVANS, DANIEL J(ACKSON)
b. Oct. 16, 1925; Seattle, Wash.
Governor, Wash., November 1964-January 1976.

A product of public schools, Evans joined the U.S. Navy upon high school graduation in 1943. When his tour of duty ended, he enrolled in the University of Washington, where he was awarded a B.S. in civil engineering in 1948 and an M.S. a year later. Evans worked briefly as a consultant for a private firm before he was recalled to Naval duty in 1951. After two years in Korea he joined the Mountain-Pacific chapter of the Association of General Contractors as an assistant manager. From 1959 to 1964 he served as a partner in the engineering firm of Gray and Evans.

Evans began his career in politics in 1956 when he won election to the Washington State House of Representatives on the Republican ticket. He soon established himself as a progressive, issue-oriented Republican, and in 1961 his Party colleagues appointed him minority floor leader. Despite the absence of statewide recognition, Evans won the governorship in 1964 and won an impressive victory.

During his first term Evans developed a program for increased spending for education and welfare and he established inducements for industrial expansion.

In 1966 Evans served as his Party's chief tactician. He sought to improve Republican chances at the polls throughout the country by "practical politicing," and under his direction the GOP secured eight governorships. In recognition of his indefatigable efforts and abilities, Evans was appointed keynote speaker at the GOP National Convention in 1968. His address called for a joint drive by "government, private enterprise and individual citizens" to combat the nation's problems. [See JOHNSON Volume]

Easily reelected in 1968, Evans directed his attention to the state's recession-wracked economy. In response to spiraling unemployment, especially among highly skilled aerospace workers, Evans negotiated aircraft trade agreements with the Soviet Union and urged private enterprise in the state to consider business exchanges with China and Russia. He mounted a campaign throughout the U.S. to attract industry to the state of Washington.

Convinced that local government was best equipped to rectify local problems, Evans increased state grants to municipalities. He also approved extensive appropriations for a school construction program and established funds for multiservice community centers in the ghetto areas.

Upon his reelection in 1972 Evans, faced with the effects of the energy crisis, imposed cutbacks on electrical consumption and encouraged the state legislature to create a mandatory energy conservation program. Committed to the preservation of the state's unspoiled natural environment, Evans formed an alliance with conservationists to prevent the development of a hydro electric dam along the Snake River. When President Ford outlined his comprehensive energy plan, Evans endorsed Ford's attempt to provide alternatives to pending congressional legislation, but he also regarded the plan as "occasionally insensitive to human needs."

When Operation Airlift went into effect to evacuate stranded Vietnamese in 1975, Evans devised a resettlement program that provided homes, jobs and temporary sponsors for the refugees. A recruitment team was established to interview Vietnamese for possible placement depending on skills and individual need. Based at the Vietnamese Assistance Center in the nation's capital, the team then solicited jobs from the private sector and informed employment agencies of the refugees' special skills. Evans was the first Governor to establish such a program.

Throughout his tenure, Evans regarded a decentralized federal government as the means by which participatory democracy can best be realized. He repeatedly balked at the label "middle of the roader" since it implied both indecison and lack of direction. In 1976 Evans decided against a fourth term in office.

[DGE]

EVERS, (JAMES) CHARLES
b. Sept. 11, 1922; Decatur Miss.
Civil rights leader.

Charles Evers was one of six children brought up in a tightly-knit family in a shack in Decatur, Miss. In 1940 he interrupted his high school education to join the Army. After his discharge in 1946 he completed his secondary schooling and studied social science at Alcorn A&M College in Lorman, Miss. Shortly after earning his BA, he moved to Philadelphia, Miss., where he became the state's first black disc jockey and opened a bar. By his own admission he was a "hustler, who ran numbers, bootlegged whiskey and managed brothels." Evers also helped his brother Medgar recruit blacks for the NAACP. As a result of continued harassment, he moved to Chicago.

On June 12, 1963, Medgar Evers, the NAACP Mississippi field director, was assassinated and Charles took his place. In 1966 he organized the crippling "black Christmas" boycott of white merchants in Fayette, Miss. Evers himself profited from the boycott by opening the Medgar Evers Shopping Center, which became an immediate success. After six months he won agreement from city officials to a list of black demands. These included the desegregation of public facilities, the hiring of black policemen, the integration of juries, the abolition of segregated rest rooms and the use of courtesy titles by city employees addressing blacks. The flamboyant Evers launched a voter registration drive during the mid-1960s that dramatically increased black voting in Mississippi. [See JOHNSON Volume]

In the spring of 1968 Evers lost a race for a U.S. House seat. That May he was made state cochairman for Sen. Robert Kennedy's campaign for the Democratic presidential nomination. In July, Evers was elected mayor of the small town of Fayette. He was the first black in the state to assume this position. During his tenure he put the town government on a sound footing, improving educational facilities and establishing a medical care center. He attempted to combat unemployment and lower the high infant mortality rates in the area. Evers lobbied for federally funded food and recreation programs for senior citizens, created a day care center for the benefit of parents on welfare seeking to find employment, and promoted continued education for blacks.

In 1972 Evers lost the race for the governorship but took heart because "for me to be running for governor in a state where my brother was killed and for none of us to get our heads bashed in—it's a hell of a lot. We changed the whole political system in this state." During the mid-1970s Evers became a subject of controversy. The Justice Department accused him of tax evasion in 1974. His trial ended in a mistrial, however. He defended Watergate as a "parking ticket crime," and maintained that he could support George Wallace [q.v.] for vice president in 1976.

[SB]

FARMER, JAMES L(EONARD)
b. Jan. 12, 1920; Marshall, Tex.
Assistant Secretary of Health, Education and Welfare, March 1969-December 1970. Civil rights leader

The son of the first black man in Texas to hold a Ph.D. degree, Farmer graduated from Wiley College in 1938 and received a bachelor of divinity degree from Howard University in 1941. Refusing ordination because the Methodist Church in the South was then segregated, he turned his energies toward social activism. From 1941 to 1945 Farmer was race relations secretary for the Fellowship of Reconciliation, a pacifist organization. Later in the 1940s and 1950s he worked as a labor organizer for a number of trade unions, served as a program director for the NAACP and was a commentator on a United Automobile Workers radio program in Detroit. Farmer also wrote and lectured extensively on race relations.

In 1942 Farmer, with some students at the University of Chicago, founded CORE, the Congress of Racial Equality. An interracial group pledged to the eradication of racial discrimination, it applied Gandhian techniques of nonviolence to the struggle for racial equality. CORE staged its first successful sit-in at a Chicago restaurant in 1943, and thereafter grew slowly until the 1960s. From 1961 to 1966 Farmer was the organization's national director. He led its efforts to achieve desegregation of public facilities, to register black voters in the South and to end discrimination in employment and housing in the North. On March 1, 1966 Farmer resigned from CORE's directorship, expecting to receive an Office of Economic Opportunity grant to establish a nationwide program to improve literacy and job skills among unemployed blacks. The proposal was never approved, however, and in September 1966 Farmer joined the faculty of Lincoln University as a professor of social welfare. [See KENNEDY, JOHNSON Volumes]

Farmer surprised many of his friends in the civil rights movement when he joined Black Independents and Democrats for Rockefeller in July 1968. When Nixon received the Republican nomination, Farmer denounced his civil rights record as "apathetic at best and negative at worst." Shortly before his inauguration, however, Nixon met with several black leaders and promised to do "more for the underprivileged and more for the Negro than any President has ever done." He offered Farmer the position of assistant secretary of Health, Education, and Welfare (HEW) with special responsibility for relations with black youth. Farmer accepted the offer and was confirmed by the Senate in March 1969. Of all the blacks appointed to office by Nixon, Farmer was by far the most prominent.

It quickly became apparent, however, that the Nixon Administration's policies were antagonistic to the goals of the civil rights movement. In January 1969 HEW Secretary Robert Finch [q.v.] announced that he was extending the deadline for Southern school districts to comply with desegregation guidelines. In June the Administration presented a substitute proposal for extension of the 1965 Voting Rights Act that would have seriously weakened the legislation. The nomination of Clement Haynsworth [q.v.] and G. Harrold Carswell [q.v.], both of whom had poor civil rights records, to the Supreme Court was a further blow to Farmer and others who had placed faith in the new Administration.

In late February 1970 a memo by White House adviser Daniel Patrick Moynihan [q.v.], in which he urged a policy of "benign neglect" toward blacks, was leaked to the press. Several days later Farmer and 36 other black officials in the Administration conferred with Nixon on civil rights. They reported that they were feeling heavy pressure from the black community and that only stronger presidential action on behalf of civil rights would relieve it. Farmer asked Nixon in particular "to clarify his posture" on school desegregation, one of the more volatile issues.

Farmer resigned from HEW on Dec. 7, 1970. At the time he declined to criticize Nixon and cited personal reasons for his resignation. Farmer said that the "ponderous bureaucracy" prevented him from achieving gains "sufficient, or fast enough, to satisfy my appetite for progress." In January 1973, however, Farmer acknowledged that he had had "great difficulty" remaining in the Administration because the President isolated himself from blacks and instead relied on white aides for advice on racial matters.

After resigning from government office, Farmer pursued his idea of a training program for blacks. Still unable to obtain funding for a community-organizing project, he announced in July 1973 the formation of the Public Policy Training Institute in conjunction with Howard University. The purpose, he said, was to study the impact of government policy on blacks and to bring teachers from black colleges to Washington to gain understanding of how public policy is set.

In February 1976 Farmer quit his membership in CORE after its director Roy Innis announced that CORE was recruiting black mercenaries to assist anti-Communist forces fighting in the Angolan civil war.

Throughout the late 1970s Farmer continued his involvement in civil rights causes.

[JD]

FINCH, ROBERT H(UTCHINSON)
b. Oct. 9, 1925; Tempe, Ariz.
Secretary of Health, Education and Welfare, January 1969-June 1970.

Robert Finch, the son of an Arizona state legislator, was a Republican Party activist beginning with his organization of 13 Young Republican clubs while a student at Occidental College in Los Angeles. After graduating in 1947 Finch went to Washington as administrative aide to California Rep. Norris Paulson. Working in the House he met freshman Congressman Richard Nixon and began a long political and personal relationship. After graduating from the University of Southern California Law School in 1951, Finch made two unsuccessful bids for the U.S. House and became a local Party chairman. He returned to Washington in 1958 as administrative assistant to Vice President Nixon.

During the 1960s Finch concentrated on building a strong Republican Party in California. He managed Nixon's unsuccessful presidential campaign in 1960, but disapproved of and kept aloof from

Nixon's 1962 race against Edmund Brown for governor of California. After managing George Murphy's upset victory over Pierre Salinger in the 1964 Senate race, Finch ran for lieutenant governor of California and won the 1966 election with more votes than the newly elected Gov. Ronald Reagan [q.v.]. As lieutenant governor Finch mediated between conservative Reagan and the liberal legislature, managing to mold a bipartisan coalition behind measures to aid minorities and urban areas.

When Richard Nixon campaigned again in 1968 for the presidency, Finch was his close adviser. After Nixon won the Republican nomination, he turned down an offer to run for the vice presidency so that Nixon would not be criticized for "nepotism." After the national election President-elect Nixon offered him the job of Attorney General, but Finch wanted to be Secretary of Health, Education and Welfare (HEW) with its 250 programs and $50 billion budget. He believed that was where the tremendous social questions facing America could be addressed.

Although Finch was widely regarded as Nixon's closest political adviser in 1969, the two were poles apart in political strategy and administrative goals. Finch had remarked that 1968 would be the last election won by "the un-black, the un-poor and the un-young." Nixon, however, was constructing a permanent political coalition aimed at adding conservative white Southerners to the Republican Party. In discharging his responsibility to enforce Title VI of the Civil Rights Act, the legal authority for school desegregation, Finch vowed, "We're going to be hard. We're going to stick to the guidelines." But the President's strategy was to appease influential Southern Senators by pushing back guideline compliance dates for eliminating de jure segregation from fall 1969 to fall 1970.

In response to pressure from Sens. Strom Thurmond (D, S.C.) [q.v.] and Charles Jonas (D, N.C.) to postpone a scheduled Jan. 29, 1969, cutoff of funds to school districts in their states that failed to submit desegregation plans, Nixon prevailed on Finch to allow a 60-day delay. This new deadline was subsequently pushed back at Nixon's request to the fall of 1969. Finch, who had staffed HEW's civil rights and education offices with liberal activist reformers, was caught in the middle. The result was indecision and finally compromise.

By summer 1969 demands from Southern Senators for relief from the fall deadline became intense. On July 3 Finch and Attorney General John Mitchell [q.v.] issued a joint statement retaining the fall deadline but noting "there may be sound reasons for some limited delay."

By August the period of compromise was over. Sen. John Stennis (D, Miss.) [q.v.] told Nixon that he would abandon leadership of the fight for the anti-ballistic missile unless the federal government dropped its court advocacy of immediate school desegregation in Mississippi. Finch was forced to send a letter to Fifth Circuit Court Judge John Brown expressing disapproval of plans written by his own staff, and Attorney General Mitchell sent Justice Department lawyers into court opposing HEW plans for 33 other school districts.

Finch's staff was now openly defiant. Leon Panetta, head of the civil rights division, vigorously protested the Administration's policy on desegregation in court. Nixon aides forced Panetta's resignation. In May 1970 after Nixon's Cambodia invasion, the HEW staff demanded a meeting with Finch on the issue. Finch scheduled a May 19 meeting but was hospitalized one hour before it was to take place. HEW employes booed Finch's statement supporting the President's Cambodia policy.

By June 1970 Nixon was convinced that Finch was incapable of leading HEW. Finch had begun efforts to reorganize the Department and had extended consumer and environmental services. He had banned cyclamates, set a deadline on the use of DDT, implemented reorganization plans and family-planning services and helped develop the Administration's Family Assistance Plan. However, the press, once favorable to him, began to show its disappointment.

On June 6 Nixon announced that Finch would leave HEW to become White House counsel to the President. But it was apparent that Finch was kept on the periphery of the Nixon circle, and in December 1972 Finch resigned to resume his political career in California. In September 1974 President Ford appointed Finch to a nine-member clemency board to consider the cases of convicted Vietnam deserters and draft evaders.

In June 1976 Finch lost the Republican senatorial nomination in California to S. I. Hayakawa.

[JMP]

For further information:
Rufus E. Miles, Jr., *The Department of Health, Education and Welfare* (New York, 1974).
Robert Hutchinson Finch, *Current Biography Yearbook, 1969,* (New York, 1970) pp. 143-146.

FINDLEY, PAUL
b. June 23, 1921; Jacksonville, Ill.
Republican Representative, Ill., 1961-.

Paul Findley graduated from Illinois College and after World War II founded a county weekly, the *Pike Press,* in Pittsfield, Ill. In 1960 he was elected to the House of Representatives from Illinois's largely rural 20th district. First known as a tough conservative, Findley consistently called for a balanced budget and received high ratings from the conservative Americans for Constitutional Action. He opposed the Kennedy Administration's domestic programs and fought many of President Lyndon B. Johnson's Great Society measures, including the anti-poverty, medicare and federal aid to education bills. Throughout the early and middle 1960s, Findley led the fight against extension of food to Communist-bloc nations and opposed trade with these countries except on a direct cash basis. [See KENNEDY, JOHNSON Volumes]

During the Nixon Administration Find-

ley moved toward more moderate stands on some issues. He voted for urban renewal, child care facilities and benefits for families of black lung victims. A member of the House Agriculture Committee for most of his congressional career, Findley persistently criticized U.S. farm policy, opposing the conservative Southern cotton growers whose representatives dominated both the House and Senate Agriculture Committees. In his book *The Federal Farm Fable,* published shortly before the 1968 election, Findley attacked price supports, acreage allotments, marketing quotas and farm subsidies. Beginning in 1969 Findley, with Rep. Silvio O. Conte (R, Mass.) [q.v.], led the House floor fight to limit cash subsidies to farmers, an effort that finally resulted in the 1973 passage of a $20,000 per farmer subsidy limitation. Findley was unsuccessful, however, in tightening the loopholes in the law by which rich farmers subdivided their lands to collect more subsidy payments.

A member of the House Foreign Affairs Committee from 1966 on, Findley was a passionate advocate of the "Atlantic Union" concept, arguing that world peace and order depended on a strong union between European democracies and the U.S. He consistently opposed cuts in the number of American troops stationed in Europe and advocated giving U.S. allies in NATO a larger decision-making role, particularly with regard to the use of nuclear weapons.

Seeking to maintain free international trade, Findley testified in 1970 before the Ways and Means Committee against the imposition of import quotas on textiles and shoes. During the late 1960s he softened his views on trade with Communist-bloc nations, sponsoring bills to facilitate trade with Rumania and the USSR. Prior to President Richard M. Nixon's trip to China in 1972, Findley advocated reopening relations with Communist China in hopes of developing trade markets there.

Findley's views on the war in Southeast Asia vascillated. Prior to 1967 he supported the conflict, but by the fall of that year, he questioned the legality of U.S. involvement. Nevertheless, he voted for war appropriations and opposed attempts to set rigid timetables for U.S. withdrawal. In 1970 he proposed a substitute to the Reid Amendment that would have barred the use of funds from the military appropriations bill from financing American troops in Laos, Cambodia or Thailand. Findley's amendment, endorsed by Nixon, would have prohibited funding for troops in those areas except where the President found the lives of U.S. troops in danger and quickly informed Congress. The proposal was tentatively approved but rejected in the final vote.

Findley remained a conservative in budget matters, voting against environmental proposals. However he supported the Equal Rights Amendment (1971) guaranteeing constitutional rights to women and busing as a means of achieving school integration. He approved the Nixon Administration's wage and price controls but opposed government controls on food prices. In 1973 Findley tried to initiate impeachment proceedings against Vice President Spiro T. Agnew [q.v.] following revelations of corruption in office and in August 1974 moved to censure President Nixon for his role in the Watergate scandal.

Findley won reelection in 1974, 1976 and 1978.

[DAE]

FITZSIMMONS, FRANK E(DWARD)

b. April 7, 1908; Jeanette, Pa.
President, International Brotherhood of Teamsters, 1967 - .

Fitzsimmons, the son of a brewery worker, left school at age 17. He worked as a truck driver in Detroit, where he befriended Jimmy Hoffa [q.v.]. During the Depression, Fitzsimmons helped Hoffa organize Local 299 of the International Brotherhood of Teamsters. In 1937 he became the local's business manager and three years later its vice president. In

contrast to Hoffa's flamboyant style, Fitzsimmons, acting the role of his loyal lieutenant, quietly rose in rank behind the controversial Hoffa. He was particularly known for his organizing ability and his blind devotion to the Teamster leader. In 1961 Fitzsimmons became the International's vice president.

After Hoffa was convicted of jury tampering and misuse of union funds, he designated Fitzsimmons his successor. In 1966 the union elected Fitzsimmons general vice president, a post created to fill any vacancy in the presidency. When Hoffa went to prison in March 1967, Fitzsimmons took over his functions. He assumed power in the midst of confusion. The union was negotiating a contract with the trucking industry, and talks had been stalled as a result of Hoffa's departure. The new leader immediately negotiated a favorable contract that many observed surpassed what Hoffa had previously obtained.

Fitzsimmons's style of leadership differed from that of Hoffa. Lacking Hoffa's personal power, he restored autonomy to the regional and local heads to negotiate and authorize strikes. Complaints against trucking firms and union officials were handled at the local or regional levels rather than at the national level. This change was favorably received by a number of union heads who had chaffed under Hoffa's domination. Investigations by the press later revealed that Fitzsimmons relinquished daily control of the union to Murray Miller, the secretary-treasurer, while major union policy was made by William Presser, who had long-standing ties to the underworld and had been convicted of misuse of union funds. Before Hoffa went to jail, Fitzsimmons had promised to do anything he could to free his friend, and he later authorized the "Spring Jimmy" campaign. Yet Hoffa soon questioned Fitzsimmons's sincerity as he saw the union leader controlling his organization rather than taking orders from the jailed leader. In his autobiography, Hoffa considered the naming of Fitzsimmons as acting president, one of the worst mistakes of his life. [See JOHNSON Volume]

The issue of Hoffa's pardon became closely tied to the Nixon White House during the 1970s. When Nixon took office, the pardon was stalled as a result of efforts by White House aide Charles Colson [q.v.], a friend of Fitzsimmons. Colson observed that it would be beneficial for the new President to work with Fitzsimmons, rather than Hoffa, since it appeared that Hoffa had lost his grip on the union. Colson argued that the pardon should be delayed until after the Teamsters' 1971 summer convention so that Fitzsimmons could be elected president in his own right.

Fitzsimmons persuaded Hoffa to officially resign in June 1971, a move that Fitzsimmons argued would strengthen Hoffa's appeal for parole. Once out of jail, Fitzsimmons suggested, Hoffa could easily win reelection as the union's president. Desperate to get out of jail, Hoffa resigned. He later found that the parole board rejected his appeal. The union's executive council designated Fitzsimmons acting president and the convention elected him to that office. Hoffa's supporters later charged that Fitzsimmons, through his White House connections, was keeping Hoffa in jail and had tricked him into resigning to gain control of the union. Hoffa was eventually paroled in December 1971 with the stipulation that he could not participate in union business for nine years. His allies maintained that Fitzsimmons had arranged the provision with Colson. Fitzsimmons was the only prominent labor leader to support Nixon and in 1971 was appointed to Nixon's Wage-Price Control Board. He backed the President's economic policies and supported Nixon during Watergate. Fitzsimmons was a frequent golfing partner of Nixon, and he later developed a close personal relationship with President Ford.

Fitzsimmons's administration was marred by charges of corruption and mismanagement, particularly on the local or regional level. Leading newspapers and journalists charged that he was keeping company with organized crime figures.

His decentralized administration of the union enabled such Teamsters as William Presser and Tony Provenzano to continue shaking down truckers. Teamster pension funds were still invested in questionable activities in Las Vegas, and the pension fund system contained so many loopholes that many members found themselves without old age coverage.

Attempts to investigate the giant union often met with opposition from government officials. The *Los Angeles Times* claimed in 1973 that the Justice Department dropped charges in a fraud case against Fitzsimmons's son because of White House intervention. In the same year *The New York Times* reported "two ranking officials of the Justice Department" had halted court-approved wiretaps "that had begun to penetrate Teamster connections with the Mafia." In 1975 investigators from the Labor Department, Federal Bureau of Investigation and Internal Revenue Service probed the Teamsters financial dealings and connections with the underworld. Fitzsimmons himself was criticized for his relationship with suspected mobsters and his trusteeship of the union pension fund.

Within the union a grass roots movement, the Professional Drivers Counsel (PROD), encountered apathy and violence in its attempts to clean up the Teamsters. It maintained that the union's power amounted to "a national scandal." The PROD leaders asserted that Teamster officials were overpaid, that there had been innumerable thefts and kickbacks from the pension fund and that members support for the union was based on fear of bodily harm. PROD pressed for democracy in the union, pension reform and the purging of gangsters. At the 1976 convention a number of PROD members were beaten up. During the meeting Fitzsimmons told the rank and file, including a small PROD contingent, "For those who would say it's time to reform this organization . . . I should say to them go to hell." The union delegates voted a dues increase to help finance a 25% pay raise for officials. Fitzsimmons also pushed through authorization for an unlimited number of patronage jobs with payments set by himself. He was given a standing ovation when he denounced government "witch hunts" against the Teamsters.

During the late 1960s and early 1970s, the Teamsters engaged in a bitter struggle with the United Farm Workers Union led by Cesar Chavez [q.v.] over representation of California migrants farm workers. The use of strong-arm tactics and sweetheart contracts reflected poorly on the union, and the Teamsters failed in many of their organizing drives.

Jimmy Hoffa mysteriously disappeared in July 1975 and was probably murdered by individuals opposed to his return to office. Fitzsimmons was not connected with the incident, and he easily won election in 1976. [See CARTER Volume]

[JB]

For further information:
Lester Velie, *Desperate Bargain: Why Jimmy Hoffa Had to Die* (New York, 1977).

FLANIGAN, PETER M(AGNUS)
b. June 21, 1923; New York, N.Y.
White House Political and Economic Adviser 1969-1974.

The son of the chairman of Manufacturer's Trust Co. (later Manufacturer's Hanover), Peter M. Flanigan was raised in New York City. Following service in the Navy during World War II, Flanigan graduated from Princeton in 1947. In the same year he joined the investment banking firm of Dillon, Read, & Co. By the time he left Dillon, Read in 1969 to work in the Nixon White House, Flanigan had become a senior partner and vice president of the firm.

Flanigan's association with Nixon dated from 1960, when he headed "Citizens for Nixon" in New York. After Nixon moved to New York in 1963, Flanigan introduced him to potential campaign contributors and helped him plan strategy for the 1966 congressional elections. In 1968 Flanigan served as Nixon's deputy campaign manager. A year later he joined the

White House staff as a political and economic adviser, serving as a consultant on high-level appointments, a trade negotiator and general liaison with the business community.

As the President's chief talent scout, Flanigan brought in more than 300 senior officers to the Nixon team. Flanigan's White House responsibilities included the arrangement of foreign embassy appointments, one of the choicest of patronage plums. Flanigan's manipulative abilities acquired him a reputation as Nixon's "Mr. Fixit," responsible for shifts in presidential policy favorable to big business.

In 1970 Flanigan was accused of using improper influence to gain a Treasury Department waiver permitting an oil tanker to engage in coastal shipping trade. The tanker was owned by officials of Dillon, Read, & Co. Flanigan also held a share in the vessel and disposed of it only 5 days before the waiver was granted. The following year Flanigan directed a White House task force aimed at overturning an earlier government decision to eliminate quotas on oil imports. Anticipating repercussions from oil-rich Republican contributors who were angered by the earlier decision, Nixon had ordered a new study of oil import quotas which recommended retention of tariffs.

In 1972 Flanigan helped to arrange a favorable decision for the International Telephone and Telegraph Corp. (ITT) in an anti-trust suit brought by the Justice Department. The Department had earlier ruled ITT's acquisition of the Hartford Fire Insurance Co. illegal. Flanigan arranged for Richard J. Ramsden, a former White House aide, to prepare a study of the case. The Ramsden report stressed the "unfavorable" economic consequences that would result should ITT be forced to divest its recent acquisition. Despite the fact that Ramsden was at that time employed by Dillon, Read, which held $200,000 in ITT stock, and that his report was based on a brief authored by ITT's own attorneys, the Justice Department reversed itself and abandoned pursuit of the case.

Herbert Kalmbach [q.v.], Nixon's former personal attorney, testified at the House Judiciary Committee's impeachment inquiry in 1974 that Flanigan brokered ambassadorships in return for massive contributions to the 1972 Nixon presidential campaign. Flanigan acknowledged telling Kalmbach that a potential ambassadorial nominee, Dr. Ruth B. Farkas, was "a good prospect for solicitation." According to Kalmbach Flanigan had advised him to contact Dr. Farkas since she was interested "in giving $250,000 for Costa Rica." Dr. Farkas, Kalmbach said, thought Costa Rica not worth that much, but by contributing $300,000, she was eventually named ambassador to Luxembourg.

Flanigan resigned from the Nixon Administration in July 1974. Several months later President Ford named him ambassador to Spain. The Flanigan nomination soon ran into opposition. At a Senate Foreign Relations Committee hearing on Oct. 2, 1974, Sen. Thomas F. Eagleton (D, Mo.) denounced the nomination as "a disgrace to the United States." The White House announced the withdrawal of the Flanigan nomination Nov. 16, 1974, after Flanigan requested that it not be resubmitted because of the "current political climate." In January, 1975, Flanigan returned to Dillon, Read, as a managing director and executive officer.

[JAN]

FLETCHER, JAMES (CHIPMAN)
b. June 15, 1919; Milburn, N.J.
Director, National Aeronautics and Space Administration, April 1971-May 1977.

James Fletcher was born into a science-oriented family of Utah pioneer heritage. He majored in physics first at Brigham Young University and later at Columbia University, where he received his B.A. degree in 1940. He became a research physicist with the U.S. Navy Bureau at Fort Townsend, Wash. (1940-1941). Fletcher was awarded a teaching fellowship at Princeton University in 1942, where he

was later an instructor and research physicist. After three years at Princeton he went to the California Institute of Technology, where he attained his Ph.D. in 1948. That year Fletcher began working in the aerospace industry, first for Hughes Aircraft Company and then the Romo-Wooldridge Corporation. Ten years later he and an associate formed their own corporation. By that time Fletcher had become a millionaire. He resigned his industry positions in 1964 to become the eighth president of the University of Utah in Salt Lake City.

In 1970 President Nixon appointed Fletcher to the President's Task Force on Higher Education. The next year he was appointed administrator of the National Aeronautics and Space Administration (NASA). The Nixon Administration felt Fletcher could redirect NASA to goals that were more feasible for the 1970s. At the time Fletcher took over NASA, the public had become disenchanted with the space program. National interest had turned to more immediate concerns such as the Vietnam war and social problems at home, and NASA's budget had been cut from $6 billion to $3 billion. Even as Apollo 16 and 17 were completed successfully, it was obvious that because of the lack of financial support, the expensive Apollo program could not continue far into the 1970s.

Fletcher began his active management of the space program by initiating programs that were financially reasonable yet valuable from a scientific and technological perspective. First, however, he attempted to educate the public on the relative amount of money being spent on the space budget, explaining that of every tax dollar only 1.4 cents went for space programs, while 42 cents was expended on social programs.

The first new manned program during Fletcher's term was Skylab, an earth-orbiting space laboratory. The Skylab was utilized by three crews of astronauts over 172 days. The Skylab crews proved man could inhabit space for relatively long periods of time. They also brought back valuable medical and scientific data. President Nixon in February 1974 described the Skylab missions as "one of the most productive endeavors in the history of human exploration." Television coverage of the Skylab 3 spashdown was, however, omitted for the first time in the history of the space program because of the lessening public interest. Fletcher said "Skylab has moved the space program from the realm of the spectacular into a new phase that can be characterized possibly as almost businesslike."

The "businesslike" trend continued with the development of the space "shuttle," a vehicle planned, researched and constructed mainly during Fletcher's term as NASA administrator. The space shuttle was designed to launch like a rocket, orbit like a space craft and return to earth like a jet airplane. The craft would be reusable, thus lowering the cost of each space venture. The shuttle could be used to visit and repair orbiting satellites, to place satellites in orbit, to exchange crews and to supply orbiting space stations and laboratories, all at a fraction of preshuttle cost for such activities. The launching of the first space shuttle was scheduled for 1979.

James Fletcher resigned in 1977 as administrator of NASA. After resigning he worked as a consulting engineer.

[CLC]

FONDA, JANE
b. Dec. 21, 1937; New York, N.Y.
Actress, political activist.

Jane Fonda attended Vassar College, studied art in Paris and then enrolled at the Art Students League in New York. During the 1950s and 1960s she starred in a number of movies, including *Tall Story* (1960), *A Walk on the Wild Side* (1962), *Period of Adjustment* (1962), *Sunday in New York* (1963) and *La Ronde* (1964). By the early 1970s she had established herself as one of the nation's leading motion picture actresses.

During the late 1960s and early 1970s, Fonda became known for her outspoken opposition to the Vietnam war and her support of the feminist movement. Fonda joined other members of the film community to form Entertainment Industry for Peace and Justice. The group's major production, "Free the Army," was well received by civilian and military audiences during its international tour and was honored with an Obie award after its New York performance. Fonda's political activities won her a degree of notoriety with the American public and even inspired the Maryland General Assembly to entertain a bill declaring her persona non grata in the state. In 1972 she traveled to Vietnam, where she broadcasted on Hanoi Radio in addition to directing a film, *Viet Nam Journey*, relating her experience of the war.

In 1973 Fonda married anti-war activist Tom Hayden [q.v.]. As the war wound down, Fonda moved out of the public spotlight. But in 1977 she resumed her full-time movie career. A year later Fonda starred in *Coming Home*, the story of a Vietnam veteran whose war injury had left him a paraplegic, and in 1978 she played a leading role in *The China Syndrome*, a movie about the possibility of an accident at a nuclear power plant. After the nuclear accident at Three Mile Island in Pennsylvania, Fonda emerged as a spokeswoman of anti-nuclear power forces.

[PM]

FONG, HIRAM L(EONG)
b. Oct. 1, 1907; Honolulu, Hawaii.
Republican Senator, Hawaii, 1959-77.

Hiram Fong, the son of indentured plantation workers, worked his way through the University of Hawaii and Harvard Law School. Fong stood out among a generation of upwardly mobile Chinese-Americans who challenged the Caucasian plantation owners' economic leadership on the islands. He worked as a deputy city attorney in Honolulu and later founded the city's first multiracial law office. So successful was the firm that

Fong was able to invest in a variety of businesses. His assets totaled several million dollars by 1960. Fong was elected as a Republican to the Hawaiian Territorial Legislature in 1938 and served as speaker of that body from 1948 to 1954. During that time he developed a working relationship with the powerful International Longshoremen's and Warehousemen's Union (ILWU). When he ran for U.S. Senator in Hawaii's first general election as a state in July 1959, Fong was the only Republican candidate backed by the normally-Democratic ILWU.

Fong won the Senate race and designation as senior Senator from Hawaii with a special term that expired in 1964. Characterized as a Republican moderate he tended to take more liberal stands on domestic issues than on foreign policy. After winning reelection by a comfortable margin in 1964, Fong proved a leading supporter of civil rights legislation. He backed the 1965 Voting Rights Act and wrote a key amendment to include poll watchers in the bill. As a member of the Judiciary Committee's Immigration and Naturalization Subcommittee, Fong worked to eliminate the traditional immigration restrictions against Asians. Also during the Johnson Administration, Fong pressed for gun control legislation and was one of the few Republicans to support the President's proposal for an Administration on Aging. In 1968 he joined six other members of the Judiciary Committee in voting against Johnson's nomination of Supreme Court Justice Abe Fortas [q.v.] for Chief Justice. [See KENNEDY, JOHNSON Volumes]

Fong became highly partisan and more conservative during the Nixon years. He consistently voted for large defense appropriations and used his seat on the Judiciary's Refugees and Escapees Subcommittee to defend the Nixon Administration's Vietnam policy. He also served as ranking Republican on the Appropriations Committee's Foreign Operations Subcommittee, where he argued for the continuation of military aid programs. On the floor Fong voted against any curtailment of funds for Vietnam and against

any cutbacks in the Defense Department budget. He voted for the Safeguard anti-ballistic missile system (ABM) and the supersonic transport (SST). Fong received a 100% rating for 1969-70 from the American Security Council.

Although Fong's unstinting support of Nixon's Vietnam policy hurt his popularity in Hawaii and weakened his relationship with the ILWU, the strength of his personal organization carried him to a narrow reelection victory in 1970. During the 92nd Congress, as ranking Republican member of the Consitutional Amendments Subcommittee, Fong supported the Equal Rights Amendment. On other domestic issues, including welfare and tax bills, his voting record was mixed. In 1972 he voted against any federal action to foster busing as a means of integrating schools and in 1973 opposed voter registration by mail. Fong supported President Nixon's veto of the U.S. Information Agency bill on the grounds that its access-to-information clause was an unconstitutional encroachment on executive prerogatives.

In January 1971 Fong's office was rocked by a major scandal involving his long-time administrative assistant, Robert Carson. Fong courageously stood by his aide, who was indicted and subsequently convicted in New York federal court for allegedly trying to bribe Deputy Attorney General Richard Kleindienst [q.v.] with $100,000 in campaign funds. Though Fong emerged blameless from the scandal, he announced his retirement in 1976, at the end of his third term. He was succeeded by Spark M. Matsunaga, formerly a Democratic Representative from Hawaii.

[DAE]

FORD, GERALD R(UDOLPH)
b. July 14, 1913; Omaha, Neb.
President of the United States, August 1974-January 1977.

Raised in Grand Rapids, Mich., Ford attended the University of Michigan, where he was a college all-star football player, and Yale Law School, where he earned his law degree in 1941. After serving in the Navy during World War II, he practiced law in Grand Rapids. In 1948, at the urging of Arthur H. Vandenberg, Ford successfully challenged an isolationist incumbent U.S. representative in the Republican primary. Ford then easily defeated his Democratic opponent and, in 12 subsequent elections, always captured over 60% of the vote. During the 1950s he aligned himself with the Eisenhower internationalist wing of the Republican Party and became a staunch proponent of large defense budgets and military alliances to prevent Communist expansion. Fiercely partisan, Ford compiled a conservative voting record in domestic affairs.

During the 1960s Ford emerged as a leader of House Republicans who elected him chairman of the House Republican Conference in 1963 and minority leader in 1965. He opposed most of the social welfare legislation of the Kennedy and Johnson Administrations, and consistently voted to reduce appropriations for such programs as model cities, the War on Poverty, and aid to education. Although he was on record as a supporter of civil rights, Ford generally played an obstructionist role until the final vote when he supported enactment of civil rights protection. Ford served on the Warren Commission to investigate the assassination of President John F. Kennedy and in 1965 helped write *Portrait of the Assassin* which defended the Commission's conclusion that Lee Harvey Oswald had acted alone. He frequently spoke out against President Johnson's conduct of the Vietnam War, arguing that the United States was not prosecuting the war aggressively enough. [See EISENHOWER, KENNEDY, JOHNSON Volumes]

During Nixon's first term in office, Ford proved himself a staunch Administration loyalist and maintained his conservative voting record. In 1970 the liberal Americans for Democratic Action gave him only a 17% rating. Ford supported Nixon's decision in March 1969 to seek appropriations for deployment of the Safeguard

anti-ballistic missile system (ABM) and accused its opponents of proposing unilateral disarmament "in the face of a serious threat from the Soviet Union." Ford led a low key campaign in the House to continue funding of the controversial supersonic transport plane (SST). In May 1971 he engineered a reversal of a previous House vote to cut off funds, but the Senate ultimately killed the measure. In January 1972 Ford signed a petition to discharge an anti-busing constitutional amendment from the House Judiciary Committee.

The rejection by the Senate of Nixon's conservative Supreme Court nominees Clement Haynsworth [*q.v.*] in November 1969 and G. Harrold Carswell [*q.v.*] in April 1970 led Ford to call for an inquiry into the possible impeachment of liberal Supreme Court Justice William O. Douglas [*q.v.*]. In a speech on the House floor on April 15, 1970, Ford demanded the removal of Douglas from the Court. He accused the Associate Justice of having ties to the underworld and of publishing an article in the "hard-core pornography" magazine *Evergreen Review* that advocated "hippie-yippie-style revolution." Ford cosponsored a resolution to have the House investigate whether grounds existed for impeachment. When a subcommittee of the House Judiciary Committee released in December 1970 a report that outlined a "mountain of evidence" against impeachment, Ford labelled the investigation a "whitewash."

Ford consistently supported Nixon's Vietnam policy. In September 1969 he denounced the proposals of anti-war activists for immediate troop withdrawal as "tantamount to surrender." He voted against all efforts to curb military spending in Southeast Asia and to place a time limit on American troop involvement in the war. In 1971 he voted to extend the draft and in 1973 voted against the War Powers Act. In the spring of 1972 he defended the intensified bombing of North Vietnam as "the right course." In May, when Nixon announced the mining of North Vietnamese harbors, Ford praised the President as "generous in his bid for peace but firm in his determination that we will not surrender."

On Oct. 12, 1973, two days after the resignation of vice president Spiro T. Agnew [q.v.], President Nixon named Gerald Ford to replace Agnew. The choice was widely viewed as an effort to win congressional support for the Administration in light of the growing Watergate scandal. The initial reaction in Congress was overwhelmingly favorable since Ford, though extremely partisan, was also well-liked and admired for his extreme honesty and candor. The following day, Ford promised a complete disclosure of his personal finances and also barred a 1976 campaign for the presidency.

Although favorably disposed to him, Congress conducted a thoroughgoing investigation of Ford's record. In the Senate Rules Committee, which opened hearings on Nov. 1, Ford was repeatedly questioned about such matters as executive privilege, the separation of powers, impoundment of funds, the independence of a new special Watergate prosecutor, and whether the President had a right to withhold information concerning criminal activity in the executive branch. Ford walked a tightrope in his answers. He denied that a President had "unlimited authority" in the areas of executive privlege, said that documents concerning "serious allegations" of criminal behavior should be made available, and said that even though he was convinced of the President's innocence, an impeachment inquiry would "clear the air." When asked if in the event of Nixon's resignation he would try to halt an investigation into the President's affairs, Ford replied "I don't think the public would stand for it."

On Nov. 20 the Rules Committee unanimously approved Ford's confirmation and on Nov. 27 the full Senate voted 92 to 3 in his favor. Although some opposition to Ford emerged in the House Judiciary Committee, largely on the basis of his conservative voting record and whether he had the leadership qualities required of a President, the House on Dec. 6 voted 387 to 35 to confirm Ford. Later

that day he was sworn in as the nation's 40th vice president.

As vice president, Ford traveled widely around the country, trying to bolster the sagging fortunes of the Republican Party, which was being buffeted by the Watergate scandal. Ford unequivocally defended Nixon. The day after he was confirmed, the Vice President declared that there was "no evidence that would justify impeachment." In January he characterized the President's opponents as "a few extreme partisans" and reiterated his conviction that Nixon had "no prior knowledge of the Watergate break-in" nor "any part in the cover-up." Ford did urge the President, however, to release the White House tapes in order to lay to rest doubts about his innocence. Even after Nixon released in April 1,200 pages of transcripts that were damaging to his case and led to the defection of much of his Republican support, Ford remained loyal. As late as July he said that "the preponderance of the evidence favors the President" and that Nixon was the victim of "Democratic partisan politics."

On Aug. 9, 1974, Nixon resigned from the presidency after admitting that he had ordered a halt to the FBI probe of the Watergate break-in, and Gerald Ford was sworn in as the nation's 38th President. In addressing the country he said, "Our long national nightmare is over. Our Constitution works. Our great republic is a government of laws and not of men." He pledged an Administration of "openness and candor" and moved quickly to meet with cabinet members, congressional leaders, national security officials and economic policy advisers. Ford took office with a great reservoir of good will. The public rallied to support him and leaders of both parties predicted an extended "honeymoon" with Congress.

Ford risked much of his popularity when, on Sept. 8, he granted Nixon a full pardon for all federal crimes he may have committed while in office. The decision provoked an uproar since the previous month Ford's press secretary Gerald ter-Horst [q.v.] had reiterated the President's statement that the public would not stand for a pardon. TerHorst immediately resigned in protest. A Harris poll in October indicated that 67% of the public opposed the pardon, and Ford's approval ratings plummeted. In October he testified before a House Judiciary subcommittee that was investigating the pardon that "no deal" had been made. The following month the subcommittee voted to drop the inquiry.

Ford balanced his pardon of Nixon by announcing on Sept. 16 a program of limited amnesty for Vietnam era draft evaders and military deserters. Although he had adamantly opposed any such efforts while in Congress, as President he said he had a responsibility to "bind up the nation's wounds." His proclamation offered clemency to those who swore an oath of allegiance to the United States and agreed to perform 24 months of alternate service work. For men already convicted, Ford set up a clemency board to review cases and recommend pardons. The clemency program received the support of Congress but was condemned by veterans groups as going too far, and by anti-war groups as inadequate. When the program expired on March 31, 1975, only about one out of six who were eligible had signed up and the American Civil Liberties Union concluded that the effort was a "fraud."

The most pressing problem that Ford faced on taking office was the state of the economy. The removal of price controls in 1973 and the quadrupling of oil prices by the Organization of Petroleum Exporting Countries (OPEC) that fall led to rapidly escalating prices. The Wholesale Price Index rose almost 18% in the 12 months ending in August 1974. In a nationally televised address to Congress on Aug. 12, Ford called inflation "our domestic public enemy No. 1" and told the legislators that "my first priority is to work with you to bring inflation under control." At Ford's request, Congress quickly passed legislation establishing a Council on Wage and Price Stability to monitor wage and price increases without, however, any enforcement powers. The President also announced plans for a White House economic summit conference in late September that would make

specific recommendations for fighting inflation.

On Oct. 8, Ford presented his anti-inflation program to Congress. Offering fiscal and monetary restraint as the main cure, he pledged to keep the federal budget for 1975 under $300 billion. Ford's program avoided mandatory controls and instead relied on appeals for "self-discipline" and "voluntary restraint," urging Americans to "drive less, heat less" as a way of cutting the consumption of high-priced fuel and heating oil. He set as a goal a reduction in oil imports of one million barrels a day without specific proposals to accomplish it. He asked Congress to enact a 5% surtax on incomes of middle and upper income families and on corporate profits, to liberalize investment tax credits, create a board to develop a coherent energy policy, and extend the length of unemployment benefits. In line with his emphasis on voluntary efforts to curb inflation, Ford announced on October 15 a "great citizens mobilization" under the slogan WIN (Whip Inflation Now). Among other things he suggested that Americans plant WIN gardens to reduce the cost of food.

Ford's initial response to the nation's economic woes provoked widespread criticism, especially from organized labor and congressional Democrats. AFL-CIO President George Meany [q.v.] disputed the targeting of inflation as a priority. "We are in a recession," Meany declared and argued that job creation and economic stimuli were most needed. Speaker of the House Carl Albert [q.v.] decried the "old time religion" of fiscal and monetary restraint. Liberal Democrats almost unanimously opposed Ford's suggested tax increases and deplored the absence of programs to create new jobs. Rebelling at the President's insistence on balancing the budget, Congress in October overrode a veto of a railroad workers pension bill and in December enacted a substantial increase in veterans' educational benefits over another Ford veto.

By the end of 1974 the evidence of recession was unmistakeable. Unemployment rose from 5.3% in July to 7.2% in

December. Auto sales fell 23% below 1973 levels, real gross national product declined 2.2% for the year, the purchasing power of workers in manufacturing dropped, and productivity declined for the first time since 1947. In addition, inflation continued at a galloping pace with wholesale prices for the year up 20.9% and consumer prices 12.2% higher than a year earlier. Economic analysts agreed that the nation was in the worst recession since the 1930s and coined a new term, "stagflation," to describe the unprecedented concurrence of rising prices with declining production.

Although the depth of the recession forced a drastic shift in Ford's economic policies, the combination of inflation and recession stymied efforts to devise a coherent approach to economic recovery. Ford's difficulties were evident in his 1975 State of the Union Address to Congress. In it, he proposed a $16 billion dollar tax cut, mostly in the form of a rebate to taxpayers, in order to stimulate the economy. He also abandoned his goal of a balanced budget and instead predicted a deficit of from $30 to $50 billion for 1975 and 1976. His proposed budget for fiscal 1974 was a record $349.4 billion, but it contained no new social welfare or job producing legislation, and Ford promised to veto any new spending bills. To counter the nation's dependence on high priced foreign oil, Ford said he would invoke his emergency powers as President to raise the tariff on imported oil, increasing its price in order to discourage consumption. He also urged Congress to deregulate the price of new natural gas in order to encourage domestic exploration, and asked for authorization to lease the government's petroleum reserves to commercial development.

The effort to enact his economic program led to a serious deterioration in Ford's relations with Congress. Upset at the inflationary effect of his energy proposals, Congress passed legislation in March to suspend his powers to raise import fees, but was unable to override a presidential veto. Controversy over Ford's energy plans continued through-

out the year. In July he presented a proposal for the phased decontrol of domestic oil prices in an effort to both cut consumption and encourage exploration of domestic oil. Instead, Congress passed a bill that month to roll-back the price of domestic oil in an effort to limit the inflationary impact of fuel consumption. Ford's veto of the bill led to a stalemate with Congress that continued until December when compromise legislation was enacted. The final version of the energy bill provided for an immediate roll-back in domestic crude oil prices, while also phasing out all controls over a 40-month period. As part of the compromise Ford agreed to remove the tariff on imported oil.

There were also substantial differences between Ford and Congress over tax and spending proposals. In March Congress enacted a $22.8 billion tax cut which Ford signed even though it was significantly larger than his original request. He did, however, successfully veto in May a $5.3 billion appropriation for public works employment and a $1.2 billion emergency housing bill the following month. But by the summer unemployment had reached 9.2%, the highest post World War II level, and Congressional Democrats and liberal Republicans joined forces to override presidential vetoes of a number of domestic spending programs. Over Ford's opposition, Congress approved a $2 billion health care bill in July, a $7.9 billion education bill in September, and an expanded school lunch program in October

The recession, meanwhile, was having a particularly adverse effect on state and municipal governments. High unemployment led to a sharp decline in tax revenues, and many state and local governments, having reached the limits of their borrowing power, were forced to cut back on social welfare programs at a time when they were most needed. New York City, on the verge of default throughout the spring and summer of 1975, pleaded with federal officials to support federally guaranteed loans to save the city. Ford, strongly backed by Treasury Secretary William Simon [q.v.], adamantly opposed such guarantees and as late as October 29 promised to veto any legislation to "bail out" New York. As evidence accumulated, however, that a default might jeopardize the banking system and the nation's economic recovery, the President was forced to relent. On Nov. 26 he asked Congress for legislation to provide up to $2.3 billion annually in loans to New York and the following month signed the bill into law.

By the end of 1975 statistics indicated that the economy, though slowly recovering from the depths of the recession, was still very weak. Unemployment in December measured 8.3% of the labor force and consumer prices rose 9.1% for the year. In his January 1976 economic report to Congress Ford declared that the "underlying fact about our economy is that it is steadily growing healthier." The persistence of high rates of unemployment and inflation, however, made the recovery shaky, and it was evident that the state of the economy would weigh heavily in the 1976 election campaigns.

While coping with the problems of the economy, Ford also found himself presiding over a somewhat new era in American foreign policy. Although he had entered politics as a Cold War advocate, as President he pursued a policy of detente with the Soviet Union and sought to defuse tensions in the Middle East. The legacy of Vietnam, moreover, affected his conduct of foreign affairs. Congress was unwilling to let the President have a free hand in the making of foreign policy and public pressure against further entanglements abroad forced a generally low profile for the United States.

Ford voiced strong support for Henry Kissinger [q.v.] and kept him on as both Secretary of State and head of the National Security Council. Kissinger was viewed as the chief architect of East-West detente and in October 1974 he visited the Soviet Union in pursuit of a new arms limitation agreement. Upon Kissinger's return, Ford announced that he would travel to the Soviet port city of Vladivostok in November to meet Soviet leader Leonid Brezhnev. There, the two heads of state announced an agreement to limit the numbers of all strategic offensive nuclear weaponry including the controversial MIRV delivery system. In contrast to the 1972 Strategic Arms Limitation Agreement (SALT), the new pact set the principle of equivalency in offensive weaponry for the two nations. Ford also revealed that SALT II talks would resume in Geneva in January and described the pursuit of a further agreement as in "the best interest" of the United States. Little further progress was made, however, and a year later in November 1975 Ford was forced to concede that the "timetable doesn't look encouraging" for a new SALT pact in the near future.

Ford also encouraged Kissinger's efforts at "shuttle diplomacy" to achieve a peace settlement in the Middle East. In March 1975, after Kissinger failed to win agreement for a second Egyptian-Israeli troop withdrawal from the Sinai, Ford angrily announced that his Administration was totally reassessing Middle East policy, and pointedly said that if Israel "had been a bit more flexible" the chances for peace would have been better. In June Ford held separate meetings with Egyptian President Anwar Sadat and Israeli Premier Yitzhak Rabin which led to a revival of Kissinger's peace-making efforts in August. On Sept. 4 Ford was able to announce that a new Sinai pact had been reached that called for a further Israeli troop withdrawal from the Sinai and the stationing of U.S. civilians there to monitor the pact. The agreement received widespread approval.

In other areas of foreign policy, Ford found his freedom to maneuver hampered by increasing congressional assertiveness. Revelations by the press of massive illegal intelligence operations by the Central Intelligence Agency (CIA) led Ford, in January 1975, to appoint a commission headed by vice president Nelson Rockefeller [q.v.] to investigate the charges. The report, issued in June, acknowledged violations of law, but disputed claims that the violations were serious or widespread. Both the Senate and the House, disturbed by reports that the CIA had plotted assassinations of foreign leaders, conducted their own investigations which caused Ford to warn against "sweeping attacks" on foreign intelligence operations. In September 1975 he refused to grant the House Select Committee on Intelligence access to classified material until it yielded any right to make the information public, a concession which the House granted. Concern about CIA activities, however, remained widespread and in December 1975 Congress, over the strong objections of Ford and Kissinger, voted to cut off funds for covert CIA operations in the Angolan civil war. Ford called the decision "a deep tragedy" but was powerless to do anything about it.

Congressional wariness about military involvement abroad was also apparent in its response to the final stages of the Vietnam war. Concerned about the upsurge in fighting there, Ford asked Congress in January 1975 for an additional $522 million in military aid for South Vietnam and Cambodia. As the Communist offensive in both countries intensified and it became obvious that victory was imminent, Ford pleaded for action, but Congress remained adamant and merely approved funds for an emergency evacuation of American personnel from South Vietnam. After the capture of the capitals of Pnompenh and Saigon in April, Ford blamed Congress for the collapse but admitted that the end of hostilities "closes a chapter in the American experience."

Shortly thereafter, on May 12, 1975, Cambodian forces seized an American merchant vessel, the Mayaguez, and its American crew, in the Gulf of Siam. Ford called the action "an act of piracy" and two days later ordered a dramatic rescue operation involving air, sea and ground forces. Although the action was successful and received praise from leaders of both parties, some analysts saw it as an excessive display of force intended to symbolize the willingness of the United States to take firm action in world affairs.

In September 1975 Ford was the target of two separate assassination attempts. On Sept. 5, in Sacramento, a member of the Charles Manson cult, Lynette Fromme, standing a few feet away from Ford as he shook hands in a crowd, pointed a gun at the President. The revolver failed to fire, and Fromme was quickly subdued by Secret Service personnel. On Sept. 22, in San Francisco, Sara Jane Moore, an FBI informant, fired at the President. The gunshot was deflected by the quick action of an onlooker, and Ford escaped injury.

On July 8, 1975 Ford formally announced his candidacy for the 1976 Republican presidential nomination. Ironically, Ford faced opposition from the conservative wing of the Party with which he had been most closely identified while in Congress. His choice of Nelson Rockefeller as vice president, the huge budget deficits of his Administration, and the Vladivostok arms limitation agreement all contributed to conservative disenchantment. Ford tried to mollify the opposition by appointing a conservative Southerner, Howard Callaway [q.v.], as his campaign manager, and intensifying his attacks on a free-spending Congress. In November, moreover, Rockefeller withdrew himself from consideration for the 1976 vice presidential spot. Nonetheless, California's conservative ex-governor Ronald Reagan [q.v.] announced his candidacy on Nov. 20 and a December Gallup poll showed Ford trailing Reagan.

Early primary victories by Ford in New Hampshire, Florida (where Reagan had predicted a two to one victory for himself), and Illinois buoyed the President's campaign, and attention shifted to the May 1 Texas primary. Reagan focused on the issues of detente and defense, charging that under Ford the United States had fallen behind the Soviet Union in military strength. Ford accused Reagan of raising "false alarms" and said that the ex-governor was so "simplistic" that, as president, he would make "irresponsible and fundamentally harmful policy decisions." Ford nonetheless lost by a huge margin, suffering the worst defeat ever sustained by an incumbent. A string of losses in Indiana, Georgia, Alabama and Nebraska added to Ford's worries, but he bounced back with victories in Michigan and Maryland on May 18. In late June Ford picked up the important endorsement of conservative Sen. Barry Goldwater (R, Ariz.) [q.v.], but when the delegate selection process was completed in July neither Ford nor Reagan had enough to clinch the nomination and the decision rested with the uncommitted delegates. Ford was slightly ahead, however, and the fact that he was the incumbent gave him the edge. On Aug. 19, the Republican national convention nominated Ford on the first ballot. To mollify conservatives, he chose Sen. Robert Dole (R, Kan.) [q.v.] as his running mate.

Having defeated the conservative opposition in his own party, Ford had to confront the opposition of liberals and moderates in the general election. The slowness of the economic recovery and Ford's numerous vetoes of spending programs to create jobs and expand social welfare measures meant that organized labor and racial minorities were solidly arrayed against him. His opponent, former Georgia Governor Jimmy Carter [q.v.], capitalized on the nation's disenchantment with Washington politicians of the Vietnam and Watergate era. Avoiding as much as possible specific solutions to problems, Carter promised to bring a new morality and a new approach to the nation's affairs. The election results were close. Ford won 27 states, including most of the Middle West and all of the West except Hawaii, while Carter captured the South and most of the heavily populated industrial Northeast. Carter received 51% of the popular vote to Ford's 49%, and 297 electoral votes in contrast to 241 for Ford.

After leaving office, Ford continued to speak out frequently on major issues in an effort to retain his leadership of the party and left open the possibility of a 1980 presidential race. [See CARTER Volume]

[JD]

For further information:
Richard H. Reeves, *A Ford Not a Lincoln* (New York, 1975).
Jerald F. terHorst, *Gerald Ford* (New York, 1974).

FORD, HENRY II
b. Sept. 4, 1917, Detroit, Mich.
Chairman and Chief Executive
Officer, Ford Motor Co., 1969–.

Ford, the grandson of industrialist Henry Ford, left Yale in 1940 to learn the family business from the bottom up. Although he lacked mechanical aptitude, his "terrific appetite for knowledge" enabled him to absorb the inner workings of the company's plant. A year later he enlisted in the Navy. With the death of his father in 1943, Ford was discharged from the Navy and returned to the family's industrial empire. With his grandfather's encouragement he proceeded to learn the company business from "the top down." A year later he was officially appointed vice president in charge of sales and promotion. Subsequent promotions followed in quick succession, and in 1945, at the age of 28, Ford inherited the presidency from his grandfather.

Ford completely reorganized the company's executive staff. Job responsibilities were succinctly defined and limits of individual power established. Ford later stated that his military experience provided the foundation for his organizational skills. Unlike his familial predecessors, he accepted the inevitability of unionism in the auto industry and established a flexible policy toward the United Automobile Workers (UAW).

Under Ford's leadership the Ford Motor Co. modernized plant facilities and production techniques and by 1964 ranked fourth among the nation's largest corporations. Described as a "hard-headed, aggressive profit-seeking executive," Ford maintained a strict adherence to a philosophy of enlightened self-interest. An unrelenting defender of the free enterprise system, it was Ford's contention that the best interests of business can only be served if they reflect societal concerns: "To hire a man because he needs a job, rather than because the job needs him, is to assure him that he is useless. On the other side of the coin, to help a man because it is in your own interest to help him is to treat him as an equal." [See TRU-MAN, EISENHOWER, KENNEDY, JOHNSON Volumes.]

Ford recognized the lack of innovation in the auto industry and pressed for research to improve car safety and performance. However except for the adoption of a long-standing engineering mechanism in 1969 that made cars difficult to steal, virtually no product improvement was made. Despite governmental pressure on the industry to subsidize research in the development of a pollution-free engine, Ford contended that such a project was unfeasible.

With pressure mounting from the Environmental Protection Agency (EPA), pollution control systems were installed in 1971 car models. However consumer complaints that the systems made cars difficult to start and reduced power at certain speeds led to their replacement with emission control devices. To comply with anti-pollution legislation, Ford established plant test centers, and in 1972 he publicly announced that a number of his employees including company executives had violated provisions of the pollution laws by falsifying data and improperly servicing 1973 model cars undergoing the tests. Despite his public disclosures, in 1973 the company was held liable for all violations and fined $7 million.

Starting in the mid-1960s Ford became engaged in public affairs. He provided his influential support for the Model Cities program in 1966 and spoke out on the importance of improving the "lot of the poor" in order to create better conditions for increased consumer spending. He helped launch the National Urban Coalition, and in 1968 he organized the National Alliance of Businessmen (NAB) to promote jobs for needy youths during the summer. The program was devised to bolster Job Opportunities in the Business Sector (JOBS), which provided federal subsidies to private firms as incentive to hire and train the chronically unemployed. In 1969 Ford reported that as a result of NAB's efforts, 145,000 jobs had been made available with 87,850 recipients still employed.

At Nixon's request Ford agreed in 1973 to head the National Center for Voluntary Action, a clearinghouse that coordinated the needs of social services agencies with available volunteer workers. In addition, during that year he announced the formation of the Committee for Concerned Consumerism whose goal was to revitalize the nation's Better Business Bureaus. Ford also began work on a pilot project to increase business involvement in the search for a comprehensive national medical program. On a local level he lent his support to a $500 million program that he considered "a catalyst for the total redevelopment of Detroit's central business district."

With the exception of his 1964 endorsement of Lyndon Johnson, Ford remained a lifetime Republican who contributed $50,000 to Nixon's reelection campaign. With the enactment of Nixon's Phase Two wage and price controls, Ford expressed his wariness regarding the administrative approach to economic recovery. Phase Two policies, he felt, were not providing the necessary momentum to undermine recessionary trends. In 1974 Ford proposed a 10% income tax cut to stimulate business and called for a revival of the Reconstruction Finance Corp. of the 1930s to fight the "severe recession." In the first quarter of 1975, the auto industry had its smallest production level in 14 years, and thousands of Ford's workers were temporarily laid off. Later that year Ford stated that he had been "let down" by Nixon and as a result of Watergate "the country is in real trouble." With Nixon's resignation, Ford praised Gerald Ford's ability and called for a "national reconciliation" to reestablish economic prosperity.

[DGE]

FORTAS, ABE
b. June 19, 1910; Memphis, Tenn.
Associate Justice, U.S. Supreme Court, 1965–69.

After receiving a B.A. from Southwestern College in Memphis in 1930, Fortas attended Yale Law School, where he graduated first in his class in 1933. He taught at Yale from 1933 to 1937 while also working part-time for several New Deal agencies. After 1937 Fortas held posts in the Securities and Exchange Commission and the Interior Department, serving as undersecretary of the interior from 1942 to 1946. In the latter year he began a private practice with several other New Dealers. Arnold, Fortas & Porter was soon a flourishing and prestigious Washington firm with a roster of corporate clients including Coca Cola, Lever Brothers, Philip Morris and Pan American Airways. Fortas himself became known as a skilled corporate counselor and appellate advocate, but he and his firm also developed a reputation for their civil liberties work. They defended various individuals charged with being security risks during the McCarthy era and took several loyalty cases to the Supreme Court. Serving as court-appointed counsel, Fortas won a landmark ruling from the Supreme Court in 1963 in which the justices unanimously held that the states must supply counsel to indigent defendants accused of serious, non-capital crimes.

In 1948 Fortas secured a Supreme Court order that enabled Lyndon Johnson [q.v.] to get his name on the general election ballot in Texas. Johnson went on to win a U.S. Senate seat that November. The incident launched a long and close friendship between the two men, with Fortas becoming one of Johnson's most trusted advisers. During Johnson's presidency Fortas acted as an unofficial counselor on appointments and legislation and on issues ranging from racial controversies to the Vietnam war. He turned down several offers of appointment to public positions but, at Johnson's insistence, finally agreed to accept a Supreme Court nomination on July 28, 1965.

On the bench Fortas immediately aligned himself with the Warren Court's liberal justices. He voted with the majority in the June 1966 *Miranda* decision and wrote the opinion of the Court in a May 1967 case extending most of the criminal safeguards in the Bill of Rights to children in juvenile court proceedings. Justice Fortas voted repeatedly to sustain civil rights claims and to invalidate state loyalty oaths, but he took a more moderate position in free press and obscenity cases.

On June 26, 1968 Johnson nominated Fortas as Chief Justice to succeed Earl Warren, who planned to retire. A coalition of Republicans and conservative Democrats managed to block Senate confirmation of the appointment, and it was withdrawn early in October. Foes of the nomination objected to Fortas's liberalism, to his advisory relationship with Johnson, which had continued even after he joined the bench, and to having a "lame-duck" President select the new Chief Justice. In addition, it had been disclosed in September that Fortas had received $15,000 for teaching a summer school course in 1968 and that the money had been raised by one of his former law partners from five prominent businessmen, one of whom had a son involved in a federal criminal case. [See JOHNSON Volume]

Despite the defeat of his nomination as Chief Justice, there was every expectation as the 1968 Court term opened that Fortas would have a long, productive and influential career as an associate justice. He seemed at ease on the bench and had won respect for his intelligence and legal craftsmanship and for opinions that were thorough and scholarly yet also crisp and colorful in style. During the term Fortas wrote several significant opinions for the Court which advanced the libertarian views he espoused. In November 1968 the Justice held that Arkansas's "monkey law," which forbade the teaching of the Darwinian theory of evolution in public schools, violated the First Amendment's ban on establishment of religion. A week later Fortas ruled that a court order restraining the National States Rights Party from holding a public rally for 10 days was an unconstitutional violation of free speech because the injunction had been granted at a hearing without prior notice to party representatives. For a seven man majority in February 1969, Fortas declared that the First Amendment guaranteed public school students the right to peaceful, nondisruptive political expression such as the wearing of black armbands to protest the Vietnam war.

In another February 1969 case involving "jailhouse lawyers," Fortas's majority opinion held that the states could not bar a prisoner from giving legal aid to illiterate or poorly educated fellow inmates when no other provision was made for those inmates to receive legal assistance in appealing their convictions. In an April 1969 opinion Fortas ruled that a lineup identification of a suspect could not be used as evidence at trial when the lineup was arranged so that the defendant stood out as the likely criminal.

Off the bench Justice Fortas and his wife, a leading Washington tax attorney, enjoyed a life of comfort and culture. Their Georgetown home contained antique furniture, contemporary works of art and Chinese scrolls and paintings. They drove a Rolls Royce and had a summer house in Connecticut. An accomplished amateur violinist, Fortas played in a string quartet at least once a week.

Fortas's judicial career ended suddenly in May 1969, when he resigned from the Court in the wake of disclosures of questionable financial associations. On May 4 *Life* magazine reported that in January 1966 Fortas had accepted $20,000 from the family foundation of industrialist Louis E. Wolfson. He had returned the money in December 1966 after Wolfson was twice indicted on federal stock charges. Since then, Wolfson had been convicted and imprisoned for selling unregistered securities. On the same day, Fortas issued a statement declaring that he had "not accepted any fee or emolument" from Wolfson or his foundation but then conceding that the foundation had tendered him a fee in 1966 for research and writing services. Fortas said he had returned the fee

when he concluded that he could not undertake the assignment. He insisted that he had not intervened in any way in Wolfson's case.

Nonetheless, some members of Congress began calling for Fortas's resignation, and there was talk of impeachment. The pressure increased when *Newsweek* magazine revealed on May 11 that Attorney General John Mitchell [*q.v.*] had visited Chief Justice Warren on May 7, reportedly to tell him that the Justice Department had "far more serious" information about Fortas than had already been disclosed. Fortas submitted his resignation May 14 and made it public the next day along with a letter to Earl Warren explaining his action. In the letter Fortas stated that late in 1965 he had made an agreement with the Wolfson Foundation that gave him $20,000 a year for life in exchange for services to the Foundation. He had received the first fee in January 1966 but had canceled the agreement that June because his Court duties were taking more time than anticipated. Fortas had returned the money in December 1966 following Wolfson's indictment. The Justice declared he was resigning for the good of the Court and flatly denied any wrongdoing on his part. On May 20, 1969 the American Bar Association's Committee on Professional Ethics concluded that Fortas's association with Wolfson was "clearly contrary" to the Canons of Judicial Ethics. The Justice Department, which had been conducting its own inquiry, decided that Fortas had done nothing criminal and closed its file on the case.

The first justice ever to leave the Court under the pressure of public criticism, Fortas made no further public statement about the Wolfson episode and returned quietly to private life. He spent some time writing a book which he later decided not to publish, and he gradually undertook some legal work. By the spring of 1970 Fortas had joined in a small new law firm in Washington.

Although his tenure on the bench was brief, Fortas was well-regarded by legal scholars because of the creativity and craftsmanship of his opinions. Despite their appreciation for the high quality of his work, however, all commentators deplored Fortas's financial indiscretions which damaged the Court's reputation and cut short what had seemed a most promising judicial career.

[CAB]

For further information:
Fred Graham, "Abe Fortas," in Leon Friedman and Fred L. Israel, eds., *The Justices of the U.S. Supreme Court, 1789-1969* (New York, 1969), Vol. 4.
Robert Shogan. *A Question of Judgment: The Fortas Case and the Struggle for the Supreme Court* (Indianapolis, 1972).

FRIEDAN, BETTY
b. Feb. 4, 1921; Peoria, Ill.
President, National Organization for Women, 1966-70; Policy Board, National Women's Political Caucus, 1971-72.

Friedan graduated from Smith College in 1942. During the next two decades she married and raised three children. In 1963 Friedan gained national attention with the publication of *The Feminine Mystique,* in which she argued that during the postwar period women were taught that fulfillment was to be found in lives of complete domesticity. In 1966 she helped found the National Organization for Women (NOW), "to bring women into the mainstream . . . in truly equal partnership with men." Friedan became NOW's first president. [See JOHNSON Volume]

The rhetorical keyword of Friedan's ideology was equality. Under her presidency NOW successfully pressured the Equal Employment Opportunities Commission (EEOC) to rule that airlines could not fire stewardesses who married or reached the age of 35 and that help-wanted ads should not be listed by male or female categories. NOW also lobbied for passage of the Equal Rights Amendment (ERA), federally funded day care

centers, job protection for pregnant women, tax law revision to permit deduction for childcare expenses and the repeal of anti-abortion laws.

It was Friedan who initiated the opposition that led to the defeat of President Nixon's 1970 nominee to the Supreme Court, G. Harrold Carswell [q.v.]. Testifying before the Senate Judiciary Committee, Friedan charged that Carswell openly defied the Civil Rights Act in a 1969 ruling that sanctioned the right of employers to deny jobs to women with children.

Wary of her ability to support and lead the increasingly radical elements of NOW who emphasized the sexual domination of men over women and support of lesbian rights, Friedan, at the Organization's 1970 convention, announced she would not run for reelection. At the same meeting she called for a Women's Strike for Equality. On Aug. 26, 1970–the 50th Anniversary of the 19th Amendment–demonstrations, marches and speeches were staged in 40 major cities, and Friedan led a parade of over 10,000 down Fifth Avenue in New York City.

In July 1971 Friedan, Bella Abzug [q.v.], Shirley Chisholm [q.v.] and Gloria Steinem [q.v.] announced the formation of the National Women's Political Caucus (NWPC) to encourage women to run for public office and plan an agenda of women's issues for the 1972 national party conventions. Later Friedan bitterly accused Steinem and Abzug of dictatorial control of the NWPC, selective support of women candidates and responsibility for the weaknesses of the NWPC at the 1972 Democratic National Convention.

After her defeat in a controversial 1972 NWPC election, Friedan retreated from organizational leadership of the women's movement, wrote "Betty Friedan's Notebook" for *McCall's,* and accepted teaching positions at Temple, Yale, Queens College and the New School for Social Research.

Friedan became convinced that the defeat of the ERA in over 26 attempts at ratification from 1973 to 1977 was due to the political infighting and left-right split in the women's movement, which had been successfully exploited by such groups on the right as Stop ERA. In November 1977 at the National Conference of Women in Houston, Friedan, in a major shift, supported a plank on lesbian rights and called for the reestablishment of a healthy, wide ranging coalition of women.

[JMP]

FRIEDMAN, MILTON
b. July 31, 1912; New York, N.Y.
Economist.

The son of immigrant merchants, Milton Friedman grew up in Rahway, N.J., and graduated from Rutgers University in 1932. He did graduate work in economics at the University of Chicago, a citadel of classic economic theory. In 1935 he joined the National Resources Committee, a federal agency, as a statistician, leaving in 1937 to do a study of independent professional practice for the National Bureau of Economic Research. Friedman taught economics, and from 1941 to 1943 he was the principal tax research economist at the Treasury Department. After obtaining his Ph.D. from Columbia University in 1946, he joined the faculty at the University of Chicago, where he spent the next three decades.

By the 1960s Friedman had become the foremost academic apostle of free market economics and an iconoclastic critic of the Keynesian theories prevalent among government economists. In *Capitalism and Freedom* (1962) he made a vigorous laissez-faire case against virtually all government interference with the private market. He favored the elimination of most federal agencies, as well as tariffs and farm price supports, arguing that the best guarantee of prosperity and consumer welfare was an unfettered price system. Friedman believed that Social Security should be abolished and called for the abandonment of minimum wage legislation on the grounds that such a wage floor increased unemployment. He advocated

turning over public schools and public transportation to the private sector.

Within the academic community Friedman won prominence with his persistent and provocative advocacy of the quantity theory of money, or "monetarism" as it became known. According to this theory, the dominant factor in the economy is the amount of money in circulation, not, as the Keynesians held, the fiscal policy of the federal government. In *The Monetary History of The United States,* Friedman correlated contractions in the money supply with the occurrence of recessions and depressions. His chief policy prescription was to strip the Federal Reserve of its discretionary control of the money supply and mandate that the supply be increased at the steady rate of 4% each year.

An active supporter of the unsuccessful presidential candidacy of Sen. Barry Goldwater (R, Ariz.) [*q.v.*] in 1964, Friedman reached the peak of his influence with the election of Richard Nixon in 1968. Although he was not an official member of the Republican Administration, Friedman saw his ideas reflected in several of the new Administration's policies and personnel. Nixon's first chairman of the Council of Economic Advisers, Paul McCracken [*q.v.*], described himself as "Friedmanesque." The Administration's basic economic policy of cutting government spending and taxes to halt the inflation and stimulate investment followed the outlines of Friedman's thought. By late 1969, however, the Federal Reserve allowed a slow and steady expansion of the money supply.

The creation of an all-volunteer army and the publication by the Federal Reserve of regular reports on the money supply were other Friedman proposals implemented during the Nixon years. The Administration tried to enact Friedman's substitute for welfare, the negative income tax, as part of its Family Assistance Plan, but Congress rejected the measure. The Administration did not attempt to implement many of Friedman's favorite libertarian schemes, such as his proposal to replace public schools with a system of government-awarded tuition vouchers that would enable parents to send children to the school of their choice.

After the Nixon Administration's wage-price freeze of August 1971, Friedman regularly excoriated the controls. To Friedman the controls were not only economically unsound but "deeply and inherently immoral." "By substituting the rule of men for the rule of law and for voluntary cooperation in the marketplace," he wrote, "the controls threaten the very foundations of a free society." Friedman was also a frequent critic of the Food and Drug Administration (FDA), whose extended procedures for approving experimental drugs were, according to Friedman, costly, inefficient and self-defeating. Friedman wrote in *Newsweek* in January 1973 that the FDA's regulatory procedures "condemn innocent people to death." Friedman's confidence in the market led him to dispel fears of an energy crisis and continually escalating oil prices after the Organization of Petroleum Exporting Countries dramatically hiked oil prices in October 1973. Friedman predicted in June 1974 that the oil cartel would break up and prices would return to pre-October 1973 levels.

At the same time Friedman stimulated a lively debate with his suggestion, unusual for a conservative, that the U.S. adopt a system of automatic wage-price increases to keep pace with inflation. He cited Brazil's successful use of the mechanism, known as "indexing," in reducing its inflation without inhibiting economic growth. He maintained that indexing would give greater protection to the poor and those on fixed incomes from the inflationary spiral. Some critics charged that the Brazilian technique spawned black markets, while others criticized Friedman's idea as a surrender to inflation that would weaken the political resolve to try more orthodox techniques, such as reduced government spending.

In March 1975 Friedman visited Chile and recommended an economic "shock treatment" to combat inflation. In line with his advice, the military dictatorship instituted a rigorous economic austerity program, which included sharp government spending cuts, tax increases and regular devaluations of the currency. Friedman, who acknowledged that the program would be hardest on the poorest section of Chile's population, was severely criticized in America for associating with the repressive regime.

In October 1976 the Swedish Royal Academy of Sciences named Friedman winner of the 1976 Nobel Memorial Prize in Economics for his achievements in the fields of consumption analysis, monetary history and theory and for his demonstration of the complexity of stabilization policy. The selection was controversial, with several former Nobel Prize winners publicly protesting the award to Friedman because of his association with the Chilean regime and 2,000 leftists demonstrating outside the Stockholm ceremony.

[TO]

FULBRIGHT, J(AMES) WILLIAM
b. April 9, 1905; Sumner, Mo.
Democratic Senator, Ark., 1945-75;
Chairman, Foreign Relations
Committee, 1959-75.

The son of a wealthy businessman and banker, Fulbright was raised in Fayetteville, Ark. where his family moved in 1906. After graduating from the University of Arkansas in 1925, he studied at Oxford University on a Rhodes scholarship. He returned to the United States and studied law at George Washington University. Admitted to the bar in 1934, Fulbright became an attorney for the Justice Department, then taught law at the University of Arkansas and served as president of the University from 1939 to 1941. He was elected to the House of Representatives in 1942 and two years later won a seat in the Senate.

In the Senate, Fulbright generally supported liberal legislation in the areas of health, education, and welfare, but, reflecting the sentiments of the white majority in his state, he consistently opposed civil rights legislation.

Throughout his career in Congress,

Fulbright was concerned primarily with foreign affairs. In 1943 he introduced the "Fulbright Resolution," approved by the House, which favored the creation of an international organization to maintain world peace. Three years later he introduced the bill which set up the educational exchange program that bears his name. Becoming chairman of the Senate Foreign Relations Committee in 1959, he used his position to conduct highly publicized hearings to educate the American public on foreign affairs. Fulbright first voiced doubts about U.S. policy in Vietnam during the spring of 1965. He conducted televised hearings on the war in February 1966 and questioned the wisdom of continued escalation of the conflict. By the end of the decade, he had become the symbol of congressional opposition to the Vietnam War and was credited with making criticism of the war respectable in Congress. [See TRUMAN, EISENHOWER, KENNEDY, JOHNSON Volumes]

During the Nixon years Fulbright continued his criticism of United States foreign policy. His first major clash with the new Administration came in March 1969 after Nixon requested congressional approval of funds for the Safeguard antiballistic missile system. In hearings conducted by the Foreign Relations Committee, Fulbright accused Secretary of Defense Melvin Laird [q.v.] of using "the technique of fear" to justify deployment of the ABM. Charging that Safeguard had little military value and was "purely a political gimmick," he deplored the decision to go ahead with its deployment before completing arms limitation talks with the Soviet Union. In June 1969 Fulbright signed a statement with other members of Congress urging a moratorium on the deployment of the Safeguard system. In August he voted in favor of the Cooper-Hart amendment to a defense procurement bill to bar funds for the ABM. The amendment was defeated, however, and in November Congress finally approved the appropriation.

In 1970 Fulbright published *The Pentagon Propaganda Machine*, an expanded version of speeches he delivered in the Senate in December 1969. In it, he accused the Defense Department of waging "a coordinated high pressure propaganda and public relations campaign" to win approval of the ABM. The Pentagon was guilty of "subterfuge" he said, in its efforts to manipulate public opinion. Fulbright also warned that the "monster bureaucracy" at the Pentagon had become an active participant in making foreign policy, at the expense of both the State Department and Congress, and that militarism was "slowly undermining democratic procedure and values."

Fulbright led efforts to restore the constitutional balance between Congress and the Executive in foreign affairs. In February 1969 he introduced a "national commitments" resolution that reasserted a congressional voice in decisions pledging the United States to the defense of foreign nations. The resolution, as approved by the Senate in June, stipulated that the use of troops abroad "results only from affirmative action by the legislative and executive branches" of the government. As a sense of the Senate resolution, however, it did not have binding power on the President, and later in the year, Fulbright pushed for more forceful measures.

In December 1969, Congress voted to prohibit the commitment of U.S. ground troops to Laos and Thailand. The action came after Fulbright won acknowledgement from the Administration of a secret "contingency plan" with Thailand, and after reports surfaced of U.S. involvement in the Laotian civil war. Throughout 1969 and 1970, the Senate Foreign Relations Committee conducted an inquiry on U.S. military activities overseas. Highly critical of the extensive use of executive agreements in foreign affairs rather than treaties which required Senate approval, its final report, issued in December 1970, charged that "creeping commitments" threatened to trap the nation into global military responsibilities. In 1972 Fulbright supported legislation requiring the Secretary of State to submit to Congress the text of any international agreement made by the executive branch.

After Nixon took office in 1969, Fulbright initially muted his criticism of the Vietnam War. He praised the eight point peace plan which Nixon offered in May, and applauded the President's announced intention gradually to withdraw all U.S. troops. By the autumn, however, Fulbright had resumed his criticism of the war. In October 1969, after nationwide protests against the war captured the attention of the public, he deplored Nixon's call for a moratorium on dissent and instead urged a "moratorium on killing." The next month Fulbright declared that Nixon had taken "fully as his own the Johnson war" by acting on the assumption that the war was a fight against an international Communist conspiracy.

In a major speech in St. Louis in December, he attacked "Vietnamization" as another form of waging "a continuing war of stalemate and attrition" and warned that "every day this war goes on the sickness of American society worsens." In February and March 1970, Fulbright held extensive public hearings on the effectiveness of Nixon's Vietnamization policy. He expressed skepticism that the prospects for peace had improved, and a report by his Committee's staff cast serious doubt on the chances of Vietnamization succeeding.

Fulbright attacked the President's decision to invade Cambodia and, in June 1970, supported the Cooper-Church amendment to cut off funds for combat operations in Cambodia. In 1971, after the United States provided support for a South Vietnamese invasion of Laos, Fulbright announced that he would hold "end-the-war" hearings in order to propose legislation to curb the President's war making powers. He supported legislation aimed at that purpose which Sen. Jacob Javits (R, N.Y.) introduced. As finally passed by Congress, the 1973 War Powers Act limited to 60 days the President's ability to commit U.S. troops to combat abroad without Congressional approval.

Fulbright presented his most extreme attack on American foreign policy in his 1972 book, *The Crippled Giant.* Surveying U.S. policy abroad since World War II, he charged that the nation's policymakers seemed "driven by a sense of imperial destiny." The exercise of power had become an end in itself, he charged, "purposeless and undisciplined" in its use. "History did not prepare the American people for the kind of role we are now playing in the world," he said. Fulbright warned that the unbridled resort to force in foreign affairs would cripple the United States, leaving a "moral wasteland." Already it was destroying the constitutional balance of power between Congress and the President and unless it was stopped, the "ultimate casualty" would be democracy itself.

After Henry Kissinger [*q.v.*] became Secretary of State in 1973, Fulbright's criticism of the Nixon Administration's foreign policy lessened. Fulbright respected Kissinger's abilities and approved of his willingness to abandon Cold War myths in the conduct of foreign affairs. He supported Kissinger's pursuit of detente with the Soviet Union and approved of the friendly initiatives toward mainland China. Kissinger's reassertion of a strong role for the Department of State in making foreign policy and his obvious preference for negotiation and diplomatic initiatives over the use of force was more in line with Fulbright's own thinking. The Senator also praised Kissinger's evenhanded approach to a Middle East peace settlement.

Fulbright's preoccupation with foreign affairs put him increasingly out of touch with the voters of his state. In 1974, in his bid for a sixth term in the Senate, he lost the Democratic primary to Gov. Dale Bumpers. When Fulbright retired from the Senate, he had amassed the longest tenure as chairman of the Foreign Relations Committee of any previous senator.

[JD]

For further information:
Haynes Johnson and Bernard M. Gwertzman, *Fulbright: The Dissenter* (New York, 1968).

GALBRAITH, JOHN KENNETH
b. Oct. 15, 1908; Iona Station, Ontario
Economist

Galbraith grew up in Canada and attended Ontario Agricultural College at Guelph. He received his doctorate from Berkeley in agricultural economics. He taught at Harvard at various periods from 1934 to 1975. During World War II, he served as assistant administrator, and then deputy administrator in charge of the price division of the Office of Price Administration. He also was director of the United States Strategic Bombing Survey in 1945 and director of the State Department's Office of Economic Security Policy in 1946. A liberal Democrat, he was an adviser to Adlai Stevenson in two presidential campaigns. He also advised John Kennedy in the 1960 presidential election and served for 27 months as Kennedy's ambassador to India. In 1972 he was elected President of the American Economic Association.

As an economist Galbraith's reputation was based largely on *American Capitalism* (1952), *The Affluent Society* (1958), and *The New Industrial State* (1967). *American Capitalism* developed the idea of countervailing power, a balance among the major actors of the American economy—big industry, major retailers, unions, and the federal government. *The Affluent Society* predicted an age of private wealth and public impoverishment and pointed to the wasteful misallocation of national resources in the United States. *The New Industrial State* introduced the concept of the technostructure—the complex of engineers, accountants, lawyers, psychologists and others who ran the giant corporations and shaped the economy to their own purposes. [See TRUMAN, EISENHOWER, KENNEDY, JOHNSON Volumes]

In these books and *Economics and the Public Purpose* (1973), Galbraith established many of the themes he asserted during the Nixon and Ford Administrations. Galbraith argued for a new socialism to serve the needs of the American public better than alternative economic systems. In this regard, he contended that the free-enterprise system was no longer capable of supporting certain industries. His socialism, moreover, would be new because it would not be directed at the banks and high-technology monopolies that traditional socialists had longed to take over in the past, but rather the housing, health, and other public purpose segments of the economy which were experiencing neglect or a low-priority status.

Galbraith was a keen critic of Nixon's economic policies and called for price and wage controls as a means to control inflation. He blamed Nixon's economic policy for causing the economic crisis of the mid-1970s. He criticized Nixon's two top economic advisers, George P. Shultz [q.v.] and Herbert Stein [q.v.], whom he once described as "two of the finest 18th-century [economists] in the United States."

As a strong liberal Democrat, he was a vocal critic of the United States role in the Indochina war. He supported Eugene McCarthy's [q.v.] bid for the Democratic presidential nomination in 1968. He was a major opponent of the American military, and his book, *How to Control the Military* (1969), revealed his objections. He supported equal rights for women, an end to racism, and the need for environmental protection.

Galbraith backed George McGovern's [q.v.] bid for the Democratic presidential nomination in 1972. His name was one of many appearing on Nixon's "enemies' list." At the end of the 1974-75 academic year, Galbraith retired from Harvard as Paul M. Warburg Professor of Economics. He continued to write and engage actively in Democratic Party politics.

[HML]

GARDNER, JOHN W(ILLIAM)
b. Oct. 8, 1912; Los Angeles, Calif.
Chairman, Urban Coalition, 1968-70;
Chairman, Common Cause, 1970-77.

Gardner earned his doctorate in psychology at Berkeley in 1938 and taught at Connecticut College for Women and

Mount Holyoke. He began work at the Carnegie Corp. in 1946 and became its president in 1955. He served as Secretary of Health, Education and Welfare under Lyndon Johnson from 1965 to 1968. Gardner left the Administration in March 1968 contending that he could deal more effectively with solving urban problems from a position outside of government. To that end, he became chairman of the National Urban Coalition, a private association, organized in 1967. [See JOHNSON Volume]

In the fall of 1970, Gardner formed Common Cause, an organization that soon became one of the most effective public interest groups. According to Gardner, the agenda of Common Cause was "how to get responsive government, government that you can hold to account, government to which the citizen has access."

Under Gardner's leadership Common Cause became active in many areas of public policy and government structure. It sought, among other goals, to depoliticize the Justice Department, end illegal covert police and intelligence activities, terminate the war in Vietnam, give high priority to solving problems of poverty, reform legislative machinery, halt construction of the B-1 bomber and supersonic transport and establish a federal consumer protection agency.

Common Cause achieved much notoriety because of its early criticism of the Nixon Administration. The organization filed the lawsuit that forced Nixon to disclose the contributors to his 1972 presidential campaign. In the aftermath of Watergate, Common Cause moved with considerable success to institute election reforms dealing with limits on campaign spending and public financing of presidential elections. It played a role in weakening the seniority system in the House and in deposing the chairmen of some congressional committees.

At the height of its influence in 1973, Common Cause had 320,000 members, most articulate and well educated. Its membership declined to 250,000 by 1977, however. By 1975 it had a staff of 80 Washington employees and 14 lobbyists.

Gardner was not without his critics. His name was included on Nixon's "enemies' list." Rep. Wayne Hays [q.v.] of Ohio referred to Common Cause as "common curse." Gardner stepped down as chairman in 1977 and was succeeded by Nan Waterman, a civic activist from Muscatine, Iowa. He remained with Common Cause, however, serving as a member of the board and a lobbyist.

[HML]

GARMENT, LEONARD
b. May 11, 1924; New York, N.Y.
Special Assistant to the President, 1969-73; Acting Legal Counsel to the President, 1973.

Leonard Garment received his law degree from Brooklyn Law School in 1949 and then joined the prestigious law firm of Mudge, Rose, Guthrie, and Alexander. A specialist in litigation, Garment befriended Richard Nixon when the former Vice President joined the law firm in 1963. Frequently, Nixon visited Garment's Brooklyn Heights home. Garment introduced Nixon to his New York friends; many of them were liberals and many were active in the arts. When Nixon decided to pursue the Republican nomination for the presidency, Garment, a liberal Democrat, joined his campaign staff. Garment headed the media division throughout the primary run and the fall campaign. Following election day, Garment participated in the selection of the cabinet. Nixon asked Garment to join the Administration as a White House adviser on minority problems.

On July 12, 1969 Nixon appointed Garment director of the National Goals Research Staff. Garment also dealt with a number of civil rights problems the Administration confronted. Following a July 1970 NAACP attack on the Administration for being anti-black, Garment wrote the White House response which declared that "the President and the Administration are committed to achieving equal opportunity for every American, and are determined to maintain their efforts to reach that goal." Garment further persuaded Nixon not to veto the Voting Rights Act of 1970 which promised to continue to protect the newly enrolled one million black voters in the South and added 18-year-olds to the voting rolls. Garment argued that Nixon could not afford to alienate the young and the minorities.

As the Watergate crisis grew more ominous, Nixon consulted Garment for advice. At Garment's urging the President fired H. R. Haldeman [q.v.] and John Ehrlichman [q.v.], his top advisers, who were implicated in the coverup. Nixon asked Garment to replace John Dean [q.v.], who was also fired, as the acting counsel for the President for Watergate matters. Garment's first responsibility was to assist speechwriter Raymond Price in composing a statement announcing the ousters. Garment then joined with the other White House lawyer, J. Fred Buzhardt, to answer reporters' questions concerning the shakeup in the White House staff and Watergate.

At this press conference Garment quickly discovered that there were many gaps in the White House case. He thus requested access to presidential tapes and documents on the case so that he could prepare a better defense for the President. Nixon refused to permit him to look at the material. Throughout the remainder of 1973 Garment found it difficult to function as the President's lawyer because he could not examine the material in question. He further feared that he might be implicated in obstructing justice as long as the President denied the special Watergate prosecutor access to the material.

On Nov. 3, 1973 Garment and Buzhardt flew to Key Biscayne to confront their client on this issue. They outlined to Alexander Haig [q.v.], Nixon's chief aide, the legal problems the President faced and they argued they could not defend him as long as he denied them the right to see the evidence. Both found Nixon's position so hopeless that they requested permission to see him in order to persuade him to resign. After seeing Nixon, Haig reported

that the President would neither resign nor see them. Garment then quietly resigned his counsel position but remained on the White House staff.

President Ford appointed Garment United States representative to the United Nations Human Rights Commission in 1975. In a number of stormy sessions, Garment defended the Israeli treatment of the Arabs in the occupied territories. He also fought against passage of the "Zionism-as-Racism" resolution. In 1977 Garment returned to practice full-time law in New York.

[JB]

GENEEN, HAROLD S(YDNEY)
b. Jan. 22, 1910; Bournemouth, England.
Chief Executive Officer, International Telephone and Telegraph Corporation, 1959-77.

Geneen spent much of his youth in a Connecticut boarding school, leaving at age 16 to become a page on the New York Stock Exchange. After acquiring a degree in accounting in 1934, he rose quickly through a succession of companies, including Bell and Howell and Jones and Laughlin Steel Corp., before winning his reputation of master manager as vice president of Raytheon Manufacturing, which he joined in 1956. Dividing the large electronics firm into 12 semiautonomous units, Geneen applied a system of strict financial control and constant monitoring of each division by top management.

Geneen brought the same management principles to International Telephone and Telegraph (ITT) when he assumed the presidency of the communications carrier in 1959. Through an aggressive program of mergers, acquisitions and diversification both in the U.S. and overseas, he succeeded in boosting ITT's sales to $8.5 billion annually by the early 1970s. [See KENNEDY, JOHNSON Volumes]

During the 1970s Geneen and ITT became embroiled in several scandals implicating high Nixon Administration officials in possible conflict of interest and influence peddling. In 1970 the conglomerate purchased the Hartford Fire Insurance Co. as a consistent source of fresh revenue. The Department of Justice immediately filed an anti-trust suit. The suit was about to be appealed to the Supreme Court when it was settled in 1971 by an out-of-court agreement that permitted ITT to keep the insurance company. However the company was forced to divest itself of other holdings, including Avis Rent-a-Car and the Canteen Corp.

In February 1972 columnist Jack Anderson [q.v.] released a confidential memorandum allegedly written by ITT lobbyist Dita Beard [q.v.] linking the anti-trust settlement with an ITT pledge of $400,000 for the 1972 Republican National Convention, which was tentatively scheduled to be held in San Diego where ITT owned hotel property. On March 17 Beard denied writing the Anderson memo and called it a "forgery" and a "hoax," but the Senate Judiciary Committee launched an immediate investigation into Anderson's charges. Geneen testified before the Committee on March 29 and stated that the firm's contribution to the Republican Convention was conditional on establishment of convention headquarters for President Nixon at ITT's hotel in San Diego.

On March 20, 1972, Anderson charged that ITT had attempted to influence U.S. policy in Chile, a country where the conglomerate had six affiliates with over 7,000 employees. Anderson said his material revealed ITT efforts and "fervent hopes for a military coup" in Chile in 1970 to prevent the election of Marxist Salvador Allende as president.

In March 1973 a Senate Foreign Relations Committee special Subcommittee on Multinational Corporations began a two-year investigation of the influence of those firms on the U.S. economy and conduct of foreign policy. Testifying before the committee on March 21, John A. McCone, former director of the Central Intelligence Agency (CIA) and a director of ITT, stated that he had met with Henry Kissinger [q.v.] and CIA Director Richard Helms [q.v.] in mid-1970 to offer the U.S. government $1 million in financial aid on behalf of ITT. The money was to be used to block the runoff election of Allende as president. The funds had been authorized by Geneen, and according to McCone, they were to be channeled to people who "support the principles and programs the U.S. stands for against the programs of the Allende Marxists." He denied charges that the money was intended for "surreptitious" purposes or would be used to create "economic chaos." Instead he maintained it was to be used to support conservative politicans and for housing and agricultural projects.

The plan was rejected but Helms put Geneen into contact with William Broe, director of clandestine operations in Latin America for the CIA. Earlier testimony by ITT Vice President William Merriam had revealed that Geneen had arranged to establish a working relationship between the corporation and the CIA to prevent Allende's election and failing that to bring about the "economic collapse" of Chile. When the results of the presidential election were still in doubt, Broe and ITT worked together to put economic pressure on the nation. On April 2, Geneen, testifying before the panel, admitted offering the government money. He justified the gesture as an "emotional reaction" of fear that the U.S. government would do nothing to prevent the Allende election. He reiterated McCone's testimony that the money was to be used for social projects.

The investigations by several government agencies into ITT's anti-trust settlements with the Justice Department continued in 1973. The House Interstate and Foreign Commerce Committee's special Subcommittee on Investigations made public March 19 a confidential document prepared by the Securities and Exchange Commission (SEC) that revealed the extent and success of ITT's attempt to pressure the Administration in the 1971 Hartford Fire Insurance Co. settlement. The document implicated seven present and former Administration officials, including Vice President Spiro Agnew [q.v.], presidential assistant John D. Ehrlichman [q.v.] and former Attorney General John Mitchell [q.v.].

On July 19, 1974, two volumes of evidence on the Administration's handling of anti-trust cases against ITT were released by the House Judiciary Committee. While no evidence appeared to substantiate allegations that President Nixon had personally ordered the Justice Department to drop its appeal before the Supreme Court of the Hartford anti-trust case in 1971, the documents did reveal numerous meetings in the 1969-71 period between high Administration officials and ITT executives. The executives waged an intense lobbying campaign in an effort to have the anti-trust charges dropped. Although the case was filed for appeal with the high court, the settlement was reached before arguments could be heard.

Geneen retired as chief executive officer of ITT in 1977.

[FHM]

GESELL, GERHARD A(LDEN)
b. June 16, 1910; Los Angeles, Calif.
U. S. District Court Judge, 1968 - .

Gesell earned his law degree from Yale in 1935 and became counsel for the Securities and Exchange Commission. He left the Commission in 1941 and practiced law until 1967, when he was appointed judge in the U. S. District Court for the District of Columbia by President Lyndon Johnson.

He established a reputation as a liberal with a pair of controversial rulings. The first came in November 1969 when Gesell ruled that a law which severely restricted abortions was unconstitutional. In another decision Gesell upheld charges of mismanagement and conspiracy against the United Mine Workers' pension fund and the union-owned National Bank of Washington. An out-of-court settlement, approved by Gesell, resulted in the payment of $53 million to 17,000 retired miners and miners' widows during the first year of a reorganized fund.

This liberal reputation was enhanced in June 1971 when Gesell refused a request from the Justice Department to block the printing of the *Pentagon Papers,* classified documents describing the U. S. entry into the Vietnam war that had been leaked initially to *The New York Times.* Gesell held that to prevent publication would constitute prior restraint and violate the First Amendment. Later in the year the *Pentagon Papers* issue again came before Gesell's court when two congressmen asked the judge to compel the government to release the entire 47-volume set of documents. This time, however, Gesell refused the request, noting that the bulk of the papers had already been released and saying "the government must have some degree of privacy."

In 1973 Watergate-related cases began to appear before Gesell. The cases would take up much of his time for the next year. The first Watergate case came before the judge when Donald H. Segretti [q.v.] entered a guilty plea to three misdemeanor charges involving dirty tricks during the 1972 Florida Democratic primary. Gesell sentenced Segretti to six months in jail and three years probation. In November 1973 Gesell ruled that the firing of special Watergate prosecutor Archibald Cox [q.v.] by President Nixon was illegal, holding that Justice Department regulations establishing the position had the force of law. The regulations stipulated the prosecutor could not be removed except "for extraordinary improprieties," a condition the judge said did not exist in the firing of Cox. A plantiff in the suit, Rep. Bella Abzug [q.v.] of New York, said Gesell's ruling established obstruction of justice by the President and could be used as grounds for impeachment.

All of Gesell's rulings did not go against the President, however. When the Senate Watergate Committee subpoenaed five White House tapes in February 1974, the judge dismissed the suit, saying publicity surrounding release of the tapes could be harmful to criminal prosecutions.

Gesell heard the first case brought by the new special Watergate prosecutor,

Leon Jaworski [q.v.], in April 1974. Dwight L. Chapin [q.v.], appointments secretary to the President, was convicted on two counts of perjury after covering up for Segretti. Gesell's sentencing, as it had been with Segretti, was light, giving Chapin 10 to 30 months in jail.

Gesell's most important case related to Watergate was as trial judge in the prosecution of six members of the White House Special Investigations Unit dubbed the "Plumbers". The six were charged with planning and executing a break-in at the office of Daniel Ellsberg's [q.v.] psychiatrist with the intention of finding damaging evidence against Ellsberg, the man who leaked the *Pentagon Papers*. Charged were Egil Krogh [q.v.], aide to presidential adviser John D. Ehrlichman [q.v.] and head of the unit; Charles Colson [q.v.], special counsel to the President; Ehrlichman, White House liaison to the unit; and G. Gordon Liddy [q.v.], Bernard L. Barker and Eugenio Martinez, the convicted Watergate burglars who carried out the break-in. Krogh pled guilty well before the trial and was separated from the case after agreeing to cooperate with the Watergate prosecutors.

In pretrial hearings the defense indicated it would use national security as justification for the break-in, but Gesell immediately quashed the argument, saying that the Fourth Amendment's protection of privacy was more fundamental in the case than any national security consideration. The White House then refused to produce documents subpoenaed by Ehrlichman and Colson, drawing the wrath of the judge. He told presidential counsel James D. St. Clair [q.v.], "It is not up to the President which documents to produce." Gesell added that by withholding evidence "the President must know he is acting deliberately [in] aborting this trial," and raised the possibility that Nixon could be held in contempt of court. This eventuality was avoided when Gesell agreed to a White House plan whereby the judge privately examined the presidential documents to determine relevancy to the trial.

On the eve of the trial, Colson entered a guilty plea, leaving four defendants to face the court. After a week of testimony Gesell told the jury that "an individual cannot escape criminality because he sincerely, but incorrectly, believes his acts are justified in the name of patriotism." All of the defendants were found guilty of violating the civil rights of Lewis B. Fielding, Ellsberg's psychiatrist, and Ehrlichman was found guilty of three additional counts of making false statements. Ehrlichman received a stiff sentence of 20 months to five years, Liddy was given one to three years, and Barker and Martinez were placed on probation. Colson had previously been sentenced to one to three years and fined $5,000, and Krogh had been given a six-month sentence.

Gesell remained on the bench through the late 1970s.

[BO]

GIBSON, KENNETH A(LLEN)
b. May 15, 1932; Enterprise, Ala.
Mayor, Newark, N.J. 1970–.

Kenneth Gibson was raised in Alabama until he was eight years old. At that time his family moved to Newark, N.J., after customers indicated to his father, a butcher, that a new toilet he had built was an insult to the many white people who still did not own one. After graduating from high school, working in a factory and spending two years in the Army, he enrolled in the Newark College of Engineering. He received a degree in civil engineering in 1963 and began working as an engineer with the Newark Housing Authority. He soon became a civil rights activist and was prominent in many service organizations. Through his work on the Business and Industry Coordinating Council, Gibson labored to find jobs for blacks. At the urging of several community leaders, he ran for mayor of Newark in 1966 and finished third in a field of six. Realizing then that "a black candidate can get votes from all segments of the community," he decided to "run for the next four years."

In the late 1960s Newark's elections were nonpartisan, although its politics were strongly influenced by the Essex County Democratic Organization. While the city's population was 54% black in 1970, blacks comprised a minority of the voters. Before 1968 no sizeable city in New Jersey ever had a black mayor, but by 1972 there were four black mayors in cities numbering 25,000 or more. In his 1970 bid for Mayor of Newark, Gibson was aided by a growing black political consciousness and by the predicament of the incumbent mayor, Hugh Addonizio [q.v.], whose candidacy was backed by the Essex County Democratic Organization. Mayor Addonizio was under indictment for conspiracy to extort money from contractors doing business with the city. On the other hand many whites were disconcerted by some of Gibson's supporters, particularly black-nationalist writer Imamu Baraka. Because of this association Addonizio labeled Gibson a "radical revolutionary," but Gibson countered that it was better to have Baraka working inside than outside the system. In the election Gibson received almost all the black vote and about 20% of the white vote.

Assuming the mayor's office in 1970 was an especially formidable task. Newark was widely believed to be, as urban specialist George Sternlieb stated, "the most accelerated case of the death of the old central city as we know it." One-fourth of Newark's residents were receiving public assistance, and the city's unemployment rate was almost three times the national average. To make matters worse Newark's property tax was one of the state's highest.

Gibson's main contribution was to make Newark's plight more widely appreciated in order to obtain increased amounts of state and federal aid. With eight other big city mayors, he joined a widely publicized attack in February 1971 on the Nixon Administration budget that slashed monies for the Office of Economic Opportunity, granting funds for cities below the level of congressional authorization. The same year Newark's reve-nues were so paltry Gibson was forced to ask that Gov. William Cahill [q.v.] call a special session of the state legislature to grant additional funding. The Mayor was instrumental in organizing a long-term, multibillion-dollar project for Newark that was to be erected over a large area of downtown. In 1973 the sleek new Newark International Airport opened. Both projects were small signs of economic hope for the city.

During Gibson's first term racial issues contined to erupt in Newark, often rekindling memories of the widespread riots that convulsed the city in 1967. In 1971 an 11-week teachers' strike polarized racial feelings. Charges were made that the predominantly white teaching staff was unsympathetic to the needs of black students. Violence exacerbated the tensions. Gibson was able to end the strike after getting the school board and teachers to agree to a compromise that included provision for the establishment of a special task force to investigate the city's education problems.

In 1972 and 1973 bitter racial and political antagonism erupted around the Mayor's selection of a black police lieutenant to be police commissioner. Another emotional issue involved the construction of Kawaida Towers, a high-rise housing project in Newark's predominantly white North Ward. Although Gibson consistently supported the low-income housing project, many blacks were furious at him for not putting pressure on the courts to move the white pickets and demonstrators away from the site. Baraka began calling the Mayor a "puppet" of business interests and did not support his reelection bid in 1974, which Gibson won with 55% of the vote in a five-man contest.

On the national scene Gibson backed Sen. George McGovern of South Dakota [q.v.] for the 1972 Democratic presidential nomination. He was chairman of the Democratic Platform Committee that year, advised McGovern on his vice-presidential selection and made the nomination speech for Sen. Thomas Eagleton of Missouri [q.v.]. During the fall campaign he headed McGovern's urban affairs policy group which made proposals for $6 billion in funds for public service jobs and recommended a shift from public housing projects to housing allowances.

In 1979 Gibson was elected president of the U.S. Conference of Mayors, the first black to be so chosen. In that position he sponsored a resolution against excessive Pentagon spending at the expense of domestic problems and endorsed the Humphrey-Hawkins full-employment bill.

Gibson was reelected to a third term as Mayor in 1978. [See CARTER Volume]

[GB]

GILLIGAN, JOHN J(OYCE)
b. March 22, 1921, Cincinnati, Ohio.
Governor, Ohio, 1971-75.

John Gilligan, the son of a mortician, graduated from the University of Notre Dame in 1943. After service in the Navy during World War II, he returned to school, receiving his M.A. from Xavier University in 1947. He taught there until 1953. Gilligan was elected to the Cincinnati City Council on a fusion party ticket in 1953. He was reelected five times, the last three as a Democratic Party candidate.

In 1964 Gilligan won a seat in the House of Representatives, where he became a strong and effective advocate for President Johnson's Great Society programs. Gilligan lost his reelection bid two years later as a result of redistricting.

After returning to the Cincinnati City Council for a year, Gilligan ran unsuccessfully for the Senate in 1968. Two years later he ran for governor of Ohio. He won 60% of the primary vote and went on to win the general election against State Auditor Roger Cloud by a margin of 339,000 votes. Gilligan benefited from the whiff of scandal involving Cloud in alleged illegal loans to private corporations from state funds. During the campaign Gilligan repeatedly insisted that Ohio would need new taxes to solve its fiscal crunch and provide adequate services for the 1970s.

Gilligan's first biennial budget, presented in March 1971, called for 50% more spending than that of the last budget under Gov. James Rhodes [q.v.]. To finance it Gilligan proposed the enactment of the first income tax in Ohio's history—affecting both corporations and individuals. In November 1972 Ohio voters approved the measure. The $400 million levy enabled the state to reduce property taxes for low-income homeowners and expand services in mental health, medicare and welfare.

Gilligan was widely praised in 1973 for the passage of a new ethics law for public officials and political candidates that mandated disclosure of personal income sources and defined certain bans on conflict of interest. After many months of haggling a modest campaign reform bill was also signed by the governor in 1974. It provided for preelection contribution disclosures; a single, centralized campaign committee for each candidate and spending limits for state and local elections.

In December 1971 Gilligan endorsed the Democratic presidential candidacy of Sen. Edmund Muskie [q.v.] of Maine, aiding the Senator's campaign substantially because at the time the Governor was thought to control about 125 of Ohio's 153 delegate votes. Much of Gilligan's influence slipped away, however, as Muskie's candidacy was eclipsed by that of Sen. Hubert Humphrey of Minnesota [q.v.] and Sen. George McGovern of South Dakota in the spring primaries.

By 1974 Gilligan had created an arrogant image of himself in Ohio, especially when contrasted to the down-home image projected by his Republican opponent, former Gov. James Rhodes. Rhodes portrayed Gilligan as a big spender who taxed "everything in Ohio that walks, crawls or flies." Gilligan tried to revive old charges of scandal against Rhodes, but the former Governor successfully ignored the issue. In the end Gilligan lost by only 10,000 votes out of 3 million cast. He viewed the results as "purely and simply a repudiation of me."

In 1977 Gilligan was named director of the Agency for International Development by President Carter.

[GWB]

GLAZER, NATHAN
b. Feb. 25, 1923; New York, N.Y.
Sociologist.

Glazer, the son of a Jewish sewing machine operator, graduated in sociology from the City University of New York in 1944 and took his M.A. in anthropology and linguistics at the University of Pennsylvania. Glazer began a long association with the magazine *Commentary* after World War II. He received his Ph.D. from Columbia University in 1962.

In 1948 he collaborated with David Reisman and Reuel Denney on a Yale-sponsored research project that resulted in the widely read book on social adjustment, *The Lonely Crowd: A Study of the Changing American Character* (1950). In the late 1950s he taught at the Universities of Chicago and California at Berkeley and at Bennington and Smith Colleges. In his *Social Basis of American Communism* (1961), Glazer examined the various social and ethnic groups to which communism appealed and concluded that Americans rejected communism out of materialist self-interest. In 1963 he wrote with Daniel P. Moynihan [q.v.] the highly influential *Beyond the Melting Pot: The Negroes, Puerto Ricans, Jews, Italians and Irish of New York City*. The book's chief conclusion was that immigrant assimilation had actually not occurred to the extent generally assumed and that minority groups continued to maintain a strong ethnic identity.

As a student Glazer had considered himself a socialist. However, during the 1960s two incidents pushed him to the right. The first was a year spent in Washington in 1962-63 developing anti-poverty programs with the Housing and Home Finance Agency during which he gained a respect for bureaucracy and its ability to handle complex social problems. The second was his involvement in the campus disturbances at Berkeley where he was a faculty member from 1963 to 1969. There he tried to negotiate a compromise, which failed, between the Free Speech Movement and the administration that would have allowed any speech not directed to any "immediate act of force or violence." His experience at Berkeley and the subsequent student revolts in the late 1960s convinced him that instead of working for needed reforms on campus, discontented student radicals were really trying to destroy the universities. [See JOHNSON Volume]

In 1969 Glazer was appointed Professor of Education and Social Structure at Harvard University. Throughout the late 1960s and early 1970s, Glazer continued to deplore attacks on existing institutions as well as the breakdown of respect for authority that he said prompted such attacks. In large part he blamed the war in Vietnam for making young people grow cynical about American motives abroad and about the advantages of liberal democracy in the West. Glazer asserted that the United States did have a rational bureaucracy responsive to change and that the problem was making government units small enough to represent a community effectively.

Glazer stressed that ethnicity was the first focus of identity for most people. Although he deplored ethnic separatism, Glazer maintained that ethnicity was as important as nation or class as a basis of group mobilization. He described this pluralism as a fundamental strength of American society. He denounced the busing of school children to achieve racial balance as a denial of that strength. Writing in *Commentary* in March 1972, Glazer applauded the advances that integration had made since the 1950s but said that school busing was "a path of pointlessly expensive and destructive homogenization." He said that busing disrupted a geographically defined community by making the schools unable to function as a focus of community action.

In 1977 Glazer attacked the establishment of quotas in school admissions for minority groups. Rejecting the notion that they were needed to correct past wrongs, he said, "If it is permitted to discriminate against whites and males today, it is permitted to discriminate against anyone else tomorrow."

[FLM]

GLEASON, THOMAS W(ILLIAM)
b. Nov. 8, 1900; New York, N.Y.
President, International
Longshoremen's Association, 1963 - .

Raised in a tenement neighborhood in New York City, Gleason began working with his father on the docks at the age of 15. He joined the International Longshoremen's Association (ILA) in 1919 and was blacklisted for a time during the Depression for his union organizing activities. Gleason was named to his first union post in 1934, became a full-time ILA organizer in 1947, and was appointed to the specially created post of general organizer in 1953. In 1963 he challenged ILA President William V. Bradley for the top post in the union. After a bitter campaign Bradley withdrew on the eve of the election, and Gleason won the presidency by acclamation.

As union president, Gleason continued the ILA tradition of striking at the expiration of a contract. In 1964 he negotiated a milestone agreement with East and Gulf Coast shippers under which the shippers won a reduction in the size of work gangs, and the longshoremen won recognition as regular, rather than occasional, workers with a guaranteed wage for a minimum 1,600 working hours per year. Fiercely anti-Communist, Gleason and the rest of the ILA leadership were staunch supporters of the Cold War and frequently refused to handle trade with Communist nations.

On Dec. 20, 1968, after the expiration of the Taft-Hartley 80-day cooling off period, Gleason led his 60,000 member union on a strike of East and Gulf Coast ports. The main issue in the strike was the guaranteed annual income, won in 1964,

which the shippers were reluctant to extend. But rank-and-file support of the strike was solid, and after 57 days shippers in the port of New York agreed to raise the paid work guarantee to 2,080 hours annually. Longshoremen also won higher pensions and a six-week vacation. Contracts in other ports were not reached until April 2, however, making the strike the longest in ILA history.

Gleason was a member of the pro-Vietnam war, "hard-hat" faction of organized labor during the Nixon Administration. In October 1969 he threatened to order a boycott of Swedish ships and goods if the Swedish government went ahead with its plan to give aid to the North Vietnamese. The following year, after the U.S. invasion of Cambodia, Gleason and 21 other union leaders met with President Richard M. Nixon and urged "national support for our fighting men." In January 1973, when Australian dock workers called a boycott of U.S. ships to protest the renewed U.S. bombing of North Vietnam, Gleason retaliated with a boycott against Australian shipping.

On Oct. 1, 1971, after the ILA contract expired, Gleason announced another strike, which coincided with a strike by the West Coast International Longshoremen's and Warehousemen's Union (ILWU) in progress since July 1. It was the first time that organized labor had closed ports on both coasts simultaneously. On Oct. 4, President Nixon invoked the Taft-Hartley back-to-work provisions. The courts immediately issued an injunction to end the West Coast work stoppage but delayed issuing the injunction on the East and Gulf Coasts until Nov. 29.

Once again, the major stumbling block to reaching an agreement was the guaranteed annual income, which the shippers wished to modify. But a big question looming over the negotiations was whether the newly created federal Pay Board, established to rule on wage increases during Phase Two of Nixon's antiinflationary program, would accept whatever settlement was reached. On Oct. 27 Gleason met in New York with ILWU President Harry Bridges [q.v.]. They issued a statement pledging joint strike action if the Pay Board disallowed their contract terms. After the 80-day cooling off period, West Coast workers resumed their strike on Jan. 17, while ILA members continued to work without a contract. When settlements were finally reached, however, the Pay Board voted to cut the wage increases to what it deemed were noninflationary levels. Although both the ILA and the ILWU acquiesced to the decision, representatives of organized labor serving on the Pay Board quit in protest.

During the Nixon-Ford years the Justice Department targeted the ILA for discriminatory practices. In January 1969 the Justice Department filed suit in federal court charging that ILA locals in Texas were guilty of racial discrimination through the practice of chartering racially segregated locals in the same port. A similar suit was filed in April against ILA locals in Baltimore. The Equal Employment Opportunities Commission later joined in these suits. On April 11, 1975 the U.S. Fifth Circuit Court of Appeals in New Orleans ruled that racially segregated ILA locals must be merged in Gulf and South Atlantic ports. The court called the ILA separate-but-equal claim ludicrous and charged that the practice denied "equal employment opportunities because of the psychological harm they inflict." The ILA appealed the decision, but on Dec. 1, 1975 the Supreme Court upheld the appellate court order.

Gleason found himself at odds with the Ford Administration during 1975 over the terms of its wheat deal with the Soviet Union. On Aug. 18, the ILA refused to load grain shipments to the Soviet Union because Gleason charged the agreement was inflationary and failed to stipulate that sufficient amounts of the grain be transported on U.S. vessels. Ford called the boycott "tragic and unfortunate." Secretary of Agriculture Earl Butz [q.v.] accused the ILA of adding to inflation through "featherbedding practices that jack up those very prices." Gleason and other labor leaders met with White House officials late in August and on Sept. 9 announced an agreement that ended the boycott. The Administration had promised to negotiate a new long-term purchasing and shipping contract with the Soviet Union.

In 1977 Gleason ordered his members to strike containerized vessels in 30 ports.

[JD]

GLENN, JOHN H(ERSCHEL), JR.
b. July 18, 1921; Cambridge, Ohio.
Democratic Senator, Ohio, 1975-.

The only son of a railroad conductor and proprietor of a heating and plumbing business, Glenn enlisted in the Marines when the U.S. entered World War II. He remained on active duty through the Korean war and flew 90 missions in Korea. He earned the nickname "MiG-mad Marine" after he shot down three Communist MiGs over the Yalu River in the closing days of that war. After the war Glenn became a Navy test pilot and in 1957 he set a speed record in the first nonstop transcontinental supersonic flight. Two years later he was made a lieutenant colonel in the Marines. Glenn was among the seven men who were chosen from 110 military test pilots to become the first American astronauts. On Feb. 20, 1962, Glenn became the first American to orbit the earth, circling the globe three times in under five hours. [See KENNEDY Volume]

Glenn resigned from the space program in January 1964 and announced his candidacy for the U.S. Senate seat from Ohio, challenging incumbent Sen. Stephen M. Young. But he was forced to withdraw from the race on March 30 after a severe injury suffered in a bathroom fall. In the fall of 1964 Glenn was named vice president of corporate planning for Royal Crown Cola Co.'s domestic operations. He also bought an interest in several Holiday Inn franchises across the country. Glenn hosted a series of television programs based on historical explorations called Great Explorations, which were aired on NBC in January, 1968.

In the 1968 presidential primaries, Glenn strongly supported Robert Kennedy's campaign. Following the New York Senator's assassination, Glenn was appointed chairman of the newly formed Emergency Committee for Gun Control, a coalition of groups formed to lobby for tough firearms control. [See JOHNSON Volume]

After Young announced his decision not to seek reelection in 1970, Glenn declared his candidacy for the Senate seat. He ran his primary campaign on a platform favoring wage and price controls, busing and the withdrawal of U.S. troops from South Vietnam and Cambodia. Glenn lost the primary election to a Cleveland lawyer, Howard Metzenbaum, by over 13,000 votes. Metzenbaum outspent Glenn 5-1 during the campaign. Metzenbaum lost the general election to Robert A. Taft, Jr. [q.v.]. Stunned by his defeat, Glenn spent the next few years building a political base in his home state.

Glenn ran again for the Democratic senatorial nomination in 1974 against Metzenbaum, who had the support of Ohio Gov. John Gilligan [q.v.]. A bitter campaign followed over the issue of Metzenbaum's use of tax shelters and an IRS suit against the millionaire for back taxes owed in 1969. Glenn suggested that Metzenbaum had used legal tax shelters to avoid paying taxes in 1969. He claimed that no one should use such shelters to avoid paying taxes, even if they were legal. During the campaign Glenn called for the return of integrity in government. He went on to beat Metzenbaum in the May primary by more than 94,000 votes. Glenn scored this victory despite the fact that he lacked the support of the state Democratic organization and the local labor leaders. He swept the general election in November with a landslide 64.6% of the vote, beating Ralph Perk, the Republican mayor of Cleveland, by one million votes.

In the Senate, Glenn compiled a moderate record. On economic issues he recommended an end to deficit spending, strict enforcement of anti-trust laws and reform of the national tax system. He proposed a "countercyclical" aid program for providing federal funds to U.S. cities to enable them to maintain essential services without raising taxes during time of recession. He approved of the creation of a consumer protection agency. Always a strong advocate of education, Glenn criticized the inequity of funding education solely through property taxes. The Ohio Senator also supported the right of teachers and other public employees to organize and bargain collectively. Glenn was a strong supporter of national health insurance legislation, and he favored increasing federal grants for basic medical research and the expanded use of paramedical personnel.

Glenn was a major spokesman for campaign and congressional reform. He especially favored public financing of political campaigns. Rather than advocating a system of full or nearly complete federal financing of campaigns out of tax revenues, he supported a program that would give incentives to the small donor. He proposed the creation of a statewide campaign finance office in each state and advocated shortening the length of campaigns. A proponent of congressional reform, he criticized what he termed "the disproportionate influence lobbyists wield over members of Congress." Glenn scored the seniority system and spoke of opening up the deliberations of Congress to the public.

Glenn was an outspoken critic of the Ford Administration's Project Independence, which was designed to make the U.S. self-sufficient in energy by 1980. He spoke out against the cost of the program and claimed that it would involve shifts of income from consumers to owners of energy-related assets. Glenn played a major role in helping formulate the Democratic response to the President's energy program. As a member of the Interior and Insular Affairs Committee, he criticized the Republican gasoline tax plan, claiming it would take money from the hands of consumers and increase the profits of energy producers, possibly by as much as one trillion dollars, without guaranteeing that imports of foreign petroleum would decrease.

Glenn instead proposed a vague program of import quotas, admitting that despite intensive study of the question he did not possess a comprehensive plan. During congressional debate of the issue in the spring of 1975, his thought matured. He recommended increased production of national gas and increased use of interstate pipelines to distribute fuel and proposed enforcing ceiling prices on "new" domestic oil developed after 1972 at the same level as that existing for foreign oil imports as of Jan. 31, 1975. In April 1975 the Senate passed a bill cosponsored by Glenn that extended price controls on domestic oil until March 1, 1976, after which a federal-state energy consumption reduction plan was to be implemented. The bill gave the President emergency powers to ration gasoline, prohibit oil imports and allocate oil supplies subject to congressional veto within a 10-day period. Glenn's major contribution to the bill was the price ceiling on "new" oil produced after 1972, which had previously been uncontrolled. The bill's aim was to cut U.S. energy consumption by 4% annually through fuel conservation rules and guidelines drawn up by the Federal Energy Administration with the approval of Congress and administered by the states. The President signed the Energy Policy and Conservation Act in December.

Glenn delivered the keynote address to the Democratic National Convention in 1976. Before the meeting he was considered one of the top candidates for the vice-presidential nomination. However Glenn's uninspiring address and relative inexperience led the presidential nominee, Jimmy Carter [q.v.], to select Sen. Walter Mondale (D, Minn.) [q.v.] as his running mate. During the first two years of the Carter Administration, Glenn supported the Panama Canal treaties. [See CARTER Volume]

[GMS]

GOLDBERG, ARTHUR J(OSEPH)
b. Aug. 8, 1908; Chicago, Ill.
Political leader.

The son of Russian Jewish immigrants, Goldberg was raised on Chicago's West Side. After working his way through college and law school, he established a private practice and occasionally served as counsel for trade unions in Chicago. Appointed general counsel in 1948 for both the United Steelworkers of America and the Congress of Industrial Organizations, he played a major role in the merger of the CIO with the American Federation of Labor in 1955, and thereafter served as its special counsel.

Picked as Secretary of Labor by President Kennedy at the start of his administration, Goldberg adopted a "public interest" activist posture, frequently intervening in labor disputes to achieve a settlement. Elevated by Kennedy to the Supreme Court in October 1962, Goldberg took advanced positions on civil liberties issues. In a 1963 opinion he first raised questions about the constitutionality of the death penalty and the following year wrote the majority opinion in the landmark *Escobedo v. Illinois* case, which protected the rights of suspects under police custody. In July 1965 Goldberg stepped down from the Court to become ambassador to the United Nations. Although told by President Johnson that he would play a major part in shaping foreign policy and in ending the Vietnam war, Goldberg in fact was excluded from high echelon decisionmaking meetings regarding the war, and found his efforts to start negotiations only weakly supported. He did, however, play an important role in the March 1968 reassessment of American policy, arguing strongly for a complete halt to the bombing. Resigning from his post in April 1968, Goldberg took an active part in Hubert Humphrey's presidential campaign. [See KENNEDY, JOHNSON Volumes]

During the first years of the Nixon Administration, Goldberg remained active in public affairs, generally taking a critical stance toward the President's foreign and domestic policies. He urged the President to push for ratification of the nuclear nonproliferation treaty, and came out in favor of recognition of Communist China. In April 1969 Goldberg formed a national citizen's committee to marshal opposition to Nixon's proposal to continue funding development and deployment of an antiballistic missile system. Remaining a strong proponent of civil rights and civil liberties, he joined with NAACP executive director Roy Wilkins [q.v.] in December 1969 in forming a citizens panel to conduct a "searching inquiry" into police clashes with the Black Panther Party. In March 1970 Goldberg denounced as unconstitutional the contempt convictions of the Chicago Seven and their lawyers, and later that year he attacked Nixon's preventive detention bill for the District of Columbia as an infringement of the rights of the accused.

Goldberg became more outspoken in his criticism of the Vietnam War during Nixon's tenure in the White House. At an October 1969 moratorium rally in the nation's capital he called for a "straightforward" statement from Nixon that he accepted the principle of "a prompt withdrawal of all American forces" from Southeast Asia. The following month, when Vice President Spiro Agnew [q.v.] assailed the major television networks for their coverage of anti-war protests, Goldberg deplored his comments as "inflammatory." In 1970 he played a key role in organizing lawyers around the country to lobby against the war.

Despite earlier disclaimers, Goldberg announced his candidacy on March 19, 1970 for the Democratic nomination in the New York State gubernatorial race. Receiving the official endorsement of state party leaders, Goldberg faced a challenge in the primary from industrialist Howard J. Samuels, but defeated Samuels by a narrow margin. His opponent was three-term governor Nelson Rockefeller [q.v.] and Goldberg took the position that the New York race was "nothing less than a referendum on the Nixon-Agnew administration." He campaigned on a standard liberal platform, urging a continua-

tion and expansion of existing social welfare programs to solve urban problems, and spoke out strongly against Rockefeller's increasingly tough law-and-order stance. Although he received the endorsement of New York City Mayor John Lindsay [q.v.], who praised Goldberg for resisting the "ominous political trend to the right," Goldberg's lackluster campaign style failed to arouse the voters. Rockefeller, moreover, won the support of normally Democratic white ethnic voters who were angered by Goldberg's opposition to the war and who were reacting against the rising tide of urban disorders and student protests. Outspending Goldberg by over $800,000, Rockefeller defeated him by more than half a million votes in the November election.

After his electoral defeat, Goldberg returned to the practice of law and continued to speak out occasionally on public issues. In 1974, during the Senate confirmation hearings on Rockefeller's nomination to the vice-presidency, it was revealed that the millionaire politician had financed a derogatory biography of Goldberg during their gubernatorial race.

[JD]

GOLDWATER, BARRY M(ORSE)
b. Jan. 1, 1909; Phoenix, Ariz.
Republican Senator, Ariz., 1953–65, 1969–.

Goldwater left the University of Arizona after one year to join the family department store, Goldwater, Inc., and he became the firm's president in 1937. He served as a noncombat flyer with the Army Transport Command in the Far East during World War II. Goldwater became active in Republican politics and helped build the Party in Arizona during the 1950s when the state was almost completely dominated by the Democrats. He was elected to the Phoenix City Council in 1949. Goldwater won election to the U.S. Senate in 1952, where he established a conservative record. During the 1950s and 1960s he became the Party's most effective fundraiser and spokesman of its conservative wing. Goldwater captured the 1964 Republican presidential nomination, beating the disorganized opposition to his candidacy. He ran on a conservative platform that alienated many of the moderates in the Party. In November he lost the election to Lyndon B. Johnson in a landslide. Goldwater, who gave up his Senate seat to run for President, surrendered his Party leadership position after the election and spoke out only occasionally on political issues. In 1968 he was reelected to the Senate. [See EISENHOWER, KENNEDY, JOHNSON Volumes]

As a conservative who wanted to stop federal programs, Goldwater staunchly supported the Nixon-Ford Administrations' efforts to limit federal spending for social welfare measures. He opposed allowing striking workers to get food stamps; establishing federal standards for a uniform national no-fault auto insurance system; using federal funds for abortions; and creating a federal consumer protection agency. As a staunch anti-Communist he consistently supported defense spending and voted for every major controversial weapons system advocated by the Administration. These included the Safeguard anti-ballistic missile system, the Trident submarine and the B-1 bomber.

Goldwater was one of the Senate's strongest advocates of America's Vietnam involvement. In 1972, for example, he attacked critics of the renewed bombing offensive against North Vietnam begun by Nixon after the Communists had started an offensive in the South. When raids against the port of Haiphong raised fears about Soviet involvement if Russian ships were hit, Goldwater said the raids were better than the "dilly-dally" bombing of supply lines that had gone on before.

Goldwater opposed all congressional efforts to legislate an end to the war. These included the 1970 Cooper-Church Amendment to limit the President's authority to conduct military operations in Cambodia and the 1973 amendment by Sen. Thomas F. Eagleton (D, Mo.) [q.v.]

to halt American combat operations in Laos and Cambodia. At the same time Goldwater supported the Nixon Administration's attempts to end the war through negotiations. When a peace treaty was concluded in 1973, Goldwater warned the Saigon government not to be an obstacle to the peace agreement the U.S. had signed. Goldwater was one of the strongest congressional supporters of the Saigon government. He continued to support military aid for South Vietnam after the peace treaty was signed. When the Senate Armed Services Committee debated the Ford Administration's request for additional military aid in April 1975, two weeks before the Communists captured Saigon, Goldwater favored sending at least an additional $101 million. The Committee rejected both this proposal and a $70 million proposal, which Goldwater opposed as inadequate.

While an advocate of a strong defense posture, Goldwater was one of the leading congressional opponents of the military draft. In 1970 he was one of 12 Senators who introduced legislation to implement the recommendations of a presidential commission that studied the creation of an all-volunteer force. The commission, headed by former Secretary of Defense Thomas S. Gates, called for ending the draft when the draft law expired on June 30, 1971. As requested by the Nixon Administration, Congress extended the draft until 1973, when an all-volunteer force was established.

In 1974 Goldwater played a key role in forcing Nixon's resignation after the release of transcripts of White House conversations which showed that Nixon had discussed using the Central Intelligence Agency (CIA) to head off the FBI's Watergate probe. Goldwater had consistently defended Nixon as the Watergate scandal unfolded during 1973 and 1974. At the same time, however, he condemned the scandals and urged the President to reveal the full story. In April 1973 he warned that Watergate was hurting the Republican Party. In May 1973 he cosponsored a Senate resolution calling on Nixon to appoint a Watergate special prosecutor.

But he initially opposed suggestions made by Republicans that Nixon resign. In March 1974, when Sen. James L. Buckley (R, N.Y.) [q.v.] urged resignation, Goldwater opposed it. He defended Nixon, saying resignation would involve questions of fair play and precedent "whereby any man in the White House who was unacceptable to certain politicians and segments of the media might be forced to resign." But he also said, "If any evidence of criminal acts on the part of the President is proven, I shall change my position and support the Buckley proposal."

The August release of the incriminating tapes furnished the proof Goldwater demanded, and he ended his opposition to resignation. On Aug. 7 Goldwater, Senate Minority Leader Hugh Scott (R, Pa.) [q.v.] and House Minority Leader John J. Rhodes (R, Ariz.) [q.v.] met with Nixon to discuss the political situation in Congress. The meeting occurred the day after the Senate Republican Policy Committee had reached a consensus that the President should be told of his erosion of support in the Senate. Goldwater and Scott told the President that he had less than 15 supporters left in the Senate, far fewer than the number he needed to avoid conviction. After the meeting Goldwater said the group had not made any suggestions to the President about what he should do. But when Goldwater, who had been opposing resignation, agreed that the situation looked "damn gloomy," other words were unnecessary. Nixon announced his resignation the next day.

After Ford became President, Goldwater supported Nelson A. Rockefeller's [q.v.] nomination as vice president. He also noted, however, that Rockefeller would not be acceptable to "rank and file" Republicans in 1976 and pointed out that Rockefeller was not the one to put the Party back together again. Goldwater, however, was one of seven who eventually voted against the nomination in the Senate after congressional hearings disclosed Rockefeller's financial dealings with political figures. Goldwater did not object to Rockefeller's millions but questioned "whether or not he's used these millions of dollars to buy power. I think that's wrong."

In 1976 Goldwater backed Ford for the Republican presidential nomination, declining to support the conservative Ronald Reagan [q.v.]. Goldwater strongly opposed the Carter Administration's efforts to normalize relations with mainland China, which also ended U.S. diplomatic relations with the Nationalist government on Taiwan. [See CARTER Volume]

[AE]

GOODELL, CHARLES E(LLSWORTH), (JR.)
b. March 16, 1926; Jamestown, N.Y.
Republican Senator, N.Y., 1968-71.

The son of a Jamestown, N.Y., physician, Goodell served in the Naval Reserve during World War II. He received his B.A. degree from Williams College in 1948 and his law degree from Yale three years later. Goodell remained at Yale to receive his master's degree in political science in 1952. Following a short stay at Jamestown, where he practiced law, Goodell moved to Washington to serve from 1954 to 1955 as a congressional liaison assistant with the United States Department of Justice. He returned to his home in 1955 to become a partner in a local Jamestown law firm.

Active in local Republican politics, Goodell won election to the U.S. House in 1959. During the Kennedy and Johnson years, he compiled a record as a moderate Republican. He was a leader of the "Young Turks" who replaced the conservative Party leadership with moderates headed by Gerald Ford. [See KENNEDY, JOHNSON Volumes]

In September 1968 Gov. Nelson Rockefeller [q.v.] appointed Goodell to complete the Senate term of the late Robert F. Kennedy (D, N.Y.). Goodell's short, stormy term in the Senate from 1968 to 1970 became controversial as New Yorkers observed their Senator trying to emulate Kennedy's brand of politics. Conservative critics of Goodell defended his political move to the left by pointing out that he had supported liberal legislation in the past.

Charles Goodell thus became for Nixon one of the least reliable Republican senators the President could count on in key votes. Goodell opposed the G. Harrold Carswell [q.v.] and Clement Haynsworth [q.v.] Supreme Court nominations, voted against the anti-ballistic missile system and became the leading and most visible Republican critic of the Vietnam war. In late September 1969 Goodell introduced one of the Senate's earliest end-the-war resolutions calling on the President to withdraw all troops from Vietnam by December 1970. He then began an extensive tour of colleges, criticizing the Administration's war policy. Goodell opposed the American invasion of Cambodia in 1970 and spoke at numerous rallies against the action. He enthusiastically voted for the Cooper-Church Amendment aimed at ending the war.

Goodell's anti-war activities incensed the powerful conservative faction of New York's Republican Party. A "dump-Goodell" movement was organized to bar him from obtaining the Party's senatorial nomination in 1970, but Gov. Rockefeller's powerful control of the organization prevented Goodell from being denied a chance to run for a full term. Disgruntled Republicans thus flocked to support the state's Conservative Party candidate, James Buckley [q.v.], who pledged to vote with the Republicans if elected to the Senate. Goodell, who made no such pledge, thus found himself in a three-way race. The Democrats nominated Rep. Richard Ottinger (D, N.Y.), who questioned Goodell's commitment to liberalism by citing his often conservative votes in the House.

Vice President Spiro Agnew [q.v.] also campaigned against Goodell. In a speech in San Diego on Sept. 11, Agnew said, in reference to Goodell, "In my view, this fall, any candidate of any party who voices radical sentiments or who courts and enjoys the support of radical ele-

ments ought to be voted out of office by the American people." On Sept. 30 in South Dakota, Agnew called Goodell a "radical liberal" who "has left his Party." The following day in Salt Lake City, Agnew stated that Goodell "has strayed beyond the point of no return." Goodell defended himself by accusing Agnew of using "inflammatory and divisive rhetoric." "What is involved," said Goodell, "is the right of people to differ with official policies, and to do so with power and effectiveness." Goodell charged that the Vice President's "rhetoric suggests that people who question the Administration's views are somehow dangerous and irresponsible, have no place in public life and should be discredited in the public eye."

In response to Agnew's attempt to purge the Party of one of its leading liberals, moderate and even some conservative Republican senators came to Goodell's defense. In New York, liberals feared the Goodell candidacy would siphon from Ottinger enough votes to guarantee a Buckley victory. They failed in their attempt to persuade Goodell to withdraw from the race. The liberals' fears proved correct as Buckley garnered 39% of the vote to Ottinger's 37%. Goodell's 24%, a large percentage of it liberal, would have easily gone to Ottinger. Following his defeat, Goodell resumed his private law practice.

[JB]

GOODPASTER, ANDREW J(ACKSON)

b. Feb. 15, 1915; Granite City, Ill.
Supreme Commander, Allied Forces (NATO), Europe, July 1969-October 1974.

Andrew Goodpaster graduated second in his class from West Point in 1939. During World War II he saw combat in North Africa and Europe. Detailed to Princeton University after the war for graduate study in engineering and international relations, Goodpaster took an MSE in 1948 and a Ph. D. in political science in 1950. From 1950 to 1954 Goodpaster served with the newly formed North Atlantic Treaty Organization (NATO). In Paris, Goodpaster worked to organize the alliance's military arm and develop political aims.

Goodpaster served as White House Staff secretary from 1954 to 1961. [See EISENHOWER Volume]

During the Johnson Administration Gen. Goodpaster held a series of high level positions at the Pentagon and was often consulted by the President. He was a member of the U.S. delegation to the Paris peace negotiations from May to July 1968, when he became deputy to Gen. Creighton W. Abrams [q.v.], commander of the U.S. forces in Vietnam. Goodpaster was made a full general at the time.

At the request of President-elect Nixon, Johnson called Goodpaster to Washington in December 1968. He remained there throughout the presidential transition period, serving as chief military adviser to Nixon. At a time when the new Administration was formulating its policy on Vietnam, Goodpaster reportedly informed Nixon that a continued display of patience and determination were necessary for America to bring about an acceptable end to its role in the conflict. Reflecting the thinking of top military leaders, he counseled against the U.S. settling for anything less than the maintenance of South Vietnam. Goodpaster argued that a disadvantageous outcome in that country would precipitate political troubles in particular in other Asian countries, but also in other parts of the world, that were of interest to the U.S.

In March 1969 Goodpaster became Supreme Allied Commander of NATO forces in Europe. He arrived in Europe at a time of growing concern over NATO. The renewed interest resulted primarily from the Soviet invasion of Czechoslovakia in 1968. During the mid 1960s the support of European governments for the alliance had declined. American attention meanwhile had been focused on Vietnam. There was also the feeling in European capitals that they had not been consulted by previous administrations. Because of the failure of some European governments to contribute their quotas, Goodpaster found the forces he had helped Eisenhower organize 20 years earlier suffering from chronic troop shortages. This led to fears that NATO would be forced to rely on nuclear weapons. Goodpaster let it be known that he believed in a policy of flexible response that was not dependent on nuclear weapons alone.

Goodpaster worked to improve the communication between Washington and its European allies. In October, three months after taking command, he told an annual meeting of the North Atlantic Assembly, composed of parliamentarians from the 15 NATO countries, that the alliance "must pay the more modest costs for peace" to avoid the larger costs of war. He listed steps necessary for maintaining NATO's ability to deter a Soviet attack in Europe and the Mediterranean area. These included increasing and improving troop and war stock levels and the expansion of reinforcement capabilities.

As supreme allied commander, Goodpaster warned repeatedly against NATO troop reductions, particularly by the United States. Goodpaster asserted that the Soviet Union's armed forces constituted a concentration of military power beyond anything the world had previously seen. Congressional efforts to cut forces were rejected during the period.

The military lessons and experiences of the 1973 Arab-Israeli war brought on a reevaluation of NATO's forces and their tactics and strategy. Goodpaster began the modernization of NATO forces that resulted from the West's study of Soviet weapon systems in action during the Yom Kippur War. Improved tactical nuclear artillery weapons, electronic warfare, night-fighting capability, and anti-tank warfare received specific attention.

By 1974 the U.S. was developing miniature nuclear warheads to replace the larger warheads spread across Europe. Nevertheless, Goodpaster maintained that as the U.S. and USSR reached nuclear parity, a strong conventional capability was as important a deterrent as a nuclear capability.

President Ford named Gen. Alexander M. Haig [q.v.] to succeed Goodpaster at NATO in October 1974. Goodpaster retired from the Army and became a senior fellow in security and strategic studies at the Woodrow Wilson International Center for Scholars. In retirement he was a founder of the Committee on the Present Danger. The committee was organized to publicize the belief that the Soviet Union's military threat was underestimated and that the U.S. needed to maintain a strong defense. In 1977 President Carter called Goodpaster out of retirement to become commandant of West Point.

[SF]

GORE, ALBERT A(RNOLD)
b. Dec. 26, 1907; Granville, Tenn.
Democratic Senator, Tenn., 1953-71.

Gore, the son of a Tennessee dirt farmer, earned his law degree from the Nashville YMCA Night School, where he studied while serving as a county school superintendent. A staunch New Deal supporter, Gore was elected to the House in 1938. He won a seat in the Senate in 1952. In the Senate, Gore matched the liberalism of his fellow Tennessean, Sen. Estes Kefauver. He was a leading supporter of tax reform and backed the bulk of President Johnson's Great Society legislation. He had a mixed record on civil rights. [See TRUMAN, EISENHOWER, KENNEDY, JOHNSON Volumes]

Gore generally opposed the Nixon Administration's legislative programs. He was one of the few senators from the South who opposed the Supreme Court nominations of conservative judges Clement F. Haynsworth [q.v.] in 1969 and G. Harrold Carswell [q.v.] in 1970. In 1970 he voted against the Administration's controversial anti-crime bill that authorized "no knock" search warrants.

Gore continued his battle for tax reform into the Nixon Administration. He consistently waged battles in the Senate Finance Committee and on the Senate floor to close tax loopholes that benefited corporations and wealthy individuals and led the fight to decrease the oil depletion allowance. Gore pushed the effort to raise the personal income tax exemption when the Senate Finance Committee was considering the House-passed Tax Reform Act of 1969. Describing the $600 personal exemption as the unfairest part of the entire tax law, Gore wanted to increase it to $1,250, a move that was opposed as prohibitively expensive even by fellow tax reformers like Sen. Edward M. Kennedy (D, Mass.) [q.v.]. When the Finance Committee defeated Gore's proposal to raise the exemption to $725, he took the issue to the Senate floor and led the fight to raise the exemption to $800, a proposal that would have cut individual taxes by about $2.2 billion per year. He won despite President Nixon's threat to veto the bill if it included the $800 exemption. As enacted, the law raised the personal exemption to $750 over a three-year period.

Gore was one of the leading Senate opponents of the Safeguard anti-ballistic missile system, which the White House proposed as an alternative to the more extensive system advocated by the Johnson Administration. His disarmament subcommittee of the Foreign Relations Committee held numerous hearings on the issue during 1969 and 1970. At the hearings Gore refuted the Administration's claims that the system was needed to protect U.S. deterrent forces from a first-strike attack by the Soviet Union. He pointed out that the proposal to build two missile sites would only protect about 10% of the total U.S. deterrent forces. He asserted that the Safeguard deployment would "endanger our security" and "make an arms limitation agreement more difficult, if not impossible, to attain." Gore's subcommittee produced a mass of academic and scientific testimony opposing the deployment of the ABM system on technical and practical grounds. Congress, however, agreed to build the system in 1969, but six years later voted to dismantle it after having spent $6 billion on the project.

Gore, an early and consistent critic of

the Johnson Administration's Vietnam policy, was also an outspoken opponent of the Nixon Administration's Vietnamization program. When Nixon announced the initial withdrawal of 25,000 American troops as part of the Vietnamization program, Gore objected to the "piecemeal withdrawal" as a plan for "prolonging the war." In February 1970 he warned about increasing U.S. involvement in Laos and accused the Administration of misleading the American people about the situation. He said the White House was refusing to release congressional testimony on U.S. involvement in Laos because it would reveal that the activities violated the 1962 Geneva Accords on Laos. He consistently supported efforts to legislate an end to the war.

Gore became the Administration's number one target during the 1970 election campaign. His criticism of Nixon's Vietnam policy and his votes against the two Southern Supreme Court nominees had undermined his political popularity at home. President Nixon persuaded Rep. William E. Brock, III (R. Tenn.), a four-term House member, to challenge Gore's bid for reelection. President Nixon and Vice President Spiro T. Agnew [q.v.] both campaigned against Gore in Tennessee and strongly attacked his stand on the Supreme Court nominations and his liberalism. Brock attempted to exploit racial prejudices in a well-financed media campaign that attacked Gore for being a traitor to the South, for supporting school busing and for opposing prayer amendments to the U.S. Constitution. Gore fought back by attacking Brock's votes against medicare and the Appalachia poverty program and by pointing to his own efforts to win tax reforms and increased Social Security benefits. Gore's campaign fell short, however, and he lost the Senate race by 42,000 votes.

After his defeat Gore left public life. He became a law instructor at Vanderbilt University from 1970 to 1972, and was named chairman of the board of the Island Creek Coal Co., the nation's third largest coal producer.

[AE]

GRAHAM, BILLY (WILLIAM FRANKLIN)
b. Nov. 7, 1918; Charlotte, N.C.
Evangelist.

A descendant of pre-Revolutionary Scottish pioneers, Graham was raised on his family's prosperous dairy farm near Charlotte. He experienced a religious conversion at the age of 16 and made his "decision for Christ." After attending Florida Bible Institute and fundamentalist Wheaton College, Graham became active as a preacher on the so-called sawdust trail. A sensationally successful crusade in Los Angeles in 1949 brought him notice in the press, especially in the Hearst papers, and Graham rapidly rose to preeminence as an evangelist.

Over the next 20 years Graham conducted crusades throughout the world, addressing more than 60 million people. Through the careful use of radio, television and film, and through magazines and syndicated newspaper columns, he became perhaps the most widely-known evangelist in the world. With his fundamentalist fervor and charismatic style, Graham preached a message of repentance and faith in Christ. Often named in polls as one of the most admired men in America, Graham found himself invited to the White House by every President from Truman through Johnson. Although he claimed to avoid mixing politics and religion, Graham's rousing sermons frequently contained a strong measure of patriotic zeal. [See EISENHOWER, KENNEDY Volumes]

Graham had an especially close relationship with President Nixon. In January 1969 he gave the first of a series of White House religious services, and at Nixon's second inauguration in 1973, Graham was invited to deliver a short prayer. During Nixon's first term in office, as protests and demonstrations against the Administration's Vietnam war policy rose in size and frequency, the two men often appeared in public together, and Graham had Nixon address the friendly and enthusiastically patriotic audiences that gathered to hear the evangelist.

In May 1970 Graham invited the President to a rally of 88,000 in Knoxville, and in October of the following year, Nixon addressed a well-attended tribute to Graham in Charlotte. At a Fourth of July 1970 Honor America Day Rally in Washington, D.C., organized by the President's supporters, Graham gave the keynote address. Telling the participants that there was "too much discouragement, despair, and negativism in the nation," he said that Americans "deserve to wave the flag a bit."

Graham remained loyal to Nixon through much of the revelations surrounding Watergate, and as late as December 1973 he publicly expressed his "confidence in the President's integrity." After reading the transcripts of White House Tapes in May 1974, however, Graham called it "a profoundly disturbing and disappointing experience." When Nixon finally resigned from office, Graham urged Americans to pray for him.

In 1975 the Billy Graham Evangelical Association, with a yearly income in excess of $28 million. lost its status as a charitable gift fund in the state of Minnesota for failure to submit financial reports. Two years later the Charlotte *Observer* reported that the Association had amassed a $23 million secret fund under another corporate name. Graham quickly issued a six-page defense in *Christianity Today* in which he denied any wrongdoing and said that the fund had "some of America's most reputable businessmen in control."

[JD]

For further information:
Lowell D. Streiker and Gerald S. Strober, *Religion and the New Majority: Billy Graham, Middle America, and the Politics of the 70s* (New York, 1972).

GRAHAM, KATHARINE (MEYER)
b. June 16, 1917; New York, N.Y.
President, Washington Post Company, 1963-73; Publisher, *The Washington Post*, 1969-79.

Katharine Meyer was the daughter of an investment banker and philanthropist. In 1935, two years after her father purchased *The Washington Post*, Katharine Meyer graduated from the Madiera School in Greenway, Va., where she worked on the student newspaper. After graduation from the University of Chicago in 1938, she worked as a reporter for the *San Francisco News.*

In 1939 her father asked her to join *The Washington Post.* She became part of the editorial staff of the *Post*, and from 1939 to 1945 she worked in the circulation and editorial departments of the Sunday edition. In June 1940 she married Philip L. Graham, a brilliant Harvard Law School graduate and a law clerk for Felix Frankfurter. In 1946 Graham became publisher of the *Post.* Two years later Eugene Meyer sold all the voting stock of the company to the Grahams for one dollar. Like many women of her generation, Katharine Graham spent the 1950s raising children and entertaining friends in her stylish Georgetown home. In 1963 the Grahams' domestic tranquility was shattered when Philip Graham killed himself.

In September 1963 Katharine Graham assumed her husband's position as president of *The Washington Post.* In 1961 Philip Graham had purchased *Newsweek* and held a 50% interest in the *Los Angeles Times* with a news service wire. The Post Company also held several radio and television stations in Washington, Miami, Jacksonville, Cincinnati and Hartford. Newspeople considered Katharine Graham's most important decision to be her hiring of Benjamin C. Bradlee [q.v.], the Washington bureau chief for *Newsweek,* as the managing editor for the *Post.* Under Bradlee's direction *The Washington Post* soon became one of the best daily papers in the country.

Virtually from the beginning the liberal *Washington Post* was critical of the Nixon Administration. For instance a 1968 editorial compared the nomination of Spiro Agnew [q.v.] as Republican Vice President with Roman emperor Caligula's appointment of his horse as proconsul. The editorial fueled Agnew's attack on the news media in general and on *The Washington Post* in particular as being part of the "liberal establishment" out to get the Nixon Administration. In 1971 *The Washington Post* with *The New York Times* was sued by the Nixon Administration for publishing the *Pentagon Papers,* a study of U.S. military involvement in Vietnam during the Johnson years. In June 1971 the Supreme Court upheld the newspapers' right to publish the study.

In October 1972 two young *Washington Post* reporters, Carl Bernstein [*q.v.*] and Robert Woodward [*q.v.*], broke the story of the Donald Segretti [*q.v.*] "dirty tricks" operation during the 1972 presidential campaign. When the Nixon White House not only denied the story but attacked the reporters and the *Post,* Katharine Graham stood behind her staff. Although both Richard Nixon and John Mitchell [*q.v.*] threatened the paper with anti-trust suits if it persisted in its Watergate coverage, Katharine Graham supported the probe and insisted only that the reporters verify their information and print the truth.

In February 1973 Graham, Bernstein and Woodward from the *Post* and reporters from the *Washington Star News, The New York Times* and *Time* magazine were issued subpoenas in a civil suit brought by the Committee for the Reelection of the President (CREEP) and were ordered to surrender "all notes, tapes and story drafts in their possession regarding Watergate." They refused to comply, and Katharine Graham declared that she would go to jail as the paper's representative before she allowed the freedom of the press to be threatened in that way. The judge agreed with the press's position and disallowed CREEP's subpoenas of Graham and her staff.

Although she conceded the important role the press and the *Post* played initially in raising public awareness about the deeds of the Nixon White House and of CREEP, Graham insisted that "in the long run it was minor compared to that of the courts, the grand juries, the Judiciary Committee and the American people."

Graham announced her plans to retire as publisher of the *Post* in January 1979.

[SJT]

GRASSO, ELLA T(AMBUSSI)
b. May 10, 1919; Windsor Locks, Conn.
Governor, Conn., 1975–.

The daughter of Italian immigrants, Ella Tambussi was raised in the small town of Windsor Locks where her father was a baker. Encouraged by her mother to pursue her education, she attended Mount Holyoke College, receiving her B.A. with honors in 1940 and an M.A. in economics in 1942. She worked for the War Manpower Commission during World War II and became a member of the League of Women Voters which aroused an interest in politics. Joining the Democratic Party, Grasso, who married a school principal in 1942, became the protege of the powerful state party chairman John Bailey. She worked hard for the Party machine and in 1952 was elected to the state Assembly, where she served two terms and became assistant house leader. Elected secretary of state in 1958, she retained that position for 12 years, and turned her office into a "people's lobby" where ordinary citizens could air their complaints.

On the national level, Grasso was a member of the Democratic Party's platform committee in 1960, and co-chaired the resolutions committee at the Party's National Conventions in 1964 and 1968. At the latter convention she played a major role in the composition of a minority report which opposed continued U.S. involvement in Vietnam. Grasso was one of the delegates who walked out of the convention as a protest against the provocative tactics of the Chicago police toward anti-war demonstrators. In 1970 Grasso ran for the U.S. House in the district represented by Republican Thomas Meskill, who was running for governor, and won a narrow victory. In 1972 she was reelected by a substantial margin.

Assigned to the Education and Labor Committee, Grasso supported most social welfare legislation and was a strong advocate of increased federal spending to reduce unemployment. She was among the most active proponents of the Emergency Employment Act of 1971 and also supported a 1971 emergency aid to education bill, an increase in the minimum wage to two dollars an hour and extension of coverage under the law to an additional six million workers. Though she supported congressional efforts to limit the President's war-making powers, Grasso displeased anti-war activists by her support of military appropriations bills, a position attributed to Connecticut's heavy dependence on defense industries. A practicing Catholic, Grasso received a poor rating from the feminist Women's Lobby because of her unequivocal opposition to abortion and her failure to support child-care legislation.

A 1973 poll by the Hartford *Times* indicated that Grasso was by far the most popular choice among voters to succeed Thomas Meskill as governor. In January 1974 she announced her candidacy and in July the state nominating convention chose her by acclamation. Running against a House colleague, Robert H. Steele, Grasso won the election handily, thereby becoming the first woman in the nation's history to win a governorship in her own right. She was also the first person of Italian descent to be elected governor of Connecticut.

Grasso's first two years in office were difficult ones as Connecticut was particularly hard hit by the nationwide recession. Unemployment in the state was over 10%, and in April 1975, Connecticut was forced to borrow $106 million from the federal government to pay unemployment benefits, having exhausted its own fund the previous month. With a projected deficit of $90 million, the state also saw its credit ratings downgraded by the Standard and Poor's Corp.

In February Grasso presented the state legislature with an austerity budget that called for higher taxes, a wage freeze for state employees, a lengthening of the work week for government employees to 40 hours, and the transfer of veterans' pension funds to the general budget. Her proposals aroused widespread opposition and state civil service unions threatened to strike if the measures were enacted. Although the legislature raised the sales tax to 7%, making it the highest in the nation, they balked at the other measures. Grasso convened a special session of the legislature in the autumn, but when she failed again to win approval of her austerity measures, she announced the layoffs of several hundred state employees. The following year, with economic conditions still poor, she won a compromise extension of the work week to 37½ hours.

Taking office in the post-Watergate era, Grasso attempted to make government more responsive to the people. She bypassed normal patronage routes in making appointments to office. In 1975 she won passage of a state Freedom of Information Act. The law insured public access to government meetings and to the records of state agencies. Grasso also held public hearings throughout the state on her budget proposals, and opened her office for a number of hours each week to hear the complaints of ordinary citizens.

Long-time state party chairman John Bailey's death in April 1975 created disarray among Connecticut Democrats. In 1976 Grasso attempted to oust Bailey's successor, Assembly majority leader William A. O'Neill. Her failure to do so, coupled with the unpopularity of her two austerity budgets, raised speculation that she might not win renomination to a second term. Further opposition to Grasso came from feminist leaders in the state who were dismayed by her failure to appoint more women to state office and by her strong stand against public funding of abortions. When the U.S. Supreme Court ruled on June 20, 1977 that states were not constitutionally required to pay for abortions for poor women, Grasso immediately ordered a halt to state funding.

In January 1978 Lieutenant Governor Robert Killian announced that he would challenge Grasso for the gubernatorial nomination. Improved economic conditions, however, had decreased dissatisfaction with Grasso. The Governor won reelection in November. [See CARTER Volume]

[JD]

GRAVEL, MIKE
b. May 13, 1930; Springfield, Mass.
Democratic Senator, Alaska, 1969 -.

The son of French-Canadian immigrants, Gravel was a counterintelligence officer with the Army in Europe from 1951-54. After graduating from Columbia University in 1956 with a B.A. in economics, he moved to Alaska and went into real estate. Gravel won election to the Alaska House of Representatives in 1962, and became speaker of the House in 1965. Three years later he defeated incumbent Sen. Ernest Gruening in the Democratic primary and went on to win the election.

In the Senate Gravel generally aligned with liberal Democrats, supporting most social welfare legislation and opposing President Nixon's impounding of funds for domestic programs. Occasionally he broke ranks to back the President: in 1969 he voted to confirm Clement Haynsworth [*q.v.*] to the Supreme Court and two years later supported continued funding of the controversial SST.

Largely inconspicuous during his first two years in the Senate, Gravel suddenly received national attention in spring 1971 when he placed portions of the Pentagon Papers, a top secret Defense Department study of U.S. involvement in Southeast Asia, into the Senate record. On June 28, a federal grand jury had indicted Daniel Ellsberg, a former Defense Department aide, on charges of stealing the *Pentagon Papers.* The next day Gravel responded by calling reporters to a late-night session of his Subcommittee on Public Buildings and Grounds where he read aloud from a copy of the *Pentagon Papers* for three hours. Senate Minority Leader Hugh Scott of Pennsylvania [*q.v.*] threatened to have Gravel censured but Majority Leader Mike Mansfield of Montana [*q.v.*] blocked any such attempt. In a major court decision on congressional immunity, the Supreme Court on June 29, 1972, ruled 5-4 that although Gravel and his aides could not be subpoenaed or indicted for reading the documents to the press, immunity did not extend to the circum-

stances surrounding their acquisition. No action was taken against Gravel.

Gravel took an increasingly active role in the Senate's opposition to the war in Vietnam. During the summer of 1971 he led a three-month filibuster against extension of the draft. One of four Senators to vote against the military appropriations bill of 1971, Gravel consistently supported attempts to cut off funding for the war. In May 1972 after President Nixon announced the mining of North Vietnam's major harbors and a resumption of bombing, Gravel read portions of another classified government report on Vietnam into the Congressional Record.

Concerned about the economic development of his underpopulated state, Gravel was a strong proponent of the Alaska oil pipeline. He helped win passage in 1971 of the Alaska Native Claims Settlement Act, which provided the state's native population with 40 million acres of land and almost $1 billion in compensation. However the act prohibited the state or native Alaskans from claiming lands selected by the Secretary of the Interior for a pipeline corridor. In 1973 Congress passed a $3.5 billion appropriation to build the pipeline. The measure included an amendment introduced by Gravel barring further court challenges to the pipeline by its opponents, thus assuring construction of the pipeline.

Gravel was also a vocal critic of nuclear power. He supported passage in 1974 of the Energy Research and Development Act, which abolished the Atomic Energy Commission and created in its place a Nuclear Regulatory Commission. In 1975 he tried unsuccessfully to win passage of a bill to increase the liability of nuclear power companies in damage suits filed by private citizens. After failing to win a seat on the Joint Atomic Energy Committee, he charged in 1976 that Senate leaders had denied his request because of his opposition to the nuclear power industry.

Gravel easily won reelection to a second Senate term in 1974.

[JD]

GRAY, L(OUIS) PATRICK
b. July 18, 1916; St. Louis, Mo.
Acting Director, Federal Bureau of
Investigation, May 1972-April 1973.

The son of a railroad inspector, L. Patrick Gray grew up in Houston, where he studied at Rice University and trained with the Naval Reserve. After four years at Rice, he won an appointment to the Naval Academy at Annapolis, Md., graduating in 1940 with a B.S. and a commission as ensign. After serving aboard a submarine in the Pacific during World War II, Gray was chosen in 1946 to attend George Washington University Law School in Washington, D.C., as a Navy postgraduate student. Receiving his J.D. with honors in 1949, Gray advanced to the rank of captain during the 1950s.

In the Korean war Gray commanded three submarine combat patrols and after the war was stationed at the School of Naval Justice, Newport, R.I. In 1958 he was named military assistant to the chairman of the Joint Chiefs of Staff and special assistant to the Secretary of Defense for legal and legislative affairs. In these posts Gray served principally as a liaison between the Pentagon and Congress and had frequent dealings with the staff of Vice President Richard Nixon.

When Nixon began organizing his 1960 presidential campaign, Gray left the Navy to become an aide to Robert Finch [q.v.], head of Nixon's vice-presidential staff and chairman of his campaign. After Nixon's defeat by John F. Kennedy in 1960, Gray joined a New London, Conn. law firm and established a small-business investment company. Throughout the 1960s he maintained his political contacts with Nixon, serving as a fund raiser for the Republican Party. Early in 1968 he met with Nixon to pledge his support in the race for the presidential nomination. During the campaign Gray prepared a position paper elaborating Nixon's views on the small-business investment field.

After his victory in November 1968, Nixon recruited Gray as executive assistant to Robert Finch, who was designated

Secretary of Health, Education and Welfare (HEW). Gray quickly became known as "a very strong loyalist to the President and the Administration and the Party." In a speech given to HEW's political appointees soon after joining the Department, Gray stressed that all appointees owed their jobs to the Nixon Administration and must be willing to subjugate "personal goals to a deep personal commitment to serve our President, our Secretary and our Nation." Though not highly visible in his HEW work, Gray played a key role in the Department's internal organization and earned the President's gratitude for his service. A death in his family led Gray to leave HEW and return to his law practice in January 1970, but he continued to serve the Nixon Administration as a cabinet-level consultant on school busing and desegregation.

In December 1970 Gray was persuaded to return to Washington as assistant attorney general for the Justice Department's Civil Division. In this post he was responsible for handling anti-war demonstrations on federal property. In April 1971 he obtained a federal court restraining order to keep the Vietnam Veterans Against the War from camping on Capitol Hill. When the White House decided against forcibly evicting the veterans, many of whom were paraplegics, Gray was left the embarrassing task of asking the court to withdraw its order. Gray was also given the responsibility of enforcing the wage and price controls specified in Nixon's Economic Stabilization Act.

In February 1972 when Nixon nominated Richard G. Kleindienst [q.v.] to replace John N. Mitchell [q.v.] as Attorney General, Gray was nominated for the post of deputy attorney general. Both men were still awaiting confirmation, pending the Senate's investigation of Kleindienst's handling of an anti-trust case against International Telephone and Telegraph, when FBI Director J. Edgar Hoover [q.v.] died on May 2, 1972. It was rumored that Nixon's appointment of Gray as acting FBI director on the following day had been planned far in advance. Nixon promised to evaluate Gray's performance after several months before deciding whether to nominate him for the permanent position, which required confirmation by the Senate.

When Gray took over as head of the FBI, he faced the problem of winning the loyalty and respect of an organization that had idolized Hoover, the Bureau's tough, idiosyncratic chief, for almost 50 years. Some of Gray's immediate reforms, such as his relaxation of dress and weight codes for agents and his inclusion of agents' wives in Bureau activities, were welcomed by the FBI field offices. Many of these changes, however, including Gray's policy of hiring women as special agents, drew criticism from Hoover loyalists at Bureau headquarters. These top officials, often at odds with the agents in the field offices, resented the elevation of an outsider to the Bureau's top post and feared that Gray's background might lead him to politicize the traditionally independent FBI. Gray's selection of non-FBI people as his top staff advisers fueled the resentment of veteran Bureau officials, many of whom resigned soon after Gray's appointment. Unfamiliar with the daily operations of the FBI, Gray relied heavily on his deputy director, W. Mark Felt, to deal with the vast amount of paperwork that crossed his desk. Instead of concentrating on learning FBI routines, Gray spent much of his time visiting the Bureau's 59 field offices and fulfilling speaking engagements in what many saw as a "campaign" for the Bureau's permanent directorship.

In February 1973 Nixon announced Gray as his choice for permanent FBI director. During 10 days of confirmation hearings before the Senate Judiciary Committee, the Senators attacked such controversial areas of FBI policy as the handling of fingerprints and arrest records, the Bureau's efforts against organized crime, its secret files on government officials and the gathering of domestic intelligence on U.S. citizens who had never been charged with a crime.

Most damaging to Gray, however, was the review of the FBI's Watergate investigation. The Committee exploded when it learned that during the initial investigation of the break-in at Democratic headquarters in the Watergate, Gray had regularly provided John Dean [q.v.], the President's special counsel, with copies of "raw" unevaluated investigative materials, including summaries of the telephone conversations that were originally intercepted with the electronic devices illegally installed at Democratic headquarters in the Watergate complex. In addition Gray had allowed attorneys at the Committee to Re-Elect the President (CREEP) to sit in on FBI interviews of CREEP employees and had agreed to the White House demand that John Dean monitor the FBI's interviews of 14 White House aides.

Defending his actions Gray stated that "you've got to operate on a basic presumption of regularity," pointing out that Dean was, after all, counsel to the President. Yet Gray was unable to explain why his dealings with Dean had been carried out in secrecy, to the extent that Gray had insisted Dean personally pick up packets of Watergate materials, instead of having them delivered by Justice Department courier. When Gray offered, during his confirmation hearings, to provide the Judiciary Committee with the same "raw" Watergate materials he had given to Dean, he incurred the wrath of the White House as well. After Gray testified on March 22 that John Dean had probably lied to FBI agents about the activities of Howard Hunt [q.v.], a former White House aide who had helped engineer the Watergate break-in, the Judiciary Committee met secretly to dispose of Gray's nomination by indefinitely postponing action on it. In early April Gray wrote to President Nixon asking that his name be withdrawn.

Following his disastrous confirmation hearings, Gray told Sen. Lowell Weicker (R, Conn.) that John Dean and presidential aide John Ehrlichman had, in June 1972, given Gray two envelopes from Howard Hunt's files, suggesting that they were "political dynamite" which "should not see the light of day." Gray told Weicker that he had burned the files, which were later revealed to have contained

State Department cables doctored by Hunt to demonstrate that John F. Kennedy had ordered the assassination of South Vietnamese President Ngo Dinh Diem during the early stages of U.S. involvement in the Vietnam war. The documents were to have been used in the event that Sen. Edward Kennedy (D, Mass.) [q.v.] challenged Nixon in the 1972 presidential election.

The story, which was leaked to the press by Weicker, made banner headlines on April 27, 1973. Gray immediately resigned as acting director of the FBI and returned to his private law practice in Connecticut. Later Gray revealed to the Senate Watergate Committee that he had warned President Nixon of the Watergate cover-up effort on July 6, 1972, about three weeks after the break-in.

[DAE]

For further information:
Sanford J. Ungar, *FBI* (Boston, 1976).

GRAYSON, C(HARLES) JACKSON, JR.
b. Oct. 8, 1923, Fort Necessity, La.
Chairman, Federal Price
Commission, February 1972-January 1973.

The son of a Louisiana dirt farmer, Grayson graduated Tulane University with a degree in business administration in 1944. He joined the Navy for the duration of World War II and then returned to graduate school. After securing an M.B.A. from the Wharton School of Finance at the University of Pennsylvania in 1947, Grayson returned to Tulane to teach business. In 1949 he joined the New Orleans *Item* as an obituary writer, and later he covered city hall. From 1950 to 1952 Grayson was an FBI agent. Dissatisfied with the Bureau's authoritarian atmosphere, he returned to the family farm for a year before becoming an assistant professor at Tulane in 1953.

After receiving a D.B.A. in 1959 from the Graduate School of Business Ad-

ministration at Harvard, Grayson returned to Tulane. In 1961 he was appointed assistant dean, and two years later dean of the school. Grayson remained at Tulane until 1968, when he assumed a similar post at Southern Methodist University (SMU) in Texas.

An educational reformer Grayson revised SMU's curriculum and disposed of specific prerequisites for courses because he felt self-determination in educational development led to better academic understanding. An early exponent of college credit for actual experience in one's discipline, Grayson devised a program whereby students received credit for the successful operation of campus businesses.

In 1971 Nixon appointed Grayson chairman of the Federal Price Commission (FPC) under Phase Two of his economic program. The purpose of the Price Commission, according to the President was, "to restrain prices and rent increases to the necessary minimum and to prevent windfall profits." With a well-educated advisory staff Grayson mapped out his approach for circumventing potential crises in several areas of the economy.

Shortly before Nixon's Phase Two was implemented, the Commission outlined in November 1971 its program for limiting price increases to a maximum 2.5% per year in an effort to bring about economic stabilization. According to the Commission's guidelines a company's profit margin could be no greater than the highest average of the two most profitable years of the firm's three previous years. Price increases were restricted to production costs minus expansion in productivity. Grayson stated "a strong and sustained increase in the productivity of our labor force" was essential in order to legitimately increase profits and achieve economic prosperity. To facilitate the imposition of price restrictions, Grayson established "term limit pricing," which allowed a firm producing a variety of items to fix an overall percentage increase, thus eliminating unnecessary paperwork for the Commission.

In December Grayson instituted temporary restrictions on medical costs and rent increases, although municipal guidelines on rent were not suspended. Grayson's major area of concern was in the steel, coal, auto and chemical industries, where wage and price increases were pending when Phase Two was initiated. Although he permitted a 3.6% price increase by U.S. Steel, he received a commitment from the firm that no further increase would be sought until August 1972. Grayson also rejected a request for price increases in the construction industry because he considered the increases excessive and inflationary.

In 1972 the Commission expanded its efforts to regulate public utilities in coordination with state agencies. Although Phase Two guidelines were soon removed from small businesses at the request of the White House, Grayson ordered medium-sized and large firms to decrease prices by as much as 30%, since profit margins had not been reduced in the quarterly report of the preceding year. With food costs continuing to spiral, he established a "food watch unit" to monitor the rise of food prices. He criticized Secretary of Agriculture Earl Butz [q.v.] for recommending higher farm prices that would only delay a move toward stabilization. By mid-1972 most unprocessed agricultural goods were subject to governmental control.

While the Price Commission had received widespread endorsement for its "clear, effective, anti-inflationary policy," the FPC was not without its opponents. Organized labor and consumer groups charged that the actual impact of the Commission was negligible, and Ralph Nader [q.v.] regarded it as "the captive of special corporate pleaders who routinely get the price increases they want."

In January 1973 Phase Two had ended and the responsibilities for Phase Three were to be handled by Nixon's Cost of Living Council. With the dismantling of the Federal Price Commission, Grayson returned to academic life.

[DGE]

GREENBERG, JACK
b. Dec. 22, 1924; New York, N.Y.
Director-Counsel, NAACP Legal
Defense and Educational Fund,
1961- .

A graduate of Columbia University's School of Law in 1948, Greenberg was appointed assistant counsel of the NAACP Legal Defense and Educational Fund the following year. The fund, an independent agency of the NAACP, had been established in 1939 in order to challenge the constitutionality of widespread discriminatory practices as well as provide a legal arm for the civil rights movement. During the early 1950s Greenberg worked as an assistant to Thurgood Marshall [q.v.] in school segregation cases and joined Marshall and other attorneys in arguing the historic school integration suits before the U.S. Supreme Court which led to the May 17, 1954 decision in *Brown v. the Board of Education.*

In 1961 Greenberg became Director-Counsel of the Fund. From 1961 to 1966 the organization represented sit-in and freedom ride demonstrators and won more than 40 civil rights cases in the Supreme Court. Greenberg also helped in the battle to integrate several Southern universities. [See KENNEDY, JOHNSON Volumes]

In 1970, after the Nixon Administration began a covert attempt to delay desegregation in Southern schools, Greenberg won *Alexander v. Holmes County (Miss.) Board of Education* before the Supreme Court which ordered the dissolution of segregated school systems "at once." A year later in *Griggs v. Duke Power Company* he won an important decision stating that "employment or promotion tests having a differential racial impact must be shown to be job related." Under Greenberg's leadership the Fund established the Earl Warren Legal Training Program in 1972 in order to provide scholarships and internship programs to black law students who would consider settling in areas where there existed a shortage of lawyers to handle cases of concern to black citizens.

Since his earliest days with the Fund, Greenberg undertook a campaign to examine the inequitable bases by which capital punishment was administered in rape cases. The majority of those put to death had been black and the alleged victims had, almost without exception, been white. In 1972 Greenberg argued one of the cases which resulted in the Supreme Court ruling which outlawed capital punishment because it had been applied arbitrarily "falling with uneven incidence on the poor, uneducated and racial minorities." The decision culminated the Fund's seven-year program to end capital punishment.

By 1974 under Greenberg's supervision, the Fund had expanded to include 25 staff and 400 affiliated attorneys in a national program of civil rights and poverty litigation. In addition to lecturing on the role of litigation in social change, Greenberg conducted a clinical seminar on civil rights at Columbia University Law School during the 1970s.

[DGE]

GREENSPAN, ALAN
b. March 6, 1926; New York, N.Y.
Chairman, Council of Economic Advisers, September 1974-January 1977.

Greenspan was born and raised in New York City. The son of a stockbroker he took his B.S. in economics from New York University (NYU) in 1948 and acquired his M.A. in 1950. In the same year he began a doctoral program at Columbia under Arthur Burns [q.v.], but gradually lost interest in academic economics. While still a student at NYU, Greenspan had already worked as an economist for the Conference Board, a private business research organization, and in 1953, with business counselor William Townsend, Greenspan founded the consulting firm Townsend-Greenspan & Co. He also began teaching economics at NYU.

Beginning in 1952 Greenspan was influenced by Ayn Rand and her controversial philosophy of laissez-faire capitalism. Rand, he explained later, showed him "why capitalism is not only efficient and practical, but also moral." In the 1960s Greenspan published articles in Rand's magazine, The Objectivist, and in one of them characterized the modern welfare state as "nothing more than a mechanism by which governments confiscate the wealth of the productive members of a society." Greenspan's association with Rand later provoked Arthur M. Okun, former member of the Council of Economic Advisers (CEA) under Lyndon Johnson, to remark that "when Greenspan came to Washington . . . I had an image of him as the worst, flaming right-wing bastard in the world."

In 1967 Greenspan was recruited from his consulting firm to work on Richard Nixon's 1968 Presidential campaign. Greenspan had deeply mixed feelings about involving himself in national politics, and at the 1968 Republican Convention told a reporter: "I'm disturbed. Every single decision is governed by politics, and the narrowest kind of politics." After Nixon's election, Greenspan declined any full-time post with this Administration, but served as Nixon's personal representative to the Bureau of the Budget during the transition period and was also appointed chairman of the Task Force on Foreign Trade Policy.

In 1969 Greenspan returned to his consulting firm in New York City, but remained a part-time adviser to the Administration, serving on the Task Force on Economic Growth, the Commission on an All-Volunteer Armed Force and the Commission on Financial Structure and Regulation. Greenspan kept his distance from the official economic spokesmen of Nixon's Administration, correctly predicting in his newsletter, despite government optimism to the contrary, that the recession of 1969-70 would continue well into 1971. After the events of August 1971, when Nixon introduced his "New Economic Policy" and effectively became, in his own words, a "Keynesian," Greenspan was quite critical of the turn and called for the "old time religion" of conservative fiscal and monetary policies, which he would later advocate as chairman of the CEA. Despite his criticisms of Nixon's economics, Greenspan agreed to work on the President's 1972 campaign, repeatedly attacking Democratic nominee Sen. George McGovern [q.v.] for "fiscal irresponsibility." In early 1974 Nixon offered Greenspan the chairmanship of the CEA, which Greenspan declined.

After the Administration's six-month search had failed to turn up another economist for the CEA post, Federal Reserve Board Chairman Arthur Burns, Greenspan's college professor, persuaded Greenspan to reconsider, citing the dire situation of the U.S. and world economies as they entered the deep recession of 1974-75. Greenspan's nomination was pending in the Senate at the time of Nixon's resignation in August 1974, and despite some initial reluctance by the Senate to accept a Nixon appointee, Greenspan became CEA chairman on Sept. 1, 1974.

Greenspan was initially the symbol of a commitment to classic economic conservatism by the new Ford Administration. But at the time he assumed office, the tight money policies and fiscal restraint designed by Burns and Treasury Secretary William Simon [q.v.] were rapidly being made obsolete by the accelerating fall in production, giving Greenspan an opening for a more flexible economic policy. This flexibility became apparent in Greenspan's endorsement in 1975, over the objections of Burns and Simon, of Ford's proposed $23 billion tax cut to inject consumer spending power into the economy.

Greenspan was not a classic conservative. In a September 1974 meeting with AFL-CIO leaders, he produced charts and graphs showing conclusively that inflation was seriously outstripping wage gains and effectively refuting the traditional conservative claim that inflation was the product of a "wage-price spiral." Not all of his public appearances were so successful, however, and a few weeks later Greenspan committed a major public relations blunder. Speaking before hearings on the economy held by Health, Education and Welfare (HEW) officials and attended by many poverty organization representatives, Greenspan said: "Everyone is hurt by inflation. If you really want to examine percentage-wise who was hurt most in their income, it was Wall Street brokers." Jeers and catcalls drowned out the remainder of Greenspan's remarks, and the ensuing outcry, which seized on the incident to portray the Ford Administration as strictly a government of big business, compelled Greenspan to state one week later, "Obviously, the poor are suffering more."

Greenspan's stature as an Administration spokesman was based on his ability to call the turns of the economy with considerable accuracy. Greenspan had predicted a "mild" recession for 1974 before accepting the CEA chairmanship, and though he consistently underestimated the rise of the unemployment rate, he correctly predicted that the recession would "bottom out" by mid-1975. In January 1975, when U.S. production was falling at the fastest rate since 1931, Greenspan told the Joint Economic Committee (JEC) of Congress that the economic outlook for the year was "neither pleasant nor reassuring," warning that "a sharp contraction of production and employment still has several months to run" with the economy continuing to decline "into the summer." With unemployment figures approaching 9%, Greenspan said that the "recession has come upon us much more suddenly than we generally anticipated," and agreed that strong action by the government was necessary to "dissipate the extraordinary sense of uncertainty and gloom that businessmen and housewives have about the economy."

Nevertheless in early May 1975 Greenspan told the JEC that "the economy may wobble on the bottom for a while, but the worst does appear to be behind us." Production had in fact bottomed two months earlier. In June 1975 Greenspan stated definitively in a television interview that the recession was over, warning against any "overexpansion of the money supply" and echoing Treasury Secretary Simon's concern about the danger of federal borrowing "crowding out" the private sector in capital markets.

Greenspan's ability to foresee with accuracy the turns of the economy made him invaluable to the Ford Administration. One White House official stated in the spring of 1975 that "Greenspan has a unique personal relationship with Ford . . . Alan spends time alone with the President on economic policy, and on economic policy Alan is a heavyweight." By July 1975 Greenspan was able to tell the JEC that the business recovery was "ahead of schedule."

Greenspan, with Simon, was most closely associated with a general shift in economic philosophy that became apparent in the final year of the Ford Administration. Although Greenspan's backing of the 1975 tax cut had appeared to many as a surprising policy from a conservative, Greenspan and Simon felt that the real problems of the U.S. economy would not be solved until a serious revamping of U.S. industry was made possible by an investment boom in capital goods. To bring about such a boom, they felt a fundamental shift in tax incentives was necessary to encourage corporations to make large-scale investments. In the 1976 debate over extending the tax cut, Greenspan said he preferred a tax cut to a deficit increase, but looked to more fundamental changes for a long-term solution. Ford's defeat in the 1976 election, however, ended any more serious reform of corporate depreciation allowances and similar measures.

After the 1975 turnaround in production, Greenspan saw his major task as preventing a rekindling of inflation. In 1974 he had already stated that "if inflation continues, our system will not hold together in its present form," and called for a reduction in government borrowing, tightening of the money supply and a federal surplus as a means of combating inflation. In 1975-76, despite record peacetime federal deficits to finance the Ford "reflation" program, Greenspan warned Congress against "excessive" deficits or tax cuts. He also expressed concern about costly labor settlements. When the International Brotherhood of Teamsters, after a brief strike in April 1976, won a large wage increase in excess of Administration recommendations, Greenspan stated that the Teamster settlement, while "not inflationary," was "somewhat higher than I would have liked to see."

In the late summer of 1976, the recovery of the U.S. economy reached a plateau that lasted several months, leading many observers to prematurely announce the end of the 1975-76 recovery. Greenspan correctly argued that the economy had merely entered a "pause," and that "the basic recovery is solidly in place with no evidence of underlying deterioration." The economy stayed flat into the fall of 1976, however, and was an important factor in the electoral defeat of Gerald Ford.

Greenspan completed his term as CEA chairman in January 1977, and returned to Townsend-Greenspan & Co. to resume his private consulting work.

[LSG]

GRIFFIN, ROBERT P.
b. Nov. 6, 1923; Detroit, Mich.
Republican Senator, Mich., 1966-.

Following his graduation from Central Michigan College of Education in 1947, Robert Griffin obtained his law degree from the University of Michigan in 1950. He practiced law in Traverse City until 1956, when he won a seat in the House of Representatives. Griffin earned national distinction during Eisenhower's second term for his cosponsorship of the Landrum-Griffin Act in 1959 and his lobbying efforts to increase federal assistance to education. [See EISENHOWER Volume] As a Representative during the Kennedy and early Johnson years, Griffin compiled a moderate record supporting civil rights, federal aid to education and medicare. In 1963 Griffin and a number of other young Republicans, called the "Young Turks," staged a revolt against the Party hierarchy by voting for Rep. Gerald R. Ford (R, Mich.) for chairman of the House Republican Conference Committee instead of Rep. Charles Hoeven (R, Iowa). Two years later they unseated Minority Leader Charles A. Halleck (R, Ind.) in favor of Ford. [See KENNEDY Volume]

Griffin was appointed to the Senate in May 1966 following the death of Patrick McNamara. He won election to that Senate seat in November. Griffin achieved national prominence in 1968 when he led Republican opposition to President Johnson's nomination of Abe Fortas [q.v.] as chief justice of the Supreme Court. [See JOHNSON Volume]

In October 1969 the Senate Republicans elected Griffin their minority whip. Griffin thus became one of the leading congressional spokesmen for the White House. He consistently backed Nixon's Vietnam war policies, especially during the turbulent period of the spring of 1970 as demonstrations mounted against the war. Griffin opposed the Cooper-Church Amendment prohibiting the President from sending combat troops into Cambodia without the consent of Congress. On the Senate floor he stated that he knew the Amendment sponsors did not intend "to aid the enemy," "but it does aid the enemy when we tie the hands of the commander in chief."

Griffin backed Nixon's vetoes of bills to increase funds for education, health and manpower training programs because he felt they were inflationary. He also opposed increasing food stamp allotments and voted against most proconsumer legislation. In 1972 the conservative Americans for Constitutional Action gave Griffin a rating of 74 and in 1973 of 88. Nevertheless Griffin supported liberal legislation in several areas of interest to him. In 1972 he called for the elimination of monthly premiums that medicare recipients had to pay for supplementary coverage. Griffin also introduced a bill to revamp the Nation's health coverage system by requiring all employers to contribute to a privately-run health care insurance program for their workers. Those not covered by the program and ineligible for medicare would be included under a government-paid program. Griffin cospon-

sored a 1970 constitutional amendment calling for direct election of the President and vice president by popular vote. Griffin also supported the Equal Rights Amendment in 1972 and backed the stiff Federal Election Campaign Act of 1971.

In 1971 a federal court ordered Detroit and its suburban school systems to intergrate through busing. In response Griffin introduced a constitutional amendment to abolish forced busing. On Feb. 25, 1972, the Senate adopted Griffin's amendment by a vote of 43 to 40, but five days later, in another vote, the same measure was rejected 48 to 47. Griffin was successful in persuading the White House to sponsor the repeal of the 8% automobile excise tax to stimulate his state's automaking industry.

Griffin opposed the Administration on a number of issues. He voted against the nomination of Clement Haynsworth [q.v.] to the Supreme Court because of "legitimate and substantial doubt" about Haynsworth's "sensitivity to high ethical standards demanded by the bench." Griffin opposed the allocation of funds to develop the supersonic transport because of the "unresolved questions about the SST's impact upon the environment." The Michigan Senator backed his liberal friend Sen. Charles Goodell (R, N.Y.) [q.v.] against the White House attempt, led by Vice President Spiro Agnew [q.v.], to purge Goodell from the Republican Party.

During the early period of the Watergate controversy, Griffin gave the President the benefit of the doubt concerning his statements on the innocence of the White House in the cover-up. He sat in on a number of strategy sessions to discuss Nixon's best possible response to public pressure for an explanation of the President's relationship with the break-in. But Griffin soon grew disenchanted with how Nixon was handling the whole affair. In the spring of 1974 he joined with other Republican congressional leaders in privately urging the President to release all material related to the case. By failing to do so, the leaders warned, Nixon would be setting himself up for impeachment.

On Aug. 3 Griffin notified the President that if he defied a Senate demand for the tapes in the expected impeachment trial, he would vote for conviction. Two days later Griffin appeared before television cameras to call for Nixon's resignation. "I think we've arrived at a point where both the national interest and his own interest will best be served by resigning," Griffin said. "It's not just his enemies who feel that way. Many of his friends, and I count myself one of them, believe now that this would be the most appropriate course."

Griffin supported the economic and foreign policies of his friend President Ford. He endorsed Ford in his drive for the presidency and campaigned for him in the fall. During the first two years of the Carter presidency, Griffin emerged as one of the leading Republicans challenging the new President on his foreign and economic policy programs. [See CARTER Volume]

[JB]

GRIFFITHS, MARTHA W(RIGHT)
b. Jan. 29, 1912; Pierce City, Mo.
Democratic Representative, Mich., 1954-74.

The daughter of a letter carrier, Griffiths received her B.A. from the University of Missouri in 1934 and her LL.B. from the University of Michigan in 1940. Admitted to the Michigan bar in 1941, she worked in the legal department of an auto insurance company and during World War II was a contract negotiator for Army Ordnance in Detroit. In 1946 she opened a law office, which later became a partnership with husband Hicks G. Griffiths and former classmate G. Mennen Williams, who was governor of Michigan.

Griffiths served as a state representative from 1948 to 1952, fighting for unemployment compensation. In 1952 Griffiths ran unsuccessfully for the U.S. House. She won the seat two years later. Griffiths' interest in human rights and welfare surfaced early in her House career. She sponsored bills to increase the pay of Post Office workers, to promote library service in rural areas and to provide food stamps for the poor and housing for the elderly.

In 1963 the House Democratic caucus elected Griffiths to the powerful Ways and Means Committee, seats on which are reserved for representatives whose electoral strength in their own districts allows them to take independent stands. By 1970 she emerged as the fifth ranking member of the Committee, helping to write tax and welfare legislation and to decide on all other House Democratic committee assignments. In the 91st Congress she steered the Women's Rights Amendment to passage, only to see it die in the Senate. A long-time advocate of free trade, Griffiths voted against an amendment to President Richard Nixon's 1973 trade reform proposals which would have set mandatory quotas on imports that had taken over 15% or more of the U.S. market. Also in 1973 Griffiths supported the Older Americans Act, though she opposed the proliferation of welfare programs and felt such benefits should be administered by the Social Security System.

A member of the Joint Economic Committee, Griffiths ordered a survey of poverty benefits programs by the General Accounting Office. In response to the report issued May 27, 1973, which found that substantial inequities prevailed in the distribution of welfare funds, Griffiths denounced the inadequacy of the federal welfare effort, pointing to work disincentives built into the program.

During the 93rd Congress Griffiths voted with the bipartisan majority on 56% of all floor votes, supporting President Nixon on 40% and President Gerald Ford on 31% of the bills on which each had declared positions in 1974. Griffiths was one of three Ways and Means Committee Democrats to be named in 1974 to the new House Budget Committee. Also in that year she sponsored the Health Security Act, the most comprehensive national health insurance plan of its kind presented to the Ways and Means Committee. No action was taken the same year on Griffiths' plan, which called for health benefits for all Americans, without deductibles or copayments, to be financed by general federal revenues and new payroll taxes. Griffiths announced her retirement in 1974 at the end of her 10th consecutive term. She was succeeded by Democrat William M. Brodhead.

[DAE]

GROSS, NELSON
b. Jan. 9, 1932; Englewood, N.J.
Chairman, New Jersey Republican Party, 1969-70.

After graduating from Yale in 1953, Gross received his law degree from Columbia University in 1956. He served as an assistant U.S. attorney from 1956 to 1958, a New Jersey state assemblyman from 1962 to 1963 and the Bergen County, N.J., counsel from 1963 to 1966. He then became chairman of the Bergen County Republican Party from 1966 to 1969.

Gross gained prominence as a delegate during the 1968 Republican Presidential Convention when he delivered five pivotal votes to Richard Nixon that had been pledged to New Jersey Sen. Clifford Case [q.v.], a favorite-son candidate standing in for Nelson Rockefeller [q.v.]. "We don't want to wind up with a dark-horse candidate," Gross cited as his reason. He was rewarded by being named state campaign manager for the fall election and was credited with winning a 61,000-vote plurality for the future President.

In 1969 Gross became chairman of the New Jersey Republican Committee. He gathered organizational support for Rep. William Cahill's [q.v.] gubernatorial candidacy and helped him win the November election by the largest margin in the state's history.

The following year Gross resigned his state Party chairmanship to run against incumbent Democratic Sen. Harrison Williams [q.v.] in what first appeared an easy race. Williams, who had been publicly rebuked by the state NAACP for appearing at their breakfast meeting drunk, had a lackluster campaign style as well as an unspectacular legislative record.

Gross accumulated a large campaign fund, arranged appearances on his behalf by members of the Nixon family and declared his election part of the national referendum on the policies of the Nixon Administration. Following the lead of Vice President Spiro Agnew [q.v.], Gross labeled Williams a radical liberal who coddled criminals, a politician ineffective against the mass violence sweeping the nation's college campuses.

Yet the election turned out a surprise victory for Williams, whose campaign had been helped by large contributions from labor and an effective public acknowledgment of his rehabilitation from alcoholism. In addition a certain voter unease surfaced against the strident rhetoric of Nixon, Agnew and Gross in the closing days of the campaign. Gross lost all the state's Republican strongholds in the election, even his home county of Bergen, signaling a crack in what had been considered an emerging Republican majority.

From 1971 to 1973 Gross served in the State Department as a special coordinator on international narcotics, putting pressure on foreign governments to crack down on the production and export of a wide variety of dangerous drugs. He was instrumental in trying to force Turkey to stop its farmers from producing opium.

Gross resigned his position in early 1973 shortly before he was indicted in New Jersey for tax fraud, obstruction of justice and subornation of perjury. He was convicted of involvement in a conspiracy to make a $5,000 contribution to William Cahill's 1969 gubernatorial campaign appear as a business expense. After serving four months in prison in 1973, he became a business man.

[GWB]

GURNEY, EDWARD J(OHN)
b. Jan. 12, 1914; Portland, Maine.
Republican Senator, Fla., 1969-74.

Edward Gurney received his B.S. in 1935 from Colby College, his LL.B. from Harvard in 1938. He served in the Army in World War II. In 1948 Gurney established a law practice in Winter Park, Fla. His political career began four years later when he became Winter Park's city commissioner, remaining in the position for six years. In 1961 he was elected mayor of Winter Park. The following year, he won a seat in the U.S. House where he established a conservative record.

Gurney ran for the Senate in 1968, forging the same conservative Democratic–Republican coalition on a statewide level that had worked so effectively within his congressional district. On the campaign trail, he denounced the riots in the black sections of Newark and Detroit and endorsed "bombing the hell" out of Vietnam. His conservative stands, plus the active support of such prominent senators as John Tower of Texas and Everett Dirksen of Illinois, resulted in a stunning victory in November in which Gurney received the largest number of votes in Florida history.

In the Senate Gurney was a strong Nixon supporter. He backed Nixon's nomination of conservative appeals court judge Clement Haynsworth [q.v.] to the Supreme Court and sponsored the nomination of G. Harrold Carswell [q.v.], both of which met defeat. Gurney was a consistent supporter of antibusing proposals. Because his state contained a large number of elderly, he worked for the expansion of government programs for the aged.

Gurney was a particularly vocal advocate of Nixon's handling of the war in Indochina, including the President's decision to send American troops into Cambodia to attack Communist strongholds along the border in the spring of 1970. In the wake of the Cambodian incursion and the killing of four students at Kent State University during an anti-war protest, demonstrations and strikes were triggered in colleges across the country. In June, during a debate in the Senate on funds for the Office of Education, Gurney offered an amendment that would have withheld such funds from any institution of higher learning which closed or suspend-

ed classes to allow participation in non-academic political affairs, except for elections. The amendment was rejected. That same month, Gurney voted against the Cooper-Church Amendment, which set a specific cut-off date for military appropriations for use in Cambodia.

By 1973 the scandal resulting from a break-in at the Democratic Party's headquarters in Washington's Watergate complex had become a major political crisis. In February the Senate created a seven member select committee to probe the break-in and the general question of political espionage in the 1972 presidential elections. Gurney was one of the three Republican senators chosen for the committee.

The hearings began in May. Throughout the probe Gurney supported Nixon. He warned that an elaborate investigation could jeopardize the conduct of the presidency.

Gurney carefully cross-examined John Dean [q.v.], who in late June testified that Nixon knew of the cover-up. The Senator focused on Sept. 15, 1972, the date that indictments were handed down in the Watergate case. Those indicted were only minor figures in Nixon's reelection campaign organization. Dean testified that on that day, the President had commended him on "doing a good job"—which Dean asserted was further indication of Nixon's awareness of the coverup operation. Gurney countered this claim, saying to Dean, "your whole thesis on saying that the President of the United States knew about Watergate on September 15, 1972 is purely an impression. There isn't a single shred of evidence." In July, Sen. Lowell Weicker (R, Conn.) [q.v.], suggested that Nixon himself testify in rebuttal. Gurney labeled Dean a "shoddy turncoat" and said that it would be "demeaning" to respond to his charges. The following month he again urged a swift conclusion to the hearings.

But by October Gurney was facing political problems of his own. That month, he acknowledged reports that he was under investigation by the Justice Department on charges of maintaining a secret "boosters' fund" of more than $300,000 in contributions from Florida builders. One of these builders had accused Gurney aide Larry E. Williams of demanding a $5,000 contribution in exchange for federal approval of two government funded housing projects. Gurney denied any knowledge of the incident.

The *Miami Herald* reported in December that Williams gave sworn testimony to federal investigators in which he said that Gurney knew of $50,000 delivered to his office in Washington in July 1972, which was not reported as required by new federal election laws. In April 1974, Gurney was indicted by a Leon Co. grand jury in Tallahassee for violating state campaign laws. Gurney called the move a "political Pearl Harbor" engineered by Democrats seeking his seat. The indictment was dismissed in May.

Two months later a federal grand jury indicted him on seven counts of bribery, conspiracy and perjury, accusing him of using his influence in the Department of Housing and Urban Development in exchange for campaign funds. At the urging of Florida Republicans, he withdrew from his reelection campaign. That same month, the final report of the Senate Watergate Committee was issued. In his own personal statement in the report, Gurney said, "In my opinion, the evidence gathered by the Committee does not indicate that the President had knowledge of the cover-up." He attacked "careless handling of cash contributions, which should be barred from future elections," and strongly differed with the report's endorsement of a permanent special prosecutor in Washington.

Gurney was acquitted of all charges against him in 1975 and 1976.

In September 1978, he won the Republican primary contest in his attempt to win back the seat that had launched his career in Washington, but he lost the general election.

[MDQ]

HAIG, ALEXANDER M.
b. Dec. 2, 1924; Bala-Cynwyd, Pa. Assistant to the President, May 1973-September 1974; Supreme Allied Commander, North Atlantic Treaty Organization, September 1974- .

The son of a Philadelphia lawyer, Haig worked his way through high school to finance his college education. After studying at the University of Notre Dame for two years, he was admitted to the United States Military Academy in 1944. Despite his unimpressive class rank of 214th out of 310, Haig advanced rapidly after his graduation in 1947. From 1953 to 1955 while he was tactical officer at the U.S. Military Academy at West Point, he studied business administration at Columbia University. Later he took a two-year course of study at Georgetown University in international relations, which culminated in a M.A. degree awarded in 1961. Interspersed among these extensive and diverse courses of study, Haig served in Japan, Korea, and Vietnam and performed in various staff capacities at the Pentagon. During the early sixties, he was a staff officer in the Department of the Army where he attracted the attention of Joseph Califano, who was then general counsel of the Army. Califano later recommended Haig to the Secretary of the Army, Cyrus Vance, who took him on as his military assistant. When Vance became deputy defense secretary late in 1964, Haig remained with him as his deputy special assistant. In the mid 1960s Haig saw action in Vietnam as commander of the First Battalion of the 26th Infantry. Upon his return to the States in June 1967, he was appointed regimental commander of the Third Regiment of the Corps of Cadets at West Point. A month later he was promoted to the rank of colonel and in June of 1968 he became deputy commandant of cadets.

During the transition period between the Johnson and Nixon Administrations late in 1968, LBJ's domestic adviser, Joseph Califano, recommended Haig to the incoming national security assistant, Henry Kissinger [q.v.], calling Haig "one of the new breed of sophisticated Army officers." Kissinger, who was looking for a military man with field service rather than a defense intellectual, made Haig his military assistant at the National Security Council (NSC).

Haig cemented his relationship with Kissinger by being a discreetly inconspicuous and competent staff man who solidly supported his superior on controversial policies like the mining of Haiphong harbor and the bombing of Hanoi during the final phase of the Vietnam War. Haig's staff responsibilities evolved and expanded as Kissinger's prominence as a top presidential adviser became evident.

Haig reorganized the NSC staff to improve the flow of ideas and information, screened all intelligence information to prepare a daily summary for the President, served as liaison between the Pentagon and the State Department, and took charge of NSC meetings when Kissinger was absent. He quickly gained a reputation for "meticulous staff work" and was regarded by Kissinger as a virtually "indispensable deputy." This status was recognized by his promotion to the position of deputy assistant to the President in June 1970.

Haig was often used as a "diplomatic trouble shooter," particularly in Southeast Asia. As early as 1970 he began a series of visits to Vietnam to provide the President with a first-hand, on-the-spot assessment of the situation there.

Then as negotiations for a peace settlement began to gain momentum during the summer of 1972, Haig became the major diplomatic courier between President Nixon and South Vietnamese President Nguyen Thieu. Between October 1972 and January 1973 Haig made over a dozen trips to South Vietnam acting in both a fact-finding capacity and in a persuasive effort to keep President Thieu from sabotaging the Paris peace talks. He was particularly effective in explaining President Nixon's "difficult domestic situation" with a presidential election looming on

the horizon and with the conduct of the war as a major campaign issue.

Although Haig in Saigon and Kissinger in Paris worked diligently toward negotiating a diplomatic breakthrough before the 1972 presidential election, both Haig and the President "felt that the North Vietnamese would be more likely to make concessions after the election" when Nixon would have more freedom of action as a result of his expected landslide victory.

Since a settlement was not worked out before the election, Haig continued his shuttle diplomacy during the winter of 1972. Fully aware of the President's belief that the prospect of the new and more dovish incoming Senate made a speedy settlement of the Vietnam conflict imperative, Haig took a tough line with President Thieu. Yet because Thieu also respected Haig's views as "a soldier and as someone completely familiar with Communist treachery," Haig finally succeeded in securing South Vietnamese acquiesence to the January 27, 1973 ceasefire accord.

In the midst of this diplomatic troubleshooting, Haig also found time to serve as the President's advance man for the Nixon trip to China in February 1972. He made all final arrangements for the President's arrival and touring in China, personally checking-out each stop on the President's itinerary as well as providing for press coverage and a television relay system.

In these various diplomatic missions, as well as in his administrative work at the NSC, Haig had established himself as second only to Mr. Kissinger as the President's most trusted diplomatic trouble shooter. Both in recognition of his exemplary service and in deference to his desire to return to his military career, the President promoted Haig from a two-star major-general to a four-star general in September of 1972 and designated him as Army Vice Chief of Staff.

Although the President regretted Haig's departure from the White House staff, the President acted in response to the urgings of his Secretaries of Defense and of the Army to promote upwardly mobile young officers to bring new, young blood into the armed forces command structure. In order to promote Haig, the President bypassed the routine recommendation process of the Pentagon and passed over more than 240 top-ranking officers with greater seniority. Haig's assumption of the position as Vice Chief of Staff in January of 1973 took him out of the White House just as the President was beginning his second term in office. Shortly thereafter evidence of White House involvement in the Watergate affair began to develop.

By mid-1973 as politically damaging and explosive revelations about the Watergate cover-up forced the resignations of two of the President's closest top aides—H.R. Haldeman [q.v.] and John Ehrlichman [q.v.]—Haig was brought back to the White House, initially on a temporary basis, to help restore some semblance of order to the staff. Haig's appointment as assistant to the President, replacing Haldeman, was the first step in a complete reevaluation of the operations of the White House.

In appointing a military man to replace a scandal-tainted civilian chief of staff, the President was following the tactic he had seen President Eisenhower use in 1958 when he replaced a discredited Sherman Adams with Gen. Wilton P. Persons. Observers of Eisenhower's maneuver concluded that the appointment had been designed to bolster public confidence in White House operations. Nixon hoped to accomplish the same end with the appointment of a man whose service with both Republican and Democratic administrations had won him a reputation as a tough, hardworking, effective and dependable administrator.

Haig's temporary appointment soon became permanent as President Nixon came to rely on him heavily as the Watergate crisis worsened. The President had known that asking Haig to stay at the White House (and subsequently resign from the Army) would probably torpedo his bright prospects of becoming Army Chief of Staff and perhaps even Chairman of the Joint Chiefs of Staff. Haig was also

aware of the sacrifice he was making and the problems he would face in undertaking the job as presidential chief of staff. While he could joke that he was a "historical phenomenon—the first active-duty general who had to retire from military service to enter combat," a more serious evaluation of his position was that duty left him "no alternative but to come" and that having "commanded units in combat in which the ultimate sacrifice was demanded . . . [he was] conditioned to a degree."

Unlike his predecessor, Haig functioned in a relatively relaxed, open manner. Cabinet officials no longer had to work through the chief of staff to report to the President. Not under attack himself, Haig even managed to reintroduce a sense of humor and pleasantness to staff operations that had been lacking under the besieged and dour Haldeman. Leonard Garment [q.v.], another presidential assistant, commented that Haig "never lost his composure . . . but dealt with the problems of the wounded with both compassion and detachment." Despite being a military man accustomed to a clear chain of command, Haig was apparently less authoritarian than his predecessor. As one Nixon aide observed, "Haldeman issued orders. You work with Haig as an equal."

Even though President Nixon had not intended Haig to become preoccupied with the Watergate saga, he turned to Haig for advice on the matter almost as soon as he joined the White House staff. In June 1973 when John Dean [q.v.] told a Senate investigating committee that the President had discussed "hush money" for the Watergate burglars, Nixon contemplated resigning. President Nixon recalled that when he asked Haig's opinion, he got a "robust no" and was urged "to listen to the tapes of the Dean meetings and to construct an unassailable defense based on them."

A month later when the existence of a White House taping system was revealed to the Ervin Committee, Haig was again consulted. At that time the General counselled against destroying the tapes, arguing that such action "would create an indelible impression of guilt."

The more intensive the political fire on the White House became, the more Haig rallied to the President's aid and support. He took his responsibilities as chief of staff seriously and restructured staff operations to prevent any possible recurrence of the kind of mistakes that he felt had spawned the Watergate affair. In addition to these duties, he became a primary counsellor to the President on his political troubles. To handle the double load, Haig put in 12 to 14 hour days, seven days a week. Despite his importance to the President, Haig never achieved the intimacy that Haldeman had had with Nixon. Instead he maintained an air of military formality which he believed was both to his own and to the President's preference.

Soon after joining the staff, Haig saw the need for the President to begin marshalling a legal team, and he was responsible for getting Fred Buzhardt [q.v.], a Pentagon lawyer, appointed special counsel for Watergate affairs. He was also confronted with the need for extensive bureaucratic restaffing. While he moved quickly to fill the most necessary positions and to reenlist men like John Connally [q.v.], Melvin Laird [q.v.] and Bryce Harlow [q.v.], more confusion and frustration followed since almost no one knew where he fitted into the new hierarchy, or the measure of either his access or his authority.

Within a few weeks of assuming command of the staff, Haig became aware of yet another calamity brewing—the investigation of Vice President Spiro Agnew [q.v.] on charges of conspiracy, extortion, bribery, and tax fraud. Throughout the summer Haig monitored developments until Attorney General Elliot Richardson [q.v.] and special counsel Fred Buzhardt agreed that there was a solid and serious case against the Vice President. Worried at the prospect that possible impeachment hearings against the Vice President would merge with and fuel the Watergate issue, Haig and Buzhardt launched a campaign with Richardson and Agnew to negotiate a plea rather than provoke a constitutional crisis with an indictment and subsequent trial or impeachment proceedings. Much later Haig remarked that "arranging that cop-out was one of the greatest feats of bureaucratic skill in the history of the art."

As the Watergate investigation proceeded through the appointment of Archibald Cox [q.v.] as special prosecutor and more and more White House tapes were subpoenaed, it was Haig who handled negotiations between the Oval Office and Attorney General Richardson over the course of Cox's investigation and tried to work out a compromise over the tapes. When relations with Special Prosecutor Cox broke down completely during the October 1973 Arab-Israeli War, Haig tried to persuade the Attorney General not to resign in protest, or at least to delay any action until the Mideast crisis was resolved.

Though he was unsuccessful in this effort to prevent, or at least limit, the "Saturday Night Massacre," Haig immediately set about finding a new special prosecutor. After consulting with the then acting Attorney General, Robert Bork [q.v.], Haig recommended Leon Jaworski [q.v.] and within days secured the President's approval of this appointment.

Soon after the Supreme Court decision requiring Nixon to release the White House tapes in July 1974, Haig heard the infamous "smoking gun" tape of June 23, 1972. He knew that the President was doomed and set out to salvage the presidency from a state of complete collapse. Whether Haig presided over the demise of the Nixon presidency or he orchestrated the President's resignation is a matter of contention and is likely to remain so since Haig has chosen to maintain a loyally discreet silence about events that were agonizing for his Commander-in-Chief.

Throughout the first seven days of August 1974, Haig kept the government functioning as a virtually "acting President." He prepared the groundwork for the imminent transfer of power and for a short time the new President Ford retained General Haig as his White House chief of staff.

During the six weeks that Haig continued as Ford's chief of staff, the President issued the Nixon pardon and some speculation held Haig responsible for convincing Ford to grant it. Haig, however, while admitting he favored the pardon, maintained that he was not even consulted on the matter.

Despite his evident competence, Haig could not long survive the fall of Richard Nixon. He was "the most visible symbol of the continued presence of Nixon men in the White House" and until he left the White House the administration's character would remain a Nixon legacy. Indeed, to many of the new Ford men, Haig had become "a symbol of Ford's inability to get rid of the Nixon taint."

Unlike many other Nixon staff members, when Haig left the corridors of power in late September of 1974, he did so with his honor and dignity intact. President Ford recalled the General to active duty and awarded him the two most prestigious foreign military positions available for an American officer—Supreme Allied Commander, Europe and Commander in Chief, American Forces, Europe.

Once again military critics grumbled that Haig lacked sufficient command experience to head a multi-service, international force. Yet precedent and the nature of the job seemed to indicate otherwise. In an era of evolving detente and of defensive reevaluation, General Haig's primary task at NATO was seen as one of convincing the United States' "allies to remain equipped and trained to fight even as the US itself [was] beginning to debate the importance of its own military commitment in Europe." This required the talents of a soldier-statesman well versed in diplomacy, politics, and public relations—skills which Haig had honed to a fine point during his White House years.

Although there was some congressional concern over the appointment, Haig successfully weathered these reactions and assumed command of the NATO forces in December of 1974. His only comment on the politically controversial overtones of his appointment was a request "to be judged on . . . performance, and not [on] how [he] got here." Gen. Haig continued in command of NATO through the Ford and into the Carter presidencies.

[MJW]

HALDEMAN, H(ARRY) R(OBBINS)
b. Oct. 27 1926: Los Angeles, Calif.
Assistant to the President, January 1969–April 1973.

A third-generation Californian with Midwestern roots, Haldeman came from a comfortable, business-minded, conservative family. His paternal grandfather, Harry Marston Haldeman, had been an early anti-Communist and helped found the Better America Foundation after World War I to combat the purported Bolshevik threat.

His father was a shrewd businessman whose sixth sense about market trends had enabled the family to successfully weather the Depression and prosper. H.R. Haldeman inherited his grandfather's ardent anti-communism and his father's business sense.

Although of near-genius intelligence, Haldeman did not originally do well in public school and was ultimately sent to a strict private school where he acquired "a zest for regimen and rigid command structure." Just young enough to miss service during World War II, he did take part in the Navy's wartime V-1 training program during his first two years of college, first at Redlands University and then at the University of Southern California. He finished his college career at the University of California at Los Angeles (UCLA), graduating with a B.S. degree in business administration in 1948.

During his years at UCLA, Haldeman met and became friends with another future White House assistant, John Ehrlichman [q.v.]. In the late 1940s Haldeman became a Nixon enthusiast, avidly following and applauding the House UnAmerican Activities Committee investigation of Alger Hiss and Whittaker Chambers.

During the years that Nixon served in the House and the Senate, Haldeman remained a political spectator while he actively built a career in advertising. Initially a market researcher with Foote, Cone and Belding, he soon joined the advertising firm of J. Walter Thompson Co. From 1949 to 1959 he was an account executive with the firm in New York, Los Angeles and San Francisco and handled or supervised accounts like those of Disneyland, Seven-Up, Aerowax and Black Flag insecticide. In 1959 he was named vice president and manager of the Los Angeles office.

Meanwhile Haldeman began to act on his admiration for Richard M. Nixon. Although he volunteered to work for Nixon's first vice-presidential campaign in 1952, it was not until the 1956 campaign that he was taken on as one of the Vice-President's advance men. In that role Haldeman put his advertising and managerial skills to good use in Nixon's service.

He combined "crisp organization, precise attention to detail and a strong sense of image" with a "fervid personal commitment to the candidate." His work in 1956 and in the subsequent congressional campaign of 1958 impressed key Nixon advisers like Robert Finch [q.v.] and Herb Klein [q.v.]. When Finch became manager for Nixon's presidential campaign in 1960, he convinced Haldeman to take a leave of absence from the Thompson Co. to become chief advance man for the presidential campaign. Although his candidate was narrowly defeated by John Kennedy in 1960, Haldeman learned a great deal from the mistakes of that campaign and would later take care to avoid repeating them when he managed the 1968 campaign.

During the 1960 campaign Richard Nixon was only superficially acquainted with Haldeman. In the months following the electoral defeat, however, Haldeman became a Nixon intimate by volunteering to stay and help Nixon research and write the book that became *Six Crises*. In that

effort Haldeman was "a combination sounding board and cheerleader." He was a self-effacing and reassuring listener during these months, convincing Nixon of his loyalty and, in turn, winning his trust.

Haldeman tried to dissuade Nixon from running for governor of California in 1962, but when Nixon persisted, he remained faithful and managed the unsuccessful campaign. In retrospect Haldeman's part in that campaign was noteworthy for an incident similar to the kind of "dirty tricks" that came to light years later in the Watergate scandal. With Nixon's approval, Haldeman organized a mailing campaign against the Democratic opponent, incumbent Gov. Edmund "Pat" Brown. The letter, from a bogus Committee for the Preservation of the Democratic Party, was designed to discredit Brown within his own Party. When the ruse was discovered to be a violation of California's election law, the Democrats took the matter to court and won a ruling against the Republicans. But by that time the election had already ended in Nixon's defeat.

During the 1960s, when Nixon was largely out of public affairs, Haldeman advanced in the advertising world, excelling at promotional strategy and staff building. Hugh Sutherland, a boyhood friend who worked for Haldeman at J. Walter Thompson Co., observed that he "had a gift for recognizing whether or not [a product] would sell, and if so, exactly what advertising and publicity techniques would be most effective." Haldeman was also adept at recruiting and molding individuals into an efficient, enthusiastic staff. Indeed a number of his proteges from the advertising agency—men like Ronald Ziegler [q.v.], Dwight Chapin [q.v.], Larry Higby, Kenneth Cole and Bruce Kehrli—later moved with Haldeman to Washington and the Nixon White House, where they were nicknamed "the beaver patrol" because of their eagerness.

Haldeman tentatively reenlisted in political activity as Nixon began to nurture hopes of a political comeback in the wake of the crippling intraparty struggle between Barry Goldwater [q.v.] and Nelson Rockefeller [q.v.] and the subsequent Republican rout in the 1964 presidential election. Although he declined to help train some new advance men to help Nixon's midterm campaign efforts in 1966, he did suggest a substitute—his college friend John D. Ehrlichman.

During 1967 and early 1968 Haldeman cautiously monitored Nixon's chances and aided Operation Comeback on a part-time basis, helping to set general strategy and directing Nixon's travels and promotional affairs for the primary contests. Dan Rather [q.v.] in *The Palace Guard* speculated that Haldeman and Ehrlichman refrained from making a definite and full commitment to Nixon's 1968 presidential campaign effort until June of 1968 when they felt that Nixon was assured of the Republican nomination and that his Democratic opponent would not be another Kennedy (as in 1960).

Named campaign manager, Haldeman worked out a campaign for the "new" Nixon designed to rectify what he considered to be the tactical errors of the 1960 race. Knowing that Nixon tired easily and had a tendency to push too hard on the campaign trail, Haldeman plotted a restrained and highly controlled campaign designed to keep the candidate rested, relaxed and as remote as possible from both the press and from unstructured, and potentially unfriendly, audiences. He pursued this strategy by strictly controlling access to Nixon and by personally acting as liaison between the protected candidate and the official campaign apparatus. The remote and controlled campaign that the Republicans implemented in 1968 and that advertising executive Haldeman had designed to sell the "new Nixon" was tailored not only to the political situation of the moment but also to the candidate's likes, dislikes, strengths and weaknesses. It also prefigured Haldeman's operating style at the White House.

Within five weeks of the election, Haldeman emerged as the Administration's first eminence grise under the title of assistant to the President. In this capacity he was the President's gatekeeper and image overseer. This was essentially the same role he had performed during the campaign—that of "human link between the President and the machinery."

It was his job to arrange the President's schedule, screen his calls, decide who saw him and what memos, reports or papers crossed the President's desk. His most evident predecessor (although he denied the similarity) was Eisenhower's chief of staff, Sherman Adams, who had held the same title of assistant to the President.

Although the parallel to Sherman Adams was clear, there were important differences. Adams restricted himself primarily to coordination and administration, leaving command over public relations to Press Secretary James Hagerty. Within Nixon's White House, Haldeman, as chief of staff, was responsible for all administrative matters including the press. To facilitate this control, he took pains to assure that the man appointed press secretary, Ron Zeigler was one of his proteges. Whereas Adams had quickly become primus inter pares on the Eisenhower White House staff, Haldeman emerged as as one of the Nixon staff triumvirate. Although he was given an even broader administrative coordinating role than Adams, Haldeman had to share prominence with two other equally influential staff members who had substantive concerns: John Ehrlichman for domestic affairs and Henry Kissinger [q.v.] for national security-foreign affairs. These were the three men who saw the President most frequently.

Haldeman characterized his role as that of a "coordinator rather than an innovator, a technician rather than a policy man." He considered it his main mission to marshall "the use of the President's time, to make him as effective as he can be . . . [and to be] . . . the one to get done the things he wants done."

The role of coordinator was, however, not so simplistic. Although some felt that Haldeman always did what the President wanted done without argument, even when it was not in the best interest of the President, he saw himself as something of a "devil's advocate" who was responsible for presenting contrary views to the President before he made decisions. An associate said that on occasion Haldeman would even delay implementating what he considered an unwise presidential decision to give the President time to reflect on it. A short time later Haldeman would return to the President and ask if he really wanted the decision carried out. The fact that the President sometimes changed his mind seemed to support Haldeman's belief that he could serve Nixon so well because he thought like the President.

Observers suggested that Haldeman exercised such broad administrative control with little effective internal opposition because he eschewed a policy-making role. According to one White House staff member, although everything was channeled through Haldeman and Ehrlichman, "Haldeman [was] not at all interested in policy, and Ehrlichman [was]. This explains how they manage to get along." Haldeman himself maintained that "we have Moynihan and Kissinger and Burns and an entire executive apparatus to make policy" and that his job was "to make sure that the people who do make policy get a hearing with the President."

As presidential assistant, Haldeman was on virtual 24-hour call. Herb Klein [q.v.] Nixon's communications director, observed that Haldeman was "the only Nixon man who [had] no schedule of his own" tailoring his time exclusively to the President's. In his book *The Ends of Power*, Haldeman recounted that he kept "himself totally at the President's beck and call." He accompanied the President on all trips, including holiday and weekend vacations, usually pursuing his photographic hobby of taking home movies of the President and of big state events. Rarely more than a few feet away from the President during working hours, Haldeman was "in Nixon's office so often . . . he [was] usually trying to get out at the same time everyone else [was] trying to get in."

Accused of isolating the President, Haldeman's access and intimacy with Nixon and his gruff style irritated many

with less access. Indeed the prominence of individuals with a Germanic background—Haldeman, Ehrlichman and Kissinger—was quickly parodied by their antagonists and by the press. The three became known as "the Berlin Wall" around the President. Kissinger called his two compatriots "the Praetorian Guard," and Haldeman was sometimes likened to the "Iron Chancellor."

Haldeman pursued his tasks as chief of White House operations and administration with loyalty, self-righteousness and an "intellectual preoccupation with the techniques of modern management." Haldeman's fundamental loyalty was to a well-ordered American society, and he viewed Richard M. Nixon as essential to that vision. Haldeman's wife commented after the 1968 election victory, "Thank goodness Nixon won, because now Bob will have someting to devote his life to." This unswerving loyalty to a man, rather than to a set of principles represented in a political party or in a process of government, helped cultivate a White House environment that tolerated and condoned Watergate-related activities. In *The Ends of Power*, Haldeman recognized that in being a perfectionist task-master, he put too much pressure on men under him and indoctrinated them with the view that "the job must be done" and that results, not alibis, were expected of them.

Haldeman's loyalty, without personal political ambitions; his ideological compatibility with the President; and his rigid staff control gave him an almost unprecedented concentration of power. Although Haldeman seldom made his views on policy issues known, Ken Clawson said that "there is no policy that Haldeman is responsible for, yet there is no policy that he doesn't have a hand in somehow."

Added to this unswerving personal loyalty to the President was a desire to protect him not only from "the unending flow of public officials who just had to see the President" but also from his own "dark side" which was petty, vindictive, insecure, awkward and rigidly disciplined. In terms of personal style, Haldeman was ideally suited to be Richard Nixon's doorkeeper. Puritanically moral, Haldeman was incorruptible about money and neither smoked nor drank and frowned on those who did. It was thus with a certain amount of smug glee that Haldeman and other White House strategists looked forward to the reelection campaign of 1972 when their virtuous incumbent would face a weak Democratic contender like Humphrey or Muskie instead of Ted Kennedy who had been morally discredited by the Chappaquiddick incident.

Throughout the campaign of 1972, Haldeman continued to be President Nixon's primary image molder, even though this brought him into bitter dispute with Nixon's campaign manager, John Mitchell [q.v.]. In this vein, Haldeman orchestrated the presidential trip to Peking in February of 1972 as the kickoff of the reelection campaign. It was the high point of the Nixon presidency, showing him at his most self-assured and presenting a dramatic, statesmanlike contrast to the squabbling Democratic contenders who were fighting their way through the New Hampshire snows to the primaries.

Nixon thrived on Haldeman's hero worship and was impressed by his efficient management. Both men had a passion for neatness, precision and attention to detail that complimented their day-to-day working relationship. In addition the President valued Haldeman as his hatchet man. For Richard Nixon, who had always abhorred unpleasant face-to-face confrontations, a "no-man" was essential and Haldeman was just the man for the job. Haldeman liked to say that "every President needs an SOB" and that he was Nixon's. He accepted this role as a necessary part of keeping the President free from avoidable tensions and demands.

Ironically, Haldeman was in someways responsible for the downfall of the Nixon presidency. The fundamental criticism of his White House style centered on the intense concentration of power in the hands of a few presidential assistants and the indoctrination of much of the staff to follow orders, not discuss them. This resulted in

an isolation and inflexibility in the White House and a consequent inability to realistically assess public and political sentiment to Administration policies and actions. Such a system of staff operations provided fertile soil for overzealous, unscrupulous attitudes that produced the Watergate break-in and cover-up.

Haldeman was also instrumental in setting up the White House taping system that in the end proved to be Nixon's undoing. In 1970 Haldeman had convinced the President to install an elaborate taping system to provide an unparalleled historical record of his presidency. If the tapes had not existed, or if their existence had not been revealed by one of Haldeman's proteges, Alexander Butterfield, the Nixon presidency might have survived the Watergate inquiry and been saved the painful trip down the road to impeachment.

As the unorthodox and illegal means Nixon and his assistants had taken to assure the President's reelection in 1972 slowly came to light in the Senate hearings, Haldeman and other high-ranking White House officials became deeply implicated. As public scrutiny intensified, efforts to cope with or cover up the scandal preoccupied the time and attention of many presidential assistants and led to a near paralysis of the Administration. In a desperate attempt to keep his Administration afloat, the President announced the resignations of Haldeman and Ehrlichman on April 30, 1973, calling it "one of the most difficult decisions of my presidency" to accept the resignations of "two of the finest public servants it has been my privilege to know." The President went on to state that the resignations were not to be taken as an implication of any personal wrongdoing on their parts, but rather that their ability to function had been impaired by rumors, accusations, and charges generated by the Watergate investigations.

In resigning, Haldeman said he had "hoped and expected to have had an earlier opportunity to clear up various allegations and innuendos that have been raised" but it had become "virtually impossible . . . to carry on . . . regular responsibilities in the White House." He noted that he intended "to cooperate fully" with the investigation and would consult with his attorneys and with the Senate Select Committee investigating the case.

In July 1973 Haldeman's appearance before the Senate Watergate Committee caused a new flurry over the presidential claim of executive privilege regarding tapes that both the Senate Committee and the special prosecutor wanted. Haldeman testified that he had been allowed to listen to and take notes of a tape recording of the Sept. 15, 1972, conversation between himself, John Dean [q.v.] and the President in order to prepare his testimony. Subsequently Special Watergate Prosecutor Archibald Cox [q.v.] used this incidence of access by nonprivileged individuals to White House material as an argument against the President's assertion that the tapes could not be subpoenaed because they fell under the protection of executive privilege.

In his testimony Haldeman said that the Watergate scandal had not come to presidential attention until March 1973. In two days of restrained, courteous testimony, Haldeman continued to defend the President and, in his concluding statement, spoke of the "high standards Nixon set for the White House staff and of his deep regret and sorrow that in a few instances there was a failure to live up to them."

The resignations of Haldeman and Ehrlichman from the White House staff late in April 1973 marked a turning point in the Watergate investigations and seemed to indicate that Administration efforts to "stonewall" were not proving effective. The revelation of a White House taping system and Haldeman's testimony concerning such tapes during the summer of 1973 added further fuel to the public fires of indignation. This eventually culminated in the "Saturday night massacre," firings of the special prosecutor and the Attorney-General and his deputy in October. This action in turn precipitated the opening of impeachment hearings against the President. Later the March 1974 indictments of Haldeman, Ehrlichman and John Mitchell for conspiracy and obstruction of justice hastened the demise of the Nixon presidency.

Haldeman was charged, among other things, with conspiring to impede the Watergate investigation through the improper use of government agencies, the covert raising and distribution of payoff funds, and the concealment or destruction of records and documents. He was also charged with three counts of perjury relating to his testimony before the Senate Watergate Committee. Although Haldeman did not actually come to trial and sentencing until after President Nixon resigned, his indictment, with other influential former members of the White House staff, led to the establishment of presidential involvement in the Watergate cover-up.

On Jan. 1, 1975, H.R. Haldeman was convicted in a U.S. district court in Washington, D.C., of one count of conspiracy, one count of obstruction of justice, and three counts of perjury before the Senate investigating committee with regard to his own (and the President's) knowledge of the payment of "hush money" and other cover-up activities. He was originally sentenced to from two and a half to eight but this was later reduced to from one to four years. Eventually he was paroled after serving six months in the federal minimum security facility at Lompoc, Calif.

Although Haldeman never became as critical of President Nixon or his conduct of the Watergate affairs as did his former colleague and friend, John Ehrlichman, he was reportedly spurred by Nixon's television interviews with David Frost to publicly discuss his part and the President's flaws because he felt that the former President was trying "to offload the guilt for Watergate on him and Ehrlichman."

The criticisms found in his book *The Ends of Power* were restrained and appeared to be the remarks of a man who had been disappointed by his lifelong hero, but who was still loyal. Ultimately Haldeman seemed to have reached the conclusion, so typical of the Nixon circle, that the true indictment of the Nixon Administration concerning the Watergate affair was that it failed. Haldeman admits that "morally and legally it was the wrong thing to do—so it should have failed." But he goes on to say that "tactically, too many people knew too much" and that "there were many mistakes . . . [which] can be summed up in that we totally failed to get out ahead of the curves at any point."

[MW]

HAMMER, ARMAND
b. May 21, 1898; New York, N.Y.
Chairman of the Board, Occidental
Petroleum Corporation, 1957-.

Although he was trained for a career in medicine and performed with distinction as a student at the Columbia College of Physicians and Surgeons, Hammer never practiced medicine. Instead he turned his talents to business and had the golden touch from his earliest commercial efforts. He earned his first million dollars before he was ever licensed to practice medicine. His early business success was achieved in the Soviet Union, which he visited in 1921. His first deal with the Soviets involved a million tons of American wheat in exchange for furs, precious stones and caviar. He thrived under Lenin's New Economic Policy by not only negotiating trade deals but by serving as an agent for foreign companies as well. He also began to acquire a superb collection of art treasures while in the Soviet Union, and part of his wealth was derived from the acquisition and sale of these and other art works.

Hammer retired in 1956 but within the year returned to the business world to become chairman and president of Occidental Petroleum Corp., which at that time was a small oil company on the verge of bankruptcy. Under his leadership Occidental became the 11th largest oil company in the United States by 1975. In addition to art and petroleum, Hammer made millions in deals involving many prod-

ucts, such as pencils, whiskey, cattle and phosphates.

Hammer benefited from the policy of detente in Soviet-American relations pursued by President Richard Nixon and Henry Kissinger [q.v.]. For the Soviets, Hammer represented American know-now and advanced technology. For the United States, Hammer provided access to Soviet trade. Building on his contacts and experience from his early trade deals in the Soviet Union, Hammer deftly negotiated for new economic agreements. In April 1974 Hammer signed contracts with the Soviet government that involved a $20 billion fertilizer deal. The deal largely involved the exporting of American equipment and technical assistance for a fertilizer complex to be built in the Soviet Union by Occidental. Hammer was also involved in deals with other American corporations engaged in transactions with the Soviet Union.

Detente was further strengthened through Hammer's role as an art connoisseur. In 1973 he arranged for a loan of 48 post-Impressionist paintings from the Soviet Union to be shown in the United States. In addition, he organized another exchange of Soviet art treasures for the U.S. Bicentennial. Hammer contended that through his business and other dealings with the Soviet Union, he was promoting peace between the big powers.

Hammer played an unintended role in helping to shift power from the oil companies to the oil-producing countries. In 1970 the new revolutionary government in Libya successfully raised royalties and taxes on Occidental's oil holdings. This act paved the way for the major oil price increases by oil-producing countries three years later.

Hammer was implicated in the Watergate wrongdoings. In April 1976 he pleaded guilty on three counts of making and concealing $54,000 worth of illegal contributions in 1972 to the reelection campaign of Richard Nixon. He was fined $3,000 and placed on probation for one year. Federal Judge Laurence T. Lydick decided not to send Hammer to prison because of the defendant's age and poor health.

[HML]

HANKS, NANCY
b. Dec. 31, 1927; Miami Beach, Fla.
Chairwoman, National Council on the Arts, National Endowment for the Arts, October 1969-October 1979.

Hanks grew up in Miami, where her father was a corporate lawyer and the president of the Miami Water Power Co. After graduating magna cum laude from Duke University in 1949, she began a career in Washington in 1951 as a receptionist in the Office of Defense Mobilization. The following year she became a secretary for the President's Advisory Committee on Government Operations, where she became acquainted with the Committee's chairman, Nelson A. Rockefeller [q.v.]. Rockefeller retained Hanks as his assistant following his appointment as undersecretary of Health, Education and Welfare in 1953 and his assignment to President Eisenhower's Special Projects Office two years later.

In 1956 Hanks came to New York to be executive secretary of the Special Studies Project of the Rockefeller Brothers Fund. Over the ensuing years she coordinated the fund's research into foreign policy, defense, financial and educational issues. In 1963 she directed a study of the performing arts in America. Published two years later under the title *The Performing Arts: Problems and Prospects*, it was hailed as the first major report of its kind. Urging the creation of state and community arts councils across the nation, *The Performing Arts* anticipated many of the policies Hanks would pursue during her years with the National Endowment for the Arts, which was created by the Johnson Administration in September of the same year.

Hanks subsequently became a board member of the private, non-profit Associated Council of the Arts (ACA), an organization promoting and assisting arts councils around the country. In June 1968 Hanks was elected ACA president. The following year President Nixon appointed her chairman of the National Endowment for the Arts (NEA) and of its advisory body, the National Council for the Arts. The appointment was a highly popular move. The Senate swiftly confirmed her nomination, and she was sworn into office in October 1969.

The NEA's budget was $9 million dollars when Hanks became chairwoman. The conditions described in the 1965 Rockefeller Brothers Fund report—increasing costs in the arts coupled with decreasing sources of private revenue—had become even more critical. Hence in preparing the 1970–71 budget of the NEA, Hanks sought a major increase in funding to $20 million—more than double that granted her predecessor in his last year. When Congress seemed destined to cut most of her requests, Hanks and her assistant personally spoke to over 150 Senators and Representatives. Approximately 100 of them changed their previously negative votes, and most of the budget was passed.

Hank's considerable success with Congress was due not only to her personal skills as a lobbyist, but to her philosophy of a nationwide, "grass roots" approach to arts funding. During the NEA's years under Roger Stevens, the emphasis was on "rescuing" established arts institutions such as the American Ballet Theatre and the American National Theatre and Academy from financial peril. Hanks sought a wider dispersion of the arts. In her first month in office, she announced a series of grants to various performing arts groups in the theater, dance and music that would enable them to tour small communities. In subsequent years funds spent on touring dance companies and the creation of local dance troupes helped foster a major revival of interest in dance, much of it outside the New York area and other traditional arts centers.

This trend was furthered under the NEA's Expansion Arts program, which encouraged the development of local artists and arts programs outside of the large institutions. A prominent example was the Michigan Artrain; a traveling museum, jointly financed by the NEA and the Michigan Arts Council, containing exhibits on the history of the visual arts, artworks by contemporary artists, and a workshop where artists could be seen at work.

Thus, while Congress criticized the NEA's sister organization, the National Endowment for the Humanities, for "elitism," there was widespread approval on Capitol Hill for Hanks' populist approach to the arts. Some critics, however, argued that the funds should be disbursed on the basis of who could use them most effectively, rather than the politically expedient standard of geographic distribution. Uniform, top quality art could not be expected from every part of the country, it was argued, and funding practices that did not take this into account threatened to weaken the standards of excellence American art should seek to attain.

Another program that attracted some controversy in the artistic community was the NEA's Artists-in-the-Schools program, described as a "national, state-based program which places professional artists in elementary and secondary schools to work and demonstrate their artistic disciplines." The program began in 1969 on a budget of $145,000 that soon grew into the millions. While many educators were enthusiastic about the program, others complained that it was superficial and too transient to have any real effect on students. In 1973 Stanford University education professor Elliot W. Eisner urged the NEA to undertake an evaluation of the program's effectiveness. When the NEA finally commissioned such a study in 1974, the contract went to a foundation that was itself partially funded by the NEA. The resultant report was so one-sided in its praise for the program that Eisner referred to it as a "public relations document, rather than a professional evaluation of a publicly funded program."

Under Hanks the NEA budget almost doubled every year. While this represent-

ed the greatest commitment ever made by the U.S. government to the arts, it also resulted in a growing bureaucracy that frustrated many artists. The procedure for grant application became more complex, to the extent that some feared it would inhibit requests for small amounts of assistance.

Nonetheless when Hanks announced her resignation from the National Endowment for the Arts and the National Council on the Arts at the conclusion of her second term, the consensus of opinion was that she had played a major role in the growth of the arts in the U.S. "Eight years are enough," was her comment at the official White House announcement in August 1977, though there was little doubt that had President Carter chosen to reappoint Hanks, she would have accepted.

In responding to her resignation the President wrote, "Under your thoughtful and creative stewardship, the Endowment has . . . firmly established in the country's consciousness the importance of broad-based public and private support for the arts."

[MDQ]

HANNAH, JOHN A(LFRED)
b. Oct. 9, 1902; Grand Rapids, Mich.
President, Michigan State University, 1941-69; Director, Agency for International Development, 1969-73.

Hannah, the son of a poultry breeder, grew up in Grand Rapids. He graduated from the Michigan Agricultural College, which later became Michigan State University, in 1923 and spent most of his professional career working for his alma mater—first as an extension specialist in poultry raising, then as business manager and finally, beginning in 1941, as president of the university.

Hannah remained president of Michigan State for 28 years, during which time the school grew from a small land-grant college into a giant "megaversity" with an enrollment of 42,500 and an annual budget of over $100 million. Hannah proved adept at "selling" his institution to the Michigan state legislature, which provided a sizable share of the university's funds, by emphasizing popular and practical courses. In addition, during the 1930s he devised a self-liquidating loan plan that helped the university to expand its physical plant.

Hannah also served the federal government, first as advisor to the Point Four Program in the Truman Administration and later as chairman of the U.S. Civil Rights Commission under Presidents Eisenhower, Kennedy and Johnson. [See JOHNSON Volume]

In 1969 President Richard M. Nixon appointed Hannah director of the Agency for International Development (AID), the main organ of the U.S. foreign aid program. As AID director Hannah became the Nixon Administration's chief spokesman on foreign aid programs. In March 1970 testifying before the House Subcommittee on Foreign Operations, Hannah outlined the Administration's new approach to economic aid in underdeveloped countries. The program called for a concentration of economic aid in fewer countries, with the most funds going to countries where a "critical margin of assistance" was needed to blunt the influence of governments hostile to the U.S. Heavy financial commitments, called "supporting assistance," would be made to countries such as South Vietnam, Laos and Thailand, which were maintaining larger defenses against Communist subversion and infiltration than their own resources could support. Hannah spoke in favor of a reversal in what had become, by 1970, a downward trend in the level of U.S. economic aid to developing nations. In 1962 AID had operated assistance programs in 82 countries with loan authorizations of $1.3 billion; by 1970 a total of $682 million in loans was provided to only 42 nations.

Despite Hannah's commitment to increased foreign aid, the level of U.S. economic assistance to developing nations continued to drop during the Nixon Administration. A study by a European economist showed that more than half of the net AID assistance to foreign countries was in the form of private investments and export credits. In accordance with the decrease in U.S. foreign aid, Hannah ordered a major reorganization of AID in January 1972, including a one-third reduction in staff, a consolidation of bureaus within the agency, and the elimination of military aid and supporting assistance from AID's jurisdiction. Hannah retired as head of AID in 1973, though he remained associated with the agency as a consultant.

[DAE]

HANSEN, JULIA BUTLER
b. June 14, 1907; Portland, Ore.
Democratic Representative, Wash., 1960–74.

The daughter of a family active in Cathlamet, Wash., politics, Julia Hansen graduated from the University of Washington at Seattle in 1930. In 1938 she was elected to the Cathlamet City Council and the following year to the state House of Representatives. Concurrent with her political responsibilities, she managed an insurance company in her home town. In 1960 Hansen won a special election to fill a U.S. House seat vacated by the death of Russell V. Mack. She went on to win the November general election, as well as subsequent ones, by a wide margin. A coalition of labor and corporate support, plus general popularity with voters because of the federal conservation projects she brought into the area, were responsible for her victories. A liberal on domestic policies, Hansen generally supported the legislative programs of the Kennedy and Johnson Administrations.

In 1963 Hansen became the first woman ever appointed to the House Appropriations Committee. Four years later she achieved another first by assuming the chairmanship of the subcommittee that controlled the funding of the Interior Department. With such power she emerged as one of the most influential members of Congress. The chairmanship, which she conceded took up 90% of her time, involved control over allocations to such Interior Department agencies as the Bureau of Indian Affairs, the National Park Service and the Bureau of Mines, and expenditures for national projects in the arts and humanities. Calling herself "not a press release legislator," Hansen rarely introduced or cosponsored bills, even under her own Committee's jurisdiction. She preferred working behind the scenes to ensure the passage of legislation she desired. Of all the issues her subcommittee dealt with, Hansen was most concerned with the fate of the American Indian. She devoted a substantial part of her official time traveling to inspect the living conditions of the Indians. Her work to improve their plight received praise from Congress.

Hansen initially backed U.S. military involvement in the Vietnam war, although she supported a halt to bombing of the North. In 1971 she changed her position and voted for the unsuccessful Boland Amendment which called for the termination of funds to Vietnam after June 1, 1972, provided that U.S. prisoners of war had been released. Hansen voted against attempts to reduce defense appropriations, to limit the anti-ballistic missile system and to eliminate from the defense budget the B-I bomber and the F-14 fighter plane. These positions alienated her from fellow liberals.

In 1973 Richard Bolling (D, Mo.) [*q.v.*] headed a panel charged with reviewing the House's committee structure and jurisdiction. Following a year of hearings and investigation, Bolling proposed the limitation of one committee chairmanship per member, the expansion of power on the committees to the minority party and junior members and the realignment of committee jurisdiction to reflect a more accurate division of power. On May 9, 1974, the House Democratic Caucus voted to sidetrack the Bolling proposal by sending it to Hansen's Democratic Committee on Organization Study and Review for further consideration.

The following July, Hansen presented a narrower plan. It sided with those favoring the status quo by keeping the existing committee structure and permitting members to serve on more than one important committee. It also permitted legislation on one subject to be divided among several committees. However it weakened the powers of the Rules Committee by permitting committee chairman under certain circumstances to go to the floor to ask for a call up of bills kept in the Rules Committee. In commenting on her alternative to Bolling's plan, Hansen said, "Too many of us have put too many years into this institution to have it all torn apart and upset by so-called reformers, some of whom will not even be with us in the next Congress." She predicted that adoption of the Bolling resolution would create "legislative chaos" and leave "a legacy of bitterness and acrimony." After a vigorous debate, the House overwhelmingly approved Hansen's plan in October. However, as amended, the provision limiting the Rules Committee's power was dropped. Hansen did not seek reelection in 1974.

[JB]

HARDIN, CLIFFORD M(ORRIS)
b. Oct. 9, 1915, Knightstown, Ind.
Secretary of Agriculture, January 1969-November 1971.

Hardin, the son of a Quaker farmer, was raised on his father's 200-acre grain and livestock farm. He received a B.A. from Purdue in 1937, an M.A. from the university in 1939 and his Ph.D. in agricultural economics in 1941. From 1941 to 1944 he was on the University of Wisconsin faculty. In 1944 he moved to Michigan State College (later university), where he held several research and administrative posts. He was the dean of the College of Agriculture when he left Michigan in 1954 to become the chancellor of the University of Nebraska. Under Hardin's leadership the university's enrollment jumped from 7,200 to 30,000 students.

A leading international developmental economist, Hardin was always interested in the problem of world hunger and agricultural development in the less-developed countries. He was a U.S. delegate to the International Conference on Agricultural Economics in 1947; he organized agricultural training programs and educational development projects in South America, Asia and sub-Saharan Africa; and he introduced the background papers presented at the World Food Conference in New York in 1968, papers he later edited and published as *Overcoming World Hunger* (1969).

Nixon appointed Hardin Secretary of Agriculture in 1969. When Hardin assumed office, federal farm policy was governed by the Food and Agriculture Act of 1965. Under this law the government tried to regulate production by establishing acreage allotments that specified how much land a farmer could use to grow various crops. Farmers who accepted the allotment controls could get government price support loans for their crops. Farmers could either repay these loans if the market price for the crops exceeded the price support level for the loan, or they could default on the loan and turn their crop over to the government if market prices were below the price support level. The government also made direct subsidy payments to farmers who voluntarily used less than their alloted acreage. The law was scheduled to expire in 1969, but Nixon urged Republicans to support a one-year extension to give his Administration a chance to develop a new farm policy.

Hardin worked to change this policy. He favored a land retirement program as the key element of a new farm policy. He also wanted to relax the strict federal controls over agricultural production. Hardin believed that the problems of the small, marginal farmer had to be separated from those common to the large, commercial farmer. Government subsidy payments were inadequate for marginal farmers and merely encouraged them to remain on the farm in poverty. Hardin felt the government should encourage the marginal farmers to move off the farm by paying them to retire their land. At the same time

Hardin believed that the commercial farmers needed a more market-oriented policy which gave them additional flexibility in deciding what to produce and which relied more heavily on market prices to set price support levels.

The Administration program Hardin presented to the House Agriculture Committee in September 1969 retained the old acreage allotment formulas, direct subsidy payments and price support loan programs, but implemented them in a new way. Hardin proposed a "set aside" program under which farmers would agree to set aside, or leave unplanted, a portion of their acreage allotments for feed grains, wheat and cotton. Farmers who did so could then grow whatever crops they wanted on the remaining land and be eligible for price support loans on all the crops they produced. The price support levels would, however, be set at world market prices rather than at some fixed price. Farmers who agreed to set aside additional land could get direct subsidy payments in lieu of what they would have produced.

Farm groups opposed Hardin's proposals and submitted their own plans to Congress. A coalition of 24 farm groups wanted to extend the 1965 law permanently. But they also wanted to raise the price support levels. The American Farm Bureau Federation, which represented the larger commercial farmers, wanted to return to a free market in agriculture by phasing out acreage controls, marketing quotas and direct subsidy payments to wheat, feed grain and cotton growers. The Farm Bureau also wanted to reduce agricultural production to maintain free market prices by requiring the Secretary of Agriculture to retire 10 million acres from farm production during each year from 1971 through 1975. Urban legislators, on the other hand, wanted to set a ceiling on the amount of subsidy payments farmers could get. Hardin proposed a $110,000 per crop ceiling, but urban legislators wanted a $20,000 ceiling.

The Agriculture Act of 1970, which Congress enacted in November after 16 months of hearings and negotiations, was a compromise between Hardin's proposals and those made by the other groups. Congress enacted the set aside proposal and eliminated strict commodity-by-commodity production controls by allowing farmers to plant whatever they wanted after they had set aside the required acreage. Congress also gave the Administration some flexibility in setting prices for the price support loan program, but protected farmers by establishing minimum price support levels for such loans. Finally, Congress established a ceiling of $55,000 per crop on subsidy payments, which was later reduced to $20,000.

Hardin had to increase farm subsidies for corn and wheat growers less than a year after the new law went into effect. In 1971 farmers produced a record 5.4 million bushels of corn. The set aside targets Hardin announced in October 1971 increased the set aside for feed grain lands for the 1972 crop from 18.2 million acres to 38 million acres. He also increased subsidy payments for leaving land out of production, which raised the cost of the program by over $300 million.

Hardin's food stamp policies were strongly criticized in Congress, which failed to enact the Administration's food stamp reform proposals that Nixon announced in May 1969. The reforms would have limited the maximum amount paid by food stamp recipients. Hardin, however, implemented some of the reforms by revising departmental rules so that families did not have to spend more than 25% of their income for food stamps. Hardin's proposal to give free food stamps to families earning less than $30 per month was attacked by liberals, who called the program inadequate, and by conservatives, who said that dead beats who can but won't work should be prevented from getting free food stamps. But Congress enacted the program in 1970. Responding to congressional pressures, the Administration raised its funding requests for the food stamp program for fiscal 1970 and 1971. However when congressional liberals wanted to increase fiscal 1970 spending even more, Hardin thwarted their efforts by telling Congress that the Ad-

ministration could not reasonably spend more than the amount it had requested.

Hardin was sued by conservation groups in early 1970 for imposing only a partial ban on the use of DDT in November 1969. Hardin defended his action by claiming that since scientific evidence had so far failed to show DDT was an "imminent hazard to human health," he would not completely ban the use of the pesticide while his Department was still studying the question. The DDT suit and other environmental issues were, however, taken out of Hardin's hands when the Environmental Protection Agency was created by a presidential executive reorganization in 1970. Hardin opposed the creation of the new agency but was overruled by President Nixon, who insisted that a central agency was the best solution for dealing with environmental issues which cut across several jurisdictions.

Hardin vigorously advocated the Administration's $1.1 billion special revenue-sharing proposal for rural community development, which Nixon announced in 1971. Hardin testified that the program was needed to promote balanced growth between urban and rural areas. He pointed out that half the counties in the U.S. had lost population during the 1960s and that most of these counties were in rural areas. He said that the revenue-sharing proposal would consolidate federal funding and grant programs for rural areas and equitably allocate funds to the states. Congress refused to enact the proposal and adopted instead the Rural Development Act of 1972, when Hardin was no longer in office.

Hardin's action to raise milk price supports in 1971 became a major political issue the following year when Ralph Nader and three consumer groups sued the Department of Agriculture to rescind the increase. Hardin had refused to increase the price support level on March 12, 1972, claiming the hike was unjustified. But he reversed himself 13 days later and raised the price support level for milk. The Nader suit charged that the increase had been granted "illegally" in return for "promises and expectations of campaign contributions for" Nixon's reelection drive. According to the suit, Hardin's reversal occurred after milk producers had contributed $10,000 to various Republican fund-raising committees on March 22 and 16 dairy industry spokesmen had met with Hardin and the President on March 23. The suit also claimed that milk producers had donated $322,500 to GOP campaign committees by the end of 1971. The suit alleged that Hardin had received no new evidence or information bearing on the issue since his earlier denial of the price support increase.

Hardin was no longer in office when the suit came to trial. He resigned on Nov. 11, 1971. Reports of Hardin's departure had already circulated in Washington a year before he resigned. Hardin could not establish effective relations with Congress and was the sixth member of Nixon's original cabinet to leave office. He became a vice president of the Ralston-Purina company in St. Louis, Mo.

[AE]

HARLAN, JOHN MARSHALL
b. May 20, 1899; Chicago, Ill.
d. Dec. 29, 1971; Washington, D.C.
Associate Justice, U.S. Supreme Court, 1955-71.

Born into a family distinguished in the law, Harlan graduated from Princeton in 1920 and then studied law while a Rhodes Scholar at Oxford for three years. He received a degree from New York Law School in 1924 and joined a large Wall Street firm, where he became a partner in 1931. Although he held a number of public service positions, Harlan devoted himself mainly to private practice until 1954. He specialized in corporate and antitrust cases and became a leader of the New York bar. A Republican, he was named a judge on the U.S. Second Circuit Court of Appeals in January 1954. Ten months later he was appointed to the U.S. Supreme Court. Grandson of a Supreme Court justice, Harlan took his seat on March 28, 1955.

On the bench Harlan was soon aligned with Justice Felix Frankfurter in philosophy as well as votes. Like Frankfurter, Harlan believed that judges should approach issues in a dispassionate, reasoned fashion and that the Court should exercise restraint. He placed great value on adherence to precedent and thought the Court should limit its role, leaving other branches of government free to work out solutions to the nation's problems. Harlan was deeply committed to the maintenance of federalism. He believed Court interference should be minimal in areas where state power was pre-eminent. He resisted, for example, the effort to extend all of the Bill of Rights to the states and argued that the 14th Amendment's due process clause only required state criminal procedures to be "fundamentally fair." Harlan also respected the doctrine of separation of powers and was wary of invalidating federal legislative or executive action. Although he could be rigorous in his application of the Bill of Rights to the federal government, the Justice believed individual rights had to be balanced against government interests in each case. He also thought the Court should not deal with political questions such as reapportionment and vigorously protested the Court's establishment and extension of the one-man, one-vote standard. Harlan insisted that reform was a legislative and not a judicial function and criticized many of the major trends of the activist and liberal Warren Court.

Justice Harlan was no inflexible conservative, however. His judicial views on matters like due process allowed for considerable discretion and made it hard to predict his stance in particular cases. He voted in June 1963, for example, to overturn a 21-year-old precedent and require the states to supply counsel to indigent defendants accused of a felony. He also joined in a June 1965 ruling overturning a state anti-contraceptive law which he considered an invasion of the right to marital privacy. Harlan concurred in May 1967 when the Court extended certain constitutional safeguards such as the right to counsel to juvenile court proceedings. [See EISENHOWER, KENNEDY, JOHNSON Volumes]

Because of personnel changes, Justice Harlan found himself more often at the center of the Court during his final years on the bench. He remained, though, as thoughtful and dispassionate and as independent and difficult to predict as before. On criminal rights questions, for example, Harlan dissented in June 1969 when a majority applied the provision against double jeopardy to the states. Nevertheless, he concurred, when the Court extended the right to counsel to preliminary hearings in June 1970 because recent Court rulings supported such a decision, a ruling he had personally disagreed with. The Justice joined in March 1970 and June 1971 rulings guaranteeing juvenile defendants the right to have their guilt proven "beyond a reasonable doubt" but not the right to trial by jury. In two June 1971 cases Harlan's opinion for the Court held that the states did not deny due process by giving juries in capital cases complete discretion in deciding whether to impose the death penalty or by allowing such juries to determine both a defendant's guilt and his punishment in one proceeding.

Since he demanded high procedural standards in federal criminal cases, Harlan voted in January 1969 and June 1971 to overturn federal convictions where he thought there had not been sufficient cause for a search warrant to be issued. He also dissented from an April 1971 judgment upholding "third party bugging" in which a federal informer used an electronic device, without a warrant, to transmit a conversation between himself and another person. In June 1970 the Justice concurred when the Court upheld the use of six member juries in state trials. However, he objected when the majority at the same time overruled a long-standing precedent requiring 12 members for federal juries.

Harlan maintained his opposition to the one-man, one-vote standard in reapportionment cases decided in 1969 and 1970. He believed that the states had the power to set reasonable voting require-ments. Harlan, therefore, dissented in June 1969 and June 1970 when the Court invalidated state laws limiting voting for school board members and on bond issues to those considered to have the most immediate stake in the results. In December 1970 Harlan took the position that Congress could neither lower the voting age to 18 for state or federal elections nor limit state residency requirements for presidential elections to 30 days.

Justice Harlan generally supported state welfare regulations. Nevertheless, he did join the majority in March 1970 to hold that due process guaranteed welfare recipients the right to a hearing before their benefits could be terminated. He also opposed the Court's increasing use of the equal protection clause against economic rather than racial discrimination. However, his majority opinion in a March 1971 decision ruled that the states could not deny poor persons a divorce solely because they could not pay the court costs. In civil rights cases Harlan backed school desegregation orders in June and October 1969 decisions. Yet he dissented in December 1969 when the majority used an 1866 civil rights law to rule that a black family could not be excluded from membership in a community recreation club when a club share was included in their lease of a house in the neighborhood.

In April 1969 Harlan spoke for a five man majority to reverse a conviction for making derogatory statements about the American flag as a violation of the First Amendment. His majority opinion in a June 1971 case also overturned the conviction of a demonstrator who had entered a courthouse wearing a jacket inscribed with a vulgarism condemning the draft. In June 1971, when a majority refused the government's request for an injunction to halt newspaper publication of a classified study of U.S. involvement in Indochina, Harlan strongly objected to the haste with which the cases were handled. He maintained that the Court should have allowed more time for consideration of the serious issues involved. On the merits, the Justice dissented from the majority in the *Pentagon Papers* case because he thought that the Constitution gave control of foreign affairs to the executive branch and that the scope of judicial review of foreign policy matters was severely limited.

Justice Harlan retired from the Court on Sept. 23, 1971 and died three months later of cancer. His retirement came when he was at the height of his intellectual powers, and his departure from the Court was mourned by commentators of every political persuasion. A diligent and disciplined worker, Harlan had been nearly blind during his last seven years on the Court. Yet he continued to turn out meticulously crafted opinions which won universal praise. Often called a "judge's judge," Harlan wrote clear and learned opinions which analyzed the issues and opposing arguments in a case and fully explained the reasons for his decision. Both critics and admirers of the Warren Court recognized that Harlan had performed a valuable service by acting as a "conservative conscience" and a restraining influence on his activist brethren. Near the end of his career, when the Court seemed to be taking a conservative turn, many observers expected Harlan, with his unquestioned integrity and his commitment to consistency in the law, to apply the same critical standards to a new majority and to serve as a brake on any conservative activism as well. Harlan's 16 year career on the bench, wrote fellow jurist Henry J. Friendly, offered an outstanding example "of moral rectitude, of penetrating analysis, of unstinting labor" and "of utter devotion to the Constitution and respect for acts of Congress as he read them."

[CAB]

For further information:
Norman Dorsen, "John Marshall Harlan," in Leon Friedman and Fred L. Israel, eds., *The Justices of the United States Supreme Court, 1789-1969* (New York, 1969), Vol 4.
David L. Shapiro, ed., *The Evolution of a Judicial Philosophy: Selected Opinions and Papers of Justice John Marshall Harlan* (Cambridge, Mass., 1969).
J. Harvie Wilkinson III, "Justice John M. Harlan and the Values of Federalism," *Virginia Law Review,* 57 (October, 1971), pp. 1185-1221.

HARLOW, BRYCE N(ATHANIEL)
b. Aug. 11, 1916; Oklahoma City, Okla.
Assistant to the President, January–November 1969; Counselor to the President, November 1969–December 1970, June 1973–April 1974.

Bryce Harlow received his B.A. from the University of Oklahoma in 1936 and his M.A. from the same institution in 1942. In the interim he had worked as an assistant librarian for the House of Representatives. He rose to the rank of lieutenant colonel in the army during World War II. He worked on the staff of the Armed Services Committee from 1947 to 1951. President Eisenhower appointed Harlow to the White House staff in 1953. He served throughout both terms as an assistant to the President. From 1961 to 1968 Harlow was the director of governmental relations for the Procter & Gamble Manufacturing Corp. in Washington. [See EISENHOWER Volume]

When President-elect Nixon began to name key Administration aides in November 1968, his first appointee was Harlow, designated to be an assistant to the President for legislative and congressional affairs. A year later the White House announced that Harlow had been raised to counsellor with cabinet rank responsible for national affairs and relieved of operational duties. Harlow reported directly to the President. The change was coordinated with the expected departure of domestic adviser Dr. Arthur Burns [q.v.] whom Nixon had nominated to the Federal Reserve Board.

Harlow worked to generate support for the administration's domestic legislative program—federal revenue sharing, welfare reform, alterations in manpower training programs—which was bottled up in Congress. In an action typical of his responsibilities as counselor, he wrote Republican congressmen in January 1970 seeking support for Nixon's position of federal budget restraint during congressional debate of an appropriations bill the president had threatened to veto because of what he considered inflationary increases over his funding requests. Despite such lobbying, the bill and many other such measures passed the heavily Democratic Congress.

That same month it was announced that Harlow would work with a cabinet-level task force established by Nixon to counsel Southern school districts on implementation of court-ordered desegregation plans. After the U.S. military incursion into Cambodia in the spring, Harlow attempted to modify the language of many of the resolutions introduced in Congress seeking to limit U.S. involvement in that country. In June he accompanied a high-level delegation sent at the President's behest to inspect the war theater in Southeast Asia.

In December, Harlow resigned from the Administration and resumed his career with Procter & Gamble. In the spring of 1973, during the growing Watergate crisis he informally advised Nixon that White House aides John Dean [*q.v.*], H.R. Haldeman [*q.v.*] and John D. Ehrlichman would have to leave "if they have undertaken actions which will not float in the public domain." For Harlow there was "too much at stake to hang on for personal reasons." In the subsequent reorganization after their resignations, Harlow took a leave of absence from Procter & Gamble to return at Nixon's request to the White House.

Harlow, again as counselor to the President, immediately found himself involved in such controversial Watergate issues as the audits of Nixon's finances and the release of the White House tapes to the courts. Along with other close and long-time Nixon aides, he attempted to rally the President's cause. After the dismissal of special Watergate Prosecutor Archibald Cox [*q.v.*], he relayed the suggestions of Republican members of Congress to Nixon that he appoint a new special prosecutor. When the House Judiciary Committee began its proceedings early in 1974, Harlow urged that the panel adopt tighter rules to govern its hearings. At issue were Committee leaks and the fact that the procedure's format did little to distinguish accusation from evidence.

Harlow again resigned from the White House in April. He returned to Procter & Gamble as a vice-president. The following year he helped plan President Ford's 1976 campaign.

[SF]

HARRINGTON, MICHAEL J(OSEPH)

b. Sept. 2, 1936; Salem, Mass.
Democratic Representative, Mass., 1969–79.

Harrington was exposed to politics at an early age when his father was elected mayor of Salem, Mass. Educated at Harvard, Harrington received a law degree in 1961 and subsequently did graduate work in public administration. His interest in Latin America, dating back to his years at Harvard, became the focus of his concerns in the House of Representatives. Harrington had already begun his political career by the time he graduated from law school. He served on the Salem City Council from 1960 to 1963, and as state representative from 1964 to 1969. In 1969 Harrington entered the House of Representatives after winning a special election held to fill the vacancy created by the death of William H. Bates. During the campaign Harrington opposed U.S. involvement in Vietnam and heavy military spending, especially on the anti-ballistic missile system (ABM). His victory was thus regarded as a vote of no confidence for the Nixon Administration's foreign and defense policies.

Harrington maintained a vigorous anti-Administration stance during the Nixon and Ford years, receiving a rating of 100 from the liberal Americans for Democratic Action (ADA) in 1973. He was appointed to the House Foreign Affairs Committee in 1973, after serving four years as one of the few doves on the Armed Services Committee.

As a member of the Foreign Affairs Committee's subcommittee on Inter-American Affairs, Harrington was an outspoken critic of the Central Intelligence Agency (CIA). He became aware that U.S. policies of economic "deprivation" had contributed to the downfall of Chile's Marxist Allende regime in 1973. At Harrington's urging the Subcommittee on Intelligence of the Armed Services Committee called CIA Director William Colby [q.v.] to testify about his Agency's operations; Colby revealed in a closed session that the CIA spent $8 million to eliminate Allende and that this was a "laboratory experiment" in overthrowing governments.

After reviewing the transcript of Colby's secret testimony, Harrington disclosed portions of it to "unauthorized" persons in an attempt to convince the House and Senate international relations committees to investigate CIA operations. In the process Colby's revelations were leaked to the press. The resulting public outcry spurred presidential and congressional investigations of intelligence activities. In the meantime Harrington sued the CIA in federal court to enjoin its covert operations.

Harrington, after working to establish a congressional watchdog panel for intelligence activities, became a member of the newly created House Select Committee on Intelligence. However his criticism of Committee Chairman Lucien Nedzi, backed by other Committee Democrats, impaired the Committee's effectiveness. Neither Harrington nor Nedzi was reappointed when House Speaker Carl Albert [q.v.] reconstituted the Committee.

Shortly after the original leak of Colby's testimony in September 1974, the Armed Services Committee reprimanded Harrington for disregarding House secrecy rules. During the controversy between Harrington and Nedzi in June 1975, the issue was revived: the Armed Services Committee denied Harrington access to its classified files and this time brought charges before the House Ethics Committee. The Committee later dismissed the complaint against Harrington on the grounds that Colby's testimony was taken under conditions that violated House rules.

Harrington continued to criticize the CIA's covert operations, especially in Chile, although he admitted the need for covert intelligence gathering. During the Ethics Committee's later investigation of leaks by CBS news reporter Daniel Schorr [q.v.], Harrington maintained that the priorities of the House were wrong if attention could be diverted from illegal intelligence activities to congressional ability to keep secrets.

Harrington was reelected in 1976. He did not run in 1978, preferring to return to his law practice.

[PG]

HARRIS, FRED R(OY)
b. Nov. 13, 1930; Walters, Okla.
Democratic Senator, Okla., 1965-73.

Following the completion of college and law school at the University of Oklahoma, Fred Harris entered the Oklahoma state Senate at the age of 33. Within three years he headed the Democratic Party Caucus and was a leader of the civil rights movement. In 1964 Harris won a seat in the U.S. Senate. He was a loyal Johnson supporter, voting for the Great Society legislation and civil rights measures and defending the war in Vietnam. He backed the oil depletion allowances that favored the oil interests of his state. Married to a Comanche Indian, Harris was the most militant advocate of Indian rights in the Senate. In the 1968 campaign Harris worked for Hubert Humphrey [q.v.].

Following Nixon's victory Harris moved further to the left. His membership on the President's Advisory Commission on Civil Disorders under Johnson had persuaded him that a major effort must be undertaken to eliminate poverty in the nation. Harris angrily observed the Vietnam War had been diverting needed funds for domestic programs and moved into the anti-war camp. In 1970 he voted for the Cooper-Church Amendment. That same year he introduced his own welfare reform bill as an alternative to the Administration's plan. Harris proposed a national guaranteed minimum income of $3,600 a year for a family of four. The Harris program would also allow a family of four to retain additional earnings to raise its yearly income to $6,000 without losing the guaranteed payments. He maintained that the President's proposal of a $1,600 national minimum would plunge more people into poverty. The Senate rejected Harris's plan.

Harris was particularly concerned with Indian affairs. He lobbied for more land to be given to the native Americans in Alaska. In 1970 he sponsored a bill to grant the Taos Pueblo Indians title to 48,000 acres of New Mexico land which included the tribe's sacred Blue Lake. Enjoying bi-partisan support, his bill passed both houses and was signed by the President.

In early 1969 Harris became chairman of the Democratic National Committee. Aside from his role as the leading partisan critic of the Republican Administration, Harris began the implementation of the reforms in the Party that opened up greater opportunities for minorities, young people and women to participate in the 1972 Democratic National Convention. He resigned as chairman in 1970. Two years later he decided not to seek reelection because of his fear that his liberal stands had doomed his chances. Instead, Harris waged a shortlived run for the 1972 Democratic presidential nomination. Four years later Harris ran again. Campaigning from a trailer, he toured the nation promising to break up the major corporations, end tax loopholes and restore morality to American diplomacy. The neo-populist enjoyed strong grass roots support from many veterans of the 1972 McGovern campaign. Although he had found receptive audiences while campaigning, Harris's recognition in the polls remained low, and his proposals made him a weak contender. In the early

1976 primaries he did poorly, losing even his own state's party caucus to Jimmy Carter [q.v.]. Harris withdrew from the race in April for lack of funds but promised his supporters to remain active in the Party to move it further to the left.

[JB]

HARRIS, PATRICIA R(OBERTS)
b. May 31, 1924; Mattoon, Ill.
Chairwoman, Democratic National Convention Credentials Committee, 1972.

Patricia Harris, the daughter of a railroad waiter, graduated from Howard University in 1945 and held a variety of jobs before deciding to attend George Washington University Law School to become a lawyer. After her graduation in 1960, Harris worked as an attorney in the Criminal Division of the Justice Department and then taught law at Howard University until President Johnson appointed her ambassador to Luxembourg in May 1965, becoming the first black woman to hold that position. Harris returned to Howard University in 1967 to resume her teaching career and served as alternate delegate to the United Nations in 1966 and 1967.

In December 1969 the National Commission on the Causes and Prevention of Violence issued a report that in part condemned civil disobedience and nonviolent protest action. Harris, a member of the Commission and a participant in early civil rights sit-ins while a student at Howard, issued a dissenting report which argued that if persons were willing to accept the penalty, civil disobedience "can represent the highest loyalty and respect for a democratic society."

Harris had confronted such action herself as dean of Howard University Law School in February 1969 when students occupied the law building. She obtained a court injunction, and the students left the building, but Harris resigned after charging that President Nabrit had undermined her authority by negotiating with the students behind her back. [See JOHNSON Volume]

Long active in the Democratic Party, Harris had been a member of the Democratic National Committee, seconded the nomination of Lyndon Johnson at the 1964 National Convention and was appointed to a number of commissions by Presidents Kennedy and Johnson. In October 1971 the Democratic National Committee met and elected Harris temporary chairwoman of the Credentials Committee for the 1971 National Convention.

That post was considered a measure of the Party's progress toward fulfillment of reform proposals made in the wake of the 1968 Democratic Convention disruptions. Harris was backed by National Chairman Lawrence O'Brien [q.v.], labor and Party regulars including Max Kempleman, a Humphrey supporter and co-partner in Harris's law firm. Reform elements including blacks and presidential hopefuls George McGovern [q.v.], Fred Harris [q.v.], Eugene McCarthy [q.v.], and Edmund Muskie [q.v.] supported Sen. Harold Hughes (D, Iowa) [q.v.], who was nominated by Shirley Chisholm [q.v.].

When the Credentials Committee met in late June and early July 1972, Harris was elected permanent chairwoman. She faced over 80 challenges to state delegations, two of which threatened to expose Party infighting on the Convention floor. The Committee voted to invalidate California's winner-take-all primary, a setback for McGovern who had won the primary, and to oust the Illinois delegation led by Mayor Richard Daley [q.v.] in favor of a more representative delegation, a move by McGovern forces angry at the California decision. Harris's performance was assessed as strict and fair, but the struggle between Party regulars and reformers was fought out at the National Convention.

From 1970 to 1971 Harris was a partner in a Washington, D.C., law firm and was elected to the board of directors of the National Bank of Washington, Scott Paper Co. and IBM. From 1973 to 1976 she was member-at-large of the Democratic National Committee. On Jan. 20, 1977, the Senate confirmed President Carter's [q.v.]

nomination of Harris as Secretary of the Department of Housing and Urban Development.

[JMP]

HART, GARY (WARREN)
b. Nov. 28, 1937; Ottawa, Kan.
Director, Sen. George McGovern's Campaign for President, 1970-72; Democratic Senator, Colo., 1975-.

Hart received his B.A. degree in 1958 at Bethany Nazarene College and also attended Yale Divinity School. He earned a law degree from Yale in 1964 and moved to Washington, D.C., where he served as an appellate attorney in the Department of Justice and as a special assistant to Secretary of the Interior Stewart L. Udall. In the late 1960s Hart taught law in Colorado and was a consultant for the National Water Commission and the Public Land Review Commission. He also entered private law practice in Denver.

Hart volunteered his services to Sen. Robert F. Kennedy when Kennedy declared his candidacy for President in March 1968. He continued working for Democratic Party candidates following Robert Kennedy's assassination. Hart organized the Colorado hearings of the Reform Commission, also called the Commission on Party Structure and Delegate Selection. He was one of the earliest of Sen. George McGovern's supporters for the presidency and became his first full-time staff member in March 1970. He agreed to manage McGovern's national campaign in August 1970.

In organizing McGovern's national campaign, Hart promoted a policy of decentralization. Instead of giving the national staff full authority in campaign decisions, Hart delegated responsibility to volunteers on the local level. This method increased communication between national headquarters and local offices, as well as encouraging a sense of increased involvement for all the volunteers. McGovern's people worked at the grassroots level, canvassing neighborhoods and talking to voters.

McGovern announced his presidential candidacy in January 1971. Some political contributions arrived at this point, but lack of money was a continuing problem. Hart created the "McGovern for President Club," in which members contributed $10 per month and in return received current news on McGovern's campaign. It proved to be an effective strategy. Hart felt that the willingness of ordinary citizens to invest in the political process was "a revolutionary event in American politics."

McGovern captured the leadership of the liberal wing of the Democratic Party and secured the nomination for the presidency on the first ballot at the Democratic National Convention in July 1971. Hart organized the McGovern campaign by concentrating on the states that Hubert Humphrey [q.v.] had either won or narrowly lost in his campaign for President in 1968. Hart urged his field organizers to reevaluate these states and to move in with media campaigns and public appearances when the time was right.

Although he originally felt it would be easier for McGovern to beat President Richard Nixon than for the Senator to get the Democratic presidential nomination, Hart eventually concluded that the campaign was doomed after McGovern's first vice-presidential choice, Thomas Eagleton (D, Mo.) [q.v.] withdrew following revelations that he had been hospitalized for psychiatric problems. But neither Hart nor McGovern anticipated the dramatic defeat in November. Nixon was reelected by a plurality of nearly 18 million votes and carried 49 of the 50 states.

Hart returned to Denver, resumed his law practice and began work on a book recording his personal history of McGovern's campaign. In *Right From the Start* he concluded that McGovern and his advisers did not offer workable solutions to America's problems or clearly identify the national issues. Hart also felt that liberalism in the United States had become extremely removed from the problems of the working class. He proposed reestablishing effective communication with the people to develop a new generation of national leaders.

Hart won a U.S. Senate seat from Colorado in 1974. As Senator he worked for national health insurance, the restoration of run-down residential buildings in inner-city areas and the protection of Colorado's natural beauty.

[CE]

HART, PHILIP A(LOYSIUS)
b. Dec. 10, 1912; Bryn Mawr, Pa.
d. Dec. 26, 1976; Washington, D.C.
Democratic Senator, Mich., 1959-76.

Following graduation in 1937 from the University of Michigan Law School, Hart established a law practice in Detroit. He served in the Army during World War II and then returned home to resume his practice. Gov. G. Mennen Williams, a former law school classmate of Hart, appointed his friend Michigan's Corporation and Securities Commissioner in 1949. He made Hart his legal adviser in 1953. Hart was elected lieutenant governor of Michigan in 1954 and served two terms. In 1958 he won a seat in the U.S. Senate with strong labor support. In subsequent campaigns Hart was also aided by the wealth of his wife, an auto parts heiress. Hart immediately joined the liberal coalition in the Senate. An open, frank man known as the conscience of the Senate, Hart built a reputation as a quietly effective legislative technician with a special interest in civil rights, consumer protection and anti-trust matters. [See EISENHOWER KENNEDY, JOHNSON Volumes]

During the Nixon Administration, Hart earned consistently high marks from the liberal Americans for Democratic Action. In 1969 and again in 1974 the organization gave him a 100 rating. Hart voted for federal campaign subsidies, busing and government aid for abortions while opposing "no-knock" entry legislation. In defense and foreign affairs he opposed the deployment of the Safeguard anti-ballistic missile system and supported the ban on importing chrome from Rhodesia and cuts in military spending. He was an early critic of the Vietnam war and voted for attempts to limit presidential authority to conduct the war and efforts to end the conflict.

Hart's liberal voting record often proved unpopular at home. His battle for stiff air pollution and safety devices on cars angered Detroit and the auto unions. In 1972 he introduced a bill to restrict the ownership of hand guns that alienated Michigan's rural voters. Hart's most controversial stand was his support of school busing at a time when Detroit and its suburbs were embroiled in a dispute over the issue.

As chairman of the Judiciary Committee's Subcommittee on Anti-trust and Monopoly, Hart frequently challenged the power of the nation's insurance companies. In August 1972 he introduced legislation to establish a national no-fault insurance program. The Senate recommitted it, thus killing the bill. Hart then chaired hearings in the spring of 1973 to expose the questionable selling practices of life insurance companies. Hart proposed a truth-in-insurance bill, but the Senate failed to act on this also.

Hart's subcommittee also held hearings throughout the Johnson and Nixon years on the power of the largest corporations to stifle competition. Hart found that existing anti-trust and anti-monopoly laws were rarely enforced and that big business engaged in practices presumably outlawed. To rectify this situation he introduced the 1972 industrial reorganization bill aimed at breaking up monopolies in seven major industries—automobiles, chemicals and drugs, steel, electronics, energy, electrical machinery and nonferrous metals. Hart's bill stipulated that corporations would be liable to divestiture if the businesses earned over 15% of their profits after taxes, if four or fewer companies accounted for 50% of sales in a given industry or if there was a lack of price competition. To enforce these stiff requirements Hart proposed a commission to prosecute the conglomerates in a special federal court. The law would have

specifically affected such corporations as IBM, Xerox, Procter and Gamble, and Ford, Chrysler and General Motors, all with corporate headquarters in Hart's home state. Responding to charges that he was anti-business, Hart answered that on the contrary he was probusiness because he desired to return fair competition to the economy. Hart's bill was defeated, but his expose contributed to the Justice Department's decision to sue for the breakup of IBM.

Throughout 1976 Hart battled cancer. He died in December of that year. Before his death the Senate, in an unprecedented move, named its new office building after him.

[JB]

HARTKE, R(UPERT) VANCE
b. May 31, 1919; Stendal, Ind.
Democratic Senator, Ind., 1959-76.

The son of a small town Indiana postmaster, Hartke received his law degree from Indiana University in 1948. He practiced law in Evansville, where he was also active in local Democratic Party politics. In 1955 the city elected him mayor; four years later, he became the state's first Democratic Senator in 20 years. Earning high rankings by the liberal Americans For Democratic Action, Hartke supported the Great Society legislation of Lyndon Johnson. He was the principal author of the Higher Education Act of 1965 and the Adult Education Act of 1967, both of which made college education readily available to those who could not afford it. Originally a supporter of the Vietnam war, Hartke became one of the leading Senate doves after a visit to Asia in 1965. [See KENNEDY, JOHNSON Volumes]

As chairman of the Surface Transportation Subcommittee and a member of the Aviation Subcommittee, both under the Commerce Committee, Hartke was particularly concerned with improving safety features in the nation's transportation system. He led efforts for legislation to authorize the Department of Transportation to set national uniform safety standards for airlines, highways and railroads as well as natural gas pipelines. Hartke had lost a sister in a car crash and had been impressed with critics' charges that American automobiles were inherently unsafe. Beginning in 1966 Hartke unsuccessfully pressed for a mandatory prison term for those in the automobile industry who willfully violated auto safety in their designs. Hartke was also a leading critic of the Federal Aviation Administration, which he accused of failing to enforce safety precautions.

Hartke played a major role in the passage of the Rail Passenger Service Act of 1970. The measure provided for the establishment of the National Rail Passenger Corp. known as Amtrak, a quasi-public corporation providing passenger service between major cities throughout the nation. It was hoped that Amtrak would relieve the railroads of the financial burden of operating commuter routes that frequently ran deficits. Hartke's Hazardous Material Transportation Act, signed by Ford in 1975, restricted the shipments of radioactive and hazardous materials on passenger aircraft. To insure a uniform system of track maintenance, Hartke introduced in 1970 the Railroad Safety Act, which was subsequently passed. Two years later his more ambitious Interstate Railway Act provided for the rehabilitation of mainline tracks and roadbeds through a program of federal grants and loans.

In 1973 Hartke became chairman of the Veterans Affairs Committee. He obtained in 1974 cost-of-living increases for G.I. education benefits. Hartke also sponsored similiar increases in pensions given to wartime veterans and their survivors for service-connected disability and death.

Hartke was a major supporter of organized labor, which was a major power in Indiana politics. Hartke coauthored with Rep. James A. Bourke (D, Mass.) the AFL-CIO-sponsored foreign trade and investment bill that sought to safeguard American jobs and industry through a protectionist tariff system and a discriminatory tax levied on multinational

American corporations flooding the domestic market with cheap imports. This bill, as well as the one he introduced in 1971 to curb imports of steel, was defeated.

In foreign affairs Hartke opposed the Vietnam war policies of the Nixon Administration, voting, for example, for the Cooper-Church and McGovern-Hatfield Amendments. Because of Hartke's opposition to the war, the Administration made him a priority target for defeat in his 1970 campaign. The Republican Party poured money into the state to aid his rival and Vice President Spiro Agnew [q.v.] toured the state speaking for the Republican challenger. Hartke won the election in one of the closest senatorial elections in recent memory. His opponent, Rep. Richard L. Roudebush, challenged the results, but the Supreme Court in 1972 declared Hartke the winner.

In January 1972 Hartke announced his candidacy for the Democratic nomination for the presidency. Running as a liberal with little funds and no press coverage, Hartke did poorly in both the Florida and New Hampshire primaries. He withdrew in April in favor of Hubert Humphrey [q.v.]. In 1976 Hartke lost in his bid for a third term to the popular Indianapolis Mayor Richard Lugar [q.v.].

[JB]

HATFIELD, MARK O(DUM)
b. July 22, 1922; Dallas, Ore.
Republican Senator, Ore., 1967-.

After earning his master's degree in political science from Stanford University in 1948, Hatfield taught political science at Willamette University. In addition to his academic responsibilities, the Republican Hatfield concurrently served in both houses of the Oregon legislature. In 1957 Oregon voters elected him secretary of state; two years later, he became his state's youngest governor. In 1966 he won a seat in the Senate on an anti-war platform. [See KENNEDY, JOHNSON Volumes]

During the Nixon Administration Hatfield was one of the major doves in the

Senate. In June 1970 he suggested the Nixon-Agnew team might have to be replaced because it failed to deliver on its promise to end the war. In May 1970 when Nixon ordered American troops into Cambodia, Hatfield co-sponsored with Sen. George McGovern (D, S.D.) [q.v.] an amendment to the arms appropriations bill providing for the termination of funds for the Vietnam war after Dec. 31, 1971. The Hatfield-McGovern Amendment became the rallying cry for the anti-war movement among activists who collected petitions, held demonstrations and lobbied in Congress for its passage. The Senate defeated the Amendment twice, once in 1970 and again in 1971. Hatfield also lobbied for the replacement of the draft with a voluntary army. His bill, first introduced in 1967 and on a number of occasions thereafter, never passed, but the Administration eventually ended the draft on its own initiative.

Hatfield was particularly concerned with a number of major constitutional reforms. He joined the group in the Senate that had been urging the abolition of the electoral college. Hatfield further proposed special elections for the vice president and other top cabinet officials to create a "plural executive" and forestall the trend toward one-man rule. Hatfield also sponsored a constitutional amendment that sought to restrict senators to two six-year terms and representatives to 12 years. Following a mandatory sabbatical of two years, those congressmen whose terms had expired would be permitted to seek office again. Hatfield argued that this plan would restore democracy to the Congress by undermining the seniority system.

Hatfield's record during the Nixon-Ford years also revealed concern for both the conservation of natural resources and the sanctity of what he believed to be human life. Hatfield lobbied for legislation to preserve the forests and asked for the decentralization of national control over forest areas especially in his home state. In 1973 Hatfield cosponsored a constitutional amendment barring abortions except to save the life of the mother. Al-

though he opposed abortions, he was in the forefront of those who desired a stronger federal commitment to encourage family planning.

During the Carter Administration, Hatfield's interest in foreign policy and in domestic liberal legislation made him a reliable Republican vote for the new President in these areas.

[JB]

HAWKINS, AUGUSTUS F(REEMAN)
b. Aug. 31, 1907; Shreveport, La.
Democratic Representative, Calif., 1963-.

Hawkins moved to Los Angeles with his family when he was 10. He attended the University of California at Los Angeles and received a B.A. in economics in 1931. After working as a volunteer in Upton Sinclair's End Poverty in California campaign, Hawkins was elected to the state Assembly in 1934. He served there for 28 years.

In 1962 Hawkins won election to the House of Representatives. A black Representative from a predominantly black district in Los Angeles, Hawkins consistently supported President Johnson's Great Society programs. After the 1965 Watts riots, which occurred in his district, Hawkins was able to win large amounts of federal aid for his constituents. He was an early critic of the Vietnam war on the grounds that it diverted badly needed funds from anti-poverty programs. [See JOHNSON Volume]

Hawkins continued his opposition to the war during the Nixon years. In 1970 he was a member of a House fact-finding mission to Vietnam. Although the majority of the group issued a report on July 6 that was optimistic about the success of U.S. military policies, Hawkins and another member of the group, Rep. William R. Anderson (D, Tenn.), issued a report highly critical of conditions and treatment of civilian political prisoners. Hawkins described the "tiger cages" on

Con Son Island as "the worst" prison he had ever seen. The revelations led to congressional hearings on the matter and a great deal of unfavorable publicity for the South Vietnamese government.

Hawkins quickly became a vocal congressional opponent of President Nixon, whose domestic policies and appointments appeared to threaten the gains made by the civil rights movement during the 1960s. Nixon's nomination of Clement Haynsworth [q.v.] and G. Harrold Carswell [q.v.] to the Supreme Court, the extension by the Department of Health, Education and Welfare of school desegregation deadlines in the South, and Administration proposals to weaken the Equal Employment Opportunies Commission (EEOC) and to dismantle the Office of Economic Opportunities (OEO) angered Hawkins and other black members of Congress. In February 1970 they sought a meeting with Nixon but after several months were informed that it could not be fit into the President's schedule.

During the summer Hawkins released to the press a letter he had addressed to the President which said that the Administration's policies were "destined to destroy all possibilities of unity and brotherhood" between blacks and whites. With other black Representatives he announced the formation in October 1970 of a "shadow cabinet" on civil rights, and the following year, at the start of the 92nd Congress, he helped organize the Congressional Black Caucus, of which he was chosen vice chairman. Finally granted a meeting with the President on March 25, 1971, the Caucus members presented Nixon with 60 legislative goals, including a guaranteed annual income for all Americans, federal funds for minority businesses, the nationalization of welfare and expansion of the federal government's low-income housing program. The Caucus later denounced Nixon's response as disappointing and inadequate.

Hawkins, meanwhile, was working on proposals to strengthen the enforcement powers of the EEOC. In 1969 he introduced legislation to give the Commission the power to issue cease-and-desist orders in cases of job bias, but no action was taken. In 1971 he introduced a similar bill, with the cosponsorship of Rep. Ogden Reid (R, N.Y.) [q.v.]. Although approved by the Education and Labor Committee in June, it was defeated on the House floor in September. In its place was adopted a weaker Administration measure that limited the EEOC to bringing suit in federal court. The weakened bill was finally cleared by Congress in March 1972 and became law.

Hawkins also opposed efforts to dismantle OEO. In March 1971 Nixon asked for a simple two-year extension of OEO pending the development of a reorganization plan that would transfer many of its programs to other agencies. Hawkins denounced the proposal as a disguised attempt at "dismantling the OEO and stripping it of all its programs" so that there would no longer be an "advocate for the poor" among federal agencies. In 1973 Nixon attempted to scuttle OEO without congressional approval but was blocked by court order. The following year Hawkins sponsored the legislation that replaced OEO with a new independent Community Services Administration to handle federal programs for the poor. Aided by a recession and rising unemployment rates that highlighted the need for aid to the poor, the bill was approved by Congress in December 1974 and signed into law the following month by President Ford, despite his reservations.

On June 20, 1974, Hawkins proposed a full-employment bill in the House. Introduced in the Senate by Hubert Humphrey [q.v.] in October, the Humphrey-Hawkins bill quickly became a priority legislative item of liberals, blacks and organized labor. The measure called for a national unemployment rate of 3% to be achieved within 18 months of enactment for those 16 years of age and older, with the federal government as an employer of last resort. Throughout 1975 and early 1976 Hawkins and Humphrey held hearings around the country to mobilize support for the legislation.

On March 12, 1976, a revised version

was introduced extending to four years the timetable for reaching full employment. The House Education and Labor Committee approved the measure in May, and the bill had the endorsement of Democratic presidential hopeful Jimmy Carter. The Republican Party criticized the bill in its platform as a "quick-fix solution" to unemployment, and Ford attacked the measure as an "election-year boondoggle."

In response to these criticisms and in an effort to broaden support for the bill, Hawkins agreed to a compromise version approved by the Committee in September. The revised bill strengthened the anti-inflation sections, provided for a goal of 3% unemployment for workers over 20 years of age and made clear that last-resort government jobs would be low paying. Despite these compromises no action was taken on the bill by either the full House or the Senate in 1976.

In 1977 President Carter expressed further reservations about the full employment bill. In November he and Hawkins worked out a compromise that raised the unemployment target to 4%, restricted federal action to fiscal and monetary policies and established no new jobs programs or spending programs to create jobs for the unemployed. Furthermore the measure would not guarantee government jobs for the hard-core unemployed. On Oct. 27, 1978, President Carter signed a significantly weakened version of the original Humphrey-Hawkins bill based on this compromise.

Hawkins was reelected in 1978 to his ninth consecutive term in the House.

[JD]

HAYDEN, THOMAS E(MMETT)
b. Dec. 12, 1940; Royal Oaks, Mich.
Radical, anti-war leader.

Hayden, raised in a conservative suburb of Detroit, was the only child of a Chrysler Corp. accountant. After graduating from the University of Michigan in 1961, he worked full time with the Stu-dent Nonviolent Coordinating Committee in the South. Returning to Ann Arbor, he helped form a campus chapter of the newly organized Students for a Democratic Society (SDS). He wrote the initial draft of SDS's "Port Huron Statement," which became the manifesto of the New Left, and served as president of SDS in 1962 and 1963.

With the escalation of U.S. involvement in Vietnam in 1965, Hayden increasingly focused his attention on the growing anti-war movement. In December 1965 he traveled to North Vietnam with other anti-war activists. In September 1967 he attended a conference in Czechoslovakia with North Vietnamese leaders. A second trip to North Vietnam later that year led to the release of three American prisoners of war as a gesture of good faith by the Vietnamese Communists. Hayden participated in the student occupation of Columbia University in April 1968, and as project director of the National Mobilization Committee to End the War in Vietnam, he organized the anti-war demonstrations outside the Democratic National Convention in Chicago in August. During the bloody clashes between demonstrators and police, which the National Commission on the Causes and Prevention of Violence later described as a "police riot," Hayden told the crowds, "It may be that the era of organized, peaceful and orderly demonstrations is coming to an end." [See JOHNSON Volume]

On March 20, 1969, Hayden, along with seven other leaders of the anti-war movement, was indicted on charges of crossing state lines with intent to riot and conspiring to incite a riot. The indictments were the first ones issued under the anti-riot provisions of the 1968 Civil Rights Act. The trial, which opened on Sept. 24, 1969, was widely publicized as a test of the limits of dissent, and became a cause celebre for radicals. The courtroom was the scene of numerous confrontations between the defendants, their lawyers and Judge Julius Hoffman [q.v.]. When the trial ended in February 1970, Hoffman imposed heavy contempt-of-court sentences on the defendants and their lawyers, including a 14-month sentence on Hayden. The jury acquitted all of the defendants of the conspiracy charge, but found Hayden and four others guilty of crossing state lines with intent to riot.

After the verdict was announced, protests erupted in numerous cities. In November 1972 an appeals court overturned the convictions, charging Judge Hoffman with improper rulings and conduct, and the Justice Department decided not to seek a retrial. In December 1973, Hayden's contempt conviction was also overturned.

Hayden continued to be active in the anti-war movement. In May 1971 he was arrested at a demonstration in Berkeley commemorating the second anniversary of "People's Park," when a student was killed by state troopers. Hayden spoke and wrote extensively about the war and about the intensifying government repression directed at anti-war radicals and other dissenters. In 1970 he published *Trial* and in 1972 *The Love of Possession Is a Disease with Them.* In January 1973 Hayden married antiwar activist and actress Jane Fonda [*q.v.*], and together they directed the efforts of the newly organized Indochina Peace Campaign toward ending U.S. clandestine involvement in Vietnam and all U.S. aid to the Thieu regime in South Vietnam. As the Saigon government approached its final collapse in April 1975, Hayden declared, "Indochina has not fallen—it has risen."

With the end of the Vietnam conflict and the decline of the mass protest movements of the 1960s and early 1970s, Hayden turned toward electoral politics. Declaring that "the radicalism of the '60s is fast becoming the common sense of the '70s," he announced on June 2, 1975, his candidacy for the U.S. Senate seat held by John V. Tunney of California. In response to charges that he had abandoned his radicalism, Hayden answered that he had "redefined" it. Campaigning against the power of big business and big government, Hayden sought the support of minorities, blue-collar workers, the poor, and young middle-class voters from the

student movement of the 1960s. Although pollsters and professional politicians initially dismissed his candidacy, Hayden waged a vigorous campaign and won almost 40% of the vote–over 1,000,000 votes–in the June 1976 primary.

After the primary Hayden transformed his campaign organization into the California Campaign for Economic Democracy, a grass-roots coalition opposed to the concentrated wealth and power of big corporations. He was also active in the National Conference on Alternative State and Local Policies, a loose coalition of activists and progressive public officials, many of whom were leaders of the protest movements of the 1960s.

[JD]

HAYNSWORTH, CLEMENT F(URMAN) JR.
b. Oct. 30, 1912; Greenville, S.C.
Chief Judge, Court of Appeals, Fourth Circuit, 1964- .

In 1933 Haynsworth graduated from Furman University, a school founded by his great-great-grandfather. After receiving his LL.B. from Harvard Law School in 1936, Haynsworth began a 20 year career (interrupted only by his service in World War II as a Navy ensign) in a law firm founded by his great-grandfather. In 1957 Haynsworth was appointed judge of the U.S. Court of Appeals for the Fourth Circuit (Maryland, W. Virginia, Virginia, North Carolina and South Carolina), and in 1964, he became chief judge.

In August 1969, Richard Nixon nominated Haynsworth to fill the Supreme Court seat of Abe Fortas [*q.v.*] who had resigned in May following charges of financial improprieties. In nominating Haynsworth, a Southerner, a Democrat, an Episcopalian, and a conservative jurist, Nixon broke the tradition of reserving the seat for a Jewish justice. He selected a nominee consistent with his "Southern Strategy": to capture the political loyalty of the white Southerners whose historic affiliation with the Democratic Party was believed to have been weakened by that Party's support of the civil rights movement. Nixon selected a nominee acceptable to influential Southern Sens. Strom Thurmond (D, S.C.) [q.v.], James Eastland (D, Miss.) [q.v.], and John McClellan (R, Ark.) [q.v.], men who sought a halt to enforcement of guidelines for implementation of school desegregation plans and reversal of recent Supreme Court opinions in support of immediate desegregation.

The nomination provoked an angry response from civil rights organizations who argued that four of Haynsworth's opinions supported racial segregation in schools. Organized labor also denounced some of Haynsworth's decisions. Decisive opposition developed during Judiciary Committee hearings in September over Haynsworth's judicial ethics when it was revealed that the Judge had purchased stock in a corporation after he had decided but before he had announced the ruling in a suit involving that company.

Many Republicans who could not in good faith support a candidate whose ethics were as questionable as those of Abe Fortas, announced their opposition, and Robert Griffin (R, Mich.) [q.v.] led the floor fight against his nomination. On Nov. 21, Haynsworth was rejected by a vote of 55-45. Forty percent of Senate Republicans had voted nay.

Richard Nixon blamed Haynsworth's defeat on "anti-Southern, anti-conservative, anti-strict constructionist" prejudice and persuaded Haynsworth to remain at his post. In 1972 Haynsworth sided with a majority in overturning a district court order to bus students between predominately black Richmond and predominately white suburbs to achieve school desegregation.

[JMP]

HAYS, WAYNE L(EVERE)
b. May 13, 1911; Bannock, Ohio.
Democratic Representative, Ohio, 1949-76; Chairman, House Administration Committee, 1971-76.

Wayne Hays was born in the area of southeastern Ohio marked by an abundance of coal and poverty. He graduated from Ohio State University in 1933 and entered Duke University to study law. But financial conditions eventually forced him to find employment as a school teacher in Flushing, Ohio.

In 1939 Hays was elected mayor of Flushing, a position he held for three terms. In 1941 he also began a term as state senator. Shortly after the attack on Pearl Harbor by the Japanese in December of 1941, Hays volunteered for Army duty. Nine months later, however, he received a medical discharge. In 1948, after two years as a county commissioner, he won a seat in the U.S. House.

Hays attracted little attention during his early years in the House, usually siding with the Democratic majority on roll call votes. Domestically he generally supported the social policies of Truman's Fair Deal. On foreign policy matters he pursued a hawkish course that would remain a consistent theme of his entire political career. He was a strong believer in massive military aid to the North Atlantic Treaty Organization (NATO) and approved of actions taken against the Communist Party in the United States. Hays was a vocal critic of political "witch-hunting" during the 1950s. The vitriolic and abrasive style Hays employed against his opponents, directly contrary to the Capitol Hill tradition of at least outward courtesy, was to become a widely recognized trademark of the Ohio Representative. [See JOHNSON Volume]

Hays supported such civil rights legislation as the Civil Rights Act of 1964 and the Voting Rights Act of 1965. However during the Nixon years he opposed such specific remedies as busing to achieve school integration and the "Philadelphia Plan," which provided for specific minority-hiring targets at federal construction sites.

Hays was a staunch advocate of the Indochina war. Beginning in 1966 he backed all Pentagon requests for funds to fight the war, as well as the transfer of funds from other defense programs to finance the Vietnam effort. He frequently delivered scathing attacks on the war's opponents from the House floor. In October 1969, during the nationwide anti-war moratorium, he referred to a group of dovish congressional representatives as "self-appointed emissaries from Hanoi." In December of that same year, he cosponsored a resolution supporting the President's conduct of the war.

In July 1970 he opposed the Cooper-Church Amendment to limit U.S. involvement in Cambodia.

Hays competed against four other Democratic congressmen for the position of House majority leader in 1970. He came in second to last—even he conceded that the vote reflected the animosity existing between him and many of his colleagues. In January of 1971 Hays became the chairman of the House Administration Committee. Under previous chairmen the Administration Committee had been little more than a housekeeping body for the lower chamber of Congress. But Hays was able to use its various powers to reap major influence in the House. Aside from managing such pedestrian yet essential aspects of the House bureaucracy as office and stationary expenses, travel allotments and the like, the Committee determined the budget for all other committees, with the exception of Appropriations.

Hays's power was further enhanced in July of 1971 when the House granted his panel the authority to determine the benefits and allowances of representatives. This move was popular in the House because it prevented controversial increases in benefits from reaching the House floor where debate would perhaps attract adverse publicity. Coupled with his chairmanship of the Democratic Congressional Campaign Committee, Hays's control of the House Administration Committee made him one of the most powerful members of Congress.

One of the first issues Hays faced as the new chairman was campaign reform. There had been no major revision of the laws in this area since the Corrupt Practices Act of 1925. There was a particular need for legislation concerning the financing of election campaigns. In June 1971 Hays introduced to the Administration Committee a resolution setting a lim-

it on campaign spending and placing responsibility for complete disclosure of funds on the candidates themselves. The legislation was modeled after Ohio campaign laws. Proponents of campaign finance reform urged swift action on the resolution, but Hays stated he would not be pressured. The bill was finally reported out of committee in October 1971, but by this time the House had agreed to the Senate version of the same legislation and the Hays bill was dropped. Hays insisted that the vote be delayed until after the Christmas recess, and thus it was not until January of 1972 that the Federal Election Campaign Act was passed. This had the effect of delaying the date that the bill became effective.

The new law required that all campaign contributions in excess of $100 be reported and the contributor be fully identified. The House clerk, the secretary of the Senate and the comptroller general were to receive copies of the reports. Hays became involved in a bitter dispute with House Clerk Pat Jennings when Jennings appeared before the Administration Committee to request additional staff and funding to help implement the law. After a closed Committee hearing, which reportedly included threats and name-calling, Hays granted Jennings half the staff requested.

The fall of 1974 saw fresh debate on campaign financing as the House considered a new federal elections bill. Hays opposed the much-discussed concept of public financing of elections, particularly congressional races. In August he stated that the plan was "a scheme to break down the two-party system." Hays also opposed the establishment of an enforcement commission to monitor compliance with the election laws.

In 1973 the House attempted to curtail foreign travel "junkets" at taxpayers' expense by requiring that members list their traveling expenses in the Congressional Record. Hays, however, was able to render the resolution ineffective by adding an amendment that merely called for such expenses to be "available for public inspection." Hays had long possessed a reputation among congressmen as one of the most frequent users of the traveling privileges extended to representatives. Citing his responsibilities as head of the United States delegation to NATO and chairman of a House Foreign Affairs subcommittee, Hays traveled so extensively that Sen. Stephen Young of Ohio referred to Hays as the "Marco Polo of the Ohio delegation."

During a debate in October 1974 on reform of House committees, Hays opposed an amendment to prevent congressmen who were defeated in elections or retiring from using government funds to travel during the last weeks of their terms.

During the summer of 1973, Hays expressed increasing anger at the mounting Watergate scandal. In January of 1974 he would become one of the first major congressional figures to call on Richard Nixon to resign from the presidency.

The 1974 elections were held almost immediately after the resignation of President Nixon and the virtual conclusion of the Watergate scandals. The result was a dramatic increase in freshman congressmen the following January, many of whom had campaigned on promises of bringing reform to Washington. When the Democratic Caucus met in January of 1975, the new representatives were instrumental in removing such veteran committee chairmen as Rep. Wright Patman [q.v.] of the House Banking Committee and Rep. F. Edward Hebert [q.v.] of the House Armed Services Committee from their influential positions. Many observers predicted Hays would be next. But Hays was once again able to use his political clout as head of the Administration Committee to curry favor with congressmen. He was also able to gain the support of Rep. Phillip Burton [q.v.], newly elected chairman of the Democratic Caucus who owed his position in part to Hays's backing. Thus Hays retained his chairmanship. Subsequently, however, he seemed to make a determined effort to soften his well-known abrasive personality when dealing with colleagues.

In 1976 Hays divorced his wife of many years, from whom he had been sep-

arated since 1970, in order to marry Patricia Peak, head of his Ohio office. But his professional and personal life was suddenly shattered in May when Elizabeth Ray, a secretary on a Hays subcommittee, told *The Washington Post* that Hays kept her on the payroll simply in exchange for her services as a mistress. Initially Hays denied the charges, only to stand before the House later and admit them. Initially he gave up the chairmanship of the Administration Committee, but in the face of continued pressure, Hays resigned from Congress in August, bringing to an abrupt end an 18-year congressional career.

Returning to his farm in Ohio with Patricia Peak, Hays avoided the limelight for two years. In 1978, however, he won a seat in the Ohio Senate. He denied reports that he was using the post as a springboard to return to the House of Representatives.

[MDQ]

HEARST, PATRICIA C(AMPBELL)
b. Feb. 20, 1954; San Francisco, Calif.
Kidnap victim.

Patricia Hearst led a sheltered private existence, raised in luxury in Hillsborough, Calif., and attended the University of California at Berkeley, where her mother was a regent.

On Feb. 4, 1974, Hearst was kidnapped from her Berkeley apartment. On Feb. 6 the Symbionese Liberation Army (SLA) claimed responsibility for the kidnapping. The SLA was a radical Bay-area group committed to warring with what it termed "the fascist capitalist class."

A number of demands from the SLA followed—some written, some taped—all directed at Hearst's father. Randolph Hearst was at first ordered to provide food, totaling $400 million, for all of California's poor. This amount was gradually reduced to a $2 million giveaway plan, which Randolph Hearst inaugurated on Feb. 19. Two months after her abduction a message was received that Patricia

Hearst had joined the SLA of her free will and had changed her name to "Tania."

On April 15, 1974, Hearst participated with the SLA in the robbing of the Sunset branch of the Hibernia Bank. Soon after in a taped message Hearst called her parents "pigs and clowns" and said she had willingly participated in the bank holdup. On May 16, she fired a shot into a Los Angeles storefront to free fellow SLA members Emily and Will Harris who were being held for shoplifting. The next day she fled to San Francisco with the Harrises. After a final taped message on June 7, 1974, she vanished into the underground. The FBI conducted a cross-cuntry search that ended on Sept. 18, 1975, when Patricia Hearst was captured with Emily and Bill Harris in San Francisco.

Hearst was wanted in San Francisco for bank robbery and for the use of a weapon during the commission of a felony. She was also wanted in Los Angeles for several offenses, ranging from kidnapping to the illegal use of firearms. The Hearsts considered several lawyers to defend their daughter before deciding on F. Lee Bailey and Albert Johnson. The trial became a battle of the psychiatrists, the central issue being whether Hearst had been coerced into her activities with the SLA or had acted voluntarily.

On March 20, 1976, Patricia Campbell Hearst was found guilty in San Francisco of bank robbery and the illegal use of firearms. She was sentenced on April 12, 1976, to provisional maximum terms of 25 years for the robbery and 10 years for the use of weapons. After her conviction pressure built to get Hearst to testify against her former SLA associates. Originally her lawyers said she had no plans to testify for the prosecution. But after formal charges in the Hearst kidnapping case were brought against Emily and Will Harris, she agreed to testify against the couple and other SLA members in an apparent move to gain judicial leniency.

The American public was split in its feelings about Patricia Hearst. Some felt sympathy for her. Others felt that she was properly sentenced, that she should suffer the same consequences anyone else

would under the given circumstances. An appeal was launched on claims that the trial judge should not have permitted the introduction of evidence concerning Hearst's actions following her participation in the bank robbery and not allowed the prosecution to ask questions which forced Hearst to use the Fifth Amendment. On Nov. 19, 1976, Patricia Hearst was freed on bail, pending the appeal of her federal conviction.

On April 18, 1977, Hearst was sentenced to five years probation for charges against her in Los Angeles. A three-judge panel of the Ninth Circuit Court of Appeals unanimously upheld Hearst's bank robbery conviction on April 24, 1978, and she was returned to the federal prison in Pleasanton, Calif., to complete her sentence. In September 1978 Hearst's attorneys filed a petition for presidential clemency. Hearst's sentence was commuted by President Carter on Jan. 29, 1979, and she was freed from prison on Feb. 1, 1979.

[CE]

HEBERT, F(ELIX) EDWARD
b. Oct. 12, 1901; New Orleans, La.
Democratic Representative, La., 1941-77; Chairman, House Armed Services Committee, 1971-75.

A newspaperman from 1919 to 1940, Hebert helped expose corruption in the administration of Louisiana Gov. Richard W. Leche in 1939. Capitalizing on his fame Hebert successfully ran for the U.S. House in 1940 and in subsequent elections faced little opposition. Hebert, a member of the Southern Democratic bloc, opposed liberal domestic programs and supported the 1948 presidential campaign of Sen. Strom Thurmond (D, S.C.) [q.v.], who ran on the States Rights Democratic ticket. As chairman of the House Armed Services Special Investigations Subcommittee, Hebert led an investigation of Defense Department procurement procedures during the 1950s. During the 1960s he opposed the Kennedy and the

Johnson Administrations' attempts to impose stronger civilian control over the Pentagon. Hebert was a strong supporter of the war in Vietnam. [See TRUMAN, EISENHOWER, KENNEDY Volumes]

With the death of Mendel Rivers (D, S.C.) [q.v.], Hebert rose to the chairmanship of the Armed Services Committee in January 1971, proclaiming that "my goal is the same as his . . . that the United States have an uncontestable military defense and overwhelming offensive power." As chairman he was considered to be less dictatorial than Rivers, but his control stayed firm into 1973.

Hebert remained a staunch supporter of the Vietnam War, backing the President's requests for defense funds, voting against the Dec. 31, 1971, deadline for mandatory withdrawal of troops and favoring the resumption of the bombing of North Vietnam in January 1973. In 1972 he forced the Armed Services to stop sending military personnel to study at universities that had banned ROTC. It was a move aimed against the schools of the Northeast, which he said was "where most of the draft-dodgers come from." He opposed the President's plans for an all-volunteer army as impractical.

Hebert's control of military spending began to erode in 1973. In July Pentagon critics and fiscal conservatives joined forces to pass an amendment to Hebert's defense procurement budget that restricted funds for weapons research and acquisition during fiscal 1974 to the same levels as 1973. The passage of the amendment, which left the Pentagon with $1.5 billion less than it had requested, marked the first time a recommendation for defense spending by the Armed Services Committee had been reversed by the House. The passage of a similar bill the following year and a rejection by the House in April 1974 of an Administration request for increased military aid to South Vietnam marked further defeats for Hebert. In 1975 the Armed Services Committee rejected President Ford's request for emergency military aid to the falling government of South Vietnam despite Hebert's efforts.

In January 1975 opponents of the seniority system, given further impetus by newly elected Democrats who regarded the Louisiana Democrat as too amenable to Pentagon pressure, succeeded in stripping Hebert of his chairmanship.

In 1976 Hebert retired after serving 36 years in the House.

[FLM]

HELMS, JESSE A.
b. Oct. 18, 1921; Monroe, N.C.
Republican Senator, N.C., 1973–.

Jesse Helms was educated at Wingate Junior College and Wake Forest College. During World War II Helms served four years in the Navy. Following the war he became city editor of the *Raleigh Times* and director of news and programs for the Tobacco Radio Network and WRAL Radio in Raleigh. In the early 1950s Helms was an administrative assistant to Sen. Willis Smith and Alton Lennon in Washington. From 1953 until 1960 Helms was executive director of the North Carolina Bankers Association. Elected to the Raleigh City Council in 1957, Helms was reelected in 1959 and served as chairman of the Law and Finance Committee. As a television commentator for WRAL-TV in Raleigh and the Tobacco Radio Network Helms criticized President Nixon for "appeasing Red China" when Nixon visited Peking.

In 1972 Helms ran for the U.S. Senate. Helms handily defeated his Democratic opponent, Rep. Nick Galifianakis, in what had been forecast as a close race. Helms won by more than 12,000 votes with 56% of the vote. Not only did Helms carry the Piedmont and western part of North Carolina, where Republicans have historically been a factor, but he carried the traditionally Democratic eastern counties by a 53% to 47% margin. Helms was assisted in the election with a campaign stint by President Nixon.

In his first term of office, Helms was one of the most conservative members of the Senate. The conservative Americans for Constitutional Action gave Helms a

100 rating in both 1973 and 1974 and again in 1976. He voted against busing, the licensing of handguns and efforts to give the President discretionary power to deal with the energy crisis. He also opposed the establishment of a consumer protection agency and federal campaign subsidies. A fiscal conservative, he proposed a balanced budget in 1975. In foreign affairs, Helms voted against reducing troop commitments abroad, foreign aid and the ban on importing Rhodesian chrome.

A strong supporter of the Vietnam war, in May 1973 Helms introduced an amendment with Sen. Robert Dole (R, Kan.) [q.v.] to weaken a bill that called for the cut off of all funds for combat activities in Cambodia and Laos. The amendment, which failed, would have delayed the fund cutoff if President Nixon determined that North Vietnam had failed to account for U.S. soldiers listed as missing in action. Helms was one of only two senators to vote against allocating over $300 million in aid to Vietnamese refugees. As an alternative, he proposed funding the refugee program with private voluntary contributions and attached a check of $1,000 to his amendment. He proposed that each member of Congress do the same. However the Senate rejected the proposal by a vote of 75 to 5.

Helms led the fight on Capitol Hill against legalized abortions. In March 1974 he proposed a constitutional amendment aimed at rescinding the 1973 Supreme Court decision upholding a woman's right to have an abortion. The amendment set out to guarantee, without exception, the right to life at the instant of conception. Two years later he proposed another constitutional amendment that would have outlawed abortions even for those women who were raped or for those whose lives were endangered by pregnancy. The Senate tabled the measure.

In February 1975 Helms called for the drafting of a conservative platform at the second annual Conservative Political Action Conference. He also headed a group of conservative Republicans, the Committee on Conservative Alternatives,

which established a panel to research state election laws in preparation for a possible third party presidential bid in 1976. That June he was one of a group of conservative Republicans who called for an "open convention" in 1976.

In the 1976 presidential campaign, Helms threw his support initially behind the candidacy of former California Gov. Ronald Reagan [q.v.]. The Senator was nominated for the vice presidency, but he withdrew his name after using the opportunity to address the Convention and call for the upholding of conservative principles.

During the Carter Administration, Helms was one of the Senate's fiercest opponents of the Panama Canal treaties. [See CARTER Volume]

[GMS]

HELMS, RICHARD M(cGARRAH)
b. March 30, 1913; St. David's, Pa.
Director of Central Intelligence, June 1966-December 1972; Ambassador to Iran, February 1973-May 1977.

After receiving his secondary education in Europe, Helms graduated from Williams College. He then worked as a news correspondent for U.P.I. Following a short stint in the Navy in 1942, he was transferred to the Office of Strategic Services (OSS), the nation's war-time intelligence gathering agency. Following the war Helms remained in the OSS and then helped organize the Central Intelligence Agency (CIA) in 1947. He moved up in the Agency to become one of its leading operatives and administrators. From 1965 to 1966 Helms served as its deputy director. He became Director of Central Intelligence in June 1966.

During Helms's tenure the Agency was involved in numerous domestic activities that were illegal under the Agency's charter, which forbade CIA operations in the U.S. except to protect intelligence sources. These efforts included mail-opening operations, projects to obtain background information on campus radicals and probes of possible foreign links with domestic anti-war groups. [See JOHNSON Volume]

The CIA was also involved in a number of projects designed to ensure the establishment and preservation of friendly foreign governments. The most dramatic of these operations was the effort to strengthen the moderate Chilean government of Eduardo Frei and prevent the election of Marxist Salvador Allende as president. During the late 1960s the Agency gave monetary support to political and intellectual groups, established leftist splinter parties to draw support away from Allende and continued propaganda and liaison activities with Chile's internal security and intelligence services to meet any threat posed by leftists.

The effort failed, and in 1970, Allende won election. At the request of President Nixon, Helms then began a top secret program to block Allende's assumption of office. Allende had to be voted into office by the Chilean Congress since he had obtained only a plurality in the general election. The CIA was to see that he did not get the vote and, if necessary, was to turn to the Chilean military for help. Funds were allocated to bribe Chilean congressmen, but this tactic proved unworkable. The Agency then investigated the possibility of kidnapping the head of the army, Gen. Rene Schneider, the most prominent military supporter of Allende. It was thought that if he were to be removed from power, the Army might act against the Marxist. The CIA cancelled its plans because it found the organization it had contacted to carry out the kidnapping ineffective. But the group still abducted Schneider who was killed resisting. The Agency's efforts were terminated, and Allende was installed in office. The CIA continued efforts to undermine him during the early 1970s and directly subsidized the strikes by Chilean middle class groups in 1972 and 1973. The strikes helped precipitate the military coup that toppled Allende in September 1973. Allende was killed during the coup.

Helms became involved in domestic politics during the Watergate controversy.

Following identification of the Watergate burglars as former CIA agents, he ascertained that they had no current connection with the Agency and developed the CIA's fundamental strategy during the investigations of the incident that followed. Helms handed down a directive to distance the CIA from the event to every extent possible. The Agency provided responses to what it considered legitimate demands from law enforcement groups but would not volunteer information. Several days after the break-in, Helms and Deputy Director Vernon Walters [q.v.] were called to the White House. There John Ehrlichman [q.v.] ordered Walters to inform the FBI that a probe of the matter would endanger CIA operations in Latin America. Walters complied, but when FBI Director L. Patrick Gray [q.v.] asked for a written statement to the effect that CIA interests were at stake before he called off the probe, Walters, at Helms's instruction, informed him that no operations were in jeopardy. As a result of Helms's actions, the CIA was kept on the periphery of the Watergate scandal.

At the end of 1972 Helms was replaced as DCI, ostensibly because of his failure to institute needed reforms in the Agency. However, former CIA operative Victor Marchetti reported that another factor in his dismissal was his connections with liberal congressmen on President Nixon's "enemies list." His refusal to cooperate during the Watergate controversy may also have been a factor. Helms was appointed ambassador to Iran in January 1973. His confirmation hearings were stormy. He was asked about CIA activities in Chile and replied that the Agency had not attempted to overthrow the government there or to pass money to Allende's opponents. He was confirmed in February.

Helms was frequently called back from his post to defend his activities as DCI during the congressional and presidential probes of the CIA from 1973 to 1976. In contrast to Director William Colby [q.v.], Helms publicly denied the existence of covert domestic projects. He asserted that the charges remained unsupported and had been "undermined by contrary evidence in the press itself." But he admitted that in collaboration with the FBI, the CIA did discover in the late 1950s and 1960s that the upsurge in radicalism was "inspired by, coordinated with, or funded by anti-American subversion mechanisms abroad."

In January 1975 the Senate Armed Services Subcommittee on Intelligence asked Helms to reconcile his previous testimony denying CIA involvement in Chile with revelations of Agency actions published in the *New York Times* and the findings of the Senate Foreign Relations Committee. Helms replied that there was "no doubt" in 1970 that former President Nixon wanted the Allende government overthrown. He admitted that the Administration had requested a "very secret probe . . . just to see if there were any forces to oppose Allende's advent as president . . . and no further effort was made along these lines." In recognizing that he might have perjured himself, Helms said that he should have stated "off the record" during the confirmation hearings that the CIA was involved in Chile. But, he added, he felt that he did not have to provide the Foreign Relations Committee with such information. He claimed that he was only obliged to discuss such a sensitive activity with the CIA Oversight Subcommittee. Critics of Helms demanded he be indicted for perjury and the Justice Department commenced an investigation.

In the fall of 1977 the Justice Department completed its probe and planned to request a perjury indictment from the grand jury. Helms's attorney, Edward Bennett Williams, informed the Department and the White House that if a trial was held he would have to subpoena secret documents. In addition, Helms was prepared to provide names of other Americans who had been in intelligence who had misled Congress. Through the process of plea bargaining, sanctioned by President Carter and Attorney General Griffin Bell, Helms's trial was averted. Helms pleaded guilty to two misdemean-

or counts for failing to answer senatorial questions "fully, completely, and accurately." He was fined $2,000 and received a two year suspended sentence. Liberals condemned the deal while Helms's defenders pointed out that all Helms was doing was trying to protect the nation. He asserted that he should never have even been indicted.

Following his retirement as ambassador in 1977, Helms opened up a consulting firm in Washington D.C.

[JB]

For further information:
Judith F. Buncher, *The C.I.A. & the Security Debate: 1971-1975* (New York, 1976).
———, *The CIA and the Security Debate: 1975-1976* (New York, 1977).
Victor Marchetti and John D. Marks, *The C.I.A. and the Cult of Intelligence* (New York, 1974).

HESBURGH, THEODORE M(ARTIN)
b. May 25, 1917; Syracuse, N.Y.
President, University of Notre Dame, 1952—; Member, United States Civil Rights Commission, November 1957-November 1972.

Hesburgh was ordained a Roman Catholic priest in 1943 and taught theology at Notre Dame before becoming the school's president in 1952. As president, he secularized the school's faculty and administration and raised its academic reputation to match the quality of Notre Dame football. He was appointed by President Dwight D. Eisenhower to the newly founded United States Commission on Civil Rights (CRC) in 1957. Hesburgh's public fame derived primarily from his involvement with the CRC, although he simultaneously served on many committees, including the National Science Board and the President's Advisory Committee on Foreign Assistance, and as a trustee of the Rockefeller Foundation.

The CRC often recommended legislation more sweeping and progressive than any acceptable to Congress or the President. Hesburgh won special notice as one of the Commission's most outspoken members. During the Johnson Administration, when the black civil rights struggle held the nation's attention, Hesburgh wrote a report protesting the low wages and miserable living conditions of Mexican migrant workers in Texas. [See KENNEDY, JOHNSON Volumes]

Seven years before, in January 1961, the CRC had issued a report charging the federal government with "a heavy responsibility for . . . discrimination against . . . Negroes." The report recommended that all federal aid be withheld from public and private colleges and universities that practice discrimination. The demand was still unsatisfied in 1970 when the Commission issued a similar report, this time proposing that federal funds be withdrawn from suburban districts that remained all or predominantly white and were adjacent to cities with concentrated black populations. Hesburgh, at that time chairman of the CRC, said with typical passion, "This Commission has had it up to here with counties and communities that have to be dragged kicking and screaming into the U.S. Constitution."

His attacks against racial discrimination in both the South and the North made him a target for accusations of hypocrisy, however, as students demanded that he increase the enrollment of blacks at his own university and other critics cited instances of his refusing to support all civil rights issues. Hesburgh contended that increasing the enrollment of blacks in colleges would not suffice to improve their educational opportunities, and he said that no college should lower its academic standards to fill quotas. He strongly advocated busing as a solution to the "hopeless" cycle of poor education in poor neighborhoods. In accepting the first Reinhold Niebuhr Award in September 1972, Hesburgh said that "unless black children are given a chance to get out of, and away from, these schools we now finally see as so bad . . . then we have destroyed the last bridge out of the ghetto,

which we also created by prejudice and often by government-financed housing policies."

This position conflicted directly with President Nixon's legislative and administrative efforts against the use of busing to achieve desegregation of schools. The Administration requested Hesburgh's resignation as chairman of the CRC shortly after Nixon's 1972 reelection, making Hesburgh the first of over 2,000 appointed officials replaced in the massive "housecleaning" of the second Nixon Administration.

In addition to his CRC activities, Hesburgh advocated setting aside land for a Palestinian homeland as a first step toward a Mideast peace settlement, on the grounds that Israel had been created to provide a homeland for the Jews. He served as the Vatican's permanent representative to the International Atomic Energy Agency in Vienna and was a member of the Carnegie Commission on Higher Education.

[AKM]

HICKEL, WALTER J(OSEPH)
b. Aug. 18, 1919; Ellinwood, Kan.
Secretary of the Interior, January 1969-November 1970.

After spending his early life in Kansas, Walter Hickel moved to Alaska in 1940, where he made a fortune with his own construction business. He later became active in Republican politics and was a supporter of Richard Nixon for the 1964 Republican presidential nomination. He was elected governor of the state in 1966. During his one term he gave top priority to the economic development of the state, particularly opening up the Arctic for mining and drilling. He often received criticism from conservationists for his neglect of environmental issues. He was one of the first governors to support Nixon for President in 1969.

Hickel's appointment as Interior Secretary sparked immediate controversy.

Known for his conservative beliefs and strong anti-environmental opinions ("A tree looking at another tree really doesn't do anything."), his confirmation was delayed in January 1969 because of extended questioning by the Senate Interior and Insular Affairs Committee. During the hearings such organizations as the Sierra Club, American Indians United, and Eskimos of the North Slope opposed his confirmation. These groups believed that Hickel was too closely allied with oil interests. Nevertheless, the Senate Committee approved Hickel's nomination by a 14-3 vote on Jan. 20.

Hickel's most important environmental decision came shortly after he took office as a result of the Santa Barbara, Calif. oil leak that occurred on Jan. 31, 1969. 235,000 gallons of crude oil spilled into the Santa Barbara channel, destroying marine and wildlife and washing oil onto 30 miles of Southern California beaches. Controversy over the accident intensified when the president of Union Oil Co., which owned the well responsible for the disaster, was widely misquoted as saying, "I am amazed at the publicity for the loss of a few birds."

On Feb. 5 Hickel ordered all drilling and pumping stopped in the channel. Twelve days later he announced regulations making all oil firms drilling on federal leases on the continental shelf responsible for cleaning up any pollution that resulted from offshore operations, whether or not the pollution resulted from company negligence.

On Feb. 27 Hickel reversed his decision and permitted Union Oil to reactivate several wells in the channel. He stated that the authorization was a safety measure to stem seepage from the ocean floor. A Presidential task force, commissioned Feb. 11 to study the spill, recommended a resumption of drilling "to prevent forever" future blowouts, because the 11-member panel had concluded that pumping the field dry was the only way to guarantee leaks would not reoccur. On June 2 Hickel authorized unlimited drilling in the channel.

During his tenure Hickel became increasingly concerned with conservation. In June 1970 he banned the use of 16 pesticides on 534 million acres of public land controlled by the Interior Department. The Department prohibited the use of DDT, aldrin, mercury compounds, as well as other pesticides.

In May 1970 Hickel clashed with Nixon over environmental policy. Angered because the Administration was unwilling to make Earth Day—held on April 22—a national holiday, and possibly influenced by the environmental concerns of his six sons, Hickel accused the Administration of failing the nation's youth. He reserved special criticism for Vice President Spiro Agnew [q.v.], accusing him of making "a continued attack on the young."

In a letter outlining his views, Hickel also appealed to the President to meet "on an individual and conversational basis" with members of the Cabinet. In his 15 months in office, Hickel had seen the President privately on only two occasions. The letter was quickly leaked to the press. After the letter was made public, Hickel was immediately cut off from several White House functions, and White House staff members began to speak of him with contempt. Thereafter a government reorganization plan was implemented that removed all major anti-pollution programs from the Interior Department.

Despite considerable pressure from the Administration, Hickel refused to resign. On Nov. 23, during a private meeting with the President, Hickel was fired as Secretary of the Interior.

In 1972 Hickel seconded Nixon's nomination at the Republican National Convention in Miami Beach. But the next year his name appeared on the Administration's "political enemies" list. In August 1974 he lost the Alaska Republican gubernatorial nomination to conservationist Jay S. Hammond. He returned to running his construction business in Anchorage, where he later built and operated an inn.

[FHM]

HICKS, LOUISE DAY
b. Oct. 16, 1919; Boston, Mass.
Democratic Representative, Mass.,
1971–73.

The daughter of a local Democratic judge, Louise Day grew up in a tightly-knit, Irish Catholic community in South Boston. She obtained a teaching certificate from Wheelock College in 1938 and taught primary grades for two years. In 1942 she married design engineer John Hicks. Hicks completed her B.S. degree in education at Boston University in 1952 and received her law degree from the same institution in 1955.

In 1961 Hicks won a seat on the Boston School Committee on a pledge to take politics out of the school board. During her first years on the Committee, Hicks compiled a moderate record, attempting to alleviate local disputes on education. However by 1963 she had come out as a supporter of the "neighborhood school" and an opponent of forced busing to achieve integration. Until 1966 she prevented the implementation of massive busing. Hicks ran unsuccessfully for mayor of Boston in 1967 under the somewhat ambiguous slogan, "You know where I stand." She contended that the central issue in the race was the "alienated voter." Hicks lost by 10,000 votes.

In 1969 Hicks ran for and was elected to the Boston City Council. Her platform skirted the racial issue, emphasizing, instead, the problems of crowded schools, street crime and the tremendous tax burden. In 1970 she campaigned successfully for retiring House Speaker John McCormack's (D, Mass.) [q.v.] seat on a platform of law and order, contending further that money spent on military operations could be better spent on inner cities.

During her one term in Congress, Hicks focused her attention on education issues. She supported legislation designed to postpone court-ordered busing and to permit voluntary prayer in schools. She pushed bills permitting direct federal aid to needy students and allowing tax credits to parents of nonpublic school students, both of which might have assisted the large number of segregated academies that arose during the late 1960s. As a result of redistricting, she lost her 1972 reelection bid.

While still in the House, Hicks attempted a second mayoral bid in 1971. She openly promised to seek repeal or amendment of the state's stiff desegregation laws. Hicks lost by over 40,000 votes out of the 180,000 cast. Hicks won reelection to the City Council in 1977, where she continued to oppose busing.

[RLN]

HILLS, CARLA A(NDERSON)
b. Jan. 3, 1934; Los Angeles, Calif.
Secretary of Housing and Urban Development, March 1975-January 1977.

Carla Anderson grew up in a wealthy family and graduated from Stanford University in 1955. Resisting her father's wish that she enter the family's building supplies business, she fulfilled her childhood ambition to become a lawyer by obtaining her LL.B. from Yale in 1958. Hills worked as an assistant attorney in the Los Angeles civil division of the Justice Department for three years before joining her husband, Roderick Hills, in private practice where she specialized in antitrust law. In 1974 Hills was appointed assistant attorney general in charge of the civil division.

Betty Ford, advocate of placing more women in top government positions, claimed part of the credit for President Ford's nomination in February 1975 of Carla Hills to succeed Fred T. Lynn [q.v.] as Secretary of Housing and Urban Development (HUD). Some members of the housing industry and Sen. William Proxmire (D, Wisc.) [q.v.], chairman of the Senate Banking, Housing, and Urban Affairs Committee protested that this was no position for someone lacking knowledge of the severely depressed housing industry. They also pointed out that Hills had had no experience in dealing with an extensive bureaucracy. Nevertheless the Senate confirmed Hills in March by a vote of 85-5.

Carla Hills brought to HUD a philosophy shared by the Ford Administration, fiscal conservatism and restrained government intervention in the economy. Hills demonstrated how that philosophy translated into housing policy in two programs legislated during the Nixon Administration.

Section 8 of the 1974 Housing and Community Development Act appropriated monies for rental subsidies to landlords to place low and moderate income level families in existing, rehabilitated, or new housing. Hills made implementation of Section 8, which had not begun, her first priority. But her emphasis was upon existing and rehabilitated housing and the policy became to "recycle" not to subsidize new public housing. As Hills explained, HUD was "no longer emphasizing clearance and removal but . . . preservation and restoration." After demanding realistic projections and temporary deadlines, Hills was able to report the initial processing of 92,000 rental units.

Section 235 of the housing law provided interest subsidies to enable low and moderate income families to become homeowners, but the program had been abandoned by Nixon and ignored by Ford until October 1975, when a General Accounting Office law suit pressured Ford into releasing $264.1 million of the funds. Hills reshaped the program to address the moderate income groups by increasing the minimum down payment required and decreasing the interest subsidy, thus limiting the risk and the fiscal generosity of the program. Hills felt that "home ownership for the poor [was] unrealistic," that, "When the plumbing backs up, when the heating acts up . . . these people do not have the wherewithal to deal with those problems."

It was Hills's administration of these two programs which became the focal point of congressional activity in the spring 1976 housing authorization and HUD appropriation bills. Democrats fought for a revival of old public housing programs by earmarking funds for that purpose and extension of Section 235. Hills objected to the revival of public housing as wasteful and expensive and protested that the earmarking of funds would destroy flexibility in HUD administration. She recommended that Ford veto the measure. The bills which passed and Ford signed did earmark funds for new construction of housing and extend section 235. But they reduced somewhat the amount of funding for new construction that Democrats had proposed, continued to place major emphasis on Section 8 rental subsidies as Hills desired, and did not change the operation of the various programs in HUD which Hills administered.

Although Hills's leadership at HUD was essentially supportive of the Ford Administration's philosophy, she did publicly oppose Ford's recalcitrant position on aid for financially crippled New York City and backed the 1975 congressional loan guarantees because bankruptcy would have retarded the housing investment market.

Hills was criticized for underutilization of appropriations and for using the Department to further Ford's 1976 election campaign. But she had earned a reputation as a professional, exacting, thorough administrator.

After Jimmy Carter's 1976 presidential victory, Hills was elected to the Board of Directors of IBM.

[JMP]

HODGSON, J(AMES) D(AY)
b. Dec. 3, 1915; Dawson, Minn.
Secretary of Labor, June 1970–February 1973.

James Day Hodgson was the product of a small Minnesota lumber town. He graduated from the University of Minnesota and a few years later moved to California. In 1941 he started working for Lockheed Aircraft Corp. as a personnel clerk. For the next 28 years, except for three years during World War II when he was a Navy officer, Hodgson remained at Lockheed. He rose to the position of vice president for industrial relations, responsible for corporate policy regarding Lockheed's 100,000 employees. As a labor negotiator, he gained the unions' respect for being "a straight-shooting management man." Hodgson was instrumental in organizing one of the first corporate efforts to hire and train the hard-core unemployed.

Hodgson accepted Nixon's offer to become undersecretary of labor in February 1969, even though the position meant a drop in salary and a change in Party allegiance from Democrat to Republican. When Secretary of Labor George Shultz [q.v.] was elevated to the newly created White House post of director of the Office of Management and Budget in June 1970, Hodgson was moved up to Labor Secretary. He was only the second businessman to serve in that post.

Hodgson's belief in encouraging employment of the disadvantaged carried over into his tenure in public office. As undersecretary, he was a prime supporter of the Philadelphia Plan, a quota system that required contractors working on federal projects in Philadelphia, and later Washington, D.C., to hire a fixed number of minorities. In July 1970, one month after his nomination, Hodgson warned the construction industry to open up more jobs for blacks or the government would enforce federal hiring quotas. The following January he proposed quota rules that would require unions to adopt "affirmative action plans." His policy would be that "decisions on work and employment will increasingly be influenced by social and human needs rather than just private purpose." In spite of strong union opposition, by that summer the Labor Department had imposed quota plans on Chicago, San Francisco, Seattle and Atlanta. Within one year 55 other cities had voluntarily adopted "home town" plans geared to their minority populations.

Nixon's stance on this program altered drastically when he was faced with an election year. In a Labor Day speech in 1972, he opposed job quotas for minority groups, calling them "a dangerous detour away from the traditional value of measuring a person on the basis of ability." Hodgson dealt with Nixon's withdrawal of support by defining the Philadelphia Plan not as a quota system but as a system of "goals and timetables" to which a "good-faith effort" must be directed. Herbert Hill, an NAACP labor director, accused Hodgson of sending a memo that implied abandonment of the Philadelphia Plan and similar programs and charged that the reason was "in large part, part of a political payoff to the AFL-CIO for its neutrality in the presidential election."

Besides the problem of persuading the construction unions to accept more minority membership, Hodgson also attacked their inflationary wage settlements. In January 1971 the Secretary noted that while the Labor Department deplored the excessive increases, it still observed a "hands-off policy." He personally felt these settlements contributed to the high 11% unemployment rate in construction. Hodgson observed that during the first nine months of 1970, construction wage increases had averaged 15.7%, in contrast to only 8% in manufacturing. In March 1971 Nixon signed an executive order setting up a primarily industry-regulated system of "constraints" to stabilize wages and prices that Hodgson had worked out with industry representatives. The objective of the wage-price plan was to keep the industry increases to about 6%. Administration officials denied that the plan represented controls. Hodgson said that he did not regard the presidential order as a policy switch but a signal that any industry that permits its wages and prices to range "far out in front" of others is "in danger of getting itself singled out by the government." At the end of 1971, Hodgson remarked that "the level of wage increases has been brought down markedly, employment is up and the industry is generally healthier than it was before this plan was put in operation."

Construction industry strikes were rife prior to the wage-price stabilization, but they were not the only labor disturbances. There were also long strikes in the coal industry and on the docks on both the East and West Coasts. Hodgson, though a firm supporter of collective bargaining, believed that strikes in the transportation industry created emergency situations. To deal with this situation, in the beginning of 1971 the Administration proposed the emergency public interest protection bill which revised procedures for settling transportation disputes. In all forms of transportation—railroads, trucking, airlines, longshore and maritime industries—the President would be empowered to end strikes. His power would include the most drastic and final step: an imposed solution. The bill became stalled in Congress, however. The following year, after a long lobbying blitz, the White House removed the bill from the legislative priority list two days before the Teamsters Union was to vote on a presidential endorsement. After the Teamsters endorsed Nixon for reelection, Hodgson admitted at a press conference that the removal of the legislation was politically motivated.

Throughout Hodgson's term in office the economy and unemployment were front-page news. The longest sustained boom in U.S. history ended in late 1969, and 1970 was a year of economic recession and high unemployment. When Hodgson took office, the unemployment rate was 5% and climbing. By September of 1970, it had hit 5.5% and in 1971 the figure hovered around the 6% mark. The figures were so depressing that in May 1971 the Labor Department stopped holding press briefings on the unemployment figures and the consumer price index. With an increase in economic activity, the figure dropped back to 5.5% in October 1972.

Because of the jobless millions, unemployment benefits were extended, and programs were developed to increase jobs in both the public and private sectors. In August of 1971 the public service jobs bill was enacted. Hodgson was given the authority to spend $1 billion to create 120,000 jobs in state, county and city government. The life of the subsidized work, however, was limited to two years. Nixon had vetoed a similar bill the year before because it did not have this provision. Job preference was given to veterans.

With the returning Vietnam veteran entering the labor market (more than three million returned to civilian life between 1969 and 1971), the problems of the jobless were intensified. In June 1971 Nixon announced a high-priority job placement program for the Vietnam veteran. At that time about 10.8% of veterans were unemployed, compared to 8.4% of nonveterans in the same age bracket. Hodgson headed the drive which was coordinated with private industry efforts. By May of the following year, Hodgson noted that almost one-fourth of the new jobs created in the U.S. in 1971 had gone to veterans, though their jobless rate was still high at 8.6%.

In June of 1971 Hodgson announced a $20 million manpower program for migrant farm laborers. The program was immediately denounced by several migrant groups because it was to be administered by the Farm Labor Service (FLS). Critics charged that the FLS had served the growers by guaranteeing them a cheap supply of labor and that it was guilty of discrimination. Although the name of the agency was changed to the Rural Manpower Service (RMS), after a 10-month study the Labor Department found many of the charges to be true. Widespread evidence pointed to discrimination against blacks, Chicanos and women and the RMS's cooperation in the exploitation of migrant workers. Hodgson admitted that past reforms had been ineffectual but promised new efforts. Farm worker and civil rights groups were unimpressed with the proposed reforms and filed suit in October of 1972 to prevent Hodgson from giving the manpower money to the RMS. The Labor Department indicated that "implementation of the reforms has begun but everything can't be done overnight."

For much of Hodgson's time in office, he was concerned with Nixon's economic policy. First, there was the 90 day wage-price freeze imposed in August of 1971, followed by a system of wage-price controls instituted in mid-November of 1971. In both Phase One and Phase Two, Hodgson was involved as a participant as a member of the Cost of Living Council and as a defender of these policies before organized labor. At the outset labor unions came out strongly critical of the freeze, complaining that profits were not frozen but workers' earnings were. Hodgson accused George Meany, president of the AFL-CIO, of being negative and "out of step" with his union members. Asked about his personal confrontation with Hodgson, Meany commented: "I don't pay much attention to the Secretary of Labor. After all, when you have a problem with the landlord, you don't discuss it with the janitor."

In August of 1971 Hodgson made a surprise visit to AFL-CIO headquarters in Washington and pledged to Meany that organized labor would be consulted on any controls retained after the 90-day freeze. Labor was not mollified, and at the AFL-CIO Executive Council meeting in February 1972, the members attacked Nixon's economic programs. For the first time in the union's 17-year history, the Secretary of Labor was not invited to speak at the meeting. Nevertheless with adroit handling Nixon gained labor's neutrality in the upcoming November election.

Following Nixon's reelection Hodgson resigned ostensibly because he wanted to return to private life. However he appeared to have become a casualty of the President's continuing effort to dissolve labor's alliance with the Democratic Party. His replacement was a construction union president, Peter Brennan [q.v.]. In February 1973 Hodgson rejoined Lockheed as vice president for corporate relations. In June 1974 he was named ambassador to Japan and served until 1977.

[MW]

HOFFA, JAMES R(IDDLE)
b. Feb. 14, 1913; Brazil, Ind.
d. presumed, July 1975.
President, International Brotherhood of Teamsters, Chauffeurs, Warehousemen and Helpers of America, 1957-71.

Because of his father's death, Hoffa had to quit school to support his family. After moving to Detroit, he became involved in the activities of the Teamsters union, heading Local 299 at the age of 18. During the 1940s Hoffa gained control of the entire Midwestern branch of the organization as leader of the Central States Drivers Council. To achieve such power Hoffa had no reservations about using strong-arm tactics to win contracts or destroy rivals. He made alliances with Chicago's Capone mob and Detroit's Purple Gang to protect his activities and in exchange employed hoodlums as business agents and secretly channeled union dues to finance illegal activities. Businessmen that had connections with organized crime, or that solicited its help, received preferential treatment from Hoffa in contract negotiations. The terms of such "sweetheart contracts" enriched Hoffa's leaders and the mobsters. In 1952 Hoffa became a Teamsters vice president. Five years later he succeeded Dave Beck, who was indicted for tax fraud, as president of the corrupt International Brotherhood of Teamsters (IBT).

From 1957 to 1961 Sen. John McClellan's (D, Ark.) [q.v.] Permanent Investigations Subcommittee heard testimony detailing Hoffa's links with organized crime and the embezzlement and misuse of union dues and pension funds. When Robert F. Kennedy, who had served as chief counsel to the subcommittee, became Attorney General in 1961, he organized a "Get Hoffa" task force in the Justice Department to put the union leader behind bars. Meanwhile Hoffa attempted to portray himself as a reformed labor statesman and issued a ban on sweetheart contracts. In 1963 he was charged with jury tampering in Nashville. Concurrently he was indicted in Chicago for pension fraud. Found guilty of both charges, Hoffa was sentenced to 13 years in prison. He began serving his term in 1967. Hoffa left the day-to-day operation of the union to his loyal national vice president, Frank Fitzsimmons [q.v.], but he did not resign the IBT presidency formally until June 1971. Running the union from his prison cell, Hoffa coordinated contract negotiations and had the final say about the investment of pension funds. [See EISENHOWER, KENNEDY, JOHNSON Volumes]

After Nixon won the presidency, White House aide John Ehrlichman [q.v.] began to press for a pardon for Hoffa. Reports circulated that the Teamsters had secretly donated $100,000 to the Nixon campaign to secure Hoffa's release from prison. Hoffa was still popular with the union, and the Administration believed a pardon would improve Nixon's position with labor, which for the most part had been distrustful of him.

But the pardon did not come immediately. Presidential assistant Charles Colson [q.v.], a close friend of Fitzsimmons, prevailed on Nixon to keep Hoffa in jail until after the union elections in 1971 so that he could not challenge Fitzsimmons for the presidency. Colson succeeded in blocking the Hoffa pardon until Fitzsimmons won election in July. To protect Fitzsimmons from a future Hoffa challenge, Nixon issued a Christmas pardon that barred Hoffa from engaging in union activity for nine years.

Nixon's action ingratiated his standing with the union rank and file, who still revered Hoffa and were unaware of how Colson and their leader intrigued to keep him in jail. Fitzsimmons was indebted to Nixon for keeping Hoffa in jail long enough to consolidate his control of the union. A frequent golfing partner of the President, Fitzsimmons had, among union leaders, the closest relationship with the President. Teamster donations aided Nixon in his 1972 reelection campaign. For his role in the Hoffa affair, Colson became the union's general counsel in 1973.

In addition to the ban on his participation in union affairs, Hoffa was placed un-

der constant surveillance. Ostensibly he toured the nation lecturing on prison reform, but he secretly discussed Teamster activities with those disturbed by Fitzsimmons' conduct. He learned that Fitzsimmons had approved huge loans from the pension fund to gangsters, a practice Hoffa began to discourage in the 1960s. Hoffa was also angered by Fitzsimmons' refusal to continue his ban on sweetheart contracts, which had enriched the organizations of crime figures Anthony Provenzano and Anthony Giacalone, former Hoffa associates with whom Fitzsimmons had developed close relationships.

Lester Velie, author of *Desperate Bargain: Why Jimmy Hoffa Had to Die* (1977), speculated that Hoffa's reform efforts angered organized crime, which seemed to have had a lock on Fitzsimmons. In July 1975 Hoffa left his Detroit home to meet Giacalone and Provenzano. He was not heard from again and presumably was executed by mobsters. Provenzano and Giacalone denied knowledge of the meeting or the reasons for Hoffa's disappearance.

[JB]

For further information:
Walter Sheridan, *The Fall and Rise of Jimmy Hoffa* (New York, 1972).
Lester Velie, *Desperate Bargain: Why Jimmy Hoffa Had to Die* (New York, 1977).

HOFFMAN, JULIUS J(ENNINGS)
b. July 7, 1895; Chicago, Ill.
U.S. District Judge, 1953–1971.

Julius Hoffman was the son of German Jewish immigrants. Raised on Chicago's North Side, he attended Northwestern University and received his B.A. in 1912 and a law degree in 1915. He was admitted to the Illinois bar in 1915 and began a highly successful practice as a corporate lawyer. A substantial contributor to the Republican Party, Hoffman served as a superior court judge in Cook County from 1947 to 1953. Appointed to the U.S. District Court for Northern Illinois in 1953, he presided over many widely publicized trials of Chicago mobsters during the 1950s and early 1960s.

Hoffman received national attention in 1969 and 1970 as presiding judge in the famous Chicago conspiracy trial. On March 20, 1969, eight radicals and anti-war activists, including Tom Hayden [q.v.], Bobby Seale [q.v.] and David Dellinger, were indicted on charges of conspiracy and of crossing state lines with intent to riot in connection with demonstrations at the 1968 Democratic National Convention in Chicago. The indictments were the first under the anti-riot provisions of the 1968 Civil Rights Act, and the trial was seen as a test of the limits of dissent. The trial began on Sept. 24, 1969, and throughout the proceedings the courtroom was the scene of heated confrontations between Judge Hoffman and the defendants and their lawyers.

The trial opened with procedural battles between Hoffman and defense lawyers William Kunstler [q.v.] and Leonard Weinglass. Hoffman denied several pretrial motions presented by the defense and then ordered the arrest of four absent defense lawyers on charges of contempt. The lawyers, who were hired only to work on pretrial preparations, had written to Hoffman to ask that they be excused, a standard judicial procedure. Hoffman's contempt sentence was condemned by many lawyers, and on Sept. 29 over 150 attorneys picketed the court building. That same day a U.S. court of appeals overruled Hoffman and allowed the defense lawyers to be excused in writing.

During the first weeks of the trial, controversy centered around defendant Bobby Seale, national chairman of the Black Panther Party. Seale's lawyer, Charles Garry, had been unable to appear in court for the trial's opening since he was recuperating from surgery in a California hospital. Hoffman refused Seale's request for a delay and instead ordered William Kunstler, attorney for the other defendants, to represent Seale. Kunstler did so under protest, but Seale adamantly demanded to conduct his own defense. When Hoffman denied Seale's request, the defendant accused Hoffman of being

a "racist" and a "fascist." After numerous outbursts, Hoffman had Seale gagged and shackled in the courtroom, on Oct. 29, over the protests of Kunstler and the other defendants. On Nov. 5, Hoffman declared a mistrial for Seale, severed his case from the others, and set April 23, 1970, as the date for a new trial. He also convicted Seale of 16 counts of contempt of court, sentenced him to four years in prison, and denied bail pending appeal, calling Seale "a dangerous man."

Courtroom confrontations continued after the removal of Seale. Kunstler tried to demonstrate that the defendants were being tried for their political beliefs, that the police had engaged in deliberate provocation and had initiated the violence in Chicago, and that actions to oppose the Vietnam war were within the constitutional rights of the defendants. His attempts to prove his case by calling respected political figures as defense witnesses were stymied, however, by Hoffman's rulings. On Jan. 28 Hoffman denied the defense request to call former Attorney General Ramsey Clark [q.v.] as a witness. On Feb. 2 Hoffman similarly prevented civil rights leader Ralph Abernathy [q.v.] from testifying for the defendants. The decision provoked a sharp interchange with Kunstler who told Hoffman that "these men are going to jail by virtue of a legal lynching and your honor is wholly responsible."

Minutes after the jury retired to deliberate on Feb. 14, Hoffman handed down heavy contempt-of-court sentences against all of the defendants. The following day he convicted attorneys Weinglass and Kunstler of contempt, sentenced Kunstler to four years in prison, and accused him of a deliberate effort to "continuously disrupt the administration of justice and sabotage the functioning of the federal judicial system." When the jury returned a guilty verdict against five of the defendants on charges of intent to riot (all of the defendants were acquitted of conspiracy charges and two of them, John Froines and Lee Weiner, were acquitted of the riot charge), Hoffman handed down the maximum five-year sentence and refused to release the defendants and their lawyers on bail.

Hoffman's behavior and rulings during the trial received heavy criticism. The Board of Directors of the American Civil Liberties Union called his contempt sentences "extraordinary and unconstitutional," and former Supreme Court Justice Arthur Goldberg [*q.v.*] released a similar statement. On March 31, 134 Wall Street lawyers petitioned the United States Judicial Conference "to investigate and consider the censure and condemnation" of Hoffman for his courtroom actions. The contempt sentences also provoked demonstrations of student radicals in cities across the country.

Over the succeeding months and years, most of Hoffman's judicial decisions in the conspiracy trial were overturned. On Feb. 28, 1970, a U.S. court of appeals released all of the convicted defendants and their lawyers on bail pending appeal. In May 1972 an appeals court ordered a retrial on the contempt-of-court sentences, and in November the riot convictions were overturned due to improper rulings and conduct by Hoffman. In its decision, the appeals court rebuked Hoffman in unusually emphatic terms for his "deprecatory and often antagonistic attitude toward the defense." In January 1973 the Justice Department announced that it would not seek a retrial on the riot charges.

Meanwhile, District Judge Edward T. Gignoux was placed in charge of the contempt trial of the defendants and their lawyers. In November 1972 he dropped the charges against Seale and reduced the other sentences to 177 days. The following year he handed down his final decision in the case. Acquitting Froines, Weiner, Weinglass, and Hayden of contempt, he nonetheless found defendants Dellinger, Abbie Hoffman, Jerry Rubin and Kunstler guilty, but declined to impose any sentence, citing the improper behavior of Judge Hoffman as his reason.

On Dec. 1, 1971, Hoffman retired from the bench at the age of 76.

[JD]

HOLIFIELD, CHET (CHESTER) (EARL)

b. Dec. 3, 1903; Mayfield, Ky.
Democratic Representative, Calif., 1943-75; Chairman, Joint Committee on Atomic Energy, 1961-63, 1965-67, 1969-70; Chairman, Government Operations Committee, 1970-75.

After dropping out of high school, Chet Holifield ran away from home in Arkansas and became a presser in a California cleaning shop. In 1921 he helped set up a family cleaning and pressing store, which was later converted to a retail clothing concern.

Holifield became involved in local Democratic politics during the 1930s, and won his first election from California's 19th congressional district in 1942. As an incumbent he often won 60% of the vote from a district composed of both poor and affluent neighborhoods.

Holifield was considered a liberal Democrat early in his career, involving himself primarily in congressional reform and labor issues. In 1957 he helped organize and lead the Democratic Study Group, a small liberal caucus seeking to reform congressional practices. His early efforts on behalf of prolabor legislation brought Holifield continued support in his strongly blue-collar district. Although less active in labor issues during the 1970s, he received a 15-year cumulative rating from the AFL-CIO's committee on Political Education, compiled in 1971, that showed 99 votes for labor-supported bills and only three against. [See EISENHOWER, KENNEDY, JOHNSON Volume]

Holifield's support of the military, however, severely tarnished his liberal reputation. In 1966 he voted in favor of military appropriations for the war in Vietnam and signed, with 77 other Democrats, a statement supporting supplemental funding. In the early 1970s Holifield repeatedly voted against legislation limiting funds or manpower for U.S. efforts in Indochina. He also favored development of anti-ballistic missiles, B-1 bombers and the Navy's F-1 fighter; he voted against three 1971 bills inhibiting these projects. In 1972, however, he voted in favor of a Democratic resolution denouncing the U.S. bombing of North Vietnam.

A consistent advocate of nuclear power development, Holifield was appointed to the newly formed Joint Committee on Atomic Energy in 1947. He rotated the Committee's leadership with Rep. John Pastore (D, R.I.) [q.v.] throughout the 1960s until his appointment as chairman of the Government Operations Committee in 1970. He remained the panel's ranking Democrat, however.

In November 1970 Holifield publicly supported a $2 billion breeder reactor program and asked it be given "the same priority we gave to the development of nuclear weapons in the 1940s and to the space effort in the 1960s." When considering the 1974 atomic energy appropriations authorization, he argued against an amendment that would have halted construction of nuclear plants for one year pending safety studies. Said Holifield: "I am constantly amazed at people . . . who want to turn back the clock." If the "nervous Nellies and doubting Thomases had their way," he continued, "we would still be sitting in caves with our ancestors beside a wood fire. . . ."

As chairman of the Government Operations Committee, Holifield gave considerable attention to the formation of an independent consumer protection agency. In 1974 he introduced a bill that would have permitted the consumer protection agency (CPA) to represent consumer interests before other federal bureaus in both formal and informal proceedings, given the agency indirect subpoena power and allowed the CPA to appeal other agency rulings in court. Despite protests from consumer groups that the measure was not strong enough, it passed the full House. A stronger bill was killed by filibuster in the Senate, ending the possibility of the establishment of a consumer protection agency that year.

Holifield retired from the House at the end of the 93rd Congress.

[RB]

HOLLOWAY, JAMES L(EMUEL), III
b. Feb. 23, 1922; Charleston, S.C.
Chief of Naval Operations, July 1974-July 1978.

Holloway, whose father was an admiral, graduated from Annapolis and was commissioned an ensign in 1942. He served on destroyers during World War II in both the Atlantic and Pacific Fleets. After the war he gained experience in staff positions and in the Navy's air wing, serving as the executive officer of a fighter squadron in Korea. In 1961 he attended the National War College. He was given command of the aircraft carrier USS *Enterprise* in 1965 and promoted to admiral a year later. As commander of Carrier Division Six, Holloway directed operations in the eastern Mediterranean during the 1970 Jordanian crisis. He was named commander of the Seventh Fleet stationed off Vietnam in 1972 and appointed vice chief of Naval Operations the following year.

Holloway succeeded Adm. E. R. Zumwalt, Jr. [q.v.], as chief of naval operations in July 1974. At the time of his retirement Zumwalt had provoked a controversy by questioning whether the U.S. Navy would be able to preserve its control of vital sea lanes in the event of a war with the Soviet Union. Holloway responded in October that the Navy would continue to maintain its superiority over the Soviet Union's naval forces. He argued that U.S. naval power lay in its 15 aircraft carriers, superior nuclear submarines, specialized surface ships and "more imaginative, resourceful, combat-experienced personnel." He saw Soviet naval strength in the size of its submarine fleet and its anti-ship missiles. He noted, however, that Soviet naval effectiveness was lessened by a limited capacity for operations outside of the Mediterranean Sea.

As chief of naval operations Zumwalt had initiated a series of sweeping reforms. Soon after he replaced Zumwalt,

Holloway countered that policy announcing he would institute a period of consolidation. As an example he said that the accent on youth in command would be tempered by the need to maintain an experienced staff.

Faced with continuing inflation in the mid-1970s, Holloway reemphasized smaller, much faster ships with high firepower in his efforts to carry out the modernization of the surface fleet begun under his predecessor. Top Navy officials came to believe that the Department had seriously miscalculated by thinking that funds for modernization could be freed by retiring older vessels and reducing the size of the fleet. From a peak of 976 vessels in 1968, fleet strength had dropped to a low of 508 by mid-1976. Holloway's plans projected a fleet of 600 or mre vessels, including 230 major combat ships, in the 1980s. However, he eventually supported Secretary of Defense James R. Schlesinger's [q.v.] decisions to extend the timetable for the construction of Trident submarines and to construct medium-sized aircraft carriers rather than supercarriers in the future.

With the end of the U. S. military involvement in Vietnam and the fall of Saigon in 1975, the relative military strengths of the U. S. and the Soviet Union became the dominant national security issue. Holloway retreated from his previous assessment of U. S. naval preeminence in May 1976 when he told the Senate Armed Services Committee that the U. S. enjoyed "a thin margin of maritime superiority in a majority of scenarios that have the greatest vital interest to us." To preserve this lead Holloway focused on improving anti-submarine warfare systems to counter the Soviet submarine fleets, and he supported the development of tactical and strategic cruise missiles.

Holloway continued as chief of naval operations in the early years of the Carter Administration. In 1978 he was succeeded as chief of Naval Operations by Adm. Thomas B. Hayward.

[SF]

HOLTZMAN, ELIZABETH
b. Aug. 11, 1941; New York, N.Y.
Democratic Representative, N.Y., 1973–.

Elizabeth Holtzman, the daughter of a lawyer and a professor, graduated from Radcliffe in 1962 and Harvard Law School in 1965. In 1970, after two years in a New York State law firm and an appointment as mayoral assistant in the Lindsay administration, Holtzman was elected Democratic state committeewoman from Flatbush. In 1972 Holtzman ran against veteran Rep. Emanuel Celler (D, N.Y.) [q.v.], powerful chairman of the House Judiciary Committee, who had represented the 16th congressional district for 50 years. Campaigning with less than $50,000 against Celler's support of the Vietnam war, his anti-ERA vote, and his insensitivity to the needs of his constituency, she won the primary and the general election.

In the House, Holtzman established a solidly liberal record. She received a 100 rating from the liberal Americans for Democratic Action and the AFL-CIO's Committee on Political Education. Holtzman's legislative aspirations were clear: stop the war in Southeast Asia, reduce defense budget and reestablish the solution of domestic social problems as the nation's first priority. In foreign affairs and defense matters, she supported the cutoff of arms aid to Turkey and opposed the development of the anti-ballistic missile and the B-1 bomber. In domestic issues she supported busing, government aid for abortion and the Equal Rights Amendment. She backed conservation and consumer protection legislation. Coming from an area dependent on mass transit, Holtzman voted for subsidies for public transit systems.

During her first term Holtzman played a significant role in formulating the rules of evidence for federal courts. After President Nixon ordered the bombing of Cambodia in early 1973, a number of bills were introduced to prohibit bombing after Aug. 15, 1973. In addition Congress began creating legislation to define the President's power to conduct war. The result was the War Powers Act, passed over Nixon's veto in November 1973. Holtzman refused to vote for these bills because they gave congressional sanction to the bombing of Cambodia up until Aug. 15, and in stipulating what the President could do, they conferred war-making power on the President.

Instead, on April 18, 1973, Holtzman filed suit in U.S. district court in New York to enjoin the Cambodia bombings on the grounds that they had not been authorized by Congress and were therefore unconstitutional. On July 25 a federal court ordered a halt to the bombings within 48 hours and then allowed a stay of the order until the government could obtain a hearing on appeal. The decision was overturned on appeal. Convinced that a definitive ruling on the need for congressional authorization of war was vitally important, especially for an era in which a President could initiate a nuclear war, Holtzman pressed an appeal to the Supreme Court. On Aug. 13 Chief Justice Warren Burger [q.v.] denied the request for a hearing. Holtzman voted in November to override the Nixon veto of the War Powers Act. In December she successfully fought for an amendment to the National Energy Emergency Act that prohibited the export of petroleum products for military purposes in Southeast Asia.

During the nationally televised House Judiciary debates in July 1974 on the impeachment of President Nixon, Holtzman earned a reputation for her well-reasoned, competent argument in support of a broad definition of impeachment. Holtzman voted for all five of the articles of impeachment and specifically supported an article that charged the President with illegally and secretly invading Cambodia in 1970. The Committee defeated the article.

When President Ford appeared before the Criminal Justice Subcommittee in October 1974 to submit to questions on the pardon of President Nixon, Holtzman, incensed at the subcommittee's intent to conduct a mild, pro forma hearing, objected to the five-minute time limit on questions and hurled a series of politically explosive questions at Ford. "Why was no crime cited, no guilt confessed. Why was the action done in haste and secrecy without consultation with the Attorney General or the special prosecutor?"

In 1975 Holtzman won an assignment to the Budget Committee, where she fought unsuccessfully for the passage of a budget that stated national priorities. Holtzman continued her opposition to large defense appropriations and her defense of women's rights.

[JMP]

HOOVER, J(OHN) EDGAR
b. Jan. 1, 1895; Washington, D.C.
d. May 2, 1972; Washington, D.C.
Director, Federal Bureau of Investigation, 1924–72.

J. Edgar Hoover supported himself through George Washington University Law School by working days as an indexer for the Library of Congress. After obtaining his law degree, he began his lifelong association with the Justice Department as a clerk in 1916. He assisted Attorney General A. Mitchell Palmer in the roundup of Communists during the Red Scare of 1919–1920. As a result of his performance, he was appointed assistant director of the Department's Bureau of Investigation (the name was changed in 1935 to the Federal Bureau of Investigation). In 1924 Attorney General Harlan Fiske Stone appointed Hoover, known for his integrity and dedication, to take over the scandal-ridden, politicized bureau. During Hoover's long tenure as head of the Bureau, he oversaw the vast expansion of the FBI's power. In the 1930s and 1940s the Bureau was given authority to investigate all major interstate crimes and monitor those on the right and on the left suspected of subversive activities. The Bureau also kept President Franklin Roosevelt informed on the activities of his political enemies. The security needs of World War II further enhanced Hoover's power. His agents tracked down Nazi and Japanese spies, used the security pretext to spy on the activities of unions and civil rights organizations whose conduct Hoover and the Administration deemed detrimental to national unity, and kept a close surveillance on American Communists. The director promised that all these pursuits would be terminated when the national emergency had ended. America's entry into the Cold War, however, justified the retention of Hoover's power.

In the postwar period Hoover was particularly concerned about Communist infiltration of the American left, and during the McCarthy era, he played a major role in the government's loyalty programs and investigations. In the Eisenhower years the FBI continued to investigate the loyalty of civil servants with expanded authority to conduct wiretaps. Hoover, by that point the self-proclaimed expert on American communism, continued his campaign to urge Americans to ferret out subversives from the nation's life. Using Communists as a catch-all for all dissenters, Hoover questioned the patriotism of such movements as those lobbying for free speech, civil rights, disarmament, academic freedom, and increased trade and cultural contacts with the Communist world. During the 1950s Hoover's agents made a number of spectacular spy arrests and continued the policy of observing the activities of Administration opponents. [See TRUMAN, EISENHOWER Volumes]

In the 1960s the Bureau carried out a series of operations of questionable constitutionality against civil rights organizations and radical groups that Hoover considered subversive. COINTELPRO, as the operation was known, had originally begun in 1956 against the Communist Party of the United States. But in the 1960s it was expanded to include the Southern Christian Leadership Conference and the Congress of Racial Equality. It also carried out operations against the Socialist Workers Party, white-hate groups such as the Ku Klux Klan and black power groups such as the Black Panthers. COINTELPRO operations included sending anonymous

or fictitious materials to groups to create internal dissension; leaking of informant-based or nonpublic information to friendly media sources; using informants to disrupt group activities; informing employers, credit bureaus and creditors of member's activities; informing or contacting businesses and persons with whom members had economic dealings of the members' activities; attempting to use religious and civic leaders and organizations in disruptive activities; and informing family or others of radical or supposed immoral activities. Probably the most controversial activity was inciting radicals to commit illegal acts. The FBI also conducted illegal wiretaps, including the bugging of members of Congress. [See KENNEDY, JOHNSON Volumes]

Beginning in 1971 revelations of these questionable activities embarrassed Hoover and the Bureau. Anti-war activists raided the Media, Pa., FBI office and stole confidential documents damaging to the Bureau. These were published in a number of leading newspapers including *The New York Times* and *The Washington Post*. Liberal senators and representatives also began waging a campaign against the Bureau by publicizing the extra-constitutional activities of the FBI. Individuals and organizations believing they had been harassed by Hoover released anti-FBI material obtained through the Freedom of Information Act of 1966. Investigative reporting by newspapers and radio and TV networks contributed to a demand for a thorough appraisal of the Bureau and the conduct of its leader.

In response to the growing leaks, Hoover ended COINTELPRO in 1971. During his last years in office, he flatly denied any wrongdoing. President Nixon, Vice President Spiro Agnew [q.v.] and Attorney General John Mitchell [q.v.] backed Hoover's claims that the accusations were a cheap ploy by Democrats and liberals to embarrass the Administration and undermine the FBI chief. Hoover tried to distract critics of the Bureau by announcing in 1972 the existence of a plot hatched by the Rev. Philip Berrigan and other militant anti-war Catholics to kidnap Henry

Kissinger [q.v.] and blow up buildings in Washington.

Although Hoover was not adverse to the extra-constitutional activities of the Bureau, he did resist the attempts by the Nixon Administration to centralize all countersubversive operations in the White House. In July 1970 Tom Charles Huston, coordinator of security affairs for the White House, sent a memorandum to H. R. Haldeman [q.v.] suggesting the creation of a "working group consisting of the top domestic intelligence officials" of the FBI, CIA, Defense Intelligence Agency, National Security Agency and the three military services. Huston recommended an increase in "electronic surveillance and penetrations" of both "individuals and groups in the United States who pose a major threat to the internal security"; the removal of all restrictions on legal mail covers; the lifting of restrictions against surreptitious entry or burglary to obtain vitally needed material; and an expansion of the monitoring of "violence-prone and student-related groups." Hoover objected to the plan, not for constitutional reasons, but because he felt it threatened his authority. He persuaded Mitchell and Haldeman to force Huston to withdraw the recommendation.

Amidst all the turmoil surrounding his years as director, especially the growing demand that he retire or be ousted, Hoover died on May 2, 1972. President Nixon and the rest of the Administration joined leading American conservatives in eulogizing Hoover as a patriot. Yet just before his death Hoover's popularity slipped in the public opinion polls. A Harris poll reported that the American people were evenly split concerning Hoover's performance in office. Even members of the Administration had seriously contemplated forcing Hoover to retire following the 1972 election.

In 1975 and 1976 the Church Committee held hearings on intelligence activities not only of the FBI but also the CIA and other information-gathering groups. From its hearings as well as earlier accusations made against the Bureau, the nation learned of the extensive illegal operations conducted during Hoover's years in office.

[JB]

HOWE, IRVING
b. June 11, 1920; New York, N.Y.
Literary critic; editor, *Dissent*.

Born of Russian immigrant Jews, Howe was brought up in the slums of Manhattan's Lower East Side and the East Bronx. As a teenager he joined a socialist youth organization and became a Trotskyist. Upon graduation from City College in 1940, he started graduate study at Brooklyn College but left after a term to enlist in the Army. Following World War II Howe began a career as a writer and emerged during the 1950s and 1960s as a leading critic of the American social and political scene. In 1953 Howe with other socialists founded the magazine *Dissent*, which was dedicated to publishing the precepts of social democracy and democratic socialism. In the 1950s *Dissent* was involved in defending the civil liberties of American Communists and criticizing the "smug conformity" of formerly radical intellectuals to American society. *Dissent* became an organ of intellectuals on the Democratic Left.

Initially Howe and other Democratic leftists admired the New Left for its emphasis on "participatory democracy" and saw it as a means of revitalizing the Democratic Party. But later New Left denunciations of liberal policies and the Democratic Party dampened his hopes. The Vietnam war intensified the rift between the liberals and the New Left as the antiwar movement urged civil disobedience, particularly violent and general resistance to the draft, as the way to end the war. Howe condemned the anti-war demonstrators' tactics as "apocalyptic" and "kamikaze," a subordination of ideology to suit personal style and a rejection of "democracy as an indispensable part of civilized life." [See JOHNSON Volume]

After 1970 Howe became concerned

over the Arab-Israeli conflict, calling for American support and the preservation of Israel. He decried the anti-Israeli and, in some radical camps, anti-Semitic attitudes prevailing in American politics. In an article published in 1972, Howe declared the survival of democratic Israel not only essential to averting a possible world war initiated in the Middle East but an "urgent moral-political necessity." However he found disturbing Israeli partiality for the Nixon camp, which had promised U.S. military aid. Howe and his associates viewed the minority of extremely wealthy Jews and formerly radical intellectuals who shifted support to Nixon as part of the general disenchantment with the liberal-left politics of the 1960s and a rising tide of "new conservatism."

In the 1972 presidential elections, Howe questioned the endorsement of Nixon by distinguished intellectuals who saw him as a "prudent" candidate, and he actively supported Sen. George McGovern (D, S.D.) [q.v.].

The outbreak of the Watergate scandal in 1972 drew Howe's vehement criticism of former supporters of Nixon. He maintained that the scandal revealed a disintegration of the confidence and belief in formal values of American society. In highly emotional articles published in *Dissent* in 1973 and 1974, Howe denounced Nixon as a "cheap little man," "local grifter" and a "nasty petty-bourgeois" and demanded his immediate dismissal from office as essential for the preservation of American democracy and the welfare state. He used the impact of Watergate to question the credibility of the "new conservatives" and in a book he edited on the new conservatives in 1974, he accused them of condoning "a crude Marxized version of society in behalf of Nixonite politics." Following Nixon's resignation Howe continued to harangue the new right on its political and moral principles and to reiterate that democratic radicalism emphasized "rationality and intelligence, for the life of the mind as a human dedication."

Deeply interested in Yiddish literature

and culture, Howe in 1976 published a 714-page study on the experiences of Eastern European Jews in American society. *The World of Our Fathers*, which focused on Jewish socialism, their labor movement and secular cultures was widely praised by critics and became a bestseller, selling over 120,000 copies by early 1978.

[LW]

HRUSKA, ROMAN L(EE)
b. Aug. 16, 1904; David City, Neb.
Republican Senator, Neb., 1954-77.

Born in a rural Nebraska Czech community, Hruska earned his law degree from Omaha's Creighton University College of Law in 1929. He engaged in private practice until he entered the House as a Republican in 1953. The following year he won a special election to the Senate. Throughout the Eisenhower, Kennedy, and Johnson years Hruska compiled one of the most conservative records in the Upper House. He enjoyed near perfect ratings from the conservative Americans for Constitutional Action. Hruska opposed urban aid, Medicare, federal aid to housing, and gun control legislation. He voted for the major civil rights legislation but opposed busing. Sitting on the Judiciary Committee, Hruska cast votes against antitrust legislation and improved regulation of business. Hruska's strict laissez-faire beliefs did not influence his consistent support for legislation beneficial to his state's farming and cattle interests. An avowed anti-Communist, who began his political career as an admirer of Sen. Joseph R. McCarthy (R, Wisc.), Hruska opposed any attempt to relax Cold War tensions and backed the Johnson Vietnam War policies. [See EISENHOWER, KENNEDY, and JOHNSON Volumes]

During the Nixon-Ford years Hruska was the ranking Republican member of the Judiciary Committee. In this capacity, he had great power in determining the nation's legal legislation. Campaigning for Hruska in 1970, Richard Nixon called him "Mr. Law Enforcement." The Nebraska senator helped shape the Omnibus Crime Control and Safe Street Act of 1968 and, two years later, the Omnibus Crime Control Act of 1970. Both laws increased federal anticrime assistance. Hruska introduced a number of amendments to the second act which made it illegal to invest money derived from criminal activities. This, Hruska hoped, would strengthen the federal prosecution of organized crime. Hruska's opposition to gun control legislation gratified the National Rifle Association. Speaking for the sportsmen, whom Hruska believed gun control would penalize, he led the campaign that successfully prevented meaningful regulation. In his committee, Hruska also opposed attempts to provide federal aid for legal help to the poor.

Hruska gained national attention in 1970 during the congressional battle for confirmation of President Nixon's conservative nominees to the Supreme Court. During the Johnson years Hruska had voted for all the President's liberal appointments; therefore, he expected liberals to do the same with Nixon's conservative choices. The opposition to Clement Haynsworth [q.v.] incensed Hruska. He was G. Harrold Carswell's [q.v.] principal defender. Hruska found him to be "well qualified and well-suited for the post . . . learned in the law . . . experienced . . . a man of integrity." To the press Hruska responded to the charges that Carswell was mediocre by saying "Even if he were mediocre there are a lot of mediocre judges and people and lawyers, and they are entitled to a little representation aren't they? We can't have all Brandeises, Frankfurters, and Cardozos."

Hruska also waged a campaign against consumer legislation. His threat to filibuster a 1970 bill that would permit consumers to join together in class action suits against defective goods killed the measure. He unsuccessfully led the forces in 1971 to delete money from an appropriations bill for the Federal Trade Commission to enable it to study methods to improve consumer grievance procedures. Hruska thought the bill would enhance the power of bureaucrats in Washington.

In foreign and defense matters Hruska backed the Nixon-Ford policies. He remained an enthusiastic supporter of the Vietnam war. Hruska voted for all the defense spending proposals including the ABM. In 1970, running in one of the most Republican states in the nation Hruska barely won reelection. He decided to retire in 1976.

[JB]

HUGHES, HAROLD E(VERETT)
b. Feb. 10, 1922; Ida Grove, Iowa.
Democratic Sen., Iowa, 1969-75.

Born and raised in rural poverty, Harold Hughes attended the University of Iowa for a short time before being called into the Army in late 1942. Following his discharge in 1945 Hughes returned to his home state to become a truck driver. For the next seven years Hughes struggled with alcoholism, and through his involvement with the Methodist Church and Alcoholics Anonymous, he was able to overcome the habit. Hughes then made a lifelong commitment to serve his church. For a while he even contemplated entering the ministry. In the mid-1950s Hughes worked as a trucking association executive. He became involved in state politics and was elected governor in 1962. During his four years in office, Hughes was responsible for modernizing the state's services in such areas as prisons and hospitals and creating a civil rights commission. He won a seat in the Senate in 1968. [See JOHNSON Volume]

Hughes entered the Senate with two overriding interests: ending the Vietnam War and dealing with the problem of alcohol and drug abuse. His first major speech was in opposition to the war. He became one of the nation's most popular anti-war politicians. Hughes voted for the major resolutions to end the war such as the Cooper-Church, McGovern-Hatfield, and the Mansfield Amendments. Hughes was also a leading critic of the Administration's defense policies. Sitting on the

Armed Services Committee, Hughes cast numerous negative votes against new weapons systems. In 1969 he was one of the leaders against the deployment of the ABM missile system. His amendment to totally scrap the project, far more ambitious than the Cooper-Hart resolution, failed by a large measure.

As chairman of the Armed Services Subcommittee on Drug Abuse in the Armed Forces, Hughes worked for a more humane federal policy for alcoholics and drug addicts. His committee conducted hearings throughout the nation to gather material for new legislation. The Senate unanimously passed the Comprehensive Alcohol Abuse and Alcoholism Prevention, Treatment, and Rehabilitation Act of 1970 which provided funds for treatment and educational opportunities for alcoholics. Although President Nixon signed the bill, he impounded funds for its implementation. Hughes then lobbied to successfully force the President to release the money. On a personal level, Hughes helped a number of his congressional colleagues to combat drinking problems. Hughes was also concerned with the drug problem. He favored the expansion of methadone programs and the decriminalization of the possession of marijuana.

Coming from a farm-belt section, Hughes was particularly concerned with the impact of Secretary of Agriculture Earl Butz's [q.v.] policies on the small farmer. He opposed Butz's nomination, calling it "a blow to farmers not only because of Mr. Butz's devotion to agribusiness, but because of his obsession with agribusiness." In the Senate Hughes continued to press for relief for the small farmer.

In the first two years in the Senate, Hughes compiled a 97% rating from the liberal Americans for Democratic Action. His record and his prominence as an antiwar politician made him a dark-horse candidate for the Democratic presidential nomination in 1972. Hughes toured the nation following the congressional election of 1970. In the style of a Methodist preacher, he called for the restoration of

morality in American politics and blasted the Administration for continuing to wage a war that divided the people. The Iowa senator, only on the national political scene for two years, promised to unify the American people through a liberal program at home and peace abroad. Although he obtained support from the antiwar movement, especially among students, Hughes found the rank and file Democrats unresponsive to his unannounced candidacy. Part of this apathy was due to Hughes's refusal to court the party professionals. He withdrew from the race in the summer of 1971. Six months later he endorsed Edmund Muskie (D, Maine) [q.v.] for the nomination.

Hughes decided to retire in 1975 to devote the rest of his public career to serve his church. On a number of occasions he returned to the nation's capital to hold prayer breakfasts with his colleagues.

[JB]

HUGHES, HOWARD R(OBARD)
b. Dec. 24, 1905; Houston, Tex.
d. April 5, 1976; Aboard an Acapulco-Huston flight.
Industrialist.

At the age of 18, Howard Hughes inherited his father's oil well drilling equipment company, which provided the young man with an income of close to $2 million annually. Hughes turned his attention to film making and the aircraft and airline industries. In 1935 he founded the Hughes Aircraft Co., which later held a number of profitable wartime contracts, and that same year purchased Trans World Airlines (TWA), the first international air carrier. In the 1950s the onetime playboy millionaire became known as the "spook of capitalism." Hughes shunned publicity and secluded himself in a number of secret retreats in the U.S., the Caribbean and Europe. His behavior became even more eccentric in the following decade. The once tall, handsome Texan resorted to eating strange diets, taking drugs and avoiding contacts with all humans, outside of his bodyguards, for fear they were carrying germs. [See TRUMAN, EISENHOWER Volumes]

In the late 1960s Hughes was forced to sell his controlling interest in TWA when other investors won a case charging that he had used the company to finance other investments. Hughes then invested in Las Vegas hotels purchasing the Desert Inn, the Sands and the Frontier Hotels and attempting to purchase the Dunes hotel. He also began investing in Nevada mineral land. In addition, he purchased Air West, the regional airline that served Canada, the West and Mexico. [See KENNEDY, JOHNSON Volumes]

Hughes's name figured prominently in the Watergate controversy. In 1969 and 1970 a Hughes aide gave Nixon's friend Charles (Bebe) Rebozzo [q.v.] two cash donations of $50,000 each, presumably to be used to support the Republican congressional campaigns and aid Nixon's re-election bid. At the time Hughes was negotiating with the Justice Department for an anti-trust ruling that would permit him to buy the Dunes. The Department gave a favorable ruling but the deal fell through for financial reasons. Fearing disclosure of the donation, Nixon's friend placed the money in a safe deposit box. It was returned in 1973. During the Watergate controversy some investigators speculated that the money had been used to help pay for Nixon's San Clemente estate. However, no charges were brought in the case.

J. Anthony Lukas of *The New York Times*, in his book *Nightmare: The Underside of the Nixon Years*, claimed the Watergate burglars had broken into the Democratic National Committee's office to find out what the Party knew of the Hughes-Rebozzo transaction. Lawrence O'Brien [q.v.], chairman of the Democratic National Committee, had been Hughes's chief Washington representative from 1968 to 1970. Lukas speculated that O'Brien might have had in his safe damaging documents concerning the link between the donation and permission to purchase the Dunes.

In 1974 the government indicted Hughes for a major stock swindle in the purchase of Air West. At the time the industrialist was living in the Bahamas and he could not be extradited on the charge. There were charges made during the period that Hughes had used his connection with the White House to prevent extradition. In 1972 Hughes, who shunned publicity, was continually in the news when Clifford Irving announced he had written an authorized biography of the reclusive billionaire. The book was later discovered to be a hoax. In the last years of his life, Hughes lived in seclusion in the Caribbean and Mexico. He died in 1975 aboard a plane en route to Houston for emergency medical treatment. Following his death a complicated legal battle centered on the question of who would inherit his estate.

[JB]

HUMPHREY, HUBERT H(ORATIO)

b. May 27, 1911; Wallace, S.D.
d. Jan 13, 1978; Waverly, Minn.
Democratic Senator, Minn., 1949–65; 1971–78.

The son of a South Dakota druggist, Hubert Humphrey was profoundly influenced by his father's reverence for William Jennings Bryan and Woodrow Wilson. He was a star debater and class valedictorian in high school, but he had to leave the University of Minnesota early in the Depression to work in his father's drugstore. He became a registered pharmacist and managed the store while his father participated actively in South Dakota Democratic Party politics. Humphrey returned to the University of Minnesota in 1937, earning his B.A. in 1939 and M.A. in political science from Louisiana State University a year later. His master's thesis, entitled, "The Political Philosophy of the New Deal," was a glowing tribute to Franklin D. Roosevelt's response to the Depression.

Humphrey taught in college and

worked for the War Production Administration before plunging into Minnesota politics. He played a key role in the 1944 merger of the Farmer-Labor and Democratic Parties and won election as mayor of Minneapolis the next year. As mayor he waged an anti-vice war, created the first municipal fair employment practices commission in the United States, expanded the city's housing program and took an active part in settling strikes. Reelected in 1947 Humphrey helped to organize the liberal, anti-Communist Americans for Democratic Action (ADA) and fought a successful battle to purge the Communist faction from the Democratic-Farmer-Labor (DFL) Party. He gained national attention at the 1948 Democratic National Convention with a stirring oration in favor of a strong civil rights plank, one of the most memorable convention speeches of modern times. In November, Minnesota voters elected Humphrey to the Senate over the conservative Republican incumbent.

Humphrey quickly moved into the vanguard of the Senate's liberal minority, promoting a wide variety of social welfare, civil rights, tax reform and prolabor legislation. The first bill he introduced was a proposal to establish medical care for the aged financed through the Social Security system, which was finally enacted as medicare in 1965. In his early career Humphrey's aggressive debating style and effusive liberalism alienated powerful Senate conservatives, and their hostility reduced his effectiveness.

Gradually he eased his way into the Senate "Establishment," toning down his fervid ideological approach and working closely with the Democratic leader, Sen. Lyndon Johnson, who used Humphrey as his liaison with liberals and intellectuals. Humphrey, moreover, combined his advocacy of social reform with unwavering anti-communism. He introduced the Communist Control Act of 1954, which outlawed the Communist Party. In foreign affairs Humphrey leavened his anti-communism with Wilsonian idealism. He became a leading advocate of disarmament and the distribution of surplus food to needy nations. By the late 1950s Humphrey was the most outspoken Congressional champion of the welfare state, the premier symbol of postwar American liberalism.

Humphrey's first run for the presidency began in January 1959 and ended in May 1960 with his defeat in the West Virginia primary by Sen. John F. Kennedy (D, Mass.). Humphrey reached the peak of his legislative influence during the Kennedy Administration. As assistant majority leader, or majority whip, he became the Administration's most ardent ally in the Senate, working tirelessly to win passage of Kennedy programs. In the process he helped to enact several measures, such as the Peace Corps and the nuclear test ban treaty, that he himself had long promoted. Humphrey was the floor manager of the landmark Civil Rights Act of 1964, the culmination of his career-long advocacy of the cause of equal rights.

Elected vice president in 1964, Humphrey defended the Johnson Administration's domestic and foreign policies with his characteristic ebullience. His zealous support for Johnson's Vietnam policy cost him the support of many anti-war Democrats in his 1968 presidential campaign. Despite a dramatic surge in the last month of his troubled campaign, Humphrey lost the election to Republican Richard Nixon by a narrow margin. [See TRUMAN, EISENHOWER, KENNEDY, JOHNSON Volumes]

After his defeat Humphrey taught at the University of Minnesota and Macalester College. He also traveled widely on speaking engagements, wrote a $200-a-week syndicated newspaper column, and became a consultant and member of the board of directors for Encyclopedia Britannica, Inc. at a salary of $75,000 a year. He publicly expressed his approval of Nixon's Vietnam policy. With Sen. Eugene McCarthy's (D, Minn.) [q.v.] announcement that he would not seek reelection, an avenue opened for Humphrey's return to political office. He easily won the DFL's nomination in September 1970 and in November defeated his Republican opponent, Rep. Clark MacGregor (R, Minn.) with 59% of the vote, his largest percentage victory in a Senate race.

On his return to the Senate, Humphrey requested but was denied assignment to the Appropriations Committee. He was assigned to the Government Operations, Agriculture, and Joint Economic Committees instead. Lacking seniority and the institutional power he had once enjoyed, the junior Senator from Minnesota experienced frustration in pushing his usual host of legislative initiatives. In May 1971 he proposed a national domestic development bank to provide a new source of capital funds for state and local governments. His proposal received little attention, as did his bill to establish an environmental trust fund to enable communities to set up their own environmental action plans. Humphrey's call for national health insurance was eclipsed by Sen. Edward Kennedy's (D, Mass.) [q.v.] conspicuous activity in the area. He worked vigorously for passage of a new fair labor standards law in 1972 and 1973 that would have expanded coverage to another 8.4 million workers and combated age and sex discrimination in employment, but President Nixon vetoed the measure in 1973. In 1974 a compromise version raising the minimum wage and covering 7 million more workers became law.

Humphrey's backing in March 1971 of a successful Senate move to cut off further funding for the proposed $1.3 billion SST signaled a shift to the left from his centrist course. Organized labor had strongly supported the plan. At the same time he endorsed a resolution of the Democratic Policy Council condemning Nixon's Vietnam policy and calling for withdrawal of all American forces by the end of 1971. This was a critical turning point for Humphrey. A day later, in his first major speech since returning to Congress, he criticized the Administration's slow movement on arms control negotiations with the Soviet Union and urged the U.S. to accept a Soviet offer to limit deployment of the anti-ballistic missile.

In January 1972 Humphrey again became a candidate for the Democratic presidential nomination. Out of a crowded field of contenders, Humphrey's candidacy survived until the climactic California primary in June, his last chance of catching the front-runner, Sen. George McGovern (D, S.D.) [q.v.]. Humphrey's vigorous campaigning and sharp criticisms of McGovern's proposals for a guaranteed annual income and sweeping cuts in the defense budget reduced the South Dakotan's lead, but McGovern's margin of victory was still substantial, effectively ending Humphrey's candidacy. As he had done after his primary defeat in 1960, Humphrey campaigned hard for the Democratic ticket.

In his last years in the Senate, Humphrey became that body's foremost proponent of national planning. In 1973 he proposed a balanced national growth and development bill that would have created an executive office and a congressional committee to oversee policy and prepare long-range programs dealing with economic growth, population, environmental protection, housing, welfare, and other areas of national concern. The ambitious plan made little headway in Congress, however.

As sponsor of the Humphrey-Hawkins full-employment bill, Humphrey spearheaded the movement to force the federal government to create a massive number of jobs for the unemployed. First introduced in 1976, the bill committed the federal government to being the employer of last resort for the unemployed who could not otherwise find jobs. The measure was the focal point for labor and liberal agitation to combat unemployment and for Humphrey, the most prominent embodiment of governmental activism in America. Stymied during Humphrey's lifetime, the bill passed in diluted, largely symbolic form 10 months after his death in 1978. The bill declared that it was a national goal to reduce the unemployment rate to 4% by 1983, as well as cut the inflation rate to 3% by that year and reduce the federal share of the economy to the lowest possible level "consistent with national needs and priorities."

During the Watergate scandal it emerged that Humphrey had received some illegal contributions from dairy producers. Humphrey acknowledged the contributions but said he had not known they were from corporate funds and thus illegal. Jack Chestnut, Humphrey's campaign manager in 1970 and 1972, was sentenced in 1975 to four months in prison and fined $5,000 for accepting illegal campaign contributions.

In 1976 Humphrey almost made another bid for the Democratic presidential nomination, but finally decided not to enter the primaries. At the July Convention he nominated a protege, Sen. Walter Mondale (D, Minn.) [q.v.] for vice president. Reelected to the Senate in November, Humphrey made his final effort for a higher office, that of Senate majority leader. Although he held the affection and respect of his colleagues, Humphrey was unable to match the support conscientiously gathered by his foe, Sen. Robert Byrd (I, W. Va.) [q.v.], and withdrew before the vote in January 1977. As a consolation, Senate Democrats created a special post for Humphrey, that of deputy president pro tem of the Senate, which carried a $7,500 salary increase.

In October 1976 Humphrey underwent surgery for bladder cancer. In August 1977 doctors found terminal cancer in his pelvis. In the ensuing months Humphrey performed his public duties while his physical condition deteriorated. He died on Jan. 13, 1978. President Jimmy Carter [q.v.] eulogized him as the "most beloved of all Americans."

[TO]

For further information:
Albert Eisele, *Almost to the Presidency: A Biography of Two American Politicians* (Blue Earth, Minn., 1972).
Hubert H. Humphrey, *The Education of a Public Man: My Life and Politics* (New York, 1976).

HUNT, E(VERETTE) HOWARD, JR.
b. October 1918; Hamburg, N.Y.
Convicted Watergate conspirator.

Hunt's father was a lawyer with business interests in New York and Florida. A 1940 graduate of Brown University, Hunt entered the Naval Reserve and was commissioned at Annapolis in 1941. After an injury while on duty in the North Atlantic, he was given a medical discharge. Hunt wrote a novel, *East of Farewell,* based on his wartime experiences, and continued to write some 50 adventure and espionage books in the following three decades.

Hunt became a writer for the news series "The March of Time," then transferred to *Life* magazine as a South Pacific war correspondent. In 1944 he volunteered for the Office of Strategic Services and worked with partisan groups until the end of the war. After several postwar writing jobs, Hunt joined Marshall Plan Ambassador Averell Harriman [q.v.] in Paris as a press aide. While there, Hunt met his wife-to-be, Dorothy de Goutiere, and was recruited into the Central Intelligence Agency (CIA).

As a CIA agent, Hunt served in Europe, the Far East and Latin America and was a major figure behind the overthrow of the Marxist government of Guatemala in 1954. In 1961, under the cover-name Eduardo, Hunt was the CIA contact in Miami for anti-Castro Cubans involved in the abortive Bay of Pigs invasion of Communist Cuba.

After 21 years in the CIA, Hunt retired from the agency in May 1970 and began working for a Washington-based public relations firm, Mullen & Co. In July 1971, recruited by fellow Brown alumnus Charles Colson [q.v.], Hunt went to work for the Nixon White House as a part-time consultant. With presidential assistant G. Gordon Liddy [q.v.], Hunt was involved in a number of covert activities for the Administration, some of them aimed at damaging the reputations of possible Democratic presidential candidates in 1972. Hunt unsuccessfully tried to uncover damaging evidence of Sen. Edward M. Kennedy's [q.v.] culpability in the 1969 drowning death of a female campaign worker on Martha's Vineyard. At Colson's urging, Hunt also tried to fabricate State Department cables linking President John F. Kennedy to the assassination of South Vietnamese President Ngo Dinh Diem in 1963. (Hunt later stated that several cables possibly damaging to the Kennedy Administration were already missing from the files.) Hunt unsuccessfully attempted to pass off the doctored cables as authentic to a *Life* magazine reporter.

During the summer of 1971, the Nixon Administration began looking for ways to discredit former Defense Department analyst Daniel Ellsberg [q.v.], who had been indicted for leaking the *Pentagon Papers,* classified documents that detailed the U.S. buildup in Vietnam. Hunt became one of a team of officials known as the "Plumbers," assigned by the White House to investigate such leaks to the news media. Liddy and Hunt developed a plan to break into the office of Ellsberg's psychiatrist, Dr. Lewis Fielding, in order to photograph his files on Ellsberg. Nixon aides hoped to leak damaging information about Ellsberg from the files, and they feared that the Ellsberg defense might enter an insanity plea when the case went to trial. At one point, at Hunt's suggestion, a CIA psychiatric profile of Ellsberg was obtained, the first one the agency had ever prepared on a U.S. citizen. Hunt, and other White House aides, believed that Ellsberg was possibly a Soviet agent. Hunt later wrote of his suspicions, "If Daniel Ellsberg viewed the legitimate government of the United States as 'criminal,' then we perceived him as treasonist and alien." After obtaining clearance from Egil Krogh, Jr. [q.v.], and presidential adviser John Ehrlichman [q.v.], Hunt and Liddy put the break-in plan into operation. In the early morning hours of Sept. 4, 1971, they directed three Cuban Americans, Bernard Barker [q.v.], Eugenio Rolando Martinez, and Felipe De Diego, in a covert entry of Fielding's office. But the three found no records on Ellsberg. When John W. Dean [q.v.] re-

vealed the illegal break-in in 1973, charges against Ellsberg and a codefendant in the *Pentagon Papers* trial were dismissed.

In March 1972 Hunt flew to Denver to interview International Telephone and Telegraph Co. (ITT) lobbyist Dita Beard [q.v.], who was recuperating from a heart ailment. Beard had allegedly written a memo establishing a connection between the settlement of a Justice Department anti-trust suit then pending against ITT and ITT's contribution to the 1972 GOP presidential campaign. During the interview, Hunt used a disguise and a false name. After his visit Beard denied writing the memo, and ITT presented evidence disputing the memo's veracity. Hunt later claimed that after the Beard episode, he stopped accepting money for his White House consultant work.

During the spring and summer of 1972, Hunt and Liddy drew up plans for a massive political espionage campaign to be directed against President Nixon's Democratic rivals. Hunt named the plan "Gemstone." Approved by former Attorney General John Mitchell [q.v.], who left that post to head the Committee to Re-Elect the President, the Gemstone plan involved electronic surveillance, "dirty tricks" and the introduction of paid informers onto the campaign staffs of Democratic candidates. In the belief that Sen. George S. McGovern (D, S.D.) [q.v.] was receiving funds from Cuban President Fidel Castro, Hunt and Liddy arranged an entry into the Democratic National Committee's (DNC) Washington headquarters in the Watergate Office Building.

On May 27, with Hunt and Liddy stationed nearby, a team led by former CIA agent James McCord [q.v.] and recruited by Hunt entered the DNC offices and planted electronic surveillance devices and photographed files. But because of a mistake in planting the bugs, the team had to repeat the entry on June 17. This time a security guard discovered them and called the police, who arrested McCord, Barker, Martinez, Frank Sturgis and Virgilio R. Gonzalez. Hunt's name was found in the address books of two of the men arrested. He deposited some of the break-in equipment in his White House safe and fled Washington, traveling to California on the advice of Liddy.

After his departure Dean broke into Hunt's White House safe and removed the documents there. Then, with Ehrlichman present, Dean turned the materials over to acting FBI Director L. Patrick Gray [q.v.] for destruction, telling Gray that they were "political dynamite." Gray had the files burned on July 3, an action that eventually led to his resignation. Among the documents destroyed were the faked cables linking the Kennedy Administration to the Diem assassination and papers dealing with the Gemstone operation, the Plumbers unit and other covert projects. Hunt later claimed that the destruction of the documents robbed him of evidence he needed for his defense. He argued that his constitutional rights were thereby violated, and like Ellsberg, the charges against him should have been dropped. The FBI began a nationwide search for Hunt on July 1, but called it off six days later when Hunt, still in hiding, said through his lawyer that he would meet with federal authorities. Shortly afterward he was fired from his job at Mullen & Co.

On Sept. 11 he was named in a civil suit initiated by the Democratic Party against the Watergate entry team and GOP officials for conspiracy to commit political espionage. The $6.4 million suit was settled out of court in February 1974 for $775,000. On Sept. 15 the five-member burglary team, along with Hunt and Liddy, were indicted on several criminal charges in connection with the Watergate break-in. After pleading not guilty, as did the other six, Hunt was released on a $10,000 bond.

After the indictments, money for the defendants was covertly funneled through Hunt's wife Dorothy. Hunt felt the amounts were insufficient for legal costs and family support, and after Nixon's reelection in November, he felt the White House was unresponsive to his complaints. On Dec. 8, 1972, Dorothy Hunt took $10,000 in cash and boarded a flight to Chicago, but her plane crashed before landing near Midway Airport, killing her. Hunt claimed the money was earmarked for investment in a motel management company owned by friends in the Midwest. After his wife's death, Hunt's attitude underwent a marked change. Believing that he could not stand the stress of a trial and convinced that the government was concealing evidence which showed him acting in good faith, Hunt decided to plead guilty, "in the hope that leniency would be accorded me."

U.S. District Judge John J. Sirica [q.v.] refused to allow Hunt to plead guilty to three charges, as had been agreed to by chief prosecutor Earl J. Silbert. Therefore, Hunt, on Jan. 11, 1973, pleaded guilty to all six charges against him. After being freed on $100,000 bail, Hunt told reporters that he believed all of his activities were "in the best interests of my country." Sirica sentenced Hunt on March 23 to a provisional maximum prison term of 35 years and gave the other defendants similarly long sentences. Sirica recommended that they cooperate with the federal grand jury and the Senate Select Committee investigating the Watergate case.

Hunt later denied that he had been paid hush money by the White House to plead guilty and remain silent on the Administration's involvement with the Gemstone and Watergate operations. He also denied claims by Dean that he had demanded large sums of money and a guarantee of executive clemency in exchange for his silence. He claimed any requests he had made were "routine" actions to provide security for his family and to pay overdue legal fees. His portrayal as a blackmailer, Hunt contended, was a White House strategy to make him a scapegoat for the Watergate affair. Hunt disclosed that he gave $156,000 of the funds to his attorney William O. Bittman, who withdrew from the case under government pressure in August 1973.

Hunt appeared before the Watergate grand jury for three days of testimony in March 1973. The second session was interrupted to grant Hunt immunity from further prosecution so that he could answer questions. According to testimony released in May 1973 at the *Pentagon Papers* trial, Hunt had revealed his attempt to fabricate cables linking the Kennedy Administration to the Diem coup d'etat.

In September 1973 Hunt filed a petition for dismissal of the charges against him, contending that he thought he had been acting lawfully, "pursuant to the President's power to protect national security." Hunt also claimed misconduct by government officials in his case and asked to have his guilty plea withdrawn.

Also in September, Hunt went before the Senate Watergate Committee. On Sept. 24 he told the panel that he considered his actions to be "a duty to my country." He said that after a career as a spy, "following orders without question," he never thought to question the legality or propriety of the Watergate entries. While he said he regretted his role, he maintained that the break-ins were "unwise" but "lawful." He also related his personal plight in the aftermath of Watergate, noting that he had been attacked and robbed and had suffered a stroke in his six months in prison "isolated from my four motherless children." He claimed he had been "crushed by the failure of my government to protect me and my family, as in the past it has always done for its clandestine agents."

On Sept. 25 he reiterated his belief that the Watergate entries were sanctioned by high government officials for legitimate national security purposes. He also denied having sought executive clemency and repeated his denials of having accepted hush money. He suggested that the Watergate conspirators were "trapped" by a double agent and named the possible informer as former FBI agent Alfred C. Baldwin III, who acted as lookout during the break-in. Hunt's attempt to link Baldwin to the Democrats was sharply disputed by Sen. Lowell P. Weicker, Jr. (R, Conn.) [*q.v.*]. Weicker identified one of Baldwin's relatives as Raymond Baldwin, a former Republican senator and governor.

On Nov. 9 Sirica sentenced Hunt to from 30 months to eight years in prison and fined him $10,000, making him eligible for parole in the fall of 1975. Hunt was freed Dec. 28 without bail by the U.S. Court of Appeals in the District of Columbia pending the appeal of his case.

On Feb. 25, 1975, the U.S. Court of Appeals unanimously rejected Hunt's petition, and he was returned to prison April 25. Although Sirica reduced the sentences of the four Cuban Americans involved on July 11, 1975, he refused to take similar action in Hunt's case. Hunt was paroled on Feb. 23, 1977, after paying his $10,000 fine a week earlier. He had served 32 months of the sentence.

In November 1978 Hunt called a news conference in Miami to deny that he was in Dallas on the day of President John F. Kennedy's assassination in 1963 or that he was involved in any way with Kennedy's death. Hunt said he had made those denials before a subcommittee of the House Select Committee on Assassinations. Hunt had been plagued by reports linking him to the Kennedy assassination, including reports that he and Frank Sturgis were the "tramps" arrested near the scene of the killing. The House Assassinations Committee had rejected that theory and claimed a photograph taken at the time was not of Hunt and Sturgis.

[JF]

For further information:
E. Howard Hunt, *Undercover: Memoirs of an American Secret Agent* (New York, 1974).

HUNT, REED O(LIVER)
b. Oct. 12, 1904; Wollochet Bay, Wash. Chairman, President's Commission on Financial Structure and Regulation, 1970-71.

Reed Hunt grew up in the Pacific Northwest and began his working life as a sailor. In 1927, Hunt took a clerical job with the Crown Zellerbach Corp., a large paper manufacturer. At Crown Zellerbach, Hunt climbed the company hierarchy to eventually become chairman of the board in 1963. He held that post until his retirement in 1969.

Less than a year after Hunt's retirement, President Nixon appointed him chairman of the Commission on Financial Structure and Regulation. In announcing the creation of the panel, President Nixon had indicated that the Hunt Commission would study and present legislative recommendations to "improve the functioning of the private financial system."

The Hunt Commission was formed amidst widespread anxiety about the health of the U. S. financial system. The credit crunches of 1966 and 1969–70 had shown U. S. banks and capital markets more brittle than supposed. Anxiety was focused above all on the phenomenon of "disintermediation," or the flow of savings away from financial institutions subject to interest-rate ceilings by the Federal Reserve Bank in periods when short-term, money market rates, particularly those covering government securities, exceeded the legal maximum for commercial banks and so-called thrift institutions.

In 1966 and 1969 when Federal Reserve Board moves against inflation had precipitated serious disintermediation, the loss of funds by thrift institutions–savings banks and savings-and-loan associations–had severely contracted the housing and mortgage markets and created difficulties for the financing of state and local governments. Critics such as Rep. Wright Patman (D, Tex.) [q.v.] pointed to the multiple sources of short-term deposits available to large commercial banks that were closed off to the thrifts.

Thus, at the outset, Hunt and his co-commissioners were under considerable pressure from such quarters as the Council of Economic Advisers to recommend ways of preventing disintermediation and of allowing thrift institutions to compete for funds during periods of high interest rates. The Commission was aware of the power of Congressional supporters of the thrifts, headed by Patman, to stop any legislation deemed at the latter's expense. It was also quite aware of the importance of easy money for housing and consumer credit in fueling U. S. economic activity.

In December 1971 the Commission issued its *Report on Financial Structure and Regulation*. The panel found that the massive federal regulatory apparatus, largely a legacy of the New Deal era and the sweeping bank legislation of the 1933–35 period, had become an impediment to the efficient functioning of capital markets. The Commission also discovered jurisdictional overlap of the three major regulatory bodies–the Federal Reserve, the Comptroller of the Currency and the Federal Home Loan Bank (FHLB).

But their criticism centered primarily on the functioning of Regulation Q of the Banking Act of 1933. It was Regulation Q that permitted the Federal Reserve to fix maximum interest rates for commercial banks in order to prevent the excessive competition for savings deposits which many people felt had set the stage for the 1929 depression and subsequent banking collapse. A sudden rise in the Fed's discount rate in December 1965 occurring simultaneously with an increase of the Regulation Q maximum for commercial banks above the legal limit for thrift institutions had begun the credit crunch of 1966. The same phenomenon, with subsequent disintermediation, had recurred on a more serious scale in 1969–70.

The Hunt Commission recommended the abolition of Regulation Q for deposits above $100,000. This move, in the view of Hunt and others, would permit commercial banks to attract funds from large depositors while allowing savings banks to continue to compete with commercial banks for the funds of the small depositor.

The panel also recommended wide diversification of all thrift institutions, allowing them to perform services previously restricted only to commercial banks, and hence greatly increasing the economic activities they could finance. In additional recommendations the Hunt Commission proposed a reorganization of the federal regulatory apparatus, the creation of a single Federal Deposit Guarantee Administration to supercede the three existing semi-private deposit insurance agencies and the introduction of statewide branch banking across the country.

The report was viewed as a proposal for increased competition in the banking system as a whole. Critics denounced it for being solely concerned with the profitability of the private financial sector and totally uninterested in the social implications of its recommendations.

The Treasury Department issued its legislative recommendations based on the Hunt Commission report in August 1973, a time when the U. S. was entering the worst inflation in its postwar history. The recommendations were effectively forgotten in the subsequent inflation, quadrupling of oil prices and the 1973–75 economic contraction, and have had no significant impact on banking legislation to date.

After the disbanding of the Commission, Hunt went into retirement.

[LG]

INOUYE, DANIEL K(EN)
b. Sept. 7, 1924; Honolulu, Hawaii.
Democratic Senator, Hawaii, 1963–.

After serving with the all-nisei 442nd Infantry in World War II, Inouye returned to Hawaii, graduated from the University of Hawaii in 1950, and received his law degree from George Washington University Law School in 1952. In 1953 he set up private practice and was appointed assistant public prosecutor for Honolulu. After serving two terms in Hawaii's Territorial House of Representatives and one term in the Territorial Senate, Inouye won election in 1959 as the first representative from the new state of Hawaii. In Congress, Inouye, acutely aware of the discrimination against his fellow Japanese-Americans, supported attempts to pass civil rights legislation. In 1960 Inouye backed Lyndon Johnson's candidacy for the Democratic presidential nomination and, at Johnson's request, gave the seconding speech at the Democratic National Convention.

In 1962 Inouye was elected to the Senate, where he became a strong supporter of the Kennedy and Johnson Administration's policies, especially those concerning civil rights and social welfare. He also served on the Democratic Policy Committee, became vice chairman of the Democratic Senatorial Campaign Committee and was chosen assistant majority whip in 1966. In 1968 Inouye was reelected with 83% of the vote. [See JOHNSON Volume]

Inouye became opposed to the Vietnam war in the Nixon years, voting for the Cooper-Church Amendment to cut off funding for military operations in Cambodia. He cosponsored with 58 other senators the War Powers Act of 1973, which limited presidential authority to commit American forces and military aid to combat situations without congressional approval.

Inouye's major legislative initiatives during the Nixon years were promoting and protecting Hawaii's maritime and tourist industries. As chairman of the Commerce Committee's Subcommittee on Foreign Trade and Tourism, Inouye encouraged aggressive federal promotion of American commercial interests in foreign countries, supported water pollution control and land use policy legislation, and successfully sponsored in 1971 the Public Interest Protection Act, which gave Hawaii's governor the power to rent naval ships to move goods when dock strikes exceeded 30 days.

Inouye gained national prominence in the spring and summer of 1973 when he sat on the Select Committe on Presidential Campaign Activities, the "Watergate Committee." Inouye's conduct in questioning key Administration aides and officials was widely regarded as fair and competent, and Inouye evoked great outpourings of sympathy after Bob Haldeman [q.v.] and John Ehrlichman's [q.v.] lawyer, John J. Wilson, referred to Inouye before TV cameras and reporters as "that little Jap." On October 22, 1973, Inouye became one of the first members of Congress to publicly call for Nixon's resignation from the presidency. He supported and worked for the 1973 campaign reform bill and the 1974 Federal Election Campaign Amendments, the first such legislation that resulted from the Nixon Administration scandals.

Throughout the Nixon years Inouye was consistent in his advocacy of generous appropriations for social welfare programs and civil rights legislation. He voted for the Equal Rights Amendment in 1972 and supported busing to achieve integration. He opposed the Administration's strict anti-crime legislation. Reflecting the importance of organized labor in Hawaii, he promoted labor legislation and received high ratings from the AFL-CIO's Committee on Political Action.

In 1976 Inouye was assigned to the newly created Select Committee on Intelligence formed after investigations of the Nixon Administration revealed extensive illegal and suspect activities of U.S. intelligence agencies in domestic and foreign affairs. In 1977 Inouye became chairman of that Committee. [See CARTER Volume]

[JMP]

JACKSON, HENRY M(ARTIN)
b. May 31, 1912; Everett, Wash.
Democratic Senator, Wash., 1953- ;
Chairman, Interior and Insular Affairs
Committee, 1963- .

After two years in private legal practice "Scoop" Jackson won his first elective office in 1935. Five years later he was elected to the House of Representatives where he compiled a generally liberal voting record. He advanced to the Senate in 1952. As a member of the Armed Services Committee, he evolved into a prototype "Cold War liberal," advocating large defense expenditures in order to counter growing Soviet military power. He forged close ties with organized labor. [See EISENHOWER Volume]

Jackson's influence in defense matters declined under a Democratic administration. He was skeptical about Kennedy's efforts to control the arms race and even opposed the 1961 bill creating the Arms Control and Disarmament Agency. He refused to vote for the 1963 nuclear test ban treaty until his "safeguards" were added

to the treaty terms. His adherence made ratification possible. [See KENNEDY Volume]

The Senator was a staunch supporter of the Johnson Administration's Vietnam policy, although he tended to favor the Pentagon's military solutions over the Defense Department's. He also compiled a notable record in sponsoring conservationist legislation. In December 1968 President-elect Nixon approached Jackson with an offer to head the Defense Department. Jackson declined, apparently wishing to leave open more options for his political future. [See JOHNSON Volume]

Jackson, as chairman of the Interior and Insular Affairs Committee, deftly managed passage of the National Environmental Policy Act of 1969. A landmark piece of legislation, the bill established a national policy for the environment, authorized studies on natural resources and set up a three-member Council on Environmental Quality in the executive branch. All federal agencies were required to determine the environmental impact, if any, of all policies and proposals. Jackson had qualified Administration endorsement of the bill, in part because he was one of the few Senate Democrats who supported White House Vietnam and defense policy. Especially gratifying to Nixon was Jackson's support of the ABM in 1969. Not surprisingly, throughout 1969-70 Jackson fought for the Administration's decision to develop the Supersonic Transport (SST), whose prime contractor was the Boeing Co. located in Washington. The SST was defeated in March 1971.

Jackson's liberalism in the domestic social welfare area remained untainted. One example was his sponsorship of the Youth Conservation Corps, which cleared Congress in August 1970. He voted against Nixon's controversial Supreme Court nominees, Clement Haynsworth [q.v.] and G. Harrold Carswell [q.v.]. Particularly unexpected was his support of the Cooper-Church amendment in June 1970.

Jackson's *modus vivendi* with the White House bore some substantial benefits. Since 1968 antiwar Democrats had succeeded in taking over a number of local Washington Democratic organizations. Up for reelection in 1970, Jackson had to face a peace opponent in the primary and was embarrassed at the state convention by the adoption of the peace group's platform. Yet, with ample financial backing—much of it provided by Republicans—and relying on a record of service to his constituents, he won the primary, taking 84% of the vote. He received the same figure in the November election. The vote-getting feat was made easier because of pressure put on Washington Republicans by Nixon and other GOP leaders to choose a weak opponent for Jackson.

In November 1971 Jackson announced his candidacy for the 1972 presidential election. Theoretically, his primary chances looked promising. With most of the candidates taking antiwar positions, he could win most right-wing and many centrist Democratic votes, assuming that Alabama Gov. George Wallace [q.v.] did not enter the race. He appealed to diverse constituencies, including minorities, labor, large segments of industry and the military. Since 1948 he had been an unswerving supporter of Israel. Unlike most other Democratic candidates, Jackson did not believe that the war would be a viable campaign issue, since he trusted that the President was gradually ending U.S. involvement in Indochina. Rather, he thought the President most vulnerable on the issue of the economy. He advocated full employment measures and government action to prime the economy.

But there were weaknesses in Jackson as a candidate. His passion for expansion and growth was beginning to appear outdated in a decade in which the "less is more" philosophy was gaining currency. Many conservationists, in view of his SST position and support for the Alaskan oil pipeline, did not find his environmental record as perfect as had been thought. Although AFL-CIO president George Meany [q.v.] liked him, some younger labor leaders preferred other candidates. Jackson's principal shortcomings, however, were probably his lack of national recognition and his mediocre speaking voice.

Jackson fared far worse in the primaries than expected. Wallace's entry into the February 1972 Florida primary crushed the Senator's hopes of capturing the "law and order" vote and pushed him into proposing an anti-busing amendment that led to the further alienation of liberal voters. He came in third behind Wallace and Sen. Hubert Humphrey (D, Minn.) [q.v.] with 13% of the vote. In May he announced his withdrawal from future primaries following dismal showings in such industrial states as Ohio and Pennsylvania, but he indicated that he still hoped to win the presidential nomination. At the Democratic National Convention in July Jackson placed second to Sen. George McGovern (D, S.D.) [q.v.], getting most of organized labor's support after Humphrey withdrew from the race. He grudgingly agreed to support McGovern, whom he had attacked violently during the primaries. But immediately after the November election he and Humphrey backed the formation of a group designed to win back control of the Democratic Party for its more conservative elements.

During the 1970s Jackson was one of Congress's most powerful figures. He increasingly used his power to attack the Nixon Administration's policy of *detente* and detente's chief architect, Secretary of State Henry Kissinger [q.v.]. He criticized the May 1972 Strategic Arms Limitation Talks (SALT) accords on defensive nuclear weapons with the Soviets by arguing that the "agreements are likely to lead to an accelerated technological arms race with greater uncertainties, profound instabilities and considerable costs." At the same time, he claimed that they gave strategic advantages to the Soviets. Jackson's price for ratification of the treaty was an amendment which contained hard-line instructions for SALT negotiators. It requested that any future permanent treaty on offensive nuclear arms "not limit the United States to levels of intercontinental strategic forces inferior to" those of the Soviet Union. Any treaty was to be based on "the principle of equality."

Jackson's suspicions of the Soviets and his concern for Soviet Jews were made clear again in October when he and 75 Senate cosponsors introduced an amendment to the East-West Trade Relations Act aimed at denying the USSR most-favored nation status as long as it barred emigration or imposed "more than a nominal tax . . . on any citizen as a consequence of emigration." The Soviet leadership responded violently to the action, calling it unjustified interference in internal matters. Both the Soviets and the Administration were embarrassed, but in June 1974 Kissinger reportedly got a pledge from the Soviets to allow the emigration of 45,000 Jews a year. Jackson found the figure inadequate. Kissinger later carried more Soviet assurances to Jackson and in December 1974 the comprehensive trade bill with the Jackson amendment was passed by Congress. The USSR canceled the treaty the next month because of the emigration clause. Jackson claimed that Kissinger and President Ford were seeking to blame Congress, and him specifically, for their failure.

In the midst of the Watergate investigations in February 1973 the Government Operations Committee's Permanent Subcommittee on Investigations, which he chaired, initiated research on the circumstances surrounding the sale of grain to the USSR in the summer of 1972. Jackson charged the Department of Agriculture with mismanagement which led to excessive profits for the grain exporters and bargain prices for the Soviets at the expense of farmers and consumers. In the subcommittee's final report of August 1974 Jackson said that the "great grain robbery" resulted in depleted U.S. grain reserves, higher food prices and a crisis in the livestock industry. His pressure led to a temporary halt of grain shipments in October. The subcommittee also investigated the energy crisis beginning in January 1974. The sponsor of an emergency energy bill, Jackson suggested that the oil companies were manipulating the petroleum shortages to their own advantage. His bill, which proposed a 30% rollback

on domestically produced oil, was vetoed by Nixon in March.

In February 1975 Jackson announced his intention to seek the presidency again, pledging to help "the little people—little business, the elderly, the young." The polls showed him to be the frontrunner and in the Massachusetts primary of March 1976 he won his first contest outside of Washington, getting 23% of the vote. His platform included opposition to busing and detente and support for disarmament and national health insurance. As in the past, he enjoyed the support of organized labor. Yet, by the time he won the April New York primary (he won 38% of the vote, but had predicted a landslide), Jimmy Carter [q.v.], the former governor of Georgia, was gaining momentum and leading in the race for delegates. Following his loss in Pennsylvania Jackson decided to end active candidacy, since, without a win in Pennsylvania, his candidacy was no longer "viable." In June he endorsed Carter and turned his attention to winning reelection to the Senate. He received 85% of the September Democratic primary vote against two opponents and was reelected in November in another landslide.

[JCH]

For further information:
Peter J. Ognibene, *Scoop: The Life and Politics of Henry M. Jackson* (New York, 1975).

JACKSON, JESSE (LOUIS)
b. Oct. 8, 1941; Greenville, N.C.
National Director, Operation Breadbasket, 1966–71.

Reared among the poorest blacks in Greenville, Jackson secured his first job at the age of six, delivering stove wood to local homes. By the age of 11 he was elevated to a managerial position, in charge of the woodyard's finances and employee hiring and firing. While working to supplement his family's meager income, Jackson attended Greenville's public schools where he proved to be an outstanding athlete. In 1959 he entered the University of Illinois on a football scholarship, but left after one year because "Negroes were supposed to be linemen, not quarterbacks." He then returned to his home state and enrolled at the predominantly black Agricultural and Technical College at Greensboro, graduating in 1964. He relocated to Chicago in 1965 to attend a theological seminary. Jackson was ordained a Baptist Minister in 1968.

Jackson played an important role in the civil rights struggles of the 1960s and helped recruit for the Southern Christian Leadership Conference (SCLC) headed by Martin Luther King, Jr. [q.v.]. In 1966 he became head of the SCLC's Operation Breadbasket, a systematic economic boycott of businesses that exploited blacks. In 1968 he gained national prominence for his role in "Resurrection City," the shantytown set up in Washington, D.C., to dramatize the plight of the poor. [See JOHNSON Volume]

Soon after the assassination of King, which Jackson had witnessed, he petitioned the SCLC hierarchy for an appointment to a higher post but was turned down. Although disgruntled with the rejection, he continued in his leadership capacity at Operation Breadbasket. In 1969 he expanded his efforts by participating in the Black Coalition for United Community Action's attempt to secure construction jobs for blacks. As a result a program was implemented to train 4,000 blacks for skilled construction work.

Jackson's initial conflict with the SCLC leadership had created strained relations between himself and King's successor, the Rev. Ralph Abernathy [q.v.]. In 1971 Jackson was advised to relocate Operation Breadbasket to SCLC headquarters in Atlanta. Because of his conviction that the program's autonomy and his ever strengthening influence were being usurped, he refused the organization's directive. Later that year Jackson again clashed with the SCLC over his handling of $500,000 in profits earned from Black Expo, an exposition of black culture and accomplishment which he had initially organized in 1969. Charging that he had structured nonprofit corporations to run the expo without SCLC authorization, he

was given a 60-day suspension. Jackson, with his characteristic defiance, resigned and in two months announced the formation of Operation PUSH (People United to Save Humanity) and his self-appointment to the directorship of the organization.

Jackson, who was convinced of the need for black-owned businesses—"We would rather own A&P than burn it"— recruited several prominent black economists and politicians to develop a concise blueprint for attacking poverty and establish greater equality of wealth in the U.S. In 1972 PUSH had expanded to include chapters in 15 cities. By employing the strategy of massive boycotts, the organization by 1974 had succeeded in securing job placements for blacks in major corporations and advancement of black-owned businesses.

With regard to civil rights, Jackson stated: "The issue is dead now that we have legal, public accommodations, voting and other rights. Now it's civil economics— the cost factor. What good does it do to have the right to go to school when you can't afford the tuition?" In addition to overseeing Operation PUSH's expansion, Jackson led an alternative delegation to the 1972 Democratic Convention that unseated the hand-picked delegates of Chicago's Mayor Richard Daley [q.v.] based on a challenge of recently established Convention guidelines aimed at providing increased minority representation.

Jackson continued in the PUSH directorship and in the late 1970s under the auspices of the organization, he devised an innovative educational program to increase basic learning skills among minority students in Chicago's inner-city schools.

[DGE]

JAVITS, JACOB K(OPPEL)
b. May 18, 1904; New York, N.Y.
Republican Senator, N.Y., 1957–.

The son of Jewish immigrants, Jacob Javits was raised on the Lower East Side of New York City. Working his way through law school at New York University, he received his law degree in 1926 and was admitted to the bar in the following year. With his older brother he established a law firm that specialized in bankruptcy and corporate reorganization. A supporter of Mayor Fiorello La Guardia, Javits joined the Republican Party in the 1930s. After serving in the Army during World War II, he won election to the House of Representatives from the Upper West Side of New York City in 1946 and served there until 1954. In the House, Javits broke ranks with the Republicans on most issues and established a reputation as a liberal. He ran for attorney general of New York in 1954 and was the only Republican elected that year to statewide office. In 1956 he defeated New York City Mayor Robert F. Wagner, Jr., in a race for the United States Senate. Javits's liberalism, combined with his Jewish religious affiliation, made him one of the most successful candidates in New York state history, and he easily won reelection to the Senate in 1962, 1968 and 1974. During the 1960s Javits supported most of the social welfare proposals of the Kennedy and Johnson Administrations, and was an outspoken advocate of civil rights legislation. Blocked from influence in the Republican Party because of his liberal voting record, Javits tried to make up for his lack of power in the Party by serving on many committees and informing himself on a wide range of issues. [See EISENHOWER, KENNEDY, JOHNSON Volumes]

During the Nixon and Ford Administrations, Javits sponsored legislation in several areas. An early advocate of consumer protection, he introduced in 1970 with Sen. Abraham Ribicoff (D, Conn.) [q.v.] a bill to establish an independent consumer protection agency. Filibusters killed the bill on the Senate floor in 1972 and again in 1974. Finally passed by both houses of Congress in 1975, the bill died in conference because of a threatened veto by President Ford. Javits was also a prime mover behind legislation to regulate private pension plans. As a member of the Senate Labor and Public Welfare Committee, Javits first introduced such legislation in 1970. With Sen. Harrison Williams (D, N.J.) [q.v.], he conducted a two-year study of private pension plans and held hearings throughout the country to gather data on abuses. Their study showed that most workers seldom received benefits and recommended legislation to regulate funding of pension plans and to guarantee to workers at least a part of their pensions even when they changed jobs. In 1974 Congress finally passed a bill establishing minimum federal standards of investing and financing for private pension plans.

Javits also supported attempts to establish a national health insurance program and to provide federal subsidies for mass transit. In 1972 he led the fight for passage of a law that gave the Equal Employment Opportunities Commission the power to take cases of job discrimination to court. In 1973 he supported extension of unemployment compensation benefits, and in 1974, he helped win passage of the first increase in the federal minimum wage since 1967. A strong advocate of civil rights, Javits opposed attempts to slow the pace of school desegregation and to place restrictions on the use of busing to achieve integration.

During the Nixon years, Javits became increasingly critical of the war in Vietnam. In May 1969 he called Nixon's Vietnam policy "sterile" and asked the President to set a timetable for the withdrawal of U.S. troops. In 1970 he voted for the Cooper-Church Amendment to cut off funds for combat operations in Cambodia, and in 1971 supported the McGovern-Hatfield end-the-war Amendment. As a member of the Senate Foreign Relations Committee, Javits voted for a 1972 proposal to cut off funds for all combat operations in Southeast Asia by the end of 1972.

Concerned about the apparent erosion of congressional authority in the area of foreign policy, Javits introduced legislation in 1970 to limit the war-making powers of the President. Finally passed by both houses of Congress on Nov. 7, 1973, over President Nixon's veto, the War Powers Act limited to 60 days the President's ability to send U.S. troops into combat without receiving congressional approval. It marked the first time in the nation's history that Congress had undertaken to define the powers of the President as Commander-in-Chief. In 1973, Javits wrote *Who Makes War: The President versus Congress,* in which he outlined the rationale for the War Powers Act.

Javits also took an interest in other areas of foreign policy. Visiting Cuba in 1974 he called for an end to the trade embargo against Cuba, an easing of restrictions on travel to the island and a resumption of diplomatic relations with the Castro regime. In December 1975 Javits led the successful effort in the Senate to bar the use of defense appropriations in the civil war in Angola. A vocal proponent of American aid to Israel, Javits condemned the 1975 United Nations resolution that called Zionism a form of racism.

Javits found himself at odds with the Carter Administration over U.S. policy toward the Middle East. Javits was sharply critical of the State Department's call in 1977 for Israeli withdrawal from all occupied Arab lands and for Israeli agreement to the establishment of a Palestinian state as a condition for peace. In 1978 he led the unsuccessful fight against Carter's package arms deal for the Middle East. [See CARTER Volume]

[JD]

JAWORSKI, LEON
b. Sept. 19, 1905; Waco, Tex.
Special Watergate Prosecutor,
November 1973-October 1974.

The son of immigrant parents, Jaworski was born in Waco, Tex., where his father was an evangelical minister. He graduated from Baylor University and Baylor Law School and in 1925 became the youngest person ever admitted to the Texas bar. Six years later he joined the Houston firm of Fulbright, Crooker, Freeman & Bates and soon became a partner in the firm. During the 1930s he gained a reputation as a skillful courtroom strategist and

tactician. After serving as a colonel in the Army during World War II, Jaworski headed the war crimes trial section of the Judge Advocate General's office. Following the war he returned to his law partnership and gradually assumed a prominent place among the state's leading businessmen, bankers and politicians. During the 1960s he took a hard-line stance against lawlessness, and as president of the American Bar Association in 1971–72, Jaworski expressed his dismay over "errant lawyers" and the diminishing respect for the law.

In early November 1973 Jaworski succeeded Archibald Cox [*q.v.*] as the special Watergate prosecutor. President Nixon had fired Cox when he refused to accept summaries of taped White House conversations subpoenaed as possible evidence in the cover-up of the burglary at the Democratic Party's Washington headquarters in the Watergate complex on June 17, 1972. Jaworski agreed to take the job only after receiving strong assurances from White House staff members that he would have complete independence and could not be discharged by the President without the consensus of the leaders of both Parties in the House and Senate and on the House and Senate Judiciary Committees. The new prosecutor was also guaranteed the right to take the President to court.

Jaworski was sworn in Nov. 5 amidst considerable skepticism in Congress and the press about the viability of another White House-appointed prosecutor. No less skeptical were the members of the special prosecutor's staff, who were badly shaken by the firing of Cox. Shortly after Jaworski took over, however, the prosecutor's office obtained from District Judge John J. Sirica [*q.v.*] relevant portions of seven of the nine tapes Cox had subpoenaed months before. The White House reported that two tapes were missing and a third tape contained an 18½-minute gap.

Of the material provided, the tape from March 21, 1973, was the most damaging to the President's contention that he was innocent of any involvement in the Watergate cover-up. In a conversation with

White House Counsel John Dean [q.v.] and Chief of Staff H.R. Haldeman [q.v.], Nixon not only approved but urged the payment of a large amount of cash to secure the continued silence of E. Howard Hunt [q.v.], a convicted participant in the Watergate burglary. In another March 21 conversation the President coached Haldeman on how to testify untruthfully without committing perjury. From these revelations Jaworski proceeded to build a case against Nixon, and in late December he advised the President's new chief of staff, Alexander M. Haig [q.v.], to get the "finest criminal lawyer you can find" to study the tapes.

Jaworski requested additional tapes and documents that he believed relevant to the Watergate cover-up case and the 1971 break-in at the office of psychiatrist Lewis Fielding, whose patient Daniel Ellsberg [q.v.] was accused of leaking the *Pentagon Papers* to the press. The break-in had been traced to a White House investigative unit known as the "Plumbers," established to plug such leaks. By the end of January, however, Jaworski was told he had all the material he needed and that no more tapes would be forthcoming from the White House. Nevertheless, a month later the special prosecutor's office asked for indictments in both the Watergate and Fielding cases based on evidence already supplied by the President and information provided by the Senate Watergate Committee and former members of the Administration and the Committee to Re-Elect the President (CREEP). Among those who at this point had pleaded guilty and cooperated with the prosecutor in the investigations were John Dean, former Plumbers chief Egil Krogh [q.v.], ex-CREEP deputies Jeb Stuart Magruder [q.v.], Herbert Kalmbach [q.v.] and Frederick LaRue [q.v.].

On March 1 a grand jury in Washington, D.C., indicted seven former White House and CREEP officials for conspiracy to obstruct justice, to defraud the United States and to make false statements and declarations in covering up the Watergate burglary. The accused were top presidential aides H.R. Haldeman, John D. Ehrlichman [q.v.] and Charles W. Colson [q.v.]; ex-Attorney General John N. Mitchell [q.v.]; former Assistant Attorney General and CREEP officer Robert C. Mardian [q.v.]; CREEP counsel Kenneth W. Parkinson and White House assistant Gordon Strachan [q.v.]. Each of the seven pleaded not guilty to all charges.

Despite evidence of President Nixon's complicity in the conspiracy, the grand jury did not indict him because of doubts, raised by Jaworski, that the Supreme Court would allow the indictment of a sitting President for obstruction of justice. However Nixon was named an unindicted co-conspirator so that his taped statements could be used later as evidence in the trial of his former associates. At the same time the jury gave Judge Sirica, who had assigned himself to the case, a sealed report detailing all the information compiled by the special prosecutor on the President's involvement in the cover-up. After judicial review the report was transmitted, on the grand jury's recommendation, to the House Judiciary Committee, which was considering whether to impeach the President.

In a separate action on March 7, a grand jury charged Ehrlichman, Colson and four of the alleged principals in the Fielding break-in with conspiracy to violate civil rights. The four included G. Gordon Liddy [q.v.], a member of the Plumbers and CREEP, and Bernard Barker [q.v.] and Eugenio Martinez, all of whom had been convicted a year earlier in the Watergate burglary trial. Again the accused pleaded not guilty to the conspiracy.

In mid-April Jaworski obtained a subpoena from Judge Sirica for 64 presidential conversations, after the White House had repeatedly ignored his requests for additional material to be used in the cover-up trial, scheduled for the fall. The President's lawyer, James D. St. Clair [q.v.], sought to have the subpoena quashed on the grounds that the tapes were covered by executive privilege and the dispute between the special prosecutor and the President was an "intrabranch affair," not justiciable by the courts. Sirica denied the motion, and St. Clair petitioned the court of appeals for Washington, D.C. To avoid an extended delay of the trial, Jaworski took the matter directly to the Supreme Court, which agreed to bypass the appellate court and hear the case under the "imperative public importance" rule, invoked only twice since the end of World War II.

On July 24, 1974, the Supreme Court ordered President Nixon to turn over the subpoenaed conversations, ruling that the claim of executive privilege in this case "must yield to the demonstrated, specific need for evidence in a pending criminal trial." The decision also affirmed the right of the special prosecutor to take the President to court over the tapes.

Shortly after the decision Nixon released transcripts of three conversations held on June 23, 1972, in which he had instructed H.R. Haldeman to use the Central Intelligence Agency to halt the FBI's investigation of the Watergate burglary. The transcripts showed that the President actively participated in the cover-up just six days after the burglary. With this disclosure Nixon's remaining support collapsed and he resigned on Aug. 9.

Jaworski was deciding whether to prosecute the former President for obstruction of justice in the cover-up when President Ford pardoned his predecessor on Sept. 8 for all possible federal crimes committed while in office. Although he was not consulted on the move, Jaworski maintained that Ford had a constitutional right to issue the pardon. He also believed that Nixon could not have received a fair trial because of the vast publicity surrounding the Watergate affair.

Jaworski resigned as special prosecutor to return to his law practice on Oct. 25, 1974, shortly after the opening of the cover-up trial. By that time the prosecutor's staff had obtained convictions of Ehrlichman, Colson, Liddy and two other defendants in the Fielding break-in. It had successfully prosecuted Dwight L. Chapin [q.v.], President Nixon's appointments secretary, for perjury in connection with a political espionage campaign directed against the Democrats and secured guilty pleas from eight individuals and corporations charged with making illegal campaign contributions. On Jan. 1, 1975, Ehrlichman, Haldeman, Mitchell and Mardian were found guilty of covering up the Watergate burglary.

[JR]

For further information:
Leon Jaworski, *The Right and the Power* (New York, 1976).

JENNINGS, PAUL J(OSEPH)
b. March 19, 1918; New York, N.Y.
President, International Union of Electrical, Radio and Machine Workers, 1965-76.

Jennings studied electronics at the Radio Corp. of America Institute and worked as a technician for Sperry Rand. He helped organize a local of the United Electrical and Radio Workers of America (UE) there in 1939. In 1949, he joined James Carey in founding a CIO-chartered rival union, the International Union of Electrical, Radio and Machine Workers (IUE), with Carey as its president. Four years later Jennings was elected executive secretary of the union's largest district, which included New York and New Jersey and claimed one-third of the IUE's national membership.

During the late 1950s and early 1960s, the IUE suffered a steep drop in membership as the wages and working conditions of its members deteriorated relative to those of workers in other mass production industries. The central problem for labor in the industry was the division of electrical workers among many unions who negotiated individually with a few corporate giants. This lack of unity enabled General Electric (GE) to practice "Boulwarism," a bargaining tactic named for a former GE vice president under which the company made an initial offer and then refused to alter it. IUE President Carey refused to coordinate bargaining strategy with other unions, and opposition to his autocratic methods eventually crystalized around Jennings who challenged Carey's leadership at the union's 1964 national convention. Although on the initial count Jennings lost by a narrow margin, a Department of Labor recount showed him the overwhelming victor.

Seeking to end GE's intransigent negotiating policy as well as to improve wages and benefits, Jennings initiated "coalition bargaining" in which each AFL-CIO negotiating team included representatives from all interested unions. GE fought the coalition plan in the 1966 contract talks but eventually relented. [See JOHNSON Volume]

When the contract came up for renewal in 1969, GE refused to modify its original offer. This conduct precipitated a strike by an IUE coalition of 13 unions, comprising some 147,000 workers. The next day the U.S. Court of Appeals in New York upheld a 1964 National Labor Relations Board ruling that found GE guilty of unfair labor practices in its stubborn negotiating stance, a decision the Supreme Court upheld early in 1970. GE remained firm, however, and the strike dragged on for 102 days, with minor violence at some plants.

The Nixon Administration made an exception to its policy of noninterference in labor disputes when talks broke down in December and federal mediators were brought in. Finally in January of 1970 the IUE and the 12 other participating unions signed a 40-month contract that provided for a raise of $1.05 per hour in wages and benefits spread over the three-year period and an additional 3 cents per hour cost-of-living adjustment. The annual raise averaged 7.5% per year at a cost to GE of over $1 billion, the largest wage settlement in the company's history. Most importantly GE abandoned Boulwarism as a bargaining technique.

Jennings was a member of New York's Liberal Party and actively supported pro-labor candidates. In 1972 the AFL-CIO Executive Council voted overwhelmingly to remain neutral in the presidential elections, marking the first time in its 17-year history the union had not endorsed the Democratic candidate. Jennings, however, was one of the three council members who voted to support Sen. George McGovern (D, S.D.) for the nomination.

In April 1976 Jennings announced that when the IUE's contract expired in July, it planned to demand an unrestricted cost-of-living adjustment as well as substantial wage rises. But Jennings did not lead negotiations. He stepped down as head of the IUE in June on the advice of his doctor. He was replaced by his hand-picked successor David Fitzmaurice. In the contract negotiations the unions won a 21% wage boost spread over three years. They also secured an "uncapped" cost-of-living increase, i.e., an escalator clause with no ceiling, which provided an additional 40 cents per week for each 0.3% increase in the consumer price index.

[FLM]

JOHNSON, U(RAL) ALEXIS
b. Oct. 17, 1908; Falun, Kan.
Undersecretary of State for Political Affairs, January 1969–January 1973.

A career diplomat, Johnson became an expert on Far Eastern affairs. With the exception of a wartime assignment in Brazil and an ambassadorship to Czechoslovakia from 1953 to 1958, Johnson concentrated on Far Eastern affairs both prior to and after World War II. In April 1961 President John F. Kennedy appointed him deputy undersecretary of state for political affairs. During the Johnson Administration he advocated continued military escalation of the Vietnam war. From July 1966 to January 1969, Johnson served as ambassador to Japan. [See EISENHOWER, KENNEDY, JOHNSON Volumes].

In January 1969 President Richard Nixon appointed Johnson undersecretary of state for political affairs. He supported the two-year renewal treaty with Spain in June 1969 for continued use of defense sites in that country. Johnson explained the importance of the sites to American security interests in both the Mediterranean area and Western Europe.

Asian affairs, however, remained the focus of Johnson's attention. In 1969 he summarized the growing importance of the Pacific basin during the preceding 20 years. Referring to the Pacific as no longer an area of colonial empires, Johnson applauded the region's political stability and potential for future economic development. Because of the cautious mood of the American people, he advised that United States association with each country in the region should be based upon the degree of association desired by those countries. Security commitments would be maintained, and free trade and shared economic development would be encouraged. Thus Johnson supported the Nixon Doctrine, announced in November 1969, whereby Asian nations would be expected to assume a greater responsibility for their own defense and the United States would limit its role to economic and military aid and training. He also encouraged regional economic cooperative programs such as the Asian Development Bank, the Southeast Asian Economic Development Conference and the Southeast Asian Agricultural Development Conference.

Japan was of particular concern because of its economic impact on the United States. Johnson counseled the Japanese in 1969 to lift restrictions on American imports to encourage greater free trade between the two countries. He argued that equal access to each other's markets would double the current $7 billion in mutual trade. He also encouraged Japan to play an increasing role in the economic development of the Pacific region.

Johnson expressed the belief in July 1970 that because of South Korea's economic, political and military progress, less American presence was needed in that country. Thus he supported U.S. troop reduction commensurate with South Korea's defense capabilities, but not a total withdrawal.

On Dec. 29, 1972, Johnson signed, on behalf of the United States, the convention on Prevention of Marine Pollution, the first international treaty devoted to environmental protection. In January 1973

Johnson was appointed chief of the United States delegation to the Strategic Arms Limitation Talks (SALT) in Geneva. Annual negotiating sessions were held through 1976 without success. Talks were formally adjourned Nov. 20, 1976, until after the inauguration of President-elect Jimmy Carter [q.v.]. After 42 years in the Foreign Service, Johnson retired to private life in 1977.

[TML]

JONES E(VERETT) LEROI (IMAMU AMIRI BARAKA)
b. Oct. 7, 1934; Newark, N.J.
Black political activist.

Born in Newark, N.J., Jones graduated from Howard University in 1953. Following service in the Air Force, Jones attended Columbia University's graduate school. He became a prolific novelist, poet, literary critic and playwright, emphasizing the stultification and degradation to which blacks were subjected in the American cultural and social milieu. In Jones's opinion, the black American was "the only innocent in the bankruptcy of Western culture." He condemned white society's failure to appreciate beauty and the body, and its destructive proclivities. His plays, the most effective of which was *Dutchman* (1964), evoked the theme of the powerlessness of blacks in a society where the white man defines good and evil. He felt the black was the proper instrument to effect the resurrection of "masculine" feelings in an effeminate, materialistic America. [See JOHNSON Volume]

While teaching at San Francisco State College in 1967, Jones fell under the influence of black activist Ron Karenga, who imbued him with the idea that blacks should create their own local political parties and pressure groups, centered on "bread-and-butter issues." He founded the Black Community Development and Defense Organization (BCD) in Newark in January 1968: a black separatist group devoted to the restoration of the African language Swahili and traditional African dress and customs. Jones and his followers took up the orthodox Moslem faith, and he became their minister, adopting the Arabic name Imamu (Reverend) Amir Baraka.

Despite his apparent desire for black separation from the white, Italian community of Newark, Jones also sought political power for blacks and Puerto Ricans through his political action group, Committee for a United Newark. He also sought to ease racial tensions and prevent the eruption of interracial violence resulting from minor incidents, establishing a "hot line" with leaders of the Italian whites to hinder such escalations. Nevertheless he desired "a black nation," with separate values and culture from those of the whites, to restore black self-esteem.

During the Nixon Administration, Jones was a powerful force in the black nationalist movement. He was a delegate to the first Congress of African People, which met at Atlanta University in September 1970. The meeting's object was a "Pan-African" unity among blacks in those countries with large black populations. At the conference, Jones recommended the creation of a world African party consisting of a federation of local, grass roots parties in countries with black populations all over the world. This "international Pan-Africanist party" would deal with all varieties of black problems from the level of international diplomacy to the problems of neighborhoods. The aim was a feeling of black solidarity and brotherhood all over the world.

However Jones faced opposition from American blacks in his efforts to encourage black unity. His program involved the cultivation of interracial hostility and demanded sweeping social and economic reforms in the U.S. During the 11-week teachers strike in Newark in early 1971, Jones attempted to stir up racial tensions as a means of destroying the Newark Teachers Union (NTU), which he regarded as a tool of the white teacher leadership. He was condemned by the black president of NTU, Carole Graves, who said Jones was trying to convert a "labor-management fight" into an interracial struggle as a way to "break the union and get control of the schools" for neighborhood boards.

Black political consciousness progressed in March 1972 when the first National Black Political Convention met in Gary, Ind. Jones was one of the three co-chairman of the convention, attended by 3,300 delegates from 43 states. The convention set up a National Black Assembly of 427 members and a Council of 43 members to direct future political activities. Within the convention there was a conflict between the separatists who wished to work apart from the two major national political parties, opposed school busing to integrate the races, and supported redistribution of property from whites to blacks and a more conservative group led by the NAACP that wished to work within the existing social and political structure to gain power for blacks. The radicals, who admitted they did not speak for a majority of the nation's blacks, gained control of the convention, and failed to endorse a Democratic presidential nominee for 1972. Jones showed his contempt for the major parties and at the same time a willingness to negotiate with them. He said the new black political organization (whose convention would meet every four years) would "be a chief brokerage operation for dealing with the white power political institutions."

Among the convention's proposals were a $5 billion black development agency, a "reparations" program to transfer wealth from whites to blacks and a constitutional amendment mandating that the number of black congressmen be proportional to the black population in the United States. Local control of schools and police was also favored by the radical-dominated convention. In May, disturbed about a walkout by NAACP representatives, the convention moderated the wording of its "black agenda" and gave qualified support to a busing program run by blacks.

Jones was responsible for the anti-Semitic provisions of the black platform. He urged the "dismantling" of Israel and deplored its "expansionist policy," but his words were later toned down by the convention after leading black politicians spoke against them. The NAACP regarded the provisions on busing and Israel as "particularly outrageous" and condemned the convention's "separatist and nationalist intent."

When the National Black Assembly met in Chicago in October 1972, Jones was elected secretary general of the Assembly and Council. The Assembly passed a resolution of praise for Jones's efforts when it met in Detroit in March 1973 to formulate plans for a national networks of political workshops to improve political aptitudes of blacks. As President Nixon entered his second term, the attitudes of Jones and other nonviolent black activists seemed to be one of peaceful (although hostile) coexistence with the white community.

[AES]

For further information:
Theodore R. Hudson, *From LeRoi Jones to Amiri Baraka* (Durham, 1973).

JORDAN, BARBARA C(HARLINE)
b. Feb. 21, 1936; Houston, Tex.
Democratic Representative, Tex., 1973-79.

Jordan, the daughter of a Texas Baptist minister, graduated from Texas Southern University in 1956 and Boston University Law School in 1959. Back home in Houston, Jordan set up a private law practice and became active in the local Democratic Party organization. After campaigning for John F. Kennedy in 1960 and losing two bids for a seat in the state House of Representatives, Jordan, in 1966, became the first black woman ever elected state senator in Texas. She was an effective legislator; 50% of her bills, including one that created a state Fair Employment Practices Commission and another establishing the state's first minimum wage law, were enacted. Jordan was elected president pro tempore of the state Senate in March 1972. She won a seat in the U.S.

House that fall. She represented Houston's 18th district, which is 44% black and 19% Hispanic.

In the House she maintained a liberal record. During her freshman year she co-sponsored a bill with Martha Griffiths (D, Mich.) [*q.v.*] to extend Social Security coverage to housewives, actively supported the inclusion of domestics in the minimum wage bill, backed free legal aid to the poor and advocated increased appropriations for cities. In November 1973 she voted against the confirmation of Gerald Ford as vice president because of his weak civil rights record. That vote combined with her outspoken opposition to increased military expenditures and support for the attempts of Congress to halt the bombing of Cambodia earned for Jordan a 100% rating in 1973 from the liberal Americans for Democratic Action.

In 1975 she successfully fought for the inclusion of bilingual ballots for "language minorities" in the Voting Rights Act and in 1976 engineered the adoption of mandatory civil rights procedures by the Law Enforcement Assistance Administration and the Office of .Revenue Sharing. And Jordan was consistent in her views on military expenditures and foreign policy. She voted for reductions in the defense budget, opposed appropriations for the B-1 bomber and voted against arms sales to Turkey and Chile.

In 1975 and 1976 liberals criticized Jordan for her close ties to what was known as the "Texas Club" (together, Wright Patman [*q.v.*], George Mahon [*q.v.*], W.R. Poage, Olin Teague [*q.v.*], and Jack Brooks chaired one-third of the House standing committees) and for her vote in favor of the deregulation of natural gas in February 1976. To Jordan, that was practical politics. She was willing to work with her powerful conservative colleagues and support some of their proposals if she thought she could win their support for her proposals in return.

As a member of the Judiciary Committee, Jordan gained national attention during the Committee 1974 hearings into the impeachment of President Nixon. Her powerful oratory and brilliant delivery set the mood of serious deliberation, "My faith in the Constitution is whole," she said, "it is complete, it is total, and I am not going to sit here and be an idle spectator to [its] diminution." Jordan presented a case for a broad interpretation of the grounds of impeachment and argued that the charges before the Committee were a worthy test of the Constitution's value. She voted for all five articles of impeachment; three were passed.

In 1976 Jordan delivered the keynote address at the Democratic National Convention. She thrilled the meeting with a ringing call for "a national community" where everyone is equal. "We cannot improve on the system of government handed down to us by the founders of the Republic," she said, "but we can find new ways to implement that system and realize our destiny." Her own role that night, she asserted, showed "that the American dream need not forever be deferred." Jordan was the first black and the first woman ever to be the Party's keynoter.

After the overwhelming response to Jordan's speech, rumors spread about her chances for the vice-presidential nomination. But the only position Jordan would accept from Jimmy Carter [q.v.] was Attorney General, an offer that never came. In November 1977 Jordan keynoted the National Conference of Women in Houston.

On Dec. 10, 1977, Jordan, at age 41, announced that she would not seek reelection in 1978 and explained that her decision was "predicated on my internal compass directing me to do something different."

[JMP]

JORDAN, VERNON E(ULION)
b. Aug. 15, 1935; Atlanta, Ga.
Executive Director, United Negro College Fund, 1970-72; Executive Director, National Urban League, 1972—.

Jordon graduated from DePauw University in 1957 and Howard University Law School in 1960. He then worked for civil rights attorney Donald Hollowell in Atlanta. During the 1960s Jordan was active in a number of civil rights groups, helping to organize voter registration drives in the South. In 1968 he joined the Office of Economic Opportunity and two years later moved to New York to head the United Negro College Fund. In his first 10 months, Jordan helped the organization raise $8 million for its 36 predominately-black affiliated colleges. [See JOHNSON Volumes]

In January 1972 Jordan was named director of the National Urban League (NUL), succeeding the late Whitney Young. During his tenure he continued the programs begun by his predecessor. He focused on the problems of urban poverty—police-community relations, tenants' rights, welfare reform and job programs. Jordan predicted that the civil rights movement of the 1970s would be "less dramatic" and "less popular" than it had been in the 1960s. "Fair employment opportunities, a prominent issue in the 1960s can no longer be separated," he said, "from full employment of black people and equal access to every kind and level of employment up to and including top policymaking jobs. The central civil rights issue of the seventies is the restructuring of America's economic and political power so that black people have their fair share of the rewards, the responsibilities, and the decisionmaking in every sector of our common society. . . ." He also called for voter registration drives in the North and an effort to deal with drug problems among blacks.

In 1975 Jordan asked for the replacement of "a welfare system that destroys families, discourages work, demeans both giver and recipient and arouses hostility and rage." Jordan called for an annual federal tax credit "to all" with "no means tests, no work requirements, no coercive local regulations or other stigmatizing elements."

[RB]

KALMBACH, HERBERT W(ARREN)
b. Oct. 19, 1921; Port Huron, Mich.
Attorney.

Kalmbach graduated from the University of Southern California in 1949 after serving in the Navy during World War II. In 1951 he received a law degree from the same institution and the following year was admitted to the bar in California. In 1952 he became vice president of the Los Angeles Security Title Insurance Co., a position he held until 1957 when he entered law practice. Kalmbach first became involved in the political career of Richard M. Nixon when he quit his job to work on the 1960 presidential campaign. After Nixon's defeat he returned to the business world and the practice of law.

In 1968 Kalmbach was one of the chief fund raisers for Nixon's presidential campaign. A great deal of money came to Kalmbach through the Lincoln Club, an exclusive group of wealthy businessmen in Newport Beach Calif. who were staunch supporters of Nixon. Kalmbach reportedly raised more than $6 million. Nixon expressed his gratitude by offering the lawyer the post of undersecretary of commerce in the new Administration, which Kalmbach turned down. Kalmbach's practice soon expanded greatly as he became known as the "President's lawyer." In addition to local clients, his firm began to attract large corporations such as United Airlines, the Marriott Corp. and the Music Corp. of America.

Soon after Nixon was installed in the White House, Charles Colson [q.v.], special counsel to the President, formulated an "enemies list." This list contained the names of left-wing people and organizations, leading Democrats, media people and countless others who were considered to be either hostile or threatening to the President. To keep an eye on these people, presidential aide John Ehrlichman [q.v.] organized an investigative force, which originally consisted of two former members of the New York City Police Department's Bureau of Special Services, John Caulfield and Anthony Ulasewicz [q.v.]. The funds for the investigations came out of a secret trust that had been established in Kalmbach's name. The money in the trust was a surplus from the 1968 campaign, and in early 1969 it amounted to $1,668,000. Kalmbach dispersed the moneys in banks in New York, Washington and later in California, keeping ready cash in safe-deposit boxes and the rest of the money in checking accounts. Not only did Kalmbach disburse funds for the investigations but also paid Ulasewicz's salary. During the Watergate investigation, Kalmbach testified that he used the funds at the direction of H. R. Haldeman [q.v.] for others acting on his behalf.

The White House soon established another secret fund that was made possible in large part by Kalmbach's fund-raising abilities. This fund was used to aid favored candidates in the 1970 congressional campaign. Kalmbach alone raised $2.8 million dollars out of a total of $3.9 million. From the basement of a town house in Washington, funds were distributed to candidates in at least 19 states. The "Townhouse Project" was illegal because the participants were acting as a political committee and a committee could not support candidates in two or more states without having a treasurer who filed public reports with Congress.

In late 1970 Kalmbach began raising funds for the 1972 presidential campaign. He was able to elicit contributions from major corporations and organizations, such as the Associated Milk Producers, Inc. (AMPI), that were dependent on favorable government regulations. The AMPI had given money to Kalmbach in 1969, part of which he put into his secret fund and part into the Town House project. A $2 million pledge was obtained from the AMPI for the 1972 campaign. Eighteen other corporations, including American Airlines, Gulf Oil, and Goodyear Tire and Rubber, contributed a total of $754,540. Political contributions out of corporate funds were prohibited during this time. Kalmbach was also able to secure large contributions from those who were interested in government posts, usually ambassadorships. Even though the Administration was not always forthcoming after a contribution had been made, the tactic remained a successful one.

In February 1972 Kalmbach's role as fund raiser was made official when he received the title of associate chairman of the Finance Committee to Re-Elect the President. He held this post until April, when a new law requiring more stringent reporting of contributions went into effect. Kalmbach closed out his secret trust fund and transferred $915,037 to Hugh Sloan, Jr. [q.v.], treasurer of the Finance Committee.

In addition to raising large amounts of money for the 1972 campaign, the White House also developed a policy of harassing the Democratic Party and its candidates. As the incumbent, Nixon had a decisive edge over his Democratic opponent, but his paranoia and that of his aides led to the sabotage and spying which caused the downfall of his second Administration. Two White House aides, Dwight Chapin [q.v.] and Gordon Strachan [q.v.], with the approval of Haldeman, recruited a lawyer Donald Segretti [q.v.], to harass the Democrats and to foster hostility within the Party. In August 1971 Segretti met with Kalmbach who offered him a salary of $16,000 per year plus expenses. Over the next eight months he received $45,336; $22,000 was for expenses and $9,000 of that went to various agents he hired.

During the summer of 1972, Kalmbach worked secretely to raise funds for the Watergate defendants. He delivered the cash to Anthony Ulasewicz who in turn distributed it to the defendants and their families. For three months Kalmbach worked with Ulasewicz, using code names and secret drops for the hush money, until he realized what he was doing was illegal and decided that he could not take part in it any longer.

During the Watergate investigation of 1973, Kalmbach's illegal dealings came to light. In February 1974 he pleaded guilty to raising secret contributions for congressional campaigns and to promising an ambassador a better diplomatic post in return for a campaign contribution. He was sentenced to a jail term of from six to 18 months and ordered to pay a $10,000 fine for violating a federal disclosure law governing campaign funds. Kalmbach was also directed to serve a concurrent six-month prison term for promising the ambassadorial appointment. Kalmbach was freed from prison in January 1975.

[NK]

KASTENMEIER, ROBERT
b. Jan. 24, 1924; Beaver Dam, Wis.
Democratic Representative, Wis., 1959-.

Kastenmeier, whose father was a farmer, served in the Army during World War II. He received his law degree from the University of Wisconsin in 1952 and went into private practice. Kastenmeier won election to the U.S. House in 1958. His district, which centered around the University of Wisconsin at Madison with its 30,000 students, was well matched to Kastenmeier's strong liberal convictions. [See JOHNSON Volume]

Kastenmeier was an opponent of the Vietnam war, and he generally opposed the Nixon-Ford Administration legislative programs. He backed the positions of labor, consumer and conservation groups; he consistently voted to override Ford-Nixon vetoes of welfare and social programs; and strongly opposed the military draft, favoring instead a volunteer army. He often opposed Administration requests for increased military spending, foreign military aid and the development of controversial weapons programs like the B-1 bomber.

Kastenmeier's opposition to the Vietnam war continued into the 1970s. He remained a consistent opponent of the Nixon-Ford Vietnam policy. In 1969 he joined 55 other House members to vote against a resolution condemning President Nixon's efforts to achieve "peace with justice" in Vietnam. In 1972 he supported an amendment calling for an end to American involvement in Vietnam after American prisoners of war were released and those missing in action were accounted for. On May 1, 1975, the day Saigon was secured by Communist forces, he voted against a Ford Administration request for supplemental military aid to South Vietnam.

Kastenmeier served continuously on the House Judiciary and the House Internal and Insular Affairs Committees. In 1969 he became the chairman of the Judiciary's Subcommittee Three, which was renamed the Subcommittee on Courts, Civil Liberties and the Administration of Justice when the Judiciary Committee was reorganized in 1973. During his chairmanship, the subcommittee concentrated on prison reform, copyright law revision and civil liberties issues. Under his leadership, it became an unusually close-knit group that often cosponsored legislation and reported bills unanimously. His panel was the first Judiciary subcommittee to hold open mark-up sessions where members debated and voted on the actual wording of bills.

In 1971 Kastenmeier's subcommittee handled the repeal of the Emergency Detention Act, which had allowed the President to order the detention of persons who might engage in espionage or sabotage activities during a national emergency declared by the President. Calling the repeal one of the biggest victories of his career, Kastenmeier said "that it showed you couldn't have concentration camps in America." The Nixon Administration supported repeal, but it was opposed by the House Internal Security Committee (formerly the House Committee on Un-American Activities). The repeal was a rare defeat for that Committee.

In 1975 Kastenmeier publicly exposed the scope of two government operations that threatened civil liberties. On March 21 he released secret testimony given by the chief postal inspector to his subcommittee about the CIA's mail-snooping operations from the 1950s to the 1970s. On Oct. 22, he released FBI documents including a list of persons to be detained in national emergencies.

Kastenmeier's commitment to prison reform led to the enactment in 1976 of a law to reform parole procedures that his subcommittee had worked on for five years. The law reorganized the U.S. Parole Board and established procedures requiring that parole decisions be reached openly using fair and reasonable processes that granted prisoners some rights.

One of Kastenmeier's major legislative achievements was the enactment of a copyright revision law in 1976, the first major revision of the 1909 copyright law. The effort to revise the law started in 1955 when Congress authorized the Copyright Office to study comprehensive revision. Among other changes the 1976 law extended the copyright duration to 50 years beyond the death of the author and provided for a "fair use" doctrine, which had been sporadically developed by the courts. The doctrine allowed limited free use of copyrighted materials.

Kastenmeier played an important but low-key role during the House Judiciary Committee's 1974 impeachment proceedings. He was a member of the Committee's Impeachment Advisory Group, and his vote could be counted on for impeachment before most people had expressed a position on the issue. Kastenmeier firmly insisted that each article of impeachment be debated and voted on separately. Some members supporting impeachment wanted to delay the vote on all the articles until they had all been debated. Kastenmeier's firm position ensured that the Committee followed a procedure which required the members to show the public how each of them interpreted the evidence pertaining to each impeachment article and how they voted on the article following its debate.

During the Carter years, Kastenmeier maintained his liberal record. In 1977, as chairman of the Subcommittee on Courts, Civil Liberties and the Administration of Justice, he led an investigation of access to federal courts.

[AE]

KELLEY, CLARENCE M(ARION)
b. Oct. 24, 1911; Kansas City, Mo.
Chief of Police, Kansas City, Mo.,
1961-73; Director, Federal Bureau of
Investigation, July 1973-February
1978.

Clarence Kelley grew up in Kansas City, Mo. He received his B.A. from the University of Kansas in 1936 and his LL. B. from the University of Kansas City Law School in 1940. Shortly after graduating Kelley joined the FBI as a special agent. During his 21 years in the agency, Kelley served in 10 cities, handling criminal cases and administrative operations, rather than security investigations. During the late 1950s he was promoted to special agent in charge of the Birmingham, Ala., field office and in 1960 headed the Memphis, Tenn., office. When Kelley reached the optional retirement age of 50, he was recommended by, among others, Attorney General Robert F. Kennedy and various FBI officials to the Kansas City Board of Police Commissioners, who were searching for a new police chief. Kelley returned to Kansas City to take the job in 1961.

In a reorganization of the demoralized department, Kelley fired many men who had been involved in corruption scandals under his predecessor. He then began a series of innovations that made the Kansas City Police Department a national law enforcement model. In 1968 he introduced the first around-the-clock helicopter patrols in any major U.S. city and created the Automated Law Enforcement Response Team (ALERT), a system of computerized police records that eventually covered 10,000 square miles as smaller towns in the Kansas City area hooked into the system. At first the names of "mentals," activists and militants were fed into the computer with the names of convicted criminals, but pressure from civil rights groups and the local American Civil Liberties Union forced the police to purge their files.

Kelley also vetoed the practice of gathering information on student demonstrators and reprimanded officials of a suburban town for passing ALERT information about newcomers to landlords and employers. Another Kelley innovation was the "metro squad," a mini-FBI that could be called in for homicides and other major crimes. He experimented with a more open department, initiating regular discussions between patrolmen and officers as an alternative to the quasi-military precinct organization; increased police pay; and offered educational incentives. Modern equipment and the addition of 400 men to the force helped reduce Kansas City's crime rate by 24% between 1969 and 1972.

The major controversy during Kelley's tenure as Kansas City police chief centered on his handling of racial problems. By 1968 Kansas City's population was over 20% black, but its police force was 95% white. The police were distrusted in the black community, and racist attitudes in Kansas City hardened in reaction to the civil rights movement. Essentially a conservative, Kelley made little attempt to ease the situation.

On April 9, 1968, the day of the funeral of Dr. Martin Luther King, Jr. [q.v.], a group of school children marched to city hall demanding that the schools be closed in King's honor. They were dispersed with tear gas and billy clubs by police in full riot gear. Kelley requested National Guardsmen from the governor and adopted a hard-line policy, refusing to join the mayor in apologizing for the use of tear gas at city hall. During the ensuing riots six unarmed black men were shot. In retrospect Kelley admitted that some officers might have acted unwisely, but he took no disciplinary action.

When on June 7, 1973, President Richard Nixon designated Kelley permanent director of the FBI, political commentators expected Kelley's Senate confirmation hearings to center on the issue of racism. However the controversy over Kelley's handling of the 1968 riots had subsided, and members of the Senate Judiciary Committee were more concerned with establishing Kelley's freedom from involvement in the Watergate scandal and his willingness to cooperate with Congress. Traditionally the FBI had operated as an independent investigative agency with very little supervision from Congress or the executive branch.

The death in 1972 of J. Edgar Hoover [q.v.], FBI director for nearly 50 years, and the resignation of Acting Director L. Patrick Gray [q.v.] in April 1973, after his admission of burning documents connected with Watergate, left the Bureau in a state of growing crisis. Abuses during the Hoover period, including infringements of civil liberties involved in the FBI's "domestic security" investigations, were beginning to surface. The Senate wanted assurance that the new FBI director would stop these questionable practices and be willing to submit to congressional supervision.

During his confirmation hearings Kelley stated, "I have never bowed to political pressure," and informed the Committee that he would report to Congress regularly and cooperate in a strong congressional oversight relationship. After hearings that lasted only three days, Kelley was enthusiastically endorsed by the Senate Judiciary Committee and confirmed by the Senate. President Nixon flew to Kansas City to swear Kelley in on July 9, 1973.

As FBI director, Kelley disappointed those who had hoped for immediate sweeping reforms of Bureau policies. While Kelley faced external pressure from the Justice Department and Congress to reform and modernize Bureau practices, he also had to deal with considerable pressure from within the FBI hierarchy to remain true to the methods of former chief J. Edgar Hoover. Many observers saw Kelley's choice of veteran agent and Hoover-loyalist Nicholas P. Callahan as his associate director and of other Hoover supporters for key positions as an indication that he had capitulated to the traditionalists.

When Kelley appeared before the House Subcommittee on Civil Rights and Constitutional Rights, which was investigating the FBI's counterintelligence programs (COINTELPROs), he was accompanied by at least six Bureau officials. Denying pressure from within the FBI, Kelley nevertheless refused to condemn COINTELPRO activities that had taken place under Hoover during the political upheavals of the 1960s. These activities included attempts to have persons lose their jobs, their apartments and their credit ratings because of their political affiliations. Kelley issued orders in December 1973 forbidding FBI personnel to engage in investigative activities that would abridge the civil liberties of U.S. citizens. However he defended the COINTELPRO activities of the 1960s, stating that Hoover thought them necessary at the time to deal with "revolutionary elements" and that FBI agents should not be prosecuted for their participation in these activities.

While some saw Kelley as a Hoover loyalist, others felt that he was shrewdly gaining the trust of the slow-moving Bureau hierarchy in order to gradually introduce reforms. Kelley brought in independent advisers to help him run the Bureau and convened a series of regional management symposia for assistant directors, inspectors and special agents in charge of field offices. By 1976 he had redirected more FBI resources toward the prosecution of white-collar and organized crime and had cut the "internal security" investigations, which had formed a large part of Bureau activity during the 1960s, by 98%. Kelley removed the categories of "extremists" and "internal security" from the domestic intelligence division and, under new Justice Department guidelines, restricted political investigations to those who had already broken the law.

Despite Kelley's reforms, when the newly formed Senate Select Committee on Intelligence held its first FBI oversight hearings in September 1976, the Bureau faced the worst internal crisis in its history. The Committee unearthed new evidence of illegal activity, internal corruption and abuse of power. Kelley himself was almost fired by President Gerald Ford when it was discovered that he had accepted gifts of furniture and appliances from his subordinates and that carpenters from the Bureau's Exhibit Division had done some work in his apartment. Although Kelley's integrity was later vindicated, it became clear that such favors had been common under Hoover and that FBI officials had accepted kickbacks on electronic equipment. The Committee also gathered substantial evidence of illegal wiretappings and the "systematic theft" of government property by FBI agents, abuses that dated back to the 1930's when the FBI was first authorized to gather information about the political beliefs of U.S. citizens.

In January 1977 President Jimmy Carter [q.v.] and Attorney General Griffin Bell decided that the FBI needed a new director, someone free of any connection with FBI scandals. Both Carter and Bell praised Kelley's leadership and reforms, but felt he was moving too slowly in his attempts to change FBI policy. The President appointed Kelley to a special eight-man selection committee to search for his successor.

Kelley announced his intention to retire in June 1977, but when his designated successor, federal Judge Frank Johnson, had to decline the directorship due to health problems, Kelley agreed to remain in his position through February 1978. On Feb. 15, after more than four years of service, Kelley retired as director, and was replaced by federal Judge William H. Webster.

[DAE]

For further information:
Sanford J. Ungar, *FBI* (Boston, 1976).

KENNEDY, DAVID M(ATTHEW)
b. July 21, 1905; Randolph, Utah
Secretary of the Treasury, January 1969-January 1971.

Kennedy obtained his bachelor's degree from Weber College in 1928. He began a 16-year period at the Federal Reserve Bank in 1930 but continued his education at George Washington University, earning an M.A. in 1935 and an LL.B. in 1937. He completed his formal schooling with a degree from Rutgers University's Graduate School of Banking in 1939. In 1946 Kennedy was appointed vice president of the Continental Illinois National Bank and Trust Co. of Chicago. By the time he left Continental Illinois in 1969 he had risen to be chairman of the board. Under his leadership, Continental Illinois had become active in promoting business and economic opportunities for Chicago's black population. Kennedy was a special assistant to the Secretary of the Treasury in 1953-54.

Kennedy was part of the team which, in December 1969, planned the economic policy which the Nixon Administration pursued for the first two years of its existence, and which it began to abandon as Kennedy left office. The policy essentially involved a series of deflationary measures, above all manifest in a tightening of interest rates and a slowing of monetary growth, as well as a commitment to balancing the federal budget. In his confirmation hearings Kennedy fully endorsed these goals.

His nomination encountered some resistance when Sen. Albert Gore (D, Tenn.) [q.v.] accused Kennedy of conflict of interest as a stockholder of Continental Illinois, but Kennedy agreed to place his stock in trusteeship. He had also created a minor stir in December 1968 by implying that a rise in the official price of gold—for over a decade anathema to Treasury officials concerned with the prestige of the dollar—might be considered to help stabilize the U.S. currency. This remark triggered a speculative surge in the European gold markets. However, in one of his first statements after assuming office, Kennedy reaffirmed his commitment to the long-standing Treasury policy. The market price of gold in Europe immediately took a sharp fall.

Kennedy added his voice to the Administration's attempts to educate the American people to tight money after eight years of Keynesian policies. In February 1969 he called for "fiscal restraint," but also warned against a too-rapid reflation with its untoward consequences for employment. He warned against a repetition of the abrupt shift in Federal Reserve policy when the Fed had reverted to easy money even before its 1965-66 tight-money policies had borne fruit. He foresaw even larger federal surpluses for fiscal 1970 than the $3.5 billion estimated by the Administration and opposed proponents of the abolition of the 7% investment tax writeoff.

Kennedy came under fire from anti-banking members of Congress such as Wright Patman (D, Tex.) [q.v.] on several occasions. When Kennedy testified on a proposed bill which restricted bank-owned holding companies to banking activities alone, warning that without such restraint "within a few years . . . we would find ourselves in a structure dominated by some 50 to 75 centers of economic and financial power," Patman brushed aside the criticism and argued that the legislation was not tough enough. In July 1969, after a further prime-rate interest rise by commercial banks, Patman, a long-time advocate of low interest rates, criticized Kennedy for having failed to prevent it.

In late 1969 and early 1970, as the U.S. economy began to slow down in response to the Administration's measures, Kennedy continued to serve as a spokesman for these policies. He warned against possible wage-price controls if Congress failed to extend President Johnson's surtax and told the Joint Economic Committee that a 4% rate of unemployment was "acceptable" to the Administration. Shortly thereafter he reaffirmed the need to wait for a recession before undertaking any expansionary policies. He complained that the American public did not understand the need for fiscal restraint.

By the time of the November 1970 congressional elections, the Nixon Administration's tight-money policies had begun to show their effects: unemployment had risen from 4% to 6%, the stock market had fallen over 300 points, and production was falling. The Democratic Party thus made what were considered excessive gains for an off-year election. White House Press Secretary Ronald Ziegler [q.v.] did not deny that a Cabinet shakeup was in the offing. Thus in mid-December Nixon informed Congress that former Texas Gov. John Connally [q.v.], a Democrat, would succeed Kennedy at the Treasury, thereby giving economic policy a "bipartisan" quality. Although it was stated that the "soft-spoken" Kennedy—a description which was underlined to some observers by the style of his successor—had agreed to serve only two years upon assuming office, Treasury officials confirmed rumors that Kennedy had offered to resign as a "scapegoat" after the disappointing election results. Kennedy was thus appointed ambassador-at-large with Cabinet status, and left the Treasury in early 1971.

As ambassador-at-large, Kennedy was primarily involved in negotiating and signing trade agreements with major importers to U.S. markets. A growing chorus of protectionist sentiment was one major response to the recession. Thus in 1971, because of the Nixon Administration's opposition to overt protectionist measures, Kennedy signed a series of "voluntary restraint" agreements with Italy, Japan and Taiwan, affecting shoe and textile shipments to the United States.

In December 1971 Kennedy was given additional duties as ambassador to the North Atlantic Treaty Organization. One year later, he was replaced at that post by Donald Rumsfeld, [q.v.] and in early 1973, he retired to private life in Illinois.

[L G]

KENNEDY, EDWARD M(OORE)
b. Feb. 22, 1932: Brookline, Mass.
Democratic Senator, Mass., 1962–.

Edward Kennedy, brother of President John F. Kennedy and Sen. Robert F. Kennedy (D, N.Y.) entered Harvard University in 1950. After he was suspended from the university in the spring of 1951 for cheating on an examination, he served a two-year hitch in the Army. Readmitted to Harvard, he graduated in 1956 but was denied admission to the university's Law School. He earned his law degree from the University of Virginia in 1959. Kennedy worked in his brother's 1960 presidential campaign and won election to the U.S. Senate in 1962.

In the upper house Kennedy established a liberal record, supporting a wide variety of social welfare legislation as well as efforts to end the Cold War with the Soviet Union. He gradually established a reputation as an effective legislator. [See KENNEDY, JOHNSON Volumes]

During the Nixon-Ford years, Kennedy generally opposed the Administration. He regularly voted to override the Nixon-Ford vetoes of spending legislation for social and welfare measures, usually voted to cut defense spending and weapons development programs and often spoke out against the Administration on foreign policy issues. Kennedy was a strong advocate of consumer legislation, federal election reform and a vigorous supporter of gun control. In 1975 Kennedy, a Catholic, led the Senate floor opposition that prevented anti-abortion forces from attaching an anti-abortion amendment to the fiscal 1976 appropriations for health services. Kennedy, who was the floor manager for the health services bill, also tried to compromise with the Ford Administration on the funding issue by accepting the lower funding voted by the House. Ford still vetoed the bill, but Congress overrode the veto.

As a Democratic spokesman on foreign policy issues, Kennedy urged the normalization of relations with Communist China and introduced legislation to end the U.S. embargo on trade with Cuba established during his brother's presidency. He supported efforts toward international disarmament. Kennedy was an outspoken opponent of the Vietnam war and supported the congressional efforts to legislate an end to American involvement.

In 1969 Kennedy was considered the front-runner for the 1972 Democratic presidential nomination until the July 18 auto accident on Chappaquiddick Island in which a young woman drowned. Kennedy left the scene of the accident and failed to report it for 10 hours. He eventually pleaded guilty to a charge of leaving the scene of an accident and was given a two-month suspended sentence, the minimum under Massachusetts law. On July 25, he made a televised speech to Massachusetts voters in which he gave his account of the accident and appealed to voters to help him decide whether he should remain in the Senate. Polls showed that more than 80% of the voters wanted him to stay in office, and he resumed his Senate duties. On July 30 he announced that he would not run for President, that he would run for reelection to the Senate in 1970 and that he would serve out his full term if reelected.

Kennedy became known as "Mr. Health" during the 1970s when he provided strong leadership for national health insurance. He became the chairman of the Labor and Public Welfare Committee's Subcommittee on Health in 1971. Kennedy was one of the 100 members of the Committee on National Health Insurance established by United Automobile Workers President Walter P. Reuther [q.v.]. The Committee recommended a national health insurance bill that Kennedy sponsored with 14 other Senators in 1970. The comprehensive health insurance proposal, then estimated to cost $40 billion, encouraged group medical services and preventive medicine. It would have established national standards for hospitals and doctors; supplemented health manpower training programs for medical professionals and developed national health policies. The federal government would have administered the proposed program, which would have covered most personal health care services. It would have been financed partly from payroll taxes and partly from general federal tax revenues. The bill failed that year and in subsequent years.

Kennedy sponsored the Developmental Disabilities Services and Facilities Construction Amendments of 1970, which extended and broadened programs begun under the Mental Retardation Facilities Construction Act of 1963. The new program covered both mental and developmental disabilities, such as epilepsy. Also in 1970 Kennedy favored a three-year extension of the Hill-Burton hospital construction program. Nixon vetoed the bill, but the veto was overridden. Kennedy sponsored the 1973 law that provided federal funding for Health Maintenance Organizations and the 1974 act to create a network of local health systems agencies.

During the Carter Administration, Kennedy became an important critic of the President's economic and energy programs. His opposition revived speculation that he might challenge Carter for the Democratic nomination in 1980. [See CARTER Volume]

[AE]

KEOGH, JAMES
b. Oct. 29, 1916; Platte County, Neb.
Special Assistant to the President, 1969–71; Director, United States Information Agency, 1973–77.

James Keogh received his Ph.B from Creighton University in 1938 and the same year began a career in journalism with the Omaha *World-Herald.* He left the newspaper, where he had become city editor, to join *Time* magazine in 1951 as a contributing editor. Over the next two decades Keogh rose to become assistant managing editor and then executive editor. In 1956 Keogh wrote the complimentary *This Is Nixon* about the then Vice President. He took a leave of absence from *Time* in 1968 to serve as chief of the research and writing staff for the 1968 Nixon presidential campaign.

Keogh came to the White House with the Nixon Administration as a special assistant to the President. He held the same position he had occupied during the campaign. His research and writing staff was responsible for drafting Nixon's speeches, messages and remarks. Keogh's three senior writers, William Safire [q.v.], Raymond K. Price, Jr. [q.v.], and Patrick J. Buchanan, Jr. [q.v.], presented the President with the option of a variety of styles. Safire was quotable and wry, Price lyrical and Buchanan hard-hitting. According to Safire, Nixon deliberately sought the vari-

ety and would utilize a particular writer depending on the style and tone needed. The staff also worked to background and rehearse the President for his press conferences. The team would prepare briefing books for Nixon on anticipated questions and possible responses.

In December 1970 Keogh resigned as head of the research and writing staff and was replaced by Price. He returned to the President's service in 1972 to write the script for the documentary film "The Nixon Years-Change Without Chaos," shown at the Republican National Convention. The same year he published *President Nixon and the Press.* Keogh described the book's purpose as twofold: to provide an insight into the controversy at the time concerning the national media's coverage of the federal government and to attempt to remedy what the author saw as failing in his lifelong profession.

The book also reported on the efforts of Keogh's staff and the Nixon Administration to combat what it believed to be biased news coverage and to get its side of the story to the American public. Keogh claimed that never in recent times had a President encountered such obvious hostility from the working press. He discounted any theory of a conspiracy among journalists. Rather he identified what he called a condition of conformity in which the most influential of the news media tended to rely on each other and to report the news in a way which favored one political point of view. He sought to show that the one-sided coverage resulted from an imbalance in the political leanings of the news staffs of the major networks and newspapers. Keogh acknowledged that American journalism had always been marked by partisanship but argued that advocacy journalism became more dangerous in an age of electronic communication. He suggested that the press focus on its essential purpose to inform.

To document his point of view, Keogh drew on his experience while in the White House. He recounted how early in the Administration syndicated columnist Jack Anderson [q.v.] had written a column claiming that Director of the Office of Economic Opportunity Donald Rumsfeld [q.v.] had cut expenditures for the poor but had lavishly refurnished his own office. Despite protests from Rumsfeld and proof that the accusations were untrue, Anderson refused to print a correction. Keogh pointed out that the lasting impression of the incident in the media was that the Nixon Administration was indifferent to poverty.

A similar impression, Keogh believed, carried over into the way the press covered the Administration and race relations. The fixed understanding was that since Nixon had won with the help of the South and with little support from blacks, his Administration would turn back the advances of civil rights. Such mistaken attitudes, Keogh commented, prevented the accurate coverage of such accomplishments as the massive desegregation of Southern schools.

Keogh returned to government service in 1973 when he was confirmed as the head of the United States Information Agency. He remained in that post until 1977.

[SF]

For further information:
James Keogh, *President Nixon and the Press* (New York 1972).

KIRK, CLAUDE R(OY), JR.
b. Jan. 7, 1926; San Bernardino, Calif.
Governor, Fla., 1967-71.

The son of railroad clerks who later became Alabama state civil servants, Kirk graduated from Duke in 1945. After starting as a salesman, he eventually became a successful businessman in the investment banking and insurance fields. He registered as a Republican while working in Richard Nixon's 1960 presidential campaign. In 1964 he lost a Senate race to the incumbent, Spessard L. Holland. Two years later, benefiting from a split in the state Democratic Party, he was elected Florida's first Republican governor since Reconstruction.

Despite strains with the Democratic-controlled legislature and his popularly elected cabinet, Kirk quickly piled up some impressive achievements. He obtained passage of a new state constitution, supported the reorganization of the state's 170 agencies to a more streamlined 26 and ordered a review of mineral leases. At the same time, Kirk was a flamboyant governor, excellent at keeping himself in the public eye through both dramatic political gestures and the force of his own personality.

In February 1968 about half of the teachers in Florida went out on strike. The walkout lasted for almost a month, until taxes were raised $310 million to provide more funds for education. Opponents charged that the strike could have been settled earlier had the Governor not been spending so much time out of state in pursuit of the vice-presidential nomination. Hoping he would balance a ticket with a moderate or liberal presidential candidate, Kirk supported Nelson Rockefeller [q.v.] for the nomination. After the convention, he did campaign for Richard Nixon, but he was never a favorite at the White House, and observers thought his vice-presidential campaign had been foolish and ill-advised.

In 1969 Secretary of the Interior Walter Hickel [q.v.] conferred with the governor on the protection of Everglades National Park against deterioration and private development. By August Kirk also joined the opposition to the proposed Miami jetport in the Everglades, a plan which was later abandoned. He kept a firm hand on the affairs of state, improving services to the disadvantaged and, in August 1970, attempting to prevent the Army's dumping of nerve gas 250 miles off the Florida coast.

Nevertheless, his personal style came increasingly under attack. Earlier in his term, he had recruited a private detective force to drive organized crime from the state. Likened to a vigilante group since it was privately funded (by donations Kirk solicited), it was soon disbanded. But while Kirk continued to stress his anti-crime drive, he balked in 1969 when asked by the state attorney general to hand over files concerning control of Miami Beach resort hotels. Kirk had also organized a Governor's Club consisting of large private contributors. The funds donated by club members were used mainly to finance his comfortable life-style: for example, $177,000 was spent to rent a jet, and little was left for the 1970 gubernatorial campaign. Many Florida Republicans were beginning to feel that Kirk's actions in these and other matters were helping destroy the significant gains the party had made in recent years.

On racial matters, Kirk was generally considered a moderate. His handling of disturbances in black ghettos was sometimes termed harsh, but he also appointed the state's first black constable and supported integration laws.

Early in 1970 he tangled with the courts who had ordered statewide desegregation of schools, a move which the Governor thought impractical and disruptive in the middle of the school year. In April, he ordered schoolchildren in Manatee Co. to ignore a court-ordered integration plan involving widespread busing; he also dismissed the county school board, taking control of the system himself. Kirk said he intervened in the case to get the issue of busing (which he opposed) before the U.S. Supreme Court. When lower courts found him guilty of contempt, he relinquished personal control of the schools. By the end of April, the busing was underway, and the Manatee Co. schools were peacefully integrated.

Kirk further alienated state Republicans by persuading G. Harrold Carswell [q.v.] to run in the 1970 Senate primary against the organization candidate, Rep. William C. Cramer [q.v.]. Carswell lost, and Kirk himself did not win renomination until a runoff. In November, he lost his bid for a second term to Reuben Askew. Observers attributed the defeat to his personal flamboyance and his lack of enthusiastic support from party regulars. Upon leaving office, he resumed his career as a businessman, but remained active in anti-busing campaigns, both in Florida and elsewhere.

[TD]

KISSINGER, HENRY A(LFRED)
b. May 29, 1923; Furth, Germany.
Special Assistant to the President for National Security Affairs, December 1968-November 1975; Secretary of State, September 1973-January 1977.

Heinz Alfred Kissinger was born into an Orthodox Jewish family. The family fled Nazi Germany in 1938, going first to England and then to New York City, where Kissinger studied accounting at City College and worked in a shaving brush factory. He was drafted in 1943 and worked in Army intelligence. After serving as a district administrator with the military government of occupied Germany from 1945 to 1946, Kissinger enrolled at Harvard. He received a B.A. summa cum laude in 1950 and a Ph.D. in 1954. His dissertation, later published as a book, concerned European diplomacy during the post-Napoleonic period. The work sought to show how the archconservative Prince Metternich brought order, stability and an era of peace to Europe through maintenance of a balance of power in which each country had a vested interest. Kissinger admired Metternich's skillful use of personal and secret negotiations unhampered by the demands of bureaucracy and public opinion and of his occasional threat of force to preserve order. Kissinger's study reflected his own pessimism and fear of instability and served as the basis for his approach to international power politics.

In 1954 Kissinger became study director of a Council on Foreign Relations project seeking to explore alternatives to the massive retaliation policy of the Eisenhower Administration. The project report, published in 1957, accepted Eisenhower's view that the Soviet Union was an expansionist power seeking to undermine the stability of the West, but proposed a strategy based on the limited use of nuclear weapons as an alternative to massive retaliation.

In 1956 Nelson A. Rockefeller [q.v.] appointed Kissinger a director of a Rockefeller Brothers Fund special project formed to study the nation's major domestic and foreign problems. The project's final foreign affairs report, published as *The Necessity for Choice: Prospects for American Foreign Policy* (1961), warned against optimism over prospects for a Soviet-American detente and stressed the need for a strategy centered on tactical nuclear weapons. It called for an expanded nationwide civil defense system and for a major increase in defense spending to meet the expected Soviet challenge.

Kissinger returned to Harvard as a lecturer in the government department in 1957 and eventually became a professor in 1962. From 1959 to 1969 he was director of Harvard's Defense Studies Program. Kissinger also served as a consultant to the Arms Control and Disarmament Agency from 1961 to 1967 and to the State Department from 1965 to 1969. Between 1961 and 1962 he was an adviser to the National Security Council. During the late 1960s he visited South Vietnam as a State Department consultant. On the basis of personal interviews with many nongovernment Vietnamese, Kissinger concluded that an American victory was impossible, but that it was also unacceptable to withdraw from Vietnam in a manner that would cause the U.S. to lose its "honor" and credibility in the eyes of its allies. Nonetheless, he published an article that justified U.S. policy as necessary to stem Communist expansion.

Kissinger wrote speeches for Rockefeller's bid for the 1968 Republican presidential nomination. He also produced a peace plan that incorporated elements of the plan he would pursue as Nixon's foreign policy adviser, including a proposal for the gradual withdrawal of U.S. troops and their replacement by South Vietnamese. In addition, the plan recommended the withdrawal of troops on both sides, the imposition of an international peace-keeping force, internationally supervised free elections and negotiations for the reunification of Vietnam.

Rockefeller's failure to win the nomination upset Kissinger, who considered Richard Nixon a demagogue without purpose or a sense of history and a man who did not "have the right to rule." Nixon, however, had been impressed by Kissinger's work and, through his aides, induced the professor to act as a foreign policy consultant for the Republican campaign. In late November 1968 Kissinger was offered the post of head of the National Security Council (NSC) and the position of special assistant for national security affairs.

Politically the offer was a clever move aimed at hurting Nixon's old rival Rockefeller: Rockefeller was not offered a post in the new Administration and at the same time one of his closest advisers was taken from him. Moreover, the appointment added an intellectual to the White House staff and won Nixon some rare praise from liberal and academic critics.

Kissinger quickly altered his opinion of Nixon. He discovered he and Nixon agreed on their approach to foreign policy and shared a contempt for the bureaucracy and a pessimism about the limits of American power. They both believed that there was need for more flexibility, more thorough planning and a better defined philosophy in the conduct of foreign affairs. Nixon realized that the American public was tired of the Cold War rivalry with the USSR and particularly of the Vietnam war. Both men wanted to maintain an active international role for the U.S. and subtly resist what they viewed as the new isolationist tendencies of Congress and the public.

The new President claimed expertise in foreign affairs and wanted to make policy himself, not delegate the task to the traditional departments, State and Defense, as it had been under Lyndon Johnson. Both men agreed that Johnson had been hampered in foreign affairs because he had delegated authority and only heard what his advisers thought he wanted to hear. The new President wanted Kissinger to coordinate the thinking and recommendations of the various departments and then present him with a reasonable array of alternatives for a given foreign policy issue. Nixon aimed to rationalize and centralize the foreign policy bureaucracy and to make Kissinger the channel through which recommendations from below were passed, criticized and refined. From the beginning Kissinger's position was clearly superior to those of the Secretaries of Defense and State. Subsequently his skill at political infighting, his capacity for hard work and the President's growing dependence on him amplified that superiority. He quickly recruited an NSC staff, appropriating some of the most highly regarded Pentagon and State Department personnel.

The contrast between Kissinger's mode of operation and that followed during Johnson's period was evident in one of his first tasks, preparation of an options memorandum on the progress of the Vietnam war. Identical questions were directed to second-echelon staffers of various departments. Thus many officials evaluated areas outside their field of expertise. In contrast, Johnson's information about military matters always came from top people in the Pentagon. One result of the Kissinger report, called the National Security Study Memoranda (NSSM), was a wider range of opinions and therefore greater accuracy and honesty. But a further result—and one Kissinger did not foresee—was the virtual ineffectiveness of cabinet departments in determining policy. The NSC, in fact, supervised studies on a wide range of policy issues, working through an Interdepartmental Group (IG) composed of assistant secretaries or their deputies from State, Defense, Commerce, Treasury and other relevant departments. The IG never made recommendations. It produced "area" options for NSC consideration. Kissinger himself chaired the committees that reviewed the defense budget, intelligence policy, clandestine intelligence operations, as well as the Washington Special Action Group (WSAG), the top-level crisis group, and the Verification Panel, which oversaw monitoring of the nuclear arms agree-

ments with the Soviet Union. Thus, whatever went to the President had to pass through Kissinger. Unwittingly the Nixon White House became as isolated as Johnson's.

The Soviet Union was the centerpiece of Kissinger's foreign policy. In his view success in any other area of foreign policy was in some way dependent on the Administration's relations with the Soviets. While he no longer thought of the Communist world as an aggressive monolith, he still believed that the USSR was a capricious power not yet reconciled to the international status quo. It was Kissinger's aim to get the Soviet Union to act as a responsible nation-state convinced that working with the U.S. to maintain an international balance of power was in its best interest. To accomplish this he developed the concept of "linkage." If the Soviets wanted American trade and technology, Kissinger argued, then they had to make concessions. Most importantly, the Soviets would have to put pressure on the North Vietnamese to negotiate an end to the Indochina conflict.

Nuclear weapons constituted another crucial issue dividing the two powers. Aside from the realization that nuclear war between the superpowers was unthinkable, Kissinger knew that neither the U.S. nor the Soviet Union could tolerate the costs of an accelerated arms race. He also believed that it was in the mutual interest to defuse tensions in central Europe and in other trouble spots. In addition the U.S. should share some of its heavy defense burden with its allies. This was essential not only in economic terms but also because Kissinger felt that American foreign policy since World War II had been too paternalistic. Without retreating into isolationism, the U.S. no longer needed to confront international crises single handedly, although in practice Kissinger himself acted unilaterally. Nixon was in agreement on the necessity for detente with the USSR and restraint on unilateral U.S. action in local conflicts.

Nixon and Kissinger, because of their emphasis on linkage, were less disposed to rush into the Strategic Arms Limitation

Talks (SALT) than were many of their advisers, such as Secretary of State William Rogers [q.v.]. Nixon responded to early Soviet calls for SALT by saying that talks would be feasible "in a way and at a time that will promote, if possible, progress on outstanding political problems at the same time—for example, on the problem of the Middle East and other outstanding problems in which the U.S. and the USSR, acting together, can save the cause of peace." Meanwhile he supported the development of the Safeguard anti-ballistic missile and the MIRV (multiple independently targeted reentry vehicle) to strengthen America's bargaining position when talks began. The Russians took this expression of linkage to be a form of blackmail or extortion. Government bureaucrats and members of Congress, despite Kissinger's explanation of the concept, feared that it would endanger SALT's future and viewed support of weapons development as lack of interest in arms control.

Kissinger ignored early calls for wideranging discussions with the Soviets to give his staff time to prepare a study on the relative military strength of the two superpowers. One part of the study provided the basis for the President's approval of the nuclear nonproliferation treaty negotiated by the Johnson Administration. It was sent to the Senate in February 1969. The other part of the study put into question Nixon's campaign pledge to ensure "clear-cut military superiority" over the Soviet Union. Superiority was impossible in the decade ahead, especially in view of the Soviets' enormous defense budgets. Nixon accepted the findings and publicly substituted Kissinger's "sufficiency" for "superiority," asserting that the Administration would guarantee "sufficient military power to defend our interests and to maintain . . . commitments." The Helsinki SALT discussions did not begin until November 1969. Although the Soviets had not yet offered to satisfy U.S. demands in the Middle East and Vietnam, Kissinger hoped that progress in the negotiations would encourage greater Soviet accommodation.

Vietnam was the most pressing foreign—and domestic—problem inherited from the Johnson Administration. It also proved harder to resolve than Kissinger expected, because he underestimated the tenacity of Hanoi and the National Liberation Front (NLF). At the 1969 Paris peace talks, the North Vietnamese rejected Kissinger's "two track" formula, which projected a military settlement between Washington and Hanoi and a political settlement between Saigon and the NLF. Kissinger, as his former aide Roger Morris pointed out, was unable to understand the North Vietnamese position that the conflict was a civil war. It was for this reason that he insisted—until May 1972—on mutual withdrawal of troops, a proposition that Hanoi considered unreasonable and unacceptable.

Both Kissinger and Nixon recognized that a military victory was impossible in Vietnam. But they refused to consider a U.S. withdrawal, which they thought would be an ignominious act unworthy of a great power and a signal to enemies and allies that the U.S. could not be trusted to keep its commitments. Instead, in June 1969 they proposed a policy of Vietnamization, gradually giving the South Vietnamese Army the responsibility for conducting the war. But Kissinger had little faith in Saigon's military capacity and he ultimately placed his hopes in a combination of personal diplomacy and periodic "savage, punishing" military escalations. He initiated his personal diplomacy in secret Paris meetings in August 1969 and between February and April of the following year he met with Le Duc Tho, a member of Hanoi's politburo. Little was accomplished and even less was achieved in the official talks, which only served as a cover for the secret conferences. Meanwhile, the Administration pressured the North Vietnamese militarily. In March 1969 secret B-52 raids began over Cambodia, in spite of Washington's official recognition of that nation's neutrality, in an effort to keep enemy troops from moving across the border.

Kissinger's early efforts at diplomacy engendered criticism from several quarters and despite his efforts to end U.S. involvement in Vietnam, the anti-war movement remained active. As an academic in whom some intellectuals had put their hopes for a speedy settlement, Kissinger was especially subject to severe criticism from the left. His penchant for secrecy and tendency to show sympathy for the views of whatever groups or individuals to whom he was speaking earned him a reputation for duplicity. Members of Congress resented Kissinger's refusal to appear before their committees under the cloak of "executive privilege." (As a personal adviser to Nixon, he was not required to testify.) Kissinger's standing fell even further when he supported Nixon's decision to invade Cambodia in May 1970. With one exception his principal aides, who had tolerated his demanding regimen and abusive treatment because of their faith in him and in spite of their aversion to Nixon, quit. Academic colleagues advised Kissinger to resign; others asked him to "stop that madman."

That liberal critics came to view Kissinger as equally villainous as Nixon reflected a growing public awareness that Kissinger was, as some said, "the second most powerful man" in the country and that he, not Rogers, shaped U.S. foreign policy. Kissinger was deemed so important that the Harrisburg Six, a group of pacifists, were indicted in January 1971 for allegedly conspiring to kidnap him and put him on trial for war crimes. Kissinger sought to maintain contact with his critics and even spoke with members of the Harrisburg group, one of whom said, "The scary part of it is he really is a nice man."

Yet Kissinger was popular with the general public. With the exception of Nixon, he was the only member of the Administration to make the 10 "most-admired" persons list, which was compiled annually on the basis of a national poll. The admiration was due in part to the largely uncritical attitude of the national media, which was impressed by his intellectual credentials, charmed by his combination of arrogance and self-deprecating wit and aware of the marketability of his romantic secret shuttle diplomacy. Kissinger, unlike Nixon and his media-hating staff, cultivated the press. A divorced bachelor, Kissinger was photographed in the company of elegant women and was depicted as a cocktail party "swinger" who still found the time to unveil frequent diplomatic marvels. In November 1972 he ascribed his popularity to the "fact that I have acted alone. . . . The Americans love the cowboy . . . who comes into town all alone on his horse. . . ." It was not until after Watergate that the nonradical press would evaluate him somewhat more critically.

One of the least disputed triumphs of the Nixon-Kissinger era was the establishment of ties with the People's Republic of China. It was a case in which the initiative was clearly Nixon's. Both Kissinger and the President had long held the Cold War view of an irresponsible, fanatical China bent on world conquest. Kissinger, whose international bias was clearly European, admittedly knew almost nothing about China and was slower to change his views than Nixon. Yet he appreciated that an approach to China could exploit strained Sino-Soviet relations and be used as leverage in dealings with the Soviet Union, which was obsessed with a fear of the Chinese. Besides, it was consistent with Kissinger's philosophy to give powerful nations a stake in maintaining the international balance of power. Throughout 1969 Nixon put out diplomatic "feelers" to the Chinese via the French, Rumanians and Pakistanis. Kissinger applauded the President's diplomatic challenges to the Soviets—and to the cautious State Department as well—such as his August 1969 visit to Rumania, which was on bad terms with the Soviets and close to the Chinese. More substantive moves (e.g., easing restrictions on American travel to China and ending U.S. naval patrols in the Taiwan Strait) came at the same time border clashes broke out between the Russians and the Chinese. The first direct contacts with the Chinese were made in December 1969 in Warsaw, over the objections of both Soviet specialists in the State Department and hard-liners in the Chinese government. In October 1970 the

White House publicly suggested that it was ready to adopt a two-China formula in the United Nations. After Chairman Mao Tse-tung and Premier Chou En-lai were convinced that the South Vietnamese invasion of Laos in February 1971 was not the prelude to a U.S. invasion of China, they invited an American envoy to Peking, suggesting either Rogers or Kissinger. Nixon chose Kissinger.

With the exception of a group of Ping-Pong players, Kissinger was the first American to officially enter China since 1949. During a July 1971 Asian tour, he flew secretly to Peking via Pakistan. The meetings with Chou were marked by cordiality and apparently genuine personal rapport. The initial climate of goodwill that Kissinger fostered was considered to be his most important contribution to the successful approach to China. At the talks he also conceded that the Americans would now consider Taiwan a part of China, allowing its political future to be settled between the two Chinese governments. Kissinger also laid plans for Nixon's February 1972 visit.

Nixon's surprising announcement of the Peking visit won wide national support, with the exception of some extreme conservatives, and helped his popularity ratings. As Kissinger expected and even hoped, the Soviets were upset. But American allies, especially the Japanese and the Nationalist Chinese, resented not being consulted on the move. Nixon and Kissinger, however, enjoyed the theatricality of the trip and the impression it gave of diplomatic initiative and daring. The Administration proceeded to cut back its troop strength in Taiwan and supported the quest of the People's Republic for seats in the U.N. General Assembly and on the Security Council, although it publicly claimed it would oppose any effort to oust Taiwan from the international organization.

The Chinese breakthrough was combined with the adoption of a firmer policy towards the Soviet Union. Kissinger and the President had been battling with Rogers and the State Department over linkage and Nixon's hard-line approach to the

Russians. In the autumn of 1970 Kissinger, over State's objections, orchestrated the threatening U.S.-Israeli military moves that appeared to stop Moscow's client Syria from toppling the pro-Western regime of Jordan's King Hussein. During the same period Kissinger, employing "tough" language, warned the Soviets not to construct a nuclear submarine base in Cuba, since it was a violation of the post-1962 missile crisis understanding between the U.S. and the USSR. According to CIA reports, the Soviets stopped construction of the base. The Soviets, besieged by problems with China and Warsaw Pact nations, finally agreed in May 1971 to link limitation of offensive and defensive weapons in any SALT accord. Two months after Kissinger's visit to Peking, the Americans and Russians began preparations for a May 1972 Moscow summit. In April 1972 Kissinger made a secret trip to Moscow to lay plans for the May summit and to get the Soviets to pressure the North Vietnamese to become more flexible in the Paris peace talks. The summit, so important to Kissinger's grand designs, produced a large number of cultural, scientific, environmental and trade agreements and eventually the first SALT treaty, which set a limit on certain defensive weapons. SALT gave a crucial boost to Nixon's reelection chances. Larger trade arrangements, including the grain sale to the Soviets, were negotiated by Kissinger in September. In addition, a few weeks after the summit Soviet President Nikolai Podgorny flew to Hanoi to recommend more flexible negotiations with the U.S., since Moscow felt that Nixon was actually ending American involvement and the fall of Saigon was inevitable anyway.

Kissinger's strategy did not always produce the desired results. His famous "tilt" toward Pakistan in the December 1971 India-Pakistan war, conditioned by his and Nixon's emotional dislike of the Indians and their gratitude to Pakistan for its help in making contact with Peking, had disastrous results. The U.S. was put in the position of supporting a military dictatorship against the world's largest democracy and opposing Bangladesh's struggle for independence. India won; Pakistan lost Bangladesh, formerly East Pakistan; and the Soviets, who supported the Indians, claimed a victory over the Americans and Chinese (who also supported Pakistan). Biographers Marvin and Bernard Kalb reported that the policy failure led Kissinger to briefly consider resignation. Records of secret meetings about the war were leaked to Jack Anderson [q.v.] who published parts of them in his column, proving a great embarrassment to Kissinger. He reportedly suspected that White House aides John Ehrlichman [q.v.] and H.R. Haldeman [q.v.], who were jealous of his influence with the President, were responsible for the leaks.

During 1972 Kissinger focused his attention on ending the Vietnam war, which he regarded as a nuisance that kept him from more important business and which jeopardized Nixon's chances for reelection. In the months preceding the 1972 presidential election, he circled the globe in an effort to end the U.S. involvement in Vietnam. Nixon's critics, including his Democratic opponent for the presidency, Sen. George McGovern (D, S.D.) [q.v.], suggested that the President was "manipulating" public opinion and raising expectations by keeping Kissinger in the spotlight. Kissinger even appeared in a Republican campaign film in which he praised Nixon for making possible through SALT a "generation of peace." He also attended GOP contributors' dinners in a "nonpartisan" capacity. He met frequently—in highly publicized secret meetings—with Le Duc Tho, and before the election stated "peace is at hand," which many interpreted as an obvious ploy to improve the President's reelection chances. In October, Kissinger completed a peace settlement with the North Vietnamese. However, he was unable to get the North Vietnamese to accept changes that the South Vietnamese insisted on before agreeing to the proposal. In December, Nixon, with Kissinger's approval, resumed B-52 raids on the North to pressure Hanoi into resuming negotiations.

A peace agreement was signed in January 1973. It followed the one Kissinger had negotiated in October. The terms included: a cease-fire; the complete withdrawal of U.S. troops and the dismantling of U.S. bases within 60 days; and a prisoner-of-war (POW) exchange. The cease-fire allowed North Vietnamese troops to remain "in place," i.e., they were left in control of those areas in the south which they actually occupied. Foreign troops were to leave Laos and Cambodia and troop and supply movements through these countries were banned, but no deadline was set. The DMZ would be the provisional dividing line between north and south until reunification could be achieved peacefully. An international commission would deal with the release of POWs, elections, etc. and President Thieu would remain in office pending elections. The peace, as Kissinger had hoped, provided a "decent interval" between U.S. withdrawal and Communist victory. After the Americans left Indochina, however, an increasingly contentious Congress obstructed Kissinger's plans for further involvement there. In March and April 1973 Kissinger pleaded unsuccessfully for the continued bombing of Cambodia in order to force Hanoi to abide by the Paris accords and bring about a cease-fire. His support of an aid program for Hanoi struck congressional conservatives as an admission that the United States owed reparations to the enemy. In June, Kissinger concluded a round of talks with Le Duc Tho about observance of the terms of the January agreement. The resulting communique did not provide for an end to the Cambodian and Laotian conflicts. The poor results of the talks, some analysts suggested, only reflected the condition of an Administration weakened by the Watergate scandal.

One of Kissinger's greatest triumphs was his handling of the delicate situation in the Middle East, an area that occupied much of his time during Nixon's final months in the White House and during the Ford Administration. In Nixon's first Administration, the area had been left largely to the State Department, because, as analysts noted, State needed something to do and it was thought that Kissinger's Jewish ancestry might prejudice the Arabs against him. However, during the mid-1970s Kissinger handled Middle Eastern diplomacy on a personal level. His ethnic background eventually became an asset because it proved difficult to accuse him of anti-Semitism when he showed sympathy for Arab interests.

In October 1973 Egyptian President Anwar Sadat precipitated the Yom Kippur war with Israel to force the return of Egyptian land lost to the Israelis six years before. For years the U.S. had been staunchly pro-Israel. Kissinger, though not possessed of strong emotional ties to that nation, saw Israel as a U.S. ally and the Arab states, with the exception of the conservative monarchies, as Soviet clients. He blamed the Soviets for supplying offensive arms to the Arabs and encouraging the attack on Israel. Their actions, he felt, were inconsistent with detente. Yet because of Defense Department hesitation, the U.S. only slowly matched the Soviet effort in supplying military aid to its ally. Secretary of Defense James Schlesinger [q.v.], a frequent critic of Kissinger's policies, hesitated to give Israel massive support because such aid might precipitate an oil embargo threatened by the Arabs. However Nixon finally overrode Schlesinger. In view of his Watergate problems, the President realized that failure to aid Israel would result in an overwhelmingly negative public and congressional reaction and what he saw as weakness in the face of a Soviet challenge. In response to the U.S. aid to Israel, the Arab nations instituted a total ban on oil exports to supporters of Israel.

American aid made possible a spectacular Israeli counteroffensive and the Soviet Union consequently called for a cease-fire. Kissinger went to Moscow with authorization from Nixon to sign anything in his name. The Secretary of State and Brezhnev worked out a cease-fire providing for direct Egyptian-Israeli talks. The cease-fire was precarious, however, and a few days after meeting with Brezhnev, Kissinger called for a worldwide nuclear alert of U.S. forces in response to what he claimed were Soviet military moves to intervene in the conflict on the side of the Arabs. Kissinger's action, some skeptics believed, was a dangerously reckless tactic to divert domestic attention from the President's role in Watergate. Military and political analysts at least thought that the Russians' behavior, though belligerent, did not warrant preparations for nuclear war.

Soviet unwillingness to pursue an active role in achieving a Middle East settlement worked in Kissinger's favor. He was able to personally direct the negotiations. His shuttle diplomacy, rather than multilateral discussions in Geneva, provided the basis for a series of agreements leading up to the Egyptian-Israeli peace treaty of 1979. U.S. influence in the Middle East and Kissinger's prestige benefitted from the new situation.

The embargo dictated a more evenhanded U.S. policy in the Middle East. It was Kissinger's aim, then, to keep Israel from winning complete victory. Israeli victory would make the oil embargo permanent and peace impossible, since the Arab states, especially Egypt, would never resign themselves to the loss of their territory. Without the return of Arab lands, there could be no peace, and without peace, it was likely that the oil producers would refuse to sell to the United States.

Kissinger's diplomatic offensive in the Middle East began in November 1973 and lasted through 1976. He developed an apparently warm and intimate relationship with Sadat, who had shown signs of desiring better relations with the U.S. since 1972, when he expelled Soviet advisers from Egypt. Kissinger arranged two Sinai disengagements, in January 1974 and September 1975, which gave Egypt back its land and some measure of pride and offered Israel a measure of security it had been unable to attain in four wars. He also produced a disengagement on the Golan Heights between Israel and Syria in May 1974, although relations between the two nations remained hostile. The Mideast oil embargo was ended and relations with Saudi Arabia were restored. Such triumphs were as much responsible for Kissinger's international "Super K" reputation as the opening of relations with China. However in some places his achievements were viewed more critically. Jewish-American opinion, already angered that detente ignored the plight of Soviet Jews, attacked Kissinger's sympathy for the Arab position. Israeli public opinion, too, reflected the view that Kissinger had forced the Israeli government into disadvantageous settlements as the price of continued U.S. support. Moreover, some analysts noted that Kissinger had been unable to moderate sufficiently the position of the more militant Arab states, particularly Syria. Most importantly, his diplomacy ignored the question of the stateless Palestinians, who were, in fact, the key to any permanent Middle East peace.

The Middle East oil embargo gave rise to further friction in the relations between the U.S. and its traditional allies, Western Europe and Japan. Ironically it was Kissinger's reputedly less-idealistic "European" style of diplomacy that contributed to the deterioration of the alliance with Europe, which had already been adversely affected by disagreements over trade, monetary and military policies. Kissinger had once criticized American policymakers for their failure to consult with the allies on world issues and to consider those countries in terms of their national interests. Yet in his diplomatic initiatives with the Soviets and the Chinese, Kissinger usually failed to advise the governments of Western Europe and Japan beforehand. The behavior was partly due to Kissinger's stress on secrecy, but it also arose out of the assumption that the U.S. was a great power with global interests. Europe, in contrast, was considered a regional power. Conscious of the neglect, Kissinger in April 1973 announced the "Year of Europe," proposing a new Atlantic Charter that would include the Japanese and require a cooperative comprehensive policy on energy, military, monetary and commercial issues. The proposal was spurned more than once. British Prime Minister Edward Heath and French President Georges Pompidou made it clear in May that they wanted issues considered separately. European Economic Community (EEC) spokespersons warned the U.S. that Europe would act as a "distinct unity" in world affairs.

The Arab oil embargo prompted Kissinger to propose in December 1973 a cooperative effort on the part of the industrialized nations to develop long-term energy planning. The proposal conflicted with a French call for an Arab-EEC summit. Kissinger continued arguing in favor of oil consuming nations' solidarity in the face of high prices imposed by the Organization of Petroleum Exporting Countries (OPEC). He noted, however, that the burden of high prices weighed most heavily on underdeveloped nations. Kissinger recommended vigilance to ensure that "petrodollars" invested in the industrial economies did not threaten the sovereignty and security of the individual nations. Another proposal suggested that oil-consuming nations establish a $25 billion lending facility to provide funds for nations unable to meet balance of payments obligations.

European unwillingness to cooperate with the U.S. exasperated Kissinger, who in March 1974 declared that the Europeans constituted the nation's biggest foreign policy problem. The statement irritated the Europeans, who believed that it was in their self-interest to cultivate closer ties with the Arab world. Kissinger, in their view, was taking an excessively hard line against the Arabs. Particularly unwise, they thought, were statements by Kissinger and other members of both the Nixon and Ford Administrations, suggesting that the Americans might be forced to occupy Arab oil fields in case the Arabs became unreasonable in their policy on petroleum exports. In addition, the Europeans shared with the Arabs concern over the Americans' inability or unwillingness to fortify the dollar. Kissinger was never able to mend relations strained during the oil crisis and Europe remained a source of tension throughout his tenure.

Despite his triumphs and reputation,

Kissinger, like most members of the Nixon Administration was touched by Watergate and related issues. In May 1973 it was revealed that he had approved wiretaps of officials and newsmen in efforts to stem policy leaks. Kissinger admitted that he had authorized the taps, but he claimed that the idea had been suggested and put into operation by FBI Director J. Edgar Hoover [q.v.] and Attorney General John Mitchell [q.v.]. They assured him, he alleged, that the taps were legal. Besides, Kissinger argued, it was essential to stop the leaks to the press, which were damaging national security. Also harmful to Kissinger's image was information made available in 1973 and 1974 about his role in the secret bombing of Cambodia and efforts by the CIA and International Telephone and Telegraph to overthrow the democratically elected Marxist government of Salvador Allende in Chile. It appeared that Kissinger was as likely to resort to covert means to achieve his goals as were the political advisers who surrounded Nixon.

Watergate had a significant effect on Kissinger's conduct of foreign affairs. When he went to Moscow in late 1973, he found the Soviets uninterested in reaching any substantive agreements on arms control issues. They were evidently unwilling to deal with a lame-duck administration that might not be able to carry out its part of any bargain. Kissinger warned the American public that obsession with Watergate could damage the nation's international role and destroy the unique opportunity then available to ensure world peace. He privately urged the President to cut off all ties with Haldeman and Ehrlichman and to provide all the White House tapes requested by the Senate Watergate Committee and the special Watergate prosecutor. Kissinger reportedly considered resigning during the crisis, but soon decided that the best solution to a political nuisance—his view of Watergate—that was obstructing foreign policy was the resignation of the President.

Nixon made Kissinger Secretary of State in May 1973. Aside from a supposed desire to humiliate Rogers, Kissinger wanted the post to guarantee that he alone would control the direction of foreign affairs at a time when Nixon was, in his opinion, so desperate that he was liable to act irrationally. Moreover Kissinger hoped to strengthen his strategic position within the Administration against his newest White House rivals, White House Chief of Staff Alexander Haig [q.v.] and Secretary of the Treasury John Connally [q.v.]. The President also hoped that naming Kissinger Secretary of State would help lift his faltering position. Kissinger was Nixon's most prestigious aide, and his diplomatic triumphs had given luster to the Administration. The new appointment was designed to give the White House a measure of legitimacy. Without Kissinger, observers hypothesized, Nixon had no chance of survival.

In reaction to Watergate, the new Secretary of State promised that secrecy would no longer be as necessary in his work as it had been in the past. Secret diplomacy, he explained, had been essential in order to implement "some revolutionary changes," but the foundations had now been laid. The conduct of foreign policy in the future, he predicted, would be less secretive and less dramatic. Kissinger's reputation received another boost in October 1973 when he won the Nobel peace prize for his Vietnam negotiations, although the choice was not universally applauded.

Nixon, trying desperately to avoid confronting the question of his role in the Watergate cover-up, sought to take refuge in the less compromising realm of foreign policy in order to emphasize his indispensability. He specifically tried to take advantage of the enormous public acclaim Kissinger was winning through his Middle East shuttle diplomacy. In the spring of 1974, soon after Kissinger had worked out agreements between the Israelis and their Arab neighbors, Nixon toured the Middle East. The President traveled abroad as often as possible, even irritating foreign leaders by his desire to publicize the significance of routine conferences, which they thought unnecessary in the first place. The June 1974 summit meeting with Brezhnev produced nothing.

Kissinger resented Nixon's attempts to share the spotlight with him. He also feared that the President's frenetic travels could have undesirable effects on the work he had already done. Moreover, Kissinger felt that unless Nixon resigned, he too would be dragged irretrievably into Watergate.

In a June press conference in Salzburg the Secretary of State complained about "innuendos" that he had participated in illegal wiretapping. Speaking so emotionally that some critics called it a "tantrum," Kissinger said that he did not think it "possible to conduct the foreign policy of the United States under these circumstances when the character and credibility of the Secretary of State is at issue. And if it is not cleared up, I will resign." He requested that the Senate Foreign Relations Committee investigate charges against him. (In August the Committee cleared him of charges that he had perjured himself in testimony about his role in the wiretaps.) Although highly sensitive to criticism, Kissinger in this case appeared to be demanding that Nixon take responsibility for all illegalities and resign.

In Nixon's last days, however, Kissinger, whose relationship with the President had always been solely professional, sought to soothe his superior's vanity by assuring him that history would look favorably on Nixon's achievements, particularly in the area of foreign affairs. In a conversation between Nixon and Kissinger related in *The Final Days,* the Secretary of State reportedly knelt down in prayer beside the weeping President. Nixon resigned in August 1974. His successor, Gerald Ford [q.v.], asked Kissinger to remain.

Kissinger's last three years in government lacked the drama of the first five. Relations with China progressed slowly, in part because of internal political struggles in that country. The two nations agreed, however, to the establishment of liaison offices in Washington and Peking. Detente with the Soviets slowed too, and

SALT II negotiations were not completed while he was in office. However, the Ford-Brezhnev Vladivostok summit of November 1974 produced a tentative agreement on ceilings for strategic delivery vehicles and MIRV missiles. An effort to provide the Soviets with most-favored nation status in a trade treaty met with fierce congressional opposition. The legislators, led by Sen. Henry Jackson (D, Wash.) [q.v.] and supported by the American Jewish lobby, wanted any U.S. trade concessions tied to a Soviet agreement to liberalize their emigration restrictions on Soviet Jews. The furor embarrassed both Kissinger and the Soviets and led to Soviet cancellation of the treaty in January 1975. Conservatives began to regularly accuse Kissinger of "selling out" to the Russians and some extremists even referred to him as the "Jewish Communist." Liberals continued to attack what they considered his hardline attitude, and there was a wider consensus which believed that Kissinger was unconcerned about human rights and moral issues.

In 1975 the site of East-West confrontation shifted from Indochina and the Middle East to Africa. Both the State Department and the NSC had been unprepared for "destabilization" in Africa. They had not foreseen the Portuguese withdrawal from its African colonies nor the development of black liberation movements in areas controlled by whites. A 1971 NSC memorandum concluded that black insurgents were not "realistic or supportable" alternatives to white regimes. However the appearance of Cuban troops in the Angolan civil war in 1975 prompted Kissinger to employ threatening language against the Soviets and to reevaluate U.S. African policy.

In September 1975 Kissinger made a strong statement against apartheid and indicated American displeasure with South Africa's policy in Namibia, expressing support for Namibia's complete independence. He sought to identify the U.S. with the aspirations of black Africa. He realized that past American policy, exemplified by unstinting support for the Portuguese in Angola and backing of the

Biafrans's attempted secession from Nigeria, showed an inability to perceive the direction of the flow of power on the continent. A tour of black Africa in early 1976 gave evidence of the shift in U.S. sympathies. In a speech in Nairobi in May, Kissinger proposed a multibillion-dollar raw materials development program intended to benefit African nations. He also called for a $7.5 billion international drought-relief program for the sub-Sahara. Most importantly, Kissinger decided that the United States could no longer support the white supremacist regime in Rhodesia. He even promised aid to any south African nation that joined the campaign against Rhodesia. Together with the British, Kissinger put pressure on Rhodesian Prime Minister Ian Smith to agree to the end of white rule and preparations for a coalition government that would include moderate black leaders. To force Smith to accept the plan, he sought to persuade South Africa to stop supplying Rhodesia. The interim government plan for Rhodesia was accepted by Smith in November 1976.

It was not clear to political observers whether Kissinger under President Gerald Ford determined foreign policy as completely as he had in Nixon's last year in office. Ford depended on Kissinger, but he also saw the Secretary of State as more of a liability than Nixon ever had. In Ford's two years in office, there were repeated rumors that Kissinger would be replaced; the rumors were usually followed by denials from Ford and, in some cases, by a diplomatic coup that temporarily silenced Kissinger's critics. Nonetheless, in May 1976 Kissinger told a reporter that he expected to resign in 1977, even if Ford was elected to a full term. Kissinger's sins, in the opinion of his critics, were many. Even his biggest successes were interpreted as failures. Although the left remained hostile to Kissinger, particularly for his role in the overthrow of Salvador Allende's Marxist government in Chile, it was criticism from the Republican Party's radical right wing that most worried Ford.

Ironically, Kissinger, who had called the nuclear alert in 1973 and had advocated massive bombing of North Vietnam, was considered "soft" on Communism in the eyes of the right. Proponents of a big defense budget argued that SALT had given the Soviets an advantage over the United States and that Kissinger was fully conscious of what he had done. Secretary of Defense James Schlesinger [q.v.] claimed that Kissinger made too many concessions and was reluctant to accuse the Soviets of violating previous agreements. Schlesinger argued that the Vladivostok accord had set too high a limit on the number of MIRV's, thus failing to reduce the threat presented by Moscow's huge new missiles. The Kissinger-Schlesinger enmity led to the ouster of Schlesinger in November 1975. To give the appearance that Kissinger's authority was also being reduced, Ford replaced Kissinger as head of the NSC. However his successor in the NSC was known to be an adherent of Kissinger's policies and likely to carry out the recommendations of the former chief.

Congress also provided a forum for criticism of Kissinger's foreign policy. Senator Jackson, a supporter of both Israel and the defense establishment, led the attack on detente and the new Middle East policy. Supporters of Israel were especially angered by the United States condemnation in the U.N. of Israel's settlements on the West Bank of the Jordan River and its occupation of East Jerusalem. Just as the American Jewish community influenced congressional opinion, the nation's considerable Greek community stirred a sharp reaction against Kissinger's "tilt" toward Turkey on the Cyprus issue. In May 1975 Congress banned military aid to Turkey, justifying its action on the grounds that the law prevented the use of U.S. weapons for purposes other than defense (the Turks had used American weapons in the invasion of Cyprus).

Kissinger's handling of foreign policy became a major issue during the 1976 presidential campaign. Ronald Reagan [q.v.], running against Ford in the Republican primary, argued that the Helsinki accords had recognized the status quo in Eastern Europe and thus abandoned the "captive" nations of the Warsaw Pact to perpetual Soviet domination. Reagan even attacked Kissinger's position on Rhodesia for favoring "revolutionaries" at the expense of legitimate governments. In March 1976 Reagan, relying on information provided by Adm. Elmo Zumwalt [q.v.], claimed that Kissinger had once compared the United States to Athens and the USSR to Sparta. According to Reagan, Kissinger had said that the job of "Secretary of State is to negotiate the most acceptable second-best available." Reagan insisted that the United States could never be second best and that it should never abandon its ideals. Reagan was able to tap a strong chauvinist sentiment in the Republican Party that could not be reconciled to Kissinger's pragmatic approach to diplomacy. The Reagan wing of the Party still objected to relations with China and condemned Kissinger's efforts begun in 1973 to work out an agreement giving Panama control over the Panama Canal. The Democratic candidate, Jimmy Carter [q.v.], hit on the idealism-morality issue when he charged that Kissinger's foreign policy was based on "the assumption that the world is a jungle of competing national antagonisms where military muscle and economic muscle are the only things that work."

Although Kissinger left office less popular than he had once been, his views on world affairs were still widely respected and, more importantly, he had directed a radical change in post-World War II American foreign policy. He helped to end the Cold War and normalize relations with the Soviet Union and China. Despite his dubious record in Vietnam and in other areas of the underdeveloped world, Kissinger ensured that the foreign policy establishment would no longer automatically view local conflicts and civil wars as tests of strength between the U.S. and the Soviet Union. His pragmatism made it more likely that the U.S. would not always side with the forces of the status quo. Yet, as Michael Roskin warned, Kissinger's successors might not be able to

employ the balance-of-power concept as skillfully as he had.

Criticism of Kissinger ultimately focused on his lack of morality or idealism, which led him to abandon the nation's "friends." The friends included Israel, South Vietnam and Nationalist China. He was unable to stop the deterioration of the nation's relations with its allies. His balance-of-power approach, in fact, may have accelerated the process. Some analysts have argued that Kissinger's role in changing U.S. policy may have been exaggerated. Detente with the Communist world was inevitable anyway and the growing economic power of Europe and Japan made continued American domination of a Western alliance impossible.

[JCH]

For further information:
Carl Bernstein and Bob Woodward, *The Final Days* (New York, 1976).
Marvin Kalb and Bernard Kalb, *Kissinger* (New York, 1974).
Bruce Mazlish, *Kissinger: The European Mind in American Policy* (New York, 1976)
Roger Morris, *Uncertain Greatness: Henry Kissinger and American Foreign Policy* (New York, 1977).
Michael Roskin, "An American Metternich: Henry A. Kissinger and the Global Balance of Power" in *Makers of American Diplomacy,* Frank J. Merli and Theodore A. Wilson, eds. (New York, 1974).

KLEIN, HERBERT G(EORGE)
b. April 1, 1918; Los Angeles, Calif.
Director of Communications for the Executive Branch, January 1969-June 1973.

Klein received a degree in journalism from the University of Southern California and began his career as a reporter for the *Post-Advocate* in Alhambra, Calif. After service in the Navy during World War II, he returned to the *Post-Advocate*. In 1948 Rep. Richard Nixon, a friend of Klein's, asked him to be press agent for Nixon's reelection campaign. Klein accepted, thus beginning a political relationship that lasted for a quarter of a century. He served as a publicist during Nixon's successful Senate race in 1950 and his 1952 vice-presidential campaign. In the 1956 general election Klein was assistant press secretary to Nixon. He became editor of the *San Diego Union* in 1959. During the unsuccessful 1960 presidential contest and the 1962 California gubernatorial race, Klein acted as Nixon's press secretary. But his influence with the candidate declined as a result of losses in these elections.

Although Klein was again press secretary for Nixon in his 1968 presidential bid, he was significantly eclipsed by campaign chief of staff H.R. Haldeman [q.v.] and Haldeman's associates. Within weeks of Nixon's election victory, the president-elect announced that Klein would serve in the new post of Director of Communications for the Executive Branch. His responsibilities were described as including the formulation of information from all departments in the Executive Branch, not merely the White House.

California Rep. John E. Moss, a Democrat who headed the House Committee on Freedom of Information, asserted the new office amounted to an "information czar" with "awesome powers." Yet, because Klein did not have daily access to the President, his influence remained largely peripheral.

Klein was a major spokesman of the Nixon Administration. He helped write Spiro Agnew's [q.v.] 1969 address in which the Vice President accused television news organizations of reflecting the biases of a small, northeastern liberal elite. The Agnew speech represented the opening salvo in a public confrontation between the Administration and the news media. Shortly after the speech Klein said that Agnew's charges represented the widely-held view in the White House that "all of the news media needs to reexamine itself, in the format it has and in its approach to problems of news, to meet the current issues of the day."

Klein was a vigorous supporter of the Vietnam war and defended the Cambodian invasion of 1970. He was also a strong opponent of anti-war demonstrators, whom he maintained expressed the minority public opinion.

During the 1972 presidential campaign Klein was one of several Administration officials appearing as a surrogate for Nixon. He stumped the country as the President's stand-in during the early months of the race. It was part of a campaign strategy of having Nixon "act presidential" rather than directly confront Democratic opponent Sen. George McGovern (D, S.D.) [q.v.], whose candidacy was having trouble after the party's national convention.

In September Klein accused McGovern of using Sen. Edward M. Kennedy [q.v.] (D, Mass.) as a "crutch" in his campaign appearances. McGovern responded angrily, "Is he (Klein) campaigning for the presidency? Instead of sending Mr. Klein up here, the President ought to come himself."

Ralph Nader [q.v.] also objected to the surrogate strategy for different reasons. In November, he named Klein in a suit to recover government funds paid to White House aides for campaigning on behalf of Nixon. Nader said taxpayers should deplore "any attempts to have the federal government unlawfully finance a candidate for office."

Nixon won by a landslide in November. It was Klein's last campaign. In June of the following year Klein announced his resignation, saying he would have left earlier except that he did not wish to create the impression his departure was a result of the growing Watergate scandal.

Klein joined the Metromedia communications conglomerate as a vice president. In May 1974 he returned briefly to the White House to help coordinate the release of the transcripts of the White House tapes to the House Judiciary Committee.

[MDQ]

KLEINDIENST, RICHARD GORDAN

b. August 5, 1923; Winslow, Ariz.
Attorney General, June 1972-April 1973.

Richard Kleindienst, the son of a railroad brakeman who later became a minor government officer, was raised in a small town in Arizona. He entered the University of Arizona in 1941 but was called to active duty in the Army in 1943. After his discharge in 1946 from Italy he finished his last two years of college at Harvard University on the G.I. bill. He received his law degree from Harvard in 1950 and returned to Arizona to practice law.

During the 1950s and 1960 he was active in Republican politics and served on the Republican National Committee from 1961 to 1963. In 1964 he was instrumental in winning the presidential nomination for Barry Goldwater and became the Senator's national director for field operations.

In 1964 he ran unsuccessfully for governor of Arizona. Kleindienst served as the general counsel of the Republican National Committee in 1968 and was Richard M. Nixon's director of field operations. He became deputy attorney general in 1969. As Deputy Attorney General, Kleindienst was in charge of the supervision and direction of the Justice Department, formulating Department policies, and was the Department's liaison officer with Congress and other government agencies. During his tenure Kleindienst ordered the mass arrest of 7000 protestors during the 1971 May Day anti-war demonstrations, accepted wiretapping for organized criminals and in national security cases, and supported the enforcement of preventive detention legislation. He directed "Operation Intercept," which called for strict controls and stiff penalties for people caught smuggling marijuana across the Mexican border into the United States. Kleindienst was a foe of busing to achieve racial integration in city school systems, but he favored the preferential employment of minorities in government service.

In February 1972 John Mitchell resigned as Attorney General to become campaign director for the Committee to Re-elect the President (CREEP). Richard M. Nixon nominated Richard Kleindienst to take Mitchell's place. During the last weeks of February before the Kleindienst nomination reached the floor of the Senate, Jack Anderson [q.v.], a Washington columnist, broke the story that the anti-trust division of the Justice Department had been influenced by Kleindienst and the White House to settle out of court a $7 billion anti-trust suit against International Telephone and Telephone (ITT). In exchange the company was to underwrite the expenses for the upcoming Republican Convention to be held in San Diego. The ITT deal was spelled out in a memo from Dita Beard, a company lobbyist, to ITT's Washington Vice President, William Merriam. It was later learned that Kleindienst had spoken with Felix Rohatyn [q.v.], ITT director at least five times just before the suit was settled. The Watergate tapes also revealed that he had discussed the suit with President Nixon, who lambasted him for not making an easy settlement with ITT.

During his confirmation hearings, Kleindienst denied that ITT had received preferential treatment by the Justice Department, that he had had meetings with Rohatyn to discuss the anti-trust suit or that he had been pressured by the White House to settle out of court. Kleindienst was confirmed.

Although Kleindienst subordinates Robert C. Mardian [q.v.], Patrick Gray [q.v.], and Henry Peterson [q.v.] were involved in various aspects of the Watergate coverup, no evidence was ever produced which indicated that Kleindienst knew about the break-in plans or participated in the cover-up. In fact when G. Gordon Liddy [q.v.] approached him to see if he would use his influence to have the burglars released, he told Liddy that they would get no special treatment.

In April 1973 when Kleindienst found out John Mitchell [q.v.], H.R. Haldeman [q.v.] and John Ehrlichman [q.v.] were deeply involved in the Watergate burglary and coverup, he decided to resign. Although Kleindienst was cleared of any wrongdoing in the Watergate affair, the Watergate tapes revealed that he had committed perjury in his Senate testimony in the ITT case. Leon Jaworski [q.v.], special prosecutor for Watergate, let him plead guilty to a lesser charge of refusing to testify. In June 1975 Kleindienst was sentenced to one month in jail and given a suspended sentence. Although the Arizona bar voted to censure him, they did not vote to disbar him. Kleindienst returned to his law practice in Arizona.

[SJT]

KLEPPE, THOMAS S(AVIG)
b. July 1, 1919; Kintyre, N.D.
Republican Representative, N.D., 1967-71; Director, Small Business Administration, February 1971-September 1975; Secretary of the Interior, October 1975-January 1977.

Born and raised in rural North Dakota, Thomas S. Kleppe left Valley City (N.D.) State College after one year for a succession of bookkeeping jobs in several North Dakota banks. Following Army service during World War II, Kleppe became the bookkeeper for Gold Seal Co., a Bismarck firm that manufactured and marketed cleaning wax, bath soap and laundry detergent. Kleppe became the firm's president in 1958. By 1964, when he left Gold Seal to join Dain, Kalmar, & Quail, a Minneapolis-based investment bank, Kleppe had amassed a fortune of $3.5 million.

Kleppe entered politics in 1950, serving a four-year term as mayor of Bismarck. In 1964 he ran unsuccessfully for a U.S. Senate seat. Two years later Kleppe was elected to the U.S. House of Representatives from North Dakota's second congressional district. In the House he established a conservative record, consistently supporting the conservative coalition of Republicans and Southern Democrats. But he opposed the expansion of the Vietnam war into Cambodia and supported the Senate's Cooper-Church Amendment.

Encouraged by Nixon and Republican Party officials, Kleppe made a bid for a Senate seat in 1970. Despite strong backing from the Nixon Administration, he lost to the incumbent, Quentin Burdick, by a large margin. Shortly afterward, Nixon offered Kleppe a job as head of the Small Business Administration (SBA). Kleppe was confirmed by the Senate in February 1971.

Kleppe's record for integrity was brought into question when a scandal was uncovered during a 1973 investigation of SBA operations by the House Banking Committee's Subcommittee on Small Business. It was disclosed that Thomas F. Regan, the SBA's Richmond, Va., director, had approved loans of up to $11.7 million to companies with which his brother-in-law was associated. Although advised to fire Regan in 1971, Kleppe had refused to take action. Previously, House Banking Committee chairman Wright Patman [q.v.] had accused Kleppe of failing to discharge his responsibilities. Minority representatives complained that the SBA was not doing enough to help minority businesses and that the agency was a conservative and unresponsive bureaucracy.

Separate investigations by the House Banking subcommittee and the FBI revealed that White House pressure had been used to obtain SBA approval of loans for political purposes. In August 1975 a Civil Service Commission report confirmed the subcommittee's findings, concluding that under Kleppe's administration "political interests were allowed to influence appointments in a style approximating a patronage system." Although Kleppe was not charged in the report, a long-time observer of the SBA commented that management of the agency "had always been bad, but its been worse under Kleppe."

In September 1975 President Ford nominated Kleppe to succeed Stanley K. Hathaway as Secretary of the Interior. Despite criticism from environmental and conservation groups who charged him as "not qualified" for the Interior post, Kleppe was confirmed unanimously by the Senate on Oct. 17, 1975.

As head of the Interior Department, Kleppe promoted a policy of "cautious development of natural resources," yet his administration was again marked by controversy. In February 1976 Kleppe authorized the sale of offshore oil and gas leases in previously unexplored areas, despite repeated requests for an indefinite postponement by the Environmental Protection Agency. In keeping with its "accelerated program" for energy independence, the Ford Administration had held a sale in December 1975 of oil leases off Southern California. Kleppe's approval of the sale came amidst persistent criticism of the oil lease program, particularly in regard to the lack of coordination between federal and state policies and the lack of distinction between exploration and production.

In August 1976 Kleppe's last-minute requests for changes in the Jackson-Murphy oil lease bill nearly raised havoc on Capitol Hill. The sponsors of the legislation had worked out a series of compromises between the House and Senate versions that would revise the competitive bid system for oil leases and provide for greater state control over drilling decisions. Kleppe's proposed amendments (favored by the oil industry) would have, according to *The Washington Post*, "gutted every major provision of the bill." The amendments were not adopted.

Among Kleppe's other proposals for coping with the growing energy crisis was the leasing of federal lands for coal mining on a competitive basis, beginning in 1977. However in September 1977, U.S. District Judge John H. Pratt ruled against that policy, stating that he considered the government's required environmental impact statement deficient. The judge was especially critical of the role granted private industry in determining leasing sites on publicly owned land.

Following Ford's defeat in the 1976 election, Kleppe retired from public life and returned to his business career.

[JAN]

KNAUER, VIRGINIA H(ARRINGTON) (WRIGHT)
b. March 28, 1915; Philadelphia, Pa.
Special Assistant to the President for Consumer Affairs, 1969–1976.

Virginia Knauer studied art at the University of Pennsylvania where she received her B.F.A. in 1937. After graduation she spent one year doing postgraduate work at the Royal Academy of Fine Arts in Italy. During the 1940s, Knauer focused on her family and artistic pursuits; the latter included portrait painting and collecting antiques. Her political activities began in 1952 when she joined the Citizens for Eisenhower and Nixon. In 1956 she founded the Northeast Council for Republican Women and served as its president for eight years; she subsequently held high offices in the Philadelphia County Republican Committee and the Philadelphia Congress of Republican Councils. In 1959 Knauer became the first Republican woman ever elected to the Philadelphia City Council. She served two terms before losing her third bid in 1967.

After leaving the city council, Knauer was appointed to head the Bureau of Consumer Protection of the state's Justice Department. During the year she held this position, Knauer helped speed up complaint processing and pushed for two state laws strengthening her bureau: one giving the bureau permanent status and the other expanding its powers to subpoena witnesses and seek injunctions against fraud. Both bills were enacted in December 1968.

In April 1969 Knauer was appointed special presidential assistant for consumer affairs. She also assumed the chair of the President's Committee on Consumer Interest and the post of executive secretary of the Consumer Advisory Council; the former body was a government agency designed to coordinate federal activities on consumer issues, and the latter sought to bring private citizens together to represent consumer views to the President.

Knauer took over an office with very little effective power. As a presidential assistant she lacked permanent legislative authority as well as enforcement and investigative powers. The government's efforts for consumers were divided among over 400 agencies, none of which Knauer had the authority to coordinate or control. Her most effective function was processing complaints to other agencies.

During Knauer's tenure reformers and consumer advocates made several efforts to establish an independent consumer protection agency with effective powers. Knauer's reaction to these proposals reflected the Nixon Administration's changing policies on consumer affairs. In 1969 she opposed a bill establishing an independent nonregulatory agency with broad powers to represent consumer interests before federal agencies and in courts. Instead she backed an Administration bill, sponsored by Sen. Jacob Javits (R, N.Y.) [q.v.], establishing a White House Office of Consumer Affairs and a consumer protection division in the Justice Department. The White House office would have the "central responsibility for coordinating all federal activities in the consumer protection field," but major jurisdiction would be delegated to existing agencies. Knauer said this would "utilize existing programs without creating another cumbersome bureaucratic structure." Both measures failed.

Over the next few years the debate changed from whether a consumer protection agency (CPA) should be established to what powers it should have. In 1974 Knauer supported a House compromise bill which dropped consumer advocates' demands that a CPA be allowed to intervene in state and local agency and court proceedings. The bill was defeated, however, when its Senate companion proposal was filibustered to death. The following year Knauer offered President Ford's alternative suggesting a series of consumer representative plans: 17 executive departments and agencies would appoint one person each to handle complaints and comments and represent consumer interests in the agencies' activities.

The heads of five consumer groups issued a joint statement calling the proposal "toothless rhetoric." The Ford alternative failed.

Knauer supported a variety of consumer legislation, but her efforts were criticized by more liberal reformers who wanted stringent laws to protect the consumer. She backed efforts to protect the public against inaccurate consumer information, set federal standards for warranties and pass more stringent food inspection measures. In 1969 she demanded a comprehensive system of safety standards. A moderate, Knauer opposed measures giving consumers full legal recognition as a class.

Knauer left government service at the end of President Ford's term. The following year she set up Virginia Knauer and Associates, a private consumer consultant agency.

[RB]

KOCH, EDWARD I(RVING)
b. Dec. 12, 1924; New York, N.Y.
Democratic Representative, N.Y.,
1969–78.

Koch was born to Polish-Jewish immigrant parents. He served in the Army during World War II and received his law degree from New York University in 1948. For the next 20 years he was a practicing attorney in New York City, helping to found a Wall Street firm in 1963 with himself as a senior partner. He became active in Democratic politics during the 1950s and in 1966 won election to the City Council. In 1968 Koch ran for a seat in the U.S. House on a platform stressing opposition to the Vietnam war and supporting the presidential candidacy of Sen. Eugene McCarthy (D, Minn.) [q.v.]. He won the three-way Democratic primary and the general election for what was known as the "silk stocking" or the "perfumed stockade" district that ran north in Manhattan from Greenwich Village to Spanish Harlem. It was a predominantly white-collar area with the fourth highest median income of any district in the nation.

During the Nixon-Ford years Koch was both an ardent reformer in domestic affairs and a virulent critic of military spending and the Vietnam war. His rating from the liberal Americans for Democratic Action was frequently placed at 100. On numerous occasions he sought cuts in military spending and voted against the anti-ballistic missile system, the B-1 bomber and federal funding for the SST. Koch also voted against the Lockheed loan guarantees. He worked hard for passage of the Cooper-Church Amendment that sought to limit presidential authority to conduct military operations in Cambodia. He voted against appropriations legislation for support of bombing in Cambodia in 1973.

A steadfast supporter of Israel, Koch promoted aid to that country and legislation that would permit Jews to emigrate to the United States from the Soviet Union. In December of 1975, Koch voted against legislation that gave approval to United States participation in the African Development Fund as a response to the United Nations vote equating Zionism with racism. Others had argued against amendments that imposed such a general foreign policy position on such a specific piece of valuable legislation, but Koch asserted that "for these people [the Development Fund supporters] there is never a right time nor the right place."

On domestic issues Koch voted in favor of school busing, government aid for abortions, various subsidy proposals for public transit systems, increased appropriations for public broadcasting and establishment of a consumer protection agency. In a congressional district in which 56% of the population were unmarried adults, Koch, a bachelor, sought several times to bring an end to discriminatory legislation against single persons, especially regulations involving the Internal Revenue Service.

Although identified as an outspoken liberal, Koch demonstrated an ability to be independent from ideological stereotyping as well as earning the respect of conservatives in certain areas. In concert with Rep. Barry Goldwater, Jr. (R, Ariz.), Koch shared sponsorship of the bill that became the landmark Federal Privacy Act of 1974, which sought to prevent invasions of privacy by the federal government. In addition the Act established the Private Protection Study Commission to which both Koch and Goldwater belonged. The Commission investigated the problems of protecting individuals from intrusive investigation by nongovernmental sources such as banks, credit card issuers and insurance companies and made numerous recommendations in its 1977 report.

Koch was instrumental in getting federal loan guarantees for the city of New York in 1975, recognizing early that "the executive branch is not going to take any lead in this area." Koch ran for mayor of New York in 1973 on a platform that dismayed many liberals since it stressed the importance of combating street crime. He had trouble raising funds and dropped out by March 1973 because of the myriad of other candidates in the race and his own inability to gain the support of the influential New Democratic Coalition.

Koch again declared his candidacy for mayor in November 1976, a time when New York was still bickering over the severity of the financial crisis facing the city. He was not widely known outside of his own district, where his popularity was preserved by peripatetic service to his constituents and frequent personal appearances. In his second mayoral bid he again stressed crime control issues and endorsed capital punishment. He also became incumbent Mayor Abraham Beame's [q.v.] most outspoken critic. What was probably the most influential determinant in his 1977 campaign, however, was his use of consultant David Garth, a man who had crafted numerous winning political campaigns by skillful use of the media. Garth's commercials for Koch stressed the crime issue and the competence of the candidate in contrast to the clubhouse politics of Beame and the charisma of former Mayor John Lindsay [q.v.]. Koch's November general election victory was an impressive 50% share of the vote over three challengers.

Koch assumed the office of mayor in January 1978. Although immediately involved in seemingly endless squabbles over the city's financial condition, he was able to achieve a renewal of federal loan guarantees for New York.

[GB]

KORFF, BARUCH
b. 1914; Ukraine
Founder and Head of the National Committee for Fairness to the Presidency.

The son of a rabbi, Korff was five years old when his mother was killed by the Bolsheviks in a 1920 purge. During World War II Korff was a member of a group that bribed Nazis to permit Jews to escape from Germany. After the war as part of the terrorist Stern gang, he fought to drive the British from Palestine. The French arrested him in 1947 for allegedly taking part in a plot to bomb London with leaflets criticizing the British stand on Palestine. During the 1950s and 1960s Korff did rabbinical work in Rehoboth, Mass. He retired after three heart attacks.

Although he voted against Richard Nixon for President in 1960 and 1968, Korff came to Nixon's defense in 1973 during the Watergate scandal. He formed the National Citizens' Committee for Fairness to the Presidency for the purpose of "preserving the office of the presidency." Using $1,000 he had saved for a vacation, Rabbi Korff took out ads in support of the President in 25 newspapers throughout the country. By 1974 the Committee claimed a membership of two million who had donated $1 million for Nixon's defense. While the largest single contribution was $25,000 from the Teamsters Union, most of the donations were said to be $10 or less.

Korff was granted an interview with Nixon at the White House on May 13, 1974. This interview was the basis for Korff's book, *The Personal Nixon: Staying on the Summit,* which was published and distributed by the Committee for Fairness to the Presidency. In that book Korff wrote of Nixon, "I regard him as a man who has been vilified, savaged, brutalized, whose blood has been sapped by vampires. I see him holding out against willful people who are unworthy of polishing his shoes."

On June 9, 1974 the Committee held a luncheon rally at which Nixon gave a brief speech. Fourteen hundred members cheered Korff as he read a resolution declaring their faith in Nixon and the presidency and condemning the treatment Nixon had been receiving from the press and the House Judiciary Committee. Korff met with Nixon again on July 16 at which time they agreed that John Ehrlichman's conviction for conspiracy and lying was "a blot on justice."

On Aug. 7 *The Providence Journal* cited "an undaunted supporter" of the President as the source of a report that Nixon had made "an irrevocable decision" to resign from office. That source is believed to have been Rabbi Korff.

After Nixon resigned on Aug. 9, 1974, Korff said, ". . . For thirty years [Nixon] sacrificed everything for America's good [and] now he has made the supreme sacrifice."

[AB]

KROGH, EGIL (BUD), JR.
b. Chicago, Ill.
White House Aide.

Krogh graduated from Principia College in 1961 and then went on to secure a law degree from the University of Washington. He then joined a firm in Seattle where he was an associate of John Ehrlichman [q.v.]. When Ehrlichman went to Washington in 1969 to assume the post of Nixon's chief domestic council, Krogh became his assistant.

According to members of the press, White House staffers considered Krogh a man of "unusual piety" and jokingly referred to him as "Evil Krogh" because of his presumed incapacity for wrong-doing. As a White House staff official and Ehrlichman assistant, Krogh was responsible for overseeing a number of ongoing projects designed to curtail the flow of narcotics into the U.S. Krogh maintained up to the minute progress reports and served as a liaison for Ehrlichman when other pressing matters prevented his attendance. His ability to adhere to administrative priorities and his staunch loyalty to White House policy served to endear him to the President who appointed Krogh co-chairman of the Special Investigations Unit in 1971.

Because of a series of government leaks which culminated in the publication of the *Pentagon Papers* by the *New York Times* in 1971, Nixon established the unit in order to uncover the sources of confidential information. Because of its overriding concern with leaks the unit was soon referred to as the "Plumbers."

With the disclosure by former Defense Department employee Daniel Ellsberg [*q.v.*] that he was responsible for the papers leak, Nixon ordered the plumbers to uncover all available information concerning Ellsberg's motives and associates, since the FBI was handling the matter lethargically. Krogh and David Young, in need of additional staff, recruited veteran intelligence officer E. Howard Hunt [*q.v.*] and former Treasury Department official G. Gordon Liddy [*q.v.*].

Since the authenticity of the *Pentagon Papers* was never in doubt, the unit focused their attention on discrediting Ellsberg in order to undermine any possible national sympathetic response to his criminal action. When it was discovered that Ellsberg had previously undergone psychiatric care, the unit became determined to expose any potentially embarrassing information. However, Ellsberg's psychiatrist cited doctor patient confidentiality and refused to discuss Ellsberg.

According to testimony subsequently provided by John Dean [*q.v.*] in August 1971 the Plumbers then decided to burglarize the offices of the psychiatrist. Hunt, relying on his former Central Intelligence Agency connections, recruited a team of Miami based Cubans for the operation and together with Liddy they head-

ed to the West Coast to carry out their clandestine mission. Krogh had informed Ehrlichman that the burglary was the only means to secure the necessary information to mount a smear campaign against Ellsberg and Ehrlichman endorsed the operation provided it was carried out in such a fashion as to be "untraceable" to the White House. After the operation was completed, both Liddy and Hunt returned to Washington where they became involved in intelligence activities for the Committee to Re-elect the President (CREEP). Krogh and Young were then assigned to uncover the source of Jack Anderson's [*q.v.*] column which documented White House support for Pakistan in the India-Pakistan War. They were unsuccessful, and the Plumbers' unit disbanded after the Anderson probe.

Still a member of the White House domestic counsel staff, Krogh continued to function as assistant to Ehrlichman and with Nixon's re-election in 1972 he was given a Cabinet post as undersecretary of the Department of Transportation. The appointment took effect in February 1973.

As momentum began to build regarding White House connections to the Watergate burglary, an investigation of the break-in of Ellsberg's psychiatrist's office also pointed to possible White House complicity. Together with Young, Liddy and Ehrlichman, Krogh went on trial for the burglary in 1974. They cited "national security" as adequate defense. The jury was unimpressed, and Krogh, faced with an inevitable conviction for his role, entered a plea of guilty in February 1974. He received a maximum five year sentence for conspiracy.

[DGE]

KRUPSAK, MARY ANNE
b. Mar. 26, 1932; Schenectady, N.Y.
Lieutenant Governor, N.Y., 1975-79.

Mary Anne Krupsak's parents, both pharmacists, ran a drugstore in Amsterdam, N.Y. Krupsak received a B.A. in history from the University of Rochester in

1953 and an M.S. in public communications from Boston University in 1955. After working for three years as a legislative aide to W. Averell Harriman, Democratic governor of New York, Krupsak entered the University of Chicago Law School, receiving a J.D. in 1961. She was admitted to the New York state bar and practiced law briefly before returning to state government, first as assistant counsel to the president pro tempore of the New York state Senate, and later as assistant counsel to the speaker of the state Assembly.

Frustrated with her lack of power as a legislative assistant, Krupsak decided in 1968 to run for public office. A liberal Democrat, she ran for the state Assembly in the solidly conservative Republican 104th district, attacking Gov. Nelson A. Rockefeller's [q.v.] Republican administration for its expensive and unproductive patronage jobs and its generous pension plan for elected officials. Krupsak narrowly won the general election in November 1968 and was reelected in 1970.

During her two terms in the Assembly, Krupsak clashed repeatedly with the Republican leadership, denouncing the wastefulness of Rockefeller's extravagant construction projects, including the Albany Mall and the Nassau Coliseum. On Nov. 15, 1971, Krupsak and five other Assembly members brought suit against Rockefeller through the American Civil Liberties Union, charging that the Governor had rammed state budget and tax bills through the Assembly without due legislative process. Krupsak also worked for women's rights, cosponsoring a resolution calling for the creation of a joint legislative committee to study all laws relating to the health and welfare of women. A Catholic, she nevertheless voted in 1970 for a liberalized abortion bill, stating that "you cannot codify one group's religious or ethical beliefs into statutory law."

Before the 1972 campaign season the Republican legislative majority announced a reapportionment plan that eliminated Krupsak's district. Backed by the newly formed Women's Political Caucus, she ran instead for the state Senate on a platform that advocated improved mass transportation, more equitable taxation and legislative reform. In November 1972 she won election to the state Senate, where she continued to work for women's rights, introducing legislation to end sex discrimination, to increase maternity benefits and to abolish all restrictions on abortion.

In May 1974 Krupsak announced her candidacy for lieutenant governor of New York. Campaigning with the help of women volunteers, she concentrated on consumer affairs and public welfare issues. In the primary she captured 42% of the vote, becoming the first woman to win a majority party's nomination for a top-level New York state executive post. She teamed with the Democratic gubernatorial candidate, U.S. Rep. Hugh L. Carey [q.v.], to win the 1974 election in a victory that returned the New York governorship to Democratic control for the first time in 15 years.

As lieutenant governor Krupsak soon found that, despite her large operating budget, she had very little power. Carey's aides failed to consult her on major issues. She, in turn, supported several measures opposed by the Governor, including an increased income tax for New York City commuters and home rule for the city on all tax matters. She also spoke against Carey's proposed gasoline tax hike in 1975 and accused him of being "insensitive" to women's issues. Seeking to expand the functions of her office, Krupsak initiated the organization of three-day forums throughout the state to encourage communities to identify ways in which the state could help the local economy. She was instrumental in the creation of a scenic railway in the Mohawk River Valley and in opening an airport in the Catskill resort area. During 1978 she cochaired the National Women's Conference in Houston and led the fight to preserve New York's Radio City Music Hall as a landmark.

In June 1978, on the eve of the state Democratic convention, Krupsak, still frustrated with her exclusion from Carey's inner circle, withdrew as a candidate for reelection to the lieutenant governorship. Two weeks later she announced that she would challenge Carey, the Democratic Party's designate for the gubernatorial nomination, in the primary. Democratic officials feared that Krupsak's action might fragment the Party, but her campaign was hampered by weak organization and a lack of funds. Krupsak had trouble defining her differences with the incumbent governor's positions, which she had generally supported during the previous four years. In the Sept. 12 primary, Krupsak received only 34% of the vote, losing to Carey who received 52%.

[DAE]

KUNSTLER, WILLIAM M(OSES)
b. July 7, 1919; New York, N.Y.
Lawyer.

The son of middle-class Jewish parents, William Kunstler attended New York City's public schools and Yale University where he received his B.A. in 1941. After serving in the Army during World War II, he studied law at Columbia and in 1948 was admitted to the New York bar. During the 1950s he had a successful legal practice with his brother, and took on some civil liberties cases for the American Civil Liberties Union. During the 1960s he was active in the civil rights movement. [See JOHNSON Volume]

Kunstler received national attention during 1969 and 1970 as one of the defense lawyers for the Chicago Seven, anti-war activists accused of conspiracy and inciting to riot at the 1968 Democratic National Convention in Chicago. The trial, which began on Sept. 24, 1969, was the scene of numerous confrontations between the defendants and their lawyers, Kunstler and Leonard I. Weinglass, on the one hand, and Judge Julius J. Hoffman on the other. The most serious came in February after Hoffman refused to allow former Attorney General Ramsey Clark [q.v.] and civil rights leader Ralph Abernathy [q.v.] to testify for the defense. Kunstler accused Hoffman of being "wholly responsible" for the "legal

lynching" that was sending his clients to jail. The jury acquitted the defendants on the charge of conspiracy, but found five of them quilty of inciting to riot. Before the jury delivered its verdict, however, Hoffman convicted all of the defendants and their two lawyers on 160 counts of contempt of court. Kunstler, charged with 24 counts, was handed a sentence of four years and 13 days. In 1972, an Appeals Court overturned the riot convictions, accusing Judge Hoffman of improper rulings and conduct. In 1973, a court sustained half of the contempt charges against Kunstler but suspended sentence so that the lawyer did not spend time in jail.

Kunstler's experience in the Chicago Seven trial completed his transformation into what he called "a people's lawyer" working in "a partnership with the movement" for radical social change. During the 1970s he received $100 a week plus expenses from the Law Center for Constitutional Rights, which defends political activists, and supplemented his income through public lectures. In 1970, Kunstler defended Bobby Lee Williams, a black militant charged with assaulting a police officer during the 1967 racial riots in Plainfield, N.J., was an adviser in the defense of the Rev. Philip Berrigan and other Roman Catholic anti-war activists accused of conspiring to kidnap government officials, and helped coordinate the defense effort of students indicted for participating in the May 1970 demonstrations at Kent State University.

In 1973 Kunstler was asked by leaders of the American Indian movement who had occupied the village of Wounded Knee on the Pine Ridge reservation in South Dakota to represent them in negotiations with the government. Later, when two of the leaders of the occupation, Russell Means and Dennis Banks, were indicted on charges of conspiracy, theft, and assault, Kunstler took on the case. In September 1974, after a lengthy trial, Judge Fred J. Nichol dismissed all of the charges, accusing the FBI and the Justice Department of having "polluted" the system of justice, and praising Kunstler for his courtroom abilities. It was later revealed that the FBI had a paid informant on the defense team. In 1976, Kunstler again successfully defended Means against a murder charge.

Kunstler was also attorney, along with Ramsey Clark, in the 1975 trial of John Hill and Charley Pernasilice, two convicts charged with the murder of a prison guard during the 1971 uprising by inmates at Attica, N.Y. When inmates seized the prison in September and held several guards hostage, they asked Kunstler to come as an observer and to act as an intermediary with the officials. After state troopers stormed the prison, during which 43 persons were killed, Kunstler condemned the action. During the trial Kunstler argued that the prosecution had no real eyewitnesses and that the inmates testifying against his clients were perjuring themselves in exchange for lenient treatment. The jury found Hill guilty of murder and Pernasilice guilty of assault. In December 1976 New York Gov. Hugh Carey [q.v.] commuted the sentences of all the Attica defendants.

In 1977 Kunstler took on the case of Joanne Little, a black woman who had escaped to New York from a North Carolina prison. He failed, however, to prevent her extradition to North Carolina.

[JD]

LAIRD, MELVIN R(OBERT)
b. Sept. 1, 1922; Omaha, Neb.
Secretary of Defense, January 1969–January 1973.

Melvin Laird received his B.A. from Carlton College in 1942. After military service in World War II, Laird, a Republican, was elected to the Wisconsin State Senate, where he served from 1946 to 1952. In that year, he was elected to the U.S. House, where he remained until Richard Nixon made him his first Secretary of Defense in 1969. As a Representative, Laird emerged as a prominent figure in the Republican Party. He served on the House Appropriations Committee and was a member of the Republican Coordinating Committee, vice-chairman of the Platform Committee of the 1960 Republican Convention and chairman of the same Committee at the 1964 Convention. During his years in Congress, he also served as chairman of the national defense project of the American Enterprise Institute, a conservative "think tank" in Washington, D.C. He supported Nelson A. Rockefeller [q.v.] for the 1968 Republican nomination, but his backing of the Nixon presidential candidacy, combined with his background in Congress and his knowledge of defense matters, prompted the new Administration to appoint him Secretary of Defense. [See JOHNSON Volume]

Laird took office at a time when the fortunes of the U.S. armed forces were at a historical low, with anti-militarist sentiment widespread in the U.S. as the country attempted to disentangle itself from the Indochina war. A major focal point of the changing attitude towards the military was the defense budget, which liberal sentiment in Congress and at large wished to reduce substantially. Such a reduction was also implied in the "Vietnamization" of the war carried out during Laird's tenure. In March 1969 the Nixon Administration announced a $2.5 billion cut in defense spending for fiscal 1970, the first such cut since the beginning of the Vietnam war. Testifying before Congress in April 1969, Laird placed these cuts in the context of the Administration's overall anti-inflation policy, asserting that the U.S. was in an "extremely difficult and dangerous economic and fiscal situation" that made defense reductions imperative. Later that month Laird ordered the closing of 36 U.S. military installations at home and abroad, and in August 1969 announced a further $3.6 billion reduction, bringing military spending to $74.9 billion for the following year, to be achieved by a withdrawal of personnel from Southeast Asia and the deactivation of 100 Navy ships. Laird stated that these cuts would not mean "an inevitable weakening of our worldwide military position," but that further cuts would be "counterproductive."

These trends continued as the U.S. slipped into economic recession in 1970–71; Laird in January 1970 announced that 1,250,000 defense-related jobs were going to be phased out as a result. In this context Laird, with other Administration officials, proposed a one million man reduction in total armed forces strength. These trends were reversed in 1971, however, when Laird asked Congress for an $80 billion defense budget, and again the following year when he called for a massive $6.3 billion increase, so large that even pro-defense congressmen such as Sen. John Stennis (D, Miss.) [q.v.] questioned its wisdom. Many observers interpreted the 1971–72 turnabout as a move to stimulate the stagnant U.S. economy through arms production.

Laird was deeply involved in the extended controversy over the Sentinel anti-ballistic missile (ABM) system, which the Nixon Administration inherited from the Johnson era and which became the focus of a major confrontation with liberal anti-military sentiment in Congress. During early 1969 the Administration repeatedly underlined its desire to achieve "sufficiency," not superiority, relative to Soviet military capacity. In initial hearings on the ABM issue, Laird told Congress that the Soviet Union spent 3.7 times as much on similar systems as did the U.S., and in 1970 again warned against a major Soviet arms buildup to justify expenditures that many congressmen felt unwise and unnecessary.

A question closely tied to that of the ABM was the Nixon Administration's effort to reach a strategic arms limitation agreement with the Soviet Union. Laird told Congress in April 1969 that he did not feel that the Soviet Union would "be so foolish" as to make a first-strike attack against the U.S., but warned of Soviet superiority in several years if the arms buildup underway continued. At the beginning of the following year, he again cited the Soviet arms buildup and defend-

ed the ABM as a necessity if no arms limitation agreement could be reached. Laird told Congress in March 1971 that the U.S. was adopting a new defense posture, which he described as a "prudent middle course between two policy extremes— world policeman or a new isolationism." After the U.S. and the Soviet Union arrived at a treaty limiting their respective arsenals of anti-ballistic missiles in early 1972, Laird insisted that Congress approve the treaty only if it was willing to grant the Administration its requests for new weaponry.

The new world strategic conception inaugurated under Laird placed greater emphasis on regional military alliances and on enlisting U.S. allies in combat commitments. Laird was concerned about conveying this shift to the European member states of the North Atlantic Treaty Organization (NATO). In May 1969 he flew to Canada to urge the Canadian government not to reduce its NATO troop commitments. A year later he stated his aim of achieving greater sharing of costs by member countries, relieving the U.S. of untenable economic burdens. He toured U.S. bases in Spain in June and endorsed that country's entry into NATO. At the same time he assured America's allies that all treaties would be honored, and that no U.S. troops would be withdrawn precipitously from Europe. In December 1972, at the annual NATO ministers' conference in Brussels, Laird hailed the decisions of West Germany and Great Britain to increase their defense budgets.

Two major domestic issues tied to defense during Laird's tenure at the Pentagon were chemical-biological warfare (CBW) and the military draft. In July 1969 a group of congressmen called for a halt to CBW tests pending studies of their effects. A month later when the Senate voted curbs on the use of CBW, Laird supported the move but warned of the Soviet Union's high CBW capacity and the need for the U.S. to "keep up."

Laird supported a reform of the draft in September 1969 while President Nixon announced decreased induction calls for the month ahead. Laird said the reduction was the result of lower manpower needs for the war in Vietnam and a desire to lessen inequities in the 1967 draft law. In 1971 military manning requirements fell to new lows, and in January of the following year, the draft was suspended for several months. Laird nonetheless opposed amnesty for draft dodgers.

Much of Laird's efforts at Defense were consumed by the Indochina war. In March 1969 he toured Vietnam, emphasizing the Administration's desire to "Vietnamize" the war as quickly as possible by replacing American combatants with Vietnamese troops. In the spring of 1970, Laird again toured Vietnam, denying any U.S. buildup in Laos. It was rumored in May that Laird opposed the U.S. invasion of Cambodia, but publicly he fully backed the Administration's policy. The U.S. invasion of Laos in February 1971 discredited Laird's earlier denial of a buildup in that area, but Laird insisted that the invasion had the sole aim of shortening the war and protecting American lives. He also stated that there would be a prompt, scheduled withdrawal. In January 1972 Laird announced a 70,000-man withdrawal from Vietnam. Four months later he firmly endorsed the U.S. blockade and mining of Haiphong harbor. He attacked Sen. George McGovern's (D, S.D.) prisoner-of-war exchange plan put forward that summer in the latter's campaign for the presidency. In October 1972 Laird conceded that the May bombings of North Vietnam had in fact hit the French embassy in Hanoi, a charge earlier denied by the Pentagon.

Laird also had to confront the crisis in morale of the U.S. armed forces. In response to widespread drug use in the military in May 1969 he announced new tests to identify drug addiction in U.S. troops. When the Nixon Administration formed an international drug panel in September to stop the worldwide drug traffic, Laird was a prominent member. In February 1970 Laird also acknowledged widespread racism in the U.S. military stating that "the armed forces have a racial problem because the country has a racial problem." When the Pentagon released a report that November showing systematic racial discrimination within the armed services, Laird said that equality in the military was the "essence of an ordered, free society."

Laird participated in top-level defense discussions on crises in other parts of the world. During the 1970 crisis in which the troops of King Hussein and Israeli forces both attacked the Palestinian guerrillas operating in Jordan, Laird made public statements assuring Israel of U.S. support and promised to replace any equipment lost in combat by Israeli forces. In December he met with Israeli Defense Minister Moshe Dayan to discuss the results of the military campaigns against the Palestinians.

In November 1972 Laird announced his resignation at the end of Nixon's first term, and Elliot Richardson [q.v.] was appointed to replace him. Laird made his final report to Congress in January 1973 but returned to the White House five months later as a domestic adviser to President Nixon in the Watergate affair. After the resignation of Vice President Spiro Agnew [q.v.] in October, Laird was discussed as a possible successor and played a role in the eventual selection of Gerald Ford [q.v.] for that post. Two months later Laird resigned from his post, calling for an "early impeachment vote" to bring the issue to a head in Congress and to end the growing paralysis of government that Watergate had brought about.

After this final departure from the Nixon Administration, Laird became a senior counselor for the Readers' Digest Association and assumed several corporate directorships of such companies as Metropolitan Life Insurance and Phillips Petroleum. In May 1975 he met with a group of top-level Republican political experts to prepare the groundwork for Gerald Ford's 1976 electoral strategy.

[LRG]

LANDRUM, PHIL(LIP) M(ITCHELL)

b. Sept. 10, 1907; Martin, Ga.
Democratic Representative, Ga.,
1953-77.

Landrum graduated from Atlanta Law School in 1941 and a year later after an unsuccessful bid for Congress joined the Air Force in 1942. He returned in four years to serve as executive assistant to the governor of Georgia and won election to the U.S. House in 1952. He represented rural northeast Georgia's ninth district, where textile manufacturing and poultry raising were important industries. Landrum achieved a brief moment of national recognition in 1959 when he sponsored with Rep. Robert Griffin (R. Mich.) [q.v.] the Landrum-Griffin Act.

He played a decisive role in the House passage of the Equal Opportunity Act of 1964 and War on Poverty legislation. [See EISENHOWER, KENNEDY, JOHNSON Volumes]

Although Landrum frequently voted with the Southern Democratic-Republican coalition, he broke ranks by supporting a $250 million loan guarantee for financially troubled Lockheed Aircraft in 1970. The following year he opposed a constitutional amendment authorizing school prayer. As head of the unofficial House committee on textiles, he worked strenuously for import quotas on foreign cloth and clothing. The 1970 Trade Act, which provided for such import restrictions, had Landrum's backing.

Landrum had been an early proponent of the Vietnam War, but lack of progress made him reassess his position. In 1971 he opposed the war for the first time by voting against the bill to extend the draft and called upon Congress to reassert its war-making authority. His opposition remained tentative, however; he did not support stronger anti-war measures and continued to favor large defense spending.

Landrum voted against most environmental legislation, receiving in 1970–71 a zero rating from the League of Conservation Voters. In 1971 he opposed in committee a 5% increase in Social Security benefits and voted against the President's Family Assistance Plan, which would have granted a working family of four $2,400 per year. Landrum charged that the plan's job-training requirements were inadequate, making it a "guaranteed cash income plan."

During Nixon's second term Landrum was relatively inactive. In 1975–76 he supported President Ford on 49% of all major issues according to the *Congressional Quarterly*. In 1976 he retired from Congress and was replaced by Democrat Edgar L. Jenkins, a lawyer.

[FLM]

LARUE, FREDERICK C(HENEY)

Watergate figure.

Frederick C. LaRue came from a Texas family scarred by scandal and tragedy. His father, Ike Parsons LaRue, was sent to jail for banking violations. Following his release he struck oil in Mississippi. That oil strike made the family rich and led to Frederick LaRue's prominence in Mississippi as a political financier. In 1957 LaRue sold the field reportedly for $30 million. That same year Frederick LaRue shot and killed his father in a hunting accident in Canada.

In the early 1960s LaRue became active in Mississippi Republican politics and served on the Republican National Committee from Mississippi. In 1964 he was a big contributor to the Goldwater presidential bid and four years later was an early donor to the Nixon campaign. When Richard Nixon assumed the presidency in 1969, he took LaRue with him to the White House. Described as a "skilled behind-the-scenes operator," LaRue, with no title, no salary and no listing in the White House directory, became one of the most trusted members of the Nixon Administration.

In January 1972 when John N. Mitchell [q.v.] resigned as Attorney General and became campaign director for the Committee to Re-Elect the President

(CREEP), LaRue moved from the White House to the "Mitchell group" at CREEP, which included Robert C. Mardian [q.v.] and Henry S. Fleming. LaRue was present at the March 30, 1972 meeting in which Jeb Stuart Magruder [q.v.] presented G. Gordon Liddy's [q.v.] "Gemstone Plan" for the Watergate burglary to John Mitchell for final confirmation.

After the break-in, LaRue and Mardian were in charge of the CREEP cover-up. They supervised the shredding of documents and the destruction of financial records and helped to prepare key CREEP officials for their interviews with the various law enforcement agencies. LaRue was also a principal conduit for "hush money" payments from White House fund raisers to the Watergate burglars and their attorneys.

By June 28, 1972, it was clear that if the Watergate defendants were not supported, they would tell all they knew about the Watergage break-in and the other White House and CREEP "national security" operations. From September 1972 to March 1973 when James McCord [q.v.] broke his silence, LaRue raised funds and distributed the money to the burglars' lawyers. One reporter estimated that the total amount of money paid to the defendants and their lawyers came to $429,500.

On July 30, 1973, at the trial stemming from his indictment by the Watergate grand jury, Frederick LaRue pleaded guilty to one count of conspiracy to obstruct justice. He was sentenced to six months in prison. After serving his sentence, he returned to private life in Mississippi.

[SJT]

LAVELLE, JOHN D(ANIEL)
b. Sept. 9, 1916; Cleveland, Ohio.
Commander, Seventh Air Force,
Southeast Asia, 1966–72.

Lavelle graduated from John Carroll University in Cleveland in 1938 and joined the Army in 1940. He served in the Army Air Corps and after the war advanced through the grades in the Air Force. Appointed commander of the Seventh Air Force in Southeast Asia in 1966, he was given the rank of four-star general.

Lavelle was the focal point of civilian inquiries into military misconduct in Vietnam during the Nixon Administration. On May 16, 1972, the Defense Department disclosed that Lavelle had been recalled to Washington and later relieved of his post "because of irregularities in the conduct of his responsibilities." At that time Secretary of Defense Melvin R. Laird [q.v.] said that Lavelle had been dismissed because Gen. John D. Ryan, Air Force chief of staff, had "lost confidence" in his leadership ability. However, testifying before an investigations subcommittee of the House Armed Services Committee on June 12, Lavelle admitted that he was actually dismissed for ordering repeated and unauthorized bombing strikes on military targets in North Vietnam between November 1971 and March 1972. Lavelle had reported these raids as "protective reaction" missions and claimed to have taken full responsibility for the falsified reports. In June, Sens. Harold Hughes (D, Iowa) [q.v.] and Stuart Symington (D, Mo.) [q.v.] asked the Armed Services Committee to conduct a complete investigation before approving Lavelle's retirement.

On Sept. 11, 1972, the Committee opened its investigation to determine if others shared the responsibility with Lavelle for the unauthorized bombings. While the Air Force maintained that Lavelle had acted alone, Lavelle contradicted his previous statements and testified on Sept. 12 that he had received permission for a number of the raids from Gen. Creighton Abrams [q.v.], head of U.S. forces in Vietnam, and Adm. Thomas Moorer [q.v.], chairman of the Joint Chiefs of Staff. On Sept. 13 Gen. Abrams denied Lavelle's allegations and swore that he was unaware of Lavelle's air strikes and his falsified reports. Gen. Ryan then testified that he believed Lavelle to be the sole instigator of the unauthorized raids. He also stated that he did not think a court martial would be appropriate for Lavelle, removal from command being sufficient punishment.

On Oct. 5 *The New York Times* published a letter written by Lavelle on Sept. 26 in which he claimed that he had initiated the raids because of what he interpreted as private encouragement from his superiors. "It seemed clear to me," he wrote, "that higher authorities had recommended, encouraged and commended an extremely liberal policy, well beyond the literal language of the rules of engagement."

The Senate Armed Services Committee proposed that Lavelle be retired at the permanent rank of two-star major general. This demotion, however, was a symbolic gesture because of the rule that an officer's retirement pay be determined by the rank held during the officer's last active service. Thus Lavelle would continue to receive a general's full retirement pay—$27,000 annually, most of it tax free.

On Oct. 24 the Air Force concluded that a thorough investigation had been made into the unauthorized air strikes and charges should be dropped because the "interests of discipline" had already been served.

[AFB]

LEVI, EDWARD
b. June 26, 1911; Chicago, Ill.
Attorney-General, February
1975–January 1977.

The son of a scholarly family and descended from a long line of rabbis, Edward Levi was educated at the University of Chicago. He was awarded a Ph.B. degree in 1932 and a J.D. in 1935 by the University of Chicago and served as editor of the law review. He was a Sterling Fellow at Yale University, where he earned a Doctor of Juristic Science in 1938.

Appointed to the Chicago law faculty in 1939, he took a leave of absence the following year to work in Washington at the Justice Department under Thurman Arnold. Levi first served as special assistant to the Attorney General and later became first assistant in the Department's war division. In 1944 he was named first assistant of the anti-trust division, where he handled many suits against oil companies.

After leaving the Justice Department in 1945, Levi pursued an academic career at the University of Chicago while occasionally returning to government councils. Considered "one of the two most brilliant scholars in the anti-trust field in his generation," Levi was chief counsel to the House Judiciary Committee's Anti-Trust Subcommittee in 1950. From 1966 to 1967 he was a member of the White House Panel on Education and acted as a consultant to the Department of Health, Education and Welfare and the Office of Education.

Levi shunned party labels and did not even maintain the minimal party identification of registering for purposes of primary voting. His legal philosophies stressed the strict interpretation of the Constitution and balance among the different branches of government. In addition he seemed to subscribe to traditionally Republican views supporting less government intervention and strengthening states' rights.

At the University of Chicago, Levi earned a reputation as an "acerbic and articulate legal scholar" and "a hard-nose administrator." As a law professor he both dazzled and terrorized his students and had little tolerance for either dullness or misguided crusades. As dean, a post he assumed in 1950, Levi presided over an extensive revision of the curriculum, emphasizing an interdisciplinary approach joining the study of law with a knowledge of economics, sociology and political theory. His goal was to train lawyers who could pursue justice, advise on policy matters and were "capable of cutting through the cliches of [their] own time." When Levi was named university provost in 1962, one of his major concerns was faculty recruitment and by the end of his term, he had been instrumental in substantially upgrading the intellectual caliber of the faculty. In 1968 Levi became president of the university.

In December 1974 President Ford nominated Levi to be Attorney General. He was confirmed the following month. He inherited the post at a time when public confidence in the Justice Department was low and staff morale was badly shaken by the Watergate scandal and the personal involvement of Attorneys General John Mitchell [q.v.] and Richard Kleindienst [q.v.]. Five Attorneys General in as many years had left the Department directionless and badly tainted for breaking, rather than upholding, the law. Lacking partisan passions and of proven legal and administrative ability, Levi seemed well suited for depoliticizing and remotivating the Department. As a man of "unquestioned integrity and strength" whom Republican Sen. Charles Percy [q.v.] commended as "beholden to no one," Levi's appointment was another step towards dispelling the Nixon Administration's legacy of cronyism, duplicity and frequently unprincipled pragmatism.

His appointment was also significant as the first cabinet-level change of the Ford presidency. Nominated in December of 1974 to replace the controversial William Saxbe [q.v.], Levi's appointment was heralded as a sign of changes that would finally mark the evolution of a distinctive Ford Administration, rather than a Nixon holdover. Hailed by the American Bar Association as a "brilliant nomination," it seemed to demonstrate that the Ford Administration could attract an individual of high quality to its councils and would steer its own course.

During his tenure as Attorney General, Levi had to deal with the thorny issue of establishing guidelines for the FBI. He chose the rather controversial method of a study commission, a decidedly unorthodox move by FBI standards. The committee was headed by a woman, Mary Lawton, who was from the Justice Department rather than the Bureau. It also included, over FBI objections, a number of outside consultants, such as former Acting FBI Director William Ruckelshaus [q.v.], and some academics. In March of 1976 the committee issued a first set of guidelines covering domestic security investigations, White House personnel security and investigation, and reporting on civil disorders and demonstrations involving a federal interest. In April of 1976 the Attorney General formed a three-member unit to monitor the use and effectiveness of the guidelines and to suggest possible changes and refinements to them.

In other areas the Department vigorously prosecuted anti-trust cases, instituting a record number of criminal and civil suits, which reflected Levi's view that "anti-trust enforcement can promote competition without increasing government regulation." Along the same lines Levi argued that the Justice Department "should take from the CAB [Civil Aeronautics Board] its authority to sanction airline agreements and mergers that otherwise would be subject to anti-trust prosecution." Although Levi was not successful in pursuading the President to endorse such a move, the Administration did sponsor legislation that gave the Justice Department increased rights to review and intervene in CAB decisions.

In the area of civil rights, Levi was responsible for the decision not to ask the Supreme Court to reconsider a 1971 ruling that authorized busing as a means of achieving school desegration. As a result the Administration switched to a legislative tactic, and the Attorney General helped draft a bill proposing that busing be limited to cases of demonstrated de facto segregation resulting from state action and that busing orders be restricted to a three-year period followed by court review of their effectiveness.

Levi served until the end of the Ford Administration, and then he returned to the University of Chicago as Glen A. Lloyd Distinguished Service Professor.

[MW]

LIDDY, G(EORGE) GORDON B(ATTLE)
b. Nov. 30, 1930; New York, N.Y.
Watergate figure.

The son of a prominent patent attorney, Liddy spent his youth in a quiet New Jersey suburb. Following graduation from Fordham University in 1952, he joined the Army because, as a friend maintained, "he felt we had to stop the Communists in Korea." After his discharge, he entered Fordham Law School and received his degree in 1957. He then became an agent with the FBI. In 1962 he relocated to upstate New York, and after four years in private practice, he became assistant district attorney in Dutchess County. In 1968 he ran unsuccessfully for the Republican nomination for a seat in the U.S. House. He campaigned on a "law-and-order" platform.

In 1969 Liddy became special assistant to the Assistant Secretary of the Treasury, Eugene T. Rossides. His first assignment was in the Bureau of Narcotics and Firearms Control as a member of Operation Intercept, a program designed to undermine drug-trafficking at the Mexican border. Although Operation Intercept had little, if any, impact on drug trafficking, Liddy's forcefulness as a speaker and his unrelenting enthusiasm for the job impressed Egil Krogh [q.v.], the White House staff coordinator for the project.

Krogh considered Liddy an invaluable asset to the White House and in July 1971 Liddy joined E. Howard Hunt [q.v.] as a member of Nixon's Special Investigations Unit. The ad hoc agency, headed by Krogh and David R. Young, Jr., had been established only months earlier to provide a thorough investigation of Daniel Ellsberg [q.v.] and the publication of the *Pentagon Papers* and also to uncover the source of government leaks. Consequently, it became known as the "Plumbers Unit." Because of Nixon's instructions to give the Ellsberg case priority, Liddy together with Hunt began an intensive examination of Ellsberg's associates and his motives in an attempt to unearth a possi-

ble conspiracy. After a review of FBI files it was discovered that Ellsberg had undergone psychiatric care, but his physician refused to provide information, sighting patient doctor confidentiality.

Motivated by a campaign to discredit Ellsberg and uncover the full extent of the conspiracy, Liddy and Hunt, with the approval of Krogh and presidential counsel John D. Ehrlichman [q.v.], plotted a break-in of Ellsberg's psychiatrist's office. With the assistance of three expatriot Cubans, the plumbers implemented their burglary plan, but were unsuccessful in their attempted acquisition of damaging evidence. Ehrlichman, fearful of possible exposure of the bungled burglary, purportedly insisted that future plumbers work pursue a conventional means of investigation only. With the exception of a brief investigation of Jack Anderson [q.v.] due to his disclosures of White House involvement in the India-Pakistan War, by the end of 1971 the plumbers were out of business. In November 1971 Krogh recommended Liddy for a position with the Committee to Re-Elect the President (CREEP).

With a complex new campaign finance law in effect, Liddy was responsible for coordinating CREEP's expenditures in addition to meeting the requisite filing requirements of all 23 states where Nixon entered the primaries. Liddy, with the help of Hunt, also formulated a "broad-gauged intelligence plan" to secure Nixon's re-election. In January 1972 he prepared a detailed draft of his scheme which bore the code name "Gemstone" and presented it to John Mitchell [q.v.], head of CREEP, Jeb Stuart Magruder [q.v.] and John Dean, Counsel to the President. Liddy's "$1 million bottled-in-bond espionage plan" included the abduction of radical leaders in order to halt planned demonstrations at the Republican National Convention, break-ins at Democratic headquarters, wiretapping and surveillance of Democratic candidates and the use of call girls to compromise Democratic politicians. According to later testimony, everyone present was "stunned and appalled" by the plan. Liddy later informed security coordinator, James McCord that the plan was presently unaffordable and the project had to be reorganized.

In subsequent meetings, Liddy presented a scaled down version which restricted the project to wiretapping of the Democratic National Committee headquarters only. A reduced budget was submitted and later approved. Within months, Liddy, Hunt and McCord, together with a four man back-up team, plotted the break-in of the party's headquarters located at the Watergate complex.

In May 1972 the group succeeded in planting wiretaps, but the equipment began to malfunction in June and a return visit was necessitated. Because of a night watchman's suspicion, McCord together with the four man back-up team was arrested on the premises. As the Watergate episode began to unfold, Liddy was subpoenaed before a grand jury in August 1972. He was later indicted, tried and convicted for his role in the burglary. In November 1973 Liddy was sentenced to 6 to 20 years. Stubborn to the end, he refused to testify either in his own behalf or against his colleagues and superiors. President Jimmy Carter commuted his sentence and he was released from prison in September 1977.

[DGE]

LINDSAY, JOHN V(LIET)
b. Nov. 24, 1921; New York, N.Y.
Mayor, New York, N.Y., 1965-73.

The son of an investment banker, Lindsay was educated in fashionable private schools and at Yale University, which awarded him a law degree in 1948. Active in the Young Republicans as an Eisenhower stalwart, he worked as executive assistant to Attorney General Herbert Brownell from 1953 to 1956. In 1958 Lindsay was elected to the House of Representatives from Manhattan's East Side "Silk Stocking" district, a bastion of the GOP's Eastern Establishment and one of the few Republican districts in New York

City. He became one of the most liberal Republicans in Congress, sponsoring civil rights legislation and opposing anti-Communist-inspired attacks on civil liberties. [See KENNEDY Volume]

In November 1965 Lindsay upset New York's Democratic political machine by winning the mayoralty election on the Republican and Liberal lines. Once in office, he frequently found himself embroiled in difficult negotiations with the city's traditionally Democratic public service unions. Strikes were frequent. Despite winning handsome contracts from the city, many white union members, as well as other working and middle class whites, came to dislike Mayor Lindsay with growing intensity. Ironically, one reason was the dramatic increase in the city budget, which required higher taxes and transit fares. Another was the Mayor's close relationship with the black and Hispanic communities. His support of school decentralization against the demands of the United Federation of Teachers (UFT) led to the 1968 teacher strikes, increased—at least temporarily—black-white polarization and eroded his popularity among traditionally liberal Jews (a large percentage of the UFT membership was Jewish). Meanwhile, Lindsay's relationship with New York Gov. Nelson Rockefeller [q.v.], one of the major financial backers of the 1965 campaign, deteriorated, as Rockefeller occasionally exercised gubernatorial prerogatives to the detriment of the Mayor and New York City. [See JOHNSON Volume]

In 1969 Lindsay faced an uphill battle for a second term. He had to win if he hoped to fulfill early predictions that he would someday be a presidential candidate. In New York he was still popular among the nonwhite minorities and some liberals, and, as the charming host of "Fun City," among chic Manhattanites. One of the most appealing and photogenic national political figures—he was almost invariably described as "handsome" or "tall, tanned and mediagenic"—he was, as one local politician said, "the most popular mayor in the country outside of New York." Some found him arrogant and self-righteous. Scandal beset Lindsay, too, when a key aide was jailed for bribery. The Mayor therefore began his unofficial campaign early, appearing as often as possible in the news and visiting white communities in the boroughs. He repeatedly admitted making mistakes, but New Yorkers were reminded by his supporters that his was the "second toughest job in America." He deemphasized his glamorous "Fun City" image and sympathy for minorities. Instead, he stressed his administration's achievements in the areas of budget, employment, rapid transit, housing, education and the war on crime. He noted that his government had made city parks more available to the public. He took tough public stands on civil disorder.

Lindsay was defeated in the June Republican primary by John Marchi, a conservative state legislator from Staten Island. Jarred by the first electoral defeat of his career, Lindsay nonetheless benefitted from the loss. Having won the Liberal Party endorsement, he was free of the constraints imposed by the Republican label. Although Rockefeller refused to back him, New York's two liberal Republican Senators, Jacob Javits [q.v.] and Charles Goodell [q.v.], offered their support. The Mayor himself rejected "rigid party loyalty" and decided to "support candidates on the basis of their performance and record on behalf of New York City." He was also the only liberal in the field for November, since Democratic voters chose a "law and order" candidate, Mario Procaccino, in their primary. The Mayor continued to emphasize his "solid" accomplishments and made a concerted effort to win the crucial Jewish vote, but he was careful not to compromise his liberalism beyond the point of credibility. He used Vietnam as a campaign issue, arguing that the war diverted money and attention from urban and other domestic problems.

In November Lindsay won reelection with 41% of the vote running on the Liberal and a special Independent line.

Political analysts speculated whether Lindsay would switch party allegiance. But Lindsay moved slowly, declaring his intention to remain Republican and refusing to discuss future political ambitions. Meanwhile, polls showed Lindsay to be an attractive figure nationally, particularly among the young, the college educated and women.

During the Nixon Administration, the Mayor was spokesperson for the nation's cities. In March 1970 he helped unite the big cities through the U.S. Conference of Mayors to lobby for "Congressional and state actions to meet city needs." The mayors would concentrate on five areas of pending congressional legislation: revenue sharing; welfare reform; federal mass transit aid; urban renewal and Model Cities; crime control. For the next few years a task force of 17 mayors, Lindsay's creation, visited each other to publicize urban problems and kept the demand for revenue sharing alive. In December 1970 Lindsay drew a standing ovation at the National League of Cities convention by calling for a $10 billion revenue sharing program in 1971. As chairman of the Conference of Mayors' Legislative Action Committee, he led the cities' attack on Nixon's 1971 budget. He developed the concept of the "national city," which would bypass state government and deal directly with Washington.

Lindsay grew increasingly critical of Nixon Administration policies. Speaking in April 1970, he assailed Administration efforts to quash dissent as "the most significant threat to freedom from our own government in a generation." The following month he lauded the young men who refused to serve in Vietnam as he traded attacks with Vice President Spiro Agnew [q.v.]. Lindsay and Agnew chose opposite sides again in the fall, when Lindsay backed Sen. Goodell's bid for reelection, while Agnew indirectly endorsed Conservative candidate James L. Buckley [q.v.]. More surprising was Lindsay's public support for Democrat Arthur J. Goldberg [q.v.] in the gubernatorial contest against Gov. Rockefeller. This decision marked the final break with Rockefeller.

Lindsay faced recurrent municipal crises. In May 1970 construction workers, abetted by police inaction, attacked anti-war demonstrators in Manhattan. In the following month ghetto riots, punctuated by arson, erupted. In August and September inmates of four city prisons revolted and took over the jails. The prison affair generally enhanced Lindsay's stature, since the Mayor appeared to act with firmness but without an excessive use of force. Some liberal critics, however, blamed Lindsay for the riots, charging that his administration, while spending enormous amounts on the police, had done little to improve the backlogged court system, prison overcrowding and inmate medical and rehabilitation programs. More clearly damaging to Lindsay were the Knapp Commission hearings on police corruption held in late 1971. Evidence presented to the commission indicated that in 1967 the Mayor had been informed of police officers' complaints about widespread corruption in their department but had chosen to ignore their reports.

In August 1971 Lindsay announced his switch to the Democratic Party. In part because of the mixed reaction from national and state Democratic leaders, he did not immediately announce his presidential candidacy. Nonetheless, he said that he was "firmly committed to take an active part in 1972 to bring about new national leadership." He scored the Nixon Administration for "indifference" to urban problems, drug addiction, inflation and gun control. He noted the failure to end the Indochina war, but "the most troubling development" was "the government's retreat from the Bill of Rights," citing telephone tapping, military spying on citizens, mass arrests of protestors and "minimum enforcement" of minority rights. After a period spent making contact with Democrats across the nation and assessing his modest performance in the Gallup and Harris polls, the Mayor declared his presidential candidacy in December.

Lindsay pictured himself as an "outsider" competing with primary opponents who were "good and honorable men" but trapped in "a Capital closed to the ordinary citizen, but open to bankrupt corporate giants, foreign dictators and to those wealthy enough to buy privileged protection with campaign cash." Aided by friendly New York labor leaders, he made a strong effort to appeal to the blue-collar vote. Yet, unlike his primary opponents, he had no established constituency within the Democratic Party. Even a January 1972 convention of liberal New York State Democrats voted to back Sen. George McGovern (D,S.D.) [q.v.], giving Lindsay only 1.4% of the votes. His primary runs were disastrous. He won only 7% in the Florida primary in March and came in sixth with 7% in the April Wisconsin primary. He then announced his withdrawal from the race.

Lindsay campaigned actively for McGovern in the fall, heading the Mayors for McGovern Committee. He decided not to seek reelection in 1973. He took up law practice again in New York, finding time to take a bit part in a film, write a novel and serve as a political commentator on television and in the press.

[JCH]

For further information:
Barry Gottehrer, *The Mayor's Man: One Man's Struggle to Save Our Cities* (Garden City, 1975).

LING, JAMES J(OSEPH)
b. Dec. 31, 1922; Hugo, Okla.
Chairman, Ling-Temco-Vought 1961-70.

Son of an Oklahoma fireman, Ling was a high school dropout. After service in the Navy during World War II, he founded an electrical contracting firm in Dallas with an initial investment of $3,000. By the mid-1950s, Ling's firm was doing a multimillion dollar business. Ling converted it to a public corporation, issuing 450,000 shares of stock at $2.25 per share from a booth at the Texas State Fair. He acquired other electronics firms and moved into the booming aerospace and defense industries of the late 1950s and early 1960s. His 1961 acquisition of Chance Vought Aircraft completed the transformation of his initial holding into Ling-Temco-Vought (LTV), the name under which his conglomerate rose by 1969 to the position of the 14th largest U.S. nonfinancial corporation in *Fortune's* 500 list.

The key to Ling's success was his skill at the manipulation of corporate debt structures for maximum leverage. By the mid-1960s he had abandoned any direct role in the day-to-day management of production in the firms he controlled and was concerned exclusively with an artful pyramiding of credit, restructuring of portfolios and corporate takeovers. In the boom atmosphere of the late 1960s, this was profitable procedure, and the steady dividend returns on LTV stock quieted any concern from creditors or investors over the increasing exposure of Ling's conglomerate. [See JOHNSON Volume]

In the spring of 1969, however, the situation changed abruptly. A rapid tightening of credit by the Nixon Administration cut off Ling's previous easy access to sources of finance; at the same time a growing public outcry over "conglomerates" focused attention on empires such as LTV that had come to prominence in the 1960s, often in connection with "cost-plus" contracts for arms and aerospace production. Finally political factors came into play against Ling. An important backer of Lyndon Johnson, Ling was no favorite of the new Administration.

When the Justice Department began to look for likely conglomerates to attack, LTV, which was already the subject of a large dossier on potential anti-trust practices, presented a suitable target. Thus in April 1969 the Justice Department sued to divest LTV of its 63% holdings of Jones and Laughlin Steel Corp. stock. The suit immediately followed an LTV tender offer to acquire the outstanding stock of the company and was the first major government attack on the new conglomerates.

The Jones and Laughlin suit, by itself, would not have toppled Ling if it had not occurred simultaneously with a swift change in the environment in which Ling had built up his conglomerate. LTV was forced to report a $38 million loss in 1969, despite an increase of sales. The losses brought into sharp relief the extremely top-heavy indebtedness of LTV, which showed a debt-to-capital ratio of .85, the highest on the *Fortune* 500 list. This series of setbacks combined with the 1969–70 bear market in stock prices to drive the value of LTV's stock down to 7⅛ from a 1967 high of 169½.

In May 1970 the controlling shareholders of LTV joined the firm's deeply worried creditors to carry out a streamlining of management that resulted in Ling's resignation as chairman and chief executive. Ling was replaced by Robert H. Steward, III, head of Dallas' First National Bank. With the completion of the first phase of rationalization, including extensive firings and layoff of management personnel, Ling announced in July 1970 that he would relinquish all participation in LTV's activities.

Ling's personal fortune was vastly reduced, and his situation rendered even more difficult by the fact that most of his personal debts were held against the collapsed stock values of the company. His $3 million Dallas mansion was taken over by creditors. Ling managed to salvage 25% ownership of a newly organized holding company and retained his directorships in some others.

[LRG]

For further information:
Stanley H. Brown, *Ling: The Rise, Fall and Return of a Texas Tycoon* (New York, 1972).

LODGE, HENRY CABOT
b. July 5, 1902; Nahart, Mass.
Chief Negotiator, Paris Peace Talks, January 1969-December 1969;
Special Envoy to the Vatican, 1970-1975.

Lodge was born into a distinguished New England family that traced its ancestry to the Massachusetts Bay Colony and later included several cabinet members and congressmen. He was raised by his grandfather Sen. Henry Cabot Lodge, Sr., noted for his opposition to United States participation in the League of Nations in 1919. Subsequent to his graduation from Harvard in 1924, Lodge pursued a journalism career until his election to the Massachusetts House of Representatives in 1933. In 1936 he was elected to the U.S. Senate. Lodge served two duty tours during World War II.

Reelected to the Senate in 1946, Lodge identified with the Eastern wing of the Republican Party supporting bipartisan foreign policy to contain Communist expansion and federal programs to deal with selected economic and social problems. During 1951-52 Lodge worked for the election of Dwight D. Eisenhower as President. In so doing, Lodge ignored his own political career, losing his senatorial reelection bid to Rep. John F. Kennedy. Lodge served as ambassador to the U.N. until 1960, at which time he became the Republican Party's vice-presidential nominee. Lodge served as ambassador to South Vietnam twice: from August 1963 until August 1964 and from July 1965 until April 1967. From April 1968 until January 1969, Lodge served as ambassador to West Germany. [See TRUMAN, EISENHOWER, KENNEDY, JOHNSON Volumes]

In January 1969 President Nixon appointed Lodge chief negotiator to the Paris peace conference, replacing veteran diplomat W. Averell Harriman [q.v.]. Lodge's credentials marked him as an ardent anti-Communist, meaning that the North Vietnamese could anticipate few concessions from the new Administration. New York attorney Lawrence Walsh and ambassador to Indonesia Marshall Green were named Lodge's assistants. The American proposals called for complete withdrawal of all outside forces within one year, a cease-fire under international supervision and free elections under international supervision. The North Vietnamese rejected consideration of these proposals and demanded the immediate and total withdrawal of all Americans from South Vietnam. Frustrated by

Hanoi's "take it or leave it" attitude, Lodge asked to be relieved in October 1969. Nixon's failure to immediately replace Lodge upon his resignation Dec. 8, 1969, indicated that the Administration was momentarily downgrading the peace negotiations.

In July 1970 Lodge became President Nixon's special envoy to the Vatican, a position accepted without pay and not requiring residence in Rome. The post held significance because the Vatican was a center of worldwide information and provided an opportunity for possible peace negotiations with North Vietnam and inquiries concerning the fate of American prisoners-of-war there. Also in July 1970 Lodge was named chairman of a special presidential commission to study U.S. policy toward Communist China. After hearing testimony from 200 witnesses in six U.S. cities, the commission recommended in April 1971 that the United States seek Communist China's admission to the United Nations without the expulsion of Nationalist China.

During the 1970s Lodge maintained his home in Beverly, Mass., primarily tending to personal business. He attended the 1976 Republican National Convention but did not play a significant role.

[TML]

LOEB, WILLIAM
b. Dec. 26, 1905; Washington, D.C.
Publisher, *Manchester Union Leader,* 1948-.

William Loeb was brought up in upper class surroundings. He lived in Oyster Bay, Long Island, and graduated from Williams College in 1927. After a short career as a journalist he bought a share in the New Hampshire *Manchester Union Leader.* In 1948 he gained full control of the newspaper, using it as a platform for his own idiosyncratic right-wing views.

Loeb supported Robert Taft as a Republican presidential candidate in 1952 and was a great admirer of Sen. Joseph R. McCarthy. During the 1960 New Hampshire primary he refused to support John F. Kennedy on the grounds that he was "soft on Communism." In 1964 Loeb supported Sen. Barry Goldwater [q.v.], denouncing his political rival, Nelson Rockefeller [q.v.] as a "wifeswapper" (referring to Rockefeller's divorce and remarriage to a younger woman). Throughout the years Loeb has become a master of the printed personal attack as a means of furthering his own political ends.

In 1968 Loeb and his newspaper jumped into the New Hampshire primary races with relish. The *Union Leader* dubbed Lyndon Johnson, "Snake Oil Lyndon" while Eugene McCarthy [q.v.] was labeled "a skunk's skunk." Loeb spent the greatest part of his journalistic talents promoting Richard Nixon's [q.v.] candidacy. The result of the New Hampshire Republican primary race was a landslide victory for Nixon. In the 1968 general election campaign, Loeb remained a staunch Nixon supporter.

During the 1972 New Hampshire primary race Loeb's political relationship with Nixon became more complex. Loeb denounced Nixon's attempts to normalize relations with China and published an editorial which announced that the *Manchester Union Leader* would only support a candidate "who [was] dedicated to the restoration of . . . national defense and who [was] prepared to support a foreign policy designed to preserve the security and the honor of the United States."

On Feb. 24, 1972, with the New Hampshire primary only 11 days away, Loeb unleashed a bombshell on the front page of his paper in the form of a purported letter from a youth in Florida who claimed to have heard Democratic candidate Edmund Muskie [q.v.] make an ethnic slur against French speaking Canadian-Americans by referring to them as cannuks. Since 60% of Manchester's voters were of French-Canadian descent, and the Manchester vote was crucial in winning the state, Loeb's charges against Muskie were extremely damaging. However, the allegations seemed dubious. The author of the letter, a certain Paul Morri-

son, was never found and the national press reported that the real author was a Nixon White House aide named Ken Clawson. It was further reported that Clawson had been in contact with *Manchester Union Leader* editor-in-chief B.S. McQuaid at the time of the letter's appearance.

The day following the publication of the letter, Loeb continued his mounting attack on Muskie by publishing an article reprinted from the social section of *Women's Wear Daily.* In this article Mrs. Muskie was quoted as saying to reporters such things as "I can't mix booze and wine" and "Let's tell dirty jokes." Loeb's anti-Muskie campaign culminated in an unforeseen manner on Feb. 26 when Muskie delivered a speech in front of the *Manchester Union Leader* building. Muskie defended himself against Loeb's public attacks. However, when he turned to the subject of printed attacks on his wife he lost control and repeatedly sobbed. After this spectacle Muskie was finished as a national candidate.

During the presidential election Loeb turned his full fury on the Democratic candidate, Sen. George McGovern (D, S.D.) [q.v.]. In July 1977 Loeb published a series of articles alleging that McGovern was a coward while a bomber pilot in World War II. These charges were later found totally false. The day before the election Loeb attacked McGovern yet another time in a front page editorial under the headline " 'Kiss My Ass' says Sen. McGovern." The substance of the report was that the Democratic candidate had countered a youthful heckler in rather expressive language.

Loeb initially favored Nixon's resignation in light of the crisis surrounding the aftermath of the Watergate break-in. But he soon changed his mind and wrote that "President Nixon should not now resign or be impeached because to do so would take control of the nation away from the voters and give it to a small group of arrogant self-appointed rulers in the form of radio and TV commentators, newspaper publishers."

During the 1976 presidential election

Loeb declared the Republican Party "As dead as a dodo" and backed the candidacy of George Wallace [q.v.].

[MLB]

LONG, RUSSELL B(ILLIU)
b. Nov. 3, 1918; Shreveport, La.
Democratic Senator, La., 1949 - ;
Chairman, Finance Committee, 1966 -.

Russell Long, son of the populist Louisiana governor and U.S. senator Huey Long, obtained his law degree in 1942. He served in the Navy during World War II, and then entered politics by working on his uncle Earl K. Long's successful 1947 gubernatorial campaign. The following year he won a seat in the U.S. Senate. Long assumed the chairmanship of the powerful Finance Committee in 1966. As chairman, Long became the Senate's most influential voice on federal economic and tax policy. [See TRUMAN, EISENHOWER, KENNEDY, JOHNSON Volumes]

Long combined the "poor boy populist" image of his father with his own energetic and determined advocacy of policies favored by Louisiana's major industries—oil, natural gas, sulphur, sugar and shipbuilding. He fought for oil depletion allowances for the oil and natural gas industry, the deregulation of natural gas prices and price supports for the sugar industry. He opposed breaking up the large, integrated oil companies. But he also said that it would "probably be right to break up big fortunes" and that it would be beneficial to spin off Chevrolet and Buick from General Motors. He opposed what he called "giveaway" programs like the Communications Satellite Corp. (COMSAT) and government patent policies that grant patents on research results obtained under federally financed research projects. And he wanted to tighten up tax breaks given to foundations and those given for charitable contributions.

During the Nixon-Ford Administrations he worked for limited pension reform and for a national health insurance to cover catastrophic illness. In foreign affairs he supported the Vietnam war and opposed the 1970 Cooper-Church Amendment to limit the President's authority to conduct military operations in Cambodia and the 1971 Mansfield Amendment calling for American withdrawal from Vietnam within nine months of the release of U.S. prisoners. But when President Ford requested additional military aid for Vietnam during the final Communist offensive in 1975, Long opposed it.

Long played a major role in the formation of the Tax Reform Act of 1969. He guided through his Committee the bill extending the income tax surcharge and revised the House-passed tax reform measure so that it was more in line with the Administration's more limited reform proposals. The panel diluted reform measures that cut off tax loopholes and reduced individual tax relief measures. It entirely deleted reforms dealing with foreign income, especially from oil, and increased the oil depletion allowance to 23% after the House had cut it to 20%. The Senate, however, added several major floor amendments before passing the bill. These included a 15% increase in Social Security benefits and increases in the income tax exemptions for tax payers and their dependents. Long supported an unsuccessful Republican move to return the amended bill to his Finance Committee. Nixon at first threatened to veto the reform bill but eventually signed it, and the Tax Reform Act of 1969 became the most comprehensive tax reform law in the nation's history. The same year Long successfully led the opposition that defeated the Nixon Administration's Family Assistance Plan (FAP). The FAP was expected to check what were described as family welfare costs by increasing the incentive to work. The plan had two features: one aided the unemployed poor; the other aided the working poor who would be eligible for assistance payments until their annual income reached $3,920.

The House adopted the basic features of the Administration's proposals in April 1970, but the plan immediately ran into the combined opposition of liberal Democrats and conservative Republicans on

Long's Finance Committee. The liberals and welfare groups opposed the plan because the benefit levels were too low; the conservatives opposed it on principle because they saw it as the beginning of a guaranteed annual income system whose costs would increase substantially over the years. After three days of hearings in April, Long sent the measure back to the White House for redrafting. At July hearings, Long denounced the Family Assistance Plan as "a massive and costly experiment which proposes adding 14 million Americans to the welfare rolls." Instead, he proposed increasing the federal minimum wage as a way to raise living standards for the working poor and to cut federal welfare costs. The Administration rejected this idea. Welfare reform was effectively killed in the 91st Congress when Long's Committee rejected the FAP by an 8–6 vote in November 1970.

The following year Long was a major force behind attempts to include the family welfare features of the FAP in an omnibus Social Security bill. After his second defeat on the family welfare reform plan, Nixon announced in February 1973 that his Administration would not resubmit it to Congress.

During 1972 Long helped shape the Nixon-proposed federal revenue-sharing program Congress enacted in 1972. The Administration had first proposed the program in 1969. The revised 1971 proposal called for a $5 billion general revenue-sharing program, and an $11 billion special sharing program that reorganized and regrouped existing grant programs. But Congress failed to move on special revenue sharing.

Long's Finance Committee substantially revised the House-passed version of the program. They rewrote the aid distribution formula to increase the amounts made available to smaller, rural states at the expense of the more populous ones. Senators from urban states strongly opposed the aid formula. Long admitted that his bill gave less money to more populous states than did the House version. But he also claimed that his bill gave more money to the cities and poorer areas because it distributed less money to the well-to-do suburbs. The Senate accepted the Long formula.

Tax reform, national health insurance, welfare reform and energy policy were high on the Carter Administration's agenda when it took office in 1977. They all had to confront Russell Long and his Finance Committee.

Long remained an important force in the Senate during the first year of the Carter Administration.

[AE]

LOTT, TRENT
b. Oct. 9, 1941; Grenada, Miss.
Republican Representative, Miss.
1973–.

Lott graduated from the University of Mississippi with a B.A. degree in 1963. He went on to receive his law degree from Ole Miss in 1967. Following his graduation Lott was a practicing attorney and worked from 1968-72 as administrative assistant to Mississippi Rep. William Colmer (D, Miss) [q.v.], who chaired the powerful Rules Committee.

When Colmer decided not to seek reelection in 1972, Lott ran for his seat. Running as a Republican and with Colmer's backing, Lott won the race that November with 56% of the vote. Lott's victory was considered a dramatic break with tradition. He was the district's first Republican representative in the 20th century. President Richard Nixon carried the district with a whopping 87% of the vote in that election. Lott represented Mississippi's fifth congressional district, a gulf coast urban center.

In his first two terms in the House, Lott established a strong conservative record. The conservative Americans for Constitutional Action (ACA) rated him at 84 or 85 in almost every year during the period. In military affairs Lott voted for the anti-ballistic missile system and the B-1 bomber and supported the development of nuclear carriers. He voted against foreign aid, the Turkish arms cutoff, cuts in defense spending and attempts to limit the

President's war-making powers. Lott also opposed cuts in military aid to South Korea. In domestic affairs, he voted against busing, government aid for abortion and the establishment of a consumer protection agency.

Lott received national attention as a fierce defender of President Nixon during the Judiciary Committee's 1974 impeachment inquiry. After months of hearings, Lott maintained, "There is not one iota of evidence that the President had any prior knowledge of the Watergate break-in." He contended that there was also no evidence Nixon had interfered with the investigations of the FBI, the Justice Department, the special prosecutor and congressional committees, and asserted that charges that Nixon had made "false and misleading" public statements concerning the Watergate break-in were unfounded. Lott was one of the few Republicans on the Committee to vote "no" on all five articles of impeachment brought against Nixon. It was not until after the release of three incriminating recorded conversations between Nixon and H.R. Haldeman [q.v.] that Lott substantially altered his position. He said that he hoped Nixon would resign but if he did not, Lott would vote for impeachment.

Lott's strong support for Nixon did not hamper him politically. He was reelected in 1974 and 1976 by large margins.

[GMS]

LOVE, JOHN A(RTHUR)
b. Nov. 29, 1916; Gibson City, Ill.
Governor, Colo. 1962-73; Director,
Office of Energy Policy, 1973.

John Love attended the University of Denver, receiving his bachelor's degree in 1938 and his law degree in 1941. After serving in the armed forces in World War II, he practiced law in Colorado Springs. As a political novice, he entered the Colorado gubernatorial race in 1962 and won. He held that office until 1973 and, consequently, served longer than any other Colorado governor. He was regarded as a political moderate.

He resigned as governor to become President Nixon's director of a newly created Energy Policy Office. From the winter of 1972 until Love's appointment in July 1973, Nixon had already gone through four top energy advisers—Gen. George Lincoln, Peter Flanigan [q.v.] John Ehrlichmann [q.v.], and George Shultz [q.v.]. When Love was appointed, the President seemed to give the energy problem new attention.

From the outset, Love ran into trouble. He took the spotlight in the public criticism of summertime gasoline shortages and forecast of a possible heating oil and propane gas shortage. His lack of experience in energy matters combined with other factors to make his job difficult. When Nixon appointed Love, he gave him only eight persons to work in the energy office. In addition, Love found himself sidestepped on energy matters, meeting challenges from officials in the Treasury and Interior Departments.

Love was regarded by the Administration as indecisive and ineffectual. Dissatisfaction became widespread in the summer of 1973 when Love resisted mandatory allocations of heating oil supplies, a policy the Nixon Administration finally adopted after months of indecision. Love, too, changed his mind on allocations when criticism came from governors, oil distributors, and Congress.

When the Yom Kippur War broke out in the Middle East in October, the Administration became increasingly convinced that Love was not the person to take charge of the energy crisis. Nixon decided to create a Federal Energy Administration. Reports circulated in Washington in December that William E. Simon, then Deputy Secretary of the Treasury, would be the head of the new energy agency. It was reported, moreover, that Love would remain in the Administration as assistant to the President but would no longer be coordinating energy policy for President Nixon. On Dec. 3, Love resigned, causing the White House to upset its plans to announce the setting up of the Federal Energy Administration. Love apparently believed that the Energy Policy Office would be absorbed in the new energy agency and that his job would lack influence. Nixon's continuing legal problems over Watergate contributed to Love's demise. "To be honest," Love was quoted as saying after his resignation, "it's been difficult to try to do anything meaningful and even to get the attention of the President."

In 1976, Love supported the nomination of Gerald Ford on the Republican ticket. Love succeeded in blocking the at-large sweep of Colorado delegates to the Republican convention that the Ronald Reagan [q.v.] camp had predicted. Reagan received the support of 15 out of the 16 at-large convention delegates; the lone opponent was Love who sided with Ford.

[HML]

LOWENSTEIN, ALLARD K(ENNETH)
b. Jan. 16, 1929; Newark, N.J.
Democratic Representative, N.Y., 1969-70.

The son of a prominent physician and restaurateur, Allard Lowenstein grew up in the suburbs of New York City. He studied at the University of North Carolina and Yale Law School, where he received his law degree in 1954. As president of the National Student Association during the early 1950s, Lowenstein coordinated a nationwide student-volunteer effort to aid the presidential campaign of Democrat Adlai Stevenson. Later as an educational consultant to the American Association for the United Nations, he toured South-West Africa, an international territory under the jurisdiction of the Republic of South Africa. As a result of his trip, he published in 1962 *Brutal Mandate,* an impassioned indictment of South Africa's racial policies in the territory.

In 1960 he managed the successful congressional campaign of reform Democrat William Fitts Ryan of New York. Lowenstein taught political science at Stanford University and North Carolina State University. Active in the civil rights movement, he donated his legal services to jailed civil rights workers, helped organize voter registration drives in Mississippi and was an adviser to the Southern Christian Leadership Conference.

Lowenstein, an early critic of the Vietnam war, became the chief organizer of the "dump Johnson" movement in 1967-68. He used his strong ties to the student movement to bring anti-war Democrats and campus activists together. Convinced that only a change in leadership would end the war, he canvassed anti-war Senators to find a candidate willing to challenge President Johnson in the primaries. When Minnesota Sen. Eugene McCarthy [q.v.] agreed to run, Lowenstein mobilized large numbers of student volunteers to work for the Senator in the New Hampshire primary. McCarthy's impressive showing led Johnson to announce on March 31, 1968, that he would not seek reelection. [See JOHNSON Volume]

At the Democratic Convention in Chicago in August, Lowenstein worked for a strong peace plank. He also opposed Vice President Hubert Humphrey's nomination, but later supported Humphrey in the campaign. While putting a peace coalition together for the Convention, Lowenstein also ran for a seat in the House of Representatives from New York's Nassau County. Campaigning as a peace candidate and with the aid of large numbers of student volunteers, Lowenstein narrowly defeated his Republican opponent in November 1968.

In Congress Lowenstein compiled a consistently liberal voting record. He opposed the Nixon Administration's District of Columbia anti-crime bill, a proposal to cut off financial aid to student demonstrators and most military appropriation bills. He voted for tax reform, for reform of the Selective Service System and for liberalization of the food stamp program. In 1970 the Americans for Democratic Action gave him a 100% rating.

Lowenstein's primary concern while in Congress remained the Vietnam war. With Reps. Paul McCloskey (R., Calif.) [q.v.] Donald Riegle (R., Mich.) [q.v.] and Donald Fraser (D., Minn.) [q.v.] he tried to coordinate the efforts of anti-war Representatives to enact peace legislation, especially proposals to cut off funds for combat operations in Southeast Asia. But the anti-war forces in the House were much weaker than those in the Senate, and the efforts of Lowenstein and others were frequently stymied. Mendel Rivers (D., S.C.) the powerful chairman of the House Rules Committee, was a strong supporter of the war, and he generally imposed severe time limits on House debates over war-related issues.

In April 1970 when the Rules Committee restricted debate on a military procurement bill, Lowenstein attacked the lack of democratic procedures and accused the House leadership of contributing to "wide-spread erosion of faith" in democracy among the nations' youth. His remarks had little effect, however. Later that year the House Rules Committee allowed only one hour to debate the controversial Cooper-Church Amendment.

Lowenstein continued to be active in the anti-war movement outside of Congress. On Oct. 6, 1969 he released a statement with eight other members of Congress that urged all Americans to support the student-led nationwide protests planned for Oct. 15. He also endorsed the November march to Washington to protest the war. Throughout 1969 and 1970 Lowenstein spoke on college campuses and at anti-war rallies around the country.

Although he was defeated for reelection in 1970 after the Republican-controlled New York legislature gerrymandered his district, Lowenstein remained active in politics. In 1971 he formed Citizens for Alternatives Now, which tried to coordinate a "dump Nixon" campaign. In May 1971 Lowenstein was elected chairman of Americans for Democratic Action and immediately launched a nationwide drive to register 18 to 21 year olds and to mobilize them in support of peace candidates in 1972. Lowenstein traveled to hundreds of college campuses, urging students to reject violence as a political tactic and to work within the system to make it responsive to the people's will.

Lowenstein's outspoken opposition to the war and to the Nixon Administration's policies won him a place on the White House "enemies list" as a top priority target. A 1972 report issued by Sen. Sam Erwin (D., N.C.) [q.v.] revealed that Lowenstein was also a target of the Army's secret surveillance program on domestic political activity. In response to these revelations, Lowenstein urged an official inquiry, citing many "puzzling incidents" in his life during these years.

In 1972 Lowenstein unsuccessfully challenged incumbent Rep. John Rooney for the Democratic nomination to Congress from Brooklyn. He ran for a House seat from Nassau County in 1974 and 1976, but lost both times to Republican John Wydler.

He remained active in politics and practiced law in New York City through the late 1970s.

[JD]

LUGAR, RICHARD G(REEN)
b. April 4, 1932, Indianapolis, Ind.
Mayor, Indianapolis, Ind. 1968-76.

The son of prominent Indiana community leaders, Lugar received a B.A. from Denison University in 1954. He then went on to earn two advanced degrees from Oxford on a Rhodes scholarship. In 1957, after graduating from the Navy's Officers Candidate School, he was assigned as an intelligence briefer to the chief of naval operations. In 1960 Lugar returned to Indianapolis, where he joined his brother in successfully rescuing two foundering family businesses. During the 1960s he ran for a seat on the Indianapolis School Board and served as its vice president from 1965-66.

Despite little public exposure and political expertise, Lugar ran for mayor of Indianapolis in 1967 against Democratic incumbent John Barton. With a platform that decried the evils of public spending and a pledge to improve the city through sound business management, Lugar won 53.1% of the vote to become the first Republican mayor of Indianapolis in two decades.

Shortly after taking office Lugar began to examine the plight of the city's urban area. Indianapolis shared the steadily increasing problems of all expanding cities—rising crime, over-crowding, lack of public housing, and inadequate health care and welfare programs. According to Lugar, most cities were "being strangled by a ring of rich suburbs that draw wealth out but put very little back in." Lugar devised a blueprint to consolidate the city and the suburbs in order to alleviate the burden of the existing regional councils, which were unable to tackle the broad spectrum of problems facing Indianapolis. Known as Unigov, the program met with a great deal of resistance from many quarters. Inner-city blacks regarded the consolidation as a form of gerrymander that would severely restrict their political strength. Democrats saw the program as an attempt by Lugar to enhance his support through expansion into wealthy Republican suburbs. Lugar viewed Unigov as the opportunity to reduce the number of city and county agencies from 50 to six, thereby producing additional resources with which to combat urban problems independent of federal subsidy and also move toward a well-balanced budget. With the support of the Republican-controlled state legislature, Unigov became law in December 1969.

A longtime supporter of Richard Nixon, Lugar campaigned on his behalf during the 1968 presidential primaries and served as a delegate and platform committee member at the Republican National Convention. In 1969 Nixon appointed him vice chairman of the Advisory Commission on Intergovernmental Relations. He became the first mayor to serve on the Commission.

Lugar favored Nixon's revenue-sharing plan because it provided local governments with discretionary powers with respect to dispensing funds. The Unigov program received an enthusiastic reception from Nixon, especially since Indianapolis was the only major city in the hands of loyal Republican leadership. In 1970 the city received its first allocation of federal grants. Over $11,000,000 in funds were dispensed to Indianapolis through the Model Cities program, all of which were earmarked for urban renewal. The city became a virtual testing ground for the Administration's urban policy theories, and Lugar was soon deemed "Nixon's favorite mayor."

In 1970 he was elected president of the National League of Cities and immediately set out to shift the organization's focus to self-help programs and reform on a local level. That same year he represented America's cities at the NATO Conference on the Challenges of Modern Society, and chose the occasion to invite delegates to the International Conference on Cities held in Indianapolis in 1971. Close to 900 officials, including representatives from 17 foreign countries, flocked to the conference. Lugar informed the gathering that international peace was intrinsically connected to the stability of the world's big cities. In 1971 Lugar was reelected despite criticism from his opponent that Unigov served no other purpose than to guarantee Lugar a record majority in each election.

Growing accustomed to the limelight, Lugar gradually became more involved in national politics. At the Republican National Convention in 1972, he presented one of the three keynote addresses, and afterwards campaigned in major U.S. cities for Nixon. In 1974 despite repeated denials that he was not interested in seeking national office, Lugar announced his candidacy for Birch Bayh's (D, Ind.) [q.v.] senatorial seat. Citing his decisive leadership in Indianapolis, he promised to cut federal spending and put an end to federal intervention in state matters. Lugar's platform included opposition to busing as a means to achieve desegregation and support for a constitutional amendment outlawing abortion. Although Nixon's support was instrumental in Lugar's reelection in 1971, it now proved a detriment in light of the adverse publicity surrounding the Watergate scandals. Lugar lost the election by a narrow margin.

He then returned to his responsibilities as mayor and by the time his term was up in 1976, he had succeeded in reducing property taxes five times and created a budget surplus of $4,500,000.

In 1976 Lugar challenged incumbent Vance Hartke (D, Ind.) [q.v.] for a seat in the U.S. Senate. Calling for a reduction in welfare spending and tax cuts for individuals and businesses, Lugar achieved a comfortable victory with more than 59% of the votes.

[DGE]

MacGREGOR, CLARK
b. July 12, 1922; Minneapolis, Minn.
Republican Representative, Minn., 1961-71; Chairman, Committee to Re-Elect the President, July 1972-November 1972.

Raised in Minneapolis, MacGregor graduated from Dartmouth in 1946, and received a law degree from the University of Minnesota in 1948. He practiced law until 1960, when he was elected U.S. representative from Minnesota's third district.

In Congress MacGregor emerged as a conservative, opposing President Johnson's reform legislation; amending the anti-crime bill of 1967 to put the highest funding priority on thwarting domestic rioting and organized crime; and revising the 1968 gun-control bill to exclude curbs on the sale of rifle and shotgun ammunition. In 1968 MacGregor was one of 10 "surrogate candidates" who spoke on behalf of Richard Nixon's presidential candidacy.

During his last term in the House, MacGregor was a leader of the drive to oust liberal Supreme Court Justice Abe Fortas [q.v.] after *Life* magazine revealed that Fortas had accepted (and returned 11 months later) a $20,000 payment from financier Louis E. Wolfson, who was subsequently convicted of selling unregistered securities. One day after MacGregor urged a House probe of the matter, Fortas resigned.

MacGregor captured the Minnesota Republican nomination for Senator in 1970 but lost the election to Hubert H. Humphrey [q.v.], who received 59% of the vote. During the Senate race MacGregor pledged support for President Nixon's policies and Nixon campaigned for MacGregor, calling the candidate "a voice of the future."

Following his election defeat, MacGregor became Nixon's chief congressional liaison. He served on a five-member council appointed to study a wide range of recomendations by black members of the House, including stronger enforcement of civil rights legislation and more emphasis on Africa in foreign policy. After some initial fanfare, however, the council failed to produce concrete results, further alienating the Black Congressional Caucus from the Administration. In December 1971 MacGregor coauthored "Richard Nixon's Third Year," a paper describing the President's accomplishments that claimed 1971 "was a year of large conceptions, daring innovation and substantial progress."

On July 1, 1972, MacGregor became chairman of the Committee to Re-Elect the President (CREEP) in the wake of John Mitchell's [q.v.] resignation from the post two weeks after the arrest of five burglars at the Democratic National Committee headquarters in the Watergate complex in Washington, D.C. Before accepting the job—MacGregor said in a July 28, 1973, court deposition—he met with Nixon and was assured that CREEP had no involvement in Watergate. At the meeting MacGregor was informed that "no person in a position of authority had any foreknowledge of or involvement in the Watergate." During the campaign MacGregor worked closely with H.R. Haldeman [q.v.]. The White House played down the connection, choosing to present the President as a statesman above partisan politics.

MacGregor led the reelection effort in a

traditional partisan fashion. He warned of overconfidence when Nixon built an early lead in the polls; praised AFL-CIO neutrality and castigated the American Newspaper Guild's endorsement of Democratic candidate George McGovern [q.v.]; announced Nixon's refusal to debate McGovern; and labeled the Democratic candidate an advocate of "giveaway" welfare programs, "massive and reckless" defense budget cuts and a "begging" foreign policy.

MacGregor was not able to avoid entanglement in the Watergate issue. In September the Democrats raised the amount of a previous law suit against the Republicans for "blatant political espionage" from $1 million (filed three days after the Watergate break-in) to $3.2 million. MacGregor responded with a countersuit that claimed Democratic National Chairman Lawrence F. O'Brien [q.v.] was using the court "as a forum in which to make public accusations against innocent persons," and asked $2.5 million in damages. Both suits were later dismissed.

In October, MacGregor defended the Administration against charges that linked CREEP officials to a secret fund used for dirty tricks and political espionage. Earlier MacGregor had denied the existence of the fund and claimed *The Washington Post* was "maliciously linking the White House to Watergate." But on Oct. 26 he vacillated, admitting the existence of a "special fund" used for campaign planning and "in one instance" for gathering information on possible disruptions of Republican rallies in New Hampshire.

In his 1973 court deposition MacGregor said that throughout the campaign he was "misled, deceived and lied to" by his own staff in CREEP and by top White House aides regarding Watergate. This admission was in direct contradiction of a statement made by the President at a May 22, 1973, press conference in which Nixon said MacGregor was told to "conduct a thorough investigation" of CREEP's relation with the break-in. MacGregor said he did not conduct an investigation and was never told to do so by the President.

The day after Nixon's overwhelming election victory, MacGregor resigned as CREEP chairman and became chief Washington lobbyist for United Aircraft Corp. He testified before the Senate Watergate Committee Nov. 1, 1973, and repeated his court deposition.

[BO]

McCALL, TOM (LAWSON)
b. March 11, 1913; Egypt, Mass.
Governor, Ore. 1967–75.

McCall graduated from the University of Oregon in 1936 and worked for the Latah County Wildlife Association. From 1949 to 1952 he was executive assistant to Oregon Gov. Douglas McKay. McCall lost an initial bid for a seat in the U.S. House of Representatives in 1954. He won election in 1964 as secretary of state, Oregon's second ranking elective office. In the 1966 gubernatorial contest, he defeated his Democratic opponent, State Treasurer Robert Straub. [See JOHNSON Volume]

McCall won election as governor on an environmental platform. The new governor attempted to make good his campaign promises by first appointing himself interim chairman of the state's environmental commission to deal with the serious sewage and industrial pollution of the Willamette River. After the 1967 commission hearings, he implemented strict measures to control water pollution for every river in the state. The Willamette by 1969 was clean enough for swimming, fishing, boating and salmon spawning. McCall obtained increased funds for aid to education by adjusting income taxes rather than raising regressive state sales taxes and property taxes. Viewing the state's anti-abortion laws as harmful, he signed a bill in June 1969 making Oregon one of the first states to legalize abortions. That year he also succeeded in pushing through the legislature a reform bill which gave the governor unprecedented control over all state agencies.

Again stressing environmental protection as his main platform, McCall was reelected governor in 1970. During his second term he continued his campaign to preserve Oregon's natural resources. He pushed through bills preventing developers from building on the public beaches along Oregon's Pacific Ocean coastline in order to control the large influx of tourists, new residents and the type of new industries entering the state. By 1971, McCall had guided through the legislature over 100 environmental protection bills, including one of the nations first comprehensive land use plans to prohibit nonreturnable cans and bottles.

The same year McCall also formed the Office of Energy, Research and Planning to examine problems leading to power shortages and their possible remedies. In response to an energy crisis in the state in 1973, McCall declared a state of emergency and rapidly implemented measures that enlisted the public's cooperation in the conservation of fuel. The following year McCall put into effect the "Oregon Plan," which limited the sale of gasoline to drivers with either odd- or even-numbered license plates on alternate days. In 1973 he signed a bill making Oregon the first state to reduce criminal penalties for possession of less than an ounce of marijuana, making possession a violation rather than a felony. In addition McCall helped to promote a methadone program to aid the state's heroin addicts.

Although a Republican, McCall was frequently at odds with the Administration. He criticized Spiro Agnew's [q.v.] tough stand on anti-war protesters and the press in 1971 and feuded openly with conservative Ronald Reagan [q.v.] on federal funding policies. He was an early critic of Watergate. McCall declared in November 1973 that "we're not going to be housemen for the White House and try to whitewash one of the sorriest pages in American political history." In June 1974 McCall called for President Nixon's immediate resignation.

Restricted by law to two terms, McCall retired in 1975.

[LW]

McCARTHY, EUGENE J(OSEPH)
b. March 29, 1916; Watkins, Minn.
Democratic Senator, Minn., 1959–71.

McCarthy entered politics in 1948 as a supporter of Sen. Hubert H. Humphrey's (D, Minn.) [q.v.] fight against the Communist-led wing of Minnesota's Democratic Farmer-Labor Party (DFL). The following year he was elected over a Republican incumbent to the first of his five terms in the House, where he organized a caucus of liberal Democrats—later institutionalized as the Democratic Study Group—that agitated for more progressive legislation than the programs espoused by either Republicans or the Democratic leadership.

After his election to the Senate in 1958, however, McCarthy broke somewhat from his strongly liberal voting record in the House. Although he advocated medical care for the aged and other social reforms enacted by the Kennedy Administration, he voted against progressive tax policies considered by the Senate Finance Committee. Prior to 1967 McCarthy's most sustained legislative efforts promoted the reform of federal and state unemployment compensation systems and sought to increase wages for migrant farm workers. He also criticized U.S. intelligence agencies' influence in decisions affecting foreign policy and opposed the sale of U.S. arms to technologically undeveloped nations. [See EISENHOWER, KENNEDY Volumes]

Beginning mildly in 1966, then more vocally in 1967, McCarthy became the Senate's foremost opponent to the Johnson Administration's Vietnam war policy. As a candidate for the Democratic presidential nomination, he based his unorthodox campaign almost solely on his opposition to the "morally indefensible" war and President Johnson's "dangerous" domination over Congress in the making of foreign policy. Supported by an unusual army of idealistic young volunteers, he surprised Party regulars with strong showings against Johnson in the New

Hampshire primary (a chief reason for Johnson's subsequent withdrawal from the race) and a series of close battles with Sen. Robert F. Kennedy (D, N.Y.) in the spring primaries. McCarthy failed to garner Kennedy's supporters after the Massachusetts Senator's assassination, and he lost the nomination to Humphrey by a vote of 1,041 to 601 in the August Convention. [See JOHNSON Volume]

McCarthy's political energy dissipated after the presidential campaign. He answered only 61% of the roll call votes in 1969, the third lowest rating in the Senate. He resigned from the Foreign Relations Committee that year and virtually disappeared from the Congressional Record. In 1970 he reemerged to voice opposition to Nixon's "Vietnamization" policy. "Even if the South Vietnamese Army could be made into an effective military force," he said, "Asians would still be killing Asians with American arms. . . . The United States would still have moral responsibility for the war." He proposed an alternative plan for a negotiated settlement followed by a withdrawal of American military power, both contingent on Nixon's altering his policy to support a "coalition government to control the process of transition." The Administration stood firm in its insistence on free elections in South Vietnam. The only major issue on which McCarthy supported Nixon was the nomination of Minnesota Judge Harry A. Blackmun [q.v.] to be an associate justice of the Supreme Court.

McCarthy continued to fight, unsuccessfully, for extended unemployment compensation programs, joining other Senate liberals in opposition to Nixon's Family Assistance Plan in October 1970. He resigned from the Senate in 1971 and ran mediocre campaigns as an independent candidate for the presidency in 1972 and 1976. McCarthy's influence on American politics outlasted his own enthusiasm, as evidenced in the continued vivacious involvement of youth in electoral politics and the long-lived anger against U.S. military involvement in Southeast Asia.

[AM]

For further information:
Albert Eisele, *Almost to the Presidency: A Biography of Two American Politicians* (Blue Earth, Minn., 1972).

McCLELLAN, JOHN L(ITTLE)
b. Feb. 25, 1896; Sheridan, Ark.
d. Nov. 27, 1977; Little Rock, Ark.
Democratic Senator, Ark., 1943-77;
Chairman, Government Operations Committee, 1949-53, 1955-72;
Chairman Appropriations Committee, 1972-77.

McClellan never attended college, but studied law in his father's law firm for five years and gained admission to the bar in 1913 at the age of 17. He was the city attorney for Malvern, Ark., from 1920 to 1926 and a prosecuting attorney from 1927 to 1930. In 1934 he was elected to the U. S. House of Representatives, where he supported most New Deal programs. Eight years later he was elected to the Senate. He did not face another serious election challenge until 1972, when he was forced into a run-off primary election by Rep. David Pryor (D, Ark.). Despite his age McClellan won the primary and was reelected.

During his Senate career McClellan compiled a basically conservative record, although he supported some social welfare legislation. He gained national prominence during the 1950s and 1960s as a stern, efficient, fair investigator. Over the course of two decades he headed probes of corruption in labor unions, favoritism in the awarding of defense contracts, influence peddling in Congress and the causes of urban riots. (See TRUMAN, EISENHOWER, KENNEDY, JOHNSON Volumes)

McClellan continued basically conservative voting patterns during the Nixon-Ford years. In 1972 he cast the first cloture vote of his senatorial career in an unsuccessful effort to stop a filibuster by northern Senators opposing an anti-busing bill. He usually opposed federal spending for the Model Cities program, mass transit funds, aid for the handicapped and manpower training. He supported, however, continuing federal farm price subsidies for tobacco in 1972 and opposed limiting crop subsidy payments to $20,000 per grower in 1970. McClellan favored a strong defense posture, continuation of the draft, development of controversial weapons systems like the B-1 bomber and foreign military aid.

McClellan changed his position on the Vietnam war during the Nixon-Ford years. Although a supporter of the Johnson Administration's policies, McClellan voted to bar U. S. troops from Laos and Thailand in 1969. And while he opposed the 1970 Cooper-Church amendment to limit the President's authority to conduct military operations in Cambodia, he supported the 1971 Mansfield amendment which, as adopted by the Senate, called for the withdrawal of U. S. troops from Vietnam within nine months after the release of U. S. prisoners. The Administration strongly opposed the move. In 1973 after the Vietnam peace treaty had been signed, McClellan's Appropriations Committee voted unanimously to bar the use of funds for military operations by U. S. forces in Laos and Cambodia.

In August 1972, upon the death of Sen. Allen J. Ellender (D, La.)[q.v.], McClellan gave up his Government Operations Committee chairmanship to become the chairman of the Senate Appropriations Committee and of its Defense Subcommittee. Almost immediately McClellan's new authority was successfully challenged by Sen. Russell B. Long's (D, La.) Finance Committee on the issue of control over the funding of the federal revenue sharing program. The Nixon Administration had first proposed the program in 1969. Long's Committee had molded the revenue sharing bill specifically to keep the Appropriations Committee from acquiring control of the legislation and eventually the financing of the program. McClellan was rebuffed on the Senate floor by a 49–34 vote when he attempted to amend the bill so that his Committee would acquire control of it. Twenty-one of the 34 votes for the

amendment were cast by members of his own Committee.

McClellan's Appropriations Committee and Defense Subcommittee usually cut Administration defense budget requests. In 1974 he announced his Committee would cut $3.5 billion from the $87.1 billion fiscal 1975 budget request, but added that spending cuts would be proposed "only where we are convinced they can be made without unduly diminishing or weakening our defense posture." Despite his support of cuts in defense budget requests, he favored defense spending increases in certain areas. In 1976 he called the $104 billion defense budget lean, noting that the trend of disproportionate cuts could not be continued without seriously impairing national defense. McClellan suffered only occasional floor defeats on major appropriations issues. In 1975 he unsuccessfully opposed the vote to dismantle the controversial Safeguard anti-ballistic missile system and the vote to bar the use of defense funds to finance activities that could have involved the U.S. in Angola's civil war.

McClellan also headed the Appropriations Committee's Intelligence Operations Subcommittee. In 1973 that subcommittee was one of several congressional panels investigating the CIA's connections with the Watergate affair. Its probe revealed that several of Nixon's top advisers had discussed the Watergate affair with top CIA officials and told Agency members to inform FBI Director L. Patrick Gray [q.v.] that covert CIA operations would be jeopardized by the FBI Watergate investigation into the source of the money found on the Watergate burglars.

McClellan was the Senate's prime proponent of tough laws to limit protest activities. In 1969 he led a permanent investigation's subcommittee probe into campus disorders and proposed legislation to make it a federal crime to disrupt the operations of federally aided colleges and universities. That year Congress enacted a law that restricted the use of some higher-education funds by students who had participated in campus disorders. When students at Kent State University were killed in 1970, McClellan said on a network news program that "they should have mowed them all down."

As chairman of the Judiciary Committee's Criminal Laws and Procedures Subcommittee, McClellan worked closely with the Administration to shape federal anti-crime legislative programs during the Nixon-Ford years. In 1969 he introduced the legislation that later became the Organized Crime Control Act of 1970. The law narrowed the immunity granted to witnesses compelled to testify so that they would no longer be granted complete immunity from prosecution. It also broadened the grounds on which perjury convictions could be obtained. The measure generated opposition from many legal groups. The New York City Bar Association warned that it contained "the seeds of official repression."

In 1972 McClellan sponsored the Victims of Crime Act that was eventually incorporated into a broader measure enacted by Congress in 1973 as the Omnibus Crime Control and Safe Streets Act Amendments of 1973. This law provided federal funds to compensate injured law enforcement officers and their families, and innocent victims of certain crimes. McClellan had previously opposed such measures because of the inference that society was somehow responsible for crime and should start paying the bill.

McClellan undertook his most sweeping anti-crime effort in 1971 when his subcommittee began work on a measure to codify all federal criminal laws. The codification effort had begun in March 1967 when Congress created a commission to study federal criminal laws. McClellan served on the commission, which was headed by former California Gov. Edmond G. Brown. The Brown Commission submitted its report and a draft code to President Nixon on January 8, 1971. Its proposals included several revisions of federal criminal laws, including the abolishment of the death penalty, a ban on hand guns and reduction of the penalities for marijuana possession.

McClellan's subcommittee held lengthy hearings on the report in 1971 and prepared a much revised version of the proposed code, which was introduced in 1973 as SB 1. After the Nixon Administration submitted its own bill, the subcommittee held many hearings in 1973 and 1974 to reconcile the differences between the two versions. The bills drew heavy opposition from legal groups, civil libertarians and the press who charged the measures contained repressive features that could endanger political and personal liberties. Among other things the Committee bill substantially revised the crime classification and sentencing penalties for certain crimes and it reclassified many crimes as more serious offenses. But the committee also narrowed the definition of treason contained in the Commission's draft, and the definition of certain national security offenses. A new version was again introduced as SB 1 in 1975, and successor versions were introduced in 1977. Legal groups and civil libertarians continued to oppose them, and by the late 1970s none of the bills had passed.

McClellan died of a heart attack in Little Rock, Ark., on Nov. 27, 1977.

[AE]

McCLOSKEY, PAUL N(ORTON)
b. Sept. 29, 1927, San Bernardino, Calif.
Republican Representative, Calif., 1967–.

McCloskey, the son of an attorney, graduated from Stanford University in 1950. After service in the Marine Corps during the Korean conflict, he earned his law degree from the Stanford University Law School in 1953 and then became a deputy district attorney for Alameda County. He went into private practice in 1956 and founded a new law partnership that specialized in conservation cases in 1965. From 1964 to 1967 he taught legal ethics at the Santa Clara and the Stanford University Law Schools.

McCloskey was a progressive Republican and described himself as a fiscal conservative. He refused to support Sen. Barry Goldwater [q.v.] for President in 1964 and backed Democrat Pierre Salinger against his conservative Republican opponent, George Murphy, for U.S. senator that year. McCloskey also helped found the California Republican League to oppose extreme rightist factions in the Republican Party.

McCloskey was one of four Republicans who entered the primary election held in 1967 to fill the House seat vacated by the death of Rep. J. Arthur Younger (R, Calif.). He ran on an anti-war platform calling for immediate efforts to negotiate with the Hanoi government or a two-year de-escalation of the war if negotiations failed. McCloskey won the primary and went on to win the general election. He represented an upper- and middle-class suburban district.

In the House, McCloskey maintained his independence, voting with the Administration and the Republican Party less than 50% of the time. As a fiscal conservative, however, he generally supported Nixon–Ford vetoes of federal spending legislation for social welfare measures. A vigorous anti-Communist, McCloskey supported a strong defense policy. In 1971, he opposed an all-volunteer army, saying the nation was safer "when its army is made up of reluctant citizen-soldiers than by men who take pride in being professional killers." He fought the cut off of military aid to Turkey in 1974 and to Chile and South Korea in 1976. At the same time he was skeptical of the cost of defense programs and opposed the Administration on funding for the Safeguard anti-ballistic missile system and the B-1 bomber.

McCloskey always supported environmental programs, believing that conservation was the nation's most vital domestic issue. In 1969 he wrote a minority Government Operations Committee report in which he urged the complete banning of environmental testing of chemical and biological warfare agents after a gas testing accident at the Dugway Proving Grounds killed 6,000 sheep. He was named honorary cochairman of the Environmental Teach-in Group that organized nationwide activities for Earth Day in 1970. He voted to override Nixon's 1972 veto of the Federal Water Pollution Control Act Amendments, which authorized $18 billion for grants to states to construct waste treatment plants and set national water quality standards, and to override Ford's 1975 veto of a federal strip mining regulation bill. He opposed delaying the implementation of auto emmission standards in 1976.

McCloskey was one of the most outspoken congressional opponents of the Nixon Vietnam policy. Beginning in March 1969 he wrote Nixon the first in a series of five strongly worded letters urging the President to admit the error of U.S. policy and to begin troop withdrawals. He was one of only eight members of Congress who publicly supported the Oct. 15, 1969, Vietnam Moratorium demonstrations that were held in many cities across the country. After the May 1970 invasion of Cambodia, he led the fight for House passage of the Cooper-Church Amendment curtailing the President's authority to conduct combat operations in that country.

On Feb. 10, 1971, McCloskey called for a national dialogue to discuss the impeachment of President Nixon as a means of inducing him to change his Vietnam policy. He made the proposal after the South Vietnamese Army had launched an American-supported invasion into Laos that had ended in a rout. McCloskey defended his proposal saying "a reasonable argument can be made that the President's recent decision to employ American air power in the neutral countries of Laos and Cambodia exceeded his constitutional powers." McCloskey received little support for his proposal, however.

McCloskey formally announced his candidacy for the Republican presidential nomination on July 19, 1971, stating he would enter primaries in New Hampshire, California and other primary states to lead a slate of delegates to the 1972 Republican Convention who would be pledged to end the Vietnam war. McCloskey recognized that he had little chance of being nominated even if he won in the primaries, but insisted that true victory would be an early end to the war rather than his own election. His supporters hoped that McCloskey's candidacy would also help moderate Republicans win grass roots Party offices.

McCloskey's presidential campaign was also motivated by what he described as the Administration's duplicity in dealing with Congress and the American people. He said, "I am just tired of being lied to by members of the executive branch and having information concealed." In his book *In Truth and Untruth: Political Deceit in America* (1972), he charged that the Nixon Administration encouraged "concealment, deception and news management on a massive scale." Reviewers described the book as loosely-written campaign rhetoric and McCloskey's campaign platform rather than a serious examination of the issues he raised.

McCloskey also attacked the Administration's position on environmental matters. He pointed out that "we had to fight them tooth and nail to get the water pollution funding money and had to fight over [Nixon's] objections to even get the Environmental Policy Act. This Administration has been dragged into the environment issue."

McCloskey campaigned actively for the presidential nomination until the March 7 New Hampshire primary. He received slightly less than 20% of the vote, the target he had set for himself. With little money and time running out for filing to be eligible for reelection to Congress, he formally ended his campaign on March 10. But he left his name on the ballot in other primary states "as a symbolic protest."

McCloskey faced a tough primary in 1972 as a result of redistricting that robbed him of his traditional base of support. He won that contest and went on to win reelection in November. He was returned to the House again in 1974 and in 1976.

[AE]

McCLOY, JOHN J(AY)
b. March 31, 1895; Philadelphia, Pa.
Lawyer, lobbyist.

McCloy attended Amherst College and, after service in World War I, obtained a law degree from Harvard Law School in 1921. For two decades he practiced law in New York City. During World War II McCloy was assistant secretary of war. From 1947 to 1949 he served as president of the World Bank. He became U.S. high commissioner for Germany in 1949. Four years later McCloy left government and became chairman of Chase National Bank. In addition to his duties as a banker, McCloy served as a general foreign policy adviser to the Eisenhower administration and, after his retirement from the Chase in 1960, to Presidents Kennedy and Johnson. [See TRUMAN, EISENHOWER, KENNEDY, JOHNSON Volumes]

Despite his advanced years and the fact that he held no official public posts under the Nixon and Ford administrations, McCloy maintained an intensive activity at the highest levels of business and government, particularly as the legal representative of the major U.S. oil producers. Much of McCloy's behind-the-scenes activity became known through his 1974 testimony before the Church committee investigation of the oil crisis. McCloy told the committee that since 1961 he had been regularly advising U.S. presidents on how to confront the growing power of the Organization of Petroleum Exporting Countries (OPEC), which was founded in 1960. More importantly, from 1961 to 1971, McCloy had been the legal representative of U.S. oil companies in dealings with the U.S. Department of Justice over antitrust questions. McCloy felt that U.S. antitrust laws were a useless obstacle to a united front of U.S. oil majors against OPEC. McCloy's lobbying efforts to gain acceptance for joint company actions, however, came to naught.

McCloy was deeply involved, in 1970-71, in the confrontation between the Libyan government and U.S. oil companies in which the latter made their first serious concessions to an OPEC nation. The Libyan government demanded that Occidental Petroleum increase its per-barrel royalty payments to Libya, and that it increase its tax payments from 50% to 58% of revenue. Fearing that a capitulation would break their united front, the oil companies turned to McCloy. In late 1970, McCloy went to Washington, where he conferred with Secretary of State William Rogers [q.v.] and other top State Department officials, warning of the implications of the Libyan challenge but securing no promise of action. On Jan. 11, 1971, representatives of 23 oil companies met in McCloy's New York office, with two U.S. government officials waiting outside to inspect all agreements for possible antitrust violations. McCloy obtained from the Justice Department a formal letter of enforcement intention disavowing any federal antitrust action against the oil companies for their collective actions in dealing with OPEC. However, Occidental gave in to the Libyan demands, and the oil majors were forced to follow suit.

McCloy continued to pressure the U.S. government for a more far-sighted strategy on the oil question. He urged a peace settlement in the Middle East and recommended that the U.S. change its policy away from support of Israel to insure the friendship of the oil producing states.

With the outbreak of the Yom Kippur war in 1973, McCloy's worst fears were realized. On October 12, he sent a memo to Gen. Alexander Haig [q.v.], describing the "anger" and "great irritation" of Arab governments over U.S. support to Israel, and warned of a Saudi-led boycott on oil shipments with a potential "snowballing effect that could produce a major petroleum crisis." McCloy's letter was ignored, and massive U.S. military aid was sent to back up Israel, resulting several days later in the beginning of the OPEC oil embargo and the four-fold increase in oil prices.

At his 1974 Senate committee testimony, McCloy argued that the U.S. had been "living in a sort of fool's paradise" where oil was concerned. Referring to the mas-

sive public criticism of the U.S. oil companies after October 1973, and the calls for the very antitrust actions he had worked to avoid, McCloy said that "it seems that it is only in the United States that an almost masochistic attack on the position of its own oil companies persists."

In 1978 McCloy was an author of an American Bar Association report on the oil crisis. He also remained active as a director of the Olin Foundation, a private firm with a significant impact on major policy questions.

[LG]

For further information:
Anthony Sampson, *The Seven Sisters* (New York, 1975).

McCORD, JAMES
b. 1924
Watergate figure.

Unknown to the public prior to 1972, McCord had been deeply involved in U.S. aerial surveillance of the Soviet Union as an officer for the Central Intelligence Agency (CIA).

He officially retired from his duties with the CIA in 1970, and little is known of his activities prior to June 1972. Like many former employees of the agency, McCord obtained employment as a private security officer, and in early 1972 placed his services at the disposal of the Republican National Committee and of the Committee to Re-Elect the President (CREEP).

McCord was subsequently one of five men—all with previous ties to the CIA—who was arrested during the June 17 break-in at Democratic Party headquarters in Washington D.C.'s Watergate complex. Subsequent investigation revealed that from May 5 through June 17, McCord had conducted surveillance operations on Democratic Party activities in the Watergate. In September 1972, McCord and six other men, including two former White House aides, were indicted for conspiracy to break into the Democratic Party offices in the Watergate.

In January 1973 the U.S. District Court, presided over by Judge John J. Sirica [q.v.] found McCord guilty as charged, despite McCord's argument that he had participated in the Watergate break-in without "criminal intent." Just before his sentencing in March 1973, however, McCord sent a letter to Judge Sirica implying that "others" had been involved in Watergate. On March 28, in a secret session before the Senate Select Committee, McCord implicated White House counsel John Dean III [q.v.], presidential aides H.R. Haldeman [q.v.] and Charles Colson [q.v.], and former Attorney General John Mitchell [q.v.].

Throughout this period, McCord was the target of a pressure campaign directed, in his own words, "from the highest levels of the White House" to silence him with threats, offers of leniency, clemency, help with bail and outright cash. He recounted these pressure tactics in further Senate Select Committee testimony on May 18.

It was at McCord's May 22 appearance that he paraphrased a letter he had allegedly written to a former White House aide concerning the desirability of implicating the CIA in Watergate. It was this testimony which later became the object of much speculation that McCord himself was a CIA agent attempting to cover up the agency's role: "If [CIA Director Richard] Helms goes," wrote McCord, "and the Watergate operation is laid at the CIA's feet . . . every tree in the forest will fall. It will be a scorched desert. The whole matter is on the precipice right now. Pass the message that if they want it to blow, they are on exactly the right course . . ."

In November 1973, McCord received a 1-5 year sentence for his role in the break-in. By March 1974, McCord was in open revolt against the White House and its cover-up of Watergate, charging in a letter to various news services that President Nixon had "deliberately concealed and suppressed" evidence of improper government conduct. In June 1974, during hearings to have McCord's case dismissed, his attorney said "there is such a stench attached to this case that it has to be thrown out." In July 1974, the minority report of the Senate Watergate Committee on possible CIA involvement in the affair cited McCord's role and described the actions of another CIA agent who had helped McCord's wife destroy private papers immediately after McCord's arrest. Finally, in December 1974, McCord filed a $10 million "legal malpractice" suit against his own attorneys.

In March 1975, his legal options exhausted, McCord entered the minimum security Federal penitentiary in Allenwood, Pennsylvania, to begin serving his sentence. In July 1975, Judge Sirica reduced the sentences of all Watergate burglars, and McCord's time was consequently shortened to four months. On the same day, Sirica also dismissed McCord's lawsuit to have the pardon of former President Nixon ruled illegal.

McCord served out his sentence in Allenwood and was released in the late summer of 1975.

[LG]

McCORMACK, ELLEN
b. 1926.
Presidential candidate.

Ellen McCormack grew up in New York City and moved with her husband to Merrick, Long Island, N.Y., in the mid-1950s. The mother of four children and a full-time housewife, McCormack was not active in public affairs until 1970, when New York state adopted a liberal abortion reform law. A practicing Catholic McCormack helped organize a local anti-abortion group on Long Island. In 1974 she worked in the New York senatorial campaign of Barbara Keating, the Conservative Party nominee who took a strong stand against legalized abortions.

Abortion, meanwhile had become a major public issue. During the 1970s women's liberation groups across the country made the legalization of abortion one of their major goals, and several state legislatures enacted liberal abortion statutes. In January 1973 the Supreme Court struck down statutes banning abortion in 44 states, making it legal for women to obtain abortions, under most conditions, throughout the country. Thereafter the activities of anti-abortion forces increased and by 1975 the Pro-Life Action Committee, of which McCormack was a member, had chapters in 27 states.

At a Nov. 16, 1975, press conference in Boston called by the Pro-Life Action Committee, McCormack declared her candidacy for the 1976 Democratic presidential nomination. Conceding that she was "basically a one-issue candidate," she announced her intention to enter as many primaries as possible, but to restrict her campaigning to one appearance per state. The lack of serious campaigning raised suspicions that her candidacy was simply a ruse to gain publicity for anti-abortion forces. The suspicion grew stronger when Jay Bowman, the head of Georgia's Right-to-Life Committee, told the press: "She's not a serious candidate. . . . But she can get equal time for the pro-life message—and she can get the federal government to pay for the ads."

Controversy over McCormack's candidacy erupted in February 1976 when she applied for matching funds from the Federal Election Commission. Her request was immediately challenged in court by the National Abortion Rights Action League, a feminist group, which charged that "funds have been deceptively solicited for the 'right-to-life' movement and not for a presidential candidacy." The FEC ruled in McCormack's favor, however, and she eventually received over $240,000 in federal matching funds for her campaign.

McCormack fared poorly in the primaries. Although she received 9% of the vote in Vermont and 8% in South Dakota, in no other state did she receive more than 5% of the ballots. At the Democrat-

ic Convention in July, her name was placed in nomination, but she received only 22 delegate votes. After the campaign McCormack announced her intention to work for a constitutional amendment banning abortions.

[JD]

McCORMACK, JOHN W(ILLIAM)
b. Dec. 21, 1891; Boston, Mass.
Democratic Representative, Mass., 1928–71; Speaker of the House, 1962–71.

John McCormack, one of 12 children, was born into a poor Irish-American family. When McCormack was in the eighth grade, his father died and he left school to help support the family. He found work as an office boy for a law firm at $4 a week. He took the opportunity to read law books and learn the profession, passing the bar examination in 1913 at the age of 21—without the benefit of even a formal high school education.

McCormack proved to be a skillful trial lawyer, but he soon pursued a career in politics. He served two terms in the Massachusetts Assembly, followed by two terms in the state Senate. In 1926 he ran for the Boston congressional seat held by Democrat James A. Gallivan and lost, only to win the seat in a special election in 1928 following Gallivan's death. McCormack was a faithful advocate of the New Deal. In 1936 he backed Sam Rayburn's bid for majority leader. When Rayburn became Speaker of the House in 1940, he chose McCormack as the new majority leader.

From Rayburn, McCormack learned the various skills of negotiation and compromise that he used with great effect during his congressional career. During the 1940s and 1950s he promoted such liberal legislation as the Marshall Plan, school construction aid and civil rights bills. In 1962 McCormack, at age 70, became Rayburn's successor as Speaker of the House. His handling of the position evoked much criticism. Many members of Congress felt that he was too compromising, that he lacked the determination of his predecessor. His staunch anticommunism led him to support the war in Vietnam, a position that became increasingly unpopular among liberals, as was his friendship with the conservative Southern Democrats. [See TRUMAN, EISENHOWER, KENNEDY, JOHNSON Volumes]

In January 1969 McCormack faced a serious challenge to his authority as House Speaker. Utah Rep. Morris Udall [q.v.] offered himself for the position—an audacious move since no Speaker had ever been unseated while his own party was in power. Udall expressed "genuine respect and affection" for McCormack but claimed that there was "an overriding need for new directions and new leadership" in the House. But Udall failed to expand his base of support beyond the young, liberal members of the House, and after a secret balloting of the House Democratic Caucus, McCormack handily defeated his challenger.

In 1970 McCormack faced another challenge to his authority. Liberal California Representative Jerome R. Waldie, saying that the Speaker "was not responsive to the problems of the seventies," placed a resolution of no confidence in McCormack before the House Democratic Caucus. But even McCormack's critics felt that the resolution was poorly timed, so it was turned aside without coming to a vote. McCormack said the decision constituted a major victory. Nonetheless, as a concession to disgruntled liberals, the Caucus appointed a commission to study the seniority system and agreed to meet more frequently.

In October 1969 a major scandal involving Speaker McCormack erupted on Capitol Hill. Columnist Jack Anderson [q.v.] and Life Magazine revealed that Dr. Martin Sweig, a trusted administrative assistant to McCormack, and Nathan Voloshen, a Sweig associate, had used the Speaker's office as a base for influence peddling in Washington. Sweig and Voloshen had taken payments in exchange for interceding in various criminal cases and arranging government contracts.

Sweig had apparently used McCormack's phone, occasionally even impersonating the Speaker's voice.

McCormack bitterly denied any involvement or knowledge of the scheme, and said that the Life magazine article, which implicated him in at least one influence-peddling incident, constituted "unwarranted vilification." At a news conference, he stated that he would seek reelection the following year both as a representative and as House Speaker, adding that "whether I'm here any more depends on the people of my district. . . . They know that my life—personal and private—is an open book." In January 1970 Sweig and Voloshen were indicted by a federal grand jury in New York on charges of conspiracy. McCormack was not named, but he did submit a deposition.

In May 1970 McCormack announced that he would retire at the conclusion of his current term, saying his decision, partly due to the declining health of his wife, had been made during the 1968 Democratic Convention. That same month Nathan Voloshen pleaded guilty. Martin Sweig was found guilty the following month, after a trial in which McCormack testified that Sweig was a "devoted aide," and again denied knowledge that his office had been misused.

During his last months in Congress, McCormack continued to work for liberal programs. The House passed a bill lowering the voting age to 18 in June 1970, following a personal campaign by McCormack. In August, McCormack spoke out in favor of the Equal Rights Amendment. "This resolution does not undertake to change nature," he said, "but certainly changes conditions." He remained a vocal critic of the Nixon Administration, accusing it of "playing on people's fears" and "a callous disregard for the social needs of our less fortunate and disenfranchised and, despite a promise to bring our people together, a pattern of demagoguery that is dividing our nation's rich against poor, white against black, young against old."

As the congressional elections in November drew nearer, McCormack's denunciation of the Nixon Administration became more fervent. Following criticism by Nixon of Democratic federal spending policies, McCormack said that the President should "devote his attention to the real problems and quit playing his partisan political games."

McCormack left Congress after 43 years as a Representative and the second longest tenure as Speaker in the history of the House.

[MDQ]

McCRACKEN, PAUL W(INSTON)
b. Dec. 29, 1915; Richland, Iowa.
Chairman, Council of Economic
Advisers, January 1969-Jan. 1972

The son of a farmer, McCracken studied economics at Harvard, receiving his Ph.D. in 1948. He then left his position at the Federal Reserve Bank of Minneapolis for a teaching job at the University of Michigan School of Business Administration. He became a full professor in 1950. From 1956 to 1959 he served on the President's Council of Economic Advisers (CEA). He then returned to Michigan but was frequently consulted by the Kennedy and Johnson Administrations and by private concerns.

In December 1968 President Nixon named McCracken chairman of the CEA. His colleagues were to be Herbert Stein [q.v.] and Hendrik S. Houthakker. In his approach to running the national economy, McCracken represented a centrist position between those advocates of "fine tuning" who had run the CEA under the Democrats and the laissez-faire economists of the Chicago School. However, he never rejected Keynesian theory as did Milton Friedman [q.v.] and other members of the Chicago group. In interviews, he expressed his admiration for the economic performance of the Johnson Administration, but he believed that unwise monetary policy, aggravated by the Vietnam war, had overheated the economy. It

was the CEA's responsibility to curb inflation, already identified as the nation's primary domestic problem, but without increasing unemployment. McCracken called his policy "gradualism." It was intended to achieve the goals for which the CEA was originally created by President Harry Truman—full employment with low or no inflation.

In March 1969 McCracken announced the Administration's program. He rejected the Johnson Administration's policy of pressuring or "jawboning" groups to hold down wages and prices. Both the Administration, through its control over the budget, and the Federal Reserve Board, through its manipulation of credit and the money supply, would apply the brakes to inflation. Thus, the Chairman hoped the "psychology of inflation," which had led business and labor to assume its inevitability, could be broken. Yet, he believed that because of "inflation-mindedness," there would be a longer lag than one would normally expect between the introduction of new measures and a decline in inflation.

One Johnson measure McCracken favored retaining was the income tax surcharge, which could ensure a budget surplus. The Chairman hoped that less inflation would keep demand in line with productivity and lead to fewer imports, more exports and a resulting improvement in the balance of trade. The price of the inflation fight, as he admitted to the Joint Economic Committee of Congress in February, was a slower economic growth rate. He predicted a growth rate well under the 5% achieved in 1968 but did not believe that unemployment would go above 4% (it was 3.3% at the time).

As McCracken predicted, curbing inflation was not easy. In July 1969 the President ordered a $3.5 billion cut in federal expenditures to offset spending increases due to "uncontrollable" budget items and congressional action. Although by October McCracken claimed he could discern "some early evidence," such as the slowdown in the rise of the consumer price index, that the Administration's "fiscal and monetary policies of restraint" were beginning to cool the economy, critics felt that more action was required. Arthur Okun, former CEA chairman, recommended a revival of wage-price guideposts. Members of Congress, business leaders and representatives of foreign governments concurred, but the Chairman argued that such guideposts were of "unproven effectiveness," were often unfair and might divert attention from the more basic monetary and fiscal causes of inflation.

The President repeated McCracken's reasoning in his annual economic report in January 1970. He foresaw less inflation and less real growth in 1970 than in the previous year, but said that if Congress did not help to curb inflation, the Federal Reserve might feel compelled to follow a money and credit policy of "overly long and overly severe restraint." McCracken had already indicated that he favored a more liberal monetary policy than the Fed had been willing to allow, and the differences in policy outlook became clearer under the Fed's new chief, Arthur Burns [q.v.].

McCracken had not tried to hide his conviction that 1970 would be a difficult year for the nation's businesses and working people, even suggesting that the real output increase "might well be below" the historic annual average of 3-3.5%. By May progress against inflation had brought such small returns, while unemployment had risen, that the Administration's critics now included Secretary of Housing and Urban Development George Romney [q.v.], who demanded wage-price action. A few days later Rep. Henry Reuss (D, Wis.) introduced a bill requiring the CEA to set wage-price guidelines. As before, McCracken rejected the need for such measures.

When the Chairman appeared before the Joint Economic Committee in July, there was at least general agreement that the economic decline had "bottomed out." However there was now disagreement as to how to revive the economy. McCracken wanted more liquidity and thus monetary expansion. Burns and Treasury Secretary David M. Kennedy

[q.v.] opposed all stimulative measures. Liberal economists, such as Paul Samuelson [q.v.] and Gardner Ackley [q.v.], favored vigorous fiscal measures. It appeared that McCracken was destined to lose. Congress would probably adopt the Samuelson-Ackley prescription and, in retaliation, Burns would keep the lid on the money supply. Burns had already eased restrictions in March aiming for a 2% growth in the money supply, but McCracken thought the action inadequate.

Although official August 1970 figures showed a rise in second quarter GNP and the lowest inflation rate (a projected 4.3% annual rate) since the third quarter of 1968, in the same month the government issued its first "inflation alert." The alert, McCracken's creation, was viewed by some as an Administration attempt to give the appearance of doing something about wages and prices without, in fact, doing anything. Other observers saw it as Nixon and McCracken's first cautious exercise in jawboning. McCracken insisted that the alert was only intended to be informative. Much of it was an analysis of inflationary developments since the Eisenhower Administration. He hoped it would "lift the level of visibility and understanding and awareness of these complex developments in the price-cost area" and thus help form public policy. The alert cited developments in specific industries and implied criticism of, among others, the tire and cigarette industries, which had increased prices faster than costs. Yet, if the report represented an abandonment of gradualism and of a laissez-faire attitude on wages and prices, it nonetheless reiterated the Chairman's view that monetary and fiscal policy cause inflation. In addition, the report hypothesized that the longer inflation lasts, the harder it is to end. The alert, it was argued, was another measure to combat the "inflation-mindedness" that had overtaken American business and labor. There were two more inflation alerts, in December 1970 and April 1971. Both brought the Administration close to "jawboning" and both, in the opinion of union leaders, unjustly assigned too large a share of the responsibility for inflation to labor.

Continuing inflation and unemployment near 6% helped the Democrats to do extremely well in the November congressional elections, and the 1972 elections looked equally bad for Nixon and the GOP if the economy were not revitalized. McCracken, who had never been liked by White House advisers because of his unwillingness to disguise unpleasant economic realities, was replaced as the Administration's "economic spokesman." The new Treasury Secretary, John Connally [q.v.], assumed that public role, although in fact he worked in close agreement with McCracken.

Nixon, whose first deviation from a strict anti-inflationary policy was the release of $1.5 billion in frozen construction funds in March 1970, announced an "expansionary," but "not inflationary," budget in January 1971. His "full employment" budget called for the government to spend when the economy was sluggish what it would collect if business were brisk and unemployment low. The budget would show a deficit, due not only to inflation and high unemployment, but also to a liberalized depreciation allowance for business. Some Democrats applauded the "Republican conversion to Keynesian economy," but others thought the program inadequate to meet the Administration's optimistic predictions. McCracken himself did not share the Administration's enthusiastic GNP forecast. In a February report the CEA refused to choose between private predictions of a 7-7.5% rise in the 1971 GNP and the White House figure of 9%. Another move in the further abandonment of gradualism was McCracken's resort to jawboning in January, when he convinced steel industry leaders to moderate price increases.

In a June 1971 interview, McCracken admitted that the Administration was dissatisfied with its economic "game plan" in view of the persistence of high unemployment, and would soon decide whether to change its policies. The following month he announced to the Joint Economic Committee that with inflation

at 4% and unemployment at 6%, the Administration was abandoning its GNP target of $1.065 trillion. In order not to aggravate inflation, the government could not take further steps to stimulate the economy. On Aug. 15, Nixon took the last step in rejecting his original program by announcing a 90-day wage and price freeze and the creation of a Cost of Living Council to oversee the freeze. Connally was named Council chairman and McCracken vice chairman. The new economic program also included tax cuts and credits, a surtax on imports and the end of the dollar's convertibility into gold (effectively, the first devaluation of the dollar). Democrats almost unanimously attacked the program as a bonanza for the rich, but it greatly improved the President's standing in the popularity polls.

On Nov. 24, McCracken submitted his resignation, effective Jan. 1, 1972. He conceded that his policy of gradualism had failed against inflationary and psychological pressures that the CEA had underestimated. Some Washington analysts believed that McCracken was the victim of White House "political hatchet men," who wanted the chairman to bend the truth about the economy. Nonetheless, McCracken was credited with getting the President to implement the new program, since he had felt that the Administration had been without a coherent policy since it began to hedge on its anti-inflation commitment.

Under the Ford Administration, McCracken served as a senior consultant to the Treasury Department.

[JCH]

McGee, GALE W(ILLIAM)
b. March 17, 1915; Lincoln, Neb.
Democratic Senator, Wyo.,
1959-1977.

After receiving his B.A. from Nebraska State Teachers College in 1936, McGee taught American diplomatic history in various colleges. He earned an M.A. at the University of Colorado and a Ph.D. in

American diplomatic history from the University of Chicago in 1947. McGee took frequent sabbaticals from his professorship at the University of Wyoming from 1946 to 1958 to complete a study of Soviet foreign policy for the Council on Foreign Relations in 1952 and 1953 and to lecture on foreign policy. In 1958 he won election to the Senate.

McGee's support for the 1960 s Civil Rights Acts, medicare, and repeal of section 14b of the Taft-Hartley Act which permitted states to outlaw the closed shop, reflected his liberal voting record on domestic issues during the Kennedy-Johnson years. A persistent apologist for the Vietnam War and for a generous economic foreign aid program, McGee backed the Democratic Administrations' foreign policy. [See KENNEDY, JOHNSON Volumes]

But McGee's support for the Vietnam War was reflective of his belief as an internationalist in America's responsibility as a free world leader. In 1969 he won a seat on the Foreign Relations Committee where he resisted numerous efforts to restrict Nixon's policies in Southeast Asia. In 1970 he voted against the Cooper-Church Amendment which would have barred the use of appropriations for military activities in Cambodia. From 1971 to 1973, he fought unsuccessfully against the passage of the War Powers Act which he felt restricted the President's ability to wage war. In May 1972 he voted against the majority of the Democratic Caucus which for the first time backed legislation to bar the use of funds for the Vietnam War.

Consistent with his internationalist stance, McGee led the opposition to the Byrd Amendment to the 1972 Military Procurement Act which permitted the President to import Rhodesian chrome in violation of U.N. sanctions. As chairman of the Subcommittee on the Western Hemisphere, McGee, in 1974, urged support for a Panama Canal treaty after 32 senators signed a resolution opposed to relinquishment of American sovereignty. In February 1975, he called for a rapprochement between the U.S. and Cuba to strengthen U.S. posture in the western hemisphere.

McGee was more effective, legislatively, as chairman of the Post Office and Civil Service Committee. He was largely responsible for the legislation which reorganized the Post Office into an independent service in 1970. In 1973 McGee sponsored the National Voter Registration Act which would have allowed citizens to register by post card. Sen. James Allen (D, Ala.) led the opposition (who feared that easy registration would upset the political balance in their states) in a filibuster. McGee, to win enough votes to obtain cloture, began his own filibuster of a bill to extend wage and price controls which were due to expire shortly. McGee won; cloture was invoked; and the bill passed the Senate May 3. Despite McGee's effort to use his chairmanship to block measures which House members desired in order to get the bill reported to the House floor, the House refused consideration on May 8, 1974.

Despite McGee's consistent record of support for the environmental concerns of his constituency, the needs of Wyoming farmers, and his accumulation of seniority and importance in the Senate, he lost reelection in November 1976 to Malcolm Wallop who campaigned on an anti-big government platform. In 1977 McGee was appointed assistant secretary of state for Latin American affairs in the Carter Administration. He has served as ambassador to the Organization of American States and backed the passage of the Panama Canal Treaty. [See CARTER Volume]

[JMP]

McGOVERN, GEORGE S(TANLEY)
b. July 19, 1922; Avon, S.D.
Democratic Senator, S.D. 1963-.
Democratic Presidential Nominee, 1972.

The son of a Methodist minister, George McGovern attended Dakota Wesleyan University and served in the Army

Air Corps during World War II. He received his doctorate at Northwestern University in 1953, while also teaching at Dakota Wesleyan from 1949 to 1953. He resigned his professorship to become executive secretary of the Democratic Party in South Dakota and built it into a viable statewide organization. McGovern was elected to the House of Representatives in 1956 and in his two terms established a reputation as a liberal. In 1960 he unsuccessfully challenged Republican incumbent Karl Mundt for a Senate seat.

In January 1961 President John F. Kennedy appointed McGovern director of the newly created Food for Peace program. McGovern worked to develop the program as a humanitarian instrument of U.S. foreign policy. He resigned in July 1962 to run for the Senate once again and won a narrow victory becoming South Dakota's first Democratic Senator in 26 years.

McGovern was a strong supporter of the liberal social welfare and civil rights legislation of the Kennedy and Johnson Administrations. He also quickly became a critic of Cold War foreign policy and its "obsession with Communism," and urged that defense spending be cut in favor of humanitarian programs abroad and at home. As U.S. military involvement in South Vietnam escalated rapidly in the mid-1960s, McGovern emerged as one of its most vocal Senate critics. Although in the fall of 1967 he turned down a request from Allard K. Lowenstein [q.v.] that he head a "dump Johnson" movement, McGovern conducted a brief campaign for the Democratic nomination after the assassination of presidential candidate Robert F. Kennedy. At the Democratic National Convention in August, McGovern placed a distant third in the balloting. In November he was reelected to a second term in the Senate. [See KENNEDY, JOHNSON Volumes].

McGovern immediately became an outspoken critic of Nixon Administration policies. He opposed deployment of the Safeguard anti-ballistic missile (ABM) and was one of only nine Senators in November 1969 who voted against a military appropriations bill that included funding for the ABM. McGovern also voted against confirmation of Nixon's Supreme Court nominees, Clement Haynsworth [q.v.] and G. Harrold Carswell [q.v.], and in March 1971 voted to cut funding for the controversial supersonic transport plane (SST). McGovern repeatedly called for a reduction in defense spending. In February 1970, after the President promised to veto an education appropriations bill while asking funds for ABM deployment, McGovern accused him of having a "twisted sense of priorities." He also criticized Nixon's family-assistance plan as inadequate and instead endorsed in July 1971 the $6500 guaranteed annual income plan of the National Welfare Rights Organization.

McGovern received the most public attention for his continuing opposition to the Vietnam war. While other Democratic critics were willing to give Nixon a chance to develop his own policy, McGovern attacked him as early as March 1969 for persisting in the "tragic course" set by Johnson. When Nixon announced in June 1969 his first troop withdrawals, McGovern labeled the action "tokenism." In July McGovern revealed that he had conferred with North Vietnamese and Vietcong representatives in Paris during May and that they had specified a commitment to "unconditional" withdrawal of all U.S. troops as essential for a peace agreement. McGovern called for a unilateral 30-day ceasefire by the United States.

In October he spoke before the Vietnam Moratorium rally in Boston and the following month addressed a massive antiwar demonstration in Washington, D.C. During Senate Foreign Relations Committee hearings in February 1970 on the war, McGovern called Vietnamization a "political hoax" designed to "tranquilize the conscience of the American people while our government wages a cruel and needless war by proxy."

After the invasion of Cambodia by U.S. troops in April 1970, McGovern joined in legislative efforts to mandate an end to the war. In June he voted for the Cooper-Church Amendment to cut off funds for

U.S. operations in Cambodia. In July he cosponsored legislation to end the draft and to establish an all-volunteer army. With Sen. Mark Hatfield (R. Ore.) [q.v.] he introduced an "end-the-war" amendment to a military appropriations bill that would have legislated the withdrawal of all U.S. combat troops from Southeast Asia by the end of 1971. After heated debate the Senate rejected the amendment on Sept. 1 by a vote of 55–39. Although the vote was interpreted by many as an Administration victory, McGovern thought otherwise. "It is remarkable," he said, "that for the first time in history more than one-third of the U.S. Senate has voted to cut off funds for a war while we are still in battle." In January 1971 he and Sen. Hatfield reintroduced the "end-the-war" legislation, but in June the Senate again rejected it. McGovern participated in the Senate filibuster to block extension of the Selective Service Act and voted against the bill in September.

McGovern emerged during the Nixon Administration as the congressional leader of a fight against hunger in the United States. In December 1968 the Senate created a Select Committee on Nutrition and Human Needs and chose McGovern as its head. The Committee conducted extensive hearings throughout the country in 1969. After touring migrant farm workers camps in Florida during March, McGovern declared: "We have seen dirt and living conditions these past two days that one might expect to see in Asia, not America. Most of the cattle and hogs in America are better fed and sheltered than the families we have visited." When Herbert G. Klein [q.v.], the director of communications for the White House, accused McGovern of making hunger "a political cause," the Senator replied that "hunger knows no politics."

In response to the Committee's revelations, Nixon announced in May 1969 an expanded drive against hunger and malnutrition. McGovern criticized the President's proposals as "probably less than a third of what is needed." In August his Committee reported that an additional $4 billion a year was needed to close "the hunger gap." The following month McGovern scored a major victory when the Senate overruled an Agriculture Committee recommendation of $750 million for food stamps and instead approved a McGovern substitute calling for $1.25 billion and free food stamps to the poorest families.

The House failed to act on the measure until December 1970. Although the final bill provided larger funding, $1.75 billion, it included a "must work" provision for able-bodied recipients. McGovern threatened a filibuster but dropped the threat rather than risk having Congress adjourn without passing any legislation. During 1970 McGovern also led a successful fight for legislation to expand the federal government's school lunch program for needy children.

In February 1969 McGovern was chosen by Party leaders to head a special commission on Party structure and delegate selection. After extensive hearings, the commission issued a report in April 1970 declaring that popular control of the Party was "necessary for its survival." Among the recommendations accepted by the Democratic National Committee were proposals that delegates to the National Convention be chosen during the year of the Convention: that the selection process be opened to give wider representation to blacks, women and the young: and that votes be reapportioned to give fairer representation to the more populous states.

In January 1971 McGovern resigned as head of the Party's reform commission and became the first declared contender for the 1972 presidential nomination. In a speech in South Dakota on January 18, he said his campaign "will be rooted not in the manipulation of our fears and divisions but in a national dialogue based on mutual respect and common hope." He pledged to withdraw all U.S. troops from Vietnam and to shift resources from the war to the rebuilding of America.

Political analysts gave McGovern little chance of securing the nomination. He lacked the voter recognition of other Democrats like Sens. Edmund Muskie [q.v.] and Hubert Humphrey [q.v.], was perceived as too radical by many and seemed to be a single-issue candidate. Nevertheless McGovern's early declaration gave him time to build a strong campaign organization, and he concentrated his efforts on winning the allegiance of young people willing to volunteer their time to his anti-war candidacy.

By January 1972 the list of declared candidates had grown considerably with Sens. Muskie, Humphrey, Henry Jackson [q.v.], Eugene McCarthy [q.v.], and Vance Hartke [q.v.]. Alabama Gov. George Wallace [q.v.], New York Mayor John Lindsay [q.v.], and Rep. Shirley Chisholm of New York [q.v.] in the race. Muskie was widely perceived as the frontrunner and had the endorsement of important Party leaders and labor chiefs, but he fared badly in the primaries. Although he won the New Hampshire primary, Muskie trailed far behind in Florida, Wisconsin and Pennsylvania. McGovern meanwhile polled a respectable second in New Hampshire and won a decisive victory in Wisconsin. Muskie's withdrawal on April 27 and the attempted assassination of George Wallace on May 15 left McGovern and Humphrey the only serious contenders.

After McGovern won primaries in Oregon and Rhode Island on May 23, attention shifted to California where the two men were to clash on June 6. In a series of preprimary television debates Humphrey lashed into McGovern with unexpected harshness. He charged that McGovern's plan to slash the defense budget by almost one-third would make America a "second-class power" and that tax and welfare proposals revealed McGovern was out to "revolutionize the country by massive redistribution of wealth." Nonetheless McGovern scored a clear victory in the winner-take-all contest and followed it two weeks later with a big victory in New York that made him an almost certain victor in the quest for the nomination.

The Convention reflected the bitter fighting of the primaries. There were rancorous disputes in the credentials committee over the seating of delegates, especially from California and Illinois. McGovern forces won clearcut victories at the opening of the Convention, especially in the denial of representation to Mayor Richard Daley of Chicago [q.v.]. On July 12 McGovern won the nomination on the first ballot; the next day he announced that Missouri Sen. Thomas Eagleton [q.v.] was his choice of running mate.

McGovern's campaign was beset with difficulties from the outset. He was never able to shake off his public image as a "radical," and he failed to win the support of the Democratic Party's traditional sources of strength. AFL-CIO President George Meany was hostile to McGovern, and for the first time in its history, the federation's Executive Council refused to endorse a Democratic candidate for President and remained neutral. Many of the Democratic urban machines were angered by the changes in Convention rules, which weakened their influence in the Party and which they attributed to McGovern as head of the reform commission, and they remained lukewarm in their support of the candidate.

Further difficulties arose when, on July 25, Eagleton announced that he had hospitalized himself three times for psychiatric treatment of nervous exhaustion and fatigue and had received electroshock therapy. Although McGovern initially announced his unwavering support for his running mate, press reaction showed disapproval of Eagleton's retention and on July 31 McGovern announced that Eagleton would withdraw from the race. On August 8 the Democratic national Committee chose Sargent Shriver [q.v.] to replace him.

McGovern's campaign never gathered momentum. Throughout the fall attention focused more on his proposals than on President Nixon's record. His tax and welfare plans were attacked as unworkable and too radical, and he was accused of endangering national security with his proposed cuts in the defense budget. Nixon did little campaigning and allowed Vice President Agnew [q.v.] and other Administration officials to shoulder most campaign duties. Moreover McGovern's major issue, the war, was taken from him when Secretary of State Henry Kissinger [*q.v.*] announced on October 26 that "peace is at hand" in Indochina and that a final agreement on a truce and political settlement was almost worked out. Opinion polls on the eve of the election gave Nixon a commanding lead and the final results were a crushing defeat for McGovern. Nixon captured 61% of the popular vote and 521 electoral votes. McGovern carried only Massachusetts and the District of Columbia.

Investigations into the Watergate scandal by the Senate Watergate Committee and the Justice Department during 1973 revealed that McGovern and other contenders for the Democratic nomination were the victims of a concerted campaign of "dirty tricks" drawn up by White House officials and the Committee to Re-Elect the President. The aim, according to evidence presented to a grand jury during the spring, was to use political sabotage and espionage to hurt Muskie and Humphrey and to insure the nomination of McGovern, who was widely assumed to be the weakest of Nixon's potential opponents. Further investigation revealed that former Attorney General John Mitchell [*q.v.*] drew up plans to bug the McGovern headquarters and that White House Chief of Staff H.R. Haldeman [*q.v.*] coordinated the political sabotage activities. In August 1973 an Oliver Quayle opinion poll found that in a replay of the 1972 elections, the voters would choose McGovern.

Reelected to a third term in 1974, McGovern remained active in the area of nutrition and hunger. In 1975 he led the fight for passage of a $2.7 billion school lunch and child nutrition program that Congress enacted in October over a presidential veto. He also was floor manager of a bill to obstruct a Ford Administration attempt to weaken the food stamp program. On Nov. 26, 1974, Ford proposed higher payments for food stamps, and in January the Agriculture Department announced that the amount of monthly income a family was expected to pay for the stamps would be raised to approximately

30%. McGovern introduced legislation to freeze costs at the previous level of about 24%, and in February Congress approved the legislation by such a wide margin that a veto would have been fruitless.

McGovern took a leading role in urging the normalization of relations with Cuba. After visiting the island in May 1975 at the invitation of Fidel Castro, McGovern called for an immediate end to the U.S. trade embargo. In August McGovern praised the Ford Administration's decision to allow foreign subsidiaries of U.S. firms to trade with the Castro regime. McGovern visited Cuba a second time in April 1977.

Initially a supporter of Arizona Rep. Morris Udall's [*q.v.*] candidacy for the 1976 presidential nomination, McGovern switched to Jimmy Carter [*q.v.*] in June 1976. However after the election he attacked the "Republican economics" of the Carter Administration in May 1977, and the following year was vocal in his criticism of Carter's proposed cuts in domestic social welfare programs in order to expand the defense budget.

[JD]

For further information:
George Stanley McGovern, *Grassroots: The Autobiography of George McGovern* (New York, 1977).
Robert Sam Anson, *McGovern: a Biography* (New York, 1972).

McINTYRE, THOMAS J(AMES)
b. Feb. 20, 1915; Laconia, N.H.
Democratic Senator, N.H. 1963-79.

McIntyre, a small-town New Hampshire lawyer active in Democratic politics, won a special November 1962 election held to fill the seat of the late Republican Sen. Styles Bridges [*q.v.*]. He thereby became the first New Hampshire Democrat elected to the Senate since 1932. During his freshman year McIntyre generally supported the Kennedy Administration's foreign and domestic policies. McIntyre later supported key Johnson Administration legislation, including the civil rights, anti-poverty, medicare and school aid bills. He initially backed the President's Vietnam policy. [See KENNEDY, JOHNSON Volumes]

McIntyre reversed his position on the Vietnam war in 1968. That year he advocated legislation establishing a specific date for troop withdrawal, declaring that the U.S. should "get out of Vietnam with all due speed." In 1970 he was part of a Nixon-sponsored congressional fact-finding tour of the Vietnam and Cambodian war zones. He wrote the lone dissenting report arguing that while the U.S. invasion of Cambodia may have been a short-term military success, it would not hasten an end to the war.

As chairman of the Research and Development Subcommittee of the Armed Services Committee, McIntyre took a great critical interest in the development of new weapons systems. In 1969 he offered a compromise to an Administration proposal to build an anti-ballistic missile (ABM) system. The bill would have allowed development of onsite radar and electronic equipment but no actual missile deployment. The compromise failed. Just before the floor vote in 1970 McIntyre was persuaded to support the ABM by the Administration argument that the weapon would be a valuable "bargaining chip" in arms limitation talks with the Soviet Union.

During Nixon's second term McIntyre fought proponents of more sophisticated nuclear weapons systems. His bill to slow the development of the Trident nuclear submarine was defeated in 1973. The next year the Senate rejected McIntyre's bill to defer the $77 million program for a more powerful and accurate intercontinental ballistic missile (ICBM) capable of destroying Soviet missiles in their underground silos. McIntyre feared that these maneuvering re-entry vehicles (MaRVs) would "drastically and dangerously alter our national strategic policy" and would undermine the SALT talks. In 1975, however, the Senate passed Hubert H. Humphrey's (D, Minn.) [q.v.] similar amendment halting the testing of MaRVs unless the President certified to Congress that

the USSR was testing the same type of weapon.

In 1971 McIntyre introduced his National Healthcare Act, and hearings were held on it in that and subsequent years, but no action was ever taken. His plan called for a nationwide system of health insurance supported by employer-employee contributions with poor and middle-class people receiving government subsidies according to need.

During the Carter Administration McIntyre remained a foe of increased weapons development. He won his 1978 primary campaign but suffered a stunning defeat in November when he lost by only 5,000 votes to conservative Republican Gordon Humphrey.

[FLM]

McMILLAN, JOHN L(ANNEAU)
b. April 12, 1898; Mullins, S.C.
Democratic Representative, S.C., 1939-73; Chairman, District of Columbia Committee, 1949-73.

Raised in rural South Carolina, John McMillan served in the Navy during World War I before receiving his law degree from the University of South Carolina in 1923. He was elected to represent South Carolina's sixth congressional district in 1938. In the House he compiled a conservative record, and in 1948 assumed the chairmanship of the District of Columbia Committee.

As District Committee chairman, McMillan led a majority of conservative Southern Democrats who blocked home-rule legislation into the 1960s. Only by circumventing McMillan's committee did President Johnson succeed in reorganizing the city's government under an appointed commission in 1967. [See JOHNSON Volume]

McMillan continued to resist moves toward home rule for the District during the Nixon years, but in 1970 Congress passed a bill over his strong objections that provided for a nonvoting delegate to the House. That same year McMillan guided through his committee Nixon's District of Columbia Court Reform and Criminal Procedure Act. The measure, known as the D.C. crime bill, was characterized by Sen. Sam Erwin (D, S.C.) [q.v.] as a blueprint for a police state, but it passed Congress and was signed into law in July. Besides revamping the city's court system, the bill allowed wiretapping and electronic surveillance and contained a "no-knock" provision that permitted police to enter a premise if they feared that criminal evidence would be destroyed before a warrant could be obtained.

In 1971, at the opening of the 92nd Congress, liberal Democrats, in a move to reform the seniority system, sought McMillan's ouster as District Committee Chairman. A representative from the liberal lobbying group Common Cause testified that the South Carolina Congressman "had almost singlehandedly kept Washington D.C. in colonial bondage." Furthermore journalists said they had evidence that McMillan had used his position to further his private financial interests. Columnist Jack Anderson [q.v.] alleged in 1970 that McMillan "accepts favors from used-car dealers, parking lot barons and liquor lobbyists" in return for "obstructing public parking, welfare payments and home rule." Nonetheless the Democratic Caucus voted 126 to 96 to keep McMillan as chairman, a vote which, though considered a surprising show of liberal strength, caused Rep. Brock Adams (D, Wash.) to resign from the Committee in protest.

In 1970 McMillan survived a tough primary challenge and won reelection. In the 1972 elections a coalition of organized labor and black groups combined with the youth vote to force a two-man primary runoff. A deal by which a third candidate, Billy Craig, had given McMillan his endorsement in return for a signed statement supporting D.C. home rule shattered McMillan's image among his constituents, and John Jenrette, a progressive state legislator, defeated him in the primary.

[FLM]

McNAMARA, ROBERT S(TRANGE)
b. June 9, 1916; San Francisco, Calif.
President, World Bank, 1968–.

McNamara majored in mathematics, economics and philosophy, winning Phi Beta Kappa awards in his sophomore year at the University of California, from which he received a B.A. degree in 1937. He graduated with honors from the Harvard Business School in 1939. After serving in the Army Air Force during World War II, McNamara was employed by the Ford Motor Co. He became general manager, then vice president, as he helped revive the faltering company with emphasis on strict cost-accounting methods and approval of highly profitable projects. In November 1960 McNamara was named company president, but he spent little more than a month in the job. President Kennedy had offered him the position of Secretary of Defense, and McNamara accepted. He retained this post under the Johnson Administration until February 1968 when he resigned to accept an appointment as president of the World Bank. [See KENNEDY, JOHNSON Volumes]

McNamara, the first president of the World Bank to come from a nonbanking background, instituted new policies with enthusiasm and authority. In a report to the U.N. Economic and Social Council on Dec. 5, 1968, McNamara laid out his general plan for future World Bank activities. Although the Bank would continue its policy of financing large projects such as "power installations and road and rail networks," it would emphasize greater concern to "reach and affect the individual." There would be an effort to quadruple agricultural lending over a five-year period and to triple lending for educational development. In the address McNamara announced a policy revision that would allow the Bank and its affiliate, the International Development Association, to finance state-owned development banks "when we believe that they can be businesslike and self-supporting institutions." McNamara urged President-elect Richard M. Nixon to provide money for easy-term international loans to poor countries.

In July 1969 McNamara completed his first review of the Bank's activities. He concluded that it should, over a five-year period, double both its lending to poor countries and its borrowing efforts in the financial markets of rich countries to raise the necessary funds. In its first fiscal year under McNamara, the Bank completed about three-fourths of its five-year target. Its total lending during that fiscal year (ending June 30) was $1.78 billion, a record figure and an increase of 87% over the year before. In that fiscal year McNamara had obtained funds from some entirely new sources, such as Kuwait. The result was a record total of $1.22 billion raised in the world's capital markets, a 60% increase over the previous year.

In an address to the annual meeting of the World Bank, held on Sept. 21, 1970, McNamara criticized the U.S. as the "single exception" to the general acceptance by industrial nations of a new aid target of seven-tenths of 1% of the gross national product—double the then-current flow. He felt it "inconceivable" that the American public would accept for long a situation in which they—numbering 6% of the world's population, but consuming nearly 40% of the world's resources—would contribute under "their fair share" to efforts at development in the poor and emerging nations. He pointed out that the U.S. ranked 11th in terms of percentage of national product among the aid-giving countries.

In October 1972 McNamara instituted a restructuring of the World Bank's regional and technical departments. He felt that regionalization of operations would provide closer integration of the Bank's area and project activities and "establish even more firmly that the development of individual countries is the basis on which the Bank's program is built."

In the same month McNamara told the Economic and Social Council of the U.N. that the direction of economic development efforts must attack directly the personal poverty of the bottom 40% of populations in the developing countries rather than concentrating on their overall economic growth. He acknowledged that a reorientation of social and economic policy was basically a political problem and that it was up to the developing nations themselves to institute changes which would allow development efforts to reach their poorest citizens. "There is a natural tendency," he stated, "for growth to be concentrated in the modern sectors of the economy, with little current benefit to the lowest income groups." McNamara proposed a five-step program to reach the bottom 40%, an aspect of which required financing of rural and urban projects that were low skill, labor intensive, but economically useful.

From the time he took office, McNamara stressed, far more than his predecessors, the gravity of the world population problem, which he said was "seriously crippling" economic development efforts. In an effort to help alleviate this growing problem, McNamara instituted family-planning activities and established a Population Projects Department in 1971.

The executive directors unanimously reelected McNamara in 1972 for a second five-year term as World Bank president. He was again reelected to this post for five years in April 1977.

[MLB]

MADDOX, LESTER G(ARFIELD)
b. Sept. 30, 1915; Atlanta, Ga.
Governor, Ga., 1967-71.

The son of a poor Georgia steelworker, Maddox quit school in the 11th grade to help out at home. He held a variety of jobs until he opened the Pickrick restaurant in 1947. As the restaurant prospered, Maddox turned his attention to politics. He ran unsuccessfully for mayor of Atlanta in 1957 and 1961 and for lieutenant governor in 1962. Throughout these campaigns Maddox maintained an extreme right-wing platform characterized by an emphasis on states' rights and racial segregation. In 1964 Maddox received national attention by defying the provision of the newly adopted Civil Rights Act that outlawed racial segregation in public accommodations. Maddox and his supporters, armed with guns and ax handles, had threatened blacks attempting to integrate the Pickrick. In this first test of the Civil Rights Act, Maddox was ordered by a federal court to integrate the Pickrick. However he preferred to close the restaurant rather than comply with the court order. The national attention surrounding the affair served to advance Maddox's political career, and he ran for governor of Georgia in 1966. He was selected as governor by the Georgia legislature in 1967 after an election in which none of the candidates received an absolute majority.

As governor, Maddox surprised many by the moderation of his racial policies. Certain programs were initiated in Georgia to improve the lot of poor blacks and prisoners. Schools were not closed to prevent desegregation. Maddox's explanations for this change once in office were varied. One observer stated simply, "Maddox didn't practice what he preached," while others pointed to Maddox's lack of administrative experience and argued that he had given subordinates a free hand in initiating social programs.

In 1968 Maddox entered the race for the Democratic presidential nomination. He made his announcement on seeking the nomination less than two weeks before the start of the Democratic National Convention. Maddox ran on the basis of his old right-wing states' rights platform combined with newer themes of complete U.S. military victory in Vietnam and domestic law and order. Maddox's candidacy was not considered seriously at the Convention in August 1968, and he withdrew his name from consideration before the balloting began.

Maddox sustained a second political defeat at the Convention when a challenge Georgia delegation headed by civil rights activist Julian Bond was seated along with the mostly-white, conservative, "official" delegation, which had been handpicked by Maddox in his capacity as Georgia Democratic Party chairman. The Convention attempted a compromise, whereby Georgia's votes would be divided between the two delegations. However this proved unacceptable to Maddox and the majority of his delegation who resigned. After leaving the Convention Maddox characterized the Democrats as the Party of "looting, burning, killing and draft card burning." In the 1968 presidential election, Maddox supported the independent candidacy of George Wallace [q.v.].

Maddox continued to be a popular and colorful political figure in Georgia. In 1970 he even offered to ride on top of a train carrying deadly nerve gas through Georgia in order to prove its safety. Maddox was legally barred from a second consecutive term by a provision in the state constitution. After he attempted to have this provision overturned in court and failed, Maddox ran for lieutenant governor in the 1970 election and won. His running partner for governor was Jimmy Carter [q.v.].

During the 1972 presidential election Maddox continued to support the presidential aspirations of George Wallace. After the Democrats nominated George McGovern [q.v.], Maddox declared that he hoped Nixon would "devastate" McGovern in the coming election. He reasoned that a disastrous political defeat would increase the possibilities for a right-wing turn in sentiment within the Democratic Party.

Maddox was highly critical of the performance of the Nixon Administration. In a letter to President Nixon, he sharply denounced the Paris peace talks. He wrote that Nixon's "secret offer of billions of United States dollars to Communist Vietnam . . . is an act giving aid and comfort to the enemy of the first order . . . a pro-Communist act . . . an anti-American act . . . shameful and disgraceful and betrays every American military man who has fought, bled or died in battle throughout Southeast Asia and the rest of the world."

In 1974 Maddox attempted to gain the Democratic nomination for governor of Georgia once again. The primary battle between Maddox and George Busbee, a state representative, was extremely sharp. The primary was seen as a political struggle between the segregationist policies of Maddox and the racial moderation of the "New South" represented by Busbee and his supporters (which included Maddox's old political enemy Julian Bond). Maddox received the greatest number of votes cast for the dozen candidates in the primary but was defeated by Busbee in the subsequent runoff election. Tearfully admitting defeat, Maddox claimed, "People are quicker to turn out to vote against somebody than they are to vote for somebody."

Maddox entered the 1976 presidential election as the candidate of the right-wing American Independent Party. He asserted that Gerald Ford was a wishy-washy conservative and was dominated by Rockefeller. He attacked Jimmy Carter as a "leftist-socialist." Maddox's campaign had no appreciable effect on the outcome of the election.

During the mid-1970s Maddox attempted to put together a nightclub act starring himself and his black former dishwasher from the Pickrick. The act, entitled the "Governor and his Dishwasher," featured music and jokes. It was not a commercial success. In 1978 Maddox was in debt for over $125,000 and, having recovered from a heart attack, sold his political memorabilia at a public action.

[MIB]

MAGNUSON, WARREN G(RANT)
b. April 12, 1905; Moorehead, Minn.
Democratic Senator, Wash., 1945.

Orphaned at an early age, Magnuson was adopted by a Swedish family and raised in North Dakota. As a young adult he moved to Seattle where he received his law degree from the University of Washington in 1929. Magnuson was elected to the state legislature in 1932 and to the U.S. House in 1936. In 1944 he won a seat in the Senate.

In the Senate Magnuson consistently supported liberal social welfare legisla-

tion. He was an outspoken advocate of increased government spending, both for defense and for domestic programs. He also worked hard to channel federal funds to his home state which was heavily dependent on shipping, aircraft, fisheries and timber for its prosperity.

In 1962 Magnuson was reelected with only 52% of the vote. The narrowness of his victory led him to take an increasingly active role in sponsoring legislation of national significance. Magnuson played a key role in the passage of the controversial public accommodations section of the Civil Rights Act of 1964. During the Johnson Administration, he became one of the prime sponsors of consumer protection legislation. [See TRUMAN, EISENHOWER, KENNEDY, JOHNSON Volumes]

Magnuson continued his advocacy of consumer protection legislation in the Nixon years. In 1970 he drew upon the recommendations of the National Commission on Product Safety and introduced a bill to create an independent consumer product safety agency. No action was taken, but Magnuson reintroduced a similar bill in February 1971. The proposed legislation gave the independent agency broad authority to test products and to set safety standards, allowed it to ban products that constituted an unreasonable hazard, and authorized it to initiate court action against offending producers.

The bill was strongly opposed by industry and by the Nixon Administration, which prepared an alternative bill two months later. The Administration proposal retained product safety authority within the Department of Health, Education and Welfare (HEW), gave industry a role in the standard setting process and limited the disclosure of product information. Magnuson's Commerce Committee held intensive hearings on both bills in July 1971, and the following March it reported a revised version. The new bill retained the most important features of Magnuson's original legislation, including the independence of the agency, its right to set mandatory standards and ban products, and the authority to seek court orders against hazardous products. Magnuson was especially adamant about the agency's independence. He argued that HEW was already overburdened with functions and would inadequately perform its consumer protection functions. Magnuson's views prevailed, and in October 1972 Congress approved the creation of an independent Consumer Product Safety Agency with broad regulatory powers.

Magnuson sponsored several other pieces of consumer legislation with varying degrees of success. In 1969, he introduced a bill to ban cigarette advertising on radio and television and strengthening the health warning on cigarette packages. Despite pressure from the tobacco industry, Congress approved it in March 1970 and the bill became effective the following year. In 1970 he sponsored legislation which established federal standards for warranties on consumer products and strengthened the consumer protection powers of the Federal Trade Commission. Although the Senate approved the bill in 1971 and again in 1973, opposition from the Nixon Administration kept the House from taking action on it. In December 1974, both houses of Congress finally approved the legislation and President Ford signed it into law.

Magnuson had less success in his efforts to win passage of a no-fault auto insurance bill. In February 1971, he and Senator Philip Hart (D, Mich.) [q.v.] introduced legislation to require all motorists to carry insurance providing compensation for bodily injury regardless of who caused an accident. The bill also required each state to enact no-fault laws that met the minimum federal standard set by the bill. The Nixon Administration opposed Magnuson's bill, however, and argued instead that no-fault should remain a concern of the states. The Commerce Committee held hearings in 1971 and reported the bill favorably the following year. However it died in committee in the Senate. The Senate finally approved the bill in May 1974, but heavy lobbying by the American Bar Association killed it in the

House. A renewed effort by Magnuson to pass a no-fault law in 1976 also failed.

Magnuson took other legislative initiatives during the Nixon years. In 1971 and 1972 he won extensions of federal unemployment compensation benefits for states with high jobless rates. He sponsored the 1971 Emergency Health Personnel Act which authorized the Public Health Service to assign medical personnel to areas with critical shortages of health workers. In 1970 Magnuson introduced the constitutional amendment extending the vote to 18 year olds. He was a strong advocate of increased government funding of cancer research and attacked Nixon's war against cancer as "more myth than reality." Magnuson was highly critical of Nixon's impoundment of funds appropriated by Congress, and of President Ford's frequent vetoes of appropriation bills for social welfare programs.

In 1974, Magnuson easily won reelection to a sixth term in the Senate.

[JD]

MAGRUDER, JEB STUART
b. Nov. 5, 1934, New York, N.Y.
Special Assistant to the President, January 1969-May 1971; Deputy Director of the Committee to Re-Elect the President, May 1971-March 1973.

Magruder served in the Army from 1954 to 1956 and graduated from Williams College in 1958. He received an MBA from the University of Chicago in 1963. During the early 1960s he held various jobs in sales, advertising and merchandising. Magruder became active in Republican politics and in 1968 was in charge of the Nixon campaign in Southern California. Nixon intimates Robert Finch [q.v.] and H.R. Haldeman [q.v.] liked Magruder and offered him a job as special assistant to the President after the Nixon victory in 1968.

Working under Haldeman Magruder was involved in multiple political activities centered around public relations and manipulation of the news media. For instance Magruder thought of the scheme to use anti-trust policy to intimidate and coerce large media conglomerates like *The Washington Post* into giving the Nixon Administration more favorable news coverage. Magruder was most active in establishing the White House letter-writing campaigns around single issues (e.g., the Carswell Supreme Court nomination, the Cambodian invasion) and in the formation of dummy "citizens committees." These committees were supposed to create the impression that Richard Nixon's domestic and foreign policies had broader support than they did.

In May 1971 Haldeman released Magruder from his White House position and told him that as deputy director of the Committee to Re-Elect the President (CREEP), he should begin organizing the personnel on the Committee. Magruder ran CREEP until March 1972, when Attorney General John N. Mitchell [q.v.] officially resigned to become CREEP Director. The Committee was staffed primarily by former Haldeman White House assistants (35 in all made the move) and Magruder kept in touch with Haldeman on all issues.

Magruder's official job at CREEP was to direct campaign advertising, research and security operations. In practice he transferred the White House letter-writing campaigns, citizens committees and intelligence operations to CREEP.

In August 1971 Magruder and his assistant, Kenneth Rietz, planned the first in a series of "intelligence operations" to infiltrate the campaigns of the Democratic front-runners, Sens. Edmund Muskie of Maine [q.v.], Henry Jackson of Washington [q.v.] and Hubert Humphrey of Minnesota [q.v.]. The operation was intended not only to gather information but to sabotage the candidates' respective campaigns. These activities came under the immediate supervision of G. Gordon Liddy [q.v.], who was hired by CREEP in December 1971 as general counsel. Liddy was also responsible for initiating his own projects. In early 1972 Magruder ordered Hugh Sloan [q.v.] to give Liddy $250,000 from CREEP to finance the "Gemstone Plan," which was designed to get information from the Democratic National Committee.

Following the Watergate break-in on June 17, 1972, Magruder played a major role in attempts to get the burglars released and cover up Administration involvement in the plot. The cover-up of the burglary and other CREEP activities began immediately. As Magruder later testified, "I do not think there was ever any discussion that there would not be a cover-up." Magruder, Mitchell and John Dean [q.v.] worked on strategies to keep the FBI investigation contained to the five burglars, H. Howard Hunt [q.v.] and Liddy. They were afraid that if the FBI investigators probed too deeply, they would uncover the misdeeds of the Nixon Administration from 1969 onward and that the adverse publicity would lead to Richard Nixon's defeat in the fall. Magruder also tried to pressure Hugh Sloan into telling the FBI that the sum he gave for the Liddy "Gemstone Plan" was dramatically smaller than it had been. Sloan, however, refused to commit perjury.

In appearances before a grand jury in August, Magruder invented inflated dollar amounts for the expenses of the Liddy operation and claimed that Liddy was a maverick who had broken away from the control of the higher echelon in CREEP. During September 1972 in his last appearance before the grand jury, Magruder was asked about the entries in his and John Mitchell's daily logs for meetings at which the surveillance plan had been discussed. He testified that the first one was cancelled, and at the second one, they discussed the new campaign contributions disclosure law. When on Sept. 15, 1972, the Watergate grand jury returned indictments against the five burglars, Hunt and Liddy, it looked as though the efforts to contain the investigation had been successful.

However, on March 23, 1973, as the Watergate burglars were about to be sentenced, James McCord [q.v.] broke his silence and in a letter to Judge John Sirica [q.v.] claimed that pressure had been applied to the defendants to maintain their silence, that they all committed perjury and that they had been paid for their silence. The last phase of the cover-up involved the search for scapegoats among the President's men. In early April it appeared to insiders at the White House that Mitchell, Magruder and Dean were being "set up" by Ehrlichman and Haldeman to assume full responsibility for the break-in and the cover-up.

On April 14, 1973, Magruder followed John Dean to the prosecutor's office with his story to try to work out a bargain for leniency from the courts. A year later in March 1974, Magruder and six other top presidential aides including Haldeman and Ehrlichman were indicted by the Watergate grand jury. On June 4, 1974, after pleading guilty to charges of perjury and conspiring to help others commit perjury, Magruder was sentenced by Judge Sirica to from 10 months to four years in the federal prison at Allenwood, Pa. On Jan. 8, 1975, Magruder was released after serving seven months of his sentence.

[SJT]

MAHON, GEORGE H(ERMAN)
b. Sept. 22, 1900; Mahon, La.
Democratic Representative, Tex., 1935-79; Chairman, Appropriations Committee, 1964-79.

Mahon migrated with his parents from Louisiana to the Texas panhandle in 1908. After earning his law degree from the University of Texas in 1925, he entered politics and was elected judge and district attorney. In 1934, he was elected to the House from the rural, oil-producing 19th congressional district. A supporter of the Roosevelt and Truman Administrations' foreign policy and agricultural programs, Mahon steadily rose on the House seniority list. He became chairman of the powerful defense subcommittee of the House Appropriations Committee in 1949. In May 1964, upon the death of Rep. Clarence Cannon (D, Mo.), he also took over as chairman of the Appropriations Committee and became one of the

most influential leaders of the House. As head of the House Committee that scrutinized all executive department budget requests, Mahon earned the reputation of a tough budget cutter. [See EISENHOWER, KENNEDY, JOHNSON Volumes]

During the Nixon-Ford years Mahon often questioned Administration defense policies and regularly supported cutting defense budget requests to eliminate what he considered wasteful or questionable defense programs or weapons systems. At the same time, however, Mahon resisted the efforts of defense critics who wanted to slash the defense budget even further. When Secretary of Defense James R. Schlesinger [q.v.] told the Appropriations Committee in February 1974 that more than $1 billion had been added to the defense budget to help "stimulate the economy," Mahon questioned why the stimulation had to take place in the military rather than the civilian sector of the economy. In 1974 Mahon defended a $4.5 billion reduction of the Pentagon's budget request, saying it was the "best that can be reasonably done" for national defense at a time of double-digit inflation.

When President Ford unveiled his fiscal 1976 defense budget in February 1975, Mahon promised sharp reductions in the budget request. His Committee trimmed $9 billion from the request. But while Mahon supported selective cuts in the Administration's budget requests, he also supported increases in defense spending. In 1976 Mahon defended a $14 billion increase over the previous year's budget, explaining that inflation absorbed $7 billion of the increase and that the U.S. had to counter growing Soviet strength.

Mahon became one of the most vigorous opponents of the federal revenue-sharing program Congress enacted in 1972. He objected to the bill because it appropriated funds for three fiscal years without further congressional review and thus subverted the legislative process. Despite his opposition, the bill was passed in October.

Mahon opposed the Administration on its impounding of funds appropriated by Congress to finance federal programs.

The issue developed into a major confrontation between Congress and the White House in 1972. That year Nixon wanted Congress to enact a $250 billion federal spending ceiling and allow him to make selective cuts below appropriated levels. Mahon supported the spending ceiling, but proposed to limit the President's authority to make budget cuts. The House rejected his proposal and instead adopted an amendment that specifically allowed the President unrestricted authority to make cuts. The Senate, however, rejected the House measure, and Nixon then announced he would establish his own spending ceiling and impound funds already appropriated.

The following year Mahon became the chief sponsor of a bill, backed by the Democratic leadership, that would have limited the President's authority to impound funds. Although Congress failed to adopt the bill, a revised version of Mahon's proposal was included in a budget reform law Congress enacted in 1974. The measure, worded in part by Mahon, required that Congress adopt a budget resolution setting target figures for total appropriations, total spending, and tax and debt levels before it acted on specific appropriations and spending bills. The law also created new Budget Committees in the Senate and House to analyze budget options and prepare budget resolutions. The new House Budget Committee took over some of the Appropriations Committee's functions in setting spending limits, and eroded Mahon's influence in the appropriations process.

Mahon suffered a further rebuff in 1974 when the Democratic caucus forced him to reverse a jurisdictional assignment he had made in 1971. Mahon had felt that the Appropriations subcommittees were giving too much money for environmental and consumer protection programs. To correct the situation he transferred the jurisdiction over these programs to the agriculture subcommittee headed by Rep. Jamie Whitten (D, Miss.) [q.v.]. Whitten was a persistent critic of such programs. But in 1974 the Democratic Caucus gave itself the right to approve the appoint-

ment of Appropriations subcommittee chairmen, a step directed at removing Whitten. Mahon then agreed to transfer jurisdiction over consumer protection and environmental programs to another subcommittee to save Whitten's chairmanship.

In 1975 Mahon began to support some of the social welfare spending measures sponsored by the Democrats to help fight the economic recession, and voted to override several proposals that President Ford had vetoed. Mahon was the floor manager of the unsuccessful effort to override Ford's veto of the $5.3 billion emergency jobs bill. He countered Ford's budgetary arguments by pointing out that each 1% of increased unemployment raised the federal deficit by $16 billion. He supported unsuccessful efforts to override the vetoes of the emergency farm bill and the bill to extend the temporary 1975 tax cuts into 1976.

Mahon supported the Nixon-Ford Vietnam policy to the very end. In 1971 he backed Republican procedural moves to block the adoption of the Mansfield Amendment, which called for ending U.S. military operations in Vietnam by a specific date. However the moves failed, and modified versions of the Senate-passed Amendment were added to the military draft extension bill in September 1971 and to the defense procurement bill in November. In 1973 Mahon tried to revise the bombing prohibition Congress was considering so that it would apply only to American activities over Cambodia and Laos. The resolution finally adopted prohibited U.S. bombing operations over all of Indochina. On April 22, 1975, two weeks before the Communist forces captured Saigon, he introduced a bill to give $165 million in additional military aid to South Vietnam.

Mahon, who turned 76 in 1976, was challenged for reelection that year for the first time since 1964, when he had won 78% of the vote. In 1976 he polled only 55%. He did not seek reelection in 1978 and retired after serving in Congress for 44 years.

[AE]

MAILER, NORMAN
b. Jan. 21, 1923; Long Branch, N.J.
Author.

Mailer, the son of an accountant, grew up in New York City. He graduated from Harvard in 1943 with a degree in engineering and served in the Army from 1944 to 1946. His novel based on his Army experiences, *The Naked and the Dead*, was published in 1948. It was a major success, affording Mailer celebrity and prosperity at age 25.

During the 1950s Mailer published two novels. They reflected both his disillusionment with communism and his growing concern over government authoritarianism, a central theme of much of his later work.

Mailer became deeply involved in the anti-Vietnam war movement in the late 1960s. In October 1967, he was arrested during a protest rally at the Pentagon. His account of the events of that day was published in 1968 as *The Armies of the Night*. It instantly received an overwhelmingly favorable response from critics and readers. With the appearance of *Miami and the Siege of Chicago*, a chronicle of the 1968 Republican and Democratic Party Conventions, Mailer became known as a preeminent practitioner of "the new journalism"—a prose style combining nonfiction reportage with the personalized viewpoints and literary forms of fiction. [See JOHNSON Volume]

In April 1969 Mailer announced his candidacy for the Democratic nomination in New York City's mayoralty contest, with columnist Jimmy Breslin as his running mate vying for the City Council presidency. Characterizing his political stance as "left-conservative," Mailer ran an unorthodox campaign, calling for the establishment of New York City as the 51st state to give it a greater voice in the legislature. Political power within the city would then be decentralized, giving greater autonomy to the individual neighborhoods and boroughs.

Mailer's campaign, however, was never able to overcome the impression among most political observers that it was not a genuinely serious race for office. Many prominent liberals accused Mailer of siphoning votes from leading liberal contender Herman Badillo and thereby assuring the nomination of a conservative.

Norman Mailer received the Pulitzer Prize in May 1969 for *Armies of the Night*. In July he reported on the first manned landing on the moon and his own ambivalent feelings towards it in *Of a Fire On the Moon*, published in 1970. While recognizing the poetic implications of the moon landing, Mailer felt that it represented the supremacy of technology over poetry in American life.

In 1970 Kate Millett published *Sexual Politics* in which she devoted an entire chapter to a scathing critique of Mailer's work. Millet castigated Mailer for perpetuating reactionary cultural stereotypes of women and labeled him a "prisoner of the virility cult" whose attitude towards women was one of "open hostility."

Mailer responded with the 1971 publication of *The Prisoner of Sex*, a lengthy analysis of human sexuality, women and the women's movement. Mailer strongly questioned Millett's literary criticism of his works and those of other male writers. He perceived the ultimate goal of women's liberation to be the denial of any essential differences between man and woman. This, according to Mailer, could well lead to a totalitarian society where human beings would be reduced to depersonalized "units."

In 1972 Mailer again covered the Republican and Democratic National Conventions. He published *St. George and the Godfather* describing the events later that year. The book was written in the distinctive Mailer style stressing his own reactions to the proceedings as much as the events themselves. Hence he was openly sympathetic to the nomination of George McGovern, "probably the most decent presidential candidate to come along in anyone's life." The latter half of *St. George and the Godfather*, focusing on the Republican Convention, was a blistering attack on the Nixon Administration, both for its political policies and its impact on the moral climate of the nation. He viewed Richard Nixon as "the artist . . . of the mediocre."

In February 1973 Mailer held a celebration of his 50th birthday, charging couples $50 dollars a piece, which he announced would go towards the formation of an organization called "The Fifth Estate." Its function was to investigate the covert activities of the government in order to determine "how far paranoia is justified." Describing the concept as "the best political idea in my entire life," Mailer said "we have to face up to the possibility that the country may be sliding towards totalitarianism." The Kennedy assassinations and the Watergate affair were mentioned as possible areas of research.

Despite widespread skepticism over Mailer's organization and the circumstances under which it was unveiled, he spent the following months lecturing at various colleges and assemblies and compiling lists of interested parties. The following year the organization merged with the Committee for Action Research on the Intelligence Community.

Mailer supported Jimmy Carter in the 1976 presidential election, saying that he "was somewhere within range of the very good and very decent man he presented himself to be."

[MDQ]

MANDEL, MARVIN
b. 1920;
Governor, Md, 1969-77.

Marvin Mandel came from an orthodox Jewish background. His father was a clothing cutter in Baltimore. Mandel received his law degree from the University of Maryland in 1942. He was elected as a justice of the peace in 1948. His political career began to take off in 1951 after he was appointed to fill a vacancy on the Democratic Party's state central committee. He was elected to the Maryland House of Delegates, representing the politically important fifth district in 1952. He kept this office for the next 16 years.

Mandel became speaker of the House of Delegates in 1963. He replaced Gordon Boone, who had been convicted and jailed in a statewide political scandal involving savings and loan institutions. As speaker, Mandel became a major figure in Maryland power politics.

In January 1969 Mandel won the special legislative election to fill the remaining two years of Spiro Agnew's [q.v.] term as governor. A special election by the legislature was necessary because at that time the Maryland constitution did not provide for the post of lieutenant governor.

As governor, Mandel's major accomplishment was his attempt to revamp the state's judicial system. Uniform qualifications for judges were imposed and the practice of electing circuit and appellate judges was ended. Instead circuit and appellate judges had to seek reconfirmation from the state's Senate every 15 years. Mandel also successfully pressed for a state constitutional amendment that provided for the office of lieutenant governor.

In 1973 the governor's personal problems became a potential political liability. Mandel's estranged wife, Barbara, had refused to move out of the governor's mansion even after he had expressed his intention to get a divorce and remarry another woman. Barbara Mandel staged a five-month "sit-in" in the governor's mansion, and vacated only after she had concluded that their "marriage had not returned to normal." The Mandels were divorced in 1974, and the governor then remarried.

In the beginning of 1973 a federal grand jury began investigating corruption involving Maryland's politicians. A high point in the investigation was the indictment and conviction of Vice President Agnew for tax evasion. Late in 1973 the grand jury began to investigate Mandel's dealings, particularly his connections to the Tidewater Insurance Co., which was owned in part by close political supporters of Mandel. In an attempt to sidestep criticism, Mandel appointed a study group to inquire into the practice of awarding state contracts by competitive bidding. Mandel also promised to return $40,000 that had been contributed to his upcoming campaign for reelection by consultants who did business with the state.

In November 1975 Mandel and five long-standing political supporters were indicted by a federal grand jury on charges of mail fraud, bribery and "a pattern of racketeering activity." Mandel was also charged with falsifying his federal income tax return. The charges against Mandel concerned his relationship with the Tidewater Insurance Co. and racetrack interests owned by three of the codefendants. The indictment charged that Mandel had used his powers as governor to veto a bill that would have given Maryland's Marlboro racetrack profitable additional racing days. Mandel and the other five codefendants allegedly proceeded to obtain a concealed interest in the track at greatly reduced prices. According to the indictment, the governor then persuaded the legislature to override his veto, which resulted in prospective windfall profits for the six secret partners. Mandel was said to have received a 5% interest in a real estate concern for the services he rendered his partners in this deal.

The charges of mail fraud stemmed from the mailing out of transcripts of Mandel's news conferences in which he lied to newsmen. Mandel responded to his indictment by saying that it could be a positive opportunity because he could now "prove my innocence in a court of law." He also charged that his indictment had been a politically inspired vendetta motivated by "jealousy."

In December 1976 the court declared a mistrial after it was discovered that one of the jurors had been offered $10,000 to hold out against a conviction. After a new trial Mandel and his defendants were convicted on some 18 counts each of mail fraud and racketeering in August 1977. Leaving the courtroom after his conviction, Mandel was jeered by a crowd of spectators who shouted, "Lock him up" and "See you in jail, Marv." In October 1977 Mandel was sentenced to 4 years in prison, though he escaped paying a fine

because he told the court that he was broke.

Mandel refused to resign and was suspended from office. He was replaced by Lt. Gov. Blair Lee. In January 1979 the conviction was overturned on appeal on technical grounds. The case was returned to federal district court for retrial.

[MLB]

MANKIEWICZ, FRANK F(ABIAN)
b. May 16, 1924; New York, N.Y.
Political figure.

A graduate of the University of California at Los Angeles (UCLA) in 1947, Mankiewicz received an M.S. from Columbia the following year. In 1950 he ran an unsuccessful campaign for the California state legislature as a Democrat. After a brief stint as a journalist, he entered the University of California's Law School at Berkeley and was admitted to the bar in 1955. He spent the next six years in private practice.

In 1962 Mankiewicz relocated to Peru where he served as director of the Peace Corps. Two years later he was promoted to the post of Peace Corps regional director of Latin America. From his Washington office he implemented recruitment drives and supervised the agency's social and educational programs for Latin America.

In 1965 Mankiewicz joined Sen. Robert Kennedy's (D, N.Y.) staff as a press assistant. Because of his commitment to Kennedy's goals and his ability to deal with the press, he was appointed Kennedy's press secretary in 1968 and was responsible for coordinating the Senator's campaign for the Democratic presidential primary. [See JOHNSON Volume]

After recovering from Kennedy's tragic death later that year, Mankiewicz directed his support to Sen. George McGovern (D, S.D.), whom he considered closest to Kennedy in his liberal perspective. With Nixon's victory Mankiewicz returned to his earlier, brief occupation as a journalist and cowrote a liberal syndicated column. In 1969 a Ford Foundation grant subsidized his study of Peace Corps programs in Latin America and the Caribbean.

In 1971 McGovern recruited Mankiewicz to serve as press secretary for his attempt at the Democratic presidential nomination. An astute political observer and strategist extraodinaire, Mankiewicz plunged into the race with cold-blooded realism. The combination of McGovern's lack of recognition beyond the confines of his home state and his vocal opposition to the Vietnam war, undermined all possibilities of unified party support. Despite negligible resources and a slim chance for victory, Mankiewicz proceeded to map out logistics for McGovern's state primary entries. A barrage of intensive public exposure was followed by a retreat in order to analyze repercussions and restructure the campaign.

Mankiewicz formulated a progressive image-building strategy to challenge the media contention that McGovern was a mild-mannered one-issue candidate. In the interests of electability McGovern limited his statements on Vietnam and addressed himself to fundamental economic issues. As a result of campaign staff advice, he became more circumspect in his association with anti-war organizations so that his "radical" image would not foreshadow possible success in the primaries. Elevated to the position of political adviser, Mankiewicz guided his candidate through the requisite gatherings of the Party machine in each primary state. McGovern's relatively successful showing laid the foundation for his nomination at the Democratic National Convention in 1972.

Despite Mankiewicz's attempts to enhance McGovern's credibility as a presidential contender, the choice of Sen. Thomas Eagleton (D, Mo.) [q.v.] as a running mate proved irreversibly damaging to the campaign. Although Mankiewicz had been assured by Eagleton that his personal background was beyond reproach, the Senator's history of psychiatric treatment, including shock therapy, soon surfaced. After a short period of indecision, Eagleton was replaced with Sargent Shriver [q.v.], but McGovern's al-ready foundering popularity plummeted. Financial and organizational problems and the inescapable "radical" tag together with the Eagleton affair proved to be McGovern's undoing and his defeat was a harsh one.

After Nixon's victory, Mankiewicz turned to television writing and producing.

[DGE]

MANSFIELD, MIKE (MICHAEL) (JOSEPH)
b. March 16, 1903; New York, N.Y.
Democratic Senator, Mont., 1953–76;
Senate Majority Leader, 1961-77.

Following the death of his mother, Mansfield's Irish relatives sent him from New York City to live with family in Montana. From 1918 to 1922 Mansfield served in all three branches of the armed service. He then returned home to work for the next eight years as a miner and mining engineer. Mansfield quit mining to obtain both B.A. and M.A. degrees from Montana State University, in 1933 and 1934 respectively, where he remained to teach Latin American and Asian history. A Democrat in a traditional Republican state, Mansfield lost his first bid for a political office in his Party's congressional primary of 1940, but he won a House seat two years later. In acknowledgment of his specialization in Asian affairs, Mansfield was assigned to the House Foreign Affairs Committee.

Following his election to the Senate in 1952, Mansfield established a liberal record. In an unprecedented move, Senate Majority Leader Lyndon Johnson selected Mansfield, who had low seniority, to be his assistant, the Party whip. It was believed Johnson chose Mansfield because he was a moderate, trustworthy senator who would not threaten the Texan's strong hold on the Senate. In the last years of the Eisenhower Administration, Mansfield voted liberal on most issues and supported the nation's foreign policy. [See EISENHOWER Volume]

When Johnson became vice president in 1961, the Senate Democrats elected Mansfield their majority leader. During the Kennedy Administration, Mansfield worked with the White House in its battle for passage of liberal legislation. Unlike Johnson who had exercised flamboyant leadership over the Senate, Mansfield quietly, with the assistance of his whip, Sen Hubert H. Humphrey (D, Minn.) [q.v.] directed the policies of the majority Party. When Johnson took over the presidency, Mansfield watched his power gravitate to the White House. [See KENNEDY, JOHNSON Volumes]

Mansfield's legislative leadership contrasted sharply with that of Johnson. Demonstrating an inordinate amount of respect for the Senate, Mansfield refused to bully, badger, arm-twist and make deals to obtain the legislation his Party desired. Nevertheless he held great power as majority leader through his chairmanship of the Democratic Policy and Conference Committees, which formulated Party policies, scheduled legislation, and voted on and assigned committee chairmanships and positions. Mansfield could, if he desired, control the flow of legislation on the Senate floor. The Senator approached this responsibility cautiously. He delegated to his whip, Sen. Robert Byrd (D, W.Va.) [q.v.], the distasteful task of pressuring for needed votes. This enabled Mansfield to enjoy the prestige of being the aloof, distinguished, statesman legislator who finessed rather than browbeat the Senate into action. Few bills during his years as Majority leader bore his name. Mansfield preferred having other senators introduce legislation. In contrast to senators who thrived on press coverage, Mansfield shied away from publicity. Yet when issues angered him enough, Mansfield joined the political debate.

Mansfield was a particularly strong opponent of the Vietnam war. Although he initially backed the Johnson Administration's Indochina policy, Mansfield grew disillusioned with the war effort following a fact-finding trip to Vietnam in 1966. He privately tried to persuade Johnson that military victory would be impossible.

When it appeared that the President preferred to settle the war on the battlefield rather than at the conference table, Mansfield publicly criticized the war.

During Nixon's first term, Mansfield emerged as one of the leading Democratic critics of the Administration's Vietnam policy. He particularly deplored how the executive had usurped all the war-making functions from the Congress. In 1970 Mansfield enthusiastically supported the Cooper-Church and McGovern-Hatfield Amendments. The following year he introduced his own end-the-war amendment. Mansfield's measure declared that it was the policy of the United States to end military operations in Indochina at the earliest possible date and to "provide for the prompt and orderly withdrawal of all United States military forces not later than nine months after the date of [enactment of the bill] subject to the release of all American prisoners of war." The measure also requested the President to negotiate a cease-fire with North Vietnam and establish a final date for the withdrawal of American military forces. It passed the Senate but failed in the House.

Following Nixon's historic visit to China in February 1972, Mansfield, with Minority Leader Hugh Scott (R, Pa.) [q.v.], traveled in April to Peking. The Chinese Communists' economic and social progress impressed the former Asian scholar, who had visited China for President Roosevelt during World War II. Mansfield downgraded the fear expressed by many Americans that China was acting as an aggressive world revolutionary power. Finding the Peking regime conservative and pragmatic enough to be more concerned with its own internal development, Mansfield informed the American people that the Communist leadership paid only lip-service support to Third World revolutions. The Mansfield-Scott mission to China accomplished no major breakthroughs in the disputes that had divided Peking and Washington for close to 25 years; instead, Mansfield and his Chinese hosts engaged in exploratory talks to improve the two nations' economic, political and cultural contacts.

In addition to Mansfield's opposition to the Administration's Vietnam policy, he was particularly incensed about the continued presence of 600,000 U.S. troops in Western Europe. His repeated efforts to introduce legislation to scale down the size of the U.S. forces in the North Atlantic Treaty Organization were rebuffed by the Senate. Supporters of the continued large American military presence in Europe argued that the Mansfield proposal threatened Western security. Mansfield responded that the Europeans should pay for their own defense.

Mike Mansfield had a polite, businesslike relationship with both Presidents Nixon and Ford. He breakfasted with them every month to discuss upcoming legislation. But he frequently opposed the Administration particularly on domestic policy. Speaking for the Senate as majority leader, he deplored the Republicans' conservative policies, which he blamed for causing high unemployment and inflation. He quietly lobbied for the Senate to override the Nixon-Ford vetoes of social legislation. During the Watergate scandals Mansfield scored the Administration for its refusal to be honest with the American people, but his criticism was mild in comparison with the partisan attacks launched by fellow Democrats.

Mansfield decided to retire from the Senate following the 1976 election. Those who were impressed with his style of leadership praised him for restoring democracy to the Senate in contrast to Johnson's dictatorial leadership. On the other hand Mansfield's critics found him to be a weak leader whose desire to conciliate and patronize left the Senate an unruly body with no direction. Mansfield answered his critics by pointing out that the leadership techniques they called for were not consistent with his basically shy personality.

Mansfield's retirement from public life was shortlived. In 1977 President Jimmy Carter [q.v.] appointed him ambassador to Japan.

[JB]

MARDIAN, ROBERT C(HARLES)
b. Oct. 23, 1923; Pasadena, Calif.
Assistant Attorney General,
September 1970-June 1972.

Robert Mardian, the son of a California businessman, attended the University of California from 1941 to 1943. After graduating from the University of Southern California Law School in 1949, he practiced law in California. In 1964 Robert Mardian managed Barry Goldwater's [q.v.] presidential campaign in the Western states. Four years later he did the same for Richard Nixon. When Nixon was elected Mardian went to Washington as general counsel under Robert Finch [q.v.] at the Department of Health, Education and Welfare (HEW). At HEW Mardian carried out the Nixon Administration's "Southern Strategy," formulated by John Mitchell [q.v.]. The plan called for the Administration to stall on public school desegregation in the South to win conservative, segregationist Southerners into the Republican Party.

Because of his hard line anti-Communism, Robert Mardian, in 1970, was made assistant attorney general in charge of the Internal Security Division. He used the Justice Department's machinery to intimidate and harass a broad spectrum of anti-war protestors, civil rights advocates and radicals. The 1973 Senate Watergate hearings revealed that on at least two occasions, Mardian misused his powers at the request of the White House. First he gave President Nixon confidential FBI information on Daniel Ellsberg [q.v.], which was then passed on to John Ehrlichman's [q.v.] "plumbers." He also gave Ehrlichman confidential files on Sen. Thomas Eagleton (D, Mo.) [q.v.] which revealed that Eagleton had been hospitalized for "exhaustion." Ehrlichman leaked the information to sympathetic newspaper people who published the reports that led to Eagleton's removal as Sen. George McGovern's (D, S.D.) [q.v.] running mate in the 1972 election.

Mardian was involved in the Watergate cover-up from its inception. On June 17,

1972, when the seven Watergate burglars were arrested, John Mitchell told him to have G. Gordon Liddy [q.v.], the chief architect of the Watergate burglary and general counsel to the Committee to Re-Elect the President (CREEP), talk to Attorney General Richard Kleindienst [q.v.] about releasing the burglars, a ploy that Kleindienst rejected. Mardian and Frederick LaRue [q.v.] were put in charge of CREEP's "cleaning operation." They supervised the destruction of "potentially embarrassing" documents including the financial records of important campaign donors received before and after the new Campaign Contributions Disclosure Law went into effect.

Mardian and LaRue also destroyed Liddy's "Gemstone" file, which included memos describing wiretapped conversations of Democratic Party officials and their staffs. In addition the two men prepared witnesses for their FBI interviews by telling them not to volunteer information. Mardian arranged for his former associates at the FBI to question CREEP officials and staff at the CREEP office, instead of at FBI headquarters or in the privacy of their own homes.

During Mardian's 1973 trial for his activities in the Watergate cover-up, he denied participating in any discussion in which he encouraged Jeb Margruder [q.v.] to perjure himself. He also argued that he was counsel to CREEP and served in a privileged position vis-a-vis the CREEP staff members. In 1974 he was found guilty of one count of conspiracy and was sentenced to five years in prison and a $5,000 fine. However, in 1975 he won an appeal of his conviction when an appellate court found that Judge John Sirica [q.v.] should have severed Mardian's case from the other Nixon officials on trial since the evidence against him was not as strong as that against his codefendants.

Mardian was subsequently reinstated to the bar in California and Arizona and returned to private practice.

[SJT]

MARSHALL, THURGOOD
b. July 2, 1908; Baltimore, Md.
Associate Justice, U.S. Supreme Court, 1967-.

Marshall graduated first in his class from Howard University Law School in 1933 and then practiced for several years in Baltimore. He began working for the NAACP in 1936 and served as director-counsel of the NAACP Legal Defense and Educational Fund from 1940 to 1961. In that post Marshall spearheaded a legal assault on racial segregation and discrimination that transformed the law of race relations. His most significant victory came in the 1954 school desegregation decision, *Brown v. Board of Education,* but Marshall also successfully challenged discrimination in voting, housing, higher education, public accommodations and recreation. The nation's foremost civil rights attorney, Marshall was named a judge on the U.S. Second Circuit Court of Appeals in September 1961. He was appointed Solicitor General in July 1965, the first black to hold that position. Nominated for the Supreme Court in June 1967, Marshall became the first black on the high bench when he was sworn in that October. [See TRUMAN, EISENHOWER, KENNEDY, JOHNSON, Volumes]

From the start Marshall was a liberal and activist jurist who voted most often with Chief Justice Earl Warren and Justice William Brennan [q.v.]. He played a subordinate role in his first years on the bench, writing few majority opinions and rarely dissenting. As the Court became more conservative in the 1970s, however, Marshall became increasingly outspoken. The number of his dissents rose sharply, and he was identified as part of the left wing of the Burger Court.

In racial discrimination cases Marshall almost always voted to expand the civil rights of blacks. He supported school desegregation orders and dissented sharply in July 1974 when the Court upset an interdistrict busing plan to remedy school segregation in Detroit. Marshall also objected to a June 1971 decision sanctioning the closing of public swimming pools in

Jackson, Miss., to avoid desegregation and to a ruling a year later allowing private clubs with state liquor licenses to exclude blacks. Although he generally voted in favor of blacks in employment discrimination cases, Marshall wrote the majority opinion in a February 1975 case holding that an employer could fire employes who bypassed their union's effort to resolve a dispute over racial discrimination and picketed on their own.

In other equal protection cases, Marshall urged the Court to adopt a variable standard of review that would take into account the nature of the classification and of the interests involved in each case. Even under the accepted approach to equal protection claims, however, the Justice took a strong stand against all forms of discrimination. He favored making sex a suspect classification that would be subject to strict judicial scrutiny and voted in almost every instance to overturn differences in treatment between men and women. Marshall also opposed government distinctions between legitimate and illegitimate children and between citizens and aliens. However he did rule in a November 1973 majority opinion that the 1964 Civil Rights Act had not outlawed employment discrimination against aliens. He opposed discrimination against the poor and voted in March 1973 to invalidate public school financing systems based on local property taxes.

Justice Marshall supported expansions of the right to vote. His opinion in a June 1970 case held that residents of a federal enclave in Maryland could vote in state and local elections. In a March 1972 majority opinion, Marshall overturned state residency requirements for voting of three months or more. He opposed laws restricting voting on bond issues to property owners and favored a federal law lowering the voting age to 18. Marshall generally supported a strict one-man, one-vote standard of apportionment and dissented in cases which relaxed that standard at the state level.

Marshall spoke for a six man majority in June 1969 to hold the Fifth Amendment's provision against double jeopardy applicable to the states. In other criminal cases the Justice generally favored strong protection of the guarantees afforded by the Bill of Rights. He usually opposed searches without warrants and believed a warrant necessary for electronic eavesdropping. Marshall insisted that a waiver of rights was legitimate only if a defendant was fully informed and uncoerced. As Solicitor General he had argued against the *Miranda* ruling, requiring the police to inform suspects of their rights. But as a justice, Marshall opposed most attempts to cut back that decision. He dissented from rulings authorizing non-unanimous jury verdicts and juries of less than 12 members in state and federal courts and voted in several cases to expand the right to counsel. Marshall took a broad view of the Fifth Amendment's privilege against self-incrimination, and he voted in June 1972 and July 1976 to hold the death penalty totally unconstitutional as a violation of the Eighth Amendment's ban on cruel and unusual punishment.

Marshall took a liberal stance in most First Amendment cases. In a May 1968 opinion for the Court, he held peaceful labor picketing within a suburban shopping center protected by the Amendment. He dissented vigorously when the Court narrowed this ruling in June 1972 and then overturned it in March 1976. Marshall voted against prior restraints on the press. However he did favor narrowing the protection against libel suits enjoyed by the press when the case involved a private citizen rather than a public figure. In an April 1969 decision, his opinion for the Court held that the private possession of obscene materials within one's own home could not be made a crime. He also joined in a dissenting opinion in several June 1973 cases urging the Court to ban all government suppression of allegedly obscene material for consenting adults.

In March 1971, however, Marshall spoke for an eight man majority to rule that Congress could deny conscientious objector status to draft registrants who opposed only the Vietnam war, not all wars, without violating the First Amendment's guarantee of freedom of religion. In August 1973, while the Court was in recess, Marshall upheld a Second Circuit Court order allowing U.S. bombing of Cambodia to continue while the constitutionality of the action was being litigated. When Justice William O. Douglas [q.v.] intervened in the case several days later to order a halt in the bombing, Marshall immediately contacted the other members of the Court and issued an order with their support overriding Douglas's action.

Even before joining the Court, Thurgood Marshall had won a place in history because of his pathbreaking legal work for the NAACP. He stood as a symbol of the fight for black equality through legal action, and in both his NAACP post and later federal appointments, as a symbol of black achievement. As a justice, he was not highly creative or outstanding, but over the years, he became an increasingly articulate advocate of a liberal judicial position. In steadfastly opposing all forms of discrimination and supporting the protection of individual rights, Marshall maintained the Warren Court's tradition of libertarian activism.

[CAB]

For further information:
Randall W. Bland, *Private Pressure on Public Law: The Legal Career of Justice Thurgood Marshall* (Port Washington, N.Y., 1973).

MARTIN, GRAHAM A(NDERSON)
b. Sept. 22, 1912; Mars Hill, N. C.
Ambassador to South Vietnam, June 1973-April 1975.

Graham Martin, the son of a North Carolina minister, joined the Foreign Service in 1947 after a 15-year career in journalism and public administration. President Kennedy appointed Martin ambassador to Thailand in July 1963. Convinced that a lack of adequate U. S. aid had led to a full-scale war in Vietnam, Martin was instrumental in securing and increasing U. S. military and civilian assistance to Thailand in 1964-65. In January 1967 he admitted that the U. S. had leased large air bases in Thailand for bombing raids against Communist supply lines in Vietnam. Martin returned to Washington in July 1967 to become special assistant to the Secretary of State for refugee and migration affairs. He served in that post until named ambassador to Italy by President Nixon in 1969. [See JOHNSON Volume]

As ambassador to Italy Martin allegedly insisted on direct control of covert funds allocated by the CIA for the manipulation of Italian politics. According to *The New York Times* Martin contributed thousands of dollars to the faltering Christian Democratic Party in the 1972 parliamentary election campaign, thereby preventing a victory by the Italian Communists. Although he intended to retire following his tour of duty in Rome, Martin was persuaded by President Nixon in June 1973 to replace Ellsworth Bunker as ambassador to South Vietnam.

Martin's appointment to the embassy in Saigon on March 30, 1973 came six months after the signing of the Paris cease-fire agreement. The political section of the agreement had established a framework to enable the governments of South Vietnam, North Vietnam and the Provisional Revolutionary Government of South Vietnam (PRG) to work toward reconciliation and eventual reunification of the country. Martin's instructions as ambassador, however, were to reiterate unswerving U.S. support of President Thieu, rally a reluctant Congress to the backing of an unpopular Saigon government and restore Thieu's wavering faith in the U. S. This task became increasingly difficult following the congressional halt to all bombing of Cambodia and the prohibition of further military aid to Vietnam after Aug. 15, 1973.

Martin brooked no criticism of the South Vietnamese government. He distrusted the press and had several notable battles with U.S. correspondents stationed in Saigon, as well as a highly publicized flare-up with Sen. Edward M. Kennedy (D., Mass.) [q.v.] in March 1974. Martin had suggested that "it would be the height of folly" to give an "honest and detailed answer" to Kennedy's inquiry as to whether an increase in aid would amount to a new commitment to Thieu. The controversy caused a stir at the State Department when Congress killed in May 1974 an Administration plan for $474 million in supplementary aid to South Vietnam.

As the situation grew worse for the Saigon regime, it was Martin's hope that by surrendering territory of negligible military value in the northern area of South Vietnam, a political accommodation with the PRG could be reached to keep the Thieu government intact. President Thieu thought that such territorial concessions, if accepted by Hanoi, would be construed as "Communist victories" and would generate sympathy in the U. S. and support for his position in Congress. But the North Vietnamese would not cooperate. The PRG walked out of the negotiations at Joint Military Command in Saigon, North Vietnam broke off bilateral negotiations with the U. S. in Paris and in June 1973 hostilities between North and South Vietnam resumed.

Martin persisted in his belief that a political solution was possible, although he had been advised for weeks by his military analysts of the rapidly deteriorating situation and the Communist preparations for an attack on Saigon. On April 18, 1975, Martin said in an interview, "There has been no advice from Washington for Thieu to step down." At the same time, however, Martin was actively discouraging a military coup against Thieu, assuring former Vice President Nguyen Cao Ky that Thieu would soon step down. On April 21 Martin, with the help of French ambassador Jean-Marie Merillon, persuaded Thieu to resign. Martin held back, however, from recommending complete evacuation of Americans and their Vietnamese employes out of fear that such a move would panic the population and precipitate the Communist victory. The result was a chaotic final evacuation that left thousands of Vietnamese who had worked for the Americans stranded in Saigon, while thousands of others perished in hopeless attempts to seek refuge.

In 1976 the Ford White House nominated Martin for the post of ambassador-at-large, but the proposal languished in committee until after the presidential election, when it was withdrawn.

[JAN]

For further information:
Frank Snepp, *Decent Interval* (New York, 1978).

MARTIN, WILLIAM McCHESNEY
b. Dec. 17, 1906; St. Louis, Mo.
Chairman, Board of Governors of the Federal Reserve System, 1951-70.

William McChesney Martin was the son of a banker who had helped to found the Federal Reserve Bank of St. Louis. After graduating from Yale in 1928, he began the rapid rise in the U.S. financial community which won him acclaim as a "Boy Wonder." After a year as a clerk at the Federal Reserve Bank of St. Louis, Martin took over the statistics department of a St. Louis brokerage firm and in 1931 assumed the firm's seat on the New York Stock Exchange. In 1938, at the age of 31, Martin became president of the Exchange. Martin served in the Army during World War II.

In 1946 President Truman appointed him to head the Export-Import Bank. In 1949 he became assistant secretary of the Treasury for international finance, and played a mediating role in the 1951 accord between the Treasury and the Federal Reserve Bank. In the same year, Truman appointed Martin Chairman of the Board of Governors of the Federal Reserve Bank.

Known through his 19-year tenure as an advocate of tight money, Martin repeatedly became the center of controversy. During the Eisenhower years Martin was attacked by liberal Democrats who blamed his conservative money management for the recessions and economic sluggishness of these years. Martin, in turn, insisted that the only alternative to such control was increasing inflation, and several times proposed tax increases to further restrain demand. In the 1960 presidential campaign, John F. Kennedy similarly attacked Martin as part of his overall criticism of the economic stagnation of the Eisenhower years. Once in office, however, Kennedy and his successor Lyndon Johnson recognized the importance of Martin's domestic and international prestige for maintaining the soundness of the dollar.

After the mid-1960s, when inflation began to accelerate in conjunction with the Vietnam war, Martin increasingly played a "Cassandra" role with regard to the persistent problems of high government spending, balance-of-payments deficits and interest rates. Martin's June 1965 speech, in which he underlined "disquieting similarities between our present prosperity and the fabulous 20s," depressed the stock market for weeks. In December 1965 he cast the decisive vote in the Fed's move to raise the discount rate to a postwar high of 4½%, provoking "easy money" forces led by Rep. Wright Patman (D, Tex.) [q.v.] to call for his resignation. [See TRUMAN, EISENHOWER, KENNEDY, JOHNSON Volumes]

While Martin's term as Federal Reserve Board Chairman expired one year after Richard Nixon assumed office, the year was a propitious one. The new Republican Administration was determined to take serious action against inflation, which had reached 4.2% in 1968. Hence, Martin oversaw the first stages of the 1969-70 credit crunch which culminated in the bankruptcy of the Penn Central and the near-collapse of the commercial paper market.

Martin was positively disposed to the Nixon Administration's attempt to combat inflation, although he felt that the situation had deteriorated beyond the point where rising interest and discount rates alone would suffice. Martin had consistently cited expansionary economic programs, massive federal deficits and chronic balance-of-payments deficits as the real source of the problem. Nonetheless, during his last year in office, he lent support both in his public statements and in poli-

cy to anti-inflation measures. He used his February 1969 appearance before the Joint Economic Committee to lay out the Fed plans to fight inflation.

The first major step in this plan, enacted in April 1969, was a .5% hike in the discount rate to a then-record high of 6%. In the same month, the Fed imposed a similar .5% increase in member bank reserve requirements. In May 1969, during the congressional debate over the extension of the Johnson Administration surtax, Martin stated that the Fed would "try anything" to control inflation if the surtax were abolished. In June Martin warned of a financial collapse if inflation were not brought under control. In the event of further serious deterioration of the economy, Martin called for voluntary credit controls, forced savings and a higher surtax. In the late summer and early fall of 1969, Martin oversaw new moves by the Fed to impose reserve requirements on U.S. foreign branch banks, which had provided an important avenue for circumventing tight credit in the U.S. capital markets. Finally, in December 1969, the Fed also extended reserve requirements to commercial paper issued by bank affiliates.

Martin left office in January 1970, before the general tightening of credit reached its apex in the May-June 1970 corporate liquidity crisis which forced the Nixon Administration and Martin's successor, Arthur Burns [q.v.], into a reversal of monetary policy. After stepping down as Federal Reserve Board Chairman, Martin in 1971 was appointed to head a committee established to reorganize the New York Stock Exchange. He also served on the board of directors of several corporations.

[LG]

MATHEWS, (FORREST) DAVID
b. Dec. 6, 1935; Grove Hill, Ala.
Secretary of Health, Education and Welfare, July 1975-January 1977.

The son of a teacher and school superintendent, David Mathews was born and raised in Clarke County, Ala. He graduated from the University of Alabama in 1958 with a B.A. in history and the following year earned an M.A. In 1965 he received a doctorate in education from Columbia University. Mathews then returned to the University of Alabama, and after rising quickly through the administrative ranks, he was appointed president of the University in 1969.

Mathews instituted innovative programs to involve students in local affairs, including the College of Community Health Services, designed to improve rural health care, and the Law Center, a research group formulated to investigate public policy matters. He was also responsible for progressive curriculum changes, an adult education program and an "experimental university" of independent study and work-study programs. President Ford nominated Mathews to be Secretary of Health, Education and Welfare (HEW) in June 1975.

A major task facing Mathews was to curtail the steady rise in HEW's health care budget, much of which was attributed to fraud and mismanagement particularly in the medicaid program. In September the new Secretary announced a review of hospital procedures in 11 states and the District of Columbia to determine possible violations of federal rules designed to ensure that the government paid only for the care needed by medicaid patients. Reports submitted by the Joint Commission on Accreditation of Hospitals revealed that two out of three hospitals in those areas did not meet federal standards for reimbursement under medicaid. Because of an agreement with the Commission to keep the reports confidential, Mathews withheld this information from a House subcommittee looking into the matter until the panel subpoenaed the reports in November. Mathews then turned the material over to the House.

At the end of 1975 Mathews reported the formation of a new criminal investigation unit to identify medicaid fraud and abuse, which was resulting in the loss of an estimated $750 million a year. Criticism of the program mounted in January 1976 when a report by a House Govern-

ment Operations subcommittee charged that HEW's fraud detection resources were "ridiculously inadequate." Two months later Mathews outlined a new campaign that would combine an expanded force of HEW investigators with state officials focusing on criminal violations by nursing homes, clinical laboratories, pharmacists and doctors receiving medicaid funds.

But the dimensions of the problem grew even more serious with the release of another report in August by the Senate Subcommittee on Long-term Care, chaired by Sen. Frank Moss (D, Utah) [q.v.]. The report, based on a four-month investigation, concluded that "rampant" fraud and abuse together with "abysmal" administration were costing the government from one-quarter to one-half of the $15 billion a year spent on medicaid. During the investigation Moss and six Senate aides posing as patients visited numerous "medicaid mills," clinics in low-income areas providing various services, where doctors had authorized unwarranted tests, written needless prescriptions and made referrals to specialists solely to inflate charges paid for by the program. The Moss report recommended either a complete federal takeover of medicaid or a cutback in funding.

Mathews accused Moss of "grandstanding" and claimed HEW was well ahead of the Senator in identifying and resolving the problems. Nevertheless on Oct. 15 President Ford signed a bill creating an inspector general's office in HEW to investigate abuses and mismanagement in the Department's health care programs. The bill gave the inspector general the authority to issue subpoenas, use nondepartmental auditors and send reports to Congress without prior clearance from the Department.

In early spring 1976 Mathews began President Ford's plan to vaccinate the entire population against a serious new virus called swine flu. When manufacturers of the vaccine were unable to obtain liability insurance, Mathews attempted unsuccessfully to mediate the dispute. Congress intervened to settle the dispute in

August by passing legislation that made the government responsible for all suits resulting from the vaccination drive. In mid-December, after almost 40 million people had been immunized, the program was halted because of reports that several people had contracted a rare form of paralysis, known as Guillian-Barre syndrome, within three weeks of receiving the vaccine.

Mathews instituted new procedures at HEW to give interested parties the opportunity to express their views on issues before important regulations were written, rather than after they had been published, as in the past. HEW employees who wrote new regulations were required to take special English courses aimed at making bureaucratic language more understandable. From the time a proposed regulation first appeared in the Federal Register, the public was given 90 to 135 days to comment before the final version of the rule was printed.

Mathews returned to his former post as president of the University of Alabama in January 1977, following the inauguration of Jimmy Carter [q.v.] into the White House.

[JR]

MATHIAS, CHARLES McC(URDY)
b. July 24, 1922; Frederick, Md.
Republican Senator, Md., 1969-.

Mathias, the son of an attorney, served in the Navy during World War II. He received a bachelors degree from Haverford College in 1944 and a law degree from the University of Maryland in 1949. Mathias served in various local legal posts until 1958, when he won election to the Maryland House of Delegates. Two years later he was elected to the U. S. House of Representatives from the sixth congressional district, which included wealthy Washington suburbs as well as Maryland's poor western counties.

As a member of the House, Mathias exhibited great concern for the political interests and social welfare of the residents of the District of Columbia and was known as a firm supporter of civil rights. Mathias won election to the Senate in 1968 on an anti-war platform. [See KENNEDY, JOHNSON Volumes]

Mathias was not close to the Nixon Administration. At the 1968 Republican Presidential Convention. he was part of a liberal attempt to prevent the nomination of Spiro Agnew [q.v.] and to choose instead John Lindsay [q.v.] for Vice President. After the first few months of his Administration, Nixon allegedly ranked Mathias with fellow Republican Sen. Mark Hatfield of Oregon [q.v.], Charles Goodell of New York [q.v.] and Charles Percy of Illinois [q.v.] as men who attacked him personally and opposed an inordinate amount of his policies. Although Mathias had voted against the Carswell nomination to the Supreme Court and for busing and gun-control legislation, his record also showed him voting for the Rehnquist Supreme Court nomination, against the Consumer Protection Agency (he later changed his position and voted for it), for the SST and against cuts in the oil depletion allowance. Later he was to vote for the Equal Rights Amendment and against judicial review of the environmental aspects of the Alaska oil pipeline. Despite his disagreement with many of the President's policies and his open criticism of the "Southern Strategy," Mathias campaigned for Nixon's reelection in 1972.

Conflict was greatest between the Administration and Mathias over Vietnam and national defense policies. The Senator voted against the anti-ballistic missile and for numerous other cuts in defense spending. In the same year, he cosponsored with Senators Humphrey (D, Minn.) [q.v.] Javits (R, N. Y.) [q.v.], and Stevenson (D, Ill.) [q.v.] a resolution prodding the Nixon Administration to negotiate with NATO allies and the Soviet Union on mutual troop reductions in Europe. This was rejected 73-24. Mathias supported both the Cooper-Church and McGovern-Hatfield amendments to set withdrawal dates for U. S. troops in Southeast Asia. During the debate over the McGovern-Hatfield amendment, he called for the repeal of the Gulf of Tonkin Resolution, which Lyndon Johnson had used as his authority for escalating the war.

In the Senate Mathias pressed forward with several proposals to reform the traditional power base of Congress. In early 1971 he and Oklahoma Democratic Sen. Fred Harris [q.v.] led an unsuccessful move to scrap the seniority system. They sought to amend Senate Rule 24 to require that committee chairmen and the ranking minority members be nominated individually by majority vote of the party caucuses and elected individually by the majority vote of the full Senate. The proposed changes were tabled by the Senate.

In 1973 Mathias sponsored a legislative package to strengthen campaign finance laws, provide matching federal campaign funding and include the creation of a Federal Elections Commission. Many of his suggestions became law the following year.

Senator Mathias was cochairman, with Democratic Sen. Frank Church of Idaho [q.v.] of the Special Senate Committee on the Termination of National Emergency, which was prompted by the existence of legislation giving the President wide emergency powers that had been on the books since the early days of Franklin Roosevelt's Administration. A National Emergencies Act, approved by the Senate in 1974, was the result of the Committee's work. Many of the standby powers granted the President were revoked, and a process of periodic congressional review following declarations of emergency was created.

Mathias was reelected to a second term in 1974 by 57% over liberal Baltimore Councilwoman Barbara Mikulski. Angered at the prospect of having only two conservative Republican candidates, Gerald Ford and Ronald Reagan [q.v.], to choose from in 1976, Mathias made several public motions to run for President but withdrew out of fear that his candidacy would simply rebound to the benefit of the more conservative Reagan.

[GWB]

MEANS, RUSSELL C(HARLES)
b. 1940.
American Indian activist.

Of mixed white-Indian parentage, Means grew up in poverty in California. He attended California public schools and spent his summers with his grandparents, who were Sioux Indians, on the Pine Ridge reservation in South Dakota where they lived. Trained as an accountant Means spent two years as an alcoholic on skid row in Los Angeles. The rising militance of many American Indians in the late 1960s provided a motive for his rehabilitation. He joined the American Indian Movement (AIM), a radical organization founded in 1968 by Dennis Banks and Clyde Bellecourt, and became director of the American Indian Center in Cleveland, Ohio.

In November 1972 Means participated in the week-long occupation of the offices of the Bureau of Indian Affairs (BIA) in Washington, D.C. The occupation occurred after several hundred Indians marched cross-country to dramatize their grievances against the government's Indian policies. Before leaving the BIA offices, the occupiers seized files filled with "incriminating" documents.

Means was one of the leaders of the 71-day armed occupation in 1973 of Wounded Knee, a village in the South Dakota Pine Ridge reservation. Means and Dennis Banks, another AIM leader, demanded a Senate investigation of Indian treaties and the ouster of Richard Wilson, the elected tribal chief of the Oglala Sioux. On March 12 Means announced that the occupiers had "seceded" from the U.S. and would treat U.S. officials as foreign agents. With the aid of their lawyer, William Kunstler [q.v.], Means and Banks negotiated a cease-fire and went to Washington for talks with government officials. The cease-fire broke down, however, and two Indians were killed on April 27.

After the occupation ended in May, Means and Banks were indicted on charges of conspiracy, assault and theft. The trial began in St. Paul, Minn., in February 1974 and ended abruptly in September when Judge Fred J. Nichol dismissed all charges. Nichol accused the prosecutor of deceiving the court, suppressing documents, and lying about evidence and said that the FBI had "stooped to a new low" in its tactics. It was later revealed that Douglas Durham, who coordinated the Wounded Knee legal defense committee and who attended many legal strategy meetings, was a paid informant for the FBI.

In March 1975 Means was indicted for a murder that occurred during a barroom brawl in Scenic, S.D. His attorney, William Kunstler, subpoenaed FBI director Clarence Kelley [q.v.] as a defense witness in order to prove FBI harassment of Means and other AIM leaders. Kunstler argued that the government had created a climate of fear that caused Indians to arm themselves in self-defense. On Aug. 6, 1976, a jury acquitted Means of the murder charge.

[JD]

MEANY, GEORGE
b. Aug. 16, 1894; New York, N.Y.
President, AFL-CIO, 1955- .

The son of an Irish Catholic plumber and union official, George Meany entered his father's trade at the age of 16. In 1922 he began his own union career as business agent of the Plumbers Union local 463, which included the Bronx and Manhattan. From there Meany moved into the hierarchy of the American Federation of Labor (AFL), winning the posts of president of the New York state federation of labor in 1934 and secretary-treasurer of the national federation in 1940. Twelve years later he succeeded William Green as AFL president. [See TRUMAN Volume]

One of Meany's first important acts as head of the AFL was to negotiate a merger in 1955 with its longtime rival, the Congress of Industrial Organizations (CIO). Subsequently, he established virtually complete control over AFL-CIO decision-making on both domestic and foreign policy issues. Meany closely identified the

Federation both with the national Democratic Party and with the bipartisan anti-Communist foreign policy of the Cold War era. The Great Society programs of the Johnson Administration, in particular, won his enthusiastic support, and he strongly endorsed U.S. military intervention in Vietnam. Following President Johnson's decision not to run for reelection in 1968, Meany mobilized AFL-CIO resources on behalf of Vice President Hubert H. Humphrey's [q.v.] presidential candidacy. [See EISENHOWER, KENNEDY, JOHNSON Volumes]

Since the late 1950s Meany had been engaged in a feud with Walter Reuther [q.v.], head of the United Auto Workers (UAW) and of the AFL-CIO Industrial Union Department. Reuther continually criticized Meany's hard-line foreign policy posture and complained that the Federation lacked the dynamism and imagination needed to stimulate union growth. In early 1968 the UAW began to withhold its dues to the Federation, and as a result Meany suspended the 1.6-million-member union on May 16. Along with the independent International Brotherhood of Teamsters, the auto workers then formed the Alliance for Labor Action (ALA), which Meany's executive council promptly denounced as a "dual labor organization, rival to the AFL-CIO."

The split in AFL-CIO ranks was widened at the Federation's convention in October 1969, when the delegates voted to expel the Chemical Workers Union for having affiliated with the ALA. In April Meany's staff issued a report on the dispute with the UAW that condemned Reuther for having waged a "two-year campaign of public vilification" and for having refused to resolve the conflict within the "forums of the trade union movement." Meany insisted that the Federation would continue to organize the unorganized and to fight for social justice and civil rights.

Despite a long-standing personal and political antipathy to Richard Nixon, Meany's relations with the Nixon White House were marked by an ambivalence that puzzled many observers. As he took office in 1969 it seemed possible that the President might win the labor leader's confidence as a result of his aggressive Vietnam policy and his tough stand against the anti-war movement. However, after the economy began to slide into a recession late in the year, Meany criticized the Administration's failure to act forcefully to stem the slowdown. Alarmed by the simultaneous rise of unemployment and consumer prices, Meany proposed a variety of countermeasures, including credit rationing by the Federal Reserve and mandatory investment of tax-exempt funds in government-backed mortgages.

When Nixon inaugurated his new economic policy with the announcement on Aug. 15, 1971, of a 90-day wage-price freeze, Meany denounced the President's program as "patently discriminatory" against workers. While union contracts were "highly visible" and thus easy to control, he argued, the Administration had failed to establish effective machinery for regulating prices and had exempted entirely corporate profits and stockholders' dividends. Meany warned that labor would not cooperate with the freeze, and he urged unions to cancel their contracts with employers if negotiated benefits were withheld.

As consideration of the post-freeze "Phase Two" period began, Meany called on the Administration to create an independent, tripartite control board. Nixon accepted the proposal, and, after receiving assurances that the panel would have real authority, Meany agreed to serve on it as one of five labor members. When Phase Two began in mid-November, however, Meany and the other union representatives on the Pay Board immediately found themselves at odds with the business and public members over the question of implementing existing contracts. On Nov. 18, at the AFL-CIO convention in Bal Harbour, Fla., Meany bitterly attacked the Pay Board's decision not to grant retroactive payment of wage increases cancelled during the freeze and charged that the Administration was trying to destroy collective bargaining. Making a last-

minute appearance at the convention on the following day, the President received a pointedly cool reception. After his speech, in which he vowed to pursue his program even if labor refused to cooperate, Nixon's attempt to greet the delegates was cut short when Meany abruptly called the meeting to order. Later, White House aides publicly criticized Meany's "discourteous" treatment of the Chief Executive. Treasury Secretary John B. Connally [q.v.] called the labor leader boorish and arrogant.

In March 1972 the Pay Board majority voted to reduce a wage settlement won by the International Longshoremen's and Warehousemen's Union (ILWU) after a lengthy strike on the West Coast docks. Meany and three of the other labor members promptly resigned from the panel (Teamsters president Frank Fitzsimmons [q.v.] refused to join the four). In its statement announcing the withdrawal, the AFL-CIO indicated its dissatisfaction not only with the ILWU decision, but also with the whole trend of Administration pay and price policy.

The 1972 presidential campaign brought a measure of reconciliation between Meany and the Nixon Administration. At the beginning of the year the AFL-CIO Committee on Political Education (COPE) stated that labor's chief political goal would be the defeat of Nixon's reelection bid. COPE strongly opposed Sen. George McGovern's (D, S.D.) [q.v.] anti-war candidacy, however. Months before the Democratic National Convention Meany let it be known that Sen. Henry Jackson (D, Wash.) [q.v.], a firm supporter of the war in Southeast Asia and a leading critic of U.S.-Soviet detente, was his personal preference. The Federation provided a speech-writer for Jackson during the primary campaign, and at the convention he was nominated by Steelworkers president I.W. Abel [q.v.], a close ally of Meany's. After McGovern won the nomination, Meany announced on July 19 that the AFL-CIO executive council had voted to withhold endorsement from the Democratic candidate for the first time in its history, adding that personally he would not vote for either Nixon or McGovern.

Some of the Federation's major affiliates, as well as some state labor councils later defied Meany by endorsing McGovern. But the Federation's "neutrality" was an expression of the fact that the Republicans had won more labor support, whether open or tacit, in 1972 than at any time since the beginning of the New Deal. Throughout the campaign Meany criticized McGovern's position on the Vietnam war as a policy of "surrender," and in a post-election interview the South Dakota senator called Meany one of the "wreckers" of the Democratic Party.

In November Peter J. Brennan [q.v.], a building trades official, was nominated as Secretary of Labor after first receiving clearance from Meany. On Dec. 16 Meany rejoined the President's economic administration as a member of the Productivity Commission, and in January of the following year he became a member of the Cost of Living Council. Nixon's decision to drop most mandatory wage-price controls during Phase Three was reported by *The New York Times* to have been influenced by Meany's talks with Secretary of the Treasury George Shultz [q.v.].

Meany's rapproachement with the Administration proved short-lived, however. By April 1973 he was once again scoring the White House on a variety of issues, ranging from unemployment compensation to trade policy. In September Meany assailed the President's veto of an AFL-CIO-backed minimum wage bill as "a callous, cruel blow" to the nation's working poor. The bill would have extended coverage to public employees and to domestics. A long-standing tradition was broken in October when the Federation did not invite the President to address its national convention.

After Nixon's resignation, Meany continued to blast away at the Republican Administration for its failure to spur the economy. As the recession deepened in 1974, he called on Congress to lower interest rates, impose mandatory allocation of credit to priority needs, initiate large-scale public service projects, curb the ex-

port of scarce commodities, and take action to spur housing construction. At the same time, the Federation opposed reintroducing wage-price controls unless they were applied equitably to prices, dividends, and profits, as well as wages. Meany bitterly denounced President Ford's repeated vetoes of job-creating projects voted by Congress.

Early in 1976 Meany indicated that he prefered to see either Humphrey or Jackson as the Democratic presidential nominee. He took little direct part in the political campaigns of that year, however. After the election of Jimmy Carter, Meany's relations with the White House were distinctly strained.

[TLH]

For further information:
Joseph C. Goulden, *Meany* (New York, 1972).

METCALF, LEE
b. Jan. 28, 1911; Stevensville, Mont.
d. Jan. 12, 1978; Helena, Mont.
Democratic Senator, Mont., 1961-78.

The son of a bank cashier, Lee Metcalf obtained his B.A. degree from Stanford and his law degree from the Law School of Montana State University in 1936. That same year he was elected to the Montana State House of Representatives. In 1937 Metcalf was named an assistant attorney general in the state. Following service in the Army during World War II, he was elected an associated justice of the Montana Supreme Court. From 1953 to 1961 he represented Montana in the U.S. House of Representatives, where he was a major supporter of conservation measures. During this period Metcalf earned a reputation as one of the "Young Turks," an alliance of liberals pushing for progressive social legislation and reform of congressional procedures. Elected to the Senate in 1960, Metcalf supported most Kennedy and Johnson Administration domestic programs. In 1967 the Senator, who was a severe critic of private utilities and their rate structures, wrote a book entitled *Overcharge* that assailed the activities of the power companies. [See EISENHOWER, KENNEDY, JOHNSON Volumes]

During the Nixon-Ford years Metcalf maintained his record as a strong supporter of conservation and consumer legislation. A liberal on most domestic and foreign issues, Metcalf received a 95 rating from the liberal Americans for Democratic Action (ADA) in 1974. During the Nixon years he opposed the Administration's defense and foreign policy, voting against deployment of the Safeguard anti-ballistic missile and excessive defense spending. He voted for U.S. troop reduction abroad, foreign aid, busing and the establishment of a consumer protection agency. A critic of the Vietnam war, Metcalf voted against funding the conflict and supported measures such as the Cooper-Church Amendment designed to limit the President's power to carry out the war. He also voted against extension of the draft. During the Mayday demonstrations in Washington in 1971, Metcalf compared the tactics used by the D.C. police with those employed by the Nazis.

In domestic issues Metcalf cast the lone vote in 1970 against the Administration-backed omnibus crime bill, saying that he considered "the wrong way to curb crime to take away the basic rights of individuals." That same year he cosponsored a measure to establish national health insurance. He backed the formation of a consumer protection administration and maintained strong support of conservation legislation. Metcalf also urged congressional and bureaucratic reform and continued his interest in education. In the 1970s he attempted to free the independent regulatory agencies from White House budgetary control to limit the President's influence in policy decisions, but his efforts failed. He joined conservative Sam Ervin (D, S.C.) [q.v.] in opposing Nixon's impoundment policies.

Metcalf continued to campaign against public utilities in the Nixon years. During the early 1970s he repeatedly introduced a series of bills that would have established an independent agency to represent consumers in procedures involving regulatory agencies, to formulate methods of educating consumers about their rights and to develop model laws for regulation. Under the statute, companies would have had to submit detailed financial statements not only about corporate activities but also the activities and financial compensation of their chief officers. The measure was never reported out of committee.

Metcalf died in his apartment in Helena, Mont., in January 1978 after a long illness.

[GMS]

MEYER, CHARLES A(PPLETON)
b. June 27, 1918; Boston, Mass.
Assistant Secretary of State for Inter-American Affairs, March 1969–May 1973.

Meyer received a degree from Harvard in 1939 and joined Sears, Roebuck and Co. From 1939 to 1955 he was president of Sears Bogata and then was manager of foreign administration for the giant retail firm. President Nixon appointed him assistant secretary of state for inter-American affairs in March 1969.

Meyer entered the State Department during a period of change in U.S. policy toward Latin America. In July, Meyer announced termination of "additionality" regulations on foreign aid. Imposed in 1965 to aid the U.S. balance of payments situation, the regulations required any nation receiving Agency for International Development (AID) credit to agree to use the credit to buy U.S. goods or services that the country would not ordinarily have purchased in the U.S. The program had long been a source of contention between the U.S. and Latin American nations. Meyer also announced that Nixon was supporting a proposal to ease tariffs imposed on Latin products by industrialized countries and was pledging to support increased multilateralization of aid through international agencies.

In November 1969 Nixon announced his "new partnership" with Latin America. He adopted a posture of noninterference in the hemisphere, saying social and economic progress would henceforth depend less on the United States and more on initiatives by Latin Americans. He reiterated Meyer's statement that purchase requirements for AID funds would be dropped. He pledged that the Alliance for Progress would play a greater role in distributing aid funds. Nixon said that the U.S. would help but not direct, nurture but not dominate hemispheric development.

In 1971 the State Department had to defend its policy against critics who called it "benign neglect" and argued that its positions remained undefined. Meyer admitted that the Administration did not have a "Latin American policy" but insisted that it was because the infinite diversity of the nations in Central and South America precluded development of a single policy. Nixon's policy ran into further problems in August 1971 when the President announced a 90-day wage and price freeze in the U.S., a 10% hike in tariffs and a 10% reduction in foreign aid. Promised tariff preferences were abandoned, and when Latin American nations demanded they be exempt from the tariff surcharge, Meyer said no exceptions could be made. In November he reiterated the Administration's support for the "new partnership," even though America's own economic problems precluded implementation of some of the plans.

During Meyer's short tenure, he attempted, unsuccessfully, to negotiate an agreement with Ecuador covering U.S. fishing boat violations of that nation's 200-mile fishing limit. He also led efforts to work out a settlement following the nationalization of American interests by Chile's Marxist Allende government. During a 1973 probe by the Senate Foreign Relations Committee's Subcommittee on Multinationals into International Telephone and Telegraph's (ITT) role in the overthrow of the Allende government, Meyer testified that the Nixon Administration had a steadfast policy of nonintervention in Chile. William V. Broe, director of clandestine operations for the Central Intelligence Agency (CIA) in Lat-

in America, had testified that the CIA had worked with ITT to accelerate the economic deterioration of Chile in order to hasten the overthrow of the Allende government. In 1974 the staff of the Committee recommended a perjury investigation be initiated against Meyer, but no action was taken on the matter.

Meyer resigned from the State Department in May 1973. He joined the independent Committee on U.S.-Latin American Relations, a group of businessmen and scholars disturbed by Nixon's policies in Latin America. When Gerald Ford took office in August 1974, the group leveled harsh criticism at Nixon's policies and asked Ford to adopt a new posture. The panel urged Ford to work toward a restoration of human rights in Chile; called for an end to the Cuban trade embargo in effect since the 1960s; asked for a termination of all covert activities in Latin America; requested that more aid be given to poorer nations and sought a stop to retaliatory measures against nations that enforced the 200-mile fishing limit.

In addition to his work with the committee, Meyer returned to Sears, where he became vice president in charge of corporate planning.

[BO]

MILLER, GEORGE P(AUL)
b. Jan. 15, 1891; San Francisco, Calif.
Democratic Representative, Calif.,
1945–73; Chairman, Science and
Astronautic Committee, 1961–73.

Miller won election to the U.S. House of Representatives in 1944, where he represented a predominantly blue-collar suburban district. He compiled a moderately liberal voting record during the 1940s, 1950s and 1960s. Interested in scientific affairs he was a vigorous supporter of the U.S. space program and in 1961 became chairman of the Science and Astronautic Committee. He defended the program against critics who opposed large appropriations for the project and who denounced efforts to go to the moon while the nation was struggling with severe problems on earth. [See KENNEDY, JOHNSON Volumes]

During the Nixon Administration, Miller attempted to maintain spending levels for the space program in the face of growing criticism over the failure of the program to hold the nation's attention following the U.S. landing on the moon in 1969. He maintained that research behind the space program had improved the quality of life in such areas as transportation, medicine, energy production and communications. Miller warned that only by continued growth and exploration could the wealth of the U.S. grow and the problems of the nation be solved.

Miller used his power to push large appropriations through the House, but they were frequently cut in the Senate. Despite his efforts, Miller was unable to prevent cuts in spending for 1969 and 1970. He did, however, win funding for Skylab and the space shuttle. In 1971 he pushed through the House a funding measure substantially in excess of the Administration's request, including more money for space flight operations and nuclear power and propulsion programs.

Through the Nixon years Miller continued his moderate record and strong support of labor. He voted for the Safeguard anti-ballistic missile, the SST, the 18-year-old vote, family assistance and "no-knock" entry legislation. Miller opposed the end-the-war amendments of the period.

In 1972, Miller, at the age of 81, was the oldest member of his state's delegation. Political commentators expected him to win reelection easily. He also expected to win and did little campaigning, remaining in Washington. He was defeated by Fortney H. Stark, a 40-year-old banker, peace activist and former board member of Common Cause who opposed increased military spending and space appropriations.

[DBH]

MILLER, JACK (RICHARD)
b. June 6, 1916; Chicago, Ill.
Republican Senator, Iowa, 1961-73.

Miller received his A.B. from Creighton University in 1938 and his LL.B. from Columbia in 1946. He served in the Army Air Corps during World War II. After the war Miller practiced law in Sioux City and occasionally lectured on taxation law. Although largely unknown in the state despite six years in the Iowa Senate, Miller won a seat in the U.S. Senate in 1960. In the Senate, Miller was a moderate conservative, voting with the majority of his Republican colleagues on almost every issue during the 1960s. Throughout the Johnson years Miller was a consistent backer of the war in Vietnam and supported the expanded bombing of North Vietnam in 1968. At the August 1968 Republican National Convention, Miller strongly opposed the designation of Spiro T. Agnew [q.v.] for vice president. [See JOHNSON Volume]

Between 1969 and 1972 Miller steadfastly supported the Nixon Administration. Miller considered himself a "conservative in monetary and fiscal affairs" and a "liberal in the areas of education and human rights," but many Senate observers considered his record to be deliberately ambiguous. One Iowa farmers' organization said of him, "He votes to please when his vote is not needed, when he can afford it . . . not when needed." In 1971, for example, Miller voted against President Nixon's nominee for Secretary of Agriculture, Earl Butz [q.v.], because he was unpopular with Iowa farmers, yet he defended Butz's record strongly in committee.

On environmental issues Miller received a low rating of 35 from the League of Conservation Voters. He opposed aid to mass transit and favored an extension of the deadline for a reduction in auto emissions. He was, however, considered responsive to massive pressure and reversed his stand on the SST by voting against it in 1970. As a member of the Finance Committee, Miller was often criticized by fellow senators for paying too much attention to small details at the expense of a broader development of policy. Considered partial to business interests, he proposed a 1969 tax deduction for oil companies who "plowed back" their earnings into oil and gas explorations. The proposal, which would have had the same effect as a restoration of the 27.5% oil depletion allowance, was defeated.

Miller remained a supporter of the Vietnam war during the Nixon Administration. In 1970 he voiced strong support for the President's policy of Vietnamization as well as the entrance of troops into Cambodia. In 1970 he opposed the Cooper-Church anti-war amendment, which would have cut off all funds for the war after July 1, 1970, because he said it would restrict the President and could be used as Communist propaganda. He did, however, sponsor a resolution in 1971 calling for a total withdrawal of U.S. troops within one year after an exchange of POWs.

Up for reelection in 1972 Miller underrated his opposition and lost in a stunning upset. He was defeated by congressional aide Dick Clark, who chose to run only after his employer, Rep. John C. Culver (D, Iowa), had decided against what he thought would be a futile challenge to Miller's seat.

[FLM]

MILLS, WILBUR D(AIGH)
b. May 24, 1909; Kensett, Ark.
Democratic Representative, Ark.,
1939-77; Chairman, Ways and Means
Committee, 1957-74.

Mills won election to the House of Representatives in 1938, after having served as a county and probate judge. A protege of Speaker of the House Sam Rayburn (D, Tex.), he gained appointment under Rayburn's sponsorship to the Ways and Means Committee in 1943, an uncommonly swift ascension to the prestigious tax-writing Committee. Through exhaustive study and attention to the details of government finance and trade legislation,

Mills by the 1950s became the House's foremost tax expert. He assumed chairmanship of the Ways and Means Committee in 1957. That post and his expertise on tax legislation made Mills, according to some observers, "the most powerful man in Congress" during the 1960s. Mills played a prominent role in the passage of the Trade Expansion Act of 1962, which led to major tariff reductions between the United States and its trading partners. His opposition to medicare stalled that measure for years, until 1965 when Mills decided to support the proposal. [See TRUMAN, EISENHOWER, KENNEDY, JOHNSON Volumes]

Mills continued to be a major power in the House during the early Nixon Administration, although his domination was challenged both by liberals who resented his conservative fiscal policies and his control of the Ways and Means Committee and conservatives who opposed his support of spending for social welfare. A moderate, he urged budget cuts to prevent continued inflation but supported the extension of unemployment insurance and raises in Social Security payments to aid those affected by the economic problems of the period. He refused to support bills establishing a general debt limit and instead proposed setting specific ceilings on individual bills. Mills supported President Nixon's Family Assistance Plan, which would have given the poor a guaranteed income. Despite strong reservations, he believed it better than the existing Aid to Families with Dependent Children program, which he maintained promoted the breakup of families. He pushed for passage of the measure through the House in 1970, but the bill eventually died in the Senate. Mills also backed Nixon's practice of impounding funds allocated by Congress for federal programs, breaking with the Democratic leadership's position on this issue. He argued that the President had the constitutional authority to limit congressional spending for particular programs and urged the House to have faith in Nixon on this measure.

Mills played a prominent role in the

passage of the bill extending the Johnson Administration's income tax surcharge and in the formation of the Tax Reform Act of 1969. Shortly after his inauguration, Nixon formally asked Congress for a year's extension of the 10% surcharge, due to expire in June 1969, in an effort to fight inflation. Mills questioned the surcharge's effectiveness and suggested instead cutting the federal budget and implementing a tight money policy. Nevertheless he supported the measure, although ill health limited his role in committee deliberations on it. Liberals attempted to tie passage of the surtax to overall tax reform and threatened to block the bill until reform was discussed. But it won close passage in Ways and Means after provisions were added granting low-income individuals tax relief, postponing certain reductions in excise taxes and repealing a 7% tax credit for business investment.

On the House floor Mills campaigned hard for the surcharge bill, noting that a vote against the proposal was a vote for inflation. To convince liberals that the Administration would eventually propose broad tax reform, Nixon submitted reform proposals in April, and Mills promised to institute tax restructuring in all sectors. As was his usual practice, Mills got the surtax bill reported under a closed rule that permitted no changes in the measure after it went to the floor, thus forcing liberals to take a clear stand on the bill. The House passed it by five votes in May. The Senate approved it in July and it was signed into law in August 1969.

Throughout 1969 Mills held extensive hearings on tax reform and played a major role in molding the Tax Reform Act of 1969. In April, President Nixon introduced his own tax proposals, including repeal of the 7% business investment tax credit, exemption of the poor from federal income tax and a limit on tax preferences that would set a 50% ceiling on most income an individual could shield from taxation. Mills objected to a large number of the President's proposals, and the bill that finally won passage was written almost entirely by Congress. He opposed the limit on tax preferences because it merely restricted access to existing loopholes rather than actually closed them, but he supported the repeal of the 7% business investment tax credit. As passed, the Tax Reform Act provided for an increase in the personal income tax exemption by stages from $600 to $750; repealed the 7% excise tax for several manufacturing categories; lowered tax rates for single persons; provided a minimum standard deduction designed to remove over five million taxpayers from the tax rolls; placed a ceiling on the amount of individual capital gains eligible for low tax rates and raised capital gains taxes for corporations. It also tightened several loopholes. Despite Nixon's threats of a veto, he signed the bill in late December.

Mills was a vigorous opponent of the President's revenue-sharing proposals, aimed at giving federal funds to state and local governments for uses that they determined. He maintained that the governments that benefited from the monies should also be responsible for raising funds. However in 1972 he reversed his stand and announced he favored sharing that gave most benefits to urban areas and tied receipt of funds to the intent of local government taxing efforts. The final bill, passed in October, dropped Mills's emphasis on cities but tied funds to relative income and the extent of government taxing efforts.

Mills's power eroded in 1974 because of challenges by House reformers and his personal indiscretions. That year the House voted to force Mills to subdivide his Committee into four subcommittees with separate chairmen. In December the Democratic Caucus in the House took away from Ways and Means the power to assign all committee members and gave it to the Democratic Steering Committee, which consisted of House leaders and other influential Party members. The Caucus also voted to enlarge the Ways and Means Committee from 12 to 35 members—a move that allowed younger and more liberal representation.

Mills's decline in Congress owed much to his own behavior. Before 1974 Mills was one of the hardest working representatives in the House. He appeared to change considerably in the early 1970s. Reports circulated in 1974 that he was becoming a heavy drinker, and he was frequently seen in Washington, D.C., nightspots. Some people attributed his changed behavior to a difficult operation for a ruptured spinal disk in 1973. Still others explained it as a result of his ill-advised effort in 1971-72 to secure the Democratic nomination for the presidency.

In October 1974 Mills's car containing five passengers was stopped by Washington police. One of the passengers, Annabella Battistella, 38, leaped from the car and either fell or jumped into the Tidal Basin, an estuary of the Potomac River. The media revealed that Battistella was a striptease dancer in a Washington nightclub who performed under the name of Fanne Fox. Mills's career was severely damaged by the incident. Two months later he appeared for a few seconds on a Boston stage with the stripper, now billed as the "Tidal Basin Bombshell." Newspapers had a field day with the story and Mills's career was in effect ended. He checked himself into the Naval Medical Center in Bethesda, Md. House Speaker Carl Albert [q.v.] made it clear that the Steering Committee would not permit him to retain his chairmanship. Mills soon relinquished the post to Al Ullman (D, Ore.).

Mills served one more term as a member of the House before retiring from Congress in 1977. He later admitted his downfall was due to alcoholism.

[HML]

MILLETT, KATE
b. Sept. 14, 1934; St. Paul, Minn.
Author; feminist leader.

Millett was born and raised in St. Paul. Her father left home when she was 14 and her mother, a college graduate, worked for meager wages to support the family. Millett received a B.A. from the University of Minnesota in 1956. Two years later

she settled in New York City and took up painting and sculpture while working at odd jobs.

During the mid-1960s Millett became active in political causes. She was a member of CORE and took part in the civil rights and anti-war movements. But Millett's main focus soon became the nascent women's liberation movement. She joined the National Organization of Women (NOW) soon after its founding in 1966 and became head of its education committee.

In November 1968 Millett spoke before a women's liberation group at Cornell University where she delivered a paper titled "Sexual Politics." In it Millett argued that relationships between the sexes were political. The response to the paper was so positive that she decided to develop her ideas into a doctoral dissertation which was completed in March 1970 and published in book form as *Sexual Politics.*

In the book she contended that the current social order gave men "a birthright priority" and that "patriarchy," the system by which men governed women, constituted the "fundamental concept of power" in society and the "most pervasive ideology of our culture." *Sexual Politics* became an instant best-seller and catapulted Millett into the public spotlight. As the first major theoretical work of the burgeoning feminist movement, it found a wide audience and provided women liberationists with a coherent theory to buttress their demands for equality. The media seized upon Millett as a spokeswoman for the feminist movement and *Time* magazine featured her on the cover of its August 31, 1970 issue.

Millett, however, was attacked by those hostile to the new wave of feminism and became the center of controversy, particularly after her announcement in November 1970 that she was a lesbian. Although some feminists dissociated themselves from Millett and labeled the lesbian issue a "lavender herring," others rushed to her defense. On December 17, several prominent feminists, including Gloria Steinem [q.v.], Ti-Grace Atkinson, and Susan

Brownmiller, read a statement at a New York press conference in which they expressed their "solidarity with the struggle of homosexuals to attain their liberation." Thereafter, the oppression of lesbians remained a prominent issue in the women's movement. In June 1971 NOW's national convention passed a resolution pledging to fight discrimination based on sexual orientation.

Millett's quick rise from obscurity to media star took its toll. She experienced a serious depression and withdrew somewhat from political activity, devoting herself instead to her art and writing and to helping create a "feminist culture," which fused the personal and the political. In 1974 she published *Flying,* an autobiographical account of her activities in the women's movement. Three years later she wrote *Sita,* another autobiographical work about a love affair with a woman.

[JD]

For further information:
Sidney Abbott and Barbara Love, *Sappho Was a Right-On Woman* (New York, 1972).
Judith Hole and Ellen Levine, *Rebirth of Feminism* (New York, 1971).

MINK, PATSY (TAKEMOTO)
b. Dec. 6, 1927; Paia, Hawaii
Democratic Representative, Hawaii, 1965-77.

Patsy Takemoto graduated from the University of Honolulu in 1948 and received a law degree from the University of Chicago three years later. Mink served the Hawaii House of Representatives as house attorney in 1955 and in the following year became president of the Hawaii Young Democrats. She entered the state House of Representatives in 1956 and was voted into the Hawaiian Senate in 1958 and 1962. In 1964 Mink won a seat in the U.S. House.

While in Congress, Mink established a liberal record on both domestic and foreign affairs. She concentrated her attention on women's rights and education, with particular emphasis on the disabled

and minorities. During the last years of the Johnson Administration, Mink campaigned for federal funding of private and public nonprofit daycare centers. Her campaign culminated in the child development bill of 1971, which passed Congress but was vetoed by President Nixon. [See JOHNSON Volume]

Mink maintained her liberal record in Congress during the Nixon and Ford Administrations. In 1972 the liberal Americans for Democratic Action gave her a 100 rating. Mink voted for conservation legislation, busing, family assistance programs, federal aid for abortions and subsidies for mass transit while opposing much of the "law and order" legislation of the period. She continued as a champion of equality for women and urged the appointment of women to high policy-making positions in the Democratic Party. She opposed the nomination of conservative G. Harrold Carswell [*q.v.*] to the Supreme Court, maintaining that his confirmation would be "an affront to the women of America" because of his record on women's issues. In foreign and defense affairs, Mink opposed development of various weapons systems and backed foreign aid. An opponent of the Vietnam war after 1967, she supported the end-the-war resolutions of the period.

As a result of her liberal record and strong support of civil rights and equality for women, Mink was enticed by a group of Oregon Democrats to enter the 1972 presidential primary in that state. In announcing her candidacy, she said, "Without a woman contending for the Presidency, the concept of absolute equality will continue to be placed on the backburner as warmed-over lip service." In May she garnered only 2% of the vote.

Mink was a vigorous critic of President Nixon during the Watergate controversy. In 1973 she introduced a resolution that called for the impeachment of Nixon, charging his Administration with having created "a relentless decadence which had sapped the people's confidence in justice." "Stunned" by President Ford's pardon of Nixon in September 1974, Mink maintained, "I believe that not only was this action unprecedented but perhaps goes beyond the constitutional provisions with respect to executive authority."

In 1976 Mink waged an unsuccessful campaign for the Senate. She served as assistant secretary of state for oceans and international environment and scientific affairs in 1977 and 1978.

[SBB]

MITCHELL, CLARENCE M.
b. March 8, 1911; Baltimore, Md.
Director, Washington Bureau,
NAACP, 1950-78.

A graduate of Pennsylvania's Lincoln University in 1932, Mitchell spent his early career as a reporter. In 1936 he obtained the job of Executive Director of the Urban League in St. Paul. Mitchell began his career with the NAACP in 1946. While attending law school part time he was appointed to the post of labor secretary of the organization's Washington Bureau. He took over the directorship in 1950. Throughout the 1950s and 1960s Mitchell's ceaseless prodding contributed to congressional approval of the Civil Rights Act of 1957, the Voting Rights Act of 1965 and the 1968 open housing bill among others.

When the 1960s gave birth to highly visible black militant forces, Mitchell bitterly attacked the "hoodlums" who he felt endorsed violence as the only means to effect equality. He regarded black separatism as one of those "dangerous ideas" which must be counseled against. For Mitchell, the goal of the civil rights movement was to effectively integrate blacks into the mainstream of American life. [See KENNEDY, JOHNSON Volumes]

During the Nixon years Mitchell led the fight against the appointment of conservative judges Clement F. Haynsworth [q.v.] and G. Harrold Carswell [q.v.] to the Supreme Court. Mitchell then directed his efforts in 1970 to gaining congressional extension of the 1965 Voting Rights Act's ban on literacy tests. Despite Nixon's attempt to weaken some of the Act's provi-

sions such as the 18 year old vote amendment, the extension and provisions were signed into law.

With the confirmation of conservative Republican William H. Rehnquist [q.v.] to the Supreme Court in 1971, Mitchell lashed out at the Nixon Administration for its systematic efforts to undermine the achievements of the civil rights movement. When the President vetoed an extension of the anti-poverty program the same year, Mitchell decried the action as yet another example of the Administration's neglect of minority problems. Nixon's announcement in 1972 of his protracted approach to desegregation in public schools prompted Mitchell to condemn the President for his "cruel and savage attempts to use the power of federal government to bludgeon the courts into a surrender to mob rule."

Mitchell once again fought for extension of the Voting Rights Act which was approved in 1975. The following year Congress passed a resolution honoring Mitchell for "his contributions to the enhancement of life in America." Ford also commended the lobbyist extraordinaire for his efforts to eliminate injustices and institutional racism. Mitchell retired from the directorship of the NAACP in 1978.

[DGE]

MITCHELL, JOHN N(EWTON)
b. Sept. 15, 1913; Detroit, Mich.
Attorney General, January
1969–February 1972.

John Mitchell grew up in Long Island, N.Y. Although a Protestant, he attended college and law school at Fordham University, receiving his law degree in 1938. At the firm of Caldwell and Raymond he became an expert in the field of municipal bonds; he was made a partner in 1942. During World War II Mitchell commanded PT boat squadrons in the Pacific. After the war Mitchell returned to his firm, now Caldwell, Trimble, and Mitchell. As the firm prospered, Mitchell became a nationally recognized authority on public finance, a skilled intermediary between politicians seeking to finance projects and the financial community underwriting and selling the bonds. He pioneered in the use of devices such as the semiautonomous agency through which a state could borrow and build while evading its constitutional debt limitation. Mitchell played a key role in the financing of many of New York Gov. Nelson Rockefeller's [q.v.] grand construction projects.

In 1967 Mitchell's firm merged with that of former Vice President Richard M. Nixon to form Nixon, Mudge, Rose, Guthrie, Alexander & Mitchell. Nixon and Mitchell became close associates, frequently lunching and playing golf together. During Nixon's 1968 presidential campaign Mitchell played a role of growing dominance. Beginning as an adviser to his law partner, Mitchell then organized states for Nixon with a view toward the Republican Convention; he was named campaign manager in May. Many gave Mitchell credit for the smooth professionalism of the Nixon organization, in contrast with the candidate's previous electoral ventures. Nixon admired Mitchell's unflappable demeanor and decisive manner and trusted his pragmatic judgment. Mitchell was a staunch proponent of the so-called Southern Strategy, which sought to build for the Republicans a coalition of Southern and Western states by a conservative appeal heavy with "law-and-order" rhetoric.

During the campaign Mitchell had vociferously denied that he would accept a cabinet post in a Nixon Administration. Even after being named Attorney General by President-elect Nixon, Mitchell continued to protest that he had not wanted the job and would only stay two years. "This is the last thing in the world I wanted to do," he said. "I've got all the things I ever wanted. I'm a fat and prosperous Wall Street lawyer, which is just what I always wanted to be."

In his acceptance speech before the Republican Convention in August, Nixon had promised: "If we are going to restore order and respect for law in this country, there's one place we're going to begin. We're going to have a new Attorney Gen-

eral of the United States." During the campaign Nixon excoriated the liberal, reformist Attorney General Ramsey Clark [q.v.] for allegedly being "soft on crime." His selection of the conservative Mitchell as Attorney General was seen as a signal that the Administration intended to pursue a conspicuous hard line against crime, radicalism and civil disobedience.

Soon after taking office Mitchell stated that he differed from Clark in that he believed the Department of Justice was "an institution for law enforcement, not social improvement." In mid-1969 the Administration submitted its anti-crime package, which contained many elements also favored by former Administrations, such as federal court reform, an enlarged budget for legal aid and more job counseling for offenders on parole or probation. The most salient new feature was preventive detention, which would have allowed a federal judge in the District of Columbia to jail a defendant for up to 60 days before trial if the individual was charged with a serious offense and there was a "substantial probability" that he would be a danger to the community if released. Mitchell argued that the high crime rate among defendants out on bail made such legislation imperative. Civil libertarians strenuously opposed preventive detention as unconstitutional, arguing also that speedier trials, not pretrial detention, were the answer.

Other controversial parts of the bill would allow a federal judge to impose a life sentence on anyone convicted of three felonies and permit a police officer with a search warrant to enter a person's premises unannounced. The latter "no-knock" provision also aroused heated opposition. At the same time the Justice Department proposed a narcotics control bill to Congress somewhat more punitive than the existing laws.

Another departure from the Clark tenure was in the area of wiretapping. While his predecessor had refused to use the device except in national security cases, Mitchell pledged to exercise the full wiretapping authority contained in the 1968 omnibus anti-crime act. He loosened the restrictions under which the FBI and federal law enforcement officials could tap wires and targeted domestic radicals as well as organized crime.

Mitchell adopted a stern public stance against campus disturbances and civil disobedience. "When you get nihilists on campus," he said, "the thing to do is to get them into court." Against the advice of several career Justice Department lawyers, he approved the prosecution of the Chicago Seven, the radical activists whom the government accused of inciting the Chicago riots outside the Democratic National Convention in 1968. Mitchell also approved the conspiracy indictments against Daniel Ellsberg [q.v.] and the Harrisburg Seven and unsuccessfully sought to enjoin newspaper publication of the *Pentagon Papers.*

Mitchell often contended that anti-war demonstrations were inspired by Communists. In the aftermath of the mass Mayday anti-war protest in Washington, D.C., in May 1971, he charged that Communists and Communist sympathizers "have been part of the leadership and makeup of every mass demonstration." Mitchell also compared the Mayday protesters to Hitler's Brown Shirts and lauded the mass arrest tactics of the D.C. police, who locked up 13,400 demonstrators. "I hope that Washington's decisive opposition to mob force will set an example for other communities," he said. All the arrests were subsequently ruled unconstitutional.

The Nixon Administration's Southern Strategy was most apparent in the area of civil rights. In mid-1969 Mitchell announced that the Administration would not support an outright extension of the Voting Rights Act of 1965 but would propose its own modified version. The two most important revisions would have eliminated the 1965 law's requirement that states could not amend voting procedures without the Attorney General's approval and expanded the act's coverage beyond the seven Southern states to the entire country. Opponents of the Administration's bill argued that it represented a gutting of the 1965 law by en-

couraging the Southern states to institute delaying actions through the courts and by diluting enforcement efforts in the South through the extension of Justice Department jurisdiction to the entire nation. The bill's provisions, said Rep. William McCulloch (R, Ohio), "sweep broadly into those areas where the need is least and retreat from those areas where the need is greatest." In response to a group of black civil rights workers protesting the revision of the original act, Mitchell said, "You will be better advised to watch what we do instead of what we say." The House passed the Administration's version but the Senate did not, and the final measure enacted in 1970 extended the major features of the 1965 act for five years.

In addition to his duties as Attorney General, Mitchell exerted influence over a broad range of Administration policies through his position as President Nixon's foremost adviser. Mitchell worked closely with the National Security Council and the national intelligence apparatus. He sat on the Urban Affairs Council. Besides seeing the President once a day, Mitchell said in 1969: "We usually talk on the phone several more times. In the evening he frequently calls me at home." Mitchell oversaw the appointment process after Nixon's election and recommended the conservative Warren Burger [q.v.] to Nixon as chief justice. It was also on Mitchell's recommendation that Nixon nominated Clement Haynsworth [q.v.] and G. Harrold Carswell [q.v.] to the Supreme Court. Senate rejection of these nominations was embarrassing to Mitchell, but he still remained, in *Newsweek*'s words, "Mr. Nixon's political right arm—his chief domestic strategist, arm-twister and lightning rod, counselor and confidant on problems reaching across the full range of government."

In February 1972 Mitchell resigned as Attorney General to head Nixon's campaign for reelection. Mitchell's tenure as head of the Committee to Re-Elect the President (CREEP) was relatively quiet until June 17, when agents of the CREEP were arrested for breaking into the Watergate headquarters of the Democratic National Committee. Mitchell said on June 18 that none of those involved in the raid were "operating either on our behalf or with our consent." On July 1 Mitchell resigned as Nixon's campaign manager. He said that his wife Martha Mitchell [q.v.] had given him an ultimatum to give up either politics or her. "The happiness and welfare of my wife and daughter" must come first, Mitchell said.

Over the next two and a half years, Mitchell steadfastly reiterated—before FBI agents, grand jurors, reporters, Senate committees and a District of Columbia jury—that he had had no prior knowledge of or involvement in the Watergate break-in and took no part in the subsequent cover-up. Testifying before the Senate Watergate Committee on July 10-12, 1973, Mitchell emphatically repeated his denials and disputed the testimony of former aides Jeb Stuart Magruder [q.v.] and John Dean [q.v.], who had testified that Mitchell approved the break-in as part of an ambitious intelligence program to undermine the political opposition. Dean also testified that Mitchell had participated in arranging payment of hush money to the Watergate defendants.

Mitchell told the Committee that he had withheld information from Nixon in order to forestall an inquiry that might have exposed other "White House horror stories." These included the break-in at the office of Daniel Ellsberg's [q.v.] psychiatrist, the proposed firebombing of the Brookings Institution and the falsification of cables relating to the 1963 assassination of South Vietnamese President Ngo Dinh Diem.

In May 1973 Mitchell and former Secretary of Commerce Maurice Stans [q.v.] were indicted by a federal grand jury in New York for perjury and conspiracy to obstruct justice. The indictment charged that they had conspired to obstruct a Securities and Exchange Commission investigation into the mutual funds dealings of financier Robert Vesco [q.v.] in return for a secret $200,000 contribution by Vesco to the 1972 Nixon cam-paign. Both men pleaded not guilty. In April 1974 a federal jury acquitted the pair of all charges.

On March 1, 1974, Mitchell, with former Nixon aides H.R. Haldeman [q.v.], John Ehrlichman [q.v.], Charles Colson [q.v.], Gordon Strachan [q.v.], Robert Mardian [q.v.], and Kenneth Parkinson, was indicted for his role in the Watergate cover-up. Mitchell was charged with conspiracy to obstruct justice, commit perjury, and defraud the United States by manipulating the Central Intelligence Agency, the FBI and the Justice Department. Mitchell pleaded not guilty to all charges.

The trial took place during October-December 1974. The bulk of the case against Mitchell was contained in the White House tapes and in the detailed testimony of John Dean. Taking the stand in his own defense, Mitchell, adamantly denying any involvement in the criminal conspiracy, was subjected to a blistering cross-examination by prosecutor James Neal. On Jan. 1, 1975, the jury found Mitchell guilty of conspiracy, obstruction of justice and perjury. On Feb. 21 Judge John Sirica [q.v.] sentenced him to a prison term of two and a half to eight years. In July, Mitchell was disbarred in New York.

Over the next few years higher courts affirmed the convictions of Mitchell, Haldeman and Ehrlichman. In June 1977 Mitchell began serving his sentence at a minimum security prison in Montgomery, Alabama. He was the first U.S. Attorney General ever to serve a prison sentence. He was released on parole on Jan. 19, 1979, after serving 19 months. Of the 25 persons jailed in connection with Watergate, Mitchell was the last to be freed.

[TO]

For further information:
Richard Ben-Veniste and George Frampton, Jr., *Stonewall: The Legal Case against the Watergate Conspirators* (New York, 1977).
Richard Harris, *Justice: The Crisis of Law, Order and Freedom in America* (New York, 1970).
Milton Viorst, *Hustlers and Heroes* (New York, 1970).

MITCHELL, MARTHA (BEALL)
b. Sept. 2, 1918; Pine Bluff, Ark.
d. May 31, 1976; New York, N.Y.

Martha Elizabeth Beall was born on Sept. 2, 1918, in Pine Bluff, Ark. Her father was a cotton broker and her mother a teacher of clocution. Beall graduated from the University of Miami and moved to Mobile, Ala., where she taught school for a year.

During World War II she married Clyde W. Jennings, a businessman, with whom she had one son before their marriage ended in divorce. In 1954 she met John Mitchell [q.v.], a New York attorney at the time, and three years later they were married. She gave birth in 1962 to their only child together, a daughter, "Marty."

In January 1967 the Wall Street law firms of John Mitchell and Richard Nixon merged to form Nixon, Mudge, Rose, Guthrie, Alexander and Mitchell. During the following year the Mitchells and the Nixons became friendly, and Mitchell later accepted Nixon's offer to run his 1968 presidential campaign (after the first two campaign managers had resigned). In December 1968 the newly elected President Nixon appointed Mitchell Attorney General.

The Mitchells moved to Washington, D.C., and Martha Mitchell, an outspoken, willful Southern conservative, soon made it known that the traditional reserve and decorum expected of cabinet wives was not her style. She had strong, often vituperative opinions about many of the politically charged issues of the day, and she was not afraid to express them publicly. Among her favorite targets in 1969 and 1970 were anti-war protesters, whom she described as "very liberal Communists," and academics, whom she blamed in one interview for "all the troubles in this country." Even though her public statements were often politically embarrassing, during Nixon's first term John Mitchell and the President seemed more amused than threatened by her. Nixon once said he thought she was "spunky."

The tables began to turn, however, after Nixon's reelection in 1972. As before John Mitchell served as his campaign manager, but this time their success was soon marred by the Watergate scandal. In early 1973 evidence that John Mitchell was involved in the scandal began to surface. By March, Martha Mitchell was coming to his defense. In a phone call to *The New York Times* on March 31, she said somebody was trying to make her husband "the goat" for Watergate and she "was not going to let that happen." She phoned a United Press reporter to say that the Nixon Administration had turned "completely against my husband." In April she called the Associated Press to controvert the White House denial of a meeting between Nixon and her husband three days earlier.

On May 5 Martha Mitchell publicly demanded Nixon's resignation as the only way to "give credibility to the Republican Party and credibility to the United States." This time, however, John Mitchell disavowed his wife's comments. He told reporters it was "ridiculous" for anybody to take seriously her suggestion that Nixon resign, and he chided United Press for printing his wife's statements. But she was not to be silenced.

At a news conference on May 28 Martha Mitchell said she was convinced that her husband had been protecting the President. She also said the White House must bear "all the blame" for Watergate, and that if Nixon did not resign, he would be impeached. Two months later, angered by John Ehrlichman's [q.v.] testimony before the Senate Watergate Committee, she demanded to be heard by the Committee and accused Ehrlichman of being "arrogant, insolent and insipid." After being informed in September that her testimony was not wanted, she even accused the Committee members of protecting Nixon.

Throughout this period the strain on the Mitchells' marriage had grown more severe. In a United Press interview published Nov. 3, 1973, Martha Mitchell not only predicted that Nixon would have to quit and would "be out by April," but confirmed reports that her marriage "was over." In the final settlement John Mitchell retained custody of their daughter and Martha Mitchell was awarded $1,000 a week alimony. Although her public statements became less frequent and less vociferous after the divorce, she never dropped the contention that her husband had been "framed."

In October 1975 it was discovered she had a rare, terminal form of bone cancer. During her final months she sued John Mitchell for failure to keep up alimony payments. Then days before her death at the age of 57, she was awarded $36,000 in back alimony.

Martha Mitchell died in New York City on May 31, 1976.

[CP]

MONDALE, WALTER F(REDERICK)
b. Jan. 5, 1928; Ceylon, Minn.
Democratic Senator, Minn., 1965-77.

The son of a liberal church minister who was an admirer of Franklin Roosevelt, Walter Mondale graduated from the University of Minnesota in 1951 and served in the Army during the Korean War. While in college he worked in Hubert Humphrey's [q.v.] 1948 Senate campaign. He developed a close relationship with Humphrey which continued throughout his career. Following graduation from the University of Minnesota law school in 1956, Mondale joined the law firm of Gov. Orville Freeman, a Humphrey friend. Mondale ran Freeman's reelection campaign of 1958, and then served as special assistant to the state's attorney general. In 1960 Freeman appointed Mondale to complete the unexpired term of the resigning attorney general. In 1960 and 1962 Mondale won this office in his own right. When Hubert Humphrey became vice president in 1965, Mondale was appointed to complete his friend's term. In both 1966 and 1972, he won easy reelection victories.

Mondale compiled one of the most liberal records in the Senate. He supported President Johnson's Great Society legislation, voting for civil rights laws, the War on Poverty programs, and medicare. Although he originally voted for the appropriations for Vietnam, Mondale soon questioned the war for moral reasons because it diverted funds from social programs. Although he disagreed with Humphrey on the war policies, he helped manage his mentor's losing bid for the presidency in 1968. [See JOHNSON Volume]

During the Nixon-Ford years, Mondale emerged as one of the most powerful liberals in the Senate. He earned the highest ratings from the liberal Americans for Democratic Action. The farm lobby organizations also praised him for his work to help their constituency. The Mondale record included support for the continuation and expansion of anti-poverty programs in spite of Nixon and Ford vetoes. He voted for steeper corporate taxes especially for the oil companies, supported a national no-fault insurance program, and opposed the federal loan to bail out the Lockheed Corp. During the 1973-74 recession Mondale lobbied for public works programs and co-sponsored with Sen. Edward Kennedy (D, Mass.) [q.v.] a tax-cut for the middle and working class. Mondale also supported consumer and environmental legislation. In civil rights he voted against attempts to restrict the federal courts' power to force busing.

Mondale was a leading opponent of the Nixon and Ford's defense and foreign policies. He voted for the Cooper-Church and McGovern-Hatfield amendments, both designed to limit the President's freedom to carry on the Vietnam War. Mondale opposed the major defense spending programs such as the building of the B1 bomber, the Trident submarine, and the anti-ballistic missile system.

Although Mondale was considered a leading liberal activist, he often tended to compromise rather than fight for his goals. In tax and fiscal legislation, for example, Mondale frequently yielded to Sen. Russell B. Long (D, La.) [q.v.] the conservative chairman of the Senate Finance Committee. This refusal to fight to the bitter end for his programs played an important role in ending Mondale's abortive try for the 1976 Democratic presidential nomination. In late 1974 Mondale launched an exploratory campaign for the nomination. Throughout most of 1975 he toured the nation speaking at countless meetings and rallies, but he soon discovered that his public recognition level was still low. At a November 1975 news conference, Mondale withdrew his name from contention. He said, "I do not have the overwhelming desire to be President, which is essential for the kind of campaign that is required. I admire those with the determination to do what is required to seek the presidency, but I have found that I am not among them." In his book, *The Accountability of Power* (1976), Mondale reviewed his campaign, stressing how he resented the likelihood of having to be packaged by the media to be a viable candidate. He found this reduced the quality of campaigns and removed from the political process the most important reasons for running, namely the issues.

In July 1976 Jimmy Carter [*q.v.*], the Democratic presidential candidate, selected Mondale as his running mate. The former Georgia governor chose Mondale to win favor with the Northern liberals, led by Humphrey, who remained skeptical of Carter. In addition Carter found Mondale to be personally compatible, and he respected Mondale's grasp of the issues and his understanding of the workings of Congress. In the campaign Mondale blasted Gerald Ford's economic policies which he believed produced unemployment. He raised the issue of the Nixon pardon and condemned Henry Kissinger's [*q.v.*] diplomacy as secretive, counterproductive and immoral. In his historic debate with his rival, Sen. Robert Dole (R, Kan.) [*q.v.*], Mondale successfully maneuvered Dole to convey the image of a belligerent, insensitive conservative who ignored the needs of the common man. Pollsters believed Mondale's performance in this debate, as well as his anti-Ford campaign, helped Carter win the close victory. [See CARTER Volume]

[JB]

MONTOYA, JOSEPH
b. Sept. 24, 1915; Pena Blanca, N.M.
d. June 5, 1979; Washington, D.C.
Democratic Senator, N.M., 1965-77.

The son of a county sheriff, Montoya graduated from Georgetown University in 1938. He served in the state legislature and was lieutenant governor before being elected to the U.S. House of Representatives in 1957. He won a seat in the Senate in 1964. In the upper house Montoya supported the Johnson Administration's Great Society programs. He was especially concerned with poverty programs because his state had a high percentage of poor Mexican-Americans and Indians. But because New Mexico's wealthy, conservative landowners, livestock dealers and mining operators—known as "Little Texans"—were also a major political force, Montoya paid close attention to their needs as well. In foreign affairs Montoya was originally a supporter of the Vietnam war but broke with the Administration in 1967. [See JOHNSON Volume]

During the Nixon/Ford years, Montoya continued to press for legislation to assist the poor of his state. A strong defender of the Office of Economic Opportunity and the manpower training programs, Montoya supported increasing the minimum wage, extending unemployment insurance to migrant workers and establishing special programs to assist Spanish-speaking Americans and Indians. Montoya was the floor manager of the unsuccessful 1972 bill attempting to establish an Indian development commission. Montoya also proposed creating a cabinet-level commission on opportunities for Spanish-speaking peoples. Concerned with the elderly, Montoya cosponsored a bill that would have provided a 100% rebate for prescription drugs covered by medicare.

Montoya also lobbied for consumer interests. He joined in proposing legislation to insure truth in advertising, fair packaging and proper labeling of poisonous substances. Montoya introduced legislation to establish a consumer protection agency that would have been independent from the Department of Health, Education and

Welfare. On the Vietnam issue, Montoya voted for the Cooper-Church and McGovern-Hatfield Amendments to end the war.

The Administration targeted Montoya as one of the leading Democrats to defeat in 1970. Republican money and personnel assisted his conservative opponent, Anderson Carter, a wealthy cattle rancher and oilman who maintained that Montoya was ignoring the interests of the Little Texans. In the campaign Montoya stressed that he represented all of New Mexico's interests, not only those of the poor. When speaking to the state's conservative farmers, Montoya cited his record of opposing the reduction of a ceiling placed on price supports. He also reminded them that he had opposed the nomination of Earl Butz [q.v.], who, he asserted, was an enemy of the family farm. Montoya narrowly won the election with 52.3% of the vote.

Sen. Montoya was named to the Watergate panel in January 1973. During the early months of the probe, Montoya's skilled interrogation of John Dean [q.v.] and John Mitchell [q.v.] led to the development of evidence that President Nixon had known of the Watergate cover-up. As Nixon became increasingly embroiled in the controversy, Montoya managed a bill requiring the President to pay his own legal expenses. After Nixon's resignation, he opposed large government grants to help the former President through the transition.

Montoya died in Washington, D.C., in June 1979.

[JB]

MOORER, THOMAS H(INMAN)
b. Feb. 9, 1912; Mt. Willing, Ala.
Chief of Naval Operations, August 1967-July 1970; Chairman, Joint Chiefs of Staff, July 1970-July 1974.

Moorer graduated from the U.S. Naval Academy in 1933. After two years service as a gunnery officer, he took flight training and received his wings in July 1936. During World War II he saw action in both the Pacific and Atlantic theaters. After the war Moorer attended the Naval War College in Newport, R.I. He took command in 1962 of the Seventh Fleet. In June 1964 Moorer was made a full admiral and named commander in chief of the Pacific Fleet.

In April 1965 Moorer took charge of the allied naval command of the North Atlantic Treaty Organization (NATO). At the same time he became commander of all U.S. forces in the Atlantic. Later that month, with civil war erupting in the Dominican Republic, he directed the U.S. troops sent to the Caribbean nation to restore calm. U.S. forces under Moorer's supervision remained in the Dominican Republic until September.

Johnson appointed Moorer chief of naval operations in August 1967. In that role he served concomitantly as the Navy representative on the Joint Chiefs of Staff. Moorer strongly supported the Administration's Vietnam war effort. Testifying that summer before the Senate, he argued that only heavier bombing of North Vietnam would force it to the conference table. [See JOHNSON Volume]

President Nixon reappointed Moorer chief of naval operations in June 1969. To counter the growing presence of the Soviet Navy, Moorer worked for the modernization of aging U.S. naval forces and promoted the steady, yearly acquisition of new ships for the fleet. An advocate of the aircraft carrier as a crucial component of U.S. defense strategy throughout his career, he instituted the construction of a new phase of quiet, fast nuclear submarines. Pointing to the ongoing dramatic Soviet military buildup, Moorer warned that American indifference to the Soviet threat could lead to the U.S. being surpassed as a world power.

In April 1970 Nixon named Moorer to succeed Gen. Earle G. Wheeler [q.v.] as chairman of the Joint Chiefs of Staff. At the time the Nixon Administration was involved in ordering U.S. forces to attack Communist sanctuaries along the South Vietnamese border in Cambodia. Moorer helped direct the operation and participated in briefing Nixon on its progress at the end of May. In February 1971 Moorer backed the decision for the U.S. command in Vietnam to provide tactical support for the incursions by South Vietnamese troops into Laos to cut the Ho Chi Minh trail.

In keeping with the Nixon Administration's policy of winding down the war, by 1972 the American military presence in Vietnam stood at 69,000 servicemen. In April, North Vietnamese forces launched a major offensive against South Vietnam. Moorer agreed with Nixon's decision to resume bombing North Vietnam, and he orchestrated the mining of the harbors at Hanoi and Haiphong. He was given the responsibility for the military success of the B-52 bombing of the two cities ordered by Nixon in December 1972.

In his role as chairman of the Joint Chiefs, Moorer was one of the President's top assistants in matters of national security and foreign affairs. In September 1970 Moorer was among the high-level officials meeting informally to advise Nixon on the crisis in Jordan precipitated by the civil war between King Hussein and his army and Palestinian guerillas. In December of the following year, war broke out between India and Pakistan. After deliberation with his chief advisers, Nixon authorized Moorer to dispatch a task force of eight ships from Vietnam to the Bay of Bengal. While U.S. policy recognized the inevitability of an independent East Pakistan or Bangladesh, the Administration made the move to guarantee the defense of West Pakistan.

Moorer appeared before the House Armed Services Committee in March 1971 to express concern over the accelerated development of Soviet missiles. He reiterated his worry that the U.S. in five years could find itself "in a position of overall strategic inferiority." A year later Moorer told the same Committee that the emergence of China as a nuclear power meant that the U.S. had to reassess its military strategies regarding nuclear warfare.

Moorer told the Senate Armed Services Committee in June 1972 that he endorsed the first set of Strategic Arms Limitation Talks (SALT) accords so long as the U.S. continued to press forward with programs designed to protect its national security. He said the Joint Chiefs believed a number of assurances were needed to preserve U.S. security under the arms agreements. He identified them as: improvement in U.S. intelligence capabilities, continued modernization programs as allowed by the agreements, and a vigorous research and development program to maintain the U.S. lead in weapons technology.

Nixon reappointed Moorer to another two-year tour of duty as chairman of the Joint Chiefs in July 1972. In September Gen. John D. Lavelle [q.v.] told a Senate Armed Services Committee investigation that he had received permission from Moorer and Gen. Creighton W. Abrams [q.v.], commander of U.S. forces in Vietnam, for a series of unauthorized air raids against North Vietnam in late 1971 and early 1972. Both officers denied knowing that the raids violated the rules of engagement in effect at the time. The Committee later ruled that Lavelle had acted on his own without authority in ordering the raids.

The same Committee a year later cleared Moorer of charges that he had engaged in military spying on the White House. The Committee found that he was not involved in the unauthorized transfer of secret documents from the National Security Council to the Pentagon by two White House liaison officers in 1971. Moorer acknowledged receipt of the documents but thought that they had been sent to him through proper channels.

When the October 1973 Yom Kippur war broke out in the Mideast, Moorer took part in the decision to airlift U.S. military supplies to Israel. In response to the Soviet intention to intervene in the fighting, Moorer carried out Nixon's order to put all U.S. armed forces on a military alert. After the alert the Soviet Union, in diplomatic correspondence, withdrew its threat of intervention.

Moorer resigned as chairman of the Joint Chiefs in July 1974 and retired from the Navy. Nixon named Gen. George S.

Brown [q.v.] to succeed him. In retirement Moorer continued to speak out about the growth of the Soviet military.

[SF]

MORGAN, THOMAS E(LLSWORTH)
b. Oct. 13, 1906; Ellsworth, Pa.
Democratic Representative, Pa., 1945-77; Chairman, Committee on Foreign Affairs, 1958-77.

The son of a United Mine Workers organizer, Thomas Morgan grew up in Southwestern Pennsylvania, a region of coal mines and small steel mills whose workers of southern and eastern European descent voted Democratic and expected a pro-labor representative. Thomas "Doc" Morgan was a practicing physician and local Democratic leader when he was first elected to the U.S. House to represent the 22nd district in 1944.

Morgan believed in party loyalty and friendship with his constituency; he maintained a local medical practice, organized the Pennsylvania delegation to obtain more federal funds, compiled a strong pro-labor legislative record and won his next 15 elections easily. In 1958, because of his seniority, Morgan became Chairman of the House Foreign Affairs Committee. He believed that the threat of Communism in the postwar world and America's responsibility to her allies necessitated the search for bipartisanship in support of a foreign policy set by the executive branch. [See EISENHOWER, KENNEDY Volumes]

Despite the intensification of American involvement in Southeast Asia during the Johnson Administration, Morgan, in contrast to his Senate counterpart J. William Fulbright (D, Ark.) [q.v.], continued to believe that foreign policy was the domain of the executive branch and refused to hold hearings on Vietnam. His committee was to oversee the enactment and

efficient implementation of foreign economic and military assistance programs. But by 1967 Morgan was no longer able to keep those programs divorced from the mood of the country over Vietnam, and Congress passed the lowest foreign aid authorization in history. [See JOHNSON Volume]

Morgan changed somewhat with the political realities of the early 1970s. Disenchantment with the passive congressional role in the conduct of the Vietnam War was pervasive; it was a Republican Administration, and, most important, with the invasion of Cambodia in late April 1970, there seemed to be no end to the war in sight. In March 1971 Morgan told an interviewer that it was time for his committee to develop a more independent and aggressive foreign policy role, and he opened hearings. But Morgan was still searching for the middle ground, the bipartisan solution; he was not leading, but reacting. It was the second-ranking member of his Committee, Clement Zablocki (D, Wisc.) [q.v.], who engineered the passage of the War Powers Act in 1973.

When the House Democratic Caucus voted in May 1972 to order Morgan's Committee to report out a bill to "set a date" to end the war, Morgan reluctantly assented. But in June the panel reported a resolution in support of the Nixon Administration's withdrawal terms. In August, when it was clear that a resolution to set a date for the end of the war would pass, Morgan tried to push the deadline back or include an amendment which made withdrawal conditional upon the release of prisoners of war. Morgan did, however, vote with the majority in May 1973 to cut off funds for the bombing of Cambodia.

In 1974 Morgan, who was used to winning the Democratic primary with 60-70% of the vote, won with only 48% and announced that he would not run for reelection in 1976.

[JMP]

MORTON, ROGERS C(LARK) B(ALLARD)

b. Sept. 19, 1914; Louisville, Ky.
Republican Representative, Md.,
1963-70;
Chairman, Republican National
Committee, April 1969-November
1970; Secretary of the Interior,
January 1971-March 1975; Secretary
of Commerce, March 1975-January
1976.

A descendant of the American Revolutionary leader Gen. George Rogers Clark, Morton grew up in Kentucky, where his wealthy and prominent family had long been active in Republican politics. After graduating from Yale in 1937, Morton joined the family milling and flour processing firm. When the firm merged with the Pillsbury Co. in 1951, Morton became a vice president of Pillsbury and later director of its executive committee, a position he held until 1971.

In the early 1950s Morton moved his family to a large farm in Maryland. He was elected U.S. Representative from Maryland's predominantly Democratic first district in 1962. Morton was reelected to the House four times by considerable margins. His voting record reflected the conservativeness of his Maryland district and a strict adherence to Republican policies.

Morton served as Nixon's floor manager at the 1968 Republican National Convention and made the nominating speech for Spiro T. Agnew [q.v.], Nixon's choice for vice president. Shortly after his inauguration, President Nixon chose the voluble Morton to be chairman of the Republican National Committee (RNC). Morton kept his House seat and a spot on the powerful House Ways and Means Committee while serving as Party chairman without salary.

On April 14, 1969, Morton vowed to wage a campaign on behalf of President Nixon's proposal for a Safeguard anti-ballistic missile system (ABM). Morton's support of the ABM drew criticism both from Democrats and from Republicans who viewed his plan as a "loyalty test."

When President Nixon tacitly rebuked Morton at a press conference, the new RNC chairman backed down. He nevertheless continued to closely support the President's policies.

After a poor Republican showing in the 1970 elections, Morton resigned the RNC chairmanship. In late Nov. 1970 President Nixon designated him to replace Walter J. Hickel [q.v.] as Secretary of the Interior. Hickel, a former governor of Alaska, had become a concerned environmentalist and an outspoken opponent of Nixon's Vietnam policies. Nixon counted upon Morton, a good "team player," to support Administration policies. Despite his stated commitment to the environment, opponents pointed to Morton's past indifference to ecological issues and low rating by the League of Conservation Voters while in Congress. They feared his political background might make him soft on industrial polluters.

Although Morton made efforts to strengthen and consolidate the Interior Department and to deal with important environmental problems, he failed to establish coherent national energy and land use policies. The Administration ignored Morton's 1971 recommendation to establish a Department of Natural Resources. New Interior offices of conservation, energy data, and fuel allocation created by Morton were absorbed in 1973 by the Federal Energy Administration.

A major controversy during Morton's tenure at the Department centered on the proposed construction of an 800-mile oil pipeline across Alaska. Morton announced in early 1971 that he was "a long way" from approving the trans-Alaskan pipeline. He promised that the decision to build the pipeline would be determined by national energy needs and that possible environmental damage and the rights of native Alaskans would be considered. Environmentalists attempted to block approval of the Alaskan route with a series of environmental suits beginning in 1970.

In the spring of 1972, with the nation facing what he described as a "fuel and power crisis," Morton endorsed an increase in the price of natural gas to spur exploration for new gas supplies. He warned of the possible need for gasoline rationing as the U.S. depleted its oil reserves. Critics accused the Nixon Administration of deliberately developing an oil shortage to gain support for fuel price increases and to lessen opposition to the trans-Alaskan oil pipeline.

When Morton approved the Alaskan pipeline route in May 1972, environmental groups accused him of bowing to oil interests, which had reportedly invested more than $2 billion in the project, and continued to block work on the pipeline through legal maneuvers. A bill authorizing the pipeline's construction with appropriate environmental safeguards was approved by Congress on November 13, 1973. When Morton issued the long-awaited construction permit in January 1974, he commented that the project was the first required to comply with strict environmental and technical conditions.

Morton served as a Nixon spokesman during the 1972 presidential campaign. He charged Democratic presidential candidate Sen. George McGovern of South Dakota [q.v.] with a "lack of concern" for environmental issues and attacked McGovern's peace plan for Southeast Asia. Morton remained Secretary of the Interior through the beginning of Nixon's second term.

Following Nixon's resignation in August 1974, President Gerald R. Ford appointed Morton to a four-man committee to help oversee the Administration transition. A Ford ally since the early 1960s, Morton served as a top adviser to the new President on a variety of subjects. In late August 1974 Morton delivered Ford's first environmental policy message, stressing that the energy crisis had demonstrated the need for more coal mining, offshore oil exploration, oil shale development and nuclear power plant construction, despite possible environmental damage. Morton was named chairman of the new Energy Resources Council in 1974, a post he retained after his transfer from Interior to Secretary of Commerce in March 1975. The transfer took place amid speculation that as Commerce Secretary

Morton would be in a better position to solicit business support for Ford's 1976 reelection campaign.

As Secretary of Commerce Morton resisted the demands of the House Commerce Committee's subcommittee on investigations for a list of U.S. firms participating in the Arab boycott of Israel. Subcommittee members accused Morton of shielding private corporations that were violating U.S. policy and voted in November 1975 to cite him for contempt of Congress. On Dec. 8 Morton gave the subcommittee the list of U.S. firms who had reported being asked to participate in the Arab boycott. A proponent of detente Morton opposed the Trade Act of 1974, which denied "most favored nation" trade status to the Soviets until the easing of emigration restrictions on Jews. Morton advocated a return to President Nixon's 1972 trade agreement with the Soviets, calling for unconditional elimination of discriminatory trade restrictions on Soviet-bloc nations.

When Morton resigned as Commerce Secretary in January 1976, Ford designated him a cabinet-rank counselor to the President on economic and domestic policy matters. Morton served as Ford's campaign chairman prior to the 1976 Republican National Convention. Following Ford's nomination Morton became chairman of the Ford presidential campaign committee, but resigned a few weeks later to form a steering committee to promote Party unity. After Ford's defeat in November 1976, Morton returned to the private sector.

[DAE]

MOSS, FRANK E(DWARD)
b. Sept. 23, 1911; Holladay, Utah.
Democratic Senator, Utah, 1959-77.

Moss, a devout Mormon, received his law degree from George Washington University in 1937. He then worked for the Securities and Exchange Commission until 1940, when he won election as a Salt Lake City judge. Moss served as a judge advocate in the Army Air Corps during

World War II. After the war he became Salt Lake County attorney. A liberal with strong labor support, Moss won a Senate seat in 1958. In spite of Sen. Barry Goldwater's (R, Ariz.) [q.v.] strong showing in Utah, Moss was reelected in 1964 with 57% of the vote.

In the Senate, Moss served on the Interior and Insular Affairs Committee, paying special attention to Utah's critical problem of water use. He called throughout his first two terms for a federal department of natural resources to coordinate the chaotic federal and state bureaucracy that had jurisdiction over water. Moss was a supporter of the social programs of President Johnson's Great Society and also championed consumer legislation programs for the aged and conservation. Although he voted for appropriations for the war in Vietnam in 1966, Moss urged the President that year to continue the suspension of air attacks on the North. [See KENNEDY, JOHNSON Volumes]

Throughout 1969 Moss worked steadfastly for a total ban on cigarette advertising on television and radio and for a strong health warning on cigarette packages. He rejected a proposal by the National Association of Broadcasters to phase out advertising over a four-year period and rebuffed attempts to soften the label warning. He also called for the Federal Trade Commission to establish acceptable levels of tar and nicotine in cigarettes. Finally in March of 1970 a complete TV and radio ban and a strongly worded label warning were passed by Congress. Moss continued to urge, without success, an end to price supports for tobacco farmers.

Early in President Nixon's first term, Moss became a more vocal opponent of the Vietnam war. In 1969 he called for an end to all offensive action and the next year denounced the entrance of troops into Cambodia. In 1970 when Moss faced a difficult election, the Nixon Administration threw its weight behind his opponent, but he was able to win a third term with support from labor and anti-war groups. When Congress reconvened in 1971, Moss was elected secretary of the Democratic Conference, making him the Party's third ranking member in the Senate.

During his third term Moss fought, with intermittent success, for consumer legislation. In 1969 he introduced with Sen. Philip A. Hart (D, Mich.) [q.v.] a bill to set up an independent consumer protection agency. But it failed to pass in the Senate. Hearings were held on the proposal over the next several years until 1974 when it was filibustered to death. In 1970 he introduced and Congress passed a bill requiring special packaging of potentially dangerous household goods. In 1974 President Ford signed into law Moss's Consumer Product Warranty and Guaranty Act, which set federal guidelines and minimum standards for product warranties. Moss's efforts in 1974 and 1976 to push through a no-fault automobile insurance bill met with failure, which he blamed on intensive lobbying by the American Trial Lawyers Association.

Moss focused on the problems of the elderly in his position as chairman of the Long-Term Care Subcommittee of the Special Committee on Aging. Long an advocate of national health insurance and increased Social Security benefits, he led a 1975 probe into nursing home scandals. The next year he denounced doctor fraud in the medicare program, blaming judicial leniency and reluctance of the government to prosecute. In the course of his investigation into medicaid abuses, Moss personally visited several medicaid "mills" posing as a patient, and remarked: "If you're not sick, you won't be told you're not sick. If you are sick, the odds are you won't be helped."

Up for reelection in 1976 Moss was rated an underdog because Utah was considered solid for President Ford and because the state Democratic Party was in a shambles after Rep. Allan T. Howe's (D, Utah) arrest for soliciting a prostitute in Salt Lake City. Howe had ignored Moss's call for resignation. Moss was defeated, 54% to 45%, by Orrin G. Hatch, a conservative trial lawyer who had never turn for political office. Hatch had run an anti-Washington campaign calling for a reduced government role in everyday economic life.

[FLM]

MOTT, STEWART (RAWLINGS)
b. Dec. 4, 1937; Flint, Mich.
Political activist-philanthropist.

Mott, whose father was the largest shareholder in General Motors, enrolled at M.I.T. in 1955; he later transferred to Columbia, where he graduated in 1961. After a year of teaching during the 1963-64 term at Eastern Michigan University, Mott returned to Flint to become a part of his father's foundation, the Mott Foundation.

When Mott took over his trusts in 1966 at the age of 29, he decided to adopt the role of the politically active philanthropist instead of following the anonymous donor stereotype. He publicly backed such causes as ending the Vietnam war, birth control, sex research, abortion, arms control, feminism and liberal political reform. Early in 1968 Mott hoped to persuade New York Gov. Nelson Rockefeller [q.v.] to run on the Republican ticket as a peace candidate. Mott took out full-page ads in The New York Times promoting an anti-war Rockefeller candidacy. Rockefeller ignored the campaign and Mott soon dropped the project. After Lyndon Johnson dropped out of the Democratic race, Mott joined Sen. Eugene McCarthy's [q.v.] primary campaign, contributing approximately $210,000.

Prior to the 1972 presidential primaries, Mott founded People's Politics, a reform organization that distributed funds to various groups seeking to give women, blacks and youths more representation in the upcoming Democratic Convention. Mott contributed $5,000 apiece to John Lindsay [q.v.], Eugene McCarthy and George McGovern [q.v.] in their early primary bids. While unsure of whom to back, he was adamantly opposed to the candidacy of Maine's Sen. Edmund Muskie [q.v.]. He regarded Muskie's attitude on the war and abortion to be weak. Mott sponsored a series of newspaper ads severely criticizing Muskie for failing to reveal all of his campaign contributions. Because of the vigorousness of his anti-Muskie attack, Mott was questioned in 1973 by the Senate Watergate Committee investigating 1972 campaign "dirty tricks." He was cleared of wrongdoing, however.

When the Watergate scandals began to surface following President Nixon's reelection in 1972, Mott sponsored an investigation team to look into corrupt government activities. The project, under the direction of public interest lawyer William A. Dobrovir, investigated the ITT controversy, the dairy fund scandal and the financing of President Nixon's San Clemente retreat. In 1974 Dobrovir published a proimpeachment book, The Offenses of Richard M. Nixon, discussing the work of the project.

After 1974, Mott took a less prominent role in national politics.

[RN]

MOYNIHAN, DANIEL PATRICK
b. March 16, 1927; Tulsa, Okla.
Assistant to the President for Urban Affairs, January-November 1969;
Counsellor to the President, November 1969-December 1970;
U. S.Permanent Representative to the United Nations, 1975-76.

Raised in Manhattan under difficult financial conditions, Moynihan served in the Army during World War II and received a B.A. from Tufts University in 1948. He earned an M.A. from Tuft's Fletcher School of Law and Diplomacy in 1949. Later he did postgraduate work at the London School of Economics. During the 1950s he was assistant and later acting secretary to New York Gov. W. Averell Harriman [q.v.]. From 1958 to 1960 he was secretary of the public affairs committee of the New York State Democratic Party.

During the 1960 presidential campaign,

Moynihan wrote position papers on urban affairs for John F. Kennedy. After Kennedy's election Moynihan was appointed special assistant to the Secretary of Labor, and in March 1963 he was promoted to assistant secretary of labor for policy planning and research.

Moynihan became nationally known in March 1965 when he, Paul Barton, and Ellen Broderick released a Labor Department study called *The Negro Family: The Case for National Action.* Known as the Moynihan Report, this study suggested that the poverty and social problems experienced within the black community were fundamentally related to a deterioration of the black family. The report angered many civil rights leaders who felt that it came close to asserting that the black way of life in America was inherently debilitating. In June 1966 Moynihan was named director of the Harvard-Massachusetts Institute of Technology Joint Center for Urban Studies.

Because Moynihan was widely associated with the liberal wing of the Democratic Party, his colleagues were suprised when in December 1968 he accepted a position in the upcoming Nixon Administration as assistant to the President for urban affairs. He also served as the executive secretary of the cabinet-level Urban Affairs Council. Nixon had thought of appointing Moynihan as Secretary of Labor, but the idea was vetoed by George Meany [q.v.], who felt Moynihan did not have the necessary administrative experience.

Moynihan quickly became a Nixon favorite on the White House staff, able to spend long hours in private with the President, a privilege accorded to only a select few. Moynihan charmed the President with loyalty to the Administration and a witty, flamboyant speaking style. Moynihan's wry memorandums became a special pleasure for Nixon to read. During his first year at the White House, Moynihan had an important influence on the President, who adopted many of his proposals.

Most prominent among Nixon's domestic programs was welfare reform, of which Moynihan was the chief architect.

Moynihan's ideas on welfare reform had been enumerated in a 1967 background study on social welfare called *The Crisis in Welfare.* Moynihan endorsed a form of income maintenance that included childrens allowances–fixed sums of cash paid to families on welfare for each child. Moynihan stressed to Nixon the political importance of keeping continuity with Great Society programs. To disarm the liberal Democrats, Nixon needed to enact domestic reform. Moynihan convinced Nixon that as a conservative the President would be able to pass reform legislation that a liberal "wouldn't dare to propose" and suggested that reform could win him support of elements normally allied to the Democratic Party. He persuaded Nixon that substituting cash payments for bureaucratic services was a conservative idea.

On Feb. 2, 1969, Moynihan defended his plan on television: "I feel the problem of the poor people is they don't have enough money and I would sort of put my faith in any effort that put more resources into the hands of those that don't have them . . . Cold cash–it's a surprisingly good cure for a lot of social ills." Yet he had to admit that the American public was unlikely to accept the concept of family allowance payments. At an Aug. 6, 1969 cabinet meeting at Camp David, the President made it clear that after several months of cabinet debate, he had decided to back the welfare program Moynihan had been pushing. The President announced the new program, called the Family Assistance Program (FAP), during a televised national address on Aug. 9.

FAP left the House Ways and Means Committee in February 1970 in an almost unaltered form, and was passed by the House in April. But criticism and pressure from liberals and conservatives mounted and hope for passage of the bill through the Senate faded. In his *Memoirs* Nixon quotes Moynihan as writing in July 1970 that Republicans in the Senate were not resisting efforts to kill FAP and that "increasingly the Democrats see an opportunity to deny you this epic victory and at the same time blame you for the defeat." The Senate Finance Committee voted down the bill in November 1970. When the House again passed the FAP bill, it returned to the Finance Committee where it was stalled. By 1971 Nixon no longer believed in "the political timing" of the welfare-reform proposal, and in the face of the 1972 campaign election, he decided to drop support for the bill. It subsequently died in the Finance Committee as the 91st Congress ended.

Moynihan's influence declined after 1969, as John Ehrlichman [q.v.] took control of the Nixon staff and cut off easy access to the President. The Urban Affairs Council was dissolved, and Moynihan was reappointed to the new position of counsellor to the President with cabinet rank. But Moynihan thereafter became an insignificant factor in policymaking.

In March 1970 Moynihan was the object of a barrage of criticism when a memorandum he had sent to the President was leaked to the press. In the memo Moynihan offered a general assessment of the position of blacks at the end of the first year of the Administration "and of the decade in which their position [had] been the central domestic political issue." Moynihan wrote that "the time may have come when the issue of race could benefit from a period of benign neglect." He countered adverse criticism by contending that within its context the controversial phrase meant that outspoken Administration officials, such as Vice President Spiro T. Agnew [q.v.], should cease providing "opportunities for martyrdom, heroics, histrionics or whatever" to radicals, "hysterics, paranoids, and boodlers" on both ends of the political spectrum. He said he did not mean, as many critics claimed, to recommend neglect of the racial problems besetting the U.S.

At the end of 1970 Moynihan returned to a teaching post at Harvard. In 1973 he again left academia, accepting an appointment as ambassador to India, where he remained until May 1975, when President Gerald Ford named Moynihan as chief U.S. representative to the United Nations. Moynihan lost no time in establishing himself as a highly assertive and aggressive figure in the U.N. On Oct. 3 he denounced Uganda President Idi Amin as a "racist murderer" at an address to an AFL-CIO convention in San Francisco. After the U.N. General Assembly passed a resolution declaring Zionism "a form of racism and racial discrimination," Moynihan praised the countries who had voted against the resolution and denounced the Assembly's Social, Humanitarian and Cultural Committee, which had adopted the resolution, saying, "You have degraded this world organization." Drawing increasingly hostile criticism from Third World representatives, Moynihan said in December that the General Assembly was "becoming a theater of the absurd," adopting reports "riddled with untruths." After a highly publicized effort to break up an "anti-American" voting bloc at the U.N., which led to a conflict with the State Department, Moynihan resigned his post at the U.N. in February 1976 to return to Harvard in order to maintain his tenure. He won a seat in the U.S. Senate from New York in November 1976. [See CARTER Volume]

[MLB]

MUNDT, KARL E(RNST)
b. June 3, 1900; Humboldt, S.D.
d. Aug. 16, 1974; Washington, D.C.
Republican Senator, S.D., 1949-72.

Son of Dakota pioneers, Karl Mundt taught speech and sold real estate before his election to the U.S. House in 1938. A virulent anti-Communist, Mundt first achieved nationwide recognition in 1948 as acting chairman of the House Un-American Activities Committee investigation of Alger Hiss and as the cosponsor of legislation requiring the registration of Communist groups and their officers. Mundt was elected to the Senate in 1948. He chaired the Army-McCarthy hearings and later voted against the Senate censure of Sen. Joseph R. McCarthy (R, Wis.). In the early 1960s Mundt was among the first to call for controls on nuclear weapons. Although he staunchly reflected the conservative views of his home state, Mundt supported the farm subsidy, conservation and civil rights measures of the Johnson era. In 1967 he led Senate resistance to the ratification of the U.S.-Soviet treaty establishing new consulates on the grounds that the FBI's counter-espionage work would be hampered by the treaty's diplomatic immunity provisions. [See TRUMAN, EISENHOWER, KENNEDY, JOHNSON Volumes]

While he remained active, Mundt continued to be a firm supporter of the Vietnam war. In 1969 the Senate passed a nonbinding resolution expressing its opposition to the commitment of U.S. troops to foreign lands without congressional approval. Mundt introduced a substitute resolution making exceptions if the U.S. faced a direct attack or if American citizens or property were endangered, but critics said the measure contained too many loopholes and defeated it.

In 1969 Mundt suffered a debilitating stroke that left him partially paralyzed and prevented him from appearing in the Senate. Over the next two years he occasionally voted by proxy but refused to resign. Finally in 1972 the Senate, in the first major blow to the Old Guard and the rigid seniority system, voted to relieve Mundt of his posts as ranking Republican on the Government Operations Committee and second ranking member of the Foreign Relations and Appropriations Committees. Mundt died in Washington, D.C., in August 1974.

[FLM]

MUSKIE, EDMUND (SIXTUS)
b. March 28, 1914; Rumford, Me.
Democratic Senator, Me., 1959- .

The son of a Polish emigrant tailor, Muskie grew up in Rumford, Maine. He earned his B.A. degree at Bates College in 1936 and law degree at Cornell University in 1939. His law career was interrupted by naval service during World War II. After the war, Muskie served two terms in the state legislature before becoming

Maine's first Democratic governor in 1954. In 1958, Muskie became the first popularly elected Democratic Senator in the state's history. He was re-elected in 1964, 1970 and 1976.

During Kennedy's Administration, Muskie earned a reputation as an expert at formulating workable legislation and mobilizing support for it. Through the Johnson Administration, Muskie gained recognition for his support of environmental and Great Society programs. He received national prominence as the 1968 Democratic vice-presidential candidate. [See KENNEDY, JOHNSON Volumes]

Muskie continued to concentrate upon environmental issues during the 1970s. He was a driving force behind the National Air Quality Act which called for a pollution free automobile engine by 1985 and established National Air Quality Standards for 10 major contaminants. He criticized President Nixon's 1973 suspension of air pollution emission standards as an answer to the fuel shortage. The Maine legislator played a major role in the design and congressional passage of water quality acts in 1965 and 1966, and he continued this work after 1968. His Subcommittee on Air and Water Pollution was largely responsible for the 1970 Water Pollution Act which tightened controls on oil and sewage discharge by vessels and mines and established controls of thermal pollution from atomic power plants. Amendments to the Act in 1971 set standards to maintain the natural chemical, physical and biological integrity of the nation's waters and called for an end to discharging pollutants into navigable waters by 1985. He also introduced the 1971 Ocean Dumping Act which required permits from the Environmental Protection Agency for the dumping of toxic and non-toxic wastes in the oceans and Great Lakes. Muskie also advocated use of tax incentives to encourage industry to assume their responsibility for pollution control.

Muskie continued to support federal aid to education and increased Social Security benefits. He pressed for urban reform, pointing out that social disintegration caused by lack of jobs, poor education, housing and health care remained the fundamental needs of poverty stricken Americans. He called for an end to the supersonic transport system (SST), space exploration and atomic energy research and the utilization of those funds for the social benefit of the American poor. He introduced his own Revenue Sharing Act in 1971 and voted for that passed by Congress in 1972. He remained a champion of the small businessman and was a guiding force behind the 1970 Securities Investor Protection Act.

Following Sen. Edward M. Kennedy's (D, Mass.) [q.v.] accident on Chappaquiddick Island in July 1969, Muskie emerged as the frontrunner for the Democratic Party's 1972 presidential nomination, a position he maintained through 1971. He announced his candidacy officially on Jan. 4, 1972, attacking the Nixon Administration for continued inflation and high unemployment and charging the administration with ignoring the nation's social ills. After winning only two state primaries, but not convincingly, Muskie withdrew from the race in May 1972. Analysts explained that because Muskie was the Party's early frontrunner, his staff became overconfident and conducted a cautious and vague campaign. Also while his opponents selected primaries they were most likely to win, Muskie entered all, taxing him physically and financially. It was later learned that Muskie was also the focus of a "dirty-tricks" campaign instituted by the White House.

Muskie introduced the 1972 Truth in Government Act which created an independent board authorized to lift secrecy labels from government documents without damaging national security. Believing that a democracy works best when the people have all the information national security permits, Muskie voted for the 1974 changes in the Freedom of Information Act.

Government taxation and finance policies also concerned the Maine legislator. In February 1973, he introduced a bill to amend the tax code with respect to legis-lative activity by certain tax exempt organizations. That March he proposed legislation to reform state property taxes by relieving encumbrances upon the poor and elderly. He sponsored the 1973 Tax Reform Act which altered federal income, estate and gift tax laws, worked for the 1974 Congressional Budget and Impoundment Act and subsequently became chairman of the new Senate Budget Committee. In April 1975 he defended the Committee's $365 billion budget recommendations before the full Senate. Muskie justified the dollars for social services as indispensable, the defense cuts as necessary and projected a $70 billion deficit as essential to help weather the nation through its recession.

In the mid 1960s Muskie publicly supported the Administration's Vietnam policy, although privately he took a more "dovish" position. He opposed the anti-war platform of the 1968 Democratic National Convention. After returning to Congress in 1969, Muskie described the American experience in Southeast Asia as a tragedy. Critical of President Nixon's refusal to quickly end the fighting by 1972, Muskie proposed his own peace plan which called for the setting of a firm date for U.S. troop withdrawal in return for all American POW's. In 1973, he served as Senate Floor Manager of the War Powers Act, which passed over a presidential veto. The act more clearly defined presidential and congressional authority in war-making decisions. A critic of the ever expanding weapons systems, Muskie opposed President Nixon's ABM-Safeguard system in 1969 and approved United States-Soviet arms limitation agreements. He opposed creation of an all volunteer Army and instead suggested corrections in the current system. Muskie urged that uniform codes be established for all Draft Boards to follow; that all men be selected by lottery at age 19 and given several options to choose from, including the military and other national service groups such as the Peace Corps and VISTA.

In January 1976 the Democratic Party selected Muskie as its spokesman to respond to President Ford's State of the Union Address. Muskie described Ford's proposed budget as "penny wise and pound foolish" and designed to maintain a 7% unemployment rate. He also called for national energy, environment and food policies. Late in 1976, Muskie was considered as the possible vice presidential running mate for Jimmy Carter but was dropped in favor of Sen. Walter Mondale (D, Minn.) [q.v.]. Maine voters returned Muskie to the Senate for a fourth term in November 1976.

[TML]

NADER, RALPH
b. Feb. 27, 1934; Winsted, Conn.
Consumer activist.

The youngest of four children, Ralph Nader was born into a home where political and social affairs were the stuff of dinnertime conversation. His father ran a restaurant and bakery and was heavily involved in community issues. In 1955 Nader graduated from Princeton. He entered Harvard Law School that fall. Graduating in the spring of 1958, Nader served briefly in the Army before returning to Connecticut to set up a law practice. During the ensuing years, Nader traveled extensively, writing articles for several national magazines and pleading the case for safer motor vehicles before state legislators and civic groups.

In April 1964, the Labor Department's Office of Planning and Research hired Nader to study the federal role in auto safety. He left in May 1965 to write the book *Unsafe at Any Speed: The Designed-in Dangers of the American Automobile*, published in November. It accused the motor industry of placing fashion over safety, singling out General Motors' (GM) Corvair as a serious example. Nader began to attract national attention, especially after he told a Senate subcommittee in March 1966 that GM had hired private detectives to investigate him. GM first denied then admitted the charges, publicly apologizing to Nader. The National Traffic and Motor Vehicle Safety Act became law in September, and Nader was widely acknowledged as its principal boost-

er. That fall he sued GM for 26 million dollars, charging invasion of privacy. [See JOHNSON Volume]

In the summer of 1968 Nader assembled a group of student interns in Washington to aid him in a number of projects, principally a study of the effectiveness of the Federal Trade Commission (FTC). Dubbed "Nader's Raiders" by the press, they formed the nucleus for the Center for Study of Responsive Law, the first of several Nader-affiliated organizations that were created during the Nixon years and that transformed Nader's one-man crusade into a broad consumer advocacy apparatus.

The report on the FTC was released in January 1969. It accused the Commission of "incompetence by the most modest standards and a lack of commitment to the regulatory mission . . . ." and went on to state that FTC officials were "in collusion with business interests." Chairman Paul Rand Dixon was singled out for criticism and his resignation was urged. The report created such controversy that President Nixon asked the American Bar Association (ABA) to organize an FTC study of its own.

In May Nader publicly endorsed the insurgent candidacy of Joseph "Jock" Yablonski [q.v.] for the presidency of the United Mine Workers, a post then held by W. A. Tony Boyle [q.v.]. Nader was a staunch advocate of more stringent occupational safety standards for miners. Earlier in the year he had accused Boyle of "snuggling up to the coal operators," charging that he "neglected his responsibility" to the union members. In August, Nader said that the Interior Department had suppressed a report on the harmful environmental effects of underground mining. He was one of the vocal supporters of the Coal Mine Health and Safety Act, which passed that year.

The FTC controversy flared again in September, after the American Bar Association released its study confirming substantially the "Nader's Raiders" report. Chairman Dixon defended the agency before a Senate hearing chaired by Edward Kennedy [q.v.] and called Nader a publicity seeker. Dixon was eventually succeeeded by Miles Kirkpatrick, leader of the ABA study.

The year 1970 marked further conflict between Nader and the auto industry. In January the New York state Court of Appeals ruled that Nader had valid grounds to sue GM, saying that he could sue for "defamation" and "intentional infliction of emotional distress." The following month Nader announced the beginning of "Campaign GM," an effort designed to encourage GM stockholders to influence the company's stance on pollution and safety standards. The largely unsuccessful effort was run by the recently formed Project on Corporate Responsibility, another Nader-affiliated consumer group.

Nader's Center for Responsive Law attracted some criticism when it attacked Sen. Edmund Muskie (D, Me.) [q.v.] in May, saying he had "failed the nation in the field of air pollution control." Many environmentalists considered Muskie one of their strongest allies in the Senate and felt the accusation was unjustified. Muskie himself stated that he was working that year to strengthen the 1967 Air Control Act.

In June two new Nader organizations were established. The Center for Auto Safety, funded in part by the Consumers Union, employed the services of three lawyers to monitor the National Highway Safety Bureau. The Public Interest Research Group (PIRG), described as the "action arm" of Nader's consumer conglomerate, was staffed by young lawyers who worked to counteract the influence of corporate lobbyists—in essence, a public interest law firm. Early PIRG projects included a suit against the Federal Drug Administration for improved birth control pill warnings, an investigation of large corporations paying inadequate amounts of local property taxes, and the organization of "grass roots" opposition in West Virginia to three Union Carbide plants that were polluting the air. PIRG evenutally developed a nationwide network of subsidiaries, based on college campuses where they were funded through student activity fees. Other Na-

der groups conducted probes of the medical profession and of Congress.

Nader's long-standing legal battle with GM was settled out of court in August. GM agreed to pay Nader $425,000, while stressing that the settlement was not an admission of guilt but merely a way of ending the protracted court proceedings. Nader used the money to finance Campaign GM and PIRG projects.

Nader and three consumer groups in January 1972 filed a suit in Washington alleging that federal price supports for milk had been raised the previous year as a result of "political considerations." The suit contended that the increase had been granted in return for "promises and expectations of campaign contributions for the reelection campaign of Richard Nixon," offering as evidence the fact that Secretary of Agriculture Clifford Hardin [q.v.] had at first opposed the increase but reversed himself shortly after dairy interests donated funds to the Nixon organization. The suit touched off a major scandal that ultimately led to a number of indictments.

In January 1973 Nader and the Union of Concerned Scientists held a news conference in which they requested that the Atomic Energy Commission (AEC) impose a moratorium on the construction of new nuclear power plants "until all safety-related issues are resolved." Nader said he would pursue the issue in Congress, the courts, and among electric company stockholders and charged that the AEC was deliberately concealing what he claimed was the belief held by most of the Commission's scientists that safety problems might exist. In May he petitioned a federal court in conjunction with the Friends of the Earth seeking the shut down of 20 nuclear plants because of safety hazards and charging the AEC with a "gross breach of health and safety obligations." The suit was eventually dismissed.

Nader was an early and outspoken critic of the Nixon Administration's role in the growing Watergate scandal. In May 1973 he called for the naming of a special prosecutor to investigate the affair. In August he criticized a speech made by the President in defense against charges that he was involved in the scandal, calling the speech a "cowardly and evasive performance." When Nixon fired Special Watergate Prosecutor Archibald Cox [*q.v.*] in October, Nader bitterly attacked the action, saying, "Every citizen in this land must strive to reclaim the rule of law which this tyrant has been destroying month by month, strand by strand."

President Ford was also a target of Nader action. In July 1975 Nader announced his opposition to Ford's plan to decontrol domestic oil prices, asserting that it would cost the average family over $900 dollars a year. In November he attacked Ford's consumer policies as "a transparent and phony attempt to mislead the public into thinking that the Administration's consumer activities are anything more than a window-dressing deception.

Nader had far kinder words the following year for Ford's opponent in the general elections, former Ga. Governor Jimmy Carter [*q.v.*]. In August 1976 Nader visited Carter in Plains, Ga., and lauded the candidate as more "admirable" than any presidential prospect in "decades." But once Carter was in the White House, Nader was frequently critical of what he saw as the ineffectiveness of many Carter appointees.

[MQ]

NELSON, GAYLORD A(NTON)
b. June 4, 1916; Clear Lake, Wisc.
Democratic Senator, Wisc., 1963-.

A country doctor's son, Gaylord Nelson grew up in a small Wisconsin village. His great-grandfather helped found the Republican Party in Wisconsin, and his father was a loyal supporter of Robert LaFollette's Progressive Party. After receiving his law degree from the University of Wisconsin in 1942, Nelson served in the Army during World War II and ran unsuccessfully as a Republican for the state Assembly in 1946. After moving to Madison, where he established a law practice,

Nelson switched to the Democratic Party and was elected to the state Senate in 1948, serving there for 10 years. In 1958 he became Wisconsin's first Democratic governor since 1932. As a state senator and later as governor, Nelson distinguished himself by his interest in tax reform, conservation and public education.

Elected to the Senate in 1962, Nelson quickly aligned himself with the bloc of liberal Democrats. He was a strong supporter of Lyndon Johnson's Great Society legislation and, with Senator Edward M. Kennedy, cosponsored the legislation creating the Teacher Corps. An early environmentalist, Nelson tried to have curbs placed against the industrial pollution of the Great Lakes, introduced legislation to ban DDT and worked for legislation requiring industry to restore strip-mined land. Nelson was one of the earliest Senate opponents of the Vietnam war and consistently voted against supplemental appropriation bills to finance the war.

During the Nixon years Nelson emerged as the most visible Senate proponent of the burgeoning environmental movement. In a major Senate speech in January 1970, he charged that the environmental crisis had become a threat to the constitutional rights to life, liberty and the pursuit of happiness. Using the example of the anti-war movement's national moratorium day, he suggested observation of an "Earth Day" to highlight environmental issues. The idea took hold and on April 22 demonstrations were held across the country. The following year Nelson proposed an "Earth Week" and urged environmental groups to concentrate on local issues of environmental deterioration. During April 1971 Nelson toured the country in support of Earth Week.

Nelson continued his campaign against the use of DDT and other dangerous pesticides. In 1969 he introduced legislation to ban the sale or shipment of DDT in the United States and to establish a National Commission on Pesticides to research their safety and effectiveness. Nelson was instrumental in persuading Secretary of Agriculture Clifford Hardin [*q.v.*] to impose in July 1969 a temporary ban on the use of DDT pending a study of its effects on human health. When the ban was lifted, however, environmental groups filed suit in federal court to curb the pesticide's use and in January 1971 received a favorable court ruling. Finally, on June 14, 1972, Environmental Protection Agency Administrator William D. Ruckelshaus [q.v.] announced a ban on almost all uses of DDT.

Nelson, meanwhile, with Sen. Philip Hart (D. Mich.) [q.v.] introduced a number of amendments to a pesticide control bill requested by the Nixon Administration in 1971. They succeeded in obtaining a provision compelling manufacturers to register pesticides with the EPA even if there was no proof of substantial health hazards. They failed, however, to delete a provision that granted indemnities to manufacturers whose products were removed from the market, nor did they win approval of compulsory information disclosure by a manufacturer before registration of a pesticide. As signed by President Nixon on Oct. 21, 1972, the Federal Environmental Pesticide Control Act was a compromise between industry and environmental interests.

As chairman of the Monopoly Subcommittee of the Senate Select Committee on Small Business, Nelson held extensive hearings on the health hazards of various drugs and on abuses by the drug industry. During 1970 he conducted a controversial inquiry into the dangers posed by birth control pills. Nelson widely publicized the growing body of medical evidence indicating that the pill had serious side effects, including an increased risk of death from blood-clotting disorders. He questioned whether manufacturers had deliberately underemphasized the pills' dangers. The hearings led the Food and Drug Administration to require manufacturers to include a safety warning in packages.

In 1971 Nelson held hearings on the effectiveness of over-the-counter non-prescription tranquilizers. With consumer advocate Ralph Nader, he called for an easing of restrictions on the use of generic drugs as a way of reducing costs to the consumer, and charged that the American Medical Association was fighting the move for monetary reasons. In 1975 Nelson released a government study on the dangers of "red dye 2," a coloring commonly used in foods and cosmetics, and urged the FDA to ban the dye.

Nelson led the ongoing fight by Senate Liberals to preserve anti-poverty programs against Nixon's efforts to dismantle them. In April 1969 Nixon announced the closing of 59 Job Corps centers and proposed that federal poverty programs be turned over to the states. In May a sense of the Senate resolution opposing the closings, which Nelson introduced, was defeated by one vote. As chairman of the Subcommittee on Employment, Manpower and Poverty of the Labor and Public Welfare Committee, Nelson held hearings on legislation to extend the 1964 Economic Opportunity Act and was floor manager of the bill. Under his leadership a bill was reported extending the Office of Economic Opportunity (OEO) for two years, keeping OEO programs under federal control and earmarking funds for specific programs to avoid Administrative scuttling. Nixon vetoed the bill in January 1970 and the House sustained the veto.

In 1971, Nelson sponsored a comprehensive child-development provision in the OEO extension bill, but again was unable to override the President's veto. Unwilling to risk another confrontation with the President, Nelson engineered a compromise in 1972. Declaring that "Congress has gone the extra mile to meet the President's concerns," he won a three-year extension of OEO in return for dropping the effort to create an independent legal services agency for the poor, and for including his child-development proposals in separate legislation. In September, Nixon signed the three year extension into law.

Controversy over the poverty program continued, however, when Nixon proposed in 1973 the abolishment of OEO and the transfer of its functions to other agencies. The President's preoccupation with the Watergate affair prevented him from winning approval of OEO's abolishment and in 1974, Nelson successfully sponsored legislation creating the Community Services Administration, which gave the poverty programs the status of a permanent independent federal agency.

During the Nixon years Nelson continued his opposition to the Vietnam war. He consistently voted against military appropriations for the war, supported the 1970 Cooper-Church amendment and opposed the 1971 draft-extension bill. In 1971 he introduced legislation to bar the use of draftees in combat operations without their consent, but the Senate rejected the proposal.

Nelson's outspoken opposition to Nixon's foreign and domestic policies won him a place on the infamous White House "enemies list." Nelson voted against confirmation of Gerald Ford as vice president in 1973 and condemned Ford's pardon of Nixon. In December 1974 Congress approved legislation introduced by Nelson to insure the government's custody of the Nixon tapes and to make them available to the Watergate special prosecutor. That same month Nelson was one of only seven Senators who opposed the confirmation of Nelson Rockefeller as vice president [q.v.].

In 1974 Nelson won reelection to a third Senate term with 63% of the vote. In 1975 he became chairman of the Senate Select Committee on Small Business. In 1977 the Senate appointed him chairman of a special committee charged with formulating a code of ethics for that body.

[JD]

NESSEN, RON(ALD HAROLD)
b. May 25, 1934; Rockville, Md.
White House Press Secretary, Sept 1974-January 1977.

Raised in an upper-middle class family in Washington D.C., Nessen attended West Virginia's Shepard College and graduated from American University in 1956. Nessen worked at several jobs in journalism before joining the National

Broadcasting Co. in 1962 as a Washington correspondent. He later reported on the Vietnam War and covered numerous foreign stories in such places as Borneo, Panama, Bolivia and Nigeria.

In August 1973 Nessen, assigned to Washington, D.C., began covering Vice President Spiro Agnew's [q.v.] deepening conflict with federal prosecutors investigating charges that he had accepted bribes during his years as governor of Maryland. For two months, Nessen reported on his research into Agnew's background and the investigation being launched by the Justice Department. Eventually, Agnew subpoenaed Nessen and eight other reporters to reveal their sources of information into the federal inquiry. But the case never came to court, in the wake of Agnew's sudden plea of nolo contendere to tax evasion charges and his subsequent resignation.

NBC decided to keep Nessen assigned to the vice-presidency following Nixon's selection of House Minority leader Gerald Ford as Agnew's replacement. Gradually, a friendly working relationship developed between the two men. When Richard Nixon resigned from office in August 1974 and Gerald Ford became the new President, Ron Nessen was named NBC's White House correspondent. Following the resignation of Jerald terHorst [q.v.] Nessen became Ford's press secretary.

Intent on improving the bitter relationship with the press corps that marked the Watergate era, Nessen adopted an informal, give-and-take atmosphere at his daily briefings, sometimes beginning with a humorous anecdote. He sat in on numerous presidential policy meetings and often passed on direct quotes from these meetings to the press. He increased access to the President by arranging a greater number of press conferences and interviews with Ford and by permitting follow-up questions.

However, Nessen's relations with the press gradually deteriorated. In November Ford departed on a major tour of Asia, including a stop at Vladivostok to meet with Leonid Brezhnev and discuss strategic arms limitation. Nessen's handling of the press during the trip was widely criticized. Reporters complained that he was unavailable at crucial moments during the summit meeting, that they were unable to obtain advance copies of Ford's speeches, and that their questions frequently went unanswered. There was particular resentment of Nessen's attitude towards the reporters themselves, stemming partly from an offhand comment that the journalists were "dazzled" and "amazed" by the Ford-Brezhnev agreement (which was subsequently aborted). Nessen conceded his errors, but many observers felt that the Vladivostok conference had demonstrated that Nessen would in fact be a "salesman" for the new administration. Nessen himself believed that much of the criticism was due to lingering animosity and suspicion that existed between the press and the government during the Nixon years.

The disputes continued. In the early months of 1975, Nessen's credibility was called into question on a number of occasions. He denied Ford planned on dismissing John Sawhill from his federal energy post, even after the President had personally requested Sawhill's resignation. While Ford was attempting to develop a compromise on his energy policy, Nessen told reporters that no such compromise was being considered. As Nessen's relationship with his erstwhile colleagues deteriorated, the pressroom was sometimes the scene of heated exchanges.

Nessen remained on good terms with President Ford throughout his tenure, but came into conflict with other members of the Administration, such as Secretary of State Henry Kissinger [q.v.]. In the spring of 1975, as the military forces of the South Vietnamese government began to collapse, a Kissinger staff member told Nessen that "diplomatic initiatives" were underway. Nessen passed this information on to the press, only to discover that it was not true. It was the first of several clashes between the two over the journalistic versus the diplomatic uses of information. A political feud developed when Kissinger began to accuse Nessen of being the source of anti-Kissinger news leaks. The antagonism became public during a December presidential journey to the Far East, when Nessen labeled some reporters "patsies" for agreeing to change a pool report at Kissinger's request.

In January 1976, the National Press Club issued a study of White House press relations that was strongly critical of Nessen. Although it acknowledged his efforts to increase access to the President, the report went on to cite complaints of Nessen's "arrogance" and called his performance during Ford's China trip "the most inept . . . in modern times." Nessen reacted by saying, "I'm learning as I go along, and I still hope to earn their respect."

Following Ford's departure from the White House, Nessen remained in the public eye via his numerous writings and television appearances. In 1978, his memoirs of the Ford interregnum were published.

[MDQ]

NEWSOM, DAVID D(UNLOP)
b. Jan. 6, 1918; Richmond, Calif.
Assistant Secretary of State for African Affairs, 1969-73.

Newsom received his B.A. degree from the University of California in 1938 and his M.S. degree from Columbia University in 1940. From 1940 until 1941 Newsom was a Pulitzer traveling scholar. After World War II, he was the publisher of the *Courier-Journal,* a daily in Walnut Creek, Calif.

In 1948 Newsom joined the Foreign Service and was appointed to the position of third secretary and information officer at the American embassy in Karachi, Pakistan. After serving at various American embassies and consulates in Europe and the Middle East and at the State Department and National War College in Washington, Newsom attained the rank of duputy director of the office of North African affairs at the State Department in

1962, a position he held until 1965. Newsom served as U.S. ambassador to Libya from 1965 until 1969, when he was appointed assistant secretary of state for African affairs.

The major focus of U.S. attention toward Africa during Newsom's tenure as assistant secretary was the problems of Portugese colonialism and the policies of the white minority regimes in Southern Rhodesia and South Africa. During a behind-the-scenes policy debate within the State and Defense Departments and the National Security Council (NSC) that occurred during the months after Nixon's election in 1969, Newsom played a role as chairman of the Interdepartmental Group for Africa, an interagency, assistant secretary-level committee. In response to a request by National Security Affairs Assistant Henry A. Kissinger [q.v.], the Interdepartmental Group undertook a review of southern African policy. The panel's final report recommended a move towards increased cooperation with white regimes in the area. The recommendation was made over objections of the Africanists in the State Department who opposed the shift in U.S. policy. The policy was dubbed "tar baby" by State Department officials who felt that increased cooperation and openness with the white regimes, coupled with closer relations with black African states in the area, would prove to be "sticky."

In his frequent surveys of U.S. policy and interests in Africa, issued as addresses and statements to various groups, Newsom reiterated that U.S. action toward southern Africa was essentially limited and that the use of outside military or economic force would not be sufficient to change the racist policy of apartheid in South Africa or to force the Portuguese to withdraw from their African colonies and could lead to widespread violence. He stated before the Royal Commonwealth Society in London in March 1973 that if the U.S. was to "contribute meaningfully" to change in southern Africa, it would not be "through the pressure of isolation but through keeping open the doors of communication with all

elements of the population, particularly in South Africa."

Newsom reflected State Department views when he argued against passage of the Byrd Amendment which sought to allow the U.S. to import chrome from Rhodesia, in contravention of U.N. mandatory sanctions for which the U.S. had voted. After the Amendment was passed in 1971, Newsom endorsed congressional opponents who sought its repeal. In June 1973 Newsom stated that in his four years as assistant secretary of state "the exemption on Rhodesian sanctions has been the most serious blow to the credibility of our African policy."

In December 1973 Newsom was transferred to a new diplomatic post, that of ambassador to Indonesia, which he retained through the Ford Administration.

[MLB]

NIXON, RICHARD M(ILHOUS)
b. Jan. 11, 1913; Yorba Linda, Calif.
President of the United States,
1969-74.

Born into a Quaker family of modest means, Richard Nixon grew up in Yorba Linda and Whittier, Calif. To supplement the family income, Nixon worked in his father's grocery store and held other jobs. He excelled as a student in public schools and received his B.A. from Whittier College in 1934. Nixon graduated from Duke University Law School in 1937. After rejecting a position in a New York City law firm and failing to receive an appointment as an FBI agent because of the Bureau's limited budget, Nixon returned to Whittier to start his own practice. At the outset of World War II, he worked for eight months in the Office of Price Administration (OPA); that experience forever left him distrustful of government bureaucracy. From 1942 to 1945 Nixon served as a noncombat Navy officer in the South Pacific. Upon his return he won election to the House of Representatives as a Republican, his family's Party. During his term in the House from 1947 to 1950, Nixon established a national reputation as an investigator of Communist subversives in the federal government. That image helped to secure him election to the U.S. Senate in 1950. [See TRUMAN Volume]

From 1953 to 1960 Nixon served as vice president under Dwight D. Eisenhower. In that position, Nixon assumed many of Eisenhower's obligations as leader of the Republican Party and represented the Administration in many overseas trips. Nixon's actual role in shaping policy, however, was limited. He nevertheless endeared himself to Party leaders and workers, who pressured Eisenhower into accepting Nixon as a running mate again in 1956. Four years later the GOP Convention nominated Nixon for President. He narrowly lost the election to Sen. John F. Kennedy (D, Mass.). [See EISENHOWER Volume]

During the 1960s Nixon's political fortunes fell sharply and then reversed to net him the presidency. In 1962 Nixon lost a bitter campaign for the California governorship. Despite his 1962 humiliation he enjoyed much influence as a prominent Republican leader at a time of intraparty divisions. Nixon helped to persuade GOP congressmen to support the 1963 nuclear test ban treaty as well as civil rights legislation in 1964 and 1965. After a lame attempt to win the 1964 Republican presidential nomination, Nixon campaigned diligently for the GOP standard bearer, Sen. Barry M. Goldwater (R, Ariz.) [q.v.], a staunch conservative. Goldwater lost badly and in the process wrecked the prospects of younger Republican figures, preventing them from assuming vital roles in the national Party hierarchy. In the ensuing leadership vacuum of 1965-66, Nixon reaffirmed his hold over Party officials. He enjoyed a clear lead in the race for the 1968 Republican presidential nomination.

To ensure victory, however, Nixon had to overcome the candidacy of California Gov. Ronald Reagan [q.v.], who better represented the GOP's conservative wing and enjoyed great popularity among Southern Republican delegates. Nixon frustrated Reagan's bid by successfully negotiating an alliance with Sen. Strom Thurmond (R, S.C.) [q.v.], the de facto leader of the Republican South. Informally, Nixon promised Thurmond at a March meeting that he would not name a "liberal" Republican as his vice-presidential choice; that he would appoint conservatives to the Supreme Court; that he would deemphasize federal desegregation cases and that he would increase military spending. Prior to his session with Thurmond, Nixon had been embracing most of these positions. But the Nixon-Thurmond alliance signaled the literal adoption of a Southern Strategy in which the GOP ignored black America and the urban Northeast in favor of the South and conservative West.

Nixon captured the Republican presidential nomination at the GOP's August Convention and went on to win a close contest for the presidency. Upon winning the nomination, he named Gov. Spiro T. Agnew [q.v.] of Maryland, moderately acceptable to all wings of the Party, as his running mate. Nixon tried to direct a lofty, statesmanlike campaign along the lines of his 1960 effort and that of Thomas E. Dewey in 1948. Because he was well ahead in the polls, he had every reason to follow this strategy. Soon, however, Nixon had to fight more aggressively against the Democratic nominee, Vice President Hubert H. Humphrey [q.v.]. On election eve Nixon spoke of a U.S. "security gap" in defense weaponry and the need for "law and order" amid "the worst crime wave in American history." He also stressed, without revealing the particulars, a "secret plan" to end the war in Vietnam. In results nearly as close as those eight years earlier, Nixon edged out Humphrey and a third party nominee, Alabama Gov. George C. Wallace [q.v.], with 43.4% of the total vote, to 42.7% for Humphrey and 13.5% for Wallace. Congress, however, remained in Democratic control. Upon acknowledging his victory, Nixon promised a nation torn by racial strife and anti-war protest that his "great objective" would be "to bring the American people together." He echoed that theme in his January 1969 inaugural address. [See KENNEDY, JOHNSON Volumes]

Nixon's first priority as President in 1969 was to shift U.S. strategy in Vietnam. The President ruled out speedy withdrawal in favor of a more calculated plan designed to preserve the regime of South Vietnamese President Nguyen Van Thieu, an anti-Communist and ally of the U.S. More importantly Nixon and his chief foreign policy adviser, Henry A. Kissinger [q.v.], considered it vital to bolster U.S. relations with other powers, large and small, by demonstrating America's firm stand against the threat of Communist aggression. In early 1969 Nixon directed Gen. Creighton Abrams, Jr. [q.v.], commander of U.S. forces in South Vietnam, to limit offensive operations by American land forces so as to reduce casualties. Simultaneously the President ordered U.S. air forces to escalate bombings of North Vietnam after a vigorous offensive by the North Vietnamese in February.

Perhaps most significantly, the President and Defense Secretary Melvin R. Laird [q.v.] formulated a policy of "Vietnamization" of the conflict, first suggested by Nixon during the spring of 1968. From 1969 to 1972 the U.S. gradually withdrew 555,000 armed personnel on the assumption that the well-trained and well-equipped South Vietnamese Army could take over America's vast military role. But the U.S. continued massive air strikes. Nixon assured Thieu at a June 1969 meeting on Midway Island that the U.S. would not abandon South Vietnam altogether.

At the same time, in an effort to cut off Communist infiltration and supplies into Vietnam, Nixon widened the war. Beginning in 1969 he launched secret air bombing missions over the border provinces of the neutral nations of Laos and Cambodia, where the North Vietnamese maintained supply centers. In March 1970 the U.S. encouraged a civilian-military coup that brought about a new, pro-Western regime in Cambodia. This government soon lapsed into a corrupt and unpopular military dictatorship. On April 30, 1970, Nixon announced that U.S. and South Vietnamese troops had crossed into Cambodia to wipe out enemy sanctuaries. The President asserted that the short-term action was really "not an invasion of Cambodia" because the areas entered were under North Vietnamese control.

To quiet domestic criticism of the war, the President enunciated the "Nixon Doctrine," which promised that the U.S. would restrict its use of military intervention in future international crises. The President also reformed the Selective Service System to abolish discriminatory deferments and in 1973 ended the draft entirely. He assumed that the large reduction in the number of troops and the lower casualty rates in Vietnam combined with these other reforms would satisfy those segments of the American public concerned over escalation of the fighting between 1965 and 1968, "graphically demonstrating," Nixon recalled in his memoirs, "that we were beginning to wind down the war."

Despite the President's altered approach, the mass movement against the Vietnam conflict gathered greater force in 1969 and 1970. During that period colleges were torn apart by student protests of the war, while anti-war moratoriums, mass marches and meetings were held in major U.S. cities. The greatest turbulence, however, followed Nixon's announcement of the U.S. incursion into Cambodia. Violence between police authorities and students culminated at Kent State University when Ohio National Guardsmen fired on a crowd and killed four unarmed students. The Kent State shootings rocked the nation, as did a similar incident at Jackson State College in Mississippi. Initially Nixon dubbed his young critics "bums." However early on the morning of May 9, he made an attempt to ameliorate students at the Lincoln Memorial who were preparing to march against the war. The gesture proved fruitless.

Nixon and his aides responded to mass protests by developing a "seige" mentality. Since the beginning of his Administration, Nixon's assistants had regarded violent anti-war dissidents as potential revolutionaries. Secret data gathering by the federal government commenced against anti-war groups and eventually against less strident politicians and social groups critical of the Administration's Vietnam strategy. Concerned that members of anti-war coalitions and later more moderate critics of the President might succeed in crippling Nixon's presidency and in forcing his ouster, White House aides requested government agencies to keep secret files on such individuals. Furthermore, as in the Johnson years, the Nixon foreign policy leadership worried that domestic protest of diplomatic determinations would hurt America's prestige abroad; that in the eyes of foreign leaders, the U.S. could not be relied upon in crisis situations. Thus Nixon, Kissinger and other Administration officials not only felt free but obligated to adopt, out of concern for "national security," illegal or extralegal tactics against their more resolute and radical foes.

As a result of these fears, the White House in 1971 waged a campaign against Daniel Ellsberg [q.v.], who had released the *Pentagon Papers* to *The New York Times*. The *Papers* disclosed official misrepresentation to the public about U.S. involvement in Vietnam and revealed confidential information about the formulation of American strategy there. In an extraordinary (though not unprecedented) move, the government secured a court order restraining the *Times* from continuing publication of the *Pentagon Papers*. Nixon secretly ordered staff members to portray Ellsberg as mentally ill. "Win PR [public relations], not just the court case," top White House aide John D. Ehrlichman [q.v.] noted at the time. In September agents contracted by Ehrlichman and other assistants broke into the office of Ellsberg's psychiatrist. Nixon had tried to recruit FBI Director J. Edgar Hoover [q.v.] to have the Bureau handle the operation, but Hoover refused to cooperate in extralegal measures to prevent this and other leaks.

The character and background of Nixon's White House staff had a crippling effect on his presidency. From the start of his tenure, the President followed the pattern of Kennedy and Johnson by relying more on his personal White House advisers than members of his cabinet, which included some experienced and able political leaders. Nixon's trusted staff officers came from apolitical backgrounds. His press secretary, Ronald Ziegler [q.v.], had worked for Disneyland, the California amusement park. Nixon's chief of staff, H.R. Haldeman [q.v.], had been in advertising, where "image" was highly prized. These aides had contempt for the professional politicians in the cabinet and Congress and succeeded in alienating many of them; the President's men continually betrayed an ignorance of what public officials could or could not do and the bounds that democracy imposed on such officials.

Initially Nixon assisted in partisan causes. He worked hard for GOP candidates in the 1970 elections in the hope of securing a Republican majority in the Senate. Again there were public and private White House efforts. To increase the campaign treasuries of individual Senate candidates, Nixon staff members "laundered" funds their way. Political donations were raised secretly by Nixon assistants, in violation of the law that required them to register publicly as a campaign committee, and then channeled to selected GOP Senate and House nominees. Publicly Nixon and Agnew freely associated campus dissidents and liberal Democrats with professional criminals. The tactic failed generally; the GOP gained two Senate seats, not a majority, while losing a net of nine House seats and 11 governorships. Nixon emerged from the campaign determined to distance himself from the Republican Party.

During his Administration, Nixon took important new initiatives in domestic affairs. In 1969 the President recommended the "New Federalism," the decentralization of power from Washington to state and local governments. One important aspect of this plan was "revenue sharing," whereby the federal government directly transferred revenues to states and localities to be dispensed as they wished. The concept had originated in 1958 with Rep. Melvin Laird (R, Wis.) [*q.v.*] and had been supported, in modified form, by President Johnson. Congress followed Nixon's proposal in 1972 by voting to provide state and local governments an unrestricted $30 billion over five years. The President also persuaded the Congress in 1969 to reform the Post Office Department by transforming it into a quasi-private corporation. In his January 1971 State of the Union message, Nixon espoused another current cause by championing the budding "environment" issue. With his endorsement, Congress passed measures limiting air pollution caused by cars, industries and utilities and restricting pollution from pesticides and industrial wastes. However during his second term, as economic problems continued to grow, Nixon often advocated easing pollution regulations that might increase spending by industry and local governments.

Nixon inherited a troubled economy from his predecessor. From 1965 to 1968 Lyndon Johnson had attempted a fiscal policy that allowed for expanded federal domestic programs as well as an increasingly expensive military campaign in Vietnam. As early as 1967, this spending policy began to spark inflation. The Consumer Price Index increased from 2.9% in 1967 to 4.2% in 1968. Nixon had made inflation a major issue in his presidential campaign, and in office acted to slow the high economic growth of the late 1960s. He placed his first budget in balance, a feat last accomplished in 1960. By the new conventional wisdom, a balanced budget signaled relatively smaller government expenditures and less of an increase in gross national product, less inflation and more unemployment. The President also persuaded Congress to repeal the investment tax credit for business which, initiated under John F. Kennedy, had spurred new plant expansion. He repeatedly vetoed generous social welfare appropriations and ultimately forced the Congress to establish its own budget office. In October 1969 Nixon named Arthur Burns [*q.v.*] chairman of the Federal Reserve Board; Burns acted to curb the

growth of the money supply. Nixon's 1969–71 economic policies slowed down the economy and fostered a recession. As forecast, unemployment rose from 3.5% in 1968 to 4.9% in 1970 and 5.9% in 1971. But to the surprise of economists in and outside of the White House, inflation did not abate, but increased. Continued inflation tested Nixon severely. Critics demanded price controls but the President disapproved of such measures because of his experience at the OPA. Despite his opposition Congress granted the President in August 1970 the power to freeze and otherwise control wages and profits. Nixon signed the bill, but maintained that the measure "simply does not fit the economic conditions which exist today."

As inflation continued and his prospects for reelection worsened in 1971, Nixon altered what he liked to dub his economic "game plan." As an indication of his change in policy, in February 1971 he replaced Secretary of the Treasury David Kennedy [*q.v.*] with John B. Connally [*q.v.*]. Connally insisted, for practical political reasons, that Nixon abandon his orthodox economics. In August 1971 Nixon promulgated his New Economic Policy (NEP). He imposed a 90-day freeze on all prices and wage levels (termed Phase One) and established a Cost of Living Council to approve wage and price increases thereafter (Phase Two). The anti-inflation initiatives effectively reduced inflation and helped to restore the President's popularity to a limited degree. Also in 1972 Burns increased the money supply so as to improve economic conditions by November, a policy some observers felt added to the serious inflationary spiral that occurred in 1973 and 1974.

Nixon also had to deal with the decline of the value of the dollar. America's trade deficit had contributed to domestic inflation and over the long run caused U.S. products to become overpriced abroad. High military expenditures in Western Europe and Vietnam added to the problem. By 1971 the United States had the largest balance of payments deficit in its history. Most foreign currencies were stronger or "undervalued" compared to the fixed price to gold of the U.S. dollar. Tied to Nixon's NEP of August 1971, the President set a 10% surcharge on imported goods. He also delegated sensitive international economic negotiations to Secretary Connally, who "strong-armed" concessions from trading partners. In return the U.S. removed the 10% imports surcharge and devalued the dollar by 8.6% in December 1971, the first devaluation since 1934. Fourteen months later, in February 1973, the government again devalued the dollar by 10%.

Partly to help U.S. balance of payments, Nixon twice attempted to aid aircraft manufacturers. In March 1971 Congress voted not to approve further funding of the supersonic transport (SST), thus giving to the Soviet Union and a joint venture sponsored by France and the United Kingdom the world market for such aircraft. Nixon, who had supported continued funding, termed the vote distressing and disappointing, since the United States had heretofore led in the development of aviation technology. The Administration enjoyed greater fortune in July and August when Congress agreed to an Administration bill allowing a $250 million loan to the Lockheed Aircraft Corp., a major exporter of jet planes.

The Nixon Administration developed few programs to assist poor and black Americans. During the Johnson presidency, the federal government had committed itself to a wide range of programs designed to overcome inequalities suffered by poor people and blacks in the economy and distribution of services. In his 1968 campaign Nixon had tended to ignore black voters. Unlike Johnson he named no black to his cabinet and few to subcabinet positions. Such subcabinet members as James Farmer [q.v.], James Allen and Leon E. Panetta fought for more progressive civil rights policies, only to resign in frustration. Similarly, Secretary of Health, Education and Welfare (HEW) Robert Finch [q.v.], who had supported these advocates, found himself demoted to White House counselor with an inconsequential role in policymaking. Nix-

on offered little new legislation for minorities and systematically dismantled some "Great Society" programs meant to aid the urban poor. In early 1973, for example, he ordered the abolition of the Office of Economic Opportunity, which had been created under Johnson to aid minorities in the job market. Despite warnings to the contrary, however, Nixon's lack of involvement in civil rights issues did not result in a continuation or revival of the racial rioting that occurred from 1964 to 1968. The race riots of the 1960s all but ceased during his presidency.

Welfare reform stood out as the one exception to Nixon's laissez-faire approach to the problems of blacks and the poor. In August 1969 Nixon offered a major revamping of the welfare system through a guaranteed annual income plan, formulated by the President's chief aid on urban policy, Daniel Patrick Moynihan [q.v.]. The reform, known as the Family Assistance Plan (FAP), was a departure from traditional Republican philosophy and as such was opposed by such conservative GOP leaders as Gov. Reagan and Rep. John Ashbrook (R, Ohio) [q.v.]. Black leaders and liberal Democrats looked upon the Nixon-Moynihan plan with skepticism, and Senate liberals combined with conservative Republicans and Southern Democrats to scuttle the FAP in late 1970. Fearing Reagan's rivalry for the 1972 presidential nomination, Nixon thereafter all but ignored Moynihan's reform.

The President did monitor more closely the use of busing to end racial segregation in public schools, a controversial legacy of the civil rights revolution of the 1950s and 1960s. Courts increasingly ordered school systems throughout the nation to desegregate their facilities, and Nixon's cabinet officers found themselves having to carry out the court edicts. In 1971, for example, HEW formulated a busing plan for Austin, Tex., which Nixon in turn characterized in August as "the busing of children simply for the busing of children." In June 1972 the President assailed a Detroit court busing order and encouraged legislation to curb the practice. At the same time he did nothing to discourage the violence committed by white extremists and distraught parents during implementation of busing orders. Indeed in 1972 he commanded the Justice Department to petition the courts on behalf of some school boards opposing lower court desegregation orders. Despite Nixon's stance, court decisions effectively dictated the desegregation of many school systems during his presidency.

Implicitly related to civil rights was Nixon's preoccupation with the membership of the Supreme Court. Many conservatives in the 1960s had felt that the court under Chief Justice Earl Warren had been too "activist," or liberal, in its decisions regarding school desegregation and the rights of defendants in criminal law proceedings. Nixon shared that concern and pledged to name no liberals and preferrably more Southerners to the high court. Altogether Nixon chose four justices, including Warren's successor, Warren E. Burger [q.v.] in May 1969. That month Nixon and Attorney General John N. Mitchell [q.v.] forced the resignation of Justice Abe Fortas [q.v.], after learning of improper actions by Fortas off the bench. To succeed Fortas, a court liberal, Nixon designated federal Judge Clement Haynsworth [q.v.], a conservative jurist from South Carolina. Although an able judge, Haynsworth, Senate investigators found, had decided one case for a company in which he owned stock. The Senate voted to reject Haynsworth by a 55-to-45 margin, the first Supreme Court nominee to be disapproved since 1930.

Nixon responded angrily to Haynsworth's rejection in January 1970 by naming federal Judge G. Harrold Carswell [q.v.] of Florida. Carswell did not rank highly on anyone's list of potential nominees. He had a mediocre record of court conduct and opinions reversed by higher courts. Indeed, some commentators and senators regarded his designation as a rebuke. Richard Harris of *The New Yorker* wrote that the President "was prepared to insult one branch of the government, the Senate, in order to lower the quality of a second branch, the Judiciary." Again an

extended fight over confirmation ensued. Evidence of Carswell's racist past was uncovered. A key supporter, Sen. Roman Hruska (R, Neb.) [q.v.], not only acknowledged Carswell's "mediocrity" as a jurist, but felt that the appointment should be allowed because mediocrity warranted representation on the bench. Nixon's congressional lobbyists added to the damage from Hruska's reasoning by employing clumsy or heavy-handed tactics on GOP senators. In April 1970 the Senate rejected Carswell by a vote of 51 to 45. Nixon bitterly decried the vote as an "act of regional discrimination" against Southern judges. He then named a Northerner, Judge Harry Blackmun [q.v.] of Minnesota, to the year-long Fortas vacancy; the Senate unanimously confirmed that selection. Two years later Nixon succeeded in appointing a Southerner, Lewis Powell [q.v.] of Virginia, and then placed William Rehnquist [q.v.], an Arizona conservative, on the Court.

Nixon's efforts to reshape the Court had mixed results. The Supreme Court veered away from its stands during the Warren era, though the high court's turnabout was by no means complete. The Burger court upheld some massive school desegregation edicts that employed busing, of which the President publicly disapproved. In January 1973 the court upheld the right of women to abortions during the first six months of pregnancy, a "liberal" decision, while Nixon was assiduously wooing anti-abortion groups. More importantly, the Burger court did not, as feared, reverse most of the major decisions handed down during Warren's tenure. Burger proved less persuasive than Warren in mobilizing court votes and generally preferred to be a legal administrator, calling for court expansion and procedural reforms, rather than advocating new legal initiatives.

Foreign affairs remained Nixon's favorite area and the one in which he demonstrated the greatest imagination. From the time of his 1968 campaign, Nixon had sensed a shift in the global balance of power. China emerged from its "cultural revolution" likely to assume a vital leadership role in the world, yet it was still suspicious of the Soviet Union; sporadic armed border clashes occurred along the Sino-Soviet border in 1969. Although Nixon had long been among those who opposed U.S. diplomatic recognition of China and its admission to the United Nations, the President now felt that Chinese leaders must be approached. As a Republican President with indisputable anti-Communist credentials, Nixon could slowly begin to "normalize" U.S.-Chinese relations with little fear of domestic political repercussions. Tentative discussions began soon after Nixon's inauguration. In July 1971 Kissinger secretly flew to Peking to arrange a presidential visit to China the following year. Announced officially in August, Nixon's trip in February 1972 laid the groundwork for formal relations, which were realized under President Jimmy Carter [q.v.] in December 1978.

U.S. relations with the Soviet Union improved markedly during Nixon's Administration. From the outset, Nixon favored the Strategic Arms Limitation Talks (SALT), begun under President Johnson, as a means of containing the arms race. Yet he supported continued increases in new military weapons procurement, notably during the congressional debate over the appropriation for the anti-ballistic missile system in 1969. The SALT negotiations were designed to culminate not in an overall reduction of U.S. military spending as much as a lessening in the growth rate of military expenditures. The talks ran from 1969 to 1972, when the Soviet leaders agreed to the first of several treaties to limit new armaments. When he went to Moscow in May 1972 to sign the accord, Nixon became the first President to visit the Soviet Union since 1945.

President Nixon fostered a U.S.-Soviet "spirit" of cooperation, or "detente," as Cold War tensions between the two great powers lessened. Pushed by Soviet Party Chairman Leonid Brezhnev, the USSR aggressively sought America's trade and its high technology and investment for mining Soviet natural resources. In addition a poor grain harvest forced the USSR to request the right to purchase U.S. grain in 1972. The grain transaction taxed the resources of the Agriculture Department and had the unexpected effect of raising U.S. food prices the following year. That and the question of Soviet domestic repression raised concerns about the gains to accrue from the deal. Sen. Henry M. Jackson (D, Wash.) [q.v.] delayed approval of SALT-I over the issue of Soviet denial of emigration rights to Russian Jews.

Detente or the new China policy did not, however, resolve the problem of Vietnam. From 1968 to 1972 the U.S., North and South Vietnam and the National Liberal Front (the South Vietnamese Communist faction) continued fruitless negotiations in Paris. As the U.S. de-escalated its military operations, the governments of North and South Vietnam—the one hopeful, the other terrified over what withdrawal portended—hesitated to concede much. Nixon's patience wore thin, especially in light of the upcoming 1972 election and his inability to end the conflict. Continued North Vietnamese offensive operations in early 1972 provoked expanded U.S. air missions over North Vietnam and the mining of Haiphong, the major port city. Administration sources claimed that the bombing was necessary to protect U.S. troops remaining in the South and was aimed solely at military targets. But there were persistent reports of dikes and hospitals hit by American bombs. The May 1972 offensive prevented a rout of Saigon's forces in the northern tier of South Vietnam, but the North Vietnamese remained uncooperative in the Paris talks, hoping either to wear down Thieu or see Nixon replaced in the November elections.

Nixon appeared to face a tough reelection campaign in 1972. Challenges to Nixon within his own Party by Reps. Ashbrook and Paul N. McCloskey, Jr. (R, Cal.) [q.v.], proved inconsequential. But through 1971 he lagged behind Sen. Edmund S. Muskie (D, Me.) [q.v.], the leading Democratic contender, in public opinion polls. Indeed Nixon failed to improve his position greatly even after he announced his new and dramatic policies regarding China and inflation in August 1971. The prospect of political defeat haunted Nixon, who had suffered an inordinate number of voter rebukes. His fears and those of his staff led to complicity in condoning extralegal campaign efforts. The Committee to Re-Elect the President (CREEP) determined to do what it could, legally and illegally, to assist the President. Government officials placed pressure on business executives subject to regulation, including those affected by Nixon's new environmental legislation, to contribute to CREEP. Then CREEP commenced secret political espionage or "dirty tricks" against the Democrats. Muskie was the primary target. CREEP operatives led by Donald Segretti [q.v.] sought to sabotage his campaign; in the New Hampshire primary, for example, a letter attributing a racial slur about French Canadians to Muskie was sent to the conservative *Manchester Union Leader*, which published the remark along with an anti-Muskie editorial. These and other tactics served to undermine Muskie's lead and encouraged factional rivalries among the Democratic Party's other candidates.

Sen. George S. McGovern (D, S.D.) [q.v.] won the Democratic nomination at the July 1972 National Convention. With impeccably liberal credentials, McGovern had embraced a range of positions on drug use, income redistribution and other issues that appeared to separate him, like Goldwater in 1964, from the political "mainstream." Furthermore, he secured the nomination without the support of such traditional Democratic blocs as organized labor and the South. Polls taken immediately after the Democratic Convention gave Nixon a 30% lead over the South Dakotan.

Ironically, Nixon and his CREEP managers had not anticipated such a vulnerable opponent. They had forecast a close contest along the lines of Nixon's 1960 and 1968 efforts, and had taken precautions, notably against the expertise of one man, Lawrence F. O'Brien [q.v.], chairman of the Democratic National Commit-

tee. O'Brien had engineered Humphrey's remarkable showing in 1968 and was commonly considered one of the best political strategists of the postwar period, quite capable of frustrating the President's reelection drive. Shortly before McGovern's nomination, five men hired by CREEP broke into O'Brien's offices in the Democratic headquarters at the Watergate complex in Washington. They set telephone wiretaps and rumaged for intelligence concerning O'Brien's electoral strategy and for any confidential or damaging information on the President. On June 17 these men made a return visit only to be discovered and arrested by the Washington police.

The White House and Nixon himself denied any knowledge of the Watergate break-in. It was later revealed that Nixon knew that CREEP engaged in surreptitious data-gathering operations and realized that his campaign director, John N. Mitchell, and a White House aide, Jeb Stuart Magruder [q.v.], hired the Watergate burglars. However, he chose not to risk public disapproval and reelection; a confession might have evoked old memories of the President as "Tricky Dicky" and clouded his substantive foreign policy initiatives.

Both O'Brien and McGovern attempted to make the Watergate incident a political issue, but without avail. At Nixon's direction, Haldeman and Ehrlichman prevailed on Deputy Central Intelligence Agency (CIA) Director Vernon Walters [q.v.] to have the FBI halt its probe of the burglary on the grounds that it might compromise CIA activities. Acting FBI Director L. Patrick Gray initially agreed to limit the probe but then demanded a written request from Walters, who in turn denied CIA involvement. But Gray joined the successful White House effort to frustrate the Justice Department's initial investigation of the burglary. At about the same time White House Counsel John Dean [q.v.], overseeing the "cover-up" for Nixon, requested CIA funds to pay off the captured burglars.

Nixon overwhelmed McGovern in the November balloting. Stressing his duties as chief executive, the President campaigned little and held few press conferences. Surrogate speakers represented Nixon at Republican rallies across the nation and, together with an effective advertising effort, underscored McGovern's contradictory statements and general ineptness as a national candidate. On the eve of the voting, Kissinger sealed the victory. Returning from negotiations with the North Vietnamese in Paris, Kissinger proclaimed that "peace is at hand." On Nov. 7 Nixon bested McGovern with 60.8% of the vote; he won in 49 states. Other Republican candidates, however, did not fare nearly so well. Democrats actually increased their number of Senate seats. The GOP did win an additional 13 House seats, but Congress remained in Democratic control. Sen. Robert Dole (R, Kan.) [q.v.], chairman of the Republican National Committee, termed the results "a personal triumph for Mr. Nixon but not a Party triumph."

In the aftermath of victory, Nixon moved to solidify his control over the federal government. In November the President asked for the resignations of the top 2,000 executive branch officials; he then arranged for the removal of three of his cabinet members and several federal agency chairmen. His intention was to place cabinet departments directly under the supervision of a few trusted secretaries and White House staff members, while other Nixon loyalists took positions at various levels to monitor activities within each department. Thus, Nixon would effect a plan of "supercabinets" under more direct White House control. Removed from the cabinet were two former GOP governors, George W. Romney [q.v.] and John A. Volpe [q.v.]. They were replaced by men known only for their complete loyalty to the President. Rev. Theodore Hesburgh [q.v.], president of the University of Notre Dame, was forced out as chairman of the Civil Rights Commission, which had criticized the Administration's policies towards blacks. Commerce Secretary Peter G. Peterson [q.v.] was dismissed after he was deemed less than sufficiently faithful to Nixon and

too closely allied to Sen. Charles H. Percy (R, Ill.) [q.v.], a liberal GOP leader.

In the midst of Nixon's personnel shake-up, Kissinger completed a peace agreement with the North Vietnamese. Resolution did not come as swiftly as had been implied in Kissinger's "peace is at hand" statement. Indeed the North Vietnamese proved unwilling in November and December to make changes in the document demanded by South Vietnam. In response to North Vietnam's intransigence, in late December the President ordered a "reseeding" of mines in Haiphong harbor and the most intensive bombing ever of North Vietnam. "The order to renew bombing the week before Christmas," Nixon recalled, "was the most difficult decision I made during the war." It provoked a large outcry from both anti-war spokespersons and others, such as Sen. William B. Saxbe (R, Ohio) [q.v.], who normally supported the Administration. Nevertheless the "Christmas bombing" forced Hanoi's hand. In early January, Kissinger flew to Paris to effect an agreement. On Jan. 15 all bombing and mining operations against the North ceased. North Vietnam provided for the return of U.S. prisoners of war (mainly bomber pilots). On Jan. 23 a cease-fire was announced. Nixon had "won the peace," as he liked to phrase it, and rested on a high crest of popularity. The *Wall Street Journal* reported of an effort to repeal the constitutional limit of two presidential terms so that Nixon could run again in 1976.

In his war against inflation, Nixon took issue with the Democratic Congress in late 1972 and early 1973 over government spending. Nixon began "impounding" federal monies; that is, he directed cabinet officers in such departments as HEW not to spend the funds allocated by Congress for those departments. Not content to rely on his veto power, the President wished to curb excess expenditures, which he felt contributed much to the inflationary spiral. It appeared to be a practice of doubtful legality and certainly a direct challenge to the authority and independence of the legislative branch.

Just as Nixon's personal popularity rose to new heights, his presidency appeared jeopardized by the incident at the Watergate complex. From June 1972 to March 1973, Nixon and his staff had kept the Watergate conspirators silent by cash payments, coverage of legal fees and the promise of pardons. For a while these efforts worked. Aside from *The Washington Post*, most of the news media ignored the possibility that Watergate constituted part of a larger scheme of illegal actions. Federal Judge John J. Sirica [q.v.], assigned to the Watergate trial, repeatedly asked the defendants if they had acted under authority from CREEP. The men said nothing and pleaded guilty in October; sentencing occurred in January. By that time the *Post* and several other major newspapers stepped up their investigative reportage of the possibility that CREEP or the White House was connected with the burglary. On Feb. 7, 1973, the Senate established a special Judiciary Committee panel, chaired by Sen. Sam Ervin (D, N.C.) [q.v.], to inquire about illegal campaign practices. By the month's end, Nixon assumed full charge of all Watergate matters.

Nixon decided he had to make sacrifices in the hope of diffusing the Watergate timebomb. On March 22, 1973, Ervin's committee issued its first subpoenas of White House aides and official records. The President refused to honor the requests. Four days later, James McCord [q.v.], one of the Watergate burglars, wrote to Judge Sirica asking for a private meeting. Sirica agreed and McCord told of official culpability. The next day Nixon, Haldeman and Ehrlichman realized that CREEP would have to acknowledge some guilt and decided to make Mitchell the "fall guy," to blame him for the entire matter. Early the next month John Dean, who had been handling the cover-up, began to talk to federal prosecutors. Now Nixon determined to cast Dean as the "public" culprit and on April 30 forced his resignation. That night in a televised address, the President tried to diffuse the growing scandal by taking responsibility for the Watergate affair but denying personal involvement in the episode or the attempts to cover it up. He asked the nation to let the courts deal with the scandal, urged reform of the political process and pleaded that he be permitted to continue the tasks for which he was elected.

Public interest in Watergate rose markedly, while faith in the Justice Department and Nixon's handling of the investigation fell. In May, Congress compelled Nixon to appoint a new Attorney General, Elliot L. Richardson [q.v.], and a special Watergate prosecutor, Archibald Cox [q.v.], to handle the investigation. Richardson and Nixon both agreed to cooperate with Cox and grant him independence from White House interference, which had severely restricted the Justice Department's inquiry.

Through the late spring and summer of 1973, additional revelations damaged Nixon's reputation further. In June, for example, the General Services Administration reported federal expenditures, many of them extravagant, totaling $1.9 million on Nixon's various estates. Then too, Dean testified before Ervin's committee; he implicated the President in the cover-up and revealed the existence of the White House "enemies lists." But the greatest surprise came the following month. Alexander Butterfield, a former CIA agent and White House aide, revealed that in 1969 Haldeman had an elaborate taping system installed in the White House to record all the President's conversations. So great had been his and Nixon's concern with the historical record of the Nixon presidency that they had "bugged" themselves. For the next year access to the tapes loomed as the major issue of the Watergate inquiries. Nixon refused to destroy the recordings, but also declined, under the rubric of "executive privilege," to turn any over to Sirica, Cox or congressional panels.

Suddenly another prominent member of the Administration fell into disrepute. For some time during 1973, the Justice Department had been assembling evidence indicating that Vice President Agnew had been taking bribes during his term as governor of Maryland and after his election to the vice presidency. The Justice Department's case appeared clear-cut. After a brief fight to salvage his position, Agnew pleaded "no contest" to a long list of charges and resigned on Oct. 10. Nixon named Rep. Gerald R. Ford, Jr. (R, Mich.) [q.v.], House minority leader, as his new vice president.

Ten days after Agnew's departure from office, on Oct. 20, Nixon tried to resolve the tape controversies by dismissing Special Prosecutor Cox. To Nixon's dismay, Cox had been pursuing many possible White House crimes and activities of questionable legality involving Nixon himself, and had been relentless in his quest for access to the White House tapes. When Nixon fired Cox, Attorney General Richardson felt morally obligated to resign in protest; his deputy, William Ruckelshaus [q.v.], refused to carry out Nixon's order to remove Cox, and in turn was fired even before he could submit his own letter of resignation. Gunwielding FBI agents moved in to seal Cox's office and for one terrible moment the special prosecutor's aides thought that the President was executing a coup d'etat. The incident became known as the "Saturday night massacre."

Nixon's dismissal of Cox raised a hailstorm of protest. An unprecedented number of telegrams and other messages, overwhelmingly hostile to the President, flooded congressional and White House mail rooms. The House leadership, long loathe to act prematurely and fearful of charges of partisan consideration, began organizing impeachment proceedings. Congressional and public opinion thus forced Nixon's hand. He agreed in principle to surrender the tapes, name a new special prosecutor, Leon Jaworski [q.v.], and appoint another independent-minded Attorney-General, Sen. Saxbe.

In the midst of this crisis, foreign policy considerations brought into question the President's basic capacity to govern. In October an alliance of Arab states launched a surprise attack on Israel, an ally of the U.S. Since at first the Israeli situation appeared precarious, Nixon ordered a large shipment of arms rushed to the besieged nation. He also placed U.S. armed forces on alert, a grave step apparently related to a threat by the Soviets to intervene militarily in the war. Some observers suspected, however, that the President tried to use the war to distract attention from his serious domestic struggles.

In December the oil-exporting nations of the Middle East instituted a boycott against the U.S. and other major Western powers allied to Israel. Through the years the U.S. had become increasingly dependent on the Mideast for its primary oil supply. The boycott created an energy crisis in America; gas stations shut down and thermostats in factories and homes were lowered in warlike sacrifice. In January 1974 Nixon proposed "Project Independence" to Congress, a detailed scheme for lessening America's reliance on imported oil. The quadrupling of oil prices following the boycott, which ended in March 1974, worsened America's trade deficit, fueled inflation and fostered a worldwide recession in late 1974. Nixon and Kissinger, now Secretary of State, increased their involvement in Mideast diplomacy. They wooed Anwar Sadat, president of Egypt, in an attempt to weaken his ties with the Soviet Union and the more militant Arab states and terrorist organizations. As a result, Nixon helped to lay the groundwork for an ease in tensions between Egypt and Israel in the late 1970s.

Watergate proceedings absorbed more and more of the nation's time. In November 1973 a key tape of a conversation transferred to Jaworski revealed an 18½-minute gap, inexplicably and clumsily erased. In early March the Watergate grand jury named the President an "unindicted co-conspirator" in the cover-up; the panel elected not to indict Nixon because of doubts that the Supreme Court would allow such an action against a sitting President. By the spring of 1974 the House impeachment inquiry had begun hearings and soon petitioned for 42 White House tapes. By now the President's hopes rested in withholding the tapes themselves. In an attempt to diffuse the situation, Nixon released edited transcripts of the tapes prepared in April by the White House staff under his direct supervision. The typescripts proved unreliable and the investigators sued for release of the tapes.

Public opinion clearly worsened for Nixon by mid-1974. News coverage of Watergate overwhelmed that of all other issues. Extensive television network coverage of the Ervin hearings and later the impeachment proceedings revealed for the first time the ethics and personality of Nixon's staff, which had heretofore operated with considerable anonymity. Republicans in Congress by and large remained faithful to the President, though in March Sen. James L. Buckley (R, N.Y.) [q.v.] became among the first of a few who publicly asked Nixon to resign. The Party suffered for its loyalty; GOP candidates lost in special House elections in 1973 and 1974, a portent of disaster in the November 1974 elections if Nixon remained in office.

Nixon's hopes to retain the presidency all but collapsed in late July 1974 when the Supreme Court unanimously upheld a lower court subpoena directing the President to surrender 64 taped conversations to Jaworski. Events moved swiftly thereafter. The tapes clearly demonstrated that the President had known of and participated in the obstruction of justice in the Justice Department's Watergate investigation, and that he had done so largely for personal, political reasons. These revelations provided the basis for the Judiciary Committee's approval of three articles of impeachment in July 1974. For two years the President had lied to the American people; incredibly, he had also totally deceived his own family and GOP leaders whom he had known for years and who had stoutly defended him. It was obvious by early August that the House would impeach the President and that the Senate would vote his removal from office. Republican leaders all but abandoned him. Facing a prolonged and ultimately unsuccessful Senate trial, Nixon resigned from office on Aug. 9, 1974, the first President to do so. He did not admit

to criminal wrongdoing, only to rendering "some" bad judgments. In September his successor, Gerald Ford, granted him a blanket pardon.

Disgraced in office, Nixon faced an ignominious exile at his California estate. He occasionally traveled abroad and infrequently spoke out on foreign policy, about which President Ford kept him formally briefed. In beleaguered financial condition after leaving the White House, Nixon profited much in 1977 from a special series of TV interviews with David Frost and in 1978 from the publication of his memoirs. By then Nixon had only vaguely confessed to grave errors in handling Watergate.

The Nixon scandals had lasting repercussions for American politics. The besmirched Republican Party suffered large losses in the 1974 congressional elections and lost the presidency in 1976. Already falling in the late 1960s, mass participation in the political process, especially voting, declined further as more and more Americans lost faith in democratic leadership. Rigorous new election laws came into effect to prevent future political abuses. Finally, Watergate removed most of the aura that had come to surround the presidency. The scandals created suspicions in the Congress and the news media that so weakened the power of Nixon's successors that their effectiveness in making foreign and domestic policy was much curtailed.

Nixon's defenders were quick to point out that many of the abuses of power that lead to his resignation did not originate with his Administration but were a result of the growth of the imperial presidency. Undeniably, Watergate obscured much of Nixon's achievements as President, notably in the field of foreign policy. Domestic policy initiatives were, in turn, frustrated by the Democratic Party's control of Congress throughout his presidency. Nixon also inherited an array of problems, such as the Vietnam war and the divisions it engendered, that his predecessors had been unable to resolve.

On the other hand, Nixon had exploited the imperial presidency and expanded federal powers to the fullest. While certain predecessors performed some of the same deeds, no single President had assembled such an inclusive catalog of illegalities. Many commentators considered Nixon alone the problem. They believed, as Franklin Roosevelt had said, that "such [expanded] power would provide shackles for the liberties of the people" if invested in certain ruthless men. The greatest tragedy, however, remained Nixon's and the best explanation for it was that of journalist Walter Lippmann, who in November 1962 had described him as "a politician who doesn't have the confidence of a moderate man."

[JLB]

For further information:
J. Anthony Lukas, *Nightmare; the Underside of the Nixon Years* (New York, 1976).
Richard Nixon, *RN; The Memoirs of Richard Nixon* (New York, 1978).
Jonathan Schell, *The Time of Illusion* (New York, 1976).

NOFZIGER, (FRANK)LYN C(URRAN)
b. June 8, 1924; Bakersfield, Calif.
Deputy Assistant to the President for Congressional Liaison, 1969-71.

Lyn Nofziger began his journalism career at the Glendale *News-Press* and the Burbank *Daily Review* in 1950. He became managing editor of the *Daily Review* in 1957 but moved on the following year to become a Washington correspondent for the conservative Copley newspaper chain. From 1964 to 1966 he served as the chain's national political writer. He joined Ronald Reagan's [q.v.] gubernatorial campaign in the middle of January 1966. Following Reagan's inaugural in January 1967, Nofziger was appointed communications director for California. But he emphasized that his work was for the governor, not the state. During his year at the post, Nofziger joined other close Reagan aides in promoting the governor's presidential ambitions. In the summer of 1968 Nofziger resigned his position to work for conservative Max Rafferty, the Republican candidate for the U.S. Senate seat in California. Rafferty lost the race to Alan Cranston in November.

In July 1969 Nofziger was appointed by President Nixon to work under presidential assistant Bryce Harlow [q.v.] as deputy assistant to the President and chief of congressional liaison. Two years later he became deputy chairman for communications for the Republican National Convention. He also returned to California in 1971 to oversee President Nixon's reelection campaign in that state.

During the Senate Watergate hearings in 1973, it was revealed that Nofziger was involved in an attempt to deter George Wallace [q.v.] from entering the presidential race in California; President Nixon feared Wallace would take crucial votes away from his reelection effort. Nofziger gave $10,000 from the Committee to Re-Elect the President (CREEP) to a California advertising executive who had suggested persuading members of Wallace's American Independent Party (AIP) to change their registration. (Insufficient registration would have kept Wallace's name off the ballot.) The attempt failed, however, due in part to a California law allocating a position on the ballot for parties receiving 2% of the vote in the prior gubernatorial election; the AIP had achieved this percentage. Nofziger called the effort "legal, moral and good politics" and said he would "do it again, but it was not very practical."

According to White House Counsel John Dean [q.v.], Nofziger was also involved in preparing a list of White House enemies. The list included individuals and institutions from a variety of fields who were considered hostile to the Nixon Administration and who were targeted for retaliatory action. After leaving government Nofziger became an independent political consultant. He served for a short time as manager of California Lt. Gov. Ed Reinecke's gubernatorial campaign but resigned toward the end of the year, citing differing political approaches. He organized publicity for International Brotherhood of Teamsters President Frank Fitzsimmons [q.v.] in June 1974 and worked on a Senate campaign in South Dakota. He left the latter, however, after the Democratic candidate, Sen. George McGovern (D, S.D.) [q.v.], called him "a key member of the Nixon 'dirty tricks' gang."

In 1975 Nofziger rejoined Reagan as a chief organizer of the former governor's unsuccessful campaign for the 1976 Republican presidential nomination. In 1977 Nofziger became executive director of Citizen's for the Republic, a conservative group founded to promote Reagan and his views.

[RB]

NUNN, LOUIE B.
b. March 8, 1924; Park, Ky.
Governor, Ky. 1967-71.

The son of a farmer and merchant, Nunn served in the Army during World War II and after the war received his law degree from the University of Louisville in 1950. He began his law practice in Glasgow, Ky., and in the 1950s became active in civic affairs.

Running as a Republican, Nunn was elected county judge of Barren County in 1953. During the 1956 election, Nunn was state campaign chairman of President Eisenhower's reelection bid. In 1960 Nunn managed Richard Nixon's Kentucky campaign and John Sherman Cooper's [q.v.] Senate campaign. Nunn campaigned unsuccessfully for governor in 1963. Four years later he won the office with 51.6% of the vote over his Democratic opponent Henry Ward. He became the first Republican governor in Kentucky in 20 years.

Nunn's major program was to reduce an anticipated state budget deficit of over $24 million. Nunn set out to balance the budget, and sought and received from the Democratic-dominated General Assembly a sales tax increase from 3% to 5%. He also pushed through the legislature a substantial increase in motor vehicle license fees. Nunn was less successful in guiding tax reduction legislation through the General Assembly in 1970. However he did remove the sales tax on medicine and the tax on family automobile transfers. In an effort to provide technical expertise to state agencies and localities seeking federal aid, Nunn instituted the Kentucky Program Development Office, and his administration was also involved in the expansion of the state park system.

Nunn's tenure as governor was not a tranquil time for Kentucky or for the nation. In May 1968 Nunn activated 1,200-1,300 National Guardsmen in order to quell a racial dusturbance in Louisville. The Kentucky governor called out the National Guard once again in May 1970 during demonstrations at the University of Kentucky at Lexington following the American incursion into Cambodia. In 1968 Kentucky enacted a statewide open housing law in the South following a year of demonstrations in Louisville. Nunn allowed the ordinance to become law without his signature.

During his term in office, Nunn was active in national politics. He announced his support for Richard Nixon prior to the Republican National Convention, and he served on the temporary platform committee at the Party's Convention in Miami Beach. Nunn also chaired the Convention's Subcommittee on Federal-State Relations. In addition, he served as chairman of the Republican Governor's Conference and was active in the Southern and Midwestern Governor's Conferences.

Nunn voiced some criticism of the Nixon Administration. In December 1970, as the newly elected chiarman of the Republican Governor's Association, Nunn scored the Nixon Administration's approach to economic problems, which he called "ostrich-like." In speaking of the election reverses suffered by the Republicans that fall, he said that it "might have been better to face head-on" the problems of inflation and recession.

Unable by law to succeed himself, Nunn stepped down in 1971 and returned to private life as an attorney in Lexington. In May 1972 he won the Republican primary for the U.S. Senate seat being vacated by Senator Cooper. But in what was considered at the time to be a major upset, Nunn went down to defeat that November to Democratic State Senator Walter Huddleston. Despite the fact that Kentuckians cast 64% of their vote for Richard Nixon, Huddleston chalked up about a 34,000-vote victory. Huddleston had focused his campaign on Nunn's support as governor for a 5% sales tax on food.

Nunn continued to be active in Republican national politics and was part of a committee to organize Ronald Reagan's [q.v.] presidential campaign in 1976.

[GMS]

O'BRIEN, LAWRENCE F(RANCIS)
b. July 7, 1917; Springfield, Mass.
Chairman, Democratic National Committee, February 1970–July 1972; National Campaign Chairman, McGovern for President Campaign, July–November 1972.

O'Brien, the son of Irish immigrants, grew up in a political atmosphere spawned by his father's Democratic Party activities in Springfield, Mass. After receiving his law degree from night school at Boston's Northeastern University and serving in the Army during World War II, O'Brien worked for Rep. Foster Furcola. He became John Kennedy's campaign director in 1952 and served in the same capacity in subsequent campaigns.

O'Brien, considered by some to be one of the best political strategists in the postwar period, was special assistant to the President for congressional relations during Kennedy's presidency. He continued his work under Lyndon Johnson and was the President's campaign director in the 1964 race. He was named Postmaster General in 1965, yet he continued his wide-ranging legislative efforts on the President's behalf. As Postmaster General, O'Brien oversaw the writing of the re-

port that eventually led to the creation of a quasi-public corporation, taking the Post Office Department out of the cabinet. In 1968 he worked for Robert Kennedy's presidential campaign. After Kennedy's assassination he helped Hubert Humphrey [q.v.] in his presidential campaign. After the election O'Brien joined the Wall Street brokerage house of McDonnell & Co. [See JOHNSON Volume]

In 1970 O'Brien became chairman of the National Democratic Committee, a position he assumed with some reluctance. Upon taking office O'Brien faced the unenviable task of presiding over a Party that was $9.3 million in debt with a demoralized staff. The Party was also still deeply divided ideologically between the hawks and the doves on Vietnam and reformers and the Old Guard on domestic issues. O'Brien's role was a difficult one and he was frequently viewed as a member of the Old Guard, a front for the power brokers. He attempted to avoid antagonizing any element of the Party and forged a strategy to thwart what seemed like a potential emerging Republican majority by becoming a major Party spokesman on many issues. He vigorously denounced the Nixon economic policies, which he labeled Nixonomics—a blend of inflation and high unemployment which were previously thought to be mutually exclusive. He criticized the Nixon Administration's handling of the Vietnam war and its involvement in the ITT scandal.

It was during O'Brien's tenure as Party chairman that many of the controversial reforms which later caused such discord at the 1972 Democratic National Convention were formulated. The most significant issue involved the McGovern-Fraser Commission on Party Reform, which sought to establish specific procedural control over the state delegation selection process. The effect of the Commission's rulings provided for what seemed to be quotas for youth, minority groups and women in the delegate selection process, and gave the national Party an unprecedented amount of control over state Party affairs. O'Brien summed up the national Party's commitment to the reform agenda when he said in October 1971 that "never before has a political party so totally changed its way of doing business in such a short period of time. . . . And there will be no turning back." Yet he later added that he had wanted reform which "led to Party unity, not reform that came at the price of continuing division within the Party."

O'Brien stepped down as Party chairman after the 1972 Democratic Convention. He was succeeded by Jean Woodward, George McGovern's [q.v.] choice for the post. However McGovern was desperate for the services of O'Brien in the fall campaign and pleaded with him to accept the post of national campaign chairman, which O'Brien assumed with some reluctance. He later wrote that they were "the three worst months of my life . . . a nightmare." He became angered and frustrated over the lack of coordination within the campaign organization and the resentment between the McGovern workers who had piloted their candidate through the primaries and those, like O'Brien, who were seen as latecomers.

It was O'Brien's office that the Watergate burglars bugged in the spring of 1972. Discounting many of the widely-held theories about the motivation behind the Watergate affair, O'Brien believed the "objective of Watergate was to secure all possible information that would help destroy the Democratic Party and its chairman. It is as simple as that." What particularly angered him, however, was that during the 1972 presidential campaign when he had tried to raise the break-in as a serious and legitimate political issue, the press and the public still regarded the affair as a joke or a caper "because the hard evidence was still hidden from view."

O'Brien later asserted that he was subjected to harassment long before Watergate through Internal Revenue Service audits and break-ins at his apartment from which documents were stolen. In addition friends of his were subjected to

pressures that he believed were intended to quiet him. He later wrote: "Make no mistake about it, the government can grind you down. The Nixon Administration harassment never silenced me, but I would be dishonest if I didn't admit that it hurt me financially, sapped my energies and often left me deeply depressed." What disturbed O'Brien the most was the great difficulty he had in finding a lawyer to prosecute the Republicans in a civil suit. Even his old friends from the Kennedy and Johnson Administrations "felt involvement with me would antagonize the Nixon Administration and might jeopardize their law practices." The suit was eventually settled out of court in February 1974 for $775,000.

After he left active politics at the end of 1972, O'Brien spent the next several years writing his autobiography as well as engaging in consulting work on matters of public relations in Washington and New York. In 1975 O'Brien became commissioner of the National Basketball Association.

[GWB]

For further information:
Lawrence O'Brien, *No Final Victories* (New York, 1974).

PACKARD, DAVID
b. Sept. 7, 1912; Pueblo, Colo.
Deputy Secretary of Defense, January 1969-December 1971.

Packard received his B.A. from Stanford University in 1934 and his degree in electrical engineering in 1937. He worked for two years at General Electric, and in 1939 he became a cofounder of Hewlett-Packard Co. He served as the company's president from 1947 to 1964 and as chairman of the board from 1964 to 1969. From 1958 to 1969 Packard was also director of the Stanford Research Institute, a prestigious "think tank," and sat on the advisory board of the Hoover Institute of War, Revolution and Peace. In 1969 President Nixon appointed him deputy secretary of defense.

Because of the obvious potential conflicts of interest for the ranking executive of a large defense contractor, Packard's appointment immediately provoked controversy. He moved to head off Senate opposition by having his $300 million holdings in Hewlett-Packard administered by a charitable trust while he held office. Although Sen. Albert Gore (D, Tenn.) [q.v.] attacked the arrangement as "only a bookkeeping trust," Packard was confirmed in late January 1969.

Packard served as a spokesman for a number of Administration defense proposals. Throughout 1969 he defended the Administration's proposed Safeguard anti-ballistic missile system before a skeptical Congress. In March 1969 he testified before the Senate Foreign Relations Committee, then holding hearings to build a case against the system. Packard maintained that the Soviet Union was reaching parity with the U.S. on the total number of missiles and that the system was therefore necessary. Sen. Gore countered with the view that the United States was so far ahead in the missile race that its "overkill" capacity was not jeopardized by the Soviet Union's "first-strike" capacity. Later that year he was forced to admit that the Defense Department was using funds from other programs to begin development of the system despite its promise not to initiate development until Congress approved the plan. Congress approved funds for the project in December.

In 1970 and 1971 Packard led the Administration's campaign to save the nearly-bankrupt Lockheed Aircraft Corp. In March he told the House Armed Services Committee of the "need to preserve" Lockheed's capabilities while it unraveled its financial difficulties, and in December he disclosed the $1 billion plan to resolve the Pentagon's outstanding disputes with the ailing company. During June 1971 Packard testified before the Senate Banking and Currency Committee in support of the Lockheed bailout bill by which the Nixon Administration would guarantee $250 million worth of bank loans to the faltering company.

Packard's support for Treasury Secretary John B. Connally's testimony that Lockheed could not survive without the federal loan guarantee was ambivalent. In his view, the financial health of Lockheed was more an economic than a defense matter because of the substantial unemployment and financial losses for the defense and airline industries if Lockheed failed. Under questioning, his support for the bill was diluted by his estimate that Lockheed would need to sell well over 300 aircraft to break even and by his view that the bill potentially set a dangerous precedent for "corporate bailouts" in the future. His testimony exposed a rift within the Nixon Administration over the project. Nevertheless, the loan guarantees were passed in July.

Packard also acted as Pentagon spokesman in disputes with civil rights leaders over the Defense Department's alleged failure to follow Administration anti-discrimination guidelines. On numerous occasions he also testified before Congress in support of arms sales credit overseas. In May 1970 he was called upon to explain the U.S. invasion of Cambodia. He maintained that the United States would have taken military action against Communist bases in Cambodia earlier except for political considerations dictated by the fact that Prince Sihanouk was in power.

White House Press Secretary Ronald Ziegler [q.v.] announced Packard's resignation from his Pentagon post for "strictly personal reasons" in December 1971. Packard resumed his duties with Hewlett-Packard, where he became chairman of the board in 1972. He also served, beginning in 1973, on David Rockefeller's [q.v.] Trilateral Commission, a group of concerned citizens from the United States, Western Europe and Japan who met to discuss problems of the advanced industrialized countries.

[LG]

PASSMAN, OTTO E(RNEST)
b. June 27, 1900; Washington Parish, La.
Democratic Representative, La., 1947-1977; Chairman, Foreign Operations Subcommittee of the House Appropriations Committee, 1955-1977.

Passman, the son of sharecropper parents, left grade school when he was 13 to earn a living. He started a manufacturing company in 1929 and eventually became a well-to-do businessman. He decided to enter politics while serving in the Navy during World War II and won his first campaign when he was elected to the House in 1946.

A staunch conservative and critic of most federal spending, Passman won a seat on the House Appropriations Committee in 1949. A consistent critic of foreign aid programs, he was appointed chairman of the Appropriation Committee's Foreign Operations Subcommittee in 1955. His panel had jurisdiction over all foreign aid appropriations, and he became the most powerful House opponent of the foreign aid program. He sharply cut annual foreign aid requests made by every Administration until he was successfully challenged in 1964 by President Johnson and Rep. George H. Mahon (D, Tex.) [q.v.], the newly installed head of the Appropriations Committee. That year Passman was outvoted in his own subcommittee when the fiscal 1965 foreign aid request was cut by only 7.6%. His support on the subcommittee eroded further during the following year when the foreign aid request was cut by only 7%. These were among the smallest cuts ever made in the foreign aid program. [See EISENHOWER, KENNEDY, JOHNSON Volumes]

But Passman was again able to make substantial cuts in foreign aid requests when congressional opposition to the program increased as the cost of the Vietnam war escalated during the late 1960s. Passman cut the fiscal 1969 request by almost 40%, which was then the largest reduc-

tion ever made in the foreign aid program. Passman described the cut as "about half enough."

During the Nixon-Ford years, Passman's subcommittee usually slashed foreign aid requests by more than 25%. The cuts, when coupled with the Administration's already reduced requests for foreign aid, dropped the annual funding for foreign economic and military assistance programs from the $3 billion level during the 1960s to the $2 billion level during most of the Nixon-Ford years.

Although spending for economic and military assistance was sharply curtailed, total foreign aid appropriations increased significantly after 1973 when American interests focused on the Middle East. During this period most of the increased foreign aid spending financed special programs that benefited four Middle Eastern countries—Israel, Egypt, Jordan and Syria. Although Passman initially opposed Middle Eastern aid, he eventually sponsored the bill giving $5.8 billion in military and economic assistance to the area.

Passman fully approved the $660 million that the Administration requested for Israel and Egypt for fiscal 1975. At the same time, however, he reduced the White House request for foreign economic and military assistance by 41%, the largest cut ever made in the program. These cuts reflected congressional concern over the slumping U.S. economy and the mounting federal deficit.

The following year he supported the substantially increased foreign aid appropriations that the House approved for fiscal 1976 and 1977 when it appropriated about $5 billion for all foreign aid programs. Passman argued for the fiscal 1976 increase, noting that most of it was for Middle Eastern programs which supported the Sinai disengagement agreement between Egypt and Israel.

Although Passman still favored larger foreign aid program cuts than those supported by the Senate, he no longer was the most vocal opponent of the foreign aid program. The strongest opposition to the foreign aid requests came from liberal senators on the Senate Foreign Relations Committee who were determined to use their control over foreign aid authorization bills as a lever for changing the Administration's foreign policy. Their disputes with the White House over foreign policy issues often stalled the passage of foreign aid appropriations bills during this period when the House and Senate failed to agree on foreign policy positions adopted by the Senate.

Liberal House members tried to unseat Passman as the chairman of the Foreign Operations Subcommittee in 1975 because of his opposition to most social welfare measures sponsored by fellow Democrats. He was also one of two House members publicly opposed to Nixon's impeachment after the White House released the tape transcripts which showed that Nixon had discussed using the CIA to block the FBI's Watergate probe. The liberal challenge failed when the Democratic Caucus confirmed Passman's appointment.

However Passman's 30-year House career ended the following year when he lost the primary election amid a flurry of corruption charges. In 1978 Passman was indicted on charges of accepting large bribes from South Korean businessman Tong Sun Park in return for using his position to influence federal agencies to increase loans to South Korea and pressure South Korean businessmen into using Park as their agent in dealing with the U.S. government. He was later indicted for income tax evasion. In April 1979 Passman was acquitted of the charges.

[AE]

PASTORE, JOHN O(RLANDO)
b. March 17, 1907; Providence, R.I.
Democratic Senator, R.I., 1951-76.

Pastore, the son of an immigrant tailor, earned his law degree from Northeastern University in 1931 and, after briefly practicing law, launched a career in politics. He won election as lieutenant governor of Rhode Island in 1944 and a year later was elected governor. After serving two terms, Pastore won a seat in the U.S. Senate, becoming the first Italian-American ever elected to that body. A liberal on most domestic issues, Pastore supported the Kennedy and Johnson Administrations' programs designed to eradicate poverty and discrimination in America. Representing a state that contained two important Navy facilities, he also backed President Johnson's defense spending and his conduct of the Vietnam war. [See EISENHOWER, KENNEDY, JOHNSON Volumes]

During the early years of the Nixon Administration, Pastore continued to support the President's war and defense policies. But in 1970, the same year his Senate seat was challenged by a peace candidate, he voted for the Cooper-Church and Hatfield-McGovern Amendments aimed at ending the Vietnam conflict. That year he also departed from his previous support of defense spending by joining an unsuccessful attempt to place a $66 billion ceiling on Defense Department appropriations for fiscal 1971. Although he sided with Nixon on continued development of the Safeguard anti-ballistic missile, he voted against purchasing the F-111 fighter-bomber. In 1974 Pastore endorsed the reduction of U.S. troop levels abroad and opposed the resumption of military aid to Turkey. He also took part in the losing effort to block approval of the fiscal 1975 foreign aid bill.

Throughout the Nixon-Ford years Pastore seldom strayed from the liberal record on domestic issues he had compiled throughout his tenure in the Senate. He favored gun control, establishment of a consumer protection agency, federal campaign subsidies and tax reform. An articulate supporter of civil rights legislation in the 1960s, Pastore in 1969 approved of the Administration's Philadelphia Plan to integrate the construction trades through minority hiring quotas. However he refused to endorse Nixon's Supreme Court nomination of conservative Clement Haynsworth [q.v.]. The Rhode Islander also consistently backed the use of forced busing to achieve school desegregation. He opposed "no-knock" entry legislation and favored the reduction of penalties for marijuana offenses. The major exception to Pastore's liberalism in domestic concerns was his opposition to government abortion aid. A Roman Catholic from a predominantly Catholic state, he voted for a bill in April 1975 that would have barred the use of medicaid funds for abortions except to save the life of the mother.

As chairman of the Commerce Committee's Subcommittee on Communications, Pastore wielded considerable power in the regulation of TV and other media. He was instrumental in the development of public television and sponsored the 1973 law that lifted TV sports blackouts of professional home games when all tickets were sold out 72 hours in advance. Pastore was a leader in the push for the Federal Election Campaign Act of 1971, the first major reform of campaign financing rules in 50 years. He also helped to write the law's campaign media spending limit, in response to election expenditures that had soared in the 1960s with the increased use of television. Under the new law, which took effect in the 1972 presidential and congressional elections, a candidate was allowed to spend 10 cents per voter on media advertising—including TV and radio, newspapers and magazines, and billboards. To allow for inflation, the spending limit was tied to annual increases in the Consumer Price Index, and broadcasters were required to give candidates their lowest possible advertising rates.

Pastore alternated as chairman of the Joint Committee on Atomic Energy. In this role he presided over passage of the Energy Reorganization Act of 1974, which abolished the Atomic Energy Commission (AEC) and established the Energy Research and Development Administration (ERDA) to absorb the AEC's nuclear development and promotional activities and the Nuclear Regulatory Commission to assume AEC regulatory functions. Growing criticism over the conflict between the AEC's promotional efforts and its regulatory duties and a desire to consolidate the government's widely scattered energy programs led to the bill's enactment, which President Gerald Ford had labeled his top priority energy legislation. It was signed into law Oct. 12.

At the age of 69, Pastore retired from the Senate in 1976 before the end of his term to give his successor, Republican John Chafee [q.v.], seniority.

[JR]

PATMAN, (JOHN)(WILLIAM) WRIGHT
b. Aug. 6, 1893; Patman's Switch, Tex.
d. March 7, 1976; Bethesda, Md.
Democratic Representative, Tex., 1929-76; Chairman, Banking and Currency Committee, 1963-75.

The son of a cotton farmer, Patman worked as a sharecropper to finance his legal studies and obtained his law degree from Cumberland University in Tennessee in 1916. He was elected to the Texas House of Representatives in 1920, where he served two terms. In 1924 he was elected district attorney in Texarkana. Four years later he was elected to the U.S. House on an anti-Ku Klux Klan platform.

With the onset of the Depression, Patman became part of the Southern Democratic bloc in Congress that supported the liberal social legislation of the New Deal. In 1932 Patman's call for the resignation of Secretary of the Treasury Andrew Mellon had already established his reputation as an enemy of Eastern finance capital.

Patman's anti-banking crusade was aimed at what he viewed as the excessive interest rates charged by the large Eastern banks and promoted by the policies of the Federal Reserve Bank. Patman repeatedly introduced unsuccessful legislation to subject the Fed to government ownership.

Patman became chairman of the House Banking and Currency Committee in 1963. He used this power to conduct extensive investigations into tax-exempt corporations and the interlocking ownership of Eastern banks, and published the results in highly controversial reports.

The so-called "Patman Report," as the Banking Committee's *Commercial Banks and Their Trust Activities* came to be known, appeared in 1968, revealing not only extensive control of nonfinancial corporations by the top 10 U.S. commercial banks, but also massive mutual ownership among the banks themselves. [See TRUMAN, EISENHOWER, KENNEDY, JOHNSON Volumes]

In early 1969 Patman's Committee released a new report severely critical of the power of the one-bank holding companies (OBHCs), which were then exempt from federal regulation. In his introduction to the report, Patman asserted that 34 of the largest U.S. commercial banks, with over $100 billion in assets, had established or were planning to establish such companies to avoid Federal Reserve regulations. When President Nixon announced his proposed curbs on OHBCs, Patman attacked them as too weak and filed his own bill.

In mid-1970 due to increasing attention to the U.S. banking system in the wake of the 1969-70 credit crunch, President Nixon established the Commission on Financial Structure and Regulation under Reed O. Hunt [*q.v.*] to investigate the system. Patman promptly attacked the Commission as "little more than a trade association" for the banking industry.

Because of rapidly rising interest rates and tight money sparked by inflation, Patman's lifelong vendettas were accentuated during the Nixon Administration. When commercial prime rates reached then-historic highs in mid-1969, reflecting the Administration's policies, Patman attacked Secretary of the Treasury David Kennedy [*q.v.*] for failing to roll back the rates. Immediately after Kennedy had met with major bank representatives, Patman stated that "the Secretary had the 24 largest bankers in the room for 2 1/2 hours, and he could not bring himself to speak up for the American public and ask for a rollback in interest rates."

Patman also played a key role in determining government policy toward the major corporate bankruptcies that emerged in 1970. Just before the Penn Central railroad filed for reorganization under the bankruptcy laws in June 1970, officials of the railroad met with Patman to ask his support for government-guaranteed loans to the Penn Central, which Patman adamantly refused. After the bankruptcy was made public, Patman announced that his Committee would investigate the 1950 Defense Production Act to see if aid to the railroad could be provided under its auspices.

In December 1970 Patman's Committee issued its report on the Penn Central bankruptcy, which Patman called "one of the saddest, and at times most sordid, pictures of the American business community that has ever been revealed in an official document." In March 1971 the Committee issued another report on trading in Penn Central stock prior to bankruptcy, noting that a number of banks had unloaded nearly two million shares in the three months prior to June 1970. Patman noted that "it is obvious that many of these sales were undertaken with either the greatest clairvoyance or on the basis of inside information." Later in the summer of 1971, Patman's Committee also held hearings on government aid to the ailing Lockheed Corp., which was eventually granted.

Low-cost housing was another traditional concern of Patman's that occupied his attention during the Nixon years. In January 1971 Patman's Committee issued a report charging the Federal Housing Authority with permitting "sheer fraud" and speculation in its federal home-ownership program and providing tremendous pork barrels to real estate speculators in slum housing. George Romney [*q.v.*], Secretary of the Department of Housing and Urban Development (HUD), initially called the report "inaccurate, misleading and very incomplete," and said he was shocked that Patman would resort to such tactics. Patman replied that Romney's "emotional blast" showed he was "more interested in attacking the Congress than he was in the real estate speculators and others responsible for the massive abuses in the federal housing program." A week later HUD, conceding widespread abuses uncovered by the report, was forced to suspend the program, which Patman agreed "would do much to restore confidence" in HUD. In January 1973 Romney went much further in freezing all new applications for housing subsidies, public housing and community development assistance, prompting Patman to announce that his Committee "would do everything in its power" to restore these programs on a sound basis.

Patman became increasingly concerned about the deteriorating U.S. economy, warning in July 1971 that a depression was imminent if quick action were not taken, by which Patman meant primarily lower interest rates. He called for a federal agency to regulate interest rates. In early 1973 Patman attacked Nixon's lifting of wage-and-price controls at the end of Phase Two. Weeks later he called the February 1973 dollar crisis "an international vote of no confidence in the Nixon economic program." He also warned that the U.S. was taking inadequate measures to deal with the pending energy crisis. When the commercial prime interest rate hit a record 10% in August 1973, Patman denounced the "public be damned" attitude of the banks and renewed his efforts to subject the Federal Reserve Bank to audits by the General Accounting Office (GAO). His own Committee killed Patman's proposed bill on this question. In May 1974 the House finally approved a bill for GAO audits of the Fed, but all of Patman's proposals had been removed from the legislation. When his last attempt to push through such legislation was killed by the Rules Committee in 1975, Patman announced that "it is no secret that the big business and big banking community, orchestrated by the Federal Reserve, have been working hard to kill or weaken the audit bill."

Patman played a minor role in the early stages of the Watergate scandal. In October 1972, one month before the election, he attempted to convene his Committee for hearings on possible violations of banking laws in the Watergate break-in. This move was essentially a pretext to open the affair to congressional scrutiny and to embarrass the President in the midst of the election campaign. Republican members of Patman's Committee effectively blocked such hearings, despite Patman's renewed efforts to open them a week later. Patman attributed the opposition to the hearings to interference from the highest levels of government and predicted that "the facts will come out."

In January 1975 Patman was deposed as chairman of the Banking and Currency Committee in the "Young Turks" revolt of younger Democratic liberals that also stripped two other long-standing Southern Democratic committee chairmen of their posts. Patman was succeeded by Rep. Henry Reuss (D, Wis.) [q.v.] and demoted to chairman of the Subcommittee on Domestic Monetary Policy. In this capacity he supported Reuss's controversial bill requiring the Federal Reserve Bank to expand the domestic money supply at a rate of 6% per year, but the House turned the bill into a sense-of-Congress resolution.

Shortly after announcing that he would not seek reelection in the fall, Patman contracted pneumonia and died on March 7, 1976.

[LG]

PATRICK, HARRY
Secretary-Treasurer, United Mine Workers, 1972-77.

Patrick, like Arnold Miller [q.v.] and Mike Trbovich [q.v.], was an Appalachian coal miner who, in the late 1960s, began to organize against the union machine of Tony Boyle [q.v.]. He called for improved conditions in the mines, agitated against the deleterious effects of black lung disease and demanded the decentralization and democratization of the union's power structure. In 1969 the Miners for Democracy (MFD) ran Joseph "Jock" Yablonski [q.v.] against Boyle. After being defeated by roughly one-third of the total vote, Yablonski, with his wife and daughter, was murdered in his home in December 1969.

Shortly after the Yablonski murder, the U.S. Department of Labor took legal action to have the 1969 UMW elections invalidated, and Miller, Trbovich and Patrick became the candidates on a new MFD ticket in elections held in the summer of 1972. The MFD leaders joined forces with labor attorney Joseph Rauh to use federal backing to oust the corrupt Boyle leadership, and were voted into office in the new election.

For the first two years of their term, Miller, Trbovich and Patrick, although lacking administrative experience, were able to manage the union affairs with relative success. In November 1974 Patrick, with the executive board of the UMW, participated in the contract negotiations with the Bituminous Coal Operators of America (BCOA) through which the UMW obtained for its members a 54% increase in wages and benefits over the life of the three-year contract.

After the conclusion of a strike in 1974, however, personal and political rifts within the UMW leadership began to surface. Patrick, in the initial phase of this factional warfare, found himself caught in the middle of a feud between Miller and Trbovich. The feud became public in June 1975, when Trbovich circulated a memo criticizing Miller's management of the union. The memo pointed to the considerable outlay of UMW funds under Patrick. In August 1975, when it became clear the Trbovich would oppose Miller for the UMW presidency in 1977, Miller let it be known that he would support Patrick for the job if he decided not to run for reelection himself.

By the late summer of 1976, Patrick was being touted as a possible successor to the widely discredited Miller. At a UMW Labor Day rally, Miller received only polite applause, but Patrick drew a standing ovation. From that time on tension increased between Miller and Patrick. At the September 1976 convention the anti-Miller forces pushed through a resolution rescheduling the union elections from December to June 1977, thereby maneuvering to "dump Miller" before the 1977 contract negotiations got underway. Although Patrick's chances at the time were judged to be compromised by his close ties to Miller, the UMW President complained in December 1976 that he had been "upstaged" by Patrick at the convention, and rejected efforts by UMW insiders to heal their growing rift in hopes of restoring unity at the top.

In 1977 Patrick declared himself a candidate for the UMW presidency, and shortly before the June 1977 election, was endorsed by Joseph Rauh, the former attorney for the MFD. He placed third, behind Miller and Lee Roy Patterson, an old Boyle collaborator who was backed by outgoing Vice President Mike Trbovich, with 25% of the vote. After his defeat Patrick returned to work in the Pennsylvania mines, where he remained active in UMW politics.

[LG]

PELL, CLAIBORNE (DEBORDA)
b. Nov. 22, 1918; New York, N.Y.
Democratic Senator, R.I., 1960-.

Born into a socially and politically prominent Newport family, Pell attended the fashionable St. George's School and graduated from Princeton in 1940. He served in the Coast Guard during World War II and was a special assistant to the State Department in 1945. Commissioned in the Foreign Service in 1946, he worked in various European embassies before returning to Washington in 1950 to work in the State Department. Pell left the Department in the early 1950s to return to Rhode Island, where he worked as a partner in an investment banking firm and received political recognition as a top state Democratic fundraiser. In 1960 he won a seat in the U.S. Senate.

Pell, a liberal, supported most of the Kennedy and Johnson Administration's domestic legislative programs, including all major civil rights legislation of the period. He was instrumental in the passage of legislation in 1964 that established a National Council on the Arts, and was a sponsor of legislation designed to provide high-speed intercity rail service for the busy "Northeast corridor." During the Johnson Administration, he was a firm, if not particularly vocal, opponent of the Vietnam war. [See KENNEDY, JOHNSON Volumes]

Pell received high ratings from the liberal Americans for Democratic Action (ADA) during the Nixon-Ford years. Pell frequently supported the President's foreign policy but voted against the Administration more than 50% of the time on domestic policy. Pell supported busing and government abortion aid and opposed the death penalty. He voted against the Supreme Court nominations of G. Harrold Carswell [q.v.] and Clement Haynsworth [q.v.], both of whom were rejected by the Senate. However he did vote for the nomination of William Rehnquist [q.v.] to the Supreme Court, differing with many Senate liberals. He advocated national health insurance and aid to mass transit. A supporter of campaign-financing reform, Pell cosponsored a bill in March 1974 to provide for public financing of federal election campaigns. Pell was particularly interested in education and in 1971 sponsored a bill to provide federal aid to those attending post-high school vocational and trade schools. The Senate passed the bill without a dissenting vote.

Pell voted for the Cooper-Church Amendment to limit U.S. involvement in Cambodia in 1970. Later that year he criticized U.S. bombing raids of North Vietnam, calling them "counterproductive to an ultimate peace settlement and to our national interests." In June 1972 Pell charged that the U.S. armed forces had used rain-making technology for military purposes in Indochina, causing downpours that killed thousands of people. He then introduced a draft of a treaty barring weather and climate modification activities as weapons of war. President Nixon appointed Pell as U.S. representative to the U.N. General Assembly in 1970. In that post Pell called for the U.N. to press the North Vietnamese to allow identification of war prisoners and to allow Red Cross access to those held. In the Senate he also voted for the Rhodesian chrome

ban and for a reduction in the number of U.S. troops stationed abroad.

With Sen. Jacob Javits (R, N.Y.) [q.v.], Pell visited Cuba in September 1974 on a personal fact-finding mission during which he met with Premier Fidel Castro on the possible renewal of relations between Washington and Havana. The Senators visited Cuba without the official sanction of the State Department, although they had been granted visas. Following the visit Pell recommended that the U.S. resume normal relations with Cuba and urged the State Department to lift travel restrictions to Cuba. The Administration took no action on the suggestion.

Pell was reelected in 1978 with 75% of the vote.

[GMS]

PEPPER, CLAUDE D(ENSON)
b. Sept. 8, 1900; Dudleyville, Ala.
Democratic Representative, Fla.,
1963- .

Raised in Alabama, Claude Pepper served in the Armed Forces during part of World War I before graduating from Alabama State University. After receiving his law degree from Harvard in 1924, he moved to Florida to practice and was elected to the Florida House of Representatives in 1929 as a Democrat. Pepper won a U.S. Senate seat in 1936. He served until 1951. In the Upper House he compiled a liberal record, voting for New and Fair Deal legislation. He called for a national health insurance plan as early as 1935. An opponent of the Cold War, Pepper favored accommodation with the Soviet Union and cuts in the military budget.

In 1950 big business, industry, oil companies and medical associations united to oust Pepper. George Smathers, running one of the dirtiest campaigns in U.S. history, characterized by slander and red-baiting, defeated him in the primary. [See TRUMAN Volume]

In 1962 Pepper returned to Capitol

Hill, easily winning election from Florida's newly created 11th congressional district. During the Johnson years he consistently supported programs for the elderly who comprised a large portion of his constituency. He backed Medicare, increased Social Security benefits and nutritional programs for senior citizens. A supporter of the Vietnam War in its early years, in 1968 Pepper called for a withdrawal of U.S. troops.

In 1969 Pepper introduced a resolution establishing the Select Committee on Crime with himself as its chairman. While the Committee during its three year existence was responsible for very little legislation and some critics dismissed its work as mere "publicity," Pepper asserted that its hearings, conducted nationwide, had awakened Americans to the magnitude of the drug problem. The Committee urged that possession of heroin paraphernalia be a crime, succeeded in reducing the overproduction of amphetamines and helped sponsor research for a methadone substitute. In 1971 the seven member panel recommended that Congress pass a preventive detention law to keep drug pushers from jumping bail while awaiting trial and that the U.S. work for treaties to curb the production of opium around the world.

On foreign policy Pepper's position was more middle-of-the-road during the Nixon-Ford Administrations than it had been during his Senate term. While he remained an opponent of the Vietnam war, Pepper voted against large cuts in the military budget. He fought curtailment of the ABM system, the SST and the F-14 fighter aircraft. Reflecting the feelings of his large Cuban constituency, he opposed recognition of Castro's government.

Pepper was most effective in programs to aid the elderly. He consistently supported increases in Social Security benefits and expansion of Medicare and in 1971 succeeded in amending the Older Americans Act of 1965, setting up low cost meal programs and nutritional training. Declaring that "mandatory retirement is an extravagant waste of people," Pepper guided through the House the 1978 law raising the mandatory retirement age in private industry from 65 to 70 and abolished 70 as the age at which federal employees must retire.

[FLM]

PERCY, CHARLES H(ARTING)
b. Sept. 27, 1919; Pensacola, Fla.
Republican Senator, Ill., 1967-.

The son of an office worker, Charles Percy grew up in Chicago. He worked his way through the University of Chicago, where he operated a campus equipment agency that grossed over $150,000 a year. Receiving his B.A. in economics in 1941, Percy joined Bell & Howell, a camera and photographic equipment manufacturer. After serving in the Navy during World War II, he returned to Bell & Howell as a corporate secretary and was made president of the firm in 1949. At that time he was the youngest chief executive of a major American corporation.

Under Percy's leadership the corporation grew rapidly during the 1950s and 1960s, becoming the largest camera equipment manufacturer in the country. Concerned about the welfare of his employees, Percy introduced a profit-sharing plan and developed a comprehensive retirement program. He remained president of Bell & Howell until 1963 and chairman of the board of directors until 1966.

Percy's involvement in politics began in earnest during the mid-1950s when he worked as a fundraiser for the Illinois Republican Party. At his prodding the Republican National Committee created in 1959 a Committee on Program and Progress to formulate Party goals and appointed Percy to lead it. In 1960 he was chosen to head the Party's Platform Committee at the Republican National Convention. After an unsuccessful race for the governorship of Illinois in 1964, Percy won a seat in the U.S. Senate in 1966. Entering the Senate in 1967, he quickly distinguished himself as a newcomer who spoke openly on a wide range of issues. His liberalism put him at odds with most of his fellow Republicans. Percy won reelection in 1972 with a margin of over 1,000,000 votes.

A vocal critic of the Vietnam war, Percy consistently supported Senate efforts to bring an end to the conflict. In 1970 he voted in favor of the Cooper-Church Amendment to cut off funds for combat operations in Cambodia. He opposed extension of the draft in 1971 and in the following year voted in favor of the Foreign Relations Committee's proposal to cut off funds for combat operations by the end of 1972. Percy repeatedly urged the President to set a timetable for complete withdrawal of U.S. troops and urged a unilateral American cease-fire in Vietnam. In 1973 he cosponsored with Sen. Jacob Javits (R, N.Y.) [q.v.] the War Powers Act, which limited the President's ability to commit U.S. troops to combat abroad without congressional approval.

A liberal in domestic affairs, Percy took an active legislative role on a wide range of issues. He supported the use of money from the highway trust fund for mass transit, advocated increased federal aid to education, and urged expansion of the food stamp program and stronger efforts to eradicate hunger and malnutrition. As a member of the Senate's Special Committee on Aging, Percy became an advocate of the needs of the elderly, outlining his proposals in *Growing Old in the Country of the Young* (1974). He worked hard to include special provisions for the aged in social welfare legislation and in 1972 helped win passage of a measure that tied Social Security benefits to increases in the cost of living, thus protecting the elderly against inflation. Percy also helped draft the Budget Reform Act of 1974 prohibiting the impoundment of funds by the President.

Percy was one of the earliest advocates of consumer protection. In 1972 he cosponsored with Sen. Jacob Javits and Sen. Abraham Ribicoff (D, Conn.) [q.v.] a bill to create an independent consumer protection agency. After the bill was killed by a filibuster in 1974, Percy attacked its

opponents as the "most powerful and lavishly funded lobbying group" in Washington. Although the bill gained widespread support in Congress in the following years, with both houses passing slightly different versions of the measure in 1975, the inability to override a threatened veto by President Ford kept Senate and House conferees from working out the differences in their respective bills.

During the Nixon years Percy frequently found himself at odds with the President. In addition to his opposition to the President's war policies, he voted against the nomination of Clement Haynsworth [q.v.] and G. Harrold Carswell [q.v.] to the Supreme Court, opposed continued funding of the SST and the Lockheed loan, and sharply attacked Nixon's impoundment of funds appropriated by Congress for domestic programs. His actions won him a place on Nixon's "enemies list" and made him the target of White House attacks.

A vocal critic of Nixon's handling of the Watergate affair, Percy drafted the resolution in 1973 that called for the appointment of a special Watergate prosecutor. In March 1974 Percy predicted that the House would impeach the President; the following month he said that Nixon's resignation would be good for the country, and he urged the Republican Party to reject Watergate in its entirety.

Urging the Republican Party to unite behind Gerald Ford after Nixon's resignation, Percy advised Ford to moderate the strongly conservative tone of his 1976 campaign. A member of the Governmental Affairs Committee that investigated in 1977 the financial dealings of President Carter's budget director, Bert Lance, Percy called for Lance's resignation and urged the appointment of a special prosecutor to investigate the matter further. [See CARTER Volume]

[JD]

For further information:
Robert E. Hartley, *Charles H. Percy: A Political Perspective* (Chicago, 1975).

PEROT, H(ENRY) ROSS
b. June 27, 1930; Texarkana, Tex.
Millionaire businessman, and
philanthropist.

Son of a Texas cotton broker and horse
trader, Perot graduated from the U.S. Naval Academy in 1953. After leaving the
Navy in 1957, he went to Dallas to work
as a computer salesman for International
Business Machines (IBM), where he remained until 1962. Although offered an
executive position, he decided instead to
start his own business installing and operating computers for companies by contract. Calling his firm the Electronic Data
Systems Corp. (EDS), he rented computers at wholesale rates and then distributed
them at retail prices to his clients. His
clever management made him and his associates multimillionaires by 1968, when
he incorporated his business. From September 1968 to April 1970 the price of his
stock rose from $16.50 a share to $150.
His investments in his own stock, of
which he retained nine million shares,
made him a billionaire.

Determined to make use of his new
wealth for humanitarian ends, Perot established a nonprofit philanthropic organization, the Perot Foundation, in April
1969. He donated millions of dollars to
the Dallas public school system, including funds to support a ghetto elementary
school. He contributed a million dollars
to the Boy Scouts of America so that it
could provide increased facilities for
blacks and Mexicans in the South. In
1970 he and former astronaut Col. Frank
Borman [q.v.] joined forces to form the
American Horizons Foundation, a group
that would provide money for public discussion panels on television and sound
out public opinion on national issues. A
conservative Presbyterian, Perot believed
in the strict habits of the small town and
untiringly praised the "strong family
unit" as the key to solving America's
problems.

Perot was intensely involved with helping American prisoners of war (POWs) in
Vietnam. His concern was first aroused in
1969 when four women asked him for

money with which they could travel to
the Paris peace talks to question the North
Vietnamese negotiators about the condition of their POW husbands. After granting the women's requests, Perot began a
nationwide campaign to secure the release of American POWs in Vietnam. The
group he established through EDS, called
United We Stand, spent over a million
dollars advertising the plight of the prisoners and urging Americans to stand behind President Nixon's Vietnam policies.
It collected tons of mail, clothing, food
and medicine for the POWs, but its cargo
planes were denied permission to land by
North Vietnam in December 1969.

In January 1970 the Vietnamese rejected his offer of $100 million for the release
of American POWs and would not meet
with him when he flew to Paris and Vientiane, Laos, in April 1970 to discuss POW
release, denouncing his activities as U.S.
"propaganda." Nevertheless Perot's efforts made the U.S. government and the
public more aware of the POWs' plight
and influenced the Nixon Administration
to insist on their safety at the Paris peace
talks. His activities also forced the North
Vietnamese government to improve their
treatment and increase the flow of American mail to them.

Perot favored free public discussion
and participation among Americans about
the war, but urged support of the government as the quickest way of ending the
conflict. He claimed to be nonpartisan in
politics and to have no political ambitions. The Nixon Administration did little
of an official nature to encourage his
efforts to free the POWs.

Perot's sudden wealth led him into the
world of high finance. In 1970 he lent $10
million dollars to the nation's third largest securities firm, F.I. duPont, Glore Forgan, & Co., and took over the company's
ownership to rescue it from debt. After he
incorporated the firm in 1971, he was
indemnified by the New York Stock Exchange for his efforts. Continuing his
stock speculations Perot organized the
duPont Walston, Inc., brokerage firm in
July 1973, ostensibly to save the two big
brokerage houses from bankruptcy. He

invested over $100 million in paying off their previous indebtedness when he effected the 1973 merger, creating the second largest securities firm in the country, but it went bankrupt in March 1974 and was dissolved. Despite his promises to restore the firm to solvency and efficiency, Perot acquiesced in its dismemberment, realizing he had failed.

W.J. Allegaert, trustee of the bankrupt firm, charged in July 1975 that Perot had merged the two brokerage houses to recoup his earlier losses in duPont, Glore Forgan, Inc. Allegaert filed a $90 million lawsuit against Perot, contending that he had deliberately thrust that firm's indebtedness on the stronger Walston firm, thus appeasing the Stock Exchange, which had threatened to expose duPont's inept management.

In 1974 the Senate Watergate Committee disclosed that Rep. Wilbur D. Mills (D, Ark.) [q.v.] had received a secret $100,000 campaign contribution in 1972 from the president of EDS, Milledge A. Hart, and the Dallas regional vice president. Although Perot was not directly involved, his corporation's reputation for honesty was besmirched. In early 1979 Perot again made headlines when he hired a commando team to incite a riot in Iran. The riot led to the storming of the prison and the freeing of thousands of inmates, including two representatives of EDS.

[AES]

For further information:
A.J. Mayer, "Savior or Swindler?" *Newsweek*, (July 14, 1975), p. 64.

PETERSEN, HENRY E(DWARD)
b. March 26, 1921; Philadelphia, Pa.
Assistant U.S. Attorney General, 1971-74.

Henry Petersen graduated from Catholic University, served in the U.S. Marines during World War II, and attended Georgetown University Law School before joining the FBI in 1948. Three years later he transferred to the Justice Department and eventually rose from a clerical position to become chief of the organized crime and racketeering section. His rise was particularly rapid during the late 1960s, when he was promoted successively to posts as deputy assistant attorney general and acting attorney general. Finally, he became assistant attorney general in charge of the Justice Department's Criminal Division, the post to which he was appointed, at Attorney General John Mitchell's [q.v.] urging, by President Nixon in 1971. One year later Petersen was embroiled in the Watergate scandal.

Following the grand jury indictment of the seven Watergate burglars in September 1972, Sen. George McGovern (D, S.D.) [q.v.] accused President Nixon of ordering a "whitewash" in the case and deplored the "questions left unanswered" by the grand jury. As head of the Criminal Division, which was in charge of the early Watergate investigation, Petersen responded to McGovern's charges by stating that the Justice Department's investigation of the case had been "among the most exhaustive and far-reaching in my 25 years" in the Department, and involved some 333 agents.

Throughout the Watergate scandal, Petersen's role and his closeness to the White House prior to the appointment of a special prosecutor was a source of considerable controversy. In testimony before the Senate Watergate Committee in June 1973, former presidential counsel John Dean [q.v.] implicated Petersen in the cover-up. Dean described a meeting with Petersen in early 1972 in which Petersen, Dean felt, gave the impression he "would handle the [Watergate] matter fairly and not pursue a wide open inquiry into everything the White House had been doing for four years." Dean believed this "not because of anything Petersen said, as much as the impression he gave . . . that he realized the problems a wide open investigation of the White House might create in an election year." However, under close questioning by chief Republican counsel Fred D. Thompson [q.v.], Dean admitted that Petersen "isn't the type of man who is easily pushed around," and said he knew of no impropriety on Petersen's part. But Dean later stated in his 1976 book, *Blind Ambition*, that Petersen "must have known what was going on."

In August 1973 Petersen appeared before the Senate Watergate Committee. Offering direct and outspoken testimony, he detailed how Justice Department prosecutors had proceeded in the Watergate investigations. He took credit for informing the President on April 18, 1973 that the Watergate prosecution team had learned of the 1971 burglary of the office of Daniel Ellsberg's [q.v.] psychiatrist. According to Petersen Nixon said, "I know about that. This is a national security matter. You stay out of that. Your mandate is to investigate Watergate." Petersen emphasized: "Now he [the President] didn't say he knew about the burglary. He said he knew about it—about the [prosecutor's] report. I think that is a vital distinction to be made."

Petersen told the Committee that he was dissatisfied with Nixon's instructions on the Ellsberg matter and conveyed his feelings to Attorney General Richard Kleindienst [q.v.] on April 25, 1973. Kleindienst, Petersen stated, agreed that the judge in Ellsberg's trial, William M. Byrne, Jr., should be told. Petersen told the Committee that he had been prepared to resign if Nixon did not agree with their suggested course of action. However, the President endorsed "without hesitation" their intention to pass information about the burglary to Byrne. Petersen also testified that he had a visceral reaction that a cover-up of Watergate was taking place.

Petersen's testimony conflicted with part of Nixon's April 30, 1973 statement on Watergate. Petersen denied that the President directed him on March 21 or any time before April 15 "to get all the facts." He testified that during his meeting with the President on April 15, 1973 he advised Nixon to fire White House aides H.R. Haldeman [q.v.] and John Ehrlichman [q.v.]. He recommended against firing John Dean because Dean had been cooperative with the investiga-

tion. Later that month, however, Petersen said he informed Nixon that the prosecutor's negotiations with Dean had reached an impasse and that Dean should not be retained on the White House staff.

In his testimony Petersen also expressed anger that a special prosecutor had been appointed for the Watergate case. "That case was snatched out from under us when it was 90% complete," he said.

On Nov. 4, 1974, Petersen resigned as assistant attorney general, ending a 27-year career with the Justice Department. He stated that he had no regrets about how he had handled the Watergate investigation.

[FHM]

PETERSON, PETER
b. June 5, 1926; Kearney, Neb.
Secretary of Commerce, February 1972-December 1973.

Peterson had studied at Northwestern University and then at the University of Chicago, where he obtained his MBA in 1951. He began his business career at Market Facts, Inc., a Chicago research firm, and had become assistant director by the time he moved to the advertising firm of McCann-Erickson in 1953. In 1958 Peterson went to work for the Bell & Howell Co., eventually serving as chairman of the board and chief executive officer from 1968 to 1971.

In 1971 Peterson became an adviser on international economic affairs to President Nixon, working closely with Secretary of the Treasury John Connally [q.v.]. In announcing Peterson's appointment as executive director of the newly created cabinet-level Council on International Economic Policy, a White House spokesman said the Council would attempt to provide a "clear top-level focus on international economic issues and to achieve consistency between international and domestic economic policy."

In August 1971 Peterson participated in the special economic meeting at Camp David, Md., where Nixon and his top economic advisers devised a large-scale turnabout in Administration policy known as the "New Economic Policy" (NEP). At Camp David Peterson generally supported the views of John Connally, whose aggressive plans to stabilize the dollar on international markets signaled a complete departure from the "benign neglect" policies previously advocated by Director of the Office of Management and the Budget George Shultz [q.v.] and the Council of Economic Advisors (CEA).

Peterson was also an architect of a new "get tough" policy with Third World countries that nationalized U.S. companies. In early January 1972 he announced that the U.S. would cut off aid to countries which did not swiftly compensate nationalized firms.

In late January 1972 Peterson replaced Maurice Stans [q.v.] as Secretary of Commerce. In one of his first statements as Secretary, he warned of the intensified competition facing the U.S. in the world market, and called on the United States to undertake a "worldwide economic intelligence effort" to keep abreast of foreign developments. Peterson was committed to free trade. A week before his appointment he appeared with John Connally at a meeting organized by the Conference Board, a New York research organization, to attack the proposed Hartke-Burke bill, which would have curbed certain imports and placed restrictions on the operations of U.S. companies abroad.

Peterson played a key role in laying the foundations for the expansion of U.S.-Soviet trade in the 1970s. During May 1972 he held comprehensive talks with Soviet Foreign Trade Minister Nikolai S. Patolichev, which led to the formation of a U.S.-Soviet trade commission, with Peterson as chief U.S. negotiator. Two months later he and Secretary of Agriculture Earl Butz [q.v.] signed a three-year $750 million agreement for the sale of domestic wheat, corn and other grains to the Soviet Union. During July he traveled to the Soviet Union and Poland in an effort to formulate a trade agreement.

On October 18 Peterson signed a three-year trade pact with the Soviet Union. It provided for a settlement of Russia's Lend Lease debt and included a promise by the U.S. government to ask Congress to grant "most-favored nation" status to Soviet goods. The Secretary signed a similar pact with Poland in November.

A month later Peterson resigned his post. He remained in the Administration to conduct a special study on "how the U.S. can better coordinate our trading policy with our major trading partners."

Peterson became embroiled in the ITT scandal, which enveloped many members of the Nixon Administration. In a July 1972 article Washington columnist Jack Anderson [q.v.] alleged that ITT, in October 1971, had submitted a plan to the Administration through Peterson to guarantee that the Chilean government of Salvador Allende "would not get through the critical next six months." Peterson admitted receiving the memo, but denied receiving an 18-point "action plan" and responding to the overture.

In March 1973 the Securities and Exchange Commission (SEC) published its probe of ITT, and named Peterson, with Treasury Secretary Connally, as having been "instrumental" in the delay of three government anti-trust suits against ITT. Ten days later Peterson testified before the Senate Foreign Relations Committee on ITT's role in Chile and admitted that he had met with ITT Chairman Harold Geneen [q.v.] in December 1971 to discuss ITT's "action plan" against Allende. Peterson, however, asserted that the Nixon Administration never seriously considered the ITT proposal.

Upon leaving the government in early 1973, Peterson became chairman of the board at Lehman Brothers, a New York investment bank.

[LRG]

PETERSON, RUDOLPH
b. Dec. 6, 1904; Svenljunga, Sweden
President, Bank of America, 1963-69;
Chairman, Presidential Task Force on International Development, 1969-70.

Rudolph Peterson came to the U.S. from Sweden as a youth. After obtaining a bachelor's degree from the University of

California in 1925, he began a career in finance with the Commercial Credit Co. In 1936 Peterson became district manager for the Bank of America National Trust and Savings Association in Fresno, Calif., and thereafter rose through the Bank of America hierarchy to become its president in 1963. Six years later he was succeeded by A.W. Clausen [q.v.].

In September 1969 the Nixon Administration appointed Peterson chairman of the Presidential Task Force on International Development established to reassess U.S. foreign aid and international economic development. Peterson had made worldwide headlines in April 1967 when he publicly suggested that the U.S. place an embargo on shipments of its gold reserve to foreign holders of dollars, thereby signaling an end to the period of dialogue on international liquidity between the U.S. and its trading partners. The task force, which became known as the Peterson Commission, included future Secretary of Agriculture Earl Butz [q.v.], Harvard economist Gottfried Haberler and bankers David Rockefeller [q.v.] and Robert Roosa [q.v.], as well as other businessmen and scholars. The Peterson Commission's report appeared in March 1970 amidst a spate of similar development reports, most notably the World Bank's Pearson Report and the Rockefeller Report on Latin America, all aimed at an assessment of the first "development decade" in the Third World.

Despite secondary differences the Peterson Report and its analogues emphasized the absence of serious economic development in Third World countries and called for a vast overhauling of the existing aid programs. Of particular importance, according to the report, was the crisis of U.S. foreign policy in such countries as Cuba and Vietnam and the need for a new strategy to combat insurgency in the developing world.

The overall theme of the Peterson Report was the need for a shift from bilateral to multilateral forms of aid. The report advised that the U.S. should provide "a supporting rather than a directing role in international development." Poorer countries should establish their own development priorities and receive aid "in relation to the efforts they are making on their own behalf." The report emphasized the need for a reorientation of aid through global lending organizations such as the World Bank and for U.S. aid to be "provided largely within a framework set by the international organization." The Task Force urged the creation of a U.S.-international development bank and institute, the formation of an overseas private investment corporation to guarantee the security of U.S. foreign investments and loans and the creation of a U.S. development council. It also suggested that all outright relief and welfare grants to poor nations be consolidated under the control of the State Department.

The Peterson Report posed the need for a shift in control of foreign aid from the legislative to the executive branch to avoid the increasing hostility of Congress toward the foreign aid program that had resulted from frustration over the Vietnam war. It urged a "low profile" U.S. military presence, or "Vietnamization" of the U.S. global defense network in which indigenous troops could bear the brunt of any fighting. A strategy was also outlined in the report for using the aid issue to compete with other major developed countries, particularly the European Economic Community (EEC). By connecting the proposed "multilateralism" with a call for all countries to "untie" their aid from agreements that required a receiving nation to buy only from the donor country, the Peterson Report expressed the hope that much of Europe's nonspecified aid grants to the Third World would ultimately result in purchases of U.S. goods. Finally, warning was issued by the Task Force against the dangers of social revolution abroad that could be averted by an open international investment environment, a preparation of local populations for military, police and counter-insurgency functions, and an emphasis on capital intensive development and mass population control.

In September 1970 President Nixon submitted a message on foreign aid to

Congress that closely paralleled the proposals of the Peterson Report. Many of these proposals were adopted in Congress's shift in foreign aid programs after 1970. In August 1971 Nixon recommended Peterson for the post of director of the United Nations Development Program, which Peterson assumed in January 1972. He served until 1976. In 1977 he became chairman of the policy committee of S.G. Warburg North American Ltd., and held several bank and corporate directorships.

[LG]

For further information:
Michael Hudson, *The Myth of Aid* (New York, 1971.)

PIKE, OTIS G(REY)
b. Aug. 31, 1921; Riverhead, N.Y.
Democratic Representative, N.Y.,
1961–79; Chairman, Select
Committee on Intelligence, 1975–76.

Born in Riverhead, N.Y., Pike graduated from Princeton's Woodrow Wilson School of Public and International Affairs in 1946 after military service in World War II. He received his law degree from Columbia and practiced law privately in his home town, where he also held local political office, until elected to the House of Representatives in 1960.

Pike established himself as a moderate and independent representative during his first decade in Congress. Due to his expertise in military affairs and government operations, Pike was appointed to the House Armed Services Committee, where he supported a strong defense posture while seeking to curtail unnecessary military spending; he particularly opposed cost overruns in Defense Department contracts. He also served briefly on the House Ways and Means Committee.

Pike's moderately liberal views on domestic affairs, coupled with his initial conservatism regarding foreign policy, led him to support about 70% of the Ken-

nedy and Johnson Administrations' programs. As U.S. involvement in Southeast Asia deepened, however, Pike spoke out increasingly against American defense policy. As early as 1968, when he presided over the Armed Services Committee's investigation of the *Pueblo* incident, Pike criticized the intelligence community for activities whose value "has not been worth the cost."

In July 1975 Pike was named chairman of the new House Select Committee on Intelligence, which was created to succeed the old committee of the same name after disagreements among committee Democrats rendered it inoperative. The Committee's mandate, like that of a corresponding Senate special committee, was to probe the performance and practices of the U.S. intelligence establishment. Allegations of illegal covert activities as well as its central role in intelligence gathering made the Central Intelligence Agency (CIA) a major focus of the Committee's probe.

Pike's Committee received testimony that intelligence reporting relating to several international crises had been tampered with for political reasons. Among the incidents examined were: the Communists' 1968 Tet offensive against South Vietnam, alleged Soviet violations of the 1972 strategic arms limitation agreement, the 1973 Arab-Israeli war, the 1973 coup that ousted Chile's Marxist Allende government, Turkey's 1974 invasion of Cyprus and the 1974 coup in Portugal.

The investigations of the Pike Committee were punctuated by conflicts with the Ford Administration over access to classified intelligence information. The central issue involved the extent to which secrecy regarding intelligence operations, with its resulting loss of oversight control, was necessary to preserve national security. Pike's position was that "the foreign affairs of the nation belong to the nation, not just to the executive."

When the Administration withheld subpoenaed documents, accusing the Committee of releasing sensitive information, Pike threatened contempt of Congress proceedings against Central Intelligence Agency Director William Colby [q.v.]. A compromise restored the Committee's access to classified information; however, a subsequent dispute over the testimony of midlevel State Department officials again led Pike to seek contempt-of-Congress citations, this time against Secretary of State Henry Kissinger [q.v.]. When Kissinger eventually supplied the required information, Pike recommended that the House not pursue the contempt citations.

In its final report the Committee supported increased congressional control over intelligence agencies through oversight of their budgets and proposed covert operations. A permanent intelligence oversight committee was strongly recommended as well as a method for regular declassification of information.

The Committee's final report provoked as much controversy as its hearings. Although the panel voted to release its report, the full House agreed to delay publication until the Administration certified that it contained no sensitive secrets. Rather than allow the executive branch to "censor the report," Pike favored killing it entirely; however the question became moot after the *Village Voice* published excerpts of the report that had been leaked by CBS news reporter Daniel Schorr [q.v.]. The resulting storm over House security procedures obscured the Committee's efforts at constructive reform of congressional intelligence oversight.

Pike was reelected in 1976. He declined to seek a 10th term in 1978 and returned instead to private law practice in Riverhead.

[PG]

POAGE, W(ILLIAM) R(OBERT) "BOB"

b. Dec. 28, 1899; Waco, Tex.
Democratic Representative, Tex., 1937–79.

Raised on a cattle ranch, Bob Poage was admitted to the Texas bar in 1924, the same year he received his LL.B. After serving 12 years in the state legislature, he was elected to the House of Representatives in 1936, where he represented a largely rural district given over to cotton and livestock. A member of the Agricultural Committee since 1941, Poage allied himself with the conservative Southern Democratic-Republican coalition, backing high farm subsidies and the suppression of farm labor costs through opposition to minimum wage legislation. In 1951 he sponsored the "bracero" program permitting a temporary immigration of Mexican farm workers who would accept low wages for their labor. Poage was a supporter of the Kennedy Administration's farm measures, backing its efforts to require farmers to accept stiff controls over crop yields, rather than acreage allotments, before they could benefit from government price guarantees. In 1966 he became chairman of the Agriculture Committee. During the Johnson Administration, Poage attempted to use his post to kill anti-hunger programs. [See TRUMAN, EISENHOWER, JOHNSON Volumes]

Poage continued his conservative record during the Nixon-Ford years, voting against such key proposals as busing, revenue sharing and migrant workers compensation. In defense and foreign affairs he supported the development of the B-1 bomber and opposed foreign aid. In 1976 Poage received a rating of 100 from the conservative Americans for Constitutional Action.

Poage's power declined in the 1970s because of the dwindling farm population. With only a small number of representatives coming from agricultural areas, he needed the support of urban members to pass farm bills. However, because his Committee controlled anti-hunger and environmental legislation, he was often able to trade support for votes on his farm proposals.

In 1972 Poage successfully opposed efforts to limit the amount of subsidies given to individual farmers in return for his vote against an amendment that would have prevented strikers from getting food stamps. Yet in May 1969 he had refused to take action on an Administration-proposed food stamp program. In presenting the plan, the President had stated that "something very like the honor of American democracy is at stake." Poage charged in his defense two months later that a proposal to establish a free food stamp program would lead to "socialism."

In 1971, as opposition to the seniority system mounted, the liberal lobbying group Common Cause specifically called for Poage's ouster as chairman because he "promoted the interests of influential farmers and blocked legislation to feed hungry Americans." The effort failed that year but he was unseated in 1974. Poage retired in 1979 at the age of 78 after having served 42 years in Congress.

[SBB]

POWELL, LEWIS F(RANKLIN), JR.
b. Sept. 19, 1907; Suffolk, Va.
Associate Justice, U.S. Supreme Court, 1972-.

Lewis Powell received a bachelor's degree in 1929 and a law degree in 1931 from Washington and Lee University. After another year's study at Harvard Law School, he joined an old Richmond, Va., firm in 1932, where he became a partner in 1937. A corporate attorney, Powell specialized in securities law, corporate mergers, acquisitions and reorganizations. He eventually became a director of a number of large companies such as Philip Morris and Ethyl Corp. Powell also engaged in a wide variety of public service work. He headed the Richmond Board of Education from 1952 to 1961 and helped bring peaceful school desegregation to the city at a time when other Virginia schools closed rather than integrate. Powell served on the state board of education, the Virginia constitutional revision commission and President Lyndon Johnson's National Crime Commission during the 1960s. Long active in the American Bar Association, Powell was president of the organization in 1964 and 1965. He headed the American College of Trial Lawyers from 1969 to 1970 and the American Bar Foundation from 1969 to 1971. Along with William H. Rehnquist [q.v.], Powell was nominated to the Supreme Court on Oct. 21, 1971. A recognized leader of the legal profession, Powell faced no significant opposition, and the Senate confirmed his appointment on Dec. 6 by an 89 to 1 vote. He was sworn in on Jan. 7, 1972.

As a justice, Powell was frequently compared to John Marshall Harlan [q.v.]. Like Harlan, he showed great regard for the doctrines of federalism and separation of powers. Powell also was skeptical of the Court's ability to achieve social reform and favored a policy of judicial restraint. He was sensitive to jurisdictional limitations on the Court and adopted Harlan's practice of balancing conflicting interests in deciding cases. Uncomfortable with abstract theories and absolute rules, the Justice preferred a flexible approach that allowed him to accommodate the competing values in a suit.

In First Amendment cases, for example, Powell usually weighed free expression against other societal interests. His majority opinion in a June 1972 decision upheld the private property rights of a shopping center owner over the free speech rights of anti-war protesters and sustained the owner in barring the distribution of political pamphlets on his premises. In April 1974 Powell voided the mail censorship system in California's prisons because it infringed on First Amendment rights more than was necessary to ensure prison security and discipline. Two months later, for a five man majority, the Justice balanced freedom of the press against the right of privacy. He ruled that individuals who were not public figures or officials could recover actual damages for defamatory falsehoods if they proved negligence, not the more limited "actual malice," by the press.

Justice Powell adhered to Harlan's view that state criminal procedures must be "fundamentally fair" but need not meet the standards set for the federal government in the Bill of Rights. He also balanced the claims of defendants and the government in criminal cases but tended to give greater weight to society's interests. In June 1972 Powell voted to guarantee the right to counsel in certain misdemeanor cases and to afford defendants the right to a hearing before their parole could be revoked. However, his majority opinion in a May 1972 case narrowed the scope of the immunity a person must receive before being forced to give up his privilege against self-incrimination. The Justice took a restrictive view of the Fifth Amendment in other cases as well. He also favored the government's position in most Fourth Amendment cases. However, he did speak for the Court in June 1972 to hold that the President had no authority to use electronic surveillance in domestic security cases without a warrant. He voted to uphold state death penalty laws in June 1972, arguing that capital punishment was constitutional and that the Court could only rule on the manner of execution used and the appropriateness of the death penalty for a particular crime.

In race discrimination cases, Powell urged the Court to abandon the distinction between de facto and de jure school segregation and to establish instead a uniform national desegregation rule. He voted in July 1974 against the use of interdistrict busing to remedy school segregation in Detroit but two years later favored the inclusion of suburbs in a plan to correct intentional segregation in urban public housing. For a five man majority in April 1977, Powell ruled that suburban zoning regulations, which effectively barred housing for low income minorities, were not unconstitutional unless a racially discriminatory motive for the regulations could be proven. In other equal protection cases, Powell employed a balanced approach and frequently voted to overturn government distinctions based on illegitimacy, alienage and sex. In March 1973, however, the Justice wrote for a five man majority to hold that school financing schemes based on property taxes did not violate the equal protection clause.

Powell supported a trend narrowing the Court's jurisdiction and wrote several significant opinions in this area. His May 1974 opinion for the Court made class action suits more difficult by ruling that plaintiffs in such cases must bear the full cost of notifying all members of the class on whose behalf they were suing. In a June 1975 opinion Powell tightened the requirement that plaintiffs have legal standing to bring a suit before the Court will hear their case. In July 1976 he restricted federal court review of challenges to convictions based on the Fourth Amendment brought by state prisoners.

The Justice approached due process claims on a case-by-case basis. He voted with the majority in January 1973 to overturn state laws restricting abortions during the first six months of pregnancy as a denial of due process. However, he dissented in January 1975 when the Court held that due process required public school students to receive a notice and a hearing prior to suspension. Powell was described as a friend of the businessman in Court. He often voted against the government in antitrust cases. In a June 1975 decision, Powell ruled that a labor union was subject to antitrust laws if it tried to coerce a general contractor into dealing only with union subcontractors.

A courtly man with a gentle demeanor, Powell was a conscientious and hardworking jurist. His opinions at their best were craftsmanlike products, precise, candid and cogent in argument. Many observers during his first years on the bench saw in Powell the potential for judicial leadership. Moderate and prudent by temperament, Powell was conservative but not inflexible, and he showed considerable independence of mind. Positioned near the center of the Court philosophically, he was considered capable of bringing other justices to his point of view and of acting as a spokesman for the Court on important issues.

[CAB]

For further information:
Gerald Gunther, "In Search of Judicial Quality on a Changing Court: The Case of Justice Powell," *Stanford Law Review*, 24 (June 1972), pp. 1001-1035.
A. E. Dick Howard, "Mr. Justice Powell and the Emerging Nixon Marjority," *Michigan*

Law Review, 70 (January 1972), pp. 445-468. "Hon. Lewis F. Powell, Jr.: Five Years on the Supreme Court," *University of Richmond Law Review, 11* (Winter, 1977), pp. 259-430.

PRICE, RAYMOND K(ISSAM), (JR.)
b. May 6, 1930; New York, New York.
Special Assistant to the President,
1969–73; Special Consultant to the
President, 1973–74.

Raymond Price grew up in rural Long Island and received his B.A. from Yale University in 1951. After serving as an officer in the Navy, he began a career in journalism in 1955, working at *Collier's* and *Life* magazines. He joined the New York *Herald Tribune* in 1957 and became editor of the editorial page in 1964. After the demise of that paper in 1966, he was writing a novel when asked by Richard M. Nixon in February 1967 to join a small staff planning a possible Nixon campaign for the presidency.

A month after accepting his offer, Price accompanied Nixon on a three-week round-the-world trip. The tour, the second of four such foreign study trips made in preparation for the presidential race, covered Asia including Vietnam. During the campaign Price worked as a speechwriter. The nomination assured, Nixon went to Long Island with Price during the Republican National Convention to write his acceptance speech. The address included an "I see" passage evoking Nixon's vision of America's future that had been suggested by another speechwriter, William L. Safire [*q.v.*], and ended with a "train whistle" peroration that took the audience back to the candidate's childhood and reaffirmed the American dream.

After Nixon's election, Price was charged with the responsibility of drafting his inaugural address. The President-elect asked for recommendations from such aides as newly appointed assistant for national security affairs Henry Kissinger [*q.v.*] and urban affairs adviser Daniel Patrick Moynihan [*q.v.*]. Nixon

worked closely with Price on the speech. In preparing the address Nixon defined the themes of his presidency: a reversal of the flow of power from the federal back to the local level in order to make government more effective; a desire for peace but a determination to keep America strong; and the need to bring the country together again. The address became most widely remembered for Nixon's appeal to the nation "to lower our voices" at a time of domestic protest and turmoil "so that our words can be heard as well."

Price was named a special assistant to the President in 1969. He served on the White House research and writing staff headed by James Keogh [*q.v.*]. Other senior writers on the team working on Nixon's speeches, messages and remarks were Safire and Patrick J. Buchanan, Jr. [*q.v.*]. When Keogh resigned in December 1970, Nixon named Price to succeed him. Price was among the most eloquent and persuasive of Nixon aides who were moderates on the issues of race relations. Nixon's own position supported desegregation but opposed most busing. Price wrote the white paper on school desegregation that Nixon issued in March 1970. The 8,000-word document examined the legal history and social ramifications of the problem while spelling out the subtle distinctions of Nixon's own policies. It stressed the importance of local leadership in adapting desegreation plans to local circumstances. The following year Price prepared a similar white paper on housing discrimination and in 1972 wrote Nixon's message to Congress proposing new legislation to limit busing.

Price again played an important advisory and speech-writing part in Nixon's re-election campaign. After the election he asked for and was given a new role at the White House. Named a special consultant to the President and given a small staff, Price launched what he called his "house philosopher" project. He planned mainly to pull together the disparate elements of Nixon's philosophy of government into a more readily accessible form. At the same time Price had an informal understanding with the President that he would be available for those speeches with which Nixon particularly wanted his help, beginning with the second inaugural. The speech stressed a central theme of the Nixon presidency, the need to "locate responsibility in more places," and encouraged "individuals at home and nations abroad to do more for themselves, to decide more for themselves."

After the inaugural Price, instead of returning to his project, found himself increasingly devoting his time to Nixon's statements on the growing Watergate scandal. During the remainder of the Nixon presidency, Price worked on all the President's major speeches on Watergate and finally on his resignation.

In 1977 Price published *With Nixon,* in which he expressed his feeling that the furor over Watergate was disproportionate to the issues involved. He wondered whether "America's brightest hopes since World War II for a new era of peace abroad and progress at home" had been "sacrificed in a spasm of hysteria on an altar of hypocrisy?" Price articulated what he believed to be Nixon's unfulfilled goals: a radical reorganization of the executive branch, a streamlining of the bureaucracy and implementation of the programs of his New Federalism.

To illustrate what he perceived as the unbalanced press' coverage of the Nixon Administration, Price devoted a chapter of his book to the night in 1970 that Nixon visited the Lincoln Memorial during the protests over the U.S. military incursion into Cambodia. Price tried to show that the media had covered the events of the evening incompletely and had misquoted Nixon as having called college students "bums." In Price's view, the President, troubled by the protesters, had spontaneously gone out to try to communicate with them.

As Watergate unraveled, according to Price, the reporting in the newspapers bordered on a witch-hunt. Price did not discount what he described as Nixon's darker side, but he argued that Nixon was

both an extraordinary statesman and a "tricky Dick" and that it took the latter to bring the dreams of the former to reality.

[SF]

For further information:
Raymond K. Price, Jr., *With Nixon* (New York, 1977).

PROXMIRE, (EDWARD) WILLIAM
b. Nov. 11, 1915; Lake Forest, Ill.
Democratic Senator, Wis., 1957-.

The son of a surgeon and staunch Republican, Proxmire earned his B.A. from Yale in 1938 and an M.B.A. from Harvard in 1940. He served in the counterintelligence corps of the Army during World War II and moved to Wisconsin in 1949, where he entered politics as a Democrat. Elected to the state Assembly in 1950, he made three unsuccessful bids for the governorship. In 1957 Proxmire won a special election to fill the Senate seat of the late Joseph McCarthy and in the following year was returned to the Senate for a full term.

In the Senate, Proxmire quickly won a reputation as a maverick. In 1958 he challenged the powerful Senate majority leader, Lyndon Johnson, criticizing him for his arbitrary use of authority and demanding more frequent Party caucuses. During the 1960s Proxmire supported most of the liberal social welfare legislation of the Kennedy and Johnson Administrations. But he attracted attention largely through his persistent attacks on wasteful and extravagant spending by federal agencies, especially the Pentagon. As chairman of the Joint Economic Committee's Subcommittee on Economy in Government, Proxmire was in a position to publicize his concerns, and he frequently commissioned reports by the General Accounting Office to document charges of waste and mismanagement. [See KENNEDY, JOHNSON Volumes]

Proxmire quickly antagonized the Nixon Administration by his determined fight against the controversial supersonic transport plane (SST). In September 1969 Nixon announced his support for continued funding of the plane. Proxmire, who had voted against the initial appropriation for the SST in 1963, immediately declared his opposition to the request. Opposed by the Pentagon, the aerospace industry, and the two powerful Senators from Washington, Henry Jackson [q.v.] and Warren Magnuson [q.v.], all of whom supported continued funding, Proxmire marshaled environmental groups to lobby against the SST. He won his first victory in December 1970 when the Senate killed an Administration request for $290 million. The following month the Senate reversed itself and approved a three-month extension of funds as part of a Department of Transportation appropriations bill. Proxmire, however, won a pledge from Majority Leader Mike Mansfield [q.v.] and Sen. John Stennis [q.v.] that there would be a separate SST funding vote. The campaign against the plane received a decisive boost when the President's chief environmental adviser, Russell Train [q.v.], testified before Proxmire's subcommittee that the SST posed serious health dangers since it could deplete the atmosphere's protective ozone layer. In March 1971 the Senate voted to cut off all SST funds. A final attempt in May to revive the SST was decisively defeated.

Proxmire also targeted the Air Force's C-5A jet transport plane. In May 1969 he released Air Force documents showing a $2 billion cost overrun in the production of the plane. In August the Senate rejected Proxmire's proposal to eliminate from the defense budget $533 million earmarked for C-5As, but the Air Force later cut its purchases of the plane. In 1970 the Defense Department revealed that Lockheed, the nation's largest defense contractor and the maker of the C-5A, had appealed for interim financial assistance to cover losses on the plane. When Nixon made a formal request in 1971 for a $250 million federally guaranteed loan to Lockheed to help it avoid bankruptcy,

Proxmire scheduled hearings of the Senate Banking Committee and threatened a filibuster against the bill. Nixon successfully outmaneuvered Proxmire by requesting instead a broader federal program to aid financially troubled corporations. Proxmire then agreed not to filibuster if the broader bill were dropped. In July 1971 the Senate approved the Lockheed loan by a narrow one-vote margin.

In 1970, Proxmire published *Report from Wasteland,* a blistering critique of the military-industrial complex. He attacked the common practice of retired military officers accepting executive positions with major defense contractors. Proxmire also accused the Pentagon of deliberately bloating its yearly budget request and of lax budget control procedures that led to billions of dollars wasted yearly. He attacked the lack of competition in the awarding of defense contracts, the de facto subsidization of private industry by the Pentagon and the lack of mandatory accounting procedures for military procurement.

Initially a supporter of the Vietnam war, Proxmire changed his stand during the Nixon years. He voted for the Cooper-Church Amendment in 1970 and against extending the draft in 1971, and in 1972 unsuccessfully sponsored an amendment to end U.S. bombing in Southeast Asia unconditionally.

Proxmire also opposed the Nixon Administration's economic stabilization program. In 1970 Congress passed the Economic Stabilization Act, which provided authority for the President to impose economic controls. Although Nixon initially opposed controls, he reversed himself in August 1971, imposed a 90-day wage-price freeze and announced a "Phase Two" policy of controls to follow the freeze. In October he asked Congress to expand his authority to control the economy and to extend the Economic Stabilization Act until 1973. Proxmire opposed the request, arguing that Congress should evaluate Phase Two before extending the President's powers. During the Senate debate on the bill, Proxmire attacked Phase Two as unworkable and inequitable, and charged that it controlled far more of the economy than the parts responsible for inflation. He successfully amended the bill to require the President to report to Congress on action and progress under the stabilization program, and to require Senate confirmation of the chairmen of the Pay Board and Price Commission. But he failed to defeat the extension of the act through 1973, and in December 1971 Congress complied with the President's request.

Proxmire continued to attack the stabilization program. In 1972 he conducted hearings on the economic outlook and called Phase Two a failure. After Nixon announced the lifting of wage-price controls in January 1973 and replaced it with his "Phase Three" proposal for voluntary constraints, Proxmire criticized Phase Three as "feeble and ineffective," and accused the Administration of paralysis in fighting inflation. Proxmire proposed a six-month ceiling on all wages, prices, rents and profits, but the Senate rejected it. Finally, in 1974, Congress allowed the Economic Stabilization Act to expire.

Becoming chairman of the Senate Banking Committee in 1975, Proxmire played a leading role in winning congressional approval of loans for New York City. Throughout 1975 the nation's largest city was dangerously close to defaulting on its financial obligations. City officials first requested federal aid in May, but President Ford, Treasury Secretary William Simon [q.v.], and Federal Reserve Board Chairman Arthur Burns [q.v.] all opposed it. Proxmire opened hearings on the New York situation in October. Questioning bankers and city officials closely, Proxmire concluded that federal aid was essential to avert a New York City bankruptcy that might jeopardize the nation's economic recovery. In December, Congress finally passed legislation allowing the Treasury Secretary to make loans of up to $2.3 billion a year through mid-1978.

In 1976 Proxmire won election to a fourth term in the Senate with 73% of the vote. In 1978 he presided over New York City's request for an extension of the program of federal loans.

[JD]

For further information:
Jay G. Sykes, *Proxmire* (Washington, 1972).

QUIE, ALBERT H(AROLD)
b. Sept. 18, 1923; Dennison, Minn.
Republican Representative, Minn., 1958-78.

Albert Quie was a Navy pilot during World War II. He graduated from St. Olaf's College in 1950, then served in the State Senate from 1954 until winning a special election to the United States House of Representatives in 1958. Quie, with Reps. Charles Goodell [q.v.], Gerald Ford [q.v.] and Melvin Laird [q.v.], led a group of moderate Republicans in the House who were trying to modernize the image of the GOP by presenting alternate versions of social reform, such as revenue sharing between the federal government and the states. Quie voted for the final revenue-sharing proposal that passed the House in June 1972.

On foreign policy and military matters, Quie was generally loyal to Nixon and Ford. In 1970 he opposed the Cooper-Church Amendment limiting the authority of the President to conduct military operations in Cambodia. He voted in favor of the antiballistic missile program in 1969 and the development of the B-1 bomber in 1976. In one particularly controversial action, Quie opposed a 1974 amendment to the military procurement bill that would have deleted $5.8 million for the production of binary nerve gas. He opposed the 1974 resolution calling for a complete cutoff of military aid to Turkey if that country shipped U.S. military equipment to Cyprus.

Quie's greatest influence and area of experience was in educational and social welfare legislation considered by the Education and Labor Committee, of which he became the ranking Republican member in 1971. His association with Democratic Rep. Edith Green allowed them to forge a pivotal force on the Committee between liberals and conservatives, a force that produced many compromise pieces of legislation. Quie was particularly influential in negotiating the amendments to the Older Americans Act in 1973 that cut back funding by $1 billion from earlier Senate and House-passed bills. Through sponsorship of several bills, Quie sought to widen employment in the private sector by giving tax incentives to industry instead of having federal agencies create "make work" projects.

In 1972 Quie voted against a rise in the minimum wage and offered a floor amendment that would have extended the Office of Economic Opportunity (OEO) for two years at a funding level of $4.1 billion, $1.2 billion less than recommended by committee. Quie's reasoning for such action was that Nixon would veto the proposed legislation because it provided for a legal services corporation as well as expanding funding for the Headstart program by $1.5 billion. His amendment was rejected, however, and Congress approved an extension of OEO through fiscal 1974 at $4.75 billion.

In 1975 the Minnesota Congressman unsuccessfully attempted to reduce spending for an educational aid to the handicapped bill and opposed an extension of the school lunch program because he felt it unnecessarily aided the children of the middle class. That same year he voted against the establishment of a federal consumer protection agency as well as the loan for New York City.

In 1978 Quie won the race for governor of Minnesota.

[GWB]

RANDOLPH, JENNINGS
b. March 8, 1902; Salem, W. Va.
Democratic Senator, W. Va., 1958–.

Randolph received his B.A. degree in 1924 from Salem College and then pursued a career in journalism and educa-

tion. From 1933 to 1947 he served in the U.S. House, where he established a record as a supporter of the New Deal. During the next decade he was assistant to the president and director of public relations for Capital Airlines. In 1958 Randolph won election to the Senate to fill a seat vacated by the death of Matthew M. Neely. Two years later Randolph was elected to a full term. During the Kennedy and Johnson years, he supported most of the Administration's social welfare legislation but devoted himself primarily to measures that dealt with West Virginia's economic problems. As chairman of the Public Works Committee, which was in charge of pork barrel projects, Randolph used his position to promote federal highway programs in his state. [See KENNEDY, JOHNSON Volumes]

During the Nixon-Ford Administration, Randolph continued to focus his attention on the problems of his state and of its largest industry, coal mining. He was a frequent supporter of the United Mine Workers of America and the National Coal Association. His backing elicited criticism from reformers who charged that he was unwilling to forcefully promote reform of the industry and improve the health and safety of the miners. In 1969 Randolph, in response to the Administration's proposed coal mine health and safety bill, submitted a proposal weakening a number of provisions in the Nixon measure.

He called for limited compensation for miners incapacitated by black lung disease. Critics maintained that Randolph's changes wiped "out many of the key reforms needed to cut the death toll in the mines" and failed to deal with the problem of black lung adequately. Randolph admitted that many of the changes were suggested by the National Coal Association but defended the measure, insisting that the owners had a right to be heard. During debate on the Administration measure, he warned that hundreds of small mine owners would have to lay off workers and close because of the expense of the program. Nevertheless the Nixon measure, with the Randolph amendment on black lung disease, passed Congress in December.

In 1971 Randolph, who had initially been unsympathetic to the problem of black lung, began to push harder for federal action in response to wildcat strikes and demonstrations staged in support of relief. In 1972 Congress passed a measure, sponsored by Randolph, liberalizing eligibility standards for benefits to miners with the disease.

Although Randolph's Public Works Committee had jurisdiction over environmental and conservation legislation, Randolph played only a minor role in this area. Most of that work was handled by Sen. Edmund Muskie (D, Me.) [*q.v.*], chairman of the Subcommittee on Air and Water Pollution. Randolph usually backed Muskie's actions. However he opposed the Maine Senator on the issue of using highway trust funds for mass transit. Despite Randolph's opposition, the measure passed.

During his Senate career, Randolph was also interested in measures to aid the handicapped, particularly the blind. In 1972 he sponsored the vocational rehabilitation act, which was designed to aid those with severe handicaps. The measure, which Nixon pocket-vetoed that year, would have authorized $800 million in 1973 and $975 million in 1974 for vocational training of the handicapped.

In September 1975 a report filed with the Securities and Exchange Commission named Randolph as one of several recipients of largely illegal campaign contributions from the Phillips Petroleum Corp. He had received a $1,000 contribution from that corporation in 1972. Phillips was also alleged to have made contributions to Lyndon Johnson's 1964 campaign, Richard Nixon's 1968 campaign and Gerald Ford's congressional relection campaigns of 1970 and 1972.

Randolph was considered for a time to be in political trouble during his relection campaign in 1978, but after a campaign appearance by President Jimmy Carter [*q.v.*], West Virginians chose to return Randolph to the Senate for another six years. Randolph voted against both Panama Canal treaties. [See CARTER Volume]

[GMS]

RATHER, DAN
b. Oct. 31, 1931; Wharton, Tex.
CBS News correspondent.

The son of an oil pipeliner, Dan Rather grew up in Houston, where he earned a B.A. in journalism at Sam Houston State College in 1953. He later attended the University of Houston and South Texas School of Law. During the mid-1950s he worked as a journalism instructor and wrote for United Press International and the Houston *Chronicle* before joining the staff of KTRH, the Columbia Broadcasting System (CBS) radio affiliate in Houston. In the late 1950s Rather became director of news and public affairs for KHCU-TV, CBS's Houston television affiliate.

During the 1960s Rather became known for his bold and professional reporting in chaotic and sometimes dangerous situations. As the network's chief Southern correspondent, he concentrated on the civil rights movement. He covered the rioting in Oxford, Miss., on the night of Sept. 30, 1962, when U.S. marshals escorted the first black student, James Meredith, onto the University of Mississippi campus. Rather and his camera crew were on the scene during 15 hours of fighting, in which two people were killed and scores wounded. During this period Rather developed a close relationship with black civil rights leader Martin Luther King, Jr., and was the first reporter on the scene after the assassination of NAACP field representative Medgar Evers in Jackson, Miss.

On Nov. 22, 1963, Rather was in Dallas to film an anticipated visit by President John F. Kennedy to former Vice President John Nance Garner. When the President was shot, Rather skillfully coordinated CBS's four-day round-the-clock coverage of the assassination, impressing viewers with his cool professionalism. In early 1964 CBS News named Rather its White House correspondent. After covering the Johnson Administration for 10 months, Rather, in accordance with accepted broadcasting practice, was transferred to overseas bureaus for additional on-the-spot experience. He served for a year as chief of the London bureau before moving to the battlefields of South Vietnam to cover what he termed "the most important story of this generation." Working with native technicians who doubled as interpreters, he dogged American soldiers, accompanied medical evacuation helicopters, and questioned Vietnamese leaders and civilians in an often futile effort to explain America's intervention in the war.

In September 1966 Rather returned to cover the White House. Aware of an ever-widening "credibility gap" between President Lyndon B. Johnson and the American public as the Vietnam conflict escalated, Rather became convinced that the Johnson Administration occasionally stage-managed the news. Rather relied heavily on his personal sources for news, seldom took detailed notes during interviews with government officials and often "winged" his nightly two-minute spots on "The CBS Evening News."

Although CBS usually rotated its correspondents with a change in presidential administrations, Rather asked to remain on as White House correspondent after the election of Richard M. Nixon in 1968, in the hope that the new Administration would establish more normal relations with the press. Instead the White House assignment became even more difficult as Nixon officials, openly antagonistic toward the media, often deliberately misled reporters or ignored requests for information. Many observers felt that Rather, considered by the Nixon Administration to be a "Johnson Texas Democrat," had been selected as a scapegoat. In April 1971 presidential aides John Ehrlichman [q.v.] and H. R. Haldeman [q.v.] personally accused Rather of inaccurate and biased reporting. Ehrlichman even suggested to CBS executives that Rather be assigned to

a less visible post. Under such pressures Rather took an increasingly subjective tone in his White House coverage. Rather's flippant response to a presidential remark, made during a televised press conference in March 1974, elicited a flood of protest from CBS affiliates, who demanded the reporter's resignation. By June, however, the impact of the Watergate scandal had boosted audience confidence in Rather and other liberal CBS newscasters.

As part of his daily coverage of the White House, Rather accompanied President Nixon on his domestic and foreign travels, including his historic visits to the Mideast, the Soviet Union and the People's Republic of China. In addition, he anchored dozens of CBS News specials, among them a rare person-to-person interview with the President broadcast live from the Oval Office of the White House.

In August 1974, less than a month after Nixon's resignation, CBS reassigned Rather as anchorman-correspondent on "CBS Reports," a spot filled during the 1950s by Edward R. Murrow. In 1976 Rather was also named coanchorman of "60 Minutes," a prime time weekly news show. In 1974 Rather published *The Palace Guard*, a book chronicling the events in the Nixon White House that led to the Watergate affair. Rather's autobiography, *The Camera Never Blinks*, appeared in 1977. Both books remained for several months on *The New York Times* best-seller list.

[DAE]

For further information:
Dan Rather and Mickey Herskowitz, *The Camera Never Blinks* (New York, 1977).

RAUH, JOSEPH L(OUIS), JR.
b. Jan. 3, 1911; Cincinnati, Ohio
Lawyer

Following graduation from Harvard Law School in 1935, Rauh clerked for Supreme Court Justices Benjamin Cardozo and Felix Frankfurter and then worked in a number of New Deal agencies. After serving in the Army during World War II, Rauh worked for the Veterans Emergency Housing Program. He left the Administration in 1947 in protest against the conservative direction of President Truman's policies. In 1947 Rauh began his lifelong association with the Americans for Democratic Action (ADA), largest liberal lobby in the nation. During the 1950s and 1960s Rauh was one of Washington's leading labor and civil liberties lawyers. He was also one of the most prominent white liberals involved in the civil rights movement. [See TRUMAN, EISENHOWER, KENNEDY, JOHNSON, Volumes]

An early opponent of the Vietnam war, Rauh in 1965 helped organize Negotiations Now, one of the leading anti-war organizations. Rauh campaigned in 1968 for Sen. Eugene McCarthy in the primaries and obtained for the anti-war senator the ADA endorsement. Throughout the Nixon-Ford years Rauh remained a persistent critic of the Administration's Indochina policies.

During the Nixon-Ford years Rauh represented the civil rights movement in a variety of causes. On a number of occasions he brought suit against the Justice Department and the Department of Health, Education and Welfare for not moving fast enough to desegregate U.S. schools. Rauh also spoke for the leading black rights organizations in opposition to a number of Richard Nixon's conservative Supreme Court nominations. He led the opposition to the nomination of G. Harrold Carswell [q.v.] to the Supreme Court. Rauh maintained that the President had nominated an "unknown whose principal qualification for the post seems to be his opposition to Negro rights." He presented to the Senate Judiciary Committee a list of 15 cases in which Carswell, as a district court judge, had ruled against litigants who pressed civil rights or due process claims. In each of the cases, said Rauh, Carswell's ruling had been unanimously reversed by the Fifth Circuit Court of Appeals. Rauh later denounced the American Bar Association for approving Carswell's initial appoint-

ment to lower courts and supporting his Supreme court nomination "even after the worst was known." In 1971 Rauh opposed the nomination of William Rehnquist [q.v.] to the Court because of his opposition to school desegregation in Phoenix and his alleged membership in the John Birch Society.

Rauh opposed the nominations of Rep. Gerald Ford [q.v.] as vice president in 1973 and Nelson Rockefeller [q.v.] as vice president in 1974. He contended that Ford's long and consistent opposition to civil rights and welfare legislation was sufficient to disqualify him for the office. He also charged Ford with "extreme partisanship and reckless disregard of constitutional principles" for his role in the abortive attempt to impeach Supreme Court Justice William O'Douglas [q.v.]. Rauh questioned the Rockefeller nomination because of the former New York governor's role in the Attica prison uprising.

During the 1970s Rauh represented the state of California in the *Bakke* case.

[JB]

RAY, DIXIE LEE
b. Sept. 3, 1914; Tacoma, Wash.
Member, Atomic Energy
Commission, 1972-74; Chairman,
Atomic Energy Commission,
1973-74; Governor, Wash., 1976-.

The second daughter of a commercial printer who anticipated a son, Ray had no first name until the age of 16 when she adopted Dixie Lee because of her southern heritage and admiration for Robert E. Lee. A Phi Beta Kappa graduate of Mills College in 1937 with a degree in zoology, Ray secured an M.A. the following year and became a science teacher in the California public school system. In 1942 she returned to graduate study and in 1945 was awarded a Ph.D. from Stanford in biological science. The same year she joined the faculty of the University of Washington as an instructor in zoology.

In addition to her university post, in 1945 Ray became a member of the Friday

Harbor Laboratories, which focused on the impact of various marine organisms on the environment. Her affiliation with the organization extended to 1960. She was then appointed special consultant to the National Science Foundation (NSF) in the area of biological oceanography for a period of two years. An outspoken supporter of environmental preservation, especially when related to the equilibrium of the sea, Ray cautioned her colleagues as early as 1963 about the possible repercussions of pesticides and industrial wastes on marine life. That year she served as special assistant to the director of NSF and assumed the directorship of the Pacific Science Center in Seattle. In 1964 as a visiting professor at Stanford, she joined an international expedition of the Indian Ocean. Ray was appointed to Nixon's Task Force on Oceanography in 1969, but she maintained her faculty position as well as functioning in an advisory capacity for several environmental organizations.

In 1972 she was nominated to serve on the Atomic Energy Commission (AEC). With Senate confirmation Ray became the first woman appointee to a full five-year term. "If it hadn't been for the women's liberation movement I doubt the President would have appointed me," she stated, while denying charges of tokenism.

At the AEC Ray's responsibilities included the supervision of minority hiring and the dissemination of information to the public. At Nixon's request Ray prepared an energy research and development program that would integrate federal and private industry efforts. She structured a plan coordinating the exploitation of nuclear power, coal reserves and oil shale. The plan also called for further exploration of the potential of solar energy. After AEC Chairman James R. Schlesinger [q.v.] resigned in 1973, Ray ascended to the post.

As a result of the Arab oil embargo, the AEC was faced with the problem of developing and expanding nuclear power as quickly as possible while, because of public pressure, meeting requisite safety standards. Thus development would be severely hindered. For Ray the energy crisis had focused on the importance of constructing additional nuclear plants, and she approached the task by separating safety from development and giving each its own staff and budget.

Although many considered this decision a wise move to prevent shortcuts to safety, a number of AEC employes resigned because they regarded the apportionment of funds for safety experiments as a major setback for the development of the costly atomic breeder reactor. Ray defended her move and dismissed charges that nuclear power was inherently perilous. When asked at a news conference if she would allow her two beloved dogs to sleep next to a nuclear reactor, Ray replied, "Yes and you know I sleep next to my dogs."

With the dissolution of the AEC in 1974, Ray was appointed assistant secretary of state for oceans and international environmental and scientific affairs. Although she had been informed she and the division would be the "principal voice and forum" of science-related matters in the State Department, it soon became apparent that she was only contacted for concurrence with Department views. In early 1975, Secretary of State Henry Kissinger [q.v.] informed the Japan Society that the U.S. was prepared to enter into a large-scale joint energy research and development program. The offer was made with no prior consultation with Ray. Angered by the move she handed in her resignation immediately, after only six months in the post.

She then began work on her book *Good Bye America* (1976) with a former aide. The central message, according to Ray, is "if we don't change course and get some sense into international and domestic policies we're heading for oblivion."

In 1976 Ray was elected governor of the state of Washington. She ran on the Democratic ticket and won by more than 100,000 votes.

[DGE]

REAGAN, RONALD W(ILSON)
b. Feb. 6, 1911; Tampico, Ill.
Governor, Calif., 1967-75.

Ronald Reagan's father was an Irish Catholic shoe salesman and his mother an English-Scottish Protestant with a lively interest in the theater. Graduating with a B.A. in 1932, Reagan became a radio sportscaster in Iowa. Five years later, he signed a film contract with Warner Brothers. He subsequently appeared in over 50 movies, often playing the all-American "good guy" who fails to "get the girl."

During the 1940s Reagan became active in liberal Democratic politics. However during Reagan's five consecutive terms as president of the Screen Actors Guild (1947-52), his political views began to shift to the right. He grew disillusioned with Communist influences in the liberal groups he had formerly supported and, in 1949, cooperated with the movie industry's effort to purge actors with alleged Communist Associations. In 1952 Reagan married his second wife, actress Nancy Davis, who strengthened his conservative inclinations and encouraged his political activities. When he became a Republican in 1962, Reagan was already a popular figure among California's extreme right wing. In 1966 he won election as governor, defeating liberal Democrat Pat Brown.

During his first years as governor, Reagan and his inexperienced staff struggled to implement their conservative programs. He recruited 250 prominent businessmen to serve on a Businessmen's Task Force, aimed at restructuring the state government. The Task Force made 1,500 recommendations, and many of its members stayed on as part of Reagan's management team. While a $200 million budget deficit forced Reagan to raise instead of lower taxes, he was able to blame his large budget and tax increases on Brown's administration. Working in cooperation with Democratic Assembly Speaker Jesse Unruh, Reagan made the increased levies more palatable by shifting the burden from local property taxes to sales and income taxes and levies on

banks and corporations. In addition he froze state hiring and the purchase of new equipment and cut state mental health and higher education programs. By the time Reagan left office in 1975, he was disbursing $1 billion each year in property tax relief funds to local governments. By 1973 he had a budget surplus that allowed credits of 20% to 35% on state income taxes and eliminated all such taxes for families earning less than $8,000. [See JOHNSON Volume)

Reagan most prided himself on his successful reform of the state welfare system. In the summer of 1970 he appeared before the U.S. Senate Finance Committee to testify against the Family Assistance Program (FAP), a new federal welfare program favored by President Richard Nixon and his adviser, Daniel Patrick Moynihan [q.v.]. The FAP would have provided a guaranteed federal payment of $1,600 a year for a family of four with no income, provided the head of the family registered for work or training.

Viewing the new program as another step toward state socialism, Reagan returned to California determined to design an alternative to FAP.

The Governor formed a task force of experts in law, public administration and business management to review the existing welfare system and, in 1971, proposed a series of reforms to cut the welfare rolls, increase benefits to remaining welfare recipients and require the able-bodied to take public service jobs. Reagan's staff pushed welfare reform through the state legislature by a narrow margin and obtained the necessary Social Security waivers from the federal government only after the program had been in operation for seven months. The California Welfare Reform Program, credited with a 400,000 decrease in state welfare rolls and a $4 billion saving in taxes between 1971 and 1976, proved one of Reagan's most popular measures and served as a model for other states seeking to make similar reforms.

While liberals acknowledged the success of Reagan's welfare reform and were surprised by his support of liberalized abortion, gun-control and smog-control bills, they remained generally hostile. Critics viewed as naive Reagan's incessant attacks on the evils of big government and dismissed what they regarded as his simplistic solutions to the nations economic and social problems. Robert Moretti, Democratic Speaker of the California House, described Reagan as "a total negativist," the architect of a program that consisted mostly of saying no to the legislature. The Governor's proposals for escalating the Vietnam war and punishing war dissenters further alienated liberals, as did his opposition to farm workers'unions.

After an unsuccessful last-minute bid for the presidential nomination in 1968, Reagan threw his support to Richard Nixon, campaigning vigorously for his Party's ticket. Reagan was easily reelected governor in 1970. During the last three years of his term, he established task forces to deal with the problems of street crime, taxes and the restructuring of local government. He tried unsuccessfully to amend California's constitution to limit the percentage of personal income the state could take as revenue in any one year.

Acting on his stated belief that no governor should serve more than two terms, Reagan left office in January 1975 at the end of his second term. One of the most popular Republicans on the national scene, he had proved his effectiveness as a speaker, particularly in the South, during the 1968 presidential primaries. After leaving office Reagan undertook a heavy speaking schedule, expounding on his conservative philosophy several times a week, in addition to writing a weekly syndicated column and broadcasting a network radio commentary 5 times a week.

In March 1976 Reagan declared his presidential candidacy, challenging Republican incumbent Gerald R. Ford. Reagan aimed his major criticism at the Ford Administration's policy of detente with the Soviet Union, its heavy defense spending and the secret diplomacy of Secretary of State Henry Kissinger [q.v.]. After losing five primaries to Ford, Rea-

gan scored a decisive victory in North Carolina (52% to Ford's 46%), marking the first primary victory since 1952 against an incumbent President seeking renomination. As Reagan continued his attacks on U.S. foreign policy with accusations that the U.S. was retreating from its role as world leader, he chipped away at Ford's base of support, especially in the South and West.

Reagan broke with tradition by announcing his choice for a vice-presidential running mate three weeks before the Republican Convention. He picked liberal Pennsylvania Sen. Richard Schweiker [q.v.]. Reagan supporters were dismayed by what they saw as a betrayal of conservative principles, while critics saw the announcement as a blatantly political move, belying Reagan's avowed distaste for professional politics. At the Convention in Kansas City in August, Ford supporters successfully resisted Reagan's efforts to force the President to declare his own vice-presidential choice before the balloting. Buoyed by this victory, Ford defeated Reagan on the first ballot by 117 votes. Reagan loyalists were able to force Ford, however, to accept a conservative platform, including an amended foreign policy plank.

After his defeat, Reagan returned to speech making and writing his newspaper column. Still prominent in the Party, Reagan became a leading critic of Carter Administration politics. [See CARTER Volume]

[DAE]

For further information:
Bill Boyarsky, *The Rise of Ronald Reagan* (New York, 1968).
Charles D. Hobbs, *Ronald Reagan's Call to Action* (New York, 1976).

REBOZO, (CHARLES G.) "BEBE"
b. Nov. 17, 1912; Tampa, Fla.
Businessman.

Rebozo grew up in the Tampa area and by 1964 had become a leading Florida banker and real estate man. He was president of the Key Biscayne Bank and Trust Co. and held the presidencies of several real estate firms. A friend of Richard Nixon, Rebozo loaned money to the President in 1969 for the purchase of his San Clemente home and gave the Nixon family personal gifts. Rebozo was a frequent White House guest during the last two years of Nixon's presidency, and the President and his friend often relaxed together on the yacht *Sequoia* during evening cruises down the Potomac River. They talked over strategies in the Oval Office and visited one another in Florida and at Robert H. Abplanalp's [q.v.] home in the Bahamas.

During the 1973 Watergate investigation it was revealed that Rebozo played a role in soliciting contributions to a private campaign fund set up by Nixon. One contribution came from billionaire recluse Howard Hughes [q.v.] in the form of $100,000 cash, received in July and August of 1970. The Hughes contribution was considered, by critics, a possible payment in return for a favorable Justice Department action on an antitrust suit involving Hughes. Rebozo told the Senate Watergate Committee that the money had not been spent for any purpose and had, instead, been returned to Hughes. Rebozo was also alleged to have paid $50,000 out of the fund for personal gifts to Nixon. Money funneled through various trust accounts, the Watergate Committee revealed, paid for $46,000 in improvements for Nixon's Key Biscayne home and another $4,562 paid for a pair of diamond earrings Rebozo had given Mrs. Nixon. The Committee noted, however, that Rebozo made these gifts on his own initiative. The fund was again discussed at the Watergate cover-up trial when Assistant Special Prosecutor Richard Ben-Veniste [q.v.] said it was intended to be used to pay $200,000 to $300,000 in legal fees for H.R. Haldeman [q.v.] and John D. Ehrlichman [q.v.]. No charges were brought against Rebozo as a result of his involvement in the fund.

Questions were also raised regarding presidential influence peddling when a possible competitor to Rebozo's Key Biscayne bank was denied a charter in 1973. Rep. Wright Patman (D, Tex.) [q.v.] sought an investigation of the matter, but after a White House spokesman said there had been no involvement by the President, the matter was dropped.

Rebozo continued his banking and real estate ventures in Florida throughout the 1970s.

[BO]

REHNQUIST, WILLIAM H(UBBS)
b. Oct. 1, 1924; Milwaukee, Wisc.
Assistant Attorney General, 1969-72;
Associate Justice, U.S. Supreme
Court, 1972-.

Rehnquist received a B.A. from Stanford University in 1948 and graduated first in his class from Stanford Law School in 1952. He served as a law clerk to Supreme Court Justice Robert H. Jackson in 1952 and 1953 and then moved to Phoenix, Ariz., where he practiced privately from 1953 to 1969. Rehnquist also became active in the conservative wing of Arizona's Republican Party and supported Sen. Barry Goldwater (R, Ariz.) [q.v.] for the presidency in 1964. On the recommendation of Deputy Attorney General Richard G. Kleindienst [q.v.], Rehnquist was appointed assistant attorney general in charge of the office of legal counsel in January 1969.

In that post Rehnquist gave legal advice to the Attorney General and the President and to other departments of government. Considered a brilliant attorney, Rehnquist also served as an articulate and well-informed spokesman for the Nixon Administration in Congress on a variety of controversial issues. He promoted the unsuccessful nominations of Clement F. Haynsworth, Jr. [q.v.] and G. Harrold Carswell [q.v.] to the Supreme Court. He defended the President's power to invade Cambodia, the mass arrests of anti-war demonstrators in Washington and the executive's privilege to withhold information from Congress. Rehnquist supported the Administration's criminal law proposals including authorization of wiretapping and electronic surveillance, preventive detention and "no-knock" entry. He aroused some controversy in March 1971, when he told a Senate subcommittee that the Justice Department opposed any legislation impairing the government's ability to collect information on citizens. He also said he saw no violation of the First Amendment in the Army's surveillance of civilian demonstrators.

On Oct. 21, 1971 President Nixon unexpectedly nominated Rehnquist and Lewis F. Powell, Jr. [q.v.] to the Supreme Court. Opposition to Rehnquist's appointment soon developed among civil rights, civil liberties and labor groups who criticized his conservative record on issues of individual and minority rights. Nonetheless, the Senate Judiciary Committee approved Rehnquist's nomination by a 12 to 4 vote on Nov. 23. After several days of debate, the Senate confirmed his appointment, 68 to 26. Rehnquist was sworn in as associate justice on Jan. 7, 1972.

The youngest justice at the time of his appointment, Rehnquist soon established himself as the most conservative member of the Court. He advanced a narrow conception of judicial review and insisted that policymaking was the function of the political branches of government. He argued that the Court should defer to the judgments of legislatures unless their actions were clearly unconstitutional, and he opposed expansive constitutional interpretations, which he thought allowed the justices to impose their own values on society.

Rehnquist objected, for example, to the Court's extension of the due process clause to a variety of new interests. In cases decided in 1974 and 1975, he voted against granting a right to a notice and a hearing to a federal civil service employe prior to his dismissal, to debtors prior to the seizure of their goods by creditors, and to public school students prior to a disciplinary suspension. He dissented in January 1973 when the Court overturned state laws restricting abortions during the first six months of pregnancy as a violation of the due process right to privacy. In a March 1976 majority opinion, Rehnquist stated that police did not deny due process when they identified an individual in a notice to shopkeepers as an "active shoplifter," even though he had never been convicted of theft.

Similarly, Justice Rehnquist took a limited view of the equal protection clause. It was intended, he argued, to protect blacks from racial discrimination by the state and should not be used to overturn other forms of alleged discrimination unless there was no rational basis for the government's action. As a result of this view, Rehnquist voted, often alone, to uphold laws that established different treatment for illegitimate children, aliens and women. He was the sole dissenter, for example, in May 1973, when the majority invalidated different eligibility requirements for dependency benefits for men and women in the military. He stood alone again in April 1975 when the Court overturned state laws setting a different age of majority for the sexes. Rehnquist spoke for the Court, however, in December 1976 when he ruled that an employer did not violate the 1964 Civil Rights Act, which prohibited sex discrimination in employment, by excluding pregnancy and childbirth from coverage in a disability benefit plan.

The Justice also used a rationality test to decide apportionment cases, and he wrote several significant opinions for the Court based on this standard. In February 1973 he upheld a state legislative districting plan that departed from a strict one-person, one-vote rule because the deviations helped the state achieve the goal of providing representation for local communities. For a six-man majority Rehnquist ruled in March 1973 that the one-man, one-vote standard was not required for the election of officials to a special purpose governmental body, such as the board of directors of a state water storage district.

In racial discrimination cases Rehnquist spoke for a unanimous Court in January 1973 to hold that a defendant must be allowed to question potential jurors about possible racial prejudice. However, his majority opinion in a June 1972 case ruled that racial discrimination by a private club did not violate the Constitution, even though the club received a liquor license from the state. In June 1976, for a six-man majority, the Justice declared that once school officials had complied with a desegregation order by establishing a racially neutral pupil assignment system, they could not be required to readjust attendance zones later on when population shifts caused resegregation.

Justice Rehnquist generally voted to sustain governmental actions against individual rights claims, especially in criminal cases. On Fourth Amendment issues, where he was often the Court's spokesman, Rehnquist persistently upheld police searches and seizures against challenge. In a June 1972 decision he ruled that a policeman could stop and frisk a suspect for a weapon on the basis of an informant's tip and then, after arresting him for illegal possession of a handgun, could search the suspect's car without a warrant. His opinion for the Court in a December 1973 case upheld the authority of the police to make a full personal search following a lawful custodial arrest, even for a minor offense such as a traffic violation. In two decisions in April 1973 and April 1976, Rehnquist stated that a defendant could not claim entrapment into a crime, no matter what the extent of government involvement, if he had shown a predisposition to violate the law. The Justice also voted repeatedly to sustain state laws imposing capital punishment.

In First Amendment cases Rehnquist also tended to give greater weight to society's interests than to individual free expression. He joined the majority in several June 1973 cases, for example, to set new guidelines for obscenity laws which allowed greater government control over pornography. The Justice generally resolved federal-state conflicts in favor of the states. In a June 1976 majority opinion, he overturned a 1968 precedent and held federal minimum wage laws inapplicable to state and local governments.

Rehnquist also favored cutbacks in federal court jurisdiction. His opinion for a five-man majority in January 1976 ruled that a federal district judge exceeded his jurisdiction when he ordered Philadelphia officials to establish new procedures for handling complaints of police misconduct.

Off the bench Justice Rehnquist was a frequent public speaker who agreed with Chief Justice Warren Burger [q.v.] that the Court's caseload was too heavy. On the Court he impressed all observers with his powerful intellectual ability and with opinions that were generally well-organized, able and articulate. Rehnquist's influence on the rest of the Court was a matter of debate. Some commentators believed him too dogmatically conservative in his views to sway other justices. One analyst, David Shapiro, labeled Rehnquist's judicial performance "markedly below" his "substantial capabilities," partly because of "the inflexibility of his ideological commitments." Other observers, however, suggested that the Justice's brilliance, self-confidence and persuasiveness, combined with the prospect of a lengthy tenure, made it likely that he would have a significant impact on the Court over the long run.

[CAB]

For further information:
John R. Rydell II, "Mr. Justice Rehnquist and Judicial Self-Restraint," *Hastings Law Journal*, 26 (Febuary 1975), pp.875-915.
David L. Shapiro, "Mr. Justice Rehnquist: A Preliminary View," *Harvard Law Review*, 90 (December 1976), pp. 293-357.

REID, OGDEN R(OGERS)
b. June 24, 1925, New York, N.Y.
Republican Representative, N.Y., 1963-72; Democratic Representative, N.Y., 1972-75.

Born into the wealthy and politically influential family that owned and operated the New York *Herald Tribune,* Reid served in the Army during World War II, and then received his B.A. at Yale in 1949. He joined the staff of the *Herald Tribune* as a reporter in 1950, and gradually assumed more responsibility in running the paper. In 1955 Reid succeeded his brother as president and publisher of the *Tribune.* In 1959 he became ambassador to Israel. Two years later Gov. Nelson Rockefeller appointed Reid chairman of the New York State Commission for Human Rights.

He was first elected to the House of Representatives in 1962 from a district in Westchester County, and quickly established his independence from the Republican Party regulars by compiling a liberal voting record. As a member of the House Education and Labor Committee, Reid generally voted with the Democrats in favor of the Johnson Administration's social welfare legislation and was a particularly strong proponent of federal aid to education. A consistent supporter of civil rights legislation, Reid was among a team of Northern representatives who observed the 1966 Mississippi primary elections and reported that the Voting Rights Act was being "minimally enforced" in Mississippi. Initially a supporter of the Vietnam war, Reid toured South Vietnam in 1967 with a subcommittee of the Government Operations Committee. On his return, Reid was critical of the South Vietnamese government and questioned the advisability of continued U.S. involvement without substantial governmental reforms. [See JOHNSON Volume]

During the Nixon years, Reid became more active in opposing the war and the Administration's efforts to quell dissent. In the summer of 1969, he joined liberal Democrats on the Education and Labor Committee to defeat a proposal aimed at cutting off federal aid to students who engaged in campus demonstrations. Using numerous parliamentary procedures, the group managed to stall action on the bill and finally to kill it. Reid opposed Nixon's proposal to institute a draft lottery and instead urged a reform of the entire Selective Service System. He voiced support for the anti-war demonstrations scheduled for October and November 1969 and rejected the Administration's charge that dissent was prolonging the war.

In 1970 and 1971 Reid tried unsuccessfully to block the appropriation of funds for combat operations in Southeast Asia. In June 1971 to force the government to release the entire Pentagon Papers, Reid filed suit under the 1966 Freedom of Information Act, which he had sponsored, but the suit was dismissed in December. That same year he disclosed a 1968 Army intelligence plan to spy on persons active in the anti-war movement and labeled the silence of government officials about the plan "disturbing."

Reid also found himself at odds with President Nixon on domestic issues, especially White House efforts to cut expenditures for social welfare programs and its attempts to dismantle many of the federal programs created during the 1960s to aid the poor and to protect racial minorities. In 1969 Reid attacked the President's attempts to weaken school desegregation guidelines. Siding with liberal Democrats on the Education and Labor Committee, Reid fought unsuccessfully in 1969 for a five-year extension of the Elementary and Secondary Education Act of 1965. He also initially opposed the Administration's efforts to merge the Peace Corps, VISTA and other volunteer programs into a single agency, but changed his position in 1971 after extracting a promise from the President to seek increased funding for the programs. Reid also played a key role in the successful effort in 1972 to extend the life of the Office of Economic Opportunity for three years.

In 1971, Reid introduced with Rep. Augustus F. Hawkins (D, Calif.) the Equal Employment Opportunities Enforcement Act. The bill would have vastly strengthened the EEOC, transforming it into a quasi-judicial agency with the power to issue cease-and-desist orders against employers who practiced discrimination. After extensive hearings, the Education and Labor Committee reported the bill favorably in June, but intensive lobbying by the Nixon Administration succeeded in defeating the enforcement provision of the bill. In its place the House passed a Nixon proposal to give the EEOC the right merely to bring suit in federal court against offending employers. Although the Senate initially approved Reid's tougher enforcement provisions, House-Senate conferees agreed on the weaker proposal, which Congress finally enacted in 1972.

Because of his increasing dissatisfaction with Nixon's policies at home and abroad, Reid switched to the Democratic Party in March 1972. He charged that the Republican Party had "moved to the right" and was "not showing the compassion and sensitivity to meet the problems of the average American." In November, he won reelection as a Democrat despite his opponent's heavily financed campaign, which included substantial assistance from Reid's former political ally, Governor Nelson Rockefeller. In 1974, Reid sought the Democratic nomination for governor of New York, but withdrew when it became apparent that Democrats of longer standing in the party had wider support. In 1975 Gov. Hugh Carey appointed Reid to the post of New York State Commissioner of Environmental Conservation, which he held for a year before resigning. Reid joined the business world in the late 1970s.

[JD]

REUSS, HENRY S(CHOELLKOPF)
b. Feb. 22, 1912; Milwaukee, Wis.
Democratic Representative, Wis., 1955–; Chairman, Committee on Banking and Currency, 1975–.

Reuss received his law degree from Harvard in 1936 and shortly thereafter began his public career as counsel to the Office of Price Administration. Reuss served in the Army from 1943 to 1945 and after the war was a member of the price control board of the U.S. military government in Germany. In 1949 he served as an administrator for the Marshall Plan in Paris. Returning to legal practice in Wisconsin, Reuss bolted the Republican

Party in 1950 to protest McCarthyism and in 1954 was elected to the U.S. House as a Democrat.

Reuss generally aligned himself with liberal Democrats in the House, supporting the social legislation of the Kennedy and Johnson years but emerging as an early opponent of the U.S. war effort in Southeast Asia. Reuss was a member of both the Joint Economic Committee (JEC) and the House Banking and Currency Committee. He also chaired the International Finance Subcommittee, where he sponsored "soft loans" to Latin American countries through the International Development Association. Reuss was an early supporter of environmental legislation and opposed supersonic transport (SST) proposals from 1964 onward. [See KENNEDY, JOHNSON Volumes]

One of Reuss's primary concerns during the Nixon years was inflation, for which he saw wage-price controls as an essential antidote. When Nixon, immediately after assuming office, announced cuts in the fiscal 1970 budget aimed at achieving a government surplus, Reuss attacked the cuts as "a phony war" on inflation whose sole result would be increased unemployment. In September 1969 Reuss, as a member of the House Government Operations Committee, held hearings on his own bill requiring the Administration to adopt voluntary wage-price guidelines. Although the bill cleared committee in May 1970 and drew immediate fire from the Administration, it never became law. In July 1970 Reuss stepped up his campaign, calling for "across the board freezes on wages, prices, rents, salaries, the whole works" for a three- to four-month period.

Reuss was also deeply involved in liberal tax reform. Reuss's principal target was the corporate depreciation tax writeoff, which he felt privileged business at the expense of the consumer. In early 1971 Reuss had no less than 10 tax reform bills under consideration. In July of the same year, after the Treasury issued new depreciation guidelines, Reuss filed a joint lawsuit with Ralph Nader [q.v.], the liberal lobby Common Cause, the

United Automobile Workers, the National Rural Electric Cooperative Association and a real estate developer charging the Treasury with circumventing congressional authority in taxation matters. When the Nixon Administration proposed an income tax credit in September 1971, Reuss, who felt that the 1969 tax reform bill had already opened too many loopholes for the wealthy, attacked the proposal and instead called for public works programs to combat unemployment.

Reuss was an important House arbitrator of U.S. policy in the international monetary crises and reform of the early 1970s. When the Nixon Administration concluded an agreement with South Africa permitting the sale of South African gold to the International Monetary Fund (IMF), Reuss, in January 1970, attacked the move for "institutionalizing South Africa as a supplier of gold." In June 1971 Reuss introduced a "sense of Congress" resolution to end U.S. gold sales to foreign central banks, and in August 1971, one week before President Nixon officially suspended the gold backing of the dollar, Reuss criticized any increase in the price of gold for giving "windfall profits" to gold-producing nations. Nonetheless, when the Smithsonian Agreement of December 1971 brought about a modest devaluation of the dollar and effected a small increase in the official price of gold, Reuss called the agreement "glorious." In House debate in March 1972, he called for the phasing out of the dollar as a reserve currency. Several months later when the Smithsonian Agreement was in turn threatened by new chaos in the international money markets, Reuss urged the Joint Economic Committee to permit central banks and the IMF to sell gold on the free market to "help ease the apprehension that currently exists about the viability of the Smithsonian monetary arrangements." When the Smithsonian Agreement collapsed in the spring of 1973, Reuss attacked the Nixon Administration for its "much too laggard and lackadaisical attitude" toward the U.S. balance-of-payments deficit. He also welcomed the European currency float of

March 1973, expressing his fear that the "U.S. could be conned into massive intervention" in support of the dollar.

In January 1975 Reuss became chairman of the House Banking and Currency Committee, succeeding Rep. Wright Patman (D, Tex.) [q.v.]. His focus thus turned to questions of domestic banking reform and congressional control of the Federal Reserve. As a member of the JEC, Reuss had already been involved in shaping the One-Bank Holding Company Act of 1970, attacking the banking lobby for pushing the Committee "toward wholesale exceptions for a number of bank holding giants." But in 1975, in the wake of the 1974-75 recession, Reuss felt the need for extensive reform was even more urgent. In February 1975 the Banking Committee rejected a bill introduced by Reuss that would have required the Federal Reserve Bank to force down interest rates and to expand the money supply at a set rate of 6% per year. In June 1975 Reuss's ambitious "credit reporting" bill was defeated by the House. The bill would not only have required the top 200 U.S. commercial banks to disclose their lending practices to the Federal Reserve, but would also have required them to channel credit into "national priority areas." Opponents of the bill saw it as a step in the direction of mandatory credit allocation by the government.

In January 1976, after the Comptroller of the Currency's "problem list" of top commercial banks was leaked to the press showing potential massive illiquidity in the private banking system, Reuss convened the House Banking Committee for hearings. Federal Reserve Chairman Arthur Burns [q.v.] testified to oppose renewed calls for extensive disclosure, but Reuss argued that only such disclosure, together with serious overhaul of the federal regulation of banks, would restore public confidence in the banking system.

Aside from his areas of legislative expertise, Reuss involved himself directly in other liberal issues. In 1969 and 1970 he attacked major corporations involved in pollution and held hearings on population growth. He was a consistent opponent of funds for the SST and fought to reduce allocations for new jets. In 1971 he cosponsored legislation with Sen. Hubert Humphrey (D, Minn.) [q.v.] for federal revenue sharing, aimed at achieving "modernization" of state and local governments desiring funds. In 1975, after the Ford Administration's endorsement of Vice President Nelson Rockefeller's [q.v.] $100 billion "Energy Independence" proposal, Reuss attacked the plan as "grossly inflated, fiscally irresponsible and susceptible to political manipulation." He also sponsored legislation in late 1975 to provide $4 billion in federal loan guarantees to New York City.

Reuss was reelected to a 12th term in November 1976, and in his capacity as chairman of the House Banking Committee, he continued to support and advocate liberal measures for streamlining federal regulatory control over the credit system and other sectors of the economy. [See CARTER Volume]

[LG]

REUTHER, WALTER P.
b. Sept. 1, 1907; Wheeling, W.V.
d. May 10, 1970; Pellston, Mich.
President, United Automobile
Workers, 1946-70.

Walter Reuther was the son of an immigrant German socialist and union leader. After finishing high school he became a skilled tool and die worker at the Ford Motor Co. plant in Detroit. Fired for his union activity in 1931, Reuther joined the Socialist Party and attended Wayne State University for two years. In 1935 he and his brothers Roy and Victor joined the drive to organize the new United Automobile Workers (UAW). Reuther won his first union post in 1936 as a member of the UAW executive board.

During World War II the Reuther brothers organized their own caucus which fought for control of the UAW against the Communist-supported leadership. In 1945 Reuther led the union's General Motors division in an aggressive 113-day strike, despite the continued adherence of the Congress of Industrial Organizations (CIO) to the wartime no-strike pledge. He won the support of the UAW's restive membership and, in 1946, the union presidency. Over the next decade, however, Reuther abandoned radicalism and moved towards a rapprochement with the existing structures of American politics and industrial relations. He served as president of the CIO from 1952 until its merger with the American Federation of Labor (AFL) in 1955 and became a power within the national Democratic Party. At the same time, Reuther sought incremental improvements for UAW members through an innovative collective bargaining program. [See TRUMAN, EISENHOWER Volumes]

Reuther was an enthusiastic supporter of President John F. Kennedy, and he made the UAW an effective lobbying force for the Johnson Administration's Great Society and civil rights legislation. Within the UAW, however, as local leaders and rank and file members became more concerned with non-economic grievances involving production standards and working conditions, Reuther encountered serious opposition to his policies and recurrent wildcat strikes following negotiation of each company-wide contract.

Since the late 1950s Reuther had been involved in a continuing dispute with AFL-CIO president George Meany [q.v.] over the Federation's domestic and foreign policies. Reuther complained that the AFL-CIO had become complacent and conservative, and he criticized Meany for refusing to mobilize the Federation's resources in an all-out drive to organize the majority of American workers who did not belong to unions. He also took a dim view of AFL-CIO ties to the Central Intelligence Agency and other clandestine government units. In 1967 Reuther and other UAW officials resigned from their AFL-CIO posts, and shortly afterwards the union began to withhold its dues to the Federation. In May 1968 Meany formally suspended the auto workers. [See KENNEDY, JOHNSON Volumes]

Upon leaving the AFL-CIO Reuther formed the Alliance for Labor Action (ALA) with the International Brotherhood of Teamsters. The new labor center was later joined by the Chemical Workers Union. In 1969 the ALA issued a "declaration of purpose" which included a long list of social welfare and trade union goals, with emphasis on coordinated organizing drives among white collar employes and the working poor. Reuther and Teamster president Frank Fitzsimmons [q.v.] also issued a critical statement on the Vietnam war and on the development of the anti-ballistic missile—positions standing in sharp contrast to those of the AFL-CIO leadership. The Federation, for its part, issued a 99-page report on the dispute in April, in which Reuther was denounced for failing to use the "democratic forums" of the AFL-CIO to air his differences. The ALA proved stillborn, however, largely because of the Teamsters' growing friendliness towards the Nixon Administration. After several years of relative inactivity, it was formally dissolved by the UAW in 1972.

Approaching the 1970 auto industry negotiations, Reuther drew up a set of demands that centered around wages and retirement benefits. A key feature of the union's bargaining program was the concept of "30-and-out," whereby auto workers would start collecting monthly pensions of $500 after 30 years of service, regardless of age. Before negotiations had begun, however, Reuther, his wife, and four others were killed on May 9 when their chartered plane crashed and exploded near Pellston, Mich. Leonard Woodcock [q.v.], a former Reuther assistant, was elected to the presidency by the UAW executive board.

[TLH]

Frank Cormier and William J. Eaton, *Reuther* (Englewood Cliffs, 1970).

RHODES, JAMES A(LLEN)
b. Sept. 13, 1909; Jackson, Ohio.
Republican Governor, Ohio,
1963-1971; 1975-.

Rhodes, the only son of a coal miner who was killed in a mine accident, went to work when he was 10 to earn money for his family. He began his political career in 1933 by winning an election for Republican committeeman in Columbus, Ohio. After holding a number of city posts, he was elected state auditor in 1952. He held the post until 1962, when he unseated the incumbent Gov. Michael V. DiSalle, a liberal Democrat who had angered many voters by raising state taxes. He held the governor's office for two terms. While in office, Rhodes reduced state expenditures, balanced the state budget and embarked on an industrial development program that attracted hundreds of companies to the state. He also initiated extensive highway and university construction projects, which he financed by raising $1.4 billion through state bond issues, a program his critics attacked as deficit financing. [See JOHNSON Volume]

Rhodes's political career suffered a setback in the early 1970s. Barred from seeking a third consecutive term as governor, Rhodes ran against Robert A. Taft, Jr. [q.v.], in the 1970 Republican senatorial primary. The race became the most bitter intraparty fight in 20 years. Taft ran on an "integrity" platform and indirectly alluded to a critical *Life* magazine article on Rhodes by attacking the Governor's "lifestyle." The April 1969 article criticized Rhodes for commuting the life sentence of a mobster with alleged gangland connections and claimed that Rhodes "had dipped into" campaign funds. Rhodes, on the other hand, ran on a "law and order platform."

On May 2, 1970, three days before the primary election, Rhodes ordered National Guard troops to the Kent State University campus to quell student demonstrations that had broken out in protest of the U.S. incursion into Cambodia. The next day the Kent State Student Senate charged that Rhodes had ordered the troops to the campus out of political motivations. Rhodes denounced the demonstrators as "the worst type of people we harbor in America." On May 4, the day before the primary, the troops fired their weapons in reaction to sniper shots coming from a nearby building, but later admitted they had no evidence of such action. The day after the shooting, Rhodes lost the primary by less than 5,000 votes. In November, Ohio Republicans suffered a major defeat when their entire slate of candidates for state office was defeated after the disclosure of financial scandals involving members of the Rhodes administration.

The shootings led to lengthy grand jury investigations and bitter legal controversies. Rhodes ordered the state attorney general to convene a grand jury for the purpose of investigating the shootings to determine if those involved were criminally responsible. The grand jury issued a report which found that the guardsmen had acted in self-defense, and handed down 25 indictments against demonstrators.

In 1973 a federal grand jury launched a new investigation into the shootings. Although state officials were cleared of criminal responsibility, the parents of the victims and the wounded students filed a $46 million civil damage suit against Rhodes and other state officials in 1975. At the trial Rhodes testified he had not known that the troops carried loaded weapons and described the situation as "almost a state of war." Although the federal jury exonerated Rhodes and 28 other defendants in August 1975, a new trial was ordered after the case was appealed.

When the case was finally settled out of court before the second trial was due to begin in 1979, Rhodes was again governor. He had made an unexpected political comeback by defeating incumbent Gov. John J. Gilligan [q.v.] by 11,000 votes in 1974. Rhodes was surprised by his victory since he had publicly conceded defeat after the TV networks had declared Gilligan the winner. He was reelected in 1978 to his fourth four-year term.

The Kent State suit was settled when the state agreed to pay $600,000 in damages and when, as part of the settlement, Rhodes signed a statement saying "in retrospect, the tragedy of May 4, 1970, should not have occurred." He also admitted that the protesting students "may have believed they were right" in continuing the protests in spite of a university ban on rallies.

[AE]

RHODES, JOHN J(ACOB)
b. Sept. 18, 1916; Council Grove, Kan. Republican Representative, Ariz., 1953-; Chairman, Republican Policy Committee, 1965-1973; House Minority Leader, 1973-.

Rhodes, the youngest son of a retail lumber dealer and Kansas state treasurer, was born in the tiny farming community of Council Grove, Kan. After graduating from Kansas State University in 1938, he obtained a degree from Harvard Law School. Following service in the Army Air Corps during World War II, he resettled in Mesa, Ariz., opened a law practice and helped start a firm that later became the Farm and Home Life Insurance Co.

In 1950 Rhodes, a long-time Young Republican activist, and Phoenix City Councilman Barry M. Goldwater [q.v.] jointly managed Howard Pyle's successful Republican gubernatorial nomination campaign. Pyle was elected, but Rhodes running on the ticket for attorney general lost by a narrow margin. He successfully ran for Congress two years later, becoming the first Republican elected to the House from Arizona. He represented a white, affluent, conservative district comprising parts of Phoenix and its nearby suburbs. [See KENNEDY, JOHNSON Volumes]

Rhodes consistently supported the Nixon-Ford Administrations' legislative programs, voting their positions about 75% of the time. He favored a strong defense, endorsed the Administration's Vietnam policy and backed foreign military aid.

Generally Rhodes agreed with the concepts of a balanced federal budget and economy in government. He opposed most major domestic assistance bills, such as mass transit subsidies, aid to education, and federally funded public housing projects. He regularly backed positions taken by the National Association of Businessmen, which gave him its "Watchdog of the Treasury" award for the 1969-1970 session of Congress. He supported the policies advocated by the conservative Americans for Constitutional Action more than 70% of the time, while he rarely sided with the proposals made by consumer groups or labor organizations.

Rhodes quietly but steadily worked his way up through the Republican leadership in the House. In 1965 he was elected chairman of the Republican Policy Committee, beating an opponent endorsed by newly elected House Minority Leader Gerald R. Ford (R, Mich.). When Ford became Vice-President in October 1973, Rhodes immediately announced his candidacy for minority leader. Although he had several rivals for the job, they all dropped out of the race, and Rhodes was elected by acclamation.

The emerging Watergate scandal and the impeachment inquiry dominated the first eight months of Rhodes's leadership. Initially believing in Nixon's innocence, Rhodes tried to defend the President and to disassociate the Republican Party from the scandal. When experts reported in January 1974 that one of the key Watergate tapes might have been deliberately erased, he admitted the report was harmful, but cautioned there was "no evidence to connect the President with the erasure." In February he urged the Republican Party to take the offensive since it had nothing to do with the Watergate abuses. However by April 1974 he agreed that "the continuing mystery surrounding Watergate is hurting the image of President Nixon and the Republican Party."

When the White House gave the Judiciary Committee only edited transcripts rather than the actual tapes of presidential conversations subpoenaed by the Committee, Rhodes announced that the majority of Republicans believed the White House was in substantial compliance with the subpoena. After the released transcripts had generated a public furor, Rhodes admitted on May 9 that "the contents of the tapes was devastating." He suggested that resignation was now a possible option, and said that Nixon's departure would be beneficial to the Republican Party.

Rhodes supported the Judiciary Committee's impeachment inquiry. In January 1974 he headed off Republican efforts to put an April 30 deadline on the Committee's impeachment investigation. In June 1974 he opposed conservative Republicans who wanted to turn the case against Nixon into a vote of censure rather than impeachment. Rhodes opposed the action on the grounds that it would be doing the country a great disservice to leave a censured president in office.

Rhodes joined the move towards impeachment after the Aug. 5 release of key transcripts showed Nixon had discussed using the CIA to stop the FBI's Watergate probe. He later endorsed the Nixon pardon, arguing that Nixon had paid a substantial price by resigning and that anything more would be overkill rather than justice. However he strongly opposed pardons for other Watergate figures, contending they had not suffered the "special consequences that a fallen President must bear."

Rhodes proposed a consensus-type government after the 1974 elections swept an overwhelmingly Democratic majority into Congress. He urged that Democrats cooperate with the Administration to prevent a partisan stalemate between the Republican White House and the Democratic Congress. But he warned the Democrats in January 1976 that unless their leadership worked with the Administration instead of against it, there would be more presidential vetoes than ever before. Although it was heavily outnumbered in the House, Rhodes successfully held together the Republican minority and gathered enough conservative Democrats to sustain many of President Ford's 61 vetoes.

In 1975 Rhodes unveiled a legislative agenda drafted by the House Republicans. It called for a balanced budget within three years, the automatic extension of unemployment benefits coupled with job training programs during recession periods, catastrophic illness insurance protection, a windfall energy profits tax and revisions in the food stamp program. The agenda accepted the idea of deficit spending, a position that Rhodes had long opposed. Rhodes described the measures as a full-employment budget.

In 1976 Rhodes published *The Futile System*, a highly critical examination of Congress which he describes as "a pitiful, helpless giant, devoid of coordination or purpose." He blamed the Democratic leadership that had controlled Congress for the last 22 years for the existing congressional deficiencies. Rhodes prescribed "a periodic switching of [party] control as a way to keep Congress "institutionally fit."

Rhodes continued as minority leader during the Carter Administration. [See CARTER Volume]

[AE]

RIBICOFF, ABRAHAM A(LEXANDER)
b. April 9, 1910; New Britain, Conn.
Democratic Senator, Conn., 1963—.

The son of an immigrant Jewish factory worker, Ribicoff worked his way through New York University and the University of Chicago Law School. Following graduation in 1933, he returned to Connecticut to open a law practice. In 1938 he won election to the Connecticut General Assembly, where he served two terms. He then served five years as a police court judge. In 1948 Ribicoff won a seat in the U.S. House of Representatives, where he remained until 1952, when he lost a close race for the Senate. Two years later he was elected governor of Connecticut. Ribicoff served as Secretary of Health, Education and Welfare during the Kennedy Administration and worked unsuccessfully for the passage of medicare. He resigned to run for Connecticut's Senate seat in 1962. As senator, Ribicoff devoted a great deal of attention to the passage of liberal legislation in areas that he was interested in as a member of the Administration. [See EISENHOWER, KENNEDY, JOHNSON Volume]

During the Nixon Ford years Ribicoff was a leader in the campaign for national health insurance. He opposed the ambitious health program supported by Sen. Edward Kennedy (D, Mass.) [q.v.], which promised total coverage to all Americans, because it was too expensive and would become a bureaucratic nightmare. Rather, he joined Sen. Russell Long (D, La.) [q.v.] in offering an alternative bill that provided insurance only for catastrophic illnesses. Under the plan medicaid would handle services for the poor and medicare for the elderly. The remainder of the nation would continue to participate in government-subsidized, private or union plans. Testifying on behalf of his bill, Ribicoff stated that the government did not have the administrative capacity to manage a national health care program and suggested that private insurance companies handle the program. Supporters of the Kennedy plan accused Ribicoff of opposing the more ambitious program because his state contained more national insurance companies than any other state in the nation. Congress failed to act on either the Ribicoff or Kennedy bills.

Along with his interest in improving the health delivery system of the nation, Sen. Ribicoff assisted the Administration in 1970 in its futile effort to introduce a welfare reform program. The Administration proposed a Family Assistance Program (FAP) that promised a guaranteed minimum payment of $1,600 to a family of four. The working poor were also to receive benefits. The proposal encountered stiff opposition in the Senate, where liberals denounced it as too weak and conservatives dismissed the need for the program. In an effort to reach a compromise, Ribicoff introduced an amendment to test the FAP in selected areas and then put it into effect nationally. The Senate Finance Committee voted 9 to 4 to defeat this move endorsed by the Administration. The Committee then buried the Nixon proposal by a vote of 14 to 1.

As governor of Connecticut, at HEW and as a senator, Ribicoff was hailed as one of the champions of civil rights in the nation. In 1970 he found himself allied with Southern conservatives when he announced his intention to vote for the amendment sponsored by Sen. John Stennis (D, Miss.) [q.v.] that called for a uniform policy on enforcement of school desegregation guidelines regardless of the cause of discrimination. The amendment thus sought to eliminate the distinction between de jure and de facto segregation. Ribicoff called on other Northern senators to drop their "monumental hypocrisy" and admit that Northern school systems were just as racially segregated as those in the South. But he emphasized that he would not support any anti-busing amendment that would "halt federal efforts to enforce school desegregation." Although the Stennis amendment was adopted in the Senate, a House-Senate conference committee reinstated the de jure-de facto distinction.

The following year the Connecticut Senator proposed his own two-part plan designed to significantly increase integration in the schools and housing patterns of the nation's suburban communities. The first part of Ribicoff's proposal required all schools within a metropolitan area to have a percentage of minority students at least equal to half the percentage of minority students in the entire metropolitan area. Under his proposal communities would have 12 years to accomplish this integration but would have to show progress annually. If no progress was shown, the schools would face a cutoff of federal funds. The second part of the legislation required suburban communities to maintain federally aided housing facilities for low and moderate income families. This section of his plan was to be implemented immediately. In his speech Ribicoff deplored "the seem-

ingly inexorable march toward apartheid in the North as well as the South." Citing U.S. census figures showing Northern schools as a whole were more segregated than schools in the South, he said "racial isolation is now just as pervasive in the North as it is in the South."

During the first two years of the Carter presidency, Ribicoff continued to press for national health insurance welfare reform and the creation of a consumer protection agency. Ribicoff, a pro-Zionist Jew, startled the Jewish community when he voted for the 1978 arms sales for Egypt and Syria. Ribicoff announced in 1979 he would not seek reelection the following year.

[JB]

RICHARDSON, ELLIOT L(EE)
b. July 20, 1920; Boston, Mass.
Undersecretary of State, January 1969–June 1970; Secretary of Health, Education and Welfare, June 1970–January 1973; Secretary of Defense, January 1973–April 1973; Attorney General, May 1973–October 1973; Ambassador to Great Britain, December 1974-December 1975; Secretary of Commerce, December 1975-January 1977.

Descended from early New England settlers and a family of physicians, Richardson attended Harvard College (B.A., magna cum laude, 1941) and Harvard Law School (LL. B., magna cum laude, 1947). He interrupted his studies to serve with distinction as a first lieutenant in the Army during World War II. He began his legal career with great promise, becoming editor and president of the *Harvard Law Review*, then clerking for the distinguished U.S. court of appeals judge Learned Hand in 1947–48 and for Supreme Court Justice Felix Frankfurter in 1948–49. After three years with the noted Boston law firm of Ropes, Gray, Best, Coolidge, and Rugg, he began a career in public service as an aide to Massachusetts Sen. Leverett Saltonstall in 1953.

In 1957 President Eisenhower appointed Richardson assistant secretary for legislation in the relatively new Department of Health, Education and Welfare, where he played a major part in drafting the National Defense Education Act and in developing legislation on Social Security, public health and juvenile delinquency. He returned to Boston in 1959 with an appointment as U.S. attorney for Massachusetts. In this capacity, he quickly earned a reputation as a relentless prosecutor. One of his best-known cases involved the prosecution and conviction of Bernard Goldfine for tax evasion after Goldfine's gifts to the White House Chief of Staff Sherman Adams had produced the most scandalous cause celebre of the Eisenhower Administration.

Following the defeat of the Republican national ticket in 1960, Richardson plunged into Massachusetts politics, running for (but losing) the Republican primary contest for state attorney general in 1962. In 1964 he won election as lieutenant governor. For the next two years he took an active role in the administration of Gov. John Volpe, particularly in coordinating social welfare programs. Elected state attorney general in 1966, he pursued such liberal causes as consumer protection and crime prevention measures. He was still serving in this capacity when he was tapped by the new Nixon Administration to become undersecretary of state in 1969.

Recommended by President Nixon's close friend William Rogers [q.v.] and endorsed by newly appointed Secretary of Transportation John Volpe [q.v.] Richardson came to the State Department with little experience in foreign affairs. However Secretary of State Rogers, who knew Richardson from the Eisenhower years, had confidence in his administrative ability and felt that they would be in such personal rapport that Richardson would act as his "alter ego."

During his 17 months at the State Department, Richardson undertook both public and bureaucratic tasks. Traditionally the undersecretary has the responsibility for administering the Department, and Richardson assumed these duties, immersing himself in the details and nuances of foreign affairs and introducing administrative and personnel reforms in an attempt to revitalize the Foreign Service. Soon after being sworn in, he represented the United States at the Paris meeting of the Organization for Economic Cooperation and Development, proclaiming an Administration policy of increased free trade. Late in 1969 he was actively involved in the preparations for the Strategic Arms Limitation Talks held in Helsinki. Richardson proved to be a vigorous supporter of the President's decision to invade Cambodia even though he had serious private reservations about that action. CBS TV newsman Dan Rather, in *The Palace Guard*, suggested that this support for a controversial policy established Richardson's loyalty in President Nixon's eyes and therefore helped him to receive a promotion to the cabinet as Secretary of Health, Education and Welfare (HEW) in June 1970.

The Department Richardson inherited from Robert Finch [q.v.] was badly demoralized, administratively disarrayed and often ideologically out of tune with the Nixon political orientation. An unwieldy bureaucracy when initially created, HEW had grown during the Johnson Great Society years and then been allowed to drift as that President's attention became consumed with waging the war in Southeast Asia.

When the Nixon Administration assumed office, it found HEW difficult to manage and resistant to attempts to cut back the Great Society legacy. During 1969 and 1970 the Department was further disrupted when civil rights issues and opposition to the Vietnam war caused mass resignations of liberal departmental officials. Robert Finch, who had found the task of directing HEW frustrating and exhausting, resigned to become a White House adviser.

As a progressive Republican with a reputation and a service record as a strong administrator and a loyal team member, Richardson was suited to both the President's and the Department's needs. In addition, he had had experience in HEW during the Eisenhower Administration. The combination of these assets led Richardson to declare that he was "returning to an old love," while the President commented that he was "the best qualified man in the country" to head HEW.

With his ability to absorb detail, Richardson soon mastered all of the Department's 280 programs. He then began to revitalize the personnel while trying to redirect HEW's efforts. One of Richardson's goals was to decentralize federal control of various social program funds and to streamline HEW's "resource transfer" activities. In this effort, Richardson instituted a simpler grant procedure, consolidated programs and promoted decentralization in keeping with President Nixon's concept of the "New Federalism." Although he personally favored a moderate school busing program to end segregation, he presided over Nixon's more restrained policy of holding federally imposed busing to the minimum required by the law.

Immediately after President Nixon's successful reelection campaign of 1972, he initiated a major personnel shake-up designed to maximize the managerial virtues of thrift, efficiency and loyalty among his cabinet secretaries and core staff members. As part of this round of bureaucratic musical chairs, Elliot Richardson was moved from HEW to Defense, succeeding Melvin Laird [q.v.], who retired to private life. Richardson, although trusted and valued for his versatility, was apparently too liberal to achieve the kind of domestic program retrenchment the President envisioned. President Nixon's intentions were clearly indicated by the character of Richardson's successor at HEW, Caspar Weinberger [q.v.]—a fiscal conservative who had already tried paring down the Department's budget from his preceding position as Budget director.

Richardson's appointment as Secretary of Defense achieved two other presidential purposes. Assuming command of a departmental conglomerate with a size and budget similar to HEW's, he was expected to trim and tighten the bloated Pentagon bureaucracy. His newest assignment and his replacement by Weinberger at HEW brought two ideologically suited individuals to the President's tasks: "a liberal to make cuts at the conservative Pentagon [and] a conservative [to] swing the ax at the liberal welfare agency." Secondly, the departure of a strong foreign policy-oriented and defense-experienced Melvin Laird and his replacement by the more generalist and domestic policy-oriented Richardson seemed to crown presidential assistant Henry Kissinger [q.v.] as the undisputed, paramount foreign policy adviser. The new Secretary of Defense did not, however, even have time to settle into his new role before being summoned to yet another cabinet position. After only 91 days at the Pentagon, Richardson was drafted as Attorney General in the first wave of Watergate-related personnel changes.

By May 1973 revelations regarding the original Watergate burglary, its cover-up and related political subterfuges had forced the resignations of key White House aides John Ehrlichman [q.v.] and H.R. Haldeman [q.v.], caused the firing of White House counsel John Dean [q.v.] and prompted Attorney General Richard Kleindienst [q.v.] to resign, claiming that his close friendship with certain Watergate suspects was incompatible with the "impartial enforcement of the law." As a dependably loyal Administration member, Richardson was acceptable to the President. As a liberal with a record of success at prosecuting governmental corruption, he also had a good chance of securing Senate confirmation.

Initially reluctant to accept the post of Attorney General, Richardson felt it might be more appropriate for the Administration to bring in an outsider. Even though he was not close to any of the men implicated in the scandal up to that time, the fact that he had been a key figure throughout the Nixon Administration seemed to raise fears that he might "go easy" on Administration members involved in the Watergate affair.

At his confirmation hearings (which dragged on for three weeks), Richardson encountered these same misgivings from members of the Senate Judiciary Committee who did not want the Administration choosing "one of its own men to hold final responsibility for the Watergate investigations." Indeed, the problem of securing a full and free investigation of the growing scandal led to a disagreement between Richardson and the Senate Judiciary Committee over the independence and authority of a Watergate prosecutor and, for a time, seriously jeopardized his confirmation possibilities. By acquiescing to guide-lines that would guarantee the independence of a special prosecutor and announcing the appointment of Archibald Cox [q.v.] to that sensitive position, Richardson allayed the Committee's misgivings and secured confirmation for his third cabinet post in as many years.

As the Senate Watergate investigations continued and the special prosecutor's activities gained momentum, Richardson found himself in an increasingly hot cross fire between the White House and Cox. Legally, Richardson as Attorney General bore ultimate responsibility for the special prosecutor's actions. Only he could fire Cox, and then only for "extraordinary improprieties."

As early as July 23, 1973, when the special prosecutor issued a subpoena for Watergate-related White House tapes, Richardson realized that the President intended to "get rid" of Cox as soon as possible. During the summer and early autumn of 1973, Richardson and White House Chief of Staff Alexander Haig [q.v.] were frequent intermediaries between Nixon and Cox, trying to work out a compromise on the tapes, while the tapes case worked its way through U.S. district and appeals courts. During this same period, the Justice Department, under Richardson's direct supervision, developed and pursued a case against Vice President Spiro Agnew [q.v.] for tax fraud and bribery. In October, when the evidence against Agnew was firm enough to assure an indictment (and thus precipitate a constitutional crisis), Richardson and the White House negotiated a compromise whereby the Vice President resigned

from office after pleading no contest to a charge of income tax evasion.

Two days after Agnew's resignation, a U.S. appeals court directed the President to surrender the subpoenaed White House tapes to Judge John Sirica [q.v.], touching off a new and intense round of behind-the-scenes negotiations through Richardson and Haig. The White House offered edited transcripts of the tapes; Cox refused the arrangement. Richardson proposed that a third party authenticate the transcripts, and the White House proposed that Sen. John Stennis (D, Miss.) [q.v.] be that individual and also insisted that Cox agree not to seek any additional tapes or documents from the White House.

When Cox rejected the plan as an intrusion on his independence, the President directed the Attorney General to dismiss him. Richardson, who had pledged at his Senate confirmation hearings to guarantee the independence of the special prosecutor, felt neither justified nor willing to violate that pledge or the public interest as he saw it. Feeling that "the very integrity of the governmental process . . . [he had tried] . . . to help restore" was at stake, he concluded that he "could better serve [his] country by resigning [his] public office rather than by continuing in it."

His deputy, William Ruckelshaus [q.v.], also refused to dismiss Cox and was forced to resign. Finally, Solicitor General Robert H. Bork [q.v.], who was next in line as acting Attorney General, fired Cox and abolished the office of the special prosecutor. The quartet of resignations and dismissals of Oct. 21, 1973, which became known as the "Saturday night massacre," inflamed public opinion and spurred the commencement of impeachment hearings against President Nixon.

Praised for a principled resignation in protest, Richardson acquired the aura of a folk hero and spent the year following the "Saturday night massacre" fulfilling extensive speaking commitments ranging from television interviews to the Chubb Fellowship at Yale and the Godkin lectureship at Harvard. He also directed a project at the Woodrow Wilson International Center for Scholars on the problems of "subnational governments."

Richardson sojourned in academia only long enough to see the demise of the Nixon presidency and the transition to the Ford Administration. In December 1974 he was once again summoned to public service when President Ford nominated him to one of the most prestigious diplomatic assignments available—ambassador to Great Britain.

In becoming envoy to the Court of St. James, Richardson replaced Philadelphia publisher Walter H. Annenberg, who resigned after serving in the post since 1969. At the time of his appointment, Richardson was regarded as a leader of the liberal wing of the Republican Party and was frequently mentioned as a presidential or vice-presidential contender. Service in such a distinguished ambassadorship was possibly designed to give him additional foreign experience and thus strengthen his prospects.

After slightly less than a year in London, Richardson expressed disappointment in his diplomatic assignment because, according to *The New York Times*, "he was expected to serve as a 'super-ambassador' to Western Europe but was getting what he considered only scant attention from Secretary [of State] Kissinger." Wishing to retain Richardson in some capacity and to accommodate Commerce Secretary Rogers C.B. Morton's [q.v.] desire to leave the Administration, President Ford announced Richardson's return to the cabinet as Secretary of Commerce. Nominated in November 1975, Richardson easily won Senate confirmation and served in this capacity for the remainder of the Ford presidency.

Sometimes referred to as "the Man for All Positions," Richardson described his eclectic employment history by saying that he had "never held a job for more than two years" and that just as he got to the point where he thought he knew what he was talking about, somebody offered him another position. Richardson's admirers praised such versatility and pointed to his virtually unmatched record for

holding more cabinet positions in one administration than anyone else in American history. His critics argued that his record in these offices was "rather bare of concrete and citable accomplishments," at least partially because he seldom stayed at one job long enough to create either a major policy influence or a lasting administrative impact. If his career demonstrated anything, it would seem to be that in an age of increasing specialization, there is still a prominent place for the intelligent generalist.

[MJW]

RINFRET, PIERRE
b. Feb. 1, 1924; Montreal, Canada.
Chairman, Rinfret-Boston Associates, 1967-.

Pierre Rinfret, the son of a financier, came to the United States at the age of five. After studying electrical engineering at the University of Maine in the early years of World War II, he served as an infantryman in the U.S. Army in the European theatre. Rinfret obtained a B.S. in business from New York University in 1948 and a doctorate in political economy from the University of Dijon, France, in 1950. He then began work as an economic analyst for the New York consulting firm Lionel D. Edie & Co., rising through a series of promotions to become chairman in 1965.

By the mid-1950s Rinfret's acute analysis and flamboyant style had made him a well-known economist. He predicted quite accurately the 1957-58 recession and the slowdown in growth that followed it. Almost alone among conservative economists Rinfret endorsed the 1962 tax cut proposal as a boon to private sector industry. In 1965 he warned, well in advance of most economists, of the dangers posed for the U.S. and world economies by America's balance-of-payments deficit, and later cautioned about an inflationary economy.

In 1967, Rinfret left Lionel D. Edie and Co. to found his own consulting firm, Rinfret-Boston Associates. The following year he joined Richard Nixon's presidential campaign as an economic analyst. A dedicated free-market economist, Rinfret urged Nixon to achieve the social programs advocated by liberals through the use of tax incentives for industry. After Nixon's election he became an economic adviser to the Administration.

By 1969 Rinfret had become extremely pessimistic about the long-term prospects of the U.S. economy unless the Administration was willing to take the politically unpopular steps necessary to divert money from unproductive consumer spending to real capital formation. He urged Nixon to tighten consumer credit, ban credit cards, raise the surtax and increase the investment tax incentive for private business. Although Nixon did move to tighten credit immediately after taking office, he backed away from Rinfret's more stringent proposals. By mid-1969 Rinfret had effectively broken with the Administration, attacking the President's top economic advisers for "incompetence" and for failing to understand the dangers of inflation to the U.S. economy.

Rinfret increasingly struck economists as a maverick with a somewhat apocalyptic sense of pending catastrophe. His overall emphasis on the need to promote capital formation at the expense of consumption led him to oppose the traditional Keynesian measures adopted by both Nixon and his successor, Gerald Ford. His reputation as a forecaster suffered a setback after he repeatedly insisted there would be no recession in 1970-71, and he was overly cautious in predicting the "superboom" that emerged in 1972-73. Despite his general commitment to free-market views, he hailed Nixon's wage-price controls of August 1971 as the kind of action necessary to halt inflation. Rinfret was deeply fearful of the inflationary potential of the social programs outlined by Sen. George McGovern (D, S.D.) in the 1972 presidential campaign, and vigorously opposed his candidacy. He opposed Democratic candidate Jimmy Carter in the 1976 presidential election for similar reasons, but was encouraged by Carter's first few months in office.

[LG]

RIVERS, L(UCIUS) MENDEL
b. Sept. 28, 1905; Gumville, S.C.
d. Dec. 28, 1970; Birmingham, Ala.
Democratic Representatives, S.C.,
1941-70; Chairman Armed Services
Committee, 1965-70.

Mendel Rivers graduated from the University of South Carolina in 1931. He served as a state representative until 1936, when he became a special attorney for the U.S. Department of Justice. In 1940, he was elected to the House of Representatives. In the House he was a member of the Naval Affairs Committee, the forerunner of the Armed Services Committee, of which he became chairman in 1965. A strong defender of military spending and the need for the deployment of America's armed forces around the world, Rivers came under increasing attack in the 1960s from critics of the military-industrial complex. [See TRUMAN, EISENHOWER, KENNEDY, JOHNSON Volumes]

As head of the Armed Services Committee during the first two years of the Nixon Administration, Rivers was in a strong position to aid the efforts of the President in a number of areas. He was strongly in favor of both the Sentinel and the Safeguard anti-ballistic missile systems, nudging Secretary of Defense Melvin Laird [q.v.] to make a "definite statement" sanctioning the programs. He later used his enormous influence in the House to get the Safeguard system passed. He opposed the concept of an all-volunteer Army. In April 1969 Rivers objected to a spending ceiling on the C-5A transport because he saw it as part of the effort in Congress to curb military funding.

A vigorous proponent of the war in Vietnam, Rivers lauded Nixon's various actions. In a 1969 speech he told an audience that "we have got to get over our national guilt complex at having kept the world free." Later that year at a Veteran's Day rally in support of the Vietnam war, he said: "there are more of us patriotic Americans than those pro-Hanoi-crats. Keep up the fight. Spiro Agnew [q.v.] is helping us. You back up Spiro and he will continue to throw it on."

Rivers was thought to have been instrumental in advising Nixon in September 1969 not to hold the murder trial against six Green Berets charged with killing a Vietnamese double agent. He also aggressively opposed the Army's prosecution of those implicated in the My Lai incident, contending there was no evidence that U.S. troops were guilty of massacring Vietnamese civilians.

Throughout his career Rivers was easily reelected from his conservative district because he consistently opposed civil rights and social welfare legislation. His popularity was furthered by the large amount of military installations he succeeded in having built in his district as well as the number of defense contractors who opened plants there. It was estimated that defense-related industries accounted for 35% of the payroll in the Charleston area.

His reputation in the press and among some of his colleagues was that of an alcoholic and a bully who used his position in Congress to gain special treatment from the military. Allegations of heavy drinking surfaced in the columns of Drew Pearson in the late 1960s, and some critics considered him a security risk for top secret Pentagon information. He made a convenient target for the anti-war movement. Few denied his vast knowledge of military hardware, however, or his assistance in trying to upgrade the pay scale for the military.

Rivers underwent open-heart surgery at the University of Alabama Hospital late in 1970 and died three weeks later.

[GWB]

RIZZO, FRANK L(AZZARO)
b. Oct. 23, 1920; Philadelphia, Pa.
Mayor, Philadelphia, Pa., 1972–.

The son of Italian immigrants, Rizzo was raised in a poor neighborhood of south Philadelphia. After his mother died in 1938, Rizzo dropped out of high school and joined the Navy. In 1943 he entered the Philadelphia police department as a foot patrolman. Working his way up through the ranks, Rizzo was eventually promoted to police commissioner in 1967.

Throughout his carrer Rizzo tried to live up to the title he proudly gave himself, the "toughest cop in America." His efforts occasionally resulted in charges of police brutality. As police chief he authorized the creation of special teams equipped with shotguns and machine guns to be used for rooftop duty in the event of rioting. As police commissioner he successfully opposed the establishment of a civilian complaint review board. During the late 1960s Rizzo was able to avert racial riots like those plaguing other cities by squelching possible disturbances at the earliest stages and "moving in fast with the most."

Having vowed to "crush black power," Rizzo organized a dawn raid on a Black Panther Party center in Philadelphia on Aug. 29, 1970. Several incidents of racial violence occurred in the following days resulting in the death of one policeman and the wounding of six others. Rizzo also orchestrated the quelling of the Holmesburg Prison riot in July in which 29 guards and 84 inmates were injured. Rizzo called the prison riot "a complete racial problem." During his tenure Rizzo succeeded in enlarging the department from 6,000 to 7,200; yet despite his efforts crime in Philadelphia increased 19%, or three times the national urban average, between 1969 and 1970. Rizzo blamed this increase on the leniency of the courts.

In May 1971 Rizzo won the Democratic mayoral primary with 49% of the vote. Shunning campaign debates and refusing to answer questions from the news media, Rizzo campaigned on a "law and order" platform, insisting that he was not a politician but rather a "tough cop." He also promised to lower taxes and reform city government. His style appealed to the white, blue-collar neighborhoods of Philadelphia and despite the opposition of Gov. Milton Shapp [q.v.] and of the city's two largest daily newspapers, Rizzo managed to defeat his Republican opponent, Thacher Longstreth, in the mayoral race.

During the early months of his administration, Rizzo undertook an investigation of the use of federal funding. The probe resulted in the prosecution of the head of the Philadelphia Housing Authority's residents advisory board for alleged misappropriation of funds. He gave more disciplinary discretion and power to classroom teachers, appointed blacks to senior city jobs, closed down pornographic movie houses and investigated the issuing of city contracts. In addition to moving against organized crime, he increased the police department's budget and added to its manpower.

Two Philadelphia newspapers, the *Inquirer* and the *Bulletin*, printed stories on Aug. 3, 1973, alleging that Rizzo deployed a secret, 33-man police squad to spy on City Council President George X. Schwartz and Peter J. Camiel, chairman of the Democratic city committee. Learning of this, Camiel revealed that Rizzo and Deputy Mayor Phillip Carrol tried to bribe him on Feb. 27, 1973. According to Camiel, Rizzo and Carrol offered him control over the selection of architects and engineering firms for city contracts in return for his endorsement of Rizzo's candidate for district attorney, incumbent Arlen Specter. Camiel challenged Rizzo and Carrol to submit themselves to a lie detector test administered by an expert hired by the *Philadelphia Daily News*. Rizzo agreed saying that "If this machine says a man lied, he lied." The test indicated that Rizzo and Carrol lied on six out of 10 questions, while Camiel lied on none. On Aug. 15, 1973, Philadelphia District Attorney Arlan Specter announced that a grand jury would investigate charges that Rizzo used a police spy unit for his own purposes and attempted to bribe Camiel.

The Pennsylvania Crime Commission released a 1,404-page report on March 10, 1974, charging that police corruption in Philadelphia was "ongoing, widespread, systematic and occurring at all levels." The report also accused the Rizzo administration of actively trying to hinder the 18-month investigation by arresting the Commission's special agents and failing to act when presented with evidence of corruption. However, after federal district and appellate courts ordered Philadelphia city officials to institute new procedures for handling complaints of police misconduct, the Supreme Court overturned these rulings in a five-to-three decision. The opinion held there was insufficient proof that city officials were responsible for police misconduct.

Rizzo's popularity began to wane when 211,000 signatures were collected on petitions demanding his recall, but the Pennsylvania Supreme Court barred a special recall vote from being included on the Nov. 2, 1974, ballot. Nonetheless, Rizzo was able to recapture his office in November 1975 with 57% of the vote. In this election the mayor once again campaigned as a "law and order" candidate.

[AFB]

ROCHE, JAMES M(ICHAEL)
b. Dec. 16, 1906; Elgin, Ill.
Chairman of the Board, General
Motors Corp., 1967-71.

Roche started working at the age of 12 when his father died. Graduating from high school in 1923, he was unable to attend college but did take correspondence classes in business administration and accounting. He began working in the General Motors' (GM) Cadillac Motor Car Division in 1927, making gradual advancements until his selection as president of the corporation in 1965. In 1967 he succeeded Frederic G. Donner as chairman of the board.

During his years as president and chairman of GM, Roche became involved in a series of highly publicized disputes with consumer advocate Ralph Nader [q.v.]. In

1965 the young lawyer wrote *Unsafe at Any Speed,* which condemned the U.S. auto industry for concentrating on style rather than safety. In the book he attacked GM's Corvair directly. The following year Nader appeared before a Senate Commerce Committee subcommittee and charged that GM had investigated his personal life with harmful intent. Roche appeared before the panel and apologized for the harassment, although he said it had been done without his knowledge. In April 1970 Nader received $425,000 in an out-of-court settlement of an invasion of privacy suit he had filed against GM. Nader said the money would be used to legally monitor GM activity in pollution, safety and consumer relations areas. [See JOHNSON Volume]

GM continued to be the target of government and consumer group action in the late 1960s and early 1970s. In January 1969 the Justice Department filed a suit against the four major auto manufacturers on charges of conspiring to delay the development and use of anti-pollution devices. An out-of-court settlement was reached in September. In return for the Justice Department agreeing to drop charges, the car manufacturer, while not admitting guilt, promised not to conspire to obstruct development of pollution-control equipment and offered to give royalty-free patent licenses on air pollution inventions and technical information to any company seeking to install such devices.

The following year Nader launched "Campaign GM," a national drive coordinated by the Project for Corporate Responsibility (PCR) to make the corporation more responsive to public interests. Nader claimed that General Motors contributed 35% of the nation's air pollution, that it violated safety laws, manufactured cars that produced high repair bills, and that its design and marketing practices were fraudulently agreed upon.

The project, which bought a token amount of GM stock so that it could vote at shareholders' meetings, attempted to enlist the support of such organizations as banks, unions and churches behind its actions. In one of its first moves, it presented a series of resolutions to make the company more responsible. GM management, led by Roche, ignored them. However the Securities and Exchange Commission ordered Roche to present two of the nine resolutions directly to the company stockholders. The resolutions called for placing three new members on the board to represent public interest and for establishing a GM shareholders' committee for corporate response. Roche successfully urged defeat of the measures, stating that passage "would restrict management's ability to meet its responsibility to its stockholders and the public."

The 1971 shareholders' meeting saw a continuation of the unsuccessful reform attempts. The Episcopal church proposed that GM end its operations in racist South Africa. Roche successfully defeated the proposal by pointing out that GM was better able to achieve racial equality by remaining in the nation and that withdrawal would create hardships for GM workers there, most of whom were black. The PCR also unsuccessfully pushed for more detailed accounting of GM efforts with regard to minorities, pollution and auto safety.

The meeting generated a full-scale debate on corporate responsibility. Defending GM's record, Roche promised to increase spending aimed at curbing auto pollution by $26 million to a record $150 million and to spend $64 million to clean up GM plants. He said that the company had already spent $119 million on pollution control.

At the annual meeting in 1970, Roche reported that the corporation faced serious financial problems. Although a low point in auto sales had passed, sales were down 19% in the first quarter and net income had also dropped. In 1969 GM had raised the price of its 1970 car models by an average of $125 per vehicle. This was the sharpest increase in automobile prices in a decade. Roche called the cost rise "modest" and attributed it to rising material and labor costs as well as falling profits. Later Roche sharply attacked social critics of business, calling them "adversary culture." He also charged that their harassment had added significantly to rising business costs.

Roche supported Nixon's 1971 wage and price freeze and announced that GM was rescinding price increases for its 1972 cars. Nader, however, charged that GM had known in advance about the economic policy and had unsuccessfully tried to ameliorate its effects by selling its new model cars earlier than usual. Roche denied the charge.

Roche retired at the end of 1971 at the mandatory age of 65.

[CE]

ROCKEFELLER, JOHN D(AVISON), III

b. March 21, 1906; New York, N.Y.
d. July 10, 1978; Tarrytown, N.Y.
Chairman, Commission on Population Growth and the American Future, 1970-1972.

Rockefeller, grandson of oil magnate John D. Rockefeller, graduated from Princeton University in 1929. He then traveled to Japan as secretary for the Institute for Pacific Relations and subsequently toured the world. He was appointed trustee of the Rockefeller Brothers Fund, Colonial Williamsburg, Inc., and Rockefeller Center during the 1930s. He served in the Navy during World War II, while also directing the United China Relief and the British War Relief Society. Upon discharge in 1945, he traveled extensively, examining social conditions, particularly in Mexico and South America. In 1952 he assumed the chairmanship of the board of trustees of the Rockefeller Foundation.

That same year Rockefeller established the Population Council. Within a decade it was operating in a dozen foreign countries on a multimillion dollar annual budget and had become the most prestigious organization in its field. However as the population issue was still a sensitive social topic, the council's work was limited to research on population and family planning. After the 1964 presidential election, Rockefeller urged the Johnson Administration to address the population issue. Three years later an advisory committee was formed to deal with the problem with Rockefeller as its chairman. This panel recommended that a commission on population be established. It was Rockefeller's knowledge and interest in social conditions, especially in Asia and South America, that prompted President Richard M. Nixon to appoint him chairman of the U.S. Commission on Population Growth and the American Future in 1970.

The Commission on Population Growth consisted of 24 persons, including executives, representatives of minority groups and members of Congress. Its final report, issued in three parts, was given in March 1973. It studied the effects of continued population growth on the quality of life in America and concluded that slowing population growth "and eventually stopping it altogether" was vital. The Commission reasoned that slower growth for 10 to 15 years would help create higher national income levels and would buy time for solving environmental problems that would be exacerbated by increased population growth.

It recommended the creation of a federal office to handle the question of population growth and asked for a complete census every five years. The report also urged the government to deal more harshly with illegal immigration. It encouraged racial and economic integration of suburbs and suggested that further migration from rural areas be channeled into small cities to help boost their economic development. The Commission supported the Equal Rights Amendment, and dealt with sex education, adoption and land use planning.

On more controversial issues the report suggested making contraceptive information and services available to minors, providing child care facilities for all in need of them and, above all, enacting "affirmative statutes creating a clear and positive framework for the practice of abortion on request." The Commission felt that preventing unwanted births would be a prime factor in retarding population growth. However these issues were in direct conflict with presidential opinion. President Nixon did not comment extensively on the report but made his strong personal objections known. He was not in favor of abortion or the accessibility of birth control information to minors.

Since the Commission's work received no support from the Nixon-Ford Administrations, Rockefeller helped form the Citizen's Committee on Population and the American Future, serving as honorary chairman. The Citizen's Commission spoke to various organizations throughout the country. It emphasized the little publicized aspects of the report, playing down the abortion issue to get better feedback on other proposals. Basically it was an effort to place the population question on the national conscience, which it helped accomplish.

In 1972 Rockefeller resigned as chairman of the Rockefeller Foundation. During the mid-1970s he continued pursuing his private philanthropic ventures and served as chairman of the National Committee for the Bicentennial Era. He died on July 12, 1978 in an automobile accident near his Tarrytown home.

[CE]

ROCKEFELLER, NELSON A(LDRICH)

b. July 8, 1908; Bar Harbor, Me.
d. Jan. 26, 1979, New York, N.Y.
Governor, N.Y., 1959-73; Vice President of the United States, 1974-77.

As the grandson of John D. Rockefeller, the Standard Oil magnate, Nelson Rockefeller was born into one of America's wealthiest families. He spent several years working in various family enterprises after graduating from Dartmouth in 1930. Through his directorship of the Creole Petroleum Co., a Latin American-based affiliate of Standard Oil, Rockefeller acquired an interest in Latin American affairs. In 1940 President Franklin D. Roosevelt appointed him to head the

office of the Coordinator of Inter-American Affairs.

Over the next 15 years Rockefeller served three Presidents in a variety of appointive posts involving both foreign and domestic affairs. From 1944 to 1945 he was assistant secretary of state for Latin American affairs, and in 1950 and 1951, he advised President Harry S Truman on the Point Four Program. President Eisenhower, whom Rockefeller had endorsed in the 1952 election, appointed him undersecretary of the Department of Health, Education and Welfare in 1954. Later that year he became a special assistant to Eisenhower on foreign affairs. [See EISENHOWER Volume].

Realizing the need for a political base to promote the programs he favored, Rockefeller ran as a liberal Republican for the governorship of New York in 1958 and defeated the incumbent, Democrat W. Averell Harriman. Rockefeller successfully sought reelection in 1962, 1966 and 1970.

As governor of New York, Rockefeller initially won a reputation as an advocate of social welfare legislation and large-scale government spending programs. He transformed an undistinguished state teachers college system into a major state-wide liberal arts university. He substantially increased the state's middle-income housing program, won passage of New York's first uniform minimum wage law in 1960 and successfully pressed for civil rights legislation to bar discrimination in housing and public accommodations. In 1965 Rockefeller won expanded powers for the State Commission on Human Rights, launched an ambitious state medicaid plan the following year and established a Narcotics Addiction Control Commission to provide treatment for addicts regardless of their wishes.

Initially Rockefeller financed these programs on a "pay-as-you-go" basis, increasing taxes to meet rising expenditures. But the enormous growth of the budget made legislators reluctant to approve the ever higher taxes needed, and Rockefeller turned to bond issues to finance such projects as water pollution control and highway construction. When voters began rejecting these, however, Rockefeller and his aides devised a scheme to create quasi-independent agencies to issue so-called moral obligation bonds. Agencies such as the State University Construction Fund and the Urban Development Corporation vastly increased the state's indebtedness through large-scale borrowing from major banks at interest rates higher than those for voter-approved bonds.

Rockefeller was repeatedly frustrated in his ambition to run for the presidency. After Nixon's defeat in 1960, Rockefeller set his sights on the 1964 presidential campaign but lost the Republican nomination to conservative Sen. Barry Goldwater (R, Ariz.) [q.v.] in a campaign that aroused much bitterness. [See KENNEDY, JOHNSON Volumes].

Initially declaring himself a "noncandidate" for the 1968 nomination, Rockefeller reversed himself on April 30, 1968, and entered the race. Still campaigning as a liberal, he was unable to catch frontrunner Richard Nixon. Rockefeller supported Nixon after his nomination, and the two men appeared to have drawn closer ideologically. After the election Nixon chose Henry Kissinger [q.v.], formerly a close aide to Rockefeller, to head the National Security Council.

Rockefeller moved substantially to the right during the latter years of his governorship. He began to speak out against government spending on social welfare programs and to take a tough stand on law-and-order issues.

In January 1969 Rockefeller presented the first of his "austerity" budgets to the state legislature. Although he requested a record $6.4 billion, the increases stemmed from mandated expenditures for existing education and welfare programs, and Rockefeller pointedly did not recommend any new ventures. Instead he warned the legislature that the state faced "a grave fiscal crisis." In his 1971 budget message, Rockefeller sounded a graver alarm. Claiming that social welfare programs had "dangerously overloaded the financial capacity of state and local gov-

ernments," he predicted a "breakdown in local government services" and declared that the state "must tighten its belt and live within its resources."

In April 1971, Rockefeller signed legislation cutting welfare payments by 10%, reducing medicaid allowances and slashing funds for drug rehabilitation programs. The actions provoked riots in New York City in May as the cutbacks were felt by the city's poor. In June Rockefeller approved a welfare residency law, despite the 1969 Supreme Court ruling that such laws were unconstitutional. (The law was voided by the courts in August.) The next month he signed a bill that required welfare recipients to work or lose their benefits. Although Rockefeller's measures received praise from President Nixon, whose own welfare proposals Rockefeller had endorsed, leaders of welfare rights groups and other liberals were extremely critical.

As demonstrations by students, blacks and other disaffected groups increased in scope and intensity, Rockefeller became an advocate of a tough law-and-order response. Two months later black students at Cornell University occupied the student union building and emerged two days later armed with rifles and shotguns. Calling the situation "intolerable," Rockefeller quickly drafted legislation, which was enacted by the state legislature, outlawing guns on school or college property. He also signed a law that required colleges and universities to adopt regulations for the "maintenance of public order" or face the loss of state financial aid.

Rockefeller came under heavy criticism for his handling of the Attica prison uprising. On Sept. 9, 1971, inmates at the Attica Correctional Facility seized 32 guards and civilian employes as hostages and issued a set of 15 demands, including coverage by the state minimum wage law, an end to censorship of reading materials and a promise of no reprisals against participants in the rebellion. On Sept. 10 New York State Commissioner of Corrections Russell G. Oswald agreed to allow a team of observers to participate in the negotiations with the inmates. Among its members were *New York Times* reporter Tom Wicker, Rep. Herman Badillo (D, N.Y.) and Clarence Jones, the publisher of the black newspaper, the *Amsterdam News.* The observer committee asked Rockefeller to intervene, but he declined.

On Sept. 13, Oswald, with the support of Rockefeller, ordered an air and ground assault of the prison by 1,500 state troopers. Forty-two were killed, including prisoners, guards and employes. Although early reports accused the inmates of murdering the hostages, autopsies revealed that all of the deaths were caused by gunshot wounds, and subsequent investigation revealed that the convicts were unarmed.

Several commissions were authorized to investigate the uprisings, including one headed by Robert B. McKay, dean of New York University Law School. The McKay Report, issued in September 1972, called the uprising a spontaneous response to legitimate grievances and concluded that Rockefeller should have visited Attica before ordering the assault. The report was also sharply critical of police behavior. A later report, issued in 1975 by Special State Investigator Bernard S. Meyer, cited "serious errors in judgment" and attacked Rockefeller for making public remarks at the time that were "inappropriate and should not have been made."

Rockefeller continued to make some liberal initiatives during these years. A strong supporter of the burgeoning environmental movement, he won passage in 1970 of a bill that established a state department of the environment, and he drafted legislation to ban the use of the pesticide DDT. In April 1970 Rockefeller signed into law a major abortion reform bill, which legalized abortions up to the 24th week of pregnancy. It was considered the most liberal in the nation. In 1972, despite intense pressure from the Roman Catholic Church in New York, Rockefeller vetoed a bill that would have repealed the state's abortion law.

Rockefeller supported most of the initiatives of the Nixon Administration. He spoke out in favor of federal revenue shar-

ing and Nixon's Family Assistance Plan and praised Nixon's 1971 imposition of wage and price controls to counter inflation. Rockefeller also supported the Administration's policy of "Vietnamization," which called for the gradual withdrawal of U.S. troops from Southeast Asia and the shifting of the military effort to South Vietnamese troops. Rockefeller, however, found himself at odds with Vice President Spiro Agnew [*q.v.*], especially over the latter's sharp attacks on the liberal anti-war Senator from New York, Charles Goodell [*q.v.*]. During Goodell's reelection campaign in 1970, Rockefeller, who endorsed Goodell, sent a message to the White House requesting that Agnew stay out of the campaign, since "outside intervention would be prejudicial to the state Republican ticket."

Rockefeller, meanwhile, retained his interest in foreign affairs. In February 1969 President Nixon announced that he had asked the Governor to make a series of visits to Latin America and to formulate policy recommendations to the Administration. Rockefeller made the first trip in May 1969, visiting Mexico and several Central American nations. The trip was marred by widespread demonstrations, however, and the Latin American press criticized the tour. Three subsequent visits to South America in May, June and July saw violent demonstrations and battles between police and protesters in almost every country Rockefeller visited. The governments of Peru and Chile withdrew their invitations to avoid violence, and Rockefeller himself canceled the trip to Venezuela. Rockefeller's report, which was released in September 1969, portrayed a sense of crisis in Latin America and pointed to a "climate of growing instability, extremism and anti-U.S. nationalism." The report recommended major trade concessions, increases in military aid and the renegotiatin of foreign debt.

On Dec. 11, 1973, Rockefeller announced his resignation from the governorship and his intention to devote his time to two national study commissions. The first, a Rockefeller family-funded

Commission on Critical Choices for America, was to make a major inquiry into the future role of the federal government in a changing society. The second, a Commission on Water Quality, was a congressionally established panel to study the problem of water pollution.

On Aug. 20, 1974, Gerald Ford, who had just succeeded Richard Nixon as President, nominated Rockefeller for the vice presidency. Under the provisions of the 25th Amendment, the nomination required confirmation by both the Senate and the House. Although the selection of Rockefeller was praised by liberals and conservatives of both Parties, concern over his wealth and the potential use of it for political purposes led to extensive public hearings on the nomination.

The Senate Rules Committee opened hearings on Sept. 23. Rockefeller promised to cooperate fully, declaring his hope that "the myth or misconception about the extent of the family's control over the economy of this country will be totally brought out and exposed and dissipated." Nonetheless his disclosures about personal wealth revealed that he, his wife and children had assets of almost $230 million, and a spokesman for the family revealed that the entire Rockefeller clan owned securities worth over $1 billion, with large interests in banks and corporations whose assets were far larger.

During October it was revealed that over the years Rockefeller had given or loaned substantial amounts of money to political associates such as Henry Kissinger; William J. Ronan, the chairman of the Port Authority of New York and New Jersey and a Rockefeller appointee; and L. Judson Morhouse, the former chairman of the New York State Republican Party. It was also disclosed that Rockefeller had financed a scurrilous biography of former Supreme Court Justice Arthur Goldberg [q.v.] during Goldberg's 1970 campaign against Rockefeller for the governorship. The Senate Rules Committee held a second set of hearings in November to explore these questions.

Despite misgivings about the propriety of Rockefeller's actions, the Committee,

on Nov. 22, unanimously recommended his confirmation. Hearings by the House Judiciary Committee reached a similar conclusion. On Dec. 19, after both the House and Senate voted overwhelmingly in favor of confirmation, Rockefeller was sworn in as the nation's 41st Vice President.

Almost immediately Rockefeller was given major responsibility by President Ford. On Dec. 22, 1974, *The New York Times* began a series of articles alleging that under President Nixon, the CIA had conducted a "massive, illegal domestic intelligence operation" against anti-war activists and other dissenters. In January the *Times* and *The Washington Post* carried further articles that charged the CIA with intercepting the mail of private citizens and labor organizations and with attempting to destroy its domestic intelligence files to stave off investigations. On Jan. 5, 1975, Ford named Rockefeller to head a special commission to investigate the allegations of domestic spying by the CIA.

The Rockefeller Commission began private, closed hearings almost immediately. Extending through the winter and into the spring, the hearings gathered evidence from a wide array of present and former CIA officials. Late in March, when the press reported that the CIA was allegedly involved in plots to assassinate foreign officials, including Fidel Castro of Cuba, Rockefeller extended the investigation. On June 2, before the commission's report was released, Rockefeller told the press that although there were some violations of law, they were not serious. His remarks provoked a sharp response from Sen. Frank Church (D Idaho) [q.v.], who had conducted a similar investigation for the Senate Foreign Relations Committee. Church said that murder plots were not "a minor matter."

Rockefeller's 299-page report was released on June 10. Although it concluded that the "great majority" of CIA activities were in compliance with the law, the report did concede that the CIA had engaged in actions that were "plainly unlawful and constituted improper invasions upon the rights of Americans." It cited the illegal opening of mail, illegal wiretaps and room buggings, break-ins and the investigation of confidential tax returns of private citizens. The report also detailed the activities of the Special Operations Group within the CIA, which, beginning in 1967, collected files on over 7,200 protestors, infiltrated domestic political groups and compiled a computerized index of over 300,000 individuals and organizations involved in political protest.

In February 1975 Ford appointed Rockefeller to head the White House Domestic Council and picked two of Rockefeller's aides for key positions on the Council. Under Rockefeller the Council shifted its focus from a day-to-day advisory role to one of studying and reviewing long-range domestic policy options. Rockefeller directed the Council to study alternative financing for the Social Security system and other approaches to federal-state revenue sharing. He also emphasized the need to free the economy from "stifling" federal regulations and urged the removal of price controls on domestic oil and natural gas.

Almost from the time of his confirmation, there was speculation over whether Rockefeller would remain on Ford's ticket for 1976. Conservative Republicans were strongly opposed to the possibility. Ford, meanwhile, publicly praised Rockefeller as "an exceptionally active and able Vice President," and in June he formally endorsed Rockefeller as his desired running mate. To win over Party leaders, Rockefeller frequently addressed Republican gatherings throughout the country. During a tour of the South in August 1975, Rockefeller spoke out in favor of states' rights and a balanced budget, and against government bureaucracy and welfare "cheats." He also repeatedly urged the Party to remain as broad-based in its appeal as possible.

Despite these efforts conservative opposition to Rockefeller remained strong. On Nov. 3, he withdrew from consideration as a possible 1976 vice presidential candidate. The decision was interpreted as a major effort to appease the conservative wing of the Party and to stem the threat to Ford's renomination posed by former California Gov. Ronald Reagan. Rockefeller campaigned for Ford during the primaries and won a majority of the New York delegation for the President. After Ford was nominated Rockefeller continued to campaign for his reelection.

Upon the expiration of his term in January 1977, Rockefeller, after a long career as a public official, retired into private life. Two years later, on Jan. 26, 1979, Rockefeller died of a heart attack in New York City.

[JD]

For further information:
Robert H. Connery and Gerald Benjamin, eds., *Governing New York State: The Rockefeller Years* (New York, 1974).
Peter Collier and David Horowitz, *The Rockefellers* (New York, 1976).
Alvin Moscow, *The Rockefeller Inheritance* (New York, 1977).

ROCKEFELLER, WINTHROP
b. May 12, 1912; New York, N.Y.
d. Feb. 22, 1973; Palm Springs, Calif.
Governor, Ark., 1967–71.

Winthrop Rockefeller, grandson of John D. Rockefeller and a Yale dropout, served five years in the Army during World War II and worked at various jobs before moving to Arkansas in 1953. Arriving in his adopted state with a reputation as a rich and troubled playboy, he promptly purchased a 50,000-acre remote mountain estate where he constructed a lavish cattle farm. In 1955 Gov. Orval Faubus persuaded him to chair the Arkansas Industrial Development Commission, through which he helped to bring much new industry to the state. Two years later during the integration crisis in Little Rock, Rockefeller publicly objected to the Governor's use of the National Guard to prevent nine black students from entering the city's Central High School.

Rockefeller's first bid for the governorship was an unsuccessful challenge of Faubus in 1964. However in 1966, he forged a coalition of blacks, liberals, urban dwellers and mountain Republicans to defeat arch-segregationist Jim Johnson, thereby becoming the state's first Republican governor since 1873. [See JOHNSON Volume]

A liberal in a conservative Southern state, Rockefeller during his first term managed to introduce Arkansas's first minimum wage law, a freedom-of-information bill and insurance reforms. In 1968, after investigators had revealed "barbaric conditions" at several penitentiaries, Rockefeller initiated education and rehabilitation programs for prisoners and forced the legislature to pour substantial tax monies into the state's prisons. However, Rockefeller's efforts to increase tax revenues for education and social services were constantly stymied by the legislature. In 1969 his package increasing tax revenues by 50% and providing the first income tax reform since that tax was introduced in 1929 was overwhelmingly defeated. That same year Rockefeller signed a limited abortion-reform bill, substantially liberalizing the state's 100-year-old statute.

Rockefeller won reelection in 1968 and during his second term continued to be a force for racial integration. In 1969 he protested when the Nixon Administration announced that it was relaxing the September 1969 deadline for compliance with the 1964 Civil Rights Act requiring desegration of school districts. That summer he sent the National Guard to Forest City as white mobs, demanding the lynching of three blacks accused of raping a 15-year-old white girl, violated a curfew. Also that year he was elected the first Republican chairman of the Southern and Border States Governors Conference and led the governors in voting down a resolution condemning school busing. At Rockefeller's initiative the Conference established a Southern Regional Environmental Conservation Council, set up in 1970 to formulate multistate agreements on ecological problems.

Up for reelection in 1970, Rockefeller's coalition fell apart as he was defeated by Dale Bumpers, a political unknown and racial moderate, who received 62% of the vote. Before leaving office he commuted the death sentences of all 15 prisoners awaiting execution to life imprisonment. (Long a foe of capital punishment, he had, after taking office in 1967, declared a moratorium on executions in the state.) In February 1973 Rockefeller died of cancer in California.

[FLM]

RODINO, PETER W(ALLACE)
b. June 7, 1909; Newark, N.J.
Democratic Representative, N.J., 1948–; Chairman, Judiciary Committee, 1973–.

Rodino was born, brought up and educated in the public schools of Newark, N.J. He attended the University of Newark and the New Jersey School of Law (now Rutgers), receiving his degree in 1938. From 1930 to 1932 he taught public speaking and citizenship classes at the Young Men's Christian Association. After setting up his law practice in Newark in the late 1930s, Rodino volunteered for military service before America's entry into World War II. After being discharged from the Army in 1946, Rodino ran unsuccessfully for the U.S. House against the incumbent Fred Hartley, Jr. The latter retired in 1948 and Rodino was able to win his seat. He represented most of Newark and several surrounding communities.

The Representative first served on the Veterans Affairs Committee and then the Judiciary Committee, where he had become the fourth-ranking Democrat by the mid-1960s. A strong supporter of immigration reform, he was influential in the House passage of a 1965 Johnson Administration bill that eliminated the old nationality quota system of immigration control. In addition he was an ardent backer of civil rights legislation, acting as floor manager for the open housing provision of the proposed Civil Rights Act of 1966. In other matters Rodino generally voted for the domestic and foreign policy initiatives of the Johnson Administration. [See JOHNSON Volume]

Rodino initially supported the Nixon Vietnam policies. However he broke with the President after the Cambodian invasion of 1970. Soon after he voted for the Cooper-Church Amendment prohibiting military involvement in Cambodia without specific congressional approval. During the first years of the decade, he voted for other measures to end the war including an unsuccessful supplemental appropriations bill in June 1973 that provided for the cut off of all funds for combat activities in Laos and Cambodia. In other foreign policy action, Rodino voted against authorizing foreign aid to fund a new squadron of F-4D jet aircraft for Nationalist China in November 1969.

On domestic issues Rodino compiled a generally liberal voting record. He supported consumer protection in various votes as well as the 1969 Nixon Administration legislation calling for the government to force the hiring of minority workers on federally financed projects, the so-called Philadelphia Plan. In 1975 Rodino voted for common-site picketing, which would allow workers striking a single subcontractor to picket an entire construction site. That same year he also voted in favor of the federal loan guarantee for financially ailing New York City. He opposed unlimited payments by the government to farmers for not growing crops as well as legislation to continue federal funding for the development of the supersonic transport plane. The Representative voted his religious convictions in opposing government aid for abortions and also took what was considered a hard-line position by voting in favor of the controversial "no-knock" provision of the District of Columbia crime bill.

Rodino became chairman of the Judiciary Committee in January 1973 after the defeat of the longtime incumbent Rep. Emanuel Celler [q.v.]. As the Watergate scandal was gaining increasing attention, there were a number of members of

Congress who began to call for the impeachment of the President. It was not, however, until Oct. 22, 1973, that the Democratic leaders of the House met to consider these demands. The Speaker, Carl Albert [q.v.], ultimately decided that instead of setting up a separate committee to deal with the matter, all impeachment resolutions would be referred to the Judiciary Committee. The impeachment proceedings were stalled, however, until the Committee held hearings on the confirmation of Rep. Gerald Ford [q.v.] as vice president. These hearings lasted until November 29.

Shortly before Christmas, Rodino named John Doar [q.v.], a nominal Republican who had led the Justice Department's Civil Rights Division during the Kennedy and Johnson Administrations, as chief counsel of the Committee. A staff was somewhat hastily assembled and grew to over 100 lawyers and investors within a short period of time.

Many of the more liberal Democratic members of the Judiciary Committee, such as John Conyers [q.v.] of Michigan and Jerome Waldie of California, became irritated by the slow pace of investigation being set by Rodino and Doar. But Rodino refused to be hurried. He was concerned that the proceedings should appear eminently just. As columnist Joseph Kraft wrote: "Mr. Rodino is having his brush with history. He is determined to do everything right. He wants to avoid the slightest hint of partisanship and be fairness itself."

In February 1974, after laying the procedural groundwork for the impeachment investigation, the Committee received House authorization to proceed with the formal constitutional process of impeachment. The Committee spent much of the spring obtaining transcripts of the tapes of presidental conversations that were believed to be relevant to an understanding of whether Nixon was involved in the Watergate cover-up and whether, in fact, he was guilty of obstructing justice. On April 4, after waiting 38 days for a reply for one group of tapes, the Committee decided to give the President five additional days to respond. After a bargaining gambit by presidential lawyer James St. Clair [q.v.] failed, the Committee voted 33-3 to issue a subpoena to the President on April 11, the first time such action was taken in American history. On April 23, two days before the deadline set by the subpoena, St. Clair asked for and got an extension of five additional days.

The tapes were finally released by the White House, but they contained numerous deletions. In addition Nixon supplied transcripts that were not accurate renderings of the tape conversations. "The President has not complied with our subpoena," Rodino told the news media," we did not subpoena a presidential interpretation of what is necessary or relevant to our inquiry." The Committee then voted 20-18 to reject the transcripts, but the White House responded by saying that it would release no more tapes or transcripts. In the middle of May, after the Committee had subpoenaed additional material, the President announced that he would refuse to comply with any "such further subpoenas as may hereafter be issued." In a letter to Rodino, the President wrote that "constantly escalating requests" for materials "constitute such a massive invasion into the confidentiality of presidential conversations that the institution of the presidency would be fatally compromised."

By early summer the Judiciary Committee seemed certain to recommend impeachment to the full House, but Rodino was determined to pick up as many Republican votes as possible to avoid the appearance of partisanship. Six weeks of closed hearings had ended on June 21. But before open hearings in front of television cameras began, the *Los Angeles Times* reported that Rodino had said all 21 Democrats would vote for impeachment. Although Rodino denied making the statement, a White House spokesman, Ken Clawson, exploded with indignation. "Now we have our worst fears confirmed out of Rodino's own mouth," Clawson said, "I'm confident that the American people will now once and for all realize that President Nixon is the subject of a witch-hunt." Press Secretary Ron Ziegler [q.v.] called the Committee a "kangaroo court." But Republican Committee member Robert McClory of Illinois came to the chairman's defense when he said that Rodino "has done a good job." All in all, as *New York Times* reporter J. Anthony Lucas wrote in his account *Nightmare* "though Rodino miscalculated a few times, he had generally been generous to a fault with the opposition, treating them with great courtesy and deference."

By mid-July the Committee released 10 volumes of evidence that in the opinion of its majority and minority counsels warranted impeachment. Televised hearings captured the public's attention in the later days of July. By this time 29 proposed articles of impeachment had been presented to the Committee, and Doar, at Rodino's urging, had at last become an impassioned advocate for impeachment. By the end of the month, the Committee voted three articles of impeachment against Nixon—obstruction of justice, abuse of presidential powers and contempt of Congress. In the case of the first article, Rodino noted that it would be reported to the House that "Richard M. Nixon has prevented, obstructed, and impeded the administration of justice . . . has acted in a manner contrary to his trust as President and subversive of constitutional government, to the great prejudice of the cause of law and justice, and to the manifest injury of the people of the United States . . . [and] warrants impeachment and trial and removal from office." Nine days before the full House was to start impeachment proceedings, Nixon resigned.

Following the presidential pardon of Nixon by Gerald Ford in September, several House members called for the revival of impeachment hearings, but Rodino strongly objected saying that the principal purpose of impeachment was removal from office and that the procedure should not be used to accomplish any other purpose.

Rodino had gained a fair degree of celebrity status from the exposure he received chairing the Judiciary Committee and it was not lost on the Democratic Party. He gave a nominating speech for Georgia Gov. Jimmy Carter [q.v.] before the National Convention in 1976 and was briefly considered to be in the running for the vice-presidential nomination. Rodino was reelected that year and in 1978.

[GWB]

ROGERS, WILLIAM P(IERCE)
b. 23 June 1913, Norfolk, N.Y.
Secretary of State, January 1969-September 1973.

William P. Rogers moved from his small-town, upstate New York beginnings through positions as assistant attorney general to a racket-busting Thomas Dewey of New York in 1938, and as counsel to the Senate Special Committee to Investigate the National Defense Program in 1947 to serve in the Eisenhower Administration as deputy attorney general from 1953 to 1957 and then as Attorney General until 1961. [See EISENHOWER Volume]

As a close friend of the then vice president, Richard Nixon, Rogers had been at Nixon's side for three of his "Six Crises"—in the Alger Hiss case he had counselled Nixon to pursue his inquiry, in the 1952 "slush fund" affair he had helped Nixon arrange his "Checkers" speech defense, and after Eisenhower's 1955 heart attack he had advised Nixon to "act scrupulously like a Vice-President—not like an Acting President." In short, William Rogers was a man Richard Nixon regarded as "a cool man under pressure . . . [with] . . . excellent judgment, a good sense of press relations, and one to whom I could speak with complete freedom."

After acting as a policy adviser during Nixon's 1960 presidential campaign, Rogers decided to drop out of politics for the first time in 15 years and to pursue the practice of law in earnest. An ambitious, self-made, and rather independent individual, Rogers felt he wanted to make it "on his own." He purposely interjected a sense of distance between himself and his old friend, Nixon, in order to dispel the notion that he was simply a Nixon crony. During the eight years of the Kennedy-Johnson presidencies, he proved himself and prospered as a senior partner in the prestigious New York-Washington-Paris law firm of Royall, Koegel, Rogers, and Wells. He did not even return to play an important role in Richard Nixon's second bid for the presidency in 1968.

Despite the drifting apart that had occurred between Rogers and Nixon during the 1960s, Nixon once again turned to his old friend in 1968, insisting that he accept the ranking cabinet position of the Secretary of State. In light of Rogers's meager experience in foreign affairs, the appointment was regarded as somewhat surprising and indicative of Nixon's intention "to call the turn" on foreign affairs. Indeed, Rogers' diplomatic experience consisted of having been representative at the independence celebrations of Togo in 1960, a member of the delegation to the United Nations in 1965, and a 10-week special representative on the Ad Hoc Committee on Southwest Africa in 1967.

His supporters maintained that since he was free of "any commitments or emotional attachments to past policies or procedures," he would be less righteous, doctrinaire or crusading than his two immediate predecessors, John Foster Dulles and Dean Rusk. In addition his reputation as one of the most glittering of the "diplomatic yet plain-spoken Hill-crawlers" was viewed as an asset to the Administration in soothing the Senate Foreign Relations Committee and thus easing the course of the new Administration's Vietnam policy. One lawyer-turned-diplomat, Nicholas Katzenbach [q.v.], argued that "technical expertise" was not required in a Secretary of State and that "the Secretary's job . . . is pulling the government together on foreign problems, dealing with Congress, and . . . dealing with representatives of other governments. All [of which] falls quite naturally in the domain of any successful lawyer. Legal training—questioning, getting at the facts, looking at alternatives—is the greatest possible training."

From the President's perspective, Rogers's appointment had the advantages of bringing in a comfortable and trusted friend, an individual who would not compete with him for the diplomatic spotlight, and a Progressive-Republican from the party's Eastern, internationalist wing.

Once confirmed, Rogers quickly began to establish good relations with Congress, soliciting the advice of influential senators and representatives and, in turn, being seen as a "force for moderation" within the Administration. He also gave more attention than any postwar Secretary of State to structural reform. In an effort to modernize and streamline bureaucratic procedures and internal communications, Rogers installed a sophisticated computer system for information storage and retrieval and initiated new personnel, training and advancement programs designed to develop and keep highly qualified specialists.

By the end of President Nixon's first term, Rogers could claim, probably justifiably, that the Department had never been in better shape. Yet management alone was not the solution, since the Department's workload was growing. The Secretary pointed out that "apart from the everyday business of diplomacy . . . we've just recently had to become involved in problems that were formerly domestic but have become international. We're dealing now with the environment, communications satellites, air-traffic control, hijacking and drug suppression."

Early in his tenure, Rogers demonstrated that his talents as a negotiator would, at least partially, compensate for his lack of substantive expertise in foreign affairs. In early trips to Europe and the Far East, Rogers created a favorable impression with his "ability to gain the quick trust of foreigners by conveying goodwill and personal warmth." However, it was soon apparent that the President looked to Rogers for guidance on the public-relations implications of his decisions rather than on policy itself.

Indeed speculation maintained that Henry Kissinger [q.v.] at the National Security Council and Melvin Laird [q.v.] at the Pentagon were more influential in formulating foreign and national security policy than Rogers and the State Department. Certainly Defense Secretary Laird and Presidential Assistant Kissinger were more conspicuous and were more aggressive bureaucratic politicians than Rogers. Both Laird and Kissinger also had more extensive backgrounds in their fields than Rogers.

By inclination disposed towards keeping a rather low profile, Rogers did not attempt to be a moderating counterweight to Laird. Although rumor and bureaucratic reality pitted Rogers against Kissinger, Rogers seemed content to serve as the top-level confidant while Kissinger acted the part of the stimulator and sifter of policy ideas. While this stance may have resulted in peace among the President's foreign affairs/national security counsellors, it also had the effect of lowering public esteem for the State Department and of demoralizing the Foreign Service. One reporter commented that under Rogers, the Department's personnel seemed "consumed by self-doubt, as if they [were] constantly asking themselves whether what they do really matters."

There is considerable controversy over the extent of Rogers' influence in formulating American foreign policy during his four and a half years as Secretary of State. Part of this debate can be attributed to Rogers contention that he and the President thought "a lot alike." Thus, according to Rogers, he and the President were usually in agreement, so the Secretary seldom had to fight for his position. This natural agreement may have given the appearance that Rogers lacked significant policy influence.

Within this likemindedness, however, it is probable that Rogers exerted a cautious and moderating influence. For instance, in April of 1969, when North Korean jets shot down an American EC-121 intelligence plane over the sea of Japan, Rogers was the voice of caution, speaking against the retaliation urged by the Defense Department and urging a diplomatic resolution saying that "in international affairs, the weak can be rash, the powerful must be restrained."

Rogers also succeeded in curbing the Administration's response to the Peruvian expropriation of American oilfields and installations in the spring of 1969. Instead of provoking a confrontation with Peru (and by extension, with Latin America generally) by a retaliatory cut-off of American foreign aid, Rogers found a loophole in the Hickenlooper Amendment to avoid applying such economic sanctions and implemented a cautious response of diplomatic negotiation.

On policy regarding Vietnam, Rogers generally supported the Administration's goal of finding a political solution for South Vietnam based on free elections and went along with the military strategy of maintaining a degree of offensive pressure on enemy forces in South Vietnam. Within this context, however, he strenuously objected, without apparent effect, to the 1970 invasion of Cambodia and was a strong proponent for the withdrawal of American forces and for the policy of "Vietnamization."

Although Rogers was clear in expressing the administration's disappointment in the 1971 expulsion of Nationalist China from the United Nations in order to admit Communist China, he was also a potent administration advocate of improving U.S. relations with Peking. In fact, the Secretary of State may have been a "decisive figure" in evolving the dramatic shift in America's China policy which culminated in President Nixon's visit to China in 1972.

In most of the dramatic foreign policy issues of the first Nixon administration, Rogers played a low-keyed, unspectacular role. The one area in which he took a prominent initiative—perhaps the issue he is principally known for—was the Rogers Plan for the Middle East.

Initially proposed to the Soviets in October 1969, Rogers publicly offered his peace proposals to the Middle Eastern belligerents in December. His plan called on Israel to withdraw from Arab territories occupied in the 1967 war in return for Arab assurances of a binding commitment to peace. Although this initial proposal was rejected by both Arabs and Israelis, Rogers persevered in his efforts and during 1970 succeeded in securing Egyptian, Jordanian, and Israeli agreement to a cease-fire and a resumption of negotiations under the auspices of UN Ambassador Gunnar Jarring. Eventually Rogers' efforts in the Middle East were eclipsed by his successor's (Henry Kissinger's) "shuttle diplomacy."

Following Nixon's reelection in 1972, rumor began to predict Rogers' imminent departure. Thus, the announcement of his resignation in September 1973 came as no surprise. Apparently everyone concerned was happy with the change—Rogers was eager to get back to his New York law practice, the President continued to regard him as a man of "unwavering good spirits, good judgment and good sense." Kissinger, who had been called the "Secretary of State in everything but title," was finally accorded that formal rank.

Rogers returned to the law firm of Rogers and Wells of New York City and effectively retired from politics.

[MJW]

ROHATYN, FELIX G(EORGE)
b. May 29, 1928; Vienna, Austria.
Chairman, Municipal Assistance Corporation, 1975-79.

Rohatyn left his native Austria for France in 1933 and emigrated with his family to the United States in 1942, where he was naturalized in 1950. He graduated from Middlebury College in Vermont in 1948, and, through a relative connected with the Paris office of Lazard Freres, took a job with the New York branch of the firm. After service in the U.S. Army in Korea from 1950 to 1952, Rohatyn was assigned to the Paris office of Lazard, where he worked in foreign exchange. He returned to the U.S. in 1955, and shortly thereafter moved into the area of corporate reorganization, where he later made his reputation. Rohatyn became a partner at Lazard in 1960.

Rohatyn first emerged as a public figure in the years from 1969 to 1971 when he was chairman of the so-called Crisis Committee set up by the New York Stock Exchange. The credit crunch of 1969-70 had put an end to the boom years on Wall Street, and dozens of brokerages were being driven to the wall. Doubt about general stability was further increased when it came to light that over $4 billion in stock certificates had simply been misplaced during large-scale conversion to computerized operations and through slipshod bookkeeping.

In March 1972 Rohatyn became embroiled in the scandal surrounding the settlement of a government anti-trust action against International Telephone and Telegraph (ITT), in which the suit had been dropped in exchange for a pledge from ITT to underwrite a large part of the funds needed to hold the 1972 Republican Party Convention in San Diego. In the midst of confirmation hearings for Attorney General-designate Richard G. Kleindienst [q.v.], Washington reporter Jack Anderson [q.v.] asserted in his column that Kleindienst had negotiated the deal with ITT and quoted Rohatyn, a member of ITT's board of directors, who stated that he had discussed the deal with Kleindienst on several occasions. Kleindienst, for his part, denied any wrongdoing. Two weeks later former Attorney General John Mitchell [q.v.] stated that Rohatyn had indeed attended meetings in the Attorney General's office in April 1971 but said that the ITT case had not been discussed. In early April 1972 an associate of consumer advocate Ralph Nader [q.v.] charged that hundreds of thousands of shares of ITT stock had been sold to the public in July 1971 just before the anti-trust settlement was announced and prices fell. Because Lazard Freres had handled the sale for ITT and since Rohatyn was associated with both firms, his

role in the affair was again subject to some scrutiny.

In June 1975 the New York state legislature created the Municipal Assistance Corp. (MAC), known as "Big MAC," to underwrite further issues of New York City paper and to ensure their marketability, which had been totally undermined by the city's unfolding fiscal crisis. New York Gov. Hugh Carey [q.v.] appointed Rohatyn, as a spokesman for the New York banking community, to an advisory panel on the crisis. Rohatyn promptly informed city officials that the banks would not "roll over," i.e. extend, $280 million in short-term notes falling due on June 11 unless the city consented in full to the MAC plan for the redressment of the city's finances.

In September 1975 Rohatyn became chairman of MAC, and was effectively the most visible spokesman for the New York City banks throughout the crisis. In July 1975 the dollar price of the initial $1 billion issue of MAC notes fell by 10%, indicating that the market had no confidence in the restructured finances of the city. A second $1 billion issue, scheduled for August, had to be canceled. At that point, Rohatyn turned to Secretary of the Treasury William Simon [q.v.] and asked for federal guarantees for the next MAC issue. Simon refused. By early August, however, $900 million in MAC paper had been sold to meet the city's short-term cash needs.

A new setback for the marketability of MAC bonds emerged in September when city officials announced that the budget deficit for fiscal 1976 would be $3.3 billion instead of the $641 million previously forecast. Rohatyn called the revelation "shocking", and predicted that default was a "good possibility" with the city's pending $150 million payroll.

Rohatyn also served on the Emergency Financial Control Board (EFCB), a body created by the state legislature to oversee the city's finances at the same time as MAC was established to underwrite new issues. The EFCB, which was characterized by critics as a virtual "bankers' dictatorship," had effective veto power over the city's budget. During the summer of 1975, under Rohatyn's leadership, the EFCB exacted major budget cuts and revisions from New York City, including the end of free tuition at the city's university system, an increase in bus and subway fares from 35 to 50 cents and layoffs of thousands of New York City employees.

A complex political process surrounded the possible default of New York City throughout the crisis from May 5 to November 1975, when federal guarantees were obtained for the city's security issues. President Gerald Ford and leading government economic spokesmen such as Arthur Burns [q.v.], William Simon and Alan Greenspan [q.v.] were initially inclined to let the city default. Rohatyn, on the other hand, was more convinced about the ultimate dangers of default to U.S. and international capital markets. In September 1975 almost all cities in the Northeast region, whatever their local financial situation, were finding it almost impossible to market securities in the shadow of the New York crisis. As Rohatyn put it, "If the market looks this way without a default, think what it will be like with a default."

After the congressional legislation of late 1975, combined with large purchases of MAC bonds by New York City's unions, had temporarily resolved the crisis, Rohatyn continued to serve as chairman of MAC and to work at Lazard Freres. He played an instrumental role in the 1978 congressional legislation, signed by President Carter, which gave further federal assistance to the city.

[LG]

For further information:
Jack Newfield and Paul Du Brul, *The Abuse of Power* (New York, 1977).
Robert Sobel, *NYSE: A History of the New York Stock Exchange, 1935-1975* (New York, 1975).

ROMNEY, GEORGE W(ILCKEN)
b. July 8, 1907; Chihuahua, Mex.
Governor, Mich. 1963-69; Secretary of Housing and Urban Development, January 1969-November 1972.

The son of an American Mormon family living in Mexico, George Romney grew up in California and Idaho and worked his way through Latter-Day Saints University in Utah. After serving two years as a Mormon missionary in England and Scotland, he studied taxation and tariffs at George Washington University. In 1930 Romney joined the Aluminum Corporation of America, returning to Washington in 1932 as a lobbyist for the aluminum industry. As general manager of the Automobile Manufacturers Association from 1942 to 1948, Romney served as chief auto industry spokesman during World War II. Appointed special assistant to the chairman of Nash-Kelvinator in 1948, Romney became president and board chairman of its successor firm, American Motors, six years later.

A Republican, Romney served as governor of Michigan from 1963 to 1969. A member of the liberal wing of the Party, Romney was a front-runner for the 1968 presidential nomination. However a series of political blunders, including a statement that he had been "brainwashed" by U.S. officials during a 1965 Vietnam tour cut short his campaign. [See KENNEDY, JOHNSON Volumes]

Following his election in November 1968, Nixon appointed Romney Secretary of Housing and Urban Development (HUD). During his first months in office, Romney announced a major reorganization of the Model Cities program, giving more direct authority to mayors and local governments in the planning and administration of the federally financed model neighborhoods. A serious shortage of affordable housing, aggravated by a high rate of inflation, led to Romney's announcement in May 1969 of Operation Breakthrough, a plan to build low-cost housing for the poor by mass production methods. In a *New York Times* article in January 1970, Romney described Operation Breakthrough as a blueprint for developing a housing industry capable of producing more than 2 million new units each year. Romney hoped to enlist the cooperation of government, industry and labor to eliminate such barriers to volume housing construction as the high costs of land and materials, restrictive building codes, zoning ordinances, tax constraints and labor shortages.

Romney was never entirely comfortable in his cabinet post, where he was restricted to dealing only with housing problems, and broke with the Administration on several occasions. In a speech in May 1970, Romney criticized President Nixon's handling of inflation and called for new Administration intercession to restrain the wage-price spiral. As his personal contribution to the fight against inflation, Romney announced his intention to return 25% of his HUD salary to the U.S. Treasury, suggesting that other business and labor leaders follow suit.

Acting counter to Administration housing policy, Romney helped develop plans for the construction of federally subsidized housing outside of inner-city ghettos. President Nixon subsequently declared that his Administration would not use the power of the federal government to force integration of suburban communities. Romney denied rumors in November 1970 that he had been asked to resign his HUD post, saying that he remained "deeply involved" in Administration policy. A year later Romney gave final approval to the Forest Hills project, a plan to build low-income housing in a white middle-class section of New York City.

After suggesting that all federal housing subsidy programs be abolished and that the Federal Housing Administration be made a private agency, Romney resigned as Secretary of HUD on Nov. 27, 1972. In his resignation speech Romney complained that neither President Nixon nor his Democratic opponent in the 1972 election, Sen. George McGovern (D, S.D.) [q.v.], had dealt with the "real issues." Romney stated his intention to form a "coalition of concerned citizens" to en-

lighten the American public on "life and death" issues. In January 1973 Romney agreed to become chairman and chief executive of the National Center for Voluntary Action, a nonprofit organization he had helped found in 1970 to encourage greater voluntary initiative by individual citizens and groups in solving national problems.

[DAE]

ROONEY, JOHN J(AMES)
b. Nov. 29, 1903; New York, N.Y.
d. Oct. 26, 1975; Washington, D.C.
Democratic Representative, N.Y., 1944-75.

The son of Irish immigrants, Rooney received his education from local Catholic schools and then earned his law degree from Fordham University in 1925. For the next 14 years he had a prosperous law practice. In 1940 Rooney was appointed assistant district attorney of New York City. Four years later he won a seat in the U.S. House. Rooney represented a polyglot district of mixed ethnic groups ranging rom Irish to Hasidic Jews to wealthy third-generation Americans. But during the 1960s and 1970s, the district changed with an influx of minority groups and became overwhelmingly poor.

Rooney compiled a liberal record on domestic legislation during his tenure, voting for extensive programs to aid the growing number of poor in his district. From 1949 until his retirement he chaired the House Appropriations subcommittee that oversaw the budgets of the State and Justice Departments and the federal courts. A close friend of J. Edgar Hoover [q.v.], Rooney gave the FBI all the funds it requested. The Brooklyn Representative never questioned some of the Bureau's more controversial operations, of which he was kept informed by Hoover. However, he was extremely parsimonious in doling out funds to other branches, which frequently had difficult times receiving money needed for specific programs. [See TRUMAN, EISENHOWER, KENNEDY Volumes]

Rooney's conduct as chairman of his subcommittee frequently proved an irritant in diplomacy. In 1971-72 he blocked payment of America's dues to the International Labor Organization because a Russian occupied one of the assistant directorships. This United Nations agency carried out international foreign aid programs and tried to persuade member nations to improve the lives of working people. As a result of Administration and congressional pressure, Rooney restored funds for the program in 1973, but he continued to cut American contributions to other United Nations agencies.

Toward the end of his career, Rooney faced strong election challenges from those opposed to his vigorous support of the Vietnam war. He defeated an anti-war challenger in the 1968 primary. Two years later Peter Eikenberry, a local lawyer, mounted an impressive campaign against him with the help of hundreds of student volunteers. Rooney undercut his opponent by announcing that his support of the war was for patriotic reasons and at the same time introducing a resolution in the House requiring the approval of Congress for any future involvement in Cambodia. Rooney won by 1,600 votes.

Allard Lowenstein [q.v.], the national chairman of Americans for Democratic Action and a leader of the dump-Johnson movement, challenged Rooney in 1972. Backed by the Democratic Party machine and labor unions such as the International Longshoremen's Association, Rooney waged an aggressive campaign in which he characterized his opponent as a carpetbagger and a "treasonous peace-nik." Rooney defeated Lowenstein in the primary by 1,000 votes in a contested election. Lowenstein presented evidence of voting irregularities including machine breakdowns in anti-Rooney districts, 1,300 voters who voted with lapsed registrations, 500 voters who had either moved or died but seemed to have voted anyway, and at least 100 voters who cast their ballots twice. The federal court ordered a new primary which Rooney won by 1,200 votes.

The contested primary came after revelations of impropriety in earlier Rooney campaigns. In 1970 and 1972 Rooney had obtained illegal campaign contributions from unions and shipping interests important in his district. Both the Seafarers Union and the Prudential Grace Co., for example, had been fined for such misconduct. In addition, it was disclosed that J. Edgar Hoover had made available to his congressional benefactor information about his rivals in past primaries. To avoid a grueling third party, Rooney decided, with the friendly persuasion of the Brooklyn machine, to retire at the end of his term in 1975. He died in October of that year.

[JB]

ROOSA, ROBERT V(INCENT)
b. June 21, 1918; Marquette, Mich.
Member, President's Task Force on International Development, 1969-70; Member, Advisory Board on International Monetary Reform, August, 1973.

Robert Roosa began his career on the research staff of the Federal Reserve Bank. Trained as an economist at the University of Michigan, Roosa worked for the "Fed" from 1946-60, when President John F. Kennedy appointed him undersecretary of the treasury for monetary affairs. During the Kennedy years Roosa sought to solve the U.S. "gold drain," which was undermining the status of the dollar as an international reserve currency. He was the architect of the "Roosa bond," a Treasury security used to encourage foreign central banks to recycle their surplus dollars to the U.S. Roosa testified before Congress on the potential for a serious world depression inherent in the "dollar crisis." In late 1964, he left the Treasury to become a partner in the influential Wall Street investment firm of Brown Brothers Harriman, and thereafter emerged as a major spokesman of the private banking sector on international monetary matters. [See KENNEDY volume]

In the fall of 1969 President Nixon appointed Roosa to serve on the Task Force on International Development, which included David Rockefeller [q.v.], president of the Chase Manhattan Bank; Rudolf Peterson [q.v.], president of the Bank of America; and Harvard economist Gottfried Haberler. The task force issued its findings, known as the Peterson Report, in 1970. It recommended greater power for the executive branch in foreign policy to bypass cumbersome congressional controls, a reduced U.S. military presence abroad and an effort to involve Europe and Japan in alleviating the indebtedness of underdeveloped countries.

Roosa acted primarily as a Wall Street spokesman and critic of economic policy during the Nixon Administration. In late 1969 he had already publicly urged President Nixon to impose an immediate six-month, wage-price freeze and expressed pessimism about the effectiveness of the Administration's early moves against inflation. He renewed this call in May 1970. A few days later, in the midst of the uproar following the U.S. invasion of Cambodia, Roosa told an anti-war rally of 1,000 students in the Wall Street area of New York City that the Vietnam war was "ruining the U.S. economy."

In early August 1971, in light of the deepening international monetary crisis, a congressional committee issued a report urging an increase in the official price of gold, or an effective devaluation of the dollar. The report prompted an immediate speculative run on the dollar in Europe. On Aug. 10 Roosa attacked the report as "impractical" and repeated his criticisms in September before congressional hearings on Nixon's "New Economic Policy" and its foreign consequences. There was no need, asserted Roosa, "to glue back together some pieces of the broken idol through a highly contrived 'return to gold' . . . " Instead, Roosa proposed that the dollar be allowed to depreciate against other currencies, and also attacked the 10% surcharge as a

step toward an international trade war. By November 1971, however, as international negotiations were underway to develop new currency parities, Roosa admitted that the U.S. should not be "fastidious" about a gold-price change if that would break the "logjam" with its trading partners.

After new parities were established in the "Smithsonian Agreements" of December 1971, Roosa clashed with Federal Reserve Board Chairman Arthur Burns [q.v.] over Fed policy in upholding the agreement. In February 1972 Roosa maintained that the U.S. was "torpedoing" the Smithsonian accords by failing to raise interest rates and attract capital to the U.S. Several days later in congressional testimony, Burns conceded that the repatriation of dollars was going slowly, but insisted that the U.S. was acting in harmony with other central banks to bolster the dollar.

After the second dollar crisis and devaluation of March 1973, which wrecked the Smithsonian accords, Roosa warned against any hasty attempts to solve the crisis. He praised the European Economic Community for its float against the dollar but expressed doubts about a long-term solution. Although his criticisms of the Vietnam war had already earned him a place on President Nixon's "enemy list," Roosa was appointed by Secretary of the Treasury George Shultz [q.v.] in August 1973 to serve on a presidential advisory committee on international monetary reform.

Roosa was a prominent participant in the international debate over "petrodollar recycling" and its impact on the world financial system in the wake of the October 1973 quadrupling of oil prices. In June 1974 Roosa stated in a public speech that the world banking system could not handle the new masses of Arab oil revenues, and in January 1975 he coauthored a widely discussed article in *Foreign Affairs* that proposed steps by governments and international agencies to facilitate the recycling process which would otherwise swamp the private banking sector. In December 1974 Roosa called for a government planning effort in the U.S. to set priorities in "commanding areas" of the economy. Two years later, in August 1976, he urged the Senate Finance Committee to recommend the establishment of a council of governors for the International Monetary Fund (IMF) to insure surveillance of international capital flows.

During the late 1970s Roosa worked at Brown Brothers Harriman, while serving on the board of directors of numerous other companies and of the National Bureau of Economic Research. Roosa was also a member of the Council on Foreign Relations and a trustee of the Rockefeller Foundation.

[LG]

RUCKELSHAUS, WILLIAM D(OYLE)

b. July 24, 1932; Indianapolis, Ind.
Director, Environmental Protection Agency, December 1970-April 1973; Acting Director, FBI, April 1973-June 1973; Deputy Attorney General, July 1973-October 1973.

William Ruckelshaus came from a family with strong Republican ties. His father had attended every Republican convention between 1920 and 1960 and played a role in writing Party platforms. Ruckelshaus graduated from Princeton cum laude in 1957, and received his law degree from the Harvard Law School in 1960. He served in the Indiana attorney general's office and helped to write the Indiana Air Pollution Control Act. His work in the state's environmental protection prosecutions gave him the experience he would eventually use as a federal administrator. In 1966 he was elected to the Indiana House of Representatives and became the first freshman representative in Indiana to be elected majority leader. He ran unsuccessfully against Birch Bayh [q.v.] for the Senate in 1968.

He was brought into the Nixon Administration as assistant attorney general and head of the Justice Department's civil division. He directed 200 lawyers dealing with 20,000 cases, and was regarded as a good administrator. He became a protege of Attorney General John Mitchell [q.v.]. While in the Justice Department, he made a point of visiting college campuses to give the Administration side on Vietnam–a task he dubbed as the "kamikaze tour."

He was appointed to head the new Environmental Protection Agency (EPA) in 1970. He had to walk carefully between environmental activists who wanted legal action taken against polluters and businessmen who were critical of the high costs of environmental protection. He was able to act with some degree of independence in part because Nixon had hoped to take away attention from a potential Democratic presidential candidate, Edmund Muskie [q.v.], who had made environmental protection one of his big issues.

Ruckelshaus acted quickly in his first few weeks to prosecute polluters. He moved against Atlanta, Detroit and Cleveland threatening to take federal court action if those cities did not stop dumping raw sewage into waterways. Later he filed suit against major industrial polluters, such as Republic Steel, Jones & Laughlin and the Kennebec River Pulp and Paper Co. His strategy was to go after the biggest polluters, using a variety of techniques: 180-day notices, enforcement conferences, and civil or criminal suits brought under the revised Refuse Act of 1889. Suits were brought against hundreds of corporations and a few cities. One of his decisions received much criticism from environmental activists, however: the compromise in which he gave auto manufacturers a one-year extension of a 1975 deadline to install anti-pollution devices on new model automobiles.

On April 27, 1973, Nixon named Ruckelshaus to replace L. Patrick Gray [q.v.] as acting director of the FBI after Gray had become involved in the Watergate cover-up scandal. Ruckelshaus gave up his EPA post to take the FBI job, although he agreed to be acting director temporarily.

Nixon next appointed Ruckelshaus deputy attorney general, and Ruckelshaus was sworn in on Sept. 26, 1973. He served under Elliot Richardson [q.v.], and was one of the victims of the "Saturday night massacre," those removals from office that occurred when President Nixon sought to fire Archibald Cox [q.v.] as Watergate prosecutor.

Nixon had ordered Richardson to fire Cox on Saturday, Oct. 20. Richardson refused. He then ordered Ruckelshaus to fire Cox. Ruckelshaus also refused. Although he was never directly informed of his dismissal, Ruckelshaus felt obliged to resign after serving only 24 days in that post. Only when Solicitor General Robert Bork [q.v.] was appointed acting attorney general was Cox fired.

After Ruckelshaus left government service, he entered private law practice. In 1976 he supported Gerald Ford for President and was one of the people mentioned as a possible Ford running mate. During the campaign he served as a representative for Ford in negotiations over television arrangements for debates with Jimmy Carter [q.v.].

[HML]

RUMSFELD, DONALD
b. July 9, 1932; Chicago, Ill.
Director, Office of Economic Opportunity, April 1969-December 1970; Counsellor to the President, December 1970-October 1971; Director, Cost of Living Council, October 1971-February 1973; Ambassador to the North Atlantic Treaty Organization, February 1973-September 1974; Assistant to the President, September 1974-November 1975; Secretary of Defense, November 1975-January 1977.

The son of a Chicago real estate man, Donald Rumsfeld grew up in the conservative suburbs of Winnetka and Glenview. He won a scholarship to study at Princeton University, became captain of both the football and wrestling teams there, and graduated in 1954 with a major

in politics. Contemplating a military career, he joined the Navy and spent the next three years as a Navy pilot and flight instructor. In 1957 he left the service to test the political waters of Washington.

In 1957 he joined the staff of Ohio Representative David Dennison as an administrative assistant. Although Dennison was defeated for reelection in 1958, Rumsfeld had the opportunity to gain much practical experience as his campaign manager that year. Rumsfeld spent the next year as administrative assistant to Michigan Rep. Robert Griffin (R, Mich.), then managed Dennison's unsuccessful attempt to make a comeback in 1960.

Initiated to the legislative waters of Capitol Hill and seasoned in the practice of campaign politics in Illinois, Rumsfeld returned to Chicago to lay the groundwork for his own electoral bid. After two years with the investment banking firm of A. G. Becker & Co. he entered the Republican primary for the 13th congressional district of Illinois. Although classified as an urban district, this north Chicago area was comprised mostly of highly mobile, well-educated, young Republicans—an ideal constituency for an ambitious, young conservative Republican such as Rumsfeld. Exuding a style suggestive of a Republican Kennedy, Rumsfeld put together a highly personal and enthusiastic campaign organization staffed with numerous young volunteers. He went on to win the primary and handily defeated his Democratic opponent by a tally of 134,442 to 73,998.

In Congress, he quickly established his credentials as a conservative. Serving during the hey-day of the liberal New Frontier-Great Society presidencies, Rumsfeld consistently voted against the extension of government services, against much progressive legislation, and in favor of holding down government spending and taxation. His voting record for his first year won him a 100% perfect rating from the conservative Americans for Constitutional Action and a verdict of only 4% from the liberal Americans for Democratic Action. In his six years in the House his conservative stance put him on record against mass transit aid, the anti-poverty bill, student loans, federal aid for city and suburban libraries, against monies for the arms control and disarmament agency, against creating an executive department of urban affairs. At the same time, this conservative record was moderated by strong support for civil rights and a penchant for fighting to reform and modernize the Republican Party. These reform activities included participation in the 1965 transfer of Minority Leadership from Representative Charles W. Halleck to Gerald Ford, as well as an unsuccessful 1968 crusade to reform House rules. Such activities, coupled with the outright "dislike" of senior Illinois Rep. Les Arends, earned Rumsfeld enough resentment from the Republican old guard in the House to block his advancement. His defeat in seeking the chairmanship of the House Republican Research Committee in early 1969 clearly indicated the ill-will he had generated among his colleagues.

Thus the new Nixon administration's offer of the directorship of the Office of Economic Opportunity (OEO) in the spring of 1969 came as a welcome option to a stalled congressional career. Rumsfeld had tendered valuable campaign service during 1968 as one of ten surrogate speakers for Mr. Nixon and the new President needed someone capable and dependable to take on the controversial and the likely to be onerous task of "de-escalating the war on poverty." Speculation that Rumsfeld would dismantle the agency was understandable in light of the facts that the administration was hostile to OEO, that as a Congressman, Rumsfeld had voted against the creation of OEO, and that his opinion of the agency was that it "ought to be kept around if for no other reason than that it is important to maintain at least one credible national symbol and program which demonstrates our Government's commitment to the poor."

Since he was unwilling, however, to resign a safe seat in Congress simply to preside over the liquidation of OEO, Rumsfeld was simultaneously named a presidential assistant with cabinet rank,

made a member of the President's Urban Affairs Council, and paid a salary equal to his congressional rate. In addition, Rumsfeld asserted his mission was not to demolish, but to transform OEO from an "activist" agency to an "initiating agency—an incubator for . . . programs during their initial experimental phases."

During the 19 months of his tenure at OEO, Rumsfeld tried to reorganize the agency into a more efficient bureaucracy, with emphases on a lower public profile, on teamwork, and on administrative, mechanical matters and bureaucratic matters. Pursuant to these ends, activists in Vista were summarily dropped. Terry Lenzer, the highly committed social activist head of OEO's Legal Services, was fired and similar "advocate types" were weeded out. Rumsfeld was criticized for bowing to political pressure from Nixon's private circle and the ABA Legal Services Advisory Committee called his dismissal of Lenzer "highly duplicitous." Although under Rumsfeld various OEO programs and activities were farmed out, transferred, or merged to other cabinet departments or agencies, OEO was not dismantled but streamlined. Rumsfeld viewed his job at the agency as a challenge to make it work in a new way that was more compatible to the Nixon Administration.

Pleased with Rumsfeld's performance at OEO, President Nixon rewarded him with the post of counsellor to the President in December 1970, thus taking him off the firing line at OEO before the actual dismantling occurred. Rumsfeld's successor at OEO, Howard Phillips, succeeded not only in demolishing the agency but his own career as a result of the enemies he made in the process.

Rumsfeld's duties and status as counsellor were variable and somewhat tenuous since he shared the title of counsellor with former Secretary of Health, Education, and Welfare Robert Finch [q.v.], who was gradually being moved to the outer circles of power. This changed in October of 1971 when the President entrusted Rumsfeld with another controversial task—administering Phase II of the

Nixon economic program as director of the Cost of Living Council. Rumsfeld approached the task of maintaining wage and price controls as a matter of efficient organization which was precisely the managerial rather than political image the Council required. The effort to remain as a-partisan as possible while directing the Cost of Living Council also had the results of keeping Rumsfeld away from active involvement in the 1972 presidential campaign.

His position at the Council brought Rumsfeld onto the Domestic Council where he encountered problems with H. R. Haldeman [q.v.] and John Ehrlichman [q.v.]. In addition, his well-developed sense of timing and instinct for moving on while circumstances were still favorable led Rumsfeld to seek to put distance between himself and both the Cost of Living Council and the White House. His nomination as ambassador to the North Atlantic Treaty Organization (NATO) in December 1972 had the twin advantages of removing him from the Cost of Living Council before prices began to soar and taking him out of the White House before the Watergate scandal began to surface.

In announcing that Rumsfeld had been chosen to replace David Kennedy at NATO, Press Secretary Ron Ziegler [q.v.] stated that the appointment had been prompted by the belief that since Rumsfeld was "considering a return to politics" such a post "would round out" his background and provide him with a "firm base for challenging Adlai E. Stevenson's bid for a second Senate term in 1974." In addition, the President was said to feel that Rumsfeld's "extensive and varied background in American domestic affairs" would be particularly useful "at a time when the United States and Europe are increasingly interdependent economically and socially as well as militarily." Rumsfeld spent the next 18 months acquiring diplomatic and military-related experience and reorganizing his mission to operate more efficiently.

Within hours of Nixon's resignation, President Ford summoned his former House colleague and friend to head a five-man transition group to revise the White House staff and its organization. Rumsfeld, drawing on previous White House experience, quickly assessed the situation, saw the difficulties of trying to shift power from the Nixon appointees, and decided that he did not want to confront those problems by joining the Ford staff. He made his recommendations to the new President and flew back to Brussels. He was at NATO headquarters when Ford made one of the most decisive moves of his presidency—he pardoned Richard Nixon. Once again, Rumsfeld was well out of range of any politically damaging taint.

In the aftermath of the Nixon pardon, Ford began to clean out Nixon staffers. Alexander Haig [q.v.] was dismissed as chief of staff. In the process NATO gained Haig as a commander and lost Rumsfeld as an ambassador. In September 1974, Rumsfeld was appointed assistant to the President, replacing Haig as chief of staff in function although he preferred the title of staff coordinator.

Although all nine senior advisers of the Ford staff were theoretically equal, Rumsfeld was a bit more equal than most. While his title of coordinator was less "imperial" than Haig's or Haldeman's, he was as central and influential as they had been. He installed his own team both within the White House and throughout the administration. He held the reins of access and information to the President. His network of allies in the wider administration included Attorney General Edward Levi [q.v.] and Secretary of Transportation William Coleman [q.v.]. Rumsfeld himself spent more time with the President than any other aide, including Henry Kissinger. Rumsfeld used his organizational system to diminish the influence of all potential rivals at the White House. Although the Vice President chaired the Domestic Council, Rumsfeld headed off Nelson Rockefeller's [q.v.] hopes for "heavy involvement" in domestic policy-making by rigidly controlling the day-to-day operations of the Council. He was also instrumental in bringing in Howard "Bo" Callaway [q.v.] as Ford's campaign manager and in inducing the conservative Callaway to criticize Rockefeller as a "liability" to the national ticket. Rumsfeld took special pains to solicit counter-arguments to Kissinger's position papers, to orchestrate rumors of Kissinger's declining influence and eventually have him deprived of his White House position as national security assistant.

Rumsfeld, nonetheless, chafed at being staff and wanted to be his own man. President Ford gave him that chance in November 1975 when he appointed him Secretary of Defense as part of a startling personnel shake-up that ousted James Schlesinger [q.v.] from Defense, William Colby [q.v.] from the Central Intelligence Agency, and Henry Kissinger from his job as presidential assistant for national security affairs. Ford had long been personally uncomfortable with Schlesinger and the growing public controversy between the defense chief and Kissinger over detente policy. In appointing Rumsfeld, Ford got a man more personally agreeable to him as well as an able and diversified administrator. Rumsfeld was also a lifelong proponent of a strong military who had long been suspicious of Kissinger's brand of detente and who wanted "parallel policies of deterrence and detente." Such perspectives put him in agreement with his predecessor—a similarity the Administration took every opportunity to underline.

Despite his NATO experience, Rumsfeld's appointment to the cabinet was criticized as bringing a highly partisan novice to the Pentagon. His supporters argued that since he had the President's confidence and shared Schlesinger's views, he might prove a more effective counter-balance to Kissinger than his predecessor. In addition, the President hoped that Rumsfeld's political savvy would make him more successful in securing legislative approval for defense programs, and indeed, Rumsfeld's first order of business as Secretary was to steer the Defense budget through Congress. Critics argued that Rumsfeld had neither the intellectual capacity nor strategic

breadth to succeed Schlesinger or compete with Kissinger. Concern also abounded (even at his Senate confirmation hearings) that he would merely use the Defense Department as a stepping stone to the vice presidential nomination.

Despite such speculation, Rumsfeld was quickly and easily confirmed within two weeks of his nomination. As in all his other executive positions, Rumsfeld proceeded to move in his own team and set about a process of piecemeal immersion in the details and workings of his department in an effort to master the administration of the Pentagon. Given his short tenure in office, the magnitude of the task, and the political environment of the Ford Administration, it was no surprise that his secretaryship was not characterized by any substantive changes of policy.

Shortly after the Ford administration left office in 1977, Rumsfeld returned to his native Chicago and assumed the presidency of the financial and legally beset pharmaceutical company of G.D. Searle.

[MJW]

RUSH, (DAVID) KENNETH
b. Jan. 17, 1910; Walla Walla, Wash.
Ambassador to West Germany, July 1969-January 1972; Deputy Secretary of Defense, February 1972-November 1972; Deputy Secretary of State, February 1973-May 1974; Counselor to the President for Economic Affairs, May 1974-September 1974; Ambassador to France, September 1974-May 1977.

Rush received his bachelor's degree from the University of Tennessee in 1930 and his law degree from Yale two years later. He practiced law in New York City from 1932 to 1936 and taught law at Duke University in 1936-37, where Richard Nixon was one of his pupils. Rush then joined Union Carbide Corp., eventually becoming president of the company in

1966. In 1969 Nixon made his former law professor ambassador to West Germany. During his short tenure there, Rush continued to assert American resolve to protect West Berlin in the face of Soviet attempts to change its status. Rush served as deputy secretary of defense from February to November 1972 and in February 1973 was confirmed as deputy secretary of state. At that post he became a major spokesman for U.S. policy around the world. He defended increasing trade with Eastern Europe and opposed U.S. unilateral troop withdrawal from the North Atlantic Treaty Organization. Rush was frequently sent on missions to reaffirm U.S. support of Vietnam and to appease Pacific allies disturbed by various defense policy changes.

In May 1974 Rush left the State Department to become counselor to the President for economic affairs with the role of coordinating domestic and international economic policy. Rush encountered criticism from Congress because he refused invitations to testify formally before the Joint Economic Committee and the Subcommittee on Multinational Corporations, saying that he would meet them only informally. He maintained that formal testimony would inhibit his ability to give President Nixon candid advice. Sen. William Proxmire (D, Wis.) [q.v.] said that Rush's position was "unacceptable and ridiculous" and "based on the same arrogance of power and immaturity of thought that led to Watergate." Rush supported the Administration's opposition to congressional efforts to win tax cuts for individuals. "A tax cut for individuals means increased demands without increased productivity." However he maintained that tax incentives for business would be "noninflationary" if they spurred output.

Rush was named chairman of the eight-member Council on Wage and Price Stability by President Ford in August 1974. The following month he became ambassador to France. He resigned that post at the end of the Ford Administration.

[AFB]

RUSSELL, RICHARD B(REVARD)
b. Nov. 2, 1897; Winder, Ga.
d. Jan. 21, 1971; Washington, D.C.
Democratic Senator, Ga., 1933-71;
President Pro Tempore of the Senate,
1969-71.

Long one of the Senate's most influential members, Russell was the fourth son in a patrician Georgia family. He served as state assemblyman and governor before his election to the Senate in 1932. Russell generally supported New Deal Programs, but as he once said: "I'm a reactionary when times are good. In a depression I'm a liberal." After World War II, he was an opponent of civil rights and most social welfare legislation. By the late 1940s Russell had solidly established himself as the leader of the Southern bloc. His astute parliamentary skills combined with a dignified and gracious manner made him widely respected in the Senate.

Russell rose to chairman of the Armed Services Committee in 1951, and from that position criticized the Eisenhower and Kennedy Administrations for their heavy reliance on a strategy of nuclear deterrence at the expense of conventional weaponry. He headed Southern resistance to the Civil Rights Acts of 1957 and 1960. Besides his regular House committee positions, Russell was a member of the Democratic Policy Committee and led the conservative majority on the Democratic Steering Committee, which distributed committee assignments. As a key member of what one writer called "an interlocking directorate" of Southern power in the Senate, Russell successfully thwarted attempts by liberals in 1965 to reform the Steering Committee.

Russell had opposed Eisenhower's sending arms and technicians to aid the French in Indochina and held strong reservations as Johnson escalated the conflict during the mid 1960s. But believing that America's commitment, once made, must be honored, he helped sponsor the Gulf of Tonkin Resolution in the Senate and supported the President's requests for additional manpower for the war.

However, Russell criticized the Administration for pursuing a policy that did not promise victory and in 1968 declared that he would not support the sending of additional troops without a drastic escalation of the air war. [See TRUMAN, EISENHOWER, KENNEDY, JOHNSON Volumes]

In 1969 Russell stepped down as chairman of the Armed Services Committee to head the Appropriations Committee. That year he also became President Pro Tempore of the Senate, which made him third in line for the presidency. During the Nixon Administration Russell supported such liberal measures as aid to mass transit, increased funds for school lunches and establishment of uniform water quality control. He opposed efforts to ease requirements for invoking cloture and was one of two Democrats to vote against amendments to the tax reform bill of 1969 that increased Social Security benefits and personal tax exemptions and opened or expanded loopholes for certain categories of taxpayers.

Russell continued his battle against forced desegregation. In 1969 he condemned a Justice Department suit to integrate Georgia schools, but he said that court action was preferable to the arbitrary action of the "fanatical bureaucrats" of the Department of Health, Education and Welfare. Russell opposed forced busing and in 1970 supported efforts to require that racial standards in schools be applied uniformly throughout the country. This proposal would have outlawed the defacto segregation in the North as well as the de jure segregation in the South. Russell believed that the measure would, for the first time, make the North bear the same burden in attempting desegregation as the South bore.

Russell applauded President Nixon's Supreme Court nominations of Clement Haynsworth [q.v.] and G. Harrold Carswell [q.v.], who were opposed by many liberals because of their conservative stands on civil rights.

Russell continued his support of the Vietnam war during his last years in the Senate. He was one of three senators to support the U.S. invasion of Cambodia in 1970 and backed an amendment which provided that limiting U.S. involvement in Cambodia would not preclude the President from taking action necessary to protect U.S. forces in South Vietnam. Russell opposed the Administration on the deployment of the Safeguard anti-ballistic missile system. In 1969 he urged additional development and research on the project rather than immediate deployment.

Once a heavy smoker, Russell had first developed emphysema in 1957. On Jan. 21, 1971, he died of respiratory insufficiency after six weeks of hospitalization.

[FLM]

RUSTIN, BAYARD
b. March 17, 1910; West Chester, Pa.
Civil rights leader.

Raised by his grandparents in West Chester, Pa., Rustin was influenced by the Quaker pacifism of his grandmother and by his personal experiences with the injustices of segregation. After five years of work for the Young Communist League, Rustin left the organization in 1941 because of its prowar stance during World War II. Rustin served more than two years in jail for his conscientious opposition to the war. An early civil rights activist, he became a close associate of Martin Luther King [q.v.] and played a leading role in directing the early mass protests of the civil rights movement. He served as an adviser to King throughout the 1950s and 1960s. Rustin was the chief organizer of the 1963 March on Washington, which attracted 250,000 persons to protest discrimination.

In the mid-1960s Rustin, who had previously devoted most of his energies to behind-the-scenes organizing of civil rights protests, began to promote his political views in numerous magazine articles and public speaking engagements. He argued that advances made during the past decade had effectively destroyed the legal basis for discrimination but that in order to effect basic changes in the lives of blacks, the civil rights movement had to shift its focus to fundamental economic problems. He wrote that poor economic backgrounds had put many blacks at a disadvantage in a job market requiring increasingly sophisticated skills. It was crucial, then, for blacks to promote federal programs for full employment, the abolition of slums and the reconstruction of the educational system.

Black separatism, he argued, would only isolate blacks politically and foster anti-black sentiments. Instead, he urged black organizations to form a coalition with the AFL-CIO and work through the Democratic Party. In 1964 he formed the A. Philip Randolph Institute to promote political programs for this labor-liberal-black coalition. [See EISENHOWER, KENNEDY, JOHNSON Volumes]

In the late 1960s and early 1970s Rustin became increasingly isolated from a black leadership disillusioned with integrationist and coalition politics. In this period his support of the United Federation of Teachers and its president, Albert Shanker [q.v.] during disputes in New York City over school decentralization and black control was widely denounced within the black community.

Rustin was one of the major critics of the Nixon Administration's civil rights policies. In 1970 he joined other blacks in denouncing a memo by Daniel P. Moynihan [q.v.], a domestic adviser to President Nixon, which claimed that blacks had made great strides in the past 20 years and called for a period of "benign neglect" on the race issue. The next year Rustin attacked the Administration's housing policy. Nixon, in a major policy statement, had differentiated between "racial" and "economic" forms of discrimination, saying the latter was outside the government's domain. Rustin considered the distinction racist in effect and the whole policy "chaotic" and "a disaster."

In a May 1971 article for *Harper's Mag-*

azine, Rustin criticized the President's Philadelphia Plan, ostensibly designed to increase the number of construction jobs available to blacks, as illusionary since it would merely shift black workers from one site to another. Nixon's suspension of the 1931 Davis-Bacon Act, allowing non-union labor to be hired at less than union rates, was denounced by Rustin as an anti-union device with the effect of pitting black worker against white and placing deflationary pressure on wages. Rustin charged in the same article that near the end of Nixon's first term in office, the Administration had "engaged in an assault on the advances of the past decade" with the "intent of building a political majority on the basis of white hostility to blacks."

In the late 1960s and early 1970s, Rustin continued to oppose separatist tendencies. In 1969 he denounced college officials for capitulating to black student demands for "soul courses," contending that black studies would not provide blacks with economically usable skills. In 1972 Rustin became cochairman of the newly merged Socialist Party-Democratic Socialist Federation (later Social Democrats U.S.A.), a group dominated by trade union leaders and others who favored the type of black-labor-union coalition he advocated. The Federation had endorsed Democratic presidential nominee George McGovern [q.v.], but it criticized both his foreign and domestic policy proposals as "casual" and "vague."

In the mid-1970s Rustin turned his attention to what he considered to be the errors of white liberals. He argued, in his *Strategies for Freedom: The Changing Patterns of Black Protest* (1976), that during the past decade the civil rights movement had failed to shift from social to economic issues in part because of liberal preoccupation with the Vietnam war, political corruption, the environment and feminism. In a May 1976 article in the *New York Times Magazine*, he called the "anti-growth" ideas of the environmentalist movement a middle-class elitist tendency that would stunt the economic gains necessary for black equality.

[FM]

RYAN, WILLIAM FITTS
b. June 28, 1922; Albion, N.Y.
d. Sept. 17, 1972; New York, N.Y.
Democratic Representative, N.Y.,
1961-72.

After serving under Manhattan District Attorney Frank S. Hogan from 1950-57, Ryan helped found an anti-Tammany Democratic Club and became the leading figure in Manhattan reform politics. He was elected by large majorities in his eclectic district throughout his political career and was the only well-supported candidate outside the established Party leadership. Ryan vociferously opposed appropriations for the House Un-American Activities Committee during the Kennedy and Johnson Administrations. His outspoken support for civil rights and desegregation culminated in 1964 when he led 22 representatives in challenging, unsuccessfully, the all-white Mississippi delegation to Congress.

Under the Johnson Administration, Ryan began his unrelenting opposition to U.S. involvement in Southeast Asia. In May 1965 Ryan's vote was one of seven against Johnson's supplementary military appropriation, the first request for funds specifically to fight the Vietnam war. Although Ryan supported most of Kennedy's legislation, he disagreed strongly with Johnson on many domestic issues and was critical of the U.S. declaration of neutrality during the 1967 war in the Middle East, favoring a declaration of support for Israel. [See KENNEDY, JOHNSON Volumes]

Ryan's liberalism became more marked during the Nixon years. While the Administration requested annual increases in defense appropriations to fuel the Vietnam war, Ryan proposed amendment after amendment to eliminate or drastically reduce funds for Vietnam-related operations. Every year his amendments were overwhelmingly defeated. Ryan said the Administration's policy was "a product of the outdated Cold War mentality, the excessive growth of the military-industrial complex, and, most of all, the war in

Vietnam, which is the culmination of disastrously mistaken policies."

Before 1969 most of the issues of defense appropriations were hammered out in committee and behind the closed doors of the Pentagon. But that year nationwide protest against the war and the agitation of a small minority of congressmen, including Ryan, brought Vietnam into unusually open debate in Congress. Ryan said the central issue of the war was who participated in the government of Vietnam; he was one of the first members to identify the conflict as a civil war.

Ryan seldom found himself among the majority of Congress. He and Bella Abzug (D, N.Y.) [q.v.] were the sole opponents to the 1972 Atomic Energy Commission's (AEC) appropriations bill, which provided for an AEC license to operate a nuclear reactor in New York City and increased funding for nuclear weapons and reactor development. His amendment to eliminate funds for the nuclear rocket NERVA, designed to transport people and materials into "deep space," was defeated. He said that since the National Aeronautics and Space Administration had proposed no clear mission for the project, it should not receive funds. For similar reasons he repeatedly opposed substantial appropriations for the House Internal Security Commission, which he said was overstaffed, inefficient, and not entirely aboveboard in its dealing with the information it received.

Ryan's liberal politics also found expression in environmental issues. As a member of the Interior and Insular Affairs Committee, he consistently favored the expansion of national park properties and the limitation of their commercial and residential development. In 1970 and 1971 he sought to establish an office of noise abatement and control within the Environmental Protection Agency (EPA) to study noise pollution and its effects. The measure failed but was later incorporated into a more general EPA noise pollution program.

President Nixon's conservative requests for urban renewal angered Ryan, who accused the Administration of "misguided" priorities for approving $290 million to finance the construction of the SST while vetoing the House's original requested budget for social services. He was one of three dissenters against an Administration bill to strengthen federal laws on the sale and use of explosives; he said the bill was "another dreary episode in the ponderous assault on freedom."

Growth elsewhere in the state of New York necessitated the elimination of Rep. Abzug's district for the 1972 election. After painful deliberation, she decided to run against Ryan, who was gravely ill at the time. Despite Abzug's popularity the endorsements went heavily in Ryan's favor, and he won the primary by a 2-1 margin. Three months later, however, he died of cancer; another campaign ensued between Ryan's widow, the Liberal Party's choice to replace Ryan, and Abzug, the Democratic committee's candidate. Abzug won with 56% of the vote.

After Ryan's death, Congress broke precedent with the National Parks Service to name the Gateway National Urban Recreation Area after him, honoring Ryan as the principal sponsor of the bill that established the park.

[AM]

SAFIRE, WILLIAM L.
b. Dec. 17, 1929; New York, N.Y.
Special Assistant to the President, February 1969-April 1973.

A native New Yorker, William Safire left Syracuse University for financial reasons in 1949 to return to New York to work as a reporter for the *Herald Tribune*. After a stint as a correspondent in Europe and the Middle East for WNBC radio and WNBT TV in 1951, Safire was inducted into the Army the following year, where he was assigned to public relations work. He returned to NBC in 1954, A year later he was named a vice president of Tex McCrary, Inc., a public relations firm.

Safire went to Moscow to represent a homebuilding firm at the American National Exhibition, which was officially opened by Vice President Richard M. Nixon on July 24, 1959. As the press agent for the company's "typical American house," Safire saw the opportunity to turn Nixon's presence to advantage. By maneuvering the spectators and newsmen trailing after Nixon and Soviet Premier Nikita S. Krushchev as they toured the exhibit, he directed the two leaders into the kitchen showroom, prompting the famous "kitchen debate" on the relative merits of capitalism vs. communism. An Associated Press photographer, blocked by the crowds, tossed his camera to Safire who snapped a widely reproduced picture of the historic encounter.

As he later wrote, Safire decided at that moment to work for Nixon's 1960 presidential campaign. He served as chief of special projects. His photograph of a no-nonsense Nixon besting the Soviet leader was heavily used during the campaign to promote the candidate's tough Cold War image. He wrote and edited promotional materials for Republican volunteers and for Nixon administrative assistant Robert Finch [q.v.].

Safire resigned from the McCrary organization in 1960. He established Safire Public Relations, Inc., in January 1961. His accounts ranged from an ice cream manufacturer to a motor oil firm. Fascinated by politics and the public relations aspects of political campaigns, Safire, in the first half of the decade, worked for such New York Republican candidates as Sen. Jacob Javits [q.v.], Gov. Nelson Rockefeller [q.v.] and Mayor John V. Lindsay [q.v.].

In his first book, published in 1963, *The Relations Explosion,* Safire presented the emerging public relations concepts. *Plunging into Politics,* written in collaboration with Marshall Loeb in 1964, offered candidates a manual for organizing, staffing and financing political campaigns. His *The New Language of Politics,* originally published in 1968, contained approximately 1,200 carefully researched entries. Safire described the book in Orwellian terms as a "dictionary of the words and phrases that have misled millions, blackened reputations, held out false hopes, oversimplified ideas to appeal to the lowest common denominator, shouted down inquiry, and replaced searching debate with stereotypes that trigger approval or hatred."

Convinced that Nixon was the best possible Republican candidate for the 1968 presidential race, Safire contacted Nixon at his New York law office in November 1965 and volunteered his services as an unpaid speechwriter. Nixon assigned him to help Patrick J. Buchanan, Jr. [q.v.] with Nixon's syndicated newspaper column. Safire took part in Nixon's campaign efforts on behalf of Republican candidates in the 1966 elections as Nixon reestablished himself as a force in the party and built up momentum for his 1968 drive.

For the 1968 campaign Safire composed Nixon's "new alignment" speech in which the candidate talked about a "new majority" that was coming into being and affirmed his belief that such disparate groups as traditional Republicans, new liberals, black militants and progressive Southerners "thinking independently, have all reached a new conclusion about the direction of our nation." The speech maintained that the new direction chosen was away from increased federal power and toward more decentralization, local control and personal freedom. Safire contributed to the form of Nixon's emotive acceptance address at the Republican National Convention. Throughout the presidential campaign he prepared speeches on labor, the economy, youth and the "American spirit." After the election, Nixon, in a victory speech drafted by Safire, outlined among the major objectives of the new Administration his determination "to bring the American people together."

In February 1969 Safire moved into a White House office as a special assistant to the President. He became part of a research and writing staff headed by James Keogh [q.v.] that included Buchanan and Raymond K. Price, Jr. [q.v.]. The team wrote formal speeches, drafted presidential messages to Congress and prepared material for Nixon's press conferences.

Safire's areas of responsibility encompassed the economy and the Vietnam war.

At the same time Safire was called on to articulate the Administration's domestic philosophy as reflected in its programs. Advisers such as Daniel Patrick Moynihan [q.v.], Arthur Burns [q.v.] and George P. Shultz [q.v.] were in the process of working out initiatives on family assistance, revenue sharing and desegregation that became known as the "New Federalism." In his "New Federalist Paper #1, written under the pseudonym "Publius," Safire attempted to reconcile traditional Republicanism with Nixonian innovations. The paper advocated a selective decentralization of power, leaving to the federal government the power to set the standards of fairness and to decide what to do and allowing local government to determine how to do it according to their different circumstances. According to Safire, the paper expressed "a need both for national unity and local diversity; a need to establish equality and fairness at the national level and uniqueness and innovation at the local level." The paper provoked vigorous debate within the White House and a rebuttal signed "Cato" by aide Tom Charles Huston.

Safire assisted Vice President Spiro T. Agnew [q.v.] as he campaigned during the 1970 off-year elections. First exposed in 1960 to what he considered the biased reporting of the press in its pro-Kennedy coverage, Safire wrote many of the famous "Agnewisms" used by the Vice President to criticize the news media. Agnew identified the national press as "nattering nabobs of negativism" who monopolized the way national news was presented to the country.

During the 1972 campaign Safire abandoned the speechwriter's traditional obscurity to write a series of signed articles for a debate in *The Washington Post* with Frank Mankiewicz [q.v.], Sen. George S. McGovern's [q.v.] campaign manager. Impressed by Safire's style and political expertise, *The New York Times* offered him a permanent position as a columnist which Safire accepted. His biweekly column first appeared on the newspaper's

Op-Ed page April 16, 1973. Almost immediately Safire turned to defending the President's position in the Watergate crisis. When he learned, however, that his telephone had been tapped while he was a White House employee, he responded with "restrained fury." He commended Nixon for putting personal liberty ahead of social security, but condemned him for putting national security too far above personal liberty.

Safire's column quickly became controversial. He led the investigation into "Koreagate" and the influence peddling of South Korean Tongsun Park in the U.S. Congress. He won a Pulitzer Prize for a series of columns that led to the resignation of President Carter's budget director, Bert Lance.

In 1975 Safire published *Before The Fall*. He wrote the book in an attempt "to figure out what he [Nixon] was trying to do and how well he succeeded" and as "an effort not to lose sight of all that went right in examining what went wrong." He distinguished between the goals and accomplishments of President Nixon and his Administration and Nixon's personal mistakes and failures. Safire summed up Nixon in his "Epilogue" as a President whose greatest achievements were as a peacemaker and whose greatest disappointment was his failure to rally and inspire his countrymen.

[SF]

For further information:
William Safire, *Before The Fall* (New York, 1975).

ST. CLAIR, JAMES D(RAPER)
b. April 14, 1920; Akron, Ohio.
Presidential Watergate Counsel,
January-August 1974.

After graduating from the University of Illinois in 1941, St. Clair entered Harvard Law School. He interrupted his law studies to serve in the Navy during World War II. Following the war he returned to Harvard, graduating in 1947. He joined the prestigious law firm of Hale & Dorr. As chief assistant to Joseph Welch, special counsel for the U.S. Army in the televised Army-McCarthy hearings of 1954, St. Clair was credited with an important behind-the-scenes role in the struggle that helped destroy Sen. Joseph McCarthy. St. Clair became known as a meticulous and effective trial lawyer whose clients spanned a broad ideological spectrum. He defended the Boston school committee in its long struggle against mandatory school desegregation. William Sloan Coffin, whom he helped gain acquital for conspiracy to encourage draft evasion, criticized St. Clair as "all case and no cause."

On the advice of Charles Colson [*q.v.*], President Nixon chose St. Clair as his chief Watergate defense counsel in January 1974. St. Clair replaced Fred Buzhardt [*q.v.*], who nevertheless remained on the legal staff. In an interview St. Clair said he did not represent Nixon "individually" but rather "the office of the presidency." He defined his role as defending the office of the presidency against any unwarranted incursions. Not only did St. Clair lead President Nixon's legal defense in the courts, but he also personally defended the President before the House Judiciary Committee conducting an inquiry into impeachment.

On Feb. 28 St. Clair presented the President's legal position on the nature of presidential impeachment. According to the report, "a President may only be impeached for indictable crimes" and those crimes must be of "a very serious nature" and committed in one's governmental capacity. It maintained that "the use of a predetermined criminal standard for the impeachment of a President [was] also supported by history, logic, legal precedent, and a sound and sensible public policy which demands stability in our form of government."

St. Clair argued that the impeachment clause, although drafted in the context of English precedents, rejected the British distinction between two types of impeachment—one for "reaching great offenses committed against the government by men of high station," and the other for a politically motivated purpose of maintaining the absolute political supremacy of Parliament. The framers of the Constitution accepted only the former type. St. Clair maintained that the phrase "high crimes and misdemeanors" meant to the framers "such criminal conduct as justified the removal of an officeholder from office." And in light of precedent, there was "no evidence to attribute anything but a criminal meaning" to the phrase. The framers had, according to St. Clair, "emphatically rejected 'maladministration' as a standard for impeachment," and their debates clearly indicated a purely criminal meaning for "other high crimes and misdemeanors."

In the beginning of May, St. Clair went to court to quash a subpoena by Leon Jaworski [q.v.], special watergate prosecutor, for 64 recordings of White House conversations. St. Clair argued that since Jaworski was an employee of the executive branch, the dispute was an "intra-branch" affair in which the courts should play no role. Jaworski protested that such a doctrine would "make a farce of the special prosecutor's charter." Judge John Sirica [q.v.] upheld Jaworski's argument, refused to quash the subpoena and ordered Nixon to turn the 64 tapes over to the court. At the end of May the Supreme Court agreed to review the decision.

At the end of May, St. Clair tried to quash subpoenas by John Ehrlichman [q.v.] and Charles Colson for use in the Ellsberg break-in trial. St. Clair argued that the scope of the subpoenas was too broad and brought a note from Nixon in which the President claimed executive privilege on the documents. U.S. District Court Judge Gerhard A. Gesell [q.v.] sternly lectured St. Clair that it was not up to the President to decide what documents to produce.

In July St. Clair cross-examined John Dean [q.v.] before the Judiciary Committee but failed to break Dean as a witness. St. Clair presented President Nixon's rebuttal on impeachment to the Committee in a 242-page report. He relied heavily on the lack of a "smoking gun," arguing that

the Committee had no positive proof of Nixon's participation in the cover-up. To support this point, St. Clair tried to introduce evidence from a conversation that Nixon had refused to supply to the Committee. This provoked an outraged reaction from Republicans and Democrats alike, who charged that the President was playing games with the evidence.

Arguments before the Supreme Court on Jaworski's suit for the 64 tapes were heard in July. The Court also heard a countersuit filed by St. Clair contesting the right of the grand jury to charge an incumbent President as "an unindicted co-conspirator" in criminal proceedings. St. Clair argued that such a citation has a prejudicial and damaging effect on the constitutional powers of impeachment vested in the House of Representatives.

St. Clair, in his first appearance before the Supreme Court, contended in the tapes case that the President was not above the law but the only way the law could be applied to him was through impeachment. If the courts could subpoena confidential White House conversations, St. Clair noted, the presidency would be irrevocably weakened. The next day St. Clair said that the President might, for the sake of the "public interest," defy the Supreme Court if it ordered him to give up the tapes.

At the end of July, the Supreme Court ruled 8-0 that President Nixon must provide the tapes and documents subpoenaed by Jaworski "forthwith." While acknowledging that the generalized claim of executive privilege was "constitutionally based," the justices concluded that in this case it "must yield to the demonstrated, specific need for evidence in a pending criminal trial." The Court left standing the grand jury citation of Nixon as an unindicted coconspirator. The day the decision was announced, St. Clair read a statement to the press that the President would comply with the decision "in all respects."

Judge Sirica ordered St. Clair and Jaworski to work out a timetable for delivery of the tapes. St. Clair listened to the tapes to authenticate them and delivered them to Sirica. St. Clair was forced to admit several times to Sirica that there were gaps, and even whole conversations, missing from the tapes he delivered. This was the first time St. Clair had heard the tapes that were so damaging to his client's case. It became clear that Nixon had withheld important evidence from his own counsel.

In the first week of August, St. Clair spoke to eight Republicans on the Judiciary Committee who remained Nixon supporters. He told them what was on the tapes and said that it made the President's case hopeless. They then withdrew their support from Nixon.

On Aug. 8 President Nixon resigned. The next day St. Clair said he no longer represented Nixon because Nixon was no longer President. St. Clair remained on the White House payroll for several weeks to deal with the final details of complying with the Supreme Court's decision.

St. Clair returned to private practice in Boston with his old firm of Hale & Dorr.

[TFS]

For further information:
J. Anthony Lukas, *Nightmare: The Underside of the Nixon Years* (New York, 1973).

SAMUELSON, PAUL A(NTHONY)
b. May 15, 1915; Gary Ind.
Economist.

Samuelson obtained his B.S. from the University of Chicago in 1935 and his Ph.D. from Harvard in 1941. In 1940 he obtained a teaching position at the Massachusetts Institute of Technology, where he remained through the 1970s. During World War II he worked as a consultant on the National Resources Planning Board, and later on the Wage and Price Board. From 1945 to 1952 he was retained as a consultant by the Federal Reserve Board. When the Eisenhower Administration took over the government, Samuelson moved to the Bureau of the Budget for a year. In 1960 he was appointed to President Kennedy's Council of Econom-

ic Advisers, and during the 1960s served under Kennedy and Johnson as an adviser to the Brookings Institute, a consultant to the Joint Economic Committee (JEC) of Congress and chairman of the Presidential Task Force for Maintaining Economic Prosperity. He was also a permanent consultant to the RAND Corporation from 1948 to 1975. [See KENNEDY, JOHNSON Volumes]

After a lifetime's association with Democratic Administrations, Samuelson was reduced to the status of a critic during the Nixon years. In July 1970 he appeared before the Joint Economic Committee to attack the Nixon Administration's anti-inflationary tight credit policy and to call for an expansionary fiscal policy, warning of a recession if such measures were not taken. In March 1971 he testified again on the supersonic transport (SST), attacking the proposal as "colossal economic folly" and as perhaps "the biggest lemon ever devised." In the wake of President Nixon's dramatic speech on the economy of Aug. 15, 1971, in which the Administration had gone over to the expansionary policies long advocated by Samuelson and other liberal Keynesians, the MIT professor broadly approved the moves but criticized what he felt was an unsatisfactory increase in federal spending.

In July 1972 Samuelson again appeared before the JEC, praising the Administration's stabilization program for the economy but continuing to criticize the government's $250 billion limit on federal spending. Samuelson said in this regard that "the administration can stand everything but success. In the summer of our healthy advance, they look forward to the winter of our excess." Samuelson's consistent criticism of the White House won him a place on Nixon's "enemies list," revealed to Congress in June 1973.

In June 1974, as the U.S. economy was entering the worst recession in postwar history, Samuelson commented on the disarray of professional economists and their inability to predict developments, "It is a terrible blemish on the mixed economy and a sad reflection on my generation of economists that we're not the

Merlins that can solve the problem." Admitting that the Keynesian economics he had done so much to propagate was in crisis, Samuelson said that "there are no signs that we are converging toward a philosopher's stone that will cause all the pieces to fall neatly into place."

In October 1970 Samuelson became the second economist to receive the Nobel Prize. His published works included *Foundations of Economic Analysis* (1947) and a textbook, *Economics,* which went through numerous editions since it first appeared in 1948.

[LG]

SANDMAN, CHARLES W(ILLIAM), JR.
b. Oct. 23, 1921; Philadelphia, Pa.
Republican Representative, N.J., 1967-75.

Sandman graduated from Temple University in 1942, and after service in the Army Air Corps during World War II, he received his law degree from Rutgers in 1948. He practiced law in New Jersey until elected to the state Senate in 1956. He served in that body for 10 years, eventually becoming majority leader and president and acting governor from 1962 to 1965, when he ran unsuccessfully for the Republican gubernatorial nomination.

In 1966 Sandman was elected to the U.S. House of Representatives. While a member of the House, Sandman voted a conservative line, receiving an approval rating of from 63 to 96% from the Americans for Conservative Action. During the Nixon years he voted for the anti-ballistic missile system in 1969, the SST in 1971 and against the 1970 Cooper-Church Amendment, an attempt to extricate the U.S. from military involvement in Southeast Asia.

On domestic issues he opposed busing, establishing a consumer protection agency, lowering the voting age to 18 and funding the Clear Water Act of 1969. He also voted for the controversial state veto provision over the policies of the Office of Economic Opportunity in 1969.

Sandman ran as a fiscal conservative for the New Jersey Republican gubernatorial nomination in 1969 but lost to the more liberal, urban-oriented candidate, William Cahill [*q.v.*], by only 13,000 votes. Cahill won the general election. Later his administration was rocked by the indictment of Secretary of State Paul Sherwin, a close associate of the Governor's. With Cahill losing support, Sandman challenged him for the gubernatorial nomination again in 1973. Stressing his opposition to high spending on social welfare and to the proposed state income tax, Sandman beat Cahill. He lost the general election, however, to Judge Brenden T. Byrne [*q.v.*], who received a margin of 721,000 votes in what was widely viewed as a repudiation of Sandman's conservatism as well as the waning political appeal of the Nixon Administration.

Sandman gained national prominence as a member of the House Judiciary Committee during the 1974 impeachment hearings. There he emerged as one of Nixon's strongest supporters. He openly scorned the televised hearings as a farce. Although in late May Sandman and eight other Republican Committee members warned President Nixon that failure to produce the subpoenaed White House tapes might result in his impeachment, by July Sandman had hardened into a belligerent Nixon defender. Eventually he voted against all the articles of impeachment.

Because of his strong identification with Nixon, Sandman lost his reelection bid in 1974, winning only about two-thirds of the votes he had received just two years earlier. Shortly after leaving Congress in 1975, he was hired as township solicitor for Cape May County, N.J., at $4,000 a year. He practiced law in a private capacity.

[GWB]

SANFORD, (JAMES) TERRY
b. Aug. 20, 1917; Laurinburg, N.C.
President, Duke University, 1970-.

The son of a hardware salesman, Sanford attended the University of North Carolina before entering the Army during

World War II. In 1946 he received a law degree from the University of North Carolina and during the 1950s he practiced law and became active in state politics. In 1960 Sanford won the election for the North Carolina governorship with the help of urban-based support from blacks, organized labor and liberal businessmen. His term as Governor was characterized by educational reform and increased state expenditures. [See JOHNSON Volume]

During the 1968 presidential campaign Sanford was considered as a possible vice-presidential running mate for Hubert Humphrey [q.v.]. His image as a link between the new and old South was seen to have considerable political value. However Humphrey chose Sen. Edmund Muskie (D, Me.) [q.v.] and Sanford had to settle for a minor role in the Democratic campaign. He served as the National chairman of the Citizens for Humphrey-Muskie committee.

In 1970 Sanford took over the presidency of Duke University. The Durham, N.C., campus had for several years been the scene of militant student protest against the Vietnam war. These continued demonstrations culminated in the resignation of Sanford's predecessor, Dr. Douglas Knight. Sanford's policies on student protest were marked by moderation, in contrast to the Administration's view that universities should crack down on radicals. In a speech made shortly after his appointment as president of Duke, he stated: "With the self-righteousness of oligarchs the leaders of repression are commanding college presidents to put down the students to shut off the protest and silence dissent. I would suggest that they do not understand young people, do not understand society and have forgotten the lessons of history." Positions such as these led many to believe that Sanford might become the Democratic vice-presidential nominee in 1972 as a contrast to conservative Vice President Spiro Agnew [q.v.], who had led the call for action against demonstrators.

Sanford entered the race for the Democratic presidential nomination in March 1972. From the beginning he was a "dark horse" candidate who based his election strategy on the expectation that the primary races would prove indecisive and the convention would need a "fresh face" to break out of political deadlock. Sanford ran on a liberal platform advocating speedy U.S. withdrawal from Vietnam. However on such domestic issues as busing, his stand was less clear. He supported federal legislation that would make desegregated education a national goal but would leave actual desegregation plans in the hands of local government.

Sanford's presidential aspirations were dashed by his defeat in the North Carolina primary in May 1972. He received only 37% of the vote in his home state compared to that of the 50% cast for George Wallace [q.v.]. The candidacy of Shirley Chisholm [q.v.] hurt Sanford's chances from the beginning because it had split the black vote that would have ordinarily gone to Sanford. George Wallace's strong position against busing attracted blue-collar and rural voters and was a major obstacle Sanford could not overcome. In his statement accepting defeat, Sanford said about the busing issue, "To win, I would have to take positions I would be unwilling to take." Sanford continued to work for the Democratic Party during the 1972 election as chairman of the Democratic Charter Commission.

Sanford again made an attempt at gaining his Party's presidential nomination in 1976. His chances seemed good in light of the prevailing political current after the Nixon presidency. As one supporter stated: "Terry is clean. Watergate and things like that make a candidate like him more attractive." However, Sanford's hopes were again crushed when, after only three weeks of full-time campaigning, he was hospitalized for chest pains leading to his withdrawal as a candidate.

[MLB]

SAUNDERS, STUART T(HOMAS)
b. July 16, 1909; McDowell, W. Va.
Chairman of the Board, Penn Central
Railroad, 1968-70.

Saunders attended Roanoke College
and Harvard Law School, where he
earned a degree in 1934. He practiced law
in Washington D.C. for five years, and in
1939 became assistant general solicitor
for the Norwalk and Western Railway, rising to the post of general counsel in 1954.
In 1963 Saunders became chairman of the
board of the Pennsylvania Railroad. Five
years later, when it merged with the New
York Central to form Penn Central, Saunders became chairman of the board of the
new organization.

The merger was an attempt to achieve
an economy of scale permitting both
lines, which had been losing money since
the 1950s, to become profitable. Under
Saunders' guidance, however, the situation declined further. In 1969 Penn Central's extensive nonrailroad investments,
which had previously carried the ailing
Pennsylvania Railroad, began to lose
money. Extensive infighting between the
newly merged managements increased
the paralysis at the top. Saunders was
publicly attacked for the deplorable state
of the Penn Central's passenger and commuter services, which were the major
drain on the company's cash flow, and
which Penn Central's management made
repeated attempts to divest through petitions to the Interstate Commerce Commission (ICC).

The tactic of Penn Central's management under Saunders was to maintain appearances of stability through "creative
accounting" practices, paying consistent
healthy stock dividends while the railway's equipment, stations and service
continued to deteriorate. In 1969 and
1970 Penn Central became the first U.S.
railway to issue commercial paper to raise
short-term cash, which at a time of rising
interest rates meant a steep rise in the
company's already considerable interest
payments. Moreover an investigation by
Saunders of the company's financing beginning in early 1970 revealed that a

group of company insiders were using
Penn Central's good credit rating with
commercial banks to obtain millions of
dollars in loans for a "private investors'
club" they had constituted, and were diverting Penn Central investments to bolster the fortunes of the "club's" holdings.

The final phase of Saunders' tenure began in January 1970, when an extremely
cold winter began to wreak havoc on
Penn Central's aging equipment, bringing its service to a halt in many areas. The
situation was further complicated by over
$100 million in short-term commercial
paper that the railroad had to refinance
during the year. When the company posted massive losses for the first quarter of
1970, ostensibly due to the bad weather,
public attention was drawn to the gravity
of the railroad's plight. In May 1970, during a general corporate credit squeeze,
Penn Central's stock began to plummet. A
near-panic selloff of its commercial paper
began and Saunders began to press for
government aid. On June 3 a top-level
White House meeting was held to discuss
the possible effects of a Penn Central default on its commercial paper and of the
railroad's bankruptcy. On the same day
Saunders met with Walter Wriston [q.v.],
chairman of Citibank, the bank that had
provided the most loans to the railroad.
Wriston told Saunders that further credit
would require government guarantees of
loans and a top-level reshuffling of Penn
Central management. Immediately after
the meeting Wriston began to press for
Saunders' ouster. By June 8, when the
Penn Central's board of directors met to
discuss the crisis in Philadelphia, all the
banks involved with the railroad insisted
on Saunders' departure as a basis for any
rescue. His resignation was accepted on
the same day.

During the following two weeks bankers, politicians and government officials
attempted to prepare government-guaranteed loans for Penn Central, but strong
opposition from Rep. Wright Patman (D,
Tex.) chairman of the House Banking
Committee, ended any hopes of a bailout.
On June 21, 1970, the railroad filed for
bankruptcy, and the Federal Reserve

Bank was successfully mobilized by Chairman Arthur Burns [q.v.] to prevent a financial panic.

In March 1971 Wright Patman issued a report on the unloading of Penn Central stock by major banks in the months prior to the bankruptcy, noting major sales by Chase Manhattan and indicating Saunders' directorship with Chase as evidence of possible use of illegal insider information in the dumping of the shares. A year later the ICC's Bureau of Enforcement issued a brief strongly criticizing Saunders for his personal role in the Penn Central collapse. In May 1974 the Securities and Exchange Commission filed fraud charges, naming Penn Central, 12 top officials, including Saunders, and a former auditor as parties to a massive fraud scheme that led to the railroad's collapse.

Saunders was effectively retired by his June 1970 ouster, but was retained as a consultant for the reorganization of the railroad's assets during bankruptcy proceedings.

[LG]

For further information:
Joseph R. Daughen and Peter Binzen, *The Wreck of the Penn Central* (New York, 1971).

SAWHILL, JOHN C(RITTENDEN)
b. June 12, 1936; Cleveland, Ohio.
Administrator, Federal Energy Administration, June 1974-January 1975.

John Sawhill graduated from Princeton in 1958 and began a career in business on Wall Street. In 1960 he returned to academia at New York University, where he received his Ph.D. and became a professor and associate dean. He reentered the business world in 1963 to serve as the director of credit research and then senior vice president for a commercial credit company in Baltimore.

Sawhill entered government service in 1973 when he was named associate director of the Office of Management and Budget for the Nixon Administration. In December of that year he was named deputy director of the new Federal Energy Office (FEO) headed by Deputy Secretary of the Treasury William E. Simon [q.v.]. President Nixon had created the office in December by executive order in response to the developing energy crisis sparked by the 1973 Arab oil embargo. At the time Nixon announced that a Federal Energy Administration (FEA) would be established by statute.

The newly enacted FEO turned to devising fuel allocation rules. The guidelines were published Jan. 15 and became effective immediately. Noting that industrial and public service users were favored over those requiring fuel for home heating and private automobiles, Sawhill remarked at the time that the allocation program's aim was "to preserve jobs rather than to have homes at 75 degrees." He prophetically warned, "There will have to be changes in the American life-style over the next several years." Sawhill also released details of the Administration's contingency plan for gas rationing by coupon in the face of the ongoing Arab oil embargo, but insisted that no decision had been made on whether to adopt the plan and voiced hope that rationing could be avoided.

In April, Nixon named Simon to succeed George P. Shultz [q.v.] as Treasury Secretary. Sawhill was nominated to become head of the recently established FEA. He was confirmed in June. As the nation's new "energy czar," Sawhill found himself at the center of controversy. At the end of the month, he accused major oil companies of "foot-dragging and calculated resistance" to the government's regulations requiring them to share their crude oil supplies with independent refiners. At issue, he stated, was the statutory mandate designed "to protect the viability of small and independent sectors of the petroleum industry." Sawhill's criticism of the major oil companies marked the first break in a previously close, cooperative relationship between the industry and the energy agency. A proponent of the deregulation of natural gas prices, a move unpopular with consumer advocates, Sawhill argued that allowing market conditions to determine prices would stimulate the exploration needed to provide adequate supplies of this energy resource.

Sawhill opposed the strictness of the federal regulations governing the strip mining of coal that were passed by Congress in July. The following month he resumed his confrontation with the oil industry. In a letter to the nation's top 20 oil firms, Sawhill charged the industry with making "efforts to coax the public into buying gasoline that it has indicated it doesn't want or need" while the government was urging stepped-up conservation measures. Sawhill called for an end to "hard-sell tactics" and warned that the agency would take "strong action" to hold down fuel consumption.

The strong action turned out to be administrative proceedings brought by the FEA on Aug. 20 against 14 oil companies accused of inflating prices by roughly $200 million. The next day four of the firms complied with the government's directive to make up overcharges by rolling back prices. Six other firms had previously rolled back prices voluntarily. In a letter on Sept. 13 to Sen. Henry Jackson (D, Wash.) [q.v.] chairman of the Permanent Investigations Subcommittee, Sawhill said a continuing investigation of about 10 major oil firms revealed that they had profited to the extent of possibly $300 million from the agency's "double-recovery" rule, which, until revised in May, allowed refiners to "double-dip" or charge twice for their costs on the volume of crude oil they were required to sell to other refiners under government allocation regulations. To preclude possible conflicts of interest with the oil industry, Sawhill instituted strict standards of conduct for FEA employees requiring that high-and middle-level officials file financial disclosure reports.

President Ford announced on Oct. 29 the appointment of a "new team that will be in charge of the energy problem." Sawhill was the principal victim of the administrative shake-up. Before leaving office he oversaw the presentation of the FEA's 800-page "Blueprint for Project Independence." Differences in the Nixon and Ford Administrations over energy affairs resulted in a lack of continuity on policy matters and diluted the report's impact as a policy-setting document. In November, Sawhill told a congressional committee he believed that the oil industry had lobbied for his ouster but added he did not know if its influence had played any part in President Ford's decision to dismiss him.

Sawhill returned to New York University to become president of the financially troubled institution. Under his leadership, the university executed a series of adroit financial moves that restored its budget's integrity.

[SF]

SAXBE, WILLIAM B(ART)

b. June 24, 1916; Mechanicsburg, Ohio.
Republican Senator, Ohio, January 1969-December 1973; U.S. Attorney General, January 1974- December 1974.

Saxbe took a bachelor's degree in political science from Ohio State University in 1940. During World War II he served for five years in the Army Air Force. While studying law at Ohio State, he was elected to the Ohio House of Representatives, where he served four terms and was elected speaker in the 1953-54 session.

After three years practicing law in Columbus, Saxbe was elected state attorney general in 1957, and was subsequently reelected to four additional two-year terms. His reputation as a "tough, capable crime fighter," who favored capital punishment and long prison sentences for gun-related offenses, helped him to become the Republican candidate for the U.S. Senate in 1968. His opponent was liberal Democrat John J. Gilligan [q.v.], who campaigned against the Vietnam war, while Saxbe stressed the law-and-order issues. Saxbe won by 100,000 votes.

Upon taking office in January 1969, he was assigned to the Aeronautical and

Space Sciences Committee; the Labor and Public Welfare Committee; and the Special Committee on Aging. In his first year he accumulated one of the lowest scores for individual participation in roll-call votes for the first session of the 91st Congress. He also confounded liberal critics by compiling a moderate 61% rating from the Americans for Democratic Action (ADA) in 1969. However Saxbe gradually moved to the right politically, until in 1972 he was down to a 15% ADA rating.

In 1969 Saxbe took a strong stand against the Pentagon's deployment of anti-ballistic missiles. He asserted that the nation was becoming "militaristic" and a "national security state." In November of the same year, he voted to reject the nomination of conservative Clement F. Haynsworth [q.v.] to be an associate justice of the Supreme Court. He denied that there had been any "arm-twisting" from the Administration but admitted that "we got tens of hundreds of threatening letters from people in the state [Ohio] who have contributed to his [Nixon's] campaign. It's as strong as anything we've seen." The next year Saxbe was a strong supporter of G. Harrold Carswell's [q.v.] unsuccessful nomination to the Supreme Court despite charges that Carswell was a segregationist. On April 1, 1970, he received a widely publicized letter from President Nixon reaffirming "total support" of Carswell. In the letter Nixon went on to term the charges of segregationist beliefs against the nominee "specious." Saxbe also voted in 1971 to confirm the nomination of William H. Rehnquist to the Supreme Court.

In April 1970 Saxbe joined in an attack against critics of the Administration's Vietnam war policies. He declared that while he was "sick and tired" of the war, he was also "sick and tired" of "those who continually played politics with the war." On April 15 Saxbe returned from a trip to Vietnam and told the Senate that the U.S. pullout from that country was proceeding much faster than generally realized. He opposed setting a deadline for complete withdrawals because it

might give the enemy an advantage. Saxbe also supported continued funding for the war.

Yet the Congressman did not fully support the Administration's Vietnam policy. In June 1970 following the invasion of Cambodia, he voted for the Cooper-Church Amendment that repealed the Gulf of Tonkin resolution. In February of the next year he cosponsored with Sen. Walter Mondale (D, Minn.) [q.v.] legislation to bar U.S. participation or support of any South Vietnamese ground invasion of North Vietnam without explicit approval of Congress. In December 1972 Saxbe delivered a particularly harsh criticism of the bombing of North Vietnam: "I have followed President Nixon through his convolutions and specious arguments, but he appears to have left his senses on this issue. I can't go along with him on this one." On July 20, 1973, the Defense Department admitted that it had knowingly provided the Senate Armed Services Committee, of which Saxbe was a member, with a false report the previous month that did not reveal the secret bombing of Cambodia. Saxbe said he thought that there were stronger grounds for the impeachment of the President because of the secret air war than because of the growing Watergate scandal.

During the early 1970s Saxbe grew increasingly disenchanted with the Senate and the Administration, which he considered the "most inept" in history. He was particularly critical of the slow pace of the legislative process. As a result of his frustration, Saxbe decided to take as many junkets as possible. Explaining why he took advantage of the often-criticized trips, he stated, "I like to travel."

In October 1973 Saxbe announced that he would retire from the Senate and return to his law practice in Mechanicsburg, Ohio. In so doing he criticized the Administration once again. In explaining his decision, he announced: "Nixon had a chance to put businessmen back in the saddle and make the free enterprise system respected again. He blew it. From now on, this town will be full of social planners like Walter Mondale." The next month President Nixon announced he would appoint Saxbe to replace Elliot L. Richardson [q.v.] as U.S. Attorney General. Richardson resigned after Special Watergate Prosecutor Archibald Cox [q.v.] and Deputy Attorney General William Ruckelshaus were fired on Oct. 20 in the so-called Saturday night massacre. The President chose Saxbe because he was not "out to get Nixon" but was not "soft" on him either. In addition, by choosing the maverick, he hoped to avoid a lengthy confirmation battle. Nixon described Saxbe as "eminently qualified" and "an individual who wants this position and who will do everything that he possibly can to serve the nation as the first lawyer in the nation." Saxbe said that he was happy to tackle the job, understanding that the country was in "difficult times" and undergoing a "crisis of leadership." He delayed assuming the office until January 1974 so that he would be eligible to collect a Senate pension.

At his swearing-in ceremony, Saxbe called himself a "law-and-order man," predicated on his belief in "a society operated in a manner to give each individual the opportunity to express himself without the fear of Big Brother taking over [or] interfering in his personal life." Saxbe also affirmed the independence of the special Watergate prosecutor, Leon Jaworski [q.v.].

Despite his hope of remaining clear of the controversy, Saxbe gradually became embroiled in Watergate. On March 27, 1974, he asked the U.S. court of appeals in Washington to uphold a lower court's refusal to give the Senate Watergate Committee access to five White House tape recordings. Committee Chairman Sam J. Ervin [q.v.] said the next day that Saxbe's action was a violation of the "solemn agreement" the Attorney General had made before his confirmation that he would leave all matters relating to Watergate to Special Prosecutor Jaworski. Saxbe denied through a spokesman that he had violated his agreement since the brief dealt with "institutional issues," rather than the merits of Nixon's refusal to comply with the Committee's subpoena.

In a public television interview on June 17, Saxbe said that President Nixon had acted improperly when he relayed secret Watergate grand jury testimony to his former aides who were interested parties in the grand jury proceedings. He implied that Nixon either had a casual attitude toward enforcing the law or lacked knowledge about grand jury proceedings.

Saxbe took office determined to raise Justice Department morale and restore its credibility. In an effort to repair relations with the press, he held frequent conferences, but his blunt, off-the-cuff remarks often caused problems. In February 1974 Saxbe became embroiled in the first of a series of controversies when he stated that police would be guilty of "dereliction of duty" if they knew where the Symbionese Liberation Army (SLA) was holding kidnapped heiress Patricia Hearst [q.v.] and did not "go get her." With regard to the SLA demand that William Randolph Hearst supply $70 worth of food to each of California's needy, Saxbe said, "I certainly wouldn't recommend compliance with such vague and unrealistic demands." Later Saxbe issued a qualifying statement that he did not want "the FBI to pursue any action which would in any way jeopardize the life of the young victim in this case."

During this period Saxbe also caused a flurry of protest when he stated at his weekly press conference that "the Jewish intellectual" of the 1950s tended to be "enamored" of the Communist Party. His comments provoked strongly worded criticism from the Anti-Defamation League (ADL) of the B'nai B'rith.

On Dec. 18, 1974, Saxbe became the first cabinet member to resign from the Ford Administration. He was nominated the same day to become ambassador to India, replacing Daniel P. Moynihan [q.v.]. Edward H. Levi [q.v.] was named as the new Attorney General by President Ford. Saxbe served at his ambassadorial post until the end of the Ford Administration.

[FHM]

SCALI, JOHN A(LFRED)
b. April 27, 1918; Canton, Ohio
Ambassador to the United Nations,
January 1973-May 1975.

Scali took his B.S. degree in journalism
in 1942 at Boston University, where he
had been editor-in-chief of the campus
newspaper during his senior year. After
graduation he joined the Boston bureau of
United Press as a general assignment reporter. Looking for foreign assignments,
Scali went to Associated Press (AP) in
1944. He became a diplomatic and roving
correspondent who primarily covered the
State Department. In 1961 Scali joined
ABC News. During the Cuban missile crisis of 1962, he acted as unofficial liaison
between the White House and Kremlin.
[See KENNEDY Volume]

In April 1971 Scali accepted the position of senior White House consultant on
foreign affairs information policy. The
appointment puzzled many because Scali, a registered Democrat, had been a vocal critic of the Nixon Administration's
press policies and had denounced "blun-
derbuss attacks" on the media made by
Vice-President Spiro T. Agnew [q.v.].
Scali explained that his acceptance of the
newly-created post was due to the fact
that it would be "a unique opportunity to
see what it's like on the inside after 29
years of watching it from the outside."

Although he agreed with the general
goals of Nixon's foreign policy, he opposed the Administration's secret diplomacy. Scali hoped to close the "credibility gap" between government and public by allowing maximum disclosure of
information to the public. Despite his
efforts, the Administration continued to
suffer from lack of trust by the media and
large segments of the population. As a
media consultant Scali accompanied Nixon on his official foreign visits, including
the historic 1972 trip to China.

In 1973 Scali was appointed ambassador to the United Nations. During his two
years at the U.N., Scali had little impact
on foreign policy. The U.N. received
scant attention from the Administration,
which was increasingly preoccupied with
Watergate. In the General Assembly, Scali faced an assertive Third World bloc
which limited the power many of the major Western nations had once had in the
world body. In December the U.S., joined
by other Western nations, denounced the
Third World majority. Scali said that the
Assembly majority was endangering the
future of the U.N. by passing "one-sided,
unrealistic resolutions that cannot be implemented" and that disregarded the U.N.
Charter. Examples given by Scali were
Assembly votes to suspend South Africa
from the remainder of the 1974 session, to
grant to the Palestine Liberation Organization observer status and to limit Israel's
right to speech during a debate on the
Palestine issue. "Many Americans are
questioning their belief in the United Nations," Scali stated.

In September 1975 Scali returned to
ABC News as a Washington based correspondent.

[MLB]

SCHAUFELE, WILLIAM E(VERETT), JR.
b. Dec. 7, 1923: Lakewood, Ohio.
Assistant Secretary of State for
African Affairs, December 1975-July
1977.

Schaufele was educated at Yale University from which he received a B.A. degree
in 1948 and at the School of International
Affairs at Columbia University from
which he received an M.I.A. degree in
1950, when he joined the U.S. Foreign
Service. During the 1950s Schaufele was
stationed at various posts in Germany. In
1959 he was first assigned to an African
post as consul in Bukavu, Republic of the
Congo, thereafter serving at several African posts in the field and at the State Department. During the early 1970s Schaufele held positions as senior adviser to the
U.S. permanent representative to the U.N.

(1971–73); and as U.S. deputy representative to the Security Council (1973–75). In 1975 he was made inspector general of the U.S. Foreign Service.

In December 1975 Schaufele was appointed assistant secretary of state for African affairs. Within two weeks of his confirmation, he was sent on the first of many trips to Africa for behind-the-scenes talks and negotiations. He visited several African countries, including Zaire and Senegal, for talks that were seen as part of an attempt by the U.S. to rally African nations to withhold recognition of the Popular Movement for the Liberation of Angola (MPLA) at an emergency meeting of the Organization of African Unity set for January 1976. The MPLA was the Soviet-backed nationalist faction that won the civil war in Angola.

During 1976 Schaufele was primarily involved in U.S. efforts, led by Secretary of State Henry A. Kissinger [q.v.], to find a "solution" to the problem of minority rule in Rhodesia. During closed discussions on southern Africa between South African Prime Minister John Vorster and Kissinger held in Germany in June, Schaufele attended as part of the U.S. delegation.

Throughout the year Schaufele made various trips for behind-the-scenes talks with African officials and leaders in an effort to develop a workable plan for a settlement in Rhodesia, which was victim to an increasingly violent guerrilla war. In September he met with Tanzanian President Julius Nyerere to brief him on recent Kissinger-Vorster talks held in Zurich, and to prepare the groundwork for discussions between Kissinger and Nyerere.

At the end of October Schaufele arrived in Geneva to serve as a contact for Kissinger during a conference on majority rule in Rhodesia. By the beginning of November, the talks collapsed when the Rhodesian government refused to agree to nationalist demands for an early date for majority rule.

Schaufele continued as assistant secretary until July 1977 when he was appointed ambassador to Greece.

[MLB]

SCHLAFLY, PHYLLIS S(TEWART)
b. Aug. 15, 1924; St. Louis, Mo.
Chairman, Stop ERA; author; lecturer.

The daughter of working-class parents, Phyllis Stewart attended St. Louis Catholic schools and worked in an arms plant at night while earning her B.A. at Washington University in 1944. After receiving an M.A. in political science from Radcliffe in 1945, she worked as a research librarian and in 1949 married Fred Schlafly, a wealthy St. Louis lawyer. While raising six children, Schlafly ran unsuccessfully for the U.S. House in 1952, was research director of the Cardinal Mindszenty Foundation from 1958 to 1963, and did commentary for the "America Wake Up" radio program from 1962 to 1966.

As author and coauthor of nine books, vice president of the National Federation of Republican Women (NFRW) from 1965 to 1967 and delegate to Republican National Conventions, Schlafly molded a political career around ultraconservative causes. Her first book, *A Choice Not An Echo*, served as a tract for the 1964 Goldwater campaign. A best-seller, the book accused Eastern liberal Republicans of successfully conspiring to subvert the majority will of Party members for a conservative presidential nominee in all Conventions since 1936.

After losing a bitter fight for the presidency of the NRFW in 1967, Schlafly wrote all 500,000 Federation members and urged the diversion of a portion of their dues to a war chest to promote conservative candidates and issues. With dues of $5, Schlafly established the Eagle Trust Fund and began the publication from her home in Alton, Ill., of her newsletter "The Phyllis Schlafly Report." In

1970 she lost a bid for a House seat from Illinois's 23rd district. The following year she urged President Nixon to hand over leadership of the Republican Party to conservative Ronald Reagan [q.v.].

After a 1972 issue of her newsletter condemned the passage of the Equal Rights Amendment (ERA) as subversive of the institution of the family, Schlafly catapulted herself into leadership of the fight against state ratification. By 1973 Schlafly had formed Stop ERA to lobby against the Amendment in all state legislatures in which the ERA was up for a vote. Charging that the ERA would destroy the family, force women into combat duty, mandate unisex toilet facilities in all public buildings, promote homosexuality and dispossess women of their right to be a housewife, Schlafly testified before state legislatures, organized active lobbies in 26 states, appeared on national television and radio and lectured widely. Affiliates of the American Conservative Union, on whose board of directors Schafly served, contributed funds for this effort, and the Conservative Caucus helped to raise $50,000 through a direct-mail campaign for the anti-ratification fight in North Carolina and Florida. Schlafly claimed credit for slowing down the rapid success of the ERA in 1973 and the failure of over 26 attempts at ratification in Western and Southern state legislatures from 1973 to 1977.

By 1977 Schlafly had become a symbol and spokeswoman for the national antifeminist sentiment. Her book *The Power of the Positive Woman* (1977) set forth her belief that a woman's first priority and greatest fulfillment was in the home, that women were the "civilizing force" of history, and that a woman's primary obligation was to "safeguard the values of God, family and country." In November 1977 Schlafly staged a "profamily" rally at the Houston Astroarena in opposition to the National Women's Conference (NWC). Schlafly claimed that the NWC did not represent her constituency and would prove itself to be "radical, anti-feminine and prolesbian."

[JMP]

SCHLESINGER, JAMES R(ODNEY)

b. Feb. 15, 1929; New York, N.Y.
Chairman, Atomic Energy Commission, August 1971-January 1973; Director, Central Intelligence Agency, January-June 1973; Secretary of Defense, June 1973-November 1975

Schlesinger graduated summa cum laude from Harvard in 1950. After extended travel abroad, he resumed his graduate studies at Harvard, taking his M.A. in economics in 1952 and his Ph.D in 1956. He began teaching at the University of Virginia in 1955 and at the Naval War College two years later. In 1960 Schlesinger's first book, *The Political Economy of National Security,* impressed the staff of the RAND Corp., a defense-oriented "think tank," and consequently, Schlesinger worked from 1963 to 1967 at RAND as director of strategic studies. He left RAND in 1967 to serve as assistant director of the Bureau of the Budget. When the new Nixon Administration reorganized the Bureau into the Office of Management and Budget (OMB), Schlesinger served as acting deputy director during the transition and thereafter as assistant director.

It was at the OMB that Schlesinger first acquired his reputation as a "bureaucracy tamer" and a "budget cutter," trimming $6 billion from the Department of Defense's operating costs and overseeing a study of the U.S. intelligence services with an eye towards cost-efficiency. His background at the RAND Corporation qualified him as an expert in nuclear affairs, and this knowledge of nuclear technology made him President Nixon's choice for OMB representative on the Environmental Quality Council. From this position Schlesinger began to play a major role in the Nixon Administration's energy policy. With the rise of the environmental movement during Nixon's first term, Schlesinger became increasingly involved with energy and environmental questions. In March 1971 Nixon was prepared to make him Secretary of the Interior, but decided against the move because a number of senators from Western states insisted that Schlesinger was out of touch with their constituencies, an early sign of Schlesinger's repeated difficulties in winning congressional support for his policies.

In July 1971 Schlesinger was appointed chairman of the Atomic Energy Commission (AEC), succeeding Glenn T. Seaborg [q.v.]. In a speech made soon after his appointment, Schlesinger stated that under his leadership the AEC would become a true advocate of the public interest and not the industry's protector as it had been in the past. However he was quickly embroiled in controversy. Legal attempts to prevent a five-megaton nuclear test explosion at Amchitka Island in the Aleutians were defeated by a last-minute Surpeme Court decision. Opponents of the test had argued that it could have noxious effects on the environment and pointed to a nearby seismic fault as the source of a possible earthquake. Schlesinger replied to critics by taking his wife and two daughters to observe the test, underlining his complete faith in its safety.

In December 1971, the AEC underwent a major reorganization under Schlesinger's management. The Commission established a new office on the environment and safety and announced that it would promote research into nonnuclear sources of energy. Schlesinger defended the reorganization, saying that it marked a shift away from the AEC's old attitude of "technology purely for the sake of technology."

In January 1972 Schlesinger announced the construction of a nuclear breeder reactor for the Tennessee Valley Authority. Foreshadowing the looming energy crisis that would become the focus of public attention in later years, he said, "We are reaching the point that supplies of fossil fuel—coal, gas and oil—are recognized to be limited," and predicted that nuclear power would be preeminent as a future energy source. In keeping with this outlook, two months later Schlesinger requested an amendment to the National

Environmental Policy Act of 1969 that would permit the AEC to issue temporary operating licenses for new nuclear reactors. In December he argued for allowing private industry to build uranium enrichment facilities. At the same time the AEC published its proposals for nuclear industry regulation, allowing corporate access to secret government technology. Schlesinger argued that private industry's participation was necessary to keep the United States competitive in the export of nuclear reactors.

In December 1972, on what many observers believe was the urging of Henry Kissinger [q.v.], President Nixon appointed Schlesinger to succeed Richard Helms [q.v.] as director of the Central Intelligence Agency (CIA). Schlesinger assumed his duties at the Agency in January 1973 and began implementation of budget-trimming proposals developed during his oversight of the earlier OMB study of U.S. intelligence services. Schlesinger's move was generally interpreted as a downgrading of the "cloak-and-dagger" operations side of the CIA's activities and a bolstering of its research and intelligence-gathering work. Some 1,000 CIA "operations" personnel were scheduled for retirement or dismissal by the end of 1973. A further sign of Schlesinger's growing power over U.S. intelligence services was his appointment as chairman of the Intelligence Resources Advisory Commission, giving him responsibility over the activities of the National Security Agency and the Army Defense Intelligence Agency.

Schlesinger, although never personally linked to Watergate, was obliged to testify, as CIA director, in the spring 1973 Watergate hearings on the role of CIA agents in the burglary of the office of Daniel Ellsberg's [q.v.], psychiatrist and in the Watergate burglary itself. Schlesinger said that Agency involvement in these activities was "ill-advised" and asserted that he was against CIA involvement in covert domestic operations.

In spring 1973 Nixon once again reshuffled his cabinet in the deepening Watergate crisis. Schlesinger was appointed Secretary of Defense, succeeding Elliot Richardson [q.v.], who became Attorney General. Schlesinger had no difficulty establishing himself as a hard-liner on military and security questions, defending in early speeches the tactical bombing of Cambodia in the Indochina conflict and the 1969-70 secret raids in that country as necessary to "defend U.S. servicemen."

The weakening of the North Atlantic Treaty Organization (NATO) and its alleged lack of preparedness for war with the countries of the Warsaw Pact was a major theme for Schlesinger before and after his move to the Department of Defense. He consistently opposed NATO troop cuts and the withdrawal of U.S. military personnel from Western Europe. These concerns were further aggravated during the October 1973 Mideast crisis when the European allies of the U.S. refused to collaborate openly in the defense of Israel for fear of alienating the Arab countries on which they depended for oil. Schlesinger stated in late October that the actions of these allies would cause the U.S. to "reflect" on its concepts of military strategy. In June 1974 Schlesinger attended NATO talks in Vienna and then went on to Moscow to participate in talks on strategic arms limitation. In December of that year he warned NATO ministers not to undertake military spending cuts for reasons of economy in the belief that the U.S. would bail them out militarily. In April 1975, however, as the U.S.-backed regime in Saigon was collapsing, Schlesinger assured America's allies that they would not be abandoned.

One of Schlesinger's attempts to re-shape U.S. military strategy in the post-Vietnam world, and one linked to his downfall in October 1975, was his sponsorship of the concept of "limited nuclear warfare." In his view, growing Soviet nuclear capacity had rendered previous U.S. strategy obsolete. He expressed the fear held by many that the Soviets had reached a point where they could withstand a U.S. counterattack and still have the missiles necessary to devastate the U.S. mainland, and stated that "we are

seeking to forestall the development of an assymetrical situation which would be beneficial to the Soviet Union." To counter this situation, Schlesinger announced the U.S. was "re-targeting" Soviet missile bases and placing less emphasis on Soviet population centers.

The "limited nuclear warfare" concept came to the fore in May 1975 when the Pentagon released a paper containing a statement by Schlesinger that the U.S. was prepared to use such weapons in any general war in Western Europe. He believed a limited nuclear attack on a key Soviet installation could show U.S. determination and force the Soviets to negotiate short of all-out war. Opponents of limited nuclear warfare in Congress argued that such conceptions made nuclear warfare all the more likely. In June 1975 the Stockholm-based Institute of Peace Research charged Schlesinger with promoting the long-term deployment of "mini-nukes" to replace conventional nuclear weapons. In July, Schlesinger defended a possible "first strike" with limited nuclear weapons.

Schlesinger's views on such matters won him a reputation as a hard-liner and a general foe of detente with the Soviet Union. After visiting Japan in August 1975 for top-level talks, he described that nation as an "indispensable partner in the Pacific" but "too much of a passive partner." He urged Japan to intensify its re-armament efforts. In early October he toured the NATO capitals of Western Europe, again warning against defense cuts.

On Nov. 3, 1975, in a massive shake-up at the top of the Ford Administration, Schlesinger was dismissed from his position as Secretary of Defense, William Colby [q.v.] was fired from his CIA directorship, and Henry Kissinger, while remaining Secretary of State, relinquished his post as head of the National Security Council. Schlesinger's firing in partiuclar was interpreted as a conciliatory gesture to the Soviet Union. *The Washington Post* commented: "Nowhere else in the world is the departure of James Schlesinger likely to be more closely watched—or as warmly received—as in the Kremlin. To the Soviets, Schlesinger was a powerful and persuasive enemy of detente." The Chinese government, in a rare commentary on U.S. domestic politics, attacked Schlesinger's firing as a capitulation to the Soviets.

In the weeks after Schlesinger's firing, President Gerald Ford conceded, after initial denials of Administration infighting, that there had been "growing tension" within the government, and Henry Kissinger admitted "differences" with Schlesinger on key questions. On Nov. 23 Schlesinger appeared on "Meet the Press" and attributed his dismissal to, among other things, his opposition to limits on defense spending.

Schlesinger momentarily retired from public life. In the fall of 1976 he was visiting the People's Republic of China on the invitation of Mao Tse-tung at the time of Mao's death. When the Carter Administration took office in January 1977, Schlesinger returned to the executive branch as Carter's Secretary of Energy. Schlesinger helped draft Carter's 1977 energy program, but he drew considerable criticism, particularly in Congress, where many called for his resignation. He was eventually fired by Carter in a major cabinet shake-up in July 1979. [See CARTER Volume]

[LRG]

For further information:
Elmo Zumwalt, *On Watch* (New York, 1976).

SCHORR, DANIEL (LOUIS)
b. Aug. 31, 1916; New York, N.Y.
News correspondent.

A descendant of a Russian-Jewish immigrant family, Schorr worked his way through college. Following graduation from the City College of New York in 1939, he began his career in journalism as an assistant editor for the Jewish Telegraph Agency and then moved over to the *Journal American*. He took over the New York office of the Netherlands News Agency (ANETA) in 1941 and was draft-ed two years later. Following his discharge from the Army, Schorr moved to Amsterdam to work for ANETA until 1948 when he resigned to do free-lance work on the continent.

Schorr's work impressed Edward R. Murrow, who invited him to join the CBS news staff in 1953. Two years later Schorr was appointed CBS's first Moscow correspondent. He remained in the Soviet Union until 1957 when Soviet authorities refused to issue him a return visa following a U.S. vacation. Schorr's broadcasts were denounced by the Russians as being anti-Soviet, and Schorr was accused of being a "provocateur." From 1957 to 1966 Schorr served as a roving diplomatic correspondent reporting from the United Nations and the major capitals of the world. He transferred to the domestic desk in 1966.

Schorr continued to cover domestic politics during the early Nixon years. His program "Don't Get Sick in America," in April 1970, criticized the Nixon Administration's failure to develop a national health care program. Two months later Schorr exposed the existence of "only paper" programs in the U.S. effort to combat hunger abroad. During the debates on the Safeguard anti-ballistic missile, Schorr uncovered evidence that Dr. James C. Fletcher, a science adviser to the White House, had expressed misgivings to the President about the effectiveness of the system. Schorr informed the evening news viewers that Fletcher personally told him that Nixon also had doubts concerning the program. The following day, at a press conference, President Nixon denied the meeting with Fletcher had ever occurred and, in a very charitable manner, called Schorr a liar.

On Aug. 17, 1971, President Nixon promised in an address to the Knights of Columbus a government program to assist Catholic schools. Following a thorough investigation, Schorr found no evidence that such a program was being considered. His revelation infuriated the White House. On the morning of Aug. 20, an FBI agent visited Schorr to request an interview because he was being considered for a "position of confidence and trust." Schorr refused to answer questions. He soon learned from relatives, friends, colleagues and former employees that the FBI had contacted them to investigate his background. Schorr found no evidence that he was being considered for a post and came to believe that the investigation was carried out in retribution for his anti-Administration broadcasts. *The Washington Post* broke the FBI-Schorr story on Nov. 10. In response, the White House announced that the investigation was a routine background check for a possible job in the $40,000-a-year range "in the area of the environment." Subsequent Watergate investigations revealed that the White House never intended to offer Schorr a position but that this was one of many ways it used to intimidate its critics.

In August 1972 CBS assigned Schorr to cover the growing Watergate scandal. Of the three national networks, CBS devoted the widest coverage to the story, with Schorr handling most of the reporting. His reports complimented the disclosures made by Woodward and Bernstein of *The Washington Post* and Seymour Hersh of *The New York Times.* After many of Nixon's television appearances to try to exonerate the White House in the Watergate controversy, Schorr would appear and point out the inconsistencies in the President's position. He was considered the leading enemy of the Administration on television.

CBS was pressured by a number of its conservative affiliates and Republicans to remove Schorr from the Watergate assignment on the grounds that he lacked objectivity in his reports. For the climax of the Watergate crisis in the summer of 1974, CBS began to divide the coverage assignments among different correspondents. Schorr, for example, did not exclusively report on the impeachment hearings in the House. On the day Nixon resigned, CBS instructed its reporters to "go easy" on the President in their analysis of his speech. In his 1977 book *Clearing the Air,* Schorr suggested that CBS began to soften the Watergate coverage because of fears of White House retaliation and problems with affiliates.

After Watergate, CBS shifted Schorr to cover the growing controversy surrounding the Central Intelligence Agency (CIA). On Feb. 28, 1975, Schorr reported that an internal CIA inquiry had developed evidence of Agency involvement in assassination plots against at least three foreign leaders. Schorr said that President Ford was concerned that public disclosure of the plots would embarrass the U.S. and damage relations with one foreign nation. Schorr then covered the Senate's hearings on illegal action by intelligence agencies.

The House Intelligence Committee, headed by Rep. Otis Pike (D, N.Y.) [q.v.], also conducted an investigation of the FBI and the CIA. Schorr obtained sections of the panel's final report before it was scheduled to be released, but he did not reveal its contents because most of the information had been revealed during the Senate probe. On Jan. 29, 1976, in response to a White House request, the House voted not to open the report to the public. Angered at the action, Schorr secretly gave a copy of the classified report to the *Village Voice* for publication. Schorr announced that he had acted on "an inescapable decision of journalist conscience." His action ired the House, which voted on Feb. 19 to conduct an investigation to determine who leaked the material to him. CBS suspended Schorr from reporting until the House completed the investigation, but it did provide him with a lawyer and continued to pay his salary. Testifying before the House Ethics Committee, he refused to divulge his source because of his "professional conscience" as well as the First Amendment rights of freedom of the press. To reveal the source of the report, he contended, would "dry up many future sources for many future reporters." One week later the Committee voted to end the probe and recommended that the House not prosecute Schorr for failure to answer its questions. The majority called Schorr's conduct "reprehensible" and urged the House to hire professionals to guard secret materials.

The leaking of the Pike report created

additional problems for Schorr within CBS. The network affiliates broadcasting in conservative areas, as well as many of Schorr's colleagues, were incensed with his conduct and demanded his ouster. On Sept. 28 he resigned stating: "I would doubt my ability to function effectively if reinstated. . . . My reinstatement would be a source of tension within an organization whose future success I still care about."

Schorr then published his account of covering the Nixon-Ford years entitled *Clearing the Air* (1977). He went on a nationwide lecture tour expressing his views about government secrecy and the media.

[JB]

For further information:
Daniel L. Schorr, *Clearing the Air* (Boston, 1977).

SCHWEIKER, RICHARD S(CHULTZ)
b. June 26, 1926, Norristown, Pa.
Republican Senator, Pa., 1969-.

The son of a wealthy tile manufacturer, Schweiker, at age 17, enlisted in the Navy during World War II. Following his discharge Schweiker attended Pennsylvania State University, graduating in 1950. After college he joined his family's business and a few years later became involved in local Republican politics in the affluent Main Line suburbs of Philadelphia.

In 1960, Schweiker won a seat in the U.S. House. Cautious and noncommittal as a freshman representative, Schweiker adopted a more liberal stance in his next three terms. Schweiker voted for civil rights legislation, Medicare, Social Security increases, federal rent subsidies and welfare reform. Schweiker initially supported U.S. involvement in Vietnam, but by 1967 began to question the Johnson Administration's handling of the conflict. Eventually Schweiker became one of the most determined foes of the war, supporting such end-the-war measures as the Cooper-Church and McGovern-Hatfield amendments in 1970 and 1971.

Schweiker's election to the Senate in 1968 was considered something of a surprise, as he beat incumbent liberal Democrat Joseph S. Clark, whose defense of gun control legislation had angered many voters. In the Senate Schweiker established a reputation as a maverick who disregarded partisan politics and opposed the Nixon Administration on a number of crucial issues. A founding member of the Senate's Wednesday Club of liberal and moderate Republicans, he voted against the Administration's Safeguard anti-ballistic missile system, and opposed the President's nominations of Clement Haynsworth [*q.v.*] and G. Harrold Carswell [*q.v.*] to the Supreme Court. *Congressional Quarterly* listed Schweiker among the Republican senators who most consistently voted against the Nixon Administration's programs. The strained relations between the President and the Senator led to Schweiker's inclusion on the White House "enemies list." When confronted with mounting evidence implicating Nixon in the Watergate cover-up, Schweiker, in May 1974, became the third Republican Senator to call for his resignation. Having disassociated himself from the President, Schweiker won re-election in 1974 by defeating Pittsburgh's Democratic Mayor Peter F. Flaherty by 247,000 votes.

Overshadowed in some measure by his colleague Hugh Scott [*q.v.*], the Senate Minority Leader, Schweiker remained in relative obscurity until his selection in January 1975 to the bipartisan Senate Select Committee on Intelligence Operations. Schweiker drew headlines on July 20, 1975, when he called for a reopening of the investigation of President John F. Kennedy's assassination. But Schweiker's contention of a connection between President Kennedy's death and a CIA plot to murder Cuban Premier Fidel Castro was dismissed by other Senate members as a publicity stunt. Subsequently the Senate voted to kill further funding for the Committee, leaving Schweiker's allegations unresolved.

Schweiker's voting record was considerably more liberal than the policies endorsed by the Ford Administration. Yet Schweiker supported Ford's candidacy and announced in April 1976 that he would vote for the President at the Republican National Convention in Kansas City. But on July 26, 1976, Ronald Reagan [q.v.], Ford's rival for the nomination, stunned political observers by nominating Schweiker as his running mate. Schweiker's selection was part of a Reagan plan to force Ford to come out with his vice presidential choice, and presumably antagonize some part of his fragile coalition in the process. Arguing that Schweiker could draw off Ford's liberal support in the Northeast, Reagan strategists maintained that a balanced ticket could unite the Party and insure victory. But the plan backfired badly. Schweiker's liberal record enraged Reagan supporters, while at the same time Schweiker could not move a significant number of Pennsylvania delegates to support Reagan.

Schweiker offered to withdraw from the ticket, but Reagan refused. On August 19, 1976, Ford narrowly defeated Reagan on the first ballot, ending a six-month intraparty struggle. In the weeks following the Convention, Schweiker mended his political fences and endorsed the Ford candidacy.

Despite his liberal voting record Schweiker took a decidedly conservative position on certain issues. He favored abortion only in cases when the mother's life was in danger, disapproved of blanket amnesty for draft evaders, and supported the concept of neighborhood schools and only limited busing to achieve racial integration. In general, however, Schweiker's voting reflected his urban, industrial, Northeast constituency. Americans for Democratic Action gave Schweiker an 89 rating in 1975 (the same as ADA President George McGovern), while the AFL-CIO's Committee on Political Education awarded Schweiker a 100 rating, the only perfect score in the Senate that year.

In 1977 Schweiker became the second ranking Republican on the Senate Human Resources Committee.

[JAN]

SCOTT, HUGH D(OGGETT)
b. Nov. 11, 1900; Fredericksburg, Va.
Republican Senator, Pa., 1959-77.

After receiving his law degree from the University of Virginia in 1922, Scott entered private practice in Philadelphia and served as an assistant district attorney there from 1926 to 1941. Elected to the House of Representatives in 1940 and 1942, he served in the Navy during World War II. In 1946 he won reelection to the House and remained a member until 1959. A moderate Republican, Scott was an ardent supporter of Dwight D. Eisenhower in 1952 for the Republican presidential nomination and worked in the general's campaign headquarters.

First elected to the Senate in 1958, Scott successfully challenged the conservative leadership of the Pennsylvania Republican party in 1962 in his sponsorship of the liberal Republican William Scranton [q.v.] for the governorship. In 1964 he helped form a "stop-Goldwater" movement and, after the collapse of Nelson Rockefeller's [q.v.] presidential campaign effort, persuaded Scranton to challenge Goldwater at the Republican National Convention. After Goldwater's nomination, Scott remained aloof from the presidential race, refusing to campaign for the Arizona Senator.

Scott frequently broke with his own party to support liberal legislation. A staunch advocate of civil rights, he was partly responsible for Eisenhower's decision to support such legislation and voted for the civil rights measures of the Johnson Administration. Sensitive to the wishes of his liberal constituency in Pennsylvania's large cities, he often supported legislation favored by labor and low-income groups. [See TRUMAN, EISENHOWER, KENNEDY, JOHNSON Volumes]

In January 1969 Scott was elected Party whip by his Republican colleagues in the Senate and in September, after the death of minority leader Everett Dirksen, was chosen to succeed him. As a Party leader and the Nixon Administration's chief spokesman in the Senate, Scott was often asked to support measures and adopt strategies that he opposed and that he felt would hurt the Republican Party. Despite frequent statements in support of the Administration's legislative program, Scott was at odds with the President on many occasions.

Scott's differences with the Administration were especially apparent in the area of civil rights. In June 1969 the White House announced its opposition to an extension of the 1965 Voting Rights Act. Arguing that the law represented "regional legislation," Attorney General John Mitchell [q.v.] proposed a much weaker substitute. The next day Scott declared that he was willing to lead the fight for a five-year extension of the law. When the House adopted the Administration's proposal in December, Scott joined with liberal forces to map a strategy for the Senate debate. With Sen. Philip Hart (D, Mich.) [q.v.] he introduced a compromise measure that extended the act for five years, but added a change that would allow certain states an exemption from the ban on literacy tests as a face-saving device for the President. In March 1970 the Senate approved the Scott substitute, and the bill later became law.

Scott also resisted attempts to weaken the federal government's commitment to enforce school desegregation. He opposed the attempt by Sen. John Stennis (D, Miss.) [q.v.] in April 1970 to amend an education appropriation bill in order to require that desegregation guidelines be uniformly applied in cases of both de jure and de facto segregation. When President Nixon vetoed the education aid bill later that year, Scott voted with the Democratic majority to override the veto. In 1972, as sentiment against court-ordered busing increased, Scott came out publicly against both a constitutional amendment to prohibit busing and any absolute barring of federal funds for busing plans. In February 1972 he and Sen. Mike Mansfield (D, Mont.) [q.v.] engineered a Senate compromise that placed a limit on the use of busing but retained it as a tool to achieve integration in some cases.

In other domestic areas Scott's record

of support for the White House was mixed. Although he voted against Clement Haynsworth [q.v.] for the Supreme Court, he voted to confirm G. Harrold Carswell [q.v.]. Scott opposed the Nixon Administration's uncompromising stand against the Senate's 1969 tax reform bill. When White House intransigency led to the defeat of a Republican-initiated compromise measure, Scott angrily told the President and his advisers to "listen the next time we try to advise them." He supported Nixon's anti-ballistic missile proposals and defended the Administration's economic measures to control inflation.

For the Republican Party, in Scott's view, to make significant gains in the 1970 election, the Administration would have to reduce troop levels in Vietnam by at least 50%, substantially lower draft calls and reduce defense spending. Nevertheless Scott staunchly defended Nixon's war policies. When New York Republican Sen. Charles Goodell [q.v.] introduced a bill in September 1969 to cut off all funds for troops in Vietnam by the end of 1970, Scott attacked it as a "cut-and-run and bug-out" resolution. He defended the 1970 invasion of Cambodia and the 1971 invasion of Laos as efforts to end the war and in June 1970 voted against the Cooper-Church amendment to halt funds for combat operations in Cambodia.

When Senator William Fulbright (D, Ark) [q.v.] initiated hearings in February 1970 into the Administration's Vietnamization program, Scott attacked the inquiry and urged the nation to "surmount the hysteria of a limited number of critics." In a sharply partisan speech in April 1971, Scott charged Democratic critics of the war with "irresponsible mud-slinging" and with "giving comfort to the enemy" by "crying the same line of Moscow, Peking, and Hanoi." In June 1971 he urged that Democratic Sen. Mike Gravel of Alaska [q.v.] be disciplined for reading portions of the Pentagon Papers into the Senate record, and in September, he voted to extend the draft.

Scott defended Nixon during most of the revelations surrounding the Watergate scandal. In March 1973, after the Senate approved the creation of a special investigating committee, Scott declared that "the White House has nothing to hide." When Nixon announced on April 30 the resignations of his closest advisers who were implicated in the growing scandal, Scott applauded the speech as proof that Nixon was "determined to see this affair thoroughly cleaned up." In July he predicted that the President would "come out fighting" soon and "reply very, very strongly" to the allegations made at the Senate hearings.

But Scott increasingly found himself on a political limb as White House actions and revelations repeatedly called into question the wisdom of his public support for the President. Scott frequently urged Nixon to make a "full disclosure" of all pertinent information, and he praised Nixon's October 18th decision to hand over partial transcripts to Special Watergate prosecutor Archibald Cox [q.v.]. When Cox rejected the compromise and was subsequently fired by Nixon, Scott could only urge the President to hurriedly name a new special prosecutor. A few days later, when the White House made the startling revelation that tapes of two crucial meetings did not exist, Scott lamely defended the announcement by saying "this machine age isn't always perfect."

Late in November 1973 Scott admitted that he had "never been more uncomfortable" than in his current position. "I've had a terribly difficult job," he said, "trying to strike a balance as a Party leader and at the same time trying to hold the confidence of people." After the White House gave Scott assurances that evidence existed to clear the President, Scott, in January 1974, reaffirmed his confidence in Nixon's innocence. But he was angered by the refusal of the President to turn over to the House Judiciary Committee the evidence it had requested, and Scott warned Nixon in March that he would definitely be impeached if the White House tapes were not released.

On April 30 Nixon finally released over 1,200 pages of transcripts. A few days later Scott renounced his support of the President. The transcripts revealed, he said, "deplorable, disgusting, shabby, immoral performances" on the part of everyone involved, including President Nixon. After Nixon released further transcripts on August 5 indicating his knowledge of and involvement in the cover-up of the Watergate break-in, Scott met with Nixon and told him that his impeachment and conviction were a virtual certainty, and he urged the President to resign.

Scott's lengthy support of Nixon tarnished his position. On December 4, 1975, he announced that he would not seek reelection the following year. In 1976 his reputation was further hurt by revelations that he had received $45,000 in illegal campaign contributions from the Gulf Oil Corp. Scott admitted receiving the money but denied that he "knowingly" accepted illegal funds, arguing instead that he thought they came from legal, private sources. The Senate Ethics Committee conducted an investigation but decided in September 1976 not to take action against Scott.

Hugh Scott retired from Congress after more than 30 years of service.

[JD]

SCOWCROFT, BRENT
b. March 19, 1925; Ogden, Utah
Military Assistant to the President, 1972-73; Deputy Assistant to the President for National Security Affairs, 1973-75; Assistant to the President for National Security Affairs, 1975–77.

A native of Ogden, Utah, Brent Scowcroft graduated from the U.S. Military Academy at West Point in 1947 and earned his fighter pilot wings in 1948, although he never saw combat. Instead he pursued a rather scholarly military career studying international relations at Columbia University. He received his Ph.D. in 1967. He also studied at Georgetown University's School of Languages and Linguistics, acquiring a fluent knowledge of Russian and Serbian. During the middle 1950s he taught Russian history at West Point and in the early 1960s he taught political science at the Air Force Academy in Colorado.

Thereafter he held a series of Pentagon assignments. From 1964 to 1967 he was a member of the long-range planning division of the office of the deputy chief of staff for plans and operations. He then worked as staff assistant in the Western Hemisphere region of the office of the assistant secretary of defense for international security affairs during 1968–1969. The next year was spent as special assistant to the director of the staff of the Joint Chiefs of Staff. In November 1971 he was brought into the White House as military aide to the President, replacing Gen. J. D. Hughes, who had served Nixon since 1969 and was resigning to become vice-commander of the 12th Air Force in Austin, Tex.

Shortly after his appointment to the White House staff, Scowcroft headed the advance party to arrange for President Nixon's trip to Moscow—a delicate mission in view of the concurrent renewal of U.S. bombing of North Vietnam. As a career soldier-administrator with extensive academic background and capable of handing diplomatically tinged scout-and-prepare missions, Scowcroft had much in common with another soldier on the White House staff, Gen. Alexander M. Haig [q.v.]. Indeed when Haig left the White House to become Army vice chief of staff in January 1973, Scowcroft stepped into his position as deputy to presidential assistant Henry Kissinger [q.v.] at the National Security Council (NSC).

As Kissinger's assistant Scowcroft put in a hardworking and low-profile performance. Described as "one of the hardest workers in the White House," "cool under pressure" and "a straightforward and very quiet and very forceful man," he was an able administrator but not a vigorous or dominating one. He was "trained to serve totally and unswervingly the person to whom he was assigned." For more than two years that person was Henry Kissinger, who played a very prominent posi-

tion while his deputy stayed quietly, self-effacingly behind the scenes. Kissinger often had a tendency to operate in a highly personalized, secretive manner that cut out even his most trusted assistants. Scowcroft, however, was generally kept well informed, if not by Kissinger, then by his fellow-in-arms, Alexander Haig, who had returned to the White House as chief of staff in May 1973.

Not implicated in the Nixon Administration scandals, Kissinger and his staff survived intact the transition to the Ford Administration. As President Ford sought to "take hold of the foreign policy mechanism" and make it his own, he instituted a major cabinet-White House staff personnel shuffle in November 1975 that replaced Defense Secretary James Schlesinger [q.v.] with Ford's White House Chief of Staff Donald Rumsfeld [q.v.]. In other shifts George Bush [q.v.] replaced William Colby [q.v.] as the head of the Central Intelligence Agency. Elliot Richardson [q.v.] was brought back from the London embassy as Secretary of Commerce, and Secretary of State Henry Kissinger gave up his dual post as national security Affairs assistant. When Kissinger finally left the NSC in 1975, his deputy, Scowcroft, resigned his military commission in order to accept promotion to Kissinger's former post on the White House staff.

After working with Kissinger for two and a half years and essentially agreeing with Kissinger's views, Scowcroft was not expected to challenge the Secretary's foreign policy primacy. Although the judgment of his critics that he was merely "a good paper shuffler" and "Kissinger's errand boy within the White House" was harsh, it was nonetheless true that for his 14 months as national security assistant, Scowcroft was an unassuming figure while Kissinger continued to be the prominent foreign policy force of the Administration.

Scowcroft served until the end of the Ford Administration.

[MJW]

SCRANTON, WILLIAM W(ARREN)

b. July 19, 1917; Madison, Conn.
Ambassador to the United Nations,
February 1976-January 1977.

A descendant of a wealthy steel and banking family, William Scranton graduated from Yale in 1939 and then received his law degree from Yale Law School in 1946. Following service in the Army, he returned to his home town of Scranton, Pa., where he worked for his family. He also became active in local Republican politics. In 1960 he won a seat in the U.S. House. Two years later he won the governorship with 55.4% of the vote and immediately emerged as a dark-horse contender for the 1964 Republican presidential nomination. When it appeared certain that Sen. Barry Goldwater (R, Ariz.) [q.v.] would get the nomination, moderates and liberals turned to Scranton. Although the Pennsylvania governor initially had refused to run, he belatedly changed his mind and challenged Goldwater, but was defeated at the Convention. In 1966 Scranton completed his term as governor, pledging not to run "ever for any public office under any circumstances." Although he remained active in Republican politics, he devoted his attention to his family's financial interests and sat on the board of directors of a number of leading corporations. [See JOHNSON Volume]

In December 1968 Scranton visited the Middle East for President-elect Richard Nixon. He told reporters at the Jordan River that the U.S. should follow a "more evenhanded" policy towards Israel and its Arab neighbors. This statement infuriated American Jews as well as the Israeli government, and the future Administration repudiated it. But Scranton refused to retract his position.

Following the shootings of student protesters at Kent State and Jackson State in the spring of 1970, President Nixon appointed Scranton to chair the President's Commission On Campus Unrest. Eighty-seven witnesses testified at the hearings conducted throughout the summer. The final report advised the President that he "has the platform and prestige to urge all Americans at once, to step back from the battle lines into which they are forming." It urged him to "seek to convince public officials and protesters alike that divisive and insulting rhetoric is dangerous in the current political campaign and throughout the years ahead. The President should insist that no one play irresponsible politics with the issue of 'campus unrest.'" Ending the Vietnam war, promised the report, as well as a renewed commitment to "full social justice at home," would contribute to the reduction of divisiveness on the campuses. When dealing with the controversial question of violence, the report took a balanced position. It blamed student agitators and police for escalating the tensions through overreaction and intimidation of each other. The report recommended the democratization of the governance of the universities, the promulgation of clearly defined rules of permissible conduct and methods of protest, and the termination of defense and intelligence contracts between the federal government and the campuses. The Nixon Administration received the controversial report with little comment.

Soon after Gerald Ford became President, he asked Scranton to become the U.S. ambassador to the United Nations. Scranton turned down the offer. When Daniel Patrick Moynihan [q.v.], Ford's second choice, resigned in early March 1976, the President once again asked Scranton. This time he accepted. Because of his 1968 Jordan River statement, the selection of Scranton upset American and Jewish public opinion. Scranton himself added to the problem when he said in a U.N. debate that he regarded the Israeli settlements in the occupied territories "as an obstacle to the success of the negotiations for a just and final peace between Israel and its neighbors." The Israelis deplored this statement even though Scranton vetoed a U.N. resolution denouncing their occupation of the West Bank. After

Ford's defeat, Scranton left his U.N. post. He continued to be active in Republican politics.

[JB]

SEABORG, GLENN T(HEODORE)
b. April 19, 1912; Ishpeming, Mich.
Chairman, Atomic Energy
Commission, January 1961-August 1971.

Seaborg, a nuclear chemist, discovered the element plutonium in 1940 and worked on the Manhattan Project, which developed the atom bomb during World War II. He served on the Atomic Energy Commission's (AEC) General Advisory Board from 1946-51.

In 1961 Seaborg was appointed head of the AEC by President Kennedy. During his tenure he fought for the maintenance of AEC control over both regulation and development of atomic energy programs, despite criticism that the two functions were incompatible. Seabord supported the nuclear test ban treaty of 1963 and pressed for the confinement of nuclear energy to the five countries already developing their atomic potential. He encouraged the U.S. Plowshare Program designed to formulate peaceful uses of atomic explosives, including excavation and earth moving. The program, which attracted worldwide attention during the mid-1960s, involved numerous tests at the AEC's nuclear test site in Nevada. In 1970 an AEC report revealed that a 250 sq. mile area of its Nevada test site was contaminated with poisonous and radioactive plutonium 239; the area was sealed off from the public. Plowshare was suspended in the early 1970s, primarily due to environmental protest and lack of industry support. [See TRUMAN, EISENHOWER, KENNEDY, JOHNSON Volumes]

Considerable controversy and publicity surrounded the AEC during Seaborg's remaining years as head of the Commission. Its handling of radioactive wastes attracted severe criticism, highlighted by the 1970 release of a 1966 National Academy of Science (NAS) report. The study criticized the poor geographical locations chosen for stockpiling radioactive refuse, the Commission's general policy of underground storage, and the varied criteria used to classify the materials at different plants. A subsequent report prepared for Sen. Frank Church (D, Ida.) [q.v.] also found the AEC's disposal techniques careless.

Seaborg became embroiled in a 1971 controversy involving the use of radioactive sand, known as tailings, in construction in Grand Junction, Colo. Left by companies mining uranium during the 1950s and 1960s, mounds of tailings were carted off for free landfill by both contractors and private citizens. "Elevated" levels of radioactivity were detected in the area by state and federal health officials in 1966. Although some health officials dismissed threats from the low-level radiation, tailings were removed, at state and federal cost, from numerous private homes. In a letter to Gov. John Love [q.v.], Seaborg refused to finance a chromosomal study of infants in the town to test for possible abnormalities. Supported by state money, a five-year study was begun on a federal grant at the University of Colorado Medical Center, but the contract was prematurely canceled a year later. The limited tests conducted, however, found significant increases in birth defects and in the death rate due to cancer in the county surrounding Grand Junction.

In 1969 Seaborg gave top priority to the liquid metal fast breeder reactor (LMFBR) development program. LMFBRs were designed to recycle plutonium fuel elements to produce more plutonium. Budget allcations for LMFBRs increased from $85 million (of a nearly $2.3 billion budget) for fiscal year 1970 to $285 million (of an almost $2.6 billion budget) three years later. An accident involving this type of reactor at the Enrico Fermi Atomic Power Plant near Detroit, Mich., threatened that city in 1966. Two months after it started up in August, emissions of extremely high levels of radiation caused the plant to be shut down. Delicate and tedious testing, conducted over a year and a half, determined the cause of the fuel meltdown and enabled the Power Reactor Development Co. to begin cleanup efforts. The plant resumed operation in July 1970, but financial difficulties caused the AEC to deny the company's application for a license extension in August 1972.

Dr. Seaborg resigned in 1971 to return to teaching chemistry at the University of California at Berkeley. In April 1973 he was appointed director for international relations of the French Societe International de Technologie.

[RB]

SEALE, BOBBY
b. Oct. 22, 1937; Dallas, Tex.
Black militant.

The son of working-class black parents, Seale was raised in Dallas and Oakland, Calif. After dropping out of high school, he enlisted in the Air Force but was dishonorably discharged for fighting with a white officer. Returning to Oakland he finished high school at night and entered Merritt College, where he joined the Afro-American Association. He met Huey Newton, another black student, and together they studied Afro-American and African history and the writings of black militants such as Malcolm X, who especially influenced them. In October 1966 they founded the Black Panther Party. Seale was chairman and Newton was a minister of defense for the organization.

Although the Panthers received the most publicity for their advocacy of armed self-defense for blacks against police violence, they also had a 10-point platform that emphasized self-help and community control of ghetto institutions, such as schools, housing and businesses. The Black Panthers first came to national attention in May 1967 when Seale led a group of armed Panthers to the California State Assembly to protest gun-control legislation aimed at them. The publicity helped increase the Panther's member-

ship to several thousand and branches of the group were formed in many cities. Although an all-black organization, the Panthers cooperated with white radical groups, especially in the anti-war movement.

Because of their vocal and militant stand against police brutality, the Panthers were subject to intense government harassment. In January 1969 Seale announced a campaign to rid the Panthers of FBI and police infiltrators. When the police in several cities raided Party offices in June 1969, Seale accused the government of a conspiracy "to destroy the Black Panther Party leadership." In December, after Chicago police had slain fellow members Fred Hampton and Mark Clark, Seale denounced the action as part of a plan to "commit genocide" against the Panthers. It was later revealed that the FBI and local police had indeed infiltrated the Panthers and had encouraged Party members to commit acts of violence.

On March 20, 1969, Seale was indicted with seven other leaders of the anti-war movement for violating the anti-riot provisions of the 1968 Civil Rights Act in connection with the demonstrations at the Democratic National Convention in Chicago. Their famous "Chicago Eight" conspiracy trial, which began in September 1969, became a cause celebre for radicals and was the scene of numerous confrontations between the defendants and Judge Julius Hoffman [q.v.]. When Seale vociferously demanded the right to conduct his own defense (his lawyer, Charles Garry, was sick at the time and Hoffman refused to grant a delay), the judge ordered him gagged and shackled in court, and on November 5 declared a mistrial for Seale. He also sentenced Seale to four years in prison for contempt of court. In 1970 the government dropped the conspiracy charges against him, and in 1972 a court dismissed all of the contempt charges.

Seale, meanwhile, with several other Panther members, was indicted on murder charges in the 1969 torture slaying of Alex Rackley, a former Panther. The trial, scheduled to begin in New Haven in May 1970, provoked large-scale demonstrations, and the slogan "Free Bobby" became a rallying cry for radicals. The trial of Seale and codefendant Ericka Huggins, which had been postponed until November, was the longest in Connecticut history, finally ending on May 25, 1971, when the jury reported that it was hopelessly deadlocked. The judge declared a mistrial and ordered all charges against the defendants dropped. After almost two years in prison, Seale was finally released.

With many Panthers killed or jailed over the preceding years, Seale returned to Oakland and helped redirect the Panthers away from armed self-defense and toward community organizing and self-help programs for ghetto residents. In May 1972 Seale announced that he would run for mayor of Oakland the following year. Campaigning on a platform that emphasized community control of police and low-rent housing, he placed second in a field of nine and received over 43,000 votes in the May 1973 runoff.

Soon after the election Seale quietly left the Party and retired to private life. In 1978 he published his autobiography, *A Lonely Rage*.

[JD]

For more information:
Donald Freed, *Agony in New Haven: The Trial of Bobby Seale, Ericka Huggins, and the Black Panther Party* (New York, 1973).

SEGRETTI, DONALD HENRY
b. Sept. 17, 1941; San Marino, Calif.
Watergate figure.

A native Californian, Donald Segretti graduated from the University of Southern California (USC) in 1963. Segretti was a good student and was active in class government at USC, where he attended classes with both Dwight Chapin [q.v.] and Gordon Strachan [q.v.]. He joined the Trojans for Representative Government and became their successful candidate for the student senate. The Trojans were known on the USC campus for their spe-

cial brand of "dirty tricks," which they called "ratfucking." They stuffed ballot boxes, planted spies in the opposition camp and distributed false campaign literature about their political opponents. In 1962 with another USC graduate, Ronald Ziegler [q.v.], Segretti and Chapin were drafted to work on Richard Nixon's unsuccessful gubernatorial campaign.

Segretti studied at Cambridge in 1963, and returned to California and entered law school in 1964. He graduated from the University of California at Berkeley in 1966. Segretti worked a year for the Treasury Department before he was drafted into the Army to serve as an officer in the Judge Advocate General's office. A registered Democrat Segretti was considered a radical for his attempt to integrate private housing in Charlottesville, Va. Later Segretti defended soldiers in Long Binh, Vietnam, in their petition for discharge from the Army as conscientious objectors. In his last year in the Army at Ford Ord, he helped organize the anti-war and anti-military Concerned Officers Movement.

In spring 1971 Segretti was contacted by his two college friends Chapin and Strachan who, after working under H.R. Haldeman [q.v.], in Richard Nixon's successful 1968 presidential campaign, were aides to Haldeman in the White House. Offering the chance for "some fun and travel" plus the opportunity to "work for the President," Chapin and Strachan asked Segretti if he would like to head a "clandestine political activities unit." The purpose of the unit would be to throw the 1972 Democratic primary campaign into disarray and to eliminate the most formidable Nixon rival, Edmund Muskie [q.v.]. In August Segretti met with Herbert Kalmbach [q.v.], President Nixon's personal lawyer, and was offered a salary of $16,000 a year plus expenses for his work.

Segretti took his mission seriously and enthusiastically. He hired 28 people in 17 primary states to conduct a campaign of dirty tricks that included forging letters and distributing them under the candidates' letterheads, making dossiers on the candidates' personal lives, seizing confidential files from the candidates, leaking false statements, manufacturing items for the press and throwing the candidates schedules into disarray. He plagued Muskie's campaign with a variety of damaging political literature. His first act was to distribute a leaflet in Florida that read, "If you like Hitler, you'll just love Wallace—vote Muskie." Another flier from that primary read, "Help Muskie in Busing More Children." It was signed by the "Mothers Backing Muskie." In one of the most vicious attempts to discredit the Democratic front-runners, Segretti arranged for a letter to be sent to various Democrats and the press on stolen Muskie stationery charging both Henry Jackson [q.v.] and Hubert Humphrey [q.v.] with sexual misconduct. A falsified Hubert Humphrey press release alleged that Shirley Chisholm [q.v.] had been hospitalized in a mental institution.

Segretti kept in contact with Chapin at the White House about his political activities. Altogether Segretti received and disbursed almost $45,000. Segretti's and other "internal security" operations were financed by a slush fund of more than $700,000 in cash collected as illegal campaign gifts and kept in Maurice Stans's [q.v.] safe at the Committee to Re-Elect the President (CREEP). In 1972, CREEP's deputy director, Jeb Stuart Magruder [q.v.], had insisted that the White House Segretti-Chapin operation and the CREEP internal security operation be administered by G. Gordon Liddy [q.v.], general counsel for the Committee. Although Segretti was contacted on several occasions by E. Howard Hunt [q.v.], chief contact for the Watergate burglars, there is no indication that Segretti, Liddy and/or Hunt ever worked on a project together. However, they all met in Miami, Fla., on Feb. 11, 1972. At that meeting Hunt asked Segretti what he was doing, gave him the name of a printer in Miami who would do his leaflets and promised to get him Muskie's itinerary. Hunt gave Segretti his home phone number and told him to keep in touch.

Donald Segretti's activities were among the first to be uncovered, in October 1972, by the investigation of reporters Robert Woodward [q.v.] and Carl Bernstein [q.v.] of The Washington Post. Segretti was traced through Hunt's telephone records. In 1974 Segretti was convicted of political espionage and served four months and 20 days of a six-month sentence. He was released from jail on March 25, 1974, and disappeared from public life.

[SJT]

SHANKER, ALBERT
b. Sept. 18, 1928; New York, N.Y.
President, United Federation of Teachers, 1964-. President, American Federation of Teachers, 1974-.

Born and raised in New York City Shanker grew up in a staunchly prounion family. He received a B.A. from the University of Illinois and an M.A. from Columbia University. Shanker abandoned his graduate studies to teach in the New York City public schools and he became active in the Teachers Guild, the New York affiliate of the American Federation of Teachers (AFT). In 1959 he was hired as a full-time AFT organizer.

In May 1964 Shanker was elected president of the United Federation of Teachers (UFT), the successor to the Teachers Guild, whose 55,000 members made it the largest local union in the AFL-CIO. In September 1967 Shanker led New York City's teachers on their first extended strike. Settled after 18 days, it resulted in substantial wage and benefit increases. Shanker later served 15 days in jail when a court found him guilty of violating the state's Taylor Law, which prohibited strikes by public employes.

Shanker achieved nationwide prominence in the fall of 1968 by leading New York City's teachers in a two-month strike that shut down the city's public schools. The strike was provoked by a model decentralization program, initiated in 1967, which gave community school boards in predominantly poor, nonwhite neighborhoods more power in running local schools. The strike ended on Nov. 19 in a victory for the UFT. But there were serious consequences. Racial tensions in the city rose sharply as the black and Hispanic population of New York found its goal of community-controlled schools stymied by the mostly-white teachers union. [See JOHNSON Volume]

Shanker's tough stance during the strike raised his stature enormously among the UFT members and made him a force in New York City politics. In June 1969 the New York City Board of Education agreed to a generous three-year contract settlement rather than face the prospect of another crippling strike. The pact gave public school teachers in New York the highest average salaries of any in the nation, with a top figure of $16,950 after eight years of service.

Shanker continued to oppose proposals for community control of schools that in any way interfered with guaranteed job security and seniority rights. When Harvey Scribner, a proponent of school decentralization, was named chancellor of the city's Board of Education in 1970, the UFT opposed him at every turn. Largely through Shanker's unremitting hostility, Scribner was forced out in 1973. After a state-enacted proposal to create 32 elected community school boards in New York City took effect in May 1973, UFT-backed candidates won a majority of seats, thus insuring that the boards would represent the teachers' interests.

Largely through Shanker's efforts early in 1972 almost all of New York state's teachers unions merged into the United Teachers of New York in early 1972. The new statewide union affiliated with the AFL-CIO, and Shanker, who remained president of the UFT, was elected an executive vice president of the new union.

In 1973 Shanker became an AFL-CIO vice president and a member of its executive council, the youngest person on that body and one of its few white-collar union heads. The next year he was elected president of the AFT, which had grown to over 400,000 members since 1969. Shanker, who retained his position as head of the UFT, rapidly became a most influential labor leader in the United States.

Shanker was considered by many a possible successor to AFL-CIO president George Meany.

Shanker was again a center of controversy in 1975 during the height of the New York City fiscal crisis when Mayor Abraham Beame [q.v.] was forced to impose severe austerity measures, including the firing of 4,500 teachers. On Sept. 9, at the start of the school year, Shanker called a citywide strike of UFT members that lasted for a week. The settlement Shanker won drew widespread criticism from parents who objected to the shortening of the school day for students, and minority groups, who accused Shanker of once again ignoring their interests.

However, New York state's Emergency Financial Control Board, created to oversee the city's spending, rejected the UFT contract on October 7 and sent it back for renegotiation. In retaliation Shanker refused to comply with a plan to rescue the city from default through the purchase of municipal bonds by public employee unions. Although the four other unions had agreed to the purchase, Shanker's stance threatened to wreck the scheme and drive New York City into bankruptcy. But on Oct. 17, Shanker reversed his earlier decision and approved the purchase of $150 million in municipal bonds from the UFT pension fund.

In 1977 the AFL-CIO named Shanker head of a newly created department for professional employees.

[JD]

SHAPP, MILTON J(ERROLD)
b. June 25, 1912; Cleveland, Ohio.
Governor, Pa., 1971-79.

Milton Shapiro received his B.S. degree in electrical engineering from Case Institute of Technology in 1933. It served little good at the height of the Depression, however; his first job following graduation was driving a truck for 22 cents an hour. He soon found work as a salesman in Philadelphia, and changed his name from Shapiro to Shapp when he suspected anti-Semitism was hindering his sales.

Shapp served as an officer in the Army Signal Corps during World War II. His experience in electronics led him to form Jerrold Electronics in 1948, a small manufacturer and distributor of television-related hardware. Shapp pioneered the practical application of community antenna television (CATV) in the early 1950s and made his multimillion dollar fortune in CATV franchises.

Shapp was an early supporter of John F. Kennedy and served as a consultant to the Administration. He ran in the 1964 Pennsylvania Democratic primary for senator, but dropped out when the Party organization endorsed another candidate. In 1966 he ran unsuccessfully for governor. Following his defeat, Shapp formed the Pennsylvania Democratic Study Committee, a group of economists and other social scientists, which published periodic "Shapp Reports" on various political and economic issues. Despite voter support for Sen. Eugene McCarthy [q.v.] in the 1968 Pennsylvania primary, the state delegation's leadership supported Sen. Hubert H. Humphrey [q.v.] at the National Convention. Shapp vehemently opposed this action and took to the streets to protest, with other delegates and citizens, the Democratic National Committee's handling of the Convention. Presidential primary reform became a major issue for Shapp in later years.

Shapp ran for governor again in 1970. In the general election he presented himself as the enemy of state machine politics. His mass media saturation advertising emphasized his highly successful business activity as a qualification for pulling the state out of the financial bind into which it had been led by machine bosses. To balance the state budget and increase state aid to college education, Shapp suggested a graduated state income tax. His Republican opponent, Lt. Gov. Raymond J. Broderick, fought the income tax concept as a way of balancing the budget and characterized Shapp's activities at the 1968 Democratic National Convention as being riotous and illegal. Shapp won by a landslide, carrying the

Democrats to their first state Senate majority since 1962.

At the opening of his administration, Shapp declared himself "the people's advocate." He worked to reform and regulate the state's insurance companies and worked for consumer protection.

Shapp was confronted by several controversial issues in the last years of his first term. In November 1972 he vetoed the first of several strong anti-abortion bills, citing its unenforceability. A few months later he proposed sweeping changes in private health care, making hospital budgets and rates subject to state approval, easing health insurance application standards, and providing for public representation on the boards of all health care institutions. Shapp's graduated income tax proposal was quickly adopted by the state legislature but subsequently declared unconstitutional by the conservative Pennsylvania Supreme Court. The legislature then passed a flat 2.3% tax in its place. Shapp established a statewide lottery to lessen the impact of the state income tax on the elderly, whose small, fixed incomes would suffer, and to reduce the property taxes of the elderly poor. Shapp opposed President Nixon's revenue-sharing programs, stating that he considered them part of an attempt to curtail legitimate aid to the poor.

Towards the end of 1973, many of the state's truckers went on strike to protest fuel pricing and allocation practices resulting from the Arab oil embargo; the flow of goods by truck was almost completely stopped. In the strike, marked by violence and bloodshed, Shapp acted as a mediator and helped piece together a pact acceptable to the truckers.

Shapp pushed for a no-fault insurance law for the state's automobile drivers and Pennsylvania's resulting 1974 bill was among the first in the nation.

In 1974 Shapp became the first Pennsylvania governor eligible to run for a second term. He won the Democratic primary handily, defeating an anti-abortion candidate, Republican Andrew L. Lewis, III, in the November contest with 54% of the vote.

Shapp entered the 1975 presidential primary race in September. He eschewed "political rhetoric" and stressed a "businesslike" approach to government, featuring "executive leadership and managerial skill." He entered the Florida and Massachusetts primaries and drew negligible support. In March 1976 he dropped out of the race and in June threw his support to Jimmy Carter.

Several instances of questionable activity by political allies and administration personnel marred Shapp's last few years as governor. In March 1975 the treasurer of the state Democratic Party, William Casper, was convicted on charges of extortion and conspiracy concerning his activities as a fund raiser for Gov. Shapp's 1974 campaign. Another problem surfaced in 1976 when questions were raised about a 1972 cable TV franchise granted to Shapp from which he later made a $2 million profit. Perjury and conspiracy charges were leveled against the state police commissioner, the deputy commissioner and the head of the state patrol for incidents involving the alleged falsification of records of patrolmen involved in traffic accidents while intoxicated.

Pennsylvania Attorney General Robert P. Kane dismissed Walter M. Phillips, state special prosecutor for Philadelphia, for alleged ineffectiveness in probing municipal corruption; Phillips had been investigating House Speaker Herbert Fineman, a political ally of Gov. Shapp, for possible irregularities in the awarding of contracts for the city school system. Shapp's political problems continued into 1977 with the conviction of Fineman on charges of obstructing a federal probe into alleged payoffs by parents seeking to get their children into professional schools. Adjutant General Harry J. Mier was forced to resign from Shapp's cabinet in February 1977; he was alleged to have used military aircraft for personal reasons.

Shapp was not eligible to run for a third term as governor, and Republican Richard Thornburgh took over in 1979.

[RB]

SHOCKLEY, WILLIAM B(RADFORD)
b. Feb. 13, 1910; London, England
Scientist

Although born in England, Shockley was raised and educated in California, receiving his B.S. from the California Institute of Technology in 1932. He earned a doctorate in physics from the Massachusetts Institute of Technology in 1936 and soon afterward joined the technical staff of Bell Laboratories in New Jersey. At the Bell labs, Shockley began experiments which subsequently led to the invention of the transistor by John Bardeen and Walter Brattain. For their work all three men were awarded a Nobel Prize in physics in 1956.

During the 1960s Shockley offered courses in electrical engineering at Stanford University, whose faculty he later joined. Concurrently, he ventured into the field of genetics, a discipline in which he had no background or training. Shockley was motivated by IQ test results that showed blacks scoring consistently lower than whites and which suggested that heredity, rather than environment, determined intelligence. He urged fellow scientists to ignore taboos against research on genetic differences and to investigate the IQ test results, warning that failure to do so would be irresponsible and possibly even dangerous. Shockley made his appeal to the National Academy of Science (NAS) in 1968. At first the NAS ignored Shockley's exhortations, but in 1969 appointed a special committee on genetic factors in human performance.

Shockley meanwhile conducted his own research. Through studies based for the most part on Army preinduction mental tests and on the work of the geneticist T.E. Reed, Shockley figured that the U.S. black population had lost five IQ points relative to whites since 1918 because of the progressive reduction in its caucasian gene component. He concluded that blacks were more intelligent in direct proportion to the amount of white genes they carried and therefore genetically inferior to whites. He developed a theory which he defined as "retrogressive evolution through the disproportionate reproduction of the genetically disadvantaged" and which he termed "dysgenics." Shockley's concern superceded linking intelligence and inheritance to solving human quality problems through eugenics, i.e. heredity quality improvement. He proposed a program under which people with sufficiently low IQs would receive financial incentives if they agreed to sterilization.

The validity of Shockley's views was open to serious dispute. The tests made no allowances for cultural differences, and scientists questioned their scientific value. Others, noting Shockley's inadequate experience in genetics, accused him of seeking pseudoscientific justification for race and class prejudice.

Shockley undertook a zealous campaign to press his views. He received backing from Arthur Jensen, a noted educational psychologist who had made similar IQ studies, but other colleagues offered little support. In 1971 the NAS accepted their committee's proposition that the study of human racial differences is a relevant one, but it rejected sponsoring further research in such studies.

Outside of scientific circles Shockley's views sparked furor, particularly among blacks and human rights groups. Angry protestors prevented him from speaking at scheduled appearances. In 1972 at Yale University, Shockley sustained an hour and 15 minutes of hissing and booing before leaving the platform. On other campuses across the country he was met with similar reactions. Demonstrators dressed as Ku Klux Klan members disrupted Shockley's classes, and a Nigerian graduate student filed a formal complaint of discrimination charging that Shockley had subjected him to racial slurs while discussing his academic work.

Academics also expressed disapproval of Shockley's views. When Shockley requested permission in 1971 to teach a graduate course at Stanford that would exploit his central thesis, a five-man faculty committee voted against allowing him

to offer the course. They cited the bias of Shockley's reading list and his lack of experience in genetics as the basis of their rejection. The University of Leeds, in 1973, retracted an honorary degree which it had awarded Shockley the year before for his work in electrical engineering.

Despite attacks, Shockley remained of the "inescapable opinion that the major cause of the American Negro disadvantages is racially genetic," though, at the same time, he insisted that this question was open to sound research.

Later campaigns of Shockley's involved racial and sexual quotas. In 1976 he attacked such quotas for hiring and promoting in businesses. He claimed that "urban decay has been the tragic product of a welfare system based on the premise of the national egalitarian lie—a lie that asserts the equality of the distribution of genetic potential for intelligence to all groups, regardless of sex or race."

[CJL]

SHRIVER, R(OBERT) SARGENT, JR.
b. Nov. 9, 1915; Westminster, Md.
Democratic vice-presidential candidate, 1972.

Born into a wealthy and socially prominent Maryland family, Shriver was educated at Yale, where he received an LL.B. in 1941. After serving in the Navy during World War II, he worked for Joseph P. Kennedy as assistant manager of the Chicago Merchandise Mart. He married Kennedy's daughter Eunice in 1953, served as a liaison for his brother-in-law Sen. John F. Kennedy during the 1960 presidential campaign, and was named the first director of the Peace Corps in 1961. Shriver was named director of the Office of Economic Opportunity (OEO) on Feb. 1, 1964. In February 1968 Shriver left the OEO to accept an appointment as ambassador to France. He continued in that position under President Nixon. He resigned in March 1970 and took up private law practice in Washington and New

York. [See KENNEDY, JOHNSON Volumes]

On Aug. 8, 1972, Shriver was nominated by the Democratic National Committee as the Party's candidate for vice president. He replaced Sen. Thomas F. Eagleton (D, Mo.) [q.v.] who withdrew as the nominee because of the controversy that arose after the disclosure that he had been hospitalized three times in the 1960s for psychiatric treatment. Democratic presidential candidate Sen. George McGovern (D, S.D.) [q.v.] had named Shriver as his choice on Aug. 5, after Sen. Edmund S. Muskie (D, Me.) [q.v.] declined an offer to become McGovern's running mate.

Shriver accepted the nomination with "gratitude and joy." In his acceptance speech he stated that he could "already taste the victory." He said he was not embarrassed to be the seventh choice for vice-presidential candidate. "Think of the comparison and then you can pity poor Mr. Nixon. His first and only choice was Spiro Agnew [q.v.]."

Shriver launched his campaign with an attack on the Administration. On Aug. 10 he charged that President Nixon had lost an opportunity for a Vietnam peace settlement when he took office in 1969. Shriver stated: "Nixon had peace handed to him literally in his lap. He blew it." Shriver implied strongly that a 1969 decrease in battlefield activity had signaled North Vietnam's willingness to negotiate a settlement of the war. His statement was quickly rejected by Administration officials, but Averell Harriman [q.v.] and Cyrus Vance, the two negotiators at the Paris peace talks during the Johnson Administration, issued joint statements on Aug. 12 supporting Shriver's assertion.

Ignoring predictions that the Democrats would be routed at the polls in November, Shriver waged an arduous cross-country campaign that focused primarily on maintaining traditional Democratic support for McGovern. In addition to Party gatherings, he appeared before labor and college audiences and minority and ethnic groups. His main themes were the state of the economy, unemployment, inflation and charges against the Nixon

Administration of special interest government and of political espionage. He also defended McGovern on the issues of amnesty for Vietnam war resisters and an end to the restrictions on abortion and against the Republican charge of radicalism. The McGovern-Shriver ticket lost by one of the largest electoral and popular margins in U.S. history. Shriver then returned to private life and the practice of international law.

On Sept. 20, 1975, Shriver announced that he was a candidate for the 1976 Democratic presidential nomination. He stated his intention to claim the legacy of his late brother-in-law John F. Kennedy, and denied that he was a "stalking horse" for Sen. Edward M. Kennedy (D, Mass.) [q.v.], who had said that he would not run in 1976.

The seventh Democrat to declare a candidacy, Shriver was the first to announce that he had qualified for federal matching funds under the 1974 campaign finance law, which required candidates to raise a minimum of $5,000 in sums of $250 or less in 20 states.

In a Sept. 10 speech, Shriver advocated putting Americans back to work and "putting the government—as the expression of our common will—on the side of the consumer, the taxpayer, the individual and the community." He was critical of U.S. foreign policy for having "meddled too much." On Jan. 7, 1976, Shriver issued a 9,000-word economic plan that featured a public service jobs program, tax reductions, tax credits for private employment and permanent wage-price guidelines.

At the Iowa precinct caucus held on Jan. 19, Shriver garnered only 3.3% of the vote. He placed fifth in the New Hampshire primary, third in Mississippi and third in Illinois. On March 22 he formally withdrew from the race. He asserted that he had achieved remarkable success in light of the handicaps of a late entry into the race, lack of record in elective office or government title, and his reception in some quarters as "nothing more" than a relative by marriage to the Kennedy family.

[FHM]

SHULTZ, GEORGE P(RATT)
b. Dec. 13, 1920; New York, N.Y.
Secretary of Labor, January
1969–June 1970; Director, Office of
Management and Budget, June
1970–May 1972; Secretary of the
Treasury, May 1972–April 1974.

After receiving a B.A. from Princeton in 1942, Shultz served in the Marine Corps from 1942 to 1945. He resumed his studies after the war, obtaining his Ph.D. in industrial economics at MIT in 1949. Shultz taught at MIT from 1946 until 1957, when he was appointed professor of industrial relations at the Graduate School of Business of the University of Chicago. He became dean of the business school in 1962, and remained at that post until 1968, when he left to join President Nixon's cabinet as Secretary of Labor.

Despite a long academic career, Shultz was no stranger to government. Generally associated with the monetarist "Chicago School" of Milton Friedman [q.v.], Shultz served as an economic adviser to both Republican and Democratic Administrations beginning in the mid-1950s. He had been senior staff economist on President Eisenhower's Council of Economic Advisers in 1955–56 and a consultant to the Department of Labor in 1959–60; under Kennedy, he served as staff director of a national policy study for the Committee on Economic Development and as a consultant to the President's Advisory Committee on Labor-Management Policy. In the Johnson years he chaired a task force established to review U.S. Employment Service programs. During the same period Shultz produced a steady stream of books, articles and reports on labor relations. [See JOHNSON Volume]

Shultz's 18-month tenure as Secretary of Labor coincided with one of the greatest surges of U.S. labor militancy since the immediate postwar period. Directly or indirectly, Shultz involved himself in a six-week East Coast longshoremen's strike, a bitter three-month strike at Gen-

eral Electric, and the March 1970 postal workers' strike, as well as several White House-level bargaining sessions aimed at averting strikes in other industries. Before the postal workers' strike was settled, the National Guard had been sent into New York City to sort the mail, and Shultz had been personally embarrassed by a nation-wide rank-and-file rejection of a contract negotiated between union leaders and himself.

This wave of labor militancy jeopardized the entire economic plan of the Nixon Administration, which was aimed at deflating the economy and with it the wage push that was held partly responsible for rising prices. As Secretary of Labor, Shultz was given the assignment of enlisting the trade unions in the fight against inflation. After relatively limited success in this effort, Shultz was appointed in June 1970 to head a study panel on the "blue-collar blues," which attempted to locate the sources of worker discontent.

Under Shultz, the Labor Department also became involved in controversies over manpower planning, affirmative action and union reform. In April 1969 Shultz and other government officials were named in an NAACP lawsuit charging the Nixon Administration with failure to enforce equal employment practices. Only three days later Shultz was compelled to publicly defend the Administration's $100 million cutback in the funding of the Job Corps, which provided training for unskilled and minority youths.

The Philadelphia Plan, announced by Shultz in July 1969, was a key aspect of the Nixon Administration's response to minority criticisms, combining elements of manpower, affirmative action, wage curbs and union reform in a single strategem. The plan obliged Philadelphia construction companies with federal contracts to hire a certain quota of minority workers, and permitted them to do so at nonunion wage scales. Costly labor settlements in the construction industry and record rates of contract rejections by construction workers were a special subject of concern to Shultz, who called these settlements "disastrous" for the Administration's anti-inflation strategy.

Although the U.S. Solicitor General ruled that the Philadelphia Plan violated the 1964 Civil Rights Act, a ruling by Attorney General John Mitchell [q.v.] upheld the constitutionality of the Plan in September 1969. In spite of the estrangement of AFL–CIO leaders and "hardhat" demonstrations across the country, Shultz in early 1970 warned that if there were not voluntary compliance with the Plan, he would extend its provisions to 18 other cities. After a Philadelphia federal court upheld the Plan's constitutionality, Shultz in the summer of 1970 announced a similar Washington Plan for the capital. Finally, in February Shultz played a role in the Nixon Administration's decision to suspend provisions of the 1934 Davis-Bacon Act, which required union wages to be paid on federal construction projects.

In other important actions promoting direct government involvement in union affairs, Shultz in January 1970 ordered a full-scale Labor Department investigation into the murder of Joseph A. (Jock) Yablonski [q.v.], a United Mine Workers' (UMW) reform candidate who had been defeated in elections for the union's presidency in December 1969. Two months later Shultz announced a Labor Department suit to void the UMW election results, which ultimately resulted in new, government-supervised elections in 1972 in which UMW President Tony Boyle [q.v.] was unseated by reform candidate Arnold Miller [q.v.] and later indicted for Yablonski's murder.

In June 1970, as part of a larger White House shake-up, President Nixon named Shultz to head the newly created Office of Management and Budget (OMB), which superseded the Bureau of the Budget. In the same move Shultz was appointed presidential adviser. Shultz's appointment to head the OMB marked the beginning of the second phase of Chicago School management of the U.S. economy, in the wake of the Penn Central bankruptcy, the stock market slump and the corpo-

rate liquidity squeeze of May–June 1970, which revealed the dangers inherent in overly rapid deflation and forced the Administration and the Federal Reserve Bank into an abrupt about-face in credit policy.

Shultz's move to the OMB did not end his special relationship with labor questions. While appearing more frequently before congressional committees to defend the Administration's economic policies, he continued to play a role in opening the construction industry to nonunion labor and preventing costly contract settlements. In July 1971 he called steel industry and union negotiators to the White House on the eve of contract talks in that industry and asked for increases in productivity to justify any wage boosts. In August 1971 Shultz announced a program to limit job promotions for 1.2 million government employees in order "to get control of wages in the federal government."

In late June 1971 Shultz participated, with President Nixon, Federal Reserve Chairman Arthur Burns [q.v.] and Treasury Secretary John Connally [q.v.] in the so-called Camp David I meeting on national and international economic problems. Although the U.S. economy was showing signs of recovery from the 1969–70 recession, the growing U.S. balance-of-payments deficit was putting heavy pressure on the dollar overseas. In May 1971 the countries of the Common Market jointly floated their currencies, urging the U.S. to "put its own house in order." Although the Administration's economic outlook was in rapid transition and the Chicago School's ideas, which had shown little efficacy, were losing hegemony in policy, Shultz still prevailed over urgings for a more activist intervention—specifically from Secretary Connally—with a "steady-as-you-go" approach. He argued that the immediate crisis was the result of temporary phenomena and would correct itself without precipitous action. While Shultz prevailed in this meeting, it marked the last significant policy move influenced by Chicago School ideas prior to President Nixon's conversion to Keynesianism in August 1971.

Between June and August 1971 it became clear that the Administration plan was failing. Unemployment persisted at high levels, inflation did not subside and, most importantly, the U.S. balance-of-payments deficit deteriorated still further. Thus, on Aug. 14–15, Shultz and Connally returned to Camp David for a second weekend conference on the economy with President Nixon. On Sunday evening, Aug. 15, Nixon announced on national television a complete policy turnabout toward Keynesian, statist and interventionist solutions. Nixon's program, which he called the "New Economic Policy" (NEP), included a 90-day wage and price freeze, the end of dollar convertibility into gold, a 10% surcharge on imports, a $4.7 billion budget cut, layoffs of federal employees and tax incentives for investment. As the "Chicago" economist most disposed to go along with this policy turnabout, Shultz stayed on as OMB Director, whereas monetarist Hendryk S. Houthakker left the Council of Economic Advisers in mid-July, and CEA chairman Paul W. McCracken [q.v.] followed him at the end of the year.

Although Shultz had been a consistent opponent of wage and price controls, seeing them as unnecessary and potentially harmful government interference with the laws of the market, President Nixon appointed him to the Cost of Living Council established to oversee the control apparatus. As one of the Administration's main links to the labor movement, Shultz was also appointed to the National Commission on Productivity, established to revive U.S. industry's lagging competitive position in the world market. In late September he met with Pacific coast shippers and longshoremen's representatives in an effort to settle a three-month dock strike paralyzing West Coast shipping. Shultz also appeared before various congressional committees to report on the progress of the NEP.

In May 1972 Shultz succeeded John Connally as Secretary of the Treasury. In this capacity his previous intensive involvement in labor questions gave way to the broader concerns of federal debt management, international monetary reform and defense of the successive phases of the NEP in Congress. In September 1972 Shultz informed Congress that the expiration of federal debt ceiling legislation would leave the government insolvent before the end of fiscal 1973 if an additional $15.6 billion in debt were not approved. A few days later he stated that President Nixon, if reelected, would increase taxes in his second term. Shultz warned, "If you insist on pushing spending up, it has to come out of the American people sooner or later . . . it will come out first in inflation and then we will have to be facing up to this tax issue."

After Nixon defeated George McGovern [q.v.] for a second term, Shultz was retained at his Treasury post, and White House Press Secretary Ronald Ziegler [q.v.] said that Shultz "will be the focal point and the overall coordinator of the entire economic policy decision-making process, both domestically and internationally." Shultz was also appointed to head a new cabinet-level Council on Economic Policy. To underline his admission to Nixon's closest circle of advisers, Shultz was given an office in the White House.

For the rest of his tenure at the Treasury, Shultz dealt with the two major problems: administration of economic controls and a renewed dollar crisis that broke out in February 1973. In early January Shultz had met with AFL-CIO President George Meany [q.v.], and immediately thereafter the so-called Phase Two price controls begun in November 1971 were abolished and the apparatus for overseeing them dismantled. Phase Three of the Administration's program involved voluntary, or "jawboned," wage and price controls based on informal pressure.

In the first months of 1973, with the lifting of all but essential controls, inflation once again took off at unprecedented rates. Meat prices had been a sensitive issue through 1971–72, and Shultz had earlier abolished all import quotas on meat to assure an adequate supply to the U.S. market. With a dramatic rise in meat prices, President Nixon on March 29 reimposed price controls on meat, and both he and Shultz publicly urged labor to retain the 5.5% wage guidelines of Phase Two. Shultz persuaded the commercial banks to forego a hike in the prime interest rate. In late May he announced a possible excise tax on gasoline to curb demand, as a result of sporadic gasoline shortages that anticipated the oil crisis of late 1973 and early 1974.

Shultz's attention to the problems of the domestic economy, however, was increasingly diverted to the international arena. Shultz was a key figure in a complex U.S. strategy to simultaneously prevent a strong European front on international economic questions and to seek economic detente with the Soviet Union. A massive speculative surge against the dollar in February 1973 had compelled Shultz, after consultations with other officials, to announce a 10% devaluation of the dollar below the 1971 adjustment. The weakness of the dollar on Western European markets was such that foreign governments were obliged to suspend currency trading for two weeks while international monetary officials convened in Brussels and Paris in early March to resolve the crisis. Representing the U.S. at the Paris meeting, Shultz, who was seen as a welcome change from the previous "strongarm" tactics of Connally at such international meetings, rejected European proposals for reform but indicated a cooperative attitude by the U.S. The Paris meeting abolished once and for all the fixed rate exchange system in effect since World War II, and all currencies floated.

From Paris, Shultz, who had been appointed head of the East-West Trade Policy Committee on March 6, flew to Moscow for trade discussions with Soviet officials. Before leaving Paris he briefed French Finance Minister Giscard d'Estaing on Nixon's forthcoming trade policy legislation. In May Shultz presented Nixon's trade bill to the House Ways and Means Committee, promptly drawing the fire of French Foreign Minister Michel Jobert, who saw the trade policies as an attack on the Common Market and the European Economic Community's (EEC) Common Agricultural Policy. On June 22 Shultz signed a series of trade protocols with the Soviet Union.

Further U.S. inflation once again brought Shultz back to the domestic arena. On June 13, 1973, he admitted that Phase Three voluntary controls had been a failure and announced a new 60-day price freeze. In late August, just before the publication of the latest wholesale price index figures, Shultz warned against "astounding" price increases in the wake of the freeze. August prices for certain agricultural products did in fact show increases of over 100% on an annual basis. In early September, echoing public sentiment, Shultz stated that the United States had been "burned" in the massive grain deal with the Soviet Union and linked the deal to runaway American food prices.

In the fall of 1973, Shultz resumed his global travels on behalf of U.S. economic policy. He represented the United States at the Tokyo meeting of the General Agreement on Trade and Tariffs (GATT) on Sept. 12–14. On Sept. 24–28, Shultz represented the U.S. at the Nairobi meeting of the International Monetary Fund (IMF), where reform of the system and results of the new "floating rates" were assessed. From Nairobi, Shultz flew to Moscow for further trade talks, and predicted $1.5 billion in Soviet-American trade for 1973. From Moscow, Shultz went on to Belgrade for talks with Yugoslav officials.

The Yom Kippur war of October 1973 and the subsequent quadrupling of oil prices placed, according to some observers, an unbearable strain on an already-shaky international monetary system. In November 1973 Shultz met secretly with world monetary officials in Tours, France, for further discussions on monetary reform. In January 1974 Shultz led the U.S. delegation to another IMF meeting, where his call for a rollback of "staggering" oil prices was characterized as "naive" by Arab officials.

Shultz's remaining months at the Treasury—he stepped down in April 1974—

were spent in efforts to prepare the U.S. economy for the overall effects of the oil price increase, to avert a recession and to consolidate the U.S. trade position. At the end of January, after President Nixon ended the so-called Interest Equalization Tax (IET) imposed by Lyndon Johnson to curb U.S. overseas investment, Shultz announced that abolition of the IET had been possible because of renewed dollar strength. In a Feb. 4 report to Congress, Shultz argued that the dramatic increase in 1973 oil company profits had to be viewed against low profits in the preceding years. On Feb. 14, when an international energy conference was held in Washington to discuss the oil emergency, Shultz repeated his call for a reduction in oil prices and urged both developed countries and oil exporters to provide increased aid to non-OPEC developing countries. Earlier, Shultz had issued a joint statement with Secretary of State Henry Kissinger [q.v.] deploring the House's defeat of a $1.5 billion U.S. contribution to the International Development Agency. He also appeared before Senate committee hearings on the Administration's trade bill, opposing the proposed curb on trade with the Soviet Union that tied most favored nation status to Soviet treatment of internal dissidents and Soviet Jews desiring to emigrate.

When Shultz announced his resignation in March 1974 for personal reasons, he was the last original member of President Nixon's cabinet. Although he denied any relationship between his resignation and the Watergate scandal that was slowly enveloping the Administration, Shultz was involved in July 1974 House Judiciary Committee hearings on the Administration's use of the Internal Revenue Service, a branch of the Treasury Department, for harassment of political opponents.

After leaving his post at the Treasury, Shultz became an executive vice president of the Bechtel Corp. in San Francisco, and also taught at Stanford University.

[LG]

SIMON, WILLIAM E(DWARD)
b. Nov. 27, 1927; Paterson, N.J.
Deputy Secretary of the Treasury,
January 1973-April 1974;
Secretary of the Treasury,
April 1974-January 1977.

After receiving his B.A. from Lafayette College in 1952, Simon spent his early career in a series of Wall Street firms, and from 1964 until 1972 he served as director of the municipal and government bond department at Salomon Brothers, an investment bank in which he was a senior partner. Simon's conservative views and extensive knowledge of capital markets were decisive factors in his appointment as deputy secretary of the treasury, a post he assumed in early 1973.

Simon's first year in government was spent in dealing with the incipient energy crisis. Almost immediately he was named chairman of an interdepartmental Oil Policy Committee, established to confront the first phase of oil and gasoline shortages. His initial public prominence came during a clash with the the Federal Trade Commission (FTC) in September 1973, when he asked the FTC to withdraw its anti-trust suit against eight major U.S. oil companies, asserting that the FTC's charges of company collusion were false. Shortly thereafter Simon warned that U.S. oil imports had reached a record level in 1973, reflecting the country's growing dependency on foreign oil since it ceased to be a net exporter of oil in the mid-1960s.

Simon's role in energy policy entered a new phase in the wake of the October 1973 Yom Kippur war, the subsequent quadrupling of oil prices, and the OPEC organized boycott on oil shipments to the United States. Simon, who became known as the Nixon Administration's "energy czar," replaced former Colorado Gov. John Love [q.v.] as top White House energy official in December 1973. In what many saw as a high-level shake-up in which Simon played a role behind the scenes, Love, who had been criticized as ineffectual, resigned, complaining of the Nixon Administration's lack of concern about fuel allocation and citing difficulties in even getting to see Nixon or other White House officials about these problems.

Simon's appointment signaled a new awareness of the gravity of the oil crisis, and Simon was made head of the Emergency Energy Action Group, a new cabinet-level committee, as well as director of a new Federal Energy Office. Simon moved quickly to implement tough government controls over the use of gasoline, announcing the Administration's desire to reduce private U.S. gasoline consumption by 30% in the first three months of 1974. When fuel allocation plans were announced by Simon in mid-December, top priority went to the Defense Department, essential community services, farms, industry and public transportation. The plans aimed at curtailing private auto use. At the end of the year, Simon called for a 10-gallon-per-week limit on private drivers.

In April 1974 Simon became Secretary of the Treasury, and his activities turned increasingly to the financial monetary effects, often referred to as "petrodollar recycling," of the sudden sharp increases in Middle Eastern oil revenues. The U.S., Japan and Europe were engaged in heavy competition in the Middle East to solidify political, commercial and financial relationships with the newly-rich Arab states. Thus in July 1974 Simon toured the Middle East for the U.S. government. His first stop was Egypt, where he negotiated a tax equalization treaty. He also obtained an agreement permitting the operation of four U.S. banks that under the Nasser regime had been expelled in 1957. Terms of U.S. aid to Egypt were also discussed. From Egypt, Simon flew to Saudi Arabia and Kuwait, announcing on July 20 a U.S.-Saudi economic agreement. Simon's main concern was to induce the Saudis and Kuwaitis to place their petrodollar surpluses in U.S. bank deposits and in U.S. government securities, particularly Treasury bills, while discouraging them from actual direct investment in U.S. corporations where they would have direct control over policy. Although a Kuwaiti spokesman asked, after Simon's visit, why the OPEC countries should help the U.S. with its problems when it had done nothing for the Arab states, Saudi Arabian Oil Minister Sheik Ahmed Zaki al-Yamani announced that the bulk of recycled petrodollars would be invested in U.S. capital markets.

Another problem confronting Simon in his first year as Secretary of the Treasury was the role of gold in international and domestic transactions. In the spring of 1974 he had reaffirmed the traditional Treasury position of hostility to gold as an international resource. In May 1974 he met with Dutch Finance Minister Willem Duisenberg to discuss European proposals permitting central banks to sell their gold reserves at the market price instead of the much lower official price. Simon was also in favor of the ownership of gold by private citizens, and when in the summer of 1974 Congress repealed the 40-year ban on private gold ownership, Simon announced a 2,000,000-ounce sale for early January 1975. The gold sales were seen as part of an overall U.S. strategy to fully demonetize gold.

Prior to the onset of the 1974-75 recession, Simon was a spokesman for austerity, fiscal constraint and the maintenance of stable capital markets. Although he had assured adequate flows of petrodollars into U.S. commercial banks and government securities, the accelerating inflation of mid-1974 was threatening to bring the state and municipal bond markets to a standstill. Thus in August 1974 Simon met with Citibank Chairman Walter Wriston [q.v.] and Federal Reserve Bank Chairman Arthur Burns [q.v.] to arrange for "floating rate bonds," or bonds whose interest rates could be periodically adjusted for inflation throughout the life of the bond. In late August Simon was appointed by President Ford to the Council on Wage and Price Stability, established as part of the Administration's short-lived and ill-fated "WIN" program to fight inflation. In late September Simon was appointed to a new 14-member Economic Policy Board and was identified by one commentator as the Ford Administration's "principal spokesman on economic policy matters."

Simon continued the general U.S. policy, begun under his predecessor at the Treasury, George Shultz [q.v.], of pressuring both Europe and the Eastern bloc with U.S. economic weapons, and thereby keeping international policy initiative in the hands of the U.S. In September 1974 he participated in a secret meeting of the major powers on world financial problems and, later in the same month, met again with heads of the major capitalist powers to develop a concerted plan to cope with the world energy crisis. Simon's solution was a plan to establish a $25 billion lending facility, or "safety net," to help industrial nations pay their oil deficits, but under conditions set by international bodies with preponderant U.S. influence. This proposal marked a shift from Simon's earlier position that the private capital markets were capable of financing the oil deficits themselves.

During the same period Simon was a key figure in the Ford Administration's use of the "food weapon" for international political leverage. After a meeting of Simon, Secretary of Agriculture Earl Butz [q.v.], and Ford in early October 1974, the U.S. government abruptly canceled contracts for $500 million in grain sales to the Soviet Union. A week later in Moscow, Simon represented the U.S. at the second meeting of the U.S.-USSR Economic and Trade Council, where he discussed the grain situation with Soviet leaders. Returning to Washington Simon announced a limited grain sale to the Soviet Union, in exchange for Soviet promises to make no further purchases. Pressure over grain sales, combined with U.S. attempts, through the Jackson Amendment, to link most favored nation status to Soviet treatment of internal dissidents, pushed the Soviet Union in January 1975 to abrogate the 1972 U.S.-USSR trade agreement.

The 1974-75 recession, which was the most severe contraction of industrial production since 1929-33, greatly enhanced Simon's role as a spokesman for austerity and stabilization on both the international and domestic fronts. In mid-January 1975 the Committee of 10 of the International Monetary Fund (IMF) approved Simon's proposed $25 billion oil "safety net," which effectively made access to oil credits dependent on U.S. approval of domestic austerity measures by governments, such as Italy's, making use of the facility. Simon also had a hand in increasing U.S. contributions to other international agencies, such as the $1.5 billion additional contribution to the Inter-American Development Bank and a $1 billion lending facility establshed by the World Bank to help poor nations finance their oil deficits. In each case the United States was acquiring more direct leverage in the domestic economic policies of foreign countries.

Simon also negotiated international monetary policy in preparation for the November 1975 Rambouillet summit of the major Western industrial nations. The major problem confronting the summit was an open rift between the U.S. and France about the role of gold as an international reserve. The U.S., as Simon's repeated statements had made clear, continued to favor the elimination of gold as a reserve asset. Countries like France, on the other hand, with substantial holdings, wanted to sell off their gold at the market price, at the time $150 an ounce, instead of the official rate of $42.22. In the compromise between Simon and French Finance Minister Jean-Pierre Fourcade, both the IMF and individual central banks agreed to sell off portions of their gold holdings, thus furthering the U.S. policy of demonetizing gold; on the other hand, in keeping with French wishes, they were able to do so at the market and not the official price. Finally in an additional concession to the French position, it was agreed that a major portion of the IMF's receipts from gold sales would be given to the less-developed countries.

The less-developed countries, or LDCs, constituted a third arena for Simon's international activities. In September 1975 a two-week meeting of the United Nations Commission on Trade and Development (UNCTAD) witnessed a major confrontation between spokesmen for the

LDCs, who demanded a reorganization of the world economy to benefit the poor nations, and the advanced capitalist countries, who resisted such demands. As the major U.S. representative at the UNCTAD meeting along with Secretary of State Henry Kissinger [q.v.], Simon's strategy was to drive a wedge between the Third World and those Western European nations who were more sympathetic to the Third World's call for a "new international economic order." Simon was concerned about Third World calls for a moratorium or outright cancellation of billions of dollars of LDC debt, which he felt would wreak havoc in Western capital markets. Consequently, with Kissinger, Simon floated a plan whereby the U.S. would agree to large-scale debt relief for the Third World if Western Europe and Japan, which held over $100 billion from long-standing, U.S. balance-of-payments deficits, would in turn agree to wipe out this "dollar overhang." Simon and Kissinger thereby effectively defused any potential Third World-European alliance.

Simon became an economic ambassador-at-large for U.S. international policy. He visited Rome in March 1976 and informed the Italian government that further loans to Italy would be dependent on a domestic austerity program, without which any aid would be tantamount to "throwing money down the drain." In May 1976 he met with Chilean government officials for economic talks and a month later consulted with the Spanish Minister of Finance on possible aid to post-Franco Spain. As the U.S. representative at the June 1976 meeting of the Organization for Economic Cooperation and Development, Simon remarked that "preaching moderate growth is like trying to sell leprosy."

Simon's role in domestic policy was no less oriented toward austerity. With Alan Greenspan [q.v.], who emerged as the top economist of the Ford Administration, Simon increasingly came to feel that the U.S. economy had to turn away from massive government spending to solve its long-term structural problems. Both Simon and Greenspan began to advocate a shift of tax burdens away from corporations in order to promote capital goods investment, which was the weak element in the recovery of industrial production beginning in March 1975. Simon felt that federal taxation of both corporate profits and income from dividends and sales of stock was an impediment to capital investment, a "double taxation" of enterprise. He felt that a reduction of federal spending would reduce the need for tax revenues and alleviate the competition between private and public borrowers in the nation's capital markets.

In January 1975 Simon consequently expressed his dismay at the anticipated federal deficit for that year. Several weeks later, the House Ways and Means Committee reflected similar concerns in rejecting a $109 billion increase in the federal debt ceiling, which Simon himself had requested to accommodate anticipated government spending. Simon's worries that federal borrowing would crowd out private industry in the capital markets were criticized by economist Herbert Stein [q.v.] and former Undersecretary of the Treasury Paul Volcker [q.v.], and indeed proved to be exaggerated in the 1975-76 period largely because of stagnant corporate investment.

In the summer of 1975 Simon continued in his public utterances to emphasize the need for price stability, greater discipline in government spending, the dangers of crowding out, and a new theme, tied to stagnant corporate investment, of a "capital gap" confronting U.S. industry. In May 1975 he told the Senate Finance Committee that "we need to get back to price stability in this country, or we'll go down the drain the way Great Britain is going now." Later in the same month he warned that the Social Security system would be bankrupt by 1981 if it continued to run high deficits. He attacked the food stamp program as "a well-known haven for chiselers and rip-off artists." He stated that the main obstacle to solving the energy crisis was the federal government itself and cited "problems created by the Clean Air Act, the moratorium on coal leasing . . . [and] . . .

price and supply regulation affecting oil and gas" as examples.

Simon's most controversial role in domestic economic policy, however, was in the New York City fiscal crisis of 1975. Simon, with Greenspan, President Ford and Federal Reserve Board Chairman Burns opposed federal aid to New York City through most of the crisis, reversing or modifying their position only as it became clear that the national and international repercussions of a default would be impossible to control. In May 1975 Simon rejected an initial New York City plea for aid, stating that "not only is the federal government's legal authority to provide financial assistance limited, but also that such assistance would not be appropriate." Several days later he met with Ford, Vice President Nelson Rockefeller [q.v.], New York City Mayor Abraham Beame [q.v.] and New York Gov. Hugh Carey [q.v.] to discuss the crisis, and he once again rejected pleas for federal guarantees of city bonds. Because of his eight years' experience in the state and municipal bond market at Salomon Brothers, Simon was generally seen as a spokesman for Wall Street hostility to government profligacy and to the social services financed by government borrowing.

Throughout the crisis the major issue was whether or not the federal government would underwrite New York City's municipal paper, thereby allowing the city to return to the capital markets from which its de facto bankruptcy excluded it. To circumvent this problem the Municipal Assistance Corp. (MAC), or "Big Mac" as it was widely known, and the Emergency Financial Control Board (EFCB) were created to issue further bonds and supervise the city's finances. In spite of this reorganization, Simon rejected the request of EFCB member Felix Rohatyn [q.v.], of the Lazard Freres investment bank, for federal underwriting of MAC bonds. Simon used the New York City crisis to underline his capital gap analysis, emphasizing their relationship in congressional testimony on the city fiscal question. On Sept. 16, just back from the UNCTAD conference on Third World

debt cancellation, Simon reiterated his view that a New York City default would have no grave consequences and that U.S. capital markets were "capable of handling a default with no more than moderate and relatively short-lived disruption." Simon asserted to the contrary that "there is a serious risk that the capital and credit markets would react adversely" if the federal government acted to prevent default.

Shortly thereafter, however, Simon began to shift his position when numerous New York City bankers warned of impending difficulties in the sale of New York state bonds if the city defaulted on its debts. Simon admitted that default could have a "domino effect" on the capital markets. To meet this danger, he elaborated a three-point plan, calling for an interest moratorium on the city's short-term notes, a temporary increase in the New York state sales tax, and a government study to determine the possibility of transferring local and state welfare burdens to the federal level. At the end of September, Simon told Congress that "unprecedented" government borrowing was drawing funds away from housing and business investment, and in early October, he once again opposed federal aid to New York City in testimony before the Senate Finance Committee. Only in November, when default had been narrowly averted by last-minute municipal trade union purchases of short-term city paper, did Simon, along with Ford, Greenspan and Burns, come around to the view— underlined by the personal intervention of West German Chancellor Helmut Schmidt—that the effects of a default by New York City on the capital markets could produce an international financial panic.

Simon's high political visibility as a crisis manager led many commentators to see him as a possible running mate for Gerald Ford in the 1976 elections, but such speculation proved unfounded. At the end of his term at the Treasury, Simon became president and trustee of the nonprofit John M. Olin Foundation, as well as a consultant to several Wall St. firms.

[LG]

SIRICA, JOHN J(OSEPH)
b. March 19, 1904, Waterbury, Conn.
District Court Judge, 1957-77

The son of a tubercular Italian immigrant, John J. Sirica spent his childhood wandering with his family throughout the South in search of warm climates and business opportunities. As a boy, Sirica helped support his family by greasing cars, waiting tables, and selling newspapers. After two unsuccessful attempts at law school, Sirica received his LL.B. from Georgetown University in 1926, where he supported himself as a boxing coach. From 1930 to 1934 Sirica served the Hoover Administration as an assistant U.S. attorney in Washington and then went into private practice. In 1949 he joined the prestigious Washington firm of Hogan and Hartson as chief trial attorney. Eight years later, as reward for service in five GOP presidential campaigns, President Eisenhower appointed Sirica to the U.S. District Court for Washington, D.C.

Sirica's work on the district bench earned him a reputation among Washington lawyers as a tough, forthright man of "impeccable integrity," although it was generally conceded that he was not a profound legal scholar. Sirica tried a wide range of cases, many of which were highly complex and controversial. In 1959 he presided over the contempt-of-Congress trial of Teamster vice president Frank W. Brewster, and in 1960 over a 10-month-long, $90 million anti-trust action brought against 23 railroads by a Kansas City trucking firm. Because of his firm law-and-order stance and his tendency to give the longest sentences allowed under law, Sirica acquired the nickname "Maximum John." His command of legal niceties and technicalities, however, was sometimes questioned, and he was reversed more frequently than any other judge in D.C.

By virtue of seniority, Sirica became chief judge of the U.S. District Court in April 1971. The duties of his new office being largely administrative, he tried few cases and looked forward to his impending retirement on his 70th birthday. His plans changed, however, following the June 1972 arrest of seven undercover operatives of President Nixon's reelection committee at Democratic National Committee headquarters in the Watergate. As the investigation of the incident proceeded, a growing body of evidence suggested that many close associates of Nixon were involved in a wide range of improprieties and illegal actions. Allegations were made that the President himself was personally involved and directly responsible.

Sirica was quick to grasp the full dimensions of the developing Watergate scandal. When the case of the original seven defendants came before his court in January 1973, he did not assign it to any of the 15 judges under his supervision, but decided to try it himself. He took that action because as a Republican he would be less vulnerable to charges of political bias, and because unlike other judges who had heavy caseloads, he would have more time to devote to the case.

Impatient at times with the ineffectiveness of the prosecutors and the evasive answers of the defendants, Sirica frequently took over the questioning himself, often refusing to accept the answers he received. When defendant Bernard C. Barker said that he did not know who had sent him expense money in a plain envelope, Sirica snapped: "Well, I'm sorry, but I don't believe you." When Hugh W. Sloan, Jr. [q.v.], the reelection committee's treasurer, testified that he had given $199,000 to defendant G. Gordon Liddy [q.v.] without knowing what the money was for, yet was not cross-examined, Sirica interrogated Sloan himself with the jury out of the courtroom. On another occasion, Sirica dismissed as "ridiculous, frankly," the claim by defendant James W. McCord, Jr.'s [q.v.] attorney that the bugging scheme would help detect plans to incite violence against Republicans in the 1972 campaign: "Whether the jury will believe you is another story." The jury did not, finding both McCord and Liddy guilty of burglary, wiretapping, and attempted bugging.

Going beyond normal procedure, Sirica

let the convicted men know that the severity of their sentences would depend heavily on the degree to which they cooperated with their probation officers and investigators still probing the Watergate crime. Sirica's tactics bore fruit on March 20, 1973, several hours before the sentences of the Watergate burglars were due. On that day Sirica received a letter from McCord alleging that there had been "political pressures" on the Watergate defendants to plead guilty, that perjury had been committed, and that "others higher than Liddy" were involved in a massive cover-up. Sirica then deferred sentencing McCord, but kept pressure on the other convicted conspirators to talk by meting out provisional sentences of up to 40 years. Promising to review the sentences later, Sirica recommended cooperation with the grand jury and Sen. Sam Ervin's [q.v.] investigating committee, suggesting that such cooperation would be weighed in the final sentencing.

McCord's letter was the final blow for the cover-up. White House Counsel John W. Dean [q.v.], who had helped coordinate the cover-up, subsequently resigned and testified to Nixon's prior knowledge of the conspiracy at Senate hearings. Jeb S. Magruder [q.v.], former deputy director of the Committee to Re-Elect the President (CREEP), admitted involvement in the Watergate break-in and cover-up, and implicated former Attorney General John N. Mitchell [q.v.].

Sirica's most dramatic role came later in the year, when he ruled on whether Nixon would be allowed to retain tapes subpoenaed by Special Prosecutor Archibald Cox [q.v.] pertaining to White House conversations about Watergate. Drawing on Anglo-American jurisprudence, the Federalist Papers, and particularly the rulings of Chief Justice John Marshall in the 1807 Burr treason trial, Sirica ordered Nixon on Aug. 29, 1973 to relinquish the secret tapes for a private hearing by himself. In the process, Sirica swept aside Nixon's claim that the doctrine of executive privilege placed the President beyond the reaches of the courts and the law. Watergate, in Sirica's view, was a criminal case, one which would not be short-circuited "simply because it is the President of the United States who holds the evidence."

Carving out what he called a "middle ground" between the question of privilege and wholesale delivery of the tapes to the grand jury, Sirica said that he was willing to recognize the validity of a privilege "based on the need to protect presidential privacy," but that it was up to the courts to decide whether such a privilege had been properly claimed. Sirica assigned to himself responsibility for listening to the tapes *in camera* and deciding what parts should be delivered to the grand jury. Sirica's decision was widely applauded as a "sensible compromise" between the arguments of Cox and Presidential Counsellor Charles A. Wright [q.v.]. Although the White House appealed the decision, Sirica's opinion was upheld by the Circuit Court of Appeals, which observed Oct. 12, 1973 that the President "does not embody the nation's sovereignty" and "is not above the law's commands." However, Sirica was informed by White House Counsel J. Fred Buzhardt [q.v.], following the President's dismissal of Cox on Oct. 20, 1973, that two of the nine tapes were "nonexistent" and that a conversation of Nixon with aide H.R. Haldeman was marred by an 18-minute gap. Sirica then ordered the original tapes submitted to him for safekeeping. On Nov. 26, 1973, the White House turned over to Sirica the subpoenaed tapes, along with it a document analyzing the tapes and outlining claims of executive privilege for some of the material.

Convinced that legal procedures were well in motion to get at the Watergate truths, Sirica resentenced the convicted burglars Nov. 9, 1973 to relatively light terms, mostly to time already served. Sirica played his third major role in the Watergate affair in October 1974, when he chose to preside over the cover-up trial of Mitchell, Haldeman, John Ehrlichman, Robert Mardian [q.v.] and Kenneth Parkinson [q.v.]. Again, declaring that he would pursue the "truth" rather than adhere to "strict rules of evidence," Sirica played an activist role, although he came under heated criticism for making "gratuitous remarks" regarding the defendants' characters. On Jan. 1, 1975, Haldeman, Ehrlichman, and Mitchell were found guilty and each was sentenced by Sirica to a prison term of 20 months to five years.

Sirica's conduct of the Watergate trial made him one of the best-known and most admired judges in the country. *Time* chose him as its "Man of the Year" for 1973 and saluted his performance as "particularly reassuring as a testimony to the integrity of the law." Sirica's handling of the trial did not escape criticism, however. Both civil libertarians and political conservatives felt he had been guilty of prejudicial acts against the defendants and their attorneys, and of many technical violations of proper courtroom procedure, particularly his "outrageous efforts to force the defendants to talk." Defending his trial conduct, Sirica had replied: "In a case like this one, with great public interest in it, I don't think we should sit up here like nincompoops. The function of a trial court is to search for the truth."

Sirica retired from full-time duty in 1978.

[JAN]

For further information:
"Standing Firm for the Primacy of Law," *Time*, Jan. 7, 1974.
Richard Ben-Veniste and Hugh Frampton, *Stonewall* (New York, 1977).
James Doyle, *Not Above The Law* (New York, 1977).
J. Anthony Lukas, *Nightmare* (New York, 1976).

SISCO, JOSEPH J(OHN)
b. Oct. 31, 1919; Chicago, Ill.
Assistant Secretary of State for Near Eastern and South Asian Affairs, February 1969 to April 1974; Undersecretary of State for Political Affairs, May 1974-February 1976.

The son of Italian immigrants, Joseph J. Sisco grew up in Chicago and attended Knox College, graduating with honors in 1941. After serving in the infantry in the Pacific during World War II, he attended the University of Chicago, receiving a Ph.D. as a specialist in Soviet studies in 1950. Sisco joined the State Department in 1951, and was assigned to the Office of United Nations Affairs. In 1958 he was appointed deputy director of the Office of United Nations Political and Security Affairs. He became assistant secretary for international organization affairs seven years later. Sisco also served on the U.S. delegation to the U.N. General Assembly from 1952 to 1968. He worked in close harmony with Ambassador Arthur J. Goldberg [*q.v.*] during the Six Day War in June 1967. When Goldberg left government service in 1968, Sisco became the chief U.S. negotiator in the Middle East.

Sisco was promoted in January 1969 to assistant secretary of state for Near Eastern and South Asian Affairs. He quickly formulated a position paper that became the basis for the Nixon Administration's initial Middle Eastern policy. Sisco's policy had several clear-cut objectives, foremost among these the containment of the USSR's rising influence in the area. Equally important the Arab states had to be convinced of the Administration's impartiality. Israel had to be coaxed into withdrawing from occupied Arab lands, with only "insubstantial" border changes. The U.S. therefore had to take a direct hand in arranging a "genuine" peace, and the USSR had to be persuaded to join in this effort. During 1969 and 1970 Sisco attempted to implement these ideas.

Henry Kissinger [*q.v.*] and Sisco "disagreed sharply" over the direction of U.S. policy during the 1971 India-Pakistani war. Suspecting that India intended to dismember West Pakistan as well as detach the eastern part, Kissinger wanted the U.S. "to tilt in favor of Pakistan," according to columnist Jack Anderson [*q.v.*]. Sisco disagreed, arguing that India's ambitions were limited to guaranteeing a free and independent Bangladesh. Sisco predicted a short war, with little chance of intervention by China or Russia, and argued for a policy of cool rhetoric and calm behavior. Although Sisco lost the battle, he reluctantly agreed to present Kissinger's policy to the press.

Following the outbreak of the Yom Kippur war in October 1973, Sisco joined in Kissinger's "step-by-step" diplomacy in the Middle East. Accompanying Kissinger's shuttle between the various Arab capitals and Tel Aviv, Sisco helped work out the disengagement agreement which called for an Israeli withdrawal from the West Bank of the Suez Canal. Although the agreement was criticized by many for demanding harsh concessions from Israel, it did mark the beginning of a new U.S. relationship with the Arab world and a breakthrough in establishing future Arab-Israeli agreements.

Although Sisco had intended to leave public service in early 1974, he agreed to postpone his retirement to become under secretary of state for political affairs. During his last year in office he attempted to mediate the Greek-Turkish dispute over Cyprus. Eventually a full-scale war was prevented, but not before Congress cut off most U.S. military aid to Turkey.

In February 1976 Sisco retired from the State Department to assume the presidency of the American University in Washington, D.C.

[JAN]

For further information:
Jack Anderson, *The Anderson Papers* (New York, 1973).
Matti Golan, *The Secret Conversations of Henry Kissinger* (New York, 1976).
Marvin Kalb and Bernard Kalb, *Kissinger* (New York, 1974).
Roger Morris, *Uncertain Greatness* (New York, 1977).

SLOAN, HUGH, JR.
Treasurer, Committee to Re-Elect the President
February 1972-July 1972.

Hugh Sloan, the son of a vice president of the St. Regis Paper Co., graduated from the Hotchkiss School and Princeton Uni-

versity. After service in the Army he joined the Republican Congressional Campaign Committee. Sloan rose rapidly in the Committee structure, and in 1968 he assumed the post of finance director for the upcoming presidential campaign. After the election he became assistant to the President's appointments secretary, Dwight Chapin [*q.v.*]. In early 1971 Sloan joined the Committee to Re-Elect the President (CREEP) and in February 1972 was named its treasurer.

On March 30, 1972, at a meeting attended by Jeb Stuart Magruder [*q.v.*] and Frederick LaRue [*q.v.*], John Mitchell [*q.v.*] approved G. Gordon Liddy's [*q.v.*] "Gemstone Plan" for political spying. Two days later Magruder told Hugh Sloan that Liddy was authorized to draw up to $250,000 for his political intelligence project. Sloan, unsure of his responsibilities, asked Maurice Stans [*q.v.*], CREEP Finance Committee Chairman and Sloan's immediate superior, about the validity of Magruder's request. Stans checked with John Mitchell who told him that Sloan should make the payment to Liddy. When Sloan questioned Stans about the purpose of the payments, Stans told him, "I do not want to know about it and you do not want to know about it."

In the early days following the foiled break-in at the Democratic National Campaign headquarters in the Watergate, Sloan grew fearful that CREEP was violating the law with its cash disbursements. He reported his fears to John Ehrlichman [*q.v.*]. Nixon's adviser refused to investigate the matter. In June Sloan made his final report to Stans on the cash disbursements of the pre-April contributions. Eventually the money passed through various CREEP officials into the hands of the Watergate burglars as payment for their activities and as "support money" for their silence. On June 23, at Herbert Kalmbach's [*q.v.*] urging, Sloan destroyed the cash book used to prepare his report.

During July various officials connected with CREEP suggested Sloan commit perjury by reporting that he had given only a small amount of money to Liddy instead of the quarter million dollars actually authorized. When Sloan refused to take part in the cover-up, he was forced to resign. On July 20 he met with his lawyers and the prosecutors and told them the whole story of his involvement with CREEP, including the efforts by CREEP officials to silence him.

As the various Watergate trials and hearings progressed from 1973 to 1974, the money Sloan received and disbursed was traced to various sources and destinations. For instance the $199,000 Sloan gave Liddy came from an original fund that included $30,000 which Robert Vesco [q.v.] had given to Maurice Stans hoping to stave off a Securities and Exchange Commission investigation into his finances. The Liddy money also included $89,000 in illegal campaign contributions that had been "laundered" in Mexico. Sloan disbursed $50,000 to Alexander M. Lahler, Jr., of the Maryland Republican Party to inflate the proceeds from a Spiro Agnew [q.v.] dinner to make the event look more successful to the voting public and the media than it was. He also provided $10,000 for an anti-Wallace campaign in California that included a $1,200 payment to the Nazi Party for handing out Wallace leaflets.

Because of his cooperation with the prosecutors and with other investigative bodies and agents, no charges were brought against Hugh Sloan as a result of his activities at CREEP. Sloan, frustrated in his attempts to tell the President that something was wrong and under constant pressure to perjure himself, was the only key official at either CREEP or in the White House who refused to participate in the cover-up.

[SJT]

SMITH, C(ONRAD) ARNHOLT
b. 1899
Businessman

A high school dropout, Smith began his career as a grocery clerk and then became a bank clerk. In the postwar period, after his initial business successes, Smith emerged as a key figure in the Republican Party in San Diego and was an early supporter of Richard Nixon's political career. Smith was chairman of the San Diego County Republican Finance Committee during the 1950s and 1960s and was an important fundraiser in the Nixon campaign in 1968. During the same period he built up a financial empire including the U.S. National Bank of San Diego, the 87th largest commercial bank in the U.S., and Westgate, a large conglomerate controlling hotels, airlines, taxicab companies and the San Diego Padres, a professional baseball team. In 1970 Smith's enormous political and economic power attracted the attention of a San Diego underground newspaper, which published a series of exposes about his ties to Nixon and financial maneuvers involving his bank and Westgate. Almost immediately the paper became the target of firebombings, police infiltration and other harassment.

In March 1972 Life magazine published an article charging that the Nixon Administration had "seriously tampered with justice" in San Diego "in an effort to protect certain of its important friends." The article maintained that in 1970 a federal crime strike force had been investigating Smith and his colleagues "for conspiracy to violate federal tax laws and the Corrupt Practices Act" with an illegal $2,068 contribution to Nixon's 1968 election campaign. According to Life, U.S. Attorney Harry Steward, whom Nixon had appointed on Smith's recommendation, had ordered the team to halt the investigation and had pressured the Internal Revenue Service to drop its separate probe. The Life article further charged that Smith had personally intervened with Nixon on behalf of his financier friend John Alessio, who was under federal grand jury investigation for tax evasion. Smith denied these charges.

In May 1973 Smith's empire began to crumble. The Securities and Exchange Commission (SEC) accused Smith of defrauding the U.S. National Bank of San Diego and the Westgate Corp. Shortly thereafter The Washington Post reported that a $50,000 contribution by Smith to President Nixon's 1972 election campaign had been returned to him because the SEC, the Antitrust Division of the Justice Department and the Civil Aeronautics Board were investigating his financial activities. The SEC suit charged Smith and his associates with "systematically" appropriating assets of his bank and of Westgate for their own use while issuing false and misleading financial statements. Smith, under pressure from the pending suit, had resigned his bank chairmanship only days before.

On Aug. 3, 1973 the Internal Revenue Service filed tax liens for $22.8 million against Smith, the largest claim ever filed against an individual for a single tax year. The same day, apparently to put his financial affairs in order, Smith sold his 68% ownership of the San Diego Padres. On Oct. 18, 1973, it was announced that the U. S. National Bank of San Diego was being absorbed by the Crocker Bank of San Francisco in the largest bank liquidation in U.S. history. The Federal Deposit Insurance Corp. (FDIC) had to absorb $389.3 million in questionable loans, over half of the bank's portfolio. A week later Smith agreed to relinquish the chairmanship of the Westgate Corp. in an out-of-court settlement of the SEC's charges. Three stockholders of Smith's bank then filed a $120 million civil damage suit against him for acting "to unjustly enrich himself and entities controlled by him and his relatives."

The collapse of Smith's bank immediately became a national issue. James E. Smith, comptroller of the currency, was called to testify before a House subcommittee on why the bank's insolvency had not been noticed by the comptroller's examiners despite a *Wall Street Journal* article that had publicized the bank's questionable practices as early as 1969. Smith admitted to the subcommittee that he had attempted to prevent the SEC suit, but insisted he had done so to prevent a run on the bank and denied that the Nixon Administration had pressured him to give the bank any "special consideration."

In July 1974 Smith was indicted on criminal conspiracy charges for misapplying $170 million in bank funds and fraudulently obtaining loans for Westgate. The FDIC also filed a $158.8 million suit against Westgate. That December Smith was indicted on misdemeanor charges for making illegal contributions to Nixon's 1972 presidential campaign. He was convicted in March 1975. The following month he and his colleagues were named as defendants in 17 civil suits totaling $64 million that charged Smith with "systematically looting" Westgate. Smith pleaded no contest to felony charges of defrauding his bank of $27.5 million. He received the maximum two-year sentence, which was suspended, was placed on five years' probation and paid a $30,000 fine. Finally, in December 1975, he was arrested and indicted on 58 counts of grand theft, state income tax evasion, misapplication of bank funds, forgery and conspiracy to commit theft. He was released on bail.

Smith retired from most of his business and political activities in the late 1970s.

[LG]

SMITH, GERARD C(OAD)
b. May 4, 1914; New York, N.Y.
Director, U.S. Arms Control and Disarmament Agency, January 1969–January 1973.

Smith received his B.A. from Yale in 1935 and earned his law degree there in 1938. He served with the Navy during World War II, and, after working for various law firms, joined the Atomic Energy Commission in 1950. During the Kennedy and Johnson Administrations he served as counsel to the Washington Center for Foreign Policy Research. In 1969 President Nixon appointed Smith director of the U.S. Arms Control and Disarmament Agency, making him the chief U.S. delegate to all international disarmament conferences, including the Strategic Arms Limitation Talks (SALT) with the Soviet Union.

Smith advocated approaching the talks from a position of strength. During November 1969 he testified before Congress in support of the Administration's proposed Safeguard anti-ballistic missile (ABM) system. He argued that not only would the system be a valuable "bargaining chip" in the talks but that since the Russians capability for a surprise attack would be reduced, the ABM would also be "an incentive for a responsible Soviet weapons policy." Before the Senate vote on the ABM in 1970, Smith reportedly convinced several key senators with these arguments, resulting in congressional approval of the system.

When the SALT formally opened in Vienna in April 1970, several main issues separated the two powers. First the U.S. sought a comprehensive agreement limiting all forms of offensive and defensive nuclear weaponry, including missile-launching submarines; whereas the Soviets wanted to limit the treaty to defensive arms. The U.S. demanded on-site inspection, which the Soviet Union refused to consider. Finally the Soviet Union claimed that the U.S. sought an unfair advantage by refusing to regard as "strategic," and therefore subject to negotiation, the 500 fighter bombers based in Western Europe and at sea. The U.S. replied that the bombers were needed to defend Europe against the Soviets' 700 intermediate-range missiles.

The first breakthrough came in early 1971 when the Administration, upon learning that the Soviets would consider limiting their ABM system, dropped its demand for on-site inspections. The major deadlock was broken in May, however, when Nixon announced an agreement to work on limiting the ABM systems. This agreement relieved the delegates temporarily of the need to consider the more difficult questions involving intercontinental ballistic missiles and missiles delivered by bombers and submarines, and paved the way for the separate accords that followed.

As Smith brought SALT closer to an agreement, President Nixon flew to Moscow to complete the negotiations and on May 23, 1972 signed the treaties that for the first time put limits on strategic weapons. The first defensive treaty limited each nation to two ABM systems: one centered around its capital, the other to guard part of its offensive missile force. No site could contain more than 100 interceptor missiles, and radar complexes would be limited. Violations would be monitored by surveillance satellites that would not be interfered with. The treaty was of unlimited duration. The second treaty, an interim five-year agreement, forbade any new construction of either land-based or submarine-launched offensive ballistic missiles. It specified the numbers of each type missile to be held by each nation. The treaty left the Soviets with about three times the megatonnage of the U.S. but allowed the U.S. about three times as many warheads.

During the summer Smith worked to get congressional support for the agreements. He stated that the treaties were evidence of cooperation between the two nations but warned that strategic forces must be maintained to deter attack. He supported the development of the nuclear submarine Trident and the B-1 bomber as "bargaining chips" in further talks. Congress approved the treaties in August and September.

As SALT I progressed, Smith had also been involved in other areas of arms negotiations with the Russians. In 1971 the two nations concluded the Seabed Arms Control Treaty and the Nuclear Accident Agreement. The first prohibited the installation of nuclear weapons at sea outside the 12-mile limit, and the second established cooperative procedures in the event of a nuclear mishap. Meanwhile in separate negotiations both nations agreed to ban biological agents in warfare, but the U.S. would not accede to a Soviet proposal to prohibit chemical agents, saying that their use was primarily tactical, not strategic, and that problems of surveillance made controls impossible to enforce.

In early 1973 Smith resigned his post, having won wide praise as an able negotiator possessing a special rapport with the Russians. He returned to private law practice, and headed the Trilateral Commission. He later served as ambassador-at-large for President Carter [q.v.].

[FLM]

SMITH, JAMES E.
b. Sept. 29, 1930; Aberdeen, S.D.
Comptroller of the Currency, June 1973–July 1976.

James E. Smith presided over the U.S. government's surveillance of the nation's credit system during the most difficult years experienced by American banks since the Great Depression. Smith had been recruited from the business world by the Nixon Administration, through its first Secretary of the Treasury, David Kennedy [q.v.], to serve as deputy undersecretary of the Treasury for legislation. Smith gave up that post to become Comptroller of the Currency in June 1973.

Smith was immediately pulled into the atmosphere of scandal surrounding the Nixon Administration and its ties to various banking groups. In October 1973 he was called before the House Banking and Currency Committee, headed by Rep. Wright Patman (D, Tex.) [q.v.], to explain his rejection of an application for a national bank charter from a group wishing to compete with a Key Biscayne, Fla., bank headed by Charles G. ("Bebe") Rebozo [q.v.], a personal friend of President Nixon. The lawyers for Rebozo's bank, the sole bank on the island, had argued that there was insufficient loan demand to justify a second bank, although a bank examiner's report had stated that Rebozo's bank was so conservative with loans that it barely qualified as a bank. After Smith's decision, the White House issued a statement asserting that "there was no White House involvement whatsoever" in the affair.

In November 1973 after the collapse of the U.S. National Bank of San Diego, headed by Nixon-backer C. Arnholt Smith [q.v.], Smith was again called before the Patman Committee. Although the *Wall Street Journal* had publicized ques-

tionable practices by the San Diego bank as early as April 1969, Smith claimed that his office had discovered no problems until much later. Smith told the Patman Committee that in spite of "25 separate transactions which might violate" the U.S. criminal code, he had tried to prevent the Securities and Exchange Commission (SEC) from bringing a fraud suit against C. Arnholt Smith because he feared a run on the bank. Smith also denied that he had been pressured in any way by the Administration in the affair.

Smith's next embroilment came with the Franklin National bankruptcy of 1974. Smith's position in the affair was particularly delicate because of his ties to former Treasury Secretary Kennedy, who was a financial adviser to Italian financier Michele Sindona, the major shareholder in Franklin National's parent company. When Franklin National's pending insolvency became apparent in the first two quarters of 1974, Smith announced that the bank was still solvent. Behind the scenes, however, Smith was involved in a joint investigation of Franklin National conducted by the Federal Reserve Bank, the SEC and Smith's office of the Comptroller of the Currency.

The investigation revealed that Franklin National had suffered foreign exchange losses of over $45 million in early 1974. In late May the *Wall Street Journal* revealed that 11 New York banks were involved in a rescue operation for Franklin National, and Smith told the public that the banks had been asked to submit plans for a possible merger. In early October Smith announced the insolvency of Franklin National and the absorption of its assets by the European-American Bank.

In January 1975 Smith announced yet another bank failure, that of Security National Bank of Long Island. While, as in the cases of the U.S. National Bank of San Diego and Franklin National, the failed bank's assets were immediately absorbed by a larger, financially sound bank, Smith had to admit that the 1974–75 recession was undermining the solvency of the nation's financial institutions. He conceded that the Comptroller's list of "problem banks" had lengthened considerably in 1974 and included "a few" banks with multibillion dollar assets. In August 1975 Smith announced the establishment of a national bank surveillance system designed to detect financial problems in advance and to prevent failure. A month later, in the midst of the New York City fiscal crisis, Smith warned that a default by the city would jeopardize 10–15 major New York City banks.

Worry over the U.S. financial system increased in January 1976 when the Comptroller of the Currency's problem bank list was leaked to the press. The list included both Citibank and Chase Manhattan, the second and third largest U.S. commercial banks. Although Smith "emphatically and unequivocally" defended the solvency of the two banks, he admitted his office was watching them closely. He went on to attack the press for sensationalizing "the well-known fact that loan losses in this nation's largest banks for the years 1974 and 1975 have been above historical norms." He added that the "real news" was that Chase and Citibank had weathered the 1974–75 crisis as well as they had.

Immediately after the disclosure of the list, Sen. William Proxmire (D, Wisc.) [q.v.], chairman of the Senate Banking Committee, subpoenaed Smith and reprimanded him for his "failure to do a vigorous job on bank regulation." In his Feb. 6 testimony, Smith told the Committee that the 1974–75 recession was to blame for the deterioration in bank liquidity. Proxmire rebuked Smith for allowing critical liquidity ratios to deteriorate during his period in office. A week later Smith announced the insolvency of the Hamilton National Bank of Chattanooga, the 195th largest commercial bank in the U.S., but he claimed that his office had foreseen weakness in this case as early as December 1974.

On Feb. 17 Proxmire again criticized Smith for his "laxity" in permitting bank mergers. Mentioning the Comptroller's "lush" Washington offices, Proxmire said Smith had earned the title of "King Fa-

rouk of the Potomac." In March 1976 Smith rejected a proposal allowing a House subcommittee to conduct a detailed study of the Comptroller of the Currency's regulation procedures.

Smith resigned in July 1976 and returned to his private business career.

[LG]

SMITH, MARGARET CHASE
b. Dec. 14, 1898; Skowhegan, Me.
Republican Senator, Me., 1949–73.

After graduating from Skowhegan High School and working for the telephone company, the local county newspaper and as treasurer of the New England Waste Process Co., Margaret Chase married Clyde Smith in May 1930. She was soon absorbed into politics as her husband climbed the ladder to eventually become a liberal Republican Representative in the U.S. House following the 1936 election. He died in 1940 and his widow won a special election in September for his seat from the predominantly industrial district. Smith was subsequently to sit on the Naval Affairs Committee, the first woman ever to do so. Her tenure in the House continued until 1948, when she was elected to the Senate. Two years later Smith made a highly publicized speech condemning Sen. Joseph R. McCarthy for turning the Senate into a "forum of hate." In 1964 she ran for the Republican nomination for President on a low budget and fared poorly. She was deemed the fifth most popular woman in America in a 1966 Gallup poll, the same year that she was appointed chairman of the Senate Republican Conference. [See TRUMAN, EISENHOWER, KENNEDY, JOHNSON Volumes]

During the Nixon Administration, Smith oversaw appropriations with Sen. John Stennis [q.v.] while they both served on the Defense Subcommittee of the Armed Services Committee. She ultimately became the ranking Republican member of the full Committee. Generally a proponent of Nixon's Vietnam war policies she voted against both the Cooper-Church Amendment and the more stringent McGovern-Hatfield Amendment, both attempting to fix deadlines for U.S. withdrawal from Indochina. Liberals were particularly angry at her in 1969 when she at first proposed several unsuccessful amendments to block all research and development as well as deployment funds for the Safeguard anti-ballistic missile system and then voted against the losing compromise effort, the Cooper-Hart measure, that would have allowed only research and development.

Prior to floor action, Smith would frequently withhold announcement of her voting intentions. When the nomination of G. Harrold Carswell [q.v.] to the Supreme Court was before the Senate, she publicly became furious with White House lobbyist Bryce Harlow [q.v.] for tipping off a wavering senator about her as yet unsolidified decision. She wound up voting against Carswell. Earlier she had also voted against the Supreme Court nomination of Clement Haynsworth [q.v.]. She was an early advocate of the Equal Rights Amendment, but, although the only woman in the Senate from 1967 to 1972, she never considered herself a feminist.

Although she received a 70% approval rating by the Americans for Conservative Action on her 1971 voting record, Smith generally defied easy political labeling. She voted against federal aid to big business when such issues as funding for the SST and the loan to the Lockhead Aircraft Corp. came before the Senate. She opposed busing legislation to achieve racial integration of schools and the Philadelphia Plan to integrate the construction trades, but voted for the urban-oriented Hugh Scott [q.v.] over the conservative Roman Hruska [q.v.] for the job of Senate minority whip in January 1969.

In a major address before the Senate in June 1970, which was later expanded into a book entitled A Declaration of Conscience, the Maine Senator attempted to give a clearer conception of her concerns. She contrasted her fears of repression engendered by Sen. Joseph McCarthy in

1950 with the politically charged climate existing in 1970. "We had a national sickness then from which we recovered," she said. "We have a national sickness now. . . . It is a national feeling of fear and frustration that could result in national suicide. . . ." She warned Americans that "the excessiveness of overreactions on both sides is a clear and present danger to American democracy. That danger is ultimately from the political right, even though it is initially spawned by the anti-democratic arrogance and nihilism from the political left . . . repression is preferable to anarchy and nihilism to most Americans."

In her 1972 reelection bid at age 74, Smith was considered at a disadvantage because of the heart attack suffered by her administrative assistant of 23 years, William C. Lewis, who had been the master strategist of her previous campaigns. She managed to beat a wealthy primary opponent but was upset in the November election by Rep. William Hathaway. She retired to her hometown of Skowhegan in January 1973.

[GB]

SONNENFELDT, HELMUT
b. Sept. 13, 1926: Berlin, Germany.
National Security Council Assistant,
January 1969-December 1973;
Counselor to the Department of State,
December 1973-February 1977.

The son of German-Jewish physicians who fled Nazi Germany, Helmut Sonnenfeldt was educated in England and at Johns Hopkins University. While serving in the U.S. Army during World War II, Sonnenfeldt was stationed briefly in Germany, where he met a fellow refugee from Hitler, Sgt. Henry A. Kissinger [q.v.]. Following the war Sonnenfeldt returned to Johns Hopkins, earning an M.A. in political science in 1951.

Sonnenfeldt joined the State Department in 1952. Assigned to the office of research and analysis, he quickly won recognition as a political analyst. After working briefly on disarmament negotiations, Sonnenfeldt was appointed to the international political activities division in 1961, becoming its director in 1966. In April 1967 Sonnenfeldt was appointed to the office of research analysis for the Soviet bloc, where he headed Soviet and East European research.

Although Sonnenfeldt had developed a reputation as a hard-liner on Soviet affairs, he became the object of intense suspicion by certain State Department security officers, notably Otto F. Otepka, the Department's chief security evaluator. Allegations by Otepka and others that Sonnenfeldt had leaked classified information to the press and to foreign diplomats led to surveillance and, in late 1960, to sharp interrogation. Sonnenfeldt was eventually cleared, but the taint lingered, and he remained under surveillance for much of his career in the State Department.

When Henry Kissinger was appointed special assistant for national security affairs to President Nixon in January 1969, Sonnenfeldt was the first aide he recruited. Sonnenfeldt ranked among the most experienced experts on Soviet affairs in the government. A close personal friend of Kissinger's, Sonnenfeldt shared similar political views and personality traits with his boss. He staunchly defended Kissinger's policy of detente with the Soviet Union and accompanied Kissinger on his trips to Moscow, where he was on friendly terms with Soviet leader Leonid Brezhnev. Although recognized by his colleagues as a brilliant analyst, Sonnenfeldt developed a reputation as being "difficult to work with" and a harsh and "often irascible" taskmaster. According to one colleague in 1973, "Henry can't live with Hal—nor can he live without him."

In April 1973 the Nixon Administration nominated Sonnenfeldt to become undersecretary of the treasury. Treasury Secretary George P. Shultz [q.v.] wanted Sonnenfeldt as his aide to supervise the growing U.S.-Soviet trade and to provide the Treasury Department with political advice and a link to the National Security Council. But Sonnenfeldt's reputation as a "security risk" and persistent charges that he had leaked classified documents held up the appointment for eight months. Eventually Sonnenfeldt's nomination to the Treasury was withdrawn on Dec. 19, 1973. The same day he was confirmed as counselor to the State Department and returned to work for his old boss Kissinger.

In April 1976 Sonnenfeldt became the center of a controversy over the Ford Administration's conduct of detente. Republican presidential contender Ronald Reagan [q.v.] charged in a television address that Sonnenfeldt had proposed that "in effect, captive nations should give up any claims to national sovereignty" and "simply become a part of the Soviet Union." Reagan was upset over press accounts of an off-the-record lecture Sonnenfeldt gave in December 1975 in London to European-based U.S. ambassadors. At the same meeting Kissinger had said that the U.S. favored maintaining a position of stability with the Soviet Union, "one that would exclude Communists from power in Western Europe but would also acknowledge Moscow's influence in Eastern Europe, Yugoslavia excepted." Sonnenfeldt warned against any Soviet satellite's attempt to break free of Moscow's influence, stressing not only the dubious chances of success but the possible consequences of international repercussions. Reagan claimed that this amounted to a U.S. underwriting of Soviet dominion in Eastern Europe and that it undercut East European nationalism.

According to The Washington Post, however, "the official version of the Sonnenfeldt statement suggested that the U.S. had not abandoned its efforts to influence events in the Soviet sphere." Referring to the 1,000-word text of the speech, which appeared in the London Economist, the Post suggested that Sonnenfeldt had actually argued for a more realistic interpretation of the situation in Eastern Europe. Although the USSR was becoming a global superpower, Sonnenfeldt noted, the U.S. could affect the way in which its power was developed and used by drawing it into a series of dependencies and ties with the West. Both Kissinger and Sonnenfeldt believed it more important to exclude Communists from power in Western Europe than to encourage nationalists in the satellite nations, particularly in light of the limits of the West's military forces during past uprisings. But Reagan's speech put President Ford on the defensive, opening the way to Reagan victories in North Carolina and Texas and forcing a public reappraisal by Ford of detente.

Sonnenfeldt retired from the State Department in 1977. He taught international relations at Johns Hopkins and joined the Rand Corporation in 1978.

[JAN]

For further information:
Roger Morris, *Uncertain Greatness* (New York, 1977).

SPOCK, BENJAMIN (McLAINE)
b. May 2, 1903; New Haven, Conn.
Anti-war activist.

Spock studied medicine at Yale and Columbia, where he obtained an M.D. in 1929, specializing in pediatrics and psychiatry. He practiced in New York and in 1946 wrote *The Common Sense Book of Baby and Child Care*, which by 1969 was the all-time best-seller by an American author. From 1947 to 1967 he taught psychiatry and child development alternately at the University of Minnesota and the Mayo Clinic, the University of Pittsburgh, and Case Western Reserve University. During the 1960s Spock, a liberal Democrat, became politically involved as a result of his concern about the dangers of nuclear weapons and later the Vietnam war. In 1963 be became cochairman of the National Committee for a Sane Nuclear Policy (SANE).

During the Johnson Administration Spock was an ubiquitous figure at anti-war demonstrations. He resigned his cochairmanship of SANE after the group refused to back the April 1967 anti-war protests. In 1968 Spock was convicted of

violations of the Selective Service Act, but his conviction was later overturned on appeal. [See JOHNSON Volume]

After his acquittal, Spock continued his crusade for peace. In November he participated in a Washington, D.C. anti-war demonstration of over 250,000 people, sponsored by the New Mobilization Committee, which Spock and others had created on July 4, 1969. Speaking for the group after the invasion of Cambodia in May 1970, Spock told a news conference that "the government is committing titanic violence in Vietnam and Cambodia." He further stated, "We must stand up in opposition to the government's illegal, immoral and brutal war." He was arrested May 3 during a rally near the White House sponsored by the Fellowship of Reconciliation and other religious groups. Spock was on a list of 65 radical college campus speakers prepared by the House Internal Security Committee in 1970. Nevertheless, he continued undaunted in his anti-war activities, often cooperating with radical groups whose views on personal morality and social and economic reform were far more extreme than his own. Spock was among some 7,000 demonstrators arrested in May 1971 during an anti-war protest in Washington. The People's Coalition for Peace and Justice provided the impetus behind the demonstrations, which were aimed at closing down the capital by means of traffic obstructions. On Nov. 27, 1971, a new left-wing anti-war movement, the People's Party, nominated Spock as its stand-in candidate for President. The Party hoped to attract a nationally prestigious political leader as its standard bearer should the Democrats fail to nominate a progressive, anti-war candidate in 1972. Although he did not support its more extremist views, Spock played a leading, if only titular, role in the Party's creation, focusing attention on domestic social and economic injustice as well as the persisting war in Vietnam.

Spock was officially selected the People's Party presidential nominee on July 29, 1972, at its National Convention in St. Louis. The Party platform stood for immediate withdrawal of all American troops abroad (not only in Vietnam); free medical care for all; tax reforms to eliminate loopholes for the rich; the legalization of marijuana; equal rights for women and homosexuals; legalized abortion on demand; and a guaranteed annual income of $6,500 for a family of four. Spock's name was on the ballot in only 10 states. He received 78,801 votes.

Following his defeat in the election, Spock continued to participate in left-wing causes. In 1975 he became a member of the Bertrand Russell Tribunal, a 25-member leftist organization that met to condemn violations of human rights in Latin America and Vietnam.

[AES]

For further information:
Lynn Z. Bloom, *Doctor Spock: Biography of a Conservative Radical* (Indianapolis and New York, 1972).

STAGGERS, HARLEY
b. Aug. 3, 1907; Keyser, W.Va.
Democratic Representative, W.Va., 1949–.

Staggers was born in Mineral County, W.Va., in the mountainous, rural, coal-mining district he later represented in Congress. He graduated from a small Methodist college in 1931, did some graduate work at Duke University and held a variety of jobs, including Mineral County sheriff, before serving as a Navy Air Corps navigator during World War II. Staggers first won election to the U.S. House in 1948. A liberal who voted with his Party, favoring labor legislation and federal spending for social welfare and education, he became in 1955 assistant to Majority Whip John McCormack (D, Mass.) [q.v.].

In the 1960s Staggers was considered a steadfast Kennedy and Johnson supporter. Assuming chairmanship of the powerful Commerce Committee in 1966, he sponsored important Johnson Administration health legislation, including the Comprehensive Health Planning Act and the partnership for health bill. Staggers also played a key role in the passage of President Johnson's 1966 Traffic Safety Act to establish federal safety standards for highway vehicles and sponsored the Administration bill to end the 1967 railroad strike. [See JOHNSON Volume]

During the Nixon Administration, Stagger's voting record became increasingly conservative. A staunch supporter of both the Johnson and Nixon Administration Vietnam policies, he voted against four 1971 proposals that would have set deadlines for cutting off or restricting funds for the war. He defended the Department of Defense budget and Administration defense programs, including the anti-ballistic missile program (ABM), the B-1 bomber project and increased funding for military research. Staggers did, however, support a 1971 plan to place a 30-day limit on the President's authority to induct draftees except in case of imminent attack on the U.S. This proposal, designed to guard against future involvement in undeclared wars, was defeated 96–278.

Staggers served as chairman not only of the Commerce Committee, but also of its Special Subcommittee on Investigations, charged with examining the rule-making and enforcement activities of the many regulatory commissions under the Commerce Committee's jurisdiction. With few well-developed legislative ideas and a distaste for involving himself in controversy, Staggers was not known as a strong leader. A constituency-oriented Representative who spent over 100 days each year in his district, Staggers lacked the national policy-making vision demanded of a powerful committee chairman. He often obstructed progressive consumer and environmental legislation and spent much subcommittee time investigating individual cases.

Although Stagger's subcommittee investigated T.V. news-programming practices in 1971, he chose not to propose legislation based on well-documented evidence of broadcast deception. Instead, he focused on one controversial CBS documentary, "The Selling of the Pentagon."

Seeking to examine CBS editing procedures, Staggers subpoenaed outtakes from the program. When network President Dr. Frank Stanton refused to submit the film footage on the basis of CBS's right to freedom of the press, Staggers attempted to cite Stanton for contempt of Congress. In an unprecedented repudiation of a committee chairman, the House voted 226–181 to send the citation back to committee, effectively defeating it.

The Subcommittee on Investigations again made headlines in March 1973 when Staggers made public a confidential Securities and Exchange Commission report revealing how International Telephone and Telegraph (ITT) had pressured the Nixon Administration to dismiss an anti-trust suit against them. The report implicated key Administration figures. Unable to resolve the matter, Staggers referred the ITT hearings record to the Justice Department, stating that it indicated "violations of law, including obstruction of justice and perjury."

Other matters taken up by the Subcommittee on Investigations included railroad services, aviation safety programs, drug abuse in organized sports and enforcement of Federal Power Commission safety practices. With a record of only 15 days of public hearings during the 92nd Congress, the subcommittee's activity did not serve as an effective check on the agencies under its jurisdiction. Despite his seniority Staggers was ousted in 1975 as chairman of the Special Investigations Subcommittee and replaced by the more dynamic Rep. John E. Mess (D, Calif.).

Staggers was responsible in 1974 for drafting an emergency energy bill governing oil price reductions and gas rationing and providing for congressional veto of President Nixon's energy conservation proposals. Less comprehensive than the Administration measure, the bill's provisions were passed separately by the House in February. During the 94th Congress, Staggers supported President Gerald R. Ford on only 35% of the roll call votes for which the President had announced a position. Staggers remained popular in his district through the 1970s, consistently winning reelection with more that 60% of the vote.

[DAE]

STANS, MAURICE H(UBERT)
b. March 22, 1908; Shakopee, Minn.
U.S. Secretary of Commerce, January 1969-January 1972; Chairman, Finance Committee to Re-Elect the President, 1972-73.

The son of an immigrant Belgian house painter and musician, Stans studied business administration at Northwestern University and worked as a stenographer. In 1928 he joined the small accounting firm of Alexander Grant & Co. as an office boy. In three years he was a partner and in 1938 he became managing and executive partner. By 1955 he had made Alexander Grant the tenth largest accounting firm in the country. In 1957 he became deputy director of the Bureau of the Budget and 1958 bureau chief. A fiscal conservative, Stans achieved a balanced federal budget (in fiscal 1960). He opposed public works programs as an antidote for the recession and was particularly critical of the spending habits of the Democratic Congress.

Stans returned to the business world as an investment banker at the end of the Eisenhower Administration, but remained close to politics. He wrote a syndicated column during 1961-62 and put his considerable skills as a fund raiser to use by serving as Richard Nixon's finance chairman for the 1962 California gubernatorial campaign. He was chairman of the Nixon Finance Committee and the Republican National Finance Committee in 1968, raising an impressive $34 million for the presidential campaign.

In January 1969 Stans became Nixon's Secretary of Commerce. Commerce had been an uninfluential post since Herbert Hoover's time, and, despite Stans's predictions of a "business-oriented" administration, he could not reverse the trend which had put Commerce's old functions into the hands of the State Department and the Council of Economic Advisers.

The Secretary traveled widely in an effort to improve the nation's trade deficit. His November 1971 trip to Moscow was a notable success and an important ingredient in Nixon's pursuit of detente. However, Stans's diplomatic gaffes elsewhere irritated the State Department and damaged his goal of securing trade concessions for American business. In May 1969 his table-pounding demands for voluntary restrictions on Japanese textile exports to the U.S. only alienated his Tokyo hosts. His effusive praise of the Greek government for its "attitude toward American investment" on a May 1971 visit to Athens went beyond the bounds of protocol and irritated the State Department, which had pointedly refrained from warm endorsements of the regime.

Stans maintained extremely poor relations with American black leaders. His minority small business program aimed to give "minority people a chance to become a capitalist, an employer, to become a success . . ." Yet, the Stans program, like the Administration's general approach to social issues, was distrusted by minority spokespersons. Although Nixon and Stans had projected in 1969 that there would be 100 Minority Enterprise Small Business Investment Corporations in operation by June 1970, in fact there were only 39 as of October 1971. The Secretary's unpopularity among minorities was underscored at a July 1971 NAACP meeting which greeted him with jeers.

Stans's view that the Secretary should be the advocate of business made him one of the most conservative members of the Nixon cabinet. He opposed no-fault auto insurance, product safety standards and the lifting of oil import quotas. He was able to replace a consumer protection bill backed by Attorney General John Mitchell [q.v.] with one which made it more difficult for consumers to collect in class-action suits. In July 1971 he urged the nation to "wait a minute" before banning DDT, removing phosphates from detergents, making offshore oil drilling "too difficult" and enforcing air pollution

standards without regard for economic considerations.

In January 1972 Stans resigned to become finance chairman of the Committee to Re-Elect the President (CREEP). He worked closely with Herbert Kalmbach [q.v.], the President's lawyer, whom he had taught the fine points of political fund-raising in 1968. Because the new Federal Election Campaign Act requiring extensive financial disclosures by candidates was scheduled to go into effect April 7, Stans openly encouraged big contributors who wanted to remain anonymous to act before the deadline. He recommended that big donations be parceled out in $3-4,000 blocks to "dummy" committees (they were to be abolished by the new law) in Washington and suggested that businessmen donate 1% of their profits to the President's campaign treasury. It was later learned that many anonymous contributions were "laundered" in Mexican banks. Stans's forceful, if unorthodox, money raising techniques brought in over $10 million by April 7.

The Watergate burglary occurred in June 1972. Stans was almost immediately implicated in the subsequent investigations. In July the Office of Federal Elections, a division of the General Accounting Office (GAO), charged that Stans had failed to keep adequate books on money kept in a safe in CREEP's New York headquarters, part of which was found in the possession of Watergate suspect Bernard R. Barker. The GAO believed that a total of $350,000 derived from anonymous contributions made after April 7 was kept unaccounted for so that it could be used for "wild card" purposes. Stans told the media that "none of this has anything to do with me," but in August he pointed to G. Gordon Liddy [q.v.], campaign finance counsel, as the last man to handle the check that appeared in Barker's accounts. Stans challenged the GAO report and recommended that in fairness the GAO should investigate the Democrats. In the same manner, when the Democrats in September sought to include him in their civil action suit against the burglars, Stans responded with a personal suit against former Democratic National Chairman Lawrence O'Brien [q.v.] for having "falsely and maliciously" accused him of "a number of criminal acts." Throughout the end of 1972 and all of 1973 reports and charges appeared suggesting that Stans had wrangled large contributions from companies and individuals in exchange for political favors.

Stans was soon involved in a number of lawsuits, the most important of which was a New York grand jury indictment handed down in May 1973. Stans, Mitchell, who had been Nixon's campaign manager, and Harry Sears, a New Jersey politician and associate of financier Robert Vesco [q.v.], were charged with perjury (in their grand jury testimony), conspiracy to defraud the United States and obstruction of justice. The next month Stans was summoned to appear before the Senate Watergate Committee. He sought to avoid testifying on the grounds it would prejudice his upcoming trial (it was later learned that the President wanted to prevent him from giving testimony), but failed. As he had said in public before, he told the Committee that he knew nothing about Watergate or any "dirty tricks" operations and was only concerned in collecting "enough money to pay the bills." He noted the CREEP's finance committee was separate from the campaign committee, but indicated that he was aware that G. Gordon Liddy handled money for unspecified purposes for which "Jeb" Stuart Magruder [q.v.] gave authorization.

Stans and Mitchell were the first Cabinet members in fifty years to be formally accused of criminal acts. Sears, who had been indicted with them, was tried separately since he had agreed to testify against Mitchell and Stans. The prosecution's case asserted that Robert Vesco had made a $200,000 cash contribution to the campaign in exchange for Mitchell's help in stopping a Securities and Exchange Commission (SEC) investigation into the financier's business affairs. Besides Sears, John W. Dean III [q.v.], former SEC chairman G. Bradford Cook [q.v.], and Laurence Richardson, another Vesco associate, testified for the prosecution. It was alleged that, when in March 1972 Vesco offered $500,000 to the campaign, Stans said that half that amount would suffice. He supposedly added that it must be delivered before April 7, $200,000 of it in $100 bills. The cash was delivered April 10 and put into Stans's safe to be used for CREEP's espionage activities. Mitchell then secured a meeting for Vesco with then Securities and Exchange Commission Chairman William Casey. The indictment also charged Stans with later seeking SEC general counsel Cook's aid in covering up the Vesco affair, promising to put in a "good word" for Cook (Cook in fact became SEC chairman in February 1974). Cook claimed that it was Stans who persuaded him to perjure himself in grand jury testimony the previous year.

Despite the charges, the evidence was not clear-cut. Stans was helped by the testimony of Edward Nixon, the President's brother and a friend of Vesco's, who stated that, when he relayed Vesco's request to make an anonymous contribution to Stans, the finance chairman acted annoyed but informed him that it ought to be in cash. Another point in Stans's favor was the uncontested statement that he rejected a larger offer from Vesco because he could not guarantee privacy to the donor. And, since the SEC investigation was not stopped, it was difficult to ascertain whether Stans and Mitchell actually tried to use their considerable influence in Vesco's favor. On April 28, 1974 Stans and Mitchell were acquitted. The most important factor in the defendants' favor, according to the jurors, was the lack of credibility of the prosecution witnesses, especially John Dean and Cook, who had already admitted perjuring himself.

While the trial was in progress, the Senate Watergate Committee was investigating Stans's role in the handling of payments from the dairy lobby. Corporate representatives testified that Stans and other campaign officials had extorted large contributions from them. Other violations of campaign finance laws were being investigated, including the promise of federal jobs and diplomatic posts to big contributors.

The investigations resulted in another trial. In March 1975 Stans pleaded guilty to five misdemeanor charges of violating election fund-raising laws in Washington Federal Court. The charges included three counts of failing to properly report on the handling of $150,000 in contributions and two counts of receiving $70,000 in illegal corporate contributions. A prosecution document filed with the court also said that Stans gave $81,000 to Frederick C. LaRue [q.v.], the campaign official who handled "hush money." Stans's conviction for misdemeanors instead of felonies implied that he had broken the law unwittingly. The misdemeanor charge was the result of a plea bargaining arrangement with the Watergate special prosecutor. In May Stans received his sentence: a $5000 fine.

In January 1976 the American Institute of Certified Public Accountants trial board found Stans not guilty of bringing discredit to the accounting profession.

[JCH]

STEIN, HERBERT
b. Aug. 27, 1916; Detroit, Mich.
Member, Council of Economic
Advisers, 1969-74; Chairman,
1972-74.

Stein received his bachelor's degree from Williams College in 1935 and immediately entered professional life as an economist. Between 1935 and 1948 he worked for the Federal Deposit Insurance Corp., the National Defense Advisory Commission, the Wages and Price Board and the Office of War Mobilization and Conversion. In 1945 Stein also began work for the Committee for Economic Development (CDE), a private research group sponsored by heads of large business organizations. At the CED Stein rose to the position of director of research, a job he held from 1956. He obtained a Ph.D. in economics from the University

of Chicago in 1958. Stein was an economic adviser to the presidential campaign of Republican Barry Goldwater [q.v.] in 1964. In 1966 he went to the Brookings Institution, a Washington "think tank" for analyzing policy issues. He remained at Brookings until President Nixon invited him to join his Council of Economic Advisers (CEA) immediately after the November 1968 election.

Stein, with fellow University of Chicago economist Paul McCracken [q.v.], Nixon's first CEA chairman, felt that the 4% inflation rate posted by the U.S. economy in 1968 was far too high and that it could be halted without precipitating a recession. The essential strategy they recommend to the Administration was a tightening of credit and a subsequent slowing of growth of the U.S. money supply, aimed at bringing the total money in circulation into harmony with total production. In February 1969 Stein, with CEA colleagues McCracken and Hendrik Houthakker, predicted a "slowdown" in U.S. growth rates but denied that it would be accompanied by a serious rise in unemployment.

Stein was also appointed to head up a study of the reconversion problems facing the U.S. economy after the end of hostilities in Vietnam. Stein's earlier experience studying the same problems after World War II and the Korean war made him the obvious choice for the project. When the study appeared in August 1969, its conclusions were not heartening. It argued that the Johnson Administration had gravely overestimated the funds that an end to the war would free for social programs.

Throughout 1969 the rapid rise of U.S. interest rates, carried out under Federal Reserve Chairman William McChesney Martin [q.v.], brought monetary growth to a virtual halt. From June to December 1969 the U.S. money supply expanded by 0.6%, in keeping with the "cold turkey" policies recommended by Stein, McCracken and other CEA economists. Real production turned downward in November 1969, but in early 1970 inflation was recorded at an annual rate of 6%. Stein and other Administration economists found themselves confronted with the new phenomenon of "stagflation," or simultaneous inflation and economic contraction, for which neither their monetarist views nor Keynesian theory had any explanation. Many commentators saw these trends as definitive empirical refutation of Stein's theory. But Stein in June 1970 told the Joint Economic Committee (JEC) of Congress that the U.S. economy would have to "go through a period of slack" to cure inflation. While not denying the reality of falling output, rising prices, the 350-point fall in the Dow Jones average since Nixon had taken office, and the corporate liquidity crunch of May-June 1970, Stein deflected criticism from the Administration's economic policy and asserted that "we are running below the path . . . we would have chosen," warning against any attempt to "pump up the economy" as Keynesian theory prescribed. In September 1970 when the August Consumer Price Index rise was reported at only .2% (or a 2.4% annual rate), Stein cited this as evidence that the Administration strategy was working.

Stein was an important economic spokesman for the Administration. In October 1970 he told critics in London who questioned the efficacy of the U.S. government's anti-inflation moves that the Nixon Administration was not merely using monetary and fiscal techniques, but also manpower programs, direct intervention in collective bargaining (as in the case of construction worker contracts) and a newly established Productivity Committee to improve the performance of the U.S. economy. Stein admitted that reducing U.S. unemployment from its level of 6%—compared to 3.2% when Nixon took office—by 1972 would require a 6% increase in real production, and predicted a 3% inflation rate for that year.

Another issue that weighted on the Nixon Administration in the 1969-71 recession was a wide spectrum of opinion favoring wage-price controls. Stein, a convinced free-market theorist, was strongly opposed to such measures. Late in 1970 he told a meeting of the California Bankers' Association that inflation would slow if wage increases were limited to 8% and hinted that wage-price controls might be used in an emergency. The Administration, Stein said, was against controls, but "it would be unfortunate to allow ideological purity to stand in the way of our real objectives." Stein asserted that the use of budgetary and monetary measures would be the main tools of the Administration's attempts to reach full employment by mid-1972.

By early 1971 it was clear that the Stein-McCracken strategy for the U.S. economy was a failure. The economy had registered virtual zero growth in real terms in 1970, inflation continued and unemployment hovered at 6%. In addition chronic balance-of-payments deficits were greatly straining the dollar overseas. In the course of an internal discussion of the economy throughout the first half of 1971, these advisers were shunted aside, and President Nixon, with Federal Reserve Chairman Arthur Burns [q.v.], developed a Keynesian strategy—the application of classical deficit spending techniques—to rejuvenate the U.S. economy. In August 1971 Stein participated in the top-level Camp David discussion on the economy, but he played a secondary role because of his association with the policies being discarded. He was assigned to oversee the implementation of the wage and price controls he had previously opposed. In November 1971, however, Stein succeeded Paul McCracken as CEA chairman after the latter's resignation.

Stein had a difficult task. The June-August reversal of Administration policy, summarized in President Nixon's assertion that "I am now a Keynesian," was part of a long-term strategy to bring the U.S. economy into "high gear" in time for the 1972 elections. The combined measures succeeded in producing a 5% growth rate in 1972 but a runaway inflation in 1973. In March 1972 Stein responded to foreign pressures for an interest rate hike to protect the U.S. dollar—a move that would have been counter to the entire reflation strategy—by insisting that the August 1971 moves concerning the dollar were sound and that inflation would remain under control. In July 1972 he told a Congressional panel that the only way to prevent an "explosion of demand" was "to keep the budget from exploding." In October 1972 he told the JEC that the Administration had dropped the traditional 4% unemployment target, the usual gauge of "full employment," as "counter-productive." In December, immediately after his reelection, Nixon appointed Stein to his Economic Policy Council.

In February 1973 Stein became embroiled, along with the other leading economic figures in the Administration, in the renewed dollar crisis which erupted in that month. At the same time, the takeoff of meat prices following the lifting of price controls produced a consumer boycott of meat, which Stein praised as having some downward effect. Stein generally held to his earlier free-market views, rejecting a return to wage-price controls to slow runaway inflation. After the fourfold increase in oil prices in October 1973, he also opposed gas rationing.

Stein came into open conflict with other Administration members in early 1974 when Secretary of Labor Peter Brennan [q.v.] suggested that U.S. workers should get higher wages to keep up with inflation. Stein retorted that what the country needed was productivity, asserting, "We cannot pay workers for food that was not produced and oil that we didn't get from the Arabs." After the CEA's 1974 report was released to Congress, Stein and Secretary of the Treasury George Shultz [q.v.] defended the report's conclusion that a recession could be averted in the U.S. in 1974. In doing so, however, Stein conceded that he and Shultz were redefining recession away from textbook definitions such as a fall in output. In May 1974 when Arthur Burns called for a balanced budget to stop inflation, Stein said that "we don't all talk with the language of an Old Testament prophet," likening Burns to Jeremiah.

In July 1974, three months before the beginning of the worst U.S. recession

since the Great Depression, Stein resigned from his post as CEA chairman to return to academic life. He was succeeded by economic consultant Alan Greenspan [q.v.]. Stein began a regular column with the *Wall Street Journal* and resumed his teaching duties at the University of Virginia, where he had taught since 1971.

[LG]

For further information:
Leonard Silk, *Nixonomics* (New York 1972).

STEINEM, GLORIA
b. March 25, 1934; Toledo, Ohio.
Policy Council, National Women's Political Caucus, 1971–72; Founder, Women's Action Alliance; Editor, *Ms.*

Steinem graduated from Smith College in 1956 and studied for two years in India. In 1960 Steinem moved to New York City to establish a career in journalism. After eight years of writing articles for popular magazines and a stint as a script writer for the TV show "That Was the Week That Was," Steinem was hired by Clay Felker as a contributing editor to the new magazine, *New York*. Through her column, "The City Politic," Steinem supported the causes and politics of the American left.

After reporting on a meeting of the Redstockings, a militant feminist group, in November 1968, Steinem concentrated her energies on writing, speaking and television appearances on behalf of the women's liberation movement. By 1971 Steinem was nationally recognized as the symbol of the new left feminist leadership. Her picture appeared on the cover of *Newsweek, McCall's* and *Redbook*. Steinem's feminism was based on the belief that women's biological differences "have been used . . . to mark us for an elaborate division of labor . . . [which] is continued for clear reason, conscious or not: the economic and social profit of men as a group."

In July 1971 Steinem, Bella Abzug [q.v.], Shirley Chisholm [q.v.] and Betty

Friedan [*q.v.*] announced the formation of the National Women's Political Caucus (NWPC) to encourage women to run for public office and lobby for women's issues at the 1972 national party conventions. Although endorsing George McGovern [*q.v.*] as "the best of the male candidates" for the Democratic presidential nomination, Steinem later campaigned and ran unsuccessfully as a convention delegate for Chisholm, who had entered the presidential race. As spokeswoman for the NWPC at the Democratic Convention in Miami, Steinem led unsuccessful floor fights for the inclusion of an abortion plank in the Party platform and a challenge of the South Carolina delegation because of under-representation of women. She engineered an impressive show of the political strength of women in the nomination vote of Sissy Farenthold for vice president.

In late 1971 Steinem organized and became a member of the board of the Women's Action Alliance, a national information and referral network for women that also gave organizational assistance to women's projects. During this period Steinem gathered support for the publication of a woman's magazine owned and run by women and aimed at the "liberated woman." Financed by Felker's *New York*, all 300,000 copies of the January 1972 preview issue of *Ms.* sold out on newstands. The title, *Ms.*, is a form of address preferred by feminists who consider its use a symbolic refusal to be identified by their relationship to a man. Under Steinem's editorship, *Ms.* circulation had reached 500,000 by 1977.

Despite acrimonious charges from the right in the women's movement that her rhetoric and more militant views threatened to destroy a broad coalition of women and allegations in 1975 that she had been connected with the Central Intelligence Agency, Steinem continued to be active in feminist politics. In 1975 she helped plan the women's agenda for the Democratic National Convention and in 1977 attended the National Conference of Women in Houston, Tex.

[JMP]

STENNIS, JOHN C(ORNELIUS)
b. Aug. 3, 1901; Kemper County, Miss.
Democratic Senator, Miss. 1947- ; Chairman, Armed Services Committee, 1969- .

Stennis graduated from Mississippi State College in 1923 and received his law degree from the University of Virginia in 1928. He was elected to the Mississippi House of Representatives in 1928. In 1931 he was elected prosecutor for Mississippi's 16th Judicial District. He became a circuit judge in 1937 and succeeded Theodore Bilbo in the United States Senate in 1947. Stennis was a staunch supporter of segregation and states' rights. He was one of the Senate floor leaders engaged in extended debate and filibuster in opposition to civil rights legislation. He was one of the authors of the "Southern Manifesto," proclaiming resistance to the Supreme Court school desegregation decision of 1954. [See TRUMAN, EISENHOWER Volumes]

In domestic affairs, Stennis was a conservative Democrat, opposing most of the New Frontier and Great Society social programs. He did, however, support health programs, including medical research. [See KENNEDY, JOHNSON Volumes]

Stennis continued his opposition to civil rights legislation during the Nixon-Ford years. In 1970 the Mississippian introduced the Stennis Amendment requiring uniform national application of school desegregation rules. Stennis made it clear what his objective was: "I want [Northerners] to find out whether or not they want this massive immediate integration." Stennis did not believe that they did and would, consequently, leave the South alone. The proposal which was attacked by some Northern liberals was enacted in 1972.

Stennis was a staunch supporter of national defense and backed Nixon's anti-ballistic missile program. In at least one area, however, he disappointed the military. Stennis had insisted that the total number of admirals and generals be kept close to 1,200 rather than 1,600 the military wanted in the late 1960s. This figure of 1,200 was known among military offices as "the Stennis ceiling." Stennis was a strong supporter of the Central Intelligence Agency (CIA). He was, however, critical of CIA activities in United States domestic matters and of its role in the overthrow of the Allende Government in Chile.

In foreign policy, Stennis expressed strong support of Nixon's Indochina policy. During the late 1960s he had opposed getting the United States involved in the Vietnam War. He voiced the fear that the war might create a precedent for American entry into future conflicts without congressional approval and for the conduct of such conflicts with minimal legislative involvement. However, he believed that once the nation was committed to war, Americans should stand behind the President.

Nevertheless, Stennis worked to curb the President's warmaking power. In 1971 he introduced a resolution which would have curbed the power of the President to commit the nation to war without the consent of Congress. He was a cosponsor, along with Sen. Jacob Javits (R, N.Y.) [q.v.] of the war powers bill. The measure was a synthesis of previous proposals. It defined emergency conditions under which the President could commit troops without a formal declaration of war and outlined procedures by which Congress could terminate the emergency use if it disapproved. The Vietnam war was exempt from its provisions. The Senate passed the bill in April and the House in August.

Stennis experienced a personal attack which nearly cost him his life. While returning to his home in Washington on Jan. 30, 1973, he was shot in a robbery. He underwent extensive surgery but recovered. The assailants were apprehended.

Stennis almost played a role in the Watergate affair. When in October 1973, Richard Nixon was struggling to keep the White House tapes out of the control of Watergate investigators, he proposed that Stennis listen to them and screen them to make certain that national security secrets would not be divulged. Stennis had agreed to perform this task only if a formal invitation had been tendered to do so by the President and the Senate Watergate Committee chairmen—Sam Ervin [q.v.] and Howard Baker [q.v.]. The committee refused. Stennis' relationship with Nixon was close and cordial. He supported Gerald Ford's pardon of Nixon in 1974.

During the Carter Administration Stennis opposed the President's initiatives on Panama. [See CARTER Volume]

[HML]

STEVENS, JOHN PAUL
b. April 20, 1920; Chicago, Ill.
Judge, U.S. Seventh Circuit Court of Appeals, 1970-75; Associate Justice, U.S. Supreme Court, 1975-.

Stevens received a B.A. from the University of Chicago in 1941 and graduated first in his class from Northwestern University Law School in 1947. He was law clerk to Supreme Court Justice Wiley Rutledge in 1947 and 1948. Stevens then entered private practice in Chicago, where he specialized in antitrust and corporate law. He also served in 1950 as counsel to the House Judiciary Subcommittee on Antitrust and Monopoly and as a member of the Attorney General's National Committee to Study Antitrust Laws in 1954 and 1955.

A Republican, Stevens was named a judge on the U.S. Seventh Circuit Court of Appeals in October 1970. During his five years on the appellate bench, he established an excellent reputation for judicial craftsmanship based on opinions that were consistently clear, scholarly and well-written. He was considered a generally moderate jurist with a nonideological approach to cases that made him difficult to categorize. Stevens usually emphasized the facts in each suit and applied the relevant law on a case-by-case basis. Within that framework, he tended to favor the prosecution in criminal cases but was responsive to claims of prisoners' rights. He was moderate on discrimination and free expression issues and overall favored a policy of judicial restraint.

On Nov. 28, 1975, President Gerald Ford nominated Stevens for the Supreme Court seat vacated by the retirement of Justice William O. Douglas [q.v.]. Stevens was strongly recommended for the post by Attorney General Edward H. Levi [q.v.], who had known him in Chicago, and the nomination was generally well-received. Women's rights groups objected to Stevens because he had opposed women's claims in several sex discrimination cases. However, he was confirmed by the Senate on Dec. 17 by a 98-0 vote and sworn in two days later.

Stevens proved to be an independent justice who demonstrated the same case-by-case approach to issues that he had shown on the circuit bench. Nondoctrinaire and individualistic, he was not clearly aligned with either the more liberal or conservative members of the Court. However, Stevens was more liberal in his votes than many observers had anticipated, and though hard to categorize, seemed to take a moderate to liberal approach on most issues.

During his first year on the bench, Justice Stevens concurred in an important June 1976 decision holding that a racially discriminatory purpose as well as a discriminatory effect was needed to make a government job test unconstitutional. Later the same month, however, he joined the majority to declare racial discrimination in private nonsectarian schools illegal. Stevens dissented several days later when the Court upheld a social security act provision discriminating against illegitimate children. He also objected to a December 1976 decision ruling that pregnancy and childbirth could be excluded from coverage in a company disability insurance plan without violating a federal law prohibiting sex discrimination in employment.

Justice Stevens spoke for a five man majority in June 1976 to hold that Civil Service Commission regulations barring resident aliens from federal jobs denied of due process of law. However, he also wrote the opinion in a case holding that the dismissal of a state policeman without a hearing did not deprive him of liberty or property without due process. The Justice displayed a mixed pattern in First Amendment cases during his first term. His opinion for a five man majority upheld a Detroit ordinance restricting the location of adult movie theaters. However, Stevens took a strong stand a week later against judicial "gag" orders limiting publication of information about criminal cases.

In July 1976 Stevens voted to overturn laws making death the mandatory penalty for murder. However, he joined in rulings sustaining laws that established death as one possible penalty for murder and set guidelines for the judge or jury in determining the sentence. The Justice took a conservative stance in several Fourth Amendment cases in his first months on the Court and was part of a six-man majority that limited state prisoners' right of appeal to federal courts on search and seizure issues. He showed special sensitivity to claims of illegal treatment made by prison inmates. Stevens dissented in June 1976 when the Court ruled that inmates were not entitled to a hearing before being transferred from one prison to another, even when the move was a disciplinary action or conditions in the two prisons differed substantially.

During the next few terms of the Court, Justice Stevens continued to pursue an independent and rather unpredictable course. Quiet and mild-mannered, he was considered a "swing" vote along with Justices Potter Stewart [q.v.] and Byron White [q.v.]. Of the three, he was the one most likely to join with the Court's liberals when the justices were divided. Commentators generally rated Stevens as an intelligent, thoughtful jurist who wrote well-regarded opinions.

[CAB]

STEWART, POTTER
b. Jan. 23, 1915; Jackson, Mich.
Associate Justice, U.S. Supreme
Court, 1958-.

A 1941 graduate of Yale Law School, Stewart joined a prominent Cincinnati firm in 1947. He was appointed to the U.S. Sixth Circuit Court of Appeals in April 1954 and to the Supreme Court in October 1958. In his early years on the bench, Stewart was labeled a "swing" justice who cast a pivotal vote in cases dividing the Court's liberal and conservative wings. When a liberal majority emerged on the Warren Court in the early 1960s, Stewart's position was no longer decisive, but he remained a moderate and independent jurist. He took a conservative stance on most loyalty-security, reapportionment and criminal rights issues but frequently joined the Court's liberals in cases involving civil rights, the right to counsel, obscenity and eavesdropping. [See EISENHOWER, KENNEDY, JOHNSON Volumes]

On the Burger Court, Stewart, along with Byron White [q.v.], once again became a "swing" justice whose vote was crucial in deciding close cases. He occupied a center position between the Court's liberal members and the four more conservative Nixon appointees. When those two groups disagreed in a case, Stewart was more likely to vote with the "Nixon bloc," but his progressive views on certain issues still established him as, overall, a moderate and somewhat unpredictable jurist.

Stewart tended toward a policy of judicial restraint, but he defended individual rights against government infringement when he believed there was a clear constitutional mandate for this. He regularly voted to uphold the rights of free speech and assembly. In June 1973 he went beyond his already liberal stance on obscenity to join in a dissent urging the Court to prohibit all attempts to regulate allegedly obscene material for willing adults. Stewart took a broad view of freedom of the press and dissented in June 1972 when the Court held that journalists had no First Amendment right to refuse to identify confidential sources to a grand jury. In an exception to his generally liberal First Amendment views, the Justice spoke for the Court in March 1976 to hold that a 1968 ruling which protected the right of union members to picket within a privately owned shopping center was no longer valid.

Stewart usually opposed racial and sexual discrimination. However, he did vote in June 1972 to allow private clubs with state liquor licenses to exclude blacks. He also wrote the opinion in a June 1974 case holding that a California job disability insurance program which excluded pregnancy from coverage did not deny women the equal protection of the laws. In other discrimination cases, Stewart's judicial conservatism came to the fore. He believed the Court should normally defer to policy judgments made by legislatures, and so he voted to sustain laws that discriminated against illegitimate children and the poor. In an April 1970 opinion, Stewart upheld a state ceiling on the amount of welfare benefits one family could receive and said that the economic, social and philosophical problems presented by welfare programs were not the business of the federal courts. He also voted to uphold state laws limiting voting on bond issues to property owners or taxpayers. The Justice maintained his opposition to a strict one-man, one-vote rule in reapportionment cases and supported February and June 1973 decisions relaxing that standard for state legislative districting.

Justice Stewart insisted that the government adhere to strict procedural standards, and he voted in a series of cases from 1969 on to invalidate state laws that allowed creditors to seize a debtor's wages or goods without notice or hearing. In a potentially far-reaching June 1975 opinion, Stewart held that mental patients could not be confined in institutions against their will if they were not dangerous to others and could live outside the institution on their own.

In criminal cases Justice Stewart tended to favor law enforcement authorities.

He had opposed the 1966 *Miranda* ruling requiring police to warn suspects of their rights, and in several cases in the 1970s, he supported cutbacks on that decision. He took a narrow view of the Fifth Amendment's privilege against self-incrimination and, in Fourth Amendment cases, backed police "stop and frisk" practices, third-party bugging and grand jury use of illegally obtained evidence as the basis for questioning witnesses. However, Stewart generally opposed warrantless searches, and in an important June 1969 opinion, he limited the scope of the search police could make incident to a lawful arrest. The Justice believed that many of the criminal safeguards in the Bill of Rights took effect only when formal judicial proceedings were instituted. In a June 1972 plurality opinion, he restricted the right to counsel at police lineups to those conducted after a defendant's indictment or arraignment.

Stewart voted in June 1972 to declare the death penalty as then imposed a violation of the Eighth Amendment's ban on cruel and unusual punishment. He announced the judgment of the Court in several capital punishment cases decided in July 1976. In opinions joined by only two other justices, Stewart argued that statutes making the death penalty mandatory for certain crimes were unconstitutional. However, he voted to sustain laws setting death as one possible punishment for murder so long as standards were established to guide the judge or jury in imposing sentence.

President Nixon considered appointing Stewart Chief Justice in 1969, but Stewart reportedly asked that his name be withdrawn because he believed someone from outside the Court should be given the post. The Justice, who favored precise, narrow rulings no broader than necessary to decide the case at hand, was widely praised for his tightly-reasoned, lucid and well-written opinions. He was evaluated as a "fair-minded, able judge" who respected precedent, was cautious in his use of judicial power, and followed a "progressive-conservative" course.

[CAB]

STOKES, CARL B(URTON)
b. June 21, 1927; Cleveland, Ohio.
Mayor, Cleveland, Ohio, 1967-71.

The grandson of a slave, Stokes was raised in a black district of Cleveland by his mother who supported the family on her earnings as a cleaning woman. Stokes dropped out of high school to join the Army during World War II, but continued his education after the war. He received a B.S. from the University of Minnesota in 1954 and a law degree from Cleveland Marshall Law School in 1957. He was admitted to the bar that same year, and served as an assistant city prosecutor in Cleveland. Stokes became active in the local NAACP chapter and in 1962 was the first black Democrat ever elected to the Ohio assembly. Reelected in 1964 and 1966 he compiled a generally moderate record as a legislator.

In 1965 Stokes, running as an independent, lost the race for mayor of Cleveland. Two years later, with support from nationally prominent Democrats and civil rights leaders, Stokes won the Democratic primary and defeated his Republican opponent, Seth C. Taft, in the November election. Stokes's victory made him the first black mayor of a major U.S. city.

Initially popular because of his ambitious program to attack Cleveland's economic ills, Stokes suffered a severe setback after a shootout in July 1968 between police and black nationalists and subsequent rioting in the city's predominantly black East Side. Stokes's decision to use only black police officers to quell the trouble, although successful, evoked heavy criticism from many whites, and he never again enjoyed the popularity of his first months in office. A year later the National Commission on the Causes and Prevention of Violence concluded that the Cleveland riot constituted "a new pattern" of "person-oriented violence" with "blacks and whites shooting at each other, snipers against cops." The study predicted a bleak future for race relations in the city. [See JOHNSON Volume]

Nevertheless, Stokes sought and won

reelection in 1969, narrowly defeating Republican candidate Ralph Perk. His second term was plagued by embarrassing political appointments, labor troubles and fiscal ills. In February 1970 his police chief, William P. Ellenburg, was forced to resign when a Detroit newspaper accused him of accepting Mafia payoffs. Six months later Public Safety Director Benjamin Oliver Pavis, Jr., formerly the highest ranking black in the U.S. military, quit in the aftermath of a gun battle between police and black nationalists, which produced bitter accusations that Stokes was providing "support and comfort to the enemies of law enforcement." Other problems included a 17-day wildcat strike by transit workers that resulted in a large wage settlement and forced cuts in city services, including the closing of most public recreation programs. The defeat in 1971 of mayoral candidate Harold Pinkney, whom Stokes had backed after deciding not to run, was interpreted as a repudiation of Stokes.

Despite his difficulties in Cleveland Stokes's distinction as the first black mayor of a big city gave him a certain stature in political affairs. In 1970 he helped bring together mayors from the largest cities to form a united lobby for urban legislation, particularly federal revenue sharing, welfare reform, mass transit and urban renewal. At the U.S. Conference of Mayors in June 1970, Stokes introduced a resolution attacking the Nixon Administration's handling of the Vietnam war and condemning the expenditure of funds on the war. Rumors among black leaders about Stokes as a possible candidate in the 1972 presidential primaries ended with the entry of Shirley Chisholm (D, N.Y.) [q.v.] in September 1971.

In March 1972 Stokes retired from politics to become a television news reporter with WNBC in New York City.

[JD]

For further information:
Carl Stokes, *Promises of Power: A Political Autobiography* (New York, 1973).

STRACHAN, GORDON C(REIGHTON)
b. July 24, 1943; Berkeley, Calif.
White House aide.

A graduate of the University of Southern California in 1965, Strachan's former classmates included such future associates as Donald Segretti [q.v.], Ronald Ziegler [q.v.] and Dwight Chapin [q.v.]. He received his law degree from the University of California and then joined Richard Nixon's old New York law firm, Mudge, Rose, Guthree and Alexander, to work in the area of estates and trusts. In 1970 Strachan devoted part of his time to "advance work" for the White House in the midterm elections. He left his legal practice shortly afterward and joined the staff of the Administration's communications director, Herbert G. Klein [q.v.]. Within a few months, Strachan had moved again to become a political aide to Nixon's chief of staff, H.R. Haldeman [q.v.]. Referred to by White House staffers as "Haldeman's gofer," Strachan acted as a liaison between Haldeman and the Committee to Re-elect the President (CREEP). In December he became general counsel to the U.S. Information Agency (USIA).

In October 1972 the Department of Justice released a report that linked the White House to undercover Republican political sabotage efforts launched against the Democrats. It cited Strachan and Dwight Chapin, Nixon's deputy assistant, as those responsible for hiring Donald Segretti for the purpose of directing espionage activities in September 1971. Four months later government sources made public information that named Strachan as the initial contact between Segretti and political intelligence operations. Strachan resigned from his position as general counsel to the USIA on April 30, 1973.

Preliminary grand jury evidence revealed May 2, 1973, that such espionage activities, begun in early 1971 and continuing throughout the 1972 election campaign, had been organized by Haldeman, who delegated activities to a variety of aides and minor functionaries. The group's goals entailed the establishment of a sophisticated political intelligence-gathering system and plots to sabotage the presidential campaigns of Sens. Edmund S. Muskie (D, Me.) [q.v.] and Hubert Humphrey (D, Minn.) [q.v.] and ensure the nomination for Sen. George McGovern (D, S.D.) [q.v.], whom the White House considered the weakest candidate.

In July 1973 Strachan testified under a grant of immunity before the Senate Watergate Committee. He admitted that after the Watergate break-in he had destroyed documents that might have tied Watergate burglars to the White House and reported that he had delivered hush money subsequently paid to the burglars by Fred LaRue [q.v.]. Strachan maintained that he did not know what the money was to be used for but became suspicious when LaRue "donned a pair of gloves before touching it." When asked what advice he had to offer youths wishing to enter politics, he replied, "Stay away."

On March 1, 1974, Strachan was one of seven former White House aides indicted by the grand jury for conspiring to cover up Watergate and "other illegal activities." He was charged with one count each of conspiracy, obstruction of justice and making a false declaration (based on his statement in reference to his knowledge and handling of hush money) before a grand jury. He faced a maximum of 15 years imprisonment and $20,000 in fines. Because the court had difficulty determining whether or not Strachan's indictment came as the result of his testimony delivered under the grant of immunity, Strachan's case was separated from the main trial, which took place on Jan. 1, 1975. U.S. District Judge John Sirica [q.v.] dropped all charges against Strachan on May 10, 1975.

[SBB]

STRAUSS, ROBERT S(CHWARZ)
b. Oct. 19, 1918; Lockhart, Tex.
Chairman, Democratic Party National Committee, 1972-77.

Strauss studied at the University of Texas in Austin, where he obtained his law degree in 1941. Admitted to the Texas bar the same year, he worked as a special agent for the FBI during World War II. In 1945 he became a partner in the Dallas law firm of Akin, Gump, Strauss, Hauer and Feld, where he remained a partner until 1977. Strauss was also involved in the Texas media, becoming president of his own Strauss Broadcasting Company in 1964. Years of work in state Democratic Party politics, where he was generally associated with the right-of-center Connally faction, won him the job of Democratic national chairman from Texas between 1968 and 1972. In 1969 Strauss also became a member of the Party's National Executive Committee. In 1970 he was elected Party treasurer, a post he held until 1972, when he stepped aside for an appointee of Sen. George McGovern [q.v.].

Strauss's ascendancy to the chairmanship of the Democratic National Committee was completed a month after McGovern's crushing defeat in the November 1972 presidential election that led to a wholesale ouster of McGovern supporters from positions of power. On Dec. 3 a meeting of Democratic governors endorsed Strauss for National Committee chairman. His support came primarily from the governors of Southern and Western states. Strauss also had the backing of the AFL-CIO leadership, which had distanced itself from the McGovern campaign and was eager to return prolabor politicians to power within the Party.

Strauss was elected to the national chairmanship on Dec. 9 after an acrimonious confrontation with the McGovern forces in which he had to answer accusations that his previous close association with John Connally [q.v.] (who had led Democrats for Nixon during the 1972 campaign) made him a poor choice. On the TV program "Face the Nation" following his election, Strauss stated that anyone who supported "someone other than the Democratic candidate" for President should not hold high office within the Party. "John Connally belongs to the top of the list" of such individuals. He predicted that Connally would soon change his registration to the Republican Party, which Connally did in 1973.

In a gesture of unity, Strauss announced that he had no intention of "rolling back the clock" on the Party reforms pushed though by McGovern's supporters. He also made overtures to the trade unions by indicating that United Automobile Workers (UAW) President Leonard Woodcock [q.v.] would continue to head a commission studying convention delegate selection, and that he would attempt to involve AFL-CIO Chairman George Meany [q.v.] in the commission as well.

During early 1973 both Parties openly wooed Connally. Strauss invited his longtime colleague to "return to this party and bring with him his constituency"—an admitted attempt to compensate for his earlier public criticism of Connally. In March 1973 the Democratic National Committee endorsed 25 new members appointed by Strauss in a further consolidation of control. Strauss's public duties as national chairman consisted primarily of expressing Party opinion on the actions of the Republican Administration.

In August 1973 President Nixon made a major speech on Watergate which he hoped would clear the air and bring the scandal and its repercussions to an end. Strauss commented that the speech "added nothing, and probably subtracted nothing, from what we knew." After the firing of Watergate Special Prosecutor Archibald Cox [q.v.] and Deputy Attorney General William Ruckelshaus [q.v.] Strauss stated that Nixon had "abandoned the principle of law" and "his oath of office," and expressed doubts about whether Nixon could continue to serve. Strauss advised against openly calling for Nixon's resignation, arguing: "Let us remember what this President was and did when he perceived himself a hero. I ask you what horrors await this nation if he is

able to portray himself as a resigned martyr."

Strauss presided over the national comeback of the Democratic Party in the wake of the 1972 elections. He had difficulty, however, coping with the bitter factionary struggles within the Party. In August 1974 a Democratic Charter Commission in Kansas City was interrupted by a walkout of liberal and black Democrats who accused Strauss of "stacking" a Party committee. Several months later the labor contingent at a Kansas City "mini-convention" expressed anger over what it termed the Party's sophisticated discrimination against organized labor in the high councils of the organization.

In June 1976 Jimmy Carter [q.v.], who had virtually assured himself of the nomination with victories in the major primaries, asked Strauss to stay on as Party chairman through the November election. Strauss stepped down as national chairman in January 1977. Two months later President Carter appointed him a special representative for trade negotiations with the rank of ambassador. In addition to representing the U.S. at sensitive trade talks, including the 1977-78 negotiations on tariff reductions of the Geneva-based General Agreement on Trade and Tariffs, Strauss served briefly as the Carter Administration's "anti-inflation" ombudsman. [SEE CARTER Volume]

[LRG]

STURGIS, FRANK A.
b. Dec. 9, 1924; Norfolk, Va.
Convicted Watergate burglar.

A one-time commander under Fidel Castro, Frank A. Sturgis was one of five men arrested for breaking into the Democratic National Headquarters at the Watergate in Washington, D.C., on June 17, 1972. The men were equipped with surgical gloves, cameras, electronic equipment, $6,500 in cash, and papers referring to "W. House" and "Howard Hunt." All five had previous Central Intelligence Agency (CIA) connections.

Quickly dismissed by White House Press Secretary Ronald Ziegler [*q.v.*] as a "third-rate burglary attempt," the incident was cited as "blatant political espionage" by Democratic National Chairman Lawrence O'Brien [*q.v.*] who called for an FBI probe of the affair. The Justice Department announced a full-scale inquiry on June 19. Subsequent disclosure tied the five suspects to personnel and funds of the Committee to Re-Elect the President (CREEP).

Sturgis and his associates were indicted by a federal grand jury on Sept. 15, 1972, for conspiracy, burglary and wiretapping. Two former White House aides—G. Gordon Liddy [*q.v.*] and E. Howard Hunt [*q.v.*]—were included in the indictments. In March 1973 the original five pleaded guilty to all counts and were given "provisional" maximum penalties by Judge John J. Sirica [*q.v.*] ranging from 35 to 40 years imprisonment. Although he refused to promise leniency, Sirica recommended that they cooperate fully in the investigation.

In November 1973 Sturgis received a one-to-five year sentence. He was paroled in March 1974. Sturgis was scheduled to begin another prison term at that time due to a conviction for transporting stolen cars into Mexico in 1973. In 1975 his term was set aside because he had cooperated with the authorities.

In April 1975 Sturgis testified before the Rockefeller Commission that he had been party to a 1959 CIA plot to assassinate Fidel Castro and had participated in the Agency's 1961 Bay of Pigs invasion. Sturgis and three of the other Watergate burglars brought a $2 million suit on the grounds that they had been tricked into participating in the burglary by being made to believe that they were engaged in national security work that had government approval. In 1977 the case was settled out of court with each man receiving $50,000 from former President Nixon's 1972 campaign fund.

[SBB]

SULLIVAN, LEONOR K(RETZER)
b. Aug. 21, 1904; St. Louis, Mo.
Democratic Representative, Mo., 1953-77; Chairman, Banking and Currency Committee Subcommittee on Consumer Affairs, 1963-75; Chairman, Merchant Marine and Fisheries Committee, 1973-77.

One of nine children of a second-generation German tailor, Leonor Alice Kretzer was educated in the St. Louis public school system. After graduation from high school in 1922, she began working as a clerk with the local telephone company. Within the next five years she moved on to serve as demonstrator of office machines and eventually rose to training director with the responsibility of overseeing the education of 2,000 business machine operators a year.

After her marriage to Rep. John Berchmans Sullivan (D, Mo.), she became actively involved in Democratic politics and served first as an unpaid and later a paid member of his staff. When her husband died in 1951, Sullivan hoped to succeed him, but the Democratic machine refused to back her candidacy for the special election. She won the seat in 1952. In her successive bids for reelection, she retained her congressional seat with margins ranging from 65 to 79% of the vote.

Within the course of her first congressional term, Sullivan established herself as a thorough researcher whose dogged persistence in the area of consumer issues earned her an expanded popular base both at home and in the House. As chairwoman of the Banking and Currency Committee's Subcommittee on Consumer Affairs, she played a major role in the passage of strong truth-in-lending legislation. She was also a prominent supporter of the food stamp program. [See JOHNSON Volume]

During the Nixon Administration, Sullivan served as a ranking member of the Subcommittee on Housing of the Banking and Currency Committee, secretary of the Majority Caucus and a member of the Majority Steering Committee. Because of her widespread influence she was able to champion consumer issues in the course of her own subcommittee work and in other House committees as well. As the result of her staunch, uncompromising support for consumer protection laws, Sullivan was responsible for such major legislation as the banning of cancer-inducing agents in food, requisite testing of all chemical additives used in food and tighter controls on the manufacture and distribution of a number of prescription drugs including barbiturates. She also co-sponsored the Fair Credit Reporting Act of 1970, which protected consumers against irresponsible dissemination of credit information by various credit bureaus. In 1969 she sponsored a bill to establish a permanent office of consumer protection in the White House and to give the office the right to represent consumers before federal agencies. Efforts to create the agency failed throughout the 1970s.

Although the bulk of her legislative endeavors was confined to the consumer protection sphere, Sullivan was an outspoken supporter of housing legislation as well. In 1970 she opposed the Emergency Home Finance (EHF) bill to provide additional funds for home mortgages because it was a subsidy to lenders to enable them to continue high interest rates. Her measure to create a Home Owners Mortgage Loan Corp. granting mortgages at low rates for the poor and middle class failed, and the EHF was passed in July.

Sullivan was an opponent of much of the feminist legislation of the time. A Catholic, she maintained that "a woman's most important place is in the home" and supported the belief that a wholesome family life was "the backbone of civilization." Because of her fear that the Equal Rights Amendment could "accelerate the breakup of home life," she voted against it in the 92nd Congress, the only woman to do so.

In 1975 Sullivan lost the chairmanship of the Consumer Affairs Subcommittee in an apparent power struggle with Banking and Currency Committee Chairman Henry Reuss [q.v.]. She became chairman of the Merchant Marine and Fisheries Committee in 1973. On April 6-8, 1976, Sullivan chaired the hearings of the Panama Canal Subcommittee. While declaring her support of the 1903 treaty giving the U.S. control of the canal "in perpetuity," she accused the Ford Administration of transferring sovereignty over the canal in a "veiled and piecemeal fashion" without congressional authorization.

Sullivan retired from Congress in 1977.

[AFB]

SYMINGTON, STUART W(ILLIAM)
b. June 26, 1901; Amherst, Mass.
Democratic Senator, Mo., 1953–77.

Following his graduation from Yale in 1923, Symington began a successful business career, serving as president of Emerson Electric Manufacturing Co. from 1938 to 1945. During the Truman Administration Symington held important posts in several federal agencies and from 1946 to 1950 served as secretary of the Air Force. A leading proponent of increased defense spending, he advocated the development of a large nuclear-equipped Air Force.

Symington was elected to the Senate from Missouri as a Democrat in 1952 and argued for greater military preparedness in general and the "big bomber" in particular. In 1960 he campaigned for the Democratic presidential nomination, but eventually threw his support behind the unsuccessful candidacy of Lyndon B. Johnson. During the Eisenhower Administration he chaired hearings on stockpiling abuses; backed the Defense Department in the "muzzling" probe of 1962 and supported the development of the controversial TFX fighter-bomber. [See TRUMAN, EISENHOWER, KENNEDY Volumes]

Early in the Vietnam war, Symington, a one-time hawk, became a committed dove. As the only Senator to sit on both the Foreign Relations and Armed Services Committees, Symington grew convinced that the war was not only unnecessary to U.S. security but futile, wrong and harmful to the nation's economy. In October 1967 he urged a unilateral cease-fire aimed at initiating peace negotiations. [See JOHNSON Volume]

A liberal on domestic issues Symington supported consumer protection, abortion aid and gun control, positions unpopular in Missouri. During the Nixon years he voted against the Supreme Court nominations of Clement Haynsworth [q.v.] and G. Harrold Carswell [q.v.], supported legal services for the poor and championed spending on "human welfare needs" rather than on military projects.

In 1969 Symington headed a subcommittee investigating overseas commitments in an effort to reassess U.S. foreign policy in the wake of the Vietnam war. The subcommittee found that commitments and secret agreements had been made throughout the 1960s to such countries as Ethiopia, Laos, Thailand, South Korea and Spain and that the U.S. had 429 major military bases around the world. An agreement permitting U.S. use of bases in Spain in return for grants, loans and improvements caused particular controversy.

Symington pointed out that many major military commitments of the 1960s and 1970s resulted from executive agreements made without the knowledge or consent of Congress, and pressed for a reassertion of congressional authority in foreign policy during the 1970s. For years a supporter of foreign aid, he opposed many aid measures during the Nixon years in his belief that the U.S. was economically and militarily overcommitted throughout the world. Symington stated: "There has to be a viable economy with a strong dollar. And there has to be faith in the system and confidence of the people in their government. Without the second and third, military strength is not security."

Unlike many other doves Symington did not completely turn against the "military establishment." Yet he opposed building new military bases, bombers and an expanded anti-ballistic missile (ABM) system because he believed alternative systems would be more efficient. His opposition to the ABM hurt him politically. In his 1970 reelection campaign Symington won a narrow 37,000-vote victory over his opponent, state Attorney General John C. Danforth, who had received large political contributions from McDonnell Douglas, a builder of missile components.

Symington spoke out against the extension of the Vietnam war into Cambodia and Laos, supporting the Cooper-Church and McGovern-Hatfield Amendments. In March 1975 Symington with Sens. Humphrey [q.v.], McGovern [q.v.] and Clark opposed military aid to the faltering Cambodia government of Lon Nol while supporting additional food and medical help.

Symington also favored measures to ban the importation of Rhodesian chrome ore, withdraw 76,000 U.S. troops stationed abroad and resume U.S. military aid to Turkey, which was cut off in 1974. In 1973 Symington, as acting chairman of the Armed Services Committee, conducted hearings into the possible involvement of the CIA in the Watergate scandal. According to testimony high Administration officials sought to involve the CIA in the Watergate cover-up as well as the burglary of the office of Daniel Ellsberg's psychiatrist.

In 1976 after 24 years in the Senate, Symington chose not to seek re-election.

[JAN]

For further information:
Flora Lewis, "The Education of a Senator," *Atlantic Monthly*, (December 1971).

TAFT, ROBERT, JR.
b. Feb. 26, 1917; Cincinnati, Ohio.
Republican Representative, Ohio, 1963-65, 1967-71; Republican Senator, Ohio, 1971-77.

Robert Taft, Jr., the son of Sen. Robert A. Taft, Sr. (R, Ohio), and grandson of President and Chief Justice William Howard Taft, graduated from Yale in 1939 and earned a law degree from Harvard in 1942 while an ensign in the Navy. After the war he joined the family law firm of Taft, Stettinius & Hollister. In 1954 he successfully ran for the first of four terms in the Ohio House of Representatives.

Taft was elected to the U.S. House in 1962. He gave up his House seat in 1964 to run for the Senate and lost narrowly in the Johnson landslide of that year. Two years later he was reelected to the House, when he defeated Rep. John J. Gilligan (D, Ohio) [q.v.]. [See JOHNSON Volume]

In 1970 Taft ran successfully for the Senate, barely defeating Republican Gov. James Rhodes [q.v.] in the primary and then narrowly beating Howard Metzenbaum, a wealthy businessman, in the general election. During the early Nixon years Taft generally supported the Administration in Congress, voting for its position about 60% of the time. But after 1974 he began to oppose the White House more frequently. Taft staunchly backed Nixon's Vietnam policy and opposed the 1970 Cooper-Church Amendment limiting presidential authority to conduct military operations in Cambodia. He joined other Republican senators in attacking critics of the Vietnam troop withdrawal policy in 1971, and berated the "Johnny-come-lately doves" for "the pure politics of their current dissent." Taft generally favored a strong defense program, the development of controversial weapons systems such as the Safeguard anti-ballistic missile and foreign aid including the restoration of aid to Turkey in 1975. In 1974 he opposed the reduction of American troops abroad, but the following year he voted to ban the use of funds that could have involved the U.S. in Angola's civil war.

Taft consistently supported the Republican Presidents' policies. He backed Nixon's Family Assistance Plan; the work stamps proposal, which would cut off food stamps to adults who refused to accept any job offered to them; and "no knock" warrants that allowed police to enter buildings without notice in certain circumstances. In 1971 he attempted to amend the $6 billion appropriations bill to extend the life of the Office of Economic Opportunity so that the bill would more closely reflect Administration views.

In 1972 Taft introduced legislation and a congressional amendment to allow federal tax credits for up to half the cost of private education. The Administration supported the measure as a way to provide aid for parochial education. Although in 1973 he opposed increasing the federal minimum wage, Taft successfully urged the adoption of a subminimum wage for youths to combat high unemployment among 16 and 17 year olds.

Taft moderated his Old Guard conservative Republicanism in 1974 and began to support labor on some issues. He joined critics of the freeze on new applications for housing subsidies and public housing and community development assistance announced in January 1974. He opposed cutting off food stamps to striking workers in 1974, and the following year he voted for the successful attempt to override Ford's veto of a bill to revise and extend the federal school lunch and other child nutrition programs. In 1975 he favored the labor-backed, common-site picketing bill and then urged the President to sign it in 1976. Ford vetoed the bill, although he had initially supported it.

Taft actively campaigned for Nixon and Ford during their presidential campaigns. He supported Ford against Ronald Reagan [q.v.] for the Republican nomination in 1976, but he and 11 other moderate Republican senators urged Ford to keep Vice President Nelson A. Rockefeller [q.v.] as his running mate and to moderate his tough stance against social spending.

In 1976 Taft lost a bid for a second Senate term when he was defeated by his former opponent, Howard Metzenbaum. After the election he resumed practicing law in Cincinnati and Washington.

[AE]

TALMADGE, HERMAN E(UGENE)
b. Aug. 9, 1913; McRae, Ga.
Democratic Senator, Ga., 1957–.

After receiving his law degree from the University of Georgia in 1936, Herman Talmadge joined his father's Atlanta law firm. During World War II he served with the Navy in several Pacific theater operations. In 1948 he succeeded his father, Eugene Talmadge, as Georgia's governor. In 1950 Talmadge won a seat in the U.S. Senate and quickly gained a reputation as an intelligent and well-informed legislator. During the Kennedy-Johnson years, he opposed civil rights and social welfare legislation and supported measures favoring private enterprise. [See EISENHOWER, KENNEDY, JOHNSON Volumes]

As chairman of the Agriculture and Forestry Committee, Talmadge was concerned about hunger in America, which he termed a national tragedy. He was the author of the school lunch program passed in 1970 and helped develop the food stamp plan. Beginning in 1969 he sought to improve the food stamp program by eliminating several of its shortcomings, including the high cost of coupons, inadequate food bonuses that deprived stamp program participants of a nutritionally adequate diet and the inaccessibility of food stamps caused by pay distribution procedures. Talmadge introduced the 1969 food assistance bill, which authorized $610 billion for the food stamp program and called for a review of changes in the program. He also supported the 1970 bill extending the food stamp program for five years. Talmadge applauded the bill's provision requiring all able-bodied adults to work or register for work in order for their families to be eligible for food stamps. He opposed, as financially impractical and unwise, a guaranteed nutritional income system.

In 1969 Talmadge introduced the employment opportunity bill, which granted tax credits for certain costs that employers incurred as a result of hiring individuals through work-incentive programs. According to Talmadge, the bill had a twofold purpose: (1) to encourage trained workers under existing training programs; and (2) to hire individuals through the Social Security Act's work-incentive program. He described the 1970 family assistance bill as the "welfare expansion act" because it allegedly extended welfare benefits to an additional 15 million Americans.

Talmadge's second major concern as chairman of the Agriculture Committee was the plight of rural America. He argued that the redevelopment of small towns was vital to prevent continued migration to big cities. One of his first actions as chairman was to form a subcommittee on rural development chaired by Sen. Hubert Humphrey (D, Minn.) [q.v.]. Talmadge coauthored the 1972 Rural Development Act, which was designed to encourage rural economic growth, provide jobs and income required to support better community facilities and improve the general quality of rural life.

With Sen. George Aiken (R, Vt.) [q.v.], Talmadge introduced the 1972 National Forest and Wild Areas Act, which preserved from development wild areas largely west of the Mississippi River. In 1975 Talmadge supported the Emergency Farm Bill to revise upward target prices of wheat, cotton and feed grains. He warned that farmers, in order to reach maximum productivity, must be compensated for increased production costs. He cautioned against continuing America's practice of supplying food to the world and recommended the establishment of a monitoring system to insure that U.S. agricultural needs were satisfied prior to meeting foreign demand.

Considered an expert on tax legislation, Talmadge worked laboriously for the 1969 tax reform bill. In his struggle for budget control, he supported a proposed 1973 constitutional amendment to prohibit the federal government from spending more then it took in, except in a congressionally declared national emergency. He also urged Congress to adopt a legislative program that would cap federal expenditures for each fiscal year, and if expenditures exceeded the ceiling, would require Congress to increase taxes to balance the budget. Continuing his attack on government spending in March 1976, Talmadge introduced a resolution calling for a balanced budget. He charged that continued unrestricted spending brought the nation near bankruptcy.

Talmadge consistently opposed congressional approval of civil rights legislation, believing that such measures went far beyond the Constitution. He declared that forced busing made a mockery of public education. He gained notoriety for his proposed constitutional amendment to restore state and local control over public education. Talmadge voiced no objections to the conservative civil rights records of President Nixon's Supreme Court nominees and endorsed each of them: Clement F. Haynsworth [q.v.], G. Harrold Carswell [q.v.] and William H. Rehnquist [q.v.].

As a member of the Select Committee on Presidential Campaign Activities (Watergate Committee), Talmadge described himself as an "impartial judge and juror." He maintained that the Committee's role was to bring to light the facts concerning the Watergate break-in and cover-up. He concurred with the Committee's final report which recommended 35 election campaign reforms, including the establishment of a federal elections commission with supervisory and enforcement powers.

During the early Johnson Administration, Talmadge supported America's involvement in Vietnam, but during Nixon's Administration he became an opponent of the war. He supported the 1970 Cooper-Church Amendment prohibiting further U.S. involvement in Cambodia. He subsequently cosponsored the War Powers Act of 1973, which limited presidential authority to unilaterally order military activities. Talmadge maintained that America's national defense should be second to none. He argued that the U.S. should deal with the Soviets solely from a position of strength, and therefore in 1969 he supported President Nixon's proposed anti-ballistic missile system and in 1972 demanded that any strategic arms limitation agreement guarantee U.S. superiority. Talmadge never voted for any foreign aid program, regarding such aid as a global giveaway that the U.S. did not need and could not afford. Because of this opinion, he voted for an end to all foreign aid programs.

In 1979 the Senate Ethics Committee investigated charges that Talmadge had set up a secret bank account into which campaign contributions and expense reimbursements were diverted. [See CARTER Volume]

[TML]

TERHORST, JERALD F(RANKLIN)

B. July 11, 1922; Grand Rapids, Mich.
White House Press Secretary, August 1974 - September 1974.

Jerald terHorst was the son of a carpenter who had emigrated from the Netherlands to Grand Rapids shortly before World War I. His journalism-oriented college education at Michigan State was interrupted by service as a captain in the Marines during World War II. In 1946 terHorst joined the Grand Rapids *Press* as a city hall reporter, and two years later covered Gerald R. Ford's successful race for a Michigan congressional seat.

In 1952, after a year's active service with the Marine Corps in Korea, terHorst joined the conservative Detroit *News*. For the next 22 years, as Washington correspondent and finally Washington bureau chief, he covered four Administrations, national elections and several Presidential trips abroad, earning a reputation as a competent, tireless and generous reporter.

On August 9, 1974, the day after Richard Nixon's resignation announcement, President Ford named terHorst to replace Ronald Ziegler [q.v.] as the new White House press secretary. TerHorst and Ford immediately promised a new spirit of openness in the White House, including more frequent Presidential press conferences, "pool" reporters and photographers to cover the day's presidential activities and more complete and accurate information. TerHorst's pledge of better information was supported by his daily meetings with the President and consultations with top members of the Administration. This contact stood in marked contrast to the situation of his predecessor, who was generally excluded from policy matters.

His tenure lasted exactly a month. On Sept. 9, 1974, President Ford granted former President Nixon a full pardon for all federal crimes he "committed or may have committed or taken part in" during his term in office. Nixon later issued a statement accepting the pardon. The White House also announced that the Ford Administration had concluded an agreement with Nixon (which was later reversed) giving him title to his presidential papers and tape recordings. TerHorst resigned immediately as a matter of "conscience." The next day he told a *New York Times* reporter that he would have felt "a little awkward" defending an absolute pardon for Nixon "but only a conditional pardon for young men who had fled to Canada to escape Vietnam as an act of conscience." Reportedly terHorst's written resignation reached Ford shortly before the President announced the pardon for Nixon.

After his resignation TerHorst rejoined the Detroit *News* as a national affairs columnist. In recognition of his "exemplary display of conscience and courage in resigning a highly coveted position which he felt conflicted with his integrity as a journalist," terHorst was awarded the Society of Magazine Writers' first Conscience in Media medal.

[FHM]

THOMPSON, FRED D.
b. 1943; Lawrenceberg, Tenn.
Minority Counsel, Senate Watergate Committee, February 1973–August 1974.

A 1964 graduate of Memphis State University, Thompson earned a law degree from Vanderbilt University in 1967. He then spent two years in private practice before he became an assistant U.S. attorney. An active Republican, Thompson resigned this position in 1972 to direct the successful reelection campaign of Sen. Howard Baker (R, Tenn.) [*q.v.*]. He then briefly returned to private practice.

In early 1973 Thompson accepted Baker's offer to serve as minority counsel for the Senate Watergate Committee. Although responsible to the Republican members of the Committee, Thompson coordinated his efforts along bipartisan lines with Majority Counsel Samuel Dash [*q.v.*]. In addition to recruiting staff members, Thompson examined voluminous files of Watergate material, including the transcripts from the trial of the seven original Watergate defendants.

During the Committee's private and public hearings, Thompson and Dash presented evidence implicating a number of high officials in the Watergate conspiracy and subsequent cover-up. These included Attorney General John Mitchell [*q.v.*], White House Counsel John Dean [*q.v.*] and presidential aide H.R. Haldeman [*q.v.*]. As the probe progressed and Nixon refused to release White House tapes of conversations about Watergate, Thompson could no longer accept Nixon's innocence. He later stated that "for me the question finally became not, 'are the tapes damaging?' but instead, 'how damaging are they?'"

In the spring of 1974, as a number of grand juries convened to look into various abuses of the Nixon Administration, the Watergate Committee obtained transcripts of the White House tapes, but, according to Thompson, "even though there was still room for diehards to debate whether Nixon was personally guilty of the obstruction of justice that had taken place, the die was cast." The final transcript released in August 1974 disclosed that Nixon had ordered the FBI to withdraw from an investigation of Watergate, and with this revelation, the Watergate Committee closed its files.

Thompson returned to Nashville and began work on a book outlining his role on the Senate Watergate Committee entitled *At That Point in Time* (1975).

[DGE]

THURMOND, STROM
b. Dec. 5, 1902; Edgefield, S.C.
Republican Senator, S.C., 1954–.

The son of a South Carolina politician, Thurmond was a school superintendent, city and county attorney, state senator and state circuit court judge before World War II. During the war he served in both the European and Pacific theaters. Thurmond became governor of South Carolina in 1946. Two years later he was the presidential candidate of the States Right Party, founded in reaction to the strong civil rights plank of the Democratic Party. He carried five states from the Deep South in a losing effort. Thurmond entered the Senate in 1954, becoming the first person ever elected to a major office in a write-in campaign. In 1964 he switched allegiance to the Republican Party and was instrumental in Barry Goldwater's [q.v.] 1964 victories in five Southern states. [See TRUMAN, EISENHOWER, KENNEDY, JOHNSON Volumes]

In 1968 Thurmond supported Richard M. Nixon's presidential candidacy. Reportedly, Nixon's "Southern Strategy" was based upon an agreement with Thurmond. In return for the South Carolinian's support, Nixon pledged to oppose school busing, appoint "strict constructionists" to the Supreme Court, reduce federal spending and promote a strong military establishment. Thurmond's influence in the White House was apparent; twenty of his friends and aides received administrative jobs. The Senator was a frequent supporter of the Nixon Administration. He backed the nominations of conservatives Clement Haynsworth [q.v.] and G. Harrold Carswell [q.v.] to the Supreme Court and supported the 1972 Revenue Sharing Act, maintaining that it could reverse the trend toward centralized federal government bureaucracy. As the Watergate crisis unfolded in 1973 and 1974, Thurmond remained loyal to Nixon.

In the early 1970s Thurmond continued to vote against social welfare programs, charging that those people able to work should be given the opportunity. However he made serious efforts to win housing and welfare funds for his state. In 1972 the Senator cosponsored and worked for legislation establishing a 20% increase in Social Security benefits. In the same year he voted for the Rural Development Act, which he believed would help alleviate a potential domestic crisis. The bill was designed to ease rural outmigration and improve the quality of rural life. Thurmond also cosponsored the Equal Rights Amendment, stating that it was a "genuine reflection of the needs of many people."

In 1973 Thurmond proposed modification of the Electoral College to make it more representative of the American people's will. His "district plan" provided two electoral votes to the presidential candidate carrying the majority of the popular vote in each state and one electoral vote to the candidate carrying each state district. Thurmond maintained his proposal was constitutional and reflected the "one man, one vote" concept. No action was taken on the measure.

School busing was the most controversial issue that concerned Thurmond. He charged that the liberals promoted the very evils they condemned in 1954 when they were against allowing students to attend a particular school because of race. In August 1970 he reportedly persuaded Nixon into calling off Justice Department plans to send lawyers South to supervise school openings. Thurmond argued against the 1971 Child Development Act that created Child Day Care Centers. He viewed this as a further extension of HEW's bureaucracy and implementation of desegregation guidelines. He also added that rather than parents, government behaviorists would be molding children's character.

An advocate of a strong defense posture, Thurmond was among the first senators to support Nixon's proposed Safeguard-ABM system, passed by Congress in March 1969. He continued to speak for improved weapons systems such as the B-1 bomber, TRIDENT long-range missile, F-14 Tomcat, F-15 and S-3A Viking. In 1972 he was cautious about the SALT agreement, warning against Soviet numerical superiority. He later doubted the wisdom of establishing an all-volunteer army. Thurmond pointed out that Nixon's trip to mainland China had the potential for both triumph and tragedy. He believed this visit to be the beginning of a relationship that could improve U.S. security, but might result in tragedy if America's traditional Pacific allies were abandoned.

Thurmond suggested economic foreign policy decisions be made in American interests. Thus, although he condemned the State Department's closing of the American consulate in Rhodesia in 1970, he voted for 1971 legislation lifting the import embargo on Rhodesian chrome ore because of its importance to the U.S. defense program. He advocated ending the export of American industrial technology to the Soviet Union. For the protection of the U.S. textile indistry, Thurmond urged President Gerald R. Ford to impose quotas on textile imports from Japan and other countries. From 1972 to 1976 Thurmond argued against any new Panama Canal treaties that would surrender U.S. sovereignty over the Canal Zone. Should the canal be lost, Thurmond predicted adverse effects upon U.S. commerce and defense.

Because of similar political philosophies, Thurmond supported Ronald Reagan's [q.v.] political candidacy in 1976.

[TML]

TOWER, JOHN G(OODWIN)
b. Sept. 29, 1925; Houston, Tex.
Republican Senator, Tex. 1961-.

Tower enlisted in the Army in 1942 and after his discharge, earned a B.A. in 1948 from Southwestern University. From 1948 to 1949 he worked as a radio announcer and became an insurance salesman in Dallas. In 1951 he accepted an assistant professorship of political science at Midwestern University and taught there until 1961.

A conservative, Tower entered Republican politics in the 1950s as a member of his county's executive committee. Elected to the Senate in 1961, Tower emerged to be a leading conservative Republican spokesman. He opposed Kennedy and Johnson social programs and was a vigorous supporter of the Vietnam war. [See KENNEDY, JOHNSON Volumes].

Tower developed a close relationship with Richard Nixon. He campaigned hard for Nixon in 1968 in Texas and became the President's liaison with the growing Texas Republican Party. By the early 1970s he was a leader of the Republicans in the Senate. In 1970 he took over the Republican Senate Campaign Committee, which empowered him to distribute nearly $300,000 to the Republican candidates. Three years later he left this post to head the Party's Policy Committee, an important legislative planning group.

Tower enthusiastically backed the Nixon Vietnam war policy and voted against all the attempts to limit U.S. involvement. Extremely critical of the anti-war movement, he characterized George McGovern in 1972 as "Hanoi's Choice For the President." The following year he lobbied for Congress to sustain Nixon's veto of the Javits' War Powers Act, which severely restricted the President's right to commit troops abroad. Tower supported increased defense spending and maintained his conservative stance on domestic issues. He opposed funds allocated to anti-poverty programs, spoke out against the establishment of a consumer protection agency and a constitutional amendment to ban forced busing.

Tower was critical of labor unions. In a December 1971 article in Nation's Business, he compared their power to that of the robber barons in the late 19th century. Because Tower believed that curtailing union power would reduce inflation, he introduced legislation to abolish the National Labor Relations Board (NLRB), the government agency charged with monitoring unfair labor practices. Tower accused the Board of being "an extension of organized labor." He continued to defend the inclusion of Section 14(b) in the Taft-

Hartley law that permitted states to retain "right to work laws."

As a leading Republican Senator, Tower played a role in persuading Nixon to resign. In early April 1974 he began to publicly express concern over whether the President could govern effectively as long as questions about his role in the Watergate break-in remained unanswered. He joined with the Republican leadership in warning Nixon that impeachment could result if he continued to refuse to furnish all the materials subpoenaed by the Judiciary Committee. During August Tower participated in the Senate Republican Policy Committee decision to send Sen. Barry Goldwater (R, Ariz.) [q.v.] to request that Nixon resign.

During 1975 Tower served on the Church committee investigating possible Central Intelligence Agency (CIA) and FBI abuses. He refused to sign the panel's final report citing evidence of extensive abuses and opposed publication of the report because of "the diplomatic damage" he felt would result.

In 1978 Tower won another Senate term narrowly defeating the popular Democratic Rep. Bob Krueger. He was critical of the Carter Administration's energy, anti-inflation, disarmament, China and detente policies. [See CARTER Volume]

[JB]

TRAIN, RUSSELL E(RROL)
b. June 4, 1920; Jamestown, R.I.
Chairman, Council on Environmental Quality, March 1970–September 1973; Administrator, Environmental Protection Agency, September 1973–March 1977.

The son of an admiral, Train graduated from Princeton University in 1941 and served in the Army during World War II. In 1948 he received his law degree from Columbia University and then served as counsel and adviser to various congressional committees and leaders. In 1956

Train joined the Treasury Department as head of its tax legislation staff, and the following year he accepted a judgeship on the Tax Court of the United States. During the 1950s Train became interested in conservation. In 1961 he formed and headed the African Wildlife Leadership Foundation. Train resigned his government post in 1965 to become president of the Conservation Foundation, a nonprofit group interested in research and education on a wide variety of environmental issues. Under Train's leadership the organization broadened its interest to include the problems of hunger, waste disposal and pesticides.

Shortly after his election Richard Nixon asked Train to head a task force on resources and the environment. The group's report, issued in January 1969, criticized the gap between authorized funding and actual money given for anti-pollution programs and urged the Administration to push forward existing environmental programs. The panel also recommended the appointment of an adviser on environmental affairs to resolve differences between programs and serve as leader of a proposed council on the environment.

In January 1969 Nixon announced the appointment of Train as undersecretary of the interior. The choice won the support of conservationists and at the time was seen as a move to placate environmentalists angered by the appointment of Walter Hickel [q.v.] as Secretary of the Interior. Hickel as governor of Alaska had pushed for development rather than preservation of resources.

During his first months in office, Train chaired an intergovernmental task force studying plans for the proposed Alaskan oil pipeline, and by 1970 his group had drawn up strict construction regulations to protect the environment. He also worked to coordinate government programs on the environment and resolve conflicting priorities between existing groups.

As a result of Train's encouragement, Nixon in June 1969 created a cabinet-level Environmental Quality Council, composed of the Secretaries of Agriculture;

Commerce; Health, Education and Welfare; Housing and Urban Development; the Interior; and Transportation. Critics denounced the panel as ineffective and Congress, under the leadership of Sen. Henry Jackson (D, Wash.) [q.v.], passed legislation creating an independent environmental council and making protection of natural resources a matter of national policy. Nixon signed the bill in January 1970. At the end of the month, he appointed Train chairman of the Council on Environmental Quality. Train's duties included advising the President on environmental problems, developing a means of coordinating government pollution programs and creating new programs.

The Council's first annual report was issued less than three months later. It labeled "the most out-of-hand and irreversible" environmental problem to be the misuse of the nation's available land resources, urged the development of a "strong and consistent federal policy" opposing water pollution, and recommended the monitoring of transportation and energy policies. The report also discussed the problems of noise abatement, endangered species, ocean pollution and resources and called for an increase of staff and funds to combat them.

The following year Train recommended a "national contingency plan" for the federal cleanup of oil spills at such times when the responsible party failed to act. It backed long-range planning of land and water resources, timber-cutting regulation and the banning of commercial trade involving wildlife species in danger of extinction as well as the continuation of tax incentives for those organizations engaged in preservation of the environment. Train said that one of his highest priorities was to convince Congress to authorize funds for urban areas that needed mass transit as an alternative to automobiles in order to clean the air.

Train led the U.S. effort in securing an agreement with the Soviet Union to set up a joint environmental improvement program in June 1972 and headed a U.S.-Canadian committee formed to prevent possible oil spills off Canada's west coast

resulting from the proposed Alaskan oil pipeline in September. The Council's third annual report, appearing in August 1972, stated that while progress was being made in cleaning the air, America's waterways were growing dirtier. The report warned that it would cost nearly three times the original estimates to solve the country's most pressing pollution problems.

In September 1973 Train was confirmed as administrator of the Environmental Protection Agency (EPA), an independent organization created to oversee clean air and water legislation, pesticide control and radiation-monitoring programs. He frequently clashed with the White House over its attempts to modify or stall enforcement of environmental laws. Shortly after taking the post, Train announced his opposition to a White House suggestion that air quality standards of the Clean Air Act be delayed in light of the anticipated economic consequences of a fuel shortage.

Train eventually backed a compromise between the EPA and the Office of Management and Budget (OMB), which wanted sweeping changes in the law. Under the compromise certain cities were given extensions of the 1977 deadline to meet the Act's standards and power companies were permitted to burn coal in some cases. Auto emission standards were also pushed back. But Train was able to have dropped an OMB proposal that the EPA consider the economic impact and costs of pollution control, as well as the health effects, in setting air quality standards. Another plan that would have exempted energy-related actions by federal agencies from required environmental impact statements was also dropped. His compromise was denounced by conservationists as an unnecessary weakening of the 1970 law, but it was accepted by Congress.

Near the end of his term, Train could report that although the economic slowdown and growing energy crisis had made achievement of environmental goals difficult, progress had been made. Train boasted that carbon monoxide and hydrocarbon auto emissions were down almost 85%; dust and soot pollutants were down 14%. An $18 million water improvement program had been implemented and a plan to convert trash into fuel had begun. Under his leadership the EPA had barred the sale of pesticides and the direct industrial discharge of polychlorinated biphenyls (PCBs) into waterways and had set radiation emission limits for nuclear power plants.

Train left government at the end of the Ford Administration to return to the Conservation Foundation.

[SBB]

TRBOVICH, MICHAEL
b. Nov. 19, 1920; Stewart, Pa.
Vice President, United Mine Workers, 1972-77.

Trbovich served in the Coast Guard during World War II and returned to work in the mines after the war. A long-time union activist, he was president of United Mine Workers (UMW) Local 688 from 1950 to 1959 and president of Local 6330 in 1971-72. In the late 1960s Trbovich became involved in Miners for Democracy (MFD) a rank-and-file movement formed within the UMW against the corrupt bureaucratic leadership of President Tony Boyle [q.v.]. In 1969 the MFD ran Joseph ("Jock") Yablonski [q.v.] for the UMW presidency. The MFD attacked the safety standards in the mines and the conservative Boyle leadership, while calling for democracy and decentralization of power within the union. Trbovich served as campaign manager for Yablonski. The insurgents were soundly defeated but appealed the election results because of alleged vote-tampering by the Boyle machine. In December 1969 Yablonski was murdered with his wife and daughter by men later linked to Boyle.

At Yablonski's funeral, Trbovich charged openly that the UMW leadership had killed the insurgent leader. In early 1970, responding to the pressure of public outcry about the Yablonski murder, the Department of Labor found massive irregularities in the UMW elections and began court proceedings against the Boyle leadership. In May 1972 a federal court upheld the Labor Department's charges. Several months later the MFD ticket of Arnold Miller [q.v.], Trbovich and Harry Patrick [q.v.] defeated the Boyle leadership in a federally-sponsored election.

Despite outward appearances of MFD unity, Trbovich was bitterly disappointed in 1972 when an MFD rump convention nominated Miller. The 1974 contract negotiations, in which Miller and his team secured a 54% wage and benefit increase for UMW members over a three-year period, saw the first significant showdown between Miller and an incipient anti-Miller coalition on the UMW executive board. The coalition forced the UMW president to return to the bargaining table to obtain concessions that, it was later learned, the coal operators had been prepared to grant all along. Miller's performance underlined growing signs of weakness and incompetence, and helped to push Trbovich into the anti-Miller majority.

In 1975, under the strain of the first wave of wildcat strikes that repeatedly closed down the Eastern coalfields from 1975 to 1977, Trbovich's impatience with Miller led to an open break. In June Trbovich circulated an internal memo to all members of the UMW's executive board charging Miller with gross incompetence and financial extravagance. The memo was quickly leaked, and a Trbovich candidacy for the UMW presidency in 1977 was widely expected.

In early 1975 Miller had stripped Trbovich of his personal authority within the union by removing the UMW's safety division from his control. But Trbovich, allied with former Boyle collaborators and ex-Miller supporters on the union executive board, was part of a majority that outvoted the Miller loyalists 3-1 on every important question. Although no issues of substance stood between the pro-Miller group and its dissident ex-members, Trbovich charged that Miller had filled the UMW staff with "radicals" who did little or no work to justify their salaries.

Miller supporters inside the union, however, insisted, "Nobody in the union has wasted more money than Trbovich."

Within a year of the Miller-Trbovich rift, the anti-Miller forces within the UMW had amassed sufficient power to push through a resolution at the union's 1976 convention moving the forthcoming presidential election from December to June 1977 in order to be rid of Miller before the beginning of the 1977 contract negotiations. The anticipated Trbovich presidential candidacy, however, did not materialize. Trbovich had suffered a heart attack in 1976 and was compelled to reduce his role in the union in fighting. In December 1976 he announced his support for Lee Roy Patterson, a former Boyle supporter, for UMW president. With Trbovich's endorsement Patterson ran a strong campaign against Miller, placing second with roughly 35% of the vote in the June 1977 election.

At the end of his term in 1977, Trbovich ended his activities in top-level UMW politics.

[LG]

UDALL, MORRIS K(ING)
b. June 15, 1922; St. Johns, Ariz.
Democratic Representative, Ariz., 1961-.

Morris Udall was born and raised in St. Johns, Ariz., a town founded by his grandfather who was a Mormon missionary. After serving in the Army Air Corps during World War II, he studied law at the University of Arizona and was admitted to the bar in 1949. Entering private practice in Tucson with his older brother Stewart, he also became active in local Democratic politics. In 1950 he was elected chief deputy attorney in Pima County, and in 1953 he won a race for county attorney. In the 1956 presidential campaign, Udall chaired Arizona Volunteers for Stevenson and was a delegate to the Democratic National Convention.

In May 1961 Udall won a special election to fill the House seat vacated by his brother Stewart who had resigned to become Secretary of the Interior. A supporter of the social welfare legislation of the Kennedy and Johnson Administrations, he joined the Democratic Study Group, a liberal faction within the Democratic Party. As a member of the Post Office and Civil Service Committee, Udall wrote the House version of the 1965 federal pay raise bill and in 1967 drafted legislation to set up an independent commission to pass on salary increases for members of Congress. Initially a supporter of the Vietnam war, he broke with the Johnson Administration in October 1967 when he declared in a speech given in Tucson that his support of the war had been a "mistake." [See JOHNSON Volume]

As chairman of the Subcommittee on the Environment of the House Interior Committee, Udall emerged as one of the strongest proponents of environmental legislation during the Nixon-Ford era. He supported legislation to fund a program of environmental education and advocated the establishment of a federal commission on population growth and the environment. In 1971 he introduced a resolution to make population stabilization by voluntary means a national goal. In 1974 he successfully sponsored legislation establishing a program of research and development in nonnuclear energy resources. Udall's major concerns, however, were national land use policy and the regulation of strip mining.

In 1964 Congress created the Public Land Law Review Commission and selected Udall as one of the congressional members on the Commission. After almost six years of study, it released a report in 1970 that recommended an extensive overhaul of public land legislation and management policies. The report, which urged greater commercial exploitation of federal lands, aroused the ire of environmentalists, and Udall dissented from many of its recommendations.

A national land use policy bill was first introduced in the Senate in 1970 by Henry Jackson [q.v.]. It provided grants-in-aid for states to develop and implement statewide land use plans, set federal standards to qualify for the grants and proposed creation of a federal land and water resources planning council to administer the program. No action was taken by the Senate, but Jackson introduced similar legislation in 1972, and Udall sponsored it in the House. No progress was made in the House until 1974, when Udall's subcommittee held extensive hearings on the bill, and the full Interior Committee reported it favorably. But on June 11 the House killed the legislation on a procedural vote.

In a press conference the next day, Udall blamed President Nixon for the defeat, saying that the bill was a victim of "impeachment politics," an attempt by the President to solidify conservative support against his impeachment. Udall was especially bitter because in 1973 Nixon had called land use legislation his "number one environmental priority." In 1975 Udall tried again, but this time the Interior Committee refused to report the bill to the full House. No efforts were made to pass land use legislation in 1976.

Udall also faced stiff opposition in his efforts to have legislation enacted to regulate the strip mining of coal. Although most of the nation's coal reserves were underground, strip mining was considerably cheaper, and coal companies and utilities strongly opposed its regulation. Environmentalists, however, made the regulation of strip mining one of their high-priority items, and Udall acted as their chief proponent in the House. The House passed legislation in 1972, but no action was taken by the Senate.

In 1973, both legislative bodies held extensive hearings on a strip mining bill. Udall's subcommittee held hearings throughout the summer and fall, and in May 1974, the full Interior Committee reported the bill. Its major provisions included the establishment of federal standards for the states to follow in setting up mandatory regulatory programs to control the strip mining of coal; the requirement that mining companies restore stripped land to its original contours; and a tax on every ton of coal mined, to be used for the reclamation of previously stripped and abandoned land. Udall, who was floor manager of the bill, described the legislation as an effort to end "a legacy of neglect" of the nation's land. Finally approved by a Senate-House conference on Dec. 3, and passed by Congress on Dec. 13, it was pocket-vetoed by President Ford.

The following month, at the opening of the more liberal 94th Congress, Udall reintroduced the legislation. The coal industry mounted a heavy campaign against it, including dispensing $400,000 to finance a demonstration by mine workers in April 1975. Udall accused the industry of "a mischievous and purposeful effort" to "mislead and foster fear among workers." When Congress approved the legislation in May, Ford vetoed it again, and the House failed to override the veto by three votes. In 1976 the House Rules Committee blocked revival of strip mining legislation.

In May 1974 Udall revealed that he was considering a bid for the 1976 presidential nomination. Earlier, in 1969, he had challenged John McCormack's [q.v.] tenure as Speaker of the House, and in 1971 he ran unsuccessfully for House majority leader. Encouraged by Rep. Henry Reuss (D, Wis.) [q.v.] and other House liberals, Udall declared his candidacy in November. Announcing that the "three E's— environment, economy, and energy" would dominate his campaign, he said that the major challenge facing the nation was "whether we can adapt and change from an era of abundance and cheap natural resources, to an era of scarcity." He advocated federal responsibility for full employment, comprehensive national health insurance and the federalization of welfare. His platform also included the controversial proposal to break up the huge oil companies through legislation rather than anti-trust action through the courts. By July 1975 Udall had raised enough money for his campaign to qualify for federal matching funds under the 1974 campaign finance law. In January 1976 he picked up the endorsement of House Speaker Thomas O'Neill. [q.v.]

A large number of candidates ranging across the political spectrum, including

Henry Jackson, George Wallace [q.v.], Jimmy Carter [q.v.], Fred Harris [q.v.], and Birch Bayh [q.v.], mounted campaigns for the 1976 nomination. Liberal candidates Harris and Bayh dropped out of the race early in the year, however, and Udall urged liberals to unite behind him or else face the prospect of a conservative nominee. Although he failed to win any of the early primaries, Udall placed a strong second in New Hampshire, Massachusetts, New York and Wisconsin. The race was dominated, however, by dark horse candidate Jimmy Carter, the former governor of Georgia who capitalized on the voters' post-Watergate distrust of Washington politicians.

Carter won seven of the first nine primaries. When Henry Jackson withdrew from active campaigning at the end of April, Udall declared that he and Carter were the only serious candidates left and predicted an "uphill fight" for the nomination. Despite the last-minute challenge of California Governor Edmund "Gerry" Brown, Jr. [q.v.], Carter continued to outdistance Udall in delegate strength. Early in June the count stood at 1,117 for Carter and only 327 for Udall. On June 14 Udall met with Carter and announced that he would stop campaigning. Saying that he "will not be a part of any stop-Carter drive," he released his delegates.

Despite the failure of his campaign, Udall's race for the nomination dramatically increased his visibility and gave him added stature in the Party. He won inclusion in the platform of a plank committing the Party to enact "strip mining legislation designed to protect and restore the environment." Running for reelection to his eighth complete term in the House, Udall won by a substantial majority. [See CARTER Volume]

[JD]

ULASEWICZ, ANTHONY T. (TONY)
Watergate figure.

Anthony Ulasewicz was an original member of the team put together by John Ehrlichman [q.v.] to investigate persons on the White House "enemies list." Ulasewicz received payment from Herbert Kalmbach [q.v.], a leading fund raiser for the 1968 Republican presidential campaign and later President Nixon's personal lawyer. Ulasewicz had worked earlier for the New York City Police Department's Bureau of Special Services.

Ulasewicz performed a variety of services for Ehrlichman, including illegally wire-tapping columnist Joseph Kraft's telephone in 1969. When Rep. Mario Biaggi (D, N.Y.) criticized President Nixon's 1969 call for a war against crime as being "insulting to Italian-Americans," he searched Biaggi's past for possible Mafia connections. Ulasewicz reportedly also formulated a plan to search out damaging information on Sen. Edward Kennedy [q.v.] concerning the 1969 auto accident at Chappaquiddick that involved the drowning of Mary Jo Kopechne. These and other incidents led *The New York Times* to later describe Ulasewicz as a precursor of the White House "Plumbers."

Ulasewicz first became directly involved in the Watergate cover-up by delivering a message from John Dean [q.v.] to James McCord [q.v.] concerning McCord's course of conduct during the ongoing investigation of the Watergate break-in.

On June 28, 1972, Dean approached Kalmbach for the purpose of secretly raising funds for the defense of the Watergate burglars. At Dean's instruction Ulasewicz was to distribute the money to the defendants. Kalmbach raised money during the summer and Ulasewicz distributed $220,000 always using secretive methods such as pay telephones, drops and aliases. In September when it appeared that the indictments in the Watergate case would include only those directly involved in the break-in, Kalmbach, on the advice of Ulasewicz, declined to raise additional funds for the cover-up effort.

Ulasewicz testified about his activities both during the Senate Watergate Committee hearings in July 1973 and the cover-up trial in November 1974. In April 1975 he was indicted for tax evasion regarding the reporting of his income during 1971 and 1972 while he worked for the White House. In December 1976 Ulasewicz was convicted of these charges, and in February 1977 he received the minimum sentence of one year of unsupervised probation.

[RLN]

USERY, W(ILLIE) J(ULIAN), JR.
b. Dec. 21, 1923; Hardwick, Ga.
Secretary of Labor, February 1976-
January 1977.

The son of a postal clerk, Usery enrolled in Georgia Military Academy in 1938 but left after three years to work in Navy shipyards as a welder. In 1943 he joined the Navy, and served on a repair ship in the Pacific until 1946. After his discharge, he worked as a machinist while attending night school and became active in union politics and founded a local chapter of the International Association of Machinists (IAM).

Because of his organization skills, Usery was tapped by IAM officials for a union post at Cape Canaveral, later called Cape Kennedy, in 1954. He played a decisive role in most labor negotiations involving the aerospace industry and in 1967 was appointed chairman of the Cape Kennedy Management Relations Council. While stationed in Florida he also became active in the civil rights movement of the 1960s.

In 1968 George P. Shultz [q.v.], Nixon's Secretary of Labor, offered Usery a position as assistant secretary of labor for labor-management relations. Although he felt that "it's very difficult for a labor leader to come into a Republican Administration," he took over the job effective February 1969. His responsibilities included overseeing the federal employee unions, restructuring pension fund regulations and establishing farm workers' bargaining rights.

In the spring of 1969 Usery served as Nixon's chief mediator for a threatened strike by the Brotherhood of Railroad Signalmen (BRS). Through the use of collective bargaining, he was able to avert a national strike. His decisive role in negotiations with the BRS earned him the reputation of Nixon's "number one labor troubleshooter."

Because of his mediating expertise and interventionist skills, Usery played key roles in the settlement of the 1970 Brotherhood of Railway and Airline Clerks strike and the 1971 United Transportation Union's strike against the railroads. He subsequently intervened in such deadlocked negotiations as the International Brotherhood of Teamsters and Pan American World Airways and also the dispute between black construction workers and the white-controlled building industry in Pittsburgh. In 1971 Usery was instrumental in achieving the first collective bargaining agreement in history between the Council of American Postal Employees and the U.S. Postal Service. With the exception of accusations within the labor movement that he displayed favoritism to AFL-CIO affiliates during union membership drives, Usery was virtually exempt from criticism among national labor leaders and the Department of Labor.

In 1973 the AFL-CIO Executive Council voted unanimously to appoint Usery to the post of director of the department of organization and field services, but he declined because he felt his talents were most needed in the Nixon Administration. That same year Usery became the official top labor mediator for the government when he assumed the position of director of the Federal Mediation and Conciliation Service. He continued in his directorship to encourage improved industrywide bargaining procedures and also played a significant role in the formation of joint labor-management committees throughout various industries to avoid possible strikes and deadlocks. He also strengthened his reputation as a negotiator extraordinaire by settling a variety of local labor disputes that threatened to disrupt the clothing and trucking industries. During the Arab oil embargo of 1973, Usery's expeditious handling of a contract dispute prevented a strike by thousands of airline pilots.

Upon the resignation of John T. Dunlap [q.v.] as Secretary of Labor in 1975, Usery was considered the likely candidate for the job. Shortly thereafter President Ford nominated Usery, and in February 1976 he assumed the cabinet post. His responsibilities broadened to include the administration of federal antidiscrimination laws, the regulation of government hiring procedures and job training programs as well as establishment of job safety guidelines. Usery continued in his mediating capacity, and in April 1976 he helped to settle a strike between the Teamsters and the American and General Motors Corps. His tenure with the Labor Department ended at the close of the Ford Administration.

[DGE]

VANIK, CHARLES A.
b. April 7, 1913; Cleveland, Ohio.
Democratic Representative, Ohio,
1955-.

Charles A. Vanik received both bachelor's and law degrees from Case-Western Reserve University, and served in the Navy during World War II. Entering politics at the war's end, Vanik won election to the state Senate and a municipal judgeship before unseating a 19-term House incumbent in 1954. Of Czech heritage, Vanik represented the overwhelmingly-Democratic 21st district, composed largely of second-generation Eastern European immigrants and blacks.

In January 1965 House leaders transferred Vanik, considered a Johnson Administration loyalist, from the Banking and Currency Committee to Ways and Means. The Democratic leadership moved Vanik to the powerful taxation panel because of his strong support for medicare, long opposed by Ways and Means chairman Wilbur D. Mills (D, Ark.) [q.v.]. It was Vanik's vote that forced Mills to accept a compromise med-

icare plan in 1965. While supporting many of the domestic measures of President Johnson, Vanik became highly critical of the Administration's Vietnam policy, voting against the 1968 Defense Department authorization that passed the House 213-6.

A 1967 Ohio redistricting created a large black majority in Vanik's district. Declaring that the district should now have a black representative, Vanik decided to run in the largely-white, suburban 22nd district against 82-year-old incumbent Frances P. Belton (R, Ohio). In a hotly contested election Vanik stressed the need for updating the district's political leadership and defeated the wealthy 14-term Representative with 55% of the vote. [See JOHNSON Volume]

With his solidly liberal record and excellent constituent services, Vanik easily won reelection in 1970, 1972 and 1974. He maintained two district offices, organizing many district studies and commissions. Vanik's practices of compiling yearly reports on federal aid to his district and on educational aid to his constituents were adopted by federal agencies on a nationwide basis. A strong supporter of environmental protection, Vanik pushed for the cleanup of Lake Erie, advocating improved waste treatment, stricter regulation of industrial waste and a "no discharge" goal set for 1975. Vanik joined 40 other representatives in offering a package of clean water amendments to the Water Pollution Control Act of 1972. The amendments, which would have made polluters liable to suit and set more stringent waste-dumping standards for the Great Lakes, failed in the House. Vanik also worked actively for consumer protection programs and in 1971 introduced legislation to insure equal educational and employment opportunities for the handicapped.

In December 1973 Vanik introduced an amendment to President Richard M. Nixon's comprehensive foreign trade bill. The amendment would have placed strict curbs on U.S. trade with the Soviet Union, denying the USSR most favored nation (MFN) status and commercial credit until the Soviets eased emigration restrictions on Soviet Jews. Vanik's amendment passed the House, while the Senate approved a similar amendment introduced by Sens. Henry Jackson (D, Wash.) [q.v.], Abraham Ribicoff (D, Conn.) [q.v.] and Jacob Javits (R, N.Y.) [q.v.]. In the face of strong pressure by the Administration, which considered MFN status for the USSR essential to the pursuit of detente, Sen. Jackson offered a compromise floor amendment allowing the Soviets an 18-month waiver on the ban of MFN status provided they moved toward free emigration policies. This compromise measure passed in December 1974, but its terms were later rejected by the Soviets.

A long-time advocate of congressional reform, Vanik continued through the Nixon and Ford Administrations to oppose the leadership of Ways and Means Chairman Wilbur Mills. Often among the dissenting minority on Ways and Means, Vanik supported open committee sessions and fought the "closed rule," frequently invoked by Mills to send Ways and Means bills to the House with a ban on the introduction of floor amendments. At the time of the House Legislative Reorganization Act of 1970, Vanik introduced a measure that would have abolished the seniority system. Terming the system "arbitrary," Vanik proposed the election of new standing committee chairmen every two years. Other congressional reformers opposed Vanik's amendment, fearing that it had no hope of passage and would weaken other reform efforts. In December 1974 Vanik joined other House Democrats in a successful coalition to strip Wilbur Mills of his Ways and Means chairmanship, a position Mills had held since 1958. On Dec. 19, Ways and Means established its first subcommittees, thus decentralizing the panel's authority. As chairman of the oversight subcommittee, Vanik attacked tax system inequities, citing 11 major firms that paid no income taxes in 1975. Blasting corporate tax loopholes, Vanik charged the Republican Administration with aiding the American corporation to become "a freeloader on the Amer-

ican scene." Vanik continued to win reelection by substantial majorities through the 1970's.

[DAE]

VESCO, ROBERT L(EE)
b. Dec. 4, 1935; Detroit, Mich.
International financier.

The son of an auto worker, Vesco grew up in Detroit. He dropped out of high school at 16, and took a job in an auto repair shop. Eventually he worked his way into the management of several small companies. From 1955 to 1959 he was employed by the Olin Mathieson Corporation, and from 1959 to 1965, he was a financial consultant in New York City. In 1965 he became president of the International Controls Corporation (ICC), a small New Jersey-based firm which he used as a vehicle for entering international finance.

In 1970 Vesco used the assets available to him through ICC to gain controlling interest in the foundering Investors Overseas Services, Ltd. (IOS), the large mutual fund established by Bernard Cornfeld and one of the more spectacular victims of the 1969-70 international credit crunch. A run on IOS stock, then selling at $10 per share, was the opening phase of a year-long crisis for the "offshore" mutual fund that Cornfeld had built up through the boom of the 1960s. By early September 1970 Vesco had negotiated a bailout package for IOS with conditions effectively giving him control of the conglomerate. Vesco had compelled IOS to deposit $5 million in collateral in a Vesco-controlled bank in the Bahamas, a sum which he promptly re-lent to IOS as the main ingredient of the rescue operation. In effect he used the disarray of the IOS management to take over the conglomerate with its own money. Vesco followed his successful takeover with the ouster of Cornfeld from the organization, ultimately buying for 92 cents a share Cornfeld's 6.6 million shares of IOS stock, or roughly 15% of the total stock issued.

The Securities and Exchange Commission (SEC) had intently followed the IOS crisis and Vesco's takeover, and in May 1971 won a court battle to subpoena Vesco for an inquiry into the financing of the acquisition of Cornfeld's shares in IOS, which had just been resold to a Canadian subsidiary of Vesco's International Controls. That same month, Denver oilman John M. King filed a suit for more than $1 billion against Vesco and IOS, alleging that Vesco had used illegal funds to gain control of various U.S. companies. Dissident IOS officials from Cornfeld's management team fought and lost a proxy battle in July to regain control of IOS from Vesco.

Vesco was arrested in Geneva in November 1971 on charges of misappropriating shares while serving as a director of a former IOS bank subsidiary. The charges stemmed from a complaint by an IOS dissident manager who alleged that his own shares, on deposit in IOS's International Development Bank, had been used by Vesco to defeat the dissident faction in the proxy war for control of the firm. On Dec. 1, however, Vesco and his colleagues were released on bail. Investigations later revealed that the CIA, on orders from the Nixon Administration, had intervened to obtain Vesco's release.

In November 1972 a two-year SEC investigation culminated in charges that Vesco, 20 other individuals and 21 firms they controlled had diverted more than $224 million in assets from four mutual funds holding securities of U.S. companies. The SEC charged Vesco with having controlled IOS through a "shell" corporation created to purchase the Cornfeld shares in 1971. Vesco and his entourage took refuge in Costa Rica, where they could not be extradited. Two days after the SEC civil complaint was announced, *The Wall Street Journal* reported that a company founded by the president of Costa Rica, Jose Figueres, had received a loan of more than $2 million from Vesco.

In February 1973 Harry L. Sears, a New Jersey Republican who had headed the 1972 Committee to Reelect the President (CREEP) in that state, testified in a pretrial deposition that Vesco had contributed $200,000 to CREEP in hopes of heading off the SEC inquiry into his activities. Sears said that the sum had been delivered in cash to former Secretary of Commerce Maurice Stans [q.v.] who was serving as head of the Republican Finance Committee. The contribution had never been reported to the Government Accounting Office. Sear's account was confirmed by Edward Nixon, the President's brother and a Vesco associate. CREEP announced that it had returned Vesco's contribution because of the pending SEC suit, saying that "under these circumstances, we believe it is in your best interests, as well as ours, that the contribution was returned."

In April 1973 *The Washington Post* alleged that President Nixon and his aide John D. Ehrlichman [q.v.] had promised in 1971 to use government channels to help Vesco obtain control of a Lebanese bank. The *Post* reported a December 1971 meeting in the White House involving Gilbert R. J. Straub, a codefendant with Vesco in the SEC suit as well as a friend of Edward and Donald Nixon (the President's brothers), Harry L. Sears and a man later identified as the courier who delivered Vesco's $200,000 contribution to Stans.

In May 1973 the Justice Department filed charges against the Financial Committee of CREEP for failure to report the Vesco contribution. A week later Stans and former Attorney General John Mitchell [q.v.] were indicted for their actions while serving on CREEP; the handling of Vesco's contribution was the centerpiece of the government's case against them. At the same time Vesco was indicted on one count of conspiracy and three counts of obstructing justice. In June 1973 the U.S. ambassador to Costa Rica asked the authorities of that country to extradite Vesco. Several days later, a New York grand jury indicted Vesco for attempting to defraud the International Controls Corporation. However, in July 1973 the Costa Rican Supreme Court ruled that Vesco not be extradited.

During October new grand jury indictments were brought against Vesco for his actions in the IOS takeover. A month later, he was arrested in the Bahamas in another U.S. attempt to have him extradited, but once again the local court ruled in his favor. In late November a narcotics agent told congressional investigators that Vesco had been involved in a scheme to smuggle 100 pounds of heroin into the U.S.

In the spring of 1974 Vesco emerged as the central figure in the Stans-Mitchell trial in New York City in which the government accused both defendants of having attempted to block the SEC investigation of Vesco in exchange for a large cash contribution to the Nixon campaign. In early April 1974 the U.S. prosecutor contended that Vesco's contribution had financed the Watergate break-in. Mitchell and Stans were acquitted, however, and in December 1974 Vesco went on Costa Rican television to defend himself and to portray himself as a victim of "the same political groups that eliminated President Kennedy and then President Nixon and want to eliminate all of Nixon's associates." He further denied having broken any laws in the U.S.

In March 1975 charges against Harry L. Sears stemming from his role in CREEP were dropped. Sears's pretrial deposition revealed that Attorney General Mitchell had intervened personally on Vesco's behalf to obtain his relase from a Swiss jail in 1971, and that the CIA had informed Swiss intelligence services "that there was unusual interest in higher U.S. government circles . . . in this case, and that we hoped Vesco would be released on his own recognizance." Simultaneously a Senate subcommittee report indicated the possible involvement of Vesco in a scheme to smuggle $200,000 worth of heroin into the U.S., and stockholders of International Controls Corporation filed suit against him in Costa Rican courts. During May, 1975 New Jersey courts ordered Vesco to pay $5.6 billion to stockholders of IOS Ltd. The following year Vesco was indicted yet again for conspiring to misappropriate $100 million in the assets of mutual funds he controlled.

During the 1970s Vesco made his home in Costa Rica, where he pursued his business and financial interests, while resisting the efforts of the U.S. and local forces hostile to him to achieve his extradition.

[LRG]

For further information:
Robert A. Hutchison, *Vesco* (New York, 1974).

VOLCKER, PAUL A.
b. Sept. 5, 1927; Cape May, N.J.
Undersecretary of the Treasury for Monetary Affairs, January 1969-June 1974.

After graduating summa cum laude from Princeton in 1949, Volcker received an M.A. from Harvard in 1951 and did further postgraduate work at the London School of Economics. Upon completion of his studies, he worked as an economist for the Federal Reserve Bank of New York and later for the Chase Manhattan Bank. He served an initial period at the Treasury Department in the 1961-65 period, but returned again to Chase as a vice president, remaining there until he was appointed undersecretary of the treasury for monetary affairs in 1969.

Both publicly and behind the scenes, Volcker played an important role in the international monetary crisis that provided an ever present backdrop to the Nixon Administration's economic policies. Volcker was associated with the "hard line," or assertively nationalistic wing of U.S. policymakers on international monetary questions, typified by Secretary of the Treasury John Connally [q.v.]. Like Connally, Volcker often clashed with other U.S. and foreign officials. Central to Volcker's position on such questions was a hostility to any continued significant role for gold in international settlements, which was an important source of friction between the United States and Europe, as well as an advocacy of the extended use of "special drawing rights" (SDRs), or "paper gold" certificates issued by the International Monetary Fund (IMF), which the United States introduced as an international alternative to gold in the late 1960s.

Gold, SDRs and foreign exchange rates were complexly interrelated issues with which Volcker had to deal repeatedly. In December 1969, as part of the U.S. campaign to ease out gold, Volcker met in Rome with South African officials to negotiate a compromise agreement on South African gold sales to the IMF. In June 1971, as the crisis leading to the August 1971 abrogation of the Bretton Woods Agreement intensified, Volcker, who felt that the existing exchange rate system was adequate, denied any deep structural nature to the U.S. balance-of-payments deficit and blamed the crisis on short-term capital flows. To counter these trends he called for limited mandatory capital controls and "an international open-market operation" in the burgeoning Euro-dollar markets. The balance-of-payments crisis persisted, however, and the old exchange rates had to be abandoned.

In August Volcker was sent to Europe to explain the U.S. policy to European governments. Volcker announced that the Europeans "understood and even welcomed" the U.S. unilateral action, but reactions in European capitals did not seem to bear out his optimism. In Brussels, the headquarters of the European Economic Community (EEC), Volcker was seen as representing an "uncompromising" U.S. attitude on Nixon's 10% foreign import surcharge. In September, when the IMF Group of 10 met in Paris to discuss the situation, Volcker reaffirmed his opposition to a U.S. gold revaluation and urged the U.S. trading partners to engage in "consultation, not negotiation." Shortly thereafter, Volcker disclosed a vastly increased U.S. balance-of-payments deficit, an amount that "shocked" many foreigners.

When the Group of 10 reconvened in November 1971 for new talks and to lay the basis for new fixed rates, Volcker offered America's trading partners an abolition of the 10% import surcharge if they consented to revalue their currencies by 11% against the dollar, a proposal that elicited little enthusiasm from major exporters to U.S. markets. When the Smithsonian Agreement establishing new fixed rates was finally signed by all countries in Washington in December, most nations agreed to revalue by varying amounts.

After the establishment of new fixed rates, Volcker began to advocate what was known as a "reserve indicator" in international settlements. Under Volcker's proposal, which many observers likened to a 1943 proposal by Keynes that the U.S., then a strong creditor nation, had rejected, nations running excessive trade surpluses would be penalized in the same way as deficit nations. Most U.S. trading partners viewed Volcker's plan as a transparent attempt to shift the burden of the U.S.'s chronic deficits onto the surplus producers, and it was never adopted.

Volcker was involved in the public rift, if not actual hostility, between the Treasury and the Federal Reserve Bank on international monetary questions and the Administration's so-called benign neglect of the dollar. The Treasury, under Secretary Connally, predominated in U.S. economic policy in this period, and was more closely associated with Connally's aggressive international stance, which European and Japanese commentators called "malign neglect," than was the Fed. One dramatic expression of this rift had been the exclusion of Fed Chairman Arthur Burns [q.v.] from the "Camp David II" meeting on Aug. 14-15, 1971, when the "New Economic Policy," framed in large part by Connally, had been adopted. In a May 1972 address to the American Bankers' Association in Montreal, Burns referred to the urgent need for overall monetary reform and alluded to a continued limited reserve role for gold. Speaking after Burns, Volcker told the convention that the chairman "was not speaking for the U.S. government" and warned against any "prepackaged reforms."

At the IMF annual meeting in Vienna in September 1972, Volcker attacked what he saw as European efforts to "impose" their solutions on the rest of the world, and once again asserted that "gold will have to go the way of silver." Upon his return to the U.S., Volcker told the congressional Joint Economic Committee (JEC) that gold "should and must continue to diminish" as a reserve asset, and that advocates of an increase in the official gold price—which would be a further devaluation of the dollar—were victims of a "dangerous illusion." Volcker also told the JEC that he opposed Federal Reserve Bank intervention to shore up the dollar, leaving that task to the central banks of other countries.

When the next dollar crisis erupted in February 1973, the central banks of Europe and Japan did indeed intervene buying billions of dollars to prevent new revaluations of their currencies. Volcker was sent on a secret tour of the major world capitals to confer with foreign officials, and on Feb. 12, the day of his return to the U.S., a further 10% devaluation of the dollar was announced. The move proved insufficient. Speculation against the dollar continued, and the market price of gold, in spite of Volcker's repeated statements against gold speculators, soared to $89 an ounce. On March 1, foreign exchange markets closed for two weeks. President Nixon, Volcker, Chairman Burns and Secretary Connally met to discuss the crisis. Volcker then accompanied an American delegation to Brussels on March 4 for talks with EEC officials. On March 16 in Paris, an accord was signed ending the fixed rate system in effect since 1944, and Volcker, in spite of his long-standing opposition to floating rates, announced he was "happy" with the agreement. In June 1973 he appeared before the JEC to reaffirm his satisfaction with the new floating rates system.

Volcker resigned as undersecretary of the treasury in June 1974. The following year he became president of the Federal Reserve Bank of New York.

[LG]

VOLPE, JOHN A(NTHONY)

b. Dec. 8, 1908; Wakefield, Mass.
Secretary of Transportation, January 1969–January 1973; Ambassador to Italy, February 1973–January 1977.

Volpe, the eldest son of Italian immigrant parents, rose from a hod carrier to the head of the multimillion dollar John A. Volpe Construction Co., which he founded in 1933. Volpe's government career began in 1953 when he was appointed public works commissioner for Massachusetts and started the largest highway construction program in the state's history. He served briefly as the interim federal highway administrator when President Eisenhower appointed him to the newly created post in late 1956. In 1960 he was elected governor of Massachusetts, the only Republican to win a statewide race that year. Volpe was the first Italian and Catholic ever elected governor of the state. He was defeated for reelection in 1962, but recaptured the office in 1964 and won the state's first four-year gubernatorial term in 1966. He resigned the governorship in 1969 when Nixon appointed him as the nation's second Secretary of Transportation. As secretary, Volpe headed the department that was responsible for regulating the automotive, railway and aviation sectors of the economy. He also supervised the Interstate Highway construction program, which he helped launch in 1956.

Volpe shaped the Nixon Administration's transportation policies and programs and served as the Administration's chief Capitol Hill spokesman on many transportation issues during Nixon's first term. These included providing federal loan guarantees for the Penn Central and other bankrupt railroads, reorganizing passenger rail service under Amtrak and increasing federal safety regulation of the railroads.

Volpe also had to cope with the 1970 "sick out" staged by the nation's air controllers to protest working conditions and the 123-day West Coast dock strike in 1970 which ended after the Administration pressured Congress to enact legislation to settle the dispute.

Volpe was a strong supporter of the supersonic transport (SST), which, he maintained, was needed to preserve the U.S. aviation industry. The program, however, ran into strong congressional opposition led by Sen. William Proxmire (D, Wis.) [q.v.] and Rep. Henry Reuss (D, Wis.) [q.v.]. The opponents objected to the plane's excessive development costs, the sonic booms it would create over land, its excessive operating noise on landing and takeoff and the environmental hazards it might create in the upper atmosphere.

Volpe tried to counter some of the objections to the SST by promising that it would not be flown over land until the plane's 50-mile-wide sonic boom had been reduced to acceptable limits. However the opponents were able to strengthen their case after they obtained a Department of Transportation report that opposed the plane.

Congress eventually funded the SST in 1969, but the project ran into even stronger congressional opposition during the following year when the Administration requested $290 million for fiscal 1971. Congress granted the funds but only for three-fourths of the fiscal year to permit further congressional review. The Nixon Administration opened the fight to save the plane in March 1971. Volpe accused the SST opponents of "hysterical sloganeering." He pointed to the long-range benefits of the program which employed 13,000 people to build the prototypes and which would have employed 50,000 when the plane went into full production. But both Houses voted to end the program in March 1971, after the government had spent about $840 million on the project.

Volpe was also a strong advocate of the Administration's mass transit funding proposals that Congress adopted during Nixon's first term. The White House proposed a $10 billion 12-year program financed by general revenues to upgrade urban transit systems. The program called for an initial $3.1 billion five-year contract authorization. Urban transit proponents, who favored creating an urban transit trust fund similar to the highway trust fund that financed the construction of highways, disapproved of the proposal on the grounds that it failed to ensure full funding for the mass transit program. Instead they favored earmarking the 7% excise tax on automobiles to finance an urban transit trust fund. Trust fund spending would have been automatic, as opposed to spending authorizations funded from general revenues that required prior congressional approval before the funds could be spent.

Volpe at first favored the excise tax trust fund concept. But the Administration decided against it, and Volpe supported the Administration's position. He claimed public transportation was a public responsibility and should be met by all taxpayers out of general revenues. Congress finally resolved the funding controversy without creating a trust fund, and enacted the Administration's $3.1 billion urban transit aid proposal in 1970.

The urban transit funding controversy broke out again in the next session of Congress. This time the question was whether to divert highway trust funds for mass transit construction. In March 1972 Volpe released a report calling for the diversion of highway trust funds. He proposed a single "urban fund" to be started with a $1 billion authorization from highway trust funds for fiscal 1974. This fund was to be increased to $2.25 billion in later years. The highway construction industry vigorously objected to the proposal to divert highway trust funds from highway construction. Volpe argued that "highway investments alone cannot cope with the pressing and severe problem that is so harmful to the effective functioning of urban areas. Only by proper combination of highway and transit modes can progress be made." Congress failed to pass the measure.

Volpe was a leading supporter of no-fault auto insurance and within the Administration lobbied for legislation to create a federal no-fault system. President Nixon, however, opposed the plan, recommending that reform be left to the states, and Volpe eventually presented the President's stand urging that Congress adopt a resolution to encourage states to adopt their own plans.

Volpe was appointed ambassador to Italy in 1973 when Nixon reshuffled his cabinet at the beginning of his second term. He served until 1977 when the Carter Administration took office.

[AE]

WALLACE, GEORGE C(ORLEY)
b. August 25, 1919; Clio, Ala.
Governor, Ala., 1963-67, 1970-78.

The son of a farmer, Wallace received his law degree from the University of Alabama in 1942 and served in the armed forces during World War II. Elected to the state House of Representatives in 1947, he served two terms and established a quasi-liberal record. In 1953 he was elected a circuit judge in Alabama, and became known as the "fighting judge" because of his open defiance of the U.S. Civil Rights Commission. Having unsuccessfully sought the gubernatorial nomination in 1958, Wallace ran again in 1962, campaigning as a militant segregationist and states' rights advocate. Elected governor, he lived up to his campaign rhetoric. In June 1963, with state troopers, he personally barred the entry of two black students trying to register at the University of Alabama, thereby forcing President Kennedy to federalize the Alabama National Guard. In September he ordered the closing of public schools in several cities to prevent integration. Kennedy again federalized the National Guard to open the schools. In 1965 Wallace used state troops to block Martin Luther King's [q.v.] march from Selma, forcing the federal government to provide the marchers with protection. Prevented by state law from succeeding himself as governor, Wallace ran his wife, Lurleen, who won election in 1966. Wallace was de facto governor during his wife's term.

Capitalizing on the national publicity

he received for his segregationist stand, Wallace entered Democratic primaries in Wisconsin, Indiana and Maryland in 1964. His strong showing impressed political observers and revealed the depth of the white backlash to the civil rights movement. When the Republicans nominated Barry Goldwater [q.v.], Wallace withdrew from the race. In 1968 he announced a third party candidacy. Denying that he was a racist, he posed as a defender of the working class and an opponent of the federal government's attempt to "take over and destroy the authority of the states." However he also spoke out strongly against federal civil rights legislation. Winning a place on the ballot in all fifty states, usually as a candidate of the American Independent Party, Wallace captured 13.6% of the vote and carried five states in the South. Political analysts claimed that Wallace's candidacy hurt Republican Richard Nixon more than it did Hubert Humphrey [q.v.]. [See KENNEDY, JOHNSON Volumes]

After the election Wallace supporters took steps to form a national conservative party. In February 1969 Wallace followers met in Dallas and Louisville and in May announced the creation of the American Independent Party. Although it was clearly intended as a vehicle for Wallace, he remained officially aloof from it, wishing to preserve all of his options. He did say, however, that he felt a third party movement was "still necessary," and he continued to address political rallies and speak out on issues.

Wallace quickly became a vocal opponent of the Nixon Administration, posing criticism from the right. In a July 1969 television appearance, he set out guidelines for the President: "Conclude the war honorably, give some tax reduction to the middle class of our country and cut out unnecessary spending, restore law and order and get the government out of the control of local institutions such as schools." In November, Wallace visited Vietnam and on his return attacked Nixon's policies of troop withdrawal and Vietnamization. Keeping the issue of school desegregation prominent in his speeches, he accused Nixon of breaking his campaign pledge not to bus children to achieve racial balance. In a February 1970 speech in Birmingham, Wallace urged Southern governors to disregard federal court orders to integrate schools and told his audience, "We'll see to it that Mr. Nixon is a one-term President." Shrewdly capitalizing on the Administration's so-called Southern strategy, the effort to win the South over to the Republican Party, Wallace sought to keep pressure on the Administration in the area of school desegregation.

Wallace's wife, Lurleen, had died of cancer in 1968 and was succeeded as governor by Albert Brewer. In February 1970 Wallace announced his candidacy against Brewer in the May gubernatorial primary. The outcome of the race was considered decisive for Wallace's political future and political analysts watched the race closely. Not certain of victory, Wallace turned to explicit racial appeals toward the end of the campaign, charging that Brewer was a favorite of the "bloc vote," a code word in Alabama politics for blacks. Brewer, on the other hand, subtly appealed to blacks by promising to look to the "future" instead of the past. Although Brewer placed first in the voting he failed to achieve a majority and was forced into a runoff. Wallace received the support of the Ku Klux Klan and defeated Brewer in the runoff. Immediately after his victory Wallace called on Nixon to deliver his "two-year-old unfulfilled pledges to stop busings and school closings and to reestablish freedom of choice," and pointedly declared that "the Republican Party knows it cannot win without the South in the next election."

With his eye on the 1972 presidential race, Wallace continued to exploit antibusing sentiment. In August 1971 he ordered Alabama school boards to disregard court-ordered integration plans and to keep the schools closed if necessary. The following month, however, schools opened quietly and without incident. Wallace's stand did seem to have an effect. In August, Nixon reiterated his opposition to busing and warned federal officials that they risked losing their jobs if they sought to impose busing plans on local school districts. In November the House for the first time overwhelmingly approved an amendment to an education aid bill to prohibit the use of federal money for busing to achieve racial balance.

On Jan. 13, 1972, Wallace formally announced his candidacy for the Democratic presidential nomination. He told a large rally in Tallahassee that he was the only candidate to protest busing and other intrusions of "big government" into their private lives. He also made crime prevention and tax reduction issues in his campaign and claimed to speak for the "little man." Democratic National Chairman Lawrence F. O'Brien [q.v.] immediately disavowed the Wallace candidacy and AFL-CIO president George Meany attacked him as a "bigot" and a "racist" and accused him of being "anti-labor right down to the soles of his feet." Wallace's entry into the Democratic race quickly magnified the importance of the busing issue. On Feb. 14, Nixon promised to take steps soon to limit busing, and Sen. Henry Jackson [q.v.], another presidential aspirant, proposed a constitutional amendment to prohibit busing. A nonbinding referendum on school busing was also placed on the ballot in the Florida primary.

Wallace made the March 14 primary in Florida a test of his viability as a candidate. Although expected to win, he surprised observers by the size of his victory. Capturing 42% of the vote, he had more than double the ballots of second-place finisher Hubert Humphrey. Declaring himself a "serious candidate," Wallace took his campaign North to prove that he had national appeal. In primaries in Wisconsin and Pennsylvania in April, Wallace placed an impressive second, and in Indiana the following month he won over 40% of the vote, with strong support in the suburbs and in blue-collar districts. He also easily won primaries in Alabama, Tennessee and North Carolina. The strength of his campaign led George McGovern [q.v.] and Hubert Humphrey, the only other serious candidates left, to mount last-minute "stop Wallace" drives in Michigan and Maryland, where primaries were scheduled for May 16.

On May 15 tragedy struck the Wallace campaign. While walking through a crowd of supporters in a shopping center in Laurel, Md., he was shot several times and critically wounded. His assailant, a young drifter named Arthur Bremer who had been following Wallace on the campaign trail, was immediately seized by the Secret Service. Wallace was rushed to a hospital where the bullets were removed, but doctors announced that he would be paralyzed from the waist down. The next day he won easy victories in Michigan and Maryland, but his physical condition considerably diminished the viability of his campaign. After McGovern won the California primary in June, he was virtually assured the nomination. With McGovern's first-ballot victory and the rejection by the Party's Platform Committee of an anti-busing plank, Wallace announced that he would remain neutral in the presidential campaign and barred a third party candidacy for himself.

Wallace's name figured prominently in the Senate Watergate hearings. John Dean [q.v.] revealed that Wallace was on the President's infamous enemies list, and H.R. Haldeman [q.v.] testified that secret campaign funds had been used to aid Wallace's opponents in the 1970 gubernatorial contest. It was also revealed that the Nixon Administration had used the Internal Revenue Service to try to obtain damaging information on Wallace and members of his family.

Wallace ran for reelection in 1974. The campaign, however, was far different from previous ones. The racial issue remained in the background, and Wallace actively courted black votes, declaring that if reelected he would be governor of both "whites and blacks" and promising "opportunities for all." Although national civil rights leaders opposed him, many local black politicians endorsed Wallace in recognition of his power to disperse federal and state funds and provide political appointments. Wallace easily defeated his opponents without the need for a runoff, receiving 64% of the vote, including about one-quarter of the black vote.

Wallace came under increasingly heavy criticism during his new term as governor. Opponents attacked his preoccupation with national politics at the expense of Alabama's daily affairs. Critics charged that Alabama was really run by federal Judge Frank M. Johnson who, in the absence of action from Wallace, ordered the desegregation of schools and the state police, the redrawing of the state's political boundaries to insure fair representation, the cleaning up of the state's decrepit prison system and mental hospitals and the reassessment of commercial property for tax purposes. Wallace's claim to represent working people was also challenged. Despite his many years as governor, opponents pointed out that Alabama had no minimum wage law, minimal workmen's and unemployment compensation benefits, the lowest per pupil expenditures on education of any state, and was near the bottom in personal income. Its tax system, moreover, was among the most regressive in the country. There were also charges of rampant corruption, with two major kickback convictions, a major theft conviction and several resignations under fire of top state officials.

Despite the growing disenchantment with his governorship, Wallace, in November 1975, announced his candidacy for the 1976 Democratic presidential nomination. Avoiding for the most part the race issue, he concentrated on crime and high taxes and declared that the main issue in the campaign was whether the middle class could "survive economically." A Gallup poll in December placed him second in popularity among possible candidates, behind Hubert Humphrey, who was not openly campaigning.

Wallace's 1976 race revealed both the limits and extent of his appeal. By toning down his extremism, he failed to attract the sizable number of disenchanted voters who turned to him in the past to register a protest. On the other hand, his new image did not convince those liberal and middle-of-the-road Democrats who remembered his past record. Wallace's campaign received a serious blow from which it never recovered when he lost the March 14 Florida primary to dark horse candidate Jimmy Carter [q.v.]. Wallace had predicted a repeat of his 1972 victory, but the ex-Georgia governor won the votes of Southerners motivated by regional pride but reluctant to support Wallace. Later in March Carter also defeated Wallace in North Carolina. Wallace called him a "warmed-over McGovern" and warned Carter supporters that "smiling and grinning a lot" would not bring change. But Carter continued to win primaries and amass delegate strength. In May, Wallace announced that he "could support" Carter, and the following month he withdrew from the race and endorsed his opponent.

Although a change in Alabama election law had permitted Wallace to seek a second consecutive term, the law prevented him from running again in 1978. In June 1977 he announced his intention to seek the seat of retiring Sen. John Sparkman [q.v.], but the following year he changed his mind. When Alabama's junior Sen. James Allen [q.v.] died unexpectedly on June 1, 1978, Wallace said that he was giving "serious consideration" to running in the November special election. However when November came, Wallace was not in the race.

[JD]

For further information:
Philip Crass, *The Wallace Factor* (New York, 1976).
Wayne Greenhaw, *Watch Out for George Wallace* (New Jersey, 1976).

WALTERS, VERNON A(NTHONY)
b. Jan. 3, 1917; New York, N.Y.
Deputy Director, Central Intelligence Agency, April 1972-July 1976.

Born in New York City, Vernon Walters attended Catholic schools in France and Britain. He worked for an insurance firm before entering the Army in 1941. He remained in the Army after the war and because of his proficiency in languages

(French, German, Spanish, Italian and Portuguese) served as translator for such diplomats as W. Averell Harriman [q.v.] as well as President Dwight D. Eisenhower.

After his election to the White House, President Nixon often turned to Walters as his translator. Beginning in August 1969 Walters functioned as national security adviser Henry Kissinger's [q.v.] translator at secret peace talks in Paris with the North Vietnamese. He served as a conduit for subsequent exchanges between the two parties. On the instruction of President Nixon and Kissinger, Walters maintained a strict level of secrecy about the talks. He brought Kissinger in and out of France frequently without the knowledge of the press or the public. The talks were publicized in 1972.

In June 1970 Walters delivered a message from Nixon to the Paris embassy of the People's Republic of China; the message initiated contact between the two countries. Kissinger used Walters as his translator at subsequent secret talks with the Chinese Communists. The contact between Walters and the Chinese ambassador in Paris quickly developed into a link between Washington and Peking. Eventually Walters arranged the details of the trips by Kissinger and Nixon to China.

Nixon named Walters to be deputy director of the Central Intelligence Agency (CIA) in March 1972, and he was confirmed the following month. He quickly became embroiled in the nascent Watergate scandal. On June 23, six days after the break-in at the Democratic National Committee headquarters in the Watergate office complex, Walters and CIA Director Richard M. Helms [q.v.] were summoned to a meeting at the White House with presidential aides H.R. Haldeman [q.v.] and John D. Ehrlichman [q.v.]. According to Walters, he was asked by the two advisers to inform Acting FBI Director L. Patrick Gray [q.v.] that the Bureau's investigation into Republican campaign funds channeled through a Mexican bank might jeopardize CIA activities in that country. Both officials assured Haldeman and Ehrlichman that the

CIA was not involved in the matter, but at their insistence Walters agreed to meet with Gray and relay the message.

Gray initially consented to work only around the periphery of the Watergate case, but soon became worried and told Walters he needed a written statement to the effect that CIA interests were at stake before he could call off the FBI's investigation. Walters, at Helms's instruction, then informed Gray that none of the Agency's operations were in jeopardy. The FBI investigation continued and the campaign funds were later linked to the Watergate break-in.

Walters was summoned for three consecutive days at the end of June to meet with presidential counsel John W. Dean [q.v.]. At these meetings Walters resisted Dean's overtures to involve the CIA in the Watergate cover-up. Walters ultimately testified nearly 20 times under oath about Watergate. He appeared before the House and Senate Armed Services Committees, the Senate Watergate Committee, and later at the Watergate trials in Washington. His testimony was disputed by Haldeman and Ehrlichman and supported by Helms and internal memos written by Walters at the time. He retired from the CIA and the Army in July 1976.

[SF]

For further information:
Vernon A. Walters, *Silent Missions* (New York, 1978).

WARNER, JOHN W(ILLIAM)
b. Feb. 18, 1927; Washington, D.C.
Secretary of the Navy, April
1972-April 1974.

The son of an obstetrician, John Warner grew up in Washington, D.C., served in the Navy during World War II and graduated from Washington and Lee University in 1949. After active duty with the Marines in Korea, he completed his studies at the University of Virginia Law School. Following graduation he became law clerk to E. Barrett Prettyman, chief judge of the U.S. Circuit Court of Appeals in

Washington. In 1955 he joined the Justice Department, and worked for four years as an assistant U.S. attorney prosecuting murder and gambling cases. In 1957 he married Catherine Mellon, daughter of multimillionaire Paul Mellon. From 1960 to 1968 Warner was a member of the prestigious Washington law firm of Hogan & Hartson. He also served as an advance man on the campaign staff of Richard Nixon. In 1968 he headed the Citizens for Nixon-Agnew.

In February 1969 Nixon named Warner to the post of undersecretary of the Navy. In October 1971 Warner led a 10-member U.S. delegation to Moscow to discuss means of avoiding incidents between ships and aircraft of the U.S. and Soviet Navies in international waters, especially conflicts involving vessels "shadowing" one another. The talks resulted in a preliminary understanding, although the exact nature of the terms of agreement was not made public.

In May 1972, one month after Warner's appointment as secretary of the Navy, U.S. and Soviet officials signed an agreement designed to avoid possible ocean accidents. It was the first military agreement between the two countries since World War II. Recognizing that maneuvers in open waters were subject to regulation by the 1958 Geneva Convention on the high seas, the pact forbade both ships and aircraft from engaging in "simulated attacks" that might "constitute a hazard to navigation."

A conflict arose over the Navy's handling of defense contracts under Warner. In July 1972 Warner announced the Navy would pick up out-of-pocket construction costs for five ships under contract to Litton Industries that Litton would otherwise have been forced to pay out of its own funds. However the following year Warner ruled against rewriting an aircraft contract with Grumman despite claims by company officials that to meet the original terms of the agreement would cost Grumman $100 million.

In response to racial unrest in the Navy and the Marines, Warner and Chief of Naval Operations Adm. Elmo R. Zumwalt,

Jr. [q.v.], rebuked 100 admirals and generals in November 1972 for failure to act sufficiently against discrimination in their services. Warner stated that racial clashes, such as those aboard the aircraft carriers *Constellation* and *Kitty Hawk* that month, had demonstrated "a lack of communications," but that the Navy "was not going to tolerate such things as sit-down strikes" by seamen even when provoked by genuine grievances. Warner said a top-level Human Relations Council would be established to apply "downward pressure" through the ranks. According to a survey in June 1972 blacks comprised 5.8% of the Navy's enlisted men and .7% of its officers.

In April 1974 Warner was sworn in as administrator of the American Revolution Bicentennial Administration, which replaced the Bicentennial Commission following Senate hearings into charges that the Nixon Administration was using the Commission for commercial purposes and political partisanship. In his role as administrator of the new organization, Warner cited as his greatest achievements the Bicentennial Freedom Train; the Fourth of July "Operation Sail," in which tall ships paraded up New York's Hudson River; and the loan of the Magna Charta from Britain. However he was unable to contain the atmosphere of slick commercialism that marred much of the bicentennial celebration.

Following his divorce from Catherine Mellon, he married actress Elizabeth Taylor in 1977. The next year he was narrowly elected to a U.S. Senate seat from Virginia.

[FHM]

WEINBERGER, CASPAR W.

b. Aug. 1917; San Francisco, Calif.
Chairman, Federal Trade
Commission, January 1970-June
1970; Deputy Director, Office of
Management and Budget (OMB),
June 1970-June 1972; Director, OMB,
June 1972-February 1973; Secretary
of Health, Education and Welfare,
February 1973-July 1975.

Weinberger graduated from Harvard magna cum laude and Phi Beta Kappa in 1938, and received an LL.B. there three years later. Following service in the Army during World War II, he practiced law in California.

In 1952 he was elected for the first of three terms as a member of the California State Legislature. He made a bid for the State Attorney Generalship in 1958 but lost the Republican primary to a more conservative candidate from southern California.

Following a two-year hiatus from active politics, Weinberger returned in 1960 as vice-chairman of the California Republican Central Committee. Elected its chairman in 1962, he spent the next six years threading a course between conservatives and moderates at both the state and national levels. Thus he remained neutral in the 1964 primary battle between Barry Goldwater [q.v.] and Nelson Rockefeller [q.v.] and campaigned for Ronald Reagan [q.v.] in the subsequent election. Reagan reciprocated by appointing him chairman of a California "Little Hoover Commission" and then, in February 1968, director of finance, where Weinberger "set about implementing Reagan's budget-slashing plans" with a fervor. In October 1969 Weinberger was appointed chairman of the Federal Trade Commission (FTC). He delayed active assumption of the directorship until he had seen California through its 1969 budget year.

Weinberger's desire "to direct the agency's attention more toward protection of the nation's consumers" was well attuned to the political needs of the FTC, which was being severely criticized by Ralph Nader's Raiders and the American Bar Association for inefficiency and infighting. In his six short months at the FTC, Weinberger managed to unify the agency behind a tough new program of consumer protection and streamlined the organizational set-up from five to two bureaus— the Bureau of Competition (for antitrust matters) and the Bureau of Consumer Protection. He was generally credited with revitalizing the agency.

In June 1970 Weinberger returned to

budgetary duties, as deputy director of the newly established Office of Management and Budget (OMB) that replaced the former Bureau of the Budget (BOB). His appointment was part of a major personnel shuffle in the Nixon Administration that also brought in former Labor Secretary George Shultz [q.v.] as director of OMB, former BOB director Robert Mayo as White House Counsellor to the President, and added the directorship of the new Domestic Council to John Ehrlichman's duties as presidential assistant for Domestic Affairs. Under the new set-up at OMB, director Shultz was to focus on the management and policy-making duties while Weinberger attended to the preparation of the budget.

Regarded as a "fiscal Puritan" Weinberger concentrated on containing the budget deficit. Although he never managed to balance the federal books, he did keep the 1973 budget within President Nixon's ceiling figure of $250 billion. Indeed he was so effective a budgetary pruner that he became known as "Cap the Knife."

In May 1972 he moved up to the directorship of OMB. His promotion was taken to be an indicator that the President "was serious about curbing inflation and preventing a tax increase by cutting the federal budget." Although Weinberger prepared a frugal 1974 budget, he did not manage to cut expenditures but merely pared the growth in spending to bare bones, primarily by cutting down or out appropriations for over a hundred social welfare programs.

In November of 1972, Weinberger moved his campaign to reduce spending into the biggest, and perhaps the most open-handed, government agency, the Department of Health, Education and Welfare. His nomination as Secretary of Health, Education and Welfare was part of a more extensive Administration reorganization designed to begin implementation of the Ash Council's (Advisory Council on Executive Organization) suggestions for restructuring the executive branch. Other concurrent changes moved Elliot Richardson [q.v.] from

HEW to the Defense Department and brought in Ray L. Ash [q.v.] (the aforementioned commission's chairman) as director of OMB.

Liberal congressional reaction to Weinberger's nomination to head HEW was not favorable initially since he was expected to "intensify the HEW budget cuts he tried to initiate at OMB." Despite the misgiving of several liberal senators who "questioned Weinberger's sensitivity to social needs," he was confirmed in February 1973.

Further reorganization efforts, described as an attempt to establish a "super Cabinet" to oversee and coordinate the functions of the normal cabinet departments, resulted in Weinberger's concurrent appointment as Presidential Counsellor on Human Resources in January of 1973. In this capacity he was responsible for all departmental activities concerning health, education, manpower, development, income security, social services, drug abuse programs, Indian affairs and consumer protection. The centralization of broad program coordination in a small number of people who were concurrently cabinet secretaries and White House counsellors was, perhaps, President Nixon's most overt attempt to bring the executive bureaucracy under the direction of an "administrative presidency."

As Secretary, Weinberger proved to be extremely active in pursuing cost-control measures and attempting to decentralize social program control and spending to state and local governments as part of the President's revenue sharing plan. Congress, however, as well as many interested public groups, generally regarded such proposals with suspicion and scorn, thus bringing Weinberger and the President into frequent clashes with the legislature. Congress rejected the Administration's proposal for ending narrow categorical funding grants on health and education programs which would have enabled the states to use federal money with less federal direction. Over administrative objections and occasionally over a presidential veto, the categorical grant system for health services was expanded. After a hard fight Congress eventually did agree to consolidate several elementary, secondary, and vocational educational programs into simple grants to the states, giving the local authorities more discretion over how they would allocate those federal dollars. Indeed the divergent executive and congressional perspectives on the entire "human resources" topic kept the possibility of major reform and revision at a distance and most of the administration's achievements in this area were accomplished through tighter administration.

Weinberger, while on the front line of much of this conflict because of his position as Secretary of HEW and as Human Resources Counsellor to the President, was well regarded personally. On social welfare affairs he was characterized as "not a conservative on human issues . . . [but] a moderate and compassionate man [who] . . . hates waste and ineffective handouts." Many members of Congress admired "his personal grasp of the many programs run by the mammoth department and for his tenacity." Weinberger resigned from HEW in July 1975.

[MJW]

WESTMORELAND, WILLIAM C(HILDS)
b. March 26, 1914; Spartanburg County, S.C.
Army Chief of Staff, June 1968–June 1972.

William Westmoreland graduated from West Point in 1936 and was commissioned a second lieutenant in the artillery. During World War II he saw action as a battalion commander in North Africa and Sicily. Following the war Westmoreland took paratrooper and glider training at Fort Benning, Ga., and he taught at the Army Command and General Staff College at Fort Leavenworth, Kan. He served as commander of the 187th Airborne Regimental Combat Team in Korea. In 1958 he was named commander of the elite

101st Airborne Division. Two years later President Eisenhower appointed Westmoreland superintendent of West Point.

In 1964 President Johnson named Westmoreland deputy to Gen. Paul D. Harkins, head of the U.S. Military Assistance Command in Vietnam. In June he succeeded Harkins.

During the mid-1960s Westmoreland presided over a gradual escalation of American military involvement in Southeast Asia. To counter the increased infiltration of North Vietnamese troops into South Vietnam, he made repeated requests for additional U.S. troops. By February 1968 there were more than half a million American soldiers in South Vietnam. In June 1968 Westmoreland returned to the U.S. to become chief of staff in a move widely regarded as an indication of President Johnson's refusal to escalate the conflict further.

Gen. Creighton Abrams [q.v.] succeeded Westmoreland as U.S. commander in Vietnam. As Army chief, Westmoreland in late October was among the Johnson aides who had misgivings about the Administration's complete bombing halt of North Vietnam. He doubted that the halt would lead to serious peace talks in Paris. [See JOHNSON Volume]

With the Nixon Administration came a change in war policy. As formulated broadly in the Nixon Doctrine, the new Administration implemented a policy of "winding down" the American presence in Vietnam. The Administration emphasized the strengthening of South Vietnamese forces in a program of Vietnamization, a term coined by the new Secretary of Defense, Melvin Laird [q.v.], to describe the gradually increasing role of the South Vietnamese in assuming the burden of the fighting. At the same time Laird prepared a schedule for the withdrawal of U.S. forces. The Administration saw the troop withdrawals as part of a larger attempt to break the deadlocked Paris peace talks. Nixon also understood the mood of the country to be that it would continue to support a policy of U.S. aid for South Vietnam, but that increasingly it wanted to see an end to the direct American involvement in the fighting.

Westmoreland was troubled by the decision. He felt that winding down the U.S. role in the fighting risked undoing the accomplishments of four years of American sacrifice in Vietnam. Along with Gen. Earle Wheeler [q.v.], he led an effort to at least modify the President's plan. They were particularly concerned by Nixon's decision to remove combat troops first. The generals would have preferred removal of support troops. Nixon was committed to a policy of withdrawal, though, and the first contingent of 25,000 American combat soldiers left Vietnam in August. American troops continued to withdraw at a constant pace throughout Nixon's first term in office. Westmoreland maintained his misgivings about the troop withdrawals, believing that their timing was more for political than military reasons.

Despite his opposition to the rate and nature of the troop withdrawals, Westmoreland strongly supported the Nixon Administration's program of Vietnamization. It was a policy that he had constantly advocated during his tour of duty in South Vietnam and that he believed the Johnson Administration had not pursued seriously enough. Westmoreland likewise backed President Nixon's decision in May 1970 to order American combat troops to attack Communist sanctuaries in Cambodia along the South Vietnamese border. The goal, successfully completed, was to buy one year's grace from an enemy attack against South Vietnam to allow Vietnamization needed time. Domestic political reaction against the incursion prompted the Administration to limit it to eight weeks. Again in February 1971, in pursuit of the same military results, Westmoreland agreed with the decision for the U.S. command in Vietnam to furnish much of the tactical support for the movement of South Vietnamese troops into Laos to cut the Ho Chi Minh trail.

By the spring of 1972, U.S. forces in Vietnam had been cut back to roughly 70,000 servicemen. At the end of March, North Vietnam launched a major offen-

sive across the demilitarized zone (DMZ) into South Vietnam. Westmoreland took an active part in the deliberations among top advisers on how to respond to the invasion. In early April, Nixon announced the resumption of full-scale B-52 strikes against North Vietnam.

As Army chief, Westmoreland spoke widely at civic functions and campuses to increase public support for the military. He worked to modernize the Army and to improve training in light of modern technology and the Vietnam experience. He instituted programs to combat drug abuse, alcoholism, and racial tension and conflict. In anticipation of an end to the draft in 1973, Westmoreland helped to lay the groundwork for a volunteer Army. In keeping with America in the 1970s, he oversaw a liberalization of Army rules and regulations. Westmoreland also organized the investigation of the 1968 My Lai incident in which Lt. William C. Calley [q.v.] and other Army officers were charged with the murder, or its covering up, of over 100 South Vietnamese civilians. Calley was convicted on the premeditated murder of "at least" 11 civilians in March 1971.

Westmoreland retired from the Army in June 1972. President Nixon called him to Washington in October to seek his advice on the secret peace talks between National Security Adviser Henry Kissinger [q.v.] and Le Duc Tho, North Vietnam's principal negotiator. Westmoreland urged Nixon to delay action on the new agreement and to hold out for better terms. He argued that it was vital that North Vietnamese troops be required to withdraw from South Vietnam. Accordingly, when the pact, with few modifications, went into effect in January 1973, Westmoreland claimed that it "had only two virtues: it ended the American involvement and brought the American prisoners of war home." Westmoreland felt that the agreement, because it left North Vietnamese troops in positions in South Vietnam from which they could launch attacks, paved the way for North Vietnam's final April 1975 offensive.

In July 1974 Westmoreland was defeated in a bid for the South Carolina Republican nomination for governor. In retirement he openly denounced the Johnson Administration's handling of the war. He strongly criticized its refusal, after the Tet offensive, to allow him to follow up battlefield successes with attacks on Communist sanctuaries in Cambodia and Laos and across the DMZ into North Vietnam. He argued that this action along with sustained and intensive bombing could have brought the defeat of North Vietnam.

Westmoreland defended the will and determination of South Vietnam to maintain its freedom. He condemned those at home against the war "who went beyond the bounds of reasonable debate and fair dissension." The great majority of Americans, he insisted, had remained firm in their resolve to persevere. Vietnam was lost in the end, Westmoreland asserted, because officials in Washington at first failed to vigorously wage the war and then refused to carry on. He maintained that legislation passed by the Congress in the early 1970s designed to limit the President's power to act abroad had hamstrung the Ford Administration's final efforts to aid South Vietnam.

[SF]

For further information:
William C. Westmoreland, *A Soldier Reports*, (New York, 1976).

WEYAND, FREDERICK C(ARLTON)

b. Sept. 15, 1916; Arbuckle, Calif.
Army Chief of Staff, October 1974-October 1976.

Frederick Weyand graduated from the University of California at Berkeley and received a ROTC commission as a second lieutenant in 1939. He went on active duty in late 1940 and served during World War II in India, Burma and China. After the war he made the military a career. He was a battalion commander and divisional operations officer in the Korean war. After combat duty Weyand attended the National War College in Washington, D.C. In 1964 he took command of the 25th Infantry Division in Vietnam. He became a field force commander there in 1967. Two years later President Nixon named Weyand military adviser to the U.S. delegation at the Paris peace talks. He returned to Vietnam in 1970 as the deputy commander of the U.S. military command. In 1972 Weyand was appointed Commander of the U.S. forces in Vietnam.

When the American military role in Vietnam officially ended on March 29, 1973, Weyand presided over the departure of the last U.S. troops and the deactivation of the U.S. command there. In a farewell speech delivered at formal ceremonies marking the occasion, he declared that "the rights of the people of the Republic of Vietnam to shape their own destiny and to provide their self-defense have been upheld." In a second speech addressed to the South Vietnamese in their own language, Weyand stated, "Our mission has been accomplished. I depart with a strong feeling of pride in what we have achieved, and in what our achievement represents."

That same year Weyand was named vice-chief of staff of the Army. President Ford nominated him to succeed Gen. Creighton W. Abrams [*q.v.*] as Army chief of staff when Abrams died in office in September 1974. Weyand was confirmed in October. He was the first Chief of Staff not to graduate from West Point. When Weyand took command of the Army, the impact of inflation was affecting the military's procurement of new weapons systems, and Army weapons stockpiles had been depleted by the massive airlifting of U.S. armaments to Israel during the 1973 Yom Kippur war. Weyand concentrated in particular on increasing U.S. tank strength. In November the Pentagon announced plans to increase the volunteer Army's combat divisions from 13 to 16. Continuing the work begun by his predecessor, Weyand attempted to accomplish this by converting support and headquarters troops into combat units.

In early March 1975 North Vietnam launched its final offensive against South Vietnam. Weyand arrived March 27 in Saigon at President Ford's direction to assess the military situation and recommend whether South Vietnam needed any more U.S. military aid. He conferred April 2 with President Nguyen Van Thieu on ways of saving South Vietnam from imminent collapse. Weyand reported to Ford on April 4 that the South Vietnamese Army "still has the spirit and the capability to defeat the North Vietnamese." However in briefing congressional committees on April 8, he said South Vietnam could not survive without additional military aid from the U.S. Weyand told reporters later that whether South Vietnam could survive even with the aid was "a very good question." He added that there was no doubt in his mind that South Vietnam would fight.

Over the next several weeks, as North Vietnamese forces approached Saigon, the Ford Administration pressed Congress repeatedly for $722 million in emergency military aid and $250 million in humanitarian aid for South Vietnam. Weyand supported the request and warned that South Vietnam could survive only a few months without military assistance. Congress was reluctant to grant further military aid, but did authorize a $200 million "contingency fund" that Ford could use to evacuate Americans from South Vietnam and provide humanitarian aid for the South Vietnamese. During the latter days of April the remaining Americans were evacuated from Saigon, and on April 30 South Vietnam fell to the Communists.

During his remaining tour of duty as chief of staff, Weyand continued to work to improve Army forces stationed with the North Atlantic Treaty Organization (NATO). He retired in October 1976 and was succeeded by Gen. Bernard W. Rogers. Weyand became an officer with the First Hawaiian Bank.

[SF]

WHEELER, EARLE G(ILMORE)
b. Jan. 13, 1908; Washington, D.C.
d. Dec. 18, 1975; Frederick, Md.
Chairman, Joint Chiefs of Staff, July 1964-July 1970.

A 1932 graduate of West Point who saw action in World War II as commander of an infantry battalion, Earle Wheeler rose to prominence in the Army chiefly as an administrator. A protege of Gen. Maxwell Taylor, Wheeler was assigned to the office of the Joint Chiefs of Staff as staff director in 1960. In that post he briefed presidential candidate John F. Kennedy on military affairs. Impressed with Wheeler's performance Kennedy appointed him Army chief of staff in October 1962.

As Army chief, Wheeler shared Gen. Taylor's philosophy of a balanced military force capable of fighting both conventional and nuclear war. He won the favor of Secretary of Defense Robert S. McNamara [q.v.] for his implementation of the Secretary's program of expansion and modernization of the Army and for his articulate public defense of the nuclear test ban treaty in 1963.

President Johnson named Wheeler to succeed Taylor as chairman of the Joint Chiefs of Staff in July 1964. Wheeler stressed the primacy of the country's overall military needs and strategy over the competing demands of the separate armed services. During the Johnson years he increasingly devoted his attention to the war in Vietnam both as a close adviser to the President and as a liaison between the Joint Chiefs and civilian decision-makers. Reflecting the policies of the Joint Chiefs, Wheeler advocated an extensive American military presence in Vietnam. As the U.S. escalated its involvement in the war during the mid-1960s, he consistently supported the military's requests for more troops and weapons. [See JOHNSON Volume]

Wheeler remained chairman of the Joint Chiefs of Staff under President Nixon. As formulated broadly in the Nixon Doctrine, the new Administration implemented a policy of "winding down" the American presence in Vietnam. The new

Secretary of Defense, Melvin Laird [*q.v.*], charted a schedule for the withdrawal of U.S. forces. The Administration saw the troop withdrawals as part of a larger strategy of trying to break the deadlocked Paris peace talks. Wheeler and Army Chief of Staff Gen. William Westmoreland led a struggle to reverse or at least modify the President's plan. They were especially concerned by his decision to withdraw combat troops first and not backup or support troops. Nixon stuck to his decision and the first contingent of 25,000 soldiers left Vietnam in August.

As chairman of the Joint Chiefs, Wheeler worked to carry out the Nixon Administration's program of Vietnamization. The program sought to improve South Vietnam's armed forces with the goal of having them gradually assume the burden of the fighting. Wheeler visited South Vietnam in July on a fact-finding mission for Nixon. He returned again for a second inspection tour in October. In summing up his findings, Wheeler remarked that progress in Vietnamization was being steadily and realistically achieved. At the same time he noted that U.S. forces would have to assist the South Vietnamese for "some time to come." Wheeler forcefully supported Nixon's decision in May 1970 to send American troops into Cambodia to attack Communist sanctuaries along the South Vietnamese border. The military goal, successfully accomplished by the incursion, was to provide the Vietnamization program needed time free from enemy attack.

Throughout America's involvement in Vietnam Wheeler strongly criticized those who protested the war at home. He argued that the single most important factor in prolonging the conflict was Hanoi's perception of America's weakness of purpose. Wheeler steadfastly maintained that the United States could win the war in Vietnam; reflecting the evolution in government policy during the conflict, his definition of victory changed over the years. In 1965 he thought it was possible to guarantee South Vietnam's independence by defeating the Communists on the battlefield. By 1967 he advocated the

Administration's position that the U.S. goal was to bring Hanoi to the peace table under conditions favorable to the U.S. During his service under the Nixon presidency, Wheeler endorsed America's commitment to the process of Vietnamization that would allow South Vietnam to defend itself.

Wheeler retired from the Army and from his position as chairman of the Joint Chiefs in July 1970. He was succeeded as chairman by Adm. Thomas H. Moorer [*q.v.*], chief of naval operations. Wheeler became a director of the Monsanto Corp.

In July 1973 the Senate Armed Services Committee called Wheeler to testify about allegations that senior military and civilian officials had falsified reports to conceal secret B-52 strikes against targets in Cambodia in 1969 and 1970. Wheeler told the Committee that President Nixon had personally ordered the secret bombing of Cambodia. He denied charges of any falsification of documents. He said a system of dual reports had been instituted using cover targets in South Vietnam for the missions so that they could be conducted under stringent security. Later it was revealed that the reason for such secrecy was Prince Sihanouk, the head of the Cambodian government at the time. Sihanouk privately endorsed the U.S. action against the North Vietnamese. But because of his country's neutral status, if the bombing became known publicly, he would be forced to protest it publicly. Wheeler died in December 1975.

[SF]

WHITE, BYRON R(AYMOND)

b. June 8, 1917; Fort Collins, Colo.
Associate Justice, U.S. Supreme Court, 1962-.

White graduated first in his class from the University of Colorado in 1938. A football All-America, he played professionally for several seasons before receiving a degree from Yale Law School in 1946. White practiced in Denver from 1947 until 1961, when he was named U.S.

deputy attorney general. President John F. Kennedy's first Supreme Court nominee, White took his seat on the bench in April 1962.

As a jurist White was not easy to categorize. He refrained from broad statements of philosophy in his opinions and had a pragmatic, nondoctrinaire approach that made it difficult to predict his stance in many cases. Over time, though, his votes showed that he tended to favor government authority over individual rights in First Amendment and criminal cases. White generally supported judicial deference to legislative judgments because he believed it better for the nation to resolve many controversial questions through the political process rather than the courts. The Justice also preferred to resolve cases without making dramatic changes in existing law. As a result of such views, White proved to be far more conservative on the Court than had been expected, especially on criminal rights and civil liberties issues. He compiled a more liberal record, however, in civil rights and reapportionment cases. [See KENNEDY, JOHNSON Volumes]

On the Burger Court White occupied a center position and was identified, along with Potter Stewart [q.v.], as a "swing" justice whose vote decided cases in which the Court's liberal members were at odds with the more conservative Nixon appointees. When the two groups were sharply divided, White was more likely to vote with the conservatives, especially in criminal cases. He backed police "stop and frisk" practices, upheld warrantless searches he considered reasonable and urged the Court to limit the application of the exclusionary rule that barred the use of illegally seized evidence at trial. In a March 1969 opinion, White ordered the government to let defendants examine the transcripts of illegal electronic eavedropping against them, even in national security cases. In April 1971, however, he upheld "third-party bugging" in which an informer, without a warrant, used an electronic device to transmit his conversation with another person to government agents.

White also joined in decisions cutting back on the 1966 *Miranda* ruling. In three May 1970 cases, he upheld plea bargains against charges from defendants that their guilty pleas had been involuntary or improperly induced. In a June 1970 opinion, White sustained the use of six member juries in state courts, and in May 1972, he spoke for the Court to sanction nonunanimous jury verdicts. Justice White joined the Court's liberals in June 1972 to hold the death penalty as then imposed a violation of the Eighth Amendment's ban on cruel and unusual punishment. However, he voted four years later to sustain capital punishment as the penalty for murder under newer state laws which either made the penalty mandatory or else established guidelines restricting the judge's or jury's discretion in imposing the death sentence.

Justice White opposed the Court's use of an 1866 civil rights law to overturn racial discrimination in housing and in private nonsectarian schools. His majority opinion in a significant June 1976 case held that government action must have a discriminatory purpose as well as a racially disproportionate effect in order to violate the 14th Amendment. However, White dissented in June 1971, when a majority allowed a city to close its public swimming pools rather than desegregate them and in July 1974 when the Court rejected an interdistrict remedy for school segregation in Detroit. He favored a strict standard of review in sex discrimination cases and voted to overturn most laws discriminating against women and against illegitimate children. White also dissented in March 1973 when the Court held that public school financing systems based on local property taxes did not deny children in poorer districts the equal protection of the laws.

Because he preferred political solutions of controversial issues, White opposed the Court's January 1973 decision invalidating anti-abortion laws for the first six months of pregnancy. He also supported virtually all state and federal laws providing aid to parochial schools. In

June 1973 he was part of a five man majority which granted the states greater leeway in regulating allegedly obscene material. To ensure that the political system would be responsive to the popular will, White favored expansion of the electoral process. His opinion in a June 1970 case, for example, opened voting on local bond issues to tenants as well as property owners, and the Justice supported a federal law lowering the voting age to 18 in December 1970. Although he had endorsed the one-man, one-vote rule in reapportionment cases, White objected in these years to a very strict application of that standard. For a six man majority in June 1973, he declared that the states did not have to justify minor deviations from the one-man, one-vote rule in the apportionment of their own legislatures.

In First Amendment cases Justice White most often voted to sustain government power against individual rights claims. He did vote to deny the government's request for an injunction in June 1971 to halt newspaper publication of the *Pentagon Papers*. However, he wrote the opinion in a five-to-four decision a year later holding that journalists had no First Amendment right to refuse to testify before a grand jury about information obtained from confidential sources. In June 1969 White spoke for the Court to sustain the Federal Communications Commission's "fairness doctrine" requiring radio and television stations to air both sides of important issues.

A straightforward man with a quick intellect, White wrote very direct, blunt opinions. He was not a leader on the Court and was considered an average justice by most Court observers. Although conservative on criminal rights issues, White was evaluated as an independent and a "thoughtful moderate" on other constitutional questions.

[CAB]

For further information:
Lance Liebman, "Swing Man on the Supreme Court," *New York Times Magazine*, October 8, 1972.

WHITE, KEVIN H(AGAN)
b. Sept. 25, 1929; Boston, Mass.
Mayor, Boston, Mass., 1968–.

White was the son of a politically active family from the West Roxbury section of Boston. He earned a B.A. degree from Williams College in 1952. Three years later he graduated from Boston College Law School and was admitted to the Massachusetts bar.

He was elected Massachusetts secretary of state in 1960, and during his fourth successive term in that post, White entered the 1967 race for the Boston mayoralty, facing fellow Democrat Louise Day Hicks [*q.v.*] in the general election. Hicks, a member of the Boston School Committee, was best known for her vigorous opposition to racial integration in the city's school system. White, with the backing of liberals and blacks, narrowly defeated Hicks.

White's administration quickly demonstrated its commitment to liberal reform. The new mayor appointed blacks to top-level positions, established "mini-city halls" around Boston to serve citizens' needs, set up a 24-hour complaint center and created the Boston Urban Federation to finance a major low-income housing program. However his efforts on behalf of Boston's minority groups earned him the epithet "Mayor Black" among the city's working-class white ethnics, and his decision to increase Boston's property tax, already among the highest in the nation, further alienated many Bostonians. [See JOHNSON Volume]

During the Nixon Administration, White emerged as a leading spokesman for urban America. In March 1970 he joined the mayors of other major cities in announcing a joint lobbying effort on such issues as urban renewal, crime, mass transit, welfare reform and revenue sharing. The following year at the San Francisco meeting of the U.S. Conference of Mayors, he and nine other big city mayors issued a statement condemning President Nixon's budget proposals, including the President's revenue-sharing plan, which they said would result in an overall decrease in urban aid.

After an unsuccessful bid for governor in 1970, White easily defeated former opponent Louise Day Hicks in the November 1971 mayoral election. His victory cut across all economic, ethnic and racial lines, including the "white ethnic" neighborhoods such as South Boston, a Hicks stronghold.

In January 1972 White publicly endorsed Maine Sen. Edmund S. Muskie's [q.v.] bid for the Democratic presidential nomination and headed the slate of Muskie delegates running in the Massachusetts primary. After McGovern received the nomination in July, White was briefly considered for the vice-presidential spot but was dropped due to the strong protests of John Kenneth Galbraith [q.v.], head of the Massachusetts delegation.

In March of the same year, the NAACP filed a long-expected suit charging the city of Boston with having established a willful pattern of segregation in the school system. With a court decision imminent, White reversed his previous support of the 1965 Racial Imbalance Law, which cut off state funds to schools with a nonwhite enrollment in excess of 50%. He suggested voluntary busing of black students to adjacent white suburban areas as a possible solution, arguing that economic rather than racial integration was the real problem.

On June 21, 1974, District Court Judge Arthur Garrity, Jr., in response to the NAACP suit, ruled that Boston had indeed maintained a de facto system of segregated schools and ordered implementation of the Racial Imbalance Law in the fall by whatever means necessary—including large-scale forced busing. When schools reopened in September, whites in South Boston resisted the order with increasingly violent demonstrations. Many white parents kept their children home and the violence began to spread. Mayor White ordered police escorts for buses carrying black students after they were stoned by white mobs. Despite his stated dissatisfaction with busing, he urged obedience of the law.

At White's request Republican Gov. Francis Sargent [q.v.] ordered state police to supplement Boston's police force after a refusal by Judge Garrity to send in federal marshals. But on Oct. 15, following a high school melee that resulted in the stabbing of a student, Sargent mobilized the National Guard without consulting White. The mayor, who referred to the guard as an inept militia, accused Sargent of trying to boost his ailing reelection campaign.

In the face of continued federal court intransigence, the anti-busing campaign began to subside, with opponents simply acquiescing or transferring their children to private schools. In August a report by the Commission of Human Rights criticized White's coolness to the Garrity decision in the mayor's public statements, saying that it had given support to anti-busing sentiment. When schools reopened in the fall of 1975 under an even wider busing program than that of the previous year, there were few reports of violence or protest.

Kevin White was relected in November following a bitter campaign against Joseph Timilty, a state senator who accused White of corrupt fund-raising practices. Busing was not stressed as a campaign issue, but White's margin of victory was extremely narrow.

[MDQ]

WHITTEN, JAMIE L(LOYD)
b. April 18, 1910; Cascilla, Miss.
Democratic Representative, Miss., 1941–.

Whitten, the son of a Mississippi farmer and country store owner, attended the University of Mississippi from 1926 to 1931. He then served as a school principal and state legislator until his election as county prosecutor in 1933. Whitten won a seat in the U.S. House in a special election in November 1941. He was easily reelected in all subsequent races. Whitten became chairman of the Agriculture Subcommittee of the Appropriations Committee in 1947. The panel had jurisdiction over the budget for the Department of Agriculture. Known as the "farm baron" and the "permanent secretary of agriculture," Whitten used his post to block many of the social programs of the Kennedy and Johnson years that were funded through the Agriculture Department. A defender of farm interests, Whitten regularly voted for farm subsidies. In the late 1960s he gained attention when he disputed findings that there was hunger in Mississippi. [See JOHNSON Volume]

During the Nixon and Ford Administrations, Whitten continued his conservative voting pattern and defense of the farmer. Whitten vigorously opposed efforts to cut the ceiling on the maximum farm subsidy payments to farmers. At the same time he opposed food stamps for the poor and the school breakfast programs. He opposed minimum wage legislation and unemployment compensation for farm workers as well as legal services and child care for the poor. But he supported funding the development of the SST, and he voted for the federal loan program to bail out the Lockheed Aircraft Corp. Whitten also favored a strong defense establishment and supported every major controversial weapons system proposed by the Administration, including the B-1 bomber and the Safeguard anti-ballistic missile system.

Whitten's Agricultural Subcommittee received jurisdiction over the Environmental Protection Agency and consumer protection programs in 1971. Appropriations Committee Chairman George H. Mahon (D, Tex.) [q. v.] gave jurisdiction to Whitten's panel because he felt other subcommittees had allocated too much money for these programs. Whitten generally worked to limit spending, but he did support increased funding for some consumer protection programs. In 1973, for example, the panel recommended increased allocations for food inspection programs and additive safety reviews.

Whitten became the target of liberal representatives swept into office in the 1974 Democratic landslide. After the election, the Democratic Caucus assumed the right to approve the appointment of subcommittee chairmen, a move clearly aimed at removing the conservative Whitten. In an effort to save Whitten's chairmanship, Mahon agreed to transfer jurisdiction over environmental and consumer programs to other panels.

A staunch opponent of civil rights legislation, Whitten waged a campaign in the 1960s and 1970s to prevent busing to achieve integration. On several occasions he proposed an amendment to reinstate the freedom of choice desegregation plans that had been struck down by the courts. The amendment would have prohibited the use of federal funds to promote busing unless parents agreed to the action. Whitten was narrowly defeated in 1968 when he tried to add the proposal to the fiscal 1969 appropriations bill for the Departments of Labor and Health, Education and Welfare. Whitten's amendment gradually gained support in the early 1970s as courts began to implement busing plans. The House adopted the proposal in 1970 but then also accepted Senate amendments that effectively nullified it. Many Northern representatives who had previously supported civil rights legislation began to vote for the Whitten and other anti-busing amendments by 1971. By 1972 Northern representatives assumed the leadership in the anti-busing fight, which went on until 1974, when Congress adopted a much-weakened version.

Whitten succeeded Mahon as chairman of the Appropriations Committee in 1979. [See CARTER Volume]

[AE]

WIGGINS, CHARLES E.
b. Dec. 3, 1927; El Monte, Calif.
Republican Representative, Calif., 1967-79.

Wiggins entered the Army toward the end of World War II, and served again during the Korean War. After Korea he received B.S. and law degrees from the University of Southern California, and started a private law practice in El Monte, Calif., in 1957. Beginning with the 1949 presidency of the El Monte Young Republicans, he held several California Republican Party positions and was active in local and statewide campaigns. In 1960 and 1962 he served on the campaign committee of Rep. John Rousselot (R, Calif.) of the John Birch Society. He was chairman of the El Monte Planning Commission from 1954 to 1960, city councilman from 1960 to 1964 and mayor from 1964 to 1966. Wiggins was elected in 1966 to the U.S. House from a wealthy, conservative suburban district.

In Congress Wiggins was a strong supporter of White House legislative policy. He generally sided with the Republicans on Party line votes and supported the Administration's position about 70% of the time during the late 1960s and 1970s. He received ratings of from 70 to 80 from the conservative Americans for Constitutional Action. Wiggins backed Nixon's Vietnam policy and favored a strong defense posture and foreign military aid. In 1969 he supported the development and deployment of the Safeguard anti-ballistic missile system. The following year he opposed the Cooper-Church Amendment limiting presidential authority to conduct military operations in Cambodia, and in 1974 he voted against cutting off military aid to Turkey. Two years later he supported development of the B-1 bomber.

Wiggins voted for such anti-crime measures as the "no-knock" search warrants proposed by the Nixon Administration for its war on drugs. He consistently supported Nixon-Ford vetoes of federal expenditures for the domestic aid programs proposed by the Democrats. But in 1975 he was one of 38 Republicans who voted for the federal loan program for New York City, which the Ford Aministration finally supported. He seldom supported social welfare or consumer protection programs.

Wiggins served on the House Judiciary Committee, where he became involved in two major battles that brought him to national attention. In 1971 he led the House opposition to the Equal Rights Amend-

ment (ERA) banning sex discrimination. Wiggins convinced the Judiciary Committee to add a clause to the proposed ERA that would have permitted laws which discriminated on the basis of sex in the case of the military draft and in health and safety matters. ERA proponents objected strongly to the Wiggins amendment, contending that it significantly undermined the legislation, especially in the vital occupational health and safety area where discriminatory laws might continue to bar women from certain occupations. Wiggins lost the ERA fight when the House rejected his amendment by a 265-87 vote and then overwhelmingly adopted the Equal Rights Amendment in 1971.

In 1974 Wiggins became Nixon's chief and most eloquent defender during the House Judiciary Committee's impeachment proceedings. He insisted that the evidence must directly and explicitly link the President to an impeachable offense, a requirement that became known as the "smoking gun" evidence rule. He was one of three members who voted against the first subpoena the Committee issued on April 11, 1974, for tapes of presidential conversations and other evidence. Wiggins was one of the 10 Committee Republicans who voted against all five impeachment articles, three of which were adopted by the Committee.

While he staunchly defended Nixon as long as he felt a case could be made, Wiggins gave up the defense immediately upon discovering the smoking gun he had been demanding. He thus helped precipitate the first presidential resignation in U.S. history. Wiggins found the evidence on Aug. 2, 1974, when White House Chief of Staff Alexander M. Haig [q.v.] asked him to inspect the tapes of three critical presidential conversations about Watergate. It was during these conversations, which occurred on June 23, 1973, that Nixon and his chief White House aide, H. R. Haldeman [q.v.], had discussed using the CIA to halt the FBI's Watergate probe. Wiggins, stunned by the contents, told Haig that he could no longer defend Nixon and that he would reveal the contents of the tapes unless the White House made them public.

Following the White House release of the tapes on Aug. 5, Wiggins publicly ended his defense of the President and called for Nixon's resignation or impeachment.

After the Watergate hearings, Wiggins faded from national prominence. In 1978 he decided not to seek reelection.

[AE]

WILKINS, ROY
b. Aug. 30, 1901, St. Louis, Mo.
Executive Director, NAACP, 1955-77.

Roy Wilkins was the grandson of a Mississippi slave and the son of a minister and college graduate who was forced to earn a living doing menial labor. He attended the University of Minnesota from 1919 to 1923 and, during his college days, he became recognized as an eloquent spokesman against racial injustice. In 1920 he joined the local NAACP chapter where he served as secretary. Ten years later Wilkins was appointed executive secretary of the national NAACP serving under Walter White. Throughout the 1930s and 1940s Wilkins established himself as an active arbitrator and speaker on the organization's behalf. His efforts gained him national prominence and as the NAACP representative he served as a consultant to the War Department in 1941 and to the American delegation to the United Nations conference in 1945.

With White's death in 1955 Wilkins ascended to the post of executive secretary and assumed leadership of the most influential civil rights group in America. He continued the push for effective legislation and under his tenure the NAACP's lobbying wing was instrumental in the passage of the Voting Rights Act of 1965 and the Open Housing Act of 1968. [See EISENHOWER, KENNEDY, JOHNSON Volumes]

With Richard Nixon's succession to the presidency in 1969, the black militant movement, which had become increas-

ingly vocal throughout the 1960s, gained greater momentum. Wilkins' pro-integrationist stance and rejection of black power and black nationalism as a return to "segregation and Jim Crow" made him the target of criticism both within the more dissident ranks of the NAACP and from the new generation of black separatists. Undaunted, Wilkins continued to counsel moderation as the most effective means for gaining widespread support for civil rights issues. With the rise of the Black Panther Party and the organization's subsequent clash with police around the country, Wilkins helped form the Commission of Inquiry into Black Panthers and Law Enforcement Officials in order to explore the reasons for these clashes.

Wilkins led the campaign to extend civil rights laws despite Nixon's informal moratorium on the subject. He successfully opposed Nixon's nomination of civil rights opponent Clement F. Haynsworth [q.v.] to the Supreme Court in 1969 and of conservative G. Harrold Carswell [q.v.] the following year. Frustrated over the Nixon Administration's retreat on civil rights, Wilkins mobilized the Washington based lobbying wing headed by Clarence Mitchell [q.v.] to press for broader legislation and gain extension of the 1965 Voting Rights Act's ban on literacy tests. Although the Administration unsuccessfully attempted to modify provisions of the bill, it was signed into law in 1970.

Wilkins also led the fight against Nixon's anti-busing stance. Together with the legal wing of the NAACP, he sought to challenge the constitutionality of Nixon's position and won an impressive Supreme Court ruling with the case of *Alexander v. the Holmes County (Mississippi) Board of Education* in 1969. The verdict endorsed the implementation of a desegregation program to take effect immediately.

In 1972 Nixon countered by outlining his desegregation program to Congress which imposed severe restrictions on busing and delayed school desegregation until the latter part of 1973. The NAACP denounced the Nixon program, but Congress approved the measure. Despite this setback the NAACP made progress in other areas. It succeeded in gaining passage of the Equal Employment Opportunity Act which broadened the coverage of its predecessor passed in 1964. The law forbade discrimination by federal, state and local agencies and allowed the Equal Employment Agency to go into court to obtain endorsement of the bills provisions.

Under Wilkins' leadership the NAACP expanded its fight for equal opportunity on all fronts. The organization established day care centers for low income working mothers in 1973 and coordinated programs which sponsored housing construction and counseling centers for former prison inmates. Wilkins retired as an NAACP officer in July 1977 at the age of 76.

[DGE]

WILLIAMS, HARRISON A(RLINGTON), JR.
b. Dec. 10, 1919; Plainfield, N.J.
Democratic Senator, N.J., 1959-,
Chairman, Special Committee on Aging, 1969-71; Chairman, Labor and Public Welfare Committee, 1971-.

Harrison Williams attended Plainfield, N.J., public schools and received his B.A. from Oberlin College. He was a seaman and a Navy pilot during World War II, and then became a steelworker in Ohio for a short while before attending Columbia University Law School from which he earned his degree in 1948. Elected to the U.S. House of Representatives in 1953 and 1954 but defeated in 1956, Williams revived his political fortunes and was elected in the Democratic landslide of 1958 to become the first Democratic Senator to represent New Jersey since 1936. During the Kennedy-Johnson years, he established a reputation as a low-profile urban liberal on domestic policy, favoring the extension of federal government spending for a wide variety of human services. His ratings by

lobbying groups up to 1978 showed a consistently prolabor and pro-civil rights record. [See EISENHOWER, KENNEDY, JOHNSON Volumes]

An early supporter of President Johnson's Vietnam war policies, Williams gradually shifted his stance so that by the early Nixon years he was speaking out against the extension of the war into Laos and Cambodia and voting for the Cooper-Church Amendment of 1970. Williams supported the War Powers Act of 1973, which limited the President's power to commit troops to combat without congressional approval. He also opposed what he considered to be excessive military spending on such projects as the anti-ballistic missile system.

Unlike New Jersey's other Senator, Clifford Case [q.v.], Williams concentrated on domestic rather than foreign affairs. As chairman of the Special Committee on Aging for the first two years of the Nixon Administration, Williams was concerned about the impact of inflation on the elderly. He advocated property tax relief for low-income elderly homeowners that was linked to property tax reform and supported the establishment of the national institute on aging.

As a member of the Labor and Public Welfare Committee, the New Jersey Senator was coauthor of the Coal Mine Health and Safety Act of 1969 that provided increased protection for coal miners. He became chairman of the Committee in 1971 and frequently sought increases in the minimum wage laws as well as more liberalized laws for union organizing.

In the spring of 1972 Williams released a Committee report to the public of a year-long study into private pension plan abuses. He then presented a bill calling for uniform federal standards of fiduciary responsibility, improved disclosure provisions and the maximum feasible centralization of all federal regulatory functions related to pension plans. With some modifications, the Williams bill prevailed and became public law in 1974, known as the Employee Retirement Income Security Act. During the 1975 recession Williams unsuccessfully attempted to get the Senate to authorize one million public service jobs at a cost of $7.8 billion.

A strong civil rights advocate, the Senator voted for the controversial Philadelphia plan in December 1969 which mandated that quotas of minority groups be accepted by the construction trades unions. He spear-headed the battle for job equality in 1972 by managing the amendments that gave additional legal enforcement powers to the Equal Employment Opportunities Commission. He was an important proponent of the Occupational Safety and Health Act of 1970, requiring employers to provide working conditions free from recognized hazards likely to cause death or serious physical harm to employees.

As a member of the Banking, Housing and Urban Affairs Committee, Williams worked for the creation of the Securities Investor Protection Corp. in 1970 that would provide financial protection for customers of brokerage houses, not for the houses themselves, much like the Federal Deposit Insurance Corp. created in 1934, insured bank despositors. One controversial amendment that Williams successfully sponsored in a 1970 banking reform bill prohibiting one-bank holding companies exempted at least 899 companies, including some controlled by the nation's biggest conglomerates. The Senator, up for reelection that year, subsequently received a $5,000 contribution from the Bankers Political Action Committee, a lobbying organization. He supported several measures providing for federal financing of urban mass transit as well as the 1975 bill to aid financially beleaguered New York City.

On other issues Williams voted for government abortion aid (in a state with a high proportion of Roman Catholic voters), a consumer protection agency, the licensing of handguns and against President Nixon's Supreme Court nominees G. Harrold Carswell [q.v.], Clement Haynsworth [q.v.] and William Rehnquist [q.v.].

Williams's 1970 reelection campaign was his most difficult to date. His Repub-

lican challenger was a law-and-order Nixon stalwart, Nelson Gross [q.v.]. With Vice President Spiro Agnew [q.v.], Gross attempted to paint Williams as a "radical liberal" who did "nothing to check the violence" then besetting the country. Williams faced a major problem when heavy drinking and "erratic behavior" at the NAACP state conference in October 1968 earned him that organization's censorship. But his public acknowledgment of having conquered alcoholic dependence and $250,000 in labor union support aided him in his 250,000 vote margin of victory (54% of the total) over Gross.

When up for reelection in 1976, Williams had a far easier time than in 1970, winning with 62% of the vote over David Norcross, commonly considered a sacrificial lamb. That year he also headed the slate of "uncommitted" stop-Carter delegates to the Democratic National Convention who, preferring Sen. Hubert Humphrey [q.v.] and California Gov. Edmund Brown, Jr. [q.v.], took 64 of the 81 delegates.

With a Democratic President in 1977, Williams was in a somewhat better position to push many of his pet projects involving mass transit funding, urban aid, the Humphrey-Hawkins full employment bill and labor law revision.

[GB]

WILLIAMS, JOHN B(ELL)
b. Dec. 4, 1918; Raymond, Miss.
Governor, Miss., 1968-72.

John Bell Williams attended the University of Mississippi and the Jackson (Miss.) School of Law, receiving his law degree in 1940. After service in the Army Air Corps during World War II, Williams returned to Mississippi in 1944 as prosecuting attorney for Hinds County. In 1946 he was elected to the U.S. House of Representatives from Mississippi's seventh district, and was consistently reelected with little opposition for the next two decades. On Capitol Hill, Williams emerged as a strong opponent of civil rights measures and social legislation. In 1967 he won election as governor of Mississippi on a platform emphasizing states rights and "responsible conservatism." [See KENNEDY, JOHNSON Volumes].

In his inaugural address Williams called for an end to racial violence in Mississippi and promised to seek funds for federal programs that he had frequently opposed in Congress. During the Nixon Administration Williams backed the President's proposals for federal revenue sharing and welfare reform. As governor, Williams remained a strong foe of forced integration. In August 1969 he attended a seminar in Atlanta, Ga., to defend the South's "freedom of choice" in school desegregation. Delegates from nine Southern states accepted William's resolution urging President Nixon to "voice support and institute legislation" to bring about "maximum individual freedom" in substitution for bureaucratic directives. An executive committee, headed by Williams and Gov. Lester Maddox [q.v.] of Georgia, was established to act as a clearinghouse for proposals to block school desegregation in the South. According to Reg Murphy and Hal Gulliver in *The Southern Strategy*, the Nixon Administration was willing to ease up on federally forced desegregation.

On Nov. 6, 1969, however, the U.S. Fifth Circuit Court of Appeals rejected an Administration request for "flexible guidelines" and ordered 30 Mississippi school districts to implement effective desegregation plans by Dec. 31, 1969. Williams labeled the ruling "the rawest kind of discrimination" and immediately challenged it. He was rebuffed when the Supreme Court in February 1970 refused to consider his attempts to sue Attorney General John N. Mitchell [q.v.] and Health, Education and Welfare (HEW) Secretary Robert H. Finch [q.v.] over school desegregation.

Williams backed schemes to avoid school desegregation through the promotion of all-white private "academies." In January 1970 a three-judge federal district court panel in Washington issued an injunction to stop the Internal Revenue

Service from granting tax-exempt status to segregated schools in Mississippi. Denouncing the injunction Williams asked the state legislature to grant tax credits of up to $500 for each taxpayer contributing to the all-white schools. But the state legislature adjourned its 1970 session without approving the plan.

In the aftermath of the May 14, 1970, shootings that left two dead and 12 wounded at predominantly-black Jackson State University, Williams defended the Jackson police, stating that they had acted in self-defense. After the Scranton Commission on Campus Unrest reported that the shootings were "unwarranted and unprovoked," Williams blasted the report as "another slanderous diatribe against the state of Mississippi."

Williams was a critic of forced busing as a way to achieve school desegregation. Lambasting the "hypocritical" policy of ending Southern de jure segregation while ignoring Northern de facto segregation, Williams issued, on Sept. 11, 1971, an executive order directing that no state funds be used for busing. However on Oct. 20, a U.S. district court judge issued a permanent injunction enjoining Mississippi from withdrawing funds meant for busing.

After leaving office in 1972 Williams returned to his law practice in Raymond. He continued to be politically active, however, supporting the presidential campaigns of Nixon in 1972 and Gerald R. Ford in 1976.

[JAN]

For further information:
Earl Black, *Southern Governors and Civil Rights* (Cambridge, Mass., 1976).
Reg Murphy and Hal Gulliver, *The Southern Strategy* (New York, 1971).

WILLIAMS, JOHN J(AMES)
b. May 17, 1904; Frankford, Del.
Republican Senator, Del, 1947-71.

Williams owned a chicken feed business before he entered national politics in 1946. That year he was elected to the U.S.

Senate. He ran on a platform that advocated reduction of the government's control over the economy. Representing a state whose politics were strongly influenced by the E.I. duPont de Nemours Co., Williams compiled a conservative voting record as he opposed most social welfare legislation and foreign aid.

Williams' crusades against corruption in government and his efforts to expose official hypocrisy earned him the title of "Conscience of the Senate." His private investigation into the questionable business activities of Senate majority secretary Bobby Baker led to a 16-month investigation of influence peddling and tax fraud by the Senate Rules Committee in 1963. Williams argued that the investigation should also probe into the activities of senators who were involved with Baker, but the Senate refused to go along with his plans.

Williams maintained his conservative record during the Nixon years. He opposed increasing the personal income tax exemption to $800 as part of the tax reform bill of 1969 and was one of six senators who voted against the measure enacted that year. The law cut some taxes by $9.1 billion but increased other taxes by $6.6 billion when it closed various tax loopholes that benefited corporations and wealthy individuals. He was one of the conservatives on Sen. Russell B. Long's (D, La.) [q.v.] Finance Committee who helped to defeat the Nixon Administration's welfare reform proposal in 1970. The proposal would have increased the federal government's share of national welfare costs. At the same session, he led the unsuccessful 1969 Senate fight to put a $20,000 ceiling on farm subsidy payments. He argued for the proposal by pointing to five farmers who had each received annual subsidies of $1 million.

Williams continued his campaign for high ethical standards in government and kept the spotlight on official hypocrisy. In 1969 he voted against the Supreme Court nomination of Judge Clement F. Haynsworth [q.v.], citing the need to restore public confidence in the Supreme Court. Critics of the Haynsworth nomination charged that the judge had ruled on cases in which he had a financial interest. Haynsworth had been nominated to the seat vacated when Justice Abe Fortas [q.v.] resigned from the court amid a controversy involving judicial ethics. Williams introduced legislation in 1969 to revoke the tax-exempt status of foundations that made payments to public officials. He introduced the legislation after it was revealed Justice Fortas had received payments from a foundation established by financier Louis E. Wolfson and that other justices had also received payments from various foundations.

Williams led the 1969 Senate fight to block pay raises for members of Congress and other top government officials. The pay raise had been proposed by President Johnson in 1968 under the new procedure Congress established in 1967 to help avoid the thorny issue of having House and Senate vote for their own raises. The Johnson recommendations raised congressional salaries by 41%. The increases would cost about $21 million and would go into effect automatically unless Congress vetoed the President's proposal. Williams introduced the resolution to veto the increases on the grounds that Congress should set an example in the fight against inflation. The Senate, however, defeated the resolution.

Williams opposed the Cooper-Church Amendment to end American military involvement in Cambodia, and during debate on the measure he introduced an amendment that would have also prohibited the use of funds to finance U.S. combat troops for Israel. Williams argued that his amendment was consistent with the Senate intent to restrict the use of U.S. combat troops abroad, but the Senate rejected it by a 60–20 vote.

In 1970 Williams sponsored an amendment that stopped the long-standing political practice of giving members of Congress advanced information on the selection of defense contractors. Members used this information for publicity in their home states by releasing it to the media.

Williams ended his 24-year Senate career when he retired at the end of his term in 1971. The Republicans retained his seat when William V. Roth, Jr. (R, Del.), easily defeated his Democratic opponent by winning 60% of the vote in the 1970 election.

[AE]

WILSON, BOB (ROBERT) (CARLTON)
b. April 5, 1916; Calexico, Calif.
Republican Representative, Calif., 1953-.

Wilson, a banker's son, worked for a San Diego public relations firm and participated in several right-wing causes. He won a seat in the House of Representatives in 1952 and landed a position on the powerful House Armed Services Committee. Through his efforts, major defense and aerospace contracts were channeled to San Diego.

Wilson developed a close friendship with fellow-Californian Richard Nixon. In 1956 he served as Nixon's vice-presidential campaign manager and four years later was his scheduling director. Wilson compiled a conservative record throughout the Johnson Administration, opposing medicare and federal aid to the cities. However he backed civil rights legislation. The California Representative, reflecting the military orientation of his district, was a "super hawk" on the Vietnam war. He criticized the Johnson Administration for not escalating the war to insure a military victory. [See KENNEDY, JOHNSON Volumes]

In 1961 Wilson took over the Republican Congressional Committee, which at the time gave Republican candidates token financial aid. One of the Party's leading fundraisers, Wilson traveled extensively to raise money for his colleagues. In 1970 he was able to allocate nearly $7,000 to each of those running for reelection and an additional $5,000 to novice candidates and those in questionable districts.

Wilson compiled a poor attendance rec-
ord in Congress. His 1971 percentage of house votes was 73, 14% less than the average Republican. From 1969 to 1972 he missed a substantial number of votes on key domestic legislation, but he had a high voting rate when it came to defense and foreign policy bills. During those years he voted against all attempts to ban funds for the Vietnam war. In July 1970 he praised the invasion of Cambodia as "the most successful U.S. military action since Korea." He backed the stepped-up bombing of North Vietnam and the mining of Haiphong Harbor. Wilson also opposed any effort to reduce defense spending, particularly for the anti-ballistic missile system, the B-1 bomber and the F-14 fighter. He continued to obtain lucrative military contracts for his home district.

Wilson's name figured prominently in the 1971 International Telephone and Telegraph (ITT) scandal. Columnist Jack Anderson [q.v.] cited Wilson as one possible go-between for ITT in its attempt to convince the Justice Department to drop a pending anti-trust suit against the conglomerate. ITT's president, Harold Geneen [q.v.], had been a close friend of Wilson for years. Wilson lobbied in San Diego and within the Republican Party to have the 1972 National Convention held in his city, where the Sheraton chain, an ITT subsidiary, had built a new hotel. Geneen promised to provide up to $400,000 to finance the Convention. Wilson never denied his role in the ITT anti-trust dispute, but he refused to concede the alleged link between the government's decision to stop the suit and the Geneen offer to fund the Convention.

In 1974 a Democratic liberal, Marie O'Connor, challenged Wilson for his House seat. She focused on the ITT issue and portrayed the Representative both as a militarist and a heartless conservative. Wilson countered by warning that if the defense cuts O'Connor advocated were made, San Diego would suffer a massive job loss. Wilson easily defeated O'Connor in November.

[JB]

WOODCOCK, LEONARD (FREEL)
b. Feb. 15, 1911; Providence, R.I.
President, United Automobile
Workers Union, 1970-77.

Leonard Woodcock grew up in England after his father, a manufacturer's representative, was interned in Germany during World War I. He returned to the U.S. with his family in 1926 and shortly afterwards settled in Detroit, where he attended Wayne State University. In 1933 Woodcock became a machine assembler at the Detroit Gear and Machine Co., which manufactured auto parts. There he joined a union, then affiliated with the American Federation of Labor, that later became a local of the United Automobile Workers (UAW). Woodcock served on the UAW's regional staff in Grand Rapids, Mich., from 1940 to 1944. He returned to the assembly line for two years as a punch press operator at the Continental Motors Corp. before being appointed, in 1946, first administrative assistant to Walter P. Reuther [q.v.], who had just been elected UAW president. A year later Woodcock became director of the UAW's regional division for western and upper Michigan.

Elected to an international vice-presidency in 1955, Woodcock was put in charge of the UAW's General Motors (GM) and aerospace departments. He gained a reputation as an unusually skillful bargainer, negotiating precedent-setting contracts that included such fringe benefits as dental care programs and bans on discriminatory hiring practices. At the same time, he was regarded with greater friendliness by Detroit's business community than were other members of the top UAW leadership. Like most of the "Reutherites," who had run the union since 1947, Woodcock was an ex-socialist turned left-liberal. Over the years, however, he came to project a somewhat more moderate image than his associates. As the union's chief spokesman on Michigan state politics, for example, Woodcock was the first UAW official to endorse a flat-rate income tax that precluded proportionately higher tax levels for upper-income groups.

During the 1960s Woodcock was increasingly recognized as Walter Reuther's most likely successor. On May 9, 1970, Reuther was killed in a plane crash. When the UAW executive board met 12 days later to choose a new president, Victor Reuther, Walter's brother, nominated Douglas Fraser, the head of the Chrysler and skilled trades divisions. A straw poll was taken of the board members giving Woodcock a one-vote majority, whereupon Fraser withdrew his candidacy and made Woodcock's election unanimous.

During Woodcock's presidency the rising tide of discontent among auto workers, which had begun to assume public prominence in the 1960s, became a subject of national debate. Through the early 1970s a flood of books and articles appeared, focusing on the problems of boredom, frustration, and alienation associated with the monotony and harsh discipline of assembly line work. Social scientists and managerial personnel were particularly concerned with the effects of the high rates of absenteeism and job turnover on productivity. The UAW's response was ambiguous. In general, the union was willing to back management productivity schemes in return for high wages, on the assumption that this was necessary to meet foreign competition and thus save jobs. As rank and file resistance grew, however, the UAW was increasingly forced to take the lead in job actions aimed at blunting the auto makers' rationalizing initiatives.

Shortly after taking office Woodcock led 400,000 auto workers in an eight-week-long strike against GM in the fall of 1970. Labor writer William Serrin later charged that the walkout was designed as an escape valve for the frustrations of UAW members bitter about what they considered intolerable working conditions. The strike demands, however, which had been drawn up by Reuther before his death, centered around wages and early retirement. The new three-year pacts contained a cost of living escalator clause without a ceiling, as well as provision for monthly pensions of $500 after 30 years of service if at least 58 years old.

In 1971 the newly-organized General Motors Assembly Division (GMAD) began a coordinated campaign to speed up the production of cars. GMAD's showplace, the highly-automated Chevrolet Vega factory at Lordstown, Ohio, became the scene of a widely-publicized confrontation between plant management, along with its staff of time-study engineers, and the carefully-screened, predominantly young, white workforce. In March 1972 Lordstown's UAW local went on strike. In April workers at the GMAD plant in Norwood, Ohio, struck over the same issues and ended up staying out for 174 days. In the fall the UAW national leadership coordinated a series of 17 "ministrikes," each lasting a few days.

The issues of workload and speedup formed a backdrop to the 1973 contract negotiations. In September, after a nine-day strike, the UAW arrived at an agreement with Chrysler that set the pattern for the entire industry. A key feature of the new contract was the abolition of "compulsory overtime," giving workers the right to refuse overtime work under certain conditions. The union also won recognition of its "30-and-out" retirement program, allowing retirement with full benefits after 30 years of service regardless of age. Finally, provision was made for weekly plant inspections by joint union-management health and safety teams.

Woodcock increased the UAW's traditional involvement in Democratic Party politics. During the 1972 presidential primaries the union initially backed Sen. Edmund Muskie (D, Maine) [q.v.], but it supported Sen. George McGovern (D, S.D.) [q.v.] at the National Convention. During the campaign Woodcock sharply criticized AFL-CIO president George Meany [q.v.] for calling McGovern an "apologist for the Communist world."

The UAW had suffered a major embarrassment in 1972 when Alabama governor George Wallace [q.v.] won the Michigan primary. Four years later, with busing a volatile issue in Michigan, Woodcock backed Jimmy Carter [q.v.] in the hope of

cutting down Wallace's primary vote. As early as January 1976 UAW locals had campaigned for Carter in the Iowa primary. Woodcock gave his official endorsement in May, thus providing the Carter campaign with what most commentators considered badly-needed liberal credentials. Following the Democrats' electoral victory in November, Woodcock was considered for the post of Secretary of Health, Education and Welfare in the new administration. He declined the offer, however, on the ground that his position in favor of relaxing some automobile anti-pollution controls might constitute a "credibility problem."

Under UAW retirement rules Woodcock was ineligible for reelection to the presidency in 1976, after serving his second full two-year term. At the union's national convention in May 1977 he nominated Douglas Fraser as his successor. Earlier, in March, Woodcock had led a commission that visited Vietnam and Laos in search of information on Americans missing in the Indochina war. In May President Carter appointed him head of the U.S. liaison office in Peking.

[TLH]

For further information:
William Serrin, *The Company and the Union* (New York, 1973).

WOODS, ROSE MARY
b. Dec. 26, 1917; Sebring, Ohio.
Private Secretary to the President.

Rose Mary Woods was the daughter of an Irish potter. After graduating from high school in 1935, she worked as a secretary at the Royal China factory. When her fiance died in 1943, she went to Washington to take a position with the Office of Censorship. She worked for the International Trading Administration from 1945 to 1947, when she joined Christian A. Herter's Committee on Foreign Aid, which was studying the Marshall Plan. Richard Nixon was a young

Congressman on Herter's Committee. Ms. Woods was as impressed with Nixon's honesty and frugality as he was impressed with her competence and efficiency. In 1951 after working as a secretary with the Foreign Service Educational Foundation, she began her 23-year career as Richard Nixon's secretary.

By the time Richard Nixon became President in 1969, Rose Mary Woods was one of his closest and most trusted confidants. In spite of her obvious dedication to Nixon, most people in Washington regarded her as more congenial and approachable than either presidential aides John Ehrlichman [q.v.] or H. R. Haldeman [q.v.]. Above all she was known for her scrupulous honesty.

Rose Mary Woods entered the Watergate story dramatically in 1973 after the discovery of the 18.5 minute gap on the June 20, 1972 tape, which had been subpoenaed by Judge John Sirica [q.v.]. The tape allegedly recorded President Nixon's first discussion of the Watergate break-in with White House Chief of Staff H. R. Haldeman. On Nov. 8, 1973, in routine questioning before Judge Sirica, Woods testified that although the West German Oher 5000 tape recorder was a somewhat complicated machine, she had "caught on" to its use fairly quickly. She rejected the possibility that she could have erased part of the tape.

On Nov. 28 Woods changed her previous testimony and stated that while transcribing the June 20th tape for the court, she had stretched to answer the phone accidentally pushing the record button while holding her foot on the foot pedal and thereby erasing a section of the tape. She said she reported the mistake to President Nixon, who assured her that the tape was not an essential one. Recording experts and the manufacturers of the Oher 5000 testified that the recorder was specifically designed as a "fail safe" machine, so that Ms. Woods "accident" was virtually impossible. The experts also testified that someone had tampered with the tape in at least five sections causing the erasures.

Herbert Kalmbach [q.v.], President Nixon's personal lawyer, claimed that Woods, with Donald and Edward Nixon, had received part of a $100,000 campaign contribution from Howard Hughes [q.v.]. Kalmbach testified that he gave $100,000 to Nixon's friend Charles G. "Bebe" Rebozo [q.v.] and Rebozo split the money among the three. Kalmbach's allegations were never substantiated.

Rose Mary Woods was described as a "fiercely loyal" and "totally devoted servant" of Richard Nixon. She was one of the few staff members who broke with the rigid Haldeman discipline to enjoy Washington society. After Nixon's retirement she gave few interviews to the press. Although officially retired she flew to California to help Nixon with his memoirs. Most often she remained secluded in her Washington apartment.

[SJT]

WOODWARD, ROBERT U(PSHUR)

b. March 26, 1943; Geneva, Ill.
Journalist, author.

The oldest of six children of an Illinois Circuit Court judge, Woodward was raised and educated in Wheaton, Ill. After receiving his B.A. from Yale in 1965, he entered the Navy for a four-year tour of duty. Although he had been accepted at Harvard Law School, Woodward applied for a job at The Washington Post in September 1970. After failing a two-week tryout, Woodward landed a position with the suburban Montgomery County Sentinel. Following a year of covering civic meetings and uncovering scandals in county government, Woodward was rehired by the Post in September 1971.

Assigned to the night police beat, Woodward by-lined front-page stories on medicare abuses, consumer frauds and health code violations in Washington's most exclusive restaurants. On June 17, 1972, Woodward received a call from Post city editor Barry Sussman, who told him that five men carrying expensive electronic gear had been arrested for breaking into the Democratic National Committee headquarters in the Watergate complex.

At the arraignment the next day, Woodward heard James W. McCord, Jr. [q.v.], one of the burglars, admit that he was a former security consultant for the Central Intelligence Agency (CIA). Following up an Associated Press wire item identifying McCord as a security consultant for the Committee to Re-Elect the President (CREEP), Woodward soon linked the burglars to E. Howard Hunt [q.v.], a White House consultant and a onetime CIA operative.

In July 1972 the *Post's* editors permanently assigned Woodward and Carl Bernstein [q.v.] to the Watergate story. Using the so-called circle technique of interviewing, Woodward and Bernstein hounded CREEP staffers, FBI and Justice Department employees and White House aides. Their most valuable source was "Deep Throat," so named because he was always interviewed on "deep background" and could neither be identified nor quoted. Deep Throat, a friend of Woodward's with a "sensitive position in the executive branch," seldom volunteered information but regularly corroborated the reporters' stories before publication.

For the first nine months Woodward and Bernstein pursued the labyrinthine Watergate scandal virtually by themselves. But by April 1973 their list of scoops was staggering: laundered, illegal corporate campaign contributions; the participation of the FBI and the Central Intelligence Agency in the Watergate cover-up; and the harassment of Nixon's "enemies" by the Internal Revenue Service (IRS). Yet when Nixon resigned on Aug. 9, 1974, the reporters "felt no triumph," according to journalist Leonard Downie. "They finally realized with numbing shock that they had helped force the first resignation of a President in American history."

Woodward and Bernstein followed *All the President's Men,* their best-selling recreation of Watergate, with *The Final Days,* a detailed account of Nixon's last months in office. A few days after Nixon's resignation, Woodward and Bernstein took a year's absence from the *Post* to begin six months of intensive interviews for the latter book. Despite adverse criticism of its "gossipy" nature, *The Final Days* was acclaimed by journalists and literary critics as a model of reportage and an important contribution to contemporary history.

Woodward returned to work on the *Post's* national desk in September 1975. As a full-time investigative reporter Woodward looked into Hunt's alleged plot to assassinate columnist Jack Anderson [q.v.], the National Security Administration's wiretaps of anti-war activists and the IRS's attempts to block an inquiry into Sen. Joseph M. Montoya's [q.v.] financial affairs. All three stories led to federal investigations.

[JAN]

For further information:
Carl Bernstein and Bob Woodward, *All the President's Men,* (New York, 1974).
————. *The Final Days* (New York, 1976).
Leonard Downie, Jr., *The New Muckrakers* (Washington, D.C., 1976).

WRIGHT, CHARLES A(LAN)
b. Sept. 3, 1927; Philadelphia, Pa.
Special White House Legal
Consultant on Watergate, 1973-1974.

Wright graduated from Wesleyan University in 1947 and obtained his law degree from Yale two years later. He then embarked on a teaching career at the University of Minnesota, moving to the University of Texas in 1955. Wright became a premier authority on court procedure, authoring numerous books on the subject. He represented the state of Texas before the Supreme Court in arguments against the 18-year-old vote and abolition of the death penalty. Wright characterized his political views as "conservative."

In the summer of 1973 Wright was hired as a special legal consultant to President Nixon on constitutional issues involved in the Watergate case. He specialized on issues relating to executive privilege. In his first major assignment at the end of July, Wright drafted a letter rejecting a request by Special Watergate

Prosecutor Archibald Cox [q.v.] for White House tapes relevant to Watergate court proceedings. Wright argued that Cox was part of the executive branch and therefore subject to the instructions of the President. He said the request was an intrusion of the courts into the presidency, in violation of the separation of powers doctrine in the Constitution.

Cox filed suit to obtain the tapes, and arguments were heard before U.S. District Court Judge John Sirica [q.v.] at the end of August. Wright argued that disclosure of presidential conversations would "impair very markedly" the ability of a President to "perform the constitutional duties vested in him." Sirica ruled against Wright. President Nixon was ordered to make the tapes available to Judge Sirica for a decision on their use by a grand jury. President Nixon, after conferring with Wright and two other staff members, decided to appeal the decision.

On Sept. 11 a U.S. court of appeals heard arguments by Wright and Cox over the tape recordings. Wright reiterated the same arguments as before concerning executive privilege, saying that a President was beyond the jurisdiction of the courts until impeached. Wright also strongly suggested that Nixon might not obey an adverse judicial decision.

The appeals court, in a surprise move, urged an out-of-court settlement under which Nixon, with Wright and Cox, would examine the tapes to determine what material could go to the grand jury. After three meetings Cox and Wright informed the court that they had failed to come to a compromise settlement. On Oct. 12 the appeals court in a 5–2 decision upheld Judge Sirica's ruling that Nixon must hand over the tape recordings to the U.S. district court.

President Nixon proposed a compromise in which a summary of the tapes verified by Sen. John Stennis (D, Miss.) [q.v.] would be given to Judge Sirica and the Senate Watergate Committee. Wright viewed the proposal as a generous offer. Cox refused the offer. Wright called Cox one last time and exchanged letters in an effort to come to an agreement. Cox re-

fused and was fired on Oct. 20 in the so-called Saturday night massacre. Cox later said that Wright had confronted him with a proposal drawn in such a manner that there was no way the special prosecutor could accept it.

In a surprise announcement on Oct. 23, Wright informed Judge Sirica that "the President of the United States would comply in all respects" with the order to turn over the tapes. Two of the tapes Wright agreed to hand over to the court were subsequently discovered to be "nonexistent." Wright was informed of this by a White House secretary the same day it was announced.

Wright returned to his duties at the University of Texas Law School but remained on call for further consultation with Nixon on constitutional issues. He later said he did not resent his dealings with the White House, but added that he would have been happier if he had been told of the nonexistent tapes earlier.

In January 1974 Wright returned as a legal consultant to handle executive privilege issues involved in Watergate. Wright played a low-key role in the rest of Watergate, helping to draft briefs for the White House legal defense.

After Watergate Wright returned to the University of Texas Law School.

[TFS]

For further information:
J. Anthony Lukas, *Nightmare: The Underside of the Nixon Years* (New York, 1973).

WRISTON, WALTER B(IGELOW)
b. Aug. 3, 1919; Middletown, Conn.
Chairman, First National Citicorp, 1968-; Member, National Commission on Productivity, Labor-Management Advisory Committee, 1970-74; Member, Advisory Commission on Reform of the International Monetary System, 1973-74.

Wriston took a B.A. at Wesleyan University in 1941 and did postgraduate work at the Ecole Francaise in Middlebury, Vt.

After obtaining an M.A. at the Fletcher School of International Law and Diplomacy in 1942, Wriston entered the Army. Discharged as a lieutenant in 1946, Wriston was compelled by a tight job market to accept employment as a junior inspector in the comptroller's office of First National City Bank in New York. He advanced quickly through the ranks, becoming an executive vice president in 1960. In 1961, Wriston helped to develop the "certificate of deposit," or CD, which banks used increasingly in the 1960s and early 1970s to attract corporate funds. Wriston became president of First National City Bank in 1967, and in the following year, of the reorganized one-bank holding company, First National City Corp. (Citicorp). The constitution of Citicorp under Wriston's auspices permitted a vast expansion of investment in areas closed to commercial banks. Influenced in part by Citibank's expansion and in spite of Wriston's opposition in personal testimony, Congress in 1970 passed the One-Bank Holding Company Act in an attempt to circumscribe such activities. The expansion of Citicorp was also the object of a massive investigation by the Ralph Nader Study Group, published in 1973. A year later, in Citibank's reply to the Nader study, Wriston bitterly attacked the report as a "reckless misuse of facts."

Wriston's emergence as the head of Citicorp made him a prominent spokesman for the private business sector in the early 1970s. President Nixon appointed him to the National Commission on Productivity in 1970, and in 1971 Wriston was among the business leaders invited to a White House consultation on the implementation of Phase Two controls. When these controls were lifted in January 1973, Wriston was appointed to a Labor-Management Advisory Committee formed under the auspices of the President's Cost of Living Council. In August of the same year, Wriston joined other leading bankers and monetary specialists on the Administration's Advisory Committee on International Monetary Reform.

Wriston found himself in the midst of controversy in the summer of 1974, when Citibank, in response to accelerating inflation that was driving investors out of the bond market, attempted to issue a 15-year bond with a floating rate set at 1% above the average rate on three-month U.S. Treasury bills. The Federal Reserve Bank expressed strong reservations about such an innovation, and Wriston was asked to consult with Fed Chairman Arthur Burns [q.v.] on the bond. Citibank eventually consented to a modification of the terms of the bond. After Gerald Ford assumed the presidency, Wriston was appointed to a revamped Labor-Management Advisory Committee.

Wriston played an important role in the controversy over the potential default of New York City in the summer and fall of 1975. Citibank, as one of the largest holders of the city's debt, distinguished itself by a particularly "hard line" in its call for cutbacks in city employment and services to solve the crisis, a hard line Wriston defended in statements to the press. By October 1975, however, as the potentially disastrous effects of a default on U.S. capital markets became more apparent, Wriston came out for some form of federal aid to the city. With Chase Manhattan's David Rockefeller [q.v.] and Morgan Guaranty's Ellmore Patterson, Wriston on Oct. 18 warned the Senate Finance Committee on the dire consequences of default and on Oct. 29 endorsed President Ford's plan for aid to the city.

Wriston's role throughout the crisis was retroactively highlighted a year later when The New York Times revealed that the major New York banks had quietly unloaded their own holdings of New York City paper in 1973-74, while continuing to urge small investors to buy them. Wriston and Citibank, however, denied any wrongdoing and any "inside information" on the city's crisis, and Wriston asserted that Citibank had in fact done everything possible to avert default.

After the last-minute bailout of New York, Wriston returned to the center of public attention in January 1976, when The Washington Post "leaked" a list of "problem banks" that included both Citibank and the Chase Manhattan Bank.

Wriston, however, attacked the report as "misleading, irresponsible and at variance with the facts."

Wriston remained chairman of Citibank and Citicorp through the late 1970s.

[LG]

WURF, JERRY (JEROME)
b. April 18, 1919; New York, N.Y.
President, American Federation of State, County, and Municipal Employees, 1964- .

The son of a textile jobber, Jerry Wurf attended New York University. After finishing school he worked as a cafeteria busboy and cashier. In 1947 he joined the American Federation of State, County, and Municipal Employees (AFSCME). He gradually rose in the union hierarchy, becoming president of District Council 37 in 1959. In 1964 Wurf unseated AFSCME president Arnold Zander. He was the first insurgent to topple the incumbent president of an international union since Walter Reuther [q.v.] had captured the United Auto Workers in 1946.

Upon taking office Wurf discovered and quickly severed the ties that his predecessor had established between AFSCME and the Central Intelligence Agency. Under his presidency the union grew rapidly: by 1968 it had reached 400,000 members. A major test for the union was the 1968 public-works and sanitation strike in Memphis, Tenn., during which civil rights leader Martin Luther King was assassinated. [See JOHNSON Volume]

In its early years AFSCME had placed great stress on protecting the civil service system and promoting its extension to those local government units where the patronage system still prevailed. In contrast, Wurf made collective bargaining for public employees the cornerstone of AFSCME policy. Partly as a result of the union's efforts, a large number of collective bargaining laws for state and local government workers were enacted during the 1960s, even though strikes remained

outlawed virtually everywhere. By 1970 AFSCME had negotiated more than 1,000 collective bargaining agreements, almost twice the number in 1964; these included contracts in states that lacked any statutory basis for collective bargaining. In that year the union drafted a National Public Employees Relations Act, proposing to give public employes the same rights guaranteed to workers in the private sector.

AFSCME strike activity declined in the 1970s. In 1972 the union came out in favor of compulsory arbitration in disputes involving public safety workers—firemen, policemen, and ambulance drivers—and voluntary arbitration for other essential employees. In many cases Wurf tried, but often failed, to discourage AFSCME locals from taking strike action. In 1974 an unauthorized walkout of AFSCME sanitationmen in Baltimore, Md., eventually spread to 4,000 city employees, including policemen, prompting Maryland governor Marvin Mandel [q.v.] to call out the National Guard. Mandel alleged that Wurf had threatened that Baltimore "would burn to the ground" unless the strikers' demands were met. Wurf denied the story. After 15 days the city conceded the union's wage demands. Afterwards, however, there were severe reprisals; the AFSCME locals involved were given heavy fines, 90 probation officers were fired, and the entire police force was required to resign from the union.

The decline in municipal revenues increasingly forced AFSCME locals to adopt a more conciliatory posture in their relations with city governments. Moreover, the salaries and pensions of AFSCME members themselves were often blamed for the fiscal crisis by newspapers and political figures. During the New York City fiscal crisis Wurf personally intervened to urge the union's autonomous District Council 37 to accept a pay cut for members and to invest an additional billion dollars from its pension fund in Municipal Assistance Corporation bonds.

Under Wurf's leadership AFSCME became one of the most politically liberal unions in the AFL-CIO. Elected a vice president and member of the AFL-CIO executive council in 1969, Wurf repeatedly clashed with Federation president George Meany [q.v.]. In particular, he registered his opposition to the council's many endorsements of Administration policy in Southeast Asia. In 1972 Wurf was one of only 3 out of 35 council members to vote against taking a neutral position on the presidential race. Wurf also antagonized Meany by creating in 1971 the Coalition of Public Employees Organizations (CAPE), which included the National Education Association (NEA), a 1.1-million-member professional association of teachers, principals, and school administrators. Since the NEA was a rival of the AFL-CIO's American Federation of Teachers (AFT), AFT president Albert Shanker [q.v.] immediately denounced CAPE and urged other unions not to join it.

In 1978 AFSCME merged with the independent New York State Employees Union, making it, with a million members, the largest union in the AFL-CIO.

[TLH]

YABLONSKI, JOSEPH (JOCK)
b. March 3, 1910; Pittsburgh, Pa.
d. Dec. 31, 1969; Clarksville, Pa.
Labor reformer.

The son of an Eastern European coal miner who was killed on the job in an accident, Joseph Yablonski started working in the mines at the age of 15 to help support his family. He rose in rank in the leadership of the United Mine Workers (UMW), elected as a local president in 1934 and in the late 1930s as a district leader, and from 1942 to 1969, he served on the international executive board of the union. In 1958 Yablonski was also elected president of the Pittsburgh area District Five. He served until 1966 when union president Tony Boyle [q.v.] forced him to resign under threat of placing the district in trusteeship.

Although he was originally a loyal supporter of the UMW leadership, Yablonski in the late 1960s became outraged with a number of abuses. He found, for example, Boyle collaborating with management to prevent the implementation of improved safety procedures in the mines and offering of the best possible medical care for black lung disease. Yablonski uncovered evidence of embezzlement of union funds, outrageous expense accounts for the leadership, pension fraud, and examples of nepotism and favoritism in giving out executive positions. He opposed the clauses in the union's constitution that gave the national near-dictatorial control over the locals. The conventions Yablonski attended appeared to him to be rigged in favor of Boyle. Any attempt by the miners to reform their union, Yablonski learned, was met either with slick parliamentary tricks to muzzle the insurgents or, at the mines, violence and intimidation to silence the workers.

To correct these abuses, Yablonski declared his candidacy for the UMW presidency on May 29, 1969. Boyle immediately fired Yablonski as head of the union's lobbying office in Washington, a position he held concurrent with his other responsibilities. Yablonski's lawyer, Joseph Rauh [q.v.], sued for his reinstatement charging the ouster was politically motivated. The court ordered Boyle to return Yablonski to his position. Yablonski encountered difficulty getting the requisite 50 nominations by locals needed to place his name on the presidential ballot.

In a petition to Secretary of Labor George Shultz [q.v.], Rauh listed 17 examples of illegal actions by Boyle's supporters, including violence and intimidation against the reformers, rigged meetings that denied Yablonski the nominations of locals who did favor him, and the use of patronage and bribes to lure miners away from the insurgents. Rauh also released an FBI report citing the illegal use of union funds in the Boyle campaign. But Shultz was unable to help Yablonski. Under the Landrum-Griffin law, a union election had to take place regardless of charges of irregularities. Only after the voting, upon receiving a petition documenting the charges of corruption, could the election be set aside. Rauh then tried to use the courts to help Yablonski. In one suit Yablonski charged that the *UMW Journal*, paid for by the miners, covered the Boyle campaign but ignored his. The court therefore ordered the union to send at its own expense campaign material for Yablonski.

On a June 28 rally, an unidentified miner inflicted a karate chop on the back of Yablonski's neck leaving him unconscious. Yablonski was rushed to the hospital to recover from this attempt on his life, explained by Boyle supporters as an act by an irrational man. Despite Boyle's attempts to prevent him from getting on the ballot, Yablonski obtained the 50 nominations.

During the election campaign Yablonski's life was threatened on a number of occasions. The federal government refused to act on Rauh's request for setting aside the election because of the dangers his client faced. On Dec. 9 the UMW rank and file reelected Boyle by a vote of 81,000 to Yablonski's 45,000. Yablonski immediately sued for a new election. Rauh cited in the suit 200 examples of irregularities including ballot stuffing and violence.

On Dec. 30 Yablonski, his wife and daughter were killed in an amateurish gangland-style execution. Yablonski's two sons, joined by Rauh, and the insurgent miners anxious for a new election accused the UMW leadership of being responsible for the labor reformer's death. The three who assassinated the Yablonski family were immediately arrested, and through confessions, two UMW officials were implicated in the case and eventually convicted and imprisoned. It was learned in their trial that the killing of Yablonski was planned during his election campaign but postponed because the conspirators thought the connection between their victim and his campaign would be too obvious.

In the course of the trials of those involved in the case, a mystery person named "Tony" was cited on a number of occasions. Federal investigators identified this individual to be Boyle. Follow-ing a long trial with appeals, he was convicted in 1975 as a co-conspirator in the killing of Yablonski and received a sentence of three life terms. In 1972, following a series of appeals, the UMW complied with a federal court order and held a new election in which the reformer Arnold Miller defeated Boyle.

[JB]

For further information:
Joseph E. Finley, *The Corrupt Kingdom* (New York, 1972).

YEO, EDWIN H(ARLEY), III
b. May 23, 1934; Youngstown, Ohio.
Undersecretary of the Treasury for Monetary Affairs, 1975-77.

Yeo obtained his bachelor's degree from the University of Maryland in 1959, after serving three years in the U.S. Marine Corps following graduation from high school. He immediately began work with the Pittsburgh National Bank, where he eventually served as executive vice president and vice chairman before his appointment in July 1975 as undersecretary of the Treasury for monetary affairs.

Yeo's major achievement at the Treasury was his handling of negotiations with the French Government over the future of the international monetary system. In the summer and fall of 1975, the advanced industrial countries were just emerging from the worst economic crisis since the Great Depression. Yeo was assigned to an extended series of secret meetings with Jacques de Larosiere of the French ministry of finance to arrive at an agreement on the new system of floating exchange rates and the gold question, two issues on which the French were the major adversaries of the United States. Yeo flew to France repeatedly during months of preparation for the November 1975 Rambouillet summit, at which a major breakthrough was announced between the two countries, and for the January 1976 Jamaica summit, which officially recognized the new floating-rate system.

In the agreements reached between Yeo and Larosiere, the French conceded the impossibility of an immediate return to the fixed-rate system, which had expired in the monetary crises of 1971-73. In exchange for a softening of the French position, the United States agreed to take more responsibility for maintaining the stability of the dollar. More importantly, in the view of many observers, the U.S. agreed in principle to allow central banks to buy and sell gold at market prices, instead of the artificially low official price of $42.22 per ounce. The U.S. had long been hostile to any recognition of the ongoing significance of gold as a portion of international reserves, while France had long advocated a renewed emphasis on gold in international transactions. Hence in the view of many, the French had gotten the better of the negotiations.

In a related development Yeo was a key figure in the December 1975 meeting of the Group of 20 of the International Monetary Fund (IMF), where agreement was reached to permit the IMF to sell its gold at market prices. The proceeds were to be used to establish a trust fund that would help underdeveloped countries overcome balance-of-payments difficulties, particularly those stemming from the steep rise in oil-import costs. After the Group of 20 meeting, Yeo reaffirmed the position of the U.S. Treasury that the IMF gold sales were intended only to provide aid to the underdeveloped world, and not to depress the market price of gold, as some critics insisted.

In January 1976, Yeo participated in the international economic summit in Jamaica that formalized the three-year-old system of floating exchange rates. After the conference Yeo praised its achievements and noted that the Jamaica accords showed two marked differences from the Bretton Woods agreements which established fixed rates in 1944. On one hand, according to Yeo, the new system recognized the existence of "hot money," or rapid, speculative international flows of short-term capital as a major factor in determining exchange rates, and it also took account of the much greater integration of international capital markets that had taken place since World War II. Bretton Woods, Yeo added, did not sufficiently consider the underlying economic stability of a country as the basis for maintaining favorable rates. The legitimization of floating exchange rates, Yeo felt, would stabilize the international monetary system.

Yeo also served as a spokesman for the Treasury on general economic matters. Called upon in the fall of 1975 to explain the strengthening of the U.S. dollar relative to the currencies of the nation's major trading partners, Yeo cited the advance of the U.S. economy in recovering from the 1974-75 recession relative to other countries. Yeo also publicly defended throughout the fall of 1975 the new floating-rate system, which he was officially negotiating behind the scenes. In November 1975 at the height of the New York City fiscal crisis, Yeo pointed to the great concern he had encountered abroad over the stability of U.S. capital markets and the possible impact of a New York City default on the world economy. However he had emphasized in an earlier speech that the U.S. government itself expected no great impact on foreign exchange markets or on the dollar from a default.

Yeo left the Treasury in January 1977 and took a position as chairman of the asset and liability management committee of the First National Bank of Chicago.

[LRG]

YORTY, SAM(UEL) (WILLIAM)
b. Oct. 1, 1909; Lincoln, Neb.
Mayor, Los Angeles, Calif., 1961-73.

After graduating from high school, Yorty moved to Los Angeles. He attended Southwestern University part-time to study law and was eventually admitted to the bar. He also entered politics and was elected in 1936 to the state Assembly, where he served two terms. Initially establishing a reputation as a crusading liberal who sponsored a wide range of social and economic welfare legislation, he alienated his liberal supporters by sponsoring the bill that created an un-American activities committee in California. Thereafter he was considered a maverick conservative. For the next 20 years Yorty alternated between political campaigns and his law practice. He won election to the House of Representatives in 1950 and 1952, but lost Senate campaigns in 1940 and 1954, and failed to get the Democratic nomination for the Senate in 1956. In 1960 he antagonized California Democrats by endorsing Richard Nixon for President.

Yorty was elected mayor of Los Angeles in 1961 and 1965. He governed during the city's period of rapid population growth and expansion. Although the powers of the Los Angeles mayor were more circumscribed than in most other cities, Yorty managed to lower property taxes and to undertake the renewal of the city's neglected downtown area. He came under serious criticism for his handling of the 1965 Watts riot. The California Advisory Committee to the U.S. Civil Rights Commission charged Yorty with "gross negligence" and "attitudes and actions" that contributed to the ghetto uprising. In 1966 Yorty unsuccessfully challenged Gov. Edmund Brown in the gubernatorial primary. [See JOHNSON Volume]

Yorty ran for a third term as mayor in 1969. His main challenger in the technically nonpartisan campaign was Thomas Bradley [q.v.], a black city council member and former police lieutenant who had the endorsement of state Party leaders and national figures such as Edward Kennedy [q.v.], Hubert Humphrey [q.v.] and Edmund Muskie [q.v.]. Yorty conducted a vitriolic, racially based campaign. He accused Bradley of running a "racist" campaign by appealing to the "bloc vote" of blacks and "left-wing militants." When the two men faced each other in a runoff, Yorty intensified his campaign rhetoric. "Imagine what would happen here with a Negro mayor," he warned. If Bradley won, Yorty said, the city would become "one big campus" and be taken over by "black militants and left-wing extrem-

ists." In the May 27 voting, Yorty won by a solid margin.

The following year Yorty entered the Democratic gubernatorial primary. He was defeated by Jesse Unruh, the liberal minority leader of the state Assembly, by a more than two-to-one margin. In November 1971 Yorty declared his candidacy for the Democratic presidential nomination. With an initial campaign chest of $250,000 contributed by conservative California businessmen, Yorty was outspokenly conservative. He advocated an aggressive foreign policy, favored raising taxes to increase military spending and took a tough stand on "law-and-order" issues. Given little chance of winning, Yorty concentrated his efforts on the New Hampshire primary, where he had the endorsement of William Loeb [q.v.], the ultraconservative publisher of the *Manchester Union-Leader.* Yorty hoped that a good showing in the primary would rally conservatives around his candidacy. When the returns were in, however, he had only 6% of the vote. In succeeding primaries Yorty received only a minuscule percentage of the vote, including a showing of 1.5% in his home state.

Yorty came under increasing criticism during his third term as mayor. Voters were becoming fed up with growing pollution, traffic congestion and haphazard development, and a mayor who referred to environmentalists as "kooks" and who spent one out of every four days outside of Los Angeles, including six trips to Vietnam. Quipsters remarked that Los Angeles was the only city with a foreign policy. Yorty also took his law-and-order stance to new extremes, giving virtually complete freedom of action to Los Angeles's tough police chief, Ed Davis. Davis remarked that Yorty was "an automatic champion of safety on the streets and whatever it takes to do that." Under Yorty Los Angeles was continually plagued with charges of police brutality, especially toward blacks, the city's large Chicano population and anti-war activists.

Yorty ran for a fourth term as mayor in 1973 and again faced Bradley as his main opponent. The two men were forced into a runoff and Yorty repeated the tactics of the previous campaign. He warned white neighborhoods against the "black bloc vote," and his campaign manager took out full-page newspaper ads accusing Bradley of seeking Black Panther Party support. Bradley won a court order directing Yorty to tone down his more vitriolic campaign literature. In the May 24 runoff Bradley scored a decisive victory over Yorty, who retired after his term expired.

[JD]

YOUNG, ANDREW
b. Mar. 12, 1932; New Orleans, La.
Democratic Representative, Ga., 1973-77.

Young, who was born into a middle-class black family, graduated from Howard University in 1951 and the Hartford Theological Seminary in 1955. Ordained as a minister of the United Church of Christ, he served as pastor of churches in Alabama and Georgia. He became involved in the civil rights movement when he helped organize the 1956 Montgomery, Ala. bus boycott led by Rev. Martin Luther King, Jr. [q.v.]. He then served on the staff of the National Council of Churches in New York, but left when King asked him to become his chief aide in the Southern Christian Leadership Conference (SCLC) which led the civil rights movement during the 1960s. Young was often arrested for participating in the many nonviolent protest demonstrations organized by the SCLC in the South to end discrimination against black people.

In 1969, about a year after King's assassination, Young, who was executive vice president of the SCLC, announced a shift in the organization's strategy. Instead of backing nationwide civil rights protests, the organization would use most of its funds to register black voters in order to win local elections in the South. The following year Young ran an unsuccessful campaign to unseat Rep. Fletcher Thompson, Jr. (R, Ga.), a conservative elected from an Atlanta-area district.

Young won the seat in 1972 when redistricting had consolidated a district that included most of the city of Atlanta with its black majority and some affluent white suburbs. Young won 53% of the vote and became the first black elected to the House from the Deep South since 1898.

During his four years in the House, Young generally opposed the Nixon-Ford legislative programs and regularly voted to override Nixon-Ford vetoes of social welfare legislation. He vigorously supported congressional efforts to legislate an end to the Vietnam war. He compiled a consistently liberal voting record, backing almost every position advocated by the liberal Americans for Democratic Action, the AFL-CIO's Committee on Political Education and consumer groups.

In 1974 Young opposed the Holt Amendment, which sought to prohibit the Department of Health, Education and Welfare from withholding funds from school districts to compel them to assign students and teachers to schools and classes on the basis of race, sex, creed or national origin and to keep records on such factors. Although busing was not mentioned in the Amendment, Holt intended it to be an anti-busing measure. Young argued that the Amendment would increase school busing suits because it closed the door to negotiating settlements of segregation problems. The following year Young vigorously supported extending the Voting Rights Act of 1965, which was due to expire. He pointed out that voter registration of eligible blacks had increased from 29% in 1964 to 56% in 1972 in the states affected by the law. Young also advocated broadening the law to cover discrimination against language minorities. Congress extended the Voting Rights Act for seven years, included language minorities in its coverage and permanently banned the use of literacy tests for voter registration eligibility.

Young was among Jimmy Carter's [q.v.] first supporters for the presidential nomination and actively campaigned for him. The fact that Young, a prominent civil rights leader and Rev. King's former right-hand man, supported the Carter candidacy helped convince many blacks and white liberals that Carter was not a bigot in disguise. Young had an independent power base and was able to give Carter frank and excellent advice during the election campaign. Carter publicly stated that Young was the only man to whom he owed a political debt for his election.

Young was reelected in 1976 but resigned his seat when Carter appointed him U.S. Ambassador to the United Nations in 1977. [See CARTER Volume]

[AE]

YOUNG, MILTON R(UBEN)
b. Dec. 6, 1897, Berlin, N.D.
Republican Senator, N.D., 1945-.

A prosperous farmer in North Dakota, Young served in the state legislature from 1933 to 1945, when he was appointed to the U.S. Senate to fill a seat left vacant by the death of Sen. John Moses. The following year Young won a special election to complete the term. Representing a farm belt state Young labored for farm subsidies far exceeding the amount his Party was willing to support. In other domestic legislation Young consistently voted conservative well into the 1960s, opposing anti-poverty programs and medicare. Throughout the 1960s Young was at times skeptical of the Vietnam war, but he nevertheless approved the appropriations for it. [See TRUMAN, EISENHOWER, KENNEDY, JOHNSON Volumes]

During the Nixon-Ford years Young, a senior Republican Senator, managed a low profile. He devoted most of his attention to agricultural matters, especially issues concerning his state. Young opposed the nomination of Earl Butz [q.v.] as Secretary of Agriculture because he believed Butz favored lower price supports and showed little interest in helping the small farmer. In 1972 Young was responsible for a 10¢ increase in wheat price supports. He also cosponsored legislation for rural development, crop insurance programs and measures to improve market conditions for farm goods. In 1973 Young worked with House Agriculture Committee Chairman Herman Talmadge (D, Ga.) [q.v.] to frame legislation continuing farm product supports.

Young's ambivalent attitude towards the Vietnam war continued into the Nixon years. In 1970 he voted against the Cooper-Church amendment that would have cut off funds for the Cambodian invasion, and praised the incursion as "a long overdue decision." Yet Young did support the McGovern-Hatfield amendment of 1970 and the Mansfield amendment of 1971 that sought to end the war through congressional intervention. Young consistently supported the Administration's defense policies, voting for full appropriations for the anti-ballistic missile and opposing attempts to cut the defense budget. However he did support the withdrawal of most U.S. ground troops from Western Europe.

Young consistently voted against welfare, consumer and environment legislation. He backed Nixon's nominations of Clement Haynsworth [q.v.] and G. Harrold Carswell [q.v.] to the Supreme Court. He stressed that the conservative Carswell would provide a much-needed "philosophic balance" on the Court. Young countered charges that Carswell was a mediocre judge. He said that Carswell "may be no Abraham Lincoln," but Lincoln, too, was belittled and ridiculed for not being a great intellectual. Young agreed with the Administration that the courts had been coddling criminals.

In 1974, at the age of 76, Young decided to seek reelection despite Republican Senate Campaign Committee advice to retire. In the election he faced the popular former Gov. William Guy in a spirited campaign in which most issues were avoided. Young narrowly defeated Guy in a contested election in which the December recount gave him a 186-vote majority.

[JB]

ZABLOCKI, CLEMENT J(OHN)
b. Nov. 18, 1912; Milwaukee, Wisc.
Democratic Representative, Wisc.,
1948- .

Clement Zablocki, educated in Milwaukee parochial schools, graduated from Marquette University in 1936 and taught high school before serving in the Wisconsin State Senate from 1942 to 1948. That year he was elected representative from Wisconsin's fourth district comprised of Southern Milwaukee and its adjacent suburbs. Reflecting the interests of his working class Polish-American constituency, Zablocki was an advocate of organized labor, a generous defense budget and a firm anti-Soviet Communist foreign policy. Both the AFL-CIO Committee on Political Education and the anti-Communist, pro-defense American Security Council consistently gave Zablocki high ratings.

Despite a reputation for a more conservative approach to social programs than his fellow Wisconsin Democrats, Zablocki voted for the major social welfare legislation of the Johnson Administration. As second-ranking member of the House Foreign Affairs Committee, he was of strategic importance as an apologist for the Johnson Administration's Vietnam War policy. [See JOHNSON Volume]

During the Nixon Administration Zablocki continued to support the Vietnam War effort long after the majority of the House Democrats began to vote for amendments to appropriations bills which prohibited the use of funds for combat activity in Southeast Asia. In May 1973 Zablocki voted against the successful amendment to the Second Supplemental Appropriations bill which cut off funds for bombing in Cambodia. The legislative effort eventually resulted in an Administration-congressional compromise to end the bombing by Aug. 15, 1973.

Zablocki was the principal architect and manager of the House legislative effort to define the war making powers of the President. He introduced the first such House resolution in September 1970. It merely requested the President to consult with the Congress "whenever feasible" before committing U.S. troops to combat. This resolution finally passed the House in 1972 but was rejected by Senate conferees as too weak an assertion of the congressional war-making role under the Constitution.

After Zablocki's Subcommittee on National Security reopened hearings on war powers in early 1973 and cooperated with Senate sponsors of a tougher bill, he wrote and reported a much stronger resolution in June. Its major features included a 120 day limit on presidential commitment of U.S. troops without congressional authorization and a provision for Congress to direct disengagement before that limit through passage of a concurrent resolution. In conference, major House-Senate differences focused on the granting of "prior authority," that is allowing the President to commit troops without first obtaining congressional approval. The successful compromise was a general statement of policy that the President had prior authority in emergency situations only. President Nixon vetoed the war powers bill on Oct. 24 but the House overrode on November 7th.

When asked how enough votes were obtained to override the veto (the bill had originally passed three short of the two thirds necessary to override), Zablocki said, "Some of [them] read the returns of yesterday's elections" and felt that the Watergate scandal, the tapes controversy, and the firing of Special Prosecutor Archibald Cox [q.v.] were decisive in creating the atmosphere necessary for an override.

After Chairman of the Foreign Affairs Committee Thomas Morgan (D,Pa.) [q.v.] retired in 1977, Zablocki, by virtue of seniority and his assurances that he would support continued aid to Israel, became chairman of the newly renamed International Relations Committee.

[JMP]

ZIEGLER, RONALD L(EWIS)
b. May 12, 1939; Covington, Ky.
White House Press Secretary,
1969-74.

After receiving a degree in marketing from the University of Southern California in 1961, Ziegler began a brief stint as a salesman for Procter and Gamble. A member of the Young Republicans in his college days and a active volunteer at state Republican headquarters, Ziegler left the firm in October 1961 to serve as press officer for the Republican State Committee.

In 1962 he joined Richard Nixon's gubernatorial campaign as assistant to Herbert G. Klein [q.v.], who served as chief press aide. After Nixon's defeat in late 1962 Ziegler procured an executive post with the prestigious J. Walter Thompson advertising agency, where he became attuned to various facets of television news coverage. During his years at the agency, he continued in Republican state politics under the watchful eye of H. R. Haldeman [q.v.], also an ad man at the Thompson agency. In 1968 at the urging of Haldeman, who was serving as chief of staff for Nixon's presidential campaign, Ziegler took a leave of absence from advertising to serve again as press chief Klein's assistant.

Following Nixon's victory Ziegler was appointed presidential press secretary. He became the youngest man ever to attain the post. An eager, energetic "PR man," Ziegler's youth, thoroughness, efficiency and public relations expertise made him popular at the Nixon White House. The news media, however, was less than enthusiastic about the appointment, since Ziegler lacked press credentials and his knowledge of national and world affairs was limited.

Within a matter of months his complacent, humorless and evasive approach to press briefings came under considerable attack. Ziegler was accused of intentionally passing misinformation and articulating the White House position in a confused "Madison Avenue fuzziness" that required further clarification he was never able to provide. Because of his talent for obfuscation, Ziegler was soon nicknamed "Zigzag" and his statements to the press were labeled "Ziegles." On one occasion, when asked to elaborate on his expression "the President's least likely decision," he stated, "you should not interpret by my use of 'least likely' that ultimately, or when the final decision is made, that that may not be the decision but what I'm saying is that it is only one of the matters under consideration and the decision has not been made." A number of journalists, while frustrated with Ziegler's obscurantist style, saw the problem more in terms of Nixon's "tight leash" on his press secretary, rather than Ziegler's inability to provide background data on administrative policy. Ziegler saw that the press received only what the President intended to reveal. He often admitted ignorance about available detailed information when circuitous statements failed to appease the disgruntled press corps. His ignorance was far from affected, however. He had no input into policy decisions and was seldom given information above and beyond what was to be relayed to the press.

Ziegler experienced no conflict between presidential privacy and the people's right to be kept informed. He also considered it an occupational duty to pass on misinformation to the press. A senatorial press secretary recalled his astonishment when, upon encountering Ziegler one evening, he mentioned that their jobs consisted of "lying to the reporters." After an agitated denial, Ziegler remarked, "oh come on, of course you do. We all do."

The full wrath of press interrogations began in June 1972 soon after the Watergate break-in. One judicious reporter had already compared the list of burglars with the list of executive employees at the Committee to Re-elect the President (CREEP) and pointed out that James McCord's [q.v.] name appeared on both. But Ziegler repeatedly refused comment on "a third-rate burglary attempt." As The Washington Post published its investigations of the Watergate affair and pointed an accusing finger at members of CREEP and the White House staff, Ziegler dismissed the articles as "shabby journalism." Relations between Ziegler and the press had become so strained that members of the White House refused to enter the press room, which they referred to as a "poisoned forum."

As the trial for the Watergate burglars began, a direct path of associations led to Nixon's White House counsel, John Dean [q.v.]. In March 1973 Ziegler informed the press corps that despite this latest development, the President maintained "absolute and total" trust in Dean. Ziegler stated that an investigation would rectify his ambiguous standing in the Watergate affair. When Dean's testimony implicated many in the White House, Ziegler was compelled to issue a revised statement on Watergate developments that, in essence, contradicted the President's previous reluctant statements on the matter. In an attempt to clarify the contradiction, Ziegler labeled his latest remarks the President's "operative" position. Amidst a storm of indignation a *New York Times* reporter inquired if that meant "that the other statement is no longer operative, that it is now inoperative." Ziegler replied: "The President refers to the fact that there is new material, therefore this is the operative statement. The others are inoperative."

Whatever smattering of credibility Ziegler retained throughout his tenure had now abruptly vanished. In June 1973 the National Press Club condemned Ziegler by stating: "The White House press secretary has been reduced to a totally programmed spokesman without independent authority . . . Rather than opening a window into the White House, the press secretary closes doors."

As the result of tension between Special Watergate Prosecutor Archibald Cox [q.v.] and Nixon, in October 1973 Ziegler announced grimly that Cox had been dismissed. Rather than carry out the President's order to fire Cox, Attorney General Elliot Richardson [q.v.] and Deputy Attorney General William Ruckelshaus [q.v.] resigned. The backlash from the announcements forced Nixon to inform the

media a month later, "I am not a crook." As pressure continued to build and cries of impeachment were heard in Congress, Nixon withdrew from the public eye and relied increasingly on Ziegler for solace. Although he encouraged Nixon to fight the impeachment drive, Ziegler had already given up hope. When Nixon resigned, Ziegler accompanied him to his West Coast home.

In 1975 Ziegler attempted to join his former colleagues in an effort to capitalize on Watergate through paid lectures. But Ziegler was less interested in self-vindication than his associates, and rather chose to speak in praise of Nixon. Ziegler's lectures were met with hostility, and he soon abandoned the circuit for a job in advertising later that year.

[DGE]

ZUMWALT, E(LMO) R(USSEL), JR
b. Nov. 29, 1920; Tulare, Calif.
Chief of Naval Operations, July
1970-July 1974.

Zumwalt's parents were both physicians and at one point he intended to become a military doctor. In 1939 he won an appointment to the U.S. Naval Academy and graduated after three years because of World War II. In June 1942 Zumwalt was commissioned an ensign and assigned to the destroyer USS *Phelps*. After a year on the *Phelps* Zumwalt went to the combat information center of the destroyer USS *Robinson*, where he remained until the end of the war.

After the war Zumwalt served as executive officer on several destroyers. He attended the Naval War College for a year and the National War College in Washington for 10 months. A lecture he delivered there, "The Problems of Succession in the Kremlin," attracted the attention of Paul H. Nitze, the assistant secretary of defense for international affairs. Nitze had Zumwalt assigned to his desk as a staff officer. When Nitze became secretary of the Navy in 1963, he made Zumwalt his executive assistant.

In 1965 Zumwalt was promoted to admiral and given command of a cruiser-destroyer flotilla. He went to Vietnam in 1968 as the commander of U.S. naval forces there. While in Vietnam Zumwalt "picked up a whole set of new ideas" about the way the contemporary Navy should be run.

Zumwalt was given the chance to apply his reforms after President Nixon nominated him in April 1970 to be chief of naval operations. In July 1970 he succeeded Adm. Thomas H. Moorer [*q.v.*] who became chairman of the Joint Chiefs of Staff. To implement his changes Zumwalt, the youngest chief of naval operations in U.S. history, issued a series of directives known as "Z-Grams." His goal was to bring the Navy more into line with the nation's changing lifestyles. He also sought to counter the service's declining enlistment and reenlistment rates. Regulations regarding such matters as conduct, grooming, dress, and shore leave were relaxed, and the Navy's promotion procedures were eased. Although the changes met some opposition in the Navy hierarchy, Zumwalt contended that his policies were designed "to treat our Navy personnel with dignity, discipline, compassion, maturity, and intelligence, but most of all with 20th-century commonsense."

In 1971 Zumwalt was persuaded by senior officers on his staff to rewrite or clarify some of his relaxed rules on personal appearance for sailors. He dismissed, however, the contention of Navy traditionalists who feared the new standards would cause a breakdown in discipline. Speaking to the graduating class at Annapolis, he said the Navy's problem was not lack of discipline but a need for enlightened leadership. That same year Zumwalt announced a five-year program to recruit more black officers and enlisted men. The aim was to increase the number of black Navy personnel to the level of their representation in the U.S. population. In 1973 he disclosed plans to open all Navy jobs to women, including assignments for general sea duty. A major reason for the proposed change, he

explained, was that the imminence of an all-volunteer armed force had heightened the importance of women as a personnel resource.

After a series of racial incidents between black and white sailors and marines, Zumwalt and Secretary of the Navy John W. Warner [*q.v.*] told a meeting of top admirals and Marine Corps generals in November 1972 that race relations were to be given the same priority as professional performance. Later in the month a special House Armed Services Subcommittee opened an investigation into the racial disorders aboard the aircraft carriers Constellation and Kitty Hawk. Appearing before the subcommittee Zumwalt discounted claims by Navy officials and others that a breakdown in discipline had led to the disorders. The Constellation's executive officer, Cmdr. John Schaub, testified that the racial problems could be related to the Navy's recruitment of educationally disadvantaged black youths. Speaking later to reporters he characterized the recruiting of such men as "poorly conceived and totally unfair" because it placed them in competition with other recruits from a "more favorable" background. Zumwalt maintained that the problems stemmed mostly from the failure of commands to fully implement equal opportunity programs. The servicemen involved in the incidents were eventually disciplined or discharged by the Navy.

In February 1973 the Navy disclosed that Zumwalt had ordered the discharge of roughly 3,000 enlisted men who were considered a "burden to command." At the same time the Navy announced that it was tightening its recruitment standards with a new emphasis on education and character qualifications.

Faced with budget restraints, Zumwalt supported the development of smaller high-speed craft to offset anticipated reduction in fleet size. In 1971 he initiated guidelines for modernization of the fleet. He was a strong advocate of the Navy's controversial new jet fighter, the F-14 Tomcat, and in 1974 he fought successfully for the Trident missile program.

Zumwalt became concerned about the steady growth in Soviet naval power that had begun in the 1960s. In the spring of 1971 he told the House Armed Services Committee that updating the U.S. fleet was necessary to maintain nuclear parity with the Soviet Union and to balance its increasingly active navy. In August 1972 he reported the construction of the first Soviet aircraft carrier. Shortly before his retirement Zumwalt questioned whether the Navy would be able to maintain control of the seas in the event of a war with the Soviet Union. Zumwalt left the service in July 1974; was succeeded as Chief of Naval Operations by Adm. James L. Holloway [q.v.].

In retirement Zumwalt criticized the conduct of foreign policy under Nixon and Secretary of State Henry A. Kissinger [q.v.], specifically the failure to address the issues of detente and the first Strategic Arms Limitation Talks (SALT 1) agree-ment. In December 1975 he accused Kissinger of witholding information from President Gerald Ford [q.v.] about what Zumwalt described as "gross violations" by the Soviet Union of its 1972 SALT agreement with the U.S. Kissinger denied Zumwalt's accusations and the following year refuted the quotes attributed to him in Zumwalt's book, *On Watch.* In the book Zumwalt claimed Kissinger had said the U.S. was in decline and the Soviet Union on the rise. In 1976 Zumwalt ran as the Democratic candiate for the Senate in Virginia and lost to the independent incumbent, Sen. Harry F. Byrd, Jr. [q.v.]. He became president of American Medical Buildings the following year.

[SF]

For further information:
E.R. Zumwalt, Jr, *On Watch*, (New York, 1976).

Appendix

CHRONOLOGY: THE NIXON/FORD YEARS

1969

JAN. 20—Richard M. Nixon is sworn in as the 37th President of the United States

JAN. 26—Three thousand coal miners meet in Charleston, W.Va., to demand action against "black lung" disease.

JAN. 30—North Vietnam and the National Liberation Front reject the U.S. proposal to restore neutrality to the Demilitarized Zone.

FEB. 14—A 57-day dock strike, the longest in the history of the Port of New York, ends with a new contract providing a $1.60 hourly package raise and giving longshoremen the right to repack cargo containers when consolidated shipments comprise less than full trailer loads.

FEB. 23–MARCH 2—President Nixon visits five West European nations and consults with their leaders during a tour that he said was intended to create a "new spirit of consultation" and "confidence" between the U.S. and its European allies.

MARCH 5—Edwin C. Arnett, the first soldier to be court-martialed for deserting from Vietnam to a foreign country, is convicted and sentenced to four years at hard labor.

MARCH 10—James Earl Ray pleads guilty to the assassination of Martin Luther King.

MARCH 14—President Nixon decides to proceed with a revised anti-ballistic missile (ABM) defense plan.

MARCH 19—A strike against American Airlines by members of the AFL-CIO Transport Workers Union of America, which started Feb. 27, ends with a new contract.

MARCH 26—The Women Strike for Peace pickets Washington in the first large anti-war demonstration since Nixon's inauguration.

MARCH 28—Dwight David Eisenhower dies.

MARCH 29—American combat deaths in Vietnam reach 33,641, exceeding those in the Korean war.

APRIL 2—The nation's longest maritime strike (103 days) ends with a new contract for 8,000 longshoremen in ports from Lake Charles, La., to Brownsville, Tex. Settlements for Atlantic and other Gulf Coast ports had been reached earlier. The agreements provide a $1.60 an hour package increase and give dockers the right to unpack and repack cargo containers with consolidated shipments of less than full trailer loads.

APRIL 13—A national rail strike is averted by an agreement providing a 22¢ an hour differential for skilled signalmen and a 9¢ adjustment for the semiskilled.

APRIL 15—A U.S. Navy intelligence plane is shot down over North Korea as an intruder in North Korean territorial air space.

APRIL 23—Sirhan Bishara Sirhan, convicted April 17 of the murder of Robert Kennedy, is sentenced to death.

MAY 14—President Nixon proposes an eight-point peace plan for Vietnam; it provides for mutual troop withdrawal.

MAY 15—Supreme Court Justice Abe Fortas resigns under criticism after the disclosure that he had accepted (but returned 11 months later) $20,000 from the family foundation of imprisoned financier Louis Wolfson.

JUNE 8—President Nixon announces the withdrawal of 25,000 troops from Vietnam.

JUNE 23—Warren E. Burger is sworn in as Chief Justice of the United States.

JULY 18—Sen. Edward M. Kennedy's car plunges off a bridge on Chappaquiddick Island; his companion, Mary Jo Kopechne, drowns.

JULY 22—The Pentagon reveals that the U.S. has shipped lethal nerve gas to overseas troops.

JULY 26–AUG. 3—President Nixon tours eight countries in Asia and Europe, emphasizing his belief that peace in Asia depends on Asians themselves. Highlights of the tour are an unannounced visit to South Vietnam and a stop in Rumania.

JULY 30—Neil Armstrong and Air Force Col. Edwin Eugene (Buzz) Aldrin, Jr., become the first men to land and walk on the moon.

AUG. 1—The Justice Department sues Georgia to end segregation in schools.

SEPT. 18—President Nixon, addressing the U.N. General Assembly, urges U.N. members to aid negotiations for ending the war in Vietnam.

OCT. 1—President Nixon allows draft deferments for graduate students.

OCT. 3—President Nixon blocks a rail strike by imposing a 60-day Railway Labor Act freeze in a dispute between seven railroads and four shopcraft unions.

OCT. 15—Anti-war demonstrations take place thoughout the U.S. in a massive protest coordinated by the Vietnam Moratorium Committee in Washington; among rallies, speeches and religious services, one of the largest gatherings is a meeting of about 100,000 people in Boston Common.

OCT. 27—Some 147,000 workers go on strike against General Electric Co. at plants across the country in a wage dispute.

NOV. 3—President Nixon announces a U.S.-South Vietnam plan to withdraw U.S. troops from Vietnam.

NOV. 15—In escalating anti-war protests sponsored by the New Mobilization Committee to End the War in Vietnam (the New Mobe), more than 250,000 people participate in Washington in the largest such demonstration ever held; the rally follows a three-day March Against Death in which more than 40,000 people took part.

NOV. 17—Preliminary Strategic Arms Limitation Talks (SALT) are opened by U.S. and Soviet negotiators in Helsinki, Finland.

DEC. 1—The first draft lottery since 1942 is held at Selective Service System headquarters.

1970

JAN. 1–2—Vice President Agnew visits Vietnam while on Asian tour.

JAN. 5—Joseph A. Yablonski, president of the United Mine Workers of America, is found dead at his home.

JAN. 6—President Nixon announces a major diplomatic agreement with France that will curb heroin traffic.

JAN. 14—The Supreme Court sets the deadline (Feb. 1) for pupil desegregation of public schools.

JAN. 15—Martin Luther King, Jr., is honored across the nation on the 41st anniversary of his birthday.

JAN. 19—The second session of the 91st Congress convenes.

JAN. 19—Vice President Agnew concludes a 21–day tour of Pacific and Asian countries.

JAN. 21—Three men are arrested in connection with the Joseph A. Yablonski murder.

JAN. 22—President Nixon delivers his first State-of-the-Union address.

JAN. 22—The United States rejects Soviet proposals for Middle East peace.

JAN. 30—The International Union of Electrical Workers (IUE) and the United Electrical Workers (UE) end a three-month strike against General Electric Co. by approving a new contract.

JAN. 30—Seven Black Panthers are indicted for attempted murder by a Chicago grand jury.

FEB. 2—The pretrial hearing for 13 Black Panthers in New York City opens.

FEB. 2—President Nixon presents his fiscal 1971 budget to Congress.

FEB. 6—Sen. Fred R. Harris resigns as chairman of the Democratic National Committee.

FEB. 6—Walter Cronkite's second interview with Lyndon B. Johnson is broadcast on television.

FEB. 8—Democrats rebut President Nixon's State-of-the-Union address in an hour-long national television program.

FEB. 9—The Democratic Policy Council adopts a resolution urging total withdrawal of U.S. troops from Vietnam.

FEB. 10—The U.S., British and French embassies in Moscow accept a Soviet proposal for four-power talks on Berlin.

FEB. 10—The Army charges Capt. Thomas K. Willingham with unpremeditated murder in connection with the alleged civilian massacre at Songmy (My Lai).

FEB. 10–13—Defense Secretary Melvin Laird visits South Vietnam to study Vietnamization and U.S. troop withdrawals.

FEB. 12–17—U.S. and Soviet delegates discuss the peaceful use of nuclear explosions.

FEB. 18—President Nixon submits a foreign policy outline to Congress.

FEB. 18—The "Chicago Seven" are acquitted of conspiring to incite a riot.

MARCH 2—The Lockheed Aircraft Corp. appeals to the Defense Department for interim funding.

MARCH 4—Nixon signs legislation blocking for 37 days a nationwide railroad strike.

MARCH 5—Lawrence F. O'Brien is elected Democratic national chairman.

MARCH 5—The nuclear nonproliferation treaty goes into effect.

MARCH 6—President Nixon appeals to the Soviet Union and Britain to help restore the 1962 Geneva agreements on Laos.

MARCH 6—Pro-Communist Pathet Lao rebels propose a five-point peace plan.

MARCH 9—Gravediggers in the New York metropolitan area end an eight-week strike.

MARCH 10—Thomas A. Foran (chief prosecutor in the "Chicago Seven" conspiracy trial) resigns as U.S. attorney for the northern district of Illinois. (He remains chief prosecutor in the case.)

MARCH 13–16—San Francisco's municipal workers strike successfully for higher wages.

MARCH 13—Bobby G. Seale is extradited from San Francisco to New Haven, Conn.

MARCH 14—The *Columbia Eagle,* a U.S. freighter bound for Thailand with Air Force munitions, is siezed by two armed crewmen and diverted to Cambodia. (It may be seen as an anti-war protest by the two crewmen.)

MARCH 16–22—The New Mobilization Committee to End the War in Vietnam (New Mobe) sponsors a national "anti-draft week."

MARCH 23—President Nixon orders troops to help move the mail in New York City held up by a postal strike.

MARCH 25—A week-old New York City postal strike ends with the beginning of wage negotiations.

MARCH 26—President Nixon signs a bill increasing G.I. educational monthly allowances.

APRIL 1—The Coal Mine Health and Safety Act of 1969 goes into effect.

APRIL 2—Massachusetts Gov. Francis W. Sargent signs a bill challenging the legality of the war in Vietnam.

APRIL 4—The largest Washington prowar demonstration since America's involvement in Vietnam is held.

APRIL 7—The drowning case of Mary Jo Kopechne is closed, with no indictments.

APRIL 8—The *Columbia Eagle* is released by Cambodia.

APRIL 11—Willy Brandt concludes a week-long visit to the United States.

APRIL 15—A federal pay raise for postal and civil service employees and military personnel is enacted.

APRIL 16—SALT sessions resume after a recess.

APRIL 17—Assistant Secretary of State Joseph J. Sisco cancels his trip to Jordan after anti-American riots there.

APRIL 17—The Apollo 13 crew splashes down safely in the Pacific, after experiencing trouble in space (April 13).

APRIL 20—President Nixon announces plans to withdraw more troops from Vietnam.

APRIL 20–MAY 1—The U.S. and South Vietnam extend fighting to Cambodia.

APRIL 22—Earth Day is observed across the country.

APRIL 23—President Nixon ends occupational draft deferments and deferments for fathers.

APRIL 30—President Nixon announces the major U.S. troop offensive into Cambodia.

MAY 4—Four students are killed by National Guardsmen at Kent State University in Ohio.

MAY 4—The Soviet Union and China assail Nixon's expansion of the war to Cambodia.

MAY 6—Communist delegates to the Paris peace talks boycott in protest of the U.S. bombing of North Vietnam.

MAY 6 & MAY 9—President Nixon confers with student anti-war protestors.

MAY 8—The "Chicago Seven" are freed with all charges against them dropped.

MAY 14—Two students are slain by Mississippi highway patrolmen at Jackson State University.

MAY 22—Leonard Woodcock is chosen as president of the United Automobile Workers.

JUNE 22—President Nixon signs a bill lowering the voting age for national elections to 18.

JUNE 29—U.S. ground troop withdrawal from Cambodia is completed.

JULY 1—The nation's most liberal abortion law goes into effect in New York.

JULY 2-3—The Southeast Asia Treaty Organization (SEATO) holds its annual Ministerial Council meeting.

JULY 4—Honor America Day demonstrates national unity and faith in American institutions.

JULY 29—Contracts are signed by the United Farm Workers Organizing Committee and grape growers, increasing farm workers' wages.

JULY 30—Nixon holds his first nationally televised press conference.

JULY 31—Israel joins Egypt and Jordan in accepting the U.S. Middle East peace plan.

AUG. 14—The Vienna phase of the SALT sessions ends.

AUG. 20—President Nixon and Mexican President Gustavo Diaz Ordaz meet and propose a treaty concerning U.S.–Mexican border disputes.

AUG. 26—A demonstration is staged for "Women's Strike for Equality" and to celebrate the 50th anniversary of women's right to vote in the U.S.

AUG. 30—Vice President Agnew completes a weeklong Asian tour.

SEPT. 9–12—The Young Americans for Freedom (YAF) hold a 19th anniversary meeting at the University of Hartford in Connecticut.

SEPT. 15—Railworkers strike against Southern Pacific Co., Chesapeake & Ohio Railway and the Baltimore & Ohio Railroad when contract negotiations break down. (A restraining order sends them back to work within a day.)

SEPT. 15–20—Golda Meir visits the U.S. and talks to President Nixon, Secretary of State William P. Rogers and others.

SEPT. 17—The National Liberation Front presents an eight-point peace proposal for Vietnam at the Paris talks.

SEPT. 22—President Nixon signs a bill giving the District of Columbia a nonvoting delegate in the House of Representatives.

OCT. 5—President Nixon completes an eight-day trip to Europe.

OCT. 10—North Vietnam denounces Nix-

on's five-point peace plan (made on Oct. 7).

OCT. 13—Angela Davis is seized and arrested by FBI agents in New York City. (She is charged as an accomplice in a kidnap-escape attempt in California on Aug. 7.)

OCT. 22—President Nixon and Soviet Foreign Minister Andrei A. Gromyko confer in Washington.

OCT. 23—Nixon addresses the United Nations.

NOV. 12—U.S. policy toward Communist China changes; U.S. delegates to the U.N. argue against Communist China's expulsion from the organization.

NOV. 17—The first anniversary of the SALT sessions is marked.

NOV. 20—The 67–day national strike against General Motors by the United Automobile Workers ends. (An agreement was reached on Nov. 11.)

NOV. 25—President Nixon dismisses Walter J. Hickel as Secretary of the Interior.

DEC. 8—President Nixon confers with King Hussein of Jordan at the White House.

DEC. 10—A 24–hour nationwide rail strike ends after congressional legislation defers it.

DEC. 10—The Equal Employment Opportunity Commission (EEOC) charges the American Telephone and Telegraph Co. with gross discrimination against women, blacks and Spanish-Americans.

DEC. 11—President Nixon announces the appointment of Rep. George Bush as the U.S. representative to the U.N.

DEC. 11—President Nixon confers with Israeli Defense Minister Moshe Dayan at the White House.

DEC. 21—Angela Davis is extradited from New York to California.

DEC. 21—The Supreme Court rules that the new voting rights of 18-year-olds in federal elections do not extend to state and local elections.

1971

JAN. 2—The 91st Congress adjourns.

JAN. 7—Defense Secretary Melvin R. Laird visits Thailand to assess the military situation in Indochina.

JAN. 8–11—Defense Secretary Melvin R. Laird visits South Vietnam to assess the military situation in Indochina.

JAN. 12—Rev. Philip F. Berrigan and five others are indicted on charges of conspiring to kidnap Henry Kissinger.

JAN. 14–19—About 85% of New York City's police officers go on a wildcat strike.

JAN. 15—Sen. Edmund S. Muskie confers with Soviet Premier Aleksei N. Kosygin in Moscow, exchanging views on the Middle East and Indochina.

JAN. 17—The Chicago Teachers Union accepts a new contract, ending a week-old strike.

JAN. 18—Sen. George S. McGovern opens his campaign for the 1972 Democratic presidential nomination in a televised speech.

JAN. 21—The 92nd Congress convenes.

JAN. 22—President Nixon delivers his second State-of-the Union message.

JAN. 25—The Supreme Court rules that companies cannot deny employment to women with preschool children unless the same criterion applies to men.

JAN. 26—Charles M. Manson and three of his female followers are convicted of first degree murder in the slaying of actress Sharon Tate and six other persons.

JAN. 29—President Nixon submits his budget for 1972 to Congress.

FEB. 9—Apollo 14 splashes down after a trip to the moon.

FEB. 11—A treaty prohibiting installation of nuclear weapons on the ocean floor is signed by 63 nations.

FEB. 21—The U.S. and 20 other United Nations members sign an international treaty to end illegal drug sales.

FEB. 22—A speech by Eugene J. McCarthy in Boston launches a new effort to mobilize anti-war sentiment on college campuses.

FEB. 23 & FEB. 27—The Columbia Broadcasting System broadcasts "The Selling of the Pentagon."

FEB. 25—President Nixon makes his annual State-of-the-World message.

FEB. 26—The U.S. and France sign a protocol to crack down on organized narcotics trafficking, formalizing an agreement made in January 1970.

MARCH 2—George Bush takes over as U.S. ambassador to the United Nations.

MARCH 15—The fourth round of the U.S.-Soviet SALT negiotiations begins in Vienna.

MARCH 19—Foreign Minister Abba Eban confers with Secretary of State William P. Rogers and Henry Kissinger.

MARCH 24—The Senate votes against government sponsorship of America's supersonic transport (SST), as did the House on March 18.

MARCH 29—First Lt. William L. Calley, Jr., is convicted by an Army court-martial of the premeditated murder of at least 22 South Vietnamese civilians in the My Lai "massacre" of March 16, 1968. (Calley is sentenced March 31 to life at hard labor, but the sentence is reduced Aug. 20 to 20 years.)

MARCH 29—The jury that convicted Charles M. Manson and his codefendants votes that they be executed in the gas chamber.

APRIL 1—The five-month pilots' strike against Mohawk Airlines ends.

APRIL 3—President Nixon announces that he will personally review the case of Lt. William L. Calley, Jr., before final sentence is carried out.

APRIL 7—Outtakes of the CBS TV documentary "The Selling of the Pentagon" are subpoenaed by a House subcommittee.

APRIL 14—President Nixon relaxes a 20–year embargo on trade with Communist China.

APRIL 17—The U.S. table tennis team leaves Communist China after a week-long tour.

APRIL 18—The Newark Teachers Union and the city's board of education agree to a contract settlement, ending an 11–week strike.

APRIL 18—The White House Conference on Youth is held.

APRIL 24—Marchers mass in Washington and San Francisco and hold peaceful rallies urging Congress to end the war in Indochina immediately.

APRIL 30—Rev. Philip Berrigan and seven others are indicted for plotting to kidnap Henry A. Kissinger and blow up heating tunnels in government buildings.

MAY 3–5—Anti-war protests organized by the Peoples Coalition for Peace and Justice are held in Washington.

MAY 9—Secretary of State William P. Rogers returns after his five-nation tour of the Middle East.

MAY 21—Secretary of the Army Stanley R. Resor resigns.

MAY 22—President Nixon joins Lyndon Johnson in dedicating the Lyndon Baines Johnson Library Complex on the University of Texas campus.

MAY 25—President Nixon signs a bill terminating the project to develop a commerical supersonic transport (SST).

MAY 26—A new subpoena is issued to replace the one previously issued to CBS to furnish a House subcommittee with outtakes of "The Selling of the Pentagon."

MAY 28—U.S. and Soviet negotiators conclude the fourth round of SALT in Vienna.

MAY 30—Mariner 9, a U.S. interplanetary space probe bound for Mars, is launched from Cape Kennedy, Fla.

MAY 31—Vietnam Veterans Against the War completed a 20–mile trek to protest the war, tracing in reverse the route of Paul Revere's ride, to "spread the alarm" against the current war.

JUNE 1—The Vietnam Veterans for a Just Peace condemn the protests of the Vietnam Veterans Against the War as "irresponsible."

JUNE 3—James R. Hoffa announces from prison that he is not a candidate for re-election as president of the International Brotherhood of Teamsters.

JUNE 12—David Hilliard, the Black Panther chief of staff, is convicted of assault in connection with an April 1968 shootout with police.

JUNE 15—*The New York Times* halts publication of a series of Vietnam war articles drawn from a secret Pentagon study because of a temporary court order. (Publication of the articles began on June 13.)

JUNE 16—The U.S. Conference of Mayors urges President Nixon to withdraw all troops from Vietnam by the end of the year.

JUNE 18 & JUNE 19—*The Washington Post* publishes articles on the involvement of the U.S. in the Vietnam war based on a classified Pentagon study.

JUNE 21—Communist Chinese Premier Chou En-lai says that withdrawal of U.S. support from Taiwan would facilitate better relations between the U.S. and Communist China.

JUNE 22 & JUNE 23—The *Boston Globe* and the *Chicago Sun-Times* publish articles based on the classified Pentagon study.

JUNE 30—The Supreme Court rules that articles based on classfied Pentagon material may be published by newspapers.

JUNE 30—The 26th Amendment to the Constitution—lowering the minimum voting age to 18 years for all federal, state and local elections—is ratified by the states.

JUNE 30—Twelve Black Panthers are cleared of charges of murdering a policeman and conspiracy to murder in a gun fight with police at the Party's headquarters in Detroit in October 1970.

JULY 1—David Hilliard is sentenced to a 1–10 year prison term for assault in connection with an April 1968 shootout with police.

JULY 1—President Nixon inaugurates the new volunteer agency Action, which merges the Peace Corps, VISTA and seven other volunteer service agencies.

JULY 1—The new semi-independent U.S. Postal Service goes into operation.

JULY 5–9—The NAACP holds its 62nd annual convention in Minneapolis.

JULY 7—Seven Black Panthers are indicted in New York City on charges of murder and arson in connection with the slaying of a West Coast Panther official.

JULY 8—Frank E. Fitzsimmons is elected as president of the International Brotherhood of Teamsters.

JULY 8 & JULY 13—The fifth round of the U.S.-Soviet SALT negotiations are held in Helsinki.

JULY 9—Rep. Paul N. McCloskey, Jr., announces that he will seek the Republican Party's nomination for President.

JULY 9—U.S. troops relinquish total responsibility for defense of the area just below the demilitarized zone to South Vietnamese troops.

JULY 11—President Nixon signs a $5.15 billion education appropriation bill (HR 7016), the largest of its kind in the history of the Office of Education.

JULY 12—President Nixon signs the Emergency Employment Act (S 31), authorizing $2.25 billion to provide public service jobs in the next two years for the unemployed at state and local levels.

JULY 16—Sen. Fred R. Harris announces that he will seek the Democratic nomination for President.

JULY 16 & 22—The U.S., Great Britain, France and the Soviet Union meet in Berlin to discuss the area's future.

JULY 18—The National Association of Counties (NACO) opens its annual convention in Milwaukee.

JULY 22—The Agriculture Department issues new food stamp program regulations.

JULY 28—Vice President Spiro T. Agnew returns from his 32–day diplomatic tour of 10 nations.

JULY 31–AUG. 2—Two U.S. astronauts

drive an electric car on the moon during scientific exploration and experimentation as part of the Apollo 15 mission.

AUG. 2—Railroad strikes by the AFL-CIO United Transportation Union end with a contract agreement.

AUG. 2—The U.S. ends 20 years of opposition to Communist China's presence in the United Nations by announcing future support of China's membership.

AUG. 5—The Selective Service System conducts its third draft lottery since Congress authorized the random selection of men into the armed forces in 1969.

AUG. 6—A New Orleans jury acquits 12 Black Panthers of attempted murder of five New Orleans policemen in a gun fight in September 1970.

AUG. 7—Apollo 15 splashes down safely in the Pacific. (Apollo 15 was launched from Cape Kennedy on July 26th.)

AUG. 9—President Nixon signs a bill providing a $250 million government-guaranteed loan to Lockheed Aircraft Corp.

AUG. 9—The public service jobs bill is signed by President Nixon, to provide 150,000 jobs in state, county and city governments for the unemployed.

AUG. 9—President Nixon signs a bill appropriating $20,804,622,000 for fiscal 1972 for the Departments of Labor and of Health, Education and Welfare (HEW).

AUG. 11—New York Mayor John V. Lindsay formally switches from the Republican Party to the Democratic Party.

AUG. 13—Attorney General John N. Mitchell drops the federal investigation of the shooting deaths of four students at Kent State University.

AUG. 17—The Export Expansion Finance Act of 1971 is signed by President Nixon.

AUG. 18—A labor agreement between Heublein, Inc., and the AFL-CIO United Farm Workers Organizing Committee ends a nationwide boycott against Heublein products which began Aug. 9.

AUG. 20—Lt. William L. Calley, Jr.'s, sentence of life imprisonment is reduced to 20 years.

AUG. 21—FBI agents and local police foil a Selective Service office raid in Buffalo, N.Y., arresting five young men and women.

AUG. 21—George Jackson, one of the three black convicts known as the Soledad Brothers charged with killing a Soledad Prison guard, is shot and killed as he attempts to escape from the California State Prison at San Quentin.

AUG. 22—FBI agents and local police foil a Selective Service office raid in Camden, N.J., with the arrest of 20 people.

SEPT. 13—Nearly 1,500 state troopers, sheriff's deputies and prison guards put down an uprising by 1,200 inmates at the Attica Correctional Facility in Attica, N.Y. The insurrection began on Sept. 9 and left dead 31 prisoners and nine guards and civilian employees held as hostages.

SEPT. 13—The 63rd National Governors Conference opens in San Juan, Puerto Rico.

SEPT. 21—Federal agents seize personal papers and possessions belonging to Dr. Daniel Ellsberg, with the authority of a search warrant.

SEPT. 22—The U.S. formally submits two resolutions to the U.N. bearing on the seating of a Chinese delegation (from Communist China) in the U.N.

SEPT. 24—Sen. Fred R. Harris declares himself a candidate for the Democratic nomination for President.

SEPT. 24—The fifth round of the U.S.-Soviet SALT negotiations ends in Helsinki.

SEPT. 25—Former Supreme Court Justice Hugo LaFayette Black dies.

SEPT. 26—President Nixon greets Emperor Hirohito of Japan in Anchorage, Alaska, during a stopover on the emperor's flight to Europe.

SEPT. 29–OCT. 3—The third annual Black Business and Cultural Exposition, better known as Black Expo, is held in Chicago.

OCT. 4—Secretary of State William P. Rogers addresses the U.N. General Assembly, asking for the seating of Communist China on the Security Council and speaking against the expulsion of Nationalist China (Taiwan) from the General Assembly.

OCT. 8—President Nixon becomes the first President to visit all 50 states when he attends the 35th annual Mountain State Forest Festival in Elkins, W. Va.

OCT. 9—The West Coast dock strike that began July 1 ends in compliance with a court order obtained by the Justice Department under the Taft-Hartley Act.

OCT. 12—Sen. Birch Bayh removes himself from the competition for the 1972 Democratic presidential nomination.

OCT. 12–18—Gov. Ronald Reagan tours six Asian nations as a special presidential representative, bearing personal letters from President Nixon to the leaders of those countries.

OCT. 16—H. Rap Brown, the fugitive black militant who disappeared 17 months ago, is shot and captured by police in New York City.

OCT. 16–23—Vice President Spiro Agnew visits Greece for an official conference with Premier George Papadopoulos and a private tour.

OCT. 20–25—Henry Kissinger visits Peking to arrange the agenda and itinerary for President Nixon's forthcoming trip to Communist China.

OCT. 26—About 300 anti-war demonstrators are arrested for sitting down in the middle of Pennsylvania Avenue during rush hour, after a rally at the Washington Monument.

NOV. 6—The most powerful underground nuclear test conducted by the U.S. is executed on the remote Alaskan island of Amchitka.

NOV. 13—Aubran W. Martin is sentenced to death in the electric chair for his role in the slaying of United Mine Workers official Joseph A. Yablonski and his wife and daughter.

NOV. 13—The U.S. interplanetary probe Mariner 9 goes into orbit around Mars, as the first man-made object to orbit another planet.

NOV. 16—The first working session of the sixth round of the U.S.–Soviet SALT negotiations is held.

NOV. 19—Sen. Henry M. Jackson announces his candidacy for the 1972 Democratic presidential nomination.

NOV. 28–DEC. 2—The White House Conference on Aging is held.

NOV. 29—The East and Gulf Coasts dock strike ends after return-to-work orders are issued by federal courts under provisions of the Taft-Hartley Act.

DEC. 6–8—The first national Conference on Corrections is held in Williamsburg, Va., bringing together ex-convicts, judges, lawyers, congressmen, police chiefs and prison officials.

DEC. 7—The state of Ohio drops for lack of evidence all charges against defendants in the Kent State University riot trials. (Two of the first five defendants were cleared, two pleaded guilty and charges against one were dismissed.)

DEC. 8–10—The North Atlantic Treaty Organization (NATO) Ministerial Council holds a three-day winter session in Brussels.

DEC. 13–14—President Nixon and French President Georges Pompidou confer on the devaluation of the dollar.

DEC. 17—The first session of the 92nd Congress adjourns.

DEC. 18—President Nixon signs an Alaska native land settlement bill, granting a total of $962.5 million and 40 million acres of land and mineral rights to native Alaskans.

DEC. 18—The Rev. Jesse L. Jackson announces the formation of a new black political and economic development organization, PUSH (People United to Save Humanity).

DEC. 20–21—President Nixon meets with British Prime Minister Edward Heath in Bermuda to discuss world problems.

DEC. 28—President Nixon signs a bill requiring most persons receiving welfare benefits to register for jobs or job training.

DEC. 29—President Nixon signs a bill extending unemployment benefits.

DEC. 30–31—Columnist Jack Anderson publishes reports based on secret material pertaining to formulation of the Nixon Administration's policy on the Indian-Pakistani war.

1972

JAN. 4—Sen. Edmund S. Muskie announces his candidacy for the 1972 Democratic presidential nomination.

JAN. 6—The Paris peace talks resume after a month's suspension.

JAN. 12—U.S. Rep. James H. Scheuer is questioned by Soviet police on Jan. 12 and is expelled from the USSR Jan. 14, accused of "improper activities" during his visit.

JAN. 9—Mrs. Richard M. Nixon returns from an eight-day tour of West Africa during which she met heads of government and visited local institutions, representing the President.

JAN. 10—Sen. Hubert H. Humphrey announces his candidacy for the 1972 Democratic presidential nomination.

JAN. 11—The Supreme Court rules that a prosecutor only has to show that contested confessions of criminal defendants are voluntary "by a preponderance of the evidence" to have them admitted as evidence.

JAN. 12 & 13—Yekaterina A. Furtseva, the Soviet minister of culture, opens an exhibit of Soviet arts and crafts in Washington on Jan. 12. She has tea at the White House with Mrs. Richard Nixon on Jan. 13.

JAN. 13—Sen. Edward M. Kennedy announces that he will not be a candidate for the 1972 Democratic presidential nomination.

JAN. 16—Religious leaders from 46 Protestant, Catholic and Jewish denominations, meeting in Kansas City, Mo., to discuss Vietnam, ask the Administration to withdraw all American troops and refuse aid to the Indochinese governments.

JAN. 18—The 92nd Congress reconvenes to begin its second session.

JAN. 24—President Nixon submits to Congress a $246.3 billion budget for fiscal 1973 with an estimated deficit of $25.5 billion.

JAN. 25—Rep. Shirley Chisholm, the only black woman ever to serve in Congress, formally announces that she will seek the Democratic presidential nomination.

JAN. 30—Defense Secretary Melvin R. Laird announces that no men will be called up for military duty until April.

FEB. 2—A new political party, calling itself the Liberty Party, is announced in Denver. The key planks in the Party's platform are its opposition to big government and its dedication to civil and economic freedom.

FEB. 2—The Selective Service System assigns draft lottery numbers to nearly two million men born in 1953.

FEB. 4—The sixth round of the U.S.-Soviet Strategic Arms Limitations Talks (SALT) adjourns in Vienna.

FEB. 7—President Nixon signs into law the Federal Election Campaign Act, requiring that candidates report all campaign contributions that are received and spent, and limiting campaign spending for media advertising and from the personal funds of the candidate.

FEB. 9—President Nixon delivers his third annual State-of-the-World message to Congress.

FEB. 11—Rep. Wilbur D. Mills announces that he is a candidate for the Democratic presidential nomination.

FEB. 11–13—An anti-war rally in Versailles, France, denounces American policy in Indochina and pledges support for the Vietnamese Communists' plans for ending the war.

FEB. 15—Attorney General John N. Mitchell resigns (effective March 1) to head President Nixon's campaign for re-election.

FEB. 18—A seven-month statewide strike by plant craftsmen against the New York Telephone Co. ends.

FEB. 18—Delegates from 34 states attend the opening day of the 20th National Convention of the Communist Party, U.S.A., in New York.

FEB. 18—The California State Supreme Court votes to end the death penalty, thus sparing Sirhan Sirhan and Charles Manson, among others.

FEB. 21—President Nixon arrives in China.

FEB. 21—West Coast longshoremen end a 134-day strike, the nation's longest dock walkout.

FEB. 22 & 23—President Nixon meets with Chinese Premier Chou En-lai for policy discussions.

FEB. 27—President Nixon and Premier Chou En-lai release a joint communique showing the results of their talks.

FEB. 28—President Nixon returns from China.

FEB. 28—The Nationalist Chinese Foreign Ministry (of Taiwan) issues a statement denouncing the Sino-U.S. communique.

MARCH—A collection of documents on political surveillance stolen from the FBI's Media, Pa., office a year ago is printed in this month's issue of *Win*, an anti-war magazine.

MARCH 1 & 2—Paul E. Gilly is found guilty of first-degree murder for the 1969 murders of Joseph A. Yablonski, his wife and daughter, on March 1. Gilly is sentenced on March 2 to die in the electric chair.

MARCH 2—Pioneer 10, a U.S. space probe designed to go past Jupiter, is launched from Cape Kennedy, Fla.

MARCH 8—President Nixon signs an executive order to limit the practice of classifying government documents as secret and to speed the process of declassification.

MARCH 10–12—The first National Black Political Convention is held in Gary, Ind.

MARCH 11—The Socialist Party and the Democratic Socialist Federation merge at a New York convention, ending a 35-year split.

MARCH 23—The U.S. delegation to the Paris peace talks announces an indefinite suspension of the conference, until North Vietnamese and National Liberation Front representatives enter into "serious discussions" on concrete issues determined beforehand.

MARCH 27—Two so-called Soledad Brothers (Fleeta Drumgo and John Cluchette) are found innocent of the 1970 slaying of a guard at Soledad Prison.

MARCH 28—The U.S.-Soviet SALT negotiations begin a seventh round of discussions in Helsinki.

MARCH 31—President Nixon signs executive orders blocking for 60 days two impending railroad strikes by the AFL-CIO United Transportation Union (UTU) and the AFL-CIO Sheet Metal Workers' International Association.

APRIL 3—President Nixon signs into law a bill devaluing the dollar by raising the price of gold from $35 to $50 an ounce.

APRIL 15–20—Hundreds of anti-war demonstrators are arrested in incidents across the country as the escalation of the bombing in Indochina provokes a new wave of protests.

APRIL 20–23—Navy Capt. John Watts Young and Air Force Lt. Col. Charles Moss Duke, Jr., spend a record 71 hours 2 minutes on the moon during the first manned mission to the mountains of the moon, Apollo 16.

APRIL 20–24—Henry A. Kissinger, President Nixon's adviser on national security, secretly visits the Soviet Union to confer with Leonid I. Brezhnev, the Soviet Communist Party leader.

APRIL 27—Sen. Edmund S. Muskie announces his withdrawal from the presidential primaries.

APRIL 27—The Paris peace talks resume after a one-month break.

MAY 2—J. Edgar Hoover, the first and only director of the FBI, dies.

MAY 4—The U.S. and South Vietnam call

an indefinite halt to the Paris peace talks after the 149th session.

MAY 8—The International Monetary Fund (IMF) formally announces a reduction in the parity of the U.S. dollar to 0.818513 grams of fine gold from 0.888671 grams.

MAY 11—Interior Secretary Rogers C.B. Morton grants a permit for construction of the controversial trans-Alaska oil pipeline.

MAY 12—North Vietnam's chief negotiator, Le Duc Tho, rejects President Nixon's four-part peace plan.

MAY 15—Gov. George Wallace is shot and seriously wounded in an assassination attempt. The result is paralysis below the waist.

MAY 15—The Supreme Court rules that the Amish are entitled to exemption from state compulsory education laws.

MAY 18—Vice President Agnew returns from a six-day visit to Thailand, Japan and South Vietnam.

MAY 22—The Supreme Court rules that juries need not return unanimous verdicts to convict defendants in state criminal court cases.

MAY 26—President Nixon and Soviet General Secretary Brezhnev sign agreements limiting offensive and defensive strategic weapons.

JUNE 4—Angela Davis is acquitted on all charges of murder, kidnap and conspiracy in Santa Clara County Superior Court in San Jose, Calif.

JUNE 5–7—The National Governors Conference meets in Houston.

JUNE 9–12—Henry Kissinger makes a private visit to Tokyo, but also meets with Japanese government and political leaders to discuss Asian security and Japan's economic differences with the U.S.

JUNE 27–28—The Council of Ministers of the Southeast Asia Treaty Organization (SEATO) holds its annual meeting in Canberra, Australia.

JULY 3–7—The NAACP holds its 63rd annual convention in Detroit.

JULY 6–17—U.S. and Soviet space planners meet at the U.S. Manned Spacecraft Center in Houston, Tex.

JULY 7—The U.S. and the USSR sign an agreement detailing the first areas of study in science and technology in which scientists of both nations will cooperate.

JULY 8—President Nixon announces the sale of at least $750 million of American wheat, corn and other grains to the Soviet Union.

JULY 11—Sens. Hubert H. Humphrey and Edmund S. Muskie withdraw from the Democratic presidential nomination race.

JULY 12—Sen. George McGovern wins the Democratic presidential nomination.

JULY 13—The Paris peace talks resume after a 10-week suspension.

JULY 14—Jean M. Westwood is selected as the new chairman of the Democratic National Committee.

JULY 14—Sen. Eagleton is nominated as the Democratic candidate for vice president.

JULY 16—Thomas Eboli, a reputed East Coast Mafia leader, is shot and killed in New York City.

JULY 19—Henry Kissinger holds a private meeting with Le Duc Tho, North Vietnamese Politiburo member and chief adviser to his country's delegation at the peace talks.

AUG. 1—Sen. Thomas F. Eagleton withdraws as the Democratic vice presidential candidate.

AUG. 4—Arthur H. Bremer is found guilty of shooting Gov. George C. Wallace and sentenced to 63 years in prison.

AUG. 8—R. Sargent Shriver is nominated by the Democratic National Committee as the Party's candidate for vice president.

AUG. 22—President Nixon is renominated as the Republican presidential candidate at the Party's 30th National Convention in Miami Beach.

SEPT. 1—President Nixon and Japanese Premier Kakuei Tanaka had two days of summit talks in Hawaii.

SEPT. 15—A federal grand jury in the District of Columbia indicts seven persons, including two former White House aides, on charges of conspiring to break into the Democratic national headquarters in the capital.

SEPT. 21—President Nixon signs into law a bill to improve the benefits program for the widows, widowers and children of retired U.S. military personnel.

SEPT. 26–27—Henry Kissinger holds more private talks with North Vietnamese representatives in Paris.

SEPT. 27–31—The fourth annual Black Expo is held in Chicago under the auspices of Operation PUSH.

OCT. 3—President Nixon and Soviet Foreign Minister Andrei A. Gromyko conclude two days of talks in Washington by signing documents that put into effect the two arms accords reached in Moscow in May.

OCT. 13-Dec. 14—The United Auto Workers undertake a series of 17 "ministrikes" against 10 General Motors Corp. plants.

OCT. 18—The U.S. and the Soviet Union sign a three-year trade pact.

OCT. 19–20—Henry Kissinger and other U.S. officials hold meetings with South Vietnamese President Nguyen Van Thieu in Saigon.

OCT. 28—President Nixon signs a bill to expand consumer protection.

OCT. 30—President Nixon signs a bill to improve Social Security benefits.

NOV. 7—Richard M. Nixon is reelected President.

NOV. 20 & 21—Henry Kissinger and Le Duc Tho hold more private discussions to work out a final Indochina peace agreement.

DEC. 4—Henry Kissinger and Le Duc Tho resume private Indochina peace talks near Paris after a nine-day recess.

DEC. 4—U.S. and Soviet representatives sign an agreement authorizing each nation to construct a new embassy complex in the other's capital.

DEC. 8—Foreign ministers of the NATO states conclude their regular two-day winter session in Brussels.

DEC. 8—The *Pentagon Papers* trial in Los Angeles of Daniel Ellsberg and Anthony J. Russo is declared a mistrial.

DEC. 11-14—Navy Capt. Eugene Andrew Cernan and Dr. Harrison Hagan (Jack) Schmitt explore a mountainous site on the moon during the final Apollo flight, Apollo 17.

DEC. 13—Paris peace talks recess with no agreement.

DEC. 15—Arnold R. Miller is elected president of the United Mine Workers (UMW) union ousting W. A. Boyle.

DEC. 18—The Supreme Court strikes down a Social Security law which gave a smaller share of a dead father's survivors benefits to illegitimate children than that given to legitimate offspring.

DEC. 21—The U.S.-Soviet SALT negotiators adjourn in Geneva after establishing a four-man consultative commission to insure adherence to the arms pacts signed in May.

DEC. 26—Harry S. Truman dies.

1973

JAN. 2—Rafael Hernandez Colon is sworn in as Puerto Rico's fourth elected governor.

JAN. 3—The 93rd Congress convenes.

JAN. 8-12—Henry Kissinger and Le Duc Tho hold more secret Indochina peace talks.

JAN. 10—The Watergate trial opens.

JAN. 11—E. Howard Hunt, Jr., pleads guilty to all six charges against him relating to Watergate.

JAN. 20—President Nixon is inaugurated for his second term.

JAN. 22—Lyndon B. Johnson dies.

JAN. 26—An agreement is reached between the Chicago school board and the Chicago Teachers Union, ending a 12-day strike.

JAN. 30—G. Gordon Liddy and James W. McCord, Jr., are convicted by a jury in U.S. district court in the District of Columbia of attempting to spy on the Democrats during the 1972 presidential campaign.

FEB. 8—Congress enacts legislation imposing a status quo in the labor stalemate at the Penn Central Railroad, ending a one-day strike.

FEB. 9—The U.S. Circuit Court of Appeals forthe District of Columbia orders that a lower court prevent Interior Secretary Rogers C.B. Morton from issuing permits for construction of the trans-Alaska oil pipeline.

FEB. 9–11—The first convention of the National Women's Political Caucus (NWPC) is held in Houston.

FEB. 12—The dollar is devalued by 10%.

FEB. 15—The U.S. and Cuba sign a five-year agreement to curb the hijacking of aircraft and ships between the two countries.

FEB. 21—Laos and the Communist Pathet Lao rebels sign a cease-fire agreement aimed at ending the 20-year war in Laos.

FEB. 26—Two of the 15 counts against defendants Daniel Ellsberg and Anthony J. Russo, Jr., are dropped.

MARCH 29—H. Rap Brown and three codefendants are convicted in New York of robbery and assault with a deadly weapon.

MAY 1–2—President Nixon and West German Chancellor Willy Brandt confer in Washington.

MAY 2—Former Texas Gov. John B. Connally, Jr., joins the Republican Party.

MAY 8—The 70-day confrontation at Wounded Knee, S.D., between militant supporters of the American Indian Movement (AIM) and federal agents ends.

MAY 4—U.S.-Soviet SALT sessions resume in Geneva.

MAY 9—Henry Kissinger completes four days of intensive talks with Soviet leaders at the estate of Leonid I. Brezhnev.

MAY 11—Charges against Daniel Ellsberg and Anthony J. Russo, Jr., are dismissed in the *Pentagon Papers* trial.

MAY 14—NATO begins talks on the reduction of military forces in Central Europe.

MAY 14—The Supreme Court rules that female members of the armed services are en-titled to the same dependency benefits for their husbands as are servicemen for their dependent wives.

MAY 22—Henry Kissinger and Le Duc Tho end their talks on implementation of the Vietnam truce agreement.

MAY 29—President Nixon refuses to give oral or written testimony to the grand jury or the Senate select committee investigating the Watergate case.

JUNE 13—A new accord aimed at strengthening the Jan. 27 cease-fire agreement in South Vietnam is signed in Paris by the U.S., North Vietnam, South Vietnam and the National Liberation Front.

JUNE 20—The Finance Committee to Re-Elect the President is found guilty on three misdemeanor counts of concealing a $200,000 cash contribution.

JUNE 22—The three U.S. Skylab 1 astronauts return from a record 28 days living, working and performing scientific experiments in space.

JUNE 23—A Soviet consulate general is opened in San Francisco.

JUNE 25—Soviet Communist Party General Secretary Leonid Brezhnev ends his visit to the U.S.

JULY 6—A U.S. consulate general is officially opened in Leningrad.

JULY 9—Secretary of State William P. Rogers and Czechoslovak Foreign Minister Bohuslav Chnoupek sign a consular convention in Prague to help normalize trade and travel between the two countries.

AUG. 3—Oklahoma officials regain complete control of the state penitentiary at McAlester following an outbreak that left four inmates dead and most of the prison's physical plant in ruins.

AUG. 3—The Justice Department reopens

its investigation of the fatal shootings of four students at Kent State University.

AUG. 7—The Senate Select Committee on Presidential Campaign Activities recesses.

AUG. 14—Vice President Agnew makes his personal finance records available to the U.S. attorney's office in Baltimore.

AUG. 29—U.S. District Court Judge John J. Sirica orders President Nixon to turn over to him for private examination the tape recordings of presidential conversations involving the Watergate case.

SEPT. 22—Henry A. Kissinger is sworn in by U.S. Chief Justice Warren E. Burger as the 56th Secretary of State.

SEPT. 24—Production resumes at Chrysler Corp. plants with the ratification of a new three-year contract, ending a 10-day strike.

SEPT. 25—The crew of Skylab 2 returns to earth after 59½ days in space, the longest manned mission so far.

SEPT. 25—SALT negotiations resume in Geneva after a summer recess.

SEPT. 26—President Nixon signs a vocational rehabilitation bill for the handicapped.

OCT. 5—Oregon becomes the first state to remove criminal penalties for possession of less than one ounce of marijuana.

OCT. 10—Spiro T. Agnew resigns as vice president and pleads no contest to one charge of income tax evasion. By plea bargaining, he escapes imprisonment on the tax charge and prosecution on charges of bribery and conspiracy.

OCT. 17—President Nixon holds talks with the foreign ministers of Saudi Arabia, Morocco, Kuwait and Algeria at the White House to end fighting in the Middle East.

DEC. 6—Gerald R. Ford is sworn in as vice president after confirmation by both houses of Congress. President Nixon had chosen him for the post after Vice President Agnew resigned.

DEC. 6—President Nixon signs a bill providing a 10% cost-of-living boost to the monthly pension payments for veterans and their dependents.

DEC. 10–11—Henry Kissinger attends the annual NATO winter ministerial meeting in Brussels.

DEC. 11—Nelson A. Rockefeller resigns as governor of New York. He is succeeded by Lt. Gov. Malcolm Wilson.

DEC. 11—The Supreme Court rules that a person who has been properly arrested for a minor offense might subsequently be searched for evidence relating to a more serious but unrelated crime.

DEC. 19—President Nixon signs a bill ordering the release of approximately $1 billion in impounded funds for education and health programs.

DEC. 22—The 93rd Congress adjourns its first session.

DEC. 28—President Nixon signs a comprehensive manpower training and jobs bill, authorizing needed funding.

DEC. 29—President Nixon signs the Health Maintenance Organization (HMO) Act.

1974

JAN. 4—President Nixon refuses to comply with subpoenas for tapes and documents issued him by the Senate Watergate Committee.

JAN. 15—Experts examining the Watergate tape recordings surrendered by President Nixon report that an 18½-minute gap had been caused by at least five separate erasures, rather than a single accidental one as the White House had contended.

FEB. 4–5—Soviet Foreign Minister Andrei A. Gromyko confers with President Nixon and Secretary of State Henry Kissinger in Washington.

FEB. 5—Patricia Hearst is kidnapped by the Symbionese Liberation Army (SLA).

FEB. 8—Three astronauts complete a record 84-day space flight as the third and final Skylab crew.

FEB. 12—The trial of militant Indian leaders Russell Means and Dennis Banks in connection with the occupation of Wounded Knee, S.D., begins.

FEB. 13—Thirteen major oil-consuming nations endorse a U.S. proposal for international cooperation to fight the world's energy crisis.

FEB. 20—J. Reginald Murphy, editor of the *Atlanta Constitution,* is kidnapped by the American Revolutionary Army.

FEB. 23—J. Reginald Murphy is released by his captors, and an Atlanta couple is arrested in connection with his kidnapping.

FEB. 28—The U.S. and Egypt resume full-scale diplomatic relations, which were severed in 1967.

MARCH 6–7—The winter meeting of the National Governors Conference is held in Washington.

MARCH 9–APRIL 16—Hawaii's sugar industry is closed during a strike by field workers.

MARCH 24–28—Henry Kissinger talks with Leonid Brezhnev, Andrei Gromyko and other Soviet officials in Moscow.

APRIL 3—The White House announces that President Nixon will pay back taxes and interest totaling $465,000 to the Internal Revenue Service.

APRIL 7–29—Hawaii's pineapple industry is closed during a strike by cannery workers.

APRIL 8—President Nixon signs a bill increasing the minimum wage in stages to $2.30 an hour.

APRIL 16—Howard H. Callaway, secretary of the Army, halves the 20-year prison sentence being served by Lt. William L. Calley, Jr.

APRIL 28–MAY 2—Henry Kissinger confers with officials from the Soviet Union, Algiers, Egypt and Israel in an effort to promote an Israeli-Syrian troop disengagement.

MAY 2—Former Vice President Spiro T. Agnew is barred from the practice of law by the Maryland Court of Appeals.

MAY 3–9—Henry Kissinger holds talks with Middle East leaders in continuing efforts to end Israeli-Syrian fighting.

MAY 21—Jeb Stuart Magruder, former deputy director of the Committee to Re-Elect the President, is sentenced to a prison term of 10 months to four years after being found guilty on charges of plotting the Watergate break-in and cover-up.

MAY 31—Israeli and Syrian military officials sign a cease-fire agreement in Geneva brought about by Henry Kissinger.

JUNE 1–12—The AFL-CIO Amalgamated Clothing Workers of America strike manufacturers of men's and boys' clothing until a new contract is agreed upon.

JUNE 2–5—The National Governors Conference is held in Seattle.

JUNE 3—The Supreme Court rules that an employer's retention of night shift pay differentials favoring male employees over female employees violates the Equal Pay Act.

JUNE 7—Former Attorney General Richard Kleindienst receives a suspended sentence for his criminal offense in connection with Watergate.

JUNE 8—The U.S. and Saudi Arabia sign an agreement in Washington for economic and military cooperation.

JUNE 12–18—President Nixon visits Egypt, Saudi Arabia, Syria, Israel and Jordan.

JUNE 14—President Nixon and President Anwar Sadat sign an accord in Cairo by which the U.S. will provide Egypt with nuclear technology for peaceful purposes.

JUNE 18–19—NATO meets in Ottawa.

JUNE 26—Government leaders of NATO member nations sign a declaration on Atlantic relations.

JUNE 27–JULY 3—President Nixon and Soviet Communist Party General Secretary Leonid Brezhnev hold summit meetings in Moscow.

JUNE 28—A three-week strike by 4,400 nurses at 43 northern California hospitals ends after ratification of a two-year labor agreement increasing salaries.

JUNE 30—Alberta Williams King, mother of slain civil rights leader Dr. Martin Luther King, Jr., is shot and killed.

JULY 9—Former U.S. Chief Justice Earl Warren dies.

AUG. 2—John W. Dean, III, is sentenced to one to four years in prison for his role in the Watergate cover-up.

AUG. 5—President Nixon signs a bill authorizing $22.2 billion for military weapons research and procurement for fiscal 1975.

AUG. 9—Richard M. Nixon resigns as President. Gerald R. Ford is sworn in.

AUG. 19–23—The United Mine Workers hold a "memorial week" for men killed or maimed in mines, shutting down the nation's coal mines.

AUG. 22—President Ford signs an $11.1 billion housing and community development bill.

SEPT. 4—The U.S. and the German Democratic Republic (East Germany) establish formal diplomatic relations.

SEPT. 8—President Ford grants former President Nixon a full pardon.

SEPT. 16—Charges against militant Indian leaders Dennis Banks and Russell Means are dismissed by a federal district court judge.

SEPT. 16—President Ford signs a proclamation offering clemency to Vietnam war era draft evaders and military deserters.

SEPT. 18—The second round of the Strategic Arms Limitation Talks (SALT II) resumes in Geneva after a six-month recess.

SEPT. 23—Sen. Edward M. Kennedy announces that he will not be a presidential candidate in 1976.

SEPT. 25—The conviction of Lt. William L. Calley is overturned by U.S. District Court Judge J. Robert Elliott.

OCT. 21—President Ford and President Luis Echeverria Alvarez of Mexico meet at the border.

OCT. 31—A strike by the AFL-CIO International Association of Machinists (IAM), which had grounded flight operations of National Airlines since July 15, ends.

NOV. 5—SALT II sessions recess.

NOV. 5–7—Henry Kissinger visits five Middle East capitals to discuss Arab-Israeli conflict.

NOV. 8—Eight former Ohio National Guardsmen are acquitted of charges stemming from the shooting deaths of four students at Kent State University May 4, 1970.

NOV. 18–22—President Ford becomes the first U.S. chief executive to travel to Japan.

NOV. 18–24—Drivers and terminal workers for Greyhound Lines Inc. strike, temporarily closing down the nation's largest intercity bus system.

NOV. 19–20—President Ford and Premier Kakuei Tanaka of Japan confer in Japan.

NOV. 21—Sen. Walter F. Mondale withdraws from the race for the 1976 Democratic presidential nomination.

NOV. 23—Rep. Morris K. Udall announces his candidacy for the 1976 Democratic presidential nomination.

NOV. 23–24—President Ford and Leonid Brezhnev hold talks in Vladivostok to discuss the limitation of nuclear weapons.

DEC. 5—United Mine Workers President Arnold R. Miller signs a new national coal contract, ending a 24-day strike.

DEC. 13—Attorney General William B. Saxbe resigns.

DEC. 19—Nelson A. Rockefeller is sworn in as the 41st vice president of the United States.

DEC. 19—President Ford signs into law a bill giving the federal government custody of the official tapes and papers of former President Nixon.

DEC. 20—The 93rd Congress adjourns.

DEC. 22—Construction workers of the United Mine Workers end a five-week strike, which had blocked the return to work of United Mine Workers coal miners since Dec. 6.

1975

JAN. 3— President Ford signs the Trade Reform Act.

JAN. 4—President Ford signs a bill extending community action programs for the poor.

JAN. 11—Former Sen. Fred R. Harris declares his candidacy for the Democratic nomination for President in 1976.

JAN. 12—Former Sen. Eugene McCarthy announces that he will campaign as an independent for the presidency backed by the Committee for a Constitutional Presidency.

JAN. 14—The 94th Congress convenes.

JAN. 15—President Ford delivers a State of the Union message to Congress.

JAN. 22—President Ford signs two international agreements banning chemical and biological warfare.

JAN. 31—SALT II resumes in Geneva after a three-month recess.

FEB. 5—The United Automobile Workers union sponsors a job rally in Washington.

FEB. 6—Sen. Henry M. Jackson declares himself a candidate for the 1976 Democratic presidential nomination.

FEB. 7—The Labor Department reports the nation's unemployment rate to be 8.2%, the highest since 1941.

FEB. 10–15—Secretary of State Henry Kissinger visits the Middle East to determine the possibility of further negotiations.

FEB. 16–17—Henry Kissinger and Soviet Foreign Minister Andrei Gromyko meet in Geneva to discuss the Middle East conflict.

FEB. 17—Sen. Lloyd M. Bentsen enters the race for the 1976 Democratic presidential nomination.

FEB. 21—John N. Mitchell, H.R. Haldeman and John D. Ehrlichman are sentenced to two and a half to eight years in prison each for their roles in the Watergate cover-up.

FEB. 24—The U.S. ends its 10-year arms embargo against India and Pakistan.

MARCH 5—Postmaster General Benjamin Franklin Bailar issues an order prohibiting the Central Intelligence Agency from having access to the mail without authorization.

MARCH 14—Frederick C. LaRue is sentenced to six months in prison for his role in the Watergate cover-up.

MARCH 17—The Supreme Court rules that the federal government, not the individual states along the Atlantic Coast, have the exclusive right to exploit oil and reserves beneath the continental shelf seabed beyond the three-mile territorial limit.

MARCH 22—Henry Kissinger suspends his latest efforts to achieve a second Israeli-Egyptian troop disengagement agreement.

MARCH 29—The withdrawal of all American troops from South Vietnam and release of the last of the U.S. war prisoners held by the Communists are completed.

APRIL 5—John B. Hill and Charley Joe Pernasilice are convicted of criminal charges stemming from an uprising at Attica State Prison while they were inmates there in September 1971.

APRIL 12—The U.S. closes its embassy in Pnompenh, Cambodia, as Khmer Rouge rebel troops take over.

APRIL 14—The American airlift of homeless children to the U.S. from South Vietnam ends. A total of about 14,000 children had arrived.

APRIL 16—President Ford invokes the Railway Labor Act to avert a nationwide railroad strike by the AFL-CIO Brotherhood of Railway and Airline Clerks.

APRIL 26—About 60,000 participate in a Washington rally, sponsored by the AFL-CIO's Industrial Union Department.

MAY—Unemployment rates reach 9.2%, the highest since 1941.

MAY 11—About 50,000 people gather in the Sheep Head Meadow in Central Park in New York City to celebrate the end of war in Vietnam and Cambodia.

MAY 11—Members of the AFL-CIO International Association of Machinists ratify a three-year contract, ending a 13-week strike at McDonnell Douglas Corp.

MAY 12—The blue-ribbon presidential commission investigating charges of illegal domestic activities by the Central Intelligence Agency (CIA) completes its probe.

MAY 14—U.S. air, sea and ground forces battle Cambodian forces to free the 39 crewmen of the *Mayaguez,* an American merchant ship, after its seizure May 12.

MAY 19–20—Henry Kissinger and Soviet Foreign Minister Andrei Gromyko hold talks in Vienna.

MAY 22–23—NATO holds its semiannual talks in Brussels.

MAY 27—The Supreme Court rules that federal judges do not have the power to block a congressional subpoena issued in connection with an authorized committee investigation.

MAY 28–29—NATO holds its summit meeting in Brussels, attended by President Ford.

MAY 28–JUNE 3—President Ford makes his first trip as President to Europe.

MAY 29—Terry Sanford, president of Duke University, announces his candidacy for the 1976 Democratic presidential nomination.

JUNE 11–12—Israeli Prime Minister Yitzhak Rabin confers with President Ford and

Secretary of State Henry Kissinger in Washington on the possibility of reviving peace negotiations with Egypt.

JUNE 16—The Supreme Court rules that the setting of uniform minimum fee schedules by lawyers is price fixing and a violation of U.S. anti-trust laws.

JUNE 28—Dock workers end a strike for a higher guaranteed annual wage that had closed the port of Boston since May 31.

JUNE 29—The National Women's Political Caucus ends a four-day meeting in Boston.

JUNE 30—President Ford signs a bill extending the unemployment compensation program through 1975 for a maximum duration of 65 weeks of aid.

JULY 1—The U.S. Treasury Department sells 499,500 ounces of gold at auction at $165.05 an ounce.

JULY 1—Laid-off New York City policemen demonstrate because of the city's financial crisis.

JULY 1-3—New York City sanitation workers strike because of the city's financial crisis.

JULY 4—The NAACP ends its 66th annual convention in Washington.

JULY 8—President Ford officially announces his candidacy for the Republican nomination for President in 1976.

JULY 11—U.S. Judge John J. Sirica reduces the sentences of four Cuban-Americans involved in the original Watergate break-in.

JULY 12—U.S. Army Col. Ernest R. Morgan is released in Beirut after being held hostage for 13 days by a left-wing faction of the Palestine Liberation Army.

JULY 16—A major purchase of wheat by the Soviet Union from U.S. exporters is announced.

JULY 17—Spacecraft from the U.S. and the Soviet Union link together in space.

JULY 18—A nationwide rail strike is averted when a contract agreement is reached between the nation's railroads and the AFL-CIO Brotherhood of Railway Clerks.

JULY 21—The Postal Service and its employees agree on a new contract, averting a strike.

JULY 28—A strike by Teamsters that stopped publication of Pittsburgh's two newspapers for a month ends.

JULY 29—A $2 billion health bill is enacted into law by Congress over a presidential veto.

JULY 30—Cuban Premier Fidel Castro charges the Central Intelligence Agency with at least 24 assassination attempts on himself and other Cuban leaders.

JULY 30—Leaders of 35 nations meet in Helsinki, for the largest summit conference in European history, to sign the final document of the Conference on Security and Cooperation in Europe (CSCE).

JULY 30—The National Urban League ends its annual four-day conference in Atlanta.

JULY 31—Former Teamsters President James R. Hoffa is reported missing by his family.

AUG. 15—Joanne Little is acquitted of murder in connection with the 1974 killing of a jailer, Clarence Alligood.

AUG. 18—Soviet Communist Party General Secretary Leonid Brezhnev meets with a group of 18 U.S. congressmen at Yalta on the Crimean Coast.

AUG. 21—Henry Kissinger arrives in Israel to resume shuttle diplomacy toward attaining Middle East peace.

AUG. 27 & 28—A federal court jury in Cleveland exonerates defendants in connection with the 1970 shooting of students by National Guardsmen at Kent State University.

AUG. 30—The Libertarian Party nominates Roger L. MacBride as its candidate for President in the 1976 election.

AUG. 31—The People's Party nominates Margaret Wright as its candidate for President in the 1976 election.

SEPTEMBER—The reopening of many schools is held off by a rash of teachers' strikes, affecting at least 961,000 students.

SEPT. 1—Frank Aeidler is nominated by the Socialist Party U.S.A. as its candidate for President in the 1976 election.

SEPT. 1-5—The International Monetary Fund and the World Bank hold their 30th annual joint meeting in Washington.

SEPT. 4—Israel and Egypt sign a U.S.-mediated interim agreement.

SEPT. 5—Lynette Alice Fromme is arrested after pointing a pistol at President Ford in Sacramento.

SEPT. 9—New York state legislature passes a $2.3 billion aid bill in a last-ditch effort to save New York City from financial collapse.

SEPT. 10—The Senate overrides President Ford's veto and passes a $7.9 billion education appropriations bill.

SEPT. 16—The New York City teachers' strike ends.

SEPT. 18—Patricia Hearst is arrested by agents of the Federal Bureau of Investigation in San Francisco.

SEPT. 20—R. Sargent Shriver announces that he is a candidate for the Democratic nomination for President in 1976.

SEPT. 20—U.S. astronauts from the Apollo-Soyuz Test Project meet with the Soviet cosmonauts from the flight in Moscow for a two-week tour of the Soviet Union.

SEPT. 30—Teachers in Boston's public schools end an illegal six-day-old strike after reaching a new contract agreement.

OCT. 2-7—The AFL-CIO holds its convention in San Francisco.

OCT. 7—President Ford signs a $3.96 billion military construction authorization bill for fiscal 1976 and the July–September budget transition period.

OCT. 16—The Federal Reserve Board issues final regulations barring discriminatory credit practices against women.

NOV. 3—Vice President Nelson A. Rockefeller withdraws from consideration as President Ford's running mate in 1976.

NOV. 12—Gov. George C. Wallace announces his candidacy for the Democratic presidential nomination in 1976.

NOV. 14—President Ford signs legislation raising the temporary ceiling on the national debt to $595 billion.

NOV. 26—Lynette Alice Fromme is convicted by a federal jury in Sacramento of attempting to assassinate President Ford.

DEC. 1-5—President Ford visits the People's Republic of China, holding four days of talks with Chinese leaders including Chairman Mao Tse-tung and Deputy Premier Teng Hsiao-ping.

DEC. 8—A veto by the U.S. blocks a United Nations Security Council resolution condemning Israel for its air raid on Palestinian refugee camps in Lebanon Dec. 2.

DEC. 9—President Ford signs a bill authorizing the Treasury to loan New York City $2.3 billion annually until 1978.

DEC. 17—Lynette Alice Fromme is sentenced to life imprisonment for attempting to assassinate President Ford.

DEC. 17—The 30th session of the General Assembly of the United Nations ends.

DEC. 20—The program to resettle Vietnamese refugees in the U.S. ends.

DEC. 22—President Ford signs an energy bill providing for an immediate rollback in oil prices and an end to price controls in 40 months.

1976

JAN. 4—Flight attendants at National Airlines sign a new labor agreement and end a 127-day strike.

JAN. 9—Sen. Robert C. Byrd announces that he is a candidate for the Democratic presidential nomination in 1976.

JAN. 15—Sara Jane Moore is sentenced to life in prison for having attempted to assassinate President Ford.

JAN. 19—The second session of the 94th Congress convenes.

JAN. 21-23—Henry Kissinger attends meetings with Leonid Brezhnev, Andrei Gromyko and other Soviet officials in Moscow to discuss SALT.

JAN. 26—The U.S. vetoes a United Nations Security Council resolution on the Middle East.

JAN. 30—The Supreme Court upholds government financing of presidential campaigns and campaign contribution disclosure requirements.

FEB. 5—President Ford signs a railroad aid bill.

FEB. 8—Public school teachers in Newark ratify a new contract, ending a five-day strike.

FEB. 10—Sen. Lloyd Bentsen ends his quest for the Democratic presidential nomination.

FEB. 15—The American Federation of State, County and Municipal Employees (SCME) withdraws from the AFL-CIO's Public Employee Department.

FEB. 16-24—Henry Kissinger visits Venezuela, Peru, Brazil, Colombia, Costa Rica and Guatemala to confer with their presidents on trade and other issues.

FEB. 20—SEATO formally disbands.

FEB. 25—The Supreme Court rules that states can outlaw the hiring of illegal aliens when such hiring makes it more difficult for legal residents to obtain jobs.

MARCH 16—The U.S. State Department halts U.S.–Soviet talks because of actions taken by the Soviet Union in Angola.

MARCH 26—Henry Kissinger and Turkish Foreign Minister Ihsan Sabri Caglayangil sign an accord allowing the reopening of U.S. military installations in Turkey in return for military and economic assistance.

MARCH 30-31—King Hussein of Jordan conducts an official visit to Washington.

APRIL 1—A last-minute settlement averts a New York City subway and bus strike.

APRIL 3—The trucking industry and the Teamsters sign a new contract, ending a three-day strike.

APRIL 12—Patricia Hearst is sentenced to serve 25 years in prison for her conviction on bank robbery charges and 10 years for using a weapon while committing a felony.

APRIL 20—The Supreme Court rules that federal courts can order low-income public housing to be located in white suburbs.

MAY 20-21—NATO holds its semiannual meeting in Oslo, Norway.

MAY 24—Supersonic transport (SST) service to Dulles International Airport is inaugurated by the British-French Concorde jetliner.

JUNE 3—The AFL-CIO Amalgamated Clothing and Textile Workers Union is established when the Amalgamated Clothing Workers of America and the Textile Workers Union merge.

JUNE 14—Sen. Frank Church withdraws his candidacy for the Democratic presidential nomination.

JUNE 16—Francis E. Meloy, Jr., the U.S. ambassador to Lebanon, and Robert O. Waring, his economic counselor, are kidnapped and shot to death in Beirut.

JUNE 16—Frank E. Fitzsimmons is re-elected as president of the Teamsters union.

JUNE 21—Henry Kissinger addresses the annual ministerial meeting of the Organization for Economic Cooperation and Development (OECD) in Paris.

JUNE 23-24—Henry Kissinger and South African Prime Minister John Vorster hold talks in West Germany.

JUNE 24—The Supreme Court rules that federal minimum wage laws are not binding on state and local governments.

JULY 1—Kenneth A. Gibson is elected the first black president of the U.S. Conference of Mayors.

JULY 1—The Supreme Court rules that states cannot require a woman to obtain her husband's consent before having an abortion.

JULY 2—The Supreme Court rules that the death penalty does not violate the Constitution's ban on "cruel and unusual" punishment.

JULY 8—Former President Richard M. Nixon is ordered disbarred in New York state, effective Aug. 9.

JULY 14—President Ford signs a bill authorizing $32.5 billion in fiscal 1977 for arms procurement and research.

JULY 14—Jimmy Carter is declared the Democratic presidential nominee. Sen. Walter F. Mondale, his choice of a running mate, is approved.

JULY 17—West German Chancellor Helmut Schmidt concludes a three-day visit to Washington, during which he held talks with President Ford.

JULY 20—The unmanned U.S. spacecraft Viking 1 lands on Mars, beginning its mission to add to man's knowledge of the planet.

JULY 31—An 11–day strike by California cannery workers ends with a new contract.

AUG. 6—Russell C. Means is acquitted of murder in the slaying of Martin Montileaux.

AUG. 9—William and Emily Harris are convicted of kidnapping in the case of Patricia Hearst.

AUG. 14—President Ford signs a bill raising the price of domestic oil.

AUG. 16—A wildcat miners' strike in the East that began July 19 in West Virginia ends.

AUG. 19—Gerald Ford is nominated as the Republican Party's presidential candidate. Sen. Robert J. Dole, his choice as a running mate, is approved.

AUG. 28—Members of the United Rubber Workers union end a 130-day strike against Goodyear Tire and Rubber Co.

AUG. 28 & 31 & SEPT. 1—U.S. and North Korean representatives of the Mixed Armistice Commission meet at Panmunjom to discuss easing tension in the Demilitarized Zone.

AUG. 31—William and Emily Harris are sentenced to serve 11 years to life in prison for kidnapping and robbery.

SEPT. 3—Viking 2 lands on Mars.

SEPT. 4-6—Henry Kissinger meets with South African Prime Minister John Vorster in Zurich, Switzerland, for a second round of talks.

SEPT. 6—The U.S.-led United Nations Command and North Korea agree to partition the Joint Security Area in the Demilitarized Zone.

SEPT. 7 & SEPT. 8—The AFL-CIO United Rubber Workers sign new contracts with Uniroyal (Sept. 7) and with B.F. Goodrich Co. (Sept. 8), ending a strike that began April 21.

SEPT. 14—Henry Kissinger arrives in Tanzania to begin a series of talks with African leaders.

SEPT. 20—NATO holds a training exercise to simulate rescue operations against an enemy attack at Namsos, Norway.

SEPT. 21—The U.S.-Soviet SALT II sessions resume in Geneva after summer recess.

SEPT. 21—SALT II adjourns temporarily.

SEPT. 23—President Ford and Jimmy Carter hold the first of three debates in the presidential campaign on national television.

SEPT. 23-OCT. 2—The United Mine Workers of America hold their convention in Cincinnati.

SEPT. 24—Rhodesian Prime Minister Ian Smith accepts a proposal presented by Henry Kissinger for transfer of power to Rhodesia's black majority.

OCT. 4-8—The International Monetary Fund and the World Bank convene in Manila for their 31st annual meeting.

OCT. 6—President Ford and Jimmy Carter have their second nationally televised debate.

OCT. 15—Sens Robert J. Dole and Walter F. Mondale engage in a nationally televised debate, the first campaign debate ever between vice-presidential nominees.

OCT. 22—President Ford and Jimmy Carter hold their third and last televised debate.

NOV. 2—Jimmy Carter is elected President.

NOV. 15—The U.S. vetoes the admission of Vietnam into the United Nations.

DEC. 6-10—NATO holds year-end meetings in Brussels.

DEC. 13—A strike by the International Brotherhood of Teamsters against United Parcel Service of America Inc., which began Sept. 16, ends.

CONGRESS
1969–1976
SENATE

Alabama

James B. Allen (D) 1969-78
John Sparkman (D) 1946-

Alaska

Mike Gravel (D) 1969-
Ted Stevens (R) 1968-

Arizona

Paul J. Fannin (R) 1965-77
Barry Goldwater (R) 1953-65; 1969-

Arkansas

Dale Bumpers (D) 1975-
J. William Fulbright (D) 1945-75
John L. McClellan (D) 1943-78

California

Alan Cranston (D) 1969-
John V. Tunney (D) 1971-77
George Murphy (R) 1964-71

Colorado

Gary Hart (D) 1975-
Floyd K. Haskell (D) 1973-
Gordon Allott (R) 1955-73
Peter H. Dominick (R) 1963-75

Connecticut

Thomas J. Dodd (D) 1959-71
Abraham Ribicoff (D) 1963-
Lowell P. Weicker, Jr. (R) 1971-

Delaware

Joseph R. Biden, Jr. (D) 1973-
J. Caleb Boggs (R) 1961-73

William V. Roth, Jr. (R) 1971-
John J. Williams (R) 1947-70

Florida

Lawton Chiles (D) 1971-
Spessard L. Holland (D) 1946-71
Richard Stone (D) 1975-
Edward J. Gurney (R) 1969-74

Georgia

David H. Gambrell (D) 1971-73
Sam Nunn (D) 1973-
Richard B. Russell (D) 1933-71
Herman E. Talmadge (D) 1957-

Hawaii

Daniel K. Inouye (D) 1963-
Hiram L. Fong (R) 1959-77

Idaho

Frank Church (D) 1957-
Len B. Jordan (R) 1962-73
James A. McClure (R) 1973-

Illinois

Adlai E. Stevenson, III (D) 1970-
Everett M. Dirksen (R) 1951-69
Charles H. Percy (R) 1967-
Ralph T. Smith (R) 1969-70

Indiana

Birch Bayh (D) 1963-
Vance Hartke (D) 1959-77

Iowa

Dick Clark (D) 1973-
John C. Culver (D) 1975-

Harold E. Hughes (D) 1969-75
Jack Miller (R) 1961-73

Kansas

Robert J. Dole (R) 1969-
James B. Pearson (R) 1962-

Kentucky

Wendell H. Ford (D) 1974-
Walter Huddleston (D) 1973-
Marlow W. Cook (R) 1968-74
John Sherman Cooper (R) 1946-49; 1952-55;
   1956-73

Louisiana

Allen J. Ellender (D) 1937-72
J. Bennett Johnston, Jr. (D) 1972-
Russell B. Long (D) 1948-

Maine

William D. Hathaway (D) 1973-
Edmund S. Muskie (D) 1959-
Margaret Chase Smith (R) 1949-73

Maryland

Joseph D. Tydings (D) 1965-71
James Glenn Beall, Jr. (R) 1971-77
Charles McC. Mathias, Jr. (R) 1969-

Massachusetts

Edward M. Kennedy (D) 1962-
Edward W. Brooke (R) 1967-

Michigan

Philip A. Hart (D) 1959-76
Robert P. Griffin (R) 1966-

Minnesota

Hubert H. Humphrey (D) 1949-64; 1971-78
Eugene J. McCarthy (D) 1959-71
Walter F. Mondale (D) 1964-77

Mississippi

James O. Eastland (D) 1941; 1943-
John Stennis (D) 1947-

Missouri

Thomas F. Eagleton (D) 1968-
Stuart Symington (D) 1953-77

Montana

Michael J. Mansfield (D) 1953-77
Lee Metcalf (D) 1961-

Nebraska

Carl T. Curtis (R) 1955-
Roman L. Hruska (R) 1954-77

Nevada

Alan Bible (D) 1954-74
Howard W. Cannon (D) 1959-
Paul Laxalt (R) 1975-

New Hampshire

John A. Durkin (D) 1975-
Thomas J. McIntyre (D) 1962-
Norris Cotton (R) 1954-74; 1975

New Jersey

Harrison A. Williams, Jr. (D) 1959-
Clifford P. Case (R) 1955-

New Mexico

Clinton P. Anderson (D) 1949-73
Joseph M. Montoya (D) 1964-77
Pete V. Domenici (R) 1973-

New York

James L. Buckley (R) 1971-77
Charles E. Goodell (R) 1968-71
Jacob K. Javits (R) 1957-

North Carolina

Sam J. Ervin, Jr. (D) 1954-74
B. Everett Jordan (D) 1958-73
Robert Morgan (D) 1975-
Jesse A. Helms (R) 1973-

North Dakota

Quentin N. Burdick (D) 1960-
Milton R. Young (R) 1945-

Ohio

John Glenn (D) 1974-
Howard M. Metzenbaum (D) 1974-
Stephen M. Young (D) 1959-71
William B. Saxbe (R) 1969-74
Robert Taft, Jr. (R) 1971-77

Oklahoma

Fred R. Harris (D) 1964-73
Dewey F. Bartlett (R) 1973-
Henry Bellmon (R) 1969-

Oregon

Mark O. Hatfield (R) 1967-
Robert W. Packwood (R) 1969-

Pennsylvania

Richard S. Schweiker (R) 1969-
Hugh Scott (R) 1959-77

Rhode Island

John O. Pastore (D) 1950-76
Claiborne Pell (D) 1961-
John Chafee (R) 1976-

South Carolina

Ernest F. Hollings (D) 1966-
Strom Thurmond (D) 1954-56; 1956-64;
(R) 1964-

South Dakota

James Abourezk (D) 1973-

George McGovern (D) 1963-
Karl E. Mundt (R) 1948-73

Tennessee

Albert Gore (D) 1953-71
Howard H. Baker, Jr. (R) 1967-
William E. Brock, III (R) 1971-77

Texas

Lloyd M. Bentsen, Jr. (D) 1971-
Ralph Yarborough (D) 1957-71
John G. Tower (R) 1961-

Utah

Frank E. Moss (D) 1959-77
Wallace F. Bennett (R) 1951-74
Edwin Jacob (Jake) Garn (R) 1974-

Vermont

Patrick J. Leahy (D) 1975-
George D. Aiken (R) 1941-75
Winston L. Prouty (R) 1959-71
Robert T. Stafford (R) 1971-

Virginia

Harry F. Byrd, Jr. (D) 1965-71; (I) 1971-
William B. Spong, Jr. (D) 1966-73
William Lloyd Scott (R) 1973-

Washington

Henry M. Jackson (D) 1953-
Warren G. Magnuson (D) 1944-

West Virginia

Robert C. Byrd (D) 1959-
Jennings Randolph (D) 1958-

Wisconsin

Gaylord Nelson (D) 1963-
William Proxmire (D) 1957-

Wyoming

Gale W. McGee (D) 1959-77
Clifford P. Hansen (R) 1967-

HOUSE OF REPRESENTATIVES

Alabama

George W. Andrews (D) 1944-71
Tom Bevill (D) 1967-
Walter Flowers (D) 1969-
Robert E. Jones, Jr. (D) 1947
William Nichols (D) 1967-
John H. Buchanan (R) 1965-
William L. Dickinson (R) 1965-
W. Jack Edwards (R) 1965-

Alaska

Nick Begich (D) 1971-1972
Howard W. Pollock (R) 1967-71
Donald Young (R) 1973-

Arizona

Morris K. Udall (D) 1961-
John B. Conlan (R) 1973-77
John J. Rhodes (R) 1953-
Sam Steiger (R) 1967-77

Arkansas

William Alexander (D) 1969-
Wilbur D. Mills (D) 1939-77
David Pryor (D) 1966-73
Ray Thornton (D) 1973-
John P. Hammerschmidt (R) 1967-

California

Glenn M. Anderson (D) 1969-
George E. Brown, Jr. (D) 1963-
Yvonne Braithwaite Burke (D) 1973-
John L. Burton (D) 1974-
Phillip Burton (D) 1964-
Jeffery Cohelan (D) 1959-71
James C. Corman (D) 1961-
George E. Danielson (D) 1971-
Don Edwards (D) 1963-
Richard T. Hanna (D) 1963-75
Mark W. Hannaford (D) 1975-
Augustus F. Hawkins (D) 1963-
Chet Holifield (D) 1943-75
Harold T. Johnson (D) 1959-
John Krebs (D) 1975-
Robert L. Leggett (D) 1963-
James Lloyd (D) 1975-

John J. McFall (D) 1957-
George P. Miller (D) 1945-73
Norman Y. Mineta (D) 1975-
John E. Moss (D) 1953-
Jerry M. Patterson (D) 1975-
Thomas M. Rees (D) 1965-77
Edward Roybal (D) 1963-
Leo J. Ryan (D) 1973-
B. F. Sisk (D) 1955-
Fortney H. (Pete) Stark (D) 1973-
John V. Tunney (D) 1965-71
Lionel Van Deerlin (D) 1963-
Jerome R. Waldie (D) 1966-75
Henry A. Waxman (D) 1975-
Charles H. Wilson (D) 1963-
Alphonzo Bell (R) 1961-77
Clair W. Burgener (R) 1973-
Donald H. Clausen (R) 1963-
Delwin Clawson (R) 1963-
Ronald V. Dellums (R) 1971-
Barry M. Goldwater, Jr. (R) 1953-65; 1969-
Charles S. Gubser (R) 1953-75
Andrew J. Hinshaw (R) 1973-77
Craig Hosmer (R) 1953-75
William M. Ketchum (R) 1973-
Robert J. Lagomarsino (R) 1974-
Glenn P. Lipscomb (R) 1953-70
William S. Mailliard (R) 1953-74
R. B. (Bob) Mathias (R) 1967-75
Paul N. McCloskey, Jr. (R) 1967-
Carlos J. Moorhead (R) 1973-
Jerry L. Pettis (R) 1967-75
Shirley N. Pettis (R) 1975-
Edwin Reinecke (R) 1965-69
John H. Rousselot (R) 1961-63; 1970-
John G. Schmitz (R) 1970-73
H. Allen Smith (R) 1957-73
Burt L. Talcott (R) 1963-77
Charles M. Teague (R) 1953-70
James B. Utt (R) 1953-70
Victor V. Veysey (R) 1971-75
Charles E. Wiggins (R) 1967-
Robert Wilson (R) 1953-

Colorado

Wayne N. Aspinall (D) 1949-73
Frank E. Evans (D) 1965-
Byron G. Rogers (D) 1951-71
Patricia Schroeder (D) 1973-
Timothy E. Wirth (D) 1975-
William L. Armstrong (R) 1973-
Donald G. Brotzman (R) 1963-65; 1967-75

James P. (Jim) Johnson (R) 1943-
James D. McKevitt (R) 1971-73

Connecticut

William R. Cotter (D) 1971-
Emilio Q. Daddario (D) 1959-71
Christopher J. Dodd (D) 1975-
Robert N. Giaimo (D) 1959-
Ella T. Grasso (D) 1971-75
Anthony Moffett (D) 1975-
John S. Monagan (D) 1959-73
William L. Saint Onge (D) 1963-70
Stewart B. McKinney (R) 1971-
Thomas J. Meskill (R) 1967-71
Ronald A. Sarasin (R) 1973-
Robert H. Steele (R) 1970-75
Lowell P. Weicker, Jr. (R) 1969-71

Delaware

Pierre S. du Pont, IV (R) 1971-77
William V. Roth, Jr. (R) 1967-70

Florida

Charles E. Bennett (D) 1949-
William Chappell, Jr. (D) 1969-
Dante B. Fascell (D) 1955-
Donald Fuqua (D) 1963-
Sam M. Gibbons (D) 1963-
William D. (Bill) Gunter, Jr. (D) 1973-75
James A. Haley (D) 1953-77
William Lehman (D) 1973-
Claude D. Pepper (D) 1963-
Paul G. Rogers (D) 1955-
Robert L. F. Sikes (D) 1941-44; 1945-
Louis Arthur (Skip) Bafalis (R) 1973-
J. Herbert Burke (R) 1967-
William C. Cramer (R) 1955-71
Louis Frey, Jr. (R) 1969-
Richard Kelly (R) 1975-
C. W. Bill Young (R) 1971-

Georgia

Jack Brinkley (D) 1967-
John W. Davis (D) 1961-75
John J. Flynt, Jr. (D) 1954-
Ronald Bryan "Bo" Ginn (D) 1973-
G. Elliot Hagan (D) 1961-73
Phillip M. Landrum (D) 1953-
Elliott H. Levitas (D) 1975-77
Dawson Mathis (D) 1971-

Lawrence McDonald (D) 1975-
Maston O'Neal (D) 1965-71
Robert G. Stephens, Jr. (D) 1961-77
W. S. (Bill) Stuckey, Jr. (D) 1967-77
Andrew Young (D) 1973-77
Benjamin B. Blackburn (R) 1967-75
S. Fletcher Thompson (R) 1967-73

Hawaii

Spark M. Matsunaga (D) 1963-
Patsy Takemoto Mink (D) 1965-

Idaho

Orval H. Hansen (R) 1969-
James A. McClure (R) 1967-73
Steven D. Symms (R) 1973-

Illinois

Frank Annunzio (D) 1965-
Cardiss Collins (D) 1973-
George Washington Collins (D) 1970-72
William L. Dawson (D) 1943-70
John Fary (D) 1975-
Kenneth J. Gray (D) 1955-75
Timothy L. Hall (D) 1975-77
Ralph H. Metcalfe (D) 1971-
Abner J. Mikva (D) 1969-73
Morgan M. Murphy (D) 1959-71
Melvin Price (D) 1945-
Roman C. Pucinski (D) 1959-73
Daniel J. Ronan (D) 1965-69
Daniel D. Rostenkowski (D) 1959-
Martin A. Russo (D) 1975-
George E. Shipley (D) 1959-
Paul Simon (D) 1975-
Sidney R. Yates (D) 1949-63; 1965-
John B. Anderson (R) 1961-
Leslie C. Arends (R) 1935-75
Harold R. Collier (R) 1957-75
Philip M. Crane (R) 1969-
Edward J. Derwinski (R) 1959-
John N. Erlenborn (R) 1965-
Paul Findley (R) 1961-
Robert P. Hanrahan (R) 1973-75
Henry J. Hyde (R) 1975-
John C. Klucgynski (R) 1951-75
Edward R. Madigan (R) 1973-
Robert McClory (R) 1963-
Robert H. Michel (R) 1957-
George M. O'Brien (R) 1973-
Tom Railsback (R) 1967-
Charlotte T. Reid (R) 1963-71

Donald Rumsfeld (R) 1963-69
William L. Springer (R) 1951-73
Samuel H. Young (R) 1973-75

Indiana

John Brademas (D) 1959-
Floyd J. Fithian (D) 1975-
Lee H. Hamilton (D) 1965-
Philip H. Hayes (D) 1975-77
Andrew Jacobs, Jr. (D) 1965-73
Ray J. Madden (D) 1943-77
J. Edward Roush (D) 1959-69; 1971-77
Philip R. Sharp (D) 1975-
E. Ross Adair (R) 1951-71
William G. Bray (R) 1951-75
David W. Dennis (R) 1969-75
Elwood H. Hillis (R) 1971-
William H. Hudnut, III (R) 1973-75
Earl F. Landgrebe (R) 1969-75
John T. Myers (R) 1967-
Richard L. Roudebush (R) 1961-71
Roger H. Zion (R) 1967-75

Iowa

Berkley Bedall (D) 1975-
Michael T. Blouin (D) 1975-
John C. Culver (D) 1965-75
Tom Harkin (D) 1975-
Edward Mezvinsky (D) 1973-77
Neal Smith (D) 1959-
Charles E. Grassley (R) 1975-
Harold R. Gross (R) 1949-75
John Kyl (R) 1959-65; 1967-73
Wiley Mayne (R) 1967-75
William J. Sherle (R) 1967-75
Fred Schwengel (R) 1955-65; 1967-73

Kansas

Martha Elizabeth Keys (D) 1975-
William R. Roy (D) 1971-75
Chester L. Mize (R) 1965-71
Keith G. Sebelius (R) 1969-
Garner E. Shriver (R) 1961-77
Joe Skubitz (R) 1963-
Larry Winn, Jr. (R) 1967-

Kentucky

John Breckinridge (D) 1973-
Carroll Hubbard, Jr. (D) 1975-
Romano L. Mazzoli (D) 1971-

William H. Natcher (D) 1953-
Carl D. Perkins (D) 1949-
Frank A. Stubblefield (D) 1959-1975
John C. Watts (D) 1951-71
Tim Lee Carter (R) 1965-
William O. Cowger (R) 1967-71
Marion G. Snyder (R) 1963-65; 1967-

Louisiana

Corinne C. Boggs (D) 1973-
Hale Boggs (D) 1941-43; 1947-72
John B. Breaux (D) 1972-
Patrick T. Caffery (D) 1969-73
Edwin W. Edwards (D) 1965-72
F. Edward Hebert (D) 1941-77
Gillis W. Long (D) 1973-
Speedy O. Long (D) 1965-73
Otto E. Passman (D) 1947-76
John R. Rarick (D) 1967-75
Joe D. Waggonner, Jr. (D) 1961
W. Henson Moore (R) 1975-
David C. Treen (R) 1973-

Maine

William D. Hathaway (D) 1965-73
Peter N. Kyros (D) 1967-75
William S. Cohen (R) 1973-
David F. Emery (R) 1975-

Maryland

Goodloe E. Byron (D) 1971-
George H. Fallon (D) 1945-71
Samuel N. Friedel (D) 1953-71
Edward A. Garmatz (D) 1947-73
Clarence D. Long (D) 1963-
Parren J. Mitchell (D) 1971-
Paul S. Sarbanes (D) 1971-
Gladys Noon Spellman (D) 1975-
Robert E. Bauman (R) 1973-
J. Glenn Beall, Jr. (R) 1969-71
Lawrence J. Hogan (R) 1969-75
Marjorie S. Holt (R) 1973-
William O. Mills (R) 1971-73
Rogers C.B. Morton (R) 1963-71

Massachusetts

Edward P. Boland (D) 1953-
James A. Burke (D) 1959-
Harold D. Donohue (D) 1947-75
Robert F. Drinan (D) 1971-

Joseph D. Early (D) 1975-
Michael J. Harrington (D) 1969-
Louise Day Hicks (D) 1971-73
Torbert H. MacDonald (D) 1955-76
John W. McCormack (D) 1928-71
John J. Moakley (D) 1973-
Thomas P. O'Neill, Jr. (D) 1953-
Philip J. Philbin (D) 1943-71
Gerry E. Studds (D) 1973-
Paul E. Tsongas (D) 1975-
William H. Bates (R) 1950-69
Silvio O. Conte (R) 1959-
Paul W. Cronin (R) 1973-75
Margaret M. Heckler (R) 1967-
Hastings Keith (R) 1959-73
F. Bradford Morse (R) 1961-72

Michigan

James J. Blanchard (D) 1975-
William M. Brodhead (D) 1975-
Milton Robert Carr (D) 1975-
John R. Conyers, Jr. (D) 1965-
Charles C. Diggs, Jr. (D) 1955-
William D. Ford (D) 1965-
Martha W. Griffiths (D) 1955-75
Lucien N. Nedzi (D) 1961-
James G. O'Hara (D) 1959-
Richard F. Vander Veen (D) 1974-77
Robert Traxler (D) 1974-
William S. Broomfield (R) 1957-
Garry Brown (R) 1967-
Elford A. Cederberg (R) 1953-
Charles E. Chamberlain (R) 1957-75
Marvin L. Esch (R) 1967-77
Gerald R. Ford, Jr. (R) 1949-73
James Harvey (R) 1961-74
Robert J. Huber (R) 1973-75
Jack H. McDonald (R) 1967-73
Donald W. Riegle, Jr. (R) 1967-73; (D) 1973-
Philip E. Ruppe (R) 1967-
Guy Vander Jagt (R) 1966-

Minnesota

Robert Bergland (D) 1971-77
John A. Blatnik (D) 1947-75
Donald M. Fraser (D) 1963-
Joseph E. Karth (D) 1959-77
Richard Nolan (D) 1975-
James L. Oberstar (D) 1975-
William Frenzel (R) 1971-
Tom Hagedorn (R) 1975-
Odin Langen (R) 1959-71
Clark MacGregor (R) 1961-71
Ancher Nelson (R) 1959-75

Albert H. Quie (R) 1958-
John M. Zwach (R) 1967-75

Mississippi

Thomas G. Abernathy (D) 1942-73
David R. Bowen (D) 1973-
William M. Colmer (D) 1933-73
Charles H. Griffen (D) 1968-73
G.V. (Sonny) Montgomery (D) 1967-
Jamie L. Whitten (D) 1941-
William Thad Cochran (R) 1973-
Chester Trent Lott (R) 1973-

Missouri

Richard Walker Bolling (D) 1949-
William D. Burlison (D) 1969-
William L. Clay (D) 1969-
Durward G. Hall (D) 1961-73
W. R. Hull, Jr. (D) 1955-73
William L. Hungate (D) 1964-77
Richard H. Ichord (D) 1961-
Jerry Litton (D) 1973-76
William J. Randall (D) 1959-77
Leonor K. Sullivan (D) 1953-77
James W. Symington (D) 1969-77
Gene Taylor (R) 1973-

Montana

Max S. Baucus (D) 1975-
John Melcher (D) 1969-77
Arnold Olsen (D) 1961-71
James F. Battin (R) 1961-69
Richard G. Shoup (R) 1971-75

Nebraska

Glenn Cunningham (R) 1957-71
Robert V. Denney (R) 1967-71
David T. Martin (R) 1961-75
John Y. McCollister (R) 1971-77
Virginia Dodd Smith (R) 1975-
Charles Thone (R) 1971-

Nevada

Walter S. Baring (D) 1949-53; 1957-73
James Santini (D) 1975-
David Towell (R) 1973-75

New Hampshire

James C. Cleveland (R) 1963-
Norman E. D'Amours (D) 1975-
Louis C. Wyman (R) 1963-65; 1967-75

New Jersey

Dominick V. Daniels (D) 1959-77
James J. Florio (D) 1975-
Cornelius E. Gallagher (D) 1959-73
Henry Helstoski (D) 1965-77
James J. Howard (D) 1965-
William J. Hughes (D) 1975-
Charles S. Joelson (D) 1961-69
Gene Andrew Maguire (D) 1975-
Helen S. Meyner (D) 1975-
Joseph G. Minish (D) 1963-
Edward J. Patten (D) 1963-
Peter W. Rodino, Jr. (D) 1949-
Robert A. Roe (D) 1969-
Frank Thompson, Jr. (D) 1955-
William T. Cahill (R) 1959-70
Florence P. Dwyer (R) 1957-73
Millicent Fenwick (R) 1975-
Edwin B. Forsythe (R) 1970-
Peter H. B. Frelingheuysen (R) 1953-75
John E. Hunt (R) 1967-75
Joseph Maraziti (R) 1973-75
Matthew J. Rinaldo (R) 1973-
Charles W. Sandman, Jr. (R) 1967-75
William B. Widnall (R) 1950-75

New Mexico

Harold L. Runnels (D) 1971-
Ed Foreman (R) 1963-65 (Texas); 1969-71
Manuel Lujan (R) 1969-

New York

Bella Abzug (D) 1971-77
Joseph P. Addabo (D) 1961-
Jerome Ambro, Jr. (D) 1975-
Herman Badillo (D) 1971-78
Mario Biaggi (D) 1969-
Jonathan B. Bingham (D) 1965-
Frank J. Brasco (D) 1967-75
Daniel E. Button (D) 1967-71
Hugh L. Carey (D) 1961-75
Emanuel Celler (D) 1923-73
Shirley Chisholm (D) 1969-
James J. Delaney (D) 1945-47; 1949-
John G. Dow (D) 1965-69; 1971-73
Thomas J. Downey (D) 1975-

Thaddeus J. Dulski (D) 1959-75
Leonard Farbstein (D) 1957-71
Jacob H. Gilbert (D) 1960-71
James M. Hanley (D) 1965-
Elizabeth Holtzman (D) 1973-
Edward I. Koch (D) 1969-78
John J. LaFalce (D) 1975-
Stanley Lundine (D) 1976-
Richard D. McCarthy (D) 1965-71
Matthew F. McHugh (D) 1975-
John M. Murphy (D) 1963-
Henry J. Nowak (D) 1975-
Richard L. Ottinger (D) 1965-71; 1975-
Edward W. Pattison (D) 1975-
Otis J. Pike (D) 1961-
Bertram L. Podell (D) 1968-75
Adam Clayton Powell (D) 1945-67; 1969-71
Charles B. Rangel (D) 1971-
Frederick W. Richmond (D) 1975-
John J. Rooney (D) 1944-74
Benjamin S. Rosenthal (D) 1962-
William Fitts Ryan (D) 1961-72
James H. Scheuer (D) 1965-73
Stephen J. Solarz (D) 1975-
Samuel S. Stratton (D) 1959-
Lester L. Wolff (D) 1965-
Leo C. Zeferetti (D) 1975-
Barber B. Conable, Jr. (R) 1965-
Hamilton Fish, Jr. (R) 1969-
Benjamin A. Gilman (R) 1973-
James R. Grover, Jr. (R) 1963-75
Seymour Halpern (R) 1959-73
James F. Hastings (R) 1969-76
Frank J. Horton (R) 1963-
Jack F. Kemp (R) 1971-
Carleton J. King (R) 1961-74
Norman F. Lent (R) 1971-
Robert C. McEwen (R) 1965-
Martin B. McKneally (R) 1969-71
Donald J. Mitchell (R) 1973-
Peter A. Peyser (R) 1971-
Alexander Pirnie (R) 1971-
Ogden R. Reid (R) 1963-72; (D) 1972-75
Howard W. Robison (R) 1958-75
Angelo D. Roncallo (R) 1973-75
Henry P. Smith, III (R) 1965-75
John H. Terry (R) 1971-73
William F. Walsh (R) 1973-
John W. Wydler (R) 1963-

North Carolina

Ike F. Andrews (D) 1973-
L. H. Fountain (D) 1953-
Nick Galifianakis (D) 1967-73
Willie G. Hefner (D) 1975-
David N. Henderson (D) 1961-77

Walter B. Jones (D) 1966-
Alton Lennon (D) 1957-73
Stephen L. Neal (D) 1975-
L. Richardson Preyer (D) 1969-
Charles G. Rose, III (D) 1973-
Roy A. Taylor (D) 1960-77
James T. Broyhill (R) 1963-
Charles R. Jonas (R) 1953-73
James Grubbs Martin (R) 1973-
Wilmer D. Mizell (R) 1969-75
Earl B. Ruth (R) 1969-75

North Dakota

Mark Andrews (R) 1963-
Thomas S. Kleppe (R) 1967-71

Ohio

Thomas Ludlow Ashley (D) 1955-
Charles J. Carney (D) 1970-
Michael A. Feighan (D) 1943-71
Wayne L. Hays (D) 1949-76
Michael J. Kirwan (D) 1937-70
Thomas A. Luken (D) 1974-
Ronald M. Mottl (D) 1975-
John F. Seiberling, Jr. (D) 1971-
Louis Stokes (D) 1969-
Charles A. Vanik (D) 1955-
John M. Ashbrook (R) 1961-
William H. Ayres (R) 1951-71
Jackson E. Betts (R) 1951-73
Frank T. Bow (R) 1951-72
Clarence J. Brown, Jr. (R) 1965-
Donald D. Clancy (R) 1961-
Samuel L. Devine (R) 1959-
Willis D. Gradison, Jr. (R) 1975-
Tennyson Guyer (R) 1973-
William H. Harsha (R) 1961-
William J. Keating (R) 1971-74
Thomas N. Kindness (R) 1975-
Delbert L. Latta (R) 1959-
Donald E. Lukens (R) 1967-71
William M. McCulloch (R) 1947-73
Clarence E. Miller (R) 1967-
William E. Minshall (R) 1955-75
Charles A. Mosher (R) 1961-77
Walter E. Powell (R) 1971-75
J. William Stanton (R) 1965-
Robert Taft, Jr. (R) 1963-65; 1967-71
Charles W. Whalen, Jr. (R) 1967-
Chalmers P. Wylie (R) 1967-

Oklahoma

Carl Albert (D) 1947-77

Ed Edmondson (D) 1953-73
Glenn English (D) 1975-
John Jarman (D) 1951-75; (R) 1975-77
James R. Jones (D) 1973-
Clem Rogers McSpadden (D) 1973-75
Tom Steed (D) 1949-
Theodore M. Risenhoover (D) 1975-
Page Belcher (R) 1951-73

Oregon

Les AuCoin (D) 1975-
Robert Duncan (D) 1963-67; 1975-
Edith Green (D) 1955-74
Al Ullman (D) 1957-
James Weaver (D) 1975-
John R. Dellenback (R) 1967-75
Wendall Wyatt (R) 1964-75

Pennsylvania

William A. Barrett (D) 1945-47; 1949-76
James A. Byrne (D) 1953-73
Frank M. Clark (D) 1955-75
John H. Dent (D) 1958-
Robert W. Edgar (D) 1975-
Joshua Eilberg (D) 1967-
Daniel J. Flood (D) 1945-47; 1949-53; 1955-
Joseph Gaydos (D) 1968-
William J. Green, III (D) 1964-77
William S. Moorhead (D) 1959-
Thomas E. Morgan (D) 1945-77
John P. Murtha (D) 1974-
Robert N. C. Nix, Sr. (D) 1958-
Fred B. Rooney (D) 1963-
Joseph P. Vigorito (D) 1965-
Gus Yatron (D) 1969-
Robert J. Corbett (R) 1939-41; 1945-71
R. Lawrence Coughlin (R) 1969-
James G. Fulton (R) 1945-71
George A. Goodling (R) 1961-65; 1967-75
William F. Goodling (R) 1975-
H. John Heinz, III (R) 1971-77
Albert W. Johnson (R) 1963-77
Joseph M. McDade (R) 1963-
Gary A. Myers (R) 1975-
John P. Saylor (R) 1949-73
Herman T. Schneebeli (R) 1960-77
Richard T. Schulze (R) 1975-
E. G. Schuster (R) 1973-
John H. Ware, III (R) 1970-75
G. Robert Watkins (R) 1965-70
J. Irving Whalley (R) 1960-73
Lawrence G. Williams (R) 1967-75

Rhode Island

Edward P. Beard (D) 1975-
Fernand Joseph Saint Germain (D) 1961-
Robert O. Tiernan (D) 1967-75

South Carolina

Mendel J. Davis (D) 1971-
Butler Derrick (D) 1975-
William Jennings Bryan Dorn (D) 1947-49;
  1951-74
Thomas S. Gettys (D) 1964-75
Kenneth L. Holland (D) 1975-
John W. Jenrette, Jr. (D) 1975-
James R. Mann (D) 1969-
John L. McMillan (D) 1939-73
L. Mendel Rivers (D) 1941-70
Floyd Spence (R) 1971-
Albert Watson (D) 1963-65; (R) 1965-71
Edward Young (R) 1973-75

South Dakota

James Abourezk (D) 1971-73
F. E. Denholm (D) 1971-75
James Abdnor (R) 1973-
E. Y. Berry (R) 1951-71
Larry Pressler (R) 1975-
Benjamin Reifel (R) 1961-71

Tennessee

Clifford Allen (D) 1975-
William R. Anderson (D) 1965-73
Ray Blanton (D) 1967-73
Robert A. Everett (D) 1958-69
Joe L. Evins (D) 1947-77
Harold E. Ford (D) 1975-
Richard Fulton (D) 1963-75
Ed Jones (D) 1969-
Marilyn Lloyd (D) 1975-
LeMar Baker (R) 1971-75
Robin L. Beard (R) 1973-
William E. (Bill) Brock (R) 1963-71
John J. Duncan (R) 1965-
Dan Kuykendall (R) 1967-75
James H. Quillen (R) 1963-

Texas

Jack Brooks (D) 1953-
Omar Burleson (D) 1947-
Earle Cabell (D) 1965-73

Robert Casey (D) 1959-76
Eligio de la Garza (D) 1965-
John Dowdy (D) 1952-73
Robert Eckhardt (D) 1967-
O. C. Fisher (D) 1943-75
Henry B. Gonzalez (D) 1961-
Sam Hall (D) 1976-
Jack Hightower (D) 1975-
Barbara Jordan (D) 1973-
Abraham Kazen, Jr. (D) 1967-
Robert Kreuger (D) 1975-
George H. Mahon (D) 1935-
Dale Milford (D) 1973-
Wright Patman (D) 1929-70
J. J. (Jake) Pickle (D) 1963-
W. R. Poage (D) 1937-
Graham B. Purcell (D) 1962-73
Ray Roberts (D) 1962-
Olin E. Teague (D) 1946-
Charles Wilson (D) 1973-
Richard C. White (D) 1965-
James C. Wright, Jr. (D) 1955-
John Young (D) 1957-
William Archer Jr. (R) 1971-
George Bush (R) 1967-71
James M. Collins (R) 1968-
Ron Paul (R) 1976-
Robert D. Price (R) 1967-75
Alan Steelman (R) 1973-

Utah

Allen T. Howe (D) 1975-
Douglas W. Owens (D) 1973-75
Wayne W. Owens (D) 1973-75
K. Gunn McKay (D) 1971-
Lawrence J. Burton (R) 1963-71
Sherman P. Lloyd (R) 1963-65; 1967-73

Vermont

James M. Jeffords (R) 1975-
Richard W. Mallary (R) 1972-75
Robert T. Stafford (R) 1961-73

Virginia

Watkins M. Abbitt (D) 1948-73
W. D. (Dan) Daniel (D) 1949-
Thomas N. Downing (D) 1959-77
Joseph L. Fisher (D) 1975-
Herbert E. Harris, II (D) 1975-
John O. Marsh, Jr. (D) 1963-71
David E. Satterfield, III (D) 1965-
Joel T. Broyhill (R) 1953-75

M. Caldwell Butler (R) 1972-
Robert W. Daniel, Jr. (R) 1973-
Standord E. Parris (R) 1973-75
Richard H. Poff (R) 1953-72
J. Kenneth Robinson (R) 1971-
William L. Scott (R) 1967-73
William C. Wampler (R) 1953-55; 1967-
G. William Whitehurst (R) 1969-

Washington

Brock Adams (D) 1965-77
Don Bonker (D) 1975-
Thomas S. Foley (D) 1965-
Julia Butler Hansen (D) 1960-74
Floyd V. Hicks (D) 1965-77
Mike McCormack (D) 1971-
Lloyd Meeds (D) 1965-
Catherine May (R) 1959-71
Thomas M. Pelly (R) 1953-73
Joel Pritchard (R) 1973-

West Virginia

Ken Hechler (D) 1959-77
James Kee (D) 1965-73
Robert H. Mollohan (D) 1953-57; 1969-

John M. Slack, Jr. (D) 1959-
Harley O. Staggers (D) 1949-

Wisconsin

Leslie Aspin (D) 1971-
Alvin Baldus (D) 1975-
Robert J. Cornell (D) 1975-
Robert Kastenmeier (D) 1959-
David R. Obey (D) 1969-
Henry S. Reuss (D) 1955-
Clement J. Zablocki (D) 1949-
John W. Byrnes (R) 1945-73
Glenn R. Davis (R) 1947-57; 1965-74
Harold V. Froelich (R) 1973-75
Robert W. Kasten, Jr. (R) 1975-
Melvin R. Laird (R) 1953-69
Alvin E. O'Konski (R) 1943-73
Henry C. Schadeberg (R) 1961-65; 1967-71
William A. Steiger (R) 1967-
Vernon W. Thomson (R) 1968-75

Wyoming

Teno Roncalio (D) 1965-67; 1971-
John Wold (R) 1967-71

SUPREME COURT

Warren E. Burger, Chief Justice 1969–
Earl Warren, Chief Justice 1953–69
Hugo L. Black 1937–71
Harry A. Blackmun 1970–
William J. Brennan, Jr. 1956–
William O. Douglas 1939–75
Abe Fortas 1965–69

John Marshall Harlan 1955–71
Thurgood Marshall 1967–
Lewis F. Powell, Jr. 1972–
William H. Rehnquist 1972–
J. Paul Stevens 1975–
Potter Stewart 1958–
Byron R. White 1962–

EXECUTIVE DEPARTMENTS

Department of Agriculture

Secretary
  Clifford M. Hardin 1969–71
  Earl L. Butz 1971–76

Undersecretary
  J. Phil Campbell 1969–75
  John A. Knebel 1975–76

Assistant Secretary—Rural Development
  Thomas K. Cowden 1969–72

William W. Erwin 1973–75
William H. Walker 1975–77

Assistant Secretary—Marketing and
Consumer Services
Richard E. Lyng 1969–73
Clayton Yeutter 1973–74
Richard Feltner 1974–77

Assistant Secretary—Department
Administration
Joseph M. Robertson 1969–71
Frank B. Elliott 1971–73
Joseph R. Wright, Jr. 1973–76

Assistant Secretary—International Affairs
and Commodity Programs°
Clarence D. Palmby 1969–72
Carroll G. Brunthaver, Jr. 1972–74
Clayton Yeutter 1974–75
Richard E. Bell 1975–77
    °The position was originally Assistant
    Secretary—International Affairs. It was
    changed in 1969 to the one listed above.

Department of Commerce

Secretary
Maurice H. Stans 1969–72
Peter G. Peterson 1972–73
Frederick B. Dent 1973–75
Rogers C. B. Morton 1975–77

Undersecretary
Rocco C. Siciliano 1969–71
James T. Lynn 1971–73
John K. Tabor 1973–75
James A. Baker 1975–76
Edward O. Vetter 1976–77

Assistant Secretary for Administration
Larry A. Jobe 1969–73
Joseph E. Kasputys 1976–77

Assistant Secretary for Domestic and
International Business
Kenneth N. Davis, Jr. 1969–70
Robert McLellan 1970–72
Andrew E. Gibson 1972
Tilton H. Dobbin 1973–75
Travis E. Reed 1975–76
Leonard S. Matthews 1976

Assistant Secretary for Science and
Technology

Myron Tribus 1969–70
James H. Wakelin, Jr. 1971–72
Betsy Ancker-Johnson 1973–77

Assistant Secretary for Economic Affairs
Harold C. Passer 1969–72
James L. Pate 1974–76
Richard G. Darman 1976–

Assistant Secretary for Economic
Development
Robert A. Podesta 1969–72
William W. Blunt, Jr. 1973–75
Wilmer D. Mizell 1975–77

Department of Defense

Secretary
Melvin R. Laird 1969–73
Elliot Richardson 1973
James R. Schlesinger 1973–75
Donald H. Rumsfeld 1975–77

Deputy Secretary°
David Packard 1969–71
Kenneth Rush 1972–73
William P. Clements, Jr. 1973–77
Robert F. Ellsworth 1975–77
    °The Defense Department received
    authorization in 1972 to have more than
    one Deputy Secretary serving at the same
    time.

Secretary of the Air Force
Robert C. Seamans, Jr. 1969–73
John L. McLucas 1973–75
Thomas C. Reed 1976–77

Secretary of the Army
Stanley R. Resor 1965–71
Robert F. Froehlke 1971–73
Howard H. Callaway 1973–75
Martin R. Hoffmann 1975–77

Secretary of the Navy
John H. Chafee 1969–72
John W. Warner 1972–74
J. William Middendorf, 1974–77

Assistant Secretary (Comptroller)
Robert C. Moot 1968–73
Terence E. McClary 1973–76
Fred P. Wacker 1976–

Assistant Secretary (Installations and
Logistics)
Barry J. Shillito 1969–73
Arthur I. Mendolia 1973–75
Frank A. Shrontz 1976–77

Assistant Secretary (International Security
Affairs)
G. Warren Nutter 1969–73
Robert C. Hill 1973–74
Robert F. Ellsworth 1974–75
Eugene V. McAuliffe 1976–77

Assistant Secretary (Manpower)
Roger T. Kelley 1969–73
William K. Brehm 1973–76
David P. Taylor 1976–77

Assistant Secretary (Public Affairs)
Daniel Z. Henkin 1969–73
Jerry W. Friedheim 1973–74
Joseph Laitin 1975
M. Allen Woods 1976–77

Assistant Secretary (Administration)°
Robert F. Froehlke 1969–71
  °The position was abolished in 1972.

Assistant Secretary (Intelligence)°
Albert C. Hall 1971–76
  °The position was created in 1971.

Assistant Secretary (Systems Analysis)°
Alain C. Enthoven 1965–69
Gardiner L. Tucker 1970–73
  °The position was abolished in 1973.

Joint Chiefs of Staff

Chairman
Gen. Earle G. Wheeler, U.S. Army
1964–70
Adm. Thomas H. Moorer, U.S. Navy
1970–74
Gen. George S. Brown, U.S. Air Force
1974–78

Chief of Staff, U.S. Army
Gen. William C. Westmoreland 1968–72
Gen. Creighton W. Abrams 1972–74
Gen. Fred C. Weyand 1974–76
Gen. Barnard W. Rogers 1976–79

Chief of Naval Operations
Adm. Thomas H. Moorer 1967–70
Adm. Elmo R. Zumwalt, Jr. 1970–74
Adm. James L. Holloway, III 1974–78

Chief of Staff, U.S. Air Force
Gen. John P. McConnell 1965–69
Gen. John D. Ryan 1969–73
Gen. George S. Brown 1973–74
Gen. David C. Jones 1974–78

Commandant of the Marines Corps
Gen. Leonard F. Chapman, Jr. 1968–71
Gen. Robert E. Cushman, Jr. 1972–75
Gen. Louis H. Wilson 1975–79

Department of Health, Education and Welfare

Secretary
Robert H. Finch 1969–70
Elliot L. Richardson 1970–73
Caspar W. Weinberger 1973–75
F. David Mathews 1975–77

Undersecretary
John G. Veneman 1969–73
Frank C. Carlucci 1973–75
Marjorie W. Lynch 1975–77

Assistant Secretary (Administration and
Management)°
James Farmer 1969–71
Rodney H. Brady 1971–72
Robert A. Marik 1973–74
John R. Ottina 1974–76
  °The position was originally Assistant
  Secretary (Administration). It was changed
  in 1973 to the one listed above.

Assistant Secretary (Education)
James E. Allen, Jr. 1969–70
Sidney P. Marland, Jr. 1972–73
Virginia Y. Trotter 1974–76

Assistant Secretary (Health)°
Roger O. Egeberg 1969–71
Merlin K. DuVal 1971–72
Charles C. Edwards 1973–75
Theodore Cooper 1975–76
  °The position was originally Assistant
  Secretary (Health and Scientific Affairs). It
  was changed in 1973 to the one listed
  above.

Assistant Secretary (Comptroller)
James F. Kelly 1966–70
James B. Cardwell 1970–73
John D. Young 1973–77

Assistant Secretary (Planning and
Evaluation)
Lewis H. Butler 1969–70
Lawrence H. Lynn, Jr. 1971–73
William A. Morrill 1973–77

Assistant Secretary (Community and Field
Services)°
Patricia Reilly Hitt 1969–73
°The position was abolished in 1973.

Assistant Secretary (Human Development)°
Stanley B. Thomas, Jr. 1973–77
°The position was created in 1973.

Assistant Secretary (Legislation)
Creed C. Black 1969–70
Stephen Kurzman 1971–76

Department of Housing and Urban Development

Secretary
George Romney 1969–72
James T. Lynn 1973–75
Carla A. Hills 1975–76

Undersecretary
Richard C. Van Dusen 1969–72
Floyd H. Hyde 1973–74
James L. Mitchell 1974–75
John B. Rhinelander 1975–77

Assistant Secretary for Housing Production
and Mortgage Credit/Federal Housing
Administration Commissioner°
Eugene A. Gulledge 1969–73
Sheldon Lubar 1973–74
David S. Cook 1975–76
°The position was originally Assistant
Secretary for Mortgage Credit and Federal
Housing Administration Commissioner. It
was changed in 1973 to the one listed above
and abolished in 1976.

Assistant Secretary for Housing
Management°
Norman Watson 1971–73

H. R. Crawford 1973–76
°The position was created in 1971 and
abolished in 1976.

Assistant Secretary for Housing/Federal
Housing Administration Commissioner°
James L. Young 1976
°The position was created in 1976 and it
absorbed the functions of Assistant
Secretary for Housing Production and
Mortgage Credit/Federal Housing
Administration Commissioner and Assistant
Secretary for Housing Management.

Assistant Secretary for Renewal and Housing
Management°
Lawrence M. Cox 1969–70
°The position was abolished in 1970.

Assistant Secretary for Administration
Lester P. Condon 1969–72
Harry T. Morley 1972–73
W. Boyd Christiansen 1973–74
Thomas G. Cody 1974–76

Assistant Secretary for Fair Housing and
Equal Opportunity
Samuel J. Simmons 1969–72
Gloria E.A. Toote 1973–75
James H. Blair 1975–77

Assistant Secretary for Model Cities°
Floyd H. Hyde 1969–71
°The position was abolished in 1971.

Assistant Secretary for Community Planning
and Development°
Samuel C. Jackson 1969–71
Floyd H. Hyde 1971–73
David O. Meeker, Jr. 1973–76
°The position was originally Assistant
Secretary for Metropolitan Planning and
Development. It was changed in 1973 to
the one listed above.

Assistant Secretary for Policy Development
and Research°
Harold B. Singer 1969–72
Michael H. Moskow 1973–75
Charles J. Orlebeke 1975–77
°The position was originally Assistant
Secretary for Research and Technology. It
was changed in 1972 to the one listed
above.

Assistant Secretary for Legislative Affairs
Sol Mosher 1973–77
°The postition was created in 1973.

Assistant Secretary for Consumer Affairs and
Regulatory Functions°
Constance Newman 1976–77
°The position was created in 1976.

Department of the Interior

Secretary
Walter J. Hickel 1969–70
Rogers C.B. Morton 1971–75
Stanley K. Hathaway 1975
Thomas S. Kleppe 1975–77

Undersecretary
Russell E. Train 1969–70
Fred J. Russell 1970–71
William T. Pecora 1971–72
John C. Whitaker 1973–75
Dale Kent Frizzell 1975–76

Assistant Secretary—Fish and Wildlife
Leslie L. Glasgow 1969–71
Nathaniel P. Reid 1971–77

Assistant Secretary—Energy and Minerals°
Hollis M. Dole 1969–73
Stephen A. Wakefield 1973–74
Jack W. Carlson 1974–76
William L. Fisher 1976–77
°The position was originally Assistant
Secretary—Mineral Resources. It was
changed in 1973 to the one listed above.

Assistant Secretary—Public Land
Management°
Harrison Loesch 1969–73
°The position was abolished in 1973.

Assistant Secretary—Water and Power
Resources°
James R. Smith 1969–73
°The position was abolished in 1973.

Assistant Secretary—Program Development
and Budget°
Laurence Lynn, Jr. 1973–74
Royston Hughes 1974–76

Ronald Coleman 1976–77
°The position was created in 1973.

Assistant Secretary—Programs°
John Larson 1971–73
°The position was created in 1971 and
abolished in 1973.

Assistant Secretary—Water Quality°
Carl L. Klein 1969–70
°The position was abolished in 1970.

Assistant Secretary—Land and Water
Resources°
Jack O. Horton 1973–77
°The position was created in 1973.

Assistant Secretary—Administration
Lawrence H. Dunn 1969–71
Richard S. Bodman 1971–73
James T. Clarke 1973–76
Albert Zapanta 1976–77

Assistant Secretary—Congressional and
Legislative Affairs°
John Kyl 1973–77
°The position was created in 1973.

Department of Justice

Attorney General
John N. Mitchell 1969–72
Richard D. Kleindeinst 1972–73
Elliot L. Richardson 1973
William Saxbe 1973–75
Edward H. Levi 1975–77

Deputy Attorney General
Richard D. Kleindeinst 1969–72
Ralph E. Erickson 1972–73
William D. Ruckleshaus 1973
Laurence H. Silberman 1974–75
Harold R. Tyler, Jr. 1975–77

Solicitor General
Erwin N. Griswold 1967–73
Robert H. Bork 1973–77

Assistant Attorney General/Antitrust
Division
Richard W. McLaren 1969–72

Thomas E. Kauper 1972–76
Donald Baker 1976–77

Assistant Attorney General/Civil Division
William D. Ruckleshaus 1969–70
L. Patrick Gray, III 1970–72
Harlington Wood, Jr. 1972–73
Carla A. Hills 1974–75
Rex E. Lee 1975–77

Assistant Attorney General/Criminal
Division
Will R. Wilson 1969–71
Henry E. Petersen 1972–74
Richard L. Thornburgh 1975–77

Assistant Attorney General/Internal Security
Division°
J. Walter Yeagley 1959–70
Robert C. Mardian 1970–72
A. William Olson 1972–73
   °Reorganized in 1973 under Assistant
   Attorney General Criminal Division.

Assistant Attorney General/Lands Division
Shiro Kashiwa 1969–72
D. Kent Frizzell 1972–73
Wallace H. Johnson, Jr. 1973–75
Peter R. Taft 1975–77

Assistant Attorney General/Tax Division
Johnnie McK. Walkers 1969–71
Scott P. Crampton 1971–76

Assistant Attorney General/Civil Rights
Division
Jerris Leonard 1969–71
David Luke Norman 1971–73
J. Stanley Pottinger 1973–77

Assistant Attorney General/Administrative
Division
Leo M. Pellerzi 1968–73
Glen E. Pommerening 1974–77

Assistant Attorney General/Office of Legal
Counsel
William H. Rehnquist 1969–71
Ralph E. Erickson 1971–72
Roger E. Cramton 1972–73
Robert G. Dixon, Jr. 1973–74
Antonin Scalia 1974–77

Assistant Attorney General/Office of
Legislative Affairs°
James D. McKevitt 1972–73

W. Vincent Rakestraw 1974–75
Michael M. Uhlmann 1975–77
   °The position was created in 1972.

Department of Labor

Secretary
George P. Shultz 1969–70
James D. Hodgson 1970–72
Peter J. Brennan 1973–75
John T. Dunlop 1975–76
W.J. Usery, Jr. 1976–77

Undersecretary
James D. Hodgson 1969–70
Laurence H. Silberman 1970–72
Richard F. Schubert 1973–75
Robert O. Aders 1975–76
Michael H. Moskow 1976–78

Assistant Secretary for Administration
Leo Wertz 1965–70
Frank Zarb 1970–73
Fred G. Clark 1973–77

Assistant Secretary for Labor-Management
Relations
W. J. Usery, Jr. 1969–73
Paul J. Fasser, Jr. 1973–76
Bernard E. DeLury 1976–77

Assistant Secretary for Occupational Safety
and Health°
John Gunther 1971–73
John H. Stender 1973–75
Martin Corn 1975–77
   °The position was created in 1971.

Assistant Secretary for Policy Evaluation and
Research
Jerome M. Rosow 1969
Richard J. Grunewald 1971–72
Michael H. Moskow 1972–74
Abraham Weiss 1974–77

Assistant Secretary for Employment and
Training°
Arnold R. Weber 1969–70
Malcolm R. Lovell, Jr. 1970–73
William H. Kolberg 1973–77
   °The position was originally Assistant
   Secretary for Manpower Administration. It
   was changed in 1973 to the listed above.

Assistant Secretary for Employment
Standards°
Arthur A. Fletcher 1969–72
Richard J. Grunewald 1972–73
Bernard E. DeLury 1973–76
John C. Reed 1976–77
> °The position was originally Assistant
> Secretary for Wage and Labor Standards. It
> was changed in 1971 to the one listed
> above.

Post Office Department°

> °Reorganized in 1970 into the U.S. Postal
> Service, effective 1971.

Postmaster General
Winton M. Blount 1969–71

Deputy Postmaster General
Elmer T. Klassen 1969–71

Assistant Postmaster General/Bureau of
Operations
Frank J. Nunlist 1969–71

Assistant Postmaster General/Bureau of
Finance and Administration
James W. Hargrove 1969–71

Assistant Postmaster General/Bureau of
Facilities
Henry Lehne 1969–71

Assistant Postmaster General/Bureau of
Personnel
Kenneth A. Housman 1969–71

Assistant Postmaster General/Research and
Engineering
Harold F. Faught 1969–71

Assistant Postmaster General/Planning and
Marketing
Ronald Lee 1969–71

U.S. Postal Service°

> °The service was established as an
> independent government-owned agency in
> 1970 by the Postal Reorganization Act of
> 1970 and was given full authority to
> operate the U.S. postal system, effective in
> 1971.

Postmaster General
Elmer T. Klassen 1972–75
Benjamin F. Bailar 1975–78

Deputy Postmaster General
Merrill A. Hayden 1971–72
William F. Bolger 1975–78

Senior Assistant Postmaster General/Mail
Processing Group°
Harold Faught 1971–73
> °The position was created and abolished in
> 1973.

Senior Assistant Postmaster
General/Operations Group°
Edward V. Dorsey 1973–79
> °The position was created in 1973.

Senior Assistant Postmaster
General/Employee and Labor Relations
Group°
James P. Blaisdell 1972–73
Darrell F. Brown 1973–74
James V. P. Conway 1975–78
> °The position was created in 1972.

Senior Assistant Postmaster General/Support
Group°
James W. Hargrove 1971–72
Benjamin F. Bailar 1972–73
> °The position was created in 1971 and
> abolished in 1973.

Senior Assistant Postmaster General/Finance
Group°
Ralph W. Nicholson 1973–74
Richard F. Gould 1975–77
> °The position was created in 1973.

Senior Assistant Postmaster
General/Administration Group°
Benjamin F. Bailar 1973–75
J. T. Ellington 1975–77
> °The position was created in 1973.

Senior Assistant Postmaster
General/Manpower and Cost Control°
Carl C. Ulsaker 1974–78
> °The position was created in 1974.

Senior Assistant Postmaster
General/Customer Services Group°
Melvin Baker 1971–73
Murray Comarow 1972–73
°The position was created in 1971 and
abolished in 1973.

Senior Assistant Postmaster
General/Executive Functions Group°
Paul N. Carlin 1972–73
°The position was created in 1972 and
abolished in 1973.

State Department

Secretary
William P. Rogers 1969–73
Henry A. Kissinger 1973–77

Undersecretary
Elliot L. Richardson 1969–70
John N. Irwin, II 1970–72
Kenneth Rush 1973–74
Robert S. Ingersoll 1974–76
Charles W. Robinson 1976–77

Undersecretary for Economic Affairs
William J. Casey 1973–74
Charles W. Robinson 1974-76
William D. Rogers 1976–77

Deputy Undersecretary for Economic Affairs
Nathaniel Samuels 1969–72

Undersecretary for Political Affairs
U. Alexis Johnson 1969–73
William J. Porter 1973–74
Joseph J. Sisco 1974–76

Assistant Secretary for Public Affairs
Michael Collins 1970–71
Carol C. Laise 1973–75
John E. Reinhardt 1975–77

Assistant Secretary for Congressional
Relations
William B. Macomber, Jr. 1967–69
David M. Abshire 1970–72
J. Marshall Wright 1973–74
A. Linwood Holton 1974
Robert J. McCloskey 1975–76

Assistant Secretary for Inter-American
Affairs

Charles A. Meyer 1969–73
Jack B. Kubisch 1973–74
William D. Rogers 1974–76

Assistant Secretary for European Affairs
Martin J. Hillenbrand 1969–72
Walter J. Stoessel, Jr. 1972–74
Arthur A. Hartman 1974–77

Assistant Secretary for Near Eastern and
South Asian Affairs
Joseph J. Sisco 1969–74
Alfred L. Atherton, Jr. 1974–78

Assistant Secretary for East Asian and Pacific
Affairs°
Marshall Green 1969–73
Robert S. Ingersoll 1973–74
Arthur W. Hummel 1976–77
°The position was originally Assistant
Secretary for Far Eastern Affairs. It was
changed in 1966 to the one listed above.

Assistant Secretary for African Affairs
David D. Newsom 1969–74
Donald Easum 1974–75
Nathaniel Davis 1975
William E. Schaufele, Jr. 1975–77

Assistant Secretary for Oceans and
International, Environmental and
Scientific Affairs°
Dixy Lee Ray 1974–75
Frederick Irving 1976–77
°The position was created in 1974.

Assistant Secretary for International
Organization Affairs
Samuel DePalma 1969–73
David Popper 1973–74
William B. Buffum 1974–1975
Samuel W. Lewis 1975–77

Assistant Secretary for Administration
Francis G. Meyer 1969–71
Joseph F. Donelan, Jr. 1971–73
John M. Thomas 1973–79

Assistant Secretary for Educational and
Cultural Affairs
John Richardson, Jr. 1969–77

Assistant Secretary for Economic and
Business Affairs°
Philip H. Trezise 1969–72

Willis C. Armstrong 1972–74
Thomas O. Enders 1974–75
Joseph A. Greenwald 1976
Julius L. Katz 1976-
°The position was originally Assistant
Secretary for Economic Affairs. It was
changed in 1972 to the one listed above.

Department of Transportation

Secretary
John A. Volpe 1969–73
Claude Brinegar 1973–75
William T. Coleman, Jr. 1975–77

Undersecretary
John Robson 1968–69
James M. Beggs 1969–73
Egil Krogh 1973
John W. Barnum 1973–77

Deputy Undersecretary
Charles D. Baker 1969–70
John P. Olsson 1970–73
Robert H. Clement 1973–75
John Snow 1975–76

Assistant Secretary for Policy Planning and
International Affairs
Paul Cherington 1969–70
Charles D. Baker 1970–71
John L. Hazard 1972–73
Robert H. Binder 1974–77

Assistant Secretary for Public Affairs°
Walter L. Mazan 1969–70
°The position was abolished in 1970.

Assistant Secretary for Congressional and
Intergovernmental Affairs°
Roger Hooker 1973–74
Robert Monaghan 1975–77
°The position was created in 1973.

Assistant Secretary for Administration
Alan L. Dean 1967–69
William S. Heffelfinger 1969–77

Assistant Secretary for Systems Development
and Technology
Secor Browne 1969
Robert Connor 1970–74
Hamilton Herman 1975–77

Assistant Secretary for Environment and
Urban Systems°

James Braman 1969–70
Herbert DiSimone 1971–72
John Hirten 1972–73
°The position was created in 1969 and
abolished in 1973.

Assistant Secretary for Environmental Safety
and Consumer Affairs°
William J. Smith 1970–71
Benjamin O. Davis 1971–75
Judith Connor 1975–77
°The position was created in 1970 and
originally titled Assistant Secretary for
Safety. It was changed in 1973 to the one
listed above.

Department of the Treasury

Secretary
David M. Kennedy 1969–71
John B. Connally 1971–72
George P. Shultz 1972–74
William E. Simon 1974–77

Undersecretary
Edwin S. Cohen 1972–73
Edward C. Schmults 1974–75
Jerry Thomas 1975–77

Undersecretary for Monetary Affairs
Paul A. Volcker 1969–74
Jack F. Bennett 1974–75
Edwin H. Yeo, III 1975–77

Assistant Secretary for Tax Policy
Edwin S. Cohen 1969–72
Frederic W. Hickman 1972–75
Charles M. Walker 1975–76

Assistant Secretary for Economic Policy
Murray L. Weidenbaum 1969–71
Edgar R. Fiedler 1971–75
Sidney L. Jones 1975–77

Assistant Secretary for Enforcement,
Operations and Tariff Affairs
Eugene T. Rossides 1969–73
Edward L. Morgan 1973–74
David R. MacDonald 1974–76

Assistant Secretary for International Affairs
John R. Petty 1968–72
John M. Hennessy 1972–74
Charles A. Cooper 1974–75
Gerald L. Parsky 1976–77

REGULATORY COMMISSIONS
AND INDEPENDENT AGENCIES

Atomic Energy Commission°

°Reorganized in 1974 into the Nuclear
Regulatory Commission.

William A. Anders 1973–74
Francesco Costagliola 1968–69
William O. Doub 1971–74
Wilfrid E. Johnson 1966–72
William E. Kriegsman 1973–74
Clarence F. Larson 1969–74
James T. Ramey 1962–73
Dixy Lee Ray 1972–74; Chairman, 1973–74
James R. Schlesinger 1971–73; Chairman,
1971-73
Glenn T. Seaborg 1961–71; Chairman,
1961–71
Gerald F. Tape 1963–69
Theos J. Thompson 1969–70

Civil Aeronautics Board

John G. Adams 1965–71
Secor D. Browne 1969–73; Chairman,
1969–73
John H. Crooker, Jr. 1968–69; Chairman,
1968–69
Whitney Gillilland 1959–75
R. Tenny Johnson 1976–77
G. Joseph Minetti 1956–78
Robert Murphy 1961–73
Richard J. O'Melia 1973-
John Robson 1975–77; Chairman, 1975–77
Robert Timm 1971–76; Chairman, 1973–74
Lee R. West 1973–78

Federal Communications Commission

Robert T. Bartley 1952–72
Dean Burch 1969–74; Chairman, 1969–74
Kenneth A. Cox 1963–70
James R. Fogarty 1976–
Benjamin L. Hooks 1972–77
Thomas J. Houser 1971–
Rosel H. Hyde 1946–69; Chairman,
1953–54; 1966–69
Nicholas Johnson 1966–73
H. Rex Lee 1968–73
Robert E. Lee 1953–

James H. Quello 1974–
Charlotte T. Reid 1971–76
Glen Robinson 1974–76
James J. Wadsworth 1965–69
Abbott M. Washburn 1974–
Robert Wells 1969–71
Margita White 1976–79
Richard E. Wiley 1972–77; Chairman,
1974–77

Federal Power Commission

Carl E. Bagge 1965–70
Albert B. Brooke 1968–75
John A. Carver 1966–72
Richard Dunham 1975–77; Chairman,
1975–77
John Holloman, III 1975–77
Tom Rush Moody, Jr. 1971–75
John N. Nassikas 1969–75; Chairman,
1969–75
Lawrence J. O'Connor, Jr. 1961–71
Don S. Smith 1973–79
William Springer 1973–75
Pinkney Walker 1971–72
James Watt 1975–77
Lee C. White 1966–69; Chairman, 1966–69

Federal Reserve Board

Andrew F. Brimmer 1966–74
Jeffrey Bucher 1972–76
Arthur F. Burns 1970–78; Chairman
1970–78
Phillip Coldwell 1974–
J. Dewey Daane 1963–74
Stephen Gardner 1976–78
Robert Holland 1973–76
Phillip Jackson 1975–78
David Lilly 1976–78
Sherman J. Maisel 1965–72
William McC. Martin, Jr. 1951–70;
Chairman, 1951–70
George W. Mitchell 1961–76
J. Charles Partee 1975–
James L. Robertson 1952–73
John E. Sheehan 1972–75
William W. Sherill 1967–71
Henry Wallich 1974–

Federal Trade Commission

David Clanton 1976–
Calvin J. Collier 1976–77; Chairman, 1976–77
David S. Dennison 1970–73
Paul Rand Dixon 1961–; Chairman, 1961–70
Philip Elman 1961–70
Lewis A. Engman 1973–75; Chairman, 1973–75
Mary Elizabeth Hanford 1973–79
Mary Gardiner Jones 1964–73
Miles W. Kirkpatrick 1970–73; Chairman, 1970–73
A. Everette MacIntyre 1961–73
James M. Nicholson 1967–69
Stephen Nye 1974–76
Mayo J. Thompson 1973–75
Caspar W. Weinberger 1969–70; Chairman, 1969–70

Nuclear Regulatory Commission*

*The Nuclear Regulatory Commission was established by law on Oct. 11, 1974. It assumed the regulatory functions of the Atomic Energy Commission, which was abolished by the same legislation.

William A. Anders 1974–76; Chairman, 1974–76
Victor Gilinsky 1975–
Richard Kennedy 1975–
Edward Mason 1975–78
Marcus Rowden 1975–77

Securities and Exchange Commission

Hamer H. Budge 1964–71; Chairman, 1969–71
William J. Casey 1971–73; Chairman, 1971–73
Manuel F. Cohen 1961–69; Chairman, 1964–69
G. Bradford Cook 1973; Chairman, 1973
John R. Evans 1973–
Ray Garrett, Jr. 1973–75; Chairman, 1973–75
Albert Sydney Herlong, Jr. 1969–73
Roderick Hills 1975–77; Chairman, 1975–77
Philip Loomis, Jr. 1973–
James J. Needham 1969–72
Hugh F. Owens 1964–73
Irving M. Pollack 1974–
Richard B. Smith 1967–71
A. A. Sommer, Jr. 1973–76
Francis M. Wheat 1964–69

GOVERNORS

Alabama

Albert P. Brewer (D) 1968–71
George C. Wallace (D) 1971–

Alaska

Walter J. Hickel (R) 1966–69
Keith H. Miller (R) 1969–71
William A. Egan (D) 1959–66; 1971–74
Jay Hammond (R) 1974-

Arizona

John R. (Jack) Williams (R) 1967–75
Raoul Castro (D) 1975–

Arkansas

Winthrop Rockefeller (R) 1967–70

Dale Bumpers (D) 1970–75
David Pryor (D) 1975–

California

Ronald Reagan (R) 1967–75
Edmund G. Brown, Jr. (D) 1975–

Colorado

John A. Love (R) 1962–73
John Vanderhoof (R) (1973–75)
Richard D. Lamm (D) 1975–

Connecticut

John N. Dempsey (D) 1961–71
Thomas J. Meskill (R) 1971–75
Ella T. Grasso (D) 1975–

Delaware

Russell W. Peterson (R) 1969–73
Sherman W. Tribbitt (D) 1973–77

Florida

Claude R. Kirk, Jr. (R) 1967–71
Reubin Askew (D) 1971–

Georgia

Lester G. Maddox (D) 1967–71
Jimmy Carter (D) 1971–75
George Busbee (D) 1975–

Hawaii

John A. Burns (D) 1962–75
George R. Ariyoshi (D) 1975–

Idaho

Don Samuelson (R) 1967–71
Cecil D. Andrus (D) 1971–77

Illinois

Richard B. Ogilvie (R) 1968–73
Daniel Walker (D) 1973–77

Indiana

Edgar D. Whitcomb (R) 1969–73
Otis R. Bowen (R) 1973–

Iowa

Robert D. Ray (R) 1969–

Kansas

Robert B. Docking (D) 1967–75
Robert F. Bennett (R) 1975–

Kentucky

Wendell H. Ford (D) 1971–74
Louis B. Nunn (R) 1967–71
Julian M. Carroll (D) 1975–

Louisiana

John J. McKeithen (D) 1964–72
Edwin W. Edwards (D) 1972–

Maine

Kenneth M. Curtis (D) 1967–75
James Longley (I) 1975–

Maryland

Marvin Mandel (D) 1969–

Massachusetts

John A. Volpe (R) 1961–63; 1965–69
Francis W. Sargent (R) 1969–75
Michael S. Dukakis (D) 1975–

Michigan

William G. Miliken (R) 1969–

Minnesota

Harold LeVander (R) 1967–71
Wendell R. Anderson (D) 1971–77

Mississippi

John Bell Williams (D) 1968–72
William L. Waller (D) 1972–76
Charles C. Finch (D) 1976–

Missouri

Warren E. Hearnes (D) 1965–73
Christopher S. Bond (R) 1973–77

Montana

Forrest H. Anderson (D) 1969–73
Thomas L. Judge (D) 1973–

Nebraska

Norbert T. Tiemann (R) 1967–71
J. James Exon (D) 1971–

Nevada

Paul Laxalt (R) 1967–71
Mike D.N. O'Callaghan (D) 1971–

New Hampshire

Walter R. Peterson, Jr. (R) 1969–73
Meldrim Thomson, Jr. (R) 1973–

New Jersey

Richard J. Hughes (D) 1962–70
William T. Cahill (R) 1970–74
Brendan T. Byrne (D) 1974–

New Mexico

David F. Cargo (R) 1967–71
Bruce King (D) 1971–75
Jerry Apodaca (D) 1975–

New York

Nelson A. Rockefeller (R) 1959–73
Malcolm Wilson (R) 1973–75
Hugh L. Carey (D) 1975–

North Carolina

Robert W. Scott (D) 1969–72
James E. Holshouser, Jr. (R) 1973–77

North Dakota

William L. Guy (D) 1961–73
Arthur A. Link (D) 1973–

Ohio

James A. Rhodes (R) 1963–71; 1975–
John J. Gilligan (D) 1971–75

Oklahoma

Dewey F. Bartlett (R) 1967–71
David Hall (D) 1971–75
David Boren (D) 1975–

Oregon

Tom McCall (R) 1967–75
Robert Straub (D) 1975–

Pennsylvania

Raymond P. Shafer (R) 1967–71
Milton J. Shapp (D) 1971–

Rhode Island

Frank Licht (D) 1969–73
Philip W. Noel (D) 1973–77

South Carolina

Robert E. McNair (D) 1965–71
John C. West (D) 1971–75
James B. Edwards (R) 1975–

South Dakota

Frank Farrar (R) 1969–70
Richard F. Kneip (D) 1971–

Tennessee

Buford Ellington (D) 1959–63; 1967–71
Winfield Dunn (R) 1971–75
Ray Blanton (D) 1975–

Texas

Preston Smith (D) 1969–73
Dolph Briscoe (D) 1973–

Utah

Calvin L. Rampton (D) 1965–77

Vermont

Deane C. Davis (R) 1969–73
Thomas P. Salmon (D) 1973–77

Virginia

Mills E. Godwin, Jr. (D) 1966–70; 1974–78
Linwood Holton (R) 1970–74

Washington

Daniel J. Evans (R) 1965–77

West Virginia

Arch A. Moore, Jr. (R) 1969–

Wisconsin

Warren P. Knowles (R) 1964–71
Patrick J. Lucey (D) 1971–77

Wyoming

Stanley K. Hathaway (R) 1967–75
Ed Herschler (D) 1975–

BIBLIOGRAPHY

THE PRESIDENCY AND THE ADMINISTRATION

A complete history of the Nixon/Ford years has yet to appear, but a good starting point is Jonathan Schell's *The Time of Illusion* (New York, 1975), which provides a political history from Nixon's 1969 inauguration until his 1974 resignation. Two other political histories of the period are Kirkpatrick Sale, *Power Shift: The Rise of the Southern Rim and its Challenge to the Eastern Establishment* (New York, 1975) and Sidney Verba, *Political Participation in America* (Ann Arbor, 1975). Most pre-Watergate studies of the Nixon Administration have been by journalists. William Safire's *Before the Fall* (New York, 1975) is an extensive, though anecdotal, work. An earlier but more critical study is Rowland Evans and Robert Novak, *Nixon in the White House* (New York, 1971). A lengthy and enlightening study is Gary Wills' *Nixon Agonistes* (New York, 1970). Less satisfying is Bruce Mazlich's effort at psycho-history, *In Search of Nixon* (New York, 1972). Fewer works have appeared regarding the Ford Administration. Ron Nessen's *It Sure Looks Different From the Inside* (Chicago, 1978) is more a personal than a political history. John Osborne's *White House Watch: The Ford Years* (Washington, 1977) provides a summary of major events. The personal memoirs of both Presidents—*RN: The Memoirs of Richard Nixon* (New York, 1978) and *A Time to Heal: An Autobiography* (New York, 1978)—are interesting, but, as can be expected, leave many questions unanswered.

The activities of the Central Intelligence Agency (CIA) became a matter of deep concern and debate during the Nixon and Ford Administrations as continued probes revealed abuses of the Agency's charter. Official investigations were combined with books written by disgruntled former agents who opposed CIA policy or methods of operation. An excellent analysis of the CIA is Harry H. Ransom's *Intelligence Establishment* (Cambridge, Mass., 1978). For an inside look at the Agency from one of its important defenders see William Colby, *Honorable Men: My Life in the CIA* (New York, 1978). Colby was Director of Central Intelligence during the mid-1970s when CIA practices became public and spent much if his time as director defending the Agency in congressional hearings.

Other Works

Abrahamsen, David, *Nixon vs. Nixon: An Emotional Tragedy* (New York, 1977).

Albright, Joseph, *What Makes Agnew Run* (New York, 1972).

Allen, Gary, *Nixon's Palace Guard* (Boston, 1971).

——, *Richard Nixon: The Man Behind the Mask* (Boston, 1971).

——, *The Rockefeller File* (Seal Beach, Calif. 1976).

Anson, Robert Sam, *McGovern* (New York, 1972).

Atkins, Ollie, *The White House Years: Triumph and Tragedy* (Chicago, 1977).

Bernstein, Carl, and Robert Woodward, *The Final Days* (New York, 1976).

Bremer, Howard F., ed., *Richard M. Nixon, 1913: Chronology, Documents, Bibliographical Aids* (New York, 1975).

Broder, David S., *The Party's Over* (New York, 1972).

Casserly, John J., *The Ford White House: The Diary of a Speechwriter* (Boulder, Colorado, 1977).

Chesen, Eli S., *President Nixon's Psychodynamic-Genetic Interpretation* (New York, 1973).

Chester, Lewis, Godfrey Hodgson and Bruce Page, *An American Melodrama: The Presidential Campaign of 1968* (New York, 1969).

Cohen, Richard M., *A Heartbeat Away: The Investigation and Resignation of Vice President Spiro T. Agnew* (New York, 1974).

Connery, Robert A., and Gerald Benjamin, *Rockefeller of New York: Executive Power in the State House* (New York, 1979).

Cook, Fred, *The FBI Nobody Knows* (New York, 1972).

Drury, Allen, *Courage and Hesitation: Inside the Nixon Administration* (New York, 1972).

Elfin, Mel, "The President at Midpassage," *Newsweek* (Jan. 25, 1971).

Ford, Gerald R., *Public Papers of the Presidents: Gerald R. Ford*, 3 vols. (Washington, 1975–77).

Gilmour, Robert, and Robert Lamb, *Political Alienation in Contemporary America* (New York, 1975).

"Governmental Control of Richard Nixon's Presidential Material (Constitutional Issues)," *Yale Law Journal* (July, 1978).

Henderson, Charles P., Jr., *The Nixon Theology* (New York, 1972).

Hersey, John Richard, *The President* (New York, 1975).

Hoffman, Paul, *New Nixon* (New York, 1970).

Karcher, Joseph T., *Summation for the Defense: The Case for Nixon* (San Diego, 1979).

Kramer, Michael, and Sam Roberts, *I Never Wanted to be Vice President of Anything: An Investigative Biography of Nelson Rockefeller* (New York, 1976).

Kurland, Gerald, *Spiro Agnew: Controversial Vice President of the Nixon Administration* (Charlotteville, N.Y., 1972).

Kutz, Meyer, *Rockefeller Power* (New York, 1974).

Lankevich, George, *Gerald R. Ford: Chronology, Documents, Bibliographical Aids* (New York, 1977).

Lehman, John, *The Executive Congress and Foreign Policy: Status of the Nixon Administration* (New York, 1976).

Leroy, L. David, *Biography of Gerald Ford* (Arlington, 1974).

Lippman, Theodore, *Spiro Agnew's America* (New York, 1972).

Lurie, Leonard, *The Running of Richard Nixon* (New York, 1972).

McGinniss, Joe, *The Selling of the President, 1968* (New York, 1969).

Mankiewicz, Frank, *Perfectly Clear: Nixon from Whittier to Watergate* (New York, 1973).

Marsh, Robert L., *Agnew the Unexamined Man: A Political Profile* (Philadelphia, 1971).

Miles, Rufus, *The Department of Health, Education and Welfare* (New York, 1974).

Mollenhoff, Clark R., *Game Plan for Disaster: An Ombudsman's Report on the Nixon Years* (New York, 1976).

Nathan, Richard P., *The Plot That Failed: Nixon and the Administrative Presidency* (New York, 1975).

Nixon, Richard M., *Public Papers of the Presidents: Richard M. Nixon*, 6 vols. (Washington, 1971–74).

Osborne, John, *The Second Year of the Nixon Watch* (New York, 1971).

——, *The Third Year of the Nixon Watch* (New York, 1972).

——, *The Fourth Year of the Nixon Watch* (New York, 1973).

——, *The Fifth Year of the Nixon Watch* (New York, 1974).

——, *The Last Nixon Watch* (Washington, 1975).

Parmet, Herbert S., *The Democrats, The Years after FDR* (New York, 1976).

Peterson, Robert W., ed., *Agnew: The Coining of a Household Word* (New York, 1972).

Phillips, Devin, *The Emerging Republican Majority* (New York, 1970).

Price, Raymond, *With Nixon* (New York, 1977).

Rather, Dan, *The Palace Guard* (New York, 1974).

Reeves, Richard, *A Ford, Not a Lincoln* (New York, 1975).

Shannon, William V., "Is Gerald Ford Really Necessary?" *Worldview* (July 17, 1974).

Sobel, Lester A., comp., *Presidential Succession: Ford, Rockefeller and the 25th Amendment* (New York, 1975).

terHorst, Jerald F., *Gerald Ford and the Future of the Presidency* (New York, 1974).

Turner, William W., *Hoover's FBI: The Man and the Myth* (Los Angeles, 1970).

Unger, Sanford J., *FBI: An Uncensored Look Behind the Walls* (Boston, 1976).

Vestal, Bud, *Jerry Ford, Up Close: An Investigative Biography* (New York, 1974).

Voorhis, Horace J., *The Strange Case of Richard Milhous Nixon* (New York, 1972).

Watters, Pat, and Stephen Gillers, eds., *Investigating the FBI* (New York, 1973).

Whalen, Richard J., *Catch a Falling Flag*

(New York, 1972).

White, Theodore H., *The Making of the President, 1968* (New York, 1969).

——, *The Making of the President, 1972* (New York, 1973).

Witcover, Jules, *Marathon: The Pursuit of the Presidency, 1972–1976* (New York, 1977).

——, *White Knight: The Rise of Spiro Agnew* (New York, 1972).

Woodstone, Arthur, *Nixon's Head* (New York, 1972).

Central Intelligence Agency

Agee, Philip, *Inside the Company: CIA Diary* (New York, 1975).

Berman, Jerry J., and Morton H. Halperin, eds., *The Abuses of the Intelligence Agencies* (Washington, 1975).

Buncher, Judith, ed., *The CIA and the Security Debate 1971–1975* (New York, 1976).

——*The CIA and the Security Debate 1975–1976* (New York, 1977).

Freedman, Lawrence, U.S. *Intelligence and the Soviet Strategic Threat* (Boulder, 1977).

Jeffers, H. Paul, *The CIA: A Close Look at the Central Intelligence Agency* (New York, 1971).

Liffers, Paul H., *The CIA: A Close Look at the Central Intelligence Agency* (New York, 1971).

McGarvey, Patrick, *CIA: The Myth and the Madness* (Baltimore, 1973).

Marchetti, Victor, and John D. Marks, *The CIA and the Cult of Intelligence* (New York, 1975).

Ross, Thomas B., and David Wise, *Invisible Government: The CIA and U.S. Intelligence* (New York, 1974).

U.S. Commission on CIA Activities within the United States (Rockefeller Commission), *Report to the President* (Washington, 1975).

U.S. Senate, Select Committee on Intelligence Activities, *Foreign and Military Intelligence* (Washington, 1975).

——, *Intelligence Activities and the Rights of Americans* (Washington, 1976).

CONGRESS

An essential source for examining Congress on a year-to-year basis is the annual *Congressional Quarterly Almanac* (Washington, 1945–). It describes major bills and traces their evolution in both chambers. Important committee investigations are examined, and roll call votes, studies of voting patterns and committee membership lists are included.

For those not familiar with the work of Congress, Dennis W. Brezina and Allen Overmeyer, *Congress in Action* (New York, 1974) is recommended. This is a case study of the 1970 Environmental Education Act from its inception to implementation. A thought-provoking study is Gary Orfield's *Congressional Power: Congress and Social Change* (New York, 1975). He critically examines three theses: that Congress is fundamentally conservative; that the only solution to problems comes from the presidency; and that Congress opposes institutional reform. This final point is the subject of Robert H. Davidson and Walter J. Oleszek, *Congress Against Itself* (Bloomington, 1977). The authors were staff members working on the limited restructuring of the House in 1974. The staffs of congressmen, committees and even the General Accounting Office are reviewed favorably in *Congressional Staffs: The Invisible Force in America* (New York, 1977), by Harrison W. Fox and Susan W. Hammond.

Relationships between the President and Congress were often less than amicable. The White House tactics and strategies to gain influence with Congress are the subject of Abraham Holtzman, *Legislative Liaison: Executive Leadership in Congress* (Chicago, 1976). In a wide range of essays, including such topics as the budget, executive appointments, and the Black Caucus, Harvey C. Mansfield's, ed.,

Congress Against The President (New York, 1975) analyzes the philosophical and practical differences between the executive and legislative.

Other Works

Abzug, Bella S., *Bella! Ms. Abzug Goes to Washington* (New York, 1972).

Asbell, Bernard, *The Senate Nobody Knows* (Garden City, 1978).

Bailey, Stephen K., *Congress in the Seventies* (New York, 1970).

Beard, Edmund, and Stephen Horn, *Congressional Ethics: The View from the House* (Washington, 1975).

Blanchard, Robert O., comp., *Congress and the News Media* (New York, 1974).

Buckley, James L., *If Men Were Angels: A View from the Senate* (New York, 1975).

Clark, Peter K., "The Effect of Inflation on Federal Expenditures," United States Congressional Budget Office (June 18, 1976).

Clausen, Aage R., *How Congressmen Decide: A Policy Focus* (New York, 1973).

Congressional Quarterly Inc., *Guide To Congress* (Washington, 1976).

——, *Inside Congress*, (Washington, 1976).

——, *Powers of Congress* (Washington, 1976).

Frye, Alton, *A Responsible Congress: The Politics of National Security* (New York, 1975).

Green, Mark J., et al., *Who Runs Congress?* (New York, 1972).

Griffith, Ernest S., and Francis R. Valeo, *Congress, Its Contemporary Role* (New York, 1975).

Harris, Joseph P., *Congress and the Legislative Process* (New York, 1972).

Jones, Charles O., *The Minority Party in Congress* (Boston, 1970).

Jordan, Barbara, *Barbara Jordan: A Self-Portrait* (Garden City, 1979).

MacCann, Richard Dyer, "Televising Congress," *American Scholar* (Summer, 1976).

McGovern, George S., *Grassroots* (New York, 1977).

Mann, Kenneth Eugene, "John Roy Lynch; U.S. Congressman From Mississippi," *Negro Historical Bulletin* (April/May, 1974).

Matsunaga, Spark, and Yung Chen, *Rulemakers of the House* (Urbana, 1976).

Matthews, Donald R., and James A. Stimson, *Yeas and Nays: Normal Decision-Making in the U.S. House of Representatives* (New York, 1975).

Mayhew, David R., *Congress: The Electoral Connection* (New Haven, 1974).

Ogul, Morris S., *Congress Oversees the Bureaucracy: Studies in Legislative Supervision* (Pittsburgh, 1976).

Ornstein, Norman J., *Congress in Change: Evolution and Reform* (New York, 1975).

Polsky, Nelson W., *Congress and the Presidency* (Englewood Cliffs, 1971).

Ralph Nader Congress Project, *The Commerce Committees*, David E. Price, director (New York, 1975).

——, *The Environment Committees* (New York, 1975).

——, *The Judiciary Committees*, Peter H. Schuck, director (New York, 1975).

——, *The Money Committees*, Lester M. Salamon, director (New York, 1975).

——, *The Revenue Committees*, Richard Spohn and Charles McCollum, directors (New York, 1975).

——, *Ruling Congress: A Study of How the House and Senate Rules Govern the Legislative Process*, Ted Siff and Alan Weil, directors (New York, 1975).

Rapoport, Daniel, *Inside the House: An Irreverent Guided Tour Through the House Of Representatives, From the Days of Adam Clayton Powell to Those of Peter Rodino* (Chicago, 1975).

Rhodes, John J., *The Futile System: How to Unchain Congress and Make the System Work Again* (McLean, 1976).

Riegle, Donald, *O Congress* (Garden City, 1972).

Rieselbach, Leroy N., *Congressional Politics* (New York, 1973).

——, *Congressional Reform in the Seventies* (Morristown, 1977).

Ripley, Randall B., *Congress: Process and Policy* (New York, 1975).

Schneider, Jerrold E., *Ideological Coalitions in Congress* (Westport, 1979).

Shapiro, David L., "Mr. Justice Rehnquist: A Preliminary View," *Harvard Law Journal* (December, 1976).

Shepsle, Kenneth A., *The Giant Jigsaw Puzzle: Democratic Committee Assignments in the Modern House* (Chicago, 1978).

Uslaner, Eric M., *Congressional Committee Assignments: Alternative Models for Behavior* (Beverly Hills, 1974).

Vatz, Richard E., "The Defeats of Judges Haynsworth and Carswell: Rejection of Supreme Court Nominees," *Quarterly Journal of Speech* (December, 1974).

Vogler, David J., *The Politics of Congress* (Boston, 1974).

STATE AND LOCAL GOVERNMENT

Of paramount concern to state and local governments from 1969 to 1976 were the problems associated with urban decay. The scope of these problems is covered by Alan K. Campbell and Roy W. Bahl, eds., in *State and Local Government: The Political Economy of Reform* (New York, 1976). The diverse demands of urban dwellers and the cities' inability to raise adequate revenue to meet those demands are the subject of two important works: William G. Coleman, *Cities, Suburbs and States: Governing and Financing Urban America* (New York, 1975); and Douglas Yates, *The Ungovernable City: The Problem of Urban Politics and Policy Making* (Cambridge, Mass., 1977).

Federal efforts to aid in the solution of urban problems are examined by Bernard Friedman and Marshall Kaplan in *The Politics of Neglect: Urban Aid from Model Cities to Revenue Sharing* (Cambridge, Mass., 1975). This study analyzes the efforts of Presidents Lyndon Johnson and Richard Nixon to aid the cities and finds that urban America saw little improvement under either Administration. Gary D. Brewer's *Politicians, Bureaucrats and the Consultant; A Critique of Urban Problem Solving* (New York, 1973) focuses on federal aid programs to San Francisco and Pittsburgh. Brewer concludes that the magnitude of urban problems was not fully appreciated by bureaucratic researchers and planners, thus reform efforts fell short of success. In contrast, Paul Terrell's *The Social Impact of Revenue Sharing* (New York, 1976) is more optimistic. This study of seven Pacific Coast areas points out that President Nixon's revenue-sharing program had positive local effects, due largely to increased citizen participation in government.

New York City's fiscal crisis evoked several pessimistic essays, including two in the 1976 journal *Society*: George Sternlieb and James W. Hughes, "New York: Future Without a Future?" and Wolfgang Quante,"Flight of the Corporate Headquarters." Both articles comment on New York's bleak economic future because of its eroding tax base and labor market.

Other Works

Allswang, John M., *Bosses, Machines and Urban Voters* (New York, 1977).

Bartley, Numan V., and Hugh D. Graham, *Southern Politics and the Second Reconstruction* (Baltimore, 1975).

Beramn, David R., *State and Local Politics* (Boston, 1975).

Berg, Larry, et al., *Corruption in the American Political System* (Morristown, 1976).

Bingham, Richard D., *Public Housing and Urban Renewal: An Analysis of Federal-Local Relations* (New York, 1975).

Bollens, John C., and Grant B. Geyer, *Yorty: Politics of a Constant Candidate* (Pacific Palisades, 1973).

Boyarsky, Bill, *Backroom Politics* (Los Angeles, 1974).

Buel, Ronald A., *Dead End: The Automobile in Mass Transportation* (Englewood Cliffs, 1972).

Bulton, James W., *Black Violence: Political Impact of the 1960's Riots* (Princeton,1978).

Callow, Alexander B., ed., *The City Boss in America: An Interpretive Reader* (New York, 1976).

Cash, Kevin, *Who the Hell is William Loeb?* (Manchester, 1975).

Connery, Robert H., and Gerald Benjamin, eds., *Governing New York State: The Rockefeller Years* (New York, 1974).

Conot, Robert, *American Odyssey* (New York, 1974).

Davidson, Chandler, *Biracial Politics: Conflict and Coalition in the Metropolitan South* (Baton Rouge, 1972).

Davies, Richard O., *The Age of Asphalt: The Automobile, the Freeway and the Condition of Metropolitan America* (Philadelphia, 1975).

Downes, Bryan T., *Politics, Change and the Urban Crisis* (North Scituate, Mass., 1976).

Dye, Thomas R., *Politics in States and Communities* (Englewood Cliffs, 1977).

Edsall, Thomas B., "Racetracks, Banks and Liquor Stores," *Washington Monthly* (October, 1974).

Eisinger, Peter K., *The Patterns of Interracial Politics: Conflict and Cooperation in the City* (New York, 1976).

Ershkowitz, Miriam, and Joseph Zikmund, II, *Black Politics in Philadelphia* (New York, 1973).

Gardiner, John A., *The Politics of Corruption; Organized Crime in an American City* (New York, 1970).

Gellhorn, Walter, "The Ombudsman's Relevance to American Municipal Affairs," *American Bar Association* (February, 1968).

Gray, Francine du Plessix, *Hawaii: The Sugar-Coated Fortress* (New York, 1972).

Harbert, Anita S., *Federal Grants-in-Aid: Maximizing Benefits to the States* (New York, 1976).

Havard, William C., ed., *Politics of the Contemporary South* (Baton Rouge, 1972).

Hawley, Willis D., *Blacks and Metropolitan Governance: The Stakes of Reform* (Berkeley, 1972).

Howard, Perry H., *Political Tendencies in Louisiana* (Baton Rouge, 1972).

Hutcheson, John D., Jr., and Jann Shevin, *Citizens Groups in Local Politics; A Bibliographic Review* (Santa Barbara, 1976).

Jones, Charles O., and Robert D. Thomas, eds., *Public Policy Making in a Federal System* (Beverly Hills, 1976).

Juster, F. Thomas, ed., *The Economic and Political Impact of General Revenue Sharing* (Ann Arbor, 1977).

Klein, Woody, *Lindsay's Promise: The Dream That Failed* (New York, 1970).

Kutz, Myer, *Rockefeller Power* (New York, 1974).

Lamb, Curt, *Political Power in Poor Neighborhoods* (Cambridge, Mass., 1975).

Levin, Melvin R., et al., *New Approaches to State Land Use Policies* (Lexington, 1974).

Liebert, Roland, J., *Disintegration and Political Action: The Changing Functions of City Government in America* (New York, 1976).

Lufkin, Dan W., *Many Sovereign States: A Case for Strengthening State Government* (New York, 1975).

Mirenghoff, William, *The Comprehensive Employment and Training Act: Impact on People, Places, Programs* (Washington, 1976).

Nathan, Richard P., et al., *Revenue Sharing: The Second Round* (Washington, 1977).

Parker, Thomas F., *Violence in the U.S.* (New York, 1974).

Petshek, Kirk R., *The Challenge of Urban Reform; Policies and Programs in Philadelphia* (Philadelphia, 1973).

Phelan, James, and Robert Pozen, *The Company State: Ralph Nader's Study Group Report On DuPont in Delaware* (New York, 1973).

Peirce, Neal R., *The Megastates of America* (New York, 1972).

——, *The Border South States* (New York, 1975).

——, *The Deep South States* (New York, 1974).

——, *The Great Plains States* (New York, 1973).

——, *The Mountain States* (New York, 1972).

——, *The Pacific States* (New York, 1974).

Putnam, Jackson, K., *Old-Age Politics in California: From Richardson to Reagan* (Stanford, 1970).

Ravitch, Diane, *The Great School Wars,*

New York City, 1805–1973: A History of the Public Schools as Battlefield of Social Change (New York, 1974).

Revesz, Etta, *Hate Don't Make No Noise: Anatomy of a New Ghetto* (New York, 1978).

Rosenthal, Alan, and John Blydenburgh, eds., *Politics in New Jersey* (New Brunswick, 1975).

Royko, Mike, *Boss: Richard J. Daley of Chicago* (New York, 1971).

Sacks, Seymour, *City Schools/Suburban Schools: A History of Fiscal Conflict* (Syracuse, 1972).

Shank, Alan, *Political Power and the Urban Crisis,* (Boston, 1976).

Steiner, Henry M., *Conflict in Urban Transportation: The People Against the Planners* (Lexington, 1978).

Sternlieb, George, "New York; Future Without a Future?" *Society* (May/June, 1976).

Widick, B.J., Jr., *Detroit: City of Race and Class Violence* (Chicago, 1972).

Wilkstrom, Gunnar, *Municipal Government Response to Urban Riots* (San Francisco, 1974).

Winter-Berger, Robert N., *The Washington Payoff* (New York, 1972).

THE SUPREME COURT

General studies of the Burger Court include Robert G. McCloskey, *The Modern Supreme Court* (Cambridge, Mass., 1972) and Archibald Cox, *The Role of the Supreme Court in American Government* (New York, 1976), which concentrates on recent Court trends in the area of liberty and equality. Since 1949 the *Harvard Law Review* has presented in every fall issue a discussion analysis of the work of the preceding Court term. *The Supreme Court Review* (Chicago, 1960-), ed. Philip B. Kurland, is an excellent annual publication containing articles on recent Court decisions and trends. Law reviews are often the best source of material on constitutional history, current legal issues and Supreme Court cases. The *Index to Legal Periodicals* allows easy location of articles on a particular topic. Stephen M. Millett, *A Selected Bibliography of American Constitutional History* (Santa Barbara, 1975) is a useful starting point for locating sources on constitutional law and history. Richard Y. Funston, *Constitutional Counterrevolution?* (New York, 1977) examines continuities and discontinuities between the Warren and Burger Courts. James F. Simon, *In His Own Image: The Supreme Court in Richard Nixon's America* (New York, 1973) is a balanced assessment of the Burger Court through the 1971–72 term. Philip B. Kurland analyzes the first three terms of the Burger Court in detail in articles in *The Supreme Court Review* for 1970, 1971 and 1972. Articles giving an overview and assessment of the Burger Court's work include William F. Swindler, "The Court, the Constitution and Chief Justice Burger," *Vanderbilt Law Review,* 27 (April, 1974), pp. 443–474; "The Burger Court: New Directions in Judicial Policy-Making," *Emory Law Journal,* 23 (Summer, 1974), pp. 643–779; "The Burger Court and the Constitution," *Columbia Journal of Law and Social Problems,* 11 (Fall 1974), pp. 35–71; and Henry J. Abraham, "Some Observations on the Burger Court's Record on Civil Rights and Liberties," *Notre Dame Lawyer,* 52 (October 1976), pp. 77–86 and A.E. Dick Howard, "From Warren to Burger: Activism and Restraint," *Wilson Quarterly* (Spring 1977), pp. 109–120. Raoul Berger, *Government by Judiciary* (Cambridge, Mass., 1977) looks at the Court's recent use of the 14th Amendment in various fields and discusses both Warren and Burger Court rulings.

Other Works

Abraham, Henry, J., *Freedom and the Court: Civil Rights and Liberties in the United States*, 3d ed. (New York, 1977).

Bell, Derrick A., Jr., *Race, Racism and American Law* (Boston, 1973).

Bosmajian, Haig A., ed., *Obscenity and Freedom of Expression* (New York, 1975).

——, *The Principles and Practice of Freedom of Speech* (Boston, 1971).

Casper, Jonathan D., *American Criminal Justice: The Defendant's Perspective* (Englewood Cliffs, 1972).

Clark, Leroy D., *The Grand Jury: The Use and Abuse of Political Power* (New York, 1975).

Dorsen, Norman, et al., *Political and Civil Rights in the United States*, 4th ed. (Boston, 1976).

Elliott, Ward E.Y., *The Rise of Guardian Democracy: The Supreme Court's Role in Voting Rights Disputes, 1845–1969* (Cambridge, Mass., 1974).

Fellman, David, *The Defendant's Rights Today* (Madison, 1976).

Galloway, John, ed., *The Supreme Court and the Rights of the Accused* (New York, 1973).

Kurland, Philip B., ed., *Free Speech and Association: The Supreme Court and the First Amendment* (Chicago, 1975).

Lawhorne, Clifton O., *Defamation and Public Officials: The Evolving Law of Libel* (Carbondale, Ill., 1971).

Lewis, Felice F., *Literature, Obscenity and Law* (Carbondale, Ill., 1976).

Levy, Leonard W., *Against the Law: The Nixon Court and Criminal Justice* (New York, 1974).

Liston, Robert A., *The Right to Know: Censorship in America* (New York, 1973).

Meltsner, Michael, *Cruel and Unusual: The Supreme Court and Capital Punishment* (New York, 1973).

Milner, Neil, *The Court and Local Law En-forcement: The Impact of Miranda* (Beverly Hills, 1971).

Morgan, Richard E., *The Supreme Court and Religion* (New York, 1972).

Paul, Arnold M., ed., *Black Americans and the Supreme Court Since Emancipation* (New York, 1972).

Paulsen, Monrad G., and Charles H. Whitebread, *Juvenile Law and Procedure* (Reno, 1974).

Pember, Don R., *Privacy and the Press: The Law, the Mass Media and the First Amendment* (Seattle, 1972).

Pennock, J. Roland, and John W. Chapman, eds., *Due Process* (New York, 1977).

Pfeffer, Leo, *Church, State and Freedom*, rev. ed. (Boston, 1967).

——, *God, Caesar and the Constitution: The Court as Referee of Church-State Confrontations* (Boston, 1975).

Pious, Richard M., ed., *Civil Rights and Liberties in the 1970s* (New York, 1973).

Regan, Richard J., *Private Conscience and Public Law: The American Experience* (New York, 1972).

Schauer, Frederick F., *The Law of Obscenity* (Washington, 1976).

Schmidt, Benno C., Jr., *Freedom of the Press vs. Public Access* (New York, 1976).

Smith, Elwyn A., *Religious Liberty in the United States* (Philadelphia, 1972).

Sorauf, Francis J., *The Wall of Separation: The Constitutional Politics of Church and State* (Princeton, 1976).

Stephens, Otis, *The Supreme Court and Confessions of Guilt* (Knoxville, 1973).

Sunderland, Lane V., *Obscenity: The Court, the Congress and the President's Commission* (Washington, 1974).

Twentieth Century Fund, Task Force on the Government and the Press, *Press Freedoms Under Pressure* (New York, 1972).

Ungar, Sanford J., *The Papers and the Papers: An Account of the Legal and Political Battle over the Pentagon Papers* (New York, 1972).

Wasby, Stephen L., ed., *Civil Liberties: Policy and Policy Making* (Lexington, 1976).

FOREIGN AFFAIRS

In the forefront of the Nixon/Ford Administraion were several global issues. Tad Szulc's *The Illusion of Peace: Foreign Policy in The Nixon Years* (New York, 1978) provides an excellent overview of the Richard Nixon-Henry Kissinger stewardship of U.S. foreign policy. A more critical analysis of the period can be found in George F. Kennan's *The Cloud of Danger* (Boston, 1977). Kennan charged that the U.S. had overcommitted itself and recommended a paring down, so as to more easily cope with important issues. In contrast, Henry Brandon in *The Retreat of American Power* (Garden City, 1973) praises the Nixon-Kissinger team for overseeing the rapid withdrawal of the United States from world domination. Secretary of State Henry Kissinger has been the subject of many writers. Marvin and Bernard Kalk, *Kissinger* (Boston, 1974) presents a favorable account of Kissinger's diplomatic efforts through 1973. A sympathetic intellectual evaluation of Kissinger's foreign policy philosophy can be found in John G. Stoessinger, *Henry Kissinger: The Anguish of Power* (New York, 1976). In his *Diplomacy For a Crowded World* (Boston, 1976), George Ball criticizes Kissinger's unilateral diplomacy, asserting that it was successful for gaining domestic political support but not in establishing lasting structures of world peace and American security.

An abundant amount of foreign policy literature focused on Asia. An excellent starting point is Peter Poole's *The United States and Indochina: From FDR To Nixon* (Hinsdale, Ill., 1973). Former Central Intelligence Agency official Robert G. Sutter describes the Chinese efforts to improve U.S. relations in his *China Watch: Toward Sino-American Reconciliation* (Baltimore, 1978). Sutter concludes that "realists" in both Peking and Washington finally won out in 1972, when both nations recognized the need to balance power. Of growing concern during the Nixon-Ford years were problems in the Middle East. Robert W. Stookey's *America and the Arab States: An Uneasy Encounter* (New York, 1975) stresses that U.S. economic health and security are linked directly to the volatile Arab states. The Arab-Israeli issue is placed into the larger context of Middle East policy by Bernard Reich in *Quest For Peace: United States-Israeli Relations and the Arab-Israeli Conflict* (New Brunswick, 1977).

General Works

Andrews, Craig Neal, *Foreign Policy and the New American Military* (Beverly Hills, 1974).

Aron, Raymond, *The Imperial Republic: The United States and the World, 1945–1973* (Englewood Cliffs, 1974).

Azyliowicz, Bard E. O'Neill, ed., *The Energy Crisis and U.S. Foreign Policy* (New York, 1975).

Barber, Stephen, *America In Retreat* (New York, 1970).

Blaufarb, Douglas S., *The Counterinsurgency Era: U.S. Doctrine and Performance, 1950 to the Present* (New York, 1977).

Buckley, William Frank, *Inveighing We Will Go* (New York, 1972).

Buncher, Judith F., ed., *Human Rights And American Diplomacy, 1975–1977* (New York, 1977).

Combs, Jerald A., comp., *Nationalist, Realist and Radical: Three Views of American Diplomacy* (New York, 1972).

Coolidge, Archibald Cary, *The United States as a World Power* (New York, 1971).

Coufoudakis, Van, "U.S. Foreign Policy and the Cyprus Question: An Interpretation," *Millennium* (Winter, 1976–77).

Edwards, David V., *Creating a New World Politics: From Conflict to Cooperation* (New York, 1973).

Falk, Richard A., *What's Wrong with Henry Kissinger's Foreign Policy* (Princeton, 1974).

Falk, Stanley L., ed., *The World in Ferment: Problem Areas for the United States* (Washington, 1970).

Falkowski, Lawrence S., *Presidents, Secretaries of State and Crises in U.S. Foreign Relations: A Model and Predictive Analysis* (Boulder, 1978).

Gilpin, Robert, *U.S. Power and the Multinational Corporation: The Political Economy of Foreign Direct Investment* (New York, 1975).

Graubard, Stephen, *Kissinger* (New York, 1973).

Gujiral, M.L., *U.S. Global Involvement: A Study of American Expansionism* (New Delhi, 1975).

Halloran, Richard, *Conflict and Compromise: The Dynamics of American Foreign Policy* (New York, 1973).

Hickman, Martin B., comp., *Problems of American Foreign Policy* (Beverly Hills, 1975).

Hoxie, Ralph Gordon, *Command Decision and the Presidency: A Study in National Security Policy and Organization* (New York, 1977).

Jones, Alan M., ed., *U.S. Foreign Policy in a Changing World: The Nixon Administration, 1969-1973* (New York, 1973).

Kaplan, Morton A., *Dissent and the State in Peace and War; An Essay on the Grounds of Public Morality* (New York, 1970).

Kintner, William Roscoe, and Richard B. Foster, eds., *National Strategy in a Decade of Change: An Emerging U.S. Policy* (Lexington, 1973).

Krasner, Stephen D., *Defending the National Interest: Raw Materials, Investments and U.S. Foreign Policy* (Princeton, 1978).

Landau, David, *Kissinger: The Uses of Power* (Boston, 1972).

Lehman, John F., *The Executive, Congress and Foreign Policy: Studies of the Nixon Administration* (New York, 1974).

Lesh, Donald R., ed., *A Nation Observed: Perspectives on America's World Role* (Washington, 1974).

Nixon, Richard, *United States Foreign Policy for the 1970's. A Report by President Richard Nixon to the Congress, February 25, 1971* (New York, 1971).

Osgood, Robert E., *Retreat from Empire? The First Nixon Administration* (Baltimore, 1973).

Owen, Henry, and Charles L. Schultze, *Setting National Priorities* (Washington, 1976).

Parenti, Michael, *The Anti-Communist Impulse* (New York, 1970).

Paul, Roland A., *American Military Commitments Abroad* (New Brunswick, 1973).

Perusse, Roland I., ed., *Contemporary Issues in Inter-American Relations* (San Juan, 1972).

Pusey, Merlo John, *The U.S.A. Astride The Globe* (Boston, 1971).

Roberts, Chalmers M., "Foreign Policy Under a Paralyzed Presidency," *Foreign Affairs* (July, 1974).

Rostow, Eugene V., *Peace in the Balance: The Future of American Foreign Policy* (New York, 1972).

Scheer, Robert, *America After Nixon; The Age of the Multinationals* (New York, 1974).

Schlafly, Phyllis, and Chester Ward, *Kissinger On The Couch* (New York, 1974).

Schneider, William, "Public Opinion: The Beginning of Ideology," *Foreign Policy* (Winter, 1974-75).

Schurmann, Herbert Franz, *The Role of Ideas in American Foreign Policy; A Conference Report* (Hanover, N.H., 1971).

Sorensen, Theodore C., "Watergate and American Foreign Policy," *World Today* (December, 1974).

Stegenga, James A., ed., *Toward A Wiser Colossus; Reviewing and Recasting United States Foreign Policy* (Lafayette, 1972).

Stern, Laurence, *The Wrong Horse: The Politics of Intervention and the Failure of American Diplomacy* (New York, 1977).

The Middle East

Alroy, Gil C., *The Kissinger Experience: American Policy in the Middle East* (New York, 1975).

Arakie, Margaret, *The Broken Sword of Justice: America, Israel and the Palestine Tragedy* (London, 1973).

Churba, Joseph, *The Politics of Defeat: America's Decline in the Middle East* (New York, 1977).

Drinan, Robert F., *Honor the Promise: America's Commitment to Israel* (Garden City, 1977).

Golan, Matti, *The Secret Conversations of Henry Kissinger: Step-By-Step Diplomacy in the Middle East* (New York, 1976).

Hakleh, Emile A., *Arab-American Relations in the Persian Gulf* (Washington, 1975).

Harris, George S., *Troubled Alliance; Turkish-American Problems in Historical Perspective, 1945–1971 (Washington, 1972).*

Klebanoff, Shoshana, *Middle East Oil and U.S. Foreign Policy, With Special Reference to the U.S. Energy Crisis* (New York, 1974).

Mangold, Peter, *Superpower Intervention in the Middle East* (New York, 1978).

Pranger, Robert J., *American Policy for Peace in the Middle East, 1969–1971: Problems of Principle, Maneuver and Time* (Washington, 1971).

Quandt, William B., *Decade of Decisions: American Policy Toward the Arab-Israeli Conflict, 1967–1976* (Berkeley, 1977).

Rostow, Eugene V., ed., *The Middle East: Critical Choices for the United States* (Boulder, 1976).

Safran, Nadav, *Israel, The Embattled Ally* (Cambridge, Mass., 1978).

Sheehan, Edward, *The Arabs, Israelis and Kissinger: A Secret History Of American Diplomacy In The Middle East* (New York, 1976).

"Step by Step in the Middle East," *Journal of Palestine Studies* (Spring/Summer, 1976).

Tucker, Robert W., "Israel and the United States: From Dependence to Nuclear Weapons?" *Commentary* (May, 1975).

Ullman, Richard H., "After Rabat: Middle East Risks and American Roles," *Foreign Affairs* (December, 1975).

Asia

Barnett, A. Doak, *China and the Major Powers in East Asia* (Washington, 1977).

———, *A New U.S. Policy Toward China* (Washington, 1971).

Brodine, Virginia, comp., *Open Secret: The Kissinger-Nixon Doctrine in Asia* (New York, 1972).

Bueler, William M., *U.S. China Policy and the Problem of Taiwan* (Boulder, 1971).

Chay, John, ed., *The Problems and Prospects of American-East Asian Relations* (Boulder, 1977).

Clough, Ralph N., *East Asia and U.S. Security* (Washington, 1975).

———, *Island China* (Cambridge, Mass., 1978).

Cohen, Jerome Alan, et al., *Taiwan and American Policy; The Dilemma in U.S.-China Relations* (New York, 1971).

Destler, I.M., *Managing an Alliance: The Politics of U.S.-Japanese Relations* (Washington, 1976).

Fairbanks, John K., *The United States and China* (Cambridge, Mass., 1971).

Fifield, Russell Hunt, *Americans in Southeast Asia: The Roots of Commitment* (New York, 1973).

Gelb, Leslie H., and Richard K. Betts, *The Irony of Vietnam: The System Worked* (Washington, 1979).

Goldstein, Martin E., *American Policy Toward Laos* (Rutherford, 1973).

Haendel, Dan, *The Process of Priority Formulation: U.S. Foreign Policy in the Indo-Pakistani War of 1971* (Boulder, 1977).

Harrison, Selig S., *The Widening Gulf: Asian Nationalism and American Policy* (New York, 1978).

Hinton, Harold C., *Three and a Half Powers: The New Balance In Asia* (Bloomington, Ind., 1975).

Hohenberg, John, *New Era in the Pacific: An Adventure in Public Diplomacy* (New York, 1972).

Hon, Eugene, *Nixon's Trip—The Road to China's Russian War* (San Francisco, 1972).

Johnson, Stuart E., *The Military Equation in Northeast Asia* (Washington, 1979).

Kalb, Marvin L., *Roots of Involvement: The U.S. in Asia, 1784–1971* (New York, 1971).

Kintner, William Roscoe, *The Impact of President Nixon's Visit to Peking on International Politics* (Philadelphia, 1972).

Kirk, Donald, *Wider War: The Struggle for Cambodia, Thailand and Laos* (New York, 1972).

Kubek, Anthony, *The Red China Papers: What Americans Deserve to Know About U.S.-China Relations* (New Rochelle, 1975).

Kunhi Krishnan, T.V., *The Unfriendly Friends, India and America* (Thompson, Conn., 1974).

MacFarquhar, Roderick, comp., *Sino-American Relations 1949-1971* (New York, 1972).

May, Ernest R., and James C. Thompson, Jr., *American-East Asian Relations: A Survey* (Cambridge, Mass., 1972).

Meyers, William, and M. Vincent Hayes, eds., *China Policy; New Priorities and Alternatives* (New York, 1972).

Moorsteen, Richard Harris, and Morton Abramovitz, *Remaking China Policy: U.S.-China Relations and Governmental Decision-making* (Cambridge, Mass., 1971).

Ravenel, Earl, ed., *Peace with China? U.S. Decisions for Asia* (New York, 1971).

Rosovsky, Henry, ed., *Discord in the Pacific: Challenges to the Japanese-American Alliance* (Washington, 1972).

Scalapinao, Robert A., *American-Japanese Relations in a Changing Era* (New York, 1972).

——, *Asia and the Road Ahead: Issues for the Major Powers* (Berkeley, 1975).

Selden, Mark, *Remaking Asia; Essays on the American Uses of Power* (New York, 1973).

Shawcross, William, *Sideshow: Kissinger, Nixon and the Destruction of Cambodia* (New York, 1979).

Sih, Paul K., ed., *Asia and Contemporary World Problems: A Symposium* (New York, 1972).

Sihanouk Varman, Norodom, *My War with the CIA: The Memoirs of Prince Norodom Sihanouk* (New York, 1973).

Simon, Sheldon W., *Asian Neutralism and U.S. Policy* (Washington, 1975).

Sullivan, Marianna P., *France's Vietnam Policy: A Study in French-American Relations* (Westport, Conn., 1978).

Van der Linden, Frank, *Nixon's Quest for Peace* (Washington, 1972).

Yung-hwan, Jo, ed., *U.S. Foreign Policy in Asia: An Appraisal* (Santa Barbara, 1978).

The Western Hemisphere

Black, Jan Knippers, *United States Penetration of Brazil* (Philadelphia, 1977).

Fox, Annette B., et al., *Canada and the United States: Transnational and Transgovernmental Relations* (New York, 1976).

Kaufman, Edy, *The Superpowers and Their Spheres of Influence: The United States and the Soviet Union in Eastern Europe and Latin America* (New York, 1977).

MacEoin, Gary, *No Peaceful Way: Chile's Struggle for Dignity* (New York, 1974).

Martin, John Bartlow, *U.S. Policy in the Caribbean* (Boulder, 1978).

Petras, James F., *The United States and Chile: Imperialism and the Overthrow of the Allende Government* (New York, 1975).

Uribe Arce, Armando, *The Black Book of American Intervention in Chile* (Boston, 1975).

Europe and the Soviet Union

Barnet, Richard J., *The Giants: Russia and America* (New York, 1977).

Beam, Jacob, *Multiple Exposure: An American Ambassador's Unique Perspective on East-West Issues* (New York, 1978).

Bell, Coral, *The Diplomacy of Detente: The Kissinger Era* (New York, 1977).

Calleo, David, P., *The Atlantic Fantasy: The U.S., Nato and Europe* (Baltimore, 1970).

Catlin, George Edward Gordon, Sir, *Kissinger's Atlantic Charter* (Gerrards Cross, Britain, 1974).

Donovan, John, ed., *U.S. and Soviet Policy in the Middle East* (New York, 1972).

Griffith, William E., *Peking, Moscow and Beyond: The Sino-Soviet-American Triangle* (Washington, 1973).

Kaiser, Karl, *Europe and the United States: The Future of the Relationship* (Washington, 1973).

Mally, Gerhard, *Interdependence: The European-American Connection in the Global Context* (Lexington, 1976).

Mazlish, Bruce, *Kissinger: The European Mind in American Policy* (New York, 1976).

Newhouse, John, *DeGaulle and the Anglo-Saxons* (New York, 1970).

Pfaltzgraff, Robert L., Jr., "The United States and Europe; Partners in a Multipolar World?" *Orbis* (Spring, 1973).

Pittman, John, "Detente-Main Stake in the

Struggle," *World Marxist Review* (October, 1974).

Sakharov, Andrei Dimitrievich, *My Country and the World* (New York, 1975).

Sheldon, Della W., ed., *Dimensions of Detente* (New York, 1978).

Sobel, Lester A., ed., *Kissinger and Detente* (New York, 1975).

Stessinger, John George, *Nation in Darkness—China, Russia and America* (New York, 1975).

Strauss, David, *Menace in the West: The Rise of French Anti-Americanism in Modern Times* (Westport, 1978).

Africa

Arkhurst, Frederick S., ed., *U.S. Policy Toward Africa* (New York, 1975).

Packenham, Robert A., *Liberal America and the Third World: Political Development Ideas in Foreign Aid and Social Science* (Princeton, 1973).

U.S. National Security Council, Interdepartmental Group for Africa, *The Kissinger Study of Southern Africa: National Security Study Memorandum 39 (Secret)* (Westport, 1976).

DEFENSE

The problem of resolving defense needs with detente was the major focus of policy formulation in the Nixon/Ford years. Detente meant an easing of tensions between Moscow and Washington, but critics were fearful that the United States was giving away too much and that the Soviets would gain an advantage. A monograph, directed to the general public, that discusses the issue in global terms is Drew Middleton's *Retreat From Victory* (New York, 1973). A pessimistic theme is pursued by Rudolph J. Rummel in *Peace Endangered: The Reality of Detente* (Beverly Hills, 1976). The questions of adjusting defense options to foreign policy is assessed by Morton H. Halperin, *Defense Strategies for the Seventies* (Boston, 1971).

Alarmed by the magnitude of global weapons expenditure, Henry Kissinger calls for clearly defined doctrines and a new international order to deal with the problem in the second edition of his *Nuclear Weapons and Foreign Policy* (New York, 1969). Adding credence to Kissinger's claim is *World Military Expenditures and Arms Control Transfers 1967–1976* (Washington, 1978), issued by the United States Arms Control and Disarmament Agency. The volume is an invaluable source of statistical data, revealing the amount of money spent by each nation on its military establishment. An excellent analysis of American and Soviet capabilities is Edward Luttwack's *The U.S.-U.S.S.R. Nuclear Weapons Balance* (Beverly Hills, 1974). Despite rhetoric to the contrary, the Senate had little influence on the Strategic Arms Limitation Talks (SALT), according to Alan Platt, *The U.S. Senate and Strategic Arms Policy 1969–1977* (Boulder, Colo., 1978).

The frustration of Vietnam contributed, in part, to the end of the draft and the creation of an all-volunteer army. Two excellent studies of the topic are: Jerald C. Bachman, et al., *The All Volunteer Force: A Study of Ideology in the Military* (Ann Arbor, 1977); and Harry A. Marion, *A Case Against a Volunteer Army* (New York, 1971).

Other Works

Andrews, Craig N., *Foreign Policy and the New American Military* (Beverly Hills, 1974).

Beard, Edmund, *Developing the ICBM: A Study in Bureaucratic Politics* (New York, 1976).

Betts, Richard K., *Soldiers, Statesmen and Cold War Crises* (Cambridge, Mass., 1977).

Bezboruah, Monorajan, *U.S. Strategy in the Indian Ocean: The International Response* (New York, 1977).

Binkin, Martin, *Support Costs in the Defense Budget: The Submerged One-Third* (Washington, 1972).

Blechman, Barry M., et al., *The Soviet Mili-*

tary Buildup and U.S. Defense Spending (Washington, 1977).

Bletz, Donald F., The Role of the Military Professional in U.S. Foreign Policy (New York, 1972).

Bottome, Edgar M., The Missile Gap (Rutherford, 1971).

Boyle, Richard, The Flower of the Dragon: The Breakdown of the U.S. Army in Vietnam (San Francisco, 1972).

Carson, Williams R., Consequences of Failure (New York, 1974).

Chase, John D., "U.S. Merchant Marine— For Commerce and Defense," U.S. Naval Institute Proceedings (May, 1976).

Clemens, Walter C., The Superpowers and Arms Control: From Cold War to Interdependence (Lexington, 1973).

Clough, Ralph N., et al., The United States, China and Arms Control (Washington, 1975).

Coffey, Joseph I., Strategic Power and National Security (Pittsburgh, 1971).

Congressional Quarterly Staff, U.S. Defense Policy: A Study of Conflict and the Policy Process (Boston, 1977).

Cox, Arthur M., The Dynamics of Detente: How to End the Arms Race (New York, 1976).

Dvorin, Eugene P., ed., The Senate's War Powers: Debate on Cambodia from the Congressional Record (Chicago, 1971).

Endicott, John E., and Roy W. Stafford, American Defense Policy (Baltimore, 1977).

Farley, Philip, Arms Across the Sea (Washington, 1978).

Fitzgerald, Frances, Fire in the Lake: The Vietnamese and the Americans in Vietnam (Boston, 1972).

Fox, T. Ronald, Arming America: How the U.S. Buys Weapons (Cambridge, Mass., 1974).

Gerhardt, James M., The Draft and Public Policy (Columbus, 1971).

Goode, Stephen, The National Defense System (New York, 1972).

Goodpaster, Andrew J., For the Common Defense (Lexington, 1977).

Greenbacker, John E., "Where Do We Go From Here?" U.S. Naval Institute Proceedings (June, 1976).

Greenwood, John, et al., American Defense

Policy Since 1945: A Preliminary Bibliography (Lawrence, Va., 1973).

Habib, Philip C., "Department of State] Urges Congressional Approval of Agreement with Turkey in Defense Cooperation," Department of State Bulletin (October, 1976).

Holst, T. T., and W. Schneider, eds., Why ABM? Policy Issues in the Missile Defense Controversy (Elmsford, N.Y., 1965).

Johnson, David T., and Barry R. Schneider, Current Issues in U.S. Defense Policy (New York, 1976).

Kaplan, Morton A., ed., Isolation or Interdependence? Today's Choices for Tomorrow's World (New York, 1975).

Keeley, John B., The All-Volunteer Force and American Society (Charlottesville, Va., 1978).

Lambeth, Benjamin, Selective Nuclear Options in American and Soviet Strategic Policy (Santa Monica, 1976).

Lansdale, Edward G., In the Midst of Wars: An American's Mission to Southeast Asia (New York, 1972).

Lens, Sidney, The Day Before Doomsday (New York, 1977).

Liska, George, Quest for Equilibrium: America and the Balance of Power on Land and Sea (Baltimore, 1977).

Littauer, Raphael, and Norman Uphoff, eds., The Air War in Indochina (Boston, 1972).

Long, Franklin A., et al., Arms, Defense Policy and Arms Control (New York, 1976).

Luttwak, Edward N., "The Defense Budget and Israel:" Commentary (February, 1975).

Marmion, Harry A., A Case Against a Volunteer Army (New York, 1971).

Martin, Lawrence, ed., The Management of Defense (New York, 1976).

Myrdal, Alva, The Game of Disarmament: How the United States and Russia Run the Arms Race (New York, 1977).

Nathan, James A., and James K. Oliver, "Public Opinion and U.S. Security Policy," Armed Forces and Society (January, 1975).

Owen, David, The Politics of Defense (New York, 1972).

Palmer, Bruce, Jr., and Tarr Curtis, "A

Careful Look at Defense Manpower," *Military Review* (September, 1976).

Philips, David Morris, "Foreign Investment in the United States: the Defense Industry," *Boston University Law Review* (November, 1976).

Quanbeck, Alton H., and Barry M. Blechman, *Strategic Forces: Issues for the Mid-Seventies* (Washington, 1973).

Reeves, Thomas, and Karl Hess, *The End of the Draft* (New York, 1970).

Russett, Bruce M., *What Price Vigilance: The Burden of National Defense* (New Haven, 1970).

Schlesinger, James R., "A Testing Time for America," *Atlantic Community Quarterly* (Spring, 1976).

Smith, Clyde A., "Constraints of Naval Geography on Soviet Naval Power," *Naval War College Review* (February, 1974).

"U.S. Defense Policy and the B-1 Bomber Controversy: Pros and Cons," *Congressional Digest* (December, 1976).

Useem, Michael, *Conscription, Protest and Social Conflict* (New York, 1973).

Weidenbaum, Murray L., *The Economics of Peacetime Defense* (New York, 1974).

Business, Labor and Economic Policy

An excessive rate of inflation played havoc with the U.S. economy through the mid-1970s. The Nixon/Ford Administration chose to deal with the problem in traditional conservative fashion, except for Nixon's efforts at controls in the early 1970s. Critics spoke of "Nixonomics": recession and inflation. In his *Nixonomics: How the Dismal Science of Free Enterprise Became the Bleak Art of Controls* (New York, 1972), Leonard S. Silk explores Nixon's basic economic conservatism, analyzing the factors, including the desire for reelection, that resulted in the President's intervention in the economy. The economic problems of the 1970s are traced to the Vietnam war by Robert W. Stevens in *Vain Hopes, Grim Realities: The Economic Consequences of the Vietnam War* (New York, 1976). Stevens argued that both Presidents Johnson and Nixon made errors in economic planning because of the war. The Vietnam war ruined chances for a full-employment cycle and a successful campaign against poverty and left a devalued dollar and a large future expenditure commitment. Whatever the cause of inflation, it remained the central problem from which all others—unemployment, recession and a confused international monetary situation—arose, according to conservative economist Ezra Solomon, *The Anxious Economy* (San Francisco, 1975). On the other hand Keynesian economist Walter Heller, *The Economy: Old Myths and New Realities* (New York, 1976) concludes that contemporary economic problems were the result of traditional Republican Party policy aggravated by OPEC decisions to increase crude oil prices.

Other Works

Abel, I. W., *Labor's Role in Building a Better Society* (Austin, 1972).

Albin, Peter S., *Progress Without Poverty: Socially Responsible Economic Growth* (New York, 1978).

Bach, George L., *Making Monetary and Fiscal Policy* (Washington, 1971).

Backman, Jules, *Business Problems of the Seventies* (New York, 1973).

Bauer, Raymond A., et al., *American Business and Public Policy: The Politics of Foreign Trade* (Chicago, 1972).

Bergsten, C. Fred, *Toward a New International Economic Order: Selected Papers of C. Fred Bergsten, 1971–1974* (Lexington, 1975).

Berman, Peter I., *Inflation and the Money Supply in the United States, 1956–1977* (Lexington, 1978).

Boulding, Kenneth, et al., *From Abundance to Scarcity: Implication for the American Tradition* (Columbus, 1978).

Brandis, Royall, comp., *Current Economic Problems: A Book of Readings* (Homewood, Ill., 1972).

Brenner, Philip, comp., *Exploring Contra-*

dictions; *Political Economy in the Corporate State* (New York, 1974).

Brookstone, Jeffrey M., *The Multinational Businessman and Foreign Policy: Entrepreneural Politics in East-West Trade and Investment* (New York, 1976).

Cagan, Phillip, and Robert E. Tipsey, *The Financial Effects of Inflation* (Cambridge, Mass., 1978).

Carson, Robert B., *Government in the American Economy; Conventional and Radical Studies on the Growth of State Economic Power* (Lexington, 1973).

Congressional Quarterly Staff, *The U.S. Economy: Challenges in the '70's* (Washington, 1972).

Dahlberg, Arthur Olaus, *How to Save Free Enterprise* (Old Greenwich, 1974).

Diebold, William, *The United States and the Industrial World; American Foreign Economic Policy in the 1970's* *(New York, 1972).*

Eckstein, Otto, *Parameters and Policies in the U.S. Economy* (New York, 1975).

Eyestone, Robert, *Political Economy: Politics and Policy Analysis* (Chicago, 1972).

Fatemi, Nasrollah S., ed., *Problems of Balance of Payment and Trade* (Rutherford, 1974).

Fellner, William J., et al., *Correcting Taxes for Inflation* (Washington, 1975).

Friedman, Milton, *There's No Such Thing As A Free Lunch* (La Salle, 1975).

Galbraith, John Kenneth, *Economics and the Public Purpose* (Boston, 1973).

——,*The New Industrial State* (Boston, 1978).

Goldman, Marshall I., *Detente and Dollars: Doing Business with the Soviets* (New York, 1975).

Graham, Otis L., *Toward a Planned Society: From Roosevelt to Nixon* (New York, 1976).

Harrington, Michael, *The Twilight of Capitalism* (New York, 1976).

Harris, Fred R., *The New Populism* (New York, 1973).

Jensen, Ralph, *Let Me Say This About That; A Primer on Nixonomics* (New York, 1972).

Keyserling, Leon H., *Full Employment Without Inflation* (Washington, 1975).

Lanzillotti, Robert F., et al., *Phase II in Re-

view: The Price Commission Experience* (Washington, 1975).

LaVelle, Michael, *Red, White and Blue-Collar Views: A Steelworker Speaks His Mind About America* (New York, 1975).

Leasure, J. William, *Prices, Profit and Production: How Much Is Enough?* (Albuquerque, 1974).

Leng, Shao-chuan, ed., *Post-Mao China and U.S.-China Trade* (Charlottesville, 1977).

Levison, Andrew, *The Working Class Majority* (New York, 1974).

Levitan, Sari, and Robert Taggart, *The Promise of Greatness* (Cambridge, Mass., 1976).

Levy, Harold, "Civil Rights in Employment and the Multinational Corporations," *Cornell International Law Journal* (December, 1976).

Mayer, Joseph, "Inflation Fancies Versus Facts," *Social Science* (December, 1973).

Meany, George, "Common Sense in Labor Law," *Labor Law Journal* (October, 1976).

Miller, Roger LeRoy, and Raburn M. Williams, *The New Economics of Richard Nixon: Freezes, Floats and Fiscal Policy* (New York, 1972).

Morrison, Rodney J., *Expectations and Inflation: Nixon, Politics and Economics* (Lexington, 1973).

Moynihan, Daniel P., et al., *Business and Society in Change* (New York, 1975).

National Urban Coalition, *Counterbudget: A Blueprint for Changing National Priorities 1971–1976* (New York, 1971).

Nixon, Richard Milhous, *Setting The Course, The First Years* (New York, 1970).

Nothstein, Gary Z., and Jeffrey P. Ayers, "The Multinational Corporation and the Extraterritorial Application of the Labor Management Relations Act," *Cornell International Law Journal* (December, 1976).

Parker, James E., "Inflation's Impact on Corporate Tax Rates," *Taxes* (September, 1976).

Pohlman, Jerry. E., *Inflation Under Control?* (Reston, Va., 1976).

Popkin, Joel, ed., *Analysis of Inflation: 1965–1974* (Cambridge, Mass., 1977).

Reynolds, Floyd G., comp., *Current Issues*

of Economic Policy (Homewood, Ill., 1973).

Rostow, Walt W., Getting from Here to There (New York, 1978).

Scheer, Robert, America After Nixon; The Age of the Multinationals (New York, 1974).

Schultze, Charles L., "Inflation and Unemployment: the Dilemma of the Humphrey-Hawkins Jobs Bill," Wage-Price Law and Economic Review (January, 1976).

Sichel, Werner, ed., Economic Advice and Executive Policy: Recommendations from Past Members of the Council of Economic Advisers (New York, 1977).

Simon, William E., A Time for Truth (New York, 1978).

Smith, Allen W., Understanding Inflation and Unemployment (Chicago, 1976).

Sommers, Albert T., Answers to Inflation and Recession: Economic Policies for a Modern Society (New York, 1975).

——,The Widening Cycle: An Examination of U.S. Experience with Stabilization Policy in the Last Decade (New York, 1975).

Twight, Charlotte, America's Emerging Fascist Economy (New Rochelle, 1975).

Weidenbaum, Murray L., The Economics of Peacetime Defense (New York, 1974).

——,Government-Mandated Price Increases: A Neglected Aspect of Inflation (Washington, 1975).

Woodruff, William, America's Impact on the World: A Study of the Role of the United States in the World Economy, 1750–1970 (New York, 1975).

Young, John Parke, An American Alternative: Steps Toward a More Workable and Equitable Economy (Los Angeles, 1976).

SOCIAL DISSENT, CIVIL RIGHTS AND THE WOMEN'S MOVEMENT

Student protest marked the late 1960s and early 1970s. The protests ranged from anti-war discontent to demands for continued civil rights progress and attacks upon the corporate state. Excellent surveys of the protest movement include Irwin Unger, The Movement: A History of the American New Left 1959–1972 (New York, 1974) and James L. Wood, Political Consciousness and Student Activism (Beverly Hills, 1974). Charles A. Reich's The Greening of America (New York, 1970) describes the student revolution as an effort to overcome the dominance of the corporate state and make the nation more livable. A valuable study of the draft defectors from their initial resistance to their life in Canada is Roger N. Williams, The New Exiles; American War Resisters in Canada (New York, 1971).

In the areas of civil rights and federal aid to the poor, the Nixon/Ford Administration did not receive high marks. Lawrence N. Bailis in Bread or Justice (Lexington, 1974) traces the development of welfare rights groups since the 1960s. A more recent study is Francis Piven and Richard A. Cloward, Poor People's Movement: Studies from the Contemporary United States (New York, 1977). Peter H. Ross et al., The Roots of Urban Discontent (New York, 1974) provides an analysis of the reasons why ghetto dwellers continued to mistrust politicians and municipal institutions.

Black inequality was still an area of discontent in 1976. An attack upon Nixon's first years in the White House is Leon E. Panetta and Peter Gall, Bring Us Together: The Nixon Team and the Civil Rights Retreat (Philadelphia, 1971). Less militant but pessimistic is Charles S. Bullock and Harrell R. Rodgers, Racial Equality in America (Pacific Palisades, 1975). Bayard Rustin's Strategies for Freedom: The Changing Patterns of Black Protest (New York, 1976) noted that much had been done regarding social inequities and recommended that future efforts be directed towards economic gains.

Women's rights emerged as a formidable movement during the time period. A comprehensive survey emphasizing the recent period is Barbara S. Deckard's *The Women's Movement: Political, Socio-Economic and Psychological Issues* (New York, 1975). The range of women's views on their quest for equality can be found in Leslie Tanner's, ed., *Voices from Women's Liberation* (New York, 1971). The difficulties of overcoming the social and psychological impact of the past is the central theme of Gayle G. Yates' *What Women Want: The Ideas of the Movement* (Cambridge, Mass., 1975).

Social Dissent

Adams, Elsie B., and Mary L. Briscoe, *Up Against the Wall, Mother* (Beverly Hills, 1971).

Adams, Michael Vannoy, "From Texas to Sussex: An Odyssey of Campus Protest," *Encounter* (January, 1975).

Altbach, Philip G., *Student Politics in America: A Historical Analysis* (New York, 1973).

Arendt, Hannah, *Crises of the Republic; Lying in Politics, Civil Disobedience, on Violence, Thoughts on Politics, and Revolution* (New York, 1972).

Bacciocco, Edward J., *The New Left in America: Reform to Revolution, 1956 to 1970* (Stanford, 1974).

Bannan, John F., and Rosemary S. *Law, Morality and Vietnam: The Peace Militants and the Courts* (Bloomington, 1974).

Berrigan, Daniel, *The Dark Night Resistance* (Garden City, 1971).

Bingham, Jonathan B. and Alfred M., *Violence and Democracy* (New York, 1970).

Bowers, John W., and Donovan J. Ochs, *The Rhetoric of Agitation and Control* (Reading, Mass., 1971).

Cantor, Milton, *The Divided Left: American Radicalism, 1900–1975* (New York, 1978).

Chomsky, Noam, *For Reasons of State* (New York, 1973).

Christy, Jim, *The New Refugees: American Voices in Canada* (Toronto, 1972).

Cohane, John P., *White Papers of an Outraged Conservative* (Indianapolis, 1972).

Cutler, Richard L., *The Liberal Middle Class: Maker of Radicals* (New Rochelle, 1973).

Decter, Midge, *Liberal Parents, Radical Children* (New York, 1975).

Dellinger, David T., *More Power Than We Know: The People's Movement Toward Democracy* (New York, 1975).

Dolbeare, Kenneth M. and Patricia, *American Ideologies: The Competing Political Beliefs of the 1970's* (Chicago, 1971).

Emerick, Kenneth Fred, *War Resisters Canada* (Knox, Pa., 1972).

Erskine, Hazel, "Civil Liberties and the American Public," *Journal of Social Issues* (Spring, 1975).

Evans, Mark, *Will the Real Young America Please Stand Up? The Until Now Silent, Youthful Majority's Call for a Return to the Traditional Principles That Made This Country Great* (Harrisburg, 1973).

Flacks, Richard, *Youth and Social Change* (Chicago, 1971).

Gerzon, Mark, *The Whole World is Watching: A Young Man Looks at Youth's Dissent* (New York, 1969).

Gore, Albert, *The Eye of the Storm; A People's Politics of the Seventies* (New York, 1970).

Graubard, Mark A., *Campustown in the Throes of the Counterculture (1968-1972)* (Minneapolis, 1974).

Hatfield, Mark O., et al., *Amnesty? The Unsettled Question of Vietnam* (Croton-on-Hudson, 1973).

Heath, G. Louis, ed., *Mutiny Does Not Happen Lightly: The Literature of the American Resistance* (Metuchen, 1976).

——, *Vandals in the Bomb Factory: The History and Literature of the Students for a Democratic Society* (Metuchen, 1976).

Hendel, Samuel, comp., *The Politics of Confrontation* (New York, 1971).

Horowitz, Irving Louis, *The Struggle is the Message: The Organization and Ideology of the Anti-War Movement* (Berkeley, 1970).

Jacquency, Mona G., *Radicalism on Campus: 1969-1971; Backlash in Law Enforcement and in the Universities* (New York, 1972).

Kasinsky, Renee G., *Refugees from Militarism: Draft-Age Americans in Canada*
(New Brunswick, 1976).

Keniston, Kenneth, *Youth and Dissent; The
Rise of the New Opposition* (New York,
1971).

Killmer, Richard L., et al., *They Can't Go
Home Again: The Story of America's Political Refugees* (Philadelphia, 1971).

Kruger, Marlis, and Frieda Silvert, *Dissent
Denied: The Technocratic Response to
Protest* (New York, 1975).

Lipset, Seymour Martin, *Rebellion in the
University* (Boston, 1971).

Murphy, Jeeire G., comp., *Civil Disobedience and Violence* (Belmont, Calif.,
1971).

Ramparts Magazine Editors, *Divided We
Stand* (San Francisco, 1970).

Reitman, Alan, *The Pulse of Freedom;
American Liberties: 1920-1970's* (New
York, 1975).

Rice, Donald F., comp., *The Agitator: A
Collection of Diverse Opinions from
America's Not-So-Popular Press* (Chica-
go, 1972).

Rinzler, Alan, ed., *Manifesto Addressed to
the President of the United States from
the Youth of America* (New York, 1970).

Sale, Kirkpatrick, *SDS* (New York, 1973).

Salisbury, Harrison E., comp., *The Indig-
nant Years: Art and Articles from the
Op-Ed Page of the New York Times*
(New York, 1973).

Samberg, Paul, ed., *Fire! Reports from the
Underground Press* (New York, 1970).

Stiehm, Judith, *Nonviolent Power: Active
and Passive Resistance in America* (Lexington, 1972).

Taylor, Clyde, comp., *Vietnam and Black
America: An Anthology of Protest and
Resistance* (Garden City, 1973).

Useem, Michael, *Protest Movements in
America* (Indianapolis, 1975).

Civil Rights

Bardolph, Richard, *The Civil Rights Record:
Black Americans and the Law, 1849-1970*
(New York, 1970).

Bender, Paul, "The Reluctant Court," *Civil
Liberties Review* (June/July, 1975).

Bickel, Alexander M., *The Supreme Court

and the Idea of Progress* (New York,
1970).

Billington, Monroe Lee, *The Political South
in the Twentieth Century* (New York,
1975).

Black, Earl, *Southern Governors and Civil
Rights* (Cambridge, Mass., 1976).

Bond, Julian, *A Time to Speak, A Time to
Act* (New York, 1972).

Brooks, Thomas R., *Walls Come Tumbling
Down: A History of the Civil Rights
Movement, 1940-1970* (Englewood Cliffs,
1974).

Button, James W., *Black Violence: Political
Impact of the 1960's Riots* (Princeton,
1978).

Commission on Civil Rights, "Twenty Years
After Brown: Equal Opportunity in Housing," (Washington, 1975).

Davis, Angela Yvonne, *Angela Davis: An
Autobiography* (New York, 1974).

Draper, Theodore, *The Rediscovery of Black
Nationalism* (New York, 1970).

Fogelson, Robert M., *Violence as Protest: A
Study of Riots and Ghettos* (Garden City,
1971).

Forman, James, *The Making of Black Revolutionaries* (New York, 1972).

Franklin, John Hope, *Racial Equality in
America* (Chicago, 1976).

Gregory, Dick, *Up From Nigger* (New York,
1976).

Jackson, George, *Blood in My Eye* (New
York, 1972).

Jackson, Larry R., and William A. Johnson,
*Protest by the Poor: The Welfare Rights
Movement in New York City* (Lexington,
1974).

Katz, Nick, and Mary Lynn, *A Passion for
Equality: George A. Wiley and the
Movement* (New York, 1977).

Killian, Lewis M., *The Impossible Revolution, Phase II: Black Power and the
American Dream* (New York, 1975).

Kousser, J. Morgan, *The Shaping of Southern Politics* (New Haven, 1974).

Newton, Huey P., *Revolutionary Suicide*
(New York, 1973).

Parris, Guichard, and Lester Brooks, *Blacks
in the City: A History of the National
Urban League* (Boston, 1971).

Roberts, Sylvia, "Equality of Opportunity in
Higher Education: Impact of Contract

Compliance and the Equal Rights Amendment," *Liberal Education* (Spring, 1973).

Rustin, Bayard, *Down the Line* (New York, 1971).

Seale, Bobby, *A Lonely Rage: The Autobiography of Bobby Seale* (New York, 1978).

Wolk, Allan, *The Presidency and Black Civil Rights: Eisenhower to Nixon* (Rutherford, 1971).

The Women's Movement

Altbach, Edith H., comp., *From Feminism to Liberation* (Cambridge, Mass., 1971).

Amundsen, Kirsten, *The Silenced Majority: Women and American Democracy* (Englewood Cliffs, 1971).

Andreas, Carol, *Sex and Caste in America* (Englewood Cliffs, 1971).

Babcox, Deborah, and Madeline Belkin, *Liberation Now!* (New York, 1971).

Blahna, Loretta J., *The Rhetoric of the Equal Rights Amendments* (Lawrence, 1973).

Brady, David W., and Kent L. Tedin, "Ladies in Pink: Religion and Political Ideology in the Anti-ERA Movement," *Social Science Quarterly* (March, 1976).

Brown, Barbara A., et al., *Women's Rights and the Law: The Impact of ERA on State Laws* (New York, 1977).

Chesler, Phyllis, and Emily Jane Goodman, *Women, Money and Power* (New York, 1976).

Decter, Midge, *The Liberated Woman and Other Americans* (New York, 1971).

Flexner, Eleanor, *Century of Struggle: The Women's Rights Movement in the United States* (Cambridge, Mass., 1975).

Foss, Sonja Kay, *A Fantasy Theme Analysis of the Rhetoric of the Debate on the Equal Rights Amendment, 1970-1976: Toward a Theory of Rhetoric Movements* (Evanston, 1976).

Freeman, Jo, *The Politics of Women's Liberation: A Case Study of an Emerging Social Movement and Its Relation to the Policy Process* (New York, 1975).

Giele, Janet Z., *Women and the Future: Changing Sex Roles in Modern America* (New York, 1978).

Ginsburg, Ruth Bader, "The Need for the Equal Rights Amendment," *American Bar Asociation Journal* (September, 1973).

Sedwick, Cathy, and Reba Williams, "Black Women and the Equal Rights Amendment," *Black Scholar* (July/August, 1976).

U.S. Senate, Subcommittee on Constitutional Amendments, *Women and the "Equal Rights" Amendment* (New York, 1972).

Wohl, Lisa Cronin, "White Gloves and Combat Boots: The Fight for ERA," *Civil Liberties Review* (April, 1974).

WATERGATE

The break-in at the Democratic National Committee's headquarters in the Watergate office complex resulted in a large-scale investigation of crimes linked to the White House, which became collectively known as the Watergate affair. Sensing possible impeachment and removal from office, President Richard Nixon resigned in August 1974. The incident has produced an abundance of literature, usually of a sensational nature. In *All the President's Men* (New York, 1974), *Washington Post* reporters Carl Bernstein and Robert Woodward tell how they uncovered the story behind the Watergate break-in. The book holds a distinguished place in any Watergate history. Many participants in illegal and extralegal White House activities have published their memoirs, including John W. Dean, *Blind Ambition: The White House Fears* (New York, 1977); H.R. Haldeman, *The Ends of Power* (New York, 1978) and Jeb Stuart Magruder, *An American Life* (Paterson, 1974). These personal accounts narrate similar stories. Special Watergate Prosecutor Leon Jaworski's *The Right and the Power: The Prosecution of Watergate* (New York, 1977) weaves trial briefs and other documents into a narrative about how the prosecutor successfully pursued evidence of the Watergate cover-up. The efforts of the special prosecutor's office to obtain White House materials used in the trials of presidential assistants are told by Richard Ben-Veniste and George Frampton in their *Stonewall* (New York, 1977). A personal story about the workings of the Senate Select Committee on Presidential Campaign Activities is Samuel Dash's *Chief Counsel: Inside the Ervin Committee—The Untold Story of Watergate* (New York, 1976). Following the Watergate affair many proposals to limit executive power were made. These proposals are challenged by Theodore C. Sorenson in *Watchman in the Night: Presidential Accountability After Watergate* (Cambridge, Mass., 1975).

Other Works

Anderson, John B., *Vision and Betrayal in America* (Waco, 1975).

Ball, Howard, *No Pledge of Privacy: The Watergate Tapes Litigation* (New York, 1977).

Bromwell, Dana G., *The Tragedy of King Richard: Shakespearean Watergate* (Salina, Kan., 1974).

Boyd, Marjorie, "The Watergate Story: Why Congress Didn't Investigate Until After the Election," *Washington Monthly* (February, 1973).

Candee, Dan, "The Moral Psychology of Watergate," *Journal of Social Issues* (Spring, 1975).

Caraley, Demetrios, "Separation of Powers and Executive Privilege: The Watergate Briefs," *Political Science Quarterly* (December, 1973).

Cohen, Alden, *The Women of Watergate* (New York, 1975).

Cohen, Jacob, "Conspiracy Fever," *Commentary* (April, 1975).

Colson, Charles W., *Born Again* (Tappan, N.J., 1976).

Conrad, Paul, *The King and Us: Editorial Cartoons* (Los Angeles, 1974).

Congressional Quarterly Staff, *Watergate: Chronology of a Crisis* (Washington, 1975).

Cox, Archibald, "Watergate and the Constitution of the United States," *University of Toronto Law Journal* (Spring, 1976).

Dean, Maureen, *"Mo" A Woman's View of Watergate* (New York, 1975).

Drew, Elizabeth, *Washington Journal: The Events of 1973-1974* (New York, 1975).

Evans, Fes, and Allen Myers, *Watergate and the Myth of American Democracy* (New York, 1974).

Friedman, Leon, comp., *United States v. Nixon: The President Before the Supreme Court* (New York, 1974).

Halpern, Paul J., ed., *Why Watergate?* (Pacific Palisades, 1975).

Harrell, Jackson, "Failure of Apology in American Politics: Nixon on Watergate," *Speech Monographs* (Winter, 1975).

Hendel, Samuel, "Separation of Powers Revisited in Light of 'Watergate'" *Western Political Quarterly* (December, 1974).

Higgins, George V., *The Friends of Richard Nixon* (Boston, 1975).

Hunt, Howard, *Undercover: Memoirs of an American Secret Agent* (New York, 1974).

Hurst, James Willard, "Watergate: Some Basic Issues," *Center Magazine* (January, 1974).

Knappman, Edward W., ed., *Watergate and the White House*, 3 vols. (New York, 1973–1974).

Kurland, Philip B., *Watergate and the Constitution* (Chicago, 1978).

Lasky, Victor, *It Didn't Start with Watergate* (New York, 1977).

Lukas, J. Anthony, *Nightmare: The Dark Side of the Nixon Years, 1969–1974* (New York, 1976).

Lurie, Leonard, *The Impeachment of Richard Nixon* (New York, 1973)

McGeever, Patrick J., "Guilty, Yes; Impeachment, No," *Political Science Quarterly* (June, 1974).

Magruder, Jeb S., *An American Life: One man's Road to Watergate* (New York, 1974).

Mankiewicz, Frank, *U.S. v. Richard M. Nix-*

on: *The Final Crisis* (New York, 1975).

Myers, Robert J., *The Tragedies of King Richard, the Second: The Life and Times of Richard II (1367–1400), King of England (1377–1399), Compared to Those of Richard of America in His Second Administration* (Washington, 1973).

Moseley, Clifton L., *John Smith Views Watergate* (Memphis, 1974).

Mosher, Frederick C., *Watergate: Implications for Responsible Government* (New York, 1974).

New York Times Staff, *The End of a Presidency* (New York, 1974).

New York Times Staff, *The Watergate Hearings: Break-in and Cover-up; Proceedings of the Senate Select Committee on Presidential Campaign Activities* (New York, 1973).

Nixon, Richard M., *Submission of Recorded Presidential Conversations to the Committee on the Judiciary of the House of Representatives* (Washington, 1974).

Osborne, John, *The Fifth Year of the Nixon Watch* (New York, 1974).

Pynn, Ronald, comp., *Watergate and the American Political Process* (New York, 1975).

Ripon Society, and Clifford W. Brown, Jr., *Jaws of Victory: The Game-Plan Politics of 1972, the Crisis of the Republican Party, and the Future of the Constitution* (Boston, 1974).

Robinson, Michael J., "The Impact of the Televised Watergate Hearings," *Journal of Communications* (Spring, 1974).

Rosenberg, Kenyon C. and Judith K., *Watergate: An Annotated Bibliography* (Littleton, Colo., 1975).

Royster, Vermont, "The Public Morality: Afterthoughts on Watergate," *American Scholar* (Spring, 1974).

Saffell, David C., comp., *Watergate: Its Effects on the American Political System* (Cambridge, Mass., 1974).

Sobel, Lester A., comp., *Money and Politics: Contributions, Campaign Abuses and the Law* (New York, 1974).

Stein, Howard F., "The Silent Complicity at Watergate," *American Scholar* (Winter, 1973).

"Table Talk: A British View of Watergate," *Center Magazine* (June, 1974).

Thompson, Fred D., *At That Point in Time: The Inside Story of the Senate Watergate Committee* (New York, 1975).

Tretick, Stanley, *They Could Not Trust the King; Nixon, Watergate and the American People* (New York, 1974).

U.S. Department of Justice, *Watergate Special Prosecution Force, Final Report* (Washington, 1977).

U.S. House of Representatives, *Independent Special Prosecutor* (Washington, 1973).

——, Committee on the Judiciary, *Comparison of White House and Judiciary Transcripts of Eight Recorded Presidential Conversations* (Washington, 1974).

——, ——, *Impeachment Inquiry* (Washington, 1975).

——, ——, *Testimony of Witnesses* (Washington, 1974).

——, ——, *Transcripts of Eight Recorded Presidential Conversations* (Washington, 1974).

——, Special Subcommittee on Intelligence, *Inquiry Into the Alleged Involvement of Central Intelligence Agency in the Watergate and Ellsberg Matters* (Washington, 1975).

——, Subcommittee on Criminal Justice, *Authority to Issue Final Report by Special Prosecutor* (Washington, 1975).

——, ——, *Pardon of Richard Nixon and Related Matters* (Washington, 1975).

U.S. Senate, *The Final Report of the Select Committee on Presidential Campaign Activities, United States Senate* (Washington, 1974).

——, Select Committee on Presidential Campaign Activities, *Presidential Campaign Activities of 1972* (Washington, 1973).

——, ——, *Presidential Campaign Activities of 1972* (Washington, 1974).

Van Sickle, Clifford Kenneth, *The Oral Communication of Senator Sam J. Ervin, Jr. in the Watergate Hearings: A Study in Consistency* (Michigan, 1976).

Von Hoffman, Nicholas, and Gary Trudeau, *The Fireside Watergate* (New York, 1973).

Washington Post Staff, *The Fall of a President* (New York, 1974).

"Watergate: Its Implications for Responsible Government," *Administration and Society* (August, 1974).

Watergate: The View from the Left (New York, 1973).

Weissman, Stephen R., comp., *Big Brother and the Holding Company: The World Behind Watergate* (Palo Alto, 1974).

White, Theodore H., *Breach of Faith: The Fall of Richard Nixon* (New York, 1975).

Wise, Helen D., *What Do We Tell the Children? Watergate and the Future of Our Country* (New York, 1974).

CAREER INDEX

The following is a list of individuals profiled in the *Nixon/Ford Years* according to their most important public activity. In some cases names appear under two or more categories.

House of Representatives

Abzug, Bella (D, N.Y.)
Albert, Carl (D, Okla.)
Anderson, John B. (R, Ill.)
Arends, Leslie C. (R, Ill.)
Ashbrook, John M. (R, Ohio)
Ashley, Thomas (D, Ohio)
Aspinall, Wayne (D, Colo.)
Blatnik, John J. (D, Minn.)
Boggs, Hale (D, La.)
Bolling, Richard W. (D, Mo.)
Brademas, John (D, Ind.)
Burton, Philip (D, Calif.)
Celler, Emanuel (D, N.Y.)
Chisholm, Shirley (D, N.Y.)
Cohen, William S. (R, Me.)
Colmer, William M. (D, Miss.)
Conte, Silvio O. (R, Mass.)
Conyers, John J., Jr. (D, Mich.)
Cramer, William C. (R, Fla.)
Diggs, Charles C., Jr. (D, Mich.)
Edwards, W. Don (D, Calif.)
Findley, Paul (R, Ill.)
Griffiths, Martha (D, Mich.)
Hansen, Julia B. (D, Wash.)
Harrington, Michael (D, Mass.)
Hawkins, Augustus F. (D, Calif.)
Hays, Wayne L. (D, Ohio)
Hebert, Edward F. (D, La.)
Holifield, Chet (D, Calif.)
Holtzman, Elizabeth (D, N.Y.)
Jordan, Barbara (D, Tex.)
Kastenmeier, Robert W. (D, Wis.)
Landrum, Philip M. (D, Ga.)
Lott, Trent C. (R, Miss.)
MacGregor, Clark (R, Minn.)
McCloskey, Paul N., Jr. (R, Calif.)
McCormack, John W. (D, Mass.)
McMillan, John C. (D, S.C.)
Mahon, George (D, Tex.)
Miller, George P. (D, Calif.)
Mills, Wilbur (D, Ark.)
Mink, Patsy (D, Hawaii)
Morgan, Thomas E. (D, Pa.)
Passman, Otto E. (D, La.)
Patman, Wright (D, Tex.)
Pepper, Claude (D, Fla.)
Pike, Otis (D, N.Y.)
Poage, Bob (D, Tex.)

Quie, Albert H. (R, Minn.)
Reid, Ogden R. (D, N.Y.)
Reuss, Henry (D, Wis.)
Rhodes, John J. (R, Ariz.)
Rivers, Mendel L. (D, S.C.)
Rodino, Peter (D, N.J.)
Rooney, John (D, N.Y.)
Ryan, William F. (D, N.Y.)
Sandman, Charles W., Jr. (R, N.J.)
Staggers, Harley (D, W.Va.)
Sullivan, Leonor K. (D, Mo.)
Udall, Morris K. (D, Ariz.)
Vanik, Charles A. (D, Ohio)
Whitten, Jamie L. (D, Miss.)
Wiggins, Charles (R, Calif.)
Young, Andrew (D, Ga.)
Zablocki, Clement (D, Wis.)

Senate

Aiken, George (R, Vt.)
Allen, James B. (D, Ala.)
Allott, Gordon (R, Colo.)
Baker, Howard, Jr. (R, Tenn.)
Bayh, Birch (D, Ind.)
Bennett, Wallace F. (R, Utah)
Bentsen, Lloyd (D, Tex.)
Bible, Alan (D, Nev.)
Brooke, Edward W. (R, Mass.)
Buckley, James L. (R, N.Y.)
Byrd, Harry F., Jr. (I, Va.)
Byrd, Robert C. (D, W. Va.)
Cannon, Howard W. (D, Nev.)
Case, Clifford P. (R, N.J.)
Church, Frank (D, Ida.)
Cooper, John Sherman (R, Ky.)
Curtis, Carl T. (R, Neb.)
Dirksen, Everett M. (R, Ill.)
Dodd, Thomas J. (D, Conn.)
Dole, Robert (R, Kan.)
Eagleton, Thomas (D, Mo.)
Eastland, James O. (D, Miss.)
Ellender, Allen J. (D, La.)
Ervin, Sam J., Jr. (D, N.C.)
Fong, Hiram (R, Hawaii)
Fulbright, J. William (D, Ark.)
Glenn, John (D, Ohio)
Goldwater, Barry (R, Ariz.)
Goodell, Charles (R, N.Y.)
Gore, Albert (D, Tenn.)

Gravel, Mike (D, Alaska)
Griffin, Robert P. (R, Mich.)
Gurney, Edward (R, Fla.)
Harris, Fred R. (D, Okla.)
Hartke, Vance (D, Ind.)
Hatfield, Mark O. (R, Ore.)
Helms, Jesse (R, N.C.)
Hruska, Roman (R, Neb.)
Hughes, Harold E. (D, Iowa)
Humphrey, Hubert H. (D, Minn.)
Inouye, Daniel K. (D, Hawaii)
Jackson, Henry (D, Wash.)
Javits, Jacob K. (R, N.Y.)
Kennedy, Edward M. (D, Mass.)
Long, Russell (D, La.)
McCarthy, Eugene J. (D, Minn.)
McClellan, John L. (D, Ark.)
McGee, Gale W. (D, Wyo.)
McGovern, George (D, S.D.)
McIntyre, Thomas J. (D, N.H.)
Magnuson, Warren G. (D, Wash.)
Mansfield, Michael J. (D, Mont.)
Mathias, Charles McC., Jr. (R, Md.)
Metcalf, Lee (D, Mont.)
Miller, Jack (R, Iowa)
Mondale, Walter F. (D, Minn.)
Montoya, Joseph (D, N.M.)
Moss, Frank (D, Utah)
Mundt, Karl E. (R, S.D.)
Muskie, Edward S. (D, Me.)
Nelson, Gaylord (D, Wis.)
Pastore, John (D, R.I.)
Pell, Claiborne (D, R.I.)
Percy, Charles (R, Ill.)
Proxmire, William (D, Wis.)
Randolph, Jennings (D, W. Va.)
Ribicoff, Abraham (D, Conn.)
Russell, Richard (D, Ga.)
Saxbe, William (R, Ohio)
Schweiker, Richard (R, Pa.)
Scott, Hugh (R, Pa.)
Smith, Margaret Chase (R, Me.)
Stennis, John (D, Miss.)
Stevenson, Adlai E., III (D, Ill.)
Symington, Stuart (D, Mo.)
Taft, Robert, Jr. (R, Ohio)
Talmadge, Herman E. (D, Ga.)
Thurmond, Strom (R, S.C.)
Tower, John G. (R, Tex.)
Williams, Harrison A., Jr. (D, N.J.)
Williams, John J. (R, Del.)

State & Local

Addonizio, Hugh
Alioto, Joseph
Beame, Abraham

Brown, Edmund G., Jr.
Burns, John H.
Byrne, Brendan T.
Cahill, William T.
Carey, Hugh L.
Carter, Jimmy
Daley, Richard
Evans, Daniel
Gibson, Kenneth
Gilligan, John J.
Grasso, Ella T.
Hicks, Louisa Day
Kirk, Claude R., Jr.
Koch, Edward
Krupsak, Mary Ann
Lindsay, John V.
Love, John A.
Lugar, Richard
McCall, Thomas L.
Maddox, Lester G.
Mandel, Marvin
Nunn, Louis B.
Reagan, Ronald
Rhodes, James A.
Rizzo, Frank
Rockefeller, Winthrop
Rohatyn, Felix
Sanford, Terry
Shapp, Milton
Stokes, Carl
Volpe, John
Wallace, George
White, Kevin
Williams, John B.
Yorty, Samuel

Judiciary

Black, Hugo
Blackmun, Harry A.
Brennan, William J., Jr.
Burger, Warren E.
Carswell, G. Harrold
Douglas, William O.
Fortas, Abraham
Gesell, Gerhard
Goldberg, Arthur
Harlan, John M.
Haynsworth, Clement
Hoffman, Julius
Marshall, Thurgood
Powell, Lewis F.
Rehnquist, William
Sirica, John J.
Stevens, John Paul
Stewart, Potter
White, Byron

Intellectuals, Churchmen & Journalists

Anderson, Jack
Beam, Jacob
Bernstein, Carl
Blake, Eugene
Bradlee, Benjamin
Buckley, William F., Jr.
Chomsky, Noam
Coleman, James S.
Cronkite, Walter
Ginzburg, Allen
Glazer, Nathan
Graham, Billy
Graham, Katherine
Hannah, John
Hesburgh, Theodore M.
Howe, Irving
Loeb, William
Mailer, Norman
Millett, Kate
Rather, Dan
Schorr, Daniel
Woodward, Robert

National Political Parties, Organizations & Issues

Brower, David
Bundy, McGeorge
Bush, George
Callaway, Howard
Carswell, G. Harrold
Carter, Rubin
Charren, Peggy
Clark, Ramsey
Eisenhower, Julie Nixon
Gross, Nelson
Hart, Gary
Haynsworth, Clement
Hearst, Patty
Hicks, Louisa Day
Hoffman, Julius

Korff, Baruch
Lowenstein, Allard
MacGregor, Clark
McCormack, Ellen
Mankiewicz, Frank
Mitchell, Martha
Mott, Stewart
Nofziger, Lyn
O'Brien, Lawrence
Rauh, Joseph
Rebozo, Charles
Schlafly, Phyllis
Shockley, William
Shriver, Sargent
Strauss, Robert

Watergate & Related Incidents

Barker, Bernard
Beard, Dita
Ben-Veniste, Richard
Chapin, Dwight
Cox, Archibald
Dash, Samuel
Dean, John
Doar, John
Gesell, Gerhard
Hunt, E. Howard
Jaworski, Leon
Kalmbach, Herbert
Krogh, Egil
LaRue, Frederick
Liddy, G. Gordon
McCord, James W.
Magruder, Jeb Stuart
Mardian, Robert C.
Mitchell, John
Segretti, Donald
Sirica, John J.
Sloan, Hugh
Strachan, Gordon
Sturgis, Frank
Thompson, Fred
Ulasewicz, Anthony

Index

A

ABEL, I.W.—Profile **1-2**
ABERNATHY, Ralph—Profile **2-4**
ABORTION—Bayh views on 35; Cahill views on 109; Dole views on 174; Grasso opposition to 244; J. Helms opposition to 293; Krupsak views on 367; E. McCormack as anti-abortion presidential candidate 399; New York State statute on 536; Supreme Court rulings on 55, 399, 514, 664-665
ABPLANALP, Robert H.—Profile **4-5**
ABRAMS, Gen. Creighton W.—Profile **5-6**; 373
ABZUG, Rep. Bella—Profile **7-8**; 558
ACKLEY, Gardner—Profile **8-9**
ACTION for Children's Television—122
ADDONIZIO, Hugh J.—Profile **9-10**; 228
AFRICA—168-169, 465-466, 572
AGEE, Philip—Profile **10-11**
AGENCY for International Development (AID)—270
AGNEW, Spiro T.—Profile **11-15**; Bork argues ability to try 62-63; relations with Buchanan 83-84; W. Buckley reaction to indictment of 88; Burch supports anti-press statements of 91; Buzhardt role in resignation of 105; attacks Goodell 238; Haig role in resignation of 260; Hickel criticizes 297; efforts to impeach 201; relations with Klein 359; attacks Lindsay 378; attacks media 83; 359; Nessen covers investigation of 464; Rockefeller clashes with 536; role in 1972 presidential campaign 407; Richardson's role in prosecution of 527; Safire as speechwriter for 560
AGRICULTURE—102-104, 146, 200, 499-500
AGRICULTURE, Dept. of—102-104
AIKEN, Sen. George D.—Profile **15-16**
AIR FORCE, U.S.—79-80, 373
AIRLINE Industry—64, 136
AIRWEST—314

ALASKA Oil Pipeline—452-453
ALBERT, Rep. Carl—Profile **16-17**; 14, 209
ALDRIN, Col. Edwin B.—27
ALEXANDER v. Holmes County (Mississippi) Board of Education—249, 669
ALIOTO, Mayor Joseph L.—Profile **17-19**; 78
ALLEN, Sen. James B.—Profile **19-20**; 404
ALLENDE, Salvador—126
ALLIANCE for Labor Action (ALA)—432, 520
ALLOTT, Sen. Gordon—Profile **20-21**
ALL the President's Men (book)—48
AMALGAMATED Clothing Workers of America—12
AMERICAN Council on Education—12
AMERICAN Federation of Labor–Congress of Industrial Organizations (AFL-CIO)—51, 432, 520
AMERICAN Federation of State, County and Municipal Employees—681-682
AMERICAN Federation of Teachers—588
AMERICAN Indians—279, 297, 431-432
AMERICAN Telephone and Telegraph Co.—42
AMERICANS for Democratic Action—387
AMTRAK—136
ANDERSON, Jack—Profile **21-22**; revelations on Eagleton 179; and ITT scandal 40, 225, 360; reveals purported corruption in J. McCormack's office 400
ANDERSON, Rep. John B.—Profile **22-23**
ANGLETON, James J.—Profile **23-24**
ANTI-ballistic Missile Systems—See specific systems e.g. Safeguard
ANTI-trust and Monopoly—62, 375, 380
APOLLO VIII (space capsule)—Borman 63
ANGLETON, James J.—Profile **23-24**

ARENDS, Rep. Leslie P.—Profile **24-25**
ARKANSAS—538
ARMS Control and Disarmament Agency—607
ARMSTRONG, Anne—Profile **26**
ARMSTRONG, Neil—Profile **27**
ARMY, U.S.—6, 109, 661
ARTS—67, 268-269
ASH, Roy L.—Profile **28-29**; 140
ASH Commission—28
ASHBROOK, Rep. John M.—Profile **29-30**
ASHLEY, Rep. Thomas L.—Profile **30-31**
ASPINALL, Rep. Wayne N.—Profile **31-32**
ASSASSINATION Attempts—212
ASSOCIATED Milk Producers, Inc.—336
ATKINSON, Ti-Grace—440
ATOMIC Energy Commission (AEC)—77, 510, 584
ATTICA Correctional Facility (N.Y.)—369, 535-536
AUGUSTA, Ga.—3
AUTOMOBILE Industry—136, 214, 461
AUTOMOBILE Insurance—414

B

BADILLO, Herman—39
BAKER, Sen. Howard H.—Profile **32-33**
BALL, George W.—Profile **33-34**
BALTIMORE, Md.—681
BANGLADESH—21
BANK Holding Company Act (1970)—43
BANK of America—39
BANKS and Banking—321, 342, 518, 610; See also specific individuals and institutions
BANKS, Dennis—368
BARAKA, Imamu—228
BARKER, Bernard L.—Profile **34-5**; 602, 616
BAYH, Sen. Birch E.—Profile **35-36**

775

BEALL, George—14
BEAM, Jacob—Profile 36–37
BEAME, Mayor Abraham D.—Profile 37–39; 364
BEARD, Dita—Profile 39–41; 21, 164, 225, 360
BEIRNE, Joseph A.—Profile 41–2
BELL System—42
BENNETT, Sen. Wallace F.—Profile 42–43
BENTSEN, Sen. Lloyd—Profile 43–44
BEN-Veniste, Richard—Profile 45
BERGSTEN, C. Fred—Profile 45–47
BERNSTEIN, Carl—Profile 47–48; 243, 678
BERRIGAN, Daniel—Profile 48–49
BERRIGAN, Philip—128, 368
BIBLE, Sen. Alan D.—Profile 49–50
BIEMILLER, Andrew J.—Profile 50–51
BILLY Graham Evangelical Association—242
BINH, Mme. Nguyen Thi—82
BLACK, Justice Hugo—Profile 51–54
BLACK Americans—590–591, 616; See also specific individuals and issues
BLACK Lung Disease—506–507
BLACK Panther Party—130–131, 585, 669
BLACKMUN, Justice Harry A.—Profile 54–55
BLAKE, Eugene C.—Profile 55–56
BLATNIK, Rep. John A.—Profile 56–57
BLOUNT, Winton M.—Profile 57–59
BOGGS, Rep. Hale—Profile 59–60
BOLLING, Rep. Richard—Profile 60–61; 271
BOMMARITO, Peter—Profile 61–62
BORK, Robert H.—Profile 62–63; 153
BORMAN, Frank—Profile 63–64
BOSTON, Mass.—298
BOULWARISM—330
BOYLE, William A.—Profile 64–66
BRADEMAS, Rep. John—Profile 66–67
BRADLEE, Benjamin C.—Profile 67–68
BRENNAN, Peter J.—Profile 68–70
BRENNAN, Justice William J.—Profile 70–72
BRIDGES, Harry—Profile 72–73
BRINEGAR, Claude S.—Profile 73–74
BROADCASTING Industry—12, 91; See also ACTION for Children's Television; PRESS
BROE, William—225
BROOKE, Sen. Edward W.—Profile 75–76
BROWER, David—Profile 76–77
BROWN, Edmund G., Jr.—Profile 77–79
BROWN, George S.—Profile 79–81

BROWN, Sam—Profile 81–82
BROWN Commission—394
BROWNMILLER, Susan—441
BRUCE, David K.—Profile 82–83
BUCHANAN, Patrick J.—Profile 83–84
BUCHEN, Philip W.—Profile 84–85
BUCHER, Lloyd N.—Profile 85–86
BUCKLEY, Sen. James L.—Profile 86–87;238
BUCKLEY, William F., Jr.—Profile 87–88; 30
BUILDING and Construction Trade Council of Greater New York—68, 70
BUNDY, McGeorge—Profile 88–89;191
BUNKER, Ellsworth—Profile 89–90
BURCH, Dean—Profile 90–92
BUREAU of the Budget—See OFFICE of Management and Budget
BURGER, Chief Justice Warren E.—Profile 92–94; 308
BURNS, Arthur F.—Profile 94–99; 38, 141–142
BURNS, John A.—Profile 99–100
BURTON, Rep. Phillip—Profile 100–101
BUSH, George H.—Profile 101–102
BUSING—Agnew on 12; Ashbrook's opposition to 30; Bayh views on 36; Eastland views on 180; Ford opposition to 207; Hicks opposition to 298; Kleindienst opposition to 360; Levi action on 375; Richardson actions on 526; Russell opposition to 556; Scott on 580; Supreme Court ruling on 93, 424–425; Thurmond opposition to 636; Wilkins support of 669
BUTZ, Earl L.—Profile 102–104; 249, 313
BUZHARDT, J. Fred—Profile 104–105; 15, 603
BYRD, Sen. Harry F.—Profile 105–106
BYRD, Sen. Robert C.—Profile 106–107
BYRNE, Gov. Brendan T.—Profile 107–108
BYRNE, Matthew Jr.—191–192

C

C-5A (airplane)—504
CAHILL, William P.—Profile 108–109
CALIFORNIA—78–79, 511
CALIFORNIA Welfare Reform Program—511
CALLAWAY, Howard—Profile 109–110; 111, 554
CALLEY, Lt. William L.—Profile 110–111

CAMBODIA—Agnew defends American invasion of 12; Brown role in bombing of 79–80; Buchanan drafts Nixon's speech on 84; Holtzman files suit against bombings of 308; opposition to invasion of 221; U.S. military campaign against 6
CAMPAIGN Contributions—605, 616–617
"CAMPAIGN GM"—461
CANNON, Sen. Howard W.—Profile 111–112
CAPITAL Punishment—See DEATH Penalty
CAREY, Gov. Hugh L.—Profile 113–114; 38, 367
CARSON, Robert—206
CARSWELL, G. Harrold—Profile 114–115; 51, 75, 312, 444, 509
CARTER, Gov. Jimmy—Profile 115–116; 79, 448,
CARTER, Rubin "Hurricane"—Profile 116–117
CASE, Sen. Clifford—Profile 117–118
CASTRO, Fidel—127, 537
CELLER, Rep. Emanuel—Profile 118–120
CENSORSHIP—See OBSCENITY
CENTER for Auto Safety—461
CENTER for Responsive Law—460
CENTRAL Intelligence Agency—Agee as member of 10; Anderson reveals assassination attempts by 21–22; Bush as Director of 102; Church Committee investigation of 126–127; 1976 Executive Order on 102; Harrington as critic of 278; McCord as member of 397; Pike investigation of 498–499, Rockefeller Commission investigates 537–538; possible role in Watergate 398
CHAFEE, John H.—Profile 120; 86
CHAPIN, DWIGHT—Profile 120–121; 586
CHARLESTON, S.C.—3
CHARREN, Peggy—Profile 121–122
CHAVEZ, Cesar—Profile 122–123
CHEMICAL Workers Union—432
"CHICAGO Seven"—368
"CHICAGO Eight"—585
CHILDREN—121–122
CHILE—21, 219, 225, 536; See also INTERNATIONAL Telephone & Telegraph Co.
CHINA, People's Republic of—Ball criticizes Administration on 34; Bruce heads U.S. liaison office to 82–83; Bush heads U.S. liaison office to 102; Fulbright supports normalization of relations with 221; Haig prepares Nixon visit to 258; Nixon action on 472–473; Rogers attitude on 544
CHISHOLM, Rep. Shirley—Profile 123–125; 587, 621

D